The Selfless Constitution: Experimentalism and Flourishing as Foundations of South Africa's Basic Law

The Selfless Constitution: Experimentalism and Flourishing as Foundations of South Africa's Basic Law

The Selfless Constitution:
Experimentalism and Flourishing as Foundations of South Africa's Basic Law

This edition published 2021

First edition published 2013 by Juta & Co [ISBN 978-1-4851-0007-2]

Published in South Africa on behalf of the author by
NISC (Pty) Ltd, PO Box 377, Makhanda, 6140, South Africa
www.nisc.co.za

ISBN (print): 978-1-920033-77-4
ISBN (eBook): 978-1-920033-78-1
ISBN (pdf): 978-1-920033-79-8

Contents

For My Father, *Ephraim Woolman*
Who Understood the True Meaning of *Selfless*

Acknowledgements

Ephraim Woolman.
Lenore Woolman. Michael Bishop.
Harry Woolman. Courtenay Sprague. Li Yu.
George Abraham. Lisa Ruch. Brahm Fleisch. Wendy Ngoma.
Joyce Oliphant. Michael Dorf. Ute Kuhlmann. Theunis Roux. Karin Van Marle.
Christof Heyns. Steve Allcock. Frank Michelman. Kecia Rust. Laurie Ackermann. Graeme Friedman.
Martin Brassey. Lizette Hermann. Sanele Sibanda. Hannah Fleisch. David Bilchitz. Drucilla Cornell. Ezra Fleisch.
Kim Segal. Reuben Fleisch. Nancy Schwartz. Ross Kriel. Carole Lewis. Anthony Stein. Siobahn McDermott. Arthur Danto.
Hazel Shelton Gumede. Greg Smith. Constanza Tusconi. Mthuli Ncube. Yolanda Boyseens. Charles Larmore. Hillary Hamburger.
Tracey Segal. Rhobbie Greenblum. David Friedman. Dikgang Moseneke. Sharon Hendrickse. Edwin Cameron. Richard Adelstein.
Lance Josselsohn. Susan Levine. Paul Cheney. Kristina Dahl. Ian Hyams. Patty Searle. Greg Lee. Hilda Mbele.
David Zeffertt. Judith Abraham. Etienne Mureinik. Anton Roodt. Peter Esterhuizen. Sindi Tilane.
Jack Greenberg. Kate O'Regan. Louis Henkin. Daria Roithmayr. Derek Spitz
Arthur Hertzberg. Mary Galvin. Levison Ndlovu. Stephen Ellmann
David Woolman. Vanessa Barolsky
Ephraim Woolman.

We all love to stand taller. We only do so on other people's shoulders.
Ephraim Woolman

Umuntu ngumuntu nga bantu.
A person is a person through other persons.

Citations

Acknowledgements and citations are a matter of distributive justice, the currency in which we pay our intellectuals debts. The payment is important; indeed, there is a saying in the Talmud that when a scholar acknowledges all his sources, he brings the day of redemption a little closer. But it isn't easy to make that full acknowledgement; we are probably unaware of, or unable to recognize, many of our deepest debts.

Michael Walzer

This book contains a number of different forms of recognition:

- Bibliography: Books, Articles, Book Chapters, and Government Reports
- Table of Cases, International Covenants and Legislation
- Table of Authors
- Subject Matter Index
- Endnotes (where substantive extended encounters often occur)

Even this attempt to acknowledge all the sources that made this work possible will fall far short of the mark. More importantly, these citations – and the commentary upon them – cannot capture almost twenty years of engagement with scholars, judges and practitioners in South Africa. Professor Jonathan Klaaren once called me an oralist – meaning that I learned as much from what others had to say as I did from the books, articles or cases to which I otherwise applied my mind. Professor Klaaren's tongue in cheek characterization does, however, have a particular bearing on what does and does not appear in these pages. This book cannot possibly take cognizance of the innumerable conversations that have shaped my understanding of our country's law and the lived experience of its denizens. To my friends and fellow scholars whose wise words are not reflected in the various citations found in this work, I offer both my thanks and an apology. You have made me who I am, and this monograph would not have been possible without your work, and more often than not, the observations and the apercu that tripped from your lips. This book is because you are (like it or not).

Foreword to Reissued Edition

When first published in 2013, *The Selfless Constitution* offered a novel way of thinking about South Africa's constitutional democracy as well as all other modern democracies. It still does. Grounded in interrelated theories of neuroscientific understandings of consciousness, individual identity, social and economic constructs, political institutional analysis and constitutional law, it demonstrated that small wins (based upon experimentalism and development theory) might produce the big wins that would make good on the aspirations of the post-apartheid state.

By 2021, South Africa's political, social and economic institutions have collapsed on almost every front, and the nation edges closer to becoming a failed state. Of course, that poor policies generated by poor governance leads to entrenched poverty is a cliché in the annals of political economy. Needless to say, small wins still can be translated into the big wins necessary to create an inclusive democracy with inclusive economic institutions. The hurdles required to overcome problems of collective action and wicked problems that stand in the way are discussed by me at length in *Wrecking Ball: Why Permanent Technological Unemployment, a Predictable Pandemic and Other Wicked Problems Will End South Africa's Experiment in Inclusive Democracy.**

Stu Woolman
Johannesburg
15 June 2021

* ISBN: 978-1-920033-72-9, published by NISC (Pty) Ltd, April 2021

Preface

We only think when we are confronted with a problem.

John Dewey

I have reached bedrock, and my spade is turned.
If I am now asked 'Why?' I can only say 'This is simply what I do.'

Ludwig Wittgenstein

A. The Tale of Tiahuanaco

A set of glyphs on a stone monument in the pre-Incan city of Tiahuanaco, located in the mountainous Andean region of western South America (just 45 km from La Paz, Bolivia), tells us the following story. The sun rose in the east every day. It set in the west every night. For this regular occurrence, the people of Tiahuanaco thanked their primary deity, Viracocha. Viracocha had originally revealed himself to re-establish order after the destruction wrought by a great flood. The people of the northern Andes subsequently went about repopulating the planet. The glyphs then take us forward in time to another challenge particular to the people of Tiahuanaco. Viracocha, an aquatic god, warned the people of Tiahuanaco that they faced another challenge within the next generation: a scarcity of water. Viracocha was omniscient and omnipotent. Yet not unlike Milton's own lonely god, Viracocha had mixed feelings about doing all the heavy lifting. Wasn't it enough that he had endowed the people of Tiahuanaco with the capacity to carry out their plans in action, to reflect upon the success or the failure of their work, and to determine their vision of the good in terms of a moral sensibility that emphasized the benefits that flowed from sharing rather equally the fruits of their labour? The glyphs intimate that Viracocha neither demanded sacrifices nor endowed a representative on earth with divine powers. The people of Tiahuanaco, with a well-organized co-operative of terraced vegetable plots and herds of llamas that fed from the city's surrounding commons, got by on their wits and the rich aquifers that flowed down from the peaks of the Andes. Viracocha's omen was his final gift. The elders of Tiahuanaco would be left to their own devices in arriving at solutions to their theoretically imminent desolation. The people, being people, greeted the news with fear, speculation and ennui. The elders themselves could not agree on the best way forward. They understood that the iced peaks around them would recede. They knew that without the seasonal run-off their lovely terraces and commons would dry up. Rather than bicker, or treat diminishing resources as spoils to be secured after victory in an internecine war, they agreed instead to a competition. Members of the community would be allowed to work with each other on a solution. In return, the most ingenious, successful group – as judged by its ability to ensure a sustainable supply of water to all of Tiahuanaco – would be rewarded with houses built by fellow denizens of the city and a lifetime supply of vegetables, fruit, meat and itchy llama wool. The glyphs do not spell out exactly what transpired thereafter. They do note that one group of inspired Tiahuanacians built 'man-made rivers' that stretched out to a reliable water source – Lake Titicaca – that lay a considerable way from their city. For this virtuoso turn, they were rewarded as promised. We do not know what became of this once great civilization. However, we do know that water scarcity did not bring about its demise. We know this much because the canals and, more impressively, the aqueducts built by the people of Tiahuanaco lead away from the city and dot the landscape on the road to Lake Titicaca. These ruins not only staved off the destruction of Tiahuanaco, they actually led to a new, unexpected discovery: the ability to farm fish. That big fish story belongs to another set of glyphs and the burial mounds of fossilized bones that surround this once great metropolis.

Every book, much like every individual life, or even the story of a great civilization like that of the people of Tiahuanaco, begins in the middle of things (and ends there). So we begin with the triumphant, and pedagogically rich, story of the people of Tiahuanaco. As with any archaeological find of its kind, it's a mix of myth, truth and conjecture. However, it frames the book that follows in a number of useful ways.

The people of Tiahuanaco were under no illusions that they controlled their destiny in the kind of autonomous, unshackled manner of those bewitched by the language of 'free will' and 'undetermined autonomous selves' that still exerts such control over our folk psychology, and thus our morality, politics, and constitutional jurisprudence. The people of Tiahuanaco were content to abjure that set of pretences, and the hubris that underlies them. They understood quite well that their epistemic endowments, powers of reason and their ability to run, and learn from, experiments would serve them well enough. Modest, creative folk, the people of Tiahuanaco.

Their creativity is reflected in their response to the potential disaster that awaited them. They neither ignored the problem in the hopes that it would go away nor did they blithely assume that Viracocha would, at the eleventh hour, save them. Again, they turned to a modest form of collective self-reliance: the experimental method. Whatever means that they could divine to deliver water to their terraces and their commons would be a function of an array of trials, errors and successes. That one group of Tiahuanacians hit upon canals and aqueducts – as had others elsewhere at other moments in human history – is testament to their pluck and luck. Moreover, they did not reject the body of knowledge that had been bestowed upon them, nor did they disavow the obvious benefits of the social capital that grounded their society and allowed them to work together towards solving a collective concern.

Ingenuity and creativity would have only taken the Tiahuanacians so far. The elders of Tiahuanaco had long recognized that only a decidedly significant degree of common beliefs and common property – their 'commons' – would allow all to flourish. Recognition, and even reward, might flow to those Tiahuanacians ingenious enough to solve this crisis of water scarcity. The ultimate benefits would be shared by all.

The story of the Tiahuanacians is to some degree our story. We ignore its implications at our own peril.

This book is not, however, about the manifold failures of political will required to respond adequately to a global recession, climate change and nuclear proliferation. This book, and the lessons to be learned from the Tiahuanacians, services a much more modest and parochial affair: how best to comprehend and to develop the constitutional jurisprudence of South Africa. The family resemblance of our predicament in South Africa to that of my Tiahuanacian ancestors has already enabled me, indirectly, to introduce some of the core concepts and concerns that animate this work: free will, consciousness, selfhood, social capital, spontaneous orders, nudges, flourishing, experimentalism, capabilities, participatory bubbles, reflexivity and rolling best practices. Moreover, as with the story of my Tiahuanacian ancestors, this book emphasizes the contributions that all South Africans can tender as we attempt to resolve the profound crises that confront us. The rest of the book provides a partial, modest and exploratory answer as to how we ought to go about addressing some of these quandaries from within the limited framework of constitutional politics.

B. Waldron's Wager

After a faculty lunch and talk at Columbia Law School (circa 2000), I entered an elevator with Jeremy Waldron and a number of other faculty members. Apropos of the talk just given, and speaking to no one in particular, Professor Waldron broke the silence and said: 'You know the essence of every article can be captured in two sentences. [Pause.] No. Make that one.'

Of course, some arguments are more complicated than others. And yet, at the outset of any book, an author would do well to distil her thoughts in a pithy manner.

So here goes.

When we contemplate such matters as consciousness or constitutional democracy, we find that these domains are best described in terms of (a) trial and error and feedback mechanisms that give us fresh opportunities to reflect upon experience (reflection or memory that's immediately or substantially prior) and to imagine more or less optimal courses for action (pressganged and plodding) to realize the ends and the aspirations (b) that have largely, but not irrevocably, already made us who we are.

One sentence.

Studies of consciousness ultimately identify our neural structures as designed for trial and error. Individual corporeal selves are always experimenting, attempting to divine, through reflection (memory) and action (imagination), what 'works' best. Choice architects, those persons charged with constructing environments that create greater health, wealth and happiness for their communities, regularly run experiments that attempt to (1) eliminate biases, (2) draw on the express preferences of a representative cohort of individuals and (3) ultimately, deliver policies that nudge people away from negative defaults toward more optimal ends (as the individual herself understands them.) A constitutional democracy, made up of millions of complex, heterogeneous selves (densely populated "me's" comprised of multiple ways of being in the world), constantly strives, through policy, legislation, common law, customary law and ultimately the provisions of its basic law, to determine what works best for most of its many constituents. Because our Constitution states some (and only some) of the norms that govern our lives at an extremely high level of generality, it remains for citizens and their representatives to create doctrines and institutions that serve those capaciously framed ends best. This book suggests that experiments in living that fall within the accepted parameters of the shared constitutional norms found are likely, over time, to produce practices that can be replicated by other members of the polity. The truly interesting feature of the theory of constitutionalism on display here is that these rolling best practices – bounded by a basic law order committed to flourishing and, thus, to the development and the expansion of our individual capabilities – do not merely serve the preordained ends of South Africa's denizens. Our reflexive stance toward these rolling best practices will invariably cause us, over time, to alter the content of the fundamental norms that bind us.

One paragraph.

C. Deriving an Ought from an Is

Back in 2004, I gave a paper (upon which this book is based) for the Research Unit for Constitutional and Legal Interpretation (RULCI) Conference at the University of the Western

Cape. Professor Francis Olsen and Professor Andre van der Walt asked me roughly the same question. Are the factual claims to be found in my accounts of the self and the social necessary to support my normative claims regarding the constitutional? The *first* part of my answer to their question (a weak, rehashed version of GE Moore's indefatigable 'naturalistic fallacy'[1]) was a 'no' and a 'yes'. 'No', in the sense that one can make all sorts of normative claims about how the world ought to be structured without any compelling truth propositions to support them. 'Yes', in the three-fold sense that (a) normative claims are far more compelling when supported by empirically grounded justifications; (b) true, justifiable empirical claims are normative claims because the scientific projects upon which they are based rely on normative commitments to rationality and to inference and (c) my normative claims about an optimal constitutional regime tightly fit my factual claims about the self and the social. My *second* response was an example of how an 'ought' can easily be derived from an 'is'. I asked them: 'Is brushing one's teeth twice a day and regularly flossing between meals a relatively accepted form of dental hygiene?' The answer was 'yes'. I then asked 'Is it an accepted good to strive for excellent health and is proper dental hygiene part of a regime designed to realize well-being?' The answer was 'yes'. If so, I contended, then we can derive the 'ought' of pursuing good health from the 'is' of brushing and flossing our teeth.

Professor Olsen's and Professor Van Der Walt's error has a well-established and well-regarded philosophical pedigree. David Hume is often credited with the fact/value distinction, and the counsel that flows from it. However, as a naturalist, a materialist and an ethicist, Hume intended something far more subtle in arriving at his distinction between what is and what ought to be.[2] First, reason grounds morality. Second, when Hume writes that reason 'is and only ought to be the slave of the passions',[3] he certainly meant 'passions' to embrace what he and his friends Adam Smith and Adam Ferguson meant by 'moral sentiments'. As Patricia Churchland notes, 'moral behaviour', according to the Scottish Enlightenment, while informed by 'reflection', was rooted in 'deep', 'widespread', 'enduring' and conventional understandings of human relations.[4] What concerned Hume most was not the cleavage between is and ought, but 'simple sloppy inferences' that led exponents of a particular position about what *is* to a less than desirable position about what *ought* to be.[5]

Churchland then goes on to note that, *pace* rationalists such as Kant, Hume was correct to contend that most human thought does not turn on simple or even complex algorithms, but rather on constraint satisfaction processes. 'Brains' as Churchland writes, 'navigate the [natural] causal world by recognizing and categorizing events they need to care about.'[6] The social world is much the same. Social navigation is but a subset of causal navigation. Whether we must choose between employment opportunities or universities to attend, we are quite adept at arriving at a reasonably optimal answer. From this reconceptualization of Hume's distinction between is and ought, one based upon rigour rather than rigid distinctions, Churchland draws several conclusions quite sympathetic to this book's project:

> In sum, from the perspective of neuroscience and brain evolution, the routine rejection of scientific approaches to moral behaviour based upon Hume's [misunderstood] warning against deriving ought from is seems unfortunate.[7] ... The truth seems to be that the nexus between social ends

> and social facts is quite close. ... [V]alues rooted in the circuitry for caring – for well-being of self, offspring, mates, kin, and others – shape social issues about many issues: conflict resolution, keeping the peace, defense, trade, resource distribution, and many aspects of social life in all its vast richness. Not only do these values and their material basis constrain social problem solving, they are at the same time facts that give substance to the process of figuring out what to do.[8]

Our social values are 'facts' about what it means to be human. These facts shape our solutions to various collective conundrums and determine which solutions are to be preferred to others. To that extent, then, this book's reliance on facts about how the self and the social operate are only different in degree, not kind, from the conclusions the book ultimately draws about how best to construct our constitutional politics.

My exasperation with the is/ought (fact/value) distinction is crisply captured by Kwame Anthony Appiah: 'The universes inhabited by the sophisticated realist and anti-realist, the sophisticated cognitivist and non-cognitivist, are the same universe; and what most of those thinkers want to say about first order ethics is the same.'[9] I can't think of anything of genuine ethical, political or constitutional substance that divides Olson's and Van Der Walt's views from my own.[10] As David Mamet writes: 'There. Is. A. Real. World. Out. There.' Or if you prefer Appiah: 'There is one world.' Forays into every subject traversed in this work are imbued with the same sentiment. We live in one world, and every day we learn something new about the antics of the objects that populate it, including ourselves, whether we call them facts or values.

D. A Tale Twice Told

This book contains the results of numerous experiments, qualitative case studies and true stories designed to elucidate its various theoretical components and to describe the lineaments of a South African constitutional jurisprudence based upon experimentalism and flourishing. However, not even a winning 'Waldron Wager' can accurately condense a book that draws together current findings and learning in neuroscience, cognitive psychology, consciousness studies, choice architecture, development theory, experimental philosophy, new governance jurisprudence, the capabities approach and the manifold contributions of my fellow South African legal academics. Nor will it convince you to 'lay on'.

Perhaps it was the good fortune of the elders of Tiahuanaco to lack a written language by which to be bewitched (about such matters as freedom or consciousness). We also know a fair bit more about ourselves than the Tiahuanacian people. This book brings that modern body of scholarship to bear on current constitutional theorizing in South Africa.

There is, however, a second story that may help the reader understand the book that follows. It's history. That is, my lived experience. And everyone knows what experience is: it's the hangover you wake up with in the morning. (Sometimes every morning.)

The experience upon which this book is based is decidedly personal. After returning from New York to Johannesburg in 2002 after a joyless convalescence, I picked up a book that I had read many years back – Daniel Dennett's *Consciousness Explained.* Given the nature of my illness, it came as no surprise that I had absolutely no memory of its contents. So I began reading afresh. At about the same time, I struggled to get my head around a battery of South African

Constitutional Court decisions that seemed to me wrong. Wrong, partially in terms of reasons, and partially in terms of outcomes. Wrong *primarily* in terms of the metaphysical foundations upon which they rested. The point of contact between Dennett and the Constitutional Court turned upon opposing conceptions of the self and individual autonomy.

So: a problem to be solved. Through Dennett, I identified an entry point consistent with my own first-hand experience of the self and its construction, its disintegration, and its resurrection. Dennett's fully matured body of work, along with his canvassing of the extant literature in neuroscience, cognitive psychology and philosophy of mind seemed consistent with what I knew to be true from intuition, from experience and from experiments performed (quite literally) upon me.

At the time, the gap between metaphysics, cognitive psychology, analytic philosophy, neuroscience, social theory, on the one hand, and the extant jurisprudence of the Constitutional Court, on the other, possessed all the qualities of an unbridgeable chasm: the destination clear, but no obvious way to get there. Enter Li Yu. Li and I consumed many a meal trying to piece together something of an answer to the questions thrown up by Dennett and the Court. Li's most critical contribution was his introduction of experimental constitutionalism into our discussions. Experimental constitutionalism can – without fear of contradiction – be said to be largely a product and a project of several current and former professors at Columbia Law School: a friend (then Vice Dean) Michael Dorf (now of Cornell Law School), Barry Friedman, Charles Sabel, William Simon and Susan Sturm.

An immediate fit. Dennett's conception of consciousness turns primarily on its role as a complex set of feedback mechanisms, a capacity that allows human beings to engage in *trial and error* through *thought experiments* and *real experiments*. These experiments – and the feedback we receive – improve our chances at arriving at better answers over time to questions – factual and normative – that require a more or less immediate solution. For Dorf, Freidman, Sabel, Simon, Sturm and company, experimental constitutionalism reflects an attempt to ground the answers to constitutional (and mundane political) questions in empirical findings, in best practices arrived at through trial and error, a shared commitment to forward and lateral looking analysis of solutions that serve our ends best, and reflexivity with respect to those ends themselves. Instead of grand theories that predetermine outcomes, or an annoyingly South African scepticism that promises little more for our jurisprudence than discrete decisions shorn of any deep theoretical moorings, experimental constitutionalism splits the baby. On the one hand, Dorf, Freidman, Sabel, Simon, Sturm and company recognize the need for courts, legislatures, executives and an active citizenry to interpret constitutional provisions in terms of broadly shared understandings of the basic law's general norms. On the other hand, Dorf, Friedman, Sabel, Simon, Sturm and company, having tested their theories on specific areas of law (e.g., education reform, drug treatment courts, child welfare systems, police interrogation), conclude that the norms ought to be set at a relatively high degree of abstraction. On their view, the space created by norms set at this high degree of abstraction would enable co-ordinate branches of a central government, various agencies, different states or provinces, thousands of municipalities and innumerable private parties and stakeholders to undertake alternative approaches to the problems thrown up by constitutional litigation and more humdrum matters raised tens of thousands of times over in such venues as specialized drug treatment tribunals, school systems and family courts. Over time, so the argument goes, we would be able to see which experiments undertaken by different constellations of stakeholders worked best. These best practices could then be used to revisit our previous understanding of constitutional, statutory, common law and traditional norms so as to realize a better fit between means and ends. As importantly, the general normative commitments themselves (our ends) might change as we came to see, for example, that rehabilitation for drug users (however difficult) produced better results (for all concerned) than incarceration. (It hardly seems controversial to state that the stigma that attaches to a person battling an addiction is dramatically different than the stigma that attaches to a murderer.) The similarities between the notion of feedback mechanisms operating at the level of the self in Dennett's work and the state in Dorf's writings seemed too obvious to ignore. But still ... lay there a gap.

Li Yu and I continued to speak through 2003, and I began to write. Li Yu recognized that John Stuart Mill's notion of 'experiments in living' might provide a departure point for an experimentalist social theory. This first stage of bridge-building mirrors the evolutionary epistemology of the economist Friedrich Hayek and the social scientist Donald Campbell. But the agnosticism, the political disengagement, and the classical liberalism of Mill and Hayek left us far short of the mark for a constitutional politics appropriate for contemporary South Africa (or anywhere else for that matter).[11] In time, two different bodies of social science literature provided the foundations for a more capacious and progressive experimentalist social theory. Novel notions of bonding networks and bridging networks found in the work of sociologists, political scientists and economists in the relatively new field of social capital theory offer a necessary explanation as to why we need to conserve extant stores of social capital so that we might leverage that capital in a manner that enables the majority of South Africa's denizens to flourish after years of depredation under apartheid and colonial rule.[12] A few years ago, Richard Thaler's and Cass Sunstein's *Nudge*, with its notions of choice architecture, confirmed my intuitions about the possibility of social experimentalism that could improve the lives of all at the same time that it recognized that our adaptive preferences (especially acute for the worst off) militated against dictating the exact contours of those improvements. The politics of flourishing – the Aristotelian ideal powerfully recast in recent work on development theory and the capabilities approach by Amartya Sen and Martha Nussbaum – and the concomitant commitment to that degree of material equality necessary to make flourishing meaningful had been part of my conceptual package from the outset. At this juncture, I felt confident that I could begin to connect theories of the self, the social, the political and the constitutional. What remained? Elbow grease: the chasing down of evidence that favoured my intuitions; a tightening of the line of reasoning. And, of course, unearthing the kind of examples and stories to keep a reader hooked.[13]

We arrive, for the purposes of this preface, at Wittgenstein's sword of Damocles: 'What can be said at all, can be said clearly: And whereof one cannot, thereof one must be silent.' The bar set for truth claims in the *Tractatus* remains the (unspoken) ambition of all serious scholars. Each argument must operate as an indisputable premise in an extended syllogism that proves the thesis of the book. However, as Amartya Sen has recently pointed out, good reasons may exist to question whether the younger, ascetic Wittgenstein really meant what he said. Sen notes that at the same time Wittgenstein was working on the *Tractatus*, he could write to a friend and wistfully remark that he wished that he was 'better and smarter'. Yah. Me too. I do wish that I possessed the native intelligence and the years of training that would ensure that every sentence and every section of this book would march like soldiers, one after the other. I don't. Instead, I take some comfort from the later Wittgenstein's rueful remark at the beginning of his *Philosophical Investigations.* Though unsatisfied with what he had wrought, he had done the best that he could, and that would simply have to do. He had reached bedrock. This monograph is, as the older Wittgenstein lamented about his own work, a book of 'tips' that hang together not as a formal logical system, but as a way of seeing things that draws upon the insights of those wiser than myself.[14] This book of 'tips' presses my contemporaries and betters in the South African legal academy, on the bench and in practice, to reassess their most basic assumptions about the self, the social, and the political, and to reconsider their conclusions regarding how we should engage in the practice of South African constitutional law.

This book might well be called, in Kant's sense, a 'Prolegomenon'. Whether this text remains more than an introduction depends upon its ability to elicit constructive criticism. Some readers may conclude that I should have chosen to remain silent – and worked on a far smaller, comfortable scale, free of potential embarrassment. But where, after all, is the fun in that?

Stu Woolman
April 2012
Johannesburg, South Arica

Endnotes

1. GE Moore *Principia Ethica* (1903). Moore claimed that a naturalistic fallacy is committed whenever a philosopher attempts to prove an ethical or political claim through an appeal to a definition of the term 'good' that relies in turn on the presence of a natural property or a set of natural properties. The 'good', on Moore's intuitionist account, is a simple, non-natural, ineffable property. Moore (supra) at § 10 ¶ 1. 'Natural', by contrast, means something that can be studied within a scientific discipline. Prior places the following gloss on Moore's definition: 'The naturalistic fallacy [rests] on the [implicit but unwarranted] assumption that because some quality or combination of qualities invariably and necessarily accompanies the quality of goodness ... this quality or combination of qualities is identical with goodness. ... The naturalistic fallacy is the assumption that because the words 'good' and, say, 'pleasant' necessarily describe the same objects, they must attribute the same quality to them.' A Prior *Logic and the Basis of Ethics* (1949). No number of uncontested, experimentally verified, truth claims about the world can, on this account, prove an ethical (political or constitutional) claim that rests upon them.
2. S Blackburn *How to Read Hume* (2008).
3. D Hume *A Treatise of Human Nature*: *Being An Attempt to Introduce the Experimental Method of Reasoning in Moral Subjects* ((1739) (eds) DF Norton & MJ Norton, 2000) § 2.3.3.4.
4. P Churchland *Braintrust*: *What Neuroscience Tells Us about Morality* (2011) 6 citing A Baier *A Progress of Sentiments: Reflections on Hume's Treatise* (1991).
5. P Churchland *Braintrust* (supra) at 5.
6. Ibid.
7. Ibid at 8.

8. Ibid at 8-9. After eviscerating Moore's muddled distinction, Churchland suggests that Moore would have been on far safer ground by merely contending that the relationship between facts and values is often quite complex. Ibid at 186-190.
9. KA Appiah *Experiments in Ethics* (2008) 183.
10. Neither Hume, nor Churchland, nor Appiah nor I endorse a naïve empiricism. For example, extremely good reasons exist to prefer the findings of evolutionary biology and physical anthropology to religiously inflected notions of intelligent design. At the same time, the extant conclusions about the nature and the history of our world remain incomplete in both scientific disciplines. That incompleteness hardly counts as an argument against them. The fresh unearthing of an Australopithecus fossil in South Africa that predates findings in East Africa supplements the record – even as scientists argue over the meaning and the import of the discovery. See L Berger, D Ruiter, S Churchland, P Schmid, K Carlson, P Dirks & J Kibii 'Australopithecus Sediba: A New Species of Homo-Like Australopith from South Africa' (2010) 328 *Science* 195. That said, it is important to recognize that these disciplines, as William Rehg writes, 'aim[] beyond the lab ... [E] xperimental practices are heavily oriented toward the production of public knowledge, and to reach that goal findings have to be presented in a convincing manner as ... acceptable arguments. Here public acceptability is not measured by publication alone but more pertinently by the usability of one's findings and arguments for the research of other scientists.' W Rehg *The Cogent Science in Context* (2009) 21. Rehg's two points are important for the work that follows. Contemporary neuroscientists and experimental philosophers – now working in conjunction with one another – have shown a myriad of ancient and contemporary philosophical arguments to be false. Their discoveries, still new, and in need of confirmation and extension, have turned some of the leading philosophers of just a generation ago (Colin McGinn, John Searle, David Chalmers) into a group of contrarians known as the 'new mysterians'. See, e.g., C McGinn *The Mysterious Flame: Conscious Minds in a Material World* (2002). In a recent article reviewing the work of neuroscientist VS Ramachandram (*The Tell-Tale Brain: A Neuroscientist's Quest for What Makes Us Human* (2010)), McGinn whines (with some justification) that such scientists should be philosophically trained in order to avoid elementary logical and terminological errors. C McGinn 'VS Ramachandram's *The Tell-Tale Brain*' (2011) 58 (5) *New York Review of Books* 8; C McGinn 'The Tell-Tale Brain: An Exchange' (2011) 58 (11) *New York Review of Books* 68. (McGinn's ontological kvetching seems completely at odds with the apparent third-party truth status that he accords his own phenomenological account regarding the source of the emotion of disgust: it flows, he contends, from a universal awareness of the inevitable desuetude of consciousness that presages death. See C McGinn *The Meaning of Disgust* (2011).) The charges laid by the new mysterians ostensibly immunize 'hard questions' in philosophy from scrutiny by scientists working in other domains. When the work of teams of experimental philosophers, cognitive psychologists and neuroscientists are arranged next to arguments of conventionally trained philosophers who claim that little meaningful work can be done, the conclusions to be drawn are three-fold. First, when scientists can place chips in the brain that allow individuals to issue commands and have objects (say prosthetics) in the world perform various functions, it seems implausible to deny that the scientists in question have identified genuine neural correlates of consciousness. See S Musaliam, B Corniel, B Gregor H Shermberger & R Anderson 'Cognitive Control Signals for Neural Prosthetics' (2004) 305 *Science* 258; L Hiochberg, M Serruya, G Friehs, J Mukland, M Saleh, A Caplan, A Branner, D Chen, R Penn & JP Donoghue 'Neuronal Ensemble Control of Prosthetic Devices by a Human with Tetraplegia' (2006) 442 *Nature* 164 (Brain Computer Implants (BCIs) restore damaged capacity because the cortical plasticity of the brain eventually treats implants as natural sensors or effector channels.) Second, while philosophers have long denied the capacity for third party knowledge of an individual's percepts ('qualia'), scientists have begun to break the code and show visual images that match an individual's (internal) perceptions and thoughts. See N Shinji, A Vu, T Naseralis, Yuval, B Yu & J Gallant 'Reconstructing Visual Experiences from Brain Activity Evoked by Natural Movies' (2011) 10 *Current Biology* 1016; Y Miyawaki, H Uchida, O Sato, Y Morito,

H Tanabe, N Sadato & Y Kamitani 'Decoding the Mind's Eye – Visual Image Reconstruction from Human Brain Activity using a Combination of Multiscale Image Decoders' (2008) 60 *Neuron* 915. Third, while some of McGinn's charges are correct – points that Ramachandram gracefully acknowledges – McGinn's appropriate response ought not to be to rule out such new findings tout court, but to participate in the design and the replication of the experiments themselves. Such co-operation advances knowledge within and across disciplines. As Rehg contends, collaboration makes the arguments propounded more cogent across the academy and within the public domain.

11. This project is, at some remove, an attempt to flesh out the politics that underlay a much earlier article. S Woolman & D Davis 'The Last Laugh: *Du Plessis v De Klerk*, Classical Liberalism, Creole Liberalism and the Application of Fundamental Rights under the Interim and the Final Constitutions' (1996) 12 *South African Journal on Human Rights* 361, 363 (As Judge Davis and I wrote some 16 years ago: '[T]he state has an essential role to play in determining the contours of those 'private' relationships which so fundamentally shape individual identity and in making possible a variety of life choices through support for those associations and organizations which make up society writ large. Creole liberalism envisages a state which does not exhaust the possibilities of individual lives. Its raison d'etre is to make real those possibilities through the provision of roughly equal material means for individual and group flourishing. At the same time, creole liberalism requires that the state occupy a crucial, if not always central, place in the debate about and construction of values at the same time as it supports (and rules out) a variety of different ways of being in the world.') Needless to say, while Judge Davis and I may still share quite similar political points of view, how we go about spinning out the foundations for a particularly South African constitutional jurisprudence differs. See, e.g., D Davis *Democracy and Deliberation* (2000).

12. The existence of social capital seemed so obvious that I had previously employed the term without any exposure to the literature. See S Woolman 'Freedom of Association' in S Woolman & M Bishop (eds) *Constitutional Law of South Africa* (2nd Edition, OS, December 2003).

13. A parallel story of intellectual indebtedness must be told. After my conversations with Li Yu ended, South Africa's National Research Foundation ('NRF') provided the next little prod forward. In the beginning of 2004, the NRF called for multi-disciplinary projects that spanned the natural sciences, the social sciences, the humanities and the law. At about the same time, the Research Unit for Legal and Constitutional Interpretation (a joint venture between the University of the Western Cape and the University of Stellenbosch) issued a call for papers for a conference to be held in September of 2004. I answered both calls with a paper and a presentation. Constructive criticism from the RULCI participants convinced me that while I might be on the right track, I had quite a lot of work to do in order to convince them (and others) that what might be compelling findings in an array of other seemingly far flung disciplines had a meaningful bearing on the (rather parochial) normative concerns of South African constitutional lawyers. A fifty page conference paper may have remained just that, had not my colleague, Professor Karin van Marle, convinced me to take up the challenge of writing a work that might convince my justifiably sceptical initial audience. And so, over the next few years, between other more pressing projects, I pieced together what might be called the first draft of this book. Other projects again took precedence. However, the gut level sense that I had something novel to say did not go away. Further readings across experimental philosophy, cognitive psychology, neuroscience, social theory, and South African case law and commentary started to fill in the remaining gaps. (Developments in all of these domains seem to have caught up with many of my early intuitions.) An invitation, in December 2006 to speak at Columbia Law School – and helpful suggestions from the Columbia experimental constitutionalism cabal – kept the fire alive. A big positive push from Professor Steve Ellmann at New York Law School in 2010 forced me to produce rough drafts of the first and last chapter of this book and a detailed outline of the rest of its contents. Additional interventions by Professors Andre Van Der Walt, Marius Pieterse, Henk Botha and Dennis Davis provided welcome assistance; as have extended collaborations with Professors Courtenay Sprague, Brahm Fleisch, Theunis Roux, Frank Michelman, David Bilchitz, and Drucilla Cornell.

Finally, Michael Bishop, friend, fellow editor, frequent collaborator, offered trenchant substantive critiques and identified gaps in theory, case law and the book's overarching argument. To his credit, and my benefit, Michael often filled the gaps in.

14. See L Wittgenstein *Philosophical Investigations* (1953) Book II, xi: 'Is there such a thing as 'expert judgment' … [T]here are those whose judgment is 'better' and those whose judgment is 'worse'. Corrector prognoses will generally issue from the judgments of those with better knowledge of mankind. Can one learn this knowledge? Yes; some can. Not, however, by taking a course in it, but through experience. Can someone else be a man's teacher in this? Certainly. From time to time, he gives him the right *tip*.'

Chapter One-A

The Basic Structure and the Methodology of the Argument

At every level of organization, from the presumably hard-wired level of memory organization to the level of the design of social institutions, the best possible designs, given the constraints of finitude and time pressure, … include some measure of arbitrariness and wise risk-taking. The [unconscious] organization of memory guarantees that only some approximately appropriate subset of relevant points will occur [consciously] to one in the time available. Any individual's personally developed style of self-control must buy some efficiencies at the expense of gambles on what is to be encountered. … [As a result,] we all know the [following] feeling at times: the terrible existential funk into which … we … slid[e], self-defeatingly … [*when some efficiencies and gambles have not gone our way.*] Fortunately, for most of us, these depressions soon pass, and we return to some constructive engagement … with the world. *We break out of our slump, like the golfer who finally sees the wisdom in the curious advice of the pro: keep your head down and follow through.* Since we all know this feeling, we can all appreciate the ominousness of anything that purported to be the discovery or proof that free will is impossible for us. Having good reasons for wanting free will *is not*, of course, having good reasons for believing one has free will. … What we want when we want free will is the power to decide our courses of action, and to decide them wisely, in light of our experience and desires…We want to be agents, capable of initiating, and taking responsibility for, projects and deeds. All this is ours … as a natural product of our biological endowment, extended and enhanced by our initiation into society … *There are real threats to human freedom, but they are not metaphysical.* There is political bondage, coercion, the manipulation inducible by the dissemination of misinformation, and the 'forced move' desperation of hunger and poverty. No doubt we could do a lot more to combat these impositions on our freedom, were it not for the curious sort of *self-imposed bondage* that we create by the very exercise of our freedom, and in the very acknowledgment of our responsibility for the chains, ropes, strings and threads of commitments (explicit and tacit) that tie us to our family and friends, that tie us to our life projects, and that make us increasingly immobile by appeals to radical action. … I close with some advice on how to respond to these challenges … Inquire closely about just what variety of free will is supposedly jeopardized by the argument. Is it, in fact, a variety of free will worth caring about? … Ask yourself: can I even conceive of beings whose wills are freer than our own?

Daniel Dennett

A. The Basic Thesis

The basic thesis of this text is disarmingly simple. It goes something like this ...

The way the vast majority of us think about the self, consciousness and free will is incorrect – dramatically out of step with what the majority of neuroscientists, cognitive psychologists, social theorists, economists and analytic philosophers currently have to say about those subjects. One consequence of these erroneous views is that the manner in which the majority of us understand 'freedom' – as a metaphysical term – is sharply at odds with how things actually are. We replicate similar kinds of errors when we think about how various forms of human association are constructed and how change actually occurs within such associations. Once again, epistemological fallacies with regard to social theory have the consequence of leading us to attribute far greater 'freedom' to groups (and individuals within groups) than they actually possess. This second misattribution of autonomy results in institutional political arrangements and constitutional doctrines that operate in a manner contrary to what we know about the human condition.

This book does not attempt to describe the self and the social correctly in order to establish basic truths about the world. Its descriptive efforts have a more modest, primarily instrumental end: an intuition that an accurate understanding of the self and the social will assist us in putting our constitutional theories and practises on a more solid footing. The book's dual desire to reconceptualise 'freedom' in terms of 'flourishing' and to re-describe the commitment to 'deliberation' in politics in light of the more felicitous nomenclature of 'experimentation' is driven by a single goal: to offer a reasonably novel argument for altering a number of constitutional doctrines and political institutions so that they better fit the conditions under which we live in South Africa.

The first part of the introduction lays out the structure of the thesis and its methodology. I explain how my use of intuition pumps and experimental philosophy are designed to make controversial claims easier to swallow. I then trace developments in social theory that shore up the conclusions previously drawn up about the self. By breaking metaphysical bottlenecks regarding individual autonomy, it becomes easier to demonstrate how radical change in our society is possible without recourse to outré conceptions of free will. In a similar vein, arguments mounted in favour of choice architecture, evolutionary modelling and social capital theory are meant to nudge us away from staid classically liberal constitutional doctrines.

This broad project inevitably traverses a number of controversial subjects. Human beings have navigated and negotiated virtually every conceivable argument regarding free will and determinism over the last two and a half millennia. No claim here will settle this ancient debate. Likewise, relatively new disciplines, such as neuropsychology and choice architecture, attract a fair amount of criticism with respect to their most basic presuppositions. As a non-specialist in these fields, all I can say is that the positions that I take out appear substantially more cogent than alternative arguments.

B. Structure of the Text: The Self; the Social; the Constitutional

In some ways, this text begins at the end. The next section of the introduction (Chapter 1B) engages the limitations of several dominant theories that ground South African constitutional discourse. My aim is to show how each set of working assumptions can be traced back to errant understandings of 'freedom' in the context of the self and the social. These limitations in our existing metaphysics lead to the search for better explanations of the self in Chapter 2, a description of, and a prescription for, the mechanics of constructive change in social formations in Chapter 3 and an account of the basic tenets of experimental constitutionalism when married to a politics of flourishing in Chapter 4. After rehearsing this marriage of experimentalism and flourishing, Chapter 5 looks at the two primary theoretical innovations associated with experimental constitutionalism – shared constitutional interpretation and participatory bubbles – as well as a number of other supporting hypotheses. It then identifies a dozen species of political institutions and judicial doctrines in South Africa that currently hold out the promise of experimental governance. Chapter 6 slices up South African public law somewhat differently. It narrows our focus to two sectors: housing and education. The chapter indicates how our politicians, bureaucrats, citizens, social movements, lawyers, academics and jurists have already made use of the more rudimentary forms of experimental design implicit in our basic law. Questions of whom and what this radical, but constrained, approach to constitutional theory serve are taken up at greater length in both Chapters 4 and 7. The Court's gloss on the right to dignity, the right to equality, civil and political rights, community rights and a host of socio-economic rights reveal an intention to make good the promise of both traditional forms and revolutionary forms of individual flourishing and communal flourishing. In Chapter 8, the reasoning and the holdings of a score of Constitutional Court cases are compared with results that one might expect from a mode of adjudication fully committed to both experimentalism and flourishing. Chapter 8 reminds us that we live in a democracy and that emergent experimental institutions serve us best when they invite the participation of an active citizenry. The reader may be as surprised as the author to find that the Court has moved, over the last few years, towards such commitments, and that such commitments have, in a number of cases, yielded better results.

To make clear the cash value of the conclusions reached in each part of this thought project, the book examines the antics of objects, phenomena and practices with which we are all too familiar. Chapter 2 surveys driving, the composition of music, video games, and spelling to explain the role consciousness plays in the self-correcting feedback mechanisms of human cognition. Chapter 3 utilizes psychotherapy, golf instruction, legal theory, and triple bottom line corporate strategy to explicate how critical engagement with participants in a given form of life, and the measurement of successful responses within a social practice, operate as social feedback mechanisms and increase the potential for individual and group flourishing. Chapter 4's conclusions are buttressed by examples of emergent institutional design in the United States (e.g., drug treatment fora, education reform programmes, and family courts.) Chapters 5's inferences draw support from South African rights, limitations and remedies analysis, our own quirky understanding of democracy, doctrines regarding constitutional jurisdiction, access and amici, provincial constitutions and Chapter 9 institutions. Chapter 6 constitutes an extended meditation on the fit between the theory adumbrated in this book and two well-ventilated bodies of public law. Chapter 7 spins out a theory of flourishing as old as Aristotle, but substantially recast and reinvigorated by development theory and the capabilities approach. It then maps this theory onto South Africa's extant constitutional jurisprudence. In Chapter 8, my hypotheses about how experimentalism and flourishing might advance South African constitutional jurisprudence are tested against a score of cases that our Constitutional Court has generated over the past decade.

C. Epistemic Commitments: Self, Society and State as Natural Phenomena

This book's methodology is distinct in two important ways from many similar kinds of synthetic projects in the law, the social sciences and the humanities.

First. The description of human nature and social formations strongly favours my prescriptions for South African constitutionalism. Depending upon the reader's perspective, that could be either a strength or a weakness of this project.

Second. This humanistic venture is not set in false opposition to the natural sciences. This project does not treat the human phenomena that it engages as radically different in kind from natural phenomena. Quite often when a scholar in the social sciences and the humanities makes a claim about treating theories about natural phenomena and theories about human phenomena in the same manner, it is based upon the assumption that theories in the natural sciences, like theories in the human sciences, are reducible in some way to claims about power or ideology.[1] The book adopts the opposite view. Power may, on occasion, influence what we come to study or what we claim to know.[2] (People are susceptible to all sorts of claims made by snake oil salesmen and brutal dictators. The universe is impervious to such charms or threats of violence.) The vast majority of truth claims are not reducible to, or even translatable into, ideologically inflected propositions.[3] Human beings are subject to the same causal laws that govern other physical objects in the world. Explanations of human phenomena require no special pleading – certainly none that we would otherwise accept with respect to accounts of other phenomena.[4] Moreover, the claims made on behalf of the model of the self and the social sketched herein accord with, and are often parasitic upon, recent learning in fields as diverse as genetics, neuroscience, evolutionary biology, cognitive psychology, economics, social capital theory, psychoanalysis, socio-biology and empirical and experimental philosophy. Of course, the laws which govern human phenomena are not fully reducible to laws which govern other natural phenomena.[5] Just as no one truly claims that the description of biological properties are captured entirely by chemistry, or that chemistry is captured entirely by physics, human phenomena can never be entirely explained by the laws of biology, chemistry or physics.

D. Methodological Commitments: Intuition Pumps and Experimental Philosophy

The primary audience for this book is the lawyer, jurist and legal academic working in South Africa – and for the growing number of international scholars interested in comparative constitutional law. Natural scientists will find nothing new here as pertains to their own disciplines. They may, however, find that they have more to say about matters beyond their professional silos – in particular, moral, legal and constitutional theory in South Africa.

The justification for the selective engagement with complex natural phenomena is not that the truth or the strength of the book's philosophical claims do not much matter. Quite the opposite. They do. However, this book is not primarily about the virtues of theories of determinism as opposed to the vices of doctrines that support free will, nor is it generally about the grounds for preferring choice architecture over deliberation when trying to enhance the results of collective action. That this book is ultimately about South African constitutional law doctrine – because that is my area of expertise – raises other questions about the content of this work.

Legal academics, lawyers and judges who have read this work in various forms over the past decade have often asked a single question: are the descriptive accounts of the self and the social really necessary for a work that has as its primary aim a minor re-conceptualization of the way in which we think about constitutional law in South Africa? As noted in the Preface, several fellow academics have asked whether the 'is' with respect to the self and the social entails an 'ought' with respect to the constitutional.

As I contend in the Preface, my answer to these questions about both content and method is 'Yes'. (Following Bernard Williams, I see little reason to fear what some philosophers often call, with disdain, the 'naturalistic fallacy',[6] and have no reason to think that we should not be able to draw inferences in ethical matters from non-ethical propositions. For reasons already assayed, my method seems preferable to GE Moore's naive intuitionism.[7]) At the very least, the book's non-ethical propositions can be tested, and the logical relationship of ethical to non-ethical propositions assessed. Someone could write about the subject matter traversed in chapters 4, 5, 6, 7 and 8 of this book without engaging the subject matter covered in Chapters 2 and 3. However, because a genuine re-conceptualization of South African constitutional politics turns on a better account of the self and an enhanced depiction of social phenomena, this book elucidates those improved portrayals. We have the good fortune to live at a time when these understandings of the self and the social have already been canvassed at great length across a broad array of disciplines by a large number of scholars. (The convergence of views across scholarly domains over the last decade has been both surprising and gratifying.) By first laying out some empirically compelling views about the self and the social, this book may convince at least some readers that the politics prescribed provides the best fit for the individuals, the groups and the sub-publics that populate the Republic of South Africa.

Let me put the matter slightly differently.

1. *Intuition Pumps*

The accounts of the self and the social, in Chapter 2 and Chapter 3, are – in addition to being stand-alone theories – intuition pumps. Intuition pumps are rhetorical devices, commonly used in philosophy, that are designed by their creators to draw the reader's attention to certain features of a philosophical problem. By emphasizing critical features of a problem, often isolating them from other features, the writer hopes to make it easier for the reader to see the problem and to appreciate the novel explanation proposed. My views on the self and on the social are intuition pumps in the sense that these characterizations of the self and of the social emphasize certain views about 'trial and error' and 'feedback mechanisms' that hold true not only for the self and the social, but for the political and the constitutional. (NB: If the reader wants to understand the basic conceptual framework that drives this project, then she would best keep the notions of trial and error and feedback mechanisms firmly in mind.)

Intuition pumps better serve my efforts than does a term like 'proof'. No matter how accurate my philosophical and sociological views may be, there are simply too many nation-states and too many constitutions that do not permit a theoretical fit between my account of the self and the social, on the one hand, and my account of constitutional politics, on the other.

2. *Experimental Philosophy and Empirical Philosophy*

For those readers already inclined towards support of a largely secular, radically heterogeneous, socially democratic constitutional project, my accounts of the self and the social do the necessary heavy lifting. Again: these accounts cannot prove my preferred model of constitutional politics. But they do serve as evidence of a certain kind. This evidence suggests that if 'this' is who we really are in radically heterogeneous, socially democratic constitutional states, then 'these' are the constitutional doctrines and political institutions that will serve us best.

My confidence in making such a statement has much to do with the current success of experimental philosophy. As Joshua Knobe and Shaun Nichols contend: 'The goal [of experimental philosophy] is to determine what leads us to have the intuitions we have about free will [and] moral responsibility .... The ultimate hope is that we can use this information to help determine whether the psychological sources of the beliefs undercut the warrant for the beliefs.'[8]

That thesis addresses two overlapping concerns. First, it exposes the inconsistency of the answers that well-informed lay persons – and here I mean the South African legal audience to whom this work is primarily addressed – often offer to basic metaphysical and ethical questions. Second, conclusions drawn from experimental philosophy and empirical philosophy clear away these mischaracterizations and enable the more dramatic points registered by neuroscientists, cognitive psychologists and analytic philosophers to secure greater traction.[9]

Endnotes

1. Post-structuralist accounts of science tend to conflate proposition (1) that some, if not all, scientists may be motivated by interests not intrinsic to the matter under study, with proposition (2) that the scientific method, as practiced by a community of scholars, generates verifiable truth propositions about the world. For such theorists, proposition (1) taints proposition (2) in a manner that invariably relativizes the manner in which truth propositions in terms of proposition (2) are produced. P Feyerabend *Against Method* (1975); P Feyerabend *A Farewell to Reason* (1987). As I have suggested in the Preface, and further note in Chapter 3, this account of how science operates is simply wrong, and the truth of proposition (1) and the truth of proposition (2) have no bearing on the truth of each other.
2. See W Rehg *The Cogent Science in Context* (2008).
3. S Woolman 'Language, Power and the Margin: Eliot's Philosophy of Language, Wittgenstein on Following a Rule, and Statutory Construction in *Thembekile Mankayi v Anglogold Ashanti Limited*' (2012) 128 *South African Law Journal* 434. This point is decidedly Davidsonian. As Davidson writes in his 'Introduction' to *Inquiries into Truth & Interpretation*: '"Schnee ist Weiss" is true in the mouth

of a German speaker if, and only if, "snow is white" has to be taken not merely as true, but as capable of supporting counterfactual claims. Indeed, given that the evidence for this law, if it is one, depends ultimately on certain causal relations between speakers and the world, one can say that it is no accident that "Schnee is Weiss" is true if and only is snow is white; it is the whiteness of snow that *makes* "Schnee is Weiss" true.' D Davidson 'Introduction' *Inquiries into Truth and Interpretation* (1984) xiv. (emphasis added). Davidson clearly has in his sights the claims of conceptual relativism that mark the writings of Kuhn and Feyerabend in the philosophy of science. Davidson writes: 'Philosophers of many persuasions are prone to talk of conceptual schemes. Conceptual schemes, we are told, are ways of organizing experience: they are systems of categories that give form to the data of sensation; they are points of view from which individuals, cultures or periods survey the passing scene. There may be no translating from one scheme to another, in which case the beliefs , desires, hopes, and bits of knowledge that characterize one person have no true counterparts to the subscriber to another scheme. Reality is relative to a scheme: what counts as real in one system may not in another.' D Davidson 'On the Very Idea of a Conceptual Scheme' *Inquiries into Truth and Interpretation* (1984) 183, 183. Davidson concludes: 'Conceptual relativism is a heady and exotic doctrine, or would be if we could make sense of it. The trouble is, as so often in philosophy, that it is hard to improve intelligibility while retaining the excitement.' Ibid. About the confusion associated with conceptual schemes, he argues: '[T]he only possibility at the start is to assume general agreement on beliefs … . The guiding policy is to do this as far as possible … . The method is not designed to eliminate disagreement, nor can it; its purpose is to make meaningful disagreement possible, and this depends entirely on a foundation – *some* foundation – in agreement … . We make maximum sense of the words and thoughts of others when we interpret them in a way that optimizes agreement … Where does that leave the case for conceptual relativism? The answer is, I think, that we must say much the same thing about differences in conceptual schemes as we say about differences in belief: we improve the clarity and bite of declarations of difference, whether of scheme or opinion, by enlarging the basis of shared (translatable) language or of shared opinion. … In giving up dependence on the concept of an uninterpreted reality, something outside all schemes and science, we do not relinquish the notion of objective truth – quite the contrary. … [G]iving up the dualism of scheme and world, we do not give up the world, but re-establish unmediated touch with the familiar objects whose antics make our sentences and opinions true or false.' Ibid at 197. Davidson's theories on truth and interpretation owe a direct debt to Wittgenstein. Both Davidson and Wittgenstein are concerned with what happens when 'language goes on holiday'. L Wittgenstein *Philosophical Investigations* (GEM Anscombe, trans, 3rd Ed, 1953)(original emphasis) § 38. For further argument on these points, see S Woolman 'On the Common Saying "What's True in Golf is True in Law": The Relationship between Theory and Practice across Forms of Life' (2010) 25 *Southern African Public Law* 520; S Woolman 'Between Charity and Clarity: Kibitzing with Frank Michelman on How to Best Read the Constitutional Court (2010) 25 *Southern African Public Law* 491; GPS Backer and PMS Hacker *Skepticism, Rules & Language* (1984). See also S Woolman 'Law, Power and the Margin' (supra).

4. See G Ryle *The Concept of Mind* (1949). Ryle describes the persistence of such distinctions as category mistakes. We would be rightly perplexed if a visitor to the University of the Witwatersrand, after having been shown all the lecture halls, playing fields, offices, laboratories, academics, students and staff, still asked 'But where is the University?' The mistake is in thinking the University represents something over and above its constituent parts. Something similar occurs in discussions of the self and consciousness. The mistake is in thinking that there is something – the mind – over and above the physical constituent parts that make up an individual's brain, in particular, and body, more generally, that give rise to thought and, more importantly, action. For an application of Ryle's thesis to South African constitutional law, see S Woolman 'Category Mistakes and the Waiver of Constitutional Rights: A Response to Deeksha Bhana on *Barkhuizen*' (2008) 125 *South African Law Journal* 10 as cited in *Lufuno Mphaphuli & Associates (Pty) Ltd v Andrews & Another* 2009 (4) SA 529 (CC) at para 216, fn 30.

5. It would be easy to reduce an explanation of why we hold individuals morally and legally culpable for their actions to Darwinian and utilitarian accounts of how a commitment to individual responsibility results, generally, in the increasingly successful life chances of other individuals and in the overall welfare or 'happiness' of any given society. However, such an account is insufficiently rich to explain why individuals and societies that come to accept deontological and non-instrumental explanations of moral, political and legal responsibility are justified in doing so. We shall see in Chapter 2's discussion of 'the radically heterogeneous natural self' that deontological thought has a rather archaic neurological basis (to be found in areas of the brain that have controlled flight or fight for millions of years.) It does not follow that the German disposition towards deontological thought *qua* Kant is somehow less compelling. German post-World War II constitutionalism constitutes a rather remarkable collective response to Nazi Germany's behaviour in World War II (namely, the Holocaust as well as the mass murder of non-Jewish groups – gays and lesbians, the Roma, the Poles and Soviet prisoners of war.) That the German Federal Constitutional Court has held that it would unjustifiably violate the German Basic Law's commitment to dignity and to life to allow the German military to shoot down an airplane captured by terrorists in order to save many more German lives from being lost if the hijacked plane were allowed to crash into a densely populated area in German territory is fascinating. The Federal Constitutional Court found s 14(3) of the Aviation Security Act of 2005 constitutionally infirm on the grounds that it was incompatible with the right to life under Article 2.2 of the Basic Law in conjunction with the guarantee of human dignity under Article 1.1 of the Basic Law. (2005) 115 BVerfGE 118, 1 BvR 357/05. The Court did allow that the matter legitimately fell within the purview of the Federal Government and those organs of state (the police) that handled domestic matters such as terrorism. I can't imagine that the South African Constitutional Court would reach the same outcome. A prima facie violation of FC s 10 and FC s 11: sure. An unjustifiable limitation of those rights: surely not.
6. B Williams 'The Linguistic Turn' in *Ethics and the Limits of Philosophy* (1985) 120.
7. GE Moore *Principia Ethica* (1903).
8. J Knobe and S Nichols 'An Experimental Philosophy Manifesto' in J Knobe and S Nichols (eds) *Experimental Philosophy* (2008) 3, 7. See also S Nichols and J Knobe 'Moral Responsibility and Determinism: The Cognitive Science of Folk Psychology' (2007) 41 *Nous* 663.
9. This book's claims about the self and the social, like those made by Knobe and Nichols, are meant to have an 'indirect impact'. Knobe and Nichols 'An Experimental Philosophy Manifesto' (supra) at 8. While Knobe and Nichols are interested in whether and how one can develop 'a theory about underlying psychological processes that generates people's intuitions', I am interested in whether we can use such theories to determine 'whether or not those intuitions are warranted'. Ibid.

Chapter One-B

Why Rethinking the Foundations of South African Constitutional Law is Necessary

It was in this sphere then, the sphere of legal obligations, that the moral conceptual world of 'conscience', 'duty', 'sacredness of duty' and [free will] had its origins; its beginnings were, like the beginnings of everything great on earth, soaked in blood thoroughly for a very long time … The creditor could inflict every kind of indignity and torture upon the body of the debtor.

Friedrich Nietzsche

A. The 'So What' Question

In chapters 2 through 7, this book puts forward a fairly thick conception of the self and of the social in order to support an equally thick account of the kinds of political institutions and judicial doctrines that South Africa requires to make good the promise of our basic law. The point of this sub-section is to identify a number of difficulties in metaphysical, psychological, political and legal thought that may block a reader's predisposition to credit the book's arguments. What these problems have in common is a failure to provide an accurate account of the nature of 'freedom' or an inability to account for breakdowns in collective rationality. These problems take three distinct forms: (1) the use of 19th Century classical liberal thought as a foundation for a 21st Century socially democratic aspirational constitution; (2) the folk-psychology of free will; and (3) constitutional doctrines such as judicious avoidance that underestimate the degree of shared, principled norm-setting required of state and non-state actors.

1. *How 19th Century Classical Liberalism Undercuts a 21st Century Aspirational Constitution*

As the reader is already aware, there are other intuition pumps out there, working away in support of different models of constitutional politics. The Constitutional Court has handed down a range of decisions over the past decade that suggest that it is working with at least three competing models.[1]

The first model is classically liberal:[2] explicitly on display in *Ferreira,*[3] *Du Plessis,*[4] and *Barkhuizen,*[5] influential in the early development of the equality and dignity jurisprudence of the Court,[6] and arguably decisive in the majority opinions in *Prince*, *Jordan* and *Robinson.*[7] The second is a liberal democratic model underpinned by a strong theory of individual agency:[8] such a position appears in the majority judgments in *NCGLE I* and *NCGLE II.*[9] The third is a socially democratic model married to a strong theory of individual agency found in *Khosa, Occupiers of 51 Olivia Road, Berea Township, Joe Slovo Community, Abahlali Basemjondolo Movement SA, Merafong Demarcation Forum* and *Ermelo.*[10] All three models are predicated upon a set of metaphysical commitments to individual freedom that we should make every effort to eschew. In *Ferreira*, that 'freedom' talk takes a form that may appear hard to gainsay:

> Human dignity cannot be fully valued or respected unless individuals are able to develop their humanity, their 'humanness' to the full extent of its potential. Each human being is uniquely talented. Part of the dignity of every human being is the fact and awareness of this uniqueness. An individual's human dignity cannot be fully respected or valued unless the individual is permitted to develop his or her unique talents optimally. Human dignity has little value without freedom; for without freedom personal development and fulfilment are not possible. Without freedom, human dignity is little more than an abstraction. Freedom and dignity are inseparably linked. To deny people their freedom is to deny them their dignity.[11]

But 'freedom' talk by the Court can also possess a stern, rather moralizing tone that readily reveals the flaws in the Court's thinking. In *S v Jordan & Others*, the majority reasoned as follows:

> If the public sees the recipient of reward as being 'more to blame' than the 'client', and a conviction carries a greater stigma on the 'prostitute' for that reason, that is a social attitude and not the result of the law. The stigma that attaches to prostitutes attaches to them, not by virtue of their gender, but by virtue of the conduct they engage in. That stigma attaches to female and male prostitutes alike. I am not persuaded by the argument that gender discrimination exists simply because there are more female prostitutes than male prostitutes, just as I would not be persuaded if the same argument were to be advanced by males accused of certain crimes, the great majority of which are committed by men.[12]

The majority's commitment to a very strong form of metaphysical autonomy – a form of autonomy that makes all individuals morally and legally culpable for actions that issue ineluctably from their circumstances – fails dramatically those prostitutes whose alternatives are dramatically cabined if not entirely determined. [Significant numbers of prostitutes are the victims of sexual trafficking. Sexual trafficking is about the sale and exploitation of women and children – of people who have little chance, and no choice, in life's wheel of fortune.[13]] Prostitution – irrespective of its immediate provenance – is hardly a profession that can be charitably described as chosen.[14]

One may think this characterisation of *Jordan*'s weltanschauung unfair. The majority judgement speaks for itself:

> It was accepted that they have a *choice*, but it was contended that the *choice* is limited or 'constrained'. Once it is accepted that [the criminalisation of prostitution] is gender-neutral and that by engaging in commercial sex work prostitutes *knowingly* attract the stigma associated with prostitution, it can hardly be contended that female prostitutes are discriminated against.[15]

It's hard to discern how 'knowing' that stigma attaches to an event that takes place under conditions of compulsion makes a prostitute morally and legally culpable.[16] The minority, although sympathetic to the plight of sex-workers, offers more of the same freedom-talk:

> Their status as social outcasts cannot be blamed on the law or society entirely. By engaging in commercial sex work, prostitutes *knowingly* accept the risk of lowering their standing in the eyes of the community. In using their bodies as commodities in the marketplace, they undermine their status and become vulnerable.[17]

The freedom-talk on display in *Ferreira* and *Jordan* – the Court's commitment to a form of autonomy that makes all individuals morally and legally culpable for actions that issue ineluctably from their circumstances – reflects the basic metaphysical commitments of the three dominant models of contemporary political theory in South African constitutional law.[18] All three models of contemporary political theory remain committed to free-will. None of the three theories do adequate justice to the nature of the decision-making processes of citizens in our constitutional democracy.[19] To put it differently, most of our citizens do not act – and could not act *even were it metaphysically possible* – in light of any of the models of agency or freedom upon which the Court's three dominant theories are predicated.

The three models of political theory ascribed to the Court rest upon a belief that the various rights and freedoms enshrined in the Final Constitution should enable individuals to exercise relatively *unfettered* control over decisions about the intimate relationships and the various collective practices deemed critical to their self-understanding. However, individual autonomy as a foundation for constitutional theory overemphasizes dramatically the actual space for self-defining choices. In truth, our experience of personhood, of self-consciousness, is a function of a complex set of social and natural narratives over which we exercise little in the way of (self) control. As I argue below in Chapter 2, the involuntary and *arational* nature of identity formation – at the level of both the individual and the social – deserves a constitutional theory (that supplants the model of a rational individual moral agent which undergirds much of our current jurisprudence) with a vision of the self that is more appropriately located within and determined by the networks, communities and associations to which we all belong and the universal natural grammar that we all inherit. In Chapters 4 and 7, I show how a fourth model of political theory – very much alive in our Court's jurisprudence – better fits both my conception of the self and the more congenial goal of flourishing. Flourishing recognizes simultaneously the radically heterogeneous, socially and physically constructed, nature of individual selves, the limited utility of 'freedom' as a description of individual behaviour, and the highly circumscribed nature of collective rationality.[20]

Our constitutional rights, as both constitutive of and the condition for flourishing, are not simply a constellation of negative duties owed by the state to each human subject, or a set of positive entitlements that can be claimed by each member of the polity. Rights bind us together as a polity. This rights-based polity can coalesce only under conditions of mutual recognition. This mutual recognition cannot be merely formal. The Court in *Khosa* notes that the Final Constitution commits us to an understanding of such rights as dignity, equality and social security in terms of which 'wealthier members of the community view the minimal well-being of the poor as connected with their personal well-being and the well-being of the community as a whole'.[21]

How then to comprehend constitutional rights as a collective concern (as opposed to rights against the state or some third party)? What the Court wishes us to understand is that for dignity to be meaningful in South Africa, the political community as a whole must provide that basket of goods – including such primary goods as civil and political rights – which each member of the community requires in order to flourish.[22] This conception of flourishing possesses striking similarities to Amartya Sen's development theory and Martha Nussbaum's capabilities approach. Moreover, the virtue of development theory and the capabilities approach is that one can accept the Constitutional Court's link between constitutional rights and the need for individual freedom from state intervention without accepting the proposition that the conditions for flourishing *only* demand individual freedom from state intervention. For example, Amartya Sen ties his notion of 'development as freedom' to the provision of a basic basket of goods that enables human beings to develop those 'capabilities' necessary for each individual to achieve those ends that *each* has reason to value.[23] Sen contends that the covalent norms of dignity and freedom and equality, rightly understood, are meant neither to achieve definitive outcomes nor to prescribe a univocal understanding of the good.[24] What these covalent values do require is a level of *material* support (e.g., food, water, health, housing) and *immaterial* support (e.g., the rule of law plus civil liberties as rights to fair trials, equality before the law, expression, association) that enable individuals to pursue a meaningful and comprehensive vision of the good – as those individuals understand the good.[25] Put another way, these covalent values should promote the political institutions and the material conditions required for individual and group flourishing.

2. *The Problem with the Folk Psychology of Freedom*

As RN McCauley writes:

> Folk psychology ('FP') is a network of principles which constitutes a sort of common-sense theory about how to explain human behavior. ... Folk psychology ... is deeply ingrained in our commonsense conception of ourselves as persons. Whatever else a person is, he is supposed to be a rational (at least largely rational) *agent* – that is, a creature whose behavior is systematically caused by, and explainable in terms of, his beliefs, desires, and related propositional attitudes. The wholesale rejection of FP, therefore, would entail a drastic revision of our conceptual scheme. This fact seems to us to constitute a good *prima facie* reason for not discarding FP too quickly in the face of apparent difficulties.[26]

This book's multi-faceted assault on principles of folk-psychology should loosen the tenacious hold that folk-psychological explanations of the self and the social have over us, show how that folk-psychology blocks better understandings of who we are as human beings, and demonstrate that the folk-psychology of freedom inhibits the formation of a fair and just political order in South Africa.

When it comes to explanations of the self, the social and the constitutional, the folk psychology of freedom suffers from flaws of epic proportions.[27] The standard folk psychology of freedom suggests, in a having your cake and eating it sort of way, that human beings are not subject to the laws of cause and effect to which every other object in the physical universe is subject. In a manner that goes entirely unexplained, an ostensibly immaterial entity (the soul or the mind) causes a material entity (the body) to undertake action in the world. Only by positing the presence of such an immaterial entity does the folk psychology of freedom liberate human beings from the yoke of determinism that attaches to all other material entities. But this strategy begs several other questions for which proponents of the folk psychology of freedom have no answers.

First, where is the 'mind' or the 'soul' located? It certainly is not, as Descartes suggested, located in the pineal gland. No other *scientific* answer is proffered. The scientific answer is that what we call 'self' or (its most obvious feature) 'consciousness' is actually the product of a neurological system that is (1) primarily unconscious, (2) distributed throughout the neuro-muscular system of the brain and the body, (3) engaged in multiple parallel processes, and (4) of enormous, highly under-utilized capacity.[28] The purpose of consciousness on this generally accepted account is three-fold: (a) 'durable and explicit information maintenance' (b) 'novel combinations of operations' and (c) 'intentional behavior'. As Daniel Dennett argues, our conscious beliefs function as 'idealized fictions' that enable us to engage in sophisticated 'action-predicting, action-explaining calculus'.[29]

Second, how does an immaterial entity (the self) cause a material entity (the body) to act? Once again, those who speak of the 'mind' or the 'soul' do not offer a physical explanation for this unique form of causality. Contemporary neuroscience, cognitive psychology and materialist theories of consciousness offer such an account. This explanation does away entirely with the need for an independent, immaterial entity like the soul.

Why then is the folk psychology of freedom so deeply embedded in our multiple ways of being in the world?[30] 'Free will' is essential for any system of social control. We inculcate a belief in free will – and thus in individual responsibility – in order to ensure greater compliance with the rules that the group, the society or the polity has set up to perpetuate itself. As Dennett writes:

> Instead of investigating, endlessly, in an attempt to discover whether or not a particular trait is of someone's making – instead of trying to assay exactly to what degree a particular self is self-made – we simply hold people responsible for their conduct (within limits we care not to examine too closely.) And we are rewarded for adopting this strategy by the higher proportion of 'responsible' behaviour we thereby inculcate.[31]

The Darwinian benefit (for the group, or the herd) of the myth of a community of freely willed selves flows from the action-predicting, action-explaining algorithms that the myth supplies (batteries not included.) When we operate under the myth (or even without the myth), we know what others will and will not do – if they play by the rules. Most generally do. This shared knowledge ensures greater likelihood of group success. The success of any individual is of limited concern.

However, the real breach – in so far as the folk psychology of free will is concerned – is between constructivism and experimentalism. Constructivism assumes that we, as individuals and communities, possess conscious awareness of most of the rules that govern our lives and that we can consiously plan for all future disruptions accordingly. Experimentalism, grounded in a determinist framework, recognizes that we lack such omniscience, that much of our knowledge is tacit, that we suffer from significant cognitive biases, and that the informal aggregation of knowledge along with a formal commitment to reflexivity with regard to our collective wisdom often produces better results. Most importantly, while it is modest about the limits of conscious individual and collective planning, experimentalism is quite immodest about the possibility of genuine change when multiple experiments regarding the same problems are allowed to occur and accurate information about the results of these experiments is collected and disseminated.

Advocates of constructivism and the adherents to the folk-psychology of free will would be utterly wrong to think that this Dennettian (Nietzchean) account eliminates freedom, choice or reason in any way that truly matters. Quite the opposite. As Dennett notes:

> At every level of organization, from the presumably hard-wired level of memory organization to the level of design of social institutions, the best possible designs, given the constraints of finitude and time pressure, would have to include some arbitrariness and wise risk taking. The (entirely unconscious) organization of memory guarantees that only some approximately appropriate subset of relevant points will occur to one in the time available.[32]

In this rather capacious space, in which risk and novel problem-solving often take on life and death significance, all the varieties of free will worth wanting reside. The human brain – the body as a whole – is an extraordinarily powerful problem-solving mechanism. Its uniqueness adheres in its ability to address and to overcome apparently insurmountable obstacles through complex neurological feedback mechanisms that enhance our ability to engage in abstract, future-oriented, action-predictive behaviour. Our problem-solving capacity – our regular inquiries about the nature of our environment, our ability to penetrate the future – is where our freedom ultimately resides. As a result, Dennett rightly claims that his conclusions about free will, though radically different from those explanations on offer from folk psychology, 'is optimistic'.[33] He writes:

> Free will is not an illusion, not even an irrepressible or life-enhancing illusion. When we look closely at the sources of our suspicion and dread, we find again and again that they are not indisputable axioms or overwhelmingly well-supported empirical discoveries, but unfocused images, hastily glanced at – like shadows on the bedroom wall that take on an apparent robustness and menace because we do not look at them closely. ... What we want when we want free will is the power to decide our courses of action, and to decide them wisely, in light of our expectations and desires. We want to be in control of ourselves, and not under the control of others. We want to be agents, capable of initiating, and taking responsibility for, projects and deeds. All this is ours, I have tried to show, as a natural product of our biological endowment, extended and enhanced by our initiation into society. ... We want, moreover, to have enough elbow room in the world so that when we exercise these powers, it is not always a matter of settling for the only desperate course of action that has a chance of fulfilling our desires. We can have this elbow room as well, and it is worth striving for, but not guaranteed. There are real threats to human freedom, but they are not metaphysical. There is political bondage, coercion, the manipulation inducible by the dissemination of misinformation, and the 'forced move' desperation of hunger and poverty. No doubt we could do a lot more to combat these impositions on our freedom, were it not for another sort of straightjacket we often find ourselves wearing: the curious sort of self-imposed bondage that we create by the very exercise of our freedom, and in the acknowledgement of our responsibility for the chains, ropes, strings and threads of commitment (explicit and tacit) that tie us to family and friends, that tie us to life projects, and that make us increasingly immovable by appeals for radical action.[34]

In the above paragraph, Dennett explains the power that the individual does possess: the capacity to build better mousetraps. Moreover, Dennett ties freedom to what really matters to us – the ability to *flourish*. Our efforts to eliminate poverty, hunger, coercion, manipulation and bondage are not aimed at freedom for freedom's sake. They are aimed at ensuring that all of us are able to pursue lives worth valuing. That is the essence of flourishing.

There is a sting in this tale – and one this book does not shy away from. Flourishing, in the main, is derived from active participation in the practises of the associations, communities and networks of which we are a part and the meaning with which these associations, communities and networks imbue our lives. (Flourishing likewise recognizes the extent to which our orientation toward the world is radically and naturally determined.) We do not so much choose such meaning as embrace it. So understood, flourishing forces us to steer a path between the Scylla of tradition (of the social and natural practices that give our lives meaning) and the Charybdis of revolution (the radical change in social and natural practices that will allow others heretofore subject to domination, oppression and discrimination to flourish as well.)

This account of freedom will not satisfy those wedded to the existence of a God-given soul. The reply: It coheres best with what we know about the physical world, the brain, the body, social phenomena, politics and the law.[35] It is the only account of freedom worth having.[36]

3. *Avoidance Gives Way to Empiricism*

Experimental constitutionalism relies heavily on co-operation between the co-ordinate branches of government and the citizens that they govern. The general norm-setting practiced by the courts and other branches of government is supplemented by various attempts by other state actors and non-state actors at crafting laws and policies designed to fulfil those constitutional norms. Over time, courts, state actors and non-state actors will have the opportunity to determine whether various political experiments have achieved the ends set for us by our basic law. We will, especially in instances of obvious policy failure, also have an opportunity to decide whether the norms or the ends set by the courts, the legislature, the executive and non-state actors constitute the best possible gloss on our basic law. (Finally, our circumscribed, reflexively understood experiments may tell us something critical about the virtues and the limitations of various tenets of our basic law, and suggest, in the latter case, what revisions to our basic law we ought to make.)

The embrace of the principle of avoidance by our courts and by a number of constitutional commentators poses a unique set of threats to the project of experimental constitutionalism. In its least pernicious form, the principle of avoidance has been articulated by the Constitutional Court in *Mhlungu* as follows: '[W]here it is possible to decide any case, civil or criminal, without reaching a constitutional issue, that is the course that should be followed.'[37] On its face, this salutary rule seems unobjectionable. What is objectionable, even on the Court's own terms, is turning this salutary rule into a full-blown jurisprudence in which a court must never 'formulate a rule of constitutional law broader than is required by the precise facts to which it is to be applied.'[38]

The *first objection* is that this early statement in *Mhlungu* flatly contradicts the Court's later statement in *Mhlungu* as to the nature of constitutional interpretation. The Constitutional Court in *Mhlungu* avers that constitutional interpretation takes the form of 'a principled judicial dialogue, in the first place between members of this Court, then between our Court and other courts, the legal profession, law schools, Parliament, and, indirectly, with the public at large.'[39] However, if a court refuses to say more than is necessary to decide a case on its facts, then one can hardly expect any meaningfully predictive principle to be drawn from the judgment.

That leads to the *second objection*. The lack of precision and almost casuistic approach to constitutional norm setting means that it is difficult for any actor – another lower court, a government official or a private actor – to anticipate future forms of law or conduct that would or would not satisfy the basic law's general norms. If there is no rule of law to which a state actor or private actor knows that she must conform her behaviour, then it would be surprising to find her attempting to conform her behaviour to some unarticulated and inchoate sense of a 'rule' that is consistent with the Constitutional Court's understanding of what the Final Constitution permits. (This problem continues to arise as a result of the Court's flirtation with the notion of subsidiarity.[40])

Thus, the *third objection.* The absence of rules of law undermines the ability of other branches of government to comply with the Bill of Rights. It places the court in the unnecessarily uncomfortable position of having to reject or to accept the government's positions in every case as if it were ruling *ab initio.*

Such considerations constitute some of the strongest arguments against a jurisprudence of 'judicious avoidance'.[41] The *fourth objection* against avoidance is that the absence of clearly articulated rules undermines the optimal conditions for (rational) political and social decision-making. The incompletely theorized agreements that are the mainstay of minimalism (not South African inflected 'judicious avoidance') were explained by Sunstein (almost two decades ago) as follows:

> A minimalist court settles the case before it, but leaves many things undecided. It is alert to the existence of reasonable agreement in a heterogeneous society. It knows that there is much that it does not know; it is intensely aware of its own limitations. It seeks to decide cases on narrow grounds. ... Alert to the problem of unanticipated consequences, it sees itself as part of a system of democratic deliberation; it attempts to promote the democratic ideals of participation, deliberation and responsiveness. It allows for continued space for democratic reflection from Congress and the states. It wants to accommodate new judgments about facts and values.

However, Sunstein's minimalism only secures traction because it is parasitic upon a deep and widely shared set of norms and recognizes the necessity of a solid core. 'In American constitutional law at the turn of the century', he writes, 'a distinctive set of substantive ideals now form that core'.[42]

More importantly, Sunstein no longer offers (what appeared to be) an account of judicial deliberation as the primary impediment to optimal individual, social and political decision-making.[43] Consistent with the findings of a broad array of natural and social scientists, Sunstein identifies deliberation and grand theorizing as but two of a variety of 'thought processes' subject to biases that lead to sub-optimal solutions.[44] Sunstein endorses decision-making methods – such as choice architecture – that produce more accurate assessments and better solutions to problems on substantially larger scales than those dispute-driven quandries faced by courts of law limited to binary oppositions that often yield zero-sum outcomes.[45] For the empiricist Sunstein, markets, though imperfect, often rely upon limited, shared information (sometimes no more than price) and generate substantially more efficient, and *thicker* outcomes. (He never denies, of course, that markets are often subject to devastatingly painful corrections – as we are experiencing now.) But we should always choose well-regulated socially democratic state-led corrections of market failures (read Iceland, circa 2008 – 2012) over extremely long-term corrections to hideous, centrally-planned Nazi Germany, Stalinist Russia, or Maoist China statecraft any day. Some open-source software, like Linux, produces incredibly rich results without any central planning. The web itself – the environment for Linux – produces both optimal and suboptimal outcomes, depending on how information is solicited, how it is aggregated and how further co-operative endeavours are organized.

Thinness is, therefore, no longer a virtue (if it ever was.) It may be of limited value within systems with information deficits or significant distortions in the manner in which decision-makers use the information that they possess. As the better part of this book suggests, a growing contingent of constitutional law scholars have recognized that problems of information deficit, lack of cross-cultural understanding and limited institutional competence can be 'solved' by a subtle recasting of existing constitutional doctrines and judicial remedies that extract better information, aggregate that information more effectively and thereby achieve *more mindful* results.[46]

The problem with Sunstein's initial articulation of minimalism was its propensity to be misunderstood.[47] At least one sitting justice on the South African Constitutional Court stated, in a public forum, that 'judicial avoidance' was and remains attractive for members of the Constitutional Court exactly because it does not require the eleven justices to possess a core of shared understandings.[48] Whether Sunstein should be on the hook for such misapprehensions is neither here nor there.[49]

This much can be said. Reasoned disagreement can only take place when parties agree on the general terms of the debate. The Constitutional Court must, in terms of its institutional role, establish the contours of constitutional norms and thus the general framework for contestation. The Constitutional Court abdicates this institutional responsibility to model rational political discourse when it refuses to state, in a reasonably comprehensive manner, the reasons that ground its conclusions.

A *fifth objection* is that avoidance undermines the integrity of the legal system.[50] It is impossible to create a more coherent jurisprudence without identifying the rules – and the reasons – that ground decisions.[51]

Chapters 4 through 8 demonstrate why experimental constitutionalism – with its commitment to shared constitutional interpretation and participatory bubbles – abhors a jurisprudence of avoidance. Shared constitutional interpretation relies, fundamentally, upon principled, yet reflexive, exchanges between the courts, various branches of government, and the public. The process of general norm-setting by the courts that initiates a process of rolling best practices by other parts of the state never gains sufficient traction when constitutional norms remain radically under-theorized. Participatory bubbles rely, on the other hand, on a court-initiated structure to ensure that meaningful engagement about optimal outcomes takes place. These bubbles lose their cohesion – and the pressure to produce better than zero-sum outcomes – if the courts fail to articulate the norms within which a preferred solution is meant to occur. If experimental constitutionalism and governance are judged to be an attractive set of principles by which to establish political norms (by widespread public agreement) and to assess best practices (by inviting as many stakeholders as possible to design an optimal remedy for a specific social problem) then the jurisprudence of avoidance must be one of the first judicial doctrines to go.[52]

Endnotes

1. See *Prince v President, Cape Law Society* 2002 (2) SA 794 (CC), 2002 (1) SACR 431 (CC), 2002 (3) BCLR 231 (CC)(Rastafarian use of cannabis in religious ritual justifiably impaired by criminal sanctions because the legislature has power and duty to enact legislation prohibiting conduct considered by it

to be anti-social – whether court agrees with this assessment or not)('*Prince*'); *S v Jordan (Sex Workers Education and Advocacy Task Force and others as Amici Curiae)* 2002 (6) SA 642 (CC), 2002 (2) SACR 499 (CC), 2002 (11) BCLR 1117 (CC)(Women's right to engage in commercial transactions involving sex, though private and often involving economically marginalized classes, deemed insufficient to outweigh the state's interest in proscription through criminal sanction)('*Jordan*'); *Christian Education South Africa v Minister of Education* 2000 (4) SA 757 (CC), 2000 (10) BCLR 1051 (CC)(Court assumes, for the purposes of analyzing the constitutionality of the use of corporal punishment by teachers, that FC ss 15 and 31 have been infringed; however upon proceeding to limitations analysis, the Court explains why the state is justified in barring corporal punishment and why the court is justified in not crafting an order creating a religious exemption for such punishment)('*Christian Education*').

2. Classical liberalism stresses the capacity of separate, independent selves to choose the aims and attachments by which they will define themselves. As a chooser, 'the [liberal] self', as John Rawls has written, 'is prior to the ends which are affirmed by it; even a dominant end must be chosen from among numerous possibilities.' *A Theory of Justice* (1971) 3-4. In fairness to Rawls, the quote from *Theory* may be misleading. He has never been a classical liberal as that position is described in these pages. See J Rawls *Political Liberalism* (1993); J Rawls 'The Domain of the Political and Overlapping Consensus' (1989) 64 *New York University Law Review* 233. Similar justifications for liberalism appear to rely upon comparable notions of agency. See P Lenta 'Taking Diversity Seriously: Religious Associations and Work-Related Discrimination' (2009) 125 *South African Law Journal* 828. Lenta writes: 'Another way to capture the significance of freedom [of liberty] … is to frame it as a matter of diversity.' William Galston, as Lenta notes, has argued that 'properly understood, liberalism is about the protection of diversity'. W Galston *Liberal Pluralism: The Implications of Value Pluralism for Political Theory and Practice* (2002) 111, 523. Lenta then invokes Justice William Brennan's justification for liberalism in *Roberts v United States Jaycees*: '[Not only is liberalism designed] to 'foster diversity' … 'An individual's freedom to speak [and] to worship … could not be vigorously protected from interference by the State unless a correlative freedom to engage in group effort toward those ends were not also guaranteed. According protection to collective effort on behalf of shared goals is especially important in preserving political and cultural diversity.' 468 US 609, 619, 622 (1984). Galston, Brennan and Lenta all beg the question as to why we should value diversity – especially where it runs against the grain of egalitarian desires to protect such historically disadvantaged groups such as gays and lesbians. Don't we – as constitutive liberals *and* egalitarian pluralists – know, morally and empirically, everything we need to know about a gay person's entitlement to be treated with equal dignity and respect? The answer lies in three places: (1) a person must actually have the ability to exit a repressive community; (2) we, as members of various communities and non-members of others, must have the ability to see what 'fits' or 'works' best for us; and (3) we should know generally what counts as an unjustifiable impairment of dignity. See S Woolman 'On the Fragility of Associational Life: A Constitutive Liberal's Response to Patrick Lenta (2009) 25 *South African Journal on Human Rights* 58. For all that, little distinguishes Professor Lenta's positions from my own. For a hard-charging, but slightly off the mark, radically egalitarian critique of positions adopted by Patrick Lenta and myself, see D Bilchitz 'Should Religious Associations Be Allowed to Discriminate?' (2011) 27 *South African Journal on Human Rights* 219. See, in reply, S Woolman 'Seek Justice Elsewhere: An Egalitarian Pluralist Reply to David Bilchitz on the Distinction between Differentiation and Domination' (2012) 28 *South African Journal on Human Rights* 271. Initial and remaining differences aside, I am grateful to Professor Bilchitz for pushing me to describe the egalitarian pluralism that underlies this book and other works in a far more nuanced fashion. His own more nuanced, well developed account can be found at, D Bilchitz 'Why Courts Should Not Sanction Unfair Discrimination in the Private Sphere, (2012) 28 *South African journal on Human Rights* 296.

3. *Ferreira v Levin* 1996 (1) SA 984 (CC), 1996 (1) BCLR 1 (CC)('*Ferreira*').
4. *Du Plessis v De Klerk* 1996 (3) SA 850 (CC), 1996 (5) BCLR 658(CC)('*Du Plessis*').
5. *Barkhuizen v Napier* 2007 (5) SA 323 (CC), 2007 (7) BCLR 691 (CC). See also *African Dawn Property Finance 2 (Pty) Ltd v Dreams Travel and Tours CC & Others* 2011 (3) SA 511 (SCA). For a critique of the

classically liberal politics that drive *Barkhuizen,* see D Bhana 'The Law of Contract and the Constitution: *Napier v Barkhuizen*' (2007) 124 *South African Journal on Human Rights* 269. While Professor Bhana's analysis of the politics underlying the judgment is accurate, far more persuasive arguments are available, see S Woolman 'Category Mistakes and the Waiver of Constitutional Rights: A Response to Deeksha Bhana on *Barkhuizen*' (2008) 125 *South African Law Journal* 10. For a more recent critique of the conservative common law inflected approach adopted by the Constitutional Court, the Supreme Court of Appeal and the High Courts, see F Michelman 'Eviction, Expropriation and the Gravity of the Common Law', (Constitution Hill, 21 July 2012), currently available at http://papers.ssrn.com/sol3/papers.cfm?abstract_id=2116643. (A final version of this paper will appear in (2013) 25 (2) *Stellenbosch Law Review* and a festschrift, S Woolman and K Van Marle (eds) *Frank I Michelman's Imagination and South Africa's Constitutional Jurisprudence* (2013).)

6. That this body of learning occupies such a central place in the Court's jurisprudence is poetically just. The majority of the *Ferreira* Court rejected Justice Ackermann's libertarian take of what 'freedom' in the right to 'freedom and security of the person' meant. At the very least, it rejected this analysis with respect to the text of the Interim Constitution. However, the Court's early judgments on the meaning of equality and dignity under the Final Constitution ultimately vindicate Justice Ackermann's understanding of negative liberty by recasting it in terms of dignity. In finding the common law criminalization of sodomy a violation of the right to dignity, the *NCGLE I* Court wrote, '[I]t is clear that the constitutional protection of dignity requires us to acknowledge the value and the worth of all individuals as members of society.' *National Coalition for Gay and Lesbian Equality v Minister of Justice* 1999 (1) SA 6 (CC), 1998 (12) BCLR 1517 (CC) at paras 28. Moreover, the Court argued, 'the rights of equality and dignity are closely related, as are the rights of dignity and privacy.' Ibid at para 30. Individual freedom – negative liberty – thus becomes the foundation for dignity. Dignity, in turn, becomes the basis for equality. As the Court writes in *Prinsloo*: 'In our view unfair discrimination [the linchpin of equality analysis]... principally means treating people differently in a way which impairs their fundamental dignity as human beings, who are inherently equal in dignity.' *Prinsloo v Van der Linde* 1997 (3) SA 1012 (CC), 1997 (6) BCLR 759 (CC). If the link between *individual* freedom, and dignity and then equality is still not clear, the *Hugo* Court writes: '[D]ignity is at the heart of individual rights in a free and democratic society... [E]quality ... means nothing if it does not represent a commitment to each person's equal worth as a human being, regardless of their differences. Equality means that our society cannot tolerate legislative distinctions that treat certain people as second-class citizens.' *President of the Republic of South Africa v Hugo* 1997 (4) SA 1 (CC), 1997 (1) SACR 567 (CC), 1997 (6) BCLR 708 (CC). For further analysis of the relationship between equality and dignity, see C Albertyn and B Goldblatt 'Equality' in S Woolman & M Bishop (eds) *Constitutional Law of South Africa* (2nd Edition, OS, 2006) Chapter 35; S Cowan 'Can Dignity Guide Our Equality Jurisprudence?' (2001) 17 *South African Journal on Human Rights* 34. But see S Woolman 'Dignity' in S Woolman & M Bishop (eds) *Constitutional Law of South Africa* (2nd Edition, OS, March 2006) Chapter 36 (Contends that Court's reading of dignity need not end with self-actualization, but clearly embraces a commitment to democratic solidarity in such cases as *Khosa & Others v Minister of Social Development & Others; Mahlaule & Others v Minister of Social Development & Others* 2004 (6) SA 505 (CC), 2004 (6) BCLR 569 (CC). See, more recently, *Juma Musjid Primary School & Others v Ahmed Asruff Essay NO & Others* [2011] ZACC 13, 2011 (8) BCLR 761 (CC).

7. Critics of the early Court's work contended that the dignity inflected right to equality rendered the latter too elastic to do meaningful work. See D Davis 'Equality: The Majesty of Legoland Jurisprudence' (1999) 116 *South African Law Journal* 398, 412 – 413 ('The court has given dignity both the content and scope that make for a piece of jurisprudential Lego-Land to be used in whatever form and shape is required by the demands of the judicial designer.') For the articulation of similar concerns with respect to German jurisprudence, see D Kommers *The Constitutional Jurisprudence of the Federal Republic of Germany* (2nd Edition, 1997) 300-301, 312-313 (The anteriority of the right to dignity to the state complicates judicial control of the concept); S Wermiel 'Law and Human

Dignity: The Judicial Soul of Justice Brennan' (1998) 7 *William and Mary Bill of Rights Journal* 223. See, further, C Taylor 'What's Wrong with Negative Liberty' *Philosophy and the Human Sciences: Philosophical Papers* 2 (1985) 211, 213. The classical liberal account, evinced in the Constitutional Court's early jurisprudence, defines individual autonomy primarily in terms of non-interference by other individuals or the state. This view wrongly identifies flourishing as 'a matter of what we can do, of what is open to us to do' without external restraints. Taylor (supra) at 213. If we instead identify individual flourishing with self-realization, then we may be forced to realize that such control is not solely a function of the absence of external constraints, but also involves overcoming internal barriers as well. (The explanation of, and examples of, feedback mechanisms and error correction in Chapters 2 and 3 explain why this is so.) As Charles Taylor argues, even a classical liberal view of autonomy requires us to discriminate between, and make judgments about, those restrictions which serve significant or important goals, and those which do not. For example, we do not see traffic stop signs and speed limits as significant obstacles to self-realization, but we will likely view restrictions on religion as significant obstacles to flourishing. The point is that even a constitutional state committed to negative liberty forces its citizens to identify some purposes as important for flourishing, and others as unimportant or unrelated to individual self-realization. The upshot of this thesis is that a person's claim that she is doing what she says she wants to do doesn't mean that she should be read as having flourished. Other people may have a better idea of what my own interests are and what will truly enable me to flourish. Thus, contrary to Berlin and classical liberals, Taylor contends that 'we cannot maintain the incorrigibility of the subject's judgments about his freedom, or rule out second-guessing.' Ibid at 228. (Again: the recasting of freedom discourse in terms of error correction, social feedback mechanisms and flourishing reinforces this controversial thesis.) As Taylor points out, all individual actions are in some way addressed towards other individuals and groups with whom they are involved. Since the meaning of any action is often assigned within socially determined horizons of meaning (loosely speaking), other individuals to whom the actions are addressed can have something meaningful to say about the rightness or the wrongness of those actions. *The Ethics of Authenticity* (1992) (I just happen to think that those horizons of meaning are rather broad and widely shared – and that disagreements occur primarily at the margin.) A similar constellation of arguments may be arrayed against the classically liberal position that politics is not the most suitable arena for individual and group value construction. The critique of this political position is that the classical liberal view of autonomy – that people live their lives in accordance with personal ideals - simply operates as a justification for doing what one likes without the need for rational explanation for one's acts to others. The response of a modest, naturalised account of flourishing is that while there is an undeniably justifiable attachment to the belief that the ability of each person to live (largely) as she likes and to author her own law is a necessary condition of a free society, it does not follow that every individual choice is morally or politically justifiable. See J Nedelsky 'Reconceiving Autonomy: Sources, Thoughts and Possibilities' in A Hutchinson & L Green (eds) *Law and the Community: The End of Individualism?* (1994) 219, 220–1, 223. What all persons committed to flourishing ought to say is that while value choice is a precondition of flourishing, not every choice is worthy of praise or is politically desirable. These conclusions regarding the flaws of classical liberalism and other forms of liberalism support the following propositions for experimental constitutionalism, and the modest, naturalised account of flourishing upon which it rests. First, members of a given polity can have meaningful disagreements about political ideals and the extent to which particular practices conform to the ideals to which a polity has committed itself in such public documents as a Constitution. Second, such disagreements can sometimes make a difference in the way others see us, the way we see others, and the way we live together. Third, disagreements and their resolution through deliberation alone rarely convince us to see the world differently: More often, however, it is action, and seeing how others construct their world, that makes for the most compelling argument. See M Nussbaum *Upheavals of Thought: The Intelligence of Emotions* (2001); M Nussbaum *Love's Knowledge* (1991). See also H Arendt *The Human Condition* (1961). My understanding of action, unlike Arendt's vision, is not one which requires mobilization of the citizenry around noble goals. It has the more modest aim of enabling all members of society to (a) have their basic needs met so that (b) they might engage in meaningful action that (c) would count as evidence for or against a way of living in the world and (d) at a minimum expand the range of conditioned choices available in a polity. See A Sen *Development as Freedom* (2009); A Sen *The Idea of Justice* (2010); A Sen *Commodities and Capabilities* (1985); A Sen & M Nussbaum (eds) *The Quality of Life* (1993); M Nussbaum *Creating Capabilities: The Human Development Approach* (2011); *M Nussbaum Women and Human Development: The Capabilities Approach* (2000); M Nussbaum 'Constitutions and Capabilities: Perception against Lofty Formalism' (2007) 121 *Harvard Law Review* 4.

8. For jurisprudential accounts based upon a strong agency model consistent with social democratic theory, see D Meyerson *Rights Limited* (1996); J Rawls *Political Liberalism* (1993).

9. See *National Coalition for Gay and Lesbian Equality v Minister of Justice* 1999 (1) SA 6 (CC), 1998 (12) BCLR 1517 (CC)('*NGCLE I*'); *National Coalition for Gay and Lesbian Equality v Minister of Home Affairs* 2000 (2) SA 1, 41 (CC), 2000 (1) BCLR 39 (CC)('*NGCLE II*').

10. *Merafong Demarcation Forum & Others v President of the Republic of South Africa & Others* [2008] ZACC 10, 2008 (5) SA 171 (CC), 2008 (10) BCLR 968 (CC); *Occupiers of 51 Olivia Road, Berea Township and 197 Main Street Johannesburg v City of Johannesburg & Others* [2008] ZACC 1, 2008 (3) SA 208 (CC), 2008 5 BCLR 475 (CC); *Residents of Joe Slovo Community, Western Cape v Thubelisha Homes & Others* [2009] ZACC 16, 2010 (3) SA 454 (CC), 2009 (9) BCLR 847 (CC); *Abahlali Basemjondolo Movement SA & Another v Premier of the Province of Kwazulu-Natal & Others* [2009] ZACC 31, 2010 (2) BCLR 99 (CC); *Head of Department, Mpumalanga Department of Education and Another v Hoërskool Ermelo & Another* 2010 (2) SA 415 (CC), 2010 (3) BCLR 177 (CC). For defenses of a social democratic state tied to ideal speech conditions and strong accounts of individual agency, see D Davis *Democracy and Deliberation* (2000); J Habermas *Between Facts and Norms: A Discourse Theory of Law and Democracy* (1997). The Court's dignity and socio-economic rights jurisprudence evinces a strong social democratic political theory – but one still unnecessarily pinned, in many places, to the metaphysical commitments of freedom and the unencumbered self that comes under attack in these pages. For a discussion of cases emphasizing self-actualization and self-governance, see S Woolman 'Dignity' in S Woolman & M Bishop (eds) *Constitutional Law of South Africa* (2nd Edition, OS, December 2005) Chapter 36.

11. *Ferreira* (supra) at 1013–1014.

12. *Jordan* (supra) at paras 16–17.

13. S Woolman & M Bishop 'State as Pimp: Sexual Slavery in South Africa' (2006) 23 *Development Southern Africa* 385.

14. See S Woolman 'Freedom of Association' in S Woolman & M Bishop (eds) *Constitutional Law of South Africa* (2nd Edition, OS, December 2003) Chapter 44. See also S Woolman and M Bishop 'Slavery, Servitude and Forced Labour' in S Woolman & M Bishop (eds) *Constitutional Law of South Africa* (2nd Edition, OS, December 2005) Chapter 64. My pithy point is that Constitutional Court judges, in capitalist economies, also commodify their bodies. No more or less stigma should attach to their 'lofty' work *qua* commodification than the 'dirty deeds' of sex workers.

15. *Jordan* (supra) at para 16.

16. See, further, N Fritz 'Crossing Jordan: Constitutional Space for (Un)Civil Sex?' (2004) 20 *South African Journal on Human Rights* 230. See also V Barolsky et al *Understanding the Dimensions of Human Trafficking in Southern Africa*, (2010).

17. *Jordan* (supra) paras 16–17.

18. A fourth position – largely, but not entirely, inconsistent with the space for private ordering required by South Africa's Constitution – could be described as communitarian. See, e.g., M Sandel *Liberalism and the Limits of Justice* (1982); A MacIntyre *After Virtue* (1984); M Walzer *Spheres of Justice* (1983); C Taylor 'Atomism' *Philosophical Papers II: Philosophy and the Human Sciences* (1991); IM Young 'The Ideal of Community and the Politics of Difference' in *Throwing Like a Girl and Other Essays* (1991). Only BMW Bolsheviks and Rolls Royce radicals in South Africa attempt to squeeze far left ideology into a

document that rightly recognizes a significant degree of private ordering. As a philosophical matter, communitarianism largely receded as a significant critique of liberalism because, for the most part, liberal theory absorbed the original Sandelian critique that liberalism relies upon a fiction of persons always capable of rationally ordering their preferences in a manner that maximizes utility. See, e.g., C Larmore *Patterns of Moral Complexity* (1987); J Cohen *Rules of the Game* (1986); J Cohen & J Rogers *Associations and Democracy* (1995); J Cohen, A Fung and E Elgar (eds) *Constitutionalism, Democracy, and State Power: Promise and Performance* (1996); A Gutmann *Freedom of Association* (ed)(1998). It's also important to note that communitarianism lost much of its force with the fall of the Berlin Wall and the dissolution of the Soviet Union. All of a sudden capitalist democracies, committed to human rights, had the ideological field almost entirely to themselves. China, if anything, represents classic mercantilism and a state run oligopoly. Whether the philosophical landscape will again shift as a result of the recent crisis in capitalist economies post-2008 remains to be seen. It goes without saying then, that this book falls squarely within the liberal tradition, but it's a liberalism that has absorbed the contributions of egalitarian pluralists such as Walzer and Taylor. For more on how liberalism has absorbed the critiques levelled against it by communitarianism and postmodernism, see S Benhabib *Situating the Self* (1992) (Benhabib does not argue from within the liberal tradition, but, as a feminist, who grounds her ethical theory in universal principles.) Against the classical liberal, the welfare state liberal, and the social democratic liberal, Sandel-like communitarians pit an encumbered theory of the self. In this account, individuals are born into existing political communities, and have their identities or selves created or conditioned by a vast network of political practices. The primary, and most important, difference between the social democratic politics of flourishing and experimental constitutionalism defended here and the communitarian account is how and where they locate the self in relation to the communities out of which the self's primary understandings are constructed. My account recognizes the sources of the self as radically heterogeneous. The self and its sources are made up of linguistic, religious, social, class, racial, ethnic, gender, national and political groupings which may overlap, but which are never identical, and which often conflict with one another. Communitarians (a) tend to privilege the political community over other communities, and underplay existing and historical conflicts between the various communities that source the self, or (b) entirely elide the difference between the polity and other communities that make up a society. For example, George Fletcher writes: 'In a patriotic society, where all individuals share a common past and purpose, each can identify with others and find in them an equal partner in a common cause. The rooting of the self in a culture of loyalty enables individuals to grasp the humanity of their fellow citizens and to treat them as bearers of equal rights.' *Loyalty* (1993) 21 (my emphasis). Fletcher's prose is a perfect example of what might be called the *communitarian shuffle*: the easy move back and forth between discussions about society and polity that obscures the fact that the two are not co-extensive - that polities contain multiple societies, sub-publics and cultures, and that cultures, sub-publics and societies are often rooted in a variety of different states. The difference is important. The communitarian privileging of the state over other communities within the state - or in some cases conflating the state and those communities – has significant repercussions for individual and group flourishing, as well as the construction of the self. Once shared pasts, united purposes and common causes are assumed, the state is further free to assume that important differences between its citizens and the smaller communities (or larger transnational communities) of which they are a part do not exist. Once pluralism is no longer a concern, there is no reason for individual and group flourishing to be. The state is then truly free to impose a more homogenous and standardized way of life. David Bilchitz makes a similar error in an article that extols the putative benefits of reading the South African Constitution as reflective of and committed to a radically egalitarian polity. See D Bilchitz 'Should Religious Associations be Allowed to Discriminate?' (2011) 27 *South African Journal Human Rights* 219. First, his original position begs a host of unanswered questions about a founding document committed to the simultaneous realization of three basic non-covalent values – dignity, equality and freedom – and a host of civil and political rights (from expression to religious practice to property) that require a significant degree of private ordering. Second, exactly what polity does Professor Bilchitz have in mind?

The South African polity in which the current President (then Deputy President) Jacob Zuma tells an audience in KwaZulu-Natal that he would know how to 'take care of those moffies'? The Constitutional Court as led by a Chief Justice whose express religious beliefs would make gays and lesbians pariahs in their own land? The vast majority of individual members of South Africa's heterogeneous array of sub-publics who adhere to extremely traditional (read conservative) values and who, if asked to vote directly, would likely deny gay and lesbian members of our society the equal rights vouchsafed in the Constitution? A strong democratic experimentalist, on the other hand, retains a commitment to a thinner conception of the good: the creation of institutions that vouchsafe rough equality with respect to the distribution of basic opportunities and essential goods and a pluralist's bounded toleration of other more comprehensive visions of the good. The role of the strong democratic experimentalist state thus remains the mediation of disputes between different individuals and communities with different visions of the good, and roughly equal support for decidedly different visions of the good, even as its basic law (and the institutions that support it) presses upon various publics a politics that can best be described as 'rough egalitarian pluralism'. See S Woolman 'Seek Justice Elsewhere: An Egalitarian Pluralist's Reply to David Bilchitz on the Distinction between Differentiation and Domination' (2012) 28 *South African Journal on Human Rights* 273.

19. The constitutional theories adumbrated by Davis and Habermas are perhaps closest to the mark. See D Davis *Democracy and Deliberation* (2000); J Habermas *Between Facts and Norms: A Discourse Theory of Law and Democracy* (1997). The kind of limits on individual rationality and autonomy described herein must place some meaningful limits on one's expectations regarding reasoned political discourse – especially deliberation at the margins. This book supplants a commitment to rationality and ideal speech situations with a cautious experimentalism. Of course, either way one goes, the success of the entire constitutional enterprise depends to a large degree on shared normative assumptions. See S Woolman 'On the Common Saying "What's True in Golf is True in Law": The Relationship between Theory and Practice across Forms of Life' (2010) 25 *Southern African Public Law* 520.

20. See S Woolman 'Freedom of Association' in S Woolman & M Bishop (eds) *Constitutional Law of South Africa* (2nd Edition, OS, December 2003) Chapter 44; S Woolman 'Dignity' in S Woolman & M Bishop (eds) *Constitutional Law of South Africa* (2nd Edition, OS, December 2005) Chapter 36. For a similar set of views, offered from a slightly different philosophical perspective, see K van Marle 'Law's Time, Particularity and Slowness' (2003) 19 *South African Journal on Human Rights* 239 (Van Marle shows how greater attentiveness – slowness – promotes a deeper understanding of the requirements of justice.)

21. *Khosa* (supra) at para 74. The Court's language echoes Rawls' description of a Kantian 'realm of ends' in which: 'Everyone recognizes everyone else as not only honouring their obligation of justice and duties of virtue, but also, as it were, legislating law for their moral commonwealth. For all know of themselves and of the rest that they are reasonable and rational, and that this fact is mutually recognized.' J Rawls *Lectures on the History of Moral Philosophy* (2001) 209. See also S Doctor 'Dignity, Criminal Law and the Bill of Rights' (2004) 121 *South African Law Journal* 265, 315 ('Dignity has a communitarian aspect: by requiring respect for others' claims to dignity, vindication of the human dignity of all is better assured, and a community of mutual co-operation and solidarity is fostered.')

22. See D Bilchitz *Poverty and Fundamental Rights* (2006).

23. See A Sen *Development as Freedom* (1999)('*Development*'); A Sen *Inequality Re-examined* (1992); A Sen *The Idea of Justice* (2010).

24. Sen's relationship to classical schools of political philosophy is far too subtle to be explicated meaningfully here. However, a précis of his positions may suggest why Sen, of all contemporary theorists, offers an account of dignity, equality and freedom that provides the best fit with my own take on these 'three conjoined, reciprocal and covalent values' and my ultimate commitment to flourishing. *S v Mamabolo* 2001 (3) SA 409 (CC), 2001 (5) BCLR 449 (CC), 2001 (1) SACR 686 (CC) at para 41. Sen rejects Rawls' (Kantian and deontological) contention in *A Theory of Justice* (1972) – and to a lesser degree in

Political Liberalism (1993) – that there are certain primary goods – civil liberties such as expression, assembly, the franchise – that 'cannot be compromised in any way.' Sen *Development* (supra) at 64. Sen has even less time for utilitarian frameworks that make the greatest good for the greatest number the measure of justice. In addition to offering standard criticisms of utilitarianism – its inability to arrive at an acceptable metric for interpersonal comparisons of happiness, its general indifference to radical inequality in the distribution of happiness, and its neglect of rights, freedoms and other non-utility-based concerns – Sen inveighs against the general inclination, especially amongst economists, to measure utility or happiness in terms of wealth (e.g., GNP) and wealth in terms of income (per capita). Neither wealth nor income provides adequate information about the well-being and the substantive capacities and life chances of individuals. Both liberals and utilitarians fail to take account of how individual differences – in physical ability or disability, in environment, in social practices, in family structure – create significant asymmetries in the manner in which primary goods and incomes can be exploited. Ibid. at 73. Sen's theory of distributive justice accounts for how the heterogeneity amongst individuals (both within societies and across societies) shapes the meaning of primary goods *and* incomes. For example, the meaning of a primary political good like freedom of assembly will have demonstrably different meanings for a person who is ambulatory and for a person who is not ambulatory, but housebound. Similarly, the utility of an income of R200 000 may have a demonstrably different value for a person who is ambulatory and for a person who is not ambulatory, but housebound. At a minimum, says Sen, quoting Adam Smith, our primary concern ought to be with providing individuals with those necessities of life that will give them '"the ability to appear in public without shame".' Ibid at 73 quoting A Smith *The Wealth of Nations* (1776)(RH Campbell and AS Skinner)(eds) (1976) 469 – 471. That, in just a few well-chosen words, sounds very much like South African discourse on dignity. Sen thus shifts our focus to the actual 'freedom generated by commodities', and away from 'commodities seen on their own,' to the actual freedom generated by civil liberties, and away from formal constitutionally enshrined civil rights viewed in the abstract. Ibid. at 74. Sen argues that the best measure of equality or freedom or dignity is the ability of individuals to *convert* such primary goods as *income* or *civil liberties* into the capability 'to choose a life one has reason to value' – or in simpler terms, the ability to pursue one's own ends. Ibid at 75. That is, in sum, how I understand flourishing. The virtue of Sen's approach is that it recognizes (a) the heterogeneity of capacity that people possess by virtue of biology, custom, or class; (b) the heterogeneity of critical functions – from nourishment to civic participation – that may be required to live a life one has reason to value; and (c) the heterogeneity of capabilities that people will possess – different combinations of more basic functions – which will, in turn, enable them to pursue different 'lifestyles' or different visions of the good. For an account of flourishing that gave rise to much of contemporary development and capabilities theory, see Martha Nussbaum's wonderful essay '"Finely Aware and Richly Responsible": Moral Attention and the Moral Task of Literature' (1986) 82 *The Journal of Philosophy* 516.

25. Sen *Development* (supra) at 75. See also D Cornell *Defending Ideals: War, Democracy, and Political Struggle* (2004).
26. RN McCauley 'Folk Psychology is Here to Stay' (1985) 94 *The Philosophical Review* 197, 198.
27. See P Churchland 'Eliminative Materialism and Propositional Attitudes' in SM Christensen & DR Turner (eds) *Folk Psychology and the Philosophy of Mind* (1993) 42; P Feyerabend 'Materialism and the Mind-Body Problem' in SM Christensen & DR Turner (eds) *Folk Psychology and the Philosophy of Mind* (1993) 3, 15 ('Is it then possible to reject materialism by reference to the success of a non-materialistic language? The answer is NO and the reason … is as follows: in order to discuss the weaknesses of an all-pervasive system of thought such as is expressed by the 'common' idiom, it is not sufficient to compare it with 'the facts.' Many such facts are formulated in terms of the idiom and therefore already prejudiced in its favour.') For a far more recent defence of materialism and ethics based upon a third party perspective provided by neuroscience, see Patricia Churchland's recent work: P Churchland *Braintrust: What Neuroscience Tells Us about Morality* (2011). What Feyeraband cavalierly dismissed as an 'idiom' employed by both Paul Churchland and Patricia Churchland two decades

ago now has a hefty body of evidence to support many of its original claims. Where is Feyeraband's evidence in support of non-materialistic language? Certainly, others, 'the new mysterians', have taken up his cause. See C McGinn *The Mysterious Flame: Conscious Minds in a Material World* (2000); J Searle *Making the Social World: The Structure of Human Civilization* (2010); D Chalmers *The Character of Consciousness* (2010). McGinn's theory of 'cognitive closure' runs, briefly, as follows: the multitude of tasks that the human mind or brain can carry out does not include the ability to explain how consciousness works. Given the new found capacity of individual human brains, enhanced with computer chips, to move objects or to answer questions without verbal or motor responses by the individual (but through the brain implants), it seems a little early to give up on what Descartes started. Forty odd years of experiments have demonstrated that Locke was clearly wrong about the possibility of inverted colour spectra – a belief about qualia (the stuff of consciousness) maintained by philosophers for almost 300 years. According to the Lockean view, we could never tell what colours another person experienced (is your blue, my blue?) or what colours human beings experience as truly primary. The answer to the last question is four: red, blue, yellow and green. See S Palmer 'Consciousness and Isomorphism: Can the Colour Spectrum Really be Inverted?' in B Baars, W Banks & J Newman (eds) *Essential Sources in the Scientific Study of Consciousness* (2003) 185 (The only real space for inversion is well-known to everyone: colour-blindness. The inversion of red and green occurs because of the proximity and the frequency of the cones and rods for red and green in the retina.) The jury is certainly out on McGinn's 'closure' argument. However, chips designed to carry out cognitive requests without verbal or motor interventions by an individual would suggest that the door to identifying neural correlates of consciousness has been opened. Despite daily revelations as to how consciousness emerges out of the material conditions of existence, this frontier of scientific investigation remains in its incipient stages. Our ignorance is McGinn's true source of bliss.

28. See BJ Baars 'How Does a Serial, Integrated and Very Limited Stream of Consciousness Emerge from a Nervous System that is Mostly Unconscious, Distributed, Parallel and of Enormous Capacity' in GR Bock & J Marsh (eds) *Experimental and Theoretical Studies of Consciousness* (1993) 282.
29. D Dennett *Brainstorms* (1978) 30. See also D Dennett *Freedom Evolves* (2003).
30. Nietzsche's epigram at the outset of this section of the introduction offers one answer. F Nietzsche *On the Genealogy of Morals* (1887) 64–67.
31. D Dennett *Elbow Room: The Varieties of Freedom Worth Wanting* (1984).
32. Ibid at 164. See also C Cherniak 'Rationality and the Structure of Human Memory' (1983) 57 *Synthese* 163.
33. Dennett *Elbow Room* (supra) at 169.
34. Ibid.
35. Cf J Searle 'Putting Consciousness Back in the Brain' in M Bennett, D Dennett, P Hacker and J Searle (eds) *Neuroscience and Philosophy: Brain, Mind & Language* (2003) 97.
36. Assume that this descriptive claim about freedom is true. One problem that remains is that of arationality, and the distortion of truth and politics by abuses of power. See S Woolman 'Language, Power and the Margin: Eliot's Philosophy of Language, Wittgenstein on Following a Rule, and Statutory Construction in *Thembekile Mankayi v Anglogold Ashanti Limited* (2012) 128 *South African Law Journal* 434. One form of 'arationality' has already been identified: the extent to which various ways of being in the world (including comprehensive visions of the good) determine (a) who we are as individuals and (b) the necessary conditions for flourishing. I am only concerned with this form of arationality to the extent that it prevents – through various forms of coercion – individuals from creating ways of being in the world that enable them to flourish. What we want from a politics of flourishing, ultimately, are institutional arrangements that enable individuals who are square to live in square holes, and individuals who are round to inhabit round holes. No more than that. See J Gray *Enlightenment's Wake: Politics and Culture at the Close of the Modern Age* (1997) 102 (The politics of flourishing and experimental constitutionalism are only possible against a background of common cultures that ensure the general stability of a society. Or, as John Gray argues, the institutions

of the modern social democratic state on offer in these pages 'depends far more on their political and cultural acceptability than upon the legal framework which supposedly defines and protects them.') A second form of arationality is more pernicious. This second form of arationality drives the distinction Plato offers in *The Republic* between philosophy and politics. Politics, on Plato's view, is largely the domain of the messy and the venal. It concerns itself with competitive advantages between individuals, with the distribution of the goods in life among various groups in society, with 'the instabilities engendered by changing social and economic relationships.' See LJ Biskowski 'Reason in Politics: Arendt and Gadamer on the Role of the *Eide*' (1998) 31 *Polity* 1. Politics is the enemy of stability and truth, and thus philosophy. See WE Connolly *Political Theory and Modernity* (1988)(Connolly, following Nietzsche, contends that Plato: 'discounts the sensuous world of change, growth, decay and finitude to attain the true world of ideas .... The sphere of ideas brings the pious and virtuous man to truth and it establishes a set of standards by which the mundane world must be evaluated. This is the first and most confident expression of the western will to truth, of the will to interpret the world in human terms and then to pretend that the interpretation reflects the world as it is in itself.' Ibid at 141–142.) See also S Wolin *Politics and Vision: Continuity and Innovation in Western Political Thought* (1960) 42 (Plato treats these phenomena – of competition, disagreement and instability – 'as the symptoms of an unhealthy society, as the art against which political philosophy and the political art had to contend. Political philosophy and ruling alike had as their objectives the creation of the good society, 'politics' was evil, and hence the task of philosophy and of ruling was to rid the community of politics.' Such is Plato's paradox: politics without the political.) Arendt, Dahl, Pitkin, and Young – attacking Platonic thought from a variety of very different philosophical angles – also contend that politics is inherently messy, and in the nature of all things human, unavoidable. See H Arendt *The Human Condition* (1960); RA Dahl *Democracy and Its Critics* (1989) 52; HF Pitkin *Wittgenstein and Justice* (1972) 326; IM Young *Justice and the Politics of Difference* (1990) 126-127. That said, we need not adopt the benevolent tyranny of *The Republic* to have some sympathy for Plato's concerns about arationality. For example, Gadamer's reconstruction of Plato reconnects the capacity to recognize 'Ideal Forms' with more general forms of human reasonableness and moral consciousness. See HG Gadamer *Truth & Method* (1968). It should be clear that the capacity to form reasoned judgments is critical both to flourishing – which involves a pre-commitment (grounded in reason) to tolerating some, but not all, ways of being in the world – and to experimental constitutionalism – which involves a pre-commitment (grounded in reason) to making assessments regarding the kinds of 'experiments in living' worth reinforcing and those kinds of experiments *not* worth maintaining. The concern with arationality, then, is not a concern with a failure to recognize 'the one true way'. It is, first, a concern with forms of politics that would impose a single comprehensive vision of the good on all the members of a polity. A theocracy run according to a particularly conservative variation of *shariah* (Islamic law) or *halachah* (Jewish law), or a dictatorship run according to a cult of personality, are simply the most pernicious forms of the arational in politics. Neither flourishing nor experimentalism is genuinely possible under such regimes. Eliminating the extreme examples is easy. Arationality strongly adheres to the desire to maintain the status quo. (Human beings do not like change. We seek stasis.) I want to suggest that my understanding of human flourishing and experimental constitutionalism constitute radical and persistent challenges to the status quo (defined as the commitment to leaving things as they are, and in the hands of those who currently exercise power) and requires a thicker conception of reasonableness than our current constitutional politics admits. To disentrench established interests, to challenge things as they are, demands both a more thorough-going commitment to creating the material conditions for flourishing and a revision of our political arrangements in light of the dictates of experimental constitutionalism. To accept anything less is to admit that our current political commitments are simply the product of the arational – both in the Platonic idiom and in the modern sense. As we shall see, flourishing and experimentalism connects us to intercultural attempts to extend shared understandings of the good without reifying 'the good' in a manner that allows any given conception of 'the good' to displace 'the right'.

37. *S v Mhlungu* 1995 (3) SA 867 (CC), 1995 (7) BCLR 793 (CC) at para 59.
38. *Zantzi v Council of State, Ciskei* 1995 (4) SA 615 (CC) at para 8.
39. *Mhlungu* (supra) at para 129.
40. See *Nokotyana v Ekurhuleni Metropolitan Municipality* 2010 (4) BCLR 312 (CC), [2009] ZACC 33. For trenchant critiques of the Court's adoption of subsidiarity with respect to socio-economic rights, generally, and sanitation, in particular, see M Lanford & R Stacey 'Water' in S Woolman & M Bishop (eds) *Constitutional Law of South Africa* (2nd Edition, RS3, May 2011) Chapter 56B; R Kapindu 'The Desperate Left in Desperation: A Court in Retreat – *Nokotyana v Ekurhuleni Metropolitan Municipality* Revisited' (2010) 3 *Constitutional Court Review* 201; D Bilchitz 'Is the Constitutional Court Wasting Away the Rights of the Poor?' (2010) 127 *South African Law Journal* 591.
41. See C Sunstein *One Case at a Time* (1996); I Currie 'Judicious Avoidance' (1999) 15 *South African Journal on Human Rights* 138.
42. Sunstein *One Case at a Time* (supra) at ix–x. See also C Sunstein 'Leaving Things Undecided' (1996) 110 *Harvard Law Review* 4; C Sunstein 'Incompletely Theorized Agreements in Constitutional Law' *John M Olin Law & Economics Working Paper* no 322 (January 2007), available at *https://www.law.uchicago.edu/Lawecon/wkngPprs_301–350/322.pdf* (last accessed 11 October 2007).
43. Sunstein *One Case at a Time* (supra) at x. At the time it was written, I thought that this work was a strategic (craven) attempt, by an academic with a long politically progressive paper trail, to turn the author into a viable candidate for the US Supreme Court. Not only did such a view of Sunstein's work constitute bad faith on my part, one must now read Sunstein's *One Case* as a throat-clearing exercise and as part of a long term project to think through the various possibilities for creating better judicial, political and social institutions. No other living American legal scholar can claim to have worked through and turned over such a broad array of jurisprudential problems and built up, as a consequence, a novel theory not just about judicial decision-making, but about decision-making across a broad range of institutions. Sunstein has contributed to the growth of experimentalism as a way of understanding how everything works, and how things can be made to work better.
44. See C Sunstein *Infotopia: How Many Minds Produce Knowledge* (2007).
45. See R Thaler & C Sunstein *Nudge: Improving Decisions about Health, Wealth and Happiness* (2008).
46. See, eg, M Dorf & C Sabel 'A Constitution of Democratic Experimentalism' (1998) 98 *Columbia Law Review* 267; Michael Dorf & B Friedman 'Shared Constitutional Interpretation' (2000) *Supreme Court Review* 61; C Sabel & W Simon 'Destabilization Rights: How Public Law Litigation Succeeds' (2004) 117 *Harvard Law Review* 1015. For the application of experimental constitutionalism to South African jurisprudence, see S Woolman 'Application' in S Woolman & M Bishop (eds) *Constitutional Law of South Africa* (2nd edition, OS, March 2005) Chapter 31; S Woolman & H Botha 'Limitations' in S Woolman & M Bishop (eds) *Constitutional Law of South Africa* (2nd edition, OS, July 2006) Chapter 34; S Woolman and B Fleisch *The Constitution in the Classroom: Law and Education in South Africa, 1994 – 2008* (2009); See S Woolman 'On the Common Saying "What's True in Golf is True in Law": The Relationship between Theory and Practice across Forms of Life' in S Woolman & D Bilchitz (eds) *Is This Seat Taken? Conversations at the Bar, the Bench and the Academy about the South African Constitution* (2012) 341.
47. As noted above, Sunstein seems committed to a full blown institutional empiricism that allows for the possibility of extracting and using information to build better theories and institutions. His 'libertarian paternalism' only puts certain limits on what any polity should do when it undertakes social experiments, regulation creation, and constitutional norm-setting. Sunstein abjures the tendency in the legal academy to reify deliberation as a problem solving mechanism. (I share his scepticism.) He has instead become an adherent of emergent experimental governance when it comes to building better theories about the normative content of federal law in the United States. [Sunstein's appointment in 2009 as US President Obama's administrative law Czar – responsible for tweaking, correcting or discarding regulations – reflects this turn.] We shall see below that Sunstein's movement from scepticism to problem-solving is consistent with the kind of empiricism

that got off the ground with David Hume and the Scottish Enlightenment, that lies at the heart of John Dewey's American pragmatism, and that has reappeared in a number of contemporary currents of legal realism.

48. A Sachs 'Democracy, Dignity and Deliberation', paper delivered at the *Conference on the Dignity Jurisprudence of Laurie Ackermann* (University of Cape Town, 27 July 2007)(Notes of conference on file with author.)

49. Professor Iain Currie is the only South African constitutional law scholar to have articulated an alternative full-blown theory of judicial review. It closely tracks Sunstein's earlier views on incompletely theorized agreements. Two problems with Professor Currie's decade old account warrant mention here. Professor Currie may have been correct, as a descriptive matter, to ascribe (some notion of) judicial minimalism to the Constitutional Court in its first few years of existence. The shallowness of the Chaskalson Court's judgments and the unanimity that the Chaskalson Court imposed on its potentially fractious bench are noteworthy features of its first four years. However, Professor Currie has, over time, elevated an accurate description of a small cohort of cases to a highly questionable normative account. His more recent work shows no signs of backing away. See I Currie & J de Waal (eds) *The Bill of Rights Handbook* (5th ed 2005). Currie's difficulty is that South Africa, circa 1995 to 1999, possessed no core of fully or reasonably theorized agreements about constitutional norms that would allow for meaningful incompletely theorized agreements. As of 2012, the Constitutional Court continues to offer incompletely theorized judgments in the (general) absence of theorized cores. Avoidance of the kind espoused by Professor Currie only works against a background of shared understandings. It is the absence of shared understandings – in the Court and in the society at large – that make it impossible to accept judicial avoidance as either an accurate description of or a desirable prescription for our Bill of Rights jurisprudence. (In liberal societies, this distinction between the shared assumptions necessary for society to work (and to work fairly) and more general assumptions about the correct way to live tracks the philosophical distinction between the right (justice) and the good (morality).) A constitutional democracy, with a justiciable Bill of Rights, requires a significant number of shared assumptions about the right in order to operate: it also consciously leaves space for disagreement about comprehensive visions of the good. See J Rawls *Political Liberalism* (1993). Robert Post and Reva Seigal have offered a far more nuanced set of objections to the original minimalist project. See R Post & R Seigal 'Roe Rage: Democratic Constitutionalism and Backlash' (2007) 42 *Harvard Civil Rights-Civil Liberties Law Review* 373. In response to Sunstein's original minimalism, which assiduously eschews judicial pronouncements on contentious value choices, they advance a theory called 'democratic constitutionalism': 'Democratic constitutionalism suggests that some degree of conflict may be an inevitable consequence of vindicating constitutional rights, whether rights are secured by legislation or by adjudication. [...] Democratic constitutionalism suggests ... that controversy provoked by judicial decision-making might even have positive benefits for the American constitutional order. Citizens who oppose court decisions are politically active. They enact their commitment to the importance of constitutional meaning. They seek to persuade other Americans to embrace their constitutional understandings. These forms of engagement lead citizens to identify with the Constitution and with one another. Popular debate about the Constitution infuses the memories and principles of our constitutional tradition with meanings that command popular allegiance and that would never develop if a normatively estranged citizenry were passively to submit to judicial judgments. ... [the early] Sunstein ... [was] in the grip of an image of constitutional law as "*democracy foreclosing*". Democratic constitutionalism refuses to accept this image, and it thus provides a more nuanced appreciation of the actual operation of our constitutional system. *No* court, including the Supreme Court, has the capacity to rule a controversial issue "off-limits to politics". ... Although constitutionalizing a right takes certain legislative outcomes off the table, it can also invigorate and transform politics. ... A theory of the proper relationship between adjudication and democratic politics necessarily lies coiled at the core of every judicially defined and enforced constitutional right. ... Minimalism approaches conflict with

the assumption that it is a threat to social cohesion and legitimacy. Democratic constitutionalism, by contrast, examines the understandings and practices that promote the social cohesion and legitimacy of our constitutional order. It considers the possibility that controversy over constitutional meaning might promote cohesion under conditions of normative heterogeneity. …' Ibid at 391–406. Though I'm not enamoured with this deliberative turn, what is refreshing about Post and Seigal's take on democratic constitutionalism is that conflict may, in fact, produce better results and constitutional norms over time, as well as greater normative legitimacy through broader political participation. That said, the polarization of American politics – by what would have been considered the lunatic fringe of half-baked libertarianism just 20 years ago – suggests that public discourse (infected and inflected by huge amounts of money from the wealthy) may actually undermine social stability. Post and Seigal fail to recognize how the web and a highly fragmented media have debased discourse by feeding people 'information' that conforms to, rather than challenges, their existing beliefs. See, eg, G Soros 'My Philanthropy' *The New York Review of Books* (23 June 2011) 4.

50. See, eg, *True Motives (Pty) Ltd v Mahdi and Another* 2009 (4) SA 153 (SCA), 2009 (7) BCLR 712 (CC) (Cameron J's judgment expressly recognizes this very problem and cites my own work as identifying the problem. See S Woolman 'The Amazing, Vanishing Bill of Rights' (2007) 124 *South African Law Review* 762.) See also *Makhanya v University of Zululand* 2010 (1) SA 62 (SCA) at paras 81 -88 (The *Makhanya* court, per Nugent J, was rather scathing with respect to the thinness of several of the Constitutional Court's judgments. According to Nugent J, the Constitutional Court had come to two 'mutually destructive findings' with respect to the content of the rule to be followed in lower courts and by other social actors because it had given no express statement as to the true ratio for its decisions. It had left the ratio to be gleaned by highly circumstantial inferences at best.)

51. See, especially, C Hoexter 'Clearing the Intersection? Administrative Law and Labour Law in the Constitutional Court (2008) 1 *Constitutional Court Review* 209; M Brassey 'Back Off, but Back Up: Administrative Law Rightly Yields to Labour Law (2009) 2 *Constitutional Court Review* 209; J Brickhill 'Precedent and the Constitutional Court' (2010) 3 *Constitutional Court Review* 79; A Fagan 'The Confusions of K' (2009) 126 *South African Law Journal* 154; D Davis 'Private Law after 1994: Progressive Development or Schizoid Confusion?' (2008) 24 *South African Journal on Human Rights* 318; G Penfold and D Milo 'Media Freedom and the Law of Privacy: *NM v Smith (Freedom of Expression Institute as Amicus Curiae)* 2007 5 SA 250 (CC)' (2008) 1 *Constitutional Court Review* 311; L Chenwi 'A New Approach to Remedies in Socio-Economic Rights Adjudication: *51 Olivia Road v City of Johannesburg*' (2009) 2 *Constitutional Court Review* 371.

52. For a full-blown critique of avoidance that demonstrates its incoherence when elevated to a rule of adjudication, see S Woolman 'The Amazing, Vanishing Bill of Rights' (2007) 124 *South African Law Review* 762; S Woolman 'Application' in S Woolman & M Bishop (eds) *Constitutional Law of South Africa* (2nd Edition, OS, March 2005) Chapter 31. But for a sharp response to my critique and a robust defence of the Court's Bill of Rights jurisprudence generally, see F Michelman 'On the Uses of Interpretive 'Charity': Some Notes on Application, Avoidance, Equality and Objective Unconstitutionality from The 2007 Term of the Constitutional Court of South Africa' (2009) 1 *Constitutional Court Review* 1. The colloquy between Professor Michelman and myself has closed down much of the space for disagreement. By and large, a single, question remains unanswered: are the Constitutional Court's judgments sometimes too thin to give clear direction to other members of South Africa's legal order? S Woolman 'Between Charity and Clarity: Kibitzing with Frank Michelman on How to Best to Read the Constitutional Court' (2010) 25 *Southern African Public Law* 491; F Michelman 'Old Kibitzes Never Die: A Rejoinder to Stu Woolman' (2010) 25 *Southern African Public Law* 515. A more recent work by Frank Michelman on the Court's avoidance of constitutional norms in favour of an *often* unstated reliance upon outdated, conservative common law regimes or 'practices' suggests that the Court's behaviour does indeed have the capacity to do the kind of damage to our aspirational constitutional order that sparked my initial critique and our initial discord. F Michelman 'Eviction, Expropriation and the Gravity of the Common Law' (supra).

Chapter One-C

How Rethinking Our Understanding of the Self and the Social Services a Better Constitutional Theory

'Man can do what he wills. But he cannot will what he wills.'

Arthur Schopenhauer

A. Aha Moments and Two Dominant Leitmotifs

1. *The Unchosen Conditions of Being*

'Meaning makes us'. That bumper sticker flows from two basic propositions. To be crude about it – there's rarely a thought in your head or an action that you undertake that is not directly sourced from neurological hard-wiring, or pre-existing cognitive routines and dispositional states, or shared social practices. Let's break that complex proposition into two smaller parts.

We, as a species, tend to overemphasize dramatically the actual space for self-defining choices. In truth, our experience of personhood, of self-consciousness, is a function of a complex set of narratives over which we exercise little in the way of (self) control. Our notion of 'selfness' is a function, a very useful by-product, of a complex array of semi-independent neural-muscular networks that control the body's journey through life. This complex set of dispositional states is a function of both the deep grammar of our brains (and bodies) and the social endowments that have evolved over time to determine various patterns of behaviour. It should be apparent from this brief account that the self or the mind is a valuable abstraction and not an entity that stands back from experience and then dictates to the body what it does in response to various stimuli. Each self, to use Daniel Dennett's felicitous phrase, is just 'a centre of narrative gravity'.[1] Each centre of narrative gravity – each self (you or I) – is a set of different, but overlapping narratives. Each narrative, or storyline, reflects a complex set of experiences and dispositional states organized around a particular form of behaviour. 'I' – Stu Woolman – consist of narratives that flow from my roles as a male, as an academic, as an English speaker, as a son of Ephraim, as a sexual being, as a native American, as a permanent resident of South Africa, as a golfer, as a sleeper, as a cook, as a Jew, as a disabled person, as a friend of Michael, Lisa and Brahm, as a listener, as a teacher, as a New Yorker, as bald, as the Editor-in-Chief of *Constitutional Law of South Africa*. The list of narratives is not infinite. It is, however, almost as long and diverse as my life. The self then is that centre of narrative gravity, that self-representation, which holds together and organizes information, various storylines and dispositional states that make up my sense of 'me'. It is unique. The variety of narratives that make up 'me' is different in a sufficiently large number of respects to allow me to differentiate my 'self' from any other 'self'. It is relatively stable. Though my narratives and dispositional states are always changing, my self-representations enable me to see my 'self' as remaining relatively consistent over time. But again, keep in mind that the self, and its various narratives, is thoroughly a function of physical capacities and social practices over which I have little control or choice.[2] And remember, like a necklace of pearls, this self is delicate.[3] [This general characterization of the self proves uncomfortable for most readers. In Chapter 2, I discuss the neurological basis for what I call 'core temperament' and how it provides for a 'unitary sense of self.'[4]]

We, in the western philosophical tradition, also tend to overemphasize dramatically the actual space for rational collective deliberation. We often speak of the associations that make up our lives – that give our individual selves meaning and content – as if we were largely free to choose them or make them up as we go along. I have suggested why such a notion of choice is not true of us as individual selves. It is also largely not true of associational life generally.

As Michael Walzer has argued, there is a 'radical givenness to our associational life'.[5] What he means, in short, is that most of the associations that make up our associational life are involuntary associations. We don't choose our family. We generally don't choose our race or religion or ethnicity or nationality or class or citizenship or sexual orientation. Moreover, even when we appear to have the space to exercise choice, we rarely create the associations available to us. The vast majority of our associations are already there, culturally determined entities that pre-date our existence or, at the very least, our recognition of the need for them. Finally, even when we overcome inertia and do create some new association (and let me not be understood to underestimate the value of such overcoming), the very structure and style of the association is almost invariably based upon an existing rubric. Corporations, marriages, co-edited and co-authored publications are modelled upon existing associational forms. So gay marriages may be a relatively new legal construct – but marriage itself is a publicly recognized and sanctioned institution for carrying on intimate or familial relationships. Even in times of revolution, mimicry of existing associational forms are the norm. That is, in short, what Heidegger meant when he wrote:

> [That shared practices are constitutive of 'being'] implies that the world is already given as the common world. It is *not* the case that there are first individual subjects which are at any given time have their own world; and that the task of putting them together, by virtue of some sort of arrangement, ... one would have a common world. This is how philosophers imagine things when they ask about the constitution of the intersubjective. We say instead that the first thing that is given is the common world. ... We take pleasure and enjoy ourselves as one takes pleasure, we speak ... about something as one speaks.[6]

Social practices are thus very much like the self. They are, for the most part, a function of physical capacities and entrenched group behaviour over which we have little control or choice. Our social world, as Heidegger notes, is already 'given [as] the common world'. [Again: this notion will make many readers uncomfortable. It shouldn't. To the extent that it does, this book is an extended meditation on how we might, individually and collectively, challenge and overcome deleterious social customs, habits and practices and supplant them with new, improved, experimentally-tested systems, routines, praxes, doctrines and institutions.]

As John Dewey pointed out, we often choose to ignore this inconvenient truth. Individuals, and particularly philosophers, have 'arrogated to [themselves] the office of demonstrating the existence of a transcendent, absolute or inner reality and revealing to man the nature and features of this ultimate and higher reality.[7] As Wittgenstein notes, no such transcendent, higher reality exists. Any given practice, and our ability to master it, comes first: and puts us in unmediated contact with the world.[8] He writes in the *Investigations* as follows:

> To obey a rule, to make a report, to give an, order, to play a game of chess are customs (uses, institutions). To understand a sentence means to understand a language. To understand a language means to be *master* of a technique. (§199) ... When I obey a rule, I do not choose. I obey the rule *blindly*. (§219) Would it not be possible for us, however, to calculate as we actually do (all agreeing and so on) and still at every step have a feeling of being guided by rules as by a spell, feeling astonishment at the fact that we agreed? (We might give thanks to the Deity for our agreement.) (§234) ... This merely [shows] what goes to make up what we call 'obeying a rule' in everyday

> life. (§235) … If language is to be a means of communication there must be agreement not only in definitions but also (queer as this may sound) in judgments. (§242) … One cannot guess at how a word functions. One has to *look at* its use and learn from that. But the difficulty is to remove the prejudice which stands in the way of doing this. It is not a *stupid* prejudice. (§340) … Speech with and without thought is to be compared with the playing of a piece of music with and without thought. (§341).

What Wittgenstein is saying is: (a) that we already have the material at hand to arrive at verifiable truth propositions about the world; (b) that most of these propositions are shared; (c) that most of them are true; and (d) that mastery of these propositions or capabilities precedes our capacity, or even need, for criticism.[9] Only at the margins, once we have aggressively learned all there is to be learned from one another, do our differences have any meaningful bite.[10] Perhaps Baker and Hacker can explicate, somewhat less elliptically, the order of priority between practice and theory – or more accurately, the manner in which they map on to one another:

> Wittgenstein … emphasized that behaviour is a criterion for possession of an ability, and in the specific case of understanding rules, that how one applies a rule is a criterion for how one understands it. … Using a rule correctly is also a criterion for understanding it (or more generally, how it is used is a criterion of how it is understood.) … Philosophers in the grip of the Augustinian picture [between word and world] are inclined to think that 'ultimately' explanations of expressions by definitions replacing one symbol by others must terminate in an array of 'indefinables'. These expressions, philosophers think, must somehow be *connected with reality*, for it is they that give content to the language. … In [his] criticism of the Augustinian picture, Wittgenstein … stressed … [that] understanding an explanation (understanding a rule) is just knowing how to use the explained word correctly (knowing how to apply the rule.) … Correct uses of a word are criteria both for understanding an explanation of it and for knowing how to use it correctly.[11]

Wittgenstein's astute observation that 'rule' and 'agreement' are cousins and that language, by necessity, requires agreement in both the definition of terms and the judgments that flow from the use of those terms does not forestall error. (Nor can it!) For while we are indeed endowed with a broad array of mutually supporting beliefs, theories, conditions and standards, we can neither claim that this inheritance is a seamless whole nor that all our beliefs are true. Only a hopelessly naïve epistemologist would entertain such a proposition. As Donald Davidson notes: 'Error is what gives belief its point.'[12] Yet as the result of our mastery of a broad array of techniques, we can claim to possess 'endless true beliefs'.[13]

Take two recent examples from the exploration of Mars. Does anyone even partially familiar with the years of work undertaken by a large team of scientists able to land the rover Curiosity on the red planet have any doubt regarding the team's mastery of the most complex equations in math and physics, or the engineering necessary to accomplish the unprecedented event of landing an object of its size or function? Every stage from launch to landing went exactly as expected. Expectation and realization had to mirror one another: anything less would have led to a disaster. Indeed, a basic failure to convert measurements from the Imperial units of pound-seconds into the metric system of Newton-seconds led a decade earlier to the spectacle of the Climate Orbiter crashing into the surface of Mars. Human beings make mistakes. But this colossal failure was *not* a function of a failure of human beings to match symbol to reality.

To their understandable mortification, they simply failed to demonstrate mastery of basic arithmetic. (As a result, the Orbiter entered Martian space at an improperly low altitude and disintegrated upon entry into the red planet's atmosphere.) The failure of Orbiter may have led NASA engineers to ensure that precision a magnitude of order greater would lead, to the best of their ability, to the success of Curiosity.

Error may arise in practices for another set of reasons. Our practices themselves are not entirely coherent. All traditions, institutions, games and domains of human inquiry are, as Joshua Cohen writes

> ... the result, not of legislative design by a single person acting on behalf of a coherent system of values, but of conflicts among individuals acting on behalf of diverse values and ambitions. And unlike the produce of a supreme legislative design, the outcomes of such a history are not likely to be a set of coherent social practices that completely conform to a single scheme of values.[14]

The problem with the theorist who reifies theory is that she mistakes these faults, fissures and heterogeneous layers within a practice as a problem with the practice – and its usefulness – as a whole. No one doubts that Einstein understood arithmetic as we do. Consider Einstein's contributions to the birth of both relativity theory and quantum mechanics. No working physicist argues that Einstein's views were wrong – in the main – about either basis for modern physics. And yet, with respect to an array of particular hypotheses, Einstein's views in both domains have been proven incorrect. (We often forget both how much and how little we understand about the universe around us.)

The final form of bewitchment, against which Wittgenstein warns us, is our widely shared belief that we first form theories and then test these theories against experience. Not so says Wittgenstein. It is essential – for the purposes of this book – that we get our order of priority straight. Once a practice is established (through trial and error, unconsciously and consciously), we might wish, upon reflection, to test its assumptions through experiments that do or do not confirm aspects of a practice's usefulness. (Curiosity's success constitutes proof of this order of priority and its consequences for virtually all of our endeavours.) That, to put it pithily, is why I place experimentalism at the heart of this theory of South African constitutional law.

2. *Trial and Error and Feedback Mechanisms*

If we, as individuals, are not the product of freely-willed actions by a self-made self, then what is the proper way to understand consciousness and that unitary sense of me *qua* me? As we shall see in Chapter 2, consciousness is best described as a feedback mechanism that gives us fresh opportunities to reflect upon experience and plot more or less optimal courses for action to realize the ends and aspirations that have largely, but not irrevocably, made us who we are.

Let's not overcomplicate matters just yet. Feedback mechanisms feature as a salient construct throughout this work. This book therefore demands a relatively straightforward account of this core concept that leaves readers feeling comfortable with its use within four discrete theoretical domains, as well the manner in which it connects the self to the social, and the self and the social to the political and the constitutional.

Think of feedback mechanisms in terms of the more readily understood notion of 'trial and error'. Individual selves (me's) – populated by radically heterogeneous ways of being in the world – are always experimenting, attempting to divine, through reflection (memory) and action (imagination in motion), what will work with respect to the challenges thrown up by a given environment. Consciousness enables us to focus on aspects of our current environment, and to hold them up for scrutiny, in order to form better behaviour responses to immediate and long term problems. Consciousness thus functions as a feedback mechanism in two inextricably related ways. Conscious reports create a record (though not the only available record) of our responses: the construction of our successes as well as our failures. A record of such errors (memory) enables us to respond differently – assuming we survive the error – the next time that we are faced with an appropriate test of our wiles. Put somewhat differently, consciousness, the tip of our cognitive/neural iceberg, comes into play when 'stimuli are assessed to be novel, threatening or momentarily relevant to active schemas or intentions.'[15] As Newman notes: 'The defining features of stimuli which engage conscious attention are that they: (1) vary in some significant degree from current expectations; or (2) are congruent with the current predominant intent/goal of the organism. In contrast, the processing of stimuli which are predictable, routine or over-learned is automatically allocated to non-conscious, highly-modulized cognitive systems.'[16] Dehanne and Naccache extend these observations by requiring that any theory of consciousness accommodate three critical empirical observations: '(1) a considerable amount of neural processing is possible without consciousness, (2) attention is a prerequisite of consciousness, and (3) consciousness is required for some specific cognitive tasks, including those that require durable information maintenance, novel combinations of operations, or the spontaneous generation of intentional behaviour.'[17] Once we adapt our account of consciousness so that it houses these desiderata, we arrive at the following conclusion. Although the vast majority of cognitive/neuronal processes are and must always be non-conscious, consciousness allows an individual [or networks of individuals] 'to represent a goal and to estimate the outcomes of ... actions before initiating them'.[18] The ability to undertake 'trial and error' thought experiments within the simulated framework provided by neurological structures is an enormous advance on having to undertake 'trials and errors' in an actual physical environment. Consciousness, as both a feedback mechanism and a simulator of possibilities, enables us to weed out outcomes less likely to be successful in the world and enhances our capacity to flourish.[19]

This description may seem at odds with how we normally think of the conscious and the unconscious. But it shouldn't be – and forget Freudian discourse (commonly misunderstood) for a moment. Over a century ago, Alfred North Whitehead recognized that human civilization, and its many social practices and component parts, advances by making as many dispositional states and responses to the world as possible unconscious. Why? So that we can attend to new problems as yet unsolved, and whose isolation and solution will enable us to survive and to thrive.

Let's return for a moment to the complicated task of landing the Curiosity on Mars. What a dedicated team of quite conscious individuals committed to the realization of a single (if complicated) mission did was to run simulation after simulation of how each stage of Curiosity's trip and missives back on its findings would work. Experiments – trial and error with feedback mechanisms in controlled environments designed to replicate what we already knew about space and Mars – enabled the large team of scientists and engineers to separate the chaff from the wheat in advance of the actual launch and the landing of the rover. Were they certain of success? No. But at each stage, from lift-off to landing, they received confirmation of their equations, and the various experiments conducted in advance of real-time events. It's worth recalling John Dewey's words in the Preface: 'We only think when confronted by a problem'. The Curiosity team at NASA was confronted by numerous novel problems. Given the enormous amount of knowledge that we already possess about the universe – and the unique specifications required for travel from Earth to Mars – they applied their individual and collective consciousness to the solution of each and every problem that would confront Curiosity on its voyage. Most of it may have been banal, but individual stages were unprecedented. And the team could not know – until some seven seconds after any particular event occurred – whether their predictions were correct. Extremely smart, but otherwise ordinary human beings, landed the first truly complicated rover on our neighbour's surface. Trial, some error, but ultimately great success means that when we ultimately seek to land human beings on Mars, we will have already learned what works, and what doesn't. Of course, the scale is smaller. Novel problems, including the return of the larger ship and the astronauts aboard, will throw up a host of new complications that will require conscious deliberation, simulation and the piecing together of a gigantic puzzle into a single whole.

A constitutional democracy is another kind of feedback mechanism that requires conscious engagement, simulations and the stitching together of a gigantic puzzle into a single, if ever changing, whole. A constitutional democracy – a polity comprised of millions of complex, radically heterogeneous selves – is constantly experimenting, attempting to divine through reflection and action what works best for its many constituents; what enables each and every one of us to flourish.

B. Weaving Together the Dominant Leitmotifs throughout the Text

1. *A Theory of the Self: Flourishing, Not Freedom*

Let me begin with four short stories.

On my way to 23 Forbes Street, Fellside, Johannesburg, in May 2007, I had cause to reflect upon various strands of the argument articulated in this work. The fact that I had an opportunity to engage in some form of reflective activity with regard to this project is hardly remarkable in itself. What is remarkable is that all this sophisticated reflective activity occurred while I drove my car from 82 Homestead Road, Glen Atholl, Johannesburg to the address above. As I pulled up to the house in Fellside, I realized that I had no recollection of actually driving the 6 km between the two residences. I was too busy thinking (about problems to be solved: recall again Dewey's remark.) If I was too busy thinking to be aware of the drive, then who, you might well wonder, was driving the car?

Later that same day, as I drove home from the movies, I turned off Glenhove Road in Houghton, Johannesburg and on to the M1 heading north towards Glen Atholl. There was only one problem with this chain of events. I had not wanted to take this turn on to the highway. I had wanted to go to Fellside. And yet, there I was, headed to my flat in Glen Atholl. Perhaps I was thinking about the movie I'd just seen. I don't recall. My partner, driving in the car behind me, was startled to see me peel off in an entirely unexpected direction. If we are certain that I was driving the car – and let's assume that we are – then how did this error occur? For if we are certain that that I was driving the car, then I am equally certain that the 'decision' to turn on to the highway was not a decision of which I was consciously aware.[20]

Perhaps we have all had similar experiences while driving a car.

Take a more startling account of my 'self' in action. Approximately 15 years ago, during a period of extremely debilitating illness, I telephoned a friend in New York from my office in Johannesburg. The call had been on my list of things to do all week. A normal event in the life of an émigré. Approximately 20 minutes into the call, I had the sense that my friend Adam was preoccupied. His responses seemed both canned and uneasy. As I had not been well for some time, I soon suspected that the problem lay not with Adam, but with me. So I asked Adam: 'Have we had this conversation before?' As it turns out, we had. Adam 'reminded' me that I had called him the day before and that we had covered virtually identical terrain in 45 minutes of conversation.[21]

Let's end this set of stories with something more mundane. Equipped with (something close to) my full set of faculties, and quite conscious of the orators before me in the Moot Court room at the South African Institute for Advanced Constitutional, Public, Human Rights and International Law, I banged my gavel down to signal the end of oral argument in the matter before me. Nothing strange here. Or so it seems. In addition to my role as moot court judge, however, I was also participating in a psychology experiment designed to explore the relationship between conscious awareness, neuronal impulses and physical action. As it turns out, approximately 0.6 seconds prior to my conscious awareness that I was about to bang the gavel to signal the end of oral argument – and 0.8 seconds before the event itself – a set of neuronal impulses in my brain registered my decision to bring argument to a close.

With the exception, perhaps, of the phone call to my friend Adam in New York, the experiences described above all fall within the domain of the normal. In the first two instances, we share an experience of our 'mind' being somewhere else – or more accurately, in the first case, of our mind being, at a minimum, devoted to discrete tasks, and in the second case, of being so devoted to one task, that we make an error with respect to another. Even the third experience can be made to seem more commonplace if we add a condition: the caller suffered from parasomnia (asleep yet capable of habitual physical responses), had been under anaesthesia, or had been inebriated. Although the fourth experience is not really an experience we would normally share unless we were all participants in various psychological experiments, those of us who have played sports that require quick responses are familiar with being aware of our 'reaction' only after we have already initiated – if not completed – the response. [I only become aware that I have lifted my head well after hitting a golf ball, irrespective of the outcome; I have caught a baseball hit so hard from a distance of 20 metres away that I only became aware of the catch when I looked around and then down into my glove.} This delay, between the neuronal impulses, conscious awareness and, ultimately, physical action, reflects a partial inversion of how we think traditionally of the relationship between consciousness and freedom.[22]

The traditional view of the self, consciousness and free will is one in which the individual actor surveys her options, makes a choice and then wills that choice into being. The four stories that introduce this section challenges an array of beliefs associated with traditional conceptions of the self, consciousness and free will and prepares the ground for theories that run counter to outmoded accounts.

The story of the gavel – retold from the perspective of neuroscience – is that non-conscious brain events that result in a particular physical response proceed conscious awareness of the 'decision' to respond in a particular manner. If consciousness of our action matters – that is, if particular events rise to the level of requiring attention – then we become dimly aware of the content of the unwilled intention and then – wham! – hot on the heels of consciousness, assuming we have it, comes the action itself.[23]

The story of the unconscious driver – an instance in which awareness seems unnecessary – is meant to draw our attention to the multiple narratives or selves that make up the individual – or, more precisely, the multiple processes that we individuals engage in co-temporaneously, only a few of which command our awareness or rise to the level of consciousness. And yet, despite our lack of consciousness (awareness), or perhaps, more precisely, *because of this lack of awareness*, we are able to act all the same.[24] I drove that car though I had no awareness of my actions and possess no memory of the experience.

The story of the errant driver draws our attention to multiple selves engaged in multiple processes co-temporaneously. It also signals another purpose for consciousness: error-correction. My consciousness or awareness may have initially been focussed on the movie I had just seen. However, when I was confronted with a situation that demanded attention, namely my turning on to the highway and driving in the wrong direction, that which we call 'consciousness' shifted 'its' object of attention to the road before me. Consciousness forms part of a complex set of feedback mechanisms that enable us to navigate through the world in relative safety. The sensation of singularity, as we shall see, emerges, quite incredibly, from a neurological system that is (1) primarily unconscious, (2) distributed throughout the brain and the body, (3) engaged in multiple, parallel processes, and (4) of enormous, highly under-utilized capacity.[25] The purpose of consciousness on this account is three-fold: (a) 'durable and explicit information maintenance' (b) 'novel combinations of operations' and (c) 'intentional behaviour'.[26]

The story of the repeated phone call is meant to challenge our construction of a self that is unitary, integrated and continuous over time. The gap in consciousness or self that I experienced with respect to the two phone calls is meant to emphasize the more daily and commonplace place 'gappiness' of consciousness and the self. Indeed, the self – for those persons in a fragile, parlous and frightening state – often seems to be no more than the subject of experiences that are single mental things. If you prefer metaphor, then these 'sesmets' that constitute the (fragile) self are like pearls on a string.[27] Delicate indeed.

This work is not an exercise in analytic philosophy of mind or a scientific study of consciousness. The purpose of the account of consciousness and the self that follows is to shed light upon – and change the way we understand – such basic concepts in our constitutional lexicon as 'free will', 'individual moral agent' and 'political freedom'.[28] The real upshot of the view of the self or the selves propounded here is that while we may possess far less freedom – of all kinds – than we commonly suppose,[29] we are still capable of flourishing in all ways that genuinely matter to us.[30]

2. *A Theory of the Social: Constraint, Friction and Change*

This project was animated, initially, by two apparently disparate lines of thought. The first set of thoughts addressed questions about what it is to be a person, why we have consciousness, how a self is constructed, and the extent to which that self, so constructed, exercises agency. The second set of thoughts addressed the kind of constitutional politics to which the Constitutional Court has committed us under the Final Constitution. Subsequent to those animating lines of thought appeared the express recognition of the two dominant leitmotifs in this work: the unchosen conditions of being and the virtues of feedback mechanisms properly understood.

What links these four lines of thought to a reconceptualization of freedom? The modest, naturalized account of freedom offered here first takes cognisance of the limits of individual agency. It then recasts freedom-talk in terms of the less metaphysically problematic concept of flourishing. Having supplanted freedom-talk with flourishing, this book then explains how individual flourishing and group flourishing occur. More importantly, it explains how individuals and groups so thoroughly conditioned and determined by a world of unchosen conditions of being can alter the ends they pursue, as well as the means for pursuing them, through different kinds of feedback mechanisms.[31] These feedback mechanisms allow us to learn from both negative experiences and positive experiences and create new neural and social networks that allow us to create better lives for our individual selves and for the communities to which we belong.

However, a second reason to recast freedom in terms of flourishing obtains: the mediating role that social formations play in the construction of all meaning. It is trite to note that outside society, and without language, flourishing is a meaningless notion. Only in light of the various practices, forms of life, unchosen conditions of being or language games that social groups provide do we become anything that remotely approximates what we understand to be human.

That said, the politics that I derive from flourishing is as *revolutionary* as it is traditional. As I have written elsewhere, our differences do not separate us, or merely require tolerance. They form the basis for a profound recognition that, individually and collectively, we are *radically heterogeneous creatures*.[32] That radically heterogeneous self – and the heterogeneous society in which we all find ourselves (no matter how repressive) – demands a commitment to pluralism, a deep and profound appreciation for difference. From this commitment to pluralism – the politics not of the majority but of the individual – emanates the commitment to democratic solidarity. How so? Once we recognise our own difference, sexual, religious or otherwise, and demand its recognition by others, we have no coherent choice but to recognise the difference of others. To put it more pointedly, once we recognise the otherness of others and demand such recognition for ourselves, we are committed to a society in which every member can comfortably live out that difference. Does that commit us to socialism or some particular political order? No and yes. Not socialism, but to the politics adumbrated in these pages. That politics of democratic solidarity married to experimental constitutionalism commits us to a political order in which the space we demand for ourselves is roughly equal to the space required by others. If that requires, at this particular historical moment, significant redistribution of wealth, then so be it. The bottom line: once you embrace a commitment to democratic solidarity and experimental constitutionalism, you must be willing to afford others the material and immaterial conditions in which they can recognise and express their difference. Only through such a commitment can we forge a nation that makes good the promise of its basic law.

The radical heterogeneity of the self also points out how change occurs without the attribution of free will. Each dispositional state or role has its own set of demands – its own set of responses to the surrounding environment. Again: I find myself regularly challenged by each of my roles as son, brother, friend, colleague, lover, business partner, professor, disabled person, English speaker in a land with 11 official languages, analysand, editor, author, feminist, golfer, director of a closed corporation and homeowner (just to name a few). Not only does each role or dispositional state itself pose a challenge: the attempt to reconcile all these roles without conflict is simply impossible. Change often comes – is forced upon us – when we must choose the good, the value, or the end to which we wish to give priority in a given set of circumstances. The complexity of, and the friction between, roles does not end with our own selves. We are confronted daily with equally complex radically heterogeneous selves with whom we must carry out innumerable transactions and who carry out their own roles in ways that invariably pose challenges to our current preferred ways of being. Finally, we are confronted with an environment – neither of our making or choosing – that constantly demands that we alter, ever so slightly sometimes, dramatically at others, who we are and what roles we play. Live long enough and you know how wrong F Scott Fitzgerald was when he wrote: 'There are no second acts in American lives.' The problem – to the extent that there is one – is that the play and the new acts never stop – until the play does, and the acts do, and we are but worm-meat. Disruption is a part of life, however much we try to hold change at bay.

Of course, we sometimes find that the roles we play give us little satisfaction, for reasons of which we may only be dimly aware. The trick is to try to lay down new tracks, parallel tracks, to the existing dispositional states, roles and tracks that we currently run along. It can be done. However, the work is often long, arduous and tedious. Ask my analyst. Well don't. She won't tell you a thing. I can say that, without fear of contradiction, nine years of twice a week therapy has laid down parallel tracks, tracks that have made me a somewhat happier, healthier and nominally better person.[33]

The rest (and better part) of my theory of the social contains discussions of and/or commitments (both strong and weak) to six linked components part: (1) constitutive attachments; (2) spontaneous orders; (3) evolutionary epistemology; (4) cognitive biases; (5) choice architecture;

and (6) social capital (bonding networks and bridging networks). This introduction adumbrates those arguments given full expression in Chapter 3.

As I have already noted, the constitutive nature of our attachments and practices forces us to attend to another overlooked feature of social life. We often speak of the social practices, endowments and associations that make up our lives as if we were largely free to choose them or make them up as we go along. I have already suggested why such a traditional, hidebound conception of choice is not true of our social practices (and our individual selves) and why the revolutionary account serves us best.

Again: constraints on our ways of being in the world – I prefer the word endowments – do not preclude genuine change within the small communities, the large social formations or the bonding networks of which we are a part. It does mean, however, that we must proceed with same humility and great circumspection before we proffer mechanisms that would facilitate optimal forms of change.

Given the aforementioned constraints, this theory of the social holds that constructive, collective action is best understood in terms of 'trial and error'. From simple to complex actions, groups use their cognitive modalities to test their environment, and to come up with the best possible solutions to the problem with which they are confronted. Because much of what we do as associations, communities and networks is neither consciously nor deliberatively determined, one might argue that 'a blind variation and selection retention process is fundamental to all inductive achievements, to all genuine increases in fit of system to environment.'[34]

This account of how trial and error in both cognitive and non-cognitive processes may lead to greater adaptive fit sounds a great deal like a form of evolutionary epistemology. It is. As we shall see in Chapter 3, the attraction of this account is that it simultaneously explains the ineluctability of constraint and the mechanisms for change.[35] Moreover, by attending to the mechanisms of change in blind variation and selection retention processes, it makes it possible to suggest how experiments (trials with their successes and their failures) take place on rather large playing fields of social formation,[36] and why such experiments are, as Friedrich Hayek described them, largely, but not always, the result of 'human action, but not human design.'[37]

A somewhat more powerful empirical engine for social change has come out of recent work by legal theorist and political scientist Cass Sunstein and economist and behavioural scientist Richard Thaler. For years, Sunstein appeared so consumed by doubt about grand theorizing that it led him to something akin to pyrrhonian scepticism with regard to constitutional theory. Sunstein's scepticism ultimately gave way to empirical analysis.[38] In *Infotopia*, Sunstein develops a powerful critique of deliberative politics as a constructive form of collective decision-making. Sunstein identifies four basic forms of contemporary information pooling or aggregation (discussed at length in Chapter 3): (1) statistical averages; (2) deliberation; (3) price or market systems; (4) Internet wikis. Pace the dominant pre-disposition of constitutional scholars, Sunstein's writings suggest that deliberation may well be the least useful of the four. He writes: 'Most of the time, both private and public institutions prefer to make decisions through some form of deliberation. ... Does deliberation actually lead to better decisions? Often it does not.'[39] To explain the failures of deliberation and the promise of other methods of aggregating information in the pursuit of better decision-making, Sunstein explores the consequences of two forces: 'The first consists of informational influences, which cause group members to fail to disclose what they know out of respect for the information publicly pronounced by others. … The second force involves social pressures, which lead people to silence themselves to avoid the disapproval of peers or supervisors. Even if you believe that group members are blundering, you might not want to say a word because you do not want to risk their disapproval.'[40]

Various empirical findings (even those that contradicted Sunstein's earlier assessments) led Sunstein to delve deeper into problems with deliberative political mechanisms and into everyday social biases, aversion, blunders, (false) assumptions, inertia, herd following and temptations that lead all of us to make the most mundane mistakes. Having identified good and bad social choice mechanisms in *Infotopia,* Sunstein produced a work in 'choice architecture': *Nudge.*[41] Although still committed to rooting out biases that lead to suboptimal outcomes, Thaler and Sunstein now show us how to organize social space in a manner that leads to better outcomes without forcing or coercing individual choices. As the name of the book suggests, the leitmotif of their work is enabling individuals and groups to change their deleterious choice defaults into more positive choice defaults by setting up a testing environment (an experiment) that should reveal more desirable outcomes at both an individual level and a systemic level. These experiments are conducted by choice architects – anyone who 'has the responsibility for organizing the context in which people make their decisions'.[42] Mothers, teachers, lawyers, engineers, computer programmers, customary leaders, search engine designers, bureaucrats and ballot devisers are all choice architects. Virtually any occupation with responsibility turns the responsible individual into a choice architect. Chapter 3 discloses exactly what some of these choice architects have discovered. One important theme is worth noting now. Choice architects try not to impose a comprehensive vision of 'the good' upon the people who participate in their studies. [In any event, a large body of social research and, in particular economics, demonstrates that most of us do not have genuinely 'true preferences' in many areas of social life, but often have our preferences determined by access and availability. We have, as second class citizens will confirm (and, as a person with a long-standing disability, I count myself amongst them), many adaptive preferences.[43] The choice architect naturally operates with background assumptions about optimal decisions – but even those assumptions can be overturned as the architect 'nudges' groups (and individuals) students into making more optimal choices – 'as judged by the individuals themselves'.[44] A substantial degree of reflexivity is built into the experiments.[45]

Experimentation as a way of engaging the world is *revolutionary.* Not only do experiments and the people who carry them out seek to better understand the world, but, as often as not, people who undertake experiments seek to overturn preconceived and – in their minds – incorrect ways of viewing various phenomena. Some hypotheses turn out to be incorrect. Indeed, the large majority do. The scientific method led one of its avatars, the inventor Thomas Edison, to remark that he learned more from his mistakes than he did from his successes. That said, we might be reading this book in the gloaming or by candlelight had Edison not persisted with his experiments. (Yes: someone else would likely have alighted upon the same results at a later date, and you might still have the pleasure of reading this work on a Kindle.)

At the same time, the experimentation advocated in these pages has a built in brake. A conservative streak if you must. Not every norm or institution can be subject to constant review and reformation. I have suggested several reasons, thus far, for placing brakes on how we engage and experiment upon social phenomena. The first has to do with the construction of meaning for individuals and groups. Meaning, through various endowments, makes us. A just political order recognizes that priority. The various freedoms enshrined in South Africa's basic law do exactly that. The second turns on the manner in which social norms and institutions are largely created. As Hayek wrote, these institutions and designs are primarily the product of human action, not human design. Sunstein's gloss on this agnostic approach to social projects and constitutional theory is to agree, in part, and demur, in part. Like Hayek and Campbell, Sunstein is suspicious of grand theorizing. However, as we have seen, social practices are susceptible to experimentation. For example, given a relatively weak normative goal – say, getting children to choose better food for lunch – we can construct a set of experiments that may help us identify the best way to establish the form a cafeteria lunch line takes. Sunstein, ever suspicious of built-in biases in decision-making, identifies several ways in which we can aggregate or pool information and nudge individuals and groups towards taking better decisions without dictating exactly what they do.

That leads us, finally, to another way of understanding individuals, social formations and political institutions that contain (a) the seeds for experimentation and new institution-building; and (b) a brake on the manner in which the state undermines existing social networks that provide meaning. This approach to social formations and political institutions goes by the name of social capital theory.

Social capital is – and is a function of – our collective effort to build and to fortify those things that matter. It is our collective grit and elbow grease, our relationships and their constantly re-affirmed vows of trust, loyalty and respect. Social capital emphasizes the extent to which our capacity to do anything is contingent upon the creation and maintenance of forms of association which provide both the tools and the setting for meaningful action. Social capital is often treated as ephemera. That makes sense. It is so hard to see. In fact, it is this elusive quality that makes social capital so fragile. It is made up, after all, not of bricks and mortar, but of relationships and commitments, and the trust, respect and loyalty upon which they are dependent.[46]

A positive spin on social capital can be understood to link up my justifications for flourishing and experimentation in the social realm as follows. Social capital is what keeps our intimate, economic, political, cultural, traditional, reformist and religious associations going. Without it, nothing works. Social capital explains at least part of what is at stake for both individual identity and social cohesion: the constitutive. Social capital recognizes that we store the better part of our meaning in fundamentally involuntary associations. Squander that social capital, nothing that matters *is*. Social capital recognizes both the real and the figurative sense of ownership that animates particular forms of (social) life. If anyone and everyone can claim ownership of and membership in an association, then no one owns it.

Social capital takes seriously the threat of various kinds of compelled association. Trust, respect and loyalty have no meaning where the association is coerced. These several virtues can be earned, but never commanded. No trust, respect or loyalty: no social capital.[47] No social capital: none but the most debased forms of (social) life. Finally without a comitment to preserving extant sources of social capital, we would lack the requisite conditions for the kind of social and political experimentation that makes genuine flourishing (within a modern heterogeneous polity) possible.

However, not all forms of social capital are alike – nor are they fungible. Moreover, some forms of social capital – or the associations that produce such capital – are a function of discriminatory practices that our Constitution rightly sets its face against.[48] To invoke the virtues of social capital is not to invoke an unalloyed good. Indeed, I shall try to demonstrate how a Walzerian-like understanding of egalitarian pluralism – that rests on nuanced distinctions between differentiation and discrimination, domination and tyranny – married to Bishop's rather novel notion of remedial equilibration can move communities away from mores that subordinate some of its members, or leverage their existing stores of real capital so that subordinated members have the ability to exit and to join new sub-publics that would enable these second class citizens to flourish. In short, I suggest how the courts and the state can enable individuals and groups to 'seek justice elsewhere', leave many traditional communities as they already are, and still nudge these communities and the body politic as a whole to consider more equitable and just internal arrangements regarding membership, voice and exit.[49]

For the purposes of this book, and for South African life in particular, two forms of networks (each with different degrees and dimensions of social capital) are of particular import: bonding networks and bridging networks. Robert Putnam puts the difference between these two distinct forms of social capital or social networks as follows: 'Some forms of capital are, by choice or necessity, inward looking and tend to reinforce exclusive identities and homogeneous groups. ... Other networks are outward looking and encompass people across diverse social cleavages.'[50]

It's essential to gain a slightly better grasp of these distinctions – as they shall recur again and again with respect to the constitutional boundary drawing that we shall undertake in Chapters 5, 6 and 8 when analysing the respective merits and demerits of such bonding networks as religious and cultural associations and the virtues and vices of such bridging networks as school governing bodies, universities or Black Economic Empowerment firms.

One way to distinguish the two networks would be to 'contrast the strong bonds of reciprocity and care that are found inside families and small communities (what we might call normative bonding social capital) with the [at least initial] self-interested norms that tend to predominate between relative strangers ... and through which relative strangers can cooperate successfully (what we might call normative bridging social capital.)'[51] But that's just a start. High bonding communities tend to feature well-established, historically entrenched belief sets, shared assets and rather rigid rules regarding membership, voice and exit (and rule enforcing mechanisms regarding those rules). Bridging networks are often extra-communal and bring together rather diverse groups of individuals in the pursuit of singular, generally self-interested ends. Membership, voice and exit tend to be more flexible in bridging networks.[52]

However distinct these two kinds of social capital may appear on the surface, I am going to argue – in Chapter 3 – that the success of a developmental state such as South Africa depends upon: (a) respect for the significant public goods created by private bonding networks (schools, hospitals, charities); (b) leveraging, as much as possible, admission into bonding networks for persons (and groups of persons) who would otherwise not have access to the goods made available within those networks; and (c) the use of state resources to build linking or bridging networks that, over time, produce social capital that are comparable in nature and quality to that social capital produced in bonding networks.[53] The potential for social and political revolution is truly profound if we understand how bonding and bridging networks actually function.[54]

How do these various dimensions of social theory fit together? All acknowledge the involuntariness of most social formations and the constraints that they impose on individual and group identity. They recognize that our social practices provide stores of collective wisdom about what works and what doesn't work. Evolutionary epistemologists and social capital theorists emphasize the manner in which our forms of life often constitute large playing fields against which experiments in life are played out – often unconsciously, quite often without central planning. Choice architects agree that our forms of life often constitute large playing fields against which experiments in life are played out. However, they add that we can, quite consciously, construct experiments that act as feedback mechanisms that elicit significant amounts of information about forms of behaviour that no longer work or new forms of behaviour that work 'better'. Second, even if the capacity for critique of our practices can be quite limited (recall Wittgenstein's earlier warning), all of the aforementioned theoretical orientations acknowledge that such space does exist. Third, the grander the collective exercise in experimentation is – the larger and more varied our critical community – the more varied our individual lives are likely to be. The more varied our individual lives are, the more likely we are to find successful models for what it means to be fully human. All of these social theories employ different mechanisms to *nudge* an individual in the right direction as judged by herself or himself. I then marry them to an egalitarian pluralist's commitment to a form of remedial equilibration that requires the state and various sub-publics to assist citizens and denizens into fitting their round pegs into round holes, or whatever shape flourishing takes.

Suppressing for the moment how we go about achieving and measuring success in nudging and in experimentation,[55] this brief introduction to a theory of the social suggests that we can live within communities that determine the greater part of the meaning we make, and still remain committed to the possibility of *revolutionary* change (for the better) within those communities. The next part of the two-fold argument for social revolution runs as follows. First, the more successful models of being in the world made available to us, the more likely we, and our compatriots, will possess a greater range of possibilities for our lived existence. Second, in virtually all states – developed and developmental alike – only with the intervention of the state and other powerful non-state actors will most individuals come to possess the enhanced material conditions necessary for living out their preferred forms of existence.

3. A Theory of the Constitutional: Experimentalism & Flourishing

In Chapters 4 through 8, this book goes on to explain how a commitment to experimentalism in the political domain, when married to a robust conception of basic entitlements and civil rights, services human flourishing. But let me make clear, again, why human flourishing is the goal of the state – and not freedom. The self is a 'centre of narrative gravity'. It is a place which multiple narratives, not primarily spun by the individual, call home. Not only is the individual not free to choose these narratives, she is generally not 'free', in the common-sense usage of the term, to discard old storylines and to create, out of whole cloth, new storylines. The physical and the social determination of individual action occurs both at the level of individual responses to immediate stimuli and at the level at which we tend to attribute meaning to an individual life. The social – practices, forms of life, ways of being in the world, associations – operates within the same set of constraints. However, as we have also seen, neither the self nor the social is – despite the absence of outré notions of freedom – incapable of *revolutionary* change that enhances the meaning of life.

The ability of individuals, groups and communities to give life meaning – in a variety of different ways – is what I mean by flourishing. (Flourishing in these pages possesses a decidedly modern constitutional – as opposed to neo-Aristotelian – cast.) In Chapters 4 through 7 of this work, I defend the thesis that entitlements and institutions must be set up in such a way as to enhance human flourishing. That will generally mean allowing people to continue to be what they already are – along with provision of the material resources and the immaterial economic, social and political structures necessary to sustain such ways of being in the world. The South African Constitution is designed to do just that. However, flourishing must also require the creation of an array of institutions that enable individuals and groups to undertake 'experiments in life' – along with the provision of the material resources necessary to sustain such experiments. Here, again, appear the two poles of my account of the self, the social and the constitutional: the traditional and the revolutionary. On the one hand, this project recognizes how deeply-entrenched our individual sub-routines, our social practices and our political commitments are. The meaning of these routines, practices and commitments *makes* us. At the same time, selves, practices and politics are capable of change. We are capable of error correction. We can change our ways of being to meet, *instrumentally*, changed circumstances in the world. We can, though not without great difficulty, alter 'forms of life' – and their *normative* content – in a world that currently threaten humanity's very existence. As a professor of ethics, governance and sustainable development, I am all too aware of the threats that global warming, endemic poverty, nuclear proliferation and large scale failure of international financial institutions pose to our continued existence. At the same time, we have a number of organizations, bodies and conventions – some nascent, some quite weak – that we can exploit through collective political action to alter the apparent catastrophes that loom on the horizon. To quote Dennett again:

> There are real threats to human freedom, but they are not metaphysical. There is political bondage, coercion, the manipulation inducible by the dissemination of misinformation, and the 'forced move' desperation of hunger and poverty. No doubt we could do a lot more to combat these impositions on our freedom, were it not for the curious sort of *self-imposed bondage* that we create by the very exercise of our freedom, and in the very acknowledgment of our responsibility for the chains, ropes, strings and threads of commitments (explicit and tacit) that tie us to our family and friends, that tie us to our life projects, and that make us increasingly immobile by appeals to *radical action*.

Experimental constitutionalism dovetails with a very modest, naturalized notion of flourishing and experimental social theory because all three accounts (1) take the radical givenness of existing constitutive attachments seriously; (2) recognize the boundedness of individual and collective rationality; and (3) describe various kinds of feedback mechanisms that allow for error correction. At the level of the state, experimental constitutionalism enables more citizens to see what works and what doesn't. It goes without saying that experimentalism is no cure for systemic failures. Aggregate individual behaviour can lead to outcomes that we all know to be disastrous. Increasing levels of fossil fuel consumption may lead (inexorably) to the destruction of the very environment in which most individuals live.[56] It also goes without saying that experimental constitutionalism *alone* cannot yield ways of being in the world that enhance human flourishing.

And yet, what choice do we have but to give experimental constitutionalism a shot? Its opposite numbers are on ready display throughout the world: dictatorships continue to plague Africa (still others – such as Libya, Mali and Syria – are in a terribly uncertain free fall in Northern Africa, the Maghreb and the Middle East as I write); crony capitalist states have proliferated (and sometimes failed) in the developed democratic world (Greece, Ireland), oligopolic, security states abound (Russia) alongside developing fascist, mercantalist regimes (China), and family-dominated, but democratically fractured polities (India); theocracies have an unhealthy hold on societies across the globe (Iran, Saudi Arabia, Israel, Palestine, Pakistan and Afghanistan); and outright media driven insanity, along with an unholy alliance between money and politics have driven heretofore stable states (Italy, the United States and the United Kingdom) to the very precipice of financial disaster. Chapters 4 through 7 describe the rudiments of a social democratic state committed to experimental constitutionalism both because it is the best political model available to South Africa and because the philosophical commitments that underlie experimental constitutionalism are consistent with the most fundamental principles of our basic law.

After laying out the principles of experimental constitutionalism, I then look at how this model of constitutional politics might alter a range of doctrines and the manner in which a number of institutions operate. For those who cannot wait to see how this story ends, Chapters 4, 5, 6, after setting out the principles for experimental institutional and doctrinal design, offer a number of doctrinal and institutional examples of such design. These South African innovations embrace: (1) a doctrine of constitutional supremacy that maintains a meaningful equilibrium with a doctrine of separation of powers, and thus sets relatively clear guidelines for how authority for constitutional interpretation might best be shared by the judiciary, the legislature, the executive and non-state-actors;[57] (2) the use of various standard judicial mechanisms – such as cost orders, court procedures, amici, expanded constitutional jurisdiction and structural injunctions – to create bubbles of participatory democracy better able (than courts or legislatures) to resolve various kinds of polycentric conflict;[58] (3) an approach to rights, limitations and remedies analysis (such as remedial equilibration) that provides better outcomes than balancing, zero-sum decision-making or abject deference to co-ordinate branches of government;[59] and (4) greater roles for Chapter 9 Institutions with respect to investigation, information-sharing and norm-setting.[60] Chapter 6 mines the brief historical record of two important policy areas – Education[61] and Housing.[62] It suggests how the principles of experimental constitutionalism have, sometimes unwittingly, sometimes quite consciously, already been put to work and why we might witness even greater improvement in the Housing and Education sectors if the principles of experimental constitutionalism were employed on a more consistent and explicit basis.

C. Connections that Hold This Book Together

1. *Connections: Experimental Spaces*

In some sense, what global neuronal workspace theories, spontaneous orders, nudges and participatory bubbles all share in common is a belief that the information required for polycentric problem-solving is rather diffuse and that processes that solicit participation from multiple-stakeholders will offer more optimal solutions to everyday problems with which the self, social entities or the state are confronted. All of these approaches resist models of consciousness, social theory or constitutionalism based upon central command and control.

As we shall see, consciousness in global neuronal workspace theory occupies transient locations (in the brain). These locations or neuronal networks are designed to solve the immediate problem that has captured our attention. (Though to be clear: human consciousness – given the limits of speed – attends to problems, and is good at solving problems, that require long term planning.) Various sensory inputs and a host of potential experts – neural networks – assist (and sometimes compete to assist) in the solution of the problem that has captured an individual's attention.[63] These teams of 'experts' encompass neural networks that possess particular linguistic skills, relevant memories, or trained responses. As Blackmore puts it, the global neuronal workspace 'recruits processors for ongoing tasks, facilitates executive decisions and enables voluntary control over automatic action routines.'[64] After the problem has been solved, the unique neural network responsible for the solution will go silent until it is needed once more.

Spontaneous orders offer a similar characterization of knowledge-sharing and problem-solving. Markets, for example, require no central planner, no Hercules arriving at optimal judgments, in order to arrive at efficient outcomes. Indeed, limited amounts of information – often captured by price – are sufficient to enable large numbers of participants in a market to assist each other (and sometimes to compete with one another) with respect to the solution of a social problem. However, as soon as the problem is solved, the components of the market – individuals and firms alike – turn their attention to other problems and new solutions.

Nudges possess a family resemblance to neural networks and spontaneous orders. The experiments that realize nudges rely upon a large numbers of participants in a social formation to assist (experts) in the solution of a given problem. The important difference from related forms of social experimentation is that choice architects deliberately and consciously create a space within which participants are given incentives, and provide feedback, that encourage them to choose options more optimal for themselves, others and for society writ large.

Talk of participatory bubbles offers more of the same. The physical metaphor of bubbles is meant to convey three qualities of such small-scale institutional processes. First, processes of political engagement by ordinary citizens are understood to be a natural part of on-going social interactions. They originate when challenges to a given political authority accumulate and finally come to a boil: just as bubbles form after pressure builds up in a liquid and escape to the surface. Second, bubbles are meant to suggest limits on the scope of deliberation. Bubbles only enclose a small amount of space – both in terms of the issues contested and the number of participants. Third, most bubbles are ephemeral. After satisfactory resolutions emerge from processes of participatory engagement, the raison d'etre for such political (or judicial) processes ceases to exist. The bubbles burst. Participants can return to their more routine lives. And yet, importantly, the burst bubbles leave behind a residue from which other actors can learn and lessons that may apply to future problems. Indeed, not all bubbles should be treated as ephemera. Certain problems are so complex that the only way to solve them is by permanent experimentation and feedback. We may never truly understand how to best regulate carbon dioxide because new technologies and market forces may alter the manner in which carbon dioxide is produced. A community may not realise the negative consequences of a chosen approach to sulphur dioxide control unless some entity continues to monitor the problem. Only an array of permanent systems, devoted to specific challenges, and, designed to encourage experimentation, feedback and information-sharing, will allow communities, states and international institutions to stay on top of seemingly intractable problems.

This comparison of global neuronal workspace theory, spontaneous orders, nudges and participatory bubbles reinforce a conclusion already drawn in the Preface and first part of the Introduction. That is this: the gap between *is* and *ought* is not as great as some of my early readers suggested. To the extent that the descriptions of the self, the social, the political and the constitutional are accurate, they are all meant to depict what 'is'. Ultimately, it is the 'fit' of these various descriptions with one another that should count as one of the strengths of the theory of South African constitutionalism put forward in these pages.

2. *Connections: Experimental Competition*

A similar set of family resemblances are on display in my discussion of neuronal network competition, universal selection theory, libertarian paternalism, and shared constitutional interpretation. What links all four constructs at a meta-theoretical level are the mechanisms for the identification of best practices, and the reflexive nature of the selection process.

With respect to the self and consciousness, neuronal network competition describes the actual competition between different neuronal networks for primacy of place in response to environmental stimuli. As we shall see below in Chapter 2, what we, as individuals, become 'aware' or 'conscious' of is a creation, one hopes, of the neuronal network that best 'fits' the current environment. That does not mean, of course, that such a neuronal network will remain dominant or always provide the best 'fit'. It may well not provide the appropriate response to the current environment. A new neuronal network will, one hopes, supplant an out-moded network in the face of this disruption.

With respect to the social, universal selection theory offers a similar account of cognitive and non-cognitive processes. Some practices better 'fit' the social environment within which they operate. That does not mean, of course, that such a practice will remain dominant or always provide the best 'fit'. A better practice – for the environment in question – may come along and offer the possibility of greater success (or in theoretical domains, greater explanatory power). Moreover, the environment itself may change, altering the desiderata for 'fit'.

Thaler and Sunstein's libertarian paternalism is not as agnostic about individual and social choice as the universal selection theories of Campbell and company. They begin their monograph with a bold assertion:

> The false assumption [about choice, and thus selection over time] is that almost all people, almost all the time, make choices that are in their best interest or, at the very least, better choices are better than the choices that would be made by someone else. We claim that this assumption is false – indeed obviously false.[65]

Moreover, they claim that no one truly believes 'the false assumption' upon appropriate reflection. They then offer an easy example of their thesis: a chess match between a chess novice and a grandmaster. No novice, no spectator, would expect the novice to beat the grandmaster simply because the novice possessed the autonomy to decide which move to make. What is true about individual (and collective) choice is that it improves 'in contexts in which [people] have experience, good information and prompt feedback.'[66]

The relationship between experimentation and feedback is evident in an activity to which we shall return time and again in this work: golf. Though perhaps not the most obvious candidate (to most readers) for an exegesis on the relationship between theory and practice, and experimentation and feedback, sustained improvement in golf – as I shall argue later – requires constant 'nudging' by someone with greater experience – generally a coach. (If skilled, the player over time can become adept at nudging herself. But we shall see why a coach is a preferred source of *experience, good information and prompt feedback* in chapters 2 and 3.) Thaler and Sunstein themselves note how 'feedback' – a term of art for the quality of a golf club (which allows the user to immediately experience whether a stroke was crisply, accurately or poorly struck) as well as the result of any given particular stroke in golf – is a critical component for improvement:

> Learning is most likely if people get immediate, clear feedback after each try. Suppose you are practising your putting ... on a ... green. If you hit ten balls toward the same hole, it is easy to get a sense of how hard to hit the ball ... . Suppose instead you were putting ... but not getting to see where [the balls] were going. In that environment, you could put all day and never get any better.[67]

For Thaler and Sunstein, choice architects employ a number of techniques to ensure that individuals and groups flourish.[68] They create spaces that feature incentives to make optimal choices.[69] The spaces must lay out all pertinent information for optimal decision-making.[70] The architects must understand the defaults or the heuristics that take the inherent bias toward repetitive behaviour (laziness) into account so that the default or the heuristic in a system is set toward the outcome likely to enhance the individual's and the group's welfare.[71] They must construct feedback mechanisms that allow individuals: (a) to learn from their behaviour and to make better or more optimal choices when faced with an identical or a similar setting in the future,[72] and, (b) in a related manner, to send clear error signals so that, again, individuals see what works and what doesn't.[73] They must take great care to frame complex choices in a manner that enables participants to compare, rather easily, potential outcomes. Finally, choice architects cannot be normative agnostics. They must have some conception of a more optimal outcome. Why? They must be able to nudge the chooser toward choices that they might have been less likely to make. Consistent with the overall theme of this work, the more Millian 'experiments in living' we undertake, the more likely we are to find a way of being in the world that better 'fits' with our preferences (something we often know only after we have tried out a new way of doing things.) The better the nudges, the more likely we are to flourish. (Of course, the feedback will tell us quite a bit about the normative content of the nudge. So nudges too are subject to revision.)

With respect to the constitutional, 'shared constitutional interpretation' offers a comparable account of the development of constitutional doctrines and political policies. What we want from courts – that set constitutional doctrine – and co-ordinate branches of government – that set various policies – is the best possible 'fit' in the political and social environment within which they operate. A court's gloss on a constitutional norm or the policies pursued by a particular government will not always provide the best 'fit'. That would assume an unchanging environment. What we hope for from a politics of experimental constitutionalism is the ability of all branches of government – aided by an informed, engaged citizenry and a reasonably competent bureaucracy – to remain open to understanding our basic law differently and to devising policies most likely to realize our preferred (and adaptive) ends.

What links neuronal network competition, libertarian paternalism and shared constitutional interpretation is a commitment to the notion that choices at the level of the individual, the social, and the constitutional are largely about fit, at the same time as that fit remains open-ended, partial and occasionally, sub-optimal. At each level, there is a constant interrogation of means and ends (reflexivity) and a commitment to rolling best practices that offer the greatest opportunity for flourishing over time.

3. *Connections: Experimental Selves*

The theory of the self (and selves) offered in these pages takes a number of different forms. Each form has as its goal the displacement of the dominant Cartesian notion of the self as a fully integrated, rational, freely-willed chooser of its ends. However, each of these theoretical displacements of the Cartesian notion of the self (with its folk-psychology of freedom) takes place at a different level of generality.

The account of the determined self takes two forms. The first account of the determined self is a standard materialist argument. The determined self is subject to the same laws of cause and effect as all other corporeal entities. According to this incompabilist position on free will, it is impossible to be both a physical entity subject to the same deterministic framework as all other physical entities and an incorporeal entity that freely wills its actions in an otherwise determined physical universe. The second account of the determined self concentrates on providing an explanation for how consciousness, the experience of an integrated, choosing, unified self and a subjective experience of free will arise out of a thoroughly determined physical entity. A significant amount of space in Chapter 2 is devoted to the current neuroscience of consciousness because this new discipline provides the best explanation of what consciousness is and how it operates. This empirical account of consciousness offers the best hope of breaking the tenacious hold that the folk psychology of free will *qua* freedom has upon us.

The account of the conditioned self also takes two forms. At the level of the individual, the account of the conditioned self explains how our physical and social endowments create a variety of roles or dispositional states that cohere – or overlap – in a manner that enables (some of) us to experience a sense of integrity or singularity. The point again is to narrow dramatically the space for freely-willed action by calling attention to the extent to which our actions are determined by the social endowments with which (or into which) we are born and the physical endowments with which we are graced (or burdened). This account places particular emphasis on the extent to which pre-existing forms of 'meaning makes us'. At the level of the social, the account of the conditioned self – described by Michael Walzer in terms of involuntary association and the 'radical givenness' of the self – explains how the meaning of an individual life is determined by the variety of communities into which the individual is born and the extent to which what gives meaning to our lives is determined and not freely-willed. Walzer's account of the conditioned self serves as a bridge from the discussion in Chapter 2 with respect to the constraints that exist with respect to the self to the discussion in Chapter 3 regarding the constraints that exist with respect to the social.

The discussion of the multiple self or the divided self serves the general assault on the folk-psychology of free-will in a number of different ways. Dennett's characterization of the self as a centre of narrative gravity, with its emphasis on how different selves co-exist within a single corporeal individual, and Baars' global neuronal workspace theory and its description of the actual architecture of the brain, explain how consciousness and our multiple selves emerge. They work together to displace the Cartesian view of the self as a fully integrated, rational, freely-willed chooser of its ends. However, the multiple self or the divided self does not simply offer a materialist account of consciousness and an argument against the folk-psychology of freedom. It also offers, as Amartya Sen and Michael Walzer contend, a means for understanding how change (and thus the subjective experience of freedom) is possible in a determined and conditioned self. As Walzer notes, the 'self divides itself among its interests and roles … among its identities and among its ideals, principles and values.'[74] Walzer writes that there is, amongst these roles, identities and ideals

> no linearity, … and no hierarchy. The order of the self is better imagined as a thickly populated circle, with *me* in the centre surrounded by my self-critics who stand at different temporal and spatial removes (but don't necessarily stand still). Insofar as I am receptive to criticism, ready for (a little) castigation, I try to draw some of the critics closer, so that I am more immediately aware of their criticism; or I simply incorporate them, so that I become a worried self. I am like a newly

> elected president, summoning advisors, forming a cabinet. Though he is commander-in-chief, his choices are quite limited, his freedom qualified; the political world is full of givens; it has a history that pre-dates his electoral triumph. My inner world is full of givens, too, culturally bestowed or socially imposed – I manoeuvre among them insofar as their plurality allows for manoeuvring. My larger self, my worried self, is constituted and self-constituted by the sum of them all. I am the whole circle and also its embattled centre.[75]

Walzer's 'me' sounds much like Dennett's centre of narrative gravity. Dennett's cente of narrative gravity captures many of the same qualities as Walzer's 'thickly populated circle'. As I noted in the discussion of 'the social' above, radical or revolutionary change occurs as a result of the friction between the various selves that make up the 'thickly populated circle'. So here we have an account of change that is not contingent upon the existence of rational, freely-willed chooser of its ends. On this account, change flows from a radically heterogeneous self – the Whitmanian 'I am Large' self – in which different roles, identities and ideals serve as critics that support different, and sometimes incompatible, ways of being in the world.[76] These (self)critics do not merely offer us different ways of pursuing the same ends. They offer us different ends. The radically heterogeneous self makes sense of this book's commitment to the centrality of *trial and error*: success stories remain dominant so long as they bring the thickly populated circle success. Errors or failures elicit criticism from within the thickly populated circle. And with such criticism, perhaps, comes change. (Of course, experimental selves and thickly populated persons will also experience critique from without, and learn from other experimental selves and other thickly populated persons. This form of critique and learning, as we have seen, occurs within both the domain of the social sphere and the constitutional order.)

I hope to show, in the pages that follow, how each account of the self – the determined self, the conditioned self, the multiple self, the divided self, the radically, *socially*, heterogeneous self and the radically, *naturally*, heterogeneous, determined self – undermines the Cartesian view of the self and supplants it with an account that possesses greater explanatory power. However, while these various accounts of the self largely sing off the same hymn sheet, they also work at different levels of generality. That is, they reinforce one another, but are not reducible to one another. No attempt is made, therefore, to capture the social theory of the self that Walzer offers in terms of the neuroscientific theories of the self that Baars, Naccache or Churchland proffer. So, just as we do not expect the laws of biology to be reducible to the laws of chemistry – even when they have the same objects under scrutiny – so too is it wrong to expect that the language of contemporary social theory is somehow reducible to the ostensibly more basic language of contemporary neuroscience. It is sufficient that they do not contradict one another.

C. Tweaking Constitutional Doctrine: Constitutional Court Cases Revisited and Revised

In Chapter 8, I revisit 20 of the most important cases to be handed down by the South African Constitutional Court over the past decade. This re-engagement with the facts and norms underlying this score of decisions allows us to reconsider the outcomes in light of the precepts of experimental constitutionalism and flourishing. The Constitutional Court's persistent emphasis on freedom-talk, rather than flourishing, and on the deference reflected in an arid separation of powers doctrine, rather than a more fluid inter-institutional and inter-personal theory of experimental constitutionalism, continues to have untoward consequences for our constitutional jurisprudence. What may be most fascinating to readers with respect to some of the most recent cases reconstructed is that a gratifying pattern has emerged. The Constitutional Court has adopted some facets of experimental constitutionalism (without ever describing it as such or assessing the long term effects of this mode of adjudication and politics.) We can glimpse a Court that, as of early 2012, wants to 'learn aggressively' – as my friend Professor Frank Michelman has put it – not just from the parties before the court, but from individuals, communities, networks, associations and institutions with an interest and some insight into the facts and norms at play in a given matter. I would love to be able to say that less theoretical ground now separates my theories and the Court's practices than when I first began this endeavour (a controversial thesis). You certainly won't hear that from the Court. And the judgments can't speak for themselves. As to the virtue of my approach, by the end of Chapter 9, you will have made up your own m-m-m-m-minds.

Endnotes

1. For more on the self as a centre of narrative gravity, see D Dennett *Consciousness Explained* (1991) 167–171; D Dennett *Sweet Dreams: Philosophical Obstacles to a Science of Consciousness* (2005). The path-breaking experiments of empirical psychologists Benjamin Libet and W Grey Walters provided Dennett with a well-established framework for understanding delayed conscious awareness of 'unconsciously' initiated action. In layman's terms, these experiments showed how what appeared to be 'conscious, freely willed action' could, in fact, be functions of pre-determined, unconsciously initiated neural networks. See, eg, B Libet 'The Experimental Evidence for Subjective Referral of Evidence Backward in Time: Reply to PS Churchland' (1981) 48 *Philosophy of Science* 182; B Libet 'Time of Conscious Intention to Act in Relation to the Onset of Other Cerebral Activities (Readiness Potential): The Unconscious Initiation of a Freely Voluntary Act' (1983) 106 *Brain* 623; WG Walters' *Presentation to the Osler Society* (1963) as reported in D Dennett *Consciousness Explained* (1991) 167 – 171. Some readers might want to know how one would explain the fact that while a baseball travels the 60 feet and 6 inches from pitcher to hitter in 0.45 seconds, Libet's experiments seem to reflect a much more generous period of 0.8 seconds between readiness potential and action. The explanation is agent-priming. Constant habituation enables actors to shorten dramatically the period between non-conscious intention and action. Well, that may be fine for hitting a baseball (or even a more quickly delivered serve in tennis), but how does that work for such ostensibly high level cognitive activities like writing a symphony, a novel or a response to David Bilchitz? See S Dehaene & L Naccache 'Towards a Cognitive Neuroscience of Consciousness: Basic Evidence and a Workspace Framework' in S Dehaene (ed) *Cognitive Neuroscience of Consciousness* (2001) 1, 13: 'High level processes may operate unconsciously, as long as they are associated with functional neural pathways either established by evolution, laid down during development or automized by learning. Hence there is no systematic relationship between the objective complexity of a computation and the possibility of it proceeding unconsciously. For instance, face processing, word reading, and postural control all require complex computations, yet there is considerable evidence that they can proceed without attention based upon specialized neural subsystems. Conversely, computationally trivial but non-automized operations, such as solving 21 - 8, require conscious effort.'

2. See R Dawkins *The Selfish Gene* (1976); R Dawkins *The Extended Phenotype* (1982). Dawkins provides useful accounts of how patterns of learned behaviour – memes – replicate themselves over time through individuals, groups and societies.
3. The theory of self developed in these pages does not assume a unitary supervisory 'self' over time. See D Parfit *Reasons and Persons* (1984); D Parfit 'Divided Minds and the Nature of Persons' in C Blackmore and S Greenfield (eds) *Mindwaves* (1987) 19. For the classic statement of such a disaggregated view of self, see D Hume *A Treatise of Human Nature*: *Being An Attempt to Introduce the Experimental Method of Reasoning in Moral Subjects* ((1739)(eds) DF Norton & MJ Norton, 2000)) ('[W]hen I enter most intimately into what I call *myself,* I always stumble upon some particular perception or other, of heat or cold, light or shade, love or hatred, pain or pleasure. I can never catch myself at any time without a perception and can never observe anything but the perception.')
4. From the experience of having lost almost all of the selves listed above, I know that, during this period of debilitating desuetude, I experienced a tiny, but still extant, conception of 'me'. It occurred most often in conversations with my friend Robert Greenblum, and our longstanding ability to make each other laugh. He got 'me' as I got 'him'. Laughing with him created conditions that enabled me to retrieve, or at least experience, that 'core temperament'. The neurological basis for this unitary sense of self can be traced in part to the activity of the dorso-medial frontal lobe. See VS Ramachandran *The Tell Tale Brain: A Neuroscientist's Quest for What Makes Us Human* (2011) 265. Many families bemoan the fact that while a family member who suffers damage to this portion of the brain continues to be capable of carrying out virtually all high level cognitive functions, she is no longer 'herself'. Ibid. Most of us are familiar with the story of railway foreman Phineas Gage, who, in 1848, had a crowbar driven through his skull (and left prefrontal lobe) and survived. He not only survived but continued to function. However, the damage to his brain was so profound that his friends no longer recognized him as the person they once knew. See, further, A Damasio, B Everitt and D Bishop 'The Somatic Marker Hypothesis of the Brain and the Possible Functions of the Prefrontal Cortex' (1996) 351 *Philosophical Transactions of the Royal Society of London – Series B, Biological Sciences* 1413.
5. M Walzer 'On Involuntary Association' in A Gutmann (ed) *Freedom of Association* (1998) 64, 67.
6. M Heidegger *Lectures on the History of the Concept of Time* (1926).
7. J Dewey *Reconstruction in Philosophy* (1920) 23. See also W James 'Does Consciousness Exist' in *Essays in Radical Empiricism* (1912)(James contends that consciousness is not a thing, but a process, that there is no 'aboriginal stuff or quality of being, contrasted with that of which material objects are made, out of which our thoughts of them are made ... [T]he entity known ... as consciousness ... is fictitious, while thoughts in the concrete are fully real. But thoughts in the concrete are made of the same stuff as things are.') See also W James *The Heart of William James* (R Richardson (ed))(2011).
8. L Wittgenstein *Philosophical Investigations* (1953).
9. See S Woolman 'Language, Power and the Margin: Eliot's Philosophy of Language, Wittgenstein on Following a Rule, and Statutory Construction in *Thembekile Mankayi v Anglogold Ashanti Limited* (2012) 128 *South African Law Journal* 434. Here, I re-articulate the rather banal – but too often ignored – proposition that most beliefs that human beings hold are true, and that distortions occur at the margins. Were it otherwise, translation that occurs every day would be impossible, and we would find it similarly impossible to navigate our way through a world in we were constantly misunderstood – or not understood at all. This proposition does not merely hold for homogeneous societies. In the radically heterogeneous and stratified society in which I live, South Africa, I can move between townships such as Alexandra to wealthy peri-urban areas in nearby Sandton to my extremely diverse setting at the University of the Witwatersrand without experiencing misunderstanding. The moral salience of everyday life here in Johannesburg – where every exchange (not matter how small) carries a moral charge – has taught me that most 'misunderstandings' are wilful (and flow from distortions of power.)

10. We would do well to follow Wittgenstein and his efforts in *Philosophical Investigations* to draw us back to the everyday world. Much of that effort takes the form of his desire to demonstrate how we have inverted the order of action and language: 'A picture [has] held us captive. And we could not get outside it, for it lay in our language and language seemed to repeat it to us inexorably (§115). ... What *we* do is to bring words back from their metaphysical to their everyday use. (§116) ... . Now, however, let us suppose that after some efforts on the teacher's part [the student] continues the series correctly, that is, as we do it. So now we can say he has *mastered* the system – But how far need he continue the series for us to have the right to say that? Clearly you cannot state a limit here. (§145) ... The grammar of the word 'knows' is evidently closely related to that of 'can', 'is able to'. But also closely related to that of 'understands' [and to] '*mastery*' of a technique (§150).' (Emphasis added).
11. GP Baker & PMS Hacker *Scepticism, Rules & Language* (1984) 115, 117, 119, 122, 123.
12. D Davidson 'Thought and Talk' *Inquiries into Truth and Interpretation* (1984) 155, 168.
13. Ibid.
14. J Cohen 'Review of Michael Walzer's *Spheres of Justice: A Defense of Pluralism and Equality* (1986) 82 *The Journal of Philosophy* 457.
15. See JB Newman, BJ Baars and SB Cho 'A Neural Global Workspace Model for Conscious Attention' (1997) 10 *Neural Networks* 1195.
16. JB Newman 'Reticular-Thalamic Activation of the Cortex Generates Conscious Contents' (1995) 18 (4) *Behavioral and Brain Sciences* 691.
17. S Dehaene & L Naccache 'Towards a Cognitive Neuroscience of Consciousness (supra) at 1.
18. Ibid at 30.
19. Dehaene and Naccache are quick to point out that this ability to check one's immediate responses and to come up with what one believes to be an optimal response should not be confused with being able to 'freely will' a response in the standard compatibalist sense. As Spinoza wrote: 'Men are mistaken in thinking themselves free; their opinion is made up of consciousness of their own actions, and ignorance of the causes by which they are conditioned. Their idea of freedom, therefore, is simply their ignorance of any cause of their actions.' *Ethics*, II, 35. (How consciousness has emerged, out of numerous non-conscious neuro-muscular systems and biological and socially constructed dispositions – as the wetness of water arises out of the aggregation of H_2O molecules – is something that must be left to future interrogations by scientists in various domains of inquiry.)
20. What happened, as we shall see in Chapter 2, is that I experienced 'brain freeze'. In the first example, no cost attached to the occurrence of brain freeze. With respect to everyday events, our brains often get 'lazy'. We assume (not consciously) that an ordinary cognitive process can be undertaken without reflection. Then, some other process (or self or dispositional state) commandeers our conscious awareness. We discover, much to our horror, that this new chain of conscious thought has crowded our other processes, and led us into a preformative error. As a Republican aspirant for the US Presidency, Rick Perry, discovered in 2011, his inability to recall (in front of roughly 50 million viewers) one of the three federal agencies he had promised to eliminate if elected was probably caused by the distractions of a nationalized televised debate and an assumption that he could recall his 'script' without difficulty. His pushing of one cognitive process off the stage, while another attentive process took over (say, engaging in eye contact with another contender Ron Paul), probably cost him the nomination. In short, as neuroscientist's explain, the prefrontal cortex, with the assistance of the medial temporal lobe, normally bears responsibility for the retrieval of memories and simple dispositional routines. Stress – quite high in a debate – can interfere with the medial temporal lobe's retrieval function or the hippocampus' role in memory retrieval. During more monotonous activity, such as driving, MRIs have shown that the brain does indeed get 'lazy' and falls into a 'default mode network'. T Parker-Hope 'Rick Perry's Brain Freeze' *The New York Times* (10 November 2011). Defaults are a colloquial way of describing what the social science and philosophical literature call 'heuristics'. See G Gigerenzer 'Moral Intuition = Fast and Frugal Heuristics' in W Sinnott-Armstrong (ed) *Moral Psychology, Volume II - The Cognitive Science of Morality: Intuition and Diversity*

(2008) 1. Heuristics can be far more dangerous than the examples of brain freeze offered above. Gigerenzer discusses the infamous case of a Nazi officer, well aware of the atrocity that he was about to commit, who extended the following offer to his men: 'Those of you who do not wish to participate in this action are excused.' Only a few men took up this offer. The heuristic that led them to stay in formation had little to do with evil and everything to do with the fact that this brigade, drawn from the same police force, had learned to stick together. That 'thick blue line' was one of their most powerful heuristics or defaults. Had the officer posed the problem differently – 'You are hereby relieved from any obligation to carry out this task, however those who wish to do so may stay and participate in these brutal executions' – the response might have been different. Why? The default has been changed. Under the alternative proposition, the officer would have released the men from their existing heuristic of solidarity, foregrounded the mass killing that would soon take place, and strongly insinuated their culpability in that slaughter.

21. It is important to note at the outset that my views of the self – the limits of consciousness as well as the plasticity of the brain – are drawn from personal experience. (My experience does not, of course, make my conclusions any more or less true.) My own experience of cognitive dysfunction, the awareness of my own inability to form coherent thoughts or to recall simple words or names of friends and colleagues – as any person with something akin to incipient stages of Alzheimer's disease can tell you – is truly chilling. The self is fragile – a string of pearls. I have been fortunate to have people assist me in putting Humpty Dumpty back together again. It is equally chilling to watch persons one loves – such as my Uncle Harry – experience severe post-stroke aphasia. Depending on the area and extent of brain damage, someone suffering from aphasia may be able to speak but not write, or vice versa, or display any of a wide variety of other deficiencies in language comprehension and production, such as being able to sing but not speak. I myself lost the capacity to sign my name correctly; a capacity that returned as my health improved. My Uncle Harry fades in and out – he recognizes me (I think) – but cannot say my name in my presence (without my brother's prompting). My experience, and that of my Uncle, suggests how complicated and diffuse the neural organization of language is. It seems clear to me that language, and the thought that goes with it, is not the product of some small, circumscribed region of the brain. As we shall see in Chapter 2, we require five main categories of neuronal systems to collaborate for the self and consciousness to function: (1) 'perceptual circuits that inform about the present state of the environment'; (2) 'motor circuits that allow the preparation and controlled execution of actions'; (3) 'long-term memory-circuits that can re-instate past workspace states'; (4) 'evaluation circuits that attribute {percepts} a valence in relation to previous experience'; and (5) 'attentional or top-down circuits that selectively gate the focus of interest'. The interaction of these five kinds of neural systems requires no central co-ordination. Instead, neural networks are established for the purpose of conscious action by virtue of their adequacy with respect to the demands of the environment and the task at hand. It is clear that my uncle and I possess varying degrees of consciousness and selfhood. Whether the plasticity of my brain will ever allow me to connect (with ease) names with faces or whether my uncle will regain his powerful capacity for original and humorous thought remains to be seen. But that we each have complex spatially distributed neural networks in need of repair – or rewiring – I have no doubt.

22. As I noted above, and discuss below in Chapter 2, the work of empirical psychologists Benjamin Libet and W Grey Walters has provided a well-established framework for understanding delayed conscious awareness of 'unconsciously' initiated action. See B Libet 'The Experimental Evidence for Subjective Referral of Evidence Backward in Time' (supra); 2; B Libet 'The Unconscious Initiation of a Freely Voluntary Act' (supra); WG Walters' *Presentation to the Osler Society* (supra). I am indebted to John Ostrovick for sharing his work on this subject with me and for his explanation of the findings. See J Ostrovick 'The Timing Experiments of Libet and Walters' (2004)(Unpublished manuscript on file with author.) Libet's experiments demonstrate that a readiness potential – 'a change in the voltage in the brain' – occurs 0.6 seconds before' what we describe commonly as a conscious awareness and 0.8 seconds before action. Only conscious awareness prior to readiness potential would demonstrate

consciously willed action. Again, no empirical evidence exists for such awareness. WG Walters' experiments bolster conclusions about non-conscious determination of action and the importance of maintaining an apparent causal connection between awareness and action. Walters' subjects were brain surgery patients asked to press a button to change a viewing-slide at any time. The button, however, was not connected to the slide projector. Instead, the slide-projector was rotated by an amplification of the readiness potential signal from the patient's brain. Walters' subjects reported the experience of an unsettling form of precognition – on the part of the projector. That is, they found that the slide projector had rotated the slides prior to their conscious intention to press the button. Indeed, the significant time gap between non-conscious readiness potential, slide change and intent-consciousness was sufficiently large to cause the subjects to report that they were concerned that 'they might, accidentally, advance the slide twice.' See Ostrovick (supra) at 8. See also WG Walters (supra) at 171.

23. The ability of a hitter to connect solidly with a baseball that travels the 60 feet and 6 inches from pitcher to hitter in 0.45 seconds, while Libet's experiments reflect a much more generous period of 0.8 seconds between readiness potential and consciousness, is explained by agent-priming. Constant habituation enables actors to shorten dramatically the period between non-conscious intention and action. But even time overtakes that old trick. In 2011, Derek Jeter, age 37, and one of the best hitting and fielding shortstops in baseball (history) found that he could not hit for power. Why? Age. Everything was slowing down – except for the world around him. M Sokolove 'For Derek Jeter, on His 37th Birthday' *The New York Times* (23 June 2011), available at www.nytimes.com (accessed on 30 June 2011). Robert Adair, author of *The Physics of Baseball* (3rd Edition, 2002), notes that it takes a ball traveling 90 miles per hour *400 milliseconds* to travel the 56 feet from the moment it is released from the pitcher's hand to time it arrives at home plate. During the initial period of the ball's flight, sensory cells in the retina must 'encode information and send it to the brain.' *75 milliseconds gone.* The ball has travelled nine feet. The brain must then relay signals to the spinal code to initiate muscle response. Usually, the legs initiate a stride, if the batter intends (unconsiously) to hit the ball. Quite tellingly – without knowing the science of baseball – Jeter tried, this year, to hit without a stride. He was, without awareness of the underlying physiology, trying to buy a few extra milliseconds. After the legs begin their stride, arm muscles and the upper torso bring the bat around. Here's the thing. By the time the ball has travelled 30 feet, it's too late for the batter to make any adjustments at all to the plane of his swing. Believe it or not, the batter might as well have his eyes closed for the remainder of his swing and the ball's journey home. Now you might understand why pitches that 'break late' – pitches whose 'radical' movements are delayed until the ball is near home plate – make batters look terribly foolish. The time for adjustment has long past. Even if habituation, careful study of a pitcher's tendencies and strengths, understanding the pitch count and the game situation gives the batter a clue as to what to expect, and milliseconds to (unconsciously) adjust, all things being equal, the battle still favours the pitcher. Now add age. By 37, eyesight, visual processing and fast-twitch muscles are all in decline. Work-out all you like. All it takes to turn a solid line drive into a weak, dribbling, worthless, foul ball is .01 seconds. And so, Derek Jeter, one of only 28 major league players in the history of a 125 year old league to have collected 3,000 hits, one of a tiny percentage to possess a lifetime batting average above .314, was hitting a meagre .260 through the middle of 2011 and ranked near the bottom of the league in statistics that speak to his ability to hit with power. Conscious adjustment is generally unlikely to make a palpable difference. Every pitcher will note Jeter's age, his average, his attempts to compensate – and throw the ball where he is now far less likely to hit it. If consciousness is best understood as a feedback mechanism, then Derek Jeter's most important feedback mechanisms – sight and fast twitch muscles – have begun to abandon him. Consciously, he knows that time is catching up. (As this book went through its natural editorial phases, Jeter managed to hit raise his average for the 2011 season to .298: a significant feat. And so, though he hit a measly 6 home runs, it's clear that Jeter still remains capable of making some adjustments. By 2012, he had largely righted his ship. He has maintained his ability to hit for

average, .321, though not for power. Jeter, it seems, did a little extra studying himself to tip the scales back in his favour at age 38.)

24. See S Dehaene & L Naccache 'Towards a Cognitive Neuroscience of Consciousness: Basic Evidence and a Workspace Framework' in S Dehaene (ed) *Cognitive Neuroscience of Consciousness* (2001) 1, 13.
25. See BJ Baars 'How Does a Serial, Integrated and Very Limited Stream of Consciousness Emerge from a Nervous System that is Mostly Unconscious, Distributed, Parallel and of Enormous Capacity' in GR Bock and J Marsh (eds) *Experimental and Theoretical Studies of Consciousness* (1993) 282. See also BJ Baars *In the Theatre of Consciousness: The Workspace of the Mind* (1997) 142.
26. S Dehaene & L Naccache 'Towards a Cognitive Neuroscience of Consciousness: Basic Evidence and a Workspace Framework' in S Dehaene (eds) *Cognitive Neuroscience of Consciousness* (2001) 1, 9–12. See also A Damasio *Self Comes to Mind: Constructing the Conscious Brain* (2010).
27. See G Strawson 'The Self' (1997) 4 *Journal of Consciousness Studies* 405.
28. At least part of the reason most of us continue to adhere to a conception of free will is that we view human behaviour in terms of 'agents' and other phenomena in terms of 'causation'. The former concept is a fundamentally ethical precept. It enables us to attach responsibility for actions to particular individuals and groups. The latter concept is a physical precept. It enables us to discuss and analyze regularities. The refusal to see human behaviour in terms of determined cause and determined effect is the only way in which a full-blown theory of free-will gains any purchase. See JCC Smart 'Free Will, Praise and Blame' (1961) 70 *Mind* 291. These basic errors do not mean that the notions of praise and blame that attach to human action serve no purpose. It is simply not the purpose that we most readily suppose. They are primarily mechanisms for social control. Reward reinforces the inclination towards certain behaviour. Punishment creates disincentives. The efficacy of reward and punishment is not contingent upon the existence of free will.
29. The argument, as it is developed in Chapter 2, is not just about the meaning of freedom and the meaning of consciousness. Rather the argument is that the mistakes we make about the nature of 'consciousness' share a strong family resemblance to the mistakes we make about the nature of 'freedom'. See D Dennett *Sweet Dreams: Philosophical Obstacles to a Science of Consciousness* (2005). To correct a misunderstanding of the one may lead to a correction in a misunderstanding of the other.
30. Flourishing has always been at the heart of contemporary liberal constitutional thought. John Locke's *A Letter Concerning Toleration* (1689) speaks directly to one dimension of human flourishing: religious faith. Flourishing largely owes its current revival in the philosophical literature to the neo-Aristotelian turn of Martha Nussbaum's writings. See, eg, M Nussbaum *Love's Knowledge* (1991). The notion of flourishing defended in these pages is, perhaps, closest in form to the capabilities approach of more recent work by Nussbaum and development theory first expounded by Amartya Sen. See A Sen 'More Than 100 Million Women are Missing' (1992) 37 *New York Review of Books* 61; A Sen 'More Than 100 Million Women are Missing' (1992) 367 *The Lancet* 185; A Sen *Development as Freedom* (1999). Sen contends that the conditions for flourishing – an open and democratic society based upon dignity, equality and freedom (in the language of the Final Constitution) – are, rightly understood, meant neither to achieve definitive outcomes nor to prescribe a univocal understanding of 'the good'. What these semi-covalent values do require – as conditions for flourishing – is a level of material support (e.g., food) and immaterial support (e.g., civil liberties) that enable individuals to pursue a meaningful and comprehensive vision of the good – as they understand it. Sen *Development* (supra) at 75.
31. See D Dennett *Freedom Evolves* (2003).
32. S Woolman '"I am Large": Sachs, Whitman and Democracy' (2010) 25 *SA Public Law* 58.
33. J Schedler 'The Efficacy of Psychodynamic Psychotherapy' (2010) 65 *American Psychologist* 98, 98 ('Empirical evidence supports the efficacy of psychodynamic-therapy. Effect sizes for psychodynamic therapy are as large as those reported for other therapies that have been actively promoted as "empirically supported" and "evidence-based." In addition, patients who receive psychodynamic therapy maintain therapeutic gains and appear to continue to improve after treatment ends.') See,

especially, F Leichsenring & S Rabung, 'Effectiveness of Long-Term Psychodynamic Psychotherapy: A Reply' (2009) 301 *Journal of the American Medical Association* 932; F Leichsenring, & S Rabung, 'Effectiveness of Long-Term Psychodynamic Psychotherapy: A Meta-Analysis' (2008) 300 *Journal of the American Medical Association* 1551. But see BD Thombs, M Bassel & LR Jewett 'Analyzing Effectiveness of Long-Term Psychodynamic Psychotherapy' (2009) 301 *Journal of the American Medical Association* 930 (Criticizing the methodology of the Leichsenring/Sabung study). Of course, laying down new tracks does not mean the current winner remains the dominant dispositional state. As Dennett notes, Driver and Vuileumier's work on 'the fate of extinguished stimuli shows that "multiple competitions" … leave not only singles winners but lots of powerful semi-finalists or also-rans, whose influence can be traced even when they don't achieve the canonical – indeed operationalized – badge of fame: subsequent reportability (consciousness).' D Dennett *Sweet Dreams* (2005) 139–140 citing J Driver and P Vuilleumier 'Perceptual Awareness and Its Loss in Unilateral Neglect and Extinction' in S Dehaene (ed) *The Cognitive Science of Neuroscience* (2001) 39. Indeed, after years of therapy, these regularly contested elections are what 'conscious experience' feels like. On some days, the neuronal tracks laid down at infancy, and later during a period of physical desuetude of varying degrees of severity, can make life feel overwhelming. So it goes. However, after years of cutting edge medical treatment, continued rehabilitation and grit and determination, other days approach normality and last for longer fed by the recognition that my current level of disability does not mean that that small tasks and large projects cannot be pulled off.

34. D Campbell 'Blind Variation and Selection Retention in Creative Thought as in Other Knowledge Processes' (1960) 67 *Psychological Review* 380.

35. See KM Kim 'DT Campbell's Social Epistemology of Science: Vicarious Selection, Epistemological Fallabilism, and Sociology of Scientific Validity (1997) 3 *Evolution and Cognition* 75; KM Kim 'Nested Hierarchies of Vicarious Selectors' in C Heyes and D Hull (eds) *Selection Theory and Social Construction* (2001) 101. See also HJ Eysenck 'Creativity and Personality: Suggestions for a Theory' (1993) 4 *Psychological Inquiry* 147.

36. See G Cziko 'Universal Selection Theory and the Complementarity of Different Types of Blind Variation and Selective Retention' in C Heyes and D Hull (eds) *Selection Theory and Social Construction* (2001) 15, 18. See also D Campbell 'Evolutionary Epistemology' in PA Schlipp (ed) *The Philosophy of Karl Popper* (1974) 421.

37. FA Hayek 'The Use of Knowledge in Society' (1945) 35 (4) *American Economic Review* 519, 520. See also FA Hayek 'The Results of Human Action, But Not of Human Design' *Studies in Philosophy, Politics and Economics* (1967) 96, 97.

38. Sunstein's (public) turn appears to begin with a study published in the *University of Virginia Law Review* about how initial political differences or similarities of three judge panels in US Circuit Courts led to different kinds of decisions and extremely different kinds of judgments. The differences did not turn on deliberation as much as the predispositions of the judges and the tendency of personal biases to be reinforced by like-minded judges and to be challenged (and diminished) by judges of different political stripes. A panel made up entirely of judges appointed by Democrats tended to produce quite progressive decisions. A panel made up entirely of judges appointed by Republicans tended to hand down quite conservative judgments. However, decisions handed down by panels made up of both Democrats and Republicans, in 2 to 1 break-downs, tended to be more moderate in outcome. See C Sunstein, D Schkade, & L Ellman 'Ideological Voting on the Federal Courts of Appeals: A Preliminary Investigation' (2004) 90 *University of Virginia Law Review* 304. See also C Sunstein, D Schkade, L Ellman and A Sawicki *Are Judges Political?* (2006).

39. Sunstein *Infotopia* (supra) at 11. In their interesting thought experiment on giving voters a day to discuss issues and candidates, *Deliberation Day* (2004), Ackermann and Fishkin do not pay sufficient attention to the limits of such Socratic interaction. The real value of such interaction likely lies in the greater normative legitimacy that flows from participation in such a deliberative practice. As any professor can tell you, students – like the voters in whom Ackerman and Fishkin place such

faith – are often great at articulating their opinions, but quite limited in capacity when it comes to absorbing the points being made by others. Drawing out opinions is not enough – some form of mediation is necessary. (Or at least that is what I tell myself before and after class.) Thaler and Sunstein's 'choice architecture' constitutes but one form of such mediation.

40. Ibid at 14. See also S Woolman, E Fishman and M Fischer 'Evidence of Patent Thicket Effects in Complex Biopharmaceutical Technologies' (2013) 53 *IDEA: The International Journal of Intellectual Property* 1. Eliot Fishman, Michael Fisher and I have identified similar kinds of failures in deliberation when it comes to patent thickets or anti-commons effects in the biopharmaceutical industry. Several reasons exist for the failure of perfectly 'rational' actors to fail to deliver well-designed intellectual property to downstream markets: (1) high transaction costs, (2) the heterogeneous interests of rights holders, (3) cognitive biases of license holders and (4) attributive biases of the participants. In sum, human beings generally tend, just like ordinary owners of upstream biomedical research patents, to overvalue their own contributions and property. See also SM Maurer 'Inside the Anticommons: Academic Scientists' Struggle to Build a Commercially Self-Supporting Human Mutations Database, 1999-2001' (2006) 35 (6) *Research Policy* 839; RR Nelson 'The Market Economy and the Scientific Commons' (2004) 33 (3) *Research Policy* 455; M Heller and R Eisenberg 'Can Patents Deter Innovation? The Anticommons in Biomedical Research' (1998) *Science* 280 (5364); OE Williamson 'The Economics of Organization: The Transaction Cost Approach' (1981) 87(3) *American Journal of Sociology* 548.
41. R Thaler & C Sunstein *Nudge: Improving Decisions about Health, Wealth and Happiness* (2008).
42. Ibid at 3.
43. Ibid at 5.
44. Ibid at 11.
45. Thaler and Sunstein call their social theory 'libertarian paternalism'. First, the 'libertarian aspect of our strategies lies in the straightforward insistence that people, in general, should be free to do what they like … . When we use the term libertarian to modify paternalism, we simply mean liberty preserving.' Ibid at 5. Second, the 'paternalistic aspect lies in the claim that it is legitimate for choice architects to try to influence people's behaviour in order to make their lives longer, healthier and better. In other words, we argue for self-conscious efforts, by institutions in the private sector and also by government, to steer people's choices in directions that will improve their lives. … Drawing on some well-established findings in social science, we show that in many cases, individuals make pretty bad decisions – decisions they would not have made if they had paid full attention and possessed complete information, unlimited cognitive abilities and complete self-control.' Ibid at 5.
46. See D Halpern *Social Capital* (2005) 11–12.
47. A Baier 'Trust and Antitrust' in *Moral Prejudices* (1995) 95, 96, 98, 128–129.
48. See D Bilchitz 'Should Religious Associations be Allowed to Discriminate?' (2011) 27 *South African Journal on Human Rights* 219.
49. See S Woolman 'Seek Justice Elsewhere: An Egalitarian Pluralist Reply to David Bilchitz on the Distinction between Differentiation and Domination' (2012) 28 *South African Journal on Human Rights* 271.
50. R Putnam (2000) *Bowling Alone: The Collapse and Revival of American Community* 22–23. See also R Gittel and A Vidal *Community Organizing: Building Social Capital as a Development Strategy* (1998).
51. D Halpern *Social Capital* (2005) 20.
52. Lists of nouns and adjectives – culled from the social capital literature – also provide a handy way to distinguish one kind of network from the other. Bonding networks are often said to embrace parents, siblings, love, care (as well as the withdrawal of affection), neighbourhoods, workplaces, shared customs (as well as exclusion from the community), nation, religion, ethnic group, patriotism, loyalty, honour, and trust (as well as excommunication or criminal sanction.). Bridging networks are often said to encompass acquaintances, colleagues, shame, reputation, links, generosity, mutual respect, diplomacy, negotiation as well as wartime allies.

53. South African political scientist Ivor Chipkin has argued that social cohesion is essential for long-term economic stability in South Africa. See I Chipkin 'Social Cohesion as a Factor in Development' Symposium for Office of the President (11–12 June 2007); I Chipkin 'Social Cohesion as a Factor in Development' in K Gupta, G Svendsen & P Maiti (eds) *Social Capital, Volume II* (2008) Chapter 8. For another version of this argument, see I Chipkin & B Ngqulunga 'Friends and Family: Social Cohesion in South Africa' (2007) 34(1) *Journal of Southern African Studies* 310. Brahm Fleisch and I have offered a similar argument in a favour of viewing school governing bodies as a critical fourth tier of governance – critical in the sense that SGBs enable parents and learners to determine the shape of the school community and through collective action create a sense of community that heretofore did not exist. See S Woolman & B Fleisch *The Constitution in the Classroom: Law & Education in South Africa, 1994–2008* (2009). But see B Fleisch & S Woolman 'The Problem of the 'Other Tongue: Official Languages Equal Citizenship and an Integrated South Africa' (Legal Resources Centre Conference on Law and Education, July 2012, on file with author.)
54. Understanding social capital or associational life as generic terms is insufficient for the radical aims of this project. Bridges must be built between associations that wield enormous amounts of power and associations that do not. See M Edwards *Civil Society* (2004) 47 ('Large differentials in the power of associations to make their voices heard, advance their own agendas and consolidate their own interpretation of shared norms in the public sphere are the enemy of the good society, and of democracy. That is why reducing inequality is a crucial part of any solution to the civil society puzzle.') Powerful social networks with pernicious ends are the social capital equivalent of 'group-think' institutions that tend to produce biased or pre-ordained results. Neither experimentalism nor flourishing can occur within such frameworks.
55. The notion of an experimenting society and the social science that supports such a notion is developed at length in Chapter 3. It is largely parasitic on Donald Campbell's efforts to describe the role of the social scientist in constructing assessment criteria that would make the various experiments in an 'experimenting society' meaningful. See D Campbell & MJ Russo *Social Experimentation* (1999). These principles are consistent with the notions of legal and political institutional design expounded by Michael Dorf in his work on experimental constitutionalism. See, eg, M Dorf 'Legal Indeterminism and Institutional Design' (2004) 78 *New York University Law Review* 875; M Dorf and C Sabel 'A Constitution of Democratic Experimentalism' (1998) 98 *Columbia Law Review* 267.
56. See R Hamman, S Woolman & C Sprague (eds) *The Business of Sustainable Development in Africa: Human Rights, Partnerships and Alternative Business Models* (2008).
57. See M Dorf and B Friedman 'Shared Constitutional Interpretation' (2000) 2000 *Supreme Court Review* 61; S Woolman 'Application' in S Woolman & M Bishop (eds) *Constitutional Law of South Africa* (2nd Edition, OS, March 2005) Chapter 31.
58. See A Fung and EO Wright 'Deepening Democracy: Innovations in Empowered Participatory Governance' (1998) 29 (1) *Science & Society* 5; O Fiss 'The Supreme Court 1978 Term Foreword: Forms of Justice' (1979) 93 *Harvard Law Review* 1.
59. See S Woolman and H Botha 'Limitations' in S Woolman & M Bishop (eds) *Constitutional Law of South Africa* (2nd Edition, OS, March 2006) Chapter 34.
60. See J Klaaren 'South African Human Rights Commission' in S Woolman & M Bishop (eds) *Constitutional Law of South Africa* (2nd Edition, OS, December 2005) Chapter 24C; C Albertyn 'Commission for Gender Equality' in S Woolman & M Bishop (eds) *Constitutional Law of South Africa* (2nd Edition, OS, December 2003) Chapter 24D.
61. See S Woolman & M Bishop 'Education' in S Woolman & M Bishop (eds) *Constitutional Law of South Africa* (2nd Edition, RS4, December 2011) Chapter 58; S Woolman & B Fleisch 'Democracy, Social Cohesion and School Governing Bodies' (2008) 20(1) *Education and the Law* 56; S Woolman 'Defending Discrimination: On the Constitutionality of Independent Schools that Promote a Particular, if not Comprehensive, Vision of the Good' (2007) 18 *Stellenbosch Law Review* 31; S Woolman & B Fleisch 'South Africa's Education Legislation, Quasi-Markets and School Choice' (2006) 24 (2) *Perspectives in*

Education 1; B Fleisch & S Woolman 'The Constitutionality of Single Medium Public Schools' (2007) 23 (1) *South African Journal on Human Rights* 34; S Woolman & B Fleisch 'South Africa's Unintended Experiment in School Choice: How the National Education Policy Act, the South Africa Schools Act and the Employment of Educators Act Create the Enabling Conditions for Quasi-Markets in Schools' (2006) 18(1) *Education and the Law* 31; B Fleisch & S Woolman 'On the Constitutionality of School Fees: A Reply to Roithmayr' (2004) 22 (1) *Perspectives in Education* 111.

62. See K McLean 'Housing' in S Woolman & M Bishop (eds) *Constitutional Law of South Africa* (2nd Edition, OS, July 2006) Chapter 55; K Rust 'No Shortcuts: South Africa's Progress in Implementing its Housing Policy, 1994 – 2002 (Institute for Housing of South Africa, 2003)(Manuscript on file with author).

63. Indeed, Baars recognizes that the notion of a 'theatre audience' is far too passive to capture the engagement various parts of the brain and neural processes will have with the conscious contents of the global workspace: '[T]he global workspace resembles more a deliberative body than a theatre audience. Each expert has a certain degree of 'influence', and by forming coalitions with other experts can contribute to deciding which issues receive immediate attention and which are 'sent back to the committee'. Most of the work of the deliberative body is done 'off-stage' (ie, non-consciously). Only matters of greatest relevance 'in the moment' gain access to consciousness.' See Newman, Baars and Cho (supra) at 1132 – 1133. Consciousness is not a particular thing or even a particular kind of feeling, but rather the architecture that enables discrete and disparate neurological processes to solve a host of pressing (but also important medium term and long term) problems. Baars' depiction sounds virtually identical (with far greater understanding of the actual mechanics) to the description of consciousness (articulated in the footnote above) by William James over a century ago. Pragmatism describes the self, the social and the constitutional in a manner that James, Dewey and Pierce anticipated, but lacked the tools to investigate and to prove.

64. Blackmore *Consciousness* (supra) at 72.

65. Thaler and Sunstein (supra) at 9. Following the early work of Charles Taylor, I make the same argument at great length in Chapter 1B, fn 7.

66. Ibid (emphasis added). It doesn't take much to see that Thaler and Sunstein's emphasis on experience, good information and prompt feedback fits the experimentalist model that undergirds each section of the book and the work as a whole.

67. Not exactly true. You can listen for the ball entering the cup without looking. It's a common form of putting instruction and improvement. I use it. The reason: it keeps one's putter on line. But the example is close enough for our immediate purposes. As a golfer who uses the game as a metaphor for the relationship between theory and practice, I appreciate Thaler and Sunstein's acknowledgement of the role of 'feedback' in the game. But they obviously don't play the sport. Any golfer willing to put in the time to learn how to putt better may actually spend a day just working on the rhythm of the putting stroke or finding a comfortable way to hold the club that generates either a pendulum like motion or a more classical motion in which the club moves on an arc. A golfer looking for consistency might actually spend time just rolling the ball in order to train herself or himself to do something better – and out of habit – under the pressure of actual play. Or she may spend a long session working with tools designed to ensure a pendulum stroke – and never hit a ball. Hopefully, I can nudge Thaler and Sunstein toward a better understanding of golf over the course of this book. But even here, they are close enough to the mark. All the practice in the world *without* a ball (and without watching how a ball moves on a green) will never make one a good putter. Following Wittgenstein, mastery of this technique is not reducible to a few rules or drills – it's about feel, feel that comes through tens of thousands of putts. Eventually, your body offers feedback for all the information required to make a good putt.

68. On the proximity of my account of flourishing to Thaler and Sunstein's commitment to libertarian paternalism, the following can be said. First, we all hold the preferences of individuals and groups to be a primary source of value and concern: at the same time as we recognize that such preferences are

somewhat plastic, even when they make us who we are. Second, the paternalism Thaler and Sunstein defend is not dramatically different from my commitment to flourishing. I am interested, like Sen or Nussbaum, in ensuring that people pursue lives worth valuing: whether through the maintenance of existing arrangements, the creation of more hospitable social formations or the improvement of the material conditions of being. The 'paternalism' of which Thaler and Sunstein write promotes bounded 'choice': it does not determine (entirely) the ends people pursue, nor does it control (expressly) the means for their realization. It does however coax them toward more optimal ends and the manner in which they pursue them. Neither Thaler or Sunstein speak of the preferences (they analyze) as beyond reformation. However, they do suggest that appropriate forms of information aggregation (or even, on occasion, reliance on people with greater expertise, say a chess grandmaster) have something to say about the quality of the lives that we pursue.

69. Markets often offer useful ways of aggregating information that would otherwise remain 'trapped' within individual or collective holders of both express and tacit knowledge. They do so in the form of a 'price'. The price elicits information about the value of a good by prompting individuals to purchase the good at a price (relative to comparable goods) that reflect its quality or the efficiency of manufacture. At the same time, producers of a good, armed with information about its construction and associated costs, receive immediate information about the 'value' of the good in the marketplace in the form of how many units purchasers wish to buy. Firms generally then have to work at producing or distributing the good more efficiently to get it to market at a lower cost or they may have to improve its quality in order to attract more consumers. Or they may create something new, that executes a task more effectively.

70. The relationship between a person's choice and their ultimate welfare is known as mapping. Price alone does not enable us to make optimal selections when the understanding of the various good is clouded by technical information beyond our ken. Can a man with prostate cancer really understand the trade-offs to be made between three forms of treatment: seed radiation, surgery and watch and wait? (My late father couldn't.) Given the close proximity in outcome, after some 20 years of study, one must ask what it means to take a 33% risk of incontinence or impotence from surgery and an increase of life-expectancy of 3.2 years over the alternative benefits of radiation? Given that the 'watch and wait approach' does not have 'specialists' – a doctor with a clock? – how is a patient to determine its respective value and risks vis-a-vis the other treatments? In such circumstances – and cell phone costs in South Africa are currently a good example – a map ought to set out for the user exactly what the fees are for each use – an sms or an international call. Such information would, in turn, enable the user to choose the best plan and make the most efficient use of that plan. As most cell phone users in South Africa know, contracts rarely come with detailed maps and, more importantly, cell phone companies rarely provide information (maps) regarding the relative cost of each cell phone function. Indeed, the companies, along with an incompetent regulatior (ICASA), have a vested interest in maintaining the ignorance of its users. Thaler and Sunstein claim that maps in such instances would force such information into the open, and allow users to make better informed choices. Put slightly differently their choice would map rather directly on to their optimal 'consumption' experience.

71. Defaults are what we usually do – or put more strikingly, what we do when we fail to think critically or creatively about what we do. Defaults reflect instances in which the decision-maker does not truly engage in critical reflection on the choice or the challenge before her. Given how powerful defaults are in our lives – when we do not actively assess ostensibly competing outcomes or goods but simply do what we always do (watch the same TV programme or take the same route to work) – it is essential for 'choice architects' to set the defaults in the optimal fashion. That is, choice architects should set up their system in such a manner that the default – the failure to choose – actually results in the best possible outcome (in so far as the architect can determine it.) As noted above, defaults are a colloquial way of describing what the social science and philosophical literature call 'heuristics'. See G Gigerenzer 'Moral Intuition = Fast and Frugal Heuristics' (supra) at 1.

72. Feedback: in short, we want the systems we operate to tell us when we are performing well and when we are performing poorly. Feedback is a leitmotif of any experimentalist system – such as the constitutional experimentalism advocated in these pages. If we are to create a political system predicated on rolling best practices, then we need to know what works best over both time and in an array of different circumstances.

73. A constitutional experimentalist must expect that a system that allows for an array of alternative choices and solutions will produce erroneous (or suboptimal) results. We want to be aware of such results so that we do not repeat them in the future or when the stakes are far higher.

74. M Walzer *Thick and Thin: Moral Argument at Home and Abroad* (2002) 85.

75. Ibid at 98–99.

76. Walzer interestingly juxtaposes his thickly populated, divided self with what he calls the 'thin self' or the 'dominating self'. He writes: 'The religious or political fanatic is the obvious example: god-possessed or ideologically driven. ... We must imagine it dominating other self-critics, repressing alternative possibilities within the self. No one growing up in the modern world is, as it were, linear before the fact. Only repression will make us so. I am not going to try to describe here the psychological mechanisms of repression. (I argued [elsewhere about] ... the role of fear in shaping a singular national identity.) I only want to insist that such mechanisms must be at work in every person whose 'true character' or 'normal condition' is singular and absolute. Within every thin self, there is a thick self-yearning for elaboration, largeness, freedom.' Ibid at 99–100. What is particularly apt, for the purposes of this work, is Walzer's connection of the divided critical self with the kind of roughly egalitarian, pluralist democracy defended in these pages. Walzer writes that 'divided selves are best accommodated by complex equality in domestic society and different versions of self-determination in domestic and international society. ... Even in my normal condition, I hear voices, I play parts, I identify myself in different ways – and so I must aim at a society that makes room for this divided self'. Ibid at 103–104. Walzer's views are confirmed to a large degree by the neuroscience and the experimental philosophy canvassed in Chapter 2, and, in particular, the discussion of 'radically heterogeneous naturally, determined selves' and a subset of that category, 'naturally determined selves'.

Chapter Two

A Theory of the Self: Consciousness and Radically Heterogeneous Selves as Feedback Mechanisms

Men are mistaken in thinking themselves free; their opinion is made up of consciousness of their own actions, and ignorance of the causes by which they are conditioned. Their idea of freedom, therefore, is simply their ignorance of any cause of their actions.

Benedict Spinoza

A. Free Will and Determinism: Their Connection to Social Theory and Constitutional Law

As we have seen in the introduction, the majority of South Africans (and the better part of humanity) find themselves in the tenacious hold of a folk psychology of free will, self and consciousness that is dramatically out of step with what a growing majority of neuroscientists, cognitive psychologists and philosophers have to say about those subjects. Put slightly differently, views shared by the majority of South Africans about the actual content of free will, self and consciousness are sharply at odds with how things actually are. In the pages that follow I argue that our experience of personhood, of consciousness, and of free will are functions of a complex set of innate and habituated neurological-physiological structures and socially imbued constructs and narratives over which we, as complex, unique individuals, exercise little control. At the same time, while outré metaphysical doctrines of 'freedom' ought to go by the board, space still remains for a chastened form of political freedom, properly understood.

The theories of the self offered in these pages take a number of different forms: the determined self, the conditioned self, the multiple self, the divided self, the radically heterogeneous natural self and the radically heterogeneous social self. Each form has as its goal the displacement of the dominant Cartesian notion of the self as a fully integrated, rational, freely-willed chooser of its ends. But each displaces the folk-psychological or Cartesian notion of the self in different ways and at different levels of generality. I spend a significant amount of space on Baars and Dehaene's neuropsychological explanations of global neuronal workspace theory and Dennett's use of these explanations to reconstruct a plausible account of the self. But far more is at stake than trashing folk-psychological accounts of the self. Not only must something with greater explanatory power be offered in its place, my preferred theory of the self must, ultimately, make more plausible my theory of South African constitutional politics.

So: how do we get there (South African constitutional politics) from here (metaphysics)? After knocking off Cartesian dualism, the chapter attempts to demonstrate that consciousness and the neural states that correlate with consciousness function primarily as feedback mechanisms that give us fresh opportunities to reflect upon experience (memory, immediate and decidedly prior) and plot more or less optimal courses for action (pressganged and plodding). Trial and error. What is true for individual human beings, as it turns out, is optimal for our politics. Trial and error. Think about it for a moment: it is no accident that Churchill wryly observed that 'democracy is the worst form of government except for all the others.' Like life, democracy proceeds, in theory and practice, in terms of 'trial and error'. What laws and policies work – which laws and policies do not. Moreover, a democratic system ostensibly gives the electorate an opportunity to 'kick the bums out of office' after two, three, four or five years if they fail to produce the goods. Individual selves – highly populated ways of being in the world – are always experimenting, attempting to divine, through reflection and action, what 'works' best. (How many 'life partners' did you have before you found the right fit – or are you still looking?) Constitutional democracies – highly populated communities with millions of complex, heterogeneous selves – are constantly experimenting, attempting to divine though reflection and action, what works best for its many constituents. To be sure, we must begin with a world of shared norms about what works best (most right, but some terribly wrong). Individuals and (most) constitutional democracies are no different in this regard. But, as I have already suggested, the point of trial and error is not simply instrumental. As we shall see in this account of the self, we are constantly looking for the round hole into which to fit our round peg. Constitutional democracies also experience such shifts in their normative frameworks over time: what works instrumentally (and what fails) often has the feedback effect of telling us what kinds of lives are worth living and how we should best order our society so that a majority of our fellow citizens may pursue those lives that they have reason to value.

But let's not get too far ahead of ourselves. The purpose of this chapter is to paint a picture of the self – one upon which countless neuroscientists, cognitive psychologists and analytic philosophers have begun to converge – that captures its largely determined, densely populated, hotly contested and reflexive character. Again, this picture of the self will, if sufficiently compelling, help shape this book's depiction of some, and only some, of the political institutions and doctrines that will serve South Africa's democracy best. In addition to the leitmotif of trial and error, keep in mind one word: 'modesty'. It serves well our chastened account of freedom: the extent to which our lives are cabined and the manner in which they can be revised. Modesty serves well this account of South Africa's constitutional democracy by reminding us of the various traditions, practices and endowments that give our lives meaning, at the same as we search for those novel political arrangements necessary for all to pursue lives worth valuing.

Let us also not lose sight of our various purposes here. First: to knock metaphysical 'freedom' and 'free-will' off the perch they currently occupy. We may find ourselves to be far 'freer' once we understand what freedom truly entails. Second: to offer an account of the self that recognizes its largely determined, yet heterogeneous character. Third: (a) to adumbrate a theory of constitutional politics that acknowledges the largely determined, yet heterogeneous character of selves, (b) to appreciate that flourishing requires normative understandings of our basic law that allow us to be largely (though not entirely) who we already are, and (c) to require emergent, experimental forms of governance that enable us to find better 'fits' for our (various) selves in the polity within which we reside. As with the account of the determined, yet radically heterogeneous self (which may have the somewhat ironic consequence of making us appreciate the freedom we actually possess), the upshot of a commitment to experimentalism and to flourishing is that it may actually loosen the unhealthy grip that many political ideologies have upon us.

1. *The Standard Metaphysical Case for Determinism and against Compatabilism*

Free will exists – so its proponents say – where an agent realistically possesses more than one possible course of action. I could, at a given intersection, turn my car left or right.

Were it a matter of chance, I would be just as likely to choose left or right.

In a determinist world, whether I turn left or right is an ineluctable function of an almost infinite number of events that have preceded my visit to the intersection.

William James claims that after the fact

> ... either universe [of free will, chance or determinism] would, to our means of observation and understanding appear just as rational as the other. There would be absolutely no criterion by which we might judge one necessary and the other matter of chance.[1]

Despite the absence of meaningful choice in this matter, James opted for a version of compatibalism. Compatiblism stands for the proposition that 'human' free will and a deterministic universe are logically and empirically consistent with one another. (See endnotes 1 and 2 for more on the varieties of compatibilism.) For James, freedom meant 'acting without external constraint'.[2] That definition was hardly novel. It tracks to a large degree David Hume's ostensible resolution of the debate between advocates of free will and defenders of determinism. In his *Enquiry into Human Understanding*, Hume's argument runs roughly as follows:

1. My action is free if it is the effect of the determinations of my own will.
2. Thus, the difference between our free acts and our other acts ... is not whether there are causes, but what those causes are.
3. If someone's action is the effect of his own choice, it is free and he bears *moral* responsibility for it ... [in fact] only because our actions are causally related to our motive do the former have any *moral* quality whatever.[3]

Hume's argument is interesting for three reasons. First, it comports with how most individuals capable of articulating a position on free will and determinism describe the matter. Second, it is wrong. As Mates notes: '(a) for the agent's act to be free, it does not suffice that it result from his own choice; (b) for if he did not choose freely, the chosen course cannot be considered free either.'[4] For Hume, an action is caused whether it be from an internal event or an external event. Choice is choice whether 'freely willed' or simply an action that can be attributed to the intention of a given agent. Third, notice that Hume introduces the word 'moral' into his account. Why should it matter that an action has a moral dimension to be described as free? As it turns out: Everything. (Religiously-inflected morality often drives our intuitions on this matter, and not always for the better.)

Chance seems an unlikely choice as an explanation – even if we use the term to describe the causation of any number of events. Chance operates as a place holder for descriptions of complex events beyond our ken.

That leaves us with determinism. A simple version of determinism runs as follows:

1. Every action or event is caused by a preceding event or action (or concatenation of events or actions);
2. Any future action, event or set of occurrences is entirely contingent upon preceding events or actions (or concatenation of events or actions);
3. All future actions, events or set of occurrences are thus entirely predetermined.

One might be inclined to describe the choice between free will and determinism as an antinomy – namely, 'a contradiction between principles or conclusions that seem equally necessary and reasonable; a paradox.'[5] In some respects the arguments regarding free will and determinism do indeed bear a strong family resemblance to solipsism/external world debates, mind/brain distinctions, dualist/materialist quarrels, endless questions about the existence of other minds, the possibility of private language and what it means to follow a rule. It does not follow that these antinomies are not susceptible to clearly reasoned elucidation.

Mates offers the following causal account of determinism:

> Every event is the effect of antecedent events, and these in turn are caused by events antecedent to them, and so on ... Human actions are no exception to this rule; for, although the causes of some of them are much less well understood than the causes of certain other types of events, it can hardly be denied that they do have causes and that these causes determine their effects with the same certainty and inevitability that are found in every other kind of case. In particular, those human actions usually called *free* are, each of them, the ultimate and inevitable effects of events occurring long before the agent was born and over which he obviously had no control; and since he could not prevent the existence of the causes, it is clear he could not avoid the occurrence of the effects. Consequently, despite appearances to the contrary, human actions are no more free than the motions of the tides, or the rusting of a piece of iron that is exposed to water and air.[6]

John Searle finds modern physics' materialist reductionism equally dispositive. He writes:

> [N]ature consists of particles and their relations with each other, and since everything can be accounted for ... [by the laws of physics that apply to] those particles and their relations, there is simply no room for freedom of the will. ... [There is] no evidence that there is or could be some mental energy of human freedom that can move molecules in directions that they were not otherwise going to move. So it really does look as if everything we know about physics forces us to some form of denial of human freedom.[7]

Given the rather compelling arguments that a doctrine of free will and compatibalism have to overcome, one question arises: why do they maintain such an insuperable grip on our imagination? The answer is rather straightforward – and we shall deal with it at greater length in the next section. Hume identified it: morality. Others might call it 'meaning'. As James wrote:

> What interest, zest, or excitement can there be in achieving the right way, unless we are enabled to feel that the wrong way is also a possible and a natural way? ... And, what sense can there be in condemning ourselves for taking the wrong way ... unless the right way was open to us as well?"[8]

But is a feeling (or a religious belief[9]) enough to justify an argument that fails on all other counts? Most readers will find Searle's recounting of the emotional content behind the belief most congenial to their own self-understanding:

> The appeal of free will [is that] ... if there is any fact of experience we are all familiar with, it's the simple fact that our own choices, decisions, reasonings and cogitations seem to make a difference to our actual behavior. There are all sorts of experiences that we have in life where it seems just a fact of our experience that though we did one thing, we feel we know perfectly well that we could have done something else. ... The first thing to know about our conception of human freedom is that it is essentially tied to consciousness. ... The characteristic experience that gives us the conviction of human freedom, and it is an experience from which we are unable to strip away the conviction

> of freedom, is the experience of engaging in voluntary, intentional human actions... .[And yet] our conception of physical reality simply does not allow for [such] radical freedom.[10]

Searle has set us the task ahead: to tease apart this need for free will from its connection to consciousness and our unitary sense of the self. What we shall see, as Lakoff and Johnson have written, is that free will operates at the level of metaphor, not as a defensible truth proposition.[11]

2. *Experimental Epistemology*

a. *Some Philosophical Evidence against the Standard Account of Free Will*

Free will is a delightful doctrine for those who possess significant autonomy (material control) over their lives. Put pithily, it works, really works, for the relatively small number of people on the planet who can do largely what they want to do. For them, it functions as a justification for their pride of position in the hierarchy of any given society. Its usefulness for the rest of us plebians is that it offers an opportunity to hold others responsible for what is wrong with our lives: *those people* are to blame for my miserable mortal coil. (No wonder so many men wind up divorced, depressed and drunk.) Free will also retains its legs because philosophy has been stripped of its prominence as other, once philosophical subjects have become independent fields of study that depend upon empirical and experimental analysis. Free will lives on, in other words, because metaphysics remains a field of study in philosophy departments. After 2,500 years of argument (since Democritus first articulated the premises of determinism), free will vs determinism continues to be a serious parlour game. (Perhaps that's exactly the status, it deserves.) But it need not be that way.

One way to loosen free will's hold upon us is to subject the belief to empirical examination. Philosophy need not remain the province of professors who parse the meaning of sentences in ordinary language looking for deeper truths. Nor, worse still, should it be the domain of post-modern hucksters who deny that everyday language can put us in unmediated contact with a real world. Kwame Anthony Appiah has added his voice to the mix of theorists who view the recent empirical turn in philosophy as desirable.[12] Appiah states that 'what's novel is not the experimental turn, but the turn away from it.'[13] From Descartes to Hume to Kant, all modern philosophers engaged in experiments designed to advance specific empirical claims. Descartes' dualism, for example, would never have gotten off the ground had he not claimed to have discovered that the pineal gland served as the bridge between the mind and the body.[14] (Whether such 'experiments' are best described as empirical, rather than experimental, is another matter.) What happened, again, is that various fields in philosophy were hived off – physics, anthropology, psychology, economics, artificial intelligence, political science, sociology, biology – as the scientific method extended its reach and demonstrated that a purely armchair philosophical approach, based largely on intuition and convention, lacked the explanatory power of theories that could be tested, and confirmed, by the responses of various objects – including human beings.

A return to the experimentalism that lies at the heart of the scientific method can offer at least a partial cure for such misguided notions as free will. Contemporary philosophers are better equipped to do so than their predecessors. Joshua Knobe and Shaun Nichols contend that:

> Unlike the philosophers of centuries past, we think that a critical method for figuring out how human beings think is to go out and run systematic empirical surveys. Hence, experimental philosophers proceed by conducting experimental investigations of the psychological processes underlying people's intuitions about central philosophical issues. Again and again, these investigations have challenged familiar assumptions, showing that people do not think about these issues in anything like the way that philosophers had assumed.[15]

Take the following proposition: 'people are more inclined to regard an agent as morally responsible when the case is described in vivid detail than they are when the case is described abstractly.'[16] I know that to be true from innumerable conversations that I have had with sophisticated interlocutors. In short, intelligent lay folk tend to be determinists when asked about the physical universe generally, but compatibilists when asked about a specific moral/ human quandary with an unfortunate outcome that has someone (an identifiable person) 'pulling the trigger' or 'pushing someone on to the railroad tracks in front of an oncoming train'. That is, they believe in determinism and free will, at the same time, with respect to the same phenomena, without any awareness of the incompatibility of the two positions or any desire to change their belief set. Experimental philosophers have run numerous tests on humans on subjects that lead to the identical conclusion: 'People's intuitions about moral responsibility are shaped by the interaction of two different systems – one that employs an abstract theory, another that relies more on immediate affective responses.'[17] Just that conclusion alone shows the extent to which experimental philosophy might enable us to draw compelling normative conclusions from the often surprising descriptive responses of normal human beings. As Knobe and Nichols write:

> The goal is to determine what leads us to have the intuitions we have about free will, moral responsibility ... The ultimate hope is that we can use this information to help determine whether the psychological sources of the beliefs undercut the warrant for the beliefs.[18]

That agenda serves two interrelated purposes. First, it may help to expose the inconsistency (the folk-psychology) of the answers that well-informed lay persons – and here I mean the South African legal audience to whom this work is primarily addressed – often offer to basic metaphysical and ethical questions. Second, experimental philosophy should clear away these mischaracterizations of the world so that more dramatic points registered by practising neuroscientists, cognitive psychologists or experimental philosophers have greater traction.[19]

Appiah employs much the same set of arguments in building his case against the intuitions and the self-evidence upon which so many folk psychologists and armchair philosophers rely.[20] In order to make apparent to readers how 'the framing effect' of a hypothetical determines the belief of an individual, Appiah deploys the well-trod trolley car case:

> In one scenario, there's a runaway trolley hurtling down the tracks, and it is on course to kill five people who are unavoidably in its path. You can save those 5 people, but only by hitting a switch that will put the trolley onto a side track - where it will kill one person. Should you do it? Philosophers generally say yes. ... [T]hat intuition is widely shared ... Most people – 80 or 90 per

> cent of us – will say 'yes' … In a second scenario, the trolley, once again, is hurtling down toward five people. This time you are on a footbridge over the tracks, next to a 300 pound man. The only way you can save those 5 people is by pushing the 300 pound man off the bridge and onto the tracks. His body mass will stop the runaway trolley, but he'll be killed in the process. Should you do it? Most … civilians alike, say 'no' … Prospect theory shows why the different frames lead to different responses, but it isn't supposed to show that different frames justify different responses; indeed it helps to undermine that claim.

It seems obvious (to me) that given that the outcomes are the same, they justify both pulling the switch and pushing over the 300 lb man. Empirical philosophy and experimental philosophy shows how and why the scenario generates different intuitive responses. Individuals do not want to be held culpable for pushing a 300 lb man to his death. They feel more comfortable with pulling a switch where there is a sufficient delay, and diminished physical proximity, between their action and the death of an individual as a result of the pull. This kind of 'negative agency bias' is reflected in most lay responses to thought experiments that test beliefs regarding free will and determinism. The more neutral or distant the cause of the ultimate harm the greater the likelihood that a respondent will adopt a determinist position (of non-culpability.) The greater the proximity of the cause of the ultimate harm, the more likely we are to place some form of blame and punishment upon the individual ostensibly responsible for the outcome. (Lawyers will notice immediately the place of 'proximate cause' from their study of delict or torts.)

b. The Consequences, for the Self, of Abandoning Free Will

Earlier on, I quoted Knobe and Nichols for the purpose of demonstrating that their goal, as experimental philosophers, 'is to determine what leads us to have the intuitions we have about free will, moral responsibility … and to help determine whether the psychological sources of the beliefs undercut the warrant for the beliefs.'[21] Another example drawn from Knobe's work demonstrates just how powerful a tool experimental philosophy can be in making good on this project. Take the following experiment and the analysis that follows:

> The vice president of a company went to the chairman of the board and said: 'We are thinking of starting of a new program. It will help us increase profits, but it will also harm the environment.' The chairman of the board answered: 'I don't care at all about harming the environment. I just want to make as much profit as I can. Let's start the new program.' They start the new program. Sure enough, the environment was harmed. Now ask yourself, did the chairman of the board intentionally harm of the environment? Faced with this question, most people (though certainly not all) say the answer is yes. And when asked why they think that the chairman intentionally harmed the environment, they tend to mention something about the chairman's psychological state – for example, that he decided to implement the program even though he specifically knew that he would be harming the environment. But it seems clear that these facts about the agent's psychological state cannot be all there is to the story. For suppose that we replace the word 'harm' with 'help', so that the vignette becomes … The vice president of a company went to the chairman of the board and said: 'We are thinking of starting of a new program. It will help us increase profits, and it will also help the environment.' The chairman of the board answered: 'I don't care at all about helping the

environment. I just want to make as much profit as I can. Let's start the new program.' They started the new program. Sure enough, the environment was helped. This one change in the vignette leads to a quite radical change in people's intuitions. Faced with this second version, most people say that the chairman did not intentionally help the environment. To confirm these claims about people's institutions, I presented the two vignettes to subjects in a controlled experiment.[22] The results were clear and compelling: 82 percent of subjects who received the story about environmental harm said that the chairman harmed the environment intentionally, whereas only 23 per cent of subjects who received the story about environmental help said that the chairman helped the environment intentionally. This result provides preliminary evidence for the view that people's beliefs about the *moral* status of a behaviour has some influence about whether or not the behaviour was performed intentionally.[23]

It would seem, then, that Nietzsche was right on the mark about the origins of, and the unjustifiable grounds for belief in, free will, when he wrote:

> It was in *this* sphere then, the sphere of legal obligations, that the moral conceptual world of 'conscience', 'duty', 'sacredness of duty' had its origins; its beginnings were, like the beginnings of everything great on earth, soaked in blood thoroughly for a very long time. [Before long] ... the creditor could inflict every kind of indignity and torture upon the body of the debtor.'[24]

Such debts, the creditors themselves began to realize, had begun to accumulate on their own books. The debts were especially high with respect to their ancestors, to whom they (creditor turned debtor) suddenly realized they owed almost everything meaningful that they possessed. And so, says Nietzsche, mankind invented the guilty conscience:

> Suddenly we stand before the paradoxical and horrifying experience that afforded temporary relief for tormented humanity, that stroke of genius on the part of Christianity: God himself sacrifices himself for the guilt of mankind, God himself makes payment to himself, God as the only being who can redeem man from what has become unredeemable for man himself – the creditor sacrifices himself for his debtor, out of love (can one credit that?), out of love for his debtor!'[25]

No account of our genealogy could be more repugnant to advocates of free will. When we know that 'there will be blood', we will seek out someone (after the fact) to hang – whether they are culpable or not.[26] In the absence of meaningful culpability, this book's views about intentionality – along with those views held by Nietzsche, Dennett, Knobe and Nichols – suggest that we bracket many of our home-spun notions about free will. Change, when it comes, may be traced to other causal factors: but individual intentionality looks to be a piece of folk psychology which we may discard.[27]

Still not convinced? Then let's look at the how the element of time relates to the description of an action as freely willed.

3 *The Illusion of Volition*

i. Libet's and Walter's Timing Experiments

The work of empirical psychologist Benjamin Libet has provided a well-established framework for understanding delayed conscious awareness of unconsciously initiated action.[28] Libet's experiments demonstrate that a readiness potential – 'a change in the voltage in the brain'

– occurs 0.6 seconds before what we describe commonly as conscious awareness of imminent action and 0.8 seconds before action.[29] One might be inclined to think that if the conscious intention were really the cause of the action, then it would antedate the action by at least 0.8 seconds. But even this intuition – unsupported by the evidence – is insufficient grounds for establishing consciously willed action.[30] Even if conscious intention were simultaneous with readiness potential, it could not be a cause of the action. It would remain epiphenomenal. Only conscious intention prior to readiness potential would demonstrate consciously willed action. No empirical evidence exists for such awareness. Moreover, as Dennett argues, there may be good reasons to believe that the 'conscious awareness' of the intention cannot be accurately determined even within the parameters of the 0.8 seconds afforded us. In his challenging and not uncontroversial account of mental events, Dennett suggests that the brain produces multiple – and often partial – drafts of phenomena and that the 'memory' or 'awareness' of intention is simply one report that facilitates future use of the information, and that the fixing of conscious time effects another kind of report that serves to maintain the connection between cause and action. In sum, Dennett's theory of multiple drafts – which plays an important role in demolishing the Cartesian theatre and explaining our experience of consciousness – explains why there is no master discriminator to organize consciousness and that without such a master discriminator it is difficult, if not impossible, to fix an exact time for when 'consciousness' of a mental event has occurred. Remember: all we have are the mental events themselves. We do not possess a separate consciousness of the mental event. All that we might possess is a separate and distinct conscious awareness of a previous mental event. But that is another mental event – fixed, if it can be fixed, at another moment in time.

W. Grey Walters' experiments bolster conclusions about non-conscious determination of action and the importance of maintaining an apparent causal connection between awareness and action. Walter's subjects were brain surgery patients. The props were a slide-projector, a screen upon which the patient viewed the slides and electrodes attached to the cerebral cortex. The patients were asked to press a button to change a viewing-slide at any time. The button, however, was not connected to the slide projector. Instead, the slide-projector was rotated by an amplification of the readiness potential signal from the patient's brain. Walters' subjects reported the experience of an unsettling form of precognition – on the part of the projector. That is, they found that the projector had rotated the slides prior to their intention to press the button. Indeed, the gap between (a) non-conscious readiness potential, (b) slide change, (c) consciousness of the volition, and (d) consciousness of the fact of the slide change, was sufficiently large to cause the subjects to report that they were concerned that 'they might, accidentally, advance the slide twice.'[31]

More recent sophisticated brain mapping bears out Walters' findings. New technology appears to enable researchers to determine whether a subject has previously seen a particular object. If she has, then the researchers witness a readiness potential for an affirmative response 0.3 seconds before the subject forms any conscious awareness of the object on view and before the subject can form an express opinion about her recognition of the object. If she has not seen the object before, then no readiness potential exhibited for a neuronal process that precedes a neural correlate of consciousness occurs. The benefits for law enforcement are obvious.[32]

Libet attempted to extend his analysis of conscious awareness, non-conscious neuronal activity and physical responses in a subsequent set of experiments. Libet himself had not been convinced that his previous experiments had demonstrated that conscious awareness followed non-conscious formation of a decision to act. In subsequent experiments, Libet believed that he had demonstrated that his subjects possessed a capacity to 'veto' their actions at approximately 0.15 seconds prior to the initiation of the original intention of which they were conscious. Libet writes that he is inclined to view this capacity as creating some elbow room for freely-willed conscious intention.[33] But given that all other actions demonstrate some readiness potential prior to conscious awareness, it does not seem plausible to have conscious 'veto' powers that somehow intervene in an otherwise non-consciously determined course of action. Such 'veto' actions are still a function of prior non-conscious readiness potential. Moreover, the difficulty of fixing time becomes apparent when one asks how a subject and an experimenter come to know that the veto occurs 0.15 seconds before an action that never occurs.

The conclusions drawn from all three sets of experiments should cause us to modify our account of free will and what we mean by freedom. First, we should now be inclined to attribute causation to non-conscious brain events. Second, we should be inclined to view the conscious awareness of the impending action as serving a purpose other than that of immediate cause. As we have already seen, the purpose of consciousness, generally, is to play the role of a feedback mechanism that enables the actor to analyze the consequences of a particular set of actions. If the action has been successful (and novel), then she may form a memory of those features of the action salient to the action's success. If the action fails to accomplish the desired end, then the actor may form a memory of those features of the action relevant to the action's failure. Such a memory of the failure may enable the actor to form, for future purposes, a better response to the problem that the world has set for her.

ii. Wegner and Wheatley's Experiments

Libet's experiments make clear that non-conscious neurological events precede conscious awareness of intention, and that a free conscious will is not the cause of the action that follow both the non-conscious brain events and the conscious awareness of intention. In light of Libet's reluctance to draw the appropriate conclusions from his experimental data, Daniel Wegner and Thalia Wheatley set about constructing an experiment that might prove his hypothesis that 'the experience of willing an act arises from interpreting one's thought as the cause of the act'.[34] Susan Blackmore captures the crucial features of the experiment in the following account:

> [A] 20 cm square board [was] mounted on a computer mouse. Movements of the mouse moved a cursor over a screen showing a picture of about 50 small objects. The experiment involved two participants: a subject and a confederate [of Wegner's team]. [To make the explanation easier [Blackmore] … call[s] them Dan and Jane [respectively]]. … Dan and Jane were seated facing each other across a small table. Dan … had no idea that Jane was a confederate. They were asked to place to place their fingers on the little board and to circle the cursor over the objects. They were asked to stop every 30 seconds or so and then rate how strongly they had intended to make that particular stop. Each trial consisted of 30 seconds of movement, during which they might hear words through

> a headphone, and 10 seconds of music, during which they were to make a stop. Dan was led to believe that Jane was receiving different words from his, but actually she had heard instructions to make particular movements. … In four trials, she was asked to stop on a particular object (e.g., swan) in the middle of Dan's music. Meanwhile, Dan heard the word 'swan' 30 seconds before, 5 seconds before, 1 second before or 1 second after Jane stopped on the swan. In all other trials, the stops were not forced and Dan heard various words 2 seconds into the music; 51 undergraduates were tested.

During the four forced stops, subjects in Dan's position gave the highest rating for the proposition 'I intended to make the stop' when the word came prior to the stop by 1 or 5 seconds. The subjects gave much lower ratings when the word in question was heard 30 seconds prior to the stop, and far lower ratings still when the word was heard 1 second after the stop. Wegner and Wheatley claim that the results support what they call the 'priority principle'. According to the priority principle, the 'effects' or the 'events' are described as intended – as freely willed – when the relevant thought – in this case stimulus – occurs just 'prior' to the 'effect' or the 'event'. The priority principle – in the context of this experiment – supports their contention that '[b]elieving that our conscious thoughts cause our action is an error based on the illusory experience of will.'[35]

Having concluded from his experiments that free will is an illusion, Wegner went on to explain that the illusion of free will can be explained in the following fashion.[36] First, our brain – non-consciously and consciously – identifies a problem and initiates a sequence of events to solve that problem and to achieve our objective. Second, we are, as we have seen, almost entirely unaware of the massive amount of non-conscious neuronal activity responsible for carrying out both internal bodily functions and external physical actions. However, where the problem to be solved is novel and requires our extant neuronal networks to respond in an equally novel fashion, then we tend to become aware of both a problem and an intention to respond to the problem in a particular fashion. We call this subsequent awareness of the non-consciously preferred solution an 'intention'. Finally, as we have seen from Libet's experiments, because the action occurs after we become conscious of our 'intention', we jump to the erroneous conclusion that our conscious intention was the cause of the action.

Wegner further concludes that this particular illusion is consistent with a related series of illusions:

> The fact is, it seems to us that we have conscious will. It seems we have selves. It seems we have minds. It seems we are agents. It seems we cause what we do. Although it is sobering and ultimately accurate to call all of this an illusion, it is a mistake to conclude that the illusory is trivial.[37]

I offer an explanation, later on, as to why these various illusions are not, in fact, trivial and why a proper understanding of these illusions may help us to understand better the self, the social and the constitutional. But first let's drive another stake through the heart of intention and volition.

iii. Tancredi's Serial Killer and Retrospective Intent

Everyone loves a good serial killer. Real, the suave Ted Bundy. Or fictional, the brilliant and even charming Hannibal Lecter, with his refined palate. Could it be that their stories do more than give us a rush of adrenaline? Might they not have something to say about the way we form and express intention – and when?

Laurence Tancredi's interviews with the serial killer Ricky Green tell us something important about time and intention. Green's story as a psychopath is rather mundane. He suffered sexual abuse at the hands of family and lovers and strangers, often mixed his encounters in later life with large amounts of alcohol and other drugs, and experienced the occasional breakdown of control – the flipping of a switch (a 'click' as he described it) – that led him to mutilate and to murder at least four lovers (if not more.)[38]

What is interesting about Green's story is not the complicated environment within which a textbook sociopath acted out his ire. More arresting phenomena reveal themselves when Green appears on the verge of committing murder ... and then suddenly stops. As Tancredi notes:

> These incidents are significant with regard to the question of free will. It would appear that when something forced Green to snap out of his murderous rage, whether it was a shadow on the ground or an empathetic awareness of consequence to a third party, a conscience concerning the moral value of his behaviour would slip back into place and inhibit impulses to further violence. But instead of being an argument for Green's free will, these incidents of slippage between murderous rage and empathetic inhibition indicate an individual whose controls slowly give way to antisocial impulses.[39]

Unlike Hannibal Lecter, who seduces detectives with his wit, intelligence, physical discipline and telepathic control over other minds, Ricky Green possesses none of these screen-worthy traits. His intentions appear backward looking. He could offer no explanation save that his 'click' of murderous intent gave way, inexplicably, to awareness of his immediate surroundings and the danger that presented itself to him and his potential victims. He showed no remorse for those he had killed. Nor could he adumbrate a moral framework that might explain what prevented him from carrying out further inhumane acts. His recounting of his tales of woe was always backward looking: events that happened to him, not events that he enacted. The toxic cocktail of severe familial abuse, alcoholic binges, and random sexual encounters led to homicides so unplanned and poorly conceived that his wife Sharon helped him clean up the mess on each occasion. His self-described 'waking dream of an unhappy life' – in which thoughts controlled him until something 'exploded in his brain' – left a trail of seemingly unintentional death and destruction in his wake.[40]

B. Self and Consciousness

1. *Traditional Views of the Self and Their Problems*

Success thus far must be measured by the extent the reader has been given pause to re-think her commitment to free will. It will be such a reconsideration that later leads to the conclusion that freedom is a political commitment (that takes various forms), and not a metaphysical truth (about human action).

This section engages in a related exercise: to dislodge our deeply held conviction that each individual is a unitary, coherent self that takes decisions (freely willed, of course) in a fully conscious, rational fashion. To that end, this section depicts human beings as made up of many selves, often in competition with one another, and whose corporeal self does the not unimportant job of holding these many dispositional states and stories together as a centre of narrative gravity.

a. My Cartesian Self

After dropping my friend C off at the OR Tambo International Airport at approximately 10:15 pm, I drove back to my abode in Fellside, Johannesburg. The trip back took me the entire running time of two Bruce Springsteen songs – 'The Meeting' and 'Jungleland'. Every light was green. Once home, I turned off the alarm, cranked up the heat and poured myself a weak cup of coffee. I settled down in bed to finish editing a chapter of *Constitutional Law of South Africa* – 'Social Security' – and to unwind by catching up on the exploits of my favourite baseball team, The New York Mets, in *The New York Times*. I had planned an early night so that I could join my friend Brahm early Sunday morning on the mashy-nibblick course we play in Roosevelt Park. Morpheus, however, did not arrive until 1:30 am.

I awoke the next morning having slept the sleep of the dead – not a good sign for an early tee time. Not surprisingly, my phone recorded the fact that Brahm had been leaving a steady stream of messages since approximately 8:30 am. Persistent but not obnoxious. I called him and promised that after my morning ablutions, I would pick him up at his house. I ran a hot bath, turned on the coffee maker and settled back into bed to read *The New York Times*. Having successfully negotiated the rites and the rituals required to make me human, I jumped in the car, picked up Brahm and headed west toward Roosevelt Park. The golf was a pleasure: even if my score left much to be desired. Lunch afterwards was surprisingly good. But best of all was the fact that with both of our partners in planes headed towards North America, Brahm and I had a chance to talk without any external limits being placed upon the length or the content of our conversation. Our golf and lunch complete, I stopped off at Brahm's house in Parkwood. I caught 5 minutes of a World Cup Match (2006) between the Netherlands and Serbia (actually Serbia and Montenegro to be exact) and then proceeded to Brahm's mother's cottage to check in on the French Open – split a set piece between Federer and Nadal. Having indulged my various pleasures, I returned home to work on what would ultimately become a very early iteration of this chapter.

On the standard or traditional account of the self, 'I' am the author of the story just told. I drove the car. I kissed C goodbye. I turned on the stereo. I turned off the house alarm. I edited the book chapter and read the newspaper. I slept and then I awoke in the morning. I made coffee. I ran a bath. I turned on the computer. I picked up my friend. I played golf. I had an extended conversation about the nature of love. I ate lunch. I watched television. I drove home – where all my stories begin and end.

But did I really do all these things? I have no doubt, mind you, that all these events occurred. Rather the doubt expressed is about the 'agent' – I – who engaged in this range of activities. As Susan Blackmore writes:

> In everyday language, we talk unproblematically about our 'self' ... It seems that we not only think of this self as a single thing, but we accord it all sorts of attributes and capabilities. In ordinary language, the self is the subject of experiences, an inner agent who carries out actions and makes

decisions, a unique personality, and the source of desires, opinions, hopes and fears. This self is 'me'; it is the reason why anything matters in my life.[41]

Few people deny that 'this' is how things appear or feel. (Indeed, I have already noted that there may even be compelling physiological and socio-biological reasons that we experience this unified sense of self.[42]) Even I will not deny that the 'I' that undertook all the actions above and the actions themselves matter to 'me'. Why else would I do them? Yet it is fair to say that fewer and fewer contemporary philosophers, cognitive psychologists, evolutionary biologists or neuroscientists defend the philosophical premises – or conclusions – upon which the unproblematic account of the self, articulated above, rests.

The unproblematic account has a venerable pedigree. Its most famous exposition, Rene Descartes, captured its essence in his *Meditations*.[43] His attempt to work out first principles from which all true propositions could be deduced led him to the conclusion that constitutes philosophy's best-known sound-bite: 'Cogito, ergo sum'. 'I think therefore I am.' This one incontrovertible maxim was grounded in incorrigible evidence provided by Descartes' extended, critical and openly sceptical process of introspection. The only thing that was not subject to doubt was the existence of his 'thinking' self.

The problem left over from Descartes' achievement in the *Meditations* was how this essentially incorporeal portion of the self could make anything transpire in the physical world, starting with actions undertaken by the human body. Descartes posited a theory of substance dualism in which the mind is constituted by one kind of substance, the body by another. When pressed to explain how physical events in the world and the brain itself gave rise to perceptions, images, ideas, emotions, decisions (those mental events we associate with the mind), and when further pushed to explain how the mind and various mental events gave rise to a welter of physical events – as manifest in the brain, the body and world about us – Descartes pointed to the pineal gland. The immaterial soul, our thinking self, was connected to the brain and thus the body in a tiny gland found at a midpoint in the brain. What occurred in the pineal gland that enabled the non-physical soul to work its magic on the brain and body, and the brain and the body back on the soul, Descartes could not say.

Nor can any substance dualist for that matter. Substance dualism relies upon linguistic alchemy and not empirical proof. The *only* philosophical defence of dualism of recent vintage was offered in the late 1970s by Karl Popper and John Eccles.[44] Despite Popper's extraordinary stature in 20th century philosophy and Eccles' recognition as a Nobel Laureate in biology, it is fair to say that their theory of dualist interactionism met with near universal derision. The theory held that the chemical processes that occur in the synaptic connections between neurons are so subtle that they could be subject to non-physical processes such as 'thinking' or 'feeling'. How such non-physical processes as 'thinking' or 'feeling' could affect even the most subtle changes in brain chemistry neither Popper nor Eccles could quite explain.[45] The tenets of dualist interactionism have the qualities of articles of faith – mysterious, untestable and, ultimately, unverifiable. The only significant difference between Descartes and Eccles/ Popper is that the bridging properties of the pineal gland (whose purpose is now properly understood) have been moved to the domain of the synapse.

The basic problem with dualist accounts of the self is that it is plagued by what we have seen Gilbert Ryle describe as 'the dogma of the Ghost in the Machine.'[46] Ryle describes as 'category mistakes' the distinctions we often make between (a) mind and body, or (b) a unitary physical location for the conscious self (the pineal gland?) and the product of significant amounts of largely unconscious, regionally distributed, parallel processing ultimately construct a transient global neuronal workspace that spans large, but ever changing, portions of the brain. Take the aforementioned unproblematic example of a category mistake. We would be rightly perplexed if a visitor to the University of the Witwatersrand, after having been shown all the lecture halls, playing fields, offices, laboratories, academics, students and staff, still asked 'But where is the University?' The mistake is in thinking that the University represents something over and above its constituent parts. Something similar occurs in discussions of the self and the mind. The mistake is in thinking that there is something – the mind – over and above the physical constituent parts that make up the human body that performs a variety of actions. Mental activities are physical processes, and the mind is a word we use to describe a set of physical properties and dispositions that belong to all human beings.[47]

b. My Cartesian Theatre

Yet the features of Cartesian dualism retain a tenacious hold over our imagination. Even amongst philosophers who reject substance dualism – or dualism in any form – there remains a sense that, as David Hume put it, '[t]he mind is a kind of theatre, where several perceptions successively make their appearance; pass, repass, glide away and mingle in an infinite variety of postures and situations'.[48] But Hume was unwilling to be bewitched:

> The comparison of the theatre must not mislead us. ... [S]uccessive perceptions *only* ... constitute the mind; nor have we a distinct notion of the place where scenes are represented, nor the material of which it is composed.[49]

What Hume warned against 250 years ago, and what Dennett has inveighed against more recently, is the notion that there is a place where 'it all comes together' – our ideas, images, perceptions and feelings – and 'consciousness happens'.[50] There is no such place. There is no 'screen' in the brain where 'it' all comes together so that 'I' can watch the events of my own mind and the world before 'me' unfold.

We may experience the relationship between consciousness and our self in this theatrical manner. That does not make it correct. Indeed, the distinction between the perceptual screen and the self that views that screen constitutes a form of dualism that Dennett describes as 'Cartesian materialism'. How do we know that this new form of dualism is incorrect? After all, each of us has this experience of watching her world.

To understand why the metaphor of a Cartesian theatre is inapt, Blackmore asks her readers to undertake a simple exercise:

> Right now, please – consciously and deliberately – take a thumb, raise it to your face and press it against the end of your nose. Feel the thumb-on-nose sensations and then let go.[51]

Where, she asks them, did consciousness happen? The Cartesian theatre – or some variant thereof – seems like an appropriate response. However, everything we now know about how our brain (and body) works tells us that such a theatre does not exist and that far more mundane explanations exist for the act and the experience of putting thumb to nose.

First, the reading of the instructions for the experiment engages the visual cortex (V1) and Wernicke's area (where much of the neural activity associated with linguistic tasks occurs). Second, as to the movement of the eyes and the thumb required to bring the thumb into contact with our nose, the neural activity associated with these actions occurs in the motor cortex. Finally, when my thumb touched my nose, it activated my sensory cortex. There is, as it turns out, no central headquarters where all the information is directed, processed, arranged and then projected up on to the screen of our Cartesian theatre. What is happening? Significant amounts of largely unconscious, regionally distributed, parallel processing ultimately construct a *transient* global neuronal workspace that spans large, but ever changing, portions of the brain.[52] If this initial description of a largely unconscious, regionally distributed, transient system parallel processing as the basis for consciousness does not convince you to give up on the Cartesian theatre model of consciousness, then consider the following two examples: (1) the 300 lb man returns; and (2) hemisphere disconnection.

Recall our earlier encounter with the 300 lb man – the man who, if pushed in front of a trolley, would prevent the trolley from killing five people just down the tracks. Let's give him a name: Bill. Let's give him a history: he has worked in your university for 15 years. You know his family. He's a good father with a tendency to eat all the strudel at the Christmas parties. At the same time, the Madlingozi family, just down the track, is also known to you. Wendy is the director of your school; her daughters, common visitors to the office.

As you pause to consider whether to push Bill in front of the train, and save the lives of the Mandlingozi family, Tancredi tells us that 'no fewer than TWENTY brain structures and their circuits are madly at work'.[53] 'Your long term memory (stored in the cerebral cortex)'[54] reminds you of Bill and his addiction to strudel, and that his daughter attends the same primary school as your daughter, Temba. Short term memory – stored in the hippocampus – reminds you of a recent chance encounter at the supermarket. Your sympathy for Bill receives 'a strong boost as your visual cortex and mirror neurons (including the superior temporal sulcus, the fusiform hyrus and the amygdala)' process Bill's facial expression as he suddenly recognizes the situation in which he has found himself.[55] Your amygdala is activated again as recognition of the potentially dangerous consequences (for both Bill and you) that follow what you may do asserts itself. 'Your ambivalence activates your premotor cortex' – which rehearses pushing Bill onto the rails. 'At the same time your frontal lobe and anterior cingulated cortex step in to stifle the [push] impulse.' Perhaps another way exists, as yet untested, to save both Bill and the Mandlingozi family. (There isn't: but that doesn't stop your brain from conjuring up alternative scenarios and consequences.) Your prefrontal cortex steps in at this moment to take command and to deliver the gentle, if undesirable, push, whilst you say the words 'I'm sorry Bill'. At this juncture, other regions of the cerebral cortex – visual (occipital cortex and superior temporal sulcus, superior colliculus), auditory (temporal cortex), language (Broca's and Weirneke's areas) are activated as 'your prefrontal lobe reviews all the sensations that you have received and develops a plan of response.'[56] Finally, your hippocampus (connecting memory to emotion), your anterior cingulated cortex (self-control) and the hypothalamus (which controls such bodily functions as sweating and increased heart rate) kick in as you register Bill's response to your obvious attempt to push him on to the tracks to stop the train.[57] That's one active largely unconscious, regionally distributed, massive parallel processing machine readying you to do the deed.

Still unconvinced that the Cartesian dualist mind provides an implausible explanation for how you come to push Bill on to the tracks? Then let's test your intuitions again with a medical procedure known as hemisphere disconnection.

It was common practice, in cases of severe epilepsy that could not be controlled through medication alone, for surgical procedures to be carried out that limited the damage done during epileptic fits to a single hemisphere of the brain. The procedure involved the division of the entire corpus callosum, the division of the anterior and hippocampal commissures and, on occasion, the division of the massa intermedia. In short, the left hemisphere and the right hemisphere of the brain were disconnected. RW Sperry reported the following results of hemisphere disconnection:

> One of the more general and also more interesting and striking features of this syndrome may be summarized as an apparent doubling in most of the realms of conscious awareness. Instead of the normally unified single stream of consciousness, these patients behave in many ways as if they have two independent streams of conscious awareness, one in each hemisphere, each which is cut off from and out of contact with the mental experiences of the other. In other words, each hemisphere seems to have its own separate and private sensations, its own perceptions, its own concepts, and its own impulses to act, with related volitional, cognitive and learning experiences. Following the surgery, each hemisphere also has thereafter its own separate chain of memories that are rendered inaccessible to the recall processes of the other.[58]

Sperry's interpretation of the consequences of this radical surgery suggests that one self, and one brain, has been carefully carved up into two selves and two brains. Without, for the moment, accepting all of Sperry's conclusions, it does appear from the responses of patients that this surgery had the consequence of creating two different physical 'realms' of consciousness. What this means, at a minimum, is that the Cartesian theatre is now a duplex. All kidding aside, the results indicate that there is no single theatre of consciousness. To the contrary, each hemisphere demonstrates the capacity, after disconnection, to form conscious thoughts, to experience conscious perceptions, and to perform conscious actions: all features that we attribute to a single human self. These features of selves – now located in two distinct hemispheres of one brain – support the previous contention that the self is not located in a single place in the brain where it then takes stock of the action presented to it and responds accordingly.

Subsequent assessments of split-brain subjects were less emphatic than Sperry with respect to the contention that the split brain led to the cleaving of one self into two. Gazzaniga located what he described as 'the interpreter' in the left hemisphere that appeared to retain the capacity for 'high-level consciousness'.[59] But neither this finding, nor MacKay's conclusion that the 'two selves' playing each other, as distinct entities, in a game of 20 questions did not possess a genuine 'duality of will',[60] displace the more general contention that any self – or consciousness – is a function of largely unconscious, regionally distributed, massive parallel processing. We may not yet know with certainty how the individual corporeal self coheres or how consciousness emerges, but we should be clear that the Cartesian theatre is an inapt theoretical construct.

Sperry, Gazzaniga and MacKay's findings all undermine the central metaphor of the Cartesian theatre – a 'little me' watching and responding to the 'bigger me' and the world about me from the comfort of a seat somewhere in the middle of the brain. However, underlying all three attempts at explaining the data is the belief that one can count the number of selves in a split-brain patient. But can we? I now want to suggest in William James' words, that 'the same brain may subserve many conscious selves'.[61]

C. Explaining (Away) the Self: Bundle Theory

We have seen that ego theorists – such as Descartes, or even Sperry, Mackay and Gazzaniga – have problems explaining how the unitary conception of the self actually operates both mechanically and phenomenologically. Descartes cannot explain how an immaterial mind or soul interacts with the body and the rest of the material world. Sperry, Mackay and Gazzaniga cannot agree amongst themselves as to whether a disconnected brain contains one self, two selves, or an upper self and a lower self.

Bundle theorists, such as Derek Parfit, view the consternation of ego theorists attempting to parse selves with a large degree of diffidence. Parfit contends that these experiments make little sense if our goal is to arrive at a clear conclusion about the numbers of selves located within an individual body or the brain. Given what we know about the responses of split-brain patients, Parfit asks us to imagine the following experiment. A split brain patient is shown two cards – one red, one blue. The left hemisphere registers red; the right hemisphere registers blue. When asked to write down the colour of the card, the hand controlled by the left hemisphere writes 'red'. The hand controlled by the right hemisphere writes 'blue'. The questions Parfit's thought experiment compels us to ask are: (1) How many selves are there? (2) How many streams of consciousness are there? The answer to the last question is two. But the answer to the first question is not, on Partfit's account, two as well. Parfit argues that our multiple experiences, thoughts, emotions, actions are related to one another as a 'bundle of sensations'. They are not, as it generally seems to us, the property of a single unified self. As a result, Parfit contends that the answer to question number 1 is not two, but none.[62]

Even if Parfit's reductionist account of the self as simply a 'bundle' of percepts is true, nothing about the data derived from the split-brain experiments proves the truth of the bundle theorists' account. What seems to interest Parfit most in the split-brain account is that ego theorists – who posit the existence of integrated continuous selves – cannot agree on whether the data supports the presence of one, two or more selves. Moreover, what seems evident, on Sperry, Mackay and Gazzaniga's own accounts, is that different parts of the brain carry out different functions contemporaneously, and that different constellations of these parallel processes can produce the phenomenon of consciousness. For a bundle theorist like Parfit, some succour can be derived from the brain's ability to produce consciousness in a number of different ways, using a number of different parts of the brain, and even producing two apparently different conscious responses simultaneously. For a bundle theorist, the data appears to support the hypothesis that at least two different forms of conscious awareness can be produced by the same brain that have no immediate awareness of the other conscious response and no subsequent mnemonic capacity to recall the content of the other stream of consciousness. The split-brain experiments seem to support the thesis that the unity of consciousness – and of the self – is not a necessary consequence of a functioning brain.

Yet, even the father of bundle theory, David Hume, knows that positing a stream of thought as all there is to selfhood runs counter to common sense and everyday experience. Most of us experience the sensation of a single self that holds all of its thoughts, feelings and emotions together. What then, assuming the truth of bundle theory, accounts for this sense of a unified continuous self and what, ultimately, is the truth about how our brain creates consciousness and a sense of self?

D. Some Plausible Theories of Consciousness and the Self

Over the past decade, various scientists, working in different disciplines, have proffered theories of the self that do not rely on any form of Cartesian dualism, but, consistent with the available data, explain how a unitary 'sense' of self can emerge from an enormous, normally disaggregated system of neurological processes that are distributed throughout the brain, that occur in parallel, and that may or may not be the subject of conscious awareness. The leading theories of the self share this aforementioned empirical understanding of how the brain operates. So it will come as no surprise that these accounts will sound very similar themes. The purpose of this section is not to interrogate these offerings in order to arrive at a preferred theory, but to proffer some reasonably solid conclusions about how the majority of neuroscientists, cognitive psychologists and philosophers understand the self and consciousness in order that I might better explain why a proper conception of the self matters for constitutional theory.

1. *The Proto-Self, the Core Self and the Autobiographical Self*

One way to understand consciousness and selfhood – from a neurophysiological perspective – is to think of it as having layers, or levels, of sophistication that depend upon the neurological complexity of the creature and the integrity of the brain and the neurological system. Antonio Damasio, a clinician and a neuroscientist, claims that even the simplest organisms have a proto-self.[63] This proto-self is no more than a set of neural patterns that enable the organism to monitor both its state and its environment on a moment-to-moment basis. However, the proto-self is not conscious, is not aware, of either its internal state or its relationship to the environment about it.[64]

A small, but still significant, number of organisms possess core consciousness, and thus a core self. This level of consciousness enables the organism to have a sense of self in the 'here and now'. However, the core self is 'a transient entity, ceaselessly recreated for each and every object with which the brain interacts'.[65] Severe amnesiacs, such as those who present with Korsakoff's syndrome (alcoholism, and the thiamine deficiency associated with it, leads to the destruction of the mimilary bodies and the dorso-medial nucleus of the thalamus, as well as more diffuse damage to the frontal lobes), suffer from anteretrograde amnesia (the inability to form new long-term memories) and retrograde amnesia (the loss of long-term memory that often stretches far into the past). Such persons – though they retain the capacity to engage in some tasks that can be done relatively quickly (dialling a telephone) – remain stuck in a very brief perpetual present. Oliver Sacks wrote of one such patient that his amnesia was 'a pit into which everything, every experience, every event, would fathomously drop, a bottomless memory-hole that would engulf the whole world.'[66] Such persons are incapable of creating memories of a unitary continuous self (or as some bundle theorists would argue, the comforting illusion of such a self.[67]) Although somewhat more complex than many core selves found in other organisms, the person who suffers from a severe case of Korsokoff's syndrome is recreated for each and every object with which she interacts.[68]

A third form of self is the autobiographical self. The autobiographical self features complex forms of cognitive and neurological organization and takes shape over the period of an organism's life. Unlike the person who suffers from Korsokoff's syndrome, a normal human being is able to form and to retain short, medium and long-term memories. As a result, she is able to learn and to retain the capacity to engage in a broad array of simple and complex tasks. This self, as Damasio is careful to note, is not a separate entity above and beyond the corporeal self. (That would make him guilty, of course, of the kind of category mistake Ryle warns against and that neuroscientists generally do not make.) The autobiographical self is the story, or rather stories, we tell of our life for as long as we have the capacity to tell stories (until, that is, we experience some form of Alzheimer's disease, senile dementia, CFIDS, or, of course, death.) Damasio's metaphor for the autobiographical self that retains its integrity runs as follows: 'You are the music while the music lasts.'[69] (But even that metaphor, which intimates a form of unity of consciousness, takes cognizance of the different movements within this symphony – an allegro, or a scherzo and more – or the different genres of music that play at very moments and stages of our short corporeal existence.)

As a physiological matter, Damasio remains committed to the proposition that all conscious experience is the result of transient connections between neural modules distributed throughout the brain – from places as diverse in function as 'the brain stem, thalamus and cerebral cortex'.[70] Like Baars, Dehaene and Dennett, and most of the other neuroscientists whose work I canvas, Damasio also has no need for a viewing self – a homunculus – who passively, or not so passively, experiences the world and herself in the comfort of a Cartesian theatre. Although Damasio does not demonstrate a clear link between the complex, parallel, massive, distributed neural processes that gives rise to consciousness and the autobiographical self, his writing suggests that it is our capacity for remembering (and ordering) the many events, skills and relationships that make up our lives that enables us to experience (feel) that 'unity of consciousness' that provides the subjective experience of being 'me'.[71] (It's also true that a distinct part of the brain has the responsibility for maintaining this sensation. When the prefrontal cortex is damaged, many individuals lose this sensation.[72])

Dehanne and Naccache offer one physiological explanation for Damasio's subjective experience of a 'unity of self'. On their account, a number of modular, non-conscious processes and structures distributed throughout the brain, can create, when they enter a global neuronal workspace, a sense of individual identity. Modular processors governing 'the face and person-processing circuits of the interior and anterior temporal lobes', other processors that govern episodic memory and modules that enable us 'to interpret and to predict *other* people's actions', when brought together in the 'conscious workspace, may suffice to account for the subjective sense of self.'[73] This speculation is supported by the absence of self experienced by persons who have Capgras syndrome, Fregoli syndrome and certain forms of autism, and thus do not possess the healthy functional neuronal module processors that Dehanne and Naccache believe are required for a subjective sense of self.

Does Damasio, ten years down the road, concur with this account?[74] By and large. In his most recent work, Damasio has arrived at the following conclusions. First, while consciousness does not reside in a particular 'brain centre', it is 'predominantly based ... in the 'early cortical regions and upper brain stem': though 'at any given moment the conscious brain works 'globally', ... in an anatomically differentiated manner.'[75] Second, to understand why consciousness requires both the cerebral cortex and the brain stem, we must return to the hard question of consciousness: why do we have that pronounced feeling of 'thereness' and 'selfness' that we associate with consciousness? To this question, Damasio points us in the direction of 'brain-stem neural systems'.[76] While he admits that he cannot, at this juncture, provide a 'comprehensive explanation for the making of feelings', he can advance 'a specific hypothesis ... which can be put to the test'.[77] That test runs as follows:

> Because of its mastery in the role of the life regulator, the [relatively small] brain stem has long been the recipient and the local processor of information necessary to 'represent' the body and control its life. ... [T]he brain stem also developed the machinery for elementary mind processes and even consciousness... On the other hand, the greater complexity of the cerebral cortex has enabled detailed image-making, expanded memory capacity, imagination, reasoning, and eventually language. Now comes the big problem: ... the functions of the brain stem were not duplicated in the cortical structures. ... This is where the thalamus came to the rescue ... The thalamus accomplishes a dissemination of signals from the brain stem to a widespread territory of the cortical mantle. In return, the hugely expanded cerebral cortex ... funnels signals to the brain stem. ... [I]n the end, the thalamus is best described as the marriage broker of the oddest couple.[78]

Damasio then proceeds to integrate neurons and neural networks into his hypothesis. That Damasio only has a working hypothesis can hardly be counted as a failure. It remains for future research projects that emphasize different aspects of activity in the brain and body from which consciousness emerges to tell us how close he currently is to the mark. However, when we return to the trolley car scenario later in this chapter, ask yourself, might the kind of consciousness that emerges from different neuronal networks be contingent upon the the kind of problem with which we are confronted?

2. *Global Neuronal Workspace Theory*

a. *Baars' Global Workspace Theory*

One distinguishing feature of Bernard Baars' Global Workspace Theory is that it embraces the metaphor of 'a theatre of consciousness' without endorsing any of the fundamental misconceptions about the self that plague Cartesian dualism.[79] For Baars, the theatre is more than just a metaphor. It accords with verifiable, replicable data generated by single cell recording,[80] EEGs,[81] computer tomography,[82] PETs,[83] fMRIs,[84] TMS[85] and other methods of recording brain activity.[86]

For Baars, the metaphor of the theatre is first employed to distinguish the tiny amount of 'spotlighted' data available to consciousness from the enormous amount of data being generated by unconscious neural processes. Baars extends this metaphorical contrast between 'focal consciousness' – what is, for the moment, 'on stage' – and the unconscious neural processes that are, sometimes for the moment, and sometimes forever, 'off-stage'. Around the 'bright spot' on stage are fringe players of whom we are only vaguely aware. Finally, in the audience for the 'theatre of consciousness' are unconscious neuronal processes that receive the information being delivered from the 'stage' and other unconscious neuronal processes that respond to the information delivered and serve to shape what happens 'on-stage'.[87] It goes without saying that the vast majority of neuronal processes are not really interested in the theatre, never appear in the play and will go on doing what they are doing without any meaningful interaction with the events on stage.

In Baars' terminology, the theatre of consciousness is better known as the 'global workspace'. So while 'the theatre' may be a nice metaphor for (some of) Baars' ruminations about consciousness and the self, the term 'global workspace' illuminates more powerfully how the brain works and why it produces consciousness.

Baars' 'global workspace' utilizes analytical tropes employed in other fields of study, e.g. speech understanding[88] and artificial intelligence.[89] As these fields of study reveal, the 'global workspace' focuses on a small number of 'problems' at a given moment. The 'global workspace' – a transient location designed to solve the immediate problem that has 'captured' our attention – is simultaneously connected to various sensory inputs and a host of potential experts – neural networks – that might assist in the solution of the problem.[90] These teams of 'experts' encompass neural networks with particular linguistic skills, relevant memories, or trained responses. As Blackmore puts it, the global workspace 'recruits processors for on-going tasks, facilitates executive decisions and enables voluntary control over automatic action routines'.[91]

If we return for a moment to the two sketches in Chapter 1, of the unconscious driver and the errant driver, then we might get a better idea of how the workspace operates. In the story of the unconscious driver, my conscious awareness is engaged with all sorts of ruminations about the nature of the self and its relationship to experimental constitutionalism. At best, the various objects that ought to concentrate the mind – other cars, traffic robots, layouts of streets – are pushed to the periphery of the stage. At worst, say we add a cell-phone to the mix, these objects of attention may appear to be pushed off the stage entirely. (But that is too strong a statement. The routine nature of driving is such that we are also trained to remain aware of objects that might cause us harm, e.g. other cars, red lights, sharp turns in the road.) Indeed, the story of the errant driver serves to show how the global workspace – its attention or focus drawn primarily to the plot devices of that night's film – can be shifted to another problem: the layout of roads. Whereas the unconscious driver had no apparent need of the neural network required to solve driving problems and could rely on an array of unconscious, distributed, parallel processes to carry him from Glen Atholl to Fellside, the errant driver

– having pushed his many driving sub-routines to the periphery of consciousness – suddenly became aware of a problem with 'driving' and returned 'driving' to its place of prominence in the global workspace in order to right the ship and redirect the car to Fellside.[92] The events depicted in the errant driver story fit Baars' and Newman's contention that 'consciousness generally comes into play when stimuli are assessed to be novel, threatening or momentarily relevant to active schemas or intentions':[93]

> The defining features of stimuli which engage conscious attention (i.e., the global allocation of processing resources) are that they: (1) vary in some significant degree from current expectations; or (2) are congruent with the current predominant intent/goal of the organism. In contrast, the processing of stimuli which are predictable, routine or over-learned is automatically allocated to non-conscious, highly-modulized cognitive systems.[94]

As Baars' analysis and Newman's explanation of the hallmarks of conscious attention suggest, the examples of the unconscious driver and the errant driver paint too Manichean a picture of consciousness. It is safer to say that in both instances, we were more conscious and less conscious of certain events. Brain scans reveal the graded character of consciousness – moving from highly conscious, to very conscious, to somewhat conscious, to barely conscious, to not conscious at all.[95] Such scans – which show the variability and motility of consciousness – also reveal a feature of consciousness to which we have already attended in previous sections: that it has no fixed location and, apparently, no fixed content.[96]

b. Dehanne and Naccache's Global Neuronal Workspace Theory

Over the past two decades, Dehanne, Naccache and others have extended Baars' hypotheses regarding global workspace theory in a manner that connects the theory more directly to empirical findings in neuroscience. This fleshing out of Baars' theses with hard data about the manner in which the brain operates explains the subtle shift in description from a global workspace theory to a global neuronal workspace theory.

Dehanne and Naccache begin by noting that any theory of consciousness must accommodate three critical empirical observations:

> (1) a considerable amount of processing is possible without consciousness, (2) attention is a prerequisite of consciousness, and (3) consciousness is required for some specific cognitive tasks, including those that require durable information maintenance, novel combinations of operations, or the spontaneous generation of intentional behaviour.[97]

They then offer a hypothesis which synthesizes these three findings: the theory of a global neuronal workspace. According to this hypothesis:

> [A]t any given time, cerebral networks are active in parallel and process information in an unconscious manner ... [Global neuronal] workspace theory operates on the assumption that] information becomes conscious ... if the neural population that represents it is mobilized by top-down attention amplification into a brain state of coherent activity that involves many neurons distributed throughout the brain. The long-distance connectivity of these 'workspace neurons' can ... make the information available to a variety of processes including perceptual categorization, long-term memorization, evaluation and intentional action. We postulate that this global availability

> of information through the workspace is what we subjectively experience as a conscious state. A complete theory of consciousness should explain why some cognitive and cerebral representations can be permanently or temporarily inaccessible to consciousness, what is the range of possible conscious contents, how they map on to particular cerebral circuits and whether a generic neuronal mechanism underlies all of them ... Neurophysiological, anatomical, and brain-imaging data strongly argue for a major role of prefrontal cortex, anterior cingulate, and the areas that connect to them, in creating the postulated brain-scale workspace.[98]

That a considerable amount of processing is possible without consciousness is evinced by studies of brain-lesioned patients,[99] prosopagnosic patients[100] and normal subjects in which the relevant stimuli is masked by surrounding stimuli.[101] The question then arises as to why, if so much information can be processed without consciousness, we require, or experience, consciousness at all.

The answer is that 'consciousness is required for specific mental operations'.[102] One such task is durable memory. In the absence of conscious amplification of a visual field, the contents of that visual field quickly decay. For example, imagine driving a golf ball 250 meters – literally out of sight, and perhaps off the fairway. When approaching the area in which the ball should have landed or stopped, consciousness has a distinct purpose: find the ball. If you are playing alone, your conscious engagement searches for and fixes upon any little white object that should appear in the area and relies upon durable data about the ball's flight to do so. It matters not whether the rain continues to pour, or the surrounding koppies contain abodes with astounding vistas: all that consciousness counts as relevant is the location of the ball. Detect the ball, and you may just experience a God-given epiphany. A second task is the ability to perform a novel or an unusual computation. A series of studies of the Stroop effect support the proposition that the 'ability to inhibit an automatic [and generally unconscious] stream of processes and to deploy a novel strategy depended crucially on the conscious availability of information.'[103] From this set of experiments and hypotheses, Dehaene and Naccache draw the following conclusion:

> [A]s a generalization, the strategic operations ... associated with planning a novel strategy, evaluating it, controlling its execution, and *correcting possible errors* cannot be accomplished unconsciously. It is noteworthy that such processes are always associated with a subjective feeling of 'mental effort', which is absent during automatized or unconscious processing and may therefore serve as a selective marker of conscious processing.[104]

A third kind of task associated with consciousness involves intentional behaviour. Dehaene and Naccache, following Dennett and Weiskrantz, note the difference in responses of normal subjects and blind-sighted subjects to visual stimuli.[105] Normal subjects can respond consciously and of their own accord to visual stimuli. Blind-sighted subjects cannot. Their absence of conscious awareness of the stimuli means that they must be guided by another – that is, by the intentional behaviour of another – in order to engage in a purposive response to the stimuli.

That we can distinguish tasks that require conscious attention from tasks that do not, returns us once again to the question of how the brain accomplishes these tasks. The hypothesis stated above by Baars and Dehaene and Naccache is that

> [B]esides specialized processors, the architecture of the human brain ... comprises a distributed neural system or 'workspace' with long-distance connectivity that can potentially interconnect multiple specialized brain areas in a co-ordinated though variable manner. Through the workspace, modular systems that do not directly exchange information in an automatic mode can nevertheless gain access to each other's content. The global workspace thus provides a common 'communication protocol' through which a particularly large potential for the combination of multiple input, output, and internal systems becomes available.[106]

Dehaene and Naccache then go on to identify five main categories of neural systems that must participate for the workspace to function: (1) 'perceptual circuits that inform about the present state of the environment'; (2) 'motor circuits that allow the preparation and controlled execution of actions'; (3) 'long-term memory-circuits that can reinstate past workspace states'; (4) 'evaluation circuits that attribute [percepts] a valence in relation to previous experience'; and (5) 'attentional or top-down circuits that selectively gate the focus of interest'.[107] The interaction of these five kinds of neural systems requires no central co-ordination. Instead, neural networks are established for the purpose of conscious action by virtue of their adequacy with respect to the demands of the environment and the task at hand. The neural systems ultimately selected are, not surprisingly, those networks that have worked previously, or based upon past experience, and those novel networks that can be expected to realize the person's goals and achieve the desired reward. Again Dehaene and Naccache take great care to emphasize that 'the resulting ... transient self-sustained workspace states follow one another in a constant stream, without requiring any external supervision.'[108] (That should sound more like Parfit's bundle theory than it does a Cartesian ego.) The process governing these transient self-sustained workspace states appears, from current computer simulations, to be one of 'neuronal Darwinism'.[109]

How does the workspace actually function anatomically in order to produce these conscious states? That is, what parts of the brain are responsible for conscious states? (Recall that Damasio has his own proto-hypothesis about how consciousness emerges and what parts of the brain bear primary responsibility for its production.) About that there is both general agreement – and wide-ranging resistance to tight theories of correspondence and causality.

Some theorists prefer not to employ the term consciousness at all. They spend their time explaining the physiological basis of neural correlates of consciousness, because they tend to believe that the term evokes deeply embedded, and wrong-headed, metaphysical beliefs that obscure more than they enlighten. They believe that with enough empirical investigation, and a better understanding of how the brain actually works, people will stop using dualist language and learn to speak of consciousness as they would any other physical phenomenon.[110] Their strong materialist orientation leads neural correlates proponents, such as Christopher Koch and Francis Crick, to assert that 'you', their reader and their audience, 'your joys and sorrows, your memories and your ambitions, your sense of personal identity and free will, are in fact no more than the behaviour of a vast assemblage of nerve cells and their associated molecules.'[111] Consciousness, on Koch and Crick's account, '*is* the behaviour of neurons'.[112] Consciousness is not to be understood as either the (epi) phenomenological product of neuronal activity, nor is it to be understood as a process that is responsible for neuronal activity.[113] For Damasio, the nexus between the brain stem, the thalamus and the cerebral cortex (and the individual neuronal networks) holds out the best *possible* explanation for why consciousness arises and feels as it does. But it is one hypothesis amongst many. Dehaene and Naccache recognize the tight correlation between the activation of particular neural circuits and a subject's reports of consciousness. However, they refuse to draw the conclusion that correlation implies causation.[114] 'Causality', they write, 'can only be established by demonstrating that alterations of ... brain state[s] systematically alter[] subjects' consciousness.'[115] For now, its sufficient that we recognize the degree of agnosticism – about how consciousness emerges – within the organized skepticism of the scientific community.

Dehaene and Naccache are not entirely agnostic on the subject of causation and consciousness. They contend that experiments carried out by McIntosh, Rajah and Lobaugh demonstrate the centrality of the prefrontal cortex ('PFC') for consciousness.[116] In their work, McIntosh, Rajah and Lobaugh separated out, after the experiment, those subjects who became consciously aware of the stimuli from those subjects that did not. The subjects who became consciously aware of the systematic relations between auditory and visual stimuli

> showed an increased activated of the PFC (and, to a lesser degree, in bilateral occipital cortices and left thalamus) ... Importantly, this activation was accompanied by a major increase in the functional correlation of the left PFC with other distant brain regions including the contralateral PFC, sensory association cortices, and cerebellum. This long distance coherence pattern appeared precisely when subjects became conscious and started to use their conscious knowledge to guide behaviour.[117]

These findings regarding the PFC have been confirmed by other experiments.[118] Additional experiments carried out over the past decade enabled Dehaene and Naccache to refine their hypotheses about the neurological architecture responsible for most conscious activity: the PFC, the anterior cingulate ('AC'), along with interconnected areas must, in turn, 'be tightly interconnected through long axons' with the five kinds of neural networks identified above ('high level perceptual, motor, long-term memory, evaluative and attentional').[119]

As interesting as these findings regarding the physical anatomy of the global neuronal workspace may be, Dehaene and Naccache's hypotheses about the purpose of consciousness are that much more important for this book's immediate purposes. Note that in the last long quotation, Dehaene and Naccache write that '[t]his long distance coherence pattern appeared precisely when subjects became conscious and started to use their conscious knowledge to guide behaviour.'[120] The purpose then of consciousness is to guide behaviour.

But how exactly does consciousness accomplish this feat? Dehaene and Naccache suggest that conscious attention enables us to modify or to withhold automatic or learned behavioural responses when confronted with novel circumstances. Consciousness, it would appear, allows an individual 'to represent a goal and to estimate the outcomes of [her] ... actions before initiating them'.[121] The ability to undertake trial and error thought experiments within the simulated framework provided for by neurological structures is an enormous advance on having to undertake trials with errors in one's actual physical environment. It enables us to weed out outcomes less likely to be successful and enhances our capacity to survive and to flourish.[122] That then is our explanation for the genesis of consciousness:

> The evolutionary advantages that this system confers to the organism may be related to the increased independence it affords. The more an organism can rely on mental simulation and internal evaluation to select a course of action, instead of acting out in the open world, the lower are risks and the expenditure of energy. By allowing more sources of knowledge to bear on this internal decision process, the neural workspace may represent an additional step in a general trend towards increasing internalization of representations in the course of evolution, whose main advantage is the freeing of the organism from its immediate environment.[123]

In keeping with the general thesis of this work, what Dehaene and Naccache have shown is that consciousness enables the individual – by herself or in concert with others – to undertake multiple thought experiments that maximize the chances of successful experiments in the outside world. Consciousness – as reflected in global neuronal workspaces – accomplishes this feat by allowing different combinations of neural networks to compete with one another until a winner is selected. A winner reflects a representation of the action deemed most likely to succeed.[124]

3. *Dennett's Self as a Centre of Narrative Gravity*

Daniel Dennett has, for quite some time, been the most influential philosopher in contemporary debates about consciousness. Much of Dennett's energy has been devoted to correcting long-standing errors in the philosophical canon (especially various species of mind/body dualism such as the hard problem of consciousness ('subjectivity'),[125] the nature of qualia,[126] as well as related arguments about the irreducibility and incorrigibility of first person reports and the possibility of heterophenomenology.[127]) His contributions have not been limited to the demolition of the Cartesian theatre and all vestiges of dualism.[128] As an analytic philosopher and cognitive scientist, Dennett was one of the first theorists to conceive of an empirical framework for consciousness that used the available data from fields as disparate as 'quantum physics and chemistry, through neuroscience and psychology, to philosophy and literature'.[129] By drawing heavily on contemporary scholarship in neuroscience, experimental psychology and artificial intelligence, Dennett was able to offer an account of consciousness in the early 1990s that has, in fact, largely been verified by subsequent investigations in the natural sciences as to the physiological origins of consciousness.[130] That account, already offered in various forms in the previous pages, runs as follows:

> At any given time, many modular (1) cerebral networks are active in parallel and process information in an unconscious manner. Any information (2) becomes conscious, however, if the neural population that represents it, is mobilized by top-down (3) attentional amplification of into a brain-state of coherent activity that involves many neurons distributed throughout the brain. The long distance connectivity of these 'workplace neurons' can, when they are active for a minimal duration (4), make the information available to a variety of processes including perceptual categorization, long term memorization, evaluation and intentional action. We postulate that this global availability of information through the workplace is (5) what we subjectively experience as a conscious state.[131]

Dennett draws attention to three additional hallmarks of the global workspace theory that are not only important for a theory of the self, but will become important to understanding the fundamental principles of flourishing and experimental constitutionalism developed later on in this work. First, it is important to remember that this post-competition 'consensus' amongst neural networks does not cause consciousness. It *is* consciousness. Second, the accessibility of Baars' discrete experts – and McCarthy's demons – to one another (horizontally, and not vertically to some imagined higher executive or central ego) may 'explain the dramatic increases in cognitive competence that we associate with consciousness: the availability to engage in deliberate reflection, the non-automaticity, in short, the open-mindedness that permits a conscious agent to consider anything in its purview in any way it chooses.'[132] Third, Dennett suggests that we should try to understand consciousness, or the conscious moment, in terms of

> political influence – a good slang term is clout. When processes compete for ongoing control of the body, the one with the greatest clout dominates the scene until a process with even greater clout displaces it... Our brains are ... democratic, indeed somewhat anarchic. In the brain there is no King, no official viewer of the State Television Program, no Cartesian Theatre, but there are plenty of sharp differences in political clout exercised by its contents over time.[133]

Consciousness, like political success or fame, is 'not an intrinsic property, not even just a dispositional property; it is a phenomenon that requires some actualization of potential'.[134] Dennett explains how competition and co-operation amongst neuronal networks in a global workspace results in consciousness by offering us a metaphor for what it means for neuronal activity not to achieve 'consciousness':

> Consider the following tale. Jim has written a remarkable first novel that has been enthusiastically read by some of the cognoscenti. His picture is all set to go on the cover of *Time Magazine*, and Oprah has lined him up for her television show. A national book tour is planned and Hollywood has already expressed interest in his book. That's all true on Tuesday. Wednesday morning, San Francisco is destroyed in an earthquake, and the world's attention can hold nothing else for a month. Is Jim famous? He would have been, if it weren't for that darn earthquake. Maybe next month, if things return to normal, he'll become famous for deeds done earlier. But fame eluded him this week, in spite of the fact that the *Time Magazine* cover story had been typeset and sent to the printer, to be yanked at the last moment, and in spite of the fact that his name was already in *TV Guide* as Oprah's guest, and in spite of the fact that stacks of his novels could be found in the windows of most bookstores. All the dispositional properties normally sufficient for fame were in place, but their normal effects didn't get triggered, so no fame resulted... Real fame is not the *cause* of all the normal aftermath; it *is* the normal aftermath.[135]

The same holds for consciousness. It is not the *cause* of the neuronal processes that give rise to a broad array of thoughts and actions. It *is* the set of neuronal processes that, for the moment, has achieved victory in our brain's regular competition amongst neural networks for attention (in the service of the greater good of our survival and flourishing.)

E. Selves and Heterogeneity

On my account, the various theories on offer by Baars, Damasio, Dehaene, Koch and Dennett converge on a conception of consciousness in which various networks distributed throughout the brain (a) act in parallel, (b) process substantial amounts of information in an unconscious manner, (c) compete for the awareness that constitutes the content of consciousness, and (d) then amplify that information to the rest of the brain in a manner that enables us to solve an immediate problem or to continue to carry out a critical long-term task. But what sense then are we to make of the 'self', given that consciousness itself is not fixed in a given place, that the contents of consciousness are the product of competition (and co-operation) between parallel, mostly non-conscious and widely distributed neural networks, that the winners of such competitions – like politicians in a democracy – will have tenures of varying length, and that there is no single entity, no executive programme, no master discriminator that brings all the winners to heel in the service of a single master narrative?

The proceeding account(s) of consciousness supports the claim that our notion of 'selfness' is a function, a very useful by-product, of a complex array of semi-independent and often overlapping neural networks that control the body's journey through life. This complex set of dispositional states is a function of both the deep grammar of our brains and the social endowments that have evolved over time to determine various patterns of behaviour. Once again, it should be apparent from this brief account that the self is a valuable abstraction and not an entity – neither an internal observer nor a boss – that stands back from experience and then dictates to the body what it does in response to various stimuli.[136]

1. *Socially, Radically Heterogeneous, Determined Selves*

Each self then is, in Dennett's felicitous phrase, just 'a centre of narrative gravity'. Each centre of narrative gravity – each self – is a set of different, but overlapping narratives. Each narrative, or storyline, reflects a complex set of experiences and dispositional states organized around a particular form of behaviour. As I noted in the Introduction, the "I" that goes by the name of Stu Woolman consists of such diverse narratives as male, heterosexual, academic, caucasian, son, brother, nephew, cousin, English speaker, American citizen, golfer, Jew, 'little brother' of Brahm, South African citizen (in waiting), New Yorker, and, well ... yada, yada, yada (you've already seen sufficient variations on this list of selves.) The list of narratives is not infinite. But it is almost as long and as varied as any life (and far longer than this list or those lists offered previously. The self then is that centre of narrative gravity, that self-representation, which holds together and organizes information, various storylines and dispositional states that make up a sense of 'me'. It is unique – the variety of narratives that make up 'me' is different in a sufficiently large number of respects to allow a person to differentiate his 'self' from any other 'self'. It is relatively stable – though a person's narratives and dispositional states are always changing, a person's self-representations enable him to view his 'self' as remaining relatively consistent over time. It is socially and physically determined. The self, and its various narratives, is thoroughly a function of physical capacities and social practices of which we have little control or choice.

2. *Naturally, Radically Heterogeneous Determined Selves*

I have already made the case that we, as socially conditioned creatures, are highly populated 'me's, radically heterogeneous concatenations of selves, and centres of narrative gravity. Current studies in contemporary neuroscience and experimental philosophy support the contention that we are hard-wired to be radically heterogeneous creatures. That is, analysis of activity in various parts of the brain, and the different networks that connect those parts, suggest that the human brain itself produces radically heterogeneous creatures accountable for the countless roles that we play, and sometimes dictates different *(competing), (moral)* outcomes under roughly the same circumstances. Though the forthcoming account may have the ring of socio-biology, it should and it shouldn't. For nothing in what follows undermines my contention that our social endowments create radically heterogeneous selves. Instead, this literature review simply deepens the thesis that we are radically heterogeneous determined selves – and that much of what we call freedom and progress is a function of the competition between these socially-endowed selves and our natural hard-wired selves.

To make this contention easier to understand, let's return to our trolley-car scenario. Recall that most people, when confronted with a trolley care scenario, will pick one of two 'moral' options depending on how the scenario is framed. Most individuals confronted with the switch case – in which they are asked if they would to pull a switch that will send the train in a direction that will lead to the death of one person, but will save the lives of five others – will choose to pull the switch. They neither witness the events nor know the persons whose lives are at stake. In moral philosophy, such a choice (again quite dominant) would be described as utilitarian or consequentialist. In the 'push the 300lb man in front of the trolley car' scenario, the relationship of the moral agent to the action is altered. Instead of pulling a switch at some distance from the ultimate consequences, individuals surveyed are asked to push a very large man in front of the trolley. This action stops the trolley. In stopping the trolley, the individual saves the same five persons down the track. One might think that having done the math, these same individuals would invariably push the large man on to the tracks. Not so. A significant number of individuals would not. In moral philosophy, their choice might be described as deontological. They would be unwilling to use an individual human being as a means to save the lives of five others.

Why the shift? In both scenarios, the death of one individual – let us say the same individual – will save the lives of five others. From a deontological perspective, the difference can be explained by the refusal of a person to be the agent of an act in which another individual is treated as a means and not an end. But, of course, that misses the point of both scenarios. If I pull the switch or push the man, then one person dies and another five survive. If I were to refuse to pull the switch or push the man, then the five persons down the tracks would die. The outcome remains the same irrespective of the proximity of my action. The sole difference is that pulling the switch allows for a distance from – not a difference in knowledge about – the outcome. Again: why the difference? No normative arguments would appear to offer an explanation.[137]

Joshua Greene and his collaborators offer a hypothesis. They propose that the difference in emotional pitch of each scenario explains the divergent outcomes: 'That is, people tend toward consequentialism in the case when the emotional response is low and tend toward deontology in the case in which the emotional response is high.'[138] To put it slightly differently, and in terms of trolley scenario, the 'the thought of pushing someone to his death in an "up close and personal manner" ... is more emotionally salient than the thought of bringing about similar consequences in a more impersonal way (e.g., hitting the switch).'[139]

Why the difference in emotional salience? Evolution. As Green and others contend, up close and personal violence 'reaches far back into our primate lineage.'[140] Sophisticated abstract reasoning arrives much later on. Greene and his cohorts believe that the greater the impersonal nature of a moral scenario, the less likely that the fear or flight brain apparatus associated with the 'up close and personal manner' would kick in, and the more time individuals would have to respond in a more reflective manner. In terms of our trolley car scenario, the pushing of a man to his death should activate more primitive responses. Pulling the switch, with its distance from any death, and its opportunity for reflection, should engage areas of the brain associated with higher cognition. That, indeed, is what Greene and others have found.[141]

Highly emotionally charged moral scenarios tend to activate the amygdala, the posterior cingulate cortex and the medial prefrontal cortex.[142] These areas of the brain are associated with rapid flight or fight responses. On the other hand, the more dispassionate moral scenarios – with less proximity to the action – activate 'two classically "cognitive" brain areas, the dorsolateral frontal cortex and inferior parietal lobe.'[143] Greene's point is not to prove the normative preference of the cognitive response over the emotional response: neural correlates of consciousness do no such work. What he and his colleagues have done is demonstrate why we might have these two different responses to roughly the same moral scenarios.

For the purposes of this chapter and this book, Green's work suggests that we are hard-wired to be both consequentialists and deontologists. We have at least these two moral selves competing for primacy of place within us. It's hardly surprising then that utilitarianism and deontological thought continue to vie for primacy of place within the philosophical academy: we are hard-wired for such disputes.[144] (Indeed, two of the most important 20th century works in political philosophy – John Rawls' *A Theory of Justice* and Amartya Sen's *Development as Freedom* – attempt to reconcile (in their own way) these two dominant lines of thought.)

Deontological thought and utilitarianism hardly have the field to themselves. The domain of ethics over the last 30 years has been deeply influenced by the feminist-inflected relationship theorizing of Carol Gilligan. *In a Different Voice*, Gilligan contends that men and women tend to think differently about moral dilemmas.[145] In short, while men tend to build highly abstract regimes that ought to govern any given moral situation, women tend to be more concrete and emphasize the importance of the relationship involved and the stakes of any given dilemma. So while Kant might argue that stealing can never be justified because it violates the principle of universalizability at the very heart of the categorical imperative, Gilligan claims that women (more so than men) would ask 'Why has the theft taken place?' For example, if a daughter broke into a pharmacy to procure drugs to save the life of her ailing mother, then women would, ostensibly, place a higher premium on the mother's life and the relationship between mother and daughter than more abstract thinkers. Gilligan's answer to the ethical dimensions of the hypothetical is that the daughter might well be justified in following her course of action – irrespective of what the law (as it currently stands) might have to say.

Gilligan's voice has been a powerful addition to ethical thought. But its truth, as compared to its competitors, is again not of interest here. Of greater interest, of course, is the underlying explanation for why relational ethics should exert such a powerful command on current moral philosophy.

Patricia Churchland has an answer.[146] Women, to a much greater degree than men, are hard-wired for 'care' – caring for themselves, but more importantly caring for others. As bearers of children and (historically) primary care-takers, the 'other-caring' typical of women flows, Churchland contends, from the 'maternalization' of the female brain. She writes that:

> In all pregnant mammals, humans included, the placenta of the fetus releases a variety of hormones into the mother's bloodstream that have the effect of 'maternalizing' her brain. These hormones ... act mainly on subcortical structures. ... Human females ... respond to a "nesting" urge as the time for delivery draws near, and (I can personally attest) begin energetically to houseclean and finalize preparations for the new baby. OXT [the neuropeptide oxytocin] is up regulated (made more plentiful) during pregnancy; at birth release of OXT plays a role in causing the uterus to contract. OXT is also essential in the ejection of milk during lactation. In the brain, the release of OXT triggers full maternal behaviour, including preoccupation with the infants, suckling, and keeping the infants warm, clean and safe. ... Cocaine-abusing human mothers [on the other hand] have lower levels of OXT than non-addict controls, and display less maternal behaviour.[147]

Men do not produce oxytocin [OXT] in the amounts found in pregnant women. However, they do respond to OXT in a similar manner. In a control group, men fell into three distinct classes: '52% were egoists, 20% were in-group co-operators and 28% were out-group haters.'[148] In the group of men who received intranasal OXT, two numbers shifted dramatically: '17% were egoists, 58% were in-group co-operators and 25% were out-group haters.'[149] Although a substantial body of men retained high levels of aggression toward out-groups, OXT clearly increased the levels of in-group care and co-operation. What should we make of these findings? What bearing do these OXT studies have on our understanding of caring, co-operation and our morality?

The findings do provide some comfort for Gilligan's stance. Women with maternalized brains do indeed appear to place a premium on caring for others – first children, then kin, and then other close associates. Men whose brains are dosed with OXT also demonstrate a markedly increased degree of caring for and co-operation with others. Churchland's review of the extant studies of OXT suggests that a neurological basis for a 'caring' self that places a significant emphasis on relationships exists to a greater degree in women than men. Men, if we were to concentrate on OXT studies alone, seem hard-wired to be egotists, limited co-operators and aggressive toward members of out-groups.

But are men as bad as the absence of a maternalized brain suggests? A very recent longitudinal study of men from young adulthood through fatherhood clearly shows a dramatic drop in testosterone levels once men become fathers.[150] Moreover, the more engaged men become in caring for their children, the further their testosterone levels drops. Commentators on the study suggest that drop in testosterone points up the importance of male parental care: 'It's important enough that it's actually shaped the physiology of men,'[151] notes Peter Ellison. Contrary to popular belief, the high dependency of human infants on adult care requires that mothers receive help from the fathers of their children. So strong is the correlation between male parental care and the drop in testosterone is that men who spent more than three hours a day caring for children had the lowest testosterone levels.

These findings are consistent with other smaller studies of the effects of testosterone levels, and the effect of the relational circumstances of men on their levels of testosterone. While a drop in testosterone correlates directly with the beginning of family life, the end of family life through divorce correlates with a subsequent increase in testosterone.[152] Men in committed relationships have lower testosterone levels than men who were not in long-term relationships.[153] Moreover, culture plays a role in the level of male care and the reciprocal effect of testosterone levels. In a study conducted in Tanzania, men in a community with entrenched practices of significant male parental care had markedly lower testosterone levels than men in a nearby community without a practice of engaged fathering.[154]

What do these studies tell us? That long term human evolution – re-enforced by culture over the last few millennia – has led to a demonstrable pattern of caring selves amongst fathers and less caring selves amongst bachelors and divorcees. Since all men experience bachelorhood, most experience fatherhood and many experience divorce, these testosterone studies demonstrate that individual men will possess different kinds of caring selves over time. They may actually possess different kinds of caring (and less caring) selves simultaneously.

How do these studies, from trolley cars to oxytocin to testosterone, advance the basic thesis of this chapter and the book as a whole?

First, they provide additional support for the proposition that an individual corporeal self is a constellation of radically heterogeneous, *naturally* determined selves. All of us, men and women alike, share neurological and hormonal systems that give rise to divergent and to competing 'moral' selves. (I have consciously limited myself to a discussion of a select number of selves determined and created by neurological and endocrine systems: needless to say, our corporeal selves make meaning for us in a variety of different ways. For example, the auditory selves of aboriginal peoples in Australia enable them to create songlines that carry them across the arid hinterlands of that continent.)

Second, as the experimental philosophical, neurological and hormonal studies suggest, none of these 'moral' selves has clear primacy of place. Instead, they support a view that I have held since studying ethics and politics under Charles Larmore a quarter century ago.[155] No single ethical system plausibly explains the 'best' response to each and every moral dilemma that we confront. Were it otherwise, one would have assumed that ethics as a field of inquiry would be far more settled than it is. We understand that 'truth-telling' is an essential social practice – categorically imperative as Kant would have it. Yet we also know that when the Nazis are knocking at our door, and Anne Frank is hiding in the attic, we have a moral obligation to dissemble in order to save her life. Would our caring selves promote this response? Would our rule-utilitarian selves – replete with general norms and exceptions that do not swallow up the rule – justify turning the Nazis away knowing that our own lives hang in the balance?

Third, the complexity of our moral make-up (bracketing, of course, for the many socially determined, comprehensive views of the good that suppress natural moral selves) suggests that as enticing as any algorithm might be, the actual practice of moral behaviour requires the ability to negotiate the thicket of possible responses that hard ethical dilemmas throw up. If this non-reductive view seems plausible, then we have good reason to think that one of the two pillars of this book – flourishing – provides a partial, but essential, account of how we ought to construct our constitutional order.

Contemporary notions of flourishing, as expounded by Amartya Sen and Martha Nussbaum, emphasize the radically heterogeneous nature of what it means to 'pursue lives worth valuing'. Not only will different groups and different individuals within a given polity possess different conceptions of the good, individuals themselves may pursue different conceptions of the good from time to time. We are hard-wired to do so. Flourishing recognizes this multiplicity of goods. Rather than concentrate on which conception of the good is to be preferred, flourishing (or development theory or the capabilities approach) envisages a political order that creates the space and that provides the material means for the pursuit of different lives worth living. Flourishing, as we shall see in Chapters 4 and 7, is not a form of hedonism. Far from it. The pursuit of lives worth valuing has both a subjective cast and an objective dimension. A constitutional order based upon flourishing must give priority to some goods, or ways of being in the world, and rule out others.

As our own Constitutional Court noted in *Mamabolo*, reconciling our basic law's 'three conjoined, reciprocal and covalent values' – dignity, equality and freedom – is no easy matter.[156] Our Constitution's commitment to flourishing means that we must reject the Rawlsian claim that 'there are certain primary goods – civil liberties such as expression, assembly, the franchise – that cannot be compromised in any way.'[157] Likewise, our constitutional order leaves determinations of the good to individuals and sub-publics, and rejects Peter Singer-like radical utilitarian frameworks as the sole measure of justice.[158] The Constitution, through a commitment to rights, and especially third generation rights, sets its face against more mainstream utilitarianism's general indifference to radical inequality in the distribution of happiness.[159] Assessments of happiness in terms of domestic wealth (GNP) or per capita income provide inadequate information about the material well-being and the substantive opportunities available to individuals (or groups within the larger community). Both liberals and utilitarians fail to take account of how individual differences – in physical ability or disability, in environment, in social practices, in family structure – create significant asymmetries in the manner in which primary goods and incomes can be exploited.[160] As Sen notes, the heterogeneity amongst individuals (both within societies and across societies) shapes the meaning of primary goods *and* incomes. For example, the meaning of a primary political good like freedom of assembly will have demonstrably different meanings for a person who is ambulatory and for a person who is not ambulatory, but housebound. Similarly, the utility of an income of R200 000 will have a demonstrably different value for a person who is ambulatory and for a person who is not ambulatory, but housebound: the former may spend it on a car and tertiary education; the latter may be required to spend the better part of his disposable income on health care. At a minimum, says Sen, quoting Adam Smith, our primary concern ought to be providing individuals with those necessities of life that will, in fact, give them '"the ability to appear in public without shame".'[161] That, in just a few well-chosen words, sounds very much like South African constitutional discourse on dignity.

Flourishing demands more than raising our fellow citizens out of abject poverty. It must provide them with the ability to pursue lives worth valuing.

This section gazes beyond the horizon of the self and the social to the political and the constitutional. (It's a gentle tease regarding the constitutional theory to follow.) As we have just seen, the physical architecture of human beings supports different moral selves. This hard, but heart-warming, fact about every human being provides evidence that the basic premises of a well-ordered society ought to reflect the (sometimes conflicting, sometimes co-operating) constituencies of 'caring selves', 'deontological selves' and 'utilitarian selves' that make it up. Failure to recognize our heterogeneity constitutes a failure to recognize how both socially constructed meaning and naturally constructed ends make us who we are. Recognition of that heterogeneity holds out the promise that in a future South Africa all of its denizens will be able, in Nussbaum's words to 'convert' primary goods, such as income or civil liberties, into the capability 'to choose a life one has reason to value'.

3. *What a 'Free', 'Conscious' Self Is*

The preceding account of consciousness and the self will have several important consequences for the theories of the social and the constitutional that shall follow. The preceding account emphasized (a) that consciousness is not 'a thing', but rather what emerges – in different parts of the brain – from competition and co-operation among parallel, mostly non-conscious and widely distributed neural networks; and (b) that the self is best understood as a centre of narrative gravity in which the content of our neural networks and their cognitive correlates are held together by a broad array of socially and physically determined narratives that remain – if we stay in reasonably good health – relatively stable over time. One immediate consequence is that anyone who grants the validity of either (a) or (b) or both (a) and (b) will be in a position that will require him or her to accept certain further conclusions about what it means to exercise agency and whether or not such agents exercise what we commonly refer to as 'free will'.

The above variations on the thesis that consciousness is a complex, physiological phenomenon contrasts sharply with the folk psychological attribution of unity and of immateriality to consciousness. If the reader has come around to the views about free will, consciousness and selves propounded thus far, then this chapter should have softened the reader up for the big punch. That punch – if you haven't seen it coming – looks something like this:

1. Consciousness is not located in a single place in the brain, nor is there ever a time when everything comes together as 'consciousness'. As a result, there cannot be a master discriminator or a homunculus viewing and co-ordinating the display of precepts, thoughts, actions or emotions – the unfolding movie of our lives – from a comfortable seat in the middle of our brain.
2. Selfhood is, similarly, not located in a single place in the brain, and like consciousness, lacks the unitary character that would support an 'I' that somehow stands over and above the particular experiences we have in the world and then decides how 'I' should respond to each and every phenomenological state. The widely distributed, primarily non-conscious, parallel neuronal processing that underlies consciousness supports a view of the corporeal self in which an extremely large number of selves (if you feel the need to count) play an equally large

number of roles in our lives. While these selves will, quite naturally, overlap and cohere – at various points in time – there is no self that stands above the fray directing these lower selves in the appropriate direction. To think that the self is anything more than a centre of narrative gravity – where all my storylines and my dispositional states reside and create my 'autobiographical self' – is just a comfortable illusion. (Or, in Gilbert Ryle's words – it's a category mistake.)

3. If consciousness emerges – in no specific location (within the brain) – from widely distributed, primarily non-conscious, parallel neuronal processes, and if the self is no more than an array of diverse, often non-conscious, parallel narratives, then it makes little sense to speak of an individual moral agent that exercises free will in the physical universe. The extended version of argument number 3 follows in the section below.

F. A Chastened Account of Freedom, Consciousness and Selfhood

1. *Consciousness, Selves and Error Correction*

It makes sense to talk about consciousness as the result of competing, and yet co-operative, feedback mechanisms meant to address and to solve various problems with which we are confronted at any given moment. It makes sense to speak of the self as a set of narratives – made up of different dispositional states and socially constructed purposes – meant to achieve a variety of objectives in the world and to address, and to overcome, a variety of problems that the world will throw up along the way.

However, while we are error-correcting and problem-solving organisms, it would be incorrect to assume that the conscious processes and narrative selves that address these problems commits us to the proposition that we 'freely will' a solution to any given problem. In important respects, this observation returns us to the problem of Cartesian dualism with which I opened up this chapter. Recall that the primary (and insuperable) argument against Cartesian dualism turned on Cartesian dualism's inability to explain how an immaterial soul could interact with and direct the material body.

As we saw at the outset of this chapter, those who claim that we can will freely an action must explain how, in a world of physically determined events, individual human beings can exercise volition in a manner that is free of the same physical laws that we believe hold for all other events in the world.[162] Compatibalists must offer a theory of freely-willed human agency consistent with a deterministic theory of the physical world. Like Descartes, compatibalists must explain how an 'immaterial' act of human agency is free from the set of physical laws that determine the movement of rocks, rivers, rhinos and the rest of the universe.[163] We began this chapter by suggesting why the philosophical arguments for compatibalism, whether offered by Descartes or James, remain unconvincing. The preceding materialist account of consciousness goes some distance toward demonstrating that we do not need some 'additional' immaterial agent to explain what 'causes' us to think and to act. But it does not go all the way.

In the next few pages, I review several recent studies in neuroscience and cognitive psychology that provide additional support for the proposition that the near universal experience of free will is a useful illusion. After recounting these findings, I offer a more modest account of freedom which dispenses with the problems that plague the compatibalist account and yet retains meaningful *practical* space for individual moral agency. This space for individual moral agency is, in turn, critical for my account of flourishing as a constitutional ideal.

2. *A Chastened, Forward-looking Account of Freedom and the Role of Trial and Error*

Given that we cannot explain how a human being can be free of the chain of physical events in the world, it might now come as something of a surprise to hear Daniel Dennett claim that 'free will is indeed quite real, but just not quite what you probably thought it was'.[164]

That consciousness is a physical state subject to the same laws of nature as other physical states means that when we discuss whether I 'could have done otherwise in a given set of circumstances', we do not really mean that I could have done otherwise. This position signals a clear break from those who believe that a physically determined world is compatible with a human will that stands outside the chain of physical events in the world.[165] However, the rejection of the compatibilist account does not make our discussion of whether I could have done otherwise meaningless. The point is that the self (or selves), on my account, can still analyze a problem, and either recognize it as susceptible to solution by existing dispositional states or conclude that its novelty requires a different response in order to achieve a preferable result.

Freedom, on this more modest, naturalized account, does not refer to actions that occurred in the past. Rather, it is forward looking, and recognizes that human beings have the capacity to alter their behaviour in light of error. Recall from our discussion of Dehaene and Naccache that the purpose of consciousness is that it allows an individual 'to represent a goal and to estimate the outcomes of [her] ... actions *before* initiating them'.[166] Recall that the extent to which we could then recognize that our ability to undertake 'trial and error' within the simulated framework of mental activity constitutes an enormous advance on being limited to 'trial and error' in one's actual, immediate physical environment. (Of course, we do ultimately have to engage in various trials in our immediate physical environment. Here again, consciousness, and the ability to remember what works and what doesn't, provides human beings with an enormous survival, adaptation and flourishing advantage over other beings, that whilst physically more imposing, lack our cognitive capacity.) Freedom, then, rightly understood, means an expansion of conditioned choice and an expansion of the possibilities for action in life.

To get a sense of what this means, consider the difference in the contours of freedom for a human being 10,000 to 20,000 years ago. These beings had the choice of hunting, gathering or both and lived roughly 30 years. A human being with a certain level of material wealth and education today will, over the course of a lifetime twice as long, enjoy a variety of different vocations, avocations and ways of being in the world. Moreover, a human being today is a participant in a large number of critical and discursive practices which enable her as an individual, and as a member of various groups, to reflect upon what has happened in the past and alter her pre-determined or pre-existing routines in the future.

Freedom so understood changes the rationales for attribution of responsibility to individual human agents. If individuals and their actions are as much a part of the great chain of physical events in the world as any other physical phenomena, then their actions are as fundamentally determined as the actions of any other physical phenomena. Why then attribute culpability to any individual if that individual's actions were caused in the same way that an ant is caused to move away from a torrent of water from a tap or a flower is caused to bend towards the sun?

First, as self-correcting entities – shaped to be such by biological evolution and by cultural advancements – we have the capacity to alter our behaviour in response to both negative and positive reinforcement from our environment. Holding individual agents responsible for their actions creates incentives for positive responses by the individual in the future and maximizes the likelihood for success of the system of reinforcement as a whole. Moreover, if the system of reinforcement exacts penalties that outweigh any potential positive benefit then individuals will begin resisting existing patterns of reinforcement. Though the benefits of such resistance may or may not accrue to mavericks, such individuals will test the general success of the system of which they are a part. Thus, the first rationale for moral and legal culpability is the utility of forcing individuals qua to make use of their own capacity for self-correction and the utility of forcing individuals qua members of society to make use of self-correction mechanisms that benefit the community as a whole.

Second, the utility of a form of behaviour – in very Darwinian terms – need not exhaust the reasons for holding individuals accountable. We are beings bathed in language, and in concepts that place a value on goods that have little or nothing to do with our survival. Goods such as truth, love and justice have come to be regarded as goods equal in value to decidedly more utilitarian ends of sex, food or money. As Matthew Elton suggests:

> Could it be through language, the constant trading of ideas, that we come to be creatures that see the commitment to the existence of genuine responsibility, of genuine praise and blame, genuine right and wrong, as a condition without which we would not be fully human.[167]

Such reasoning does not break the chain of determined events, it only provides grounds potentially independent of pure utility for identifying ourselves and others as responsible moral agents.[168]

G. Consciousness and Constitutional Doctrine: Freedom as Political, not Metaphysical

The conclusions I draw from the foregoing accounts of consciousness, self and freedom for understanding constitutional theory are fairly straightforward. These accounts are meant to bracket, if not dispel, the notion that individuals are best understood as rational choosers of the ends they seek. The self should be seen as the inheritor and the executor of a rather heterogeneous set of practices – of ways of responding to or acting in the world. The centrality of social endowments, as well as natural dispositional states, for both the creation and the maintenance of identity introduces an ineradicable element of *arationality* into the domain of individual decision-making. That is, despite the dominance of the enlightenment vision of the self as a rational agent, the truth of the matter is that the majority of our responses to the world are *arational:* they are not reflective; they are not critical; they are not chosen; they just are. It is this heterogeneous variety of associations and practices into which we are born and in which we continue to reside that determine substantially our responses to various events or phenomena. If this is so, then as a constitutional matter, the model of a rational individual moral agent which undergirds much of our current jurisprudence ought to be supplanted with a vision of the self that is more appropriately located within the relationships and associations to which we all belong.

Take for example the way in which the Court has dealt with Rastafarians in *Prince*, sex workers in *Jordan* and pornography in *De Reuck*. What links all of the Court's judgments is the model of the self as an autonomous, rational, integrated moral agent that freely-wills its actions. The result of this dominant mode of analysis is that it overestimates the capacity of the individual to choose his or her own ends. Conversely, it underestimates the centrality of relationships, associations, networks, endowments and practices for the formation of individual identity. If we were to frame our constitutional analysis in terms of the relationships and the associations that are constitutive of the self, and if we were to be somewhat more modest about the extent and the nature of the freedom we humans exercise, then we might be willing to treat those individuals who participate in non-dominant forms of behaviour with greater respect. Eliminate the notion that individual Rastafarians 'choose' to smoke an illicit substance and supplant it with the assessment that Rastafarians simply engage in a marginal, but not especially dangerous, form of life.[169] The result should be that we are willing to take more seriously the need to create a space for what many in our society view as aberrant practices. Exemptions for other ways of being in the world supplant the desire to sanction non-conformist or non-dominant forms of behaviour. Judicial solicitude for rational individual choice is displaced by judicial solicitude for the arational, constituitive attachments that form the better part of our identity. The difference is clear. On the rationalist, free will account, individuals, groups and minorities suffer little loss when constitutional politics turns against them. On the 'meaning makes us' view, these groups do not merely lose a legal wrangle: they lose a world.

A similar move could be made that would rectify the wrong done to many sex workers in *Jordan.* As I noted in Chapter 1, the Constitutional Court in *S v Jordan & Others* falls into 'an autonomy trap'. In rejecting equality, dignity, privacy and freedom of profession challenges to those sections of the Sexual Offences Act that criminalise prostitution,[170] the majority reasoned as follows:

> If the public sees the recipient of reward as being 'more to blame' than the 'client', and a conviction carries a greater stigma on the 'prostitute' for that reason, that is a social attitude and not the result of the law. The stigma that attaches to prostitutes attaches to them, not by virtue of their gender, but by virtue of the conduct they engage in. That stigma attaches to female and male prostitutes alike. I am not persuaded by the argument that gender discrimination exists simply because there are more female prostitutes than male prostitutes, just as I would not be persuaded if the same argument were to be advanced by males accused of certain crimes, the great majority of which are committed by men.[171]

The Court's commitment to a very strong form of metaphysical fails dramatically the large percentage of prostitutes who are literally coerced into prostitution. It also fails to do justice to the vast number of sex-workers for whom the alternatives are, quite starkly, starvation or prostitution.

Another Constitutional Court judgment hints at a way out of the kind of autonomy trap on display in *Jordan*. In *Khosa v Minister of Social Development; Mahlaule v Minister of Social Development*, the Constitutional Court found unconstitutional, as a violation of both FC s 9 and FC s 27 (1), the exclusion of permanent residents from the class of persons entitled to a variety of social security grants: old age, disability, veterans, child-support and foster care. Mokgoro J writes:

> The exclusion of permanent residents in need of social security programmes forces them into relationships of dependency upon families, friends and the community in which they live, none of whom may have agreed to sponsor the immigration of such persons to South Africa ... Apart from the undue burden that this places on those who take on this responsibility, it is likely to have a serious impact on the dignity of the permanent residents concerned who are cast in the role of supplicants.[172]

Mokgoro J could well have added that permanent residents are, as supplicants, not merely dependent on family members, but quite literally at their mercy. *Khosa* stands for the broader proposition that FC s 7(2) places the state under an obligation to protect and to fulfil the rights of all persons in South Africa.[173] As the *Khosa* Court rightly recognises, legal regimes that offer incentives to inhabitants to become members of the political community but then punish those inhabitants who cannot act on such incentives are perverse. These disincentives deny the affected person exactly that which the state is obliged to provide. The *Khosa* Court indicates that where meaningful choice is severely curtailed, the state bears a much greater responsibility with respect to creating the material conditions for genuine agency. *Khosa* recognizes that freedom, properly understood, refers to the material conditions of existence in which individuals and groups can actually learn from their errors and genuinely possess meaningful opportunities to pursue alternative ways of being in the world.[174]

Let me not be misunderstood. The recognition of the self as a function of arational, constitutive attachments does not mean that we must give each of these attachments our imprimatur of constitutional approval. Within the constraints of these social and natural endowments, we still possess the capacity to make critical assessments. Within the constraints of these social endowments, we still possess the capacity to make reasoned judgments about right and wrong, good and evil.[175] Indeed, it is the varied forms of attachments and dispositions that make up the radically heterogeneous self which provide each of us, and our society collectively, with at least some of the critical leverage necessary for discriminating between more and less valuable forms of behaviour.[176]

The recognition of the extent to which social practices and deep neurological structures determine the contours of the self does not mean that we can avert hard constitutional choices. It means, rather, that we ought to think twice before we differentiate invidiously between our preferred way of being in the world and that way of being preferred by others. This more modest account of freedom should force us to attend to the arationality of our most basic attachments and choices and to think twice before we accord our arational attachments and choices preferred status to the arational attachments and choices of others.[177]

H. The New Mysterians: The Claim that Consciousness Cannot Explain Itself

Dualists may have been driven from the field. However, it would be poor sportsmanship to deny that a new constellation of theorists have replaced them on the frontlines of debates about consciousness. Call them the New Mysterians. Colin McGinn, along with John Searle and David Chalmers, contend (and rightly so!) that extremely 'hard questions' still exist about how neural events give rise to certain kinds of mental events.[178] In response to the enthusiasm of neuroscientists and philosophers who believe that third party access to individual 'consciousness' is just around the corner, McGinn offers a theory of 'cognitive closure'. McGinn's argument runs as follows: the multitude of tasks that the 'human mind' or 'brain' can carry out does not include the ability to explain how 'consciousness' works. In short, the ability of the system to illuminate phenomena or to act in the world does not include the ability to explain how the machinery of the brain carries out these complex functions, and more importantly, produces the sensations associated with being human. In short, neither science nor philosophy provides an account for the 'internal' state of how it feels to be human.

With respect, McGinn and company seem to be wrong on a number of accounts. The cognitive closure argument looks quite like 'the problem of other minds'. If, following Wittgenstein, we don't really have doubts about the existence of other minds – and how they function – why should we continue to doubt that they experience the world – consciously – much as we do? Knocking down such arguments is not new. The field of consciousness studies has, in fact, had some success in further diminishing their powerful grip on our imagination.

When McGinn talks about consciousness, he has an entire repertoire of 'qualia' questions in mind. Qualia are such things as my experience of the blueness of the ocean, the sting of the salt-water against my cheek while on the deck of a boat, or the thrill I get from finally seeing land after weeks at sea. Ostensibly, these experiences are mine and mine alone, and there is no way of confirming or denying the quality of my experience. (That is why some describe qualia as being a species within the larger genus of what are known as problems of other minds.) John Locke thought this proposition so incontrovertible that he made it a linchpin of his epistemology.[179] Locke claimed that our perceptions were so incorrigible that my colour spectrum could be completely inverted with respect to yours and we would have no way of knowing that your blue is my blue, or more disturbing still, whether your blue is actually my orange. This claim regarding the inverted colour spectrum was thought to be immune to scientific contestation. However, over 40 years' worth of investigation into colour experience has, in fact, yielded data that suggests that we experience the same colour when we see the colour blue. Steven Palmer lays out an evidentiary record that demonstrates that all human beings experience 4 pure colours – red, yellow, blue and green – and that other colours could not – without contradicting the 'purity' of those four colours – be mapped on to them in an inverted colour scheme.[180] The only candidates for inversion are – for clear physiological reasons – red and green. First, they are both pure. Secondly, the cones for red and green are close in size and in proximity on the retina. Thirdly, the work done on colour-blindness supports this hypothesis.

As I noted in the introduction, neuroscientists can provide individual human brains, enhanced with computer chips connected to networks of neurons, with the capacity to move prosthetic devices or other objects or to answer questions without verbal responses or motor action.[181] Ever more recent efforts have enabled neuroscientists to identify neurons and neuronal networks that can capture visually, from an external third person perspective, what a person sees or that of which she is conscious.[182] We can now see, to a limited degree, what you see as you see it. Given these recent, albeit simple breakthroughs, it seems a little early to give up on Descartes' efforts to interrogate and to reveal the nature of consciousness.

The jury, then, is very much out on McGinn's 'closure' argument. Indeed silicon chip implants in the brain capable of carrying out cognitive requests without verbal or motor interventions by an individual would suggest that the door to theories regarding the neural correlates of consciousness has been opened. Once we are rid of the problem of other minds, and once we can comprehend the conscious experience of others from a third party perspective, McGinn, Searle, Chalmers and others are left with the central claim that much work remains to be done before we can have that quintessential third party experience of consciousness – why I feel like Stu Woolman.

The remaining arguments of the New Mysterians often possess a curmudgeon-like quality. As McGinn has recently written about the path-breaking work of VS Ramachandram:[183] 'It would be nice if we neuroscientists were also trained philosophers.'[184] Such remarks suggest the death knell of yet another branch or two of philosophy – metaphysics or philosophy of mind – even as they remind us that much work remains to be done by neuroscientists, cognitive psychologists, and empirical philosophers attempting to offer that 3rd party perspective on consciousness.

To be fair, McGinn is correct in his analysis of Ramachandram's absence of philosophical sophistication. Ramachandram's lucid explanations of how the brain functions sometimes miss their mark with respect to answering questions about consciousness, selfhood or free will. McGinn's response to Ramachandram should have been: work with me or another well trained philosopher to make the connection between empirical findings and age old questions. The proper riposte to the New Mysterians: Who is actually doing the work?

One of the New Mysterians is aware of the unassailable truth in the above riposte. In responding to a hard core mysterian on the undeniable connection between the firing of neurons and consciousness, Searle writes:

> [B]efore we despair, we should remind ourselves of two things. First, we know it happens. We know that brain processes cause all of our conscious experience. If it happens, we should try to figure out how it happens. Second, we have been through such mysteries before. There have frequently been phenomena that seemed utterly mysterious but eventually received an explanation. Two famous examples: first, the problem of life once seemed mysterious. How could mere chemical processes, brute lifeless chemical reactions, produce life. It is hard for us today to discover the passion with

which this issue was once debated. A second example is electromagnetism. By the principles of Newtonian physics, electromagnetism seems positively mysterious, even spooky. Advances in knowledge have removed the sense of mystery from life and electromagnetism. … [W]e have no reason to suppose that consciousness is inexplicable.[185]

I. Consciousness as a Feedback Mechanism for Error Correction that Enhances Freedom qua Flourishing

So did we get there (constitutional politics) from here (metaphysics)? After knocking off Cartesian dualism, the chapter characterized consciousness as a feedback mechanism that give us fresh opportunities to reflect upon experience (immediate and long-term) and plot more or less optimal courses for action (immediate and long-term). Trial and error. What is true for individual human beings, as it turns out, is optimal for our politics. Individual selves – highly populated ways of being in the world – are always experimenting, attempting to divine, through reflection and action, what 'works' best. Constitutional democracies – highly populated communities with millions of complex, heterogeneous selves – are (or should be) constantly experimenting, attempting to divine through reflection and action, what works best for its many constituents.

The same holds true for contemporary accounts of the social. When we discuss nudges and choice architecture, we shall see that policy makers are capable of creating environments that test our (adaptive) preferences and constructing environments that create greater health, wealth and happiness – based upon our own responses to the environments the choice architects construct. Social scientists and policy-makers, in conjunction with willing participants, are able to use a variety of environments that function as feedback mechanisms that give us fresh opportunities to reflect upon experience (immediate and long-term) and plot more or less optimal courses for action (immediate and long-term). Trial and error. It enables us to find better and better ways to fit our round pegs into round holes. In all three domains (the self, the social and the constitutional), we find that what works instrumentally (and what fails) also influences our normative frameworks: successful feedback tells us what lives are worth valuing and how we should best order our society so that a majority of our fellow citizens may pursue such lives.

In the following sections, I want to make the case that feedback mechanisms not only offer the best explanation for why we have consciousness, but that constructive feedback mechanisms play a critical role in all of our conscious and unconscious undertakings. The more errors we correct (though conscious trial and error), the more freedom we truly possess.

1. *Trial and Error in Video Games*

Initially, the mis-en-scene of your average video game is a miasma of moving objects, whose actions appear unpredictable, their purposes opaque. Over time, and with greater experience, the player begins to note certain regularities in the movement of the game's objects and is able to predict how those objects will respond to her engagement with them. As time goes on, certain kinds of responses – how to move the controls to effect desired movement and action – become 'second nature'. That is, they become dispositional states with regard to the game that require absolutely no conscious awareness of those states and their attendant consequences. In empirical psychology, this first simpler kind of awareness is often described as behavioural awareness. (One recognizes and reacts to stimuli without any conscious awareness of the stimuli or the reaction.) Consciousness enables us to attend to those novel details of the game playing that require attention: in other words, narrative awareness attends to problems in the game that need to be solved. (It should be clear that narrative awareness can, over time, become behavioural awareness. Indeed, civilization advances, to once again paraphrase Alfred North Whitehead, to the extent that we can turn tasks that require narrative awareness into tasks that require only behavioural awareness.)

Though behavioural awareness and narrative awareness will necessarily overlap, it is also the case that behavioural awareness will often not generate any narrative awareness at all. Where the demands of one's environment will be satisfied by a routinized response, behavioural awareness is all we need. That is, 'narrative awareness is ... not required for control of action. Behavioural awareness will often suffice on its own.'[186] Conscious or narrative awareness enables us to focus on aspects of our environment – and hold them up for scrutiny – in order to form better behaviour responses to the environment. Consciousness is, again, a kind of feedback mechanism. The conscious report constitutes a record of our response, and perhaps the nature of our error. A record of such errors enables us to respond differently – assuming we survive any given error – the next time we are faced with the appropriate set of circumstances. Video games provide lots of easy, uncontroversial evidence of these two different but entirely compatible kinds of awareness. The more we play the game, the more our actions take the form of behavioural awareness. Indeed, once appropriately primed for all the variations a simple video game provides, it is often possible to play a game with only the slightest narrative awareness of the action. Once the possibility for error is largely contained – and almost extinguished – it is possible to play as if one were on remote control.

2. *Trial and Error in Driving*

Learning how to drive a car reflects a similar set of experiences and offers a largely identical account of the relationship between behavioural awareness and conscious awareness. Initially, many driving activities – hitting the gas, clutching, signalling – require conscious awareness. All the relevant experts in our global neuronal workshop – portions of the brain responsible for motor control, visual concentration, memory – receive the information that create our conscious state. As we learn to drive, new neuronal pathways and processes are established. Over time, these new neuronal pathways and processes become routine non-conscious pathways and processes. Indeed, so many of the routines associated with driving become routine that one can drive a car without conscious awareness. That, of course, was the point of the story of the unconscious driver. I am not endorsing non-conscious driving practices. Retaining conscious awareness remains necessary in order to account for unpredictable changes in the driving environment caused by other drivers, dysfunctional traffic robots, small children playing in the street and even falling trees.

3. *Trial and Error in Spelling*

At this point in our respective lives, spelling as we write is a largely non-conscious activity. However, as anyone who can recall spelling bees can attest, spelling a word correctly is often a contest.

Moreover, as anyone who writes for a living will tell you, spelling as an adult is not always a non-conscious activity. Questions often arise when the word being written is arcane or technical. But it is also possible to move spelling from a non-conscious to a conscious activity by pausing to stare at the word. The attention itself may well raise doubts about the spelling – or it may, on another occasion, create some disquiet about the relation of the written symbol to the word that was 'in' our head.

Sometimes questions arise with phonemes like 'where' and 'wear', or closely related words in form, such as 'were'. Sometimes we only become aware – conscious – that we are spelling words as we write when we make an obvious error, or when the computer tells us that we have either erred or used a word with which it is unfamiliar. Spelling, it seems to me, is a good activity by which to measure the usefulness of the description of consciousness in terms of a global neuronal workspace in which consciousness emerges from the massive array of parallel, widely distributed non-conscious neuronal processes. For the most part, the adult author need not use the global neuronal workspace for spelling and can attend to more complex and novel tasks associated with writing – sentence construction, the rhythm of language, the fit between the concept one wishes to express and the words being used to express them. Not much writing would occur were we forced to attend to the spelling of each and every word that appeared on a printed page or a computer screen. Indeed, computer programmers are sufficiently aware of this need to turn spelling into an almost entirely non-conscious neuronal process that most contemporary computer programmes correct our spelling mistakes without our even noticing our error or the computer's correction.

4. *Trial and Error in Music*

We have a tendency to be 'Mysterians' – in the McGinnian and Chalmerian sense – when it comes to the conscious processes that create great music. Mozart's ability to compose ingenious pieces at the age of 3 baffles us. It shouldn't. While geniuses certainly exist – and the historical record is replete with idiot savants who could play a portion of Bach's Goldberg Variations after hearing the piece just once[187] – that difference in kind should not lead us to conclude that great composers do not operate in much the same way all human beings operate when engaged in novel and sophisticated processes: through trial and error.

Leonard Bernstein, one of the 20th Century's great composers and conductors, revealed just how hard the greatest classical composers had to work to create their most sublime symphonies and sonatas. In a recent television series, we find Bernstein

> ... intent on demonstrating that the inevitable doesn't just happen. It comes from intense work [and trial and error]. ... To show this, [Bernstein] restores a handful of Beethoven's discarded sketches to the score so that we can hear how the Fifth would have sounded if Beethoven had retained his first (or second or 10th) iteration. Some discarded passages are surprisingly workaday; others are interesting but lack the drama found in the music that eventually replaced them. The message

Bernstein leaves you with is that in composition, process – *trial and error*, writing and revision – is everything.[188]

Endnotes

1. W James *Essays in Pragmatism* (1907) 45. John Searle puts James' argument thus: 'There is a standard argument [called compatibilism] according to [which] free will and determinism are perfectly compatible with each other. Of course everything in the world is determined, but some human actions are nonetheless free. To say they are free is not to deny that they are determined; it is just to say they are not constrained... . Everything that happened was indeed determined. It's just that some things were determined by certain sorts of inner psychological causes ... and not by external forces or psychological compulsions.' J Searle *Minds, Brains and Science* (1984) 91. The problem with James' account is that James' compatibalism '... denies the substance of free will while maintaining its verbal shell. ... The problem about freedom of the will is not about whether or not there are inner psychological causes and inner compulsions. Rather, it is about whether or not the causes of our behaviour, whatever they are, are sufficient to determine the behaviour so that things have to happen the way they do.' Ibid. According to Searle, James' reliance on 'inner' causes commits James to determinism – whether he likes it or not.
2. Ibid at 75. Compatibalism, in its intuitive non-professional form, reflects the widespread belief that human being's possess the freedom (free will) to choose the ends that they wish to pursue, while all other events in the universe are governed by deterministic rules of cause and effect. More sophisticated forms of compatibalism allow compatibilists to claim that their definitions of determinism and free will are not logically inconsistent. Perhaps the most appealing form of 'soft' compatibalism has been put forward by David Hume and Harry Frankfurt. In short, compatibilism, so understood, does not mean that an agent could have chosen to act otherwise in the identical situation. The soft compatibilist still believes that a person could only make a single decision, but finds 'freedom' in the notion that she cannot as yet know what the future will hold. See, eg, H Frankfurt 'Alternative Possibilities and Moral Responsibility' (1969) 66 *Journal of Philosophy* 829.
3. B Mates *Skeptical Essays* (1981) 60 (Numbering added).
4. Ibid at 61.
5. *American Heritage Dictionary* (2010).
6. Mates (supra) at 59.
7. J Searle *Minds, Brains and Science* (1984) 87. Were quantum mechanics and its reliance on statistical probability to displace determinism, it would ostensibly do so with randomness (on the thin, public misunderstanding of quantum mechanics). Randomness (with respect to sub-atomic particles) hardly provides any succour for those who argue in favour of free will and the individual's unconstrained ability to shape her life. The presence of the as yet ill understood dark matter and dark energy in the universe has led some physicists to posit the existence of multiverses – in which the laws of physics that govern different universes may vary. Again: that hardly supports the proposition that the standard determinist conceptions of cause and effect in our universe are incorrect.
8. James (supra) at 59. Mates captures James' vexation as follows: '[W]e are morally responsible only for those of our actions that are freely done ... we are not responsible for actions we cannot help doing, [so by the arguments of determinism] then it follows that nobody is morally responsible for anything.' Mates (supra) at 60. That such a conclusion is unpalatable to James is germane to the vice-like grip free will has upon us. First, the absence of moral culpability for actions would make social control of human actions either impossible or random or unfair (or all three.) Second, the western tradition is simply not constructed to accept a determinist account. As God made clear to Moses at Sinai – someone must always be called to book for wrongs done by one human being to another. The following account makes clear that although we do not need free will to explain consciousness or the self, it is a handy device (if wrong) to explain what is going on. That we do not need this piece

of folk psychology does not mean that it does not serve a number of important purposes – for both the individual and the group.

9. For as long as religions cast an omnipotent God as affording human beings free will – to do good or ill – most metaphysical arguments regarding determinism that undercut religious doctrines of sin and virtue are unlikely to gain much traction.
10. Searle (supra) at 89.
11. G Lakoff & M Johnson *Metaphors We Live By* (1980).
12. KA Appiah *Experiments in Ethics* (2008).
13. Ibid at 6.
14. Of Descartes, Appiah notes: 'Much of his attention ... was devoted to geometry and optics, and for a period he was revered among scholars as a mathematical physicist. In *The Passions of the Souls*, Descartes' empirical interests revealed themselves in the manner in which he discusses how the 'movements of ... muscles ... depend on the nerves ... coming from the brain.' Ibid. See R Descartes *The Passions of the Souls* (1649) in *Selected Writings* (trans. J Cottingham, R Stoothoff and D Murdoch, 1988) 331. As for David Hume, the subtitle for *Treatise on Human Nature* was: *Being an Attempt to Introduce the Experimental Method of Reasoning into Moral Sciences*. But more to the point of this book, Hume contended in his *Enquiry into Human Understanding* that: 'Nothing is more usual than ... to distinguish between reason and experience. But not withstanding that this distinction be thus universally received ... I shall not scruple to pronounce that it is, at bottom, wrong, at last, superficial ... It is experience which is ultimately the foundation of inference and conclusion.' *Enquiry into Human Understanding* (1688)(ed) LA Selby-Bigge (1902) 43–44. Kant, the uber-rationalist, produced more empirical studies than he did works of 'pure' philosophy. See, e.g., I Kant *Investigation of the Question as to Whether the Rotation of the Earth on its Axis Has Undergone Any Modification* (1754); I Kant *The Question as to Whether the Earth is Growing Old from the Angle of Physics* (1754); I Kant *Universal Natural History and Theory of the Heavens* (1755); I Kant *A Brief Outline of Some Meditations on Fire* (1755); I Kant *Consideration of Recently Perceived Earthquakes* (1756); I Kant *Enquiry into Diseases of the Head* (1764); I Kant *Concerning the Volcanoes on the Moon* (1785); I Kant *Definition of the Concept of a Human Race* (1785); I Kant *Anthropology from the Pragmatic Viewpoint* (1798). The reason we no longer view Kant as an empiricist is that we no longer study his empirical work. It has long been overtaken by time and the findings of others. His ethics, metaphysics, politics and epistemology remain alive because: (a) philosophy departments still exist; (b) they retain their original rhetorical force.
15. J Knobe & S Nichols 'An Experimental Philosophy Manifesto' in J Knobe and S Nichols (eds.) *Experimental Philosophy* (2008) 3. See also S Nichols and J Knobe 'Moral Responsibility and Determinism: The Cognitive Science of Folk Psychology' (2007) 41 *Nous* 663.
16. J Knobe & S Nichols 'Experimental Philosophy Manifesto' (supra) at 5.
17. Ibid.
18. Ibid at 7.
19. This book's claims about the self and the social are likewise meant to have an 'indirect impact'. Ibid at 8. While Knobe and Nichols are interested in whether and how one can develop 'a theory about underlying psychological processes that generates people's intuitions', I am really only interested in whether we can use such theories to determine 'whether or not those intuitions are warranted.' Ibid.
20. John Rawls' *A Theory of Justice* (1973) comes in for typical rebuke by experimental philosophers for his constant appeals to 'shared understandings' or 'common intuitions'. To understand why, think of the underlying epistemological sting of one of my – and it appears Appiah's – favourite jokes. One fine, beautiful day the Lone Ranger and Tonto find themselves alone on a butte in Wyoming. All of sudden, out of nowhere, Sioux warriors surround the butte. The Lone Ranger and Tonto have nowhere to run. The Lone Ranger turns to Tonto and ruefully remarks: 'It looks like *we* are done for this time, Tonto.' Tonto, having surveyed the same scene, says: 'What's this '*we*' shit white man?' Loyal friend or disempowered side-kick? Change the frame, change the result.
21. Ibid at 7.

22. Knobe & Nichols 'An Experimental Philosophy Manifesto' (supra) at 3; Nichols & Knobe 'Moral Responsibility' (supra) at 1.
23. J Knobe 'The Concept of Intentional Action: A Case Study in the Uses of Folk Psychology' in J Knobe and S Nichols (eds) *Experimental Philosophy* (2008) 129, 130–131.
24. F Nietzsche *On the Genealogy of Morals* (1887) 64–67.
25. Ibid at 92.
26. Evolutionary psychologists such as Laurence Tancredi agree. He writes: 'Though it is indeed a social construct, morality gets its timelessness and universality from the human brain. The community's demand for cohesiveness and continued existence – its own ideas of what is appropriate human behaviour – brought into play qualities that were already present in the human brain. We have some evidence to support this view. We know that the limbic structures of the brain ... are the physical circuitry for our emotional responses – fear, disgust, guilt – to the environment... [That said], we are not constructed to have consistent reactions of guilt or shame to specific types of behaviour.' L Tancredi *Hard Wired Behaviour: What Neuroscience Reveals about Morality* (2005) 6–7. Tancredi would not only be unphased by the results of the experiments, he would argue that as inconsistent as they may be, the responses, individual and communal, can be reshaped over time. We may, with respect to the discrepancies regarding blameworthy behaviour, be able, in time, to 'get over it'. Ibid at 7.
27. Thomas Nagel anticipated these outcomes some 3 decades ago. See T Nagel 'Moral Luck' in *Moral Luck* (1979) 24. In 'Moral Luck', he writes: 'How is it possible to be more or less culpable on whether a child gets into the path of one's car, or a bird into the path of one's bullet? Perhaps it is true that what is done depends on more than the agent's state of mind or intention. The problem then is, why is it not irrational to base moral assessment on what people do, in this broad sense? It amounts to holding them responsible for the actions of fate as well as their own – provided they made some contribution to begin with. If we look at cases of negligence ... , the pattern seems to be that overall culpability corresponds to the product of mental or intentional fault and the seriousness of the outcome. Cases of decisions under uncertainty are less easily explained in this way, for it seems that the overall judgment can even shift from positive to negative depending on the outcome. ... *If the object of moral judgment is the person, then to hold them accountable for what has been done in the broader sense is akin to strict liability, which may have its legal uses but seems irrational as a moral position.*' Ibid at 31 (Emphasis added).
28. See, eg, B Libet *Mind Time: The Temporal Factor in Consciousness* (2004); B Libet 'The Experimental Evidence for Subjective Referral of Evidence Backward in Time: Reply to PS Churchland' (1981) 48 *Philosophy of Science* 182; B Libet 'Time of Conscious Intention to Act in Relation to the Onset of Other Cerebral Activities (Readiness Potential): The Unconscious Initiation of a Freely Voluntary Act' (1983) 106 *Brain* 623; J Ostrovick 'The Timing Experiments of Libet and Walters' (2004) (Unpublished manuscript on file with author).
29. See B Libet 'Unconscious Cerebral Initiative and the Role of Conscious Will in Voluntary Action' (1985) 8 *Behavioural and Brain Sciences* 529; Ostrovick (supra) at 1.
30. See Ostrovick (supra) at 5.
31. Ibid at 8. See also WG Walters' 'Presentation' (supra) at 167–171 (Emphasis added).
32. S Silberman 'Don't Even Think About Lying: How Brain Scans are Re-Inventing the Science of Lie Detection' (2006) 14 (01) *Wired* 1, available at www.wired.com/wired/archive/14.01/lying.html (accessed on June 18 2006).
33. See Ostrovick (supra) at 10.
34. D Wegner & T Wheatley 'Apparent Mental Causation: Sources of the Experience of Will' (1999) 54 *American Psychologist* 480.
35. Wegner & Wheatley (supra) at 490.
36. D Wegner *The Illusion of Conscious Will* (2002).
37. Ibid at 342.
38. Tancredi (supra) at 51.
39. Ibid at 59.

40. Ibid at 60 – 61. Interestingly, Tancredi connects his views on backwards intentionality or involuntary action to the views expressed by Daniel Dennett and the experiments conducted by Benjamin Libet. Their arguments – and the evidence they offer – provide mutual reinforcement.
41. S Blackmore *Consciousness* (2004) 94.
42. Dehanne and Naccache suggest, as I discuss below, that a number of modular, non-conscious processes and structures distributed throughout the brain, can account, when they enter the global neuronal workspace, for a 'sense' of individual identity. S Dehaene & L Naccache 'Towards a Cognitive Neuroscience of Consciousness' (supra) at 31.
43. R Descartes *Meditations on First Philosophy* (1641).
44. K Popper & JC Eccles *The Self and Its Brain* (1977).
45. JC Eccles *How the Self Controls Its Brain* (1994); JC Eccles *The Brain and the Unity of Conscious Experience* (1965).
46. See G Ryle *The Concept of Mind* (1949) iv.
47. T Metzinger *Being No-One: The Self Model Theory of Subjectivity* (2004) 1 ('No such things as selves exist in the world: Nobody ever was or had a self. All that ever existed were conscious self-models that could not be recognized as models. The phenomenal self is not a thing, but a process – and the subjective experience of *being someone* emerges if a conscious information processing system operates under a transparent self-model. You are such a system right now. Because you cannot recognize your self-model as a model, it is transparent: you look right through it. You don't see it. But you see with it.') See, further, M Minksy *Society of Mind* (1986) 287 ('Minds are simply what brains do'); G Claxton (1994) *Noises from the Darkroom* 37 ('Mind is designer language for the functions the brain carries out'); S Greenfield *Brain Story* (2000) 14 (Mind is 'the personification of the brain.')
48. D Hume *A Treatise of Human Nature: Being an Attempt to Introduce the Experimental Method of Reasoning into Moral Sciences* (1739).
49. Ibid.
50. Dennett *Consciousness Explained* (supra) at 39.
51. Blackmore *Consciousness* (supra) at 66.
52. See A Damasio 'Time-Locked Multi-Regional Retro-activation: A Systems Proposal for the Neural Substrates of Recall and Recognition' (1989) 33 *Cognition* 25; W Singer and C Gray 'Visual Feature Integration and Temporal Correlation Hypothesis' (1995) 18 *Annual Review of Neuroscience* 555; G Tononi and G Edelman 'Consciousness and Complexity' (1998) 282 *Science* 1846; BJ Baars 'How Does a Serial, Integrated and Very Limited Stream of Consciousness Emerge from a Nervous System that is Mostly Unconscious, Distributed, Parallel and of Enormous Capacity' in GR Bock & J Marsh (eds) *Experimental and Theoretical Studies of Consciousness* (1993) 282.
53. Trancredi (supra) at 41.
54. Ibid.
55. Ibid.
56. Ibid at 42.
57. Ibid.
58. RW Sperry 'Hemisphere Deconnection and Unity in Conscious Awareness' (1968) 23 *American Psychologist* 723.
59. MS Gazzaniga *Nature's Mind* (1992) 122 (Higher level functions: language use, belief construction and attribution of intentionality.)
60. D MacKay 'Divided Brains – Divided Minds?' in C Blackmore and S Greenfield (eds.) *Mindwaves* (1987) 5.
61. W James *The Principles of Psychology: Volume I* (1890) 401.
62. D Parfit 'Divided Minds and the Nature of Persons' in C Blackmore and S Greenfield (eds) *Mindwaves* (1987) 19, 20.
63. A Damasio *The Feeling of What Happens: Body, Emotion and the Making of Consciousness* (1999)('*Feeling*'). See also A Damasio *Descartes' Error: Emotion, Reason and the Human Brain* (1994).

64. Dennett would say that the proto-self is exhibiting intentionality – the ability to act on information and regulate its responses to the world in light of such information. Dennett is not concerned with whether such a simple organism can describe an internal state – only that from a third-person perspective the proto-self shares the capacity for intentionality that we attribute to beings with core selves and autobiographical selves.
65. Damasio *Feeling* (supra) at 17.
66. O Sachs *The Man Who Mistook His Wife for His Hat* (1985)('*Hat*') 34.
67. See Sachs *Hat* (supra) at 34 ('If a man has lost a leg or an eye, he knows he has lost a leg or an eye; but if he has lost a self – himself – he cannot know it, because he is no longer there to know it.')
68. The picture of memory and its relationship to self is more complicated than can be described in these pages. For example, persons with severe autonoemic amnesia – and no autonoemic consciousness – may still possess kinds of memory and kinds of recall, but absolutely no sense of subjective or personal time (past or future), and no capacity to form a sense of self over time. They lack an autobiographical self. See E Tulving 'Memory and Consciousness' (1985) 26 *Canadian Psychology* 1.
69. Damasio *Feeling* (supra) at 191.
70. Ibid at 73.
71. This autobiographical self is similar then, in some important respects, to the notion of the 'centre of narrative gravity' that Daniel Dennett employs to describe how 'self-hood' takes shape. Dennett, unlike Damasio, remains a sceptic as to whether there is anything to 'consciousness' above and beyond this densely woven tapestry of narratives. Damasio accepts the evidence of first person reports of those of his patients and subjects who report 'feeling' that they possess a unitary consciousness and compares such reports with the first person reports of patients who lack such a 'feeling' of unitary experience. Moreover, Damasio's evidentiary record supports a third person account that suggests that there is a difference. What makes it hard for many people to accept Dennett's thesis is his contention that the data found in all first person accounts could, ultimately, be accounted for in third person accounts. But as recent success with brain implants demonstrates, we already possess some idea of what another person 'sees'.
72. See A Damasio, B Everitt & D Bishop 'The Somatic Marker Hypothesis of the Brain and the Possible Functions of the Prefrontal Cortex' (1996) 351 *Philosophical Transactions of the Royal Society of London – Series B, Biological Sciences* 1413.
73. S Dehaene & L Naccache 'Towards a Cognitive Neuroscience of Consciousness' (supra) at 31.
74. A Damasio *Self Comes to Mind: Constructing the Conscious Brain* (2010).
75. Ibid at 241.
76. Ibid at 242.
77. Ibid at 243.
78. Ibid at 250 – 25.
79. The metaphor places Baars somewhat at odds with theorists who eschew descriptions of consciousness that rely upon 'movies in the brain'.
80. Single cell recording employs the use of electrodes inserted directed into living cells to measure electrical activity.
81. Electroencephalograms (EEGs) track changes in electrical potential in the brain, and though a rather old technology, it remains a useful tool to measure such events as the readiness potentials that proceed both physical action and conscious awareness.
82. Computer tomography (CT) scans generate images of different tissue densities, and are useful for determining the deterioration of various parts of the brain and, thus, any concomitant loss of cognitive capacity.
83. Positron emission tomography (PET) scans track radioactive substances introduced into the body in a manner that enables us to measure brain metabolism and blood flow, and to develop pictures of what and where brain activity occurs during certain forms of stimulation.

84. Nuclear magnetic resonance imaging (fMRI) provides vivid displays from all imaginable angles. Its limitations are that it reflects metabolic or haemodynamic responses to neural activity, and thus only indirectly measures neuronal activity.
85. Transcranial magnetic stimulation (TMS) creates a magnetic field that stimulates neural activity in motor areas that cause certain kinds of involuntary movement. Along with scanning, this technique enables investigators to map areas of the brain responsible for motor coordination.
86. See, generally, BJ Baars *In the Theatre of Consciousness: The Workspace of the Mind* (1997); JB Newman, BJ Baars & SB Cho 'A Neural Global Workspace Model for Conscious Attention' (1997) 10 *Neural Networks* 1195 as reprinted in BJ Baars, W Banks & JB Newman (eds.) *Essential Sources in the Scientific Study of Consciousness* (2003) 1131; BJ Baars 'In the Theatre of Consciousness: Global Workspace Theory, A Rigorous Scientific Theory of Consciousness' (1997) 4(4) *Journal of Consciousness Studies* 292; BJ Baars *A Cognitive Theory of Consciousness* (1988).
87. See AD Baddeley 'Short-term and Working Memory' in E Tulving and FIM Craik (eds.) *The Oxford Handbook of Memory* (2000) 77.
88. See Newman, Baars & Cho (supra) at 1131 citing DR Reddy, LD Erman, RD Fennell and RB Neely 'The Hearsay Speech Understanding System: An Example of the Recognition Process' (1973) *Proceedings of the International Conference on Artificial Intelligence* 185: 'The Hearsay model was one of the earliest attempts to simulate a massively parallel interactive computing system. The notion of a global workspace was initially inspired by this architecture, consisting of a large number of knowledge modules, or 'local experts', all connected to a single blackboard, or problem-solving space. Activated experts could post 'messages' (or hypotheses) on the blackboard for all other experts to read. Incompatible messages would tend to inhibit each other, while the output of co-operating messages would gain increasing access to the blackboard until a global solution emerged. Blackboard architectures are relatively slow, cumbersome and error-prone, but are capable of producing solutions to problems too novel or too complex to be solved by any extant modular knowledge source. Once such 'global solutions' are attained, however, the original problems can be allocated to modular processors for 'non-conscious' solution.'
89. See Newman, Baars & Cho (supra) at 1131–1132 quoting EH Durfee 'Cooperative Distributed Problem Solving between (and within) Intelligent Agents' in P Rudomin (ed) *Neuroscience: From Neural Networks to Artificial Intelligence* (1993) 84, 84 ('[D]istributed artificial intelligence [DAI] [is] the study of 'how intelligent agents coordinate their activities to collectively solve problems that are beyond individual capabilities.' ... DAI models would appear to balance competitive self-interest and co-operative problem solving that is essential to optimizing outcomes in complex 'social' organizations.)
90. Baars recognizes that the notion of a 'theatre audience' is far too passive to capture the engagement various parts of the brain and neural processes will have with the conscious contents of the global workspace: '[T]he global workspace resembles more a deliberative body than a theater audience. Each expert has a certain degree of 'influence', and by forming coalitions with other experts can contribute to deciding which issues receive immediate attention and which are 'sent back to the committee'. Most of the work of the deliberative body is done 'off-stage' (i.e., non-consciously). Only matters of greatest relevance in the moment gain access to consciousness.' Baars *In the Theatre of Consciousness* (supra) at 86. See also Newman, Baars & Cho (supra) at 1132–1133 (Consciousness is not a particular thing or even a particular kind of feeling, but rather the architecture that enables discrete and disparate neurological processes to solve a host of pressing problems (as well as important medium term and long term problems. The writing of this book has been one of those long term problems to be solved.)
91. Blackmore *Consciousness* (supra) at 72.
92. For more on the relationship between consciousness and error-correction, see JL McClelland 'The Programmable Blackboard of Reading' in JL McClelland & DE Rummelhart (eds) *Parallel Distributing Processing* (1986) 121, 151–152.

93. See Newman, Baars & Cho (supra) at 1131.
94. JB Newman 'Reticular-Thalamic Activation of the Cortex Generates Conscious Contents' (1995) 18 (4) *Behavioral and Brain Sciences* 691.
95. Baars and his colleagues rely on a wide ranging body of evidence to support their claim that global attention – and thus its shifting location and variable levels of intensity – is reflected in measurements (and models) of changes in the thalamus-NRT-cortex complex. See Newman, Baars and Cho (supra) at 1134 citing JG Taylor and FN Alavi 'Mathematical Analysis of a Competitive Network for Attention' in JG Taylor (ed) *Mathematical Approaches to Neural Networks* (1993) 34182; C Koch and T Poggio Multiplying with Synapses and Neurons' in T McKenna, J Davis and SF Zornetzer (eds) *Single Neuron Computation* (1992) 315; AB Schiebel 'Anatomical and Physiological Substrates of Arousal: A View from the Bridge' in JA Hobson and MAB Brazier (eds) *The Reticular Formation Revisted* (1980) 55. Although their findings are not based upon analysis of dendro-dendritic connections, Llinas and Pare used high frequency EEG oscillation to produce a model – like Baars – in which loops of 'non-specific' nuclei 'operate in parallel with specific loops' in a manner that appears to 'provide the basis for "perceptual unity ... by which different sensory components are gathered into one global image".' Newman, Baars and Cho (supra) at 1137 quoting RR Llinas, U Ribary, M Joliot & XJ Wang 'Content and Context in Temporal Thalmocortical Binding' in G Busaki et al (eds) *Temporal Coding in the Brain* (1994) 251. Llinas, Ribary, Joliot and Wang then go on to describe their neurological evidence for the kind of multi-centred, parallel processing that undergirds both their and Baars' account of how conscious emerges: 'When the interconnectivity of these nuclei is combined with the intrinsic properties of the individual neurons, a network for resonant neuronal oscillations emerges in which specific corticothalmic circuits would tend to resonate at 40 Hz. According to this hypothesis, neurons at the different levels, and particularly those in the reticular nucleus, would be responsible for the synchronization of 40 Hz oscillations in distant thalamic and cortical sites ... [and] these oscillations may be organized globally over the CNS [central nervous system], especially as it has been shown that neighbouring reticular cells are linked by dendrite-dendritic and intra-nuclear axon collaterals.' Llinas et al (supra) at 253 – 254 citing M Deschenes, A Madariage-Domich & M Steriade 'Dendrodendritic Synapses in the Cat Reticularis Thalami Nucleus: A Structural Basis for Thalmic Spindle Synchronization' (1985) 334 *Brain Research* 165. See also RR Llinas & D Pare 'Of Dreaming and Wakefulness' (1991) 44 (3) *Neuroscience* 521.
96. However, Baars does not discount data that suggests that the neural correlates of consciousness are preferred convergence zones for 'consciousness' that facilitate the construction of a global workspace. Such hypotheses are testable: though we may not, as yet, possess an adequate map of what occurs in each part of the brain for a sufficiently sophisticated account of how neural networks form over vast spaces within the brain. See C Koch *The Quest for Consciousness: A Neurobiological Approach* (2004).
97. S Dehaene & L Naccache 'Towards a Cognitive Neuroscience of Consciousness (supra) at 1.
98. Ibid at 1–2.
99. See E Poppel, R Held & D Frost 'Residual Visual Function after Brain Wounds Involving the Central Visual Pathways in Man' (1973) 243 *Nature* 295 (Patients with partial blindness were able to detect visual stimuli without having any conscious awareness of the stimuli.)
100. B Renault, JL Signoret, B Debouille, F Breton & F Bolgert 'Brain Potentials Reveal Covert Facial Recognition in Prosopagnosia' (1989) 27 *Neuropsychologia* 905 (Although patients failed to register consciously, and thus to report recognition of familiar faces, 'an electrical waveform indexing process, the P300', reflected the greater intensity associated with recognition of familiar faces.)
101. PJ Whalen, SL Rauch, NL Etcoff, SC McInerney, MB Lee, MA Jenike 'Masked Presentations of Emotional Facial Expressions Modulate Amygdala Activity Without Explicit Knowledge' (1998) 18 *Journal of Neuroscience* 411 (Subjects demonstrated a response – in the amygdala – to masked expressive faces.)
102. Dehaene & Naccache (supra) at 8.
103. Ibid at 9

104. Ibid at 11. See also S Dehaene, M Kerzberg & JP Changeux 'A Neuronal Model of a Global Workspace in Effortful Cognitive Tasks' (1998) 95 *Proceedings of the National Academy of Sciences USA* 14529.
105. L Weiskrantz *Consciousness Lost & Found: A Neuropsychological Exploration* (1997).
106. Dehaene & Naccache (supra) at 13.
107. Ibid at 14.
108. Ibid at 15.
109. S Dehaene & JP Changeux 'A Hierarchical Neuronal Network for Planned Behaviour' (1997) 94 *Proceedings of the National Academy of Sciences USA* 13293 – 13298.
110. See, generally, C Koch *The Quest for Consciousness: A Neurobiological Approach* (2004); C Koch & G Laurent 'Complexity and the Nervous System' (1999) 284 *Science* 96; C Koch & RB Tootell 'Stimulating Brain, But No Mind' (1996) 383 *Nature* 301; F Crick & C Koch 'Consciousness and Neuroscience' (1998) 8 *Cerebral Cortex* 97; F Crick & C Koch 'A Framework for Consciousness' (2003) 6 *Nature Neuroscience* 119; F Crick & C Koch 'Why Neuroscience May Be Able to Explain Consciousness' (1995) 273 *Scientific American* 84.
111. F Crick *The Astonishing Hypothesis* (1994).
112. Blackmore *Consciousness* (supra) at 72.
113. At some level, this stance absolves Koch and Crick of the obligation to explain to students gathered round a vivisection table how a lump of grey matter gives rise to notions of self, consciousness and free will, or to tie the read-outs of an EEG to the actual texture of lived experience. Their response is, in fact, not to ignore the problem entirely, but rather to state, with some modesty, that the neuroscience that will yield a full account of physical basis for consciousness is still in its incipient stages. As things stand, they argue, grand hypotheses about how consciousness actually emerges outstrip the conclusions that can be reasonably drawn from the limited amount of data we possess. As Koch writes: 'For now, science should rise to the occasion and explore the basis of consciousness in the brain. Like the partially occluded view of a snow covered mountain summit during a first ascent, the lure of understanding the puzzle is irresistible.' Koch *Quest* (supra) at 20. As a result, Crick and Koch concentrate their much more modest efforts on identifying the neural correlates of consciousness, and, in particular, the neural correlates of consciousness associated with vision. What are neural correlates of consciousness (NCCs)? The basic premise is that we can study – and measure – various forms of neural functioning and determine how they correlate with first person accounts of conscious experience. See T Metzinger (ed) *Neural Correlates of Consciousness* (2003). In their early work, Crick and Koch made three important and illuminating admissions. First, they have concentrated their efforts on the NCCs of visual experience because it enables them 'to avoid the more difficult aspects of consciousness, such as self-consciousness and emotion'. F Crick 'Forward' in Koch *Quest* (supra) at xiv. Second, they narrowed their focus to NCCs of visual experience – as opposed to NCCs of other experiences – because there is both a vast amount of largely undisputed evidence regarding visual perception available from 'visual psychology, brain scans, neurophysiology and neuroanatomy' that extends all the way down to the simplest of components 'neurons, synapses and molecules'. Ibid. Third, they located 'no single region in which the neural activity corresponds exactly to the vivid picture of the world we see in front of our eyes', but that, instead, 'at any moment in time, consciousness will correspond to a particular type of activity in a transient set of neurons that are a fraction of a much larger set of potential candidates.' Crick *Hypothesis* (supra) at 159, 207. This third admission tells us two very important things – even if they come as something of a disappointment for Koch and Crick. NCCs are distributed throughout various parts of the brain, even when the scope of analysis for NCCs is limited to the NCCs of visual percepts. The general physical architecture of consciousness has begun to distinguish itself from the architecture in the brain responsible for other kinds of neuronal processes and bodily functions. Thus, while some neurons, like mirror neurons, appear to directly correlate with particular phenomena (mirror neurons appear to allow humans, other primates and birds to imitate the observed actions of other beings), many neuronal processes that result in conscious awareness appear to rely on changing networks of

neurons. However, VS Ramachandran contends that mirror neurons played a special role in human evolution and still do most of the heavy lifting associated with learned behaviour and cultural practices. VS Ramachandran *The Tell-Tale Brain: A Neuroscientist's Quest for What Makes Us Human* (2011) 117–135. Of course, imitation and consciousness rely on different neuronal processes. '[T]he self seems to emerge from a ... cluster of brain areas that are linked into an amazingly powerful network.' Ibid at 249. The networks that allow for the emergence of consciousness and selfhood may, of course, draw upon the information stored in mirror neurons. The last few observations accord with the evidence Baars and Dehaene have marshalled in support of global workspace theory's two primary propositions: 'First, the vast majority of cognitive functions are carried out, non-consciously, via changing arrays of specialized modular processors. [Second,] GW theory also reminds us that conscious functions operate on an information load about the size of working memory. Thus, we are talking about a highly coarse-grained level of processing. In this context, global attention is ... a second order operation, acting upon a highly selective stream of information. All this is to say that a relatively low density of widely distributed, yet highly convergent, circuits could be all that are required to create a conscious system; and these are the very characteristics of the neural model we have described.' Newman, Baars & Cho (supra) at 1140. Not all working neuroscientists sign on to Crick and Koch's project of identifying the smallest units that could, reliably, be responsible for conscious experience. For example, Edelman and Tononi reject Crick and Koch's central contention – that a limited number of neuronal circuits or cortical regions could play a privileged role with respect to consciousness. See GM Edelman & G Tononi *A Universe of Consciousness* (2000); G Tononi and GM Edelman 'Consciousness and Complexity' (1998) 282 *Science* 1846. Instead, they prefer to explain the neuronal basis for conscious experience in terms of a 'dynamic core'. This dynamic core consists of a large cluster of thalamo-cortical neurons – a large coalition, if you will. The dynamic core – when viewed as a dominant coalition of neurons whose constituent parts are spread throughout the brain – does not look all that different than those theories offered by Baars, Dennett, Dehaene and Changeux in which the NCC is made up of a 'dominant coalition of neurons stretching halfway across the cortex.' Koch *Quest* (supra) at 311. So although these neuroscientists share a general view about how apparently unified serial consciousness emerges from massive, distributed, parallel and primarily non-conscious neuronal process, they have smaller and larger disagreements about how and where these processes (might) occur. Crick and Koch's later work generates conclusions that remain consistent with global workspace theory. Koch himself summarizes their conclusions as follows: '1. Consciousness deals with broader, less commonplace, and more taxing aspects of the world or a reflection of these in imagery. Consciousness is necessary for planning and choice among multiple courses of action... The function of consciousness is to summarize the current state of the world in a compact representation and make this 'executive summary' available to the planning stages of the brain... The content of this summary is the content of consciousness.' Koch *Quest* (supra) at 305. 2. 'The slower, conscious system may interfere with simultaneously active zombie agents. By means of sufficient repetition, specific sensory-motor behaviours that initially require consciousness, such as hitting a backhand in tennis, can be carried out effortlessly by an automatic zombie agent.' Ibid. 3. 'Any one percept, real or imagined, corresponds to a coalition of neurons. ... The dynamics of coalitions will not be easy to understand, though it is clear that a winner take all competition plays a key role.' Ibid at 305–306. 4. 'At any one moment, the winning coalition, expressing the actual content of consciousness, is somewhat sustained. A very short-lived coalition corresponds to a fleeting moment of consciousness. A useful metaphor is the hustle and bustle underlying the electoral process in a democracy.' Ibid at 315. This last metaphor for 'the mind' ties this account to the theory of the social and the constitutional developed later in these pages.

114. Dehaene & Naccache (supra) at 23.

115. Ibid.

116. AR McIntosh, MN Rajah & NJ Lobaugh 'Interactions of the Prefrontal Cortex in Relation to Awareness in Sensory Learning' (1999) 284 *Science* 1531.

117. Dehaene & Naccache (supra) at 25.
118. See E Rodriguez, N George, JP Lachaux, J Martinerie, B Renault & FJ Varela 'Perception's Shadow: Long-Distance Synchronization of Human Brain Activity' (1999) 397 *Nature* 430; C Tallon-Baudry & O Betrand 'Oscillatory Gamma Activity in Humans and Its Role in Object Representation' (1999) 3 *Trends in Cognitive Science* 151.
119. Ibid at 26. Dehaene and Naccache, following the work of Goldman-Rakic on monkeys, postulate a global neuronal workspace that has something like the following physical structure: 'A dense network of long-distance reciprocal connections linking the dorsolateral PFC with premotor, superior temporal, inferior parietal, anterior and posterior cingulated cortices as well as deeper structures including the neostratium, parahippocampal formation and thalamus. This connectivity pattern ... provides a plausible substrate for fast communication amongst the five categories of processors that we postulated contribute primarily to the conscious workspace. Temporal and parietal circuits provide a variety of high level perceptual categorizations of the outside world. Premotor, supplementary motor and posterior parietal cortices, together with the basal ganglia (notably the candate nucleus), the cerebellum and the speech production circuits of the left interior lobe, allow for the intentional guidance of actions, including verbal reports, from workspace contents. The hippocampal region provides an ability to store and retrieve information over the long term. Direct or indirect connections with the orbitofrontal cortex, AC, hypothalamus, amygdala, striatum, and mesence-phalic neuro-modulatory nuclei may be involved in computing the value or the relevance of current experiences in relation to previous experience. Finally, parietal and cingulated areas contribute to the attentional gating and shifting of focus of interest. Although each of these systems, in isolation, can probably be activated without consciousness, we postulate that their coherent activity, supported by their interconnectivity, coincides with the mobilization of a conscious content into the workspace.' Ibid at 26 – 28 citing PS Goldman-Radic 'Topography of Cognition: Parallel Distributed Networks in Primate Association Cortex' (1988) 11 *Annual Review of Neuroscience* 137.
120. Dehaene & Naccache (supra) at 27.
121. Ibid at 30.
122. Dehaene and Naccache are quick to point out that this ability to check one's immediate responses and to come up with what one believes to be an optimal response should not be confused with being able to 'freely will' a response in the standard compatibalist sense.
123. Dehaene & Naccache (supra) at 31.
124. VS Ramachandran's recent fascinating, and frustrating, work – *The Tell-Tale Brain: A Neuroscientist's Quest for Makes Us Human* – sounds a cautionary note to those of us who would like to believe that neuroscientists and philosophers are on the verge of cracking the code of consciousness. This admonition actually appears on the last page of his work, where, after siding with Darwin, Dawkins, Gould and Pinker (and all evolutionary biologists) in the puerile debate instigated by creationists about 'intelligent design', he goes on to state that we must proceed with humility about regarding questions of ultimate origins (no matter 'how deeply we understand the brain and the cosmos it creates.') We did not, and do not, create the cosmos. Ramachandran's remark recalls a kind of cheap-dime store spiritual self-help book replete with asides that rightly drives serious philosophers of mind such as Colin McGinn absolutely crazy. Remember: 'There. Is. A. Real. World. Out. There.' And neuroscientists such as Ramachandran have done an extraordinary job in the last decade of peeling back layer after layer of the brain (and the rest of our body) in order to demonstrate how different cognitive processes – from emotions to imitation to consciousness to a unitary sense of the self (whether it is an illusion or not) – are created by different neural (and neuromuscular) networks. His brief tour of the brain introduces the reader to the most important players: the cortex (higher learning), the medulla, pons and midbrain (basic bodily functions such as breathing and blood pressure), the cerebellum (fine motor co-ordination), the thalamus (relays sensory inputs to more sophisticated parts of the brain for analysis), basal ganglia (control of automatic movements subject to 'volitional alteration'), the four lobes of the cerebral cortex (temporal lobe – 'higher

perceptual function'; occipital lobe – 'visual processing'; parietal lobe – aggregates multiple forms of sensory perception and bodily functions to generate a rich sense of the corporeal self and the physical environment within which the corporeal self is located, and also contains the left angular gyrus and right angular gyrus that are responsible for higher order mathematics, abstraction, language and orchestrated skill movements; frontal lobe – simple motor commands, mid-to-long term planning, and working memory) and the prefrontal lobe (which, not to put too fine a point on it, appears to shape our individual personality.) Ibid at 17–21. Having introduced us to the brain's primary component parts (and later critical features such as motor neurons responsible for absorbing behavioural and cultural practices), Ramachandran can then describe the different, widely distributed networks activated for different mental processes. Emotions engage the amygdala, the temporal lobe, the superior temporal sulcus, the parietal lobe and the insula. Higher cognitive processes – say language use – will require the participation of the gyrus, the inferior parietal lobe, the temporal lobe, the superior parietal lobe, the anterior cingulate and Wernicke's area. Ibid at 276–277. Because these processes would appear to require the participation of less than the entire brain (and neurological system), Ramachandran writes that defining features of human cognition require a surprisingly small number of discrete portions of the brain. However, while Ramachandran does not engage alternative models – say of Baars or Dehaene and Naccache – he describes similarly broad, and highly differentiated, networks for a range of tasks. Moreover, when it comes to 'the self', he grants, expressly following Dennett, that the self is best described as a 'centre of narrative gravity' in which a variety of brain-based dispositional states, capacities, cultural endowments and learned behaviour dispersed over a range of neural networks overlap. Ibid at 271. Ramachandran subscribes to the view that that there is no single seat of consciousness or selfhood. Ibid.

125. According to David Chalmers, the 'hard problem' in consciousness studies is why we have the experience of subjectivity, that a set of percepts belong to me, that no one else has access to these subjective experiences, and that a set of brain processes give rise to subjective experiences of blueness or love. Chalmers explains the hard problem as follows: 'Even when we have explained all the cognitive and behavioural functions in the vicinity of experience – perceptual discrimination, categorization, internal access, verbal report – there may still be a further unanswered question: Why is the performance of all these functions accompanied by experience? Why doesn't all this information-processing go on 'in the dark' free of any inner feel?' D Chalmers 'Facing Up to the Problem of Consciousness' (1995) 3(1) *Journal of Consciousness Studies* 200, 203. See also D Chalmers *The Conscious Mind* (1996). The answer is found in global workspace theory itself. 'Consciousness' is simply the winner in a neuronal competition for attention that serves as a broadcast to the rest of the apposite neuronal processes in the brain about a problem that needs a solution. Others claim that such a solution is not a solution at all. See C McGinn *The Mysterious Flame: Conscious Minds in a Material World* (2000). McGinn describes the gap between the objective world, subject to scientific inquiry, and the subjective world, which we as individuals inhabit, as separated by a 'yawning conceptual divide.' Ibid at 51. That chasm is unbridgeable because, he says, '[y]ou can look into your mind until you burst, and you will not discover neurons and synapses and all the rest; and you can stare at someone's brain from dusk til dawn and you will not perceive the consciousness that is so apparent to the person whose brain you are so rudely eye-balling.' Ibid at 47. Chalmers, McGinn and others invariably begin and end with an argument that a 'naturalist' account of consciousness leaves something out – namely the feeling of consciousness (or internal mental states called *qualia* – discussed below). D Chalmers 'Absent Qualia, Fading Qualia, Dancing Qualia' *The Conscious Mind* (1996). But is that an argument or merely an intuition for which no empirical answer as yet exists? Let's flip the question: why should consciousness qua feeling be anything more than the feeling of a stubbed toe – an experience that we would attribute to animals as well as humans that possessed toes? From which it follows, as Dennett writes, that 'If you [as Chalmers and company do] believe that consciousness sunders the universe in twain, into those things that have it and those things that don't, and you believe that this is a fundamental distinction, then the demand

for fundamental laws that enforce and explain the sundering makes some sense, but we naturalists think that this elevation of consciousness is itself suspect, supported by tradition and nothing else.' D Dennett *Sweet Dreams* (2005) 16. The argument over consciousness virtually mirrors the argument over free-will and determinism previously engaged. Proponents of free will often argue from internal states – 'I' am aware of being the cause of the action, therefore free will – the self as causal agent – exists. The naturalist (or determinist) response is to proffer, in return, the following question: why are human beings any less determined than the waves of the ocean? A reason may exist, but as a rule, compatibalists do not offer a testable hypothesis to prove that the naturalist account is wrong. They rely instead on deeply ingrained traditions – about a unified self and an ineffable soul. What differentiates the naturalists from the new mysterians (e.g., Chalmers and McGinn) is that naturalists are willing to acknowledge that '[c]onsciousness, like locomotion and predation, is something that comes in different varieties, with some shared functional properties, but many differences, owing to different evolutionary histories and circumstances. We have no use for fundamental laws in making these distinctions.' Dennett (supra) at 16. What we want, instead, is empirical proof regarding the nature of different forms of consciousness. Engaging the responses of life forms from amoeba, to fish, to dolphins, to chimpanzees to humans offers fertile ground for such proof and a better understanding of the different kinds of consciousness that exist (and what purpose they serve.) Anthony Damasio lays out – perhaps as much as a research programme for the study of consciousness as anything else – a variety of 'consciousnesses' and the physiological basis for the experience of consciousness (drawn largely from the broad array of conscious experiences human beings report.) See A Damasio *The Feeling of What Happens: Body and Emotion in the Making of Consciousness* (1999); A Damasio *Descartes' Error* (2005). According to Damasio, proto-selves, core consciousness, extended consciousness, the autobiographical self, and even the limits of consciousness can be tied back to the biology of the brain and the neurological structures that support different cognitive and non-cognitive processes. While such engagement with the biological substructures of consciousness differentiates naturalists from mysterian philosophers, the truly important distinction between these two camps is that the former believe that consciousness, like all other natural phenomena, is susceptible to empirical interrogation, while the latter, generally speaking, do not. See A Damasio *Self Comes to Mind: Constructing the Conscious Brain* (2010)(In his latest work, canvassed briefly above, Damasio lays out yet another research programme for the study of consciousness.)

126. Qualia are such things as my experience of the blueness of the ocean, the sting of the salt-water against my cheek while on the deck of a boat, or the thrill I get from finally seeing land after weeks at sea. Ostensibly, these experiences are mine and mine alone, and there is no way of confirming or denying the quality of my experience. (That is why some describe qualia as being a species within the larger genus of a philosophical conundrum known as the 'problem of other minds'.) See J Locke *An Essay Concerning Human Understanding* (1690). Cf. L Wittgenstein *Philosophical Investigations* (1953) (Regards the problem of other minds as one of many lines of philosophical inquiry where language can be said to have gone on holiday.) For compelling evidence that suggests that Locke's claim that our perceptions were so incorrigible that my colour spectrum could be completely inverted is *incorrect*, see S Palmer 'Can the Color Spectrum Really be Inverted?' (1999) as reprinted in BJ Baars, W Banks and JB Newman (eds.) *Essential Sources in the Scientific Study of Consciousness* (2003) 185.

127. Those who believe in the hard problem of consciousness are going to be inclined to believe that first-person reports are essential to any science of consciousness. For some, like John Searle, 'consciousness has a first person or subjective ontology and so cannot be reduced to anything that has third-person or objective ontology.' J Searle (ed) *The Mystery of Consciousness* (1997) 212. They would be apt to say that even when we discover a way to collect effectively first-person reports about consciousness ('I feel pain when my skin is pinched') and connect them directly to third person reports (the skin is red and the somatosensory cortex registered a measurable response during an fMRI), something real, if ineffable, will be left out of our account. Likewise, David Chalmers, whose agenda for a future science of consciousness rests on the ability to make such connections, insists that because 'it's a manifest

fact that there is something it is like to be us – that we have subjective experiences – and [that] [o]ur direct knowledge of subjective experiences stems from our first person access to them', the content of conscious experience cannot be captured entirely in terms of third-person explanations.' D Chalmers 'First-Person Methods in the Science of Consciousness' (1999) *Consciousness Bulletin*, available at http://www.u.arizona.edu/chalmers/papers/firstperson.html as cited in Blackmore *Consciousness* (supra) at 372 - 373. Another way of articulating the 'hard problem' of conscious is to compare, invidiously, human consciousness with what either qualifies as bat consciousness or simply batness. See T Nagel 'What Is It Like to be a Bat?' *Mortal Questions* (1979) 165. Our lack of access to 'bat experience' and the clear differences in their sensory structure leads Nagel to draw two conclusions. First, we cannot say, meaningfully, what it is like to be a bat. Second, we can say, subjectively, what it is like to be human. That we can offer this subjective account serves as an argument in favour of the 'hard problem': namely, the inability to capture in an objective, third person account the subjective sense of what it is like to be me or a bat. Others contend that a sufficiently sophisticated objective physical science which adopts science's standard third person stance could arrive at a phenomenological account that does justice to 'most private and ineffable subjective experiences'. D Dennett *Consciousness* (supra) at 72. Indeed, studies of bird behaviour, particularly jays, show that birds understand the problem of other minds – that is, they have discarded it. Jays that 'know' that a higher ranking jay looms above will move to cover their horde of nuts. Should the other jay above be of a lower rank in the group hierarchy, the jay in question will not make a discernable effort to protect his nuts. The jay doesn't have to do so: it knows that the other lower ranking jay will not dare to steal a nut.

128. See Dennett *Consciousness* (supra) at 134: 'When you discard Cartesian dualism, you really must discard the show that would have gone on in the Cartesian theatre, and the audience as well, for neither the show nor the audience is to be found in the brain, and the brain is only real place to look for them.' The crucial move is the elimination of 'a master discriminator', a single homunculus sitting comfortably in the cortex of the brain, who *has* the experiences. (There is no mini-me inside the larger-me.) As Susan Blackmore explains, on Dennett's account – and this holds true for the global workspace theory worked out by Baars, Newman, Dehaene, Naccache and others – 'all kinds of mental activity, including perceptions, emotions, thoughts, are accomplished in the brain by parallel, multitrack processes of interpretation and elaboration of sensory inputs, and they are all under continuous revision. ... [C]ontents arise, get revised, affect behaviour and leave traces in memory, which then get overlaid by other traces, and so on.' Blackmore *Consciousness* (supra) at 74 – 75. These multiple drafts, as Dennett calls them, do, in fact, produce various narratives. However, it would be a mistake to conclude from the existence of such narratives 'that there are facts – unrecoverable but actual facts – about just which contents were conscious and which were not at the time.' Dennett *Consciousness* (supra) at 407.

129. Dennett *Sweet Dreams* (supra) at 131.

130. See S Dehaene & L Naccache (eds) *The Cognitive Neuroscience of Consciousness* (2001). Dennett notes that the authors marshal a powerful body of evidence to support the contention that the previous decade has witnessed convergence – from various quarters – on a global neuronal workspace model. Dennett *Sweet Dreams* (supra) at 131. Dennett does not, in fact, claim credit for the dominance of global workspace theory. Baars' first major work on global workspace theory – *A Cognitive Theory of Consciousness* (1988) – preceded Dennett's *Consciousness Explained* (1991) by a few years. Dennett traces the current dominant neuro-scientific theory of consciousness to work in artificial intelligence by McCarthy in the late 1950s. See J McCarthy 'Pandemonium: A Paradigm for Learning' *Symposium on the Mechanization of Thought Processes* (1959). McCarthy wrote: 'I would like to speak briefly about some of the advantages of the pandemonium model as an actual model of conscious behaviour. In observing a brain, one should make a distinction between that aspect of the behaviour which is available consciously, and those behaviours, no doubt equally important, but which proceed unconsciously. If one conceives of the brain as a pandemonium – a collection of demons – perhaps what is going on within the demons can be regarded as the unconscious part of thought, and what

the demons are publicly shouting for each other to hear, as the conscious part of thought.' McCarthy (supra) at 147.

131. Dennett *Sweet Dreams* (supra) at 133 citing S Dehaene & L Naccache (eds) *The Cognitive Neuroscience of Consciousness* (2001) 1 - 31. Dennett warns against taking the top-down imagery invoked by Dehaene and Naccache too seriously, since there is not an organizational summit in the brain. What they mean by 'top-down', says Dennett, is the result of 'competitive, cooperative, collateral activities whose emergent net result is what we may lump together and call top-down influence.' Dennett *Sweet Dreams* (supra) at 133. Indeed, 'in an arena of opponent processes (as in a democracy) the 'top' is distributed, not localized.' Ibid. The comparison to 'democracy' is important not only for understanding how conscious states occur. The competition and the coalitions that form in the brain – and whose winner *is* the conscious state – has important repercussions for how we come to understand why experimental constitutionalism in a democratic state 'fits' who we are as conscious selves.

132. Dennett *Sweet Dreams* (supra) at 136.

133. Ibid at 137. Although there is a tendency in current neuro-scientific writing to discuss consciousness in political parlance as a winner-take-all phenomenon, Baars' earlier description of fringe players in the 'theatre of consciousness' and recent work by Parvizi and Damasio suggests that the competition for consciousness 'leaves not only single winners, but lots of quite powerful semi-finalists or also-rans, whose influences can be traced even when they don't achieve the canonical ... badge of fame: subsequent reportability.' Ibid at 139 – 141 citing J Parvisi and A Damasio 'Consciousness and the Brain Stem' (2001) 79 *Cognition* 135. The persistence and continued existence of semi-finalists or also-rans makes sense if one accepts that such an also-ran network does not simply disappear, even if it has yet to rise to the level of consciousness. The basis for another run at the top-spot has already been laid. See J Driver and P Vuilleumer 'Perceptual Awareness and Its Loss in Unilateral Neglect and Extinction' in S Dehaene & L Naccache (eds) *The Cognitive Neuroscience of Consciousness* (2001) 39.

134. Dennett *Sweet Dreams* (supra) at 141.

135. Ibid at 141 – 142.

136. See, especially, D Dennett *Elbow Room: The Varieties of Free Will Worth Wanting* (1986); D Dennett *Consciousness Explained* (1991); D Dennett *Kinds of Minds* (1996); D Dennett *Freedom Evolves* (2003); D Dennett *Sweet Dreams: Philosophical Obstacles to a Science of Consciousness* (2005). See also D Parfit *Reasons and Persons* (1984). Cf A Bilgrami 'Notes toward a Definition' (2006) 135 (4) *Daedulus: Journal of the American Academy of Arts & Sciences* 5; C Rovane 'Why Do Individuals Matter?' (2006) 135 (4) *Daedulus: Journal of the American Academy of Arts & Sciences* 49; T Feiberg 'Our Brains, Our Selves' (2006) 135 (4) *Daedulus: Journal of the American Academy of Arts & Sciences* 72. This 'de-centred' characterization of the self also features in many post-modern theories of personhood. However, this book's naturalized account of the self does not share many of the epistemic commitments – and the anxieties of doubt – of much of what counts as post-modern. For useful accounts of the 'de-centred self' as it features in post-modern thought, see F Meredith *Experiencing the Post-Metaphysical Self: Between Hermeneutics and Deconstruction* (2005); RM Strozier *Foucault, Subjectivity, and Identity: Historical Constructions of Subject and Self* (2002); LH Martin, H Gutman, and PH Hutton *Technologies of the Self: A Seminar With Michel Foucault* (1988); C Mouffe *Deconstruction and Pragmatism* (1996).

137. See JM Fischer & M Ravizza (eds) *Ethics: Problems and Principles* (1992).

138. J Greene 'The Secret Joke of Kant's Soul' in W Sinnot-Armstrong (ed.) *Moral Psychology, Volume 3: The Neuroscience of Morality: Emotion, Brain Disorders and Disorder* (2008) 35, 43.

139. Ibid.

140. See R Wringham & D Peterson *Demonic Males: Apes and the Origins of Human Violence* (1996).

141. See J Green, R Sommerville, L Nystrom, J Darley & J Cohen 'An fMRI Investigation of Emotional Engagement in Moral Judgment' (2001) 293 *Science* 2105; J Green, L Nystrom, A Engell, J Darley & J Cohen 'The Neural Basis for Cognitive Conflict and Control in Moral Judgment' (2004) 44 *Neuron* 389.

142. Greene 'The Secret Joke of Kant's Soul' (supra) at 44.
143. Ibid at 44.
144. Greene's ironic article title – 'The Secret Joke of Kant's Soul' – refers to the interesting twist that experimental philosophy married to neuroscience reveals: namely, that the hyper-rationalism of Kant's deontological ethics appears to be sourced in those rather archaic (reptilian) parts of our brain responsible for emotions, affective reactions and survival responses.
145. C Gilligan *In a Different Voice: Psychological Theory and Women's Development* (1982). Not surprisingly, Gilligan was critiqued for the post-modern no-no of 'essentialism' by theorists who claim that women's roles are no more than contingent social constructions. See C Sommers *The War against Boys: How Misguided Feminism is Harming Our Young Men* (2000). The empirical data puts paid to that standard post-modern canard. Of course, we can alter responsibilities for parenting – so that they demand greater male participation – and hypothesize that they may have long term consequences for our moral inclinations (and, more importantly lead to more egalitarian gender roles.) Dorothy Dinnerstein made that very argument prior to Gilligan's work. D Dinnerstein *The Mermaid and the Minotaur* (1976). Dinnerstein's work was grounded in a Kleinian approach to the different degrees of separation experienced by male and female infants and children from their mothers. Dinnerstein noted that male differentiation occurs relatively early – when male infants recognize that they possess a penis and their mothers do not. Because female infants do not recognize palpable physical differences between themselves and their mothers at an early age, according to Dinnerstein they are less apt to see difference generally. The male infant differentiates himself from his mother at an early age: as soon as he recognizes that he possesses a penis and his mother does not. According to Dinnerstein, this early separation from the mother – the recognition of her 'otherness' – accounts for a male's generally tendency towards differentiation from other members of a family or from other members of society writ large. How can social arrangements that result in discrimination be changed if they are constructed so early on in our development? Dinnerstein suggests that equal male participation in childrearing might diminish the earlier differentiation of boys from mothers and make men, as a result, more relational, less inclined to differentiate between themselves and others, and thus more egalitarian generally. Of course, there's no beating the breast.
146. P Churchland *BrainTrust: What Neuroscience Has to Tell Us about Morality* (2011).
147. Ibid at 33 – 34 citing K Light et al 'Deficits in Plasma Oxytocin Responses and Increased Negative Affect, Stress, and Blood Pressure in Mothers with Cocaine Exposure during Pregnancy' (2004) 29 *Addictive Behaviours* 1541.
148. Ibid at 75 citing C De Dreu 'The Neuropeptide Oxytocin Regulates Parochial Altruism in Intergroup Conflict among Humans' (2010) 328 *Science* 1408.
149. Ibid.
150. L Gettler, T McDade, A Feranil & C Kuzawa 'Longitudinal Evidence that Fatherhood Decreases Testosterone in Human Males' (2011) 108 (39) *Proceeding of the National Academy of Sciences* 16194
151. P Belluck 'In Study, Fatherhood Leads to Drop in Testosterone' *The New York Times* (12 September 2011).
152. A Mazur & J Michalek 'Marriage, Divorce and Male Testosterone' (1998) 77 *Social Forces* 315.
153. T Burham, J Chapman, P Gray, M McIntyre, S Lipson & P Ellison 'Men in Committed, Romantic Relationships have Lower Testosterone' (2003) 44 *Hormones and Behaviour* 119.
154. M Muller, F Marlowe, R Bugumba & P Ellison 'Testosterone and Parental Care in East African Foragers and Pastoralists' (2009) 276 *Proceedings of the Royal Academy: Biological Sciences* 347.
155. C Larmore *Patterns of Moral Complexity* (1986).
156. *S v Mamabolo* 2001 (3) SA 409 (CC), 2001 (5) BCLR 449 (CC), 2001 (1) SACR 686 (CC) at para 41.
157. Sen *Development* (supra) at 64.
158. See, eg, P Singer 'Famine, Affluence and Morality' (1972) 1 *Philosophy and Public Affairs* 229 (1972).
159. Sen's approach, a hybrid of virtually all the major schools of modern ethical and political philosophy, had already been presaged, as I have noted, by Charles Larmore's efforts in *Patterns of Moral*

Complexity. Though writing with Rawls, McIntyre and Sandel in mind, Larmore makes the case for a non-reductive approach to deontological, utilitarian and communitarian thought. Each has its place: each identifies salient features of moral and political dilemmas. Unsatisfying as that might sound, it does seem to capture our basic intuitions about political thought. More importantly, it now squares with what we know about the relationship between the structure of our brain and different forms of moral thought. See W Sinnott-Armstrong (ed.) *Moral Psychology II – The Cognitive Science of Morality: Intuition and Diversity* (2008); W Sinnott-Armstrong (ed.) *Moral Psychology III – The Neuroscience of Morality: Emotion, Brain Disorders and Development* (2008). As I have explained in the text, Patricia Churchland's review of experiments conducted on men given intranasal doses of oxytocin demonstrates a substantial increase in caring and co-operative behaviour by men within the group to which they belong, but does not reflect a similar reduction in antagonism toward outsiders. It would appear that we are hard-wired for all three kinds of ethical responses. P Churchland *Braintrust: What Neuroscience Has to Tell Us about Morality* (2011) 75.

160. Sen *Development* (supra) at 73.

161. Ibid at 73 quoting Adam Smith *The Wealth of Nations* (1776)(RH Campbell and AS Skinner (eds) 1976) 469 – 471 (By 'necessities', Smith means 'not only the commodities which are indispensably necessary for the support of life, but whatever the customs of the country renders it indecent for creditable people, even the lowest order, to be without.')

162. See S Weinberg 'The Universes We Still Don't Know: Stephen Hawking's and Leonard Mlodinow's *The Grand Design*' (10 February 2011) 58 *New York Review of Books* 24. (Persons who borrow metaphors borrowed from quantum mechanics – like Schroedinger's Cat – in order to buttress claims about 'indeterminacy' in other disciplines simply fail to understand what it means for physicists to be incapable of locating a particular position of a sub-atomic particle in four dimensional space-time at any given moment.)

163. For contemporary accounts of the compatibalist positions on free will, see R Chisholm 'Human Freedom and the Self' in G Watson (ed) *Free Will* (2003) 27; R Taylor *Action and Purpose* (1966). Defences of pure compatibalism are difficult to find in the philosophical academy. Libertarian accounts often rely upon the unique capacity of human beings to reason and to order their ends in a manner that differs, importantly, from that of an inanimate object such as a rock. See, e.g., T O'Conner (ed) *Agents, Causes and Events* (1995); R Clarke 'Toward a Credible Agent-Causal Account of Free Will' (1993) 27 *Nous* 191.

164. D Dennett *Freedom Evolves* (2003) 223.

165. For a clear account of the incompatibalist position, see P Van Iwagen 'An Argument for Incompatabilism' *An Essay on Free Will* (1983). For other variations on the incompatibalist position on free will, see the collection of essays in G Watson (ed) *Free Will* (2003).

166. Ibid at 30.

167. M Elton *Daniel Dennett: Reconciling Science and Our Self-Conception* (2003) 265.

168. The difference between living entities to which responsible moral agency can be pinned and living entities to which responsible moral agency cannot be attributed may turn on the difference between behavioural awareness and narrative awareness. Human beings possess both kinds of awareness. Only narrative awareness – the ability to report on what one's experience of the world is like – is an exciting form of awareness. Behavioural awareness – and thus intentionality – can be attributed to one-cell organisms. Narrative awareness requires the capacity to give some kind of verbal report (and that includes any kind of sign or written language) of what an experience is actually like. As far as we can tell only humans definitively possess this kind of language. That said, the ability of apes to make use of symbols not of their own making to communicate apparent 'interior' states seems to push the envelope. (I use the term 'interior' in scare quotes because there is nothing more on the inside than the verbal report itself – the same event as is apparent on the exterior.) If we adopt an intentional stance toward other beings – and rely on descriptions and analysis of what happens, as opposed to verbal reports from the creature under observation – then

it would seem that individual dolphins have the ability to distinguish themselves from other dolphins and from previous 'narrative' awareness of their own appearance. See D Reiss & L Marino 'Self-recognition in the Bottlenose-Dolphin: A Case of Cognitive Convergence' (2001) 98 (10) *Proceedings of the National Academy of Sciences* 5937. See also M Hauser *Wild Minds: What Animals Really Think* (2000)(Hauser found that cotton-top tamarins responded to seeing in a mirror that the tufts of hair on their head had been dyed by touching their own tufts by altering the angle of the mirror to get a posterior view. Both actions suggest self-awareness and the ability to differentiate the physical state of the self at Time 1 from the physical state of the self at Time 2.) Dolphins may possess what Damasio describes as an autobiographical self. This narrative awareness is evinced through actions that reflect their recognition that a recently painted fin on their own body is their own fin and that this newly painted fin constitutes a signal difference in their own appearance over time. (Most animals lack the capacity to recognize themselves in a mirror and tend to behave as if the animal in the mirror were another creature.) Of course, while we readily adopt the intentional stance with respect to other humans because we can have our attribution of thoughts, hopes, fears and desires confirmed by both verbal accounts and observations of their actions, our current reliance on description and analysis alone – without corroborating verbal reports – currently limits the confidence we have in attributing narrative awareness to dolphins. But our present inability to translate dolphin signals fully does not rule out the possibility that one day we shall be able to translate dolphin communication in a manner that confirms our attribution of narrative awareness. It is possible that our possession of language and other sophisticated symbolic systems makes the kind of consciousness and freedom that we possess uniquely human. Even an enthusiastic user of the intentional stance like Daniel Dennett admits that it is possible that 'the kind of mind you get when you add language to it is so different from the kind of mind you can have without language, that calling them both minds is a mistake.' See D Dennett *Kinds of Minds* (1996) 17. Using the intentional stance can also have interesting consequences when we are asked to compare the actions of robots and the actions of humans so as to decide whether or not robots possess consciousness and freedom in a manner comparable to the consciousness and freedom we attribute to humans. Soda machines are like one-celled organisms. Even if we adopt an intentional stance towards the soda machine and note that its purpose seems to be able to collect 5 rand coins and to produce soda, we are unlikely to attribute consciousness or freedom to it. But what of a sophisticated computer – say like HAL in the movie *2001* – that can undertake cognitive tasks that dwarf the capacity of human beings and direct physical actions of complex machinery that human beings could not, on their own, operate? If, adopting the intentional stance, we say that HAL's purpose was to guide the spaceship from Earth to Jupiter, to take decisions that made the likelihood of success greater, to learn from mistakes made on route and to communicate with the astronauts about the mission, then what else would we require before we would attribute consciousness and freedom to HAL? Assume HAL had been programmed to speak about its mission and its on-going success – and to express pride in that success. If HAL engages in error-correction, can distinguish itself from other computers and, of course, human beings, and offers verbal reports about its own internal states – Drive D is failing – then what, save for our inability to say what an internal state of a computer feels like, would cause us to withhold the attribution of consciousness to HAL? At the moment, the evidentiary record suggests that we ought to remain agnostic as to whether animals and computers possess self, consciousness and freedom even in the modest form described in these pages. But see BJ Baars 'There are No Known Differences in Fundamental Brain Mechanisms of Sensory Consciousness Between Humans and Other Animals' (2001) 10 *Animal Welfare* 31 (Given that there is no significant difference between the basic architecture of the human brain and that of many animal brains, Baars believes the onus is on those who object to the attribution of consciousness to animals to demonstrate that their near identical architecture is incapable of producing consciousness.) However, the purpose of adopting the intentional stance with respect to dolphins or highly sophisticated computers – and the fact that questions remain about the level of consciousness and the degree of freedom they possess – serves as a challenge to our conception of what 'consciousness' is and closes the gap between humans, animals and robots when it comes to discussions of freedom. Are there conscious machines? John Searle's response is yes – but his affirmative response is not what you might expect. He writes: 'We have known this answer for a century. The brain is a machine. *It is a conscious machine.* The brain is a biological machine just as much as the heart and the liver. So of course some machines can think and be conscious. Your brain and mine for example.' J Searle *The Mystery of Consciousness* (1997) 202. But that is where Searle draws the line. Alan Turing originally set the test for whether a machine could be said to think. He asked, suggesting that the answer would be in the negative, whether a machine could 'be kind, resourceful, beautiful, friendly, have initiative, have a sense of humour, tell right from wrong, make mistakes ... fall in love, enjoy strawberries and cream, learn from experience ... use words properly, be the subject of its own thought ... do something really new.' See A Turing 'Computing Machinery and Intelligence' (1950) 59 *Mind* 433 as reprinted in DR Hofstadter and D Dennett (eds.) *The Mind's I: Fantasies and Reflections on Self and Soul* 53, 61. As it stands now, 50 years later, machines can do many of the things on that list that Turing suggested that they could not. Would we deny a machine consciousness if the only thing it could not do was taste strawberries and cream? Would we then deny consciousness to a man that had no tongue? Koch and Tononi have recently stated that no reason exists to deny *ex ante* the hypothesis that consciousness might emerge out of silicon based computer systems. They have offered their own simple test for determining whether a computer is sentient. C Koch & G Tononi 'A Test for Consciousness' *Scientific American* (June 2011)(The test turns upon whether a computer could make sense of what was 'right' or 'wrong' about a given array of features of a photograph. They contend that since a room full of the most powerful supercomputers still cannot identify what is 'right' or 'wrong' with, say, a doctored photograph of an elephant perched upon the Eiffel Tower, computers lack the ability to make sense of the world in a manner that would suggest that they are sentient. Close, but no cigar.)

169. Not surprisingly, the late Chief Justice Ismail Mohamed saw matters exactly that way. Had he lived long enough to craft a decision, the Supreme Court of Appeal would have likely decided *Prince* differently: that is, in favour of Mr Prince. (Conversation with Judge Ralph Zulman, 15 September 2011.) As an advocate of Indian extraction, who often had to eat his lunch alone in chambers, Chief Justice Mohamed understood the difference that difference makes.
170. See s 20(1)(aA) of the Sexual Offences Act 23 of 1957.
171. *Jordan* (supra) at para 16–17.
172. *Khosa* (supra) at para 76.
173. On the meaning of FC s 7(2), see further, *Glenister v President of the Republic of South Africa & Others* 2011 (3) SA 347 (CC), 2011 (7) BCLR 651 (CC).
174. Another version of the autonomy trap – or should I say the flip side of the autonomy trap – is reflected in *Case & Curtis. Case v Minister of Safety and Security; Curtis v Minister of Safety and Security* 1996 (3) SA 617 (CC), 1996 (5) BCLR 609 (CC). In finding that Section 2(1) of the Indecent or Obscene Photographic Matter Act 37 of 1967 violated the right to privacy by prohibiting the possession of 'indecent' or 'obscene' materials in one's own home, Didcott J, for a majority of the Court, wrote: 'What erotic material I may choose to keep within the privacy of my home, and only for my personal use there, is nobody's business but mine. It is certainly not the business of society or the state. Any ban imposed on my possession of such material for that solitary purpose invades the personal privacy which section 13 of the interim Constitution guarantees that I shall enjoy. *Case & Curtis* (supra) at para 91 citing with approval *Bernstein* (supra) at paras 67 – 69 (Right to privacy protects 'the inner sanctum of a person' that lies within 'the truly personal realm.') See also *Investigating Directorate: Serious Economic Offences v Hyundai Motor Distributors (Pty) Ltd: In re Hyundai Motor Distributors (Pty) Ltd v Smit* NO 2001 (1) SA 545 (CC), 2000 (10) BCLR 1079 (CC) at para 18 (Right to privacy protects intimate space because such a space is a prerequisite for human dignity.) The problem, so far as my account of freedom is

concerned, is not the result, but how the Court arrived at it. The Court appears to suggest that there exists – physically and metaphysically – a space in which the individual self has no exchange, no intercourse, with other members of society. Somehow, however, within the hermetically-sealed domain of his castle, the individual citizen is 'free' to receive and to enjoy pornographic material. But how, one might ask, did the pornographic material appear in the home in the first-place? Once again, the Court, by sealing off the individual from the society in which he is fundamentally conditioned, accords him a metaphysically implausible degree of 'freedom'. In her concurrence in *Case & Curtis*, Mokgoro J once again, in her own modest way, suggests a way out of the Court's autonomy trap: 'I would, however, respectfully part company from Justice Didcott to the extent that any part of his opinion might be read to suggest that it is not in any circumstances the business of the state to regulate the kinds of expressive material an individual may consume in the privacy of her or his own home. It may be so that, as in England, a "South African's home is his (or her) castle." But I would hesitate to endorse the view that its walls are impregnable to the reach of governmental regulation affecting expressive materials.' *Case & Curtis* (supra) at para 65. See also *S v Dube* 2000 (2) SA 583 (N)(High Court holds that the right to privacy does not embrace the right not to be secretly photographed while engaging in criminal activity. Such an extravagant notion of privacy even if constitutionally protected would have to yield before the overwhelmingly more important interests of the polity as a whole). Justice Mokgoro recognizes the self as fundamentally conditioned by, and inextricably connected to, the community of which s/he is a member. The Robinson Crusoe account of the self on offer from the majority, detached as he is from the larger world, would only be entitled to the pornography that washed up on to the island with him. That seems, upon reflection, like a cramped conception of freedom indeed.

175. The emphasis in this section on the arational sources of the self invariably brackets the place of reason in ethical, political and legal thought (or most fields of human inquiry for that matter). However, bracketing reason and diminishing its efficacy to the vanishing point are two entirely different things. First, the place of instrumental reason and the ability of human beings to recognize regularities in the world means, at the very least, that we are able to discriminate between better and worse ways of realizing our preferred ends. Second, the more varied forms of life the self draws upon, the more tools the self will have when deciding upon her preferred vision of the good. Third, this account is not averse to the existence of some deep grammar of human reason – married to long-standing social conventions – that commits us to such varied ends as the good of the family, the clan, the community and the individual. Some may think it convenient that such a species of naturalism results in a commitment to such imperfectly reconcilable goods as freedom, equality, dignity and democracy. However, putting aside the current dominance in political theory (and life) of liberal and social democracies, these values or ends have competed with one another for primacy of place for several millennia. How one settles, in a rational manner, the differences between these ultimate ends is the very meat of ethical and political thought. Fourth, though there may be plenty of instances in which the evidence for our beliefs about the world leaves room for a certain amount of theoretical indeterminacy, I take it as given that most of our beliefs about the world are true and that we share most of those beliefs. Only under such general conditions of shared understanding does it even begin to make sense to talk about disagreement. Thus, though Ptolemy and I may not share certain theories about the solar system, we certainly would share most other beliefs about things in this world. This near identity of belief sets between Ptolemy and ourselves would be obvious if you were able to watch – and to interrogate – both what we do and say. Moreover, the near identity of belief sets would enable us to settle many an apparent dispute. After we have aggressively learned all there is to be learned from each other, we would be able to establish what critical bite of difference remains. See, for example, D Davidson 'On the Very Idea of a Conceptual Scheme' (1974) 47 *Proceedings and Addresses of the American Philosophical Association* 1; WVO Quine *Word and Object* (1960); D Dennett *The Intentional Stance* (1987). The use of the term arational may likewise strikes some as deeply counterintuitive. It may seem to sweep into the ambit of the arational, various processes most people are apt to describe as falling within the domain of the rational. The point is

the authorship of the processes themselves. We employ many natural and social processes in a fashion clearly intended to secure various ends. The fit between our means and ends, as well as the choice of the ends themselves, is often just what we mean by rational. We did not, as individuals, and often as groups, consciously create many of these processes. They are not the product of any one person's capacity to reason (though various individuals will have contributed to this vast array of processes). In this respect, they are arational. So when I say these responses 'just are', I am not denying that there might not be good reasons for them being so. I only deny that the ultimate source of the reasons, evolutionary adaptation or social adaptation, lies within the individual alone. Cf. Edmund Burke 'Speech on Conciliation with America' (22 March 1775). Burke wrote that 'it is a great mistake to imagine that mankind follows up practically any speculative principle, either of government or freedom, as far as it will go in argument or logical illation.' Burke is simply sceptical of reasoning from the bottom up a la Descartes. And while committed to rational discourse about all things that matter, Burke recognized that abuses of, and vast differences in, power, often block our ability to reach agreement about the our ends and the means that we employ to pursue them. See S Woolman 'Language, Power and the Margin: Eliot's Philosophy of Language, Wittgenstein on Following a Rule and Statutory Construction in *Thembekile Mankayi v Anglogold Ashanti Limited* (2012) 128 *South African Law Journal* 434. See also S Woolman 'Seek Justice Elsewhere: An Egalitarian Pluralist's Reply to David Bilchitz on the Distinction between Differentiation and Domination' (2012) 28 *South African Journal on Human Rights* 273.

176. On our ability to create meaningful political freedom shorn of outré metaphysical commitments, see K Jackson 'A Colony with a Conscience' *The New York Times* (27 December 2007) available at www.nytimes.com (accessed on 4 July 2010)('Three hundred and fifty years ago today, religious freedom was born on [the North American] continent. Yes, 350 years. Religious tolerance did not begin with the Bill of Rights or with Jefferson's Virginia Statute of Religious Freedom in 1786. With due respect to Roger Williams and his early experiment with "liberty of conscience" in Rhode Island, this republic really owes its enduring strength to a fragile, scorched and little-known document that was signed by some 30 ordinary citizens on Dec. 27, 1657. It is fitting that the Flushing Remonstrance should be associated with Dutch settlements, because they were the most tolerant in the New World. The Netherlands had enshrined freedom of conscience in 1579, when it clearly established that "no one shall be persecuted or investigated because of his religion." And when the Dutch West India Company set up a trading post at the southern tip of Manhattan in 1625, the purpose was to make money, not to save souls. Because the founding idea was trade, the directors of the firm took pains to ensure that all were welcome. For example, while the Massachusetts Bay Colony was enforcing Puritan orthodoxy, there were no religious tests in the Dutch colony. So open was New Amsterdam that at least 16 languages were being spoken there by the 1640s; by 1654, the first Jews in what is now the United States had been able to settle there peaceably. … . The Flushing Remonstrance [average citizens backing up the Quakers' right to practice their faith in New Amsterdam] was remarkable for four reasons. First, it articulated a fundamental right that is as basic to American freedom as any we hold dear. Second, the authors backed up their words with actions – they did not whisper their opposition among themselves or protest in silence. Rather, they signed the document and sent it to the most powerful official in the colony, [Peter Stuyvesant,] a man not known for toleration or for an easy-going or gracious manner. Third, they stood up for others; none of the signers was himself a Quaker. The Flushing citizens were articulating a principle that was of little discernible benefit to themselves. And fourth, like all great documents, the language of the remonstrance is as beautiful as the sentiments they express. "If any of these said persons come in love unto us, we cannot in conscience lay violent hands upon them, but give them free egress and regress unto our town," its authors wrote in the conclusion. "For we are bound by the law of God and man to do good unto all men and evil to no man." So what was the result? As expected, Stuyvesant arrested Hart and the other official who presented the document to him, and he jailed two other magistrates who had signed the petition. Stuyvesant also forced the other signatories to recant. But

ultimately, the citizens won their case. Thus did religious toleration become the law of the colony [and part of the 1st Amendment in the US Bill of Rights almost 150 years later, in 1791].') Such freedom, such elbow room, is the variety of freedom that we so desperately need. See S Woolman My Tea Party, Your Mob, Our Social Contract: Freedom of Assembly and the Constitutional Right to Rebellion in *Garvis v SATAWU (Minister for Safety & Security, Third Party)* 2010 (6) SA 280 (WCC) (2011) 27 *South African Journal on Human Rights* 450. It's not at all clear that the Constitutional Court has understood the import of this right – and the panoply of freedoms that work in concert to support it. See *Garvis v SATAWU (Minister for Safety & Security, Third Party)* [2012] ZACC 13. Indeed, the Constitutional Court's failure to recognize the state's responsibility for creating space for prayer and protest can, without much difficulty, be tied to subsequent events such as the massacre at Marikana in which the state was culpable for the immediate harm and partly responsible for the conditions that brought about the massacre. See S Woolman 'You Break It, You Own It: Freedom of Assembly after *Garvis* (2012)(Presentation at Panel Discussion on *Garvis*, Public Interest Law Group Symposium, University of the Witwatersrand School of Law)(Manuscript on file with author).

177. That this conclusion may share some attributes of contemporary liberal theories – those predicated upon finding neutral grounds for political institutions – is coincidental. Such contemporary liberal theories have actually shied away from any meta-theoretical commitments because of the fear of making some new epistemological error that might leave them open to the kinds of attack levelled by Michael Sandel against John Rawls' theory of justice. The irony of such twice-shy liberalism is that it may have left itself with far less worth defending. The level of deference accorded non-dominant choices – the freedom accorded non-dominant ways of being – echoes the egalitarian liberalism of Ronald Dworkin. To the extent that it matters: the difference between Dworkin's epistemological commitments and my own are three-fold. To some extent, Ronald Dworkin is a methodological individualist. He is also committed to a moral cognitivism that ostensibly generates uniquely specifiable right answers in the political domain. The basis for equal concern and respect on Dworkin's account is ground in the capacity of each person to reason. As my account of the self, social choice and politics suggests, I do not make the capacity to reason the basis for meaningful decision-making. I certainly do not assume uniquely specifiable answers – in advance – in the political realm. The self that I describe here is fundamentally conditioned by memes and genes and has his or her choices circumscribed by an array of constitutive attachments. Often its is the friction between competing roles or different constituitive attachments, that drives the individual to undertake a novel approach to a problem and to arrive at what she or he believes to be an optimal course of action.

178. See C McGinn *The Mysterious Flame: Conscious Minds in a Material World* (2000); J Searle *Making the Social World: The Structure of Human Civilization* (2010); D Chalmers *The Character of Consciousness* (2010).

179. See J Locke *An Essay Concerning Human Understanding* (1690).

180. See S Palmer 'Can the Color Spectrum Really be Inverted?' (1999) as reprinted in BJ Baars, W Banks and JB Newman (eds.) *Essential Sources in the Scientific Study of Consciousness* (2003) 185.

181. See L Hiochberg, M Serruya, G Friehs, J Mukland, M Saleh, A Caplan, A Branner, D Chen, R Penn & JP Donoghue 'Neuronal Ensembe Control of Prosthetic Devices by a Human with Tetraplegia' (2006) 442 *Nature* 164 (Brain Computer Implants (BCIs) restore damaged capacity because the cortical plasticity of the brain eventually treats implants as natural sensors or effector channels); S Musaliam, B Corniel, B Gregor H Shermberger & R Anderson 'Cognitive Control Signals for Neural Prosthetics' (2004) 305 *Science* 258.

182. See N Shinji, A Vu, T Naseralis, Yuval, B Yu & J Gallant 'Reconstructing Visual Experiences from Brain Activity Evoked by Natural Movies' (2011) 10 *Current Biology* 1016; Y Miyawaki, H Uchida, O Sato, Y Morito, H Tanabe, N Sadato & Y Kamitani 'Decoding the Mind's Eye – Visual Image Reconstruction from Human Brain Activity using a Combination of Multiscale Image Decoders' (2008) 60 *Neuron* 915.

183. *The Tell-Tale Brain: A Neuroscientist's Quest for What Makes Us Human* (2011).
184. C McGinn 'The Tell-Tale Brain: An Exchange with VS Ramachandram' (2011) 58 (11) *New York Review of Books* 68.
185. J Searle 'Reply to Barclay Martin on Antonio Damasio's *Self Comes to Mind*' (2011) 58 (14) *New York Review of Books* 101.
186. M Elton *Daniel Dennett: Reconciling Science and Our Self-Conception* (2003) 145.
187. See L Tancredi (supra) at 26.
188. See A Kozin 'Bernstein on the Mystery Behind the Music' *The New York Times* (February 15, 2011), available at www.nytimes.com (accessed on 15 February 2011)(Emphasis added).

Chapter Three

A Theory of the Social: Constraint, Friction & Change

Do I contradict myself? Very well.
I am large. I contain multitudes.

Walt Whitman

A. Introduction

In Chapter 2, we saw that the way the vast majority of us think about the self, consciousness and free will is incorrect – dramatically out of step with what the majority of neuroscientists, cognitive psychologists, social theorists, economists and analytic philosophers have to say about those subjects. One consequence of these erroneous views is that the manner in which the majority of us understand 'freedom' – as a metaphysical term and as a political concept – is sharply at odds with how things actually are. In this chapter, we'll see how we replicate similar kinds of errors when we think about how various forms of human association are constructed and how change actually occurs within such associations. Once again, epistemological fallacies with regard to social theory have the consequence of leading us to attribute far greater 'freedom' to groups, and members of groups, than they actually possess. This second form of over-valorising freedom results in institutional political arrangements and constitutional doctrines at odds with what we know about the human condition. Again, I'll press the idea that we should be more concerned with creating the material and non-material conditions for individual and collective flourishing – across the many publics that make up the republic – than on formal notions of freedom predicated upon the absence of external constraint.

Chapter 3 is divided into three parts.

The first section explains the nature of the constraints the social places upon us. This realm's rules, responsibilities and regulations make us who we are: and are the source of most of life's meaning. In attempting to come to grip with these strictures, the chapter surveys such notions as Walzer's 'unchosen conditions of being', Wittgenstein's 'forms of life' and Heidegger's 'ways of being in the world'. This same descriptive section explains how the networks of individuals that sustain our most cherished forms of life operate and why it is essential that these associations are constitutionally protected.

Having established the nature and the necessity of the constraints that are placed upon the social, the second section moves on to describe two theories of social change: spontaneous orders and evolutionary epistemology. These descriptions are valuable, but partial. They do not provide an account of the construction of all social phenomena and, more importantly, they do not accommodate the possibility of revolutionary change. Remember, *revolutionary change*, within the constraints allotted us, is one of the objectives that drives this work. Markets, for example, constitute spontaneous orders that work on the basis of trial and error and feedback mechanisms. They give us fresh opportunities to reflect upon experience (immediate and long-term) and plot more or less optimal courses for action (immediate and long-term). But, in terms of allowing for the vast majority of us to fit our round pegs into round holes, they often come up woefully short. Markets are wonderful (but only when extremely well-regulated!!)[1] at creating efficiencies and producing fortunes for those who have access to reasonably large stores of capital. The real benefit of markets, as Hayek argues, is not the making of money. It is the co-ordination of knowledge, information and goods – in an intelligent manner – without the direction of any one person or groups of persons. Put slightly differently, while spontaneous orders provide important feedback (especially about their own limitations), they are not especially well-geared toward providing the kind of feedback that tells us what lives are worth valuing and how we should best order our society so that a majority of our fellow citizens may pursue them.

The third section looks at three theories of the social that we can leverage in order to realize kind of the revolutionary change that might allow a majority of our fellow citizens to pursue lives worth valuing: (1) choice architecture and its commitment (a) to experiments that reveal what people actually need and (b) to organizational design that allows such needs to be met; (2) social capital theory and its understanding of how both bonding networks and bridging networks can realize significant change in a manner that fits the needs and the aspirations of various members of our society; and (3) a theory about the radical heterogeneity of the self and the social which demonstrates that the very friction between the selves that make up individuals and the sub-publics that populate a society can – under the appropriate conditions – create the necessary space for individuals and groups to invent new lives, sub-publics and ways of being that better fit their newfound preferences.

What links these various lines of thought to our previous re-conceptualization of freedom? The modest, naturalized account of freedom offered thus far takes cognisance of the limits of individual agency. These limits led me to recast freedom-talk in terms of the less metaphysically problematic concept of flourishing. Having supplanted freedom-talk with flourishing, I then use social capital theory, the notion of spontaneous orders and evolutionary epistemology to explain, in part, how individual flourishing and group flourishing occur without central planning or hierarchical structures. More importantly, these theoretical constructs explain how individuals and groups so thoroughly conditioned and determined by the world can alter the ends they pursue – as well as the means for pursuing them – through different kinds of feedback mechanisms.[2] Choice architecture and bridging networks press persons exercising responsibility for particular spheres of life to run experiments that generate the kind of feedback that will allow us to identify and to create social structures that better align with the preferences and the needs of individuals in various communities.

1. *Unchosen Conditions of Being and Constitutive Attachments*

It is trite to note that outside society, and without language, individual flourishing is a meaningless notion. It is only in light of the various practices, forms of life, or language games that social groups provide that we become anything that remotely approximates what we understand to be human. At the same time, these social practices and forms of life from which we derive meaning in our lives also constrain our actions and often limit our ability to behave in a manner that we believe will promote our own well-being, in particular, and human flourishing, generally. How can we recognize the value of the radical givenness of social life and still attempt to alter social structures in a manner that changes things for the better?

The answer lies somewhere in the following account of friction and disruption, and how we best respond to them.

The constitutive nature of our attachments and practices forces us to attend to an often overlooked feature of social life. We often speak of the social practices, endowments and associations that make up our lives as if we were largely free to choose them or make them up as we go along. I have suggested why such a notion of choice is not true of us as individuals. It is also largely not true of social life generally. When Michael Walzer argues that there is a 'radical givenness' to our social world and the practices that make it up,[3] what he means is that most of the practices that make up our social life are involuntary. We don't choose our family. We (generally) don't choose our race or language or ethnicity or nationality or class or religion. Moreover, even when we appear to have the space to exercise choice, we rarely create the practices available to us. The vast majority of our practices and forms of life are already there, culturally determined entities that pre-date our existence. Finally, even when we overcome inertia and do create some new practice, the very structure and style of the practice is almost invariably based upon an existing rubric. Corporations, marriages, co-edited and co-authored publications are modelled upon existing associational forms. Gay marriages may be of recent vintage. But marriage itself is a publicly recognized and sanctioned institution for carrying on intimate relationships that dates back well over three millennia. Even in times of radical transformation, mimicry of existing social practices is the norm.[4]

Perhaps Walzer's most interesting challenge flows from his invitation to think of what it might mean for individuals to lack involuntary associational ties, to be 'unbound, utterly free?'[5] One image, he suggests, might be that of wild horses. But this very image is the antithesis of what makes us human. We are human, and not feral, because of the involuntary practices into which we are born and which have been sustained and developed over time. Even schools designed to enable us to make the most of our freedom do not let us do whatever we so wish. Quite the opposite. We have to learn to be free. Flourishing – freedom rightly understood – remains predicated upon practices that are involuntary in all important respects.[6]

Stop for a moment before you resist this account. To play the piano well requires years and years of practice in a practice that is centuries old – and mastery of this wonderful instrument is not something that the individual determines. You may play the piano well or poorly: you and everyone else can hear the difference. Or take advanced mathematics – a practice several millennia old. Difference, creativity occur at the very margins of this form of life: to master the rules of various species of mathematics is to already be in agreement, to judge things in the same manner as other mathmatecians. Most participants in these practices do not think less of another participant in the practice simply because they lack the genius to do something radically new within the practice's confines. Mastery offers more than enough fulfilment to qualify as part of an individual's flourishing.

This account of the involuntariness of social life is not meant to undermine the importance of equity or *revolutionary change* for individual flourishing in any truly complex, radically heterogeneous, democratic society. Issues of access, of coercion, of choice, of voice, of exit in various communities of which we are a part must be constantly negotiated: just as we must recognize that the radical heterogeneity of each self must be constantly negotiated. (Isn't that why we, in South Africa, are so very tired after a long day? The moral salience of every exchange in everyday life with another radically, heterogeneous self in our highly stratified society is highly charged and depletes (often more than it replenishes) our reserves.) The emphasis on involuntariness in social life is, however, meant to bracket the standard account of freedom. On the standard account, any impediment to free association is a denial of that which is most fundamentally human. On my account, however, those so-called impediments are the preconditions for freedom, for flourishing. A reasonably equal and democratic society must, it would seem, mediate the givenness of our social life and the aspirations all of us have to discriminate between those social forms of life which still fit and those which do not. It is often the case that not choosing to leave an association, but to stay, is what we truly cherish as freedom.[7] And again: this conditioned outcome explains why little or no explanatory power is lost when we substitute 'flourishing' for 'freedom'. Indeed, as Walzer suggests, we ought to call such decisions to reaffirm our conditioned commitments 'freedom simply, without qualification.'[8] It is, for the most part, he concludes, 'the only "freedom" that free men and women can ever have.'[9]

Again: these constraints on our ways of being in the world does not mean that genuine change within small associations or large social formations is impossible or undesirable. (Far from it, as my Walzerian-inflected account of remedial equilibration, and it underlying distinctions between differentiation and domination, monopoly and tyranny, will demonstrate.) It does mean, however, that we must take some care in offering an account of how change occurs and even greater circumspection before we proffer prescriptions for the mechanisms that would facilitate optimal forms of change.

2. *Social Capital: How Associations and Networks Function*

As Shaun Knobe's thought experiments in Chapter 2 reveal, experimentation as a way of engaging the world is *revolutionary*. Not only do experiments and the people who carry them out seek to better understand the world, but, as often as not, people who undertake experiments seek to overturn preconceived and – in their minds – incorrect ways of viewing various phenomena. Some hypotheses turn out to be incorrect. Indeed, the large majority do. But from those that succeed, we are all the beneficiaries.

At the same time, the experimentation advocated in these pages has a built in break. A conservative streak if you must. Not every norm or institution can be subject to constant review and reformation. I will suggest several reasons, later on, for placing brakes on how we engage and experiment upon social phenomena. The first turns on the manner in which meaning makes us (through natural gifts, inherited endowments and spontaneous orders). The second turns on the dangers of grand theorizing that leads to dangerous, deadly and inhumane social projects. (The 20th century social experiments of Stalinist Russia or Maoist China – alone responsible for more than 50 million deaths over less than half a century – provide evidence enough to support that proposition: Whereas no social democracy has ever gone to war with another social democracy or imperilled and destroyed the lives of so many of its citizens.) In many respects, our experimental philosophers – of Chapter 2 – have similar aims and operate under similar limits. In a variety of different ways, we saw that such philosophers test our intuitions – metaphysical, epistemological, moral and political – so that we might come to better comprehend the socially constructed myths under which we operate as well as the cognitive errors for which we appear to be hard-wired.

That leads us, finally, to another way of understanding individuals, social formations and political institutions: social capital theory. As I shall describe it, social capital theory looks upon society as a set of phenomena that contain the seeds for (a) experimentation and new institution-building; (b) at the same time that such institutions and phenomena place a break on the manner in which state and non-state actors can undermine existing social networks that provide (i) the setting for all meaningful action, (ii) the real and figurative capital that enables individuals and societies and groups to build new institutions or improve on those organization and association that already exist and (iii) the stores of trust, stability and mutual understanding that enable us to take collective risks on building something new, something different, and even something revolutionary. (We shall return later to the revolutionary possibilities of social capital made possible through the prism of Walzerian-inflected egalitarian pluralism and the legal doctrine of remedial equilibration. In this section my concerns are largely descriptive.)

Social capital is – and is a function of – our collective effort to build and to fortify the things that matter. It is our collective grit and elbow grease, our relationships and their constantly re-affirmed vows. Social capital emphasizes the extent to which our capacity to do anything is contingent upon the creation and maintenance of forms of association which provide both the tools and the setting for meaningful action. Social capital is often treated as ephemera. That makes sense. It is so hard to see. In fact, it is this elusive quality that makes social capital so fragile. It is made up, after all, not of bricks and mortar, but of relationships and commitments, and the trust, respect and loyalty upon which they are dependent.

My take on social capital has several competitors. For example, Pierre Bourdieu defines social capital as

> made up of social obligations or connections … [and the aggregation of] actual or potential resources which are linked to possession of a durable network of institutionalized relationships of mutual acquaintance and recognition.[10]

At a certain level of abstraction that sounds something like what I have described above. But one must read everything that Bourdieu writes. For only several pages later, he states that 'economic capital is at the root of all the other types of capital' and that 'every type of capital is reducible in the last analysis to economic capital'.[11] As my varied list of associations in Chapters 1 and 2 suggest, I do not adhere to such a reductive (quasi-Marxist) definition of social capital.

On the other side of the political/disciplinary spectrum, in *Bowling Alone*, Robert Putnam defines social capital as follows:

> Whereas physical capital refers to physical objects and human capital to the properties of individuals, social capital refers to social networks and the norms of reciprocity and trustworthiness that arise from them. In that sense, social capital is closely related to what some have called 'civic virtue'. The difference is that social capital calls attention to the fact that civic virtue is most powerful when embedded in a sense network of social relations. A society of many virtuous but isolated individuals is not necessarily rich in social capital.[12]

Two more recent characterizations of social capital better accord with the theses articulated in these pages. Nan Lin writes:

> [S]ocial capital may be defined operationally as the resources embedded in social networks accessed and used by actors for actions. Thus, the concept has two important components: (1) it represents resources embedded in social relations rather than individuals, and (2) access and use of such resources reside with actors. The first characterization, socially embedded resources, allows a parallel analysis between social capital and other forms of capital ... For example, human capital, as envisioned by economists, represents investment on the part of individuals to acquire certain skills ..... that are useful in certain markets ... The second component of social capital ... must reflect that [the] ego is cognitively aware of the presence of such resources in her or his relations and networks and makes a choice in invoking the particular resources.[13]

In somewhat simpler prose, designed to reach a broader audience in the academy as well as government officials, policymakers and practitioners of the law, David Halpern offers the following gloss:

> So what is social capital comprised of? Most forms ... consist of a network; a cluster of norms, values and expectancies that are shared by group members; and sanctions – punishments and rewards – that help to maintain the norms and the networks. ... The first component is the social network ... in some cases the small rural village. The network can be further characterized by its density ... and its closure... .The second component is the social norms. These are the rules, values and expectancies that characterize the community of network members... Many of these rules are unwritten. The third component is sanctions. Sanctions are not just formal – such as punishments for breaking the law. Most are very informal, but are nonetheless effective in maintaining social norms. ... The sanction may be through someone being told directly ... More commonly, however, the sanction is indirect and subtle, such as though gossip and reputation.[14]

The efforts of Halpern, Lin and Putnam have led the avatar of capitalism, the World Bank, to acknowledge the centrality of social capital:

> Social capital refers to the institutions, relationships, and norms that shape the quality ... of a society's ... interactions. Increasing evidence shows that social cohesion is critical for societies to prosper and for development to be sustainable. Social capital is not just the sums of the institutions that underpin a society – it is the glue that holds them together.[15]

In light of Putnam, Lin and Halpern's definitions, social capital can be understood to connect flourishing to experimentation in the social realm as follows.

As I have already noted in Chapter 1, Social capital is what keeps our intimate, economic, political, cultural, traditional, reformist and religious associations going. Social capital recognizes that we store the better part of our meaning in fundamentally involuntary associations: the constituitive. Squander that social capital, nothing that matters will continue to exist. Social capital recognizes both the real and the figurative sense of ownership that animates particular forms of (social) life. If anyone and everyone can claim ownership of and membership in an association, then no one owns it. Social capital takes seriously the threat of various kinds of compelled association. Trust, respect and loyalty have no meaning where the association is coerced. These several virtues can be earned, but never commanded. No trust, respect or loyalty: no social capital.[16] No social capital: none but the most debased forms of (social) life, and no room for the kind of meaningful social and political experimentation that makes genuine flourishing (within a modern heterogeneous society) possible.

However, not all social capital formations are fungible. For South African life in particular, two forms are of particular import: bonding and bridging. Putnam puts the difference between these two distinct forms of social capital networks as follows:

> Some forms of capital are, by choice or necessity, inward looking and tend to reinforce exclusive identities and homogeneous groups. Examples of bonding social capital include ethnic fraternal organizations, church-based women's reading groups, and fashionable country clubs. Other networks are outward looking and encompass people across diverse social cleavages. Examples of bridging social capital include the civil rights movement, many youth service groups, and ecumenical religious organizations ... Bonding social capital provides a kind of sociological superglue whereas bridging social capital provides a sociological WD-40.[17]

It's essential to gain a slightly better grasp of these distinctions.[18]

One way to distinguish the two networks would be to 'contrast the strong bonds of reciprocity and care that are found inside families and small communities (what we might call normative bonding networks) with the [at least initial] self-interested norms that tend to predominate between relative strangers ... and through which relative strangers can co-operate successfully (what we might call normative bridging networks.)'[19] But that's just a start. High bonding communities tend to feature well-established, historically entrenched belief sets, shared assets and rather rigid rules regarding membership, voice and exit (as well as mechanisms for the use of those rules). As the rigidity of membership and voice should suggest, these bonding networks have their dark side: discrimination, exclusion and suppression of alternative views.[20] In a state committed to overcoming centuries of oppression, bonding communities must ensure that they exercise their associational and community rights in a manner that does not offend the dignity and equality concerns of members and non-members alike.[21] Traditional and conservative religious and cultural associations often straddle quite a fine constitutional line. Bridging networks, often mediated by the state or arms-length relationships in the market, are often extra-communal and bring together rather diverse groups of individuals in the pursuit of singular, generally self-interested ends. Membership, voice and exit tend to be both more flexible and more formal in bridging networks.[22]

However distinct these two kinds of social capital may appear on the surface, the success of a developmental state such as South Africa depends upon: (a) respect for the significant public goods created by private bonding networks (schools, hospitals, charities); (b) leveraging, as much as possible, admission into bonding networks for persons (and groups of persons) who would otherwise not have access to the goods made available within those networks; and (c) the use of state resources to build linking or bridging networks that, over time, produce social capital comparable in nature and quality to that social capital produced in bonding networks.[23] The potential for social and political revolution is radical if we understand how bonding and bridging networks actually function.[24] (We shall return to that radical capacity later. I shall also acknowledge (in other chapters and an epilogue) the chastened expectations that we can have for what the World Bank has recently described as an 'unsustainable' South Africa.[25])

B. Descriptions of Several Social Feedback Systems

This section attempts to answer two distinct, but related questions. First, how does the aforementioned account of the relationship between the individual and the social fit this book's more general account of flourishing and feedback mechanisms? Secondly, how does one best describe the possibilities for change against a background of involuntary constraint?

Feedback mechanisms come in all shapes and sizes. So while 'feedback' was initially associated with electrical engineering, not long after this neologism was coined in the physical sciences it was adopted in the social sciences.[26] Consciousness, as we saw, is one kind of reflexive feedback mechanism. The conscious report constitutes a record of our response, and perhaps the nature of our error. A record of such errors enables us to respond differently – assuming we survive the errors – the next time we are faced with the appropriate set of circumstances. The same holds true for social formations. Social practices, endowments, language games and associations provide a variety of tools for being in the world. Our social practices provide stores of collective wisdom about what works and what doesn't work. They also constitute large playing fields against which 'experiments in life' can be played out. Given their vastly increased scale, they offer systems of feedback far superior to those available to the lone individual.

For now, I will place particular emphasis on particular kinds of social formations that simultaneously provide individuals with information about their world at the same time as they extract information from them and circulate that information throughout the system. Such social formations enable all participating individuals to make more informed and better decisions about how to respond to their environment.

Of course, no guarantee exists that a society will advance flourishing by providing the individual with a sufficiently heterogeneous array of social practices and feedback mechanisms. Large societies, as well as small, can stifle the individual and the group experimentation required to advance flourishing. Because individual flourishing is parasitic upon the continued existence of social practices, and social life is often repressive, the individual often faces great difficulty in changing the means and the ends of life. Social practices create experiential bottlenecks. They restrict both the ends to be pursued and the means of achieving them. Mill and other theorists who rely heavily on individual experiments in living to drive social change often fail to appreciate the extent to which social forces are often arrayed against even minor modifications. That is why, in Chapters 4 and 7, I argue at greater length that a politics committed to both flourishing *and* experimentalism is necessary to liberate the self and the social from the 'tyranny of custom'.[27]

The capacity for critique of our practices that is imminent in our practices – and which may expand the possibilities of existence – may well exist in a notoriously small number of communities. Indeed, in some rather closed and insular societies, the capacity for critique may well be a function solely of the manner in which different selves (roles, dispositional states, identities or ideals) create friction between one another and thus force conflicts that must be resolved in favour of one way of being rather than another.[28] Although such choice may seem rather impoverished, it remains choice nevertheless. More importantly, it is choice or conflict from which we can learn, and it is choice and conflict whose lessons can be applied, profitably, to similar decisions in the future. The ultimate point is that there are always social practices – in science, in religion, in law – that expand our individual and collective capacity for critical engagement with our actions and our ends.

For the experimentalist, the grander the exercise in experimentation – the larger and more varied our critical community – the more varied our individual lives are likely to be.[29] The more varied our individual lives, the experimentalist believes, the more likely we are to find successful models. The more successful models of being in the world there are, on the experimentalist account, the more likely it is that a member of a community will be able to identify at least one of a range of possible existences that will enable her to flourish.

That said, in contemporary South Africa, it is only with the intervention of the state (and co-operation from powerful non-state actors such as businesses and traditional communities) that many individuals will come to possess the enhanced material conditions necessary for living out those possibilities. Moreover, our state, to be successful, must undertake a range of social policy experiments designed to provide its citizens with the means and the goods required to flourish.

1. Spontaneous Orders

Spontaneous orders possess two notable features. They do not rely upon a centralized form of command and control to achieve optimal outcomes. They provide, in the form of abstract rules, constraints on individual behaviour that by their very abstraction enable individuals to respond constructively – singularly and collectively – to changes in the environment. The archetypal example of a spontaneous order is the market. The real purpose of markets, as Hayek argues, is not the making of money. It is the co-ordination of knowledge, information and goods – in an intelligent manner – without the direction of any one person or groups of persons. Hayek demonstrates that markets – by drawing down on the tacit knowledge and the local intelligence of individuals and groups – generally outperform the best informed central planner. More importantly, markets provide individuals with information about their world (at the same time as they extract information from them) that enables individuals to make better and better decisions about how to respond to the environment within which they live.

Hayek's theory of spontaneous orders is not limited to markets. It applies with equal force to all other cultural institutions that are 'the result of human action, but not of human design'.[30] Spontaneous orders embrace cultural institutions as diverse as language, the common law, and open-code software that 'serve the common welfare without a common will aiming at their creation'.[31]

Before moving on to a discussion of other examples of spontaneous orders – such as language, open-code software and the common law – it is, perhaps, worth pausing for a moment to consider how such cultural structures form, and how they evolve over time. As Hayek points out:

> Culture is neither natural nor artificial, neither genetically transmitted nor rationally designed. It is a tradition of learnt rules of conduct which have never been 'invented' and whose function individuals usually do not understand. … It is here that the … Cartesian approach has made thinkers accept as good for a long time only what were either innate or deliberately chosen rules, and to regard all merely grown formations as mere products of accident or caprice. Indeed, 'merely cultural' has now to many the connotation of changeable at will, arbitrary, superficial or dispensable. Actually, however, civilization has largely been made possible by subjugating the innate animal instincts to the non-rational customs which made possible the formation of larger orderly groups of gradually increasing size. … That cultural evolution is not the result of human reason consciously building institutions, but of a process in which culture and reason developed concurrently is … beginning to be more widely understood. It is probably no more justified to claim that thinking man has created his culture than that culture created his reason. … The structures formed by traditional human practices are neither natural in the sense of being genetically determined nor artificial in the sense of being the product of intelligent design, but the result of a process of winnowing or sifting, directed by the differential advantages gained by groups from practices adopted for some unknown and perhaps purely accidental reasons. … The evolution of society and of language and the evolution of the mind raise in this respect the same difficulty: the most important part of cultural history, the taming of the savage, was completed long before recorded history begins. It is this cultural revolution which man alone has undergone that distinguishes him from other animals. … To understand this development we must completely discard the conception that man was able to develop culture because he was endowed with reason. What apparently distinguished him was the capacity to imitate and to pass on what he had learned. And much if not most of what he learnt about what to do he probably learnt by learning the meaning of words. Rules for his conduct which made him adapt what he did to his environment were certainly more important to him than knowledge about how other things behaved.[32]

So, hard-wired as we might be for language, languages themselves are social systems that are the result of collective action, but not collective design. Put another way, complex social systems, such as language, persist not because of unilateral, or mono-directional, commands, but by virtue of a complex interaction of patterns that Donald Campbell calls 'downward causation'.[33] As Henry Plotkin writes, '[d]ownward causation refers to the dynamic nature of control hierarchies, where information and causal power flow in all directions.'[34]

Languages are archetypal examples of systems that reflect downward causation. Languages are rule-driven and require, for competency, the ability to master those rules. However, no modern language has its rules set by a single authority and no modern language possesses a central authority that determines the competency of its individual users. Instead, each competent user of a language employs a system of signs that millions if not billions of individuals have made use of and contributed to over time in order to convey billions of ideas, desires or demands. In using a language, each individual further contributes to the language's growth – for each use of a word entails an extension of the word's extension to a new set of phenomena, even if the newness of that set of phenomenon turns on events that seem as trivial as the date, or the position of the sun. Of course, other institutions exist that mediate the use of the language and reinforce, or alter, the denotation of particular words. Schools, parents, books, newspapers, television, the internet, dictionaries and movies all play important roles in information flow within the linguistic community. But once again, the causal flow is inordinately complex. Each conversation constitutes a new piece of information that subtly alters the linguistic landscape, and each conversation lies beyond the control of any single authority.

To understand the power of Hayek and Campbell's description of social formations as the result of the twin forces of spontaneous ordering and evolution, one need only look at the brief and ignominious history of a modern language that was entirely the result of collective human design: Esperanto. The linguists who created Esperanto offered us a logical and coherent system that was easy to learn and universal in application. However, for the language to work, it required static and immutable rules to which all speakers were required to adhere. The failure of Esperanto stems, as least in part, from the failure of its creators to appreciate that languages work not (primarily) because their users have command of ostensive definitions or grammatical rules, but because the languages meet the ever changing needs, purposes and ends of their users. Esperanto left no room for the inevitable evolution of language that occurs with neologisms or simple, novel iterations of a word or phrase. Esperanto failed because it left no room for the large-scale changes to the entire language that flows, inexorably, from smaller, ever so subtle changes to the meaning of its constituent parts. Esperanto flopped because its creators failed to recognize that language is 'the product of *slow* evolution in the course of which more knowledge and experience has been precipitated in it than any one person can know.'[35]

A good counter-example of a modern language that works is Linux. The success of this free operating software code lies in its ability to accommodate novel contributions from users without any single authority determining the benefits or the costs of any novel contribution. The users of Linux themselves determine the success of any novel development.[36]

The common law shares many of these same features of languages, open-code software and markets. The general norms of the common law provide abstract rules that guide – and delimit – the behaviour of an entire society of individuals without specifying the actions that those individuals undertake. At the same time, the rules themselves are altered, sometimes subtlety, sometimes significantly, each time they are invoked in novel disputes between individuals, or by a court asked to dispose of a novel dispute based upon an extant common law rule. In mediating the conflicts between the expectations of the litigating parties as to the actual extension of the rule, the judge is obliged to decide which set of expectations 'is to be treated as legitimate' and 'in so doing … 'provides the basis for future expectations.'[37] Although one party will have had his trial and have been deemed to have erred, the result of the judgment is that all parties to the case – and all members of society – become aware of a shift – however small – in the standard by which their future actions will, very likely, be assessed. Without pressing the point too much further, the common law, like language and like markets, relies upon individual judges and individual litigants operating within a larger system of law (and meaning) and the ability of judges and litigants to understand the system of signals being sent throughout the system by other judges and litigants. A general commitment on the part of judges, lawyers and litigants to a coherent system of law allows the common law system to evolve in response to individual cases without any person or group of persons dictating the content of the entire system of rules. Indeed, as Richard Adelstein notes, 'the dynamic which energizes the entire [common law] process of structural adaptation is the postulated search for mutually beneficial exchange.'[38] It requires no Leviathan and no legislator for the system of rules to work and to change as individuals go about their lives and seek out Adelstein's postulated mutually beneficial exchange. All this system requires is mastery by practitioners, and the ability of various members of the polity to engage, as necessary, in critical assessments of those common law norms that enable individuals and groups in a society to flourish.[39]

The theory of spontaneous orders offers a way in which to understand how we – as fully conditioned (and constrained) as we are – are capable of making decisions that alter both ourselves and the world around us. Spontaneous orders also offer us another window onto the theory of consciousness developed in Chapters 1 and 2. As we have already seen, consciousness is not the product of a central planner, or a homunculus, who audits data and then issues commands. Consciousness is, rather, the product of mostly unconscious, multiple, parallel, distributed neural networks. These networks often compete with one another – for both attention and for the ability to determine action. The tacit knowledge or dispersed knowledge of individuals upon which markets, languages, and the common law rely is not unlike the unconscious, multiple, parallel, distributed neural networks upon which the brain relies.[40]

However, while the theory of spontaneous orders might provide a useful heuristic device for demonstrating striking similarities in consciousness, language, markets, software and law as feedback mechanisms, it does not follow that this descriptive account entails a particular set of political commitments. Indeed, it should be clear that the political quietism and the commitment to classical liberal principles closely associated with Hayek's theory of spontaneous orders is fundamentally incompatible with the politics of human flourishing and experimental constitutionalism adumbrated above in Chapter 1 and below in Chapters 4, 5, 6, 7 and 8. Donald Campbell puts his critique of classical liberalism, from the perspective of the 'experimenting society', thus:

> Within western democratic capitalism, there are a number of favourable features. These include the legal tradition, the successful achievement of changes in government through elections, and the genuine pluralism of decision-making units. The so-called 'market mechanisms' of capitalist economic theory can be regarded in ideal form as self-regulatory cybernetic feedback systems implementing the collective aspects of the preferences of individual decision-makers. But the ideological justification and effective practice of the accumulation of great inequalities in individual and corporate wealth, and the role of wealth in providing uneven weightings of some persons' preferences over those of others, provide great obstacles that ... [will often] effectively sabotage ... decision-making genuinely [designed to realize] the public good.[41]

In sum, while primarily market driven economies and polities offer some capacity for human flourishing and for feedback on 'best practices' over a wide range of social institutions, the benefits flow to far too small a portion of the overall population to contribute, meaningfully, to individual flourishing and to effective social experimentation.[42] (A mere 400 Americans possess approximately the same degree of wealth as 150 million of their brethren – or 1% possess 25% of the nation's wealth. It's impossible to contend that every American has equally meaningful opportunity to flourish. Similarly, a far less wealthy South Africa still possesses one of the highest gini-co-efficients in the world. It's impossible to contend that our society – with up to 40% unemployment and horrific primary and secondary schooling offers a truly meaningful opportunity to flourish for the majority of its denizens.)

The next section looks at John Stuart Mill's commitment to flourishing and to experimentation. As we shall see, Mill's theoretical commitment to flourishing and experimentation is undermined by his refusal, like Hayek, to accord a sufficiently important role to the polity to ensure desirable outcomes at both the level of the individual and the collective.

2. *Mill's Experiments in Living*

John Stuart Mill's notion of 'experiments in living' unearths the potential of experimentation within private ordering. Instead of assuming that leaving people to their own devices will only maintain the status quo, Mill believed that people, once freed from the yoke of rigid legal constraints, would undertake 'experiments in living.' These 'experiments' should, according to Mill, enable individuals to explore their ideals in a manner that produces practices that better fit their identities.[43] As a good utilitarian, the promise of such voyages of self-discovery for Mill lay not just with individual changes in behaviour. He quite naturally believed that individual change, in the aggregate, would produce a more progressive polity.[44]

The potential for experimentation and social dynamism that Mill identified provides an intuitively plausible, if incomplete, method for reconciling the conflicting demands of progressive social transformation and liberal private ordering. Mill's commitment to negative liberty, and its concomitent guarantee of some individual and group independence from state coercion with respect to value formation and re-inscription, is certainly a necessary condition for human flourishing and social dynamism. It is simply not sufficient. Once we recognize the significant natural (and social) limitations on our capacity for reflection and autonomy, we come to understand that fostering novel forms of private ordering requires sustained structural, public intervention aimed at creating social institutions that promote collective experimentation and error correction.[45]

a. Mill and the Limits of Private Ordering

While *On Liberty* is typically identified with Mill's advocacy of individual rights, what often goes unnoticed is his powerful account of ethical empiricism. Drawing on his own experience of personal crisis, enervating depression, a nervous breakdown, exploration and recovery,[46] Mill's second line of argument ties the grounds for protecting individual freedom to more general 'experiments in living'.[47]

For Mill, his personal experience of crisis, depression, and adjustment marked a prototype for the process of 'experiments in living.' He believed that this process could be replicated throughout a society with the appropriate political arrangements, namely, maximum individual liberty. Such experiments, according to Mill, promote human flourishing because they help us to narrow the distance between our ideals, our characters, and our circumstances.[48]

However, Mill did not believe that this potential for change based on reflection, self-critique, and adjustment was limited to individuals. A similar potential for dynamism – based on reflection, critique, and adjustment – also existed within social formations. Allowing individuals greater freedom for experimentation was, for Mill, a way of overthrowing the bondage of irrational customs and social conformity. Although Mill did not indicate clearly the link between individual experimentation and progressive social change, the details can be gleaned from his writings. The process would take the shape of the following ever-expanding virtuous cycle. Personal crises prompt individuals to reflect upon their ideals and circumstances. Personal reflection produces shifts in personal ethical ideals. Upsurges of new personal ethical ideals challenge and transform existing customs. Regular transformation of customs and norms encourages the process of personal experimentation and reflection.

A crucial part of Mill's belief in the possibility of progressive social change was his theory of ethical empiricism. This theory provides a bridge between individual experimentation and the transformation of social norms. Despite his commitment to the existence of a hierarchy of values and the intrinsically greater worth of some existing social norms over others, Mill nonetheless held that such norms must be evaluated in light of their capacity for promoting individual flourishing under reasonably hospitable conditions. Accordingly, Mill deemed all ethical ideals and social norms open to assessment, critique, and adjustment on the basis of our lived experience. Two questionable assumptions about individual potential lie beneath his ethical empiricism. First, his version of ethical empiricism requires that we be creatures with the capacity for sustained, rational reflection upon our beliefs and experiences. Second, it requires the ability to change our beliefs and practices on the basis of our reflection.[49]

Given my earlier reversal of the traditional relationship between consciousness, freedom and action, it must be said that Mill dramatically overestimated the extent of our capacity for rational reflection on our experience.[50] In times of crisis that are supposed to trigger personal reflection, we are more than likely to fall back on strategies that attempt to soften the pain of the problem at hand rather than put ourselves in a position to experience epiphanies that might reveal more fundamental flaws in our self-understanding.[51] Moreover, as I have repeatedly observed, each life is often a composite of many, often competing, narratives over which we have little control as authors. A person's ethical orientation is inevitably dictated by such pre-determined roles. Given the radical givenness of our radically heterogeneous determined selves, we can never take the synoptic view of our own lives. The promise of self-analysis, through psychoanalysis with an adept, properly trained second party, may well initiate positive change. That very few individuals actually embark on such a course of radical reconstruction points up the significant limits of reflection as an engine for change.[52] We are constrained by forms of external regulation – social mores and legal norms – and our own personal entropy.[53] Even those of us who have successfully re-evaluated their beliefs through reflection may find their capacity for self-initiated changes in behaviour or beliefs limited by natural or social constraints.[54] Like Ulysses, who could not refuse the sirens' calls, we cannot simply will ourselves into adopting a belief that runs counter to deeply ingrained dispositions.[55] The cost associated with trying to alter fundamentally, upon reflection, one's beliefs is much greater than the discomfort of lashing oneself to the mast for a day. Why? It often involves severing entire aspects of one's identity.[56]

Mill also failed to appreciate fully the tenacity of social norms in resisting conscious change due to the extent to which social norms, legal rules and individual identities are linked in contemporary societies. The connection between norms and individual identities invariably entrenches social authority in a manner that dampens effective individual reflection and adjustment.[57] The presence of entrenched private power undermines Mill's political vision because such obstacles to experimentation do not depend on direct government sanctions.

Entrenched private power creates a two-fold barrier to experimentalism. First, it aligns existing custom and practices with one's individual identity. It thereby makes critical self-reflection difficult and redefinition painful. It thwarts attempts at reflection and adjustment by increasing its costs. That is, entrenched private power forces individuals to choose *between* preserving their membership in a community by muting their demands *or* alienation if they choose to speak up. Second, it enables individuals or institutional practices supported by entrenched authority to suppress new ideas and alternative points of views on the basis of authority instead of merit.[58] Entrenched private power creates a 'bottleneck' and prevents individual experimentation from leading to corresponding changes in social norms. Mill's insistence on the private order as the engine for social transformation fails to account for this inevitable brake on change.

Accordingly, one should refine Mill's political theory in several respects while retaining the essential spirit of his experimentalist vision. Chapter 2 and Chapter 3's initial recognition of the natural constraints and social limits on the individual capacity for reflection and adjustment calls for the creation of an alternative set of political mechanisms designed to realize Mill's vision of a dynamic, virtuous cycle of progressive change. To this end, we should add the following corollary to Mill's vision: experimentalism requires public intervention, not government abstention. Such public intervention entails (a) historical redress for marginalized communities; and (b) both public and private institutions that promote reflexivity and increase our individual and collective capacity to challenge the tyranny of custom. Chapters 4, 5, 6, 7 and 8 identify an array of institutional arrangements and judicial doctrines that distinguish a polity committed to experimentalism and flourishing from those jurisdictions that over-valorise either private ordering or central planning.

b. From Private Ordering to Experimentalism

Private ordering, conceived as permitting individual interaction with minimal official intrusion, can never truly be free from public ordering. Rules of contract, of delict, and of property – that often determine private ordering – can only be enforced with the backing of state authority. The distinction, then, between different levels of public intervention is a matter of degree, rather than kind.[59]

Given that private ordering inevitably entails the use of state power, questions of (conservation and) transformation of existing social formations ultimately reduce to issues of political institutional design and judicial doctrines. Generally, public intervention can either be imposed from above, via direct state action, or originate from below, through the initiative of individual stakeholders.[60] Direct state action offers the virtue of speed. It suffers, however, from two important drawbacks: information deficiency and lack of participation. First, reconfiguring social institutions requires a certain amount of inside information. If trained anthropologists find understanding the cultures they study exceedingly difficult, how much greater is the challenge, and less likely a solution, for a largely untrained, unsupported and poorly remunerated South African bureaucracy who are often asked to solve pressing polycentric social problems. Second, by relying on a bureaucratic process, a top-down approach faces the peril of excluding the participation of the people most directly affected. Not only does such exclusion fuel the information deficit already discussed, it can also undermine an essential part of the political project of transformation – to change the mind-set of those who govern. Finally, the silence of those affected undermines the legitimacy of the decisions taken.

As I shall argue in more detail in Chapters 4, 5 and 7, one way of increasing participation, information-generation and legitimation is through what Robert Mangabeira Unger describes as 'destabilization rights'.[61] Destabilization rights – in their thinnest form – provide remedies for stakeholders who seek accountability from either a government agency that influences private ordering or a social institution that exercises significant public power. Such destabilization rights offer two distinct forms of relief to the stakeholders. First, they require those persons in power to account for their decisions on the basis of evidence and reasonable arguments. Second, they bestow upon stakeholders rights of participation in the processes meant to address the problems that concern them. As we shall see in Chapter 4, destabilization rights are novel but not untested. Successful constitutional challenges to existing government policy in both South Africa[62] and the United States[63] demonstrate their potential.

Another mechanism for altering discriminatory and well-entrenched private ordering – whether it occurs in traditional communities or religious associations – is what has been described by myself, Michael Bishop and others as a remedial equilibrium. Unger's rotating capital fund and my Walzerian-inflected take on remedial equilibrium could be called, 'super-liberal'. In truth, these positions best characterized as 'egalitarian pluralist'. Under an *egalitarian pluralist* constitution such as that promised by South Africa's basic law, we enjoy a well-developed body of South African jurisprudence that distinguishes the public from the private, and understand why all comparable constitutions are invariably committed to some degree of private ordering. As Walzer himself must have understood, we can 'seek justice elsewhere' – my locution – as a response to domination and tyranny.[64] Seeking justice elsewhere may take the form of peregrinations around the globe or exiting one sub-public and entering or constructing another more felicitous community within one's birth-state. With respect to the latter form of exit, I shall later contend that the community responsible for the expulsion and the impairment of an individual's dignity should, along with the state, bear some form of material obligation in order to make the creation of a more commodious sub-public a reality. Walzer's *Spheres of Justice* enables us to make critical distinctions between differentiation and domination, as well as between legitimate distributions of social goods and tyrannical abuses of economic, social and political power that invariably lead to the kind of stratified society that we inhabit in

South Africa. Walzer's felicitous description of the difference between differentiation and domination, and monopoly power and tyranny, also intimates how a commitment to a judicial doctrine such as remedial equilibration can assist us in developing a sliding scale of 'interdependent and interrelated' rights and remedies by which the rules that govern various non-state publics, communities or associations might be assessed when charges of discrimination are laid. A court order based upon remedial equilibration possesses a number of distinct virtues. Where differentiation rises to the level of unfair discrimination, remedial equilibration allows a court: (a) to acknowledge the constitutional infirmity of the conduct, (b) to appropriately remonstrate the association responsible for such conduct without necessarily eviscerating the power of the association to continue to determine its rules for membership, voice and exit, (c) to require the association, and where appropriate the state, to bear the pecuniary costs of the dismissal or expulsion, and (d) to assist the person harmed to secure employment or some other good (e.g. marriage) in a more congenial environment and thereby 'seek justice elsewhere'. Seeking justice elsewhere and remedial equilibrium, as we shall see in Chapters 4, 5 and 7, are remedies that enable individuals, groups and states to find round holes for round souls, and square apertures for square characters. At the same time, remedial equilibrium enables individuals and groups to experiment with new forms of life, even as they look over their shoulders at what they have left behind. The more sub-publics we possess, the greater chance that individuals will be able to engage in 'experiments in living' that may enable them to flourish.

3. *Evolutionary Epistemology*

Chapter 2's theory of the self contends that trial and error offers a profitable way of understanding individual behaviour, conscious and unconscious. From simple to complex actions, individuals use their cognitive modalities to sample or to test their environment, and to come up with the best possible solutions to the problem with which they are confronted. Because much of what we do as individuals is not conscious (that is, behaviour of which we are largely unaware), Donald Campbell insists that 'a blind-variation and selective-retention process is fundamental to all inductive achievements, to all genuine increases in fit of system to environment.'[65] Blind-variation and selective-retention (BVSR) processes turn, in Karl Popper's nomenclature, on 'the process of proposing conjectures (blind variation) followed by the refutation (selective elimination) of those conjectures that are empirically false.'[66] Campbell ultimately claims that BVSR explains all systems of knowledge – not merely scientific domains. More dramatically, BVSR is said to underlie all creative endeavours.

This account of how trial and error in both cognitive and non-cognitive processes leads to greater adaptive fit may sound a great deal like a form of evolutionary epistemology. It is. The attraction of this account is that it simultaneously explains the importance (ineluctability) of constraint and the mechanisms required for change.[67] By attending to the mechanisms of change in blind-variation and selective-retention processes, we can then suggest how 'experiments' (trials) ought to take place in the formation of social policy by political actors. (That prescriptive endeavour will be reflected in my account of experimental constitutionalism in Chapter 4.)

Blind-variation and selective-retention processes – or universal selection theory – fits my previous account of the constitutive nature of the self and the social, because it does not require – indeed it eschews – undetermined (or overtly 'free') accounts of how change occurs both at the level of the individual and the social. Universal selection theory – which places blind-variation and selective-retention processes at the core of human development – consists of four basic claims.

First, a blind-variation and selective-retention process is fundamental to all inductive achievements, to all general increases in knowledge, to all increases of fit of system to environment. Second, any BVSR system possesses three essential elements: mechanisms for introducing variation; consistent selection processes; and mechanisms for preserving and/or propagating the selected variations. Note that, in general, the preservation mechanisms and the variation generation mechanisms are inherently at odds, and each must be compromised. Third, the many processes which short-cut a fuller blind-variation and selective-retention process are themselves inductive achievements, containing wisdom about the environment achieved originally by blind-variation and selective-retention. Fourth, in addition, such short-cut processes contain in their own operation a BSVR process that substitutes for overt loco-motor exploration or the life and death winnowing of organic evolution.[68]

Were these four claims about BVSR processes limited to the discoveries in biology of the mechanisms which explain the emergence and the evolution of species and their adaptive characteristics, then we might have reason to be sceptical about their application to individual cognitive processes, social processes and political processes. But this explanation fits what we know from immunology about the production of effective antibodies,[69] from neuroscience about how the brain 'selects' some neuronal-synaptic connections over others,[70] and from psychology about how creative persons are able to produce novel, diverse and often more fruitful ideas.[71]

One common critique of evolutionary epistemology or 'invisible hand' explanations of knowledge processes in the natural sciences is that they ostensibly treat each actor – in this case, the scientist – as if she is a wholly autonomous individual without the need, the desire or the experience of relationships with other scientists. Mirowski rejects that contention and states the obvious: scientists operate in communities that reflect varying degrees of integration and co-operation.[72] As Hull points out, all that is necessary for 'invisible hand' explanations of knowledge processes (in the natural sciences) to work is that 'sometimes these individuals act in relative autonomy from each other with respect to the general good at issue and that within the groups that they form, an important concern is looking out for themselves.'[73] They do not require that self-interest be the only motivation, nor that all the mechanisms by which the knowledge system produces truth or useful conclusions be 'invisible' to the participants.[74] While there is little sense in comparing, on aggregate, the virtue of scientists, with the virtue of politicians, priests or philosophers, it seems worth noting that scientists are, by and large, motivated by a desire to produce knowledge for knowledge's sake. This motivation is a necessary feature of a system in which the truth – the product of a scientific experiment – is contingent upon the recognition and the acceptance of the truths established by a whole community of scholars. They are contingent in two distinct ways. First, the truth of the hypothesis is dependent upon a body of knowledge that the scientist did not create. Second, the truth of the hypothesis – its value in the broader scientific community and beyond – is dependent upon the willingness of the scientist to rely upon the findings of others (and thus give them the credit they deserve), with the expectation that they will return that respect if the scientist's own experimental result turns out to be true.

Having at once established the relative virtue of scientists, I have also drawn attention to the manner in which natural science knowledge processes fits the general model of 'invisible-hand' or 'spontaneous order' explanations. First, the scientists are still motivated by the desire to produce valuable work for which they receive express – or at least implicit – credit. This motivation underlies the many races – and consequent disputes – about who really arrived at the truth first – Darwin or Wallace, with respect to natural selection, Gallo or Montagnier, with respect to the virus that causes AIDS.[75] Second, although scientists rarely bother to replicate the experiments of others in order to prove the actual findings of others – *no glory there* – they do attempt to discover error in the work of others and do receive credit for demonstrating that previous work contains falsehoods of one sort or another. Thus, with respect to error, science operates 'as a self-policing system of mutual exploitation, or, if you prefer, co-operation'.[76] But like all invisible hand processes, no one person determines the validity or the invalidity of truth statements, and no one person organizes a regime that determines which hypotheses are tested and how. Because the commitment to truth, and the rewards and the punishments that attach to genuine discoveries and to the failure to produce reliable results, constitute the core values of the scientific community, no central authority is required for policing its individual members.[77]

How then does this epistemology of blind-variation and selective-retention in knowledge processes fit with my previous account of the involuntariness of social associations and the constraints that they impose on individual and group identity? First, our social practices – including the blind-variation and selective-retention knowledge processes in science – provide stores of collective wisdom about what works and what doesn't work. Second, individuals and groups – individual scientists and their teams – do not need to 'know' all there is to 'know' about how a particular social practice functions in order to make use of it and in order to undertake experiments within it. Third, the capacity for critique of our practices is imminent within all our practices. The space for critique in our social practices – large in science, somewhat smaller in religion – expands our individual and collective capacity for critical engagement with our beliefs. Fourth, the stronger our collective commitment to experimentation is – that is, the larger and more varied our critical community is – the more varied our individual lives are likely to be. The blind-variation and selective-retention in knowledge processes such as science provide a good example of how experimentation creates more and more successful models of the world.[78]

4. *Limits of Evolutionary Epistemology & Spontaneous Orders*

On Campbell's view, social scientists who press for an 'experimenting society' ought not to be misread as proposing that social scientists set the political agenda.[79] Social experimentalism accepts that 'preponderantly unscientific political processes' will determine 'ameliorative program initiatives'.[80] The role of the social scientist in a social experimentalist program is to help decision-makers and citizens alike assess the success of an initiative in achieving its goals and in avoiding deleterious consequences.

It is not, therefore, ironic that advocates of social experimentalism tend to be rather modest about the contributions that social science can offer politics. Where non-experimentalists tend to fall into the over-advocacy trap – offering advice, but little subsequent analysis – experimentalists generally tend to eschew advocacy. This reserve flows from the recognition that many areas of social policy construction are notoriously resistant to experimental assessment.

Given their relative agnosticism as to what the best practices in a given area of social policy ought to be, how do proponents of social experimentalism expect to advance the goals of an experimental society? At least two general answers are offered.

First, the assessment of the experiments themselves ought to be undertaken by as large a number of independent social scientists as possible. As David Hull and Donald Campbell both note, science works best under conditions of 'competitive cross-validation'. Roger Merton shows how the 'organized scepticism' of a scientific community – in which a systemic level of distrust is married to personal ambition – leads scientists, individually and as members of research teams, to monitor one another for theoretical advances that actually improve the ability to carry out their own programs. Genuine theoretical advances need not be replicated – and indeed rarely are. They need only prove useful to others. Should the alleged theoretical advance prove unreliable – and ultimately erroneous – the scientist or the scientists responsible will be subject to communal opprobrium. The 'organized distrust' that produces 'trustworthy reports' is enhanced when our independent social scientists bring their respective critical skills to bear on a data set that is apt to be analyzed by other evaluators.[81]

Second, social experimentalists tend to advocate funding numerous local programs to address chronic problems. Only once a local program announces success would it be subject to scientific evaluation. As Campbell notes:

> Evaluation research is clearly something done by, or at least tolerated by, a government in power. It presumes a stable social system generating social indicators that remain relatively constant in meaning so that they can be used to measure the program's impact. The programs that are implemented must be small enough not to seriously disturb the encompassing social measurement system. Thus the technology I have been discussing is not available to measure the social impact of a revolution.[82]

Though individual improvements may only incrementally alter an experimentalist society, the cumulative effect of myriad experiments can be fundamental and *revolutionary*.[83] That claim is a central feature of this work. We shall see it at work again below when discussing choice architecture and further on when assessing the merits of experimental constitutionalism. For now, it is enough to note that the political agnosticism of advocates of spontaneous orders and evolutionary epistemology raise flags for constitutional scholars committed to significant normative change.

C. Better Descriptions and Prescriptions for the Social: Experimentalism in State Policy

1. *Choice Architecture*

a. *Cognitive Biases in Deliberative Practices*

A far more powerful empirical engine for social change – and a theory with prescriptive charge – has come out of recent work by legal theorist and political scientist Cass Sunstein and economist and behavioural scientist Richard Thaler. For years, Sunstein appeared so consumed by doubt about grand theorizing that it led him to something akin to pyrrhonian scepticism with regard to constitutional theory.[84] But Sunstein's scepticism ultimately gave way to empirical analysis. In *Infotopia*, Sunstein developed a critique of deliberative politics as a constructive form of information aggregation and decision-making that identified four basic forms of information aggregation and two deleterious influences on the manner in which we arrive at collective decisions. Sunstein's four basic forms of contemporary information pooling are: (1) statistical averages; (2) deliberation; (3) price or market systems; (4) Internet wikis. Pace the dominant pre-disposition of constitutional scholars, Sunstein's writings suggest that deliberation may well be the least useful of the four. He writes:

> Most of the time, both private and public institutions prefer to make decisions through some form of deliberation. ... Does deliberation actually lead to better decisions? Often it does not.[85]

To explain the failures of deliberation and the promise of other methods of aggregating information in the pursuit of better decision-making, Sunstein explores the consequences of two forces:

> The first consists of informational influences, which cause group members to fail to disclose what they know out of respect for the information publicly pronounced by others. ... The second force involves social pressures, which lead people to silence themselves to avoid the disapproval of peers or supervisors. Even if you believe that group members are blundering, you might not want to say a word because you do not want to risk their disapproval.[86]

Eliot Fishman, Michael Fisher and I have identified similar kinds of failures in deliberation when it comes to patent thickets or anti-commons effects in complex biopharmaceutical technologies.[87] A patent thicket is 'a dense web of overlapping intellectual property rights that a company must hack its way through in order to actually commercialize new technology.'[88] Hypothetically, multiple parties would always negotiate in their own best interest and expect a royalty no greater (nor less) than their proportional contribution to the commercialized product. Indeed, some authors have offered algorithmic guidance with regard to the appropriate attribution of equities in respect to sequential inventions that require cross licensing in order to create a marketable good.[89] Yet, negotiations often break down. In coining the neologism 'patent thickets', Heller and Eisenberg submit that several reasons exist for the failure of perfectly 'rational' actors – the patent holders – to fail to deliver well-designed novel, commercially viable products to downstream markets: (1) high transaction costs, (2) the heterogeneous interests of rights holders, (3) cognitive biases of license holders and (4) attributive biases of the participants.[90] Not surprisingly, ordinary owners of upstream biomedical or pharmaceutical research patents tend, like human beings generally, to overvalue their own contributions and property.[91]

But let's look at another extremely well-known case of heterogeneous interests, attributive bias and cognitive bias. In 2003, the US Central Intelligence Agency provided the White House with a memorandum regarding the alleged presence of Weapons of Mass Destruction (WMDs) in Iraq. The memo concluded – wrongly as we now know – that such WMDs (or the immediate makings thereof) already existed. A popular line of thought – propagated by Sunstein himself at the time (ooops!) – is that a CIA guilty of groupthink 'caused it to fail to explore alternative possibilities and to obtain and use the information that its employees held.'[92] The US Senate Select Committee on Intelligence on Weapons of Mass Destruction in Iraq arrived at the same erroneous conclusion.[93] In point of fact, a different deliberation/information aggregation gremlin was responsible: 'the big dog in the room'. As Fulton Armstrong indisputably shows, the CIA possessed a significant number of dissenting analyses regarding WMDs in Iraq: and the responsible analysts made their scepticism known.[94] However, after some 8 visits to the CIA by then US Vice-President Cheney, and constant combat with the Department of Defence – both of whom actively sought information that would support the administration's desire to initiate a war with Iraq – the CIA gave in to the pressure and delivered the desired cover for the invasion. The doubts within the CIA and within the State Department were relegated to a single footnote. (Actually, that's only one version of the problem. As Ron Suskind writes, the CIA handed George W Bush a memorandum entitled 'Bin Laden Determined to Strike in US' a month before the successful attacks on the World Trade Centre on 11 September 2001. Bush's reply to his well-informed briefer: 'All right. You've covered your ass now.'[95] That's one big stupid dog. However, it's consistent with what we do know about the attention span and modus operandi of that US President.)

b. Overcoming Cognitive Biases

Such empirical findings (even those that contradicted Sunstein's initial assessment) led Sunstein to delve deeper into problems with deliberative political mechanisms and into everyday social biases, aversion, blunders, (false) assumptions, inertia, herd following and temptations that lead all of us to make everyday mistakes. Having identified good and bad social choice mechanisms in *Infotopia,* Sunstein produced a work in 'choice architecture': *Nudge.*[96] Although still committed to rooting out biases that lead to suboptimal outcomes, Thaler and Sunstein show us how to devise environments – for cafeterias, school choice systems, organ donation, prescription drug programmes and airport urinals – that lead to better outcomes. By better outcomes, Thaler and Sunstein mean environments that enable individuals to change their deleterious choice defaults into more positive choice defaults without forcing or coercing individual actions.

Thaler and Sunstein first introduce the notion of a 'choice architect'. A choice architect 'has the responsibility for organizing the context in which people make their decisions'.[97] Fathers, lecturers, doctors, politicians, bureaucrats, CEOs, owenrs of spaza shops, computer programmers, traditional leaders, internet portal designers, ballot devisers, are all choice architects: virtually any occupation with responsibility turns the responsible individual into a choice architect.

Two examples of choice architects are worth considering at the outset.

Thaler and Sunstein's first 'choice architect' – Carolyn – is a cafeteria supervisor for an extremely large school system (say over 50 schools). The question: how should she design cafeterias in a manner that optimizes learner choices – and makes them 'healthier'. Of course, she could also design the cafeterias in a manner that maximizes efficiency or increases a school's profit (for profit's sake alone). But such normative choices are not on the table for a school superintendent. Assuming she does not know, in advance, everything about cafeteria architecture, her best bet would be to arrange the exact same food groups and other specific items in different places within the 50 different school cafeterias. Over time, each school would reveal patterns of selection based in significant part on where the foods were placed. (Research demonstrates that students do not have genuinely 'true preferences', but often have their preferences determined by access and availability.[98]) The choice architect would, after a few months, be able to discern where to place certain foods so as to 'nudge' students into making healthier choices – 'as judged by themselves'.[99] The supervisor isn't taking food off the shelves and the racks. She is merely placing those foods in places that either maximize or diminish the likelihood of their selection. Thaler and Sunstein describe Carolyn's ingenious experiment as follows:

> Without changing any menus, [she] would run experiments in her schools to determine whether the way the food is displayed and arranged might influence the choices kids make. Carolyn gave the directors of dozens of school cafeterias instructions on how to display the food choices. In some schools the desserts were placed first, in others last, in still others a separate line. In some schools, the French fries, but in others the carrot sticks, were at eye level. ... Simply by rearranging the cafeteria, Carolyn was able to increase or decrease the consumption of food items by as much as 25 percent. Carolyn learned a big lesson: school children, like adults, can be greatly influenced by small changes in context.[100]

Carolyn, as a choice architect, has the ability to craft an environment that enables people to make more optimal choices, for themselves, without overt coercion.

A second, less seemly, instance of choice architecture was undertaken by the management of Schipol Airport in Amsterdam. After undertaking a number of experiments designed to increase hygiene in the men's bathroom, the management found that placing a picture of a large black fly on a urinal increased accurate 'aim' by 80%. Men, it would appear, like having a target. The target nudges them in the direction of good hygiene: an outcome that was of benefit to all bathroom users. (These flies have become ubiquitous in public toilets – and they work for me. Hit the fly!)

Notice that in both instances that the choice architects were able to coax 'free' agents to make choices that were better 'as judged by themselves' and better as judged by the choice architects in terms of the overall welfare of the community that they served. (The last clause reminds us that one must always have a normative departure point in any decision-making setting.)

These two improvements – better for the individual and better for the social group as a whole – is what leads Thaler and Sunstein to call their political theory 'libertarian paternalism'. They define their cheekily named theory as follows:

> The libertarian aspect of our strategies lies in the straightforward insistence that people, in general, should be free to do what they like – and to opt out of undesirable arrangements if they want to do so. ... When we use the term libertarian to modify paternalism, we simply mean liberty preserving.'[101] 'The paternalistic aspect lies in the claim that it is legitimate for choice architects to try to influence people's behaviour in order to make their lives longer, healthier and better. In other words, we argue for self-conscious efforts, by institutions in the private sector and also by government, to steer people's choices in directions that will improve their lives. In our understanding, a policy is paternalistic if it tries to influence choices in a way that will make choosers better off, as judged by themselves. Drawing on some well-established findings in social science, we show that in many cases, individuals make pretty bad decisions – decisions they would not have made if they had paid full attention and possessed complete information, unlimited cognitive abilities and complete self-control.'[102]

In the next section and at the end of this chapter, I demonstrate – with examples drawn from environmental protection to corporate strategy – how nudges work (as experiments) across a broad range of human practices.

Although I shall devote a significant amount of space in Chapters 4 through 8 to demonstrating how constitutional doctrines and political institutions can be better understood in terms of experimental constitutionalism and how a commitment to experimental constitutionalism better serves human flourishing, it is worth noting here that there is a large and varied literature in the social sciences devoted to the promotion of experimentation in statecraft. The epistemic and political foundations of this literature are very much of a piece with the core epistemic and political foundations of experimental constitutionalism. In short, both bodies of work recognize the constraints that 'the social' places on change and both bodies of work concur that the state – as things currently stand – is in the best position to break the bottlenecks in the social that prevent individuals and groups from undertaking genuine experiments in living. Both bodies of work endorse the proposition that the state – if properly organized – is in the best position both to support and to monitor these experiments in living and, ultimately, to ratify, even if it is in only the most provisional way, the best practices that arise out of these various experiments in living. Again: Though individual improvements may only incrementally alter an experimentalist society, the cumulative effect of myriad experiments can be fundamental and revolutionary.

It's worth noting, here, the broad array of experiments that have been performed to 'nudge' participants toward more 'optimal' forms of behaviour (as judged at the time of the experiment). Thaler and Sunstein identify how everything from charitable giving,[103] automatic tax returns,[104] the wearing of motorcycle helmets,[105] the tying of insurance rates to health club usage,[106] and civility check programmes on e-mails,[107] can increase the health, the wealth, the happiness and the well-being of persons who subject themselves to even the gentlest of nudges. These nudges may appear trivial, but they demonstrate the larger point that significant change is possible without broad top-down, centrally-planned, social engineering. Consistent with the theory of self, outlined in Chapter 2, we can alter 'the social' without making grand and unjustified claims about our conscious capacity to overcome deeply engrained default positions.

2. *The Virtues (and Vices) of Social Capital: Using Bonding Networks and Bridging Networks to Foster Change*

Recall Putnam's distinction between the two primary forms of social capital or networks:

> Some forms of capital are, by choice or necessity, inward looking and tend to reinforce exclusive identities and homogeneous groups. Examples of bonding social capital include ethnic fraternal organizations, church-based women's reading groups, and fashionable country clubs. Other networks are outward looking and encompass people across diverse social cleavages. Examples of bridging social capital include the civil rights movement, many youth service groups, and ecumenical religious organizations ... Bonding social capital provides a kind of sociological superglue whereas bridging social capital provides a sociological WD-40.[108]

Now consider some actual policy choices undertaken by our own National Department of Education. (These policy choices will be discussed in further detail in Chapter 6.) For example, our unintended, but clearly recognized, system of school choice enables learners to move from school to school in search of an educational environment that best fits their needs and economic status. (Learner movement in South Africa – driven by parents – across provinces and within provinces is quite significant: and the drive by parents is to find better schools for their children.) School fees, on the other hand, are governed by a scheme of exemptions that ensures that some degree of cross-subsidization and desegregation will occur in urban and peri-urban schools. (Children of live-in domestic servants have rights of equal access to local primary schools. Children of individuals who work within a given district also possess rights of access to these same primary schools.) In both instances, engagement across race and class holds out the promise of the creation of bridging networks over time. Bridging networks can, in turn, become bonding networks that create broader access to the rich stores of social capital that they contain. The powers granted School Governing Bodies recognize both the importance of grass roots democracy and the bonding networks that enable schools to maintain their ability to deliver an adequate education to learners (including those learners who cross the bridge from other communities).[109]

3. *Radically Heterogeneous Selves and Societies as Engines for Change*

In chapter 2, we discussed change that occurs through the friction created by the various selves that 'populate' a single corporeal *radically heterogeneous* determined 'me'. We saw that the multiple roles that we individuals have been conditioned to play make different demands upon us and often pull us in dramatically different directions. In this chapter, I want to begin to tease out the lineaments of a related thesis: that a *radically heterogeneous society* (such as that of South Africa) populated by a *radically heterogeneous population of individuals* can be an engine for *revolutionary change*.

But let's back up. How does this particular theory of the self and the social bring about change? Recall that the radical heterogeneity of the self shows us how change occurs without the attribution of 'free will'. Each dispositional state or role reflects its own set of responses to the surrounding environment. I find myself regularly challenged by my each of my roles as son, partner, professor, director, golfer, disabled person, English speaker, editor, author, friend, committee member, supervisor, employer, citizen, dancer, moviegoer, lawyer, consultant, Jew, New Yorker, Jo'burger, Caucasian, poet, cook, driver, professor with an endowed chair, American, South African, atheist, utilitarian, egalitarian, libertarian, 48 year old, sexually active heterosexual (without fetishes), union member, feminist, golf club member, owner of a closed corporation, homeowner and gardener – just to name a few. Not only does the discharge of the responsibilities of each role or dispositional state itself pose a challenge (they call work 'work' for a reason), the attempt to reconcile all these roles without conflict is simply impossible. Change often comes – is forced upon us – when we must choose the good or the end to which we must give priority in a given set of circumstances. The complexity – and the friction between roles – does not end with our own corporeal selves.

As part of our social life in non-totalitarian societies, we are confronted daily with *other* equally complex radically heterogeneous selves with whom we must carry out innumerable transactions and who carry out their own roles in ways that invariably pose challenges to our current preferred ways of being. We are confronted with an environment – neither of our making or choosing – that constantly demands that we alter, sometimes ever so slightly, sometimes dramatically, who we are and what roles we play. Disruption and confrontation are part of life, however much we try to hold such challenges at bay.

We have, within our own body of South African constitutional law jurisprudence, intimations as to how selves and groups can dramatically change without top-down social engineering. Such hints can be found in the opinions of Justice Emeritus Albie Sachs.

Sachs is certainly not interested in formal forms of liberalism that preserve the status quo, nor does he confine his legal imagination to the protection of all sorts of discrete and insular minorities. Sachs writes, early on in his judicial career 'that the emancipatory elimination of institutionalised prejudice against gays and lesbians will encourage amongst the heterosexual population a greater sensitivity to the variability of the human kind'.[110] Sachs places sexual difference and sexual desire – and its radical heterogeneity of form – at the heart of what it means to be human. He challenges the majority of South Africans to acknowledge the acceptance of their own inevitably idiosyncratic sexuality (and we are all idiosyncratic in and outside the bedroom) in the hope that it will connect them more powerfully to the idiosyncratic sexuality of others and thereby forge a democratic solidarity through the recognition that we are each entitled to 'equal space' to be ourselves and to explore – with the support of others – that which makes each of us unique.

Again and again, Sachs returns, in dissenting and concurring judgments, to various forms of difference and the potential they hold out for radical change. In *Daniels v Campbell NO*, he places customary Muslim marriages on an equal footing with their legally sanctioned civil counterparts.[111] In *Volks*, Sachs rejects the majority's finding that the appellant, 'having chosen cohabitation rather than marriage ... must bear the consequences' and thus could not avail herself of the benefits of the Maintenance of Surviving Spouses Act.[112] In *Prince* – a case not about sex but about the equally challenging practice of drug use in religious rituals – Justice Sachs articulates his notion of a 'right to be different'.[113] In demanding that his colleagues, the state and his fellow citizens 'walk the extra mile' when it comes to marginal publics such as the 10,000 Rastafarians that inhabit South Africa, Sachs writes:

> Intolerance may come in many forms. At its most spectacular and destructive it involves the use of power to crush beliefs and practices considered alien and threatening. At its more benign it may operate through a set of rigid mainstream norms which do not permit the possibility of alternative forms of conduct.[114]

He then comes close to accusing those who view dagga use as dangerous of being in the grip of a blinkered hypocrisy. (They hold no such prejudices about alcohol.) He writes:

> In *Christian Education* this Court held that a number of provisions in the Constitution affirmed 'the right of people to be who they [were] without being forced to subordinate themselves to the cultural and religious norms of others, and highlight the importance of individuals and communities being able to enjoy what has been called the "*right to be different*". In each case, space [had] been found for members of communities [in our democracy] to depart from a general norm.[115]

Democracy in a society of radically heterogeneous selves and radically heterogeneous communities, Sachs seems to be saying, presupposes the capability of marginalised and vulnerable minorities to challenge the normative closure into which political communities tend to lapse. A society can only remain free if it values plurality and difference, and allows out-groups to disturb and to challenge deeply held majoritarian beliefs and practices. For this reason, the critical challenge for our constitutional 'democracy' consists 'not in accepting what is familiar and easily accommodated, but in giving reasonable space to what is "unusual, bizarre or even threatening"'.

'Unusual, bizarre or even threatening' – such a vision of the social order ties the ability of individuals to *re-imagine* their own identities to the capacity of society for change, or quiet, piecemeal revolution.[116] Of the relationship between the 'romantic-liberal' view of society and the struggle of out-groups for recognition, Frank Michelman writes:

> A chief aim of the romantic-liberal constitution must be to free 'the life-chances of the individual from the tyranny of social categories' of 'classes, sexes, and nations'. The benefit accrues not only to the emancipated: it is structural and systemic, and accrues to everyone. Everyone, in the romantic view, has reason to welcome confrontation and challenge of his or her accustomed or habitual ways and values, from all quarters known and unknown. Democracy accordingly becomes not just a procedural but a substantive ideal.[117]

But what is the content of that radically heterogeneous ideal? In *Minister of Home Affairs v Fourie (Doctors for Life International, Amici Curiae); Lesbian and Gay Equality Project v Minister of Home Affairs*, Sachs (writing for a Constitutional Court finally on the Sachs J bandwagon) argues that:

> [O]ur Constitution represents a *radical rupture* with a past based on intolerance and exclusion, and the movement forward to the acceptance of the need to develop a society based on equality and

> respect by all for all. Small gestures in favour of equality, however meaningful, are not enough. ... The Constitution thus acknowledges the variability of human beings (genetic and socio-cultural), affirms the right to be different, and celebrates the diversity of the nation. Accordingly, what is at stake is not simply a question of removing an injustice experienced by a particular section of the community. At issue is a need to affirm the very character of our society as one based on tolerance and mutual respect. The test of tolerance is not how one finds space for people with whom, and practices with which, one feels comfortable, but how one accommodates the expression of what is discomfiting.[118]

What stands out in these various judgments is that the society Sachs has in mind takes us beyond the franchise, beyond formal equality, beyond tolerance for each group doing its own thing. In his radically heterogeneous democracy, only the actual recognition and material support for difference across individuals, groups and the country as a whole is sufficient. But it does more than require an appreciation for difference. It views, as Frank Michelman suggests, difference as an engine for change. How so? As both Sachs and Michelman write, it occurs through the regular confrontation with ways of being in the world that are not like our own default positions. A truly democratic society made up of radically heterogeneous selves constantly forces us to acknowledge that there are other, perhaps better, ways of doing things with respect to all the various roles we undertake and all the forms of life in which we participate. Constant friction forces constant experimentation with alternative ways of being. Such constant friction at the level of 'the social' constitutes a potent engine for constructive change. (As I noted above: it is also true that a self's expression through action of multiple roles correlates closely with greater happiness. Where one role fails, another role steps in, as it were, to give life meaning. So consider multiple roles in a heterogeneous society as a recipe for both change and happiness.[119])

D. Shared Consciousness and Feedback Mechanisms

In this final section, I offer several accounts of social feedback mechanisms in action. They take us out of the confines of theory and place us back in the real world where we belong.

1. *Psychotherapy*

One initiates therapy because one believes that the manner in which one engages the world is flawed and leads to less-than-optimal outcomes. One might even borrow the language of our initial encounter with a video game: our life might appear to us as a miasma of moving objects, whose actions, including our own, appear unpredictable, their purpose opaque. The goals of therapy then are three-fold: to enable us to see, more clearly, what we do; to understand why we do it; and, where necessary, to change our orientation towards the world. We could engage in this reflective process by ourselves. Quite often, for many matters, we can engage in the kind of sustained self-reflection and critique that would otherwise count as therapy. But even if it were it possible for us to engage in that sort of endeavour, there are benefits to therapy that outstrip self-reflection.

The therapist provides two goods that the individual alone cannot provide. First, she presents a relationship – a safe, containing space – in which the patient can act out deeply ingrained patterns of behaviour in the world, patterns often rooted in early experience.[120] Second, her observant but critical voice sets out the individual's maladaptive behaviour in sharp relief. While there is no substitute for the internalisation of this critical voice, we must be able to see the errors first before we can respond constructively to them.

Again, the parallels to playing a video game jump out. Over time and with greater experience of the therapeutic process, the patient begins to note certain regularities in her behaviour and how she and the world respond to her various modes of engagement. As time goes on in therapy, certain kinds of responses to the world should become understood (if not unlearned, so deep do they run) and preferred ways of being should become 'second nature' and the default position. In therapy, and over significant stretches of time, we replace existing maladaptive dispositional states with beneficial dispositional states in such a manner that – if all goes to plan – we ultimately require no conscious awareness of those states.[121] We don't (can't) undo the extant networks, because, as I have noted in Chapter 2, our brain is a democracy with extant neural networks regularly competing for dominance. What we can do is lay down parallel neural tracks that compete with existing tracks (and try to remember to pull the right switch.[122])

2. *Legal Practice and Legal Theory*

Therapy is simply one of many conscious critical practices that enable us to focus on aspects of our environment – and hold them up for scrutiny – in order to form better behavioural responses to the environment. Legal academic life is another such practice.

This book, as I noted in the preface, is a product of such a practice. It relies to a significant degree on the legal, philosophical and scientific contributions of others. (Indeed, the originality of the book lies primarily in the application and the synthesis of these other contributions to constitutional law in South Africa.) More importantly for the argument in this section, legal academia functions as a social feedback mechanism. In 2004, I offered the first draft of the paper upon which this book is based at the Research Unit in Legal and Constitutional Interpretation Conference at the University of the Western Cape. The academic discussion there pointed up concerns about the necessity of foregrounding normative arguments regarding constitutional doctrine with a descriptive account of consciousness. The same process was repeated at the Columbia Law School Experimentalism Workshop in 2006. Concerns were the extent to which South Africa provided a desirable environment within which to establish experimental political structures. A talk at Birkbeck College, University of London, in 2008, led to a cordial, but bracing set of exchanges. Over the last few years, colleagues from the University of Pretoria, the University of the Witwatersrand and the University of Stellenbosch have all offered useful appraisals of the arguments in these pages. A visit to New York Law School in 2010 to present two new chapters provided further feedback – and the impetus to complete this book. I have managed, as a result of these various trials and interventions, to correct some of the limitations in both the individual arguments and the overall structure of the book. In my experience, sharp elbowed legal academic settings offer feedback mechanisms for error correction and truth propagation. At a minimum, the system points up logical or empirical flaws. At its best, this knowledge system initiates individual and collective efforts designed to forge new and better ways of understanding the world. Whether this particularly novel contribution leads to improved legal arrangements, or just convinces some of its audience of its truth, is another matter entirely.[123]

3. *Golf Instruction*

I have a magic Uncle Harry. Three years ago, he made a little white ball disappear. Standing on the 15th tee at the Riverside Golf Course, approximately 140 meters from the green, Harry hit a solid five iron that covered the flag. It bounced once, twice, and rolled straight into the cup. His playing buddies, Irwin and Jake, shouted: 'It went in!!!! It went in!!!' My uncle, the master of prestidigitation, had seen nothing. His failing eyesight made it impossible for him to watch his 'lucky dunk'. But the ball never lies in golf – and when Harry, Irwin and Jake reached the 15th green, Harry's ball reappeared – nestled snugly at the bottom of the hole. He has the plaque on his wall at home to prove it.

Harry is, was, a natural. A schoolyard legend in Brooklyn. When I picked up the game a few years ago – after a hiatus of 25 years – I did not have my Uncle's untutored, unstudied magic upon which to draw. I struggled. I wish that I could say that all that my coach Costanza Trusconi and I had to do was fix what was broken. But that would assume that we really had something with which to work. As it turns out, there is nothing natural or magical about the golf swing.

Constanza's first attempt at helping me to create a repeatable, effective swing failed. My body had a default position – developed from years of playing baseball, tennis and football – that ran counter to the requirements of a repeatable golf swing. So we started again.

First, we began with my address. We kept my feet planted and still – throughout the swing. Second, we further refined my address. Now I stood straight and bent slightly at the hips, 'eyes over the ball', ass out. Only the slightest flex of the knees was allowed. For the untrained body, this exercise was hard: for all the tension (work) lay in my lower back, glutes, hamstrings and quadriceps. Third, we allowed my hands to hang down, relaxed, before I initiated my takeaway with my left shoulder. Fourth, we began to work on undoing the flatness of my swing. Here's a truth about the body: it will lie to you. It could never lie to Stansi. So while it seemed to me (on the course) that my backswing was vertical – and though it even appeared okay on videotape – Stansi could see – on the range – what I could not. My shoulders, arms and hands were not where they were supposed to be. So we worked on my takeaway – a solid feature of my swing. Now, however, my arms and hands came up and away from my sternum, and my wrists cocked at the top. It felt – and looked – from my perspective on the range – entirely wrong. The videotape does not lie. They were where they were supposed to be. We worked still more on my finish: hips and chest turned toward the target, arms relaxed behind my head, weight posted firmly on my left side. (I had learned to rotate my body around a single axis. What makes the golf swing so difficult is that a truly good swing requires rotation around three discrete axes.)

Solution. Success. No so fast. After many, many months, we had reprogrammed my body and my brain so as to create a repeatable swing. But after a year of hard academic work and almost no golf, my defaults returned with a vengeance. And so we started again – keeping what was still good: remembering to stay rooted and quiet in my lower body, turning along the same axis back and through the ball to a proper finish. Constanza, my teacher, could apply her keen eye and understanding of golf theory to the movement of my body. But it remains up to me to make the practice and the theory meaningful. The ball never lies. If it flies on an errant course, however, I know enough to ask several questions: Where did I finish? Were my feet rooted? Did I cock my wrists prior to reaching the top of the swing? Was the tempo of my swing (roughly) the same going forward as going back? Did I finish with my weight on a straight left leg, arms relaxed, with club and hands behind my head and back. Instant empirical *feedback* and an opportunity to put a little theory back into practice.[124]

The First Moral of the Story: We can all use a good coach – in golf and in virtually all of our endeavours. We need feedback supplied by coaches and critics who can see what we cannot – just as we saw in our analysis of legal theory – where we are going, and where we are going wrong. We need exercises designed so as to train ourselves not to constantly fall back into our unhelpful default positions. What's true in golf is true in law.[125]

The Second Moral of the Story: Watch yourself swing a golf club on film. Then bring the insights and collective wisdom of millions of golfers – and your professional golf coach Stansi – to bear on what you are doing right and what you are doing wrong. Go out and repeat the drills designed to bring it all together. Suddenly you are part of a social practice in which centuries of *trial and error* put us in a position to correct mistakes – at the individual level. Go down to the pro shop and look at the new range of clubs designed to improve play. All of a sudden you are part of a social practice in which centuries of trial and error have put manufacturers of equipment in a position to make improvements to ball and club design – at the collective level. Golf, so understood, reveals itself to be a social practice in which the downward causation of multiple participants enables all boats to rise – at least a little – without any one person or any one authority responsible for such a rise.[126]

Therapy, legal theory and golf – forms of shared consciousness – are just three examples of social feedback mechanisms. In our highly differentiated, extraordinarily heterogeneous society, innumerable other individual and collective efforts will allow us to reflect more effectively upon our actions and, where necessary, to come up with better solutions to the way in which we engage the world. One not so surprising source of experimentation and successful innovation are corporations. They are forced, when markets work efficiently and are regulated properly, to find better, cheaper ways of producing products than their competitors. Or, they are forced to produce new products that perform better than extant products on the market. As I shall suggest below, the benefits of such innovation often flow to the larger communities within which they operate – and not only to shareholders.

4 *Corporations and Climate Change*

We have already seen how markets enable actors to behave in a rational, self-interested fashion that does not require a central planner to solve social problems. But, as we all know, markets fail and corporations do not attempt, by and large, to provide a whole array of what we have come to know as public goods: education, roads, law enforcement, national defence, social security, a clean environment and a minimum core of basic necessities for life: water, food, health, housing. This chapter's exploration of social experimentation (and the varied uses of nudging) suggests a third way: (a) that the public sector along with a broad array of other actors – industrial partners, NGOs, academics and, of course, consumers – should take an active role in shaping the space within which corporations and companies operate and nudge them towards the realization of pressing public goods that neither the public sector nor the private sector appear to be able to realize on their own (eg, new energy generation technology that addresses climate change); (b) that incentives for co-operative incentivized arrangements can drive the private sector itself as firms recognize that their long term survival is contingent upon (i) the existence of sufficient energy sources, (ii) the creation of technologies that enable reuse of scarce natural sources such as water, (iii) a clean environment within which their employees can flourish, and (iv) stable, skilled local communities that provide the firm with on-going social licenses to operate. General Electric stands out amongst multinationals as a firm that has ostensibly shifted its strategy to align with the 'third' way described above.[127]

GE's *Ecomagination Report* reflects co-operative efforts designed to achieve triple bottom line goals of environmental protection, economic development and enhanced community participation at the same time as it fattens the single bottom line that matters most to shareholders. GE already has over half a dozen Environmental Protection Agency Energy Star endorsed products in its stable of goods.[128] It also readily acknowledges the value of other US government incentives and partnerships – such as the US Recovery and Reinvestment Act of 2009.[129] But GE – a behemoth amongst multinationals – has not been content to work with government agencies within US borders. The China Mainline Evolution Locomotive, the Kazakhstan Evolution ES44ACi Locomotive and the Russian-Built Locomotive Modernization Skids are but three co-operative green tech efforts undertaken with other governments. In 2011, South Africa purchased 10 new GE high energy efficient trains, because it knows that Eskom cannot supply current short term needs and might not be able to supply reliable long term energy requirements. The agreement with GE also calls for 90 more trains to be built in South Africa (with the parts supplied by GE) – thus creating direct economic benefits to the community within which GE conducts its business. Co-operative efforts sponsored by other states interested in green technologies and green savings often take the form of what GE calls an 'Energy Treasure Hunt'.[130] These co-operative endeavours not only serve environmentally friendly ends and GE's bottom line: the company shares its proprietary IT with partners who will, invariably, generate new green technologies.

I want to continue to emphasize for the moment the importance of collaborative efforts between the public sector and the private sector because only such 'choice architecture' is likely to lead to optimal environmental outcomes. International collective action – that rewards both hard choices and innovation – is required to solve problems associated with climate change. States alone have failed dismally to demonstrate the requisite commitment to achieving meaningful rollbacks of greenhouse-causing carbon emissions. Durban 2011 proved no better than Copenhagen on making good the promise of Kyoto. In the current economic environment (with a long term recessionary forecast), curbing consumption patterns in China, India or the United States is unlikely to secure any political traction. While Cassandra's cries may fall on deaf ears, proper regulatory regimes might be able to harness private initiatives geared toward making humanity's global footprint more and more carbon neutral.

Take GE's wind powered efforts in Europe. The EU is committed to a 20% reduction in gashouse emissions by 2020: wind turbines supply one answer. GE ScanWind turbines currently operating in Hundhammerfjellet will soon be able to meet a sizeable amount of Norway's electricity demands. (And Norway is already an oil-rich country.) In co-operation with the largest utility in Central Europe, GE recently supplied 139 giant 2.5xl wind turbines. In the next phase, GE Energy will supply 101 more. When complete, this site will produce enough wind-generated electricity to meet the needs of more than 400,000 EU homes. Finally, two projects in Romania will generate more than 600 megawatts of wind power by 2011. GE itself notes that

> A key reason for the new wind farm's location is Romania's new pro-renewables legislation. The Romanian government has created legislation that is favourable to the development of renewable energy resources, granting significant incentives for wind farms and other renewable energy projects through 2015. [These incentives] have encouraged investors and developers to pursue projects in the country.[131]

Once again, co-operation between the public sector and the private sector has driven innovation, and served both the public good and the bottom line. The takeaway: when governments overcome problems of collective action and create regulatory and legislative structures attractive to corporations and companies, private initiatives often rush in to fill the gap. Choice architecture can be the mother of invention.[132]

At the same time, GE recognizes that all the new green technology in the world will be of little use unless governments create adequate incentives for their use by the public:

> Water reuse technologies can help public and private sector decision-makers in water-scarce regions throughout the world successfully tackle the growing problem of water scarcity. However, these technologies cannot be deployed in sufficient quantities as long as withdrawing water from a river or a well is less expensive than conserving or reusing it. So the next big challenge lies in identifying and implementing institutional, legal and regulatory reforms that boost the price and marketability of water supplies while providing adequate social and environmental safeguards.[133]

Here again is the space that 'choice architects' in the public sector and the private sector need to fill – with the kinds of incentives that nudge producers and users of scarce resources in substantially more optimal directions. GE has heard the music and sees the future. That future will remain bleak without the right kinds of public-private partnerships.[134] I will hedge my bets here and note that until greater international collective political action occurs on climate control, environmental benefits are likely to be segmented and insufficient to bring the world's ecology back into balance. Collective action on the scale required must take us far beyond what Thaler and Sunstein's smaller scale 'nudges' can accomplish.

Endnotes

1. But they are often not well-regulated. Take, for example, the use of coal as an energy source. Most regulatory schemes prod electricity generators that use coal toward environmentally friendly results through subsidies. Such subsidies serve primarily as tax havens. If the externalities of (extremely

dirty) coal-driven electricity production – pollution, health care and green-house gas climate change – were made a part of the cost of coal-fired electricity through taxation, South Africa could probably eliminate all its debts and fund its natural health insurance scheme. In the United States, coal generated electricity, if appropriately taxed just to account for the costs associated with pollution, would rise from 9.0 cents to 15.2 cents per kilowatt hour. According to the National Health Council's Committee on Health, Environmental and Other External Costs and Benefits of Energy Production and Consumption, a tax that captured all the social costs of pollution would make a substantial dent in the US federal debt (paying it off in roughly a decade), lower consumption and prompt the creation of greener, competitive technologies. *Hidden Costs of Energy: Unpriced Consequences of Energy Production and Use* (2011). But that route is profoundly political – and few countries, South Africa or the United States, possess politicians with the stomach for such hard choices. See, eg, W Nordhaus *Warming the World: Economic Models of Global Warming* (2003); W Nordhaus *Managing the Global Commons: The Economic Models of Climate Change* (1994). For the possibility of a commons in such goods in South Africa, see D Roithmayr 'Lessons from *Mazibuko*: Persistent Inequality and the Commons' (2010) 3 *Constitutional Court Review* 347.

2. See D Dennett *Freedom Evolves* (2003).
3. M Walzer 'On Involuntary Association' in A Gutmann (ed) *Freedom of Association* (1998) 64, 67.
4. The Chinese cultural revolution looked to the Jacobin period of the French Revolution (once its Athenian moment had been displaced.) The Khmer Rouge Cambodian revolution looked to its Chinese Marxist predecessors and to traditional forms of agricultural organization.
5. Walzer 'On Involuntary Association' (supra) at 70.
6. The forms of 'bewitchment' found in our accounts of free will or voluntary social practices is grounded in the mistaken belief that we first form theories about the world and then test these theories against experience. Not so says Wittgenstein. It is essential that we get our order of priority straight. Once a practice is established (through trial and error), we might wish, upon reflection, to test its assumptions through experiments that do or do not confirm aspects of the practice's usefulness. But that is not how those academics who reify theory and deliberative discord operate. Wittgenstein writes: 'If language is to be a means of communication there must be agreement not only in definitions but also (queer as this may sound) in judgments (§250).' L Wittgenstein *Philosophical Investigations* (1953).
7. We commit and recommit to marriages, friendships, religions, countries, employers. We stay with people or institutions out of loyalty: because this is just who we are. Sometimes we fight for our country. At other times, we resist injustice, generally peaceably, within our own country.
8. Walzer 'On Involuntary Association' (supra) at 73.
9. Ibid at 73. See also M Oakeshott 'Political Education' *Inaugural Lecture at the London School of Economics* (1961)('Our determination to improve our conduct does not prevent us from recognizing that the greater part of what we have is not an incubus to be thrown off, but an inheritance to be enjoyed. And a degree of shabbiness is joined with every real convenience.') Hume, like Walzer and Oakeshott, argued that freedom – properly understood – only becomes meaningful as a descriptive and a prescriptive term when we appreciate fully that it is contingent on tradition and custom. Hume writes: 'Custom is the great guide of human life. It is the principle alone which renders our experience useful to us, and makes us expect for the future a similar train of events with those that have appeared in the past. Without the influence of custom, we should be entirely ignorant of every matter of fact … We should never know how to adjust means to ends or to employ natural powers in the production of any effect. There would be an end at once of all action, as well as the chief part of speculation.' D Hume *An Enquiry Concerning Human Understanding* (1739) 29. It is interesting to note that radical social democrats such as Walzer and political conservatives such as Oakeshott share, along with Hume, a commitment to the premise that our beliefs, generally, 'are neither natural in the sense of innate … nor a deliberate invention of human reason, but an artifact, … a product

of cultural evolution.' FA Hayek 'The Legal and Political Philosophy of David Hume' *Studies in Philosophy, Politics and Economics* (1967) 111.

10. P Bourdieu 'Forms of Capital' in JC Richards (ed) *Handbook of Theory and Research for the Sociology of Education* (1986) 241, 248.
11. Ibid at 241, 248, 252–253.
12. R Putnam *Bowling Alone: The Collapse and Revival of American Community* (2000) 19. See also R Putnam *Making Democracy Work: Civic Traditions in Modern Italy* (1993). Putnam does offer a better definition of social capital elsewhere – one more congenial to the purposes of this book: 'Features of social life – networks, norms and trust – that enable participants to act more effectively together to pursue shared objectives … Social capital, in short, refers to social connections and the attendant norms and trust.' R Putnam 'Tuning In, Tuning Out: The Strange Disappearance of Social Capital in America' (1995) 28 *Political Science and Politics* 1, 20. There is a signal difference between Putnam's account of social capital and the one developed in these pages. First, in this book, social capital is not assumed to be desirable primarily because of its instrumental link to civic virtue and the well-ordered society (though it may operate in such a manner.) Social capital is simply both a cause and an effect of all stable associational frameworks. It is a predicate good for most other social goods. Second, because associational life is the necessary setting for most meaningful action, it makes little sense to speak, as Putnam does, of virtuous individuals in isolation. Virtue is a feature of human life that can exist only in the context of a densely woven fabric of social practices that define the good. Third, our deployment of our social capital is how we get various things done. In the absence of significant stores of social capital, the only tool for collective action is coercion.
13. N Lin *Social Capital: A Theory of Social Structure and Action* (2002) 24–25.
14. D Halpern *Social Capital* (2005) 11–12.
15. World Bank *Poverty and Social Capital* (1999) available at www.worldbank.org/poverty/scapital. See also D Naravan 'Bonds and Bridges: Social Capital and Poverty' Poverty Group, World Bank (July 1999).
16. A Baier 'Trust and Antitrust' in *Moral Prejudices* (1995) 95, 96, 98, 128–129.
17. R Putnam (2000) *Bowling Alone: The Collapse and Revival of American Community* 22- 23. See also R Gittel and A Vidal *Community Organizing: Building Social Capital as a Development Strategy* (1998).
18. As de Tocqueville was first to note, medium to large scale democracies only flourish in an environment with a rich associational life. A de Toqueville *Democracy in America* (1835). Social theorists have come to recognise that there is a direct correlation between (a) the availability (or the lack of availability) of social capital, (b) the presence (or absence) of bonding networks and bridging networks and (c) the virility (or the sterility) of political life. This syllogism is not the product of armchair philosophers. As David Halpern and colleagues have demonstrated, Nordic countries – such as Sweden, Norway and Denmark – often possess social capital or mutual trust ratios of over 65 per cent. That means, in short, that two-thirds of the citizens of these countries tend to 'trust' – and thus be able to work effectively with – fellow citizens. Even the US, the land of the free, autonomous (allegedly fragmented and isolated) individual, boasts social capital or mutual trust ratios of over 50 per cent. South Africa posts a dismal 15 per cent. Brazil – with an equally long history of social strife and economic stratification – is one of the few democracies to advertise a lower mark: 2 per cent. The other danger to social capital in any open society is capture. Concerns about what I call 'capture' lie, like constitutive attachments, at the very heart of associational life. Indeed, concerns about capture are, essentially, a function of – one might even say a necessary and logical consequence of – the very structure of associational life. In short, 'capture' refers to and justifies the ability of associations to control their association through selective membership policies, the manner in which they order their internal affairs and the discharge of members or users. Without the capacity to police their membership policies, as well as their internal affairs, associations would face two related threats. First, an association would be at risk of having its aims substantially altered. To the extent the original or the current

raison d'être of the association matters to the extant members of the association, the association must possess the ability to regulate the entrance, voice and exit of members. Without built-in limitations on the process of determining the ends of the association, new members, existing members and even outside parties could easily distort the purpose, the character and the function of the association. Second, an association's very existence could be at risk. Individuals, other groups or a state inimical to the beliefs and practices of a given association could use ease of entrance into and the exercise of voice in an association to put that same association out of business. In sum, by 'capture', I mean that in order for most associations to function as associations, they must possess a substantial degree of control over who belongs to the association and some degree of control over the ends the association pursues. So long as the association, and its members, as currently constituted possesses a figurative and/or real sense of ownership, so long as there is real social capital at stake, a court (and the state) must cede associations a significant level of control over entrance, voice and exit. For more on this discussion of 'internal' capture, see S Woolman 'On the Fragility of Associational Life: A Constitutive Liberal's Response to Patrick Lenta' (2009) 25 *South African Journal on Human Rights* 280; S Woolman 'Freedom of Association' in S Woolman & M Bishop (eds) *Constitutional Law of South Africa* (2nd Edition, RS5, 2012) Chapter 44. According to constitutive liberals, or egalitarian pluralists (with its Walzerian ring), it is easy to conclude that golf clubs that have been the bastion of white male Christian privilege must open their doors to persons of all colours, all sexes and all religions. But what of religious secondary schools that discriminate on the basis of an applicant's willingness to accept a prescribed religious curriculum and, at the same time, offer a better education than that generally available in our public schools? It would be foolish to dismantle such institutions solely on the grounds that either some form of exclusion takes place or that some re-inscription of privilege occurs. Almost all meaningful human labour occurs within the context of self-perpetuating social networks of various kinds. Taking a sledgehammer to social institutions that create and maintain large stores of real and figurative capital is a recipe for a very impoverished polity. More delicate forms of intervention – remedial equilibrium – are available to courts in order leverage change within associations that engage in unfair discrimination and to enable individuals to exit often conservative communities in order to join or to form new, more egalitarian sub-publics.

19. D Halpern *Social Capital* (2005) 20.

20. See P Graeff 'Social Capital: The Dark Side' in GT Svendsen and GLH Svendsen (eds) *Handbook of Social Capital: The Troika of Sociology, Political Science and Economics* (2009) 143. See also D Bilchitz 'Should Religious Associations be Allowed to Discriminate?' (2012) 28 *South African Journal of Human Rights* 250.

21. See S Woolman 'Dignity' in S Woolman & M Bishop (eds) *Constitutional Law of South Africa* (2nd Edition, OS, 2006) Chapter 36; S Woolman 'Seek Justice Elsewhere: An Egalitarian Pluralist's Reply to David Bilchitz on the Distinction between Differentiation and Domination' (2012) 28 *South African Journal of Human Rights* 243. In 'Seek Justice Elsewhere', I develop the aforementioned doctrine of remedial equilibration in order to avoid 'external capture'. By external capture, I mean to highlight the political blowback that can occur when, say, conservative elements within a society reject progressive judgments by our courts and mobilize their political constituency in a manner that results in the appointment of conservative judges unlikely to challenge discriminatory practices in traditional communities. Remedial equilibration enables courts to rachet down the political crossfire by simultaneously recognizing instances of unfair discrimination without necessarily dismantling the traditional community at fault in the process.

22. Lists of nouns and adjectives also provide a handy way to distinguish one kind of network from the other. Bonding networks are often said to embrace parents, siblings, love, care, neighbourhoods, workplaces, shared customs, religion, ethic group affiliation, patriotism, loyalty, honour, and trust (as well as ex-communication.) Bridging networks are often said to capture acquaintances, colleagues, shame, reputation, links, generosity, mutual respect, diplomacy, and negotiation.

23. Chipkin and Ngqulunga have argued that social cohesion is essential for long-term economic stability in South Africa. See I Chipkin & B Ngqulunga 'Friends and Family: Social Cohesion in South Africa' (2007) 34(1) *Journal of Southern African Studies* 310. Building on recent debates about the importance of various kinds of social capital (especially bridging networks), Chipkin contends that state institutions – especially in a developing democracy such as South Africa – have an essential role to play in building social capital and promoting social cohesion: 'There are several ways in which such linking is achieved. It may be that churches and other religious organisations, working on the basis of charity, are the key linking mechanisms between poor and resource rich(er) communities. Various civil-society bodies, including non-governmental organisations, may play similar roles. Yet the most important institution, in this regard, is the state. This is true for several reasons. In the first place, democratic state institutions, like local governments, are able to realise benefits, not simply for members of ascriptive groups, but for communities of citizens – irrespective of religious affiliation or culture or ethnicity. What matters is the degree to which their operations are inclusive and participatory and the degree to which they are able to invest in and/or leverage resources for poor communities ... In the second place, the democratic State builds networks and creates linkages on the basis of democratic values. In other words, they encourage a culture of democratic citizenship in the country. In this regard, other kinds of 'linking' mechanisms, like the church, for example, may have important developmental effects, but they do not necessarily deepen the democratic culture.' I Chipkin 'Social Cohesion as a Factor in Development' Symposium for the Office of the President (11–12 June 2007) 3 (Paper on file with author). In sum, the state has a critical role to play in ensuring that the associational life of our extremely heterogeneous society buttresses the egalitarian goals, the utilitarian interests and the democratic ends of our polity. It can do so through economic policies – micro-financing or black economic empowerment (BEE). It can do so through school policies and school governing bodies. It can do so by ensuring that citizens are given a meaningful opportunity to participate in the decision-making processes that have a direct impact on their lives. See, eg, *Doctors for Life International v Speaker of the National Assembly* 2006 (6) SA 416 (CC) 2006 (12) BCLR 1399 (CC); *Matatiele Municipality & Others v President of South Africa & Others* 2007 (6) SA 477 (CC), 2007 (1) BCLR 47 (CC).
24. Understanding social capital or associational life as generic terms is insufficient for the radical aims of this project. Bridges must be built between associations that wield enormous amounts of power and associations that do not. See M Edwards *Civil Society* (2004) 47 ('Large differentials in the power of associations to make their voices heard, advance their own agendas and consolidate their own interpretation of shared norms in the public sphere are the enemy of the good society, and of democracy. That is why reducing inequality is a crucial part of any solution to the civil society puzzle.') See also J Alexander *The Civil Sphere* (2006) 186 ('The ideal and material hierarchies that sustain non-civil domains project themselves across the boundary of the civil society, and anti-civil domination becomes justified by ascriptions of competence and incompetence within the civil sphere itself. In this manner, the discourse of civil society [and social capital] justifies the pragmatics of domination without compromising the law's semantic integrity.')
25. The World Bank Group 'Economic Update on South Africa: Focus on Inequality of Opportunity' (2012) 3 *Africa Region – Poverty Reduction & Economic Management* viii: 'The State of Human Opportunity in South Africa. While GDP growth—if modest by global comparisons—has averaged a credible 3.2 per cent a year since 1995 (1.6 per cent per capita), it has proven insufficient to absorb the wave of new entrants into the labor market from dismantling apartheid's barriers. The potential for growth has been held back by industrial concentration, skill shortages, labor market rigidities, and chronically low savings and investment rates – the latter, despite the fairly high and improving rates of return to capital. Growth has also been highly uneven in its distribution, perpetuating inequality and exclusion. With an income Gini of around 0.70 in 2008 and consumption Gini of 0.63 in 2009, South Africa stands as one of the most unequal countries in the world. The top decile of the population accounts for 58 per cent of the country's income, while the bottom decile

accounts for 0.5 per cent and the bottom half less than 8 per cent. In large part, this is an enduring legacy of the apartheid system, which denied the non-whites (especially Africans) the chance to accumulate capital in any form—land, finance, skills, education, or social networks. At the heart of high inequality lies the inability to create employment opportunities on a large enough scale. Unemployment stands at 25.2 per cent (33.0 per cent, including "discouraged" workers), among the world's highest. No surprise then that despite an almost 30 per cent increase in per capita GDP since the late 1990s, reductions in poverty have been modest at best. This would have been untenable without the growing social assistance grants. Non-contributory and means-tested (except for foster care) financial transfers from the budget account for more than 70 per cent of the income of the bottom quintile (up from 15 per cent in 1993 and 29 per cent in 2000). With the social grants, the entire spectrum of population ranked by income percentiles saw income growth between 1995 and 2005. But without the grants as part of income, those below the 40th percentile saw a significant decline in their income. In other words, without the grants, two-fifths of the population would have seen its income decline in the first decade after apartheid. Even after accounting for the equalizing role of social assistance, income inequality remains extraordinarily high. To reduce it to more reasonable levels over the long run, social assistance is clearly not enough and needs to be complemented by other initiatives. These would include a special focus on human capital development, particularly among children and youths.'

26. See A Rosenblueth, N Wiener and J Bigelow 'Behavior, Purpose and Teleology' (1943) 10 *Philosophy of Science* 18 (Behaviour controlled by negative feedback, whether in animal, human or machine, was a determinative, directive principle in nature and human creations.)
27. See JS Mill *On Liberty* (1859).
28. See M Walzer *Thick and Thin: Moral Arguments at Home and Abroad* (2002) 103 – 104.
29. A virtually unchallengeable thesis in the domain of clinical psychology is that the more roles a person plays, the greater the likelihood of her consistent experience of happiness or well-being. The reason, simply put, is that if we fail in one role, then we still have other roles from which we can draw meaning and fulfilment. See R Biswas-Diener, E Diener & M Taya 'The Psychology of Subjective Well-Being' (2004) 133 *Daedelus* 18. M Seligman 'Can Happiness be Taught? (2004) 133 *Daedelus* 87; The Sustainable Scale Project *Understanding Human Happiness and Well-Being* (2003), available at www.sustainable.scale.org./attractive solutions, accessed 1 November 2011. This understanding of happiness closely approximates the Greek notion of eudaimonia that grounds this books commitment to flourishing.
30. FA Hayek 'The Use of Knowledge in Society' (1945) 35 (4) *American Economic Review* 519, 520. See also FA Hayek 'The Results of Human Action, but not of Human Design' *Studies in Philosophy, Politics and Economics* (1967) 96, 97.
31. FA Hayek *Counter-Revolution in Science* (1952) 49.
32. FA Hayek *Law Legislation & Liberty (Volume 3): The Political Order of a Free People* (1979) 155 – 158.
33. D Campbell 'Downward Causation in Hierarchically Organized Biological Systems' in FJ Ayala and T Dobzhansky (eds) (1974) *Studies in the Philosophy of Biology*.
34. H Plotkin 'Social Constructions and Evolution' in C Heyes and D Hull (eds) *Selection Theory and Social Construction* (2001) 119, 132.
35. FA Hayek *Law Legislation & Liberty (Volume 1): Rules and Order* (1973) 16. On the debates as to how language actually evolved, see H Plotkin 'Social Constructions and Evolution' in C Heyes and D Hull (eds) *Selection Theory and Social Construction* (2001) 119, 126–127.
36. One might contend that all computer operating systems work in a similar way. Windows, as designed by Microsoft, is constantly improved based on feedback from users. Microsoft releases updates that fix problems in the program. The primary difference is that Linux users are the code-writers and they do not operate in a top-down hierarchical manner. Microsoft may make use of non-hierarchical informational systems – but its ultimate goal must be to return profits to its shareholders. (Frankly, Microsoft's market dominance (through anti-competitive behaviour) has made Windows an on-

going nightmare. As Apple and the IPad gain market share, watch for both product lines to improve immensely – prodded further by the entrance of Google and Android, as well as Samsung, into the market. Moreover, telephones – brought out by Apple and Samsung – with their innumerable applications are already posing a threat to conventional desktops and laptops.)

37. Hayek *Law, Legislation & Liberty (Volume 1)* (supra) at 156.
38. R Adelstein 'Institutional Function and Evolution in the Criminal Process' (1981) 76 *Northwestern University Law Review* 1.
39. Unfortunately, love of the common law often works as an undesirable break on the transformation of those legal norms that govern a radically unequal constitutional democracy. For such a critique, see F Michelman 'Expropriation, Eviction and the Gravity of the Common Law' (2013) 25 *Stellenbosch Law Review* – (forthcoming)(manuscript available from author and on the SSRN at http://papers.ssrn.com/sol3/papers.cfm?abstract_id=2116643.
40. Hayek develops the connection between consciousness and spontaneous orders in an early work. FA Hayek *The Sensory Order* (1952). Hayek's theory of mind relies upon the twin concepts of classification and evolution. Classification consists of the innate, as well as the nurtured, propensity of a mind to impose regularities upon the world that enable us to act with some expectation that other entities in the world will respond in accordance with our predictions. Hayek's concept of classification largely coheres with the view that neural networks are created, reinforced and distinguished by our experiences of action in the world. Indeed, Hayek's view that synaptic connections between neurons, and larger sets of neuronal networks, are not 'invariable features of the nervous system but are subject to modification in the course of the system's operation' has been borne out by the findings of contemporary scientific studies of consciousness. Ibid at 57. Our conceptual framework evolves, on Hayek's understanding, through a process of evolution: new inputs or new experiences challenge our existing belief set. Neural networks and belief sets that continue to 'work' are reinforced. Neural networks and belief sets that fail to offer adequate responses to the world are supplanted by neural networks and belief sets that possess a higher degree of success. The change in neural networks that occurs within the individual and the change in belief sets that occur within the individual and the broader society are both 'explained' by reference to the kinds of selection theory associated with evolutionary epistemology. See, eg, D Campbell 'Blind Variation and Selection Retention in Creative Thought as in Other Knowledge Processes' (1960) 67 *Psychological Review* 380.
41. D Campbell & J Russo *Social Experimentation* (1999) 19.
42. While spontaneous order theories make much of the unintended collective benefits that flow from the actions of individual agents pursuing their own interests, these theories often ignore unintended negative consequences that flow from individual agents pursuing their own interests without regard for the collective outcome. As both Hull and Hardin have pointed out, 'the tragedy of the commons' is that 'although none of the farmers using the commons intend to destroy it, that is what they do.' DL Hull *Science and Selection: Essays on Biological Evolution and the Philosophy of Science* (2001) 140. See also G Hardin *The Limits of Altruism: An Ecologist's View of Survival* (1977).
43. See JS Mill *On Liberty* (1861) 57 ('[A]s it is useful that while mankind are imperfect there should be different opinions, so it is that there should be different experiments of living; that free scope should be given to varieties of character, short of injury to others; and that the worth of different modes of life should be proved practically, when anyone thinks fit to try them.')
44. Ibid at 70 ('[D]espotism of custom is everywhere the standing hindrance of human advancement, being in unceasing antagonism to that disposition to aim at something better than customary, which is called … the spirit of liberty, or … progress or improvement.')
45. The notion that democratic theories should emphasize detailed analysis of extant social processes rather than dictating substantive outcomes born of pure theory flows from a variety of thinkers in the American pragmatist tradition. See, eg, J Dewey *Reconstruction in Philosophy* (1926); R Rorty *Consequences of Pragmatism* (1981); B Fay *Contemporary Philosophy of Social Science* (1997). Brian Fay draws heavily on Dewey's insights to argue that the philosophy of social inquiry should refrain from relying on categories and focus on processes. Fay (supra) at 223-242. I, in turn, rely heavily on pragmatic

principles of institutional design articulated, most compellingly, in Michael Dorf's oeuvre. See, eg, M Dorf 'Legal Indeterminism and Institutional Design' (2004) 78 *New York University Law Review* 875. American pragmatists invariably emphasize the extent to which progress flows from a better understanding of the relationship between means and ends and the extent to which evolutionary improvements in means often have a reciprocal effect on the ends that individuals, groups and the state seek to realize.

46. Mill undertook a personal journey from being a young man living under the intellectual shadow of his father to becoming an independent, self-possessed thinker. This journey had both a theoretical and a practical dimension. Theoretically, Mill accepted a form of ethical incompatibilism. He recognized the existence of higher and lower pleasures, ie, a diversity of goods. See C Taylor 'The Diversity of Goods' *Philosophical Papers II: Philosophy and the Human Sciences* (1985) 230. Mill rejected the strict ethical reductionism of his father, James Mill. See E Anderson 'John Stuart Mill and Experiments in Living' 102 (1) *Ethics* (1991) 4. Consistent with the change in his theoretical views, Mill also undertook a practical process of personal exploration and experimentation. Ibid at 17–19.

47. Mill borrowed a metaphor from Sydney Smith to illustrate his vision of experimentation and greater 'fit'. If we represent lives 'by holes upon a table, of different shapes – some circular, some triangular, some square, some oblong,' and persons represented 'by [pegs] of similar shapes', Smith thought that 'we shall generally find that the triangular person has got into the square hole, the oblong into the triangular ... [T]he officer and the office, the doer and the deeds, seldom fit so exactly that we can say that they were almost made for each other.' Anderson (supra) at 19. Mill's ideas present us with a dynamic, rather than static, vision of private ordering and individual preferences.

48. See Mill (supra) at 60 ('[H]uman nature is not a machine to be built after a model, and set to do exactly the work prescribed for it, but a tree, which requires to grow and develop itself on all sides, according to the tendency of the inward forces which make it a living thing.')

49. See C Taylor 'Agency and the Self' *Philosophical Papers I: Human Agency and Language* (1985) 113.

50. See Anderson (supra) at 25–26 (Points out that Mill's theory poses daunting requirements for our capacity for self-transparency and for holding systematic views as to our vision of the good.) See also Fay (supra) at 166–174 (Argues that the dynamic relationship between our present and our past experiences precludes absolute transparency in our self-interpretations.)

51. See Dennett *Consciousness Explained* (supra) at 85–87 (Deliberation may have long-term benefits: we focus first on immediate concerns.)

52. Significant positive change has required two-day-a-week psychotherapy for the past decade. The duration of treatment reflects both the limitations of a well-entrenched character and the difficulty of laying down new neuronal tracks and dispositional states even with the best of analysts. However, all the King's horses and all the King's men have managed to put some of Humpty Dumpty back together again.

53. Put another way, we are emotional beings enmeshed in dense lattice-works of narratives, traditions, identities and social mores, and corporeal beings constrained by our physical dispositions.

54. See J Elster *Ulysses and the Sirens* (1992). See, generally, Fay (supra) at 152–154, 171–178.

55. See Fay (supra) at 146–164, 191–197 (Illustrates the limits of a purely cognitivist model of human behaviour in light of our embodiment and embededness in social relationships.)

56. Imagine, for example, that your reflections on the cruelty perpetrated on people of colour by discriminatory laws have led you to subscribe to principles of racial equality. Yet, adopting those beliefs, even if secretly, would clash with your previous identity as a member of a racial community that accepts its privileged position as a deserved entitlement. Accepting the new belief requires you not only to give up previously-held racist notions, but also to reject a host of other intertwined beliefs and relationships. The difficulty of changing one's beliefs is compounded when one seeks to change one's behaviour on account of a change in beliefs. Social psychology scholarship generally holds that because our modes of behaviour in relating to others are mediated through sub-conscious stereotypes, simply changing our conscious, overt beliefs about racism or class-based

discrimination is often insufficient to eliminate patterns of behaviour that result in racially or class-based discriminatory outcomes, such as avoiding areas with a large number of poor residents. See, generally, S Plous (ed) *Understanding Prejudice and Discrimination* (2003). To successfully combat the effects of existing patterns of discrimination requires both individual reflection, changes in belief, and gradual alterations in the patterns of social practices.

57. For instance, the leader of a religious fellowship or congregation often wields a great deal of implicit authority over her or his congregants both over core religious issues as well as over questions less central to religious doctrines, such as questions of social policy. Here, the congregants may view the act of submitting to the spiritual and political authority of their religious leader as constitutive of their identities as members of that faith. Such disparities have, it seems plain, the potential to diminish demands for change.

58. Let's extend the example in the previous footnote and assume that several members of the fellowship in question have been working on a public health campaign with a group of volunteers from a gay community organization. Based on those interactions, the members of the fellowship re-examine their beliefs about the sinfulness of homosexuality. They may come to view those beliefs as a political position propounded by the leadership of the fellowship, but without any actual basis in the faith's core religious teachings. Accordingly, they raise objections to the principles within the fellowship. In the absence of entrenched authority, this conflict would not have occurred. The inevitable presence of entrenched authority within most institutions often permits the preservation of existing norms without justification.

59. See C Sunstein 'Lochner's Legacy' (1987) 87 *Columbia Law Review* 873, 876-883 (Sunstein notes that the flaws of the United States Supreme Court's jurisprudence in the early 20th century did not flow from its alleged activism – ie, a commitment to vigorous enforcement of rights – but rather from its choice of existing common law arrangements as the baseline for social relations and its assumption that such a baseline was more 'natural' than alternative legal arrangements – i.e. progressive social welfare laws.) See also S Woolman 'Application' in S Woolman & M Bishop (eds) *Constitutional Law of South Africa* (2nd Edition, OS, March 2005) Chapter 31.

60. Neither program operates in absolute terms. To contrast them as top-down vs bottom-up merely illustrates key differences. In reality, a top-down approach requires a measure of individual participation, just as a bottom-up approach demands political oversight.

61. See R Mangabeira Unger *False Necessities: Anti-Necessitarian Social Theory in the Service of Radical Democracy* (1987).

62. See *Minister of Health & Others v Treatment Action Campaign & Others No 2* 2002 (5) SA 721 (CC), 2002 (10) BCLR 1033 (CC)('*TAC*'). See also J Klaaren 'A Remedial Interpretation of the *Treatment Action Campaign* Decision' (2003) 19 *South African Journal on Human Rights* 539.

63. See C Sabel and W Simon 'Destabilization Rights: How Public Law Litigation Succeeds' (2004) 117 *Harvard Law Review* 1015. See also M Heise 'State Constitutions, School Finance Litigation and the "Third Wave": From Equity to Adequacy' (1995) 68 *Temple Law Review* 1151 (1995).

64. See S Woolman 'Seek Justice Elsewhere: An Egalitarian Pluralist's Reply to David Bilchitz on the Distinction between Differentiation and Domination' (2012) 28 *South African Journal of Human Rights* 243.

65. See D Campbell 'Blind Variation and Selective Retention in Creative Thought as in Other Knowledge Processes' (1960) 67 *Psychological Review* 380.

66. *The Work of Donald Campbell*, available at http:en.m.wikipedia.org/wiki/Donald_T._Campbell#cite_ref-1.

67. See KM Kim 'DT Campbell's Social Epistemology of Science: Vicarious Selection, Epistemological Fallabilism, and Sociology of Scientific Validity (1997) 3 *Evolution and Cognition* 75; KM Kim 'Nested Hierarchies of Vicarious Selectors' in C Heyes and D Hull (eds) *Selection Theory and Social Construction* (2001) 101.

68. G Cziko 'Universal Selection Theory and the Complementarity of Different Types of Blind Variation and Selective Retention' in C Heyes and D Hull (eds) *Selection Theory and Social Construction* (2001) 15, 18. See also D Campbell 'Evolutionary Epistemology' in PA Schlipp (ed) *The Philosophy of Karl Popper* (1974) 421.
69. See G Cziko *Without Miracles: Universal Selection Theory and the Second Darwinian Revolution* (1995).
70. WH Calvin 'The Brain as Darwinian Machine' (1987) 330 *Nature* 33, 34; WH Calvin *How Brains Think: Evolving Intelligence, Then and Now* (1996).
71. HJ Eysenck 'Creativity and Personality: Suggestions for a Theory' (1993) 4 *Psychological Inquiry* 147; HJ Eysenck *Genius: The Natural History of Creativity* (1995).
72. P Mirowski 'A Visible Hand in the Marketplace of Ideas: Precision-Measurement as Arbitrage' (1994) 7 *Science in Context* 563, 566.
73. DL Hull *Science and Selection: Essays on Biological Evolution and the Philosophy of Science* (2001) 141. See also E Ullmann-Margalit 'Invisible-Hand Explanations' (1978) 39 *Synthese* 263, 267-268 (Contends that the explanatory value of spontaneous order explanations for social phenomena depend upon the 'the process, or mechanism, that aggregates the dispersed individual actions into the patterned outcome: it is the degree to which the mechanism is explicit, complex and sophisticated – and, indeed, in a sense unexpected – that determines the success and interest of the invisible-hand explanation.')
74. See A Sen 'The Profit Motive' (1983) 147 *Lloyds Bank Review* 1, 13.
75. A Rawling 'The AIDS Virus Dispute: Awarding Priority for the Discovery of the Human Immunodeficiency Virus' (1994) 19 *Science, Technology & Human Values* 342.
76. Hull (supra) at 144.
77. David Hull points out that scientists need not be saints to do what they do well: 'Scientists may well be as motivated to produce knowledge for its own sake as they say they are, and perhaps these admirable motivations are sufficient to bring about the production of reliable knowledge, but the really neat thing about the reward system in science is that it is so organized that, by and large, more self-serving motivations tend to have the same effect as more altruistic motivations. Virtue and benefit go hand in hand … To the extent that scientists are motivated by the high opinion of others as evidenced by the use of each other's work, they will be pressured to behave themselves.' Hull (supra) at 146.
78. The history of science itself is evidence for this claim. For almost 2,000 years of western history, science and philosophy were largely synonymous – or, at the very least, the same thinkers did both and did not differentiate between the two. However, the last 300 years has witnessed a steady winnowing of subject matter in philosophy. Three hundred and fifty years ago, philosophers from Descartes to Locke to Leibniz all retained a hand in, and made contributions to, physics, mathematics, chemistry, and biology. But as the scientific revolution increased in speed, and as thinkers within the scientific community began to specialize, domain of knowledge after domain of knowledge left its original home in philosophy. Physics, mathematics, chemistry, biology, psychology, sociology, political science, computer science, artificial intelligence, critical theory, jurisprudence all got their start in philosophy. Today, philosophy's success can be measured by how little of its original content remains distinctly philosophical.
79. See D Campbell 'The Experimenting Society' in ES Overman (ed) *Methodology and Epistemology for Social Science: Selected Papers* (1988) 290.
80. D Campbell & J Russo *Social Experimentation* (1999) 19.
81. Ibid at 26.
82. Ibid at 43–44.
83. Remember too that the experimentalist – social and constitutional – is primarily concerned with the conditions and the processes under which experiments take place. Experimentalists can be – and often are – egalitarian in their orientation and quite progressive in their politics if for no other

reason than that inegalitarian arrangements often skew experimental results in favour of those persons who possess greater power or wealth (because their preferences are given undue weight.) The experimentalist is, by orientation, committed to the proposition that better political arrangements in the world are possible for the same reason that better scientific explanations of the world are possible. The experimental method has demonstrated that better and better explanations of the world are possible. Of course, with respect to political arrangements, the questions 'for what?' and 'for whom?' a particular arrangement will be better invariably arise. Experimentalists need not be wedded to any given final outcome – and almost by nature must view any positive outcome as provisionally desirable. But the notion of 'better' must, in this age, mean 'better for all to a meaningful degree'. Otherwise, we would be entitled to ask why bother with the experimentation process at all?

84. See C Sunstein *One Case at a Time* (1996) at ix-x. See also C Sunstein 'Leaving Things Undecided' (1996) 110 *Harvard Law Review* 4; C Sunstein 'Incompletely Theorized Agreements in Constitutional Law' *John M Olin Law & Economics Working Paper* no 322 (January 2007), available at *https://www.law.uchicago.edu/Lawecon/wkngPprs_301–350/322.pdf* (last accessed 11 October 2007).
85. Sunstein *Infotopia* (supra) at 11.
86. Ibid at 14.
87. S Woolman, E Fishman & M Fischer 'Evidence of a Patent Thickets in Complex Biopharmaceutical Technologies' (2013) 53 *IDEA: The International Journal of Intellectual Property Law Review* 1. (Shows that the thicket effect appears when a seller must acquire a license from two or more patent owners in order to create a downstream commercially viable product, and that where four or more other patent owners exist, negotiations for the necessary licenses makes production of a commercially viable product impossible.)
88. C Shapiro 2001 'Navigating the Patent Thicket: Cross Licenses, Patent Pools, and Standard-Setting' in A Jaffe et al (eds). *Innovation Policy & the Economy (Vol. I)* 119.
89. JR Green and S Scotchmer 'On the Division of Profit in Sequential Innovation' (1995) 26 (1) *Rand Journal of Economics* 20.
90. M Heller and R Eisenberg 'Can Patents Deter Innovation? The Anticommons in Biomedical Research' (1998) 280 *Science* 5364.
91. Woolman, Fishman and Fischer (supra) citing SM Maurer 'Inside the Anticommons: Academic Scientists' Struggle to Build a Commercially Self-Supporting Human Mutations Database, 1999–2001' (2006) 35 (6) *Research Policy* 839; RR Nelson 'The Market Economy and the Scientific Commons (2004) 33 (3) *Research Policy* 455; M Heller & R Eisenberg 'Can Patents Deter Innovation? The Anticommons in Biomedical Research' (1998) *Science* 280 (5364); OE Williamson 'The Economics of Organization: The Transaction Cost Approach' (1981) 87(3) *American Journal of Sociology* 548; C Shapiro 'Navigating the Patent Thicket: Cross Licenses, Patent Pools, and Standard-Setting' in Innovation policy and the economy 1, Jaffe et al (eds). *Innovation Policy & the Economy (Vol. I)*(2001) 119, 120; A Galasso & M Schankerman 'Patent Thickets, Courts and the Market for Innovation' (2008) 41 *Rand Journal of Economics* 472; M Noel & M Schankerman 'Strategic Patenting and Software Innovation' CEPR Discussion Paper 5701 (2006); A Makker 'The Nanotechnology Thicket and the Path to Commercialization' (2011) 84 *Southern California Law Review* 1163; G Dandalides 'The Patentability of Isolated DNA Sequences' (2011) 14 *Tulane Journal of Technology and Intellectual Property* 283; ME McCabe & LJ Kile 'Recent Developments in Patent Law and Their Impact on the Pharmaceutical and Biotechnology Industries' (2011) 19 *University of Baltimore Intellectual Property Law Journal* 75; I Hastings 'Dynamic Innovative Inefficiency in Pharmaceutical Patent Settlements' (2011) 13 *North Carolina Journal of Law & Technology* 31. On the sometimes indeterminate nature of a patent's exclusivity, see M Paslick '"Exclusive" No Longer Means Exclusive in the Context of Patent Licenses' (2011) 19 *University of Baltimore Intellectual Property Law Journal* 167; RP Merges & RR Nelson 'On the Complex Economics of Patent Scope' (1990) 90 *Columbia Law Review* 839; PC Grindley & DJ Teece 'Managing Intellectual Capital: Licensing and Cross-Licensing in

Semiconductors and Electronics' (1997) 39 *California Management Review* 8; B Werth *The Billion Dollar Molecule: One Company's Quest for the Perfect Drug* (1995).

92. Sunstein *Infotopia* (supra) at 12.
93. Report of the Senate Select Committee on Intelligence on Weapons of Mass Destruction in Iraq (2004).
94. F Armstrong 'The CIA and WMDs: The Damning Evidence' (2010) 57 (13) *The New York Review of Books* 53. Armstrong writes: 'When we ... finally got a full read of the National Intelligence Estimate on WMDs, a couple of us expressed grave reservations about the fatally weak evidence and the obsessively one-sided interpretation of what shreds of information it contained. (We were not told that [the informant] Curveball was a solitary source of obviously questionable credibility nor that contradictory evidence was actually suppressed from the intelligence collection and dissemination process.) One colleague said it was clearly a paper written to provide a rationale for a predetermined decision to go to war. When I challenged the lack of evidence and the lack of alternative explanations, including forcing the questions raised by [the State Department] into a lowly footnote, one of the WMD promoting [intelligence officers] leaned forward and bellowed "Who are you to question this paper? Even *The Washington Post* and *The New York Times* agree with us." The irony was complete: previously respected reporters, spoon-fed by Bush administration officials, were now being used to provide cover for the [National Intelligence Officers and CIA's] similar compromise in accepting the administration's view.'
95. R Suskind *The One Percent Doctrine: Deep Inside America's Pursuit of Its Enemies since 9/11* (2006).
96. R Thaler & C Sunstein *Nudge: Improving Decisions about Health, Wealth and Happiness* (2008).
97. Ibid at 3.
98. Ibid at 5.
99. Ibid at 11.
100. Thaler and Sunstein (supra) at 1–3.
101. Ibid at 5. Thaler and Sunstein do not have classic libertarianism – a thorough-going, conservative strain of fringe politics – in mind. Well, it was on the fringe until the Tea Party Movement arrived, and Ron Paul ran a strong, explicitly libertarian campaign for the Republican nomination in 2012. Thaler and Sunstein choose the term both to attract attention and to mean nothing more than enabling people – within meaningful and desirable constraints – 'to go their own way.' Ibid.
102. Ibid at 5.
103. Thaler and Sunstein (supra) at 229.
104. Ibid at 230.
105. Ibid at 232.
106. Ibid at 233.
107. Ibid at 235.
108. R Putnam (2000) *Bowling Alone: The Collapse and Revival of American Community* 22–23. See also R Gittel and A Vidal *Community Organizing: Building Social Capital as a Development Strategy* (1998).
109. It would be ludicrous to deny that eighteen years after liberation, we are on the verge of a second lost generation in our primary and secondary schools. Standardized test based statistics of third grade students and sixth grade student demonstrate that South Africa ranks in the bottom tier of countries on this continent with respect to the delivery of an adequate education. As matters currently stand, in 2012, little more than 1 out 3 students who begin grade 1 actually complete grade 12. Moreover, a real map of apartheid South Africa mapped on to a map of post-apartheid South Africa demonstrates that little has changed with respect to economic and educational goods. South Africa, for all its efforts, seems 'locked-in' to past patterns of disadvantage based upon race and class. See B Fleisch *Primary Education in Crisis* (2009).
110. *National Coalition for Gay and Lesbian Equality & Another v Minister of Justice & Others* 1999 (1) SA 6 (CC), 1998 (12) BCLR 1517 (CC) at para 38.
111. *Daniels v Campbell NO* 2004 (5) SA 331 (CC), 2004 (7) BCLR 735 (CC).
112. *Volks v Robinson* 2005 (5) BCLR 466 (CC).

113. *Prince v President, Cape Law Society, & Others* 2002 (2) SA 794 (CC), 2002 (1) SACR 431(CC), 2002 (3) BCLR 231(CC).
114. Ibid at para 145.
115. Ibid at paras 170–172. The *Prince* majority's suppression of cultural and religious differences harms not only the individuals and the communities concerned, but society as a whole. Sachs J continues: '[F]aith and public interest overlap and intertwine in the need to protect tolerance as a constitutional virtue and respect for diversity and openness as a constitutional principle. Religious tolerance is accordingly not only important to those individuals who are saved from having to make excruciating choices between their beliefs and the law. It is deeply meaningful to all of us because religion and belief matter, and because living in an open society matters.' Ibid at para 170.
116. For a fuller elaboration of this understanding of democracy, see F Michelman *Brennan and Democracy* (1999) 68–89; F Michelman 'Law's Republic' (1988) 97 *Yale Law Journal* 1493.
117. Michelman *Brennan and Democracy* (supra) at 71.
118. *Fourie* (supra) at para 60 (emphasis added).
119. See *Pillay* (supra) at para 107: '[I]f there are other learners who hitherto were afraid to express their religions or cultures and who will now be encouraged to do so, that is something to be celebrated, not feared. As a general rule, the more learners feel free to express their religions and cultures in school, the closer we will come to the society envisaged in the Constitution. The display of religion and culture in public is not a "parade of horribles" but a pageant of diversity which will enrich our schools and in turn our country.'
120. M Klein *Love, Guilt and Reparation and Other Works* 1921–1945 (1986); M Klein *Selected Work* J Mitchell (ed) (1986).
121. F Leichsenring and S Rabung 'Effectiveness of Long-term Psychodynamic Psychotherapy ('LTPP'): A Meta-Analysis' (2008) 300 (13) *Journal of the American Medical Association* 1551 (According to comparative analyses of controlled trials, LTPP showed significantly higher outcomes in overall effectiveness, target problems, and personality functioning than shorter forms of psychotherapy ... Psychodynamic psychotherapies operate on an interpretive-supportive continuum. An emphasis is placed on more interpretive or supportive interventions depending on the patient's needs... Gunderson and Gabbard define LTPP as 'a therapy that involves careful attention to the therapist-patient interaction, with thoughtfully timed interpretation of transference and resistance embedded in a sophisticated appreciation of the therapist's contribution to the two-person field.' ... In this meta-analysis, we included studies that examined psychodynamic psychotherapy lasting for at least a year, or 50 sessions. ... A considerable proportion of patients with chronic mental disorders or personality disorders do not benefit sufficiently from short-term psychotherapy. ... In this meta-analysis, LTPP was significantly superior to shorter-term methods of psychotherapy with regard to overall outcome, target problems, and personality functioning.') But see B Thombs 'Analyzing Effectiveness of Long-Term Psychodynamic Psychotherapy' (2009) 301 (9) *Journal of the American Medical Association* 930 (Letter questions study methodology) and F Leichsenring and S Rabung 'Analyzing Effectiveness of Long-Term Psychodynamic Psychotherapy: A Reply' (2009) 301 (9) *Journal of the American Medical Association* 932 (Explains, and defends, study methodology.)
122. J Rae-Dupree 'Can You Become a Creature of New Habits?' *The New York Times* (4 May 2008)('So [while] it seems antithetical to talk about habits in the same context as creativity and innovation ... brain researchers have discovered that when we consciously develop new habits, we create parallel synaptic paths, and even entirely new brain cells, that can jump our trains of thought onto new, innovative tracks. Rather than dismissing ourselves as unchangeable creatures of habit, we can instead direct our own change by consciously developing new habits. In fact, the more new things we try, the more we step outside our comfort zone – the more inherently creative we become, both in the workplace and in our personal lives. But don't bother trying to kill off old habits; once those ruts of procedure are worn into the hippocampus, they're there to stay. Instead, the new habits we

deliberately ingrain into ourselves create parallel pathways that can bypass those old roads.') See also B Carey 'Psychoanalytic Therapy Wins Backing' *The New York Times* (30 September 2008).

123. Many legal philosophers get the relationship between legal theory and legal practice wrong. In one of his many tiffs with Ronald Dworkin on the relationship between legal theory and legal practice, Stanley Fish found himself caught up in a side-bar about the relationship between theory and practice in baseball. See S Fish 'The Jurisprudence of Richard Posner, Richard Rorty and Ronald Dworkin' in *There's No Such Thing as Free Speech, And It's a Good Thing Too!* (1994) 200, 225–230, responding to R Dworkin 'Pragmatism, Right Answers and True Banality' in M Brint and W Weaver (eds). *Pragmatism in Law and Society* (1991) 359, 368. As I explain at great length elsewhere, both get the relationship between theory and practice in baseball *terribly* wrong. S Woolman 'On the Common Saying 'What's True in Golf is True in Law': Theory and Practice across Forms of Life' in S Woolman & D Bilchitz (eds). *Is This Seat Taken? Conversations at the Bar, the Bench and the Academy about the South African Constitution* 341. Dworkin reifies theory in a manner that cannot be sustained by what we know about the limits of consciousness and awareness. Fish so abhors theory that he fails to recognize the quite sophisticated form it takes in baseball. On my account, conscious theorizing is actually a product of a neurological system and social endowments that have a three-fold purpose: (a) 'durable and explicit information maintenance' (b) 'novel combinations of operations' and (c) 'intentional behaviour'. In short: (1) memory, (2) thought experiments based upon prior experience, and (3) actions designed (subsequent to thought experiments or theoretical analysis) to realize optimal outcomes (both descriptive and prescriptive.) As Daniel Dennett argues, our conscious beliefs, about law or baseball, function as 'idealized fictions' that enable us to engage – in advance – in sophisticated 'action-predicting, action-explaining calculus.' That does not mean that theory and practice operate in an identical manner in all social practices. My aim is quite modest: it is to press practitioners and judges to take greater cognizance of 'theory' – and academic musings – in their work by demonstrating just how much work constant theorizing does in sports. If you had seen a pained New York Yankees manager Joe Girardi walk out of the stadium in October 2010 holding two thick binders full of statistics – having just made an errant set of decisions (based on the books) that cost the Yankees the American League Championship – then you might better understand the degree to which theory plays a major role in what many wrongly view as non-cognitive practices. (The next season, Tony LaRussa, who lived and died by the numbers, 'the probabilities', often extremely counterintuitive to a fan, won the World Series for the second time.) Don't like baseball, think sports are boring? Go see *Moneyball* (2011) – starring Brad Pitt. Solid movie: a true story about how stats changed the way general managers in baseball go about their craft in putting together winning teams.

124. Don't believe me? Listen to Hank Haney – Tiger Woods' previous coach – explaining what most amateurs don't do: they fail to deconstruct and reconstruct their swing when the flight of the ball tells them that something must be wrong. Here's the question asked Haney (Thursday, 8 October 2009) by Connel Barrett: 'What's the biggest mistake we mortals make in the swing?' Haney replies: 'The average golfer doesn't correctly diagnose the problem in his swing ... What you should do ... is ask, 'What's my golf ball doing? What's my ball flight?' ... You have to be a detective, and work backwards from impact.'

125. Several interlocutors contend that the practice of golf is only concerned with putting the ball in the hole, and that theory only relates to the improving a score. Kant knew that proposition to be fundamentally false. See I Kant 'On the Common Saying: While It is True in Theory, It is Not Necessarily True in Practice' in A Wood (ed) *Basic Short Writings of Immanuel Kant* (1793). Golf happens to be one of the most norm-governed, *norm-creating* and *ethically-engaged* social practices within which individuals participate. See *Royal and Ancient Golf Association of St Andrews* Rules of Golf (2010). Its history of elitism and exclusion is another – not insignificant – matter. Only this year – 2012 – did Augusta National (home of the Masters) finally admit female members. A commitment to fairness by an institution in one domain does not necessarily entail fairness in another. But it

can help us arrive there eventually. Despite problems with unfairness, economic inequality and corruption around the globe, see Transparency International *Country Enforcement of the OECD Anti-Bribery Convention, Progress Report for 2012* (2012), the march toward greater democratic solidarity seems inexorable. While recent events such as the post-2008 global recession, related increases in anti-immigrant sentiment and counter-intuitive and economically destructive austerity programmes may suggest otherwise, global movements around climate change and economic inequality, as well as the Maghreb Spring, suggest that the commitment to equality at the heart of democracy may be the greatest change in human relations of the last half century.

126. See D Campbell and J Russo *Social Experimentation* (1999); D Campbell 'Evolutionary Epistemology' in P Schipp (ed) *The Philosophy of Karl Popper* (1974). Golf is a practice that dates back several hundred years. Scientific studies of the swing tell us exactly how the body's movements can be orchestrated in a manner that produces the most consistent amount of accuracy, power and control.
127. Industrial innovation alone – driven by managers who may have a 10 to 15 year view of matters – generally does not provide for a sufficiently long enough time cycle for lasting solutions to triple bottom line problems.
128. You would expect as much when, in the first 5 years, GE invested $5 billion in clean green technology research and development and generated a whopping $70 billion in revenues from the green products created.
129. At the same time, GE claims that its private sector efforts are producing 'an unprecedented wave of energy technology innovation and entrepreneurial activity' that far outstrips the innovative technologies on offer from the public sector. GE *Ecomagination Report* (2010) 5. The US EPA approved items form a small segment of GE's stable of over 50 green tech products.
130. In July 2009, representatives of SEMARNAT (the Mexico Environmental Agency) in Saltillo, Mexico, participated in an Energy Treasure Hunt at the GE office building in Monterrey, Mexico. GE Energy also conducted a similar hunt in Hangzhou China and was asked to share its findings with over 300 Chinese companies that attended the Xiaoshan Development Zone Annual Safety, Environment Protection and Energy Saving Meeting.
131. GE *Ecomagination Report* (supra) at 50.
132. Water-scarcity is one of the most vital threats to the South African, as well as the global, environment. GE is currently working with governments in water scarce regions in the US to expand water reuse efforts. Tempe, Arizona's reuse project will result in the reuse of over 2.5 billion gallons of water a year for commercial and industrial applications. Cogentrix Energy's 120-megawatt power plant in Battleboro, North Carolina implemented a GE technology solution to conserve an estimated three million gallons of water annually – the equivalent to approximately 22 percent of its current water usage. In Oakwood, Virginia, GE is providing advanced filtration membranes and thermal water treatment technology to CONSOL Energy to treat mine water in one of the nation's largest coal mines, enabling about 99 percent of the water to be reused in part at the company's preparation plant facility. Coal may be a dirty fuel – but it need not absorb precious water reserves in the process. GE is also implementing water reuse technologies in water-intensive industries. Perhaps the most exciting projects are taking place in China. GE writes: 'Imagine a wastewater treatment process that reuses virtually 100 per cent of your wastewater stream and leaves not a single drop to discharge. The technology exists today, but its high capital costs and high energy usage are preventing widespread market adoption. However, scientists and engineers at GE Global Research in Shanghai, along with the teams from GE Water and Process Technologies, China [and GE's China Technology Center's Electrochemical Processes Lab, Technology Center's Electrochemical Processes Lab, are developing new technology to address these challenges and make Zero Liquid Discharge (ZLD) available to thousands of businesses.' Ibid.
133. General Electric *Ecomagination Report* (2010).
134. These kinds of partnerships are not the only way to meet the triple bottom line. Take General Electric's recent commitment to purchase 12,000 electric cars from General Motors in 2011, to

deploy 25000 electric vehicles in its fleet and to fleet customers by 2015 and to ensure that half of its global fleet of vehicles has gone 'electric' by 2015. General Electric 'GE Announces Largest Single Electric Vehicle Commitment, Commits to Convert Half of Global Fleet by 2015' (New York Stock Exchange, Press Release, November 11, 2010.) GE's motivation can be measured in terms of the bottom line. Its 'Ecomagination Unit' – made up of green product lines – achieved sales of $18 billion in 2009 – a 6% increase in a year marked by severe global economic downturns. In terms of its own operations, GE reduced its own environmental footprint – in terms of greenhouse gas emissions – by 22 percent between 2004 and 2009. As GE recently noted: 'By every metric, by every stretch goal we set, ecomagination has delivered. We have created more efficient and economic solutions for our customers, and a more competitive position and earnings for our shareholders.' General Electric *Ecomagination Report* (2010). Look again at the electric car purchase. GE has not simply gone green because 'green is good'. GE, through its purchase of so many electric cars, has literally jump started the electric car industry in the United States. In so doing, GE created a new market for a broad array of GE products that will service the electric car industry. GE, through its car purchase and fleet management, is priming the pump for the creation of an even larger market share for itself with respect to the electric car grid. As GE Chairman and CEO Jeff Immelt notes: 'By electrifying our own fleet, we will accelerate the adoption curve, drive scale, and move electric vehicles from anticipation to action. We make technology that touches every point of the electric vehicle infrastructure and are leading the transformation to a smarter electrical grid ... This transformation will be good for our businesses and for our shareowners. Wide-scale adoption of electric vehicles will also drive clean energy innovation, strengthen energy security and deliver economic value, General Electric *Press Release* (2010). The private-private-private partnerships driven by General Electric itself demonstrate that nudging our way toward meeting triple bottom line goals can, to a limited extent, occur through private, non-state driven innovation (or conscious capitalism). See also J Montgomery 'Here Comes Conscious Capitalism: Part IV' (August 13, 2010), available at http://www.pehub.com/76857/here-comes-conscious-capitalism.

Chapter Four

A Theory of the Constitutional: Experimental Constitutionalism

All life is an experiment. The more experiments you make, the better.

Ralph Waldo Emerson

A. Philosophical Foundations

Given the theory of the self and the theory of the social put forward in Chapter 2 and Chapter 3, it should come as little surprise that my theory of the constitutional is disposed towards experimentalism. Recall that the purpose of consciousness is problem-solving (for the various selves and dispositional states that constitute an individual) and that an individual's brain/neuro-muscular system as a whole (often unconsciously/non-consciously) identifies a problem and initiates a sequence of events to solve that problem. Where the problem to be solved is novel and requires extant neuronal networks to respond in an equally novel fashion, then we tend to become aware of both a problem and the need to form an intention to respond to the problem.[1] The global neuronal workspace – a transient location (generally dispersed throughout the brain) designed to solve the problem that has captured our attention – is simultaneously connected to various sensory inputs (from a broad array of organs in the body) and a host of neuronal network experts that might assist in the solution of the problem. These experts possess particular linguistic skills, relevant memories, and trained responses. These long distance neuronal patterns are *consciousness* and we become aware of them when we must use their expertise to direct behaviour. The first purpose of consciousness then is to guide behaviour. However, consciousness pilots our behaviour in a particular way. Consciousness allows an individual (and the heterogeneous array of selves that make it up) to represent a goal and to estimate the outcomes of her actions before initiating them. The ability to undertake multiple trials within the simulated framework of mental activity is an enormous advance on having to undertake individual trials with real errors (and successes) in one's actual physical environment. We can thereby weed out, in advance, outcomes less likely to be successful in the physical world and thereby enhance our capacity to survive and to flourish. As Dehaene and Naccache put it:

> The evolutionary advantages that this system confers to the organism may be related to the increased independence it affords. The more an organism can rely on mental simulation and internal evaluation to select a course of action, instead of acting out in the open world, the lower are risks and the expenditure of energy. By allowing more sources of knowledge to bear on this internal decision process, the neural workspace may represent an additional step in a general trend towards increasing internalization of representations in the course of evolution, whose main advantage is the freeing of the organism from its immediate environment.[2]

Consciousness enables the individual, by herself or in concert with others, to undertake multiple thought experiments and concrete enquiries that maximize the chances of successful outcomes in the world. The brain (or our entire neuro-muscular system) accomplishes this feat by allowing different combinations of neural networks to compete with one another until a winner is selected. Remember: only the winners of this competition rise to the level of consciousness. Of course, if we have time, we may run through the problem again and again. For example, we may have the luxury of taking our time to ensure that our sentences scan. So, upon reflection, and many drafts of this book, I may choose one locution over another. Or, on the golf course, we might have the time to decide that a 100 metre shot to a slightly raised green and into a light breeze requires that we take an extra club – and not the club we might ordinarily use to target the green from that distance. In both cases, note that only certain sentence arrangements or club choices attract sufficient attention (because of their novelty or complexity) for conscious awareness to emerge. A winner in these problem-solving competition thus reflects a representation of the action most likely to succeed in the world. Put slightly slightly differently, competitions enables us to create a constellation of idealized fictions that function as a sophisticated 'action-predicting, action-explaining calculus.'[3] Consciousness enables the various selves that constitute our densely populated me's to undertake forward looking thought experiments and real world experiments that increase the likelyhood that an individual will successfully navigate her way through the world.

The theory of the social replicates the theory of the self in a number of striking ways. Recall that the social is populated by a large, heterogeneous array of endowments that form the environment in which individuals and groups operate. These endowments (various systems of tacit and express knowledge or language games or forms of life) are what make us human and not just feral creatures. Our innumerable interactions and conflicts with other members of our highly differentiated, extraordinarily heterogeneous society should, at least notionally, enable us to reflect more effectively upon our actions and, where necessary, to come up with better solutions to the problems, we and other members of our society in variably confront everyday. The solutions at which we arrive are not *purely* instrumental. They are reflexive in two distinct ways. First, we may find better means to achieve our ends. That's instrumental. Second, we may find, say, that treating persons with a drug addiction as persons in need of medical assistance, as opposed to persons who deserve incarceration, alters our ends (as manifest in law) in more or less radical ways. That's decidedly normative.

Thaler and Sunstein's notion of choice architecture neatly captures this arrangement. Choice architects cannot arrive with an entirely pre-conceived answer to a problem in mind. Of course, they must operate within some prescriptive framework that seeks to elicit best practices that will achieve that framework's ends. [I see no reason why these norms should not reflect the same core of shared understandings that Sunstein identified in *One Case at a Time.*] To identify those best practices, recall that a choice architect sets up a variety of environments in which different cohorts of individuals are permitted to act as they like. By reviewing the choices made by different cohorts, the choice architect can identify the environment that works best in terms of the overall welfare of the community that she serves. In so doing, the choice architect nudges individuals toward making optimal decisions as determined by the individuals themselves. Again: the choice architects must have some *ex ante* goal in mind. A normative departure point is necessary in any decision-making setting. However, the whole point of these various experiments is to discover – *ex post* – both the kinds of ends people wish to pursue and the best way of ensuring that they achieve those ends.[4]

It should come then as no surprise that the experimentalist cast of the constitutional theory explicated in these pages resonates profoundly with the problem-solving approach to the theories of consciousness and social policy construction adumbrated above. In his provocatively entitled work, 'Toyota Jurisprudence', William Simon describes this Deweyan approach to the political realm as one that:

> (1) emphasizes the goals of learning and innovation (rather than of [binary] dispute resolution and the vindication of accepted norms), (2) combines the normative explicitness associated with formal rules with the continuous adjustment to particularity associated with informal norms (no dialectic

> of rules and standards), (3) treats normative decision-making in hard cases as presumptively collective and interdisciplinary (rather than the heroic labour of a solitary professional), (4) fosters a style of reasoning that is intentionally destabilizing of settled practices (rather than harmonizing or optimizing), and (5) attempts to bracket or sublimate issues of individual and retrospective fairness or blame.[5]

Joshua Cohen and Charles Sabel ask us to reimagine the polity – again in classically Deweyan terms – as an entity:

> ... in which sovereignty – legitimate political authorship – is neither unitary nor personified, and politics is about addressing practical problems .... In this world, a public is simply an open group of actors ... which constitutes itself as such in coming to address a common problem, and reconstitutes itself as efforts at problem solving redefine the task at hand. The polity is the public formed of these publics: this encompassing public is not limited to a list of functional tasks ... enumerated in advance, but understands its role as empowering members to address such issues as need their combined attention.[6]

The democratic character we saw as emblematic of consciousness, self-hood, bridging networks and choice architecture, emerges again in experimental constitutionalism, as it moves away from the top-down, command and control character of most contemporary forms of constitutional jurisprudence (say of a Dworkinian maximalist ilk). Rather than putting the heroic judge or judges at the centre of all things that matter,[7] experimental constitutionalists self-consciously take advantage of the heterogeneity of our society by emphasizing trial and error, reflexivity, polycentricity, and feedback enhanced decision-making in a host of institutions designed to answer mundane and critical questions about the norms that govern our polity, various subpublics within the polity, and publics that extend well beyond the generally arbitrary borders that determine national sovereignty (i.e., arenas that fly under the flag of 143 UN organizations, BRICS, NATO, the Red Cross, the Catholic Church). Put slightly differently, what differentiates the functionalism of experimental constitutionalism is the extraordinary amount of information various structures make available to all concerned parties (with the maintenance of a given practice or involved in the resolution of a particular dispute), the capacity such structures have to enable all participants to alter their behaviour based upon the available information, and the ability to pool information across various state and social structures. As we shall see in Chapter 5, these South African institutions range from Chapter 9 Institutions to Provincial Legislatures to Courts to the CCMA, while the South African constitutional doctrines cover rights interpretation, limitations analysis, remedies and public participation in law-making, and expansive approaches to amici, costs and jurisdiction. As we shall see in Chapter 6, this approach has made modest, but still discernible, contributions to sectors of our society as broken as (a) primary and secondary school education, and (b) municipal, provincial and national agencies charged with providing adequate housing. (Before we get there, we'll see how such experimentalist approaches work in the United States at the level of constitutional doctrines involving search and seizure, institutional settings such as family courts and drug treatment courts and national, state and local efforts to realize measurable improvements in basic education.[8])

Before I proceed any further with this South African inflected account of experimental constitutionalism, I want to answer an unwarranted charge that experimental constitutionalism is largely instrumental, without discernible content, and minimalist in a manner that would undermine rather than service our constitutional democracy. That charge has been generously characterized by Michael Wilkinson as follows:

> It is the [alleged] prioritizing of means over ends that sometimes gives experimentalism a technocratic flavour, suggesting that we are merely looking for more efficient solutions to common and uncontroversial problems (for example, of co-ordination) and that issues of morality, justice, or democratic legitimacy therefore do not arise. Sabel [and others] are careful to avoid this charge of celebrating technocracy, but it is impossible to ignore, particularly when levelled by those who claim that an obsession with "means" exposes new governance to a "gap" in terms of our traditional understanding of the rule of law, which is valuable not merely as a means but as an end in itself. For those who advance the "gap thesis", law has an intrinsic value that is neglected by the new governance [experimental constitutionalist] paradigm.[9]

Several readily available responses take the initial sting out of claims that experimental constitutionalism does little to challenge or to change the status quo.

First, having articulated this criticism, Wilkinson simultaneously acknowledges that

> Irrespective of our views on the Constitutional (with a capital "C") question, one of the advantages of experimentalism is the clear recognition that there is no simple one-way street between establishing the goals of integration and identifying the most appropriate means to achieve them. There is, rather, a complex interplay between means and ends because, for instance, new governance demands constant revisability of ends as these are rethought and adjusted or altered in the course of experimentation and mutual learning. In this way, the various fora of new governance act as a type of public laboratory of experimentalism, in a way that Dewey could hardly have foreseen. This is not to say that experimentalism guarantees democracy, it merely provides a more realistic democratic framework than the alternatives, *such as Habermasian discourse theory*.[10]

Given the wholesale failure of member states in the European Union to conceive of themselves as constituent parts of a constitutional order (while the current Euro crisis and potential state defaults force *actions* designed to maintain economic integration), Wilkinson's acknowledgement of experimentalism's strengths should draw the attention of those constitutional scholars who continue to reify talk over action.[11] Reverse the spin.

Second, the experimentalist critique of modern democratic orders reflects dissatisfaction with a modern legal tradition stuck with legitimation, rule of law and separation of powers doctrines that take insufficient cognizance of what is required to protect individual (and collective) rights in a world of 'rapid technological and organisational change, and cross-border transactions, migration and externalities.'[12] The standard modern democratic legal tradition has a rather blinkered view of how norms are formed, and an antiquated view as to how norms can be revised in a manner that better fits most heterogeneous democratic communities. That account runs as follows:

> The sovereign is a democratically elected government; its enactments are legitimate because of its representative status. The law-applying judgements of the government's unelected agents are legitimate only to the extent they can be traced to the enactments of the legislative principal.

> Accountability is thus a matter of pedigree ... [i]deally ... tested by an independent judiciary in proceedings that can be initiated by individual citizens. Accountability in this view is upward-and backward-looking; the court looks upward towards the sovereign and backward toward some prior authorisation.[13]

Experimental constitutionalism does not reject the tradition in its entirety but recasts it in a manner consistent with how we currently understand how optimal social systems work. Instead of 'looking backward to a prior enactment and upward to a central sovereign', Sabel and Simon claim that one of an experimentalist system's virtues is its ability to look 'forward and sideways: forward to the on-going efforts at implementation, sideways to the efforts and views of peer institutions.'[14] In short, it spreads its bets out on a variety of different efforts to improve the system and enables different participants within the system to learn from the successful trials and fatal errors of others similarly intent on improving the system. Wilkinson identifies the primary benefits of the experimentalist's functional approach – as compared with a command and control or an institutional approach to governance – in terms of its predisposition to (a) set 'framework goals and measures for assessing their attainment'; (b) bestow 'upon lower-level actors the autonomy to decide on the appropriate means for their attainment'; (c) oblige 'lower-level actors to report back on their progress and participate in peer review', and (d) engage in periodic 'revision of the framework goals by those who initially established them and the inclusion of additional participants whose views are seen to be indispensable to full and fair participation.'[15] Whatever works. But 'whatever works' is now determined not, first and foremost, by legal authorities by virtue of their authority, but by a broad array of social actors who have an interest in and a willingness to participate in the creation of the norms that govern their existence. The return to 'the social' as a site of exploration, innovation, critique and reconceptualization of norms and practices is given a powerful twist in Simon's 'Toyota Jurisprudence'. Simon captures the dissatisfaction with standard centrally planned business operations in a manner consistent with the critique of the dominant top-down, command and control of modern liberal-legal governance described above:

> TPS [Toyota Performance System] arises from dissatisfaction with a traditional mass manufacturing model that combines central planning with ad hoc shop floor adjustment. In the traditional model, a central corps of managers and engineers promulgates rules that dictate practice to a workforce that is narrowly skilled and divided among functional departments ... Central management forecasts sales and then prescribes production targets for specific products, orders materials, and schedules each phase of the production process. Typically, the plan calls for the parts of a product to be processed separately in different departments in large batches with specialized machinery. Invariably, adjustments are required as events depart from the plan. The pattern of orders is different from the forecast. Supplies fail to arrive on time, or they are defective. In the plant, machines break down, or parts are improperly machined. ... TPS proponents complain that such a system is slow in responding to unanticipated changes in the volume of customer demand or in its capacity to modify or change products. It takes a long time for centralized management to absorb information indicating that changes are needed, and a long time for it to develop and implement needed changes. The traditional system tends to be quite wasteful of labour and materials, in part, because it is slow to discover defects and, when they are discovered, slow to remedy them. In addition, the system does

> not effectively capitalize on the knowledge and potential creative effort of most of its workers. And by encouraging tolerance for errors and the expectation that they will be remedied downstream, the system fails to cultivate in workers a sense of responsibility or 'ownership'.[16]

The model of social organization and decision-making looks somewhat different under a TPS regime:

> The phrase 'kaizen', or continuous improvement, connotes that process be revised in the course of its execution. TPS diffuses responsibility for the organization of production broadly. Shop-floor teams write and revise the descriptions for their jobs, schedule their members, and arrange for maintenance and repair of their equipment. All workers are encouraged to make suggestions for improvements in the process, and such suggestions often result in changes. Inspection and quality control cease to be the exclusive preoccupation of an elite corps and become the responsibility of the entire workforce.[17]

The virtues of the Toyota Performance System as a model for experimental governance have been adumbrated by Wilkerson above. Another virtue, imminent in this model, but not expressly mentioned by Simon, is a form of 'democratic solidarity'. Distinctions between 'the bosses' and 'well-trained, flexible employees' diminish. Employees receive an education, are trained to undertake multiple tasks and become part of the decision-making process. Moreover, both management and workers on the shop-floor take on responsibility for the final outcome. The notion of a shared endeavour in which all members have greater rights and responsibilities and duties sounds not unlike the kind of mobilized and engaged citizenry contemplated by s 3 of our own South African Constitution. Not only are citizens '(a) equally entitled to the rights, privileges and benefits of citizenship', but they are '(b) equally subject to the duties and responsibilities of citizenship.' Such reciprocity drives *Toyota Jurisprudence* (and experimental constitutionalism).

Third, a return to the social need not mean political agnosticism. Experimental constitutionalism in South Africa operates within an aspirational normative framework provided by the text of the Constitution. The job of courts, legislatures, executives and citizens is to seek out those laws, policies, and social practises that will achieve the basic law's ends. To identify those best practices, experimental constitutionalists enjoin state and non-state actors to create a variety of environments in which individuals and institutions make choices that are better 'as judged by themselves' and better as determined by the judiciary, the legislature and the executive in terms of the overall welfare of South Africa. In all instances, experimental constitutionalists must have some *ex ante* goal in mind. That normative departure point is determined by the text of the Constitution and various publics, networks or associations that operate within our 'objective, normative value order'. Even as we 'fill in' their content, many of the norms in the Constitution will still operate at a fairly high level of generality.

Why should the gloss placed upon most norms by the Constitutional Court also remain rather rarefied? The whole point of the experimental constitutionalism is to find out – *ex post* – both the best way of arriving at those rarefied ends (through legislation, policy and social arrangement that are both forward-looking and lateral looking) and revising those ends (within the framework established by the Constitution) as people determine, over time and space, the ends they truly wish to pursue.

Fourth, the norms found within the South African Constitution – primarily those norms found within the Bill of Rights – are best understood in terms of a contemporary understanding of flourishing. This account of flourishing – whether described in terms of development theory or the capabilities approach – is decidedly *not* instrumental. Not only does it provide a relatively concrete view as to how individuals can pursue 'lives worth valuing' when they possess a reasonably full basket of the material and immaterial means (the capabilities) required for such pursuit, it identifies a constellation of rights (and a hierarchy within that constellation of rights) necessary to realize the invariably heterogeneous notions of flourishing that individuals and communities will pursue in our radically heterogeneous constitutional order.

This fourth feature of my South Africa twist on experimental constitutionalism possesses something of a challenge for the founders of this new school of thought. The reason: most of my experimental constitutionalist friends have a John Dewey problem.[18]

Overly concerned with intractable debates about foundationalism or essentialism, Dewey and his acolytes, such as Richard Rorty,[19] deny the need for first principles, and apparently any principled departure point. This refusal leads to a problem repeatedly slammed happily home by America's own Diogenes, Stanley Fish: 'No politics follows from [pragmatism] or is blocked by it; no morality attaches to it or is enjoined by it.'[20] I should say, however, that while it's no problem for Fish, it is a sticking point for experimental constitutionalists such as Dorf, Freidman, Sabel, Simon and Sturm.[21] You simply cannot approach constitutional theory in a meaningful fashion without having an identifiable set of normative pre-commitments. Larry Tribe's rather acerbic riposte to the structured silences of various constitutional theories a quarter century ago (e.g., Ely's process theory) applies with equal force to today's experimental constitutionalists: 'My reply is to question all formulas as concealing the constitutional choices that we must make – and that we cannot responsibly pretend to derive from any neutral method.'[22] Ira Struber suggests, constructively, that pragmatists, and therefore experimental constitutionalists, can respond in three ways: (1) they can make their ideals and aspirations explicit (and no more or less subject to scrutiny and to critique); (2) they can confess that the epistemological critique has teeth (for what that's worth), while subjecting the political consequences of their ideals to external appraisal; and (3) they can set about acknowledging that they are committed to a general normative structure, but concentrate their efforts on the creation of institutions that allow members of any given community both to test the best means of achieving those ends and to alter the very norms with which they began.[23] Neither pragmatists nor experimental constitutionalists need be embarrassed by their social democratic (or egalitarian pluralist) politics. For while social democracy may not appear to be written into the fabric of supernovas at the distant outskirts of our universe, we have good reason to believe that social democracy is written into the fabric of humanity. I take up this claim again in Chapter 7's discussion of flourishing, development theory and the capabilities approach and assert that we may actually be hard-wired for something akin to social democracy. (It's a point to which I have already strongly alluded in Chapter 2's discussion of radically heterogeneous, naturally and socially determined selves.)

B. Basic Facets of Experimental Constitutionalism

The ur-text for experimental constitutionalism is Michael Dorf and Charles Sabel's monograph-length article 'A Constitution of Democratic Experimentalism'. The authors summarize their theoretical framework as follows:

> [D]emocratic experimentalism … attempts to decentralize power [in particular domains] to enable citizens and other actors to utilize their local knowledge to fit solutions to their individual circumstances, but in which regional and national coordinating bodies require actors to share their knowledge with others facing similar problems. This information pooling, informed by the example of novel kinds of coordination within and among private firms, both increases the efficiency of public administration by encouraging mutual learning among its parts and heightens its accountability through participation of citizens in the decisions that affect them. In democratic experimentalism, subnational units of government are broadly free to set goals and to choose the means to attain them. Regulatory agencies set and ensure compliance with national objectives by means of best practice performance standards based on information that regulated entities provide in return for the freedom to experiment with solutions they prefer. … This type of self-government is, in the United States, currently emerging in settings as diverse as the regulation of nuclear power plants, community policing, procurement of sophisticated military hardware, environmental regulation, and child-protective services. … [The] combination of decentralization and mutual monitoring intrinsic to democratic experimentalism better protects the constitutional ideal than do doctrines [say] of the separation of powers, [doctrines that are] so at odds with current circumstances, that courts recognize the futility of applying them consistently in practice by limiting themselves to fitful declarations of their validity in principle. … [D]emocratic experimentalism requires … social actors, separately and in exchange with each other, to take constitutional considerations into account in their decision-making. [State structures] assist the actors even while monitoring their performance by scrutinizing the reactions of each to relevant proposals by … others. The courts then determine whether the [state] has met its obligations to foster and generalize the results of this information pooling. Agencies and courts alike use the rich record of the parties' intentions, as interpreted by their acts contained in the continuing, comparative evaluation of experimentation itself. … [T]he aim of democratic experimentalism is to democratize public decision-making from within, and so lessen the burdens on a judiciary that … awkwardly superintends the every-day workings of democracy … . [Democratic experimentalism] reconceptualizes constitutional rights. Relying … on ideas associated with early-twentieth-century American pragmatism, [democratic experimentalism] treats disagreements over rights as principally about how to implement widely shared general principles. … [T]he United States Supreme Court has recognized that there are often a variety of acceptable remedies for a violation of rights or a variety of acceptable means of achieving a constitutionally mandated end. … [Democratic experimentalism so reconceives] rights, [and] … other constitutionally entrenched principles, [so that] means and ends cannot be neatly separated … [E]xperimentation at the periphery also redefines the core, ultimately challenging the very distinction between core and periphery.[24]

The remainder of this section spins out the meaning of some of the more important facets of experimental constitutionalism. The first dominant feature of experimental constitutionalism is a commitment to shared constitutional interpretation – an invitation to the co-ordinate branches of government to engage in an on-going conversation about the meaning of the provisions found in our basic law. It directly challenges the arid doctrine of separation of powers that often substitutes for reasoned discourse about the political norms that govern our lives. The second feature, participatory bubbles, draws our attention to less rarefied but no less important constitutional conversations. While a scheme of shared constitutional interpretation introduces experimentalist elements into the upper tiers of government institutions, the notion of bubbles of participatory polyarchy directs our attention to experimentation in smaller units: at the level of the individual or the local community. (Consider again Simon's description of TPS.) Other central features of experimental constitutionalism – the nature of truth propositions in radically heterogeneous constitutional orders, a chastened commitment to deliberation, destablization rights, remedial equilibration that effects the disentrenchment of discriminatory forms of private ordering, reflexivity, and flattened hierarchies – are discussed in turn.

1. *Shared Constitutional Interpretation*

What is 'shared constitutional interpretation'? In short, it stands for four basic propositions. First. It supplants the notion of judicial supremacy with respect to constitutional interpretation. All branches of government have a relatively equal stake in giving our basic law content. Second. It draws attention to a shift in the status of court-driven constitutional doctrine. While courts retain the power to determine the content of any given provision, a commitment to shared constitutional interpretation means that a court's reading of the constitutional text does not exhaust all possible readings. To the extent that a court consciously limits the reach of its holding regarding the meaning of a given provision, the rest of the judgment should read as an invitation to the co-ordinate branches or other organs of state or to non-state actors to come up with their own alternative, but ultimately consistent, gloss on the text. Third. Shared constitutional competence married to a rather open-ended or provisional understanding of the content of the basic law is meant to increase the opportunities to see how different doctrines operate in practice and to maintain the space necessary to make revision of constitutional doctrines possible in light of new experience and novel demands. In this regard, the Constitutional Court might be understood to engage in norm-setting behaviour that provides guidance to other state actors without foreclosing the possibility of other effective safeguards for rights or other useful methods for their realization. Fourth. A commitment to shared interpretation ratchets down the conflict between co-ordinate branches of government and between the state and its citizens. Instead of an arid commitment to separation of powers – and the rhetorical flourishes about courts appropriately engaging in legal interpretation, not politics[25] – courts are freed of the burden of having to provide a theory of everything and can set about articulating a general framework within which different understandings of the basic text can co-exist. The courts and all other actors have more to gain from seeing how variations on a given constitutional norm work in practice.

The Constitutional Court has already endorsed this shared endeavour. In *National Education Health and Allied Workers Union v University of Cape Town*, the Constitutional Court recognized that the process of interpreting the Labour Relations Act in light of the demands of both FC s 39(2) and FC s 23(1) requires an appreciation of the legislature's and the courts' shared responsibility for interpreting the Final Constitution. The *NEHAWU* Court writes:

> The LRA was enacted 'to give effect to and regulate the fundamental rights conferred by s 23 of the [Final] Constitution.' In doing so the LRA gives content to s 23 of the [Final] Constitution and must therefore be construed and applied consistently with that purpose. Section 3(b) of the LRA underscores this by requiring that the provisions of the LRA must be interpreted 'in compliance with the Constitution'. Therefore the proper interpretation and application of the LRA will raise a constitutional issue. This is because the Legislature is under an obligation to 'respect, protect, promote and fulfil the rights in the Bill of Rights'. In many cases, constitutional rights can be honoured effectively only if legislation is enacted. Such legislation will of course always be subject to constitutional scrutiny to ensure that it is not inconsistent with the Constitution. Where the Legislature enacts legislation in the effort to meet its constitutional obligations, and does so within constitutional limits, courts must give full effect to the legislative purpose. Moreover, the proper interpretation of such legislation will ensure the protection, promotion and fulfilment of constitutional rights and as such will be a constitutional matter. In this way, the courts and the Legislature act in partnership to give life to constitutional rights.[26]

The creation of remedies for rights violations requires a similar sort of institutional comity. The *National Coalition for Gay and Lesbian Equality v Minister of Home Affairs* Court writes:

> It should also be borne in mind that whether the remedy a Court grants is one striking down, wholly or in part; or reading into or extending the text, its choice is not final. Legislatures are able, within constitutional limits, to amend the remedy, whether by re-enacting equal benefits, further extending benefits, reducing them, amending them, 'finetuning' them or abolishing them.[27]

Shared responsibility for interpreting the Final Constitution has its limits. The legislature – or the executive – must make a good faith attempt to revisit an issue in a new and constitutionally permissible way. In *Satchwell v President of the Republic of South Africa II*,[28] the Constitutional Court was asked to assess the constitutionality of a statutory and regulatory framework almost identical to one that it had pronounced unconstitutional only a year earlier in *Satchwell v President of the Republic of South Africa I*.[29] In *Satchwell I*, the Constitutional Court had declared ss 8 and 9 of the Judges' Remuneration and Conditions of Employment Act[30] unconstitutional because the sections discriminated against homosexual Judges' same-sex life partners. The *Satchwell I* Court ordered that the words 'or partner in a permanent same-sex life partnership in which the partners have undertaken reciprocal duties of support' be read into the provisions after the word 'spouse'. Subsequent to the judgment in *Satchwell I*, Parliament promulgated a new Act, the Judges' Remuneration and Conditions of Employment Act.[31] This Act took virtually no notice of the *Satchwell I* Court's order. In *Satchwell II*, the Constitutional Court refused to accord Parliament any deference, declared the new provisions discriminatory, and read into the new legislation the words 'or partner in a permanent same-sex life partnership in which the partners have undertaken reciprocal duties of support.'[32]

Michael Dorf and Barry Friedman use the cases of *Miranda* and *Dickerson* to great effect in explaining how shared constitutional interpretation actually works.[33] As any viewer of US police dramas knows, *Miranda* rights take, in part, the form of warnings that law enforcement officers must give detained persons prior to any custodial interrogation. What few viewers appreciate is the extent to which most of those warnings were intended as judicial guidelines and not as excavations of constitutional bedrock. The *Miranda* Court explains that it granted certiorari 'to explore some facets of the problems ... of applying the privilege against self-incrimination to in-custody interrogation, and to give concrete constitutional guidelines for law enforcement agencies and courts to follow.'[34] The US Supreme Court adumbrates its 'holding' at the outset, and that holding is only that the prosecution may not use statements made in custodial interrogation 'unless it demonstrates the use of procedural safeguards effective to secure' the privilege.[35] It then notes: 'As for the procedural safeguards to be employed, unless other fully effective means are devised to inform the accused persons of their right of silence and to assure a continuous opportunity to exercise it,' then the specific *Miranda* guidelines must be followed. At the very same time, the *Miranda* Court devotes the better part of a paragraph to prodding other governmental and law enforcement bodies into devising their own ways of safeguarding the right: 'We encourage Congress and the States to continue their laudable search for increasingly effective ways of protecting the rights of the individual while promoting efficient enforcement of our criminal laws.'[36] Twice more in the course of the judgment, the Supreme Court repeats the holding and re-extends the invitation. Congress accepted the invitation. But as the judgment in *Dickerson* reflects, it wilfully misconstrued the nature of the invitation. The US Congress did not, as the US Supreme Court suggested, come up with equally effective ways of safeguarding the right to remain silent and not to have statements made in custodial interrogation used by the prosecution unless adequate safeguards have been put in place. Congress simply enacted as legislation the pre-*Miranda* test that the voluntariness of a confession would be assessed in terms of a totality of the circumstances. The *Miranda*-specific warnings were merely included as factors to be taken into account when determining whter a confession was truly voluntary. Not surprisingly, the *Dickerson* Court rejected Congress' 'new' take on the voluntarine of custodial confessions. It did so, as Dorf and Friedman argue, because Congress had failed to take seriously the Court's concerns about the 'compulsion inherent in custodial interrogation' and had failed to offer an alternative that could be deemed 'equally effective in ameliorating this compulsion.'[37] While the 34 years between *Miranda* and *Dickerson* might have witnessed confusing dicta from the Court regarding the status and the reach of the holding in *Miranda*, Dorf and Friedman convincingly show that Congress and other government actors did indeed possess significant space to place their own gloss on the Fourth Amendment's protections.[38] What they were not free to do was ignore entirely even the narrowest possible construction of the *Miranda* Court's holding.

What shared constitutional interpretation demonstrates is that it is possible to overcome problems of information deficit, lack of cross-cultural understanding and limited institutional competence through a subtle recasting of existing constitutional doctrines, judicial remedies, and special court structures that extract better information and increase normative legitimacy through the use of more mindful interventions. Over time, courts, state actors and non-state actors will have the opportunity to determine whether various socio-political experiments have achieved the ends set for us by our basic law (as interpreted by the courts, the legislature, the executive and non-state actors). We will, in instances of policy failure, also have an opportunity to decide whether the norms or the ends set by the courts, the legislature, the executive and non-state actors constitute the best possible gloss on our basic law. Shared constitutional interpretation relies upon a principled negotiation and, perhaps more importantly, a rough and tumble engagement about norm setting between the courts, the co-ordinate branches of government, and the public.

2. *Participatory Bubbles*

In acknowledging the significant limitations of rational deliberation in bringing about radical reformation, Bruce Ackerman has offered an understanding of error-correction and political change that is restricted to a few key constitutional moments.[39] However, rather than limiting reconstruction of our basic law to a few earth-shaking moments of universal participation, the institutional design proposals contemplated by experimental constitutionalists seek to create small-scale bubbles of limited participatory democracy regarding the content of individual constitutional norms and their application to subject matter specific, and often time-sensitive, institutional contexts.

The physical metaphor of bubbles is meant to convey three qualities of such small-scale institutional processes. First, processes of participation and negotiation are a natural part of ongoing social interactions. They originate when challenges to a given institutional authority accumulate and finally come to a boil: just as bubbles form after pressure builds up and escape to the surface of a liquid. Second, bubbles are meant to suggest limits on the scope of participation. Bubbles only enclose a small amount of space – both in terms of the issues raised and the number of actors involved. Third, bubbles are ephemeral. After satisfactory resolutions emerge from processes of participatory engagement, the raison d'etre for the bubble may cease to exist. The bubble bursts. Participants can, generally speaking, return to their more routine lives. Still, various supervisory structures must often remain in place. We want to ensure that the experimental resolutions are, in fact, carried out. We want to learn as much as possible from the experiments – whether they work, and whether they alter our understanding of the norms that frame them.

How do bubbles relate to constitutional interpretation? As Robert Cover observed, interpretations of constitutional values are not confined to the courts. Instead, each community continually struggles to harmonize its internal values with the constitutional norms of the society at large.[40] Such interpretative struggles are not mere word games. They can pose serious questions of individual and group survival.[41] Does the constitutional right to shelter enable one to seek accountability from housing agencies?[42] Does the constitutional right to religious freedom allow a small and ostracized religious group to compel law enforcement agencies to accommodate their ostensibly deviant practices?[43] Does the foundational value of and right to equality permit one to challenge well-entrenched social mores – and the laws and traditional practices that flow from them – that discriminate on the basis of gender or sexuality or sexual orientation?[44]

Two important caveats.

As we saw in Chapter 3, deliberation – even when restricted to participatory bubbles – does not necessarily lead to better outcomes. As Susan Sturm and Cass Sunstein have pointed out, it can lead to greater polarization of positions.[45] However, the *negotiation* that occurs within participatory bubbles is less about reaching long-term binding consensus, and more about provisional agreement upon 'best practices'. The failure of a practice – the negative feedback from our social environment – should lead us back to the drawing board to reflect further upon the nature of our failure and the options that remain. Even here, a further caveat is in order. It seems relatively clear that many discussions between different branches of government in South Africa about 'best practices' never occur. They do not occur because the political branches of government often appear incapable of making sense of the general norms articulated by the courts and of implementing the general norms – in the form of law and policy – that they do understand.

The problem is somewhat more complicated. A lack of mutual understanding is to a large degree a function of hollow state structures (not unique to South Africa) that exist, not surprisingly, alongside an extremely thin and rather fractured civil society. A weak state and a weak civil society are the natural legacies of a racist authoritarian apartheid state that served a white minority. Our one party dominant democracy, with all its attendant problems, a largely supine business community, unions that now represent but a narrow band of class interests and the withdrawal of direct support from the international community have not helped matters. These observations are neither new nor controversial. To the extent that they have a bearing on the primary theses of this book, these claims are interrogated immediately below and again in Chapters 5, 6, 8 and 9.

The mere fact of participatory bubbles does not ensure better outcomes. Any court making use of various kinds of participatory bubbles must be alive to the possibility that the power imbalances reflected in adversarial legal processes will simply be replicated in a court-sanctioned participatory bubble. Courts must, in a Habermasian manner, attempt to craft bubbles that approximate 'ideal speech' conditions and that enable less powerful voices to be heard. In short, courts must be willing to articulate constitutional norms that enable less powerful stakeholders to have a meaningful role to play in a polycentric decision-making process.

Before we throw up our hands regarding the ability of our fellow denizens of South African polity to create such useful artefacts, we ought to consider the jurisprudence flowing out of the Constitutional Court and lower courts over the past few years. The Constitutional Court has, on numerous occasions now, set out a *very* general normative framework within which 'meaningful engagement' between conflicting parties can take place.[46] The Court's commitment to this meaningful engagement possesses three features that deserve closer attention.

First, they may not (necessarily) be limited to the initial parties to the litigation. Other interested stakeholders – amici et al – may participate in the problem-solving process.[47] The aim, again, is two-fold: greater elicitation of information; greater normative legitimacy of any decision ultimately taken.

Second, the other salient feature of these participatory bubbles is that they may not remain within the domain of the courts. We can easily imagine – and have witnessed in South Africa – greater community participation in hearings called by the South African Human Rights Commission,[48] other Chapter 9 institutions,[49] national or provincial legislatures,[50] school governing bodies,[51] and other social and political fora. The Constitutional Court has shown itself alive to the need for participatory bubbles when provincial legislatures take decisions that affect the lives of the denizens within their boundaries.[52] South Africa, despite the limits imposed by what remains a largely one party dominant state, has the tools available to make participatory bubbles the norm in norm-setting environments.

Third, participatory bubbles lose their cohesion – and the pressure to produce better than zero-sum outcomes – if the court's fail to articulate the norms within which a preferred solution is meant to occur. If experimental constitutionalism is judged to be an attractive set of principles by which to establish constitutional norms (by widespread public agreement) and to assess best practices (by inviting as many stakeholders as possible to design an optimal remedy for a specific social problem) then the jurisprudence of avoidance in the South African vernacular must be one of the first judicial doctrines to go. Several of the Constitutional Court's recent judgments must leave one concerned about the ability of the Court to articulate such norms.[53] Put somewhat differently, the process of general norm-setting by the courts that initiates a process of rolling best practices by other parts of the state never gains sufficient traction when constitutional norms remain radically under-theorized. Then again, the 2010/2011 judgements in *Glenister*[54] and *Blue Moonlight*[55] demonstrate the potential of a Constitutional Court that sets its horizons beyond a largely process-driven jurisprudence and alights upon something more substantial and substantive, decisions that model rational discourse (in a country sorely in need of it) by offering a thicker vision of the basic law that initiates discussion, engagement and action in other quarters of the republic.

However, let us assume that the courts and other political institutions adopted an experimentalist approach – replete with participatory bubbles and a commitment to shared constitutional interpretation. One must remember that one of the virtues of the experimentalist approach is that it is not static. New challenges to the general norms set by the courts, the legislative and the executive will arise. These new challenges will likely attract a host of new stakeholders – and thus new participatory bubbles. Experimentalism – especially in law and the social sciences – is a compelling answer to minimalism and absolutism because it recognizes (a) the ability to extract information to create norms that reflect the lived existence of people affected by the basic law; (b) that the circumstances governed by the basic law may change in ways unanticipated by the previous norms set by political institutions (and their stakeholders); and (c) the solutions upon which we alight may have unintended negative consequences that outstrip the apparent benefits. For example, the grnd compromise struck by the ANC, big business and the unions – which let to a peaceful transition in 1994 – has outlined its usefulness. A more capacious participatory bubble revisiting and reconstituting the content of our basic law may be in order. Here's a less troubling takeaway: the norms created by the courts or some other political body are understood to be rolling best practices that will be subject to change where and when the exigencies of the moment require such change.[56]

This kind of language is not new to South African politics and the basic law that both amplifies and constrains that politics. In one of the first white papers on primary and secondary education in post-apartheid South Africa, then Minister Bengu wrote:

> Policies are stated in general terms and cannot provide for all situations. Our legacy of injustice and mistrust continuously throws up problems which need the wisdom of Solomon to settle. In this protracted transitional period, in which new policies are being developed and implemented, the

> chances are that we shall collectively make many mistakes, either in conception or execution. They must be recognized and corrected. The possibility of damage will be reduced if new policies are based on knowledge of our charter of fundamental rights and on sufficient consultation with those who are affected by them, if compromises are negotiated, and if principled compromises are sought.[57]

Minister Bengu's approach to the problems of South African primary and secondary education in a post-apartheid dispensation fits my notion of experimental constitutionalism perfectly. The Minister understood the basic norms that governed South Africa's new constitutional order. He had consulted with all of the relevant stakeholders – simply too numerous to mention here. He, and his national Department of Education, in turn, generated a white paper that would become the South African Schools Act. At the same time, Minister Bengu recognized that the law and the policies reflected in SASA were always going to be provisional. They represented a good faith effort to solve the problems that faced primary and secondary schools in South Africa. But he could not say, in advance, which policies would best serve the general commonweal and whether the provisions of our social contract might not change over time.

In the intervening 15 years, South Africa has witnessed two kinds of participatory bubbles in education: the first court-initiated, and the second driven by NGOs attempting to revise government policy. A largely grass-roots social movement, Equal Education (EE) claims, on its own behalf, that

> In just under two years, Equal Education's campaign has forced government to acknowledge a major gap in policy [the absence of adequate school libraries], achieved the publication of the overarching policy on the equitable provision of school infrastructure, forced publishers to acknowledge their prohibitively high prices, cultivated a reading consciousness in thousands of young people ... and built a new generation of activist leaders.[58]

While EE deserves credit for initiating a new social movement, along with Section 27, the Legal Resources Centre, the Socio-Economic Rights Institute and the Centre for Child Law, those claims must be viewed with a pinch of salt – and against the background of the pre-existing dismal performance of our primary and secondary public school system. Libraries are great when teachers are capable of or interested in teaching learners to read.

In *Head of Department, Mpumalanga Department of Education and Another v Hoërskool Ermelo and Another*, a case of racial exclusion masquerading as cultural autonomy, the Constitutional Court catechised two different policy initiatives.[59] Since s 29(2) does not guarantee single medium education to any public school, the first initiative, and the central holding of the case, requires that the Mpumalanga Head of Department, the Ermelo School Governing Body, principal, teaching staff, parents and learners accept that the school is now open to speakers of both Afrikaans and English, and orders the parties to find a way to satisfy the rights of all learners to a basic education. Although the Court establishes the framework – in terms of 29(2) of the Constitution and the South African Schools Act – for the resolution of this matter and subsequent similar matters, it does not dictate how the aim of equal access is to be achieved. While the Court found that good reasons may well exist for the withdrawal of the SGB's restrictive language policies, it required both the HoD and the SGB to revisit the existing language policy of the Hoërskool Ermelo school in light of the needs of learners in the Ermelo circuit and then *report back* to the Court with regard to their findings. Secondly, the Deputy Chief Justice, in what he describes as a 'collateral irony of this case' writes that:

> Learners whose mother tongue is not English, but rather one of our indigenous languages, together with their parents, have made a choice to be taught in a language other than their mother tongue. This occurs even though it is now well settled that, especially in the early years of formal teaching, mother-tongue instruction is the foremost and the most effective medium of imparting education. Ample literature indicates that in Africa the former colonial languages have become the dominant medium of teaching. *However, I need say no more about this irony because the matter does not arise for adjudication.*[60]

Deputy Chief Justice Moseneke has tapped a growing consensus that the de facto default position of English as the primary language of instruction from primary school onwards has not served South African learners well and that school language policy ought to take on a far more multilingual cast.

One experiment in education appears to reach its denouement in *Ermelo* (the autonomy of single medium Afrikaans public schools). At the same time, the *Ermelo* Court suggests that the Court might welcome results of a new experiment: an attempt by educators to determine whether multilingualism in schools is essential for the success of most South African learners (because they will only learn effectively if mother tongue instruction is offered) and whether multilingualism (that embraces an African language) amongst existing white elites will lead to the kind of mutual respect and integration required for the South African democratic project to succeed.

These two examples demonstrate two other features of participatory bubbles. First, they are not only created by courts. Second, they constitute a form of shared constitutional interpretation.

Robert Post and Riva Segal, writing in a slightly different vein, likewise demonstrate that the current understanding of fundamental norms of a Constitution can be tested and rejected by members of the polis, when popular movements arise to contest the norms as currently read.[61] Such popular movements may not result in progressive outcomes. As Riva Segal has recently shown, the assault on the original intent of the United States' 2nd Amendment's 'right to bear arms' succeeded in bringing about a conservative outcome because a 40 year old popular movement (spurred on by the National Rifle Association) altered the accepted (200 year old) discourse within the legal system.[62] (However a recent murderous attack at a Connecticut public school has prompted several new political initiatives by states to ban assault weapons entirely. Thus, a Conservative Supreme Court may see some of its work undone by individual states over time.)

3. *Truth Propositions in Radically Heterogeneous Constitutional Orders*[63]

Recall that our account of the self and the social in chapters 2 and 3 relied heavily on the heterogeneity of the self and the social as an opportunity for experimentation and an engine for change. A question naturally exists about whether this heterogeneity of the self and the social – contingent as they are upon a broad, heterogeneous array of endowments – undercuts the veracity of the truth statements at which we arrive through our participation in common political processes or impedes the acceptance of moral, political and judicial pronouncements by various political institutions. My position: heterogeneity does not entail incommensurable conceptual schemes that preclude translation and general agreement about most truth propositions (whether scientific or ethical or constitutional.) Moreover, the kind of pragmatism adopted in these pages need not be held hostage by a Fishian anti-foundationalism.

To understand why this is so, it is necessary to take a step back and consider the theory of interpretation and truth upon which this book is grounded. On this account, 'snow is 'white' because snow is white in the world – in English, in Sepedi, in German or in Zulu – and not because snow is 'white' relative to a particular linguistic set of conventions. That does not mean that our statements about the world cannot be false. As Donald Davidson powerfully puts the point:

> But of course it cannot be assumed that speakers never have false beliefs. Error is what gives belief its point. We can, however, take it as given that *most* beliefs are correct. The reason for this is that a belief is identified by its location in a pattern of beliefs: it is this pattern that determines the subject matter of the belief, what the belief is about. Before some object in, or aspect of, the world can become part of the subject matter of a belief (true or false) there must be *endless true beliefs* about the subject matter.[64]

'Endless true beliefs'. It is this notion of 'endless true beliefs' that allows us – today – to engage texts several millennia old, or a variety of 21st century South African texts in Zulu, Sepedi, Afrikaans, Xhosa and English, or bodies of constitutional law in a variety of polities, say Germany, India and Canada. Put somewhat differently, Davidson writes:

> It isn't that any one belief necessarily destroys our ability to identify further beliefs, but the intelligibility of such identifications must depend on a background of largely unmentioned and unquestioned true beliefs ... What makes interpretation possible then is the fact that we can dismiss a priori the chance of massive error. A theory of interpretation cannot be correct that makes a man assent to very many false propositions: it must generally be the case that a sentence is true when a speaker holds it to be true. But of course the speaker may be wrong; and so may the interpreter.[65]

On this account of knowledge, interpretation and truth, we must recognize that most of our fellow human beings are generally correct about most of the statements that they make about the world. This working assumption actually allows us to sharpen areas of disagreement – so that we might later arrive at more precise propositions about the truth.'[66] Problems arise – in constitutional law, as in any other domain of thought – primarily when we refuse to state our presuppositions or our conclusions clearly (when 'language goes on holiday') and when those who make the law or control various avenues of expression abuse their positions of power (the 'big lie').[67]

Recall that Wittgenstein offers a similar account of truth propositions in his *Philosophical Investigations.*[68] For Wittgenstein, it is essential that we get our order of priority straight. Once a practice is established (through *successful regular action*[69]), only then might we wish, upon reflection, to test its assumptions and results through experiments that do or do not confirm aspects of the practice's usefulness, or our ability to extend its usefulness. Wittgenstein clearly demonstrates that: (a) regular successful action comes first; (b) we all already have the material at hand to share, verifiable truth propositions about most of what we know about the world; (c) only at the very margins of belief, once we have aggressively learned all there is to be learned from one another, do our differences have any meaningful bite. (I introduced this thesis above in Chapter 1, and develop this thesis, and its application to South African constitutional law, at greater length, elsewhere, below.[70])

The ramifications for our constitutional theory should be obvious. Seventeen years into our constitutional project in South Africa, the basic law still functions both as a social contract and as a contract about whose terms we largely agree. (Whether we have discharged the terms of that contract are another matter.[71] Many, if not a majority of South Africans, believe that we have not.) Were it otherwise, the machinery of the state would grind to a complete halt and the body of constitutional jurisprudence our courts have generated would lack the coherence that it does, in fact, possess. That does not mean all cases have been correctly decided, or that all of the constitutional doctrines developed thus far are internally coherent. As Davidson pointed out above – errors exist, and will persist. However, these errors are only intelligible against a background of endless true beliefs about the world about us and the Constitution that governs us.

4. *Chastened Deliberation*

This possession of endlessly true beliefs about the world does not mean that disagreements – and significant disagreements will not arise. Indeed, South African constitutional law as a domain of study seems especially bedevilled by disagreement. But in a highly heterogeneous society such as our own, undergoing a difficult and slow transition from a fascist racist order to a more egalitarian pluralist order, what might count as 'on the margin' of belief sets in more established democracies often forms the heart of political debate in contemporary South Africa. The question, then, is whether, and to what extent, these heated disagreements (on the nationalization of mineral wealth, expedited land reform, universal health care, and the requisite conditions for job creation) can be resolved simply by rational discourse. Given my predisposition with regard to matters of truth claims, I tend to believe that our significant disagreements flow from ongoing, radical inequalities of power and an inability to form the substratum of trust necessary to have the open, honest conversations that would enable us to act, successfully, and regularly, in manner that reflects rather obvious truths about the world we inhabit.

Given its commitment to empiricism, experimental constitutionalism is not inclined toward deep Habermasian conceptions of deliberative democracy. (How far are we today from an ideal speech situation? Perhaps our *first* goal in South Africa should be to move away from having the highest Gini co-efficient in the world.) We have already seen the extent to which our ways of being in the world are radically given. Moreover, given my theory of the social, we must also recognize the broad array of cognitive biases that appear in our deliberative processes.

A thus-chastened commitment to deliberation means that public choices should be arrived at through processes that allow for the active participation of all meaningful stakeholders and are free, to the maximum extent possible, from coercion.[72] This chastened form of deliberation promises four goods: flexibility, accountability, learning by doing and the inculcation of trial and error as part of those practices that admit of error. The last part of this chapter, as well as Chapters 5 and 6, describes in detail some of the multi-stakeholder engagement fora that create feedback mechanisms without necessarily destroying existing stores of social capital or the political institutions through which experiment and change are negotiated.

5. *Destablization Rights*

In a country such as ours, with deep divisions in class (as well as race and gender and a host of other ascriptive characteristics), the notion of destabilization rights that lie at the heart of experimental constitutional thought resonates quite strongly with the goals of our own aspirational constitution. Destabilization rights function as an extended metaphor. You won't find them expressly articulated in the Bill of Rights, nor anywhere else in the Constitution. What this term of art depicts is how actual rights and other structures can be used to challenge the status quo.

Roberto Unger's idea of a rotating capital fund is the best available intuition pump if one's aim is to enable others to come to grips rather quickly with the purpose of destabilization rights.[73] In response to the tendency of virtually all capitalist systems to lock-in access to capital, and to pass on wealth from one familial or caste generation to the next, Unger's rotating capital fund ensures that all members of and groups within a state would have access to and control over a substantial portion of a polity's available economic capital at some point in time. The fund's period of rotation – Unger suggests five years – would guarantee that people have (1) an incentive to use the existing capital to maximise immediate return and (2) an incentive to ensure that existing capital is put to long term employment that will benefit all members of society (including those persons or groups at the helm of the fund at any given moment). Given that Brazil had, during the 1970s, the world's highest gini co-efficient, Unger's idea of a rotating capital fund was meant to challenge the country's radical inequality of wealth and power.

We can contrive a similar set of incentives for other political, social and economic institutions. In order to ensure that elites do not capture state institutions, we might attempt to make provision for political arrangements that ensure that various groups and persons each have a turn at the helm. Or, at a minimum, we can create bubbles of participatory democracy. The end of such institutional arrangements is not change for change's sake. Like the rotating capital fund, these political arrangements are best characterised as super-liberal.[74] The destabilisation rights that any such super-liberal community might devise are designed to ensure that dominant beliefs do not remain dominant simply because they serve the interests of elites. For political or legal interests to remain dominant they must – as a prescriptive matter – offer solace for those who did not contrive them in the first place.[75] Even in more modest incarnations, destabilization rights allow individuals and groups to participate in the political processes that shape their lives.[76]

Destabilisation rights are profitably contrasted with negative conceptions of liberty. Negative liberty takes stability as a good even where such stability works manifest injustice and takes certainty as a good even where it creates no efficiencies.[77] Destabilisation rights make no such assumptions about stability, certainty or efficiency.[78] A political system that relies upon destabilisation rights assumes that the legitimacy of any legal doctrine depends upon its ability to serve the interests of most sectors of society (and not merely the elites that have historically controlled the various organs of state.)

Destabilization rights can take a number of different forms: a rotating capital fund is but one. In another incarnation, destabilization rights might result in a judicial remedy for stakeholders who seek accountability from a government agency that influences private ordering, or a social institution that exercises significant public power. Assertion of destabilization rights in these contexts provides two forms of relief to the stakeholders. First, they require those in power to account for their decisions on the basis of evidence and reasonable arguments. Second, they bestow upon stakeholders rights of participation in processes meant to address problems that concern them.[79]

The courts have an important role to play in establishing destabilization rights. In contrast to legislative and administrative solutions, the judiciary has a fairly low informational threshold. Under the liberal standing rules of the Final Constitution, many types of parties are eligible to initiate suit. Moreover, because courts have extensive powers for structuring the scope of discovery, their capacity for information-gathering, once a suit has begun, may be substantially greater than a legislature or administrative agencies.[80] Assuming adequate resources – a potentially tendentious assumption in South Africa – a larger range of rights-based conflicts may be brought to the attention of the judiciary[81] than to the legislature or administrative agencies.[82]

More importantly, as Unger recognized, the law has an inherently disentrenching power. Because legal norms are intrinsically linked to people's self-conceptions and social practices, judicial decisions tend to have a greater impact than more narrowly confined administrative decisions. Consider the following hypothetical case. A medical student who suffers from a disability is denied a medical licence. The denial stems in part from the substantial public opprobrium that attaches to his disability and in part from the difficultly the disability presents in performing certain procedures. The aggrieved medical student challenges the denial of his medical licence in court. The court grants an interdict requiring medical professional boards to work with that student and others similarly situated, in good faith, in order to find a meaningful accommodation.[83]

The court's disentrenching power influences the behaviour of relevant actors in two respects. The primary effect of that judicial decision is to initiate a process of negotiation and, hopefully, accommodation within the medical profession of practitioners with a particular disability. In addition, the impact of that decision and the new legal doctrines contained therein will have a cascading effect in the broader sphere of private conduct. Many other licensing organizations – such as those for nurses, attorneys, and accountants – will seek to negotiate with disabled professionals, *ex ante*, to reach mutually agreeable accommodations that avoid the costs of litigation and that create formal or informal affirmative defences in the event of litigation.

As Abraham Chayes has suggested, courts enjoy other institutional advantages relative to administrative agencies. They possess greater independence and are less likely to be subject to interest-group capture.[84] They possess greater institutional legitimacy and often benefit from a public perception of neutrality. Those qualities make it possible for courts to structure solutions intended to protect fundamental rights.[85]

6. *The Disentrenchment of Private Ordering through Remedial Equilibration*

The disentrenchment of private ordering, consistent with such destabilization rights, raises thorny questions about how and where we want such disentrenchment to occur. Constitutionalism invariably entails the protection of various forms of private ordering. Civil and political rights protect – and re-inscribe – extant ways of being. It cannot, and should not, be otherwise. Many traditional ways of being in the world are only now experiencing a collective sense of political freedom long repressed under apartheid.

And yet what are we to do when these traditional ways of being in the world re-inscribe patriarchy, racism, homophobia or capitalist inequality?[86] Experimental constitutionalism recognizes that private ordering often reinforces social hierarchies that diminish individual flourishing. Experimental constitutionalism, at least in so far as it is to have meaningful application in South Africa, must be committed to forms of state intervention that shake up existing restrictive, discriminatory hierarchies and that create the space for new ways of being to emerge.[87] As I shall argue below, the commitment to flourishing means, at a minimum, that individuals in traditional communities or conservative religious communities must be afforded the means to exit those communities when those communities fail to offer them what they deem to be 'lives worth valuing'.

I briefly suggested above how a commitment to remedial equilibration might shake up extant hierarchies in a manner that increases the chances that individuals will possess the opportunity to pursue a life worth valuing, or, at a minimum, enable them to enter the public square without experiencing shame. Walzer describes the lineaments of this kind of egalitarian pluralist order as follows:

> No more bowing and scraping, fawning and toadying; no more fearful trembling; no more high-and-mightiness; no more master, no more slaves. It is not a hope for the elimination of differences. We don't all have to be the same or have the same amounts of the same things. Men and women are one another's equals (for all important moral and political purposes) when no one possesses or controls the means of domination. But the means of domination are differently constituted in different societies, [publics, communities and associations].[88]

At the same time, he reminds us that this deep, profound and widely shared yearning does not conduce to the distribution of goods necessary for flourishing by a central, benign entity:

> [There] has never been either a single criterion, or a single set of interconnected criteria, for all distributions. Desert, qualification, birth and blood, friendship, need, free exchange, political loyalty, democratic decisions: each has had its place, along with many others, uneasily coexisting, invoked by competing groups, confused with one another.[89]

Social goods that give meaning to life, as well as those social goods that make a meaningful life possible to pursue, are produced by and maintained by a panoply of different associational forms of life (over which we have little control).[90] Since, according to Walzer, we possess no single matrix for distribution of goods and entitlements (material and immaterial), our primary concern should be to prevent monopoly power or domination with respect to the distribution of one set of goods from determining the distribution of another set of goods. Given the rather egalitarian nature of his project, it may come as a surprise to find that Walzer is not adamantly opposed to the distribution of personal property through the market. Well-regulated markets, through price and other forms of information dissemination, are generally more efficient than central planners in determining an optimal distribution of existing material goods and the creation of new technologies.[91] The problem with market distributions is not with their efficient distribution of material goods, but with the ability of natural persons and juristic persons to use their dominance and monopoly power in various segments of market economies to determine the distribution of goods in other spheres of human activity. As Walzer writes:

> Dominance describes a way of using social goods that isn't limited by their intrinsic meanings ... Monopoly describes a way of owning or controlling social goods in order to exploit their dominance. When goods are scarce and widely needed, like water in a desert, monopoly will make them dominant. Mostly, however, dominance is a more elaborate form of social creation, the work of many hands, mixing reality and symbol. Physical strength, familial reputation, religious or political office, landed wealth, capital, technical knowledge: each of these, in different historical periods, has been dominant; and each of them monopolized by some group of men and women. And then all good things come to those who have the one best thing. Possess the one, and the others come in train. Or, to change the metaphor, a dominant good is converted into another good, into many others, in accordance with what appears to be a natural process but is in fact magical, a kind of social alchemy.[92]

Leaving aside the insuperable problem of overlap between spheres and competing criteria for the distribution of the same good,[93] perhaps the most interesting outcome of the Walzerian approach to these quasi-private/quasi-public exchanges has been the recognition that constitutional litigation around sensitive issues of individual dignity and collective identity need not be a zero sum game. As the Constitutional Court recognised in *Sanderson*, rights and remedies under the South African Constitution are both linked and flexible. Justice Kriegler, on behalf of the *Sanderson* Court writes: 'Our flexibility in providing remedies may affect our understanding of the right'.[94] Such a flexible relationship between rights and remedies has not generally been the norm.

Oliver Wendell Holmes – a realist shot through and through – thought the law nothing more than a set of legitimate expectations about the order a court would grant: 'The prophecies of what the courts will do in fact, and nothing more pretentious, are what I mean by the law'.[95] In addition to this rather raw outcome-based assessment of the law, as Michael Bishop notes, stand two other traditional views of the relationship between rights and remedies – automatic remedialism and rights essentialism.[96] In terms of automatic remedialism, 'a finding that law or conduct is unconstitutional results automatically in a finding of invalidity'.[97] In the lexicon of rights essentialism, writes Lawrence Sager, 'there is an important distinction between a statement which describes an ideal which is embodied in the Constitution and a statement that attempts to translate such an ideal into a workable standard for the decision of concrete issues'.[98] Daryl Levison describes the distinction in starker terms: rights are 'ideals, ultimate value judgments that are derived from some privileged source of legitimacy'; remedies 'exist not in the realm of the ideal but ... in the domain of contingent facts'.[99]

A third relationship between rights and remedies that more closely resembles Kriegler J's intuition in *Sanderson* goes by the moniker of 'remedial equilibration'.[100] Remedial equilibration – much like Martha Nussbaum's notion of 'perceptive equilibrium'[101] – acknowledges that rights and remedies (ideal and real) are 'interdependent and inextricably intertwined'.[102] The two-sidedness of the real and the ideal, contends Paul Gewirtz, 'pervades the judicial function'.[103] The two-sidedness, continues Gewirtz, means that:

> [P]racticalities cannot be cordoned off into a separate domain to keep rights-declaring purely ideal. There is a permeable wall between rights and remedies: the prospect of actualizing rights through a remedy – the recognition that rights are for actual people in an actual world – makes it inevitable that thoughts of remedy will affect thoughts of right, that judges' minds will shuttle back and forth between right and remedy.[104]

What might this permeability of rights and remedies, this flexibility in determining the normative content of rights and the particularity of related remedies, mean for the issues surrounding findings of discrimination in a host of hierarchical ways of being in the world that preclude so many of us from flourishing? Well, for starters, those forms of life that distribute unequivocally public goods – say, our universities – are clearly subject to a no holds barred attack on discriminatory practices and equally intrusive remedies that would rectify the wrong. However, as we move away from public or quasi-public institutions toward associational forms that have a discernibly private cast, the need to distinguish between differentiation and domination, and between monopoly power and tyranny, becomes more pronounced, the likelihood of a finding of unfair discrimination less likely, and the need to consider remedies less invasive of the association, the community or the sub-public in question of greater necessity.

It's rather easy to dispatch with the conceit that an individual might have an entitlement – a right – to become a member of a pre-existing intimate relationship between Joan and John, or Peter and Paul. But what might we say about religious communities that discriminate, in terms of membership, or the distribution of other goods, on the basis of sex or sexual orientation? Here, at least, potential findings of a rights violation and remedial action are on the cards.

One possibility is that one might find that unfair discrimination has occurred in terms of s 9(4) of the Constitution or relevant provisions of the Promotion of Equality and Prevention of Unfair Discrimination Act (PEPUDA). Such a finding need not dictate an 'automatic remedy'. We might find an Orthodox Jewish Shul's partition of male members and female members of the community to constitute unfair discrimination. (The very nature of the upstairs/downstairs arrangement consigns women to second-class citizenship within that community.) However, it may be that such a finding alone is remedy enough. The finding recognises the impairment of the dignity of female members of the Orthodox Jewish Shul without interfering with the well-established distribution of goods within that community. Put differently, the political public may articulate dismay with respect to the on-going subordination of women in a religious sub-public, but refrain from dictating the rules that a particular religious community continues to hold sacred. Similarly, the discharge of a gay pianist from musical instruction at a religious private school solely on the grounds of sexual orientation might warrant a finding of unfair discrimination under s 9(4) of the Constitution or the applicable provisions of PEPUDA. Given the host of creative remedies available under PEPUDA and the Constitution, one can imagine that a court would rightly hold that neither the state nor natural or juristic persons may treat another natural person as a second-class citizen and then order (a) an apology; or (b) damages commensurate with the harm and the dislocation caused; and/or (c) assistance, along with assistance from the state, in finding the pianist new and comparable employment. All such remedies are within the power of the court to grant. The religious private school, having been remonstrated, may continue to operate in a rather restrictive manner. (It would, of course, be foolish to repeat the same error again. Such behaviour might meet with less judicial solicitude the second time around.) Over time, all South African citizens come to learn that the basic law and super-ordinate legislation does not tolerate second-class citizenship.

A remedial equilibration approach in these circumstances possesses a number of virtues. First, it recognises constitutionally-mandated tolerance for the multiple forms of private ordering of different communities within the political borders of our radically heterogeneous South Africa. Second, the notion that one might 'seek justice elsewhere' recognises the agency of ordinary South Africans with respect to exploring new homes or the construction of new communities. Two provisos attach here: (1) communities found to diminish the life opportunities of some members have an obligation to leverage existing stores of real and figurative capital to make such exit viable; (2) the state, having found the traditional community wanting, must provide the material means necessary to ensure that the citizens subject to unfair discrimination have a genuine 'opportunity' to flourish elsewhere. Third, it averts the potential for politicisation of the affairs of various minority and traditional communities that might lead to a bench or reformation of the basic law that actually works against the very discrimination one seeks to undo. This third virtue is not a grim fairy-tale. Witness recent calls for judicial reform within South Africa (bracketing for the moment the unprincipled political expediency that lies beneath them). Take as established writ that the modern religious-conservative political movement that would roll back a woman's reproductive autonomy entirely in the US was born hot on the heels of the US Supreme Court decision – *Roe v Wade* – that still constitutes the apogee of women's equal rights jurisprudence in the US.[105] We must recognise that the rise of right-wing parties in Europe that oppose the grant of entitlements to minority groups, or the success in the United States of an extremely conservative movement that would withhold benefits to undocumented persons and their children born in the United States, has gained traction through the legalization, of what one might call, a negative politics of difference. In South Africa, our current president, Jacob Zuma, regularly plays to traditional and revanchist communities by making rather demeaning remarks with respect to particular historically disadvantaged minority groups. Remedial equilibration holds out the potential for realizing a more egalitarian pluralist order, through various forms of disentrenchment of power within highly stratified private orders, without incurring the backlash associated with automatic remedies and rights essentialism.

7. *Reflexivity and Optimality*

Ethical, political and constitutional empiricism requires that we evaluate social norms and institutional arrangements against our practical experience instead of a priori norms or mere intuition.[106] In keeping with the leitmotif of this work, it follows that social norms and associational arrangements ought to be altered in light of the success or the failure of various experiments in living undertaken by the state.[107]

Experimentalism is made more coherent by a concomitant commitment to reflexivity. Operationally, reflexivity describes a political system that systematically evaluates the record of past performance and adjusts accordingly. Michael Dorf and Charles Sable, for example, see reflexivity embodied in the idea of very general, centralized standard-setting, localized experimentation, and rolling implementation of best-practices.[108] As a matter of principle, reflexivity demands that we be willing to examine and to put to the test, individually and collectively, our preferred ends and the means for achieving them. This dimension of experimentalism corresponds with the notion that, in a representative and participatory democracy, no ideas or policies should be regarded as above criticism or immune to change. (At the same, this work's commitment to flourishing means that in a constitutional democracy such as our own, one cannot speak of a constitutional project without pre-commitments to a range of capabilities and entitlements and principles: universal suffrage, the absence of slavery or servitude, access to a panoply of basic goods and a commitment to the rule of law.)[109]

As Simon notes above, achieving optimality with respect to individual and collective behaviour requires great circumspection in an experimentalist order.[110] First, given that most of our ends are chosen for us, optimality primarily means maximizing utility within a highly circumscribed value domain. The best most of us can hope for is the capacity to achieve the goals that matter to us – and not to select new ones. Second, as my discussion (in Chapters 2 and 3) of error correction with respect to the individual and the social reflects, regular experience of failure in terms of the achievement of dominant existing ends should lead to reorientation toward other ends. Third, as the discussion of Sunstein's recent work revealed, our preferences are relatively adaptive: alter the environment and one can shift expectations and change behaviour. Experimentalism is both the justification for the selection of alternative ends and the method for achieving them.

8. *Flattened Hierarchies Rather than Top-Down Command and Control*

State intervention can take two forms. Neither excludes the other. It can either be imposed from above, via direct state action, or originate from below, through the initiative of informed and trained individual stakeholders. Direct state action offers the virtue of speed. It suffers from two important drawbacks: information deficiency and lack of participation. First, reconfiguring social institutions requires a certain amount of inside information. If trained anthropologists find such an understanding of other cultures exceedingly difficult, how much greater is the challenge for an untrained and often overwhelmed bureaucratic administrative staff paid to solve pressing polycentric problems.[111] Second, by relying on a bureaucratic process, a top-down approach faces the peril of excluding the participation of the people most directly affected. Not only does such exclusion fuel the information deficit already discussed, it can also undermine an essential part of South Africa's political project of liberation – to change the mind-set of those who govern. Finally, the silence of those affected undermines the legitimacy of the decisions taken.

As we saw from Simon's analysis of Toyota's Performance System, a flattened hierarchy within most social systems possesses the benefits of 'emphasizing the goals of learning and innovation', 'treats normative decision-making in hard cases as presumptively collective and interdisciplinary (rather than the heroic labour of solitary professionals), and 'attempts to bracket or sublimate issues of individual and retrospective fairness or blame'.[112] Individual citizens and communities within an experimental constitutional democracy are viewed as sources of solutions, are made part of decision-making processes that concern them and become part of a political community that is forward and lateral looking, rather than backward, upward, and punitive.

C. Potential Limits of Experimental Constitutionalism in South Africa

It would be pollyannaish, at best, to assume that the experimental constitutionalism literature of the United States or the new governance literature in Europe could be transplanted to South Africa without limitation. These limitations warrant serious consideration, though they are by no means insurmountable.

1. *Institutional Undercapacity*

The limits of traditional legislative or administrative solutions to social ills manifest in two ways. First, a given legislature or an administrative agency will lack a panoptic view of all relevant information about a particular form of abuse. The procedural requirements of the legislative process place inherent limits on the range of issues that can be addressed within a given session. Moreover, a good deal of legislative time must be devoted to more pressing political issues: foreign policy, economic development and budget allocation. Accordingly, legislatures will rarely meet the informational threshold necessary for optimal solutions to rights-based issues. Administrative agencies, in developed countries, often have greater expertise than other branches of government with respect to the enforcement of a specific set of rights. They therefore should possess a significantly lower informational threshold for action. That said, considerations of procedural fairness, on the one hand, and interest group capture, on the other, often constrain their capacity for engaging in pro-active, rights-vindicating, fact-finding processes.

South Africa's legislatures, administrative agencies and courts face even greater challenges. First, as Sujit Choudhry, Heinz Klug and Theunis Roux have demonstrated, they operate within and are subject to the pathologies of a one party dominant democracy.[113] The dominance of the African National Congress over the first 18 years of democracy cabins contestation of its preferences – whether it be in law or policy. Second, the often dramatic under-capacity of local government and the fourth branch of government (state bureaucracies) limit the ability of the state to discharge its constitutional obligations.[114] Third, limited resources constrain effective legislative and administrative solutions. The twin forces of budgetary pressures and conflicting priorities – say between large-scale delivery of such basic goods as housing, health and education – means that while the legislature may be committed to human rights generally, it will experience little meaningful pressure to address rights violations experienced by marginal or vulnerable groups.[115] Finally, limits on the fiscus – even without conflicts in priority – will continue to constrain the legislature's capacity to make good the promise of various constitutional rights.[116]

In addition, experimental constitutionalism requires institutions – courts, legislatures, bureaucracies and the various executive branches of national, provincial and local government – capable of understanding constitutional doctrine and acting upon that understanding. Closely reasoned judgments coupled with the political branches' understanding of the Court's pronouncements should – theoretically – both constrain judicial decision-making in subsequent cases and enable state actors to anticipate whether the laws they wish to promulgate will pass constitutional muster.[117] Of course, for this last proposition to be meaningful, state actors would have to be able to follow Constitutional Court judgments and Constitutional Court judgments would have to be sufficiently well and deeply reasoned to constrain judicial and non-judicial actors.[118]

However, a Constitutional Court that takes some pride in its ability to avoid constitutional issues, and saying no more than is necessary about those issues, is unlikely to produce a corpus of judgments that constrain judicial and non-judicial actors.[119] As to whether most state actors are actually attempting to make sense of and enforce Constitutional Court judgments, Roach and Budlender's careful analysis of the state's implementation of court ordered remedies suggests that many wilfully ignore them.[120] If Roach and Budlender are correct, then the actual political environment in South Africa may force upon us more modest expectations for the court-based, or issue specific forum-based, standard-setting and rolling implementation of best-practices that Dorf, Friedman, Simon, Sturm and Sabel identify as the *sine qua non* of successful experimental constitutionalism. On the other hand, Dorf, Friedman, Simon, Sturm and Sabel give us reason to believe that by returning responsibility for decision-making to the actors most immediately affected by political, administrative or judicial edicts, we stand a better chance of fixing what is broken. (It may mean, *hold your breath*, returning responsibility for various public functions to the citizens who legitimately expect delivery of basic public or common goods.) Experimental constitutionalism relies upon (a) a relatively high degree of participatory politics and (b) a commitment to fairly flexible, standard-based judicial and non-judicial adjudication.[121] Roach and Budlender's apprehensions and recent studies conducted by Ivor Chipkin loom large.[122] They remain, however, descriptive. We retain the capacity to do and to be otherwise.

2. *Traditional Forms of Life and Radical Reformation*

This work attempts to steer a path between the conservation of traditional social orders and the commitment to radical change (in widespread areas of social life) required by our basic law. Commitments to religious freedom, cultural and linguistic community rights, property rights, associational freedom and even freedom of trade, occupation and profession ensure a relatively high degree of private ordering beyond the reach of the state, and the pluralism to which these rights are committed does not generally lead to greater heterogeneity, new experiments in living and more egalitarian outcomes. Socio-economic rights – to education, to housing, to a healthy environment, to food, to water, to health and to social security – have the potential to bring about *radical* change (even as one must acknowledge that they have only been partially vindicated.)

The conservative dimension of this work's politics reflects an initial understanding of the self and the social that acknowledges that human flourishing largely consists of doing that which we are already doing – only better. It requires the reinforcement or the creation of social space that enables the group practices upon which individual meaning is contingent to continue.[123] A conservative politics recognizes the extent to which 'meaning makes us'.

The radical dimension of this work's politics recognizes the vast inequalities in existing stocks of social and economic capital that sustain various stores of meaning in South Africa. We cannot commit ourselves to flourishing without acknowledging that all citizens must have roughly equal access to the kinds of capital needed to support practices that have been historically marginalized. The nation state is, as things stand, the preferred engine for the redistribution of those resources that will support such practices. If we tie our constitutional project too closely to tradition and conservation, then the danger exists that the state will not be able to prevent individuals and groups from using existing practices and associational forms to reinforce domination and tyrranny. Radical reformation must hold out to individuals the promise of moving away from a way of being in the world that diminishes the self, to a way of being in the world that holds out the potential for the enrichment of the self.

D. Normative Content of Experimental Constitutionalism

As I noted earlier, many pragmatist projects are often subject to a single, but harsh, indictment. They are viewed as largely instrumental and without the capacity for establishing the ends by which (any degree of) success might be measured. The proper rejoinder – crucial to the success of experimental constitutionalism in South Africa – is to lay out the contours of a commitment to flourishing. My riff on flourishing is most congenial to two of the most important advances in recent political theory: development studies and the capabilities approach.

1. *On Flourishing*

In Chapters 2 and 3, we have seen how the individual, though fundamentally conditioned by the world, can use the various critical tools at her disposal to engage in more optimal forms of behaviour. We have seen that the expansion of such tools of critical discourse through participation within different knowledge domains may lead to a greater array of ways of being in the world.[124] It is the extension of the range of desirable and valuable ways of being in the world – and the material conditions that make their exercise possible – that constitute what I mean by flourishing.[125] I discuss this modern notion of flourishing and its partial, unstated acceptance as a foundation for constitutional law in South Africa at length in Chapter 7. For now, we need only delineate a politics of flourishing in a manner that makes it a plausible match for a theory of experimental constitutionalism.

At a relatively trivial level, a picture, an image, captures the essence of this commitment to flourishing. In Raphael's famous painting 'The Academy of Athens', two figures occupy centre stage: Plato and Aristotle. Plato's right hand and his right index finger point skywards. Aristotle's right arm is outstretched, the palm of his hand face down, about waist high, inclined ever so slightly toward the ground.

Plato's hand gesture vividly captures an entire weltanschauung. As most readers know, the argument developed in *The Republic* and other works (*The Meno*) suggests that the world of human perception and experience is shadow play. Recall the metaphor of 'The Cave'. Lights and silhouettes dance on the wall. These apparitions, on Plato's account, reflect the barest outlines of objects (and propositions about those objects). The things themselves remain inaccessible to limited powers of human perception. Accurate truth propositions about the world – and what makes human lives worth living – are accessible (directly) only to those philosophers who have the capacity to go beyond mere apparitions and who possess the requisite acumen to separate the wheat from the chaff of human thought. Through the identification of 'the forms' and 'the good' by these philosopher-kings, other members of Plato's hypothetical, highly-stratified community are able to partake of the benefits of the well-ordered and just society whose lineaments have been identified by their more gifted kin.

Aristotle's gesture rejects both Plato's method of divining the good (through pure reason) and the kind of well-ordered society that Plato derives from his mobile army of metaphors. My account of flourishing is not meant to revive an Aristotelian ethic of virtue. That communitarian ethic, collapsing as it does the right and the good, has no place in a theory about (some of) the optimal features of a modern democratic constitutional order that frames our own radically heterogeneous society.

Aristotle's account of practical wisdom (*phronesis*), eudeimonia (*flourishing)* and *arête (virtue*) does, however, strike a decidedly contemporary cord, convivial to constitutional theory. These features of Aristotle's work have been regularly invoked by modern political philosophers working within the existing frameworks of development theory, the capabilities approach, constitutional law and universal human rights discourse.

What could Aristotle possibly have to offer us moderns in our radically heterogeneous, sprawling, raw and riven nation state (South Africa) committed, by its basic law, to such divergent (yet ostensibly covalent) foundational values as freedom, equality and dignity? Aristotle opens Book II of the *Nicomachean Ethics* with the following statement:

> Moral virtue ... is formed by habit ... [and] none of the moral virtues is implanted in us by nature [alone]... [T]he virtues are implanted in us neither by nature nor contrary to nature; we are by nature [unlike a stone] equipped to receive them, and habit brings this ability to completion and fulfilment.[126]

One thesis that I have reiterated again and again is the extent to which a broad array of involuntary social practices (*habits*) make us who we are and give our life meaning. We are born into these practices. They are 'the habits of our heart'.[127] They are also the habits of which Aristotle speaks. The second thesis – confirmed by the neuroscience and the experimental philosophy described in Chapter 2 – is that we are innately inclined to receive and to reiterate cultural habits and naturally ingrained dispositional states.

Some habits (endowments) may be beyond scrutiny. Indeed, they may require in order to desiderate satisfy the far appearing in public without shame. Other facts and norms, consistent with a commitment to experimentalism, must be open to review. However, I have made it patently clear: (1) that most of our perceptions of the world ought to be viewed as stable (and largely verifiable and true); (2) that our reflections upon them form an essential and desirable feature of our existence (even when, as Frank Michelman says, we still attempt to learn aggressively from alternative beliefs held by others); and (3) that these perceptions, beliefs and values, when woven together, and acted upon, define flourishing. Aristotle propounded this very three-part thesis. In Book Two of the *Nicomachean Ethics*, Aristotle begins by defending the quintessentially Davidsonian principle 'that our perceptual and cognitive faculties are basically dependable, that they for the most part put us into direct contact with the features and divisions of our world, and that we need not dally with sceptical postures before engaging in substantive philosophy.'[128] In Book Six of the *Nicomachean Ethics*, he puts this complex proposition as follows: 'We are all convinced that what we know scientifically cannot be otherwise than it is ... Therefore, the object of scientific enquiry exists of necessity and is, consequently, external.'[129] Our opinions about matters scientific may or may not be entirely true. (Even statements like 'snow is white' are subject to revision; we all now know about the black snow in the Arctic that contributes to global warming.) They remain subject to examination and to experimentation undertaken by a community of like-minded philosophers and scientists. The marriage of a world with which we are in unmediated contact and our cognitive capacity to put our beliefs about the world to the test means that Aristotle shares much in common with contemporary neuroscientists, social scientists and experimental philosophers. We can view empirical and experimental philosophers such as Appiah, Knoble and Aristotle as primarily concerned with how reason relates to action and subjecting our moral, political and legal beliefs to thorough analysis and proof (of a particular kind).

This emphasis on action intimates why it is important not to collapse ethics and science. Ethics as a *practice* requires *action*. These actions remain, through *phronesis* (practical wisdom), are subject to a particular form of critical inquiry. We learn from our betters – say Pericles or Mandela – how one should behave when confronted with certain kinds of ethical dilemmas. Yet Pericles and Mandela – and statesmen of a similar ilk – do not provide us with rules or decision-procedures that we can simply apply (sans reflection) to the moral universe or a given ethical dilemma laid out before us. Our betters may be our teachers in important respects. However, it is through our own actions that we develop practical wisdom and an ethical orientation toward the world.

The emphasis Aristotle places on the privileged views of persons such as Pericles (or Mandela), *endoxa*, ('reputable judgments', 'credible opinions', 'entrenched beliefs'), constitutes a starting point – from which we may have no reason to depart. Again, however, Aristotle's emphasis on *action* as a critical component of practical wisdom, flourishing and virtue means putting both received wisdom and our own forms of ethical and political thought consistently to the test. (Here we can discern 2500 year old glints of ethical and political experimentalism.) Action – putting reason to the test – demands working back and forth between means and ends. This reflexivity with respect to the ends that we pursue and the means that we employ gives Aristotle's thought a distinctly modern cast[130] and is consistent with the basic precepts of experimental constitutionalism. His working back and forth between means and ends shares important features with the work of Nussbaum, Sen and Sunstein. Nussbaum, in her neo-Aristotelian phase, placed particular emphasis on the construction of ethical action through relationships and the reflexive relationship between means and ends through what she described as a process of 'perceptive equilibrium'. She writes:

> The effort really to see and really to represent is 'no idle business in the face of the constant force that makes for muddlement.' So wrote Henry James on the task of moral imagination. We live amid bewildering complexities. Obtuseness and refusal of vision are our besetting vices. Responsible lucidity can be wrested from that darkness only by painful, vigilant effort, the intense scrutiny of particulars. Our highest and hardest task is to make ourselves people 'upon whom nothing is lost.' A person armed only with standing rules ... would, even if she managed to apply them to the concrete case be insufficiently equipped to act rightly in it. It is not just that all by themselves they might get it all wrong; they do not suffice to make the difference between right and wrong. ... Obtuseness is a moral failing; its opposite can be cultivated. By themselves, trusted in and of themselves, the standing terms are a recipe for obtuseness. To respond 'at the right times, with reference to the right objects, towards the right people, with the right aim, and in the right way, is what is appropriate and best ... [James' writings] allows us to see more deeply into the relationship between the finely tuned perceptions of particulars and a rule governed by concern for general obligations; how each, taken by itself, is insufficient for moral accuracy; how [and why] the particular, if insufficient, is nonetheless prior; and how a dialogue between the two [characters], prepared by love, can find a common basis for moral judgment. ... James' talk ... of 'getting the tip' shows us what moral exchange and moral learning can be, inside a morality based upon perception. Progress comes not from the teaching of an abstract law but by leading the friend, or child, or loved one – by a word, by a story, by an image – to see some new aspect of the case at hand, to see it as this or that. Giving a 'tip' is a give a gentle hint about how one might see.[131] The 'tip' here is given not in words, but in a sudden show of feeling. It is concrete, and it prompts the recognition of the concrete. ... [T]his ideal of [perceptive equilibrium] makes room ... for norms or norms of rightness and a substantial account of ethical objectivity. ... Jamesian moral perception is like this: (without denying the existence of norms), [it requires] a fine development of our human capabilities to see, to feel, to judge; an ability to miss less, to be responsible for more.[132]

We may begin with certain ethical norms as our guides. But it is, ultimately, the attempt to find a fit between the moral facts with which we are confronted and the generally accepted norms that guide our behaviour that distinguishes Nussbaum's (neo-Aristotelian) approach to ethics from neo-Kantian approaches – say Rawls' notion of 'reflective equilibrium'.[133] The facts with which we are confronted are at least as important as the norms that we bring to the table. The fundamental flaw in Rawls' account of ethical reasoning flows from his decision to relegate facts and relationships to opaque background conditions – states of the world of which we are dimly aware as we construct a perfectly just society behind a 'veil of ignorance'.[134]

To sharpen this point, an example may help. I have yet to have a student in a South African law school elect to give up the particularities of their existence, step behind the 'putative' veil of ignorance and agree to a start afresh (as any one of 50 million South Africans) with only the difference principle as an insurance policy that would ensure that every economic decision would benefit (to some degree) the worst off. Everyone knows the difference between life in Alexandra Township, on one side of the M1, and life in Sandton, directly on the other side of the M1. The thought of making that 'though experiment' a reality quickly ends discussions of reverse discrimination.

The commitment to reflexivity shares a family resemblance to the contemporary notion that we do not possess, in many matters of import, locked-in preferences. Our preferences in various arenas, as both Sen and Sunstein have demonstrated, are adaptive. While we must be committed to general norms that guide our behaviour towards more virtuous or optimal ends, otherwise no ethical inquiry can get off the ground, we may find that our initial preferences, to the extent that we possess them, may not be in accord with that which we discover is best for us and others. We need only recall how Thaler and Sunstein's nudges – or the new and improved ways of understanding the world that may impose themselves upon us on the golf course, the analyst's couch, in the academy or within the corporate boardroom – result in changes in belief and practice that we now hold to be preferable to those beliefs that we previously entertained.

Aristotle, Nussbaum, Sen and Sunstein, of course, believe that the fields of ethics and politics are grounded in a substantially large number of well-justified beliefs that remain true over time. However, what these thinkers recognize, in addition, is that a politics of flourishing requires of individual citizens, and those that govern them, a well-developed attention to, and even a willingness to experiment upon, the particular circumstances from which a practically wise judgment must issue.

2. *On the Relationship Between Flourishing and Experimentalism*

How does flourishing relate to the grander project of experimental constitutionalism?

First, for Aristotle, flourishing reflects the highest order of human activity.[135] Second, flourishing is not a static state. Third, flourishing entails the actualization, to the highest possible degree, of all of our various competences, powers, faculties or gifts. As we shall see in Chapter 7's discussion of development and capabilities, the demands of flourishing require that we (as members of a given community) must provide individuals and communities with the material means necessary to realize these core competences, powers, faculties or gifts.

A fourth feature of flourishing, on Aristotle's account, is that individuals and groups will differ substantially about the nature of 'flourishing' or 'happiness'. They may agree on core competences, powers, faculties or gifts, but disagree on the import and the contours of those competences, powers, faculties or gifts,[136] and the visions of 'the good' that they produce.

One can therefore translate Aristotle's account of flourishing into modalities more felicitous to strains of modern philosophical thought without doing violence to the original text. Flourishing is a function not only of rational deliberation (which only takes one so far), but of experience, applied wisdom, and experimentation. This practical engagement with the world and other human beings enables us to discern the correct course of action for ourselves and others. That capacity is especially important given the novel ethical situations that our world throws up daily.

For many, this discussion of Aristotle may seem far afield from our current set of enquiries – pressing up as they do against the most recent revelations in neuroscience, social theory or empirical philosophy discussed in Chapters 1, 2 and 3. But I want to push two propositions

(1) that the kind of 'experimental' or 'practical' wisdom that guides contemporary theories of the self, the social and the constitutional has a long history in western thought and that these three kinds of theorization (regarding the self, the social and the constitutional) are united by considerations Aristotle identified some 2500 years ago; and (2) that experimentalism in the related fields of epistemology, ethics and politics are connected, by a shared method, to this account of flourishing. I will try to make each part of the extended argument somewhat clearer below. For now, the connection between experimentalism and flourishing runs roughly as follows.

Both approaches to politics get off the ground through an initial acceptance of the shared practices and belief sets of the various communities into which we are born and within which we live. We recognize that these habits of the heart are what allow us to be wise (and foolish). At the same time that both experimentalism and flourishing accept the 'endless true beliefs' upon which our thoughts and actions are predicated, they emphasize the circumstances under which errant beliefs or non-optimal practices can be sifted out through action. Both experimentalism and flourishing are committed to reflexivity – a working back and forth between means and ends. In addition, having chosen the correct means to realize an end, we may find over time that the means reshape our view of our ends (or the good). For example, by approaching drug offences as opportunities for treatment rather than incarceration, we may come to see drug use as less of crime against society requiring retribution and more a function of genetic or environmental factors beyond an individual's control and with which she must fight a life-long battle. Finally, Aristotle, and moderns such as Nussbaum, Sen and Sunstein recognize the heterogeneity of goods that human beings pursue. While Aristotle may have viewed many of these pursuits as misguided, they remain facts of human existence nevertheless. Moderns committed to flourishing and experimentalism are more willing to incorporate that difference into their theories – and to make the local community, the state or the international community aware that they have obligations to ensure that individuals and various sub-publics have the ability and the capability to realize varying ends. Aristotle and the moderns whose theories I have deployed also recognize an additional truth – one that may have been lost in the empirical accounts of the self and the social that drove the first few chapters: ethics and science have different aims. As Nussbaum puts it:

> But there is a mistake made, or at least a carelessness, when one takes a method and style that have proven fruitful for the investigation and description of certain truths – say those of natural science – and applies them without further reflection or argument to a very different sphere of human life that may have a different geography and demand a different form of precision, a different form of rationality. Most of the moral philosophy that I have encountered lacked these further reflections and arguments. And frequently stylistic choices appear[] … dictated … by habit and the pressure of convention … [and] above all by the academization and professionalization of philosophy, which leads everyone to write like everyone else, in order to be published in the usual journals. Most professional philosophers [do] not … share the ancient conception of philosophy as discourse addressed to non-expert readers of many kinds who would bring [to their engagement with a text] their urgent concerns, questions, and needs, … and whose souls might in that interaction [with the text] be changed. Having lost that conception they [have] lost, too, that sense of the philosophical text as an expressive creation whose form should be part and parcel of its conception, revealing in

the shape of the sentences the lineaments of a human personality with a particular conception of life.[137]

It's human beings and what matters to them that occupies these pages, not an engineer's analysis of widgets and sprockets. The sentences in this work should scan, and paragraphs should challenge the preconceptions of the reader, all without losing precision or try reflecting an unwarranted worry that a 'literary style would evoke[] criticism or even ridicule.'[138] One's training as a philosopher and a lawyer need not bind one to an arid, formalistic representation of the basic law – even as one appreciates the rigour behind more precise forms of presentation. The trick is to maintain the commitment to rigour at the same time as the writer sustains her connection with her reader.

Armed with Aristotle's original position and Nussbaum's reconceptualization of flourishing, we should see why a commitment to recasting freedom in terms of the more modest (less comprehensive) conception of flourishing (as propounded by Nussbaum) requires a relatively modest conception of constitutional politics. Though bracketed in its reach (the book does not claim to offer a full blown constitutional theory), this work should demonstrate how one modest account of politics – flourishing – compliments another equally modest account of politics – experimental constitutionalism.[139]

This work begins with the premise that individual flourishing occurs primarily within the many, and often, competing associations into which an individual is born and of which she remains a part.[140] Experimental constitutionalism envisages a state that does not exhaust the possibilities of individual lives. To the contrary, experimental constitutionalism aims at creating the conditions under which individuals can fully realize extant sources of the self and nudge them (and their adaptive preferences) toward more optimal ways of being (as they understand them).

Put another way, an experimental constitutional state bears the dual responsibility of ruling out ways of being which threaten the core values of our polity – tolerance, dignity, rough equality, democratic participation – and of providing a framework within which competing comprehensive (and non-comprehensive) notions of the good can co-exist – if inevitably uncomfortably. To meet these minimal requirements, such a state must ensure that each individual inhabitant possesses the most basic entitlements necessary to appear in public without shame and that the general conditions for both individual and group flourishing obtain.[141] Such roles for the state are entirely consistent with both the conservative and the progressive features of the Final Constitution.[142]

Three further pre-commitments are required for this model of constitutional politics to work. First, the experimental constitutional state must commit itself to fairly robust forms of intervention. These experimental institutional arrangements should enable the state to rotate social, economic and political capital in a manner that allows the citizenry to engage in various Millian 'experiments in living.' Such experiments should, in turn, yield more and better versions and visions of the good. Second, the state must create institutions that ensure the active participation of its citizens in decision-making about the basic settings for individual and collective action. Third, only under conditions of rough equality – and other such minimal requirements such as tolerance and dignity and the rule of law – can the kind of participation that leads to the legitimation of the entire political enterprise take place. Again, the purpose of this project: the maximization of flourishing. Only by creating conditions of rough equality, of access to rotating funds of (various forms of) capital, can individuals and groups either reaffirm their vision of the good or experiment with alternative visions. The experimental constitutional state can create optimal conditions for flourishing in two notionally distinct ways. The feedback mechanisms associated with experimental constitutional doctrines and institutions can help to weed out deleterious ways of being in the world. A commitment to rolling best practices should create a range of options for being in the world that enhance our understanding of what it means to be fully human. This slowly evolving enhancement and expansion of the conditions of being constitutes the only genuinely meaningful account of political freedom.[143]

E. Emergent Experimentalist Government, Information Pooling and Rolling Best Practices in the United States

The experience of many lawyers and scholars both in the United States and South Africa is that remedial intervention contingent upon a command-and-control of state bureaucracy is fraught with difficulty and is largely a failure. The reasons have as much to do with the broad remedial sweep of the desired intervention as with the ability of lawyers to control the courts and other political agencies that must enforce court-sanctioned social change. In the United States, the past fifty years have witnessed 'a move away from remedial intervention modelled on command-and-control bureaucracy toward a kind of intervention that can be called "experimentalist."'[144] Sabel and Simon write that 'instead of top-down, fixed-rule regimes, the experimentalist approach emphasizes on-going stakeholder negotiation, continuously revised performance measures, and transparency.'[145] They further view 'public law [litigation] as core instances of "destabilization rights" - rights to disentrench an institution that has systematically failed to meet its obligations and remained immune to traditional forces of political correction.'[146]

Because my naturalized account of the self and the social takes seriously the limits on our capacity for rational reflection and collective deliberation, it is inaccurate and obscurantist to ground our politics in an alleged capacity of individuals and groups to engage regularly (let alone daily) in profound reflection over critical existential questions. Politics as reasoned discourse remains an ideal even as we recognize – doctrinally and institutionally – that it is not the common practice. My naturalized account of the self and the social does not deny our capacity to engage in meaningful deliberation. Like much of experimental discourse, it primarily questions the level at which such deliberation should take place and the degree to which we should be bound to the outcome of any single set of deliberations by, say, a Constitutional Court.

1. Educational Reform

The United States has 80 years of experience with litigation designed to determine the shape of public school education.

In the first wave of such litigation, the aim was desegregation. Though initially successful as a legal intervention with regard to the racial stratification of society and political blockages in the democratically accountable branches of government, ultimately public litigation lawyers and courts found themselves unable to address the kinds of social movements – read 'white flight' – that re-inscribed patterns of segregation.[147] As Gerald Rosenberg contends, matters only changed dramatically when extra-curial structures – the executive and individual school boards – decided to take up the cause.[148]

The next wave of litigation revolved around issues of fiscal equity. Ironically, while some of these constitutional cases secured equal funding, the ultimate result has often been diminished funding overall and the movement of many privileged learners out of the public school system into the private school system (through private funding and public vouchers). Finally, there has been no discernible improvement in the performance of schools in historically poorer districts. (Unless current projections change by 2014, the No Child Left Behind Act – with its mix of funding incentives and achievement benchmarks – will find that roughly 2/3rds of learners and schools have failed to improve in the manner lawmakers expected. The only alternative, now, consistent with an experimentalist approach, is to alter the mix of incentives, benchmarks and funding to achieve more optimal outcomes.)

These two experiments in social change have been followed by a third. This last wave of education litigation has been marked by an emphasis on adequacy. Unlike the first two waves of education litigation, the new legal regimes do not contemplate judicial micromanagement or administrative centralization. In writing about attempts at establishing adequacy baselines in Alabama, Helen Hershkoff has argued that new kinds of judicial decrees 'establish[] a structure for institutional reform, [but do] not fix[] the precise content of [the] reform.'[149] The third wave of education litigation has been influenced, note Sabel and Simon

> by the 'new accountability' movement in educational reform. That movement results from the interaction of both centralizing and decentralizing developments. The centralizing theme emphasizes the importance of comparative performance measurement and material incentives. The decentralizing theme prescribes devolution of authority … [to] districts, principals, and teachers (and sometimes parents).[150]

This last wave of education litigation fits more general arguments about 'feedback mechanisms' and 'trial and error' in a two-fold manner.[151] First, it recognizes systemic failures of previous legal experiments to effect the desired change. Second, it offers the opportunity for trying a variety of different solutions to the same problem: namely, how to improve the performance of all students while simultaneously acknowledging, addressing and redressing the deficits of the worst off. The new model of legal and political intervention in education may or may not prove fruitful. But it certainly does reflect the notion, emphasized throughout this work, that we will expand the conditions of freedom, not simply by allowing people to do as they wish, but through state-sponsored and privately-sponsored experiments in living that enable us to see for ourselves what kinds of institutions expand materially our conditions of possibility. Public interest litigation – and state responses to it – is an important political feedback mechanism. By moving back and forth between courts and legislatures, experts and parents, the wave after wave after wave of litigation may achieve the kind of experimental success that ought to be the hallmark of a politics committed to individual and group flourishing.[152]

The proof of such feedback mechanisms is in the pudding. When Sabel and Simon began their investigations of experimental constitutionalism in the context of education reform, Alabama ranked near the bottom of the 50 states in terms of literacy and numeracy. It was, perhaps, the most broken of the systems that they surveyed.

One might expect that those states whose judicial systems, legislatures, teacher unions, parent associations and students would have the most to gain from experimentalist institutions and would already have the necessary feedback systems and the ability to pool information in place. That is, the best would be better off under this new regime. It ain't necessarily so. As it turned out, the most broken of systems – such as that found in Alabama – benefitted the most from the reflexivity of experimentalist feedback mechanisms. The reasons seem clear enough. Instead of formulating rules regarding education policy and goals from the top down, new institutional designs allowed for greater participation from those groups and individuals who knew the most about what needed fixing. In most educational systems, those players are likely to be the people with the greatest day to day experience of what works and what doesn't: principals, teachers, parents and learners. So, as it turns out, by extracting more information from those groups at the coalface and reversing the flow of information upwards – from principals, teachers, parents and learners to agencies, courts and legislatures – Alabama found itself in a position to benefit more from experiences of what works and what doesn't than states whose educational systems already possessed greater reflexivity in their systems.

In describing public law litigation more generally, Sabel and Simon offer assessments consistent with the more speculative 'Toyota Jurisprudence' approach to experimental constitutionalism adumbrated above. They write that public law litigation has

> moved away from remedial intervention modelled on command-and-control bureaucracy toward a kind of intervention that can be called "experimentalist." Instead of top-down, fixed-rule regimes, the experimentalist approach emphasizes on-going stakeholder negotiation, continuously revised performance measures, and transparency. Experimentalism is evident in all the principal areas of public law intervention – schools, mental health institutions, prisons, police, and public housing. This development has been substantially unanticipated and unnoticed by both advocates and critics of public law litigation. ... The evolution of structural remedies in recent decades can be usefully stylized as a shift away from command-and-control injunctive regulation toward experimentalist intervention. Command-and-control regulation is the stereotypical activity of bureaucracies. It takes the form of comprehensive regimes of fixed and specific rules set by a central authority. These rules prescribe the inputs and operating procedures of the institutions they regulate. By contrast, experimentalist regulation combines more flexible and provisional norms with procedures for on-going stakeholder participation and measured accountability. In the most distinctive cases, the governing norms are general standards that express the goals the parties are expected to achieve–that is, outputs rather than inputs. Typically, the regime leaves the parties with a substantial range of discretion as to how to achieve these goals. At the same time, it specifies both standards and procedures for the measurement of the institution's performance. Performance is measured both in relation to parties' initial commitments and in relation to the performance of comparable institutions. This process of disciplined comparison is designed to facilitate learning by directing attention to the practices of the most successful peer institutions. Both declarations

of goals and performance norms are treated as provisional and subject to continuous revision with stakeholder participation. In effect, the remedy institutionalizes a process of on-going learning and reconstruction. Experimentalist regulation is characteristic of the "networked" and "multilevel" governance proliferating in the United States and the European Union – decision-making processes that are neither hierarchical nor closed and that permit persons of different ranks, units, and even organizations to collaborate as circumstances demand. In cases that take the experimentalist approach, the courts are both more and less involved in reconstituting public institutions than they were when Chayes wrote. They are more involved because experimentalist remedies contemplate a permanent process of ramifying, participatory self-revision rather than a one-time readjustment to fixed criteria. But the courts are less involved because the norms that define compliance at any one moment are the work not of the judiciary, but of the actors who live by them. At least in prospect, the demands on the managerial capacities of the court, and the risk to its political legitimacy, are smaller in this continuous collaborative process than in top down reform under court direction.[153]

2. *Family Courts and Child Welfare Agencies*

Family Courts are the kind of institution that would make Lon Fuller's head spin.[154] Representatives of the child, parent(s) or guardian, a foster parent or institutional representative, a social worker and an attorney acting on behalf of the state will often appear in a horse-shoe like arrangement around a specialist Family Court judge. Moreover, the rules of Family Court are such – so relaxed – that not only are these seven official voices heard, but the individual parties themselves may be heard. The law may be a blunt cudgel. Family courts can often soften the blow.[155]

The virtues of such an institutional approach for experimental constitutionalism are difficult to overstate. First, virtually every stakeholder that wishes to be heard can be heard. This fact increases the normative legitimacy of the process. Second, the plurality of voices increases the amount of information that the court can secure regarding a given family's travails (and successes) once it has been found necessary to place a child under some form of protective care. Third, the expertise of the judge and the various practitioners – who are often solely involved in family law matters – increases the court's appreciation of the kinds of problems that families and the children in the child welfare system face. That increased understanding has three virtues: (1) it enables courts to tailor their findings to the particular circumstances of the parties before them, with a better idea of what works and what doesn't in such circumstances; (2) the flexibility of the court's orders – and the relative ease with which a child and his or her family can re-enter the court – means that the judge can alter an arrangement that doesn't work, in the hope that some other measure known to the court might; and (3) the court can take cognizance of improved circumstances and alter its orders accordingly. Without gilding the lily, the family court process sometimes succeeds in reuniting families.

How did this polycentric process come to pass – especially given the preference in most jurisdictions for binary, adversarial processes with zero-sum outcomes? Of child welfare agencies, Kathleen Noonan, Charles Sabel and William Simon write:

> Programs that once focused on financial redistribution increasingly link transfer payments to services, and services are increasingly customized to the needs of individual recipients. The move to services is driven by the perception that transfer payments alone do not induce (and may inhibit) the development of skills that permit self-sufficiency. The move to individuation is driven in part by a conception of fairness that mandates response to "difference" in people's values and circumstances and by the perception that these circumstances are more fluid than they have been in the past As the welfare state becomes more individuating and more adaptive, it threatens to undermine the awkward compromise between rule-of-law values and welfare state practices worked out in the Warren Court years and their aftermath Two key features of that compromise were (1) the idea of a balance between relatively rigid rules to govern the conduct of low-status frontline workers and relatively flexible standards to govern the conduct of professionals, and (2) the idea of co-ordination between a bureaucratic accountability system for routine cases and a quasi-judicial accountability system for cases in which beneficiaries protest their treatment. In addition, the compromise distinguished two modes of court intervention into the administrative system– routine discrete intervention focused on particular practices or narrow norms and extraordinary systemic intervention designed to restructure entire programs. The core tendencies of the new programs put these arrangements under pressure. The need to customize and adapt makes rules an ineffective means of controlling discretion. Effective review of frontline efforts routinely requires the type of beneficiary participation that the old regime reserved for cases in which beneficiaries complained. Because the emerging system involves more complex co-ordination and more frequent adjustment, judicial review of discrete judgments and practices seems less practicable.[156]

That such an outcome has occurred in the child welfare system – a legal regime chronically identified with abject failure – is of even greater surprise. As of 2005, some 30 (of the 50) states had been determined to be in such 'systemic noncompliance with constitutional or statutory requirements' as to warrant structural intervention.[157] Despite these systemic failures, Noonan, Sabel and Simon note recent progress, and, in an echo of what Sabel and Simon found in the reform of educational systems, they discovered that the greatest progress has occurred in two of the states previously identified as having the worst child welfare systems. Both Utah and Alabama adopted self-reflexive programs that required the social workers to critique each other's work. Social workers not only learned from their mistakes, but adopted the best practices of their peers. With respect to these two states, the authors surmise that the 'it may be because these systems have been so deeply broken that they have lent themselves to relatively radical experimentation' and success.[158] The other possibility, Noonan, Sabel and Simon suggest, is that child welfare systems were always relatively individuated and adaptable in approach, and that this specific system was simply waiting for the individuation and adaptability reflected in experimentalist models to begin to permeate the welfare state as a whole.[159] But whether it was the chicken or the egg that came first is of little consequence. What matters, Noonan, Sabel and Simon contend, is that the Alabama and Utah models

> have implications for the debate over the proper scope of judicial intervention into chronically underperforming public institutions. Reform in these states emerged from judicial decrees mandating broad institutional form; yet, in each case the court and the parties avoided the rigidification and arbitrariness associated with 'command-and-control' type judicial intervention.[160]

The Alabama and Utah models seem to marry the benefits of shared constitutional rule-making to participatory bubble-like structures at the coalface. In something of an ironic, throwaway line of argument, Noonan, Sabel and Simon identify this kind of rights discourse and remedies delivery with the socio-economic rights regime developed by our own South African Constitutional Court in *Grootboom*: namely, claimants are not entitled to specific entitlements 'but to a process in which the relation between the claimant's interests and the values underpinning the relevant public programs can be fairly and effectively considered.'[161] Similarities certainly exist. But can even recent South African socio-economic rights jurisprudence – with its commitments to meaningful engagement and a few thin substantive entitlements that the state must grant successful claiments – be genuinely said to offer a model for US states that can draw down on the significantly greater resources available in what remains the world's largest economy? Perhaps the answer is a qualified 'yes': the qualification is that the resources in the two domains differ by an order of magnitude.

3. *Drug Treatment Courts*[162]

Could any aspect of the US public law regime be more broken than the family courts and the educational system described above? Yes. The federal and state penal systems are, by far, the harshest in the developed democratic world. Approximately 1,000 of every 100,000 citizens are behind bars. Compare that figure with only 59 of 100,000 citizens in jail in Japan or 152 of 100,000 citizens in jail in the United Kingdom. And forget the Netherlands. It is committed to drug use decriminalization generally and crafts policies 'aimed primarily at limiting the harm that long-term addicts do to themselves and those around them.'[163]

At the turn of the century, illegal drug users constituted roughly half of the US prison population. Given that illegal drug users are largely non-violent, and that incarceration does little to alleviate the addiction (or its underlying causes), and thus eliminate the high rate of recidivism, this degree of retribution is difficult to justify – in terms of rather intuitive notions of justice or success, or the amount of public money spent.

There must be a better way. As Michael Dorf and Charles Sabel go to great lengths to show, there is. Even better, it already exists. It is called a drug treatment court (or sometimes a drug court, or in other places a treatment court). About such courts, Dorf and Sabel write:

> Variations in nomenclature and the precise details of their operation aside, treatment courts around the country share the same basic pattern. Persons charged with relatively low level, non-violent criminal conduct may opt out of the criminal trial court if the prosecuting attorney consents to the filing of charges in the treatment court. In treatment court, the defendant pleads guilty or otherwise accepts responsibility for a charged offense and accepts placement in a court-mandated programme of treatment. In some model programs, offenders may initially choose among different courses of treatment – residential or outpatient – according to their needs and possibilities. The judges and court personnel closely monitor the defendant's performance in the programme and the programme's capacity to serve the mandated client. If progress in the treatment regime is unsatisfactory, courts offering various programmes may require the offender to choose another, more intensive one. Upon successful completion of the programme, the conviction is typically expunged. The drug court, moreover, will cease directing defendants to programs that show signs

> of incompetence and increase referrals to others that show greater promise. Treatment courts thus provide defendants with alternatives to incarceration without decriminalizing drug use.[164]

Whilst holding no illusions about the difficulties associated with drug addiction, including the relatively high rates of recidivism even after successful treatment, Dorf and Sabel trumpet the importance of such fora in changing not only the lives of users, but in altering what Americans regard as criminal behaviour and how such behaviour should be handled. In short, Dorf and Sabel quickly illustrate – in quintessential experimentalist fashion – how a change in effective means to realizing existing ends can ultimately alter our view of the norms in play. Dorf and Sabel are a long way from claiming that the 'war on drugs' is over or that Dutch-style space brownies will soon become available at a bodega near you. However, they initiate their discussion of drug treatment courts by suggesting how the fact of non-incarceration for drug offenses can ultimately lead to social perceptions and legal norms that no longer stigmatize drug users as criminals. That, again, is a perfect example of how the reflexivity, empiricism and pragmatism at the heart of experimentalism helps us revise both the ends we pursue and the means by which we go about pursuing them.

What makes these drug treatment courts even more extraordinary is the amount of information that (a) they make available to all parties, (b) the ability they give all participants to alter the available treatment based upon the available information, and (c) the capacity to pool information across courts, drug centres and even different legal jurisdictions. The system – for all its horrors (and incarceration for drug use is that) – looks very much like we would expect a Sunsteinian choice architect to create if she were trying to build the best drug treatment scheme. As with the theory of the social developed in chapter 3: (1) individual drug users are encouraged to make those choices from which they believe that they will benefit; (2) choice architects – judges, system personnel and treatment centres – provide both feedback and assessment that nudges the individual into making better choices; and (3) the information that flows from all parties to all parties enables officials and participants in the system to see which drug treatment rehabilitation practices work best, and which drug treatment rehabilitation practices do not work especially well.

Why does this emergent experimental institution operate so well? If we return to the beginning of this chapter, we find that it meets virtually all of the desiderata for sucessful experimental governance:

- Flourishing: Drug treatment courts enhance flourishing by offering individuals batting on a sticky wicket options that may actually improve their lives. Drug rehabilitation programmes extend that chance. Incarceration does not.
- Truth Propositions in Radically Determined Forms of Life: No one kids themselves about drug addiction being easy to kick, or that various truths about rehabilitation hold across the board. At the same time, judges, treatment centres, doctors and drug users are all encouraged to challenge accepted norms by discovering better ways of beating recidivism.
- Optimality: Recall that optimality has no known ending. Life constantly disrupts our understanding of what we can expect. Optimality in an experimentalist regime

means that the regular experience of failure, given an array of choices, ought to lead to reorientation toward other alternative means.

- Reflexivity: Have we discussed an organizational system with greater (potential) reflexivity within the state? The information about a given offender flows into the system (and is disseminated throughout the system); decisions are taken based upon the offender's history; the results of the treatment are recorded (and disseminated throughout the system); new choices about both the appropriate treatment and the appropriate treatment centre are made (or incarceration may yet await); these choices are also fed back into the system; constructive arrangements, and disappointing therapies, are reflected as best practices and worst practices; as the system discovers more and more successful arrangements and therapies – which all parties have an interest in discovering – the notion that drug use is a dangerous, morally reprehensible offense has begun to diminish. Drug treatment courts – not criminal courts – may eventually become the norm.
- Tradition and Radical Reformation: Drug use remains a criminal offense. That is unlikely to change any time soon in the US or in the South African legal system.[165] Yet the success of the system – with its lateral pooling of information on best and worst practices – holds out the promise of substantial alteration of the manner in which most drug users enter the justice system. Dorf and Sabel predicted that if drug treatment courts proved successful, then its achievements might change the justice system itself. In the decade since Dorf and Sabel published their article, their hypotheses regarding reflexivity and reformation appear to have been confirmed. Most drug use offenders now enter the justice system through drug treatment courts.
- Chastened Deliberation: This system is information intensive. Many actors participate in the choices made regarding an individual's therapy. However, when we take the synoptic view, the information is not the source of a large, collective discussion. To be sure, data must be analysed, and disagreements will exist over its meaning. However, it is the ability to pool information, and see what works under certain circumstances and what does not, that matters. The drug treatment centre system does not require large amounts of deliberation about means and ends to work effectively.
- Destabilization Rights: Dorf and Sabel might be hard pressed to find a better example of destabilization rights, with their disentrenching power. Drug treatment courts do not call for top-down, fixed-rule, command-and-control forms of remediation. They are shot through with experimentation. They employ on-going stakeholder negotiation, continuously revised performance measures and transparency. The treatment courts are likewise notable for their flexibility and the provisional nature of their norms. Indeed, in many instances, the parties to drug treatment court procedures not only enjoy the ability to determine the goals that the parties are expected to achieve, the drug treatment court 'regime leaves the parties with a substantial range of discretion as to how to achieve these goals.'[166] Finally, information pooling 'is designed to facilitate learning by directing attention to the practices of the most successful peer institutions'.[1668] In the drug treatment system, the range of remedies, and information

pooling about best (and worst) practices 'institutionalizes a process of ongoing learning and reconstruction.' Trial and error – found to do so much work at the level of the self and the social – does similar heavy lifting here in a public law regime.

- Bottoms Up instead of Top Down: Although subject to discernable standards – and with the sword of Damocles of incarceration hanging over offenders – drug treatment courts send their information up and out. To be sure, systemic failures will be recorded and may be subject to top down remediation. But the dynamic described by Dorf and Sabel is one of broad bottom level participation that percolates upwards and realizes new norm construction – at the same time as it flows laterally to other similarly situated participants.
- Possibilities of Polyarchy: Drug treatment courts would seem to prove the proposition that judges – especially in specialized courts – are capable of handling polycentric problems that engage a broad array of parties. Moreover, we have seen how these 'judge-led' institutions can identify rolling best practices and effect change across the entire legal regime.
- Novel Challenges Induce Change: To be sure, one feature of experimentalist institutions is that they are often responses to novel and unexpected problems. Novelty and surprise often require radical experimentation. Those experiments that work, stick. In the United States, a crack epidemic led to an unstable, unsustainable penal system. Drug treatment courts have turned out to be a radical, but largely successful, response.

Dorf and Sabel describe the many virtues of these experimentalist regimes somewhat more crisply:

> Treatment courts ... point one way beyond the conventional limits of courts and other oversight institutions. By pooling information on good and bad performances, the courts enable and oblige improvement by the actors both individually and as members of a complex ensemble. Judicial involvement in reform is permanent and continuous in this model. Yet it is, paradoxically, less imperious than traditional forms of court-directed reform for two reasons. First, the court in effect compels the actors to learn continuously and incrementally from each other rather by instructing them to implement a comprehensive remedial plan devised by the court alone or even in consultation with the parties. Second, the court is itself compelled to change in response to the changes it facilitates. This occurs in part through the exchanges with the treatment providers and in part in response to comparisons with experience in other jurisdictions as revealed by national pooling.[169]

The takeaway: Experimentalism can work in the manner the original theory hypothesized. Over a decade after Dorf and Sabel's prescient work, most drug users now have their initial engagement with the justice system in drug treatment courts.

Without anticipating the arguments made in Chapter 6, we can see the possibilities for emergent experimental institutions in South African public law regimes such as housing and education. The information about these regimes is widely available and accessible; parties are often obliged to engage in meaningful engagement during litigation or simple participatory democracy outside the courthouse; and courts and tribunals, though aware of what other courts or other tribunals are doing in other areas of the country, are relatively free to experiment with collectively generated solutions to polycentric problems. Moreover, policymakers in South

Africa, just as they are in the United States, are often surprised by the positive responses to, as well as the unintended (negative) consequences of, their policies. One cannot plan for successful emergent experimental institutions. But one can leave space for them.

Endnotes

1. Recall both Baars' and Newman's contention that 'consciousness generally comes in play when stimuli are assessed to be novel, threatening or momentarily relevant to active schemas or intentions.' See also S Dehaene, M Kerzberg & JP Changeux 'A Neuronal Model of a Global Workspace in Effortful Cognitive Tasks' (1998) 95 *Proceedings of the National Academy of Sciences USA* 14529.
2. Dehaene & Naccache (supra) at 31.
3. D Dennett *Brainstorms* (1978) 30. See also D Dennett *Freedom Evolves* (2003).
4. NB: Here we might wish to acknowledge how very much Sen and Sunstein have in common: both theorists recognize that different individuals and groups will still make different choices even under conditions of marginally diverse satisfaction constraints; both theorists acknowledge that a significant, shared normative understanding of the optimal choice environment is a necessary pre-condition for a just political order.
5. W Simon 'Toyota Jurisprudence: Legal Theory and Rolling Rules Regimes' in G de Búrca & J Scott (eds) *Law and New Governance in the EU and the US* (2006) 267.
6. J Cohen & CF Sabel 'Sovereignty and Solidarity: EU and US' in J Zeitlin & DM Trubek (eds) *Governing Work and Welfare in A New Economy: European and American Experiments* (2003) 345, 362.
7. For an entertaining account as to why judges are not up to these complex tasks, see E Segal 'The Court: A Conversation with Judge Richard Posner' (2011) 58 (14) *The New York Review of Books* 47. See also R Posner *How Judges Think* (2008).
8. Experimental constitutionalism is simply the North American neologism for a body of thought that now goes elsewhere, in Europe, by the name of 'new governance'. See, e.g., G de Búrca & J Scott (eds) *Law and New Governance in the EU and the US* (2006); J Scott and S Sturm 'Courts as Catalysts: Re-Thinking the Judicial Role in New Governance' (2007) 13 *Columbia Journal of European Law* 565; G de Búrca & J Scott 'Introduction to Narrowing the Gap? Law and New Approaches to Governance in the European Union (2007) 13 *Columbia Journal of European Law* 513, 514; D Trubek & L *Trubek* 'New Governance and Legal Regulation: Complementarity, Rivalry, and Transformation' (2007) 13 -*Columbia Journal of European Law* 539. Other works straddle the two converging bodies of thought, see, e.g., E Szyszczak 'Experimental Governance: The Open Method of Coordination' (2006) 12 *European Law Journal* 486; C Sabel & J Zeitlin 'Learning from Difference: The New Architecture of Experimentalist Governance in the EU' (2008) 14 *European Law Journal* 271, 274. It should be easy to see why experimental constitutionalism qua new governance has caught on in Europe. The constitutional project as a federal project has, politically, failed. So while the European Union has a Parliament, a Court that enforces the European Convention of Human Rights, and even a Central Bank, power and decision-making is rather diffuse, and left primarily to the individual nation-states that make up the Union. Comparisons across borders are both useful and common. Indeed, at the time of writing, one might want to compare how German economic policies enabled it to not only to survive the financial crisis of 2008 – while Iceland, Ireland, Greece, and Spain imploded – but actually come out politically and economically stronger than virtually all other advanced western democracies. At the time of writing, small, progressive, social democratic Iceland is witnessing a comeback. The future of the once vaunted Euro still hangs precariously in the balance. A form of currency without a sovereign state to back it should always have been viewed as vulnerable. This decades old experiment has now revealed its flaws. That's good in so far as the European jurisprudence of 'new governance' is concerned. We now have a clearer understanding of the institutions and regulatory regimes that must be in place for the Euro to work effectively and efficiently, and for the European Union to survive over the long run.

9. M Wilkinson 'Three Conceptions of Law: Towards a Jurisprudence of Democratic Experimentalism' (2010) (2) *University Of Wisconsin Law Review* 673, 691. A more stinging appraisal of pragmatist politics generally is summed up by Marion Smiley as follows: 'The presence of 'aspirations' or 'ideals' in pragmatic analysis has always been a sticking point for pragmatists since ideals have almost always been construed as antithetical to pragmatism unless they can be shown to be pragmatically useful in which case, it is argued, they can no longer be ideals of the aspirational sort.' 'Pragmatic Inquiry and Democratic Politics' (1999) 43 *American Journal of Political Science* 639, 640.
10. Ibid at 679 (emphasis added).
11. See, e.g., D Bilchitz and J Tuovinen 'Theory, Practice and the Legal Enterprise: A Reply to Stu Woolman' (2010) 25 *Southern African Public Law* 544. Talk, talk and more talk has such a vice-like grip on legal imagination that many scholars cannot imagine normative orders in which 'a grand idea' is not the dominant mode of engagement. (The 'talking cure' in psychotherapy would appear, on the surface, to be about 'conscious thought'. It is manifestly about the action in the room, the relationship between analyst and analysand, and the laying down of new neuronal tracks that rereflect the creation of new patterns of behaviour that may, over time, out compete old dysfunctional, deeply ingrained dispositional states.) The miasma of Cartesian legal thought in South Africa makes it largely impossible to discuss the constitutional order in terms other than first principles. (Everyone is on the side of the angels.) The exceptions are to be found in the turn towards subsidiarity (apparently conservative in bent if not intent with its emphasis on private law) and the legal institutional (and constitutional order neutral) analysis inspired by comparative constitutionalism and political science. On subsidiarity, see A Van Der Walt 'Normative Pluralism and Anarchy: Reflections on the 2007 Term' (2008) 1 *Constitutional Court Review* 77 (In truth, Professor van der Walt might rightly contend that his desire to reconceive property rights within the existing domain of common law/Roman Dutch property law has the potential to transform individual property relations in a manner that top-down constitutional property law simply cannot. Professor Van Der Walt's seeks to return decision-making on the proper construction of property laws to those persons most affected by them – certainly a feature in common with experimental constitutionalists.) See also L du Plessis 'Interpretation' in S Woolman & M Bishop (eds) *Constitutional Law of South Africa* (2nd Edition, OS, December 2008) Chapter 32. For a critique of the conservative elements embedded in subsidiarity, see K Klare 'Legal Subsidiarity and Constitutional Rights: A Reply to AJ Van Der Walt (2008) 1 *Constitutional Court Review* 129 (Can subsidiarity be given primacy of place where property relations are so radically unequal, the market alone is unlikely to level the playing field and the reconstruction of the deeply ingrained common law property regime is resisted by the courts themselves?) See also F Michelmann 'Expropriation, Eviction and the Gravity of the Common Law (2013) 24 (2) Stellenbosch Law Review (forthcoming).
12. C Sabel & W Simon 'Epilogue: Accountability without Sovereignty' in G de Búrca & J Scott (eds) *Law and New Governance in the EU and the US* (2006) 395, 396.
13. Ibid at 398.
14. Ibid at 400.
15. Wilkinson (supra) at 689.
16. Simon (supra) at 10–11.
17. Ibid at 12.
18. The problem to which I address myself on pragmatism and first principles appears early on in Dorf and Sabel's (otherwise) magisterial work 'A Constitution of Democratic Experimentalism': 'The backdrop of our design is the pragmatist account of thought and action as problem solving in a world, familiar to our time, that is bereft of first principles and beset by unintended consequences, ambiguity, and difference. Thus, a central theme of the pragmatism of Peirce, Dewey, and Mead is the reciprocal determination of means and ends. Pragmatists argue that in science, no less than in industry and the collective choices of politics, the objectives presumed in the guiding understandings of theories, strategies, or ideals of justice are transformed in the light of the experience of their pursuit, and these transformations in turn redefine what counts as a means to a guiding end. Art epitomized for Dewey

the essentials of pragmatist investigation, because in art means *become* ends, and the relation between them commands attention because of this immediacy: The picture is constantly reconceptualized in the painting. Pragmatism thus takes the pervasiveness of unintended consequences, understood most generally as the impossibility of defining first principles that survive the effort to realize them, as a constitutive feature of thought and action, and not as an unfortunate incident of modern political life.' M Dorf & C Sabel 'A Constitution of Democratic Experimentalism' (1998) 98 *Columbia Law Review* 267, 284–285 citing, in part, C Peirce *How To Make Ideas Clear* (1878), J Dewey *Democracy and Education: An Introduction to the Philosophy of Education* (1916), G Mead *Mind, Self, and Society: From the Standpoint of a Social Behavioralist* (1934). It's exactly this refusal to make the necessary commitments required for a normative project to get off the ground that cause latter-day curmudgeons such as Stanley Fish (see below) such glee, and experimental constitutionalists such as me, much distress.

19. See R Rorty *Contingency, Irony and Solidarity* (1989). Rorty tries to have it both ways, claiming like Donald Davidson, that grass is green because grass is green; and then claiming that the claim grass is green is only contingently true, its truth conditional upon the meaning and grammar of a particular language. While Davidson would agree with the first proposition, the second notion, that truth propositions are contingent upon conceptual schemes or languages games, is not something to which he would adhere. Indeed, Davidson rejected the second proposition outright. See, e.g., 'On the Very Idea of a Conceptual Scheme' *Inquiries into Truth and Interpretation* (1984) 219; D Davidson 'Thought and Talk' *Inquiries in Truth and Interpretation* (1984) 155. Rorty further argues his case in two collections of essays. See R Rorty 'Pragmatism without Method' in *Objectivity, Relativism and Truth: Philosophical Papers 1* (1991) 63 and R Rorty 'Heidegger, Contingency and Pragmatism' in *Essays on Heidegger and Others: Philosophical Papers 2* (1991) 27.
20. S Fish *The Trouble with Principle* (1999) 295.
21. In fairness to Professor Sturm, whose work on experimental constitutionalism dovetails with her commitment to the eradication of gender-based discrimination in a variety of settings, it may be unfair to attribute the failure to work out a clear normative base-line to her body of work. See, e.g, S Sturm 'Second Generation Employment Discrimination: A Structural Approach' (2001) 101 *Columbia Law Review* 452.
22. L Tribe 'The Pointless Flight from Substance to Procedure' *Constitutional Choices* (1985).
23. See I Struber 'Framing Pragmatic Aspirations' (2003) 35 *Polity* 491.
24. M Dorf & C Sabel 'Democratic Experimentalism' (supra) at 267 – 268.
25. S Woolman 'Humility, Michelman's Method and the Constitutional Court: Rereading the *First Certification Judgment* and Reaffirming a Distinction between Law and Politics' (2013) 24 *Stellenbosch Law Review* – (forthcoming). I actually don't believe such flourishes need be empty: as the *First Certification Judgement* reflects.
26. 2003 (3) SA 1 (CC), 2003 (2) BCLR 154 (CC) at para 14 (Emphasis added). See also *Institute for Democracy in SA & Others v ANC & Others* [2005] JOL 14201 (C) ('*IDASA*') at paras 16–18. In *IDASA*, Griesel J reinforces this understanding of the shared responsibility for constitutional interpretation, especially with regard to constitutionally-mandated super-ordinate legislation such as PAIA. The legal institutional/comparative constitutional approach generally accepts the constitutional order as a good, and asks, in an experimental mode, what has worked in different, but similar constitutional orders, and what can we learn from such comparisons.
27. *NCGLE II* (supra) at para 76.
28. 2004 (4) SA 266 (CC), 2004 (1) BCLR 1 (CC)('*Satchwell II*').
29. 2002 (6) SA 1 (CC), 2002 (9) BCLR 986 (CC)('*Satchwell I*').
30. Act 88 of 1989.
31. Act 47 of 2001.
32. *Satchwell II* (supra) at para 26.

33. See M Dorf & B Friedman 'Shared Constitutional Interpretation' (2000) *Supreme Court Review* 61, 81–83. See *Miranda v Arizona* 384 US 436 (1966)('*Miranda*'); *US v Dickerson* 530 US 428 (2000) ('*Dickerson*').
34. Dorf & Friedman (supra) at 81–83.
35. *Miranda* (supra) at 467.
36. Ibid.
37. Dorf & Friedman (supra) at 71.
38. Dorf & Sabel also note that the states did not take up the offer made in *Miranda*. M Dorf & C Sabel 'Democratic Experimentalism' (supra) at 459.
39. See B Ackerman *We The People: Foundations* (1991)(Ackermann identifies two periods of intense political mobilization – triggered by the Civil War and the Great Depression – that created radical paradigm-shifts in the United States' fundamental constitutional commitments.)
40. See R Cover '1982 Term Foreword: Nomos and Narrative' 97 *Harvard Law Review* 4, 28 (1983) (Commenting on the American Mennonites' *amicus curiae* brief in *Bob Jones University v. United States*, Cover characterizes the 'Mennonite understanding of the first amendment as not simply the 'position' of an advocate – though it is that [as well].' According to Cover, 'the Mennonites inhabit an ongoing nomos that must be marked off by a normative boundary from the realm of civil coercion, just as the wielders of state power must establish their boundary with a religious community's resistance and autonomy.')
41. See R Cover 'Violence and the Word' (1986) 95 *Yale Law Journal* 1601 (Cover reminds us of the inevitably coercive dimension of constitutional interpretation: 'legal interpretation takes place in a field of pain and death. ... A judge articulates her understanding of a text, and as a result, somebody loses his freedom, his property, his children, even his life.') See also J Van Der Walt *Law and Sacrifice* (2006).
42. See *Government of the Republic of South Africa v Grootboom* 2001 (1) SA 46 (CC), 2000 (11) BCLR 1169 (CC)('*Grootboom*').
43. See *Prince v Law Society* 2002 (2) SA 794 (CC), 2002 (3) BCLR 231 (CC)('*Prince*').
44. See *S v Jordan & Others (Sex Workers Education and Advocacy Task Force & Others as Amici Curiae)* 2002 (6) SA 642 (CC), 2002 (11) BCLR 1117 (CC)('*Jordan*'); *Minister of Home Affairs & Another v Fourie & Another; Lesbian and Gay Equality Project & Others v Minister of Home Affairs & Others* 2006 (1) SA 524 (CC), 2006 (3) BCLR 355 (CC).
45. See C Sunstein *Infotopia* (2008); S Sturm 'The Promise of Participation' (1993) 78 *Iowa Law Review* 981, 987-991, 1002-1010.
46. See *City of Johannesburg Metropolitan Municipality v Blue Moonlight Properties 39 (Pty) Ltd & Another* [2011] ZACC 33, 2012 (2) SA 104 (CC) 2012 (2) BCLR 150 (CC); *Occupiers of 51 Olivia Road, Berea Township and 197 Main Street Johannesburg v City of Johannesburg & Others.* [2008] ZACC 1, 2008 (3) SA 208 (CC), 2008 (5) BCLR 475 (CC). See also L Chenwi 'A New Approach to Remedies in Socio-Economic Rights Adjudication: *51 Olivia Road and Others v City of Johannesburg and Others*' (2009) 2 *Constitutional Court Review* 371.
47. See *Shilubana v Nwamitwa* 2009 (2) SA 66 (CC); 2008 (9) BCLR 914 (CC).
48. See South African Human Rights Commission 'Report on Equality and Voluntary Associations' available at www.sahrc.org.za.
49. SeeM Bishop and S Woolman 'Public Protector' in S Woolman & M Bishop (eds) *Constitutional Law of South Africa* (2nd Edition, OS, December 2005) Chapter 24A; C Albertyn 'Commission for Gender Equality' in S Woolman & M Bishop (eds) *Constitutional Law of South Africa* (2nd Edition, OS, December 2003) Chapter 24D.
50. See M Bishop 'Vampire or Prince? 'The Listening Constitution and *Merafong Demarcation Forum & Others v President of the Republic of South Africa & Others*' (2009) 2 *Constitutional Court Review* 313.
51. See S Woolman & Brahm Fleisch *The Constitution in the Classroom: Law and Education in South Africa, 1994–2008* (2009).

52. See *Merafong Demarcation Forum & Others v President of South Africa* [2008] ZACC 10, 2008 (5) SA 171 (CC), 2008 (10) BCLR (CC).
53. *Nokotyana v Ekurhuleni Metropolitan Municipality* [2009] ZACC 33, 2010 (4) BCLR 312 (CC); *SATAWU & COSATU v Garvis & Others* [2012] ZACC 13. See, further, D Bilchitz 'Is the Constitutional Court Wasting Away the Rights of the Poor? *Nokotyana v Ekurhuleni Metropolitan Municipality*' (2010) 127 *South African Law Journal* 591.
54. *Glenister v President of the Republic of South Africa & Others* 2011 (3) SA 347 (CC), 2011 (7) BCLR 651 (CC).
55. *City of Johannesburg Metropolitan Municipality v Blue Moonlight Properties 39 (Pty) Ltd & Another* (CC) [2011] ZACC 33, 2012 (2) BCLR 150 (CC), 2012 (2) SA 104 (CC).
56. Recall that Dorf and Friedman showed that the *Miranda* Court openly invited the US Congress to address those concerns afresh. Congress did not (genuinely) do so. When the government, in *US v Dickerson*, sought to uphold its post-Miranda legislation, the *Dickerson* Court noted that too much time had passed (34 years), and that the Court's normative position in *Miranda* had become accepted by law enforcement officials and citizens alike as legitimate. Dorf and Sabel's engagement with drug treatment courts does not deny the normative content of the law those courts enforce. Rather, they demonstrate that a court designed to engage particular kinds of problems and provided with information from (and the experience of) multiple stakeholders (counsellors, doctors, treatment facility personnel, lawyers for all concerned parties, police, and the judge herself) have a greater likelihood to overcome various cognitive deficits and arrive at a solution better for the addict (an opportunity for rehabilitation) as well as the commonweal (less recidivism and a less expensive resolution). Experimental constitutionalism recognizes that the norms themselves may change over time as participants in a form of life – say drug treatment courts – recognize the kind of interventions that work and the kinds of interventions that don't. The alteration of norms (more or less incarceration, more or less rehabilitation) will flow from the experience of various actors who have worked in this domain over time. Finally, experimental constitutionalism need not eschew a normative framework – nor even a deep, normative framework. The very word 'constitutionalism' places experimental constitutionalists within a very explicit, specific, and constraining, Western value order – one that South Africa explicitly shares (in terms of its basic law).
57. See Department of Education Draft *White Paper II: The Organisation, Governance and Funding of Schools* G-N 1229 GG 16839 (November 1995) 6.
58. Equal Education *We Can't Afford Not To: Costing the Provision of Functional Libraries in South African Public Schools* (2011) 8.
59. 2010 (2) SA 415 (CC), 2010 (3) BCLR 177 (CC)('*Ermelo*').
60. Ibid at para 58.
61. R Post & R Segal Popular Constitutionalism, Departmentalism and Judicial Supremacy' (2004) 92 *California Law Review* 1027.
62. R Segal 'Dead or Alive: Originalism as Popular Constitutionalism in *Heller*' (2008) 122 *Harvard Law Review* 191; R Segal 'Heller and Originalism's Dead Hand – in Theory and Practice (2009) 56 *University of Southern California Law Review* 1399.
63. S Woolman 'On the Fragility of Associational Life: A Constitutive Liberal's Response to Patrick Lenta' (2009) 25 *South African Journal on Human Rights* 280. Professor Lenta and I both agree that the Anglo-American political-constitutional tradition truly begins with John Locke's *A Letter of Toleration* (1689). But the meaning of that 'letter' is not altogether clear. Locke's primary concern – on my reading – was to identify a political-philosophical basis for a negotiated settlement that would prevent England from being continually riven by religious strife. The primary reason the 1st Amendment (1791) is the *first* amendment to the US Constitution is *freedom of religion* – and not, as might be commonly thought, freedom of expression. Most Americans of European dissent had fled their native lands in order to escape religious persecution, and not the practice of their faith. Alighting on American soil, many of the denizens of the 13 colonies set about producing powerful local and colonial governments committed to advancing *their* particular comprehensive vision of the good (as reflected by the tenets of

their particular Christian faith.) The genius of the 1st Amendment of the US Constitution lies not in some desiccated negative liberal theory of the polity that many attribute to it. Its radical break with any previous founding political document is reflected in a uniquely American solution to the problem of how *communities* with vastly *different conceptions of the good* could live peaceably amongst each other via a document that provided a 'theory' of a just political order that satisfied all 13 states. A social democratic constitutional order – as we have in South Africa – is primarily committed to enabling *communities* with vastly *different conceptions of the good* to live peaceably amongst one another. Here we have, on full display, in both the South African Constitution and the US Constitution, the genius of liberal/pluralist order: the ability to negotiate between the right and the good (and ability to keep reasonably stable democracies from engaging in war with one another or disintegrating into civil wars themselves.)

64. D Davidson 'Thought and Talk' in *Inquiries into Truth and Interpretation* (1984) 155, 168 (emphasis added).
65. Ibid at 168–169 (emphasis added). Here is the takeaway: in isolated cases a speaker might be mistaken about the truth of a particular proposition, but it does not follow that the entire body of knowledge possessed by the speaker is thereby undermined.
66. D Davidson 'On the Very Idea of a Conceptual Scheme' in *Inquiries into Truth and Interpretation* (1984) 183.
67. As Constitutional Court Justice Edwin Cameron has noted (when then a judge on the Supreme Court of Appeal): 'At this tender stage of our legal development, the doctrine of precedent has special importance. The CC has been accused of disregarding its own decisions without convincing reason (without, indeed, acknowledging that it has done so). That is a grave charge ...[And] this means that other courts, including the SCA, must follow the binding basis of its decisions in all cases in which it has assumed jurisdiction. *True Mhadi* 2009 (4) SA 153 (SCA), 2009 (7) BCLR 712 (CC) at para 102 fns 52 and 53, Cameron J cites, in support of his claim, 'Constitution Chapter 1, Founding Provisions, s 1 – the Republic of South Africa is founded on values that include ... (c) Supremacy of the Constitution and the Rule of Law'... and Stu Woolman 'The Amazing, Vanishing Bill of Rights' (2007) 124 *South African Law Journal* 762–794'. Cameron J then identifies a broad array of contradictory administrative law judgments in the lower courts as evidence of the deleterious consequences of Constitutional Court judgments so thinly reasoned that they lead to contradictory outcomes in the lower courts. *True Mhadi* (supra) at para 102, fn 53.
68. L Wittgenstein *Philosophical Investigations* (1946)(3rd Edition, GEM Anscombe (ed) 1953).
69. Ibid at § 243.
70. See S Woolman 'Language, Power and the Margin: Eliot's Philosophy of Language, Wittgenstein on Following a Rule and Statutory Construction in *Thembekile Mankayi v Anglogold Ashanti Limited* (2012) 128 *South African Law Journal* 434.
71. See S Woolman 'My Tea Party, Your Mob, Our Social Contract: Freedom of Assembly and the Constitutional Right to Rebellion in *Garvis v SATAWU (Minister for Safety & Security, Third Party)* 2010 (6) SA 280 (WCC)' (2011) 27 *South African Journal on Human Rights* 346.
72. See W Rehg *Insight & Solidarity: The Discourse Ethics of Jurgen Habermas* (2000) 62. See also J Habermas *Facts and Norms: Contributions to a Discourse Theory of Law and Democracy* (1998).
73. See, e.g., RM Unger *Politics: A Work in Constructive Social Theory* (1987): *Social Theory: Its Situation and Its Task (Volume I)*; *False Necessity: Anti-Necessitarian Social Theory in the Service of Social Democracy (Volume II)*; and *Plasticity into Power: Comparative Historical Studies on the Institutional Conditions of Economic and Military Societies.* A rotating capital fund bears a passing resemblance to a South African stokvel.
74. Such super-liberal political institutions take cognizance of the extent to which political power invariably shapes and reinforces the formation of group and individual identity. They also reflect the extent to which the state plays an essential role in mediating between conflicting associations and promoting rational discourse about the ends of individuals and groups.

75. The argument from immanence is one of the most attractive features of Unger's work. It suggests that rearrangement of extant institutions for the purpose of disentrenchment can occur through tweaking the existing system. See R Rorty 'Unger, Castoriadis and a National Future' *Philosophical Papers II: Essays on Heidegger & Others* (1991) 177.

76. C Sabel & W Simon 'Destabilization Rights: How Public Law Litigation Succeeds' (2004) 117 *Harvard Law Review* 1015.

77. Many traditional legal doctrines, such as stare decisis, privilege certainty over equity, even where such doctrines work manifest injustice. See S Woolman & D Brand 'Is There a Constitution in This Classroom? Constitutional Jurisdiction after *Walters* and *Afrox*' (2003) 18 *SA Public Law* 38.

78. This account of flourishing forces us to take existing ways of being in the world seriously. It does not, however, assume that any given way of being must survive or that the state is obliged to avoid intervention with respect to the internal affairs of non-state associations. For an analysis of the legitimate and the illegitimate grounds for such intervention, see S Woolman 'Freedom of Association' in S Woolman & M Bishop (eds) *Constitutional Law of South Africa* (2nd Edition, OS, December 2003) Chapter 44; S Woolman 'Seek Justice Elsewhere: An Egalitarian Pluralist's Reply to David Bilchitz on the Distinction between Differentiation and Domination' (2012) 28 *South African Journal of Human Rights* 247.

79. The Constitutional Court has accepted destabilization rights in the legislative arena. FC s 59(1)*(a)*, FC s 72(1) and FC s 118(1) promise citizens – within reason – the right to participate in and to be consulted with regard to decisions that affect their communities. See, e.g., *Matatiele Municipality & Others v President of the RSA & Others* 2006 (5) SA 47 (CC), 2006 (5) BCLR 622 (CC)('*Matatiele II*').

80. See A Chayes 'The Role of the Judge in Public Law Litigation' (1976) 89 *Harvard Law Review* 1281, 1308 (Chayes notes that the adversarial structure of litigation 'furnishes strong incentives for the parties to produce information [and] that 'the information that is produced will not be filtered through the rigid structures and preconceptions of bureaucracies' of the legislative or administrative process.)

81. But see J Dugard 'Courts and the Poor in South Africa: A Critique of Systemic Judicial Failures to Advance Transformative Justice' (2009) 25 *South African Journal on Human Rights* 214; J Dugard 'Court of First Instance? Towards a Pro-Poor Jurisdiction for the South African Constitutional Court' (2006) 22 *South African Journal on Human Rights* 261.

82. I'm not at all certain that the South African case law bears this contention out. The Constitutional Court hears but 30 cases a year. Although South Africa remains a one party dominant democracy, lots of rights based claims play themselves out in the political arena and non-political fora such as Chapter 9 Institutions. There's more politocal contestation than the new 'one party dominant democracy' literatured bears out. In part, that contestation over the content of rights comes from businesses, civil society, NGO's, unions, various forms of litigation and, yes, from within the ANC itself.

83. The Constitutional Court's commitment to a theory of meaningful engagement for both rights analysis and remedies construction, though limited in many respects, hints at the possibility of a more robust form of judicial structuring of basic norms on a rolling basis. See *Occupiers of 51 Olivia Road, Berea Township and 197 Main Street Johannesburg v City of Johannesburg & Others*; [2008] ZACC 1, 2008 (3) SA 208 (CC), 2008 (5) BCLR 475 (CC)('*51 Olivia*'); *Residents of Joe Slovo Community, Western Cape v Thubelisha Homes & Others;* [2009] ZACC 16, 2010 (3) SA 454 (CC), 2009 (9) BCLR 847 (CC) (*'Joe Slovo I'); Abahlali Basemjondolo Movement SA & Another v Premier of the Province of Kwazulu-Natal & Others;* [2009] ZACC 31, 2010 (2) BCLR 99 (CC)('*Abahlali Basemjondolo*'); *Residents of Joe Slovo Community, Western Cape v Thubelisha Homes & Others;* [2011] ZACC 8 (*'Joe Slovo II')*. The possibilities and limits of the Court's 'meaningful engagement' doctrine will be discussed in Chapters 6 and 8. See also S Liebenberg *Socio-Economic Rights: Adjudication under a Transformative Constitution* (2010).

84. Chayes (supra) at 1307–08 (A judge's 'professional tradition insulates him from narrow political pressures, but … he is likely to have some experience of the political process and acquaintance with a fairly broad range of public policy problems.')

85. That statement may possess even greater purchase within South Africa. Government officials often seem to be at a loss as to how the Final Constitution and fundamental rights ought to shape both law and policy. At the same time, South African judges are fairly conservative – in terms of their self-conception of their avocation. They resolutely resist acknowledgement of even the slightest political dimension to their role (even if they are right to maintain a distinction between law and politics.) On the distinction between law and politics, see S Woolman 'Humility, Michelmann's Method and the Constitutional Court: Re-reaching *First Certification Judgement* and Reaffirming a a Disfunction between Law and Politics, (2013) 24 (2) *Stellenbosch Law Review* – (forthcoming). South African judges are not unique in this regard. As Eric Segall and Richard Posner note regarding constitutional discourse on the bench and in the academy of the United States '[Most] law professors [and judges] are unwilling to say the Supreme Court is a political court. Why do you think that is and how can we change it?' (Eric Segall). '[A] couple of reasons ... [J]udicial opinions are public documents and public officials can't be as candid as private persons. There is an accepted rhetoric of judicial expression, and judges have to write that way ... Law professors don't labour under that constraint. Their problem is they are comfortable with legal doctrine and not ... psychology or political science.' (Richard Posner) For an entertaining account as to why judges are not up to these complex tasks, see E Segal 'The Court: A Conversation with Judge Richard Posner' (2011) 58 (14) *The New York Review of Books* 47. See also R Posner *How Judges Think* (2008). See also *Ex parte Chairperson of the Constitutional Assembly: In re Certification of the Constitution of the Republic of South Africa, 1996* 1996 (4) SA 744 (CC), 1996 (10) BCLR 1253 (CC)('First and foremost it must be emphasised that the Court has a *judicial* and not a *political* mandate. Its function is clearly spelt out in IC 71(2): to certify whether all the provisions of the [New Text] comply with the C[onstitutional] P[rinciple]s. That is a judicial function, a legal exercise.')
86. D Cornell 'The Significance of the Living Customary Law for an Understanding of Law: Does Custom Allow for a Woman to be Hosi' (2009) 2 *Constitutional Court Review* 395; C Albertyn 'The Stubborn Persistence of Patriarchy: Gender Equality and Cultural Diversity' (2009) 2 *Constitutional Court Review* 165.
87. S Woolman 'On the Common Saying 'What's True in Golf, Is True in Law': The Relationship between Theory and Practice across Forms of Life' (2010) 25 *Southern African Public Law* 521.
88. M Walzer *Spheres of Justice: A Defence of Pluralism and Equality* (1983).
89. Ibid at 4.
90. M Walzer 'On Involuntary Association' in A Gutmann (ed) *Freedom of Association* (1998); M Walzer *Thick and Thin: Moral Arguments Here and Abroad* (2002).
91. F Hayek 'The Use of Knowledge in Society' (1945) 35 *American Economic Review* 519; F Hayek 'The Results of Human Action, but not of Human Design' in *Studies in Philosophy, Politics and Economics* (1967); F Hayek 'Competition as a Discovery Procedure' in *New Studies in Philosophy, Politics and Economics* (1978).
92. Walzer (supra) at 10–11.
93. See J Cohen 'Michael Walzer's *Spheres of Justice*' (1986) 59 *The Journal of Philosophy* 464. The compartmentalisation of plural spheres of human endeavour, and the concomitant limitation of the distribution of goods by criteria intrinsic to these spheres is a lofty and noble goal, but a well-nigh impossible task. In the first place, as Joshua Cohen has remarked, spheres of human endeavour and the criteria for distribution of goods within those spheres are spontaneously ordered over time. Rarely are these spheres a discrete product of conscious, intentional and comprehensive human design at a given moment in time. Rarer still are the forms of life whose desiderata for success are mapped out once and for all. In the second place, spheres of human endeavour, as well as the criteria for distribution of goods often overlap. Is it genuinely possible to separate out the bonds of love that join individuals in a life-long partnership from the ties that bind a family together to create a home or the efforts of a clan to ensure the health, well-being and success – educational and economic – of fellow kin over time? Marriage. Family. House and home. Learning and education. The purchase of an arable piece of land adjacent to the old homestead that might extend a family farm – or perhaps 30 head of Nguni cattle to solidify the relationship between two families. Nightly readings. Trips to the Planetarium. Can one really claim that the charm that first elicited love must be limited to an initial

tryst and should play no role in the formal education of the progeny that a consequent marriage may produce? Just as densely populated selves and radically heterogenous social roles overlap, so do spheres of justice. It follows them that such strict boundaries would make little sense of the lives we lead, nor could they hope to garner support from but the tiniest segment of humanity.

94. *Sanderson v Attorney-General, Eastern Cape* 1998 (2) SA 38 (CC), 1997 (12) BCLR 1675 (CC).
95. OW Holmes 'The Path of the Law' in *Collected Papers* (1920) 173.
96. This section owes a significant debt to Michael Bishop's magisterial treatment of constitutional remedies under South African constitutional law as well as other well-established bodies of constitutional jurisprudence, see M Bishop 'Remedies' in Woolman & Bishop (supra) Chapter 9.
97. Ibid at 9-20. As Bishop astutely observes, automatic remedialism tracks traditional models of adjudication. Abraham Chayes writes: 'The scope of relief is derived, more or less logically, from the substantive violation'. A Chayes 'The Role of the Judge in Public Law Litigation' (1976) *Harvard Law Review* 1281, 1282.
98. L Sager 'Fair Measure: The Legal Status of Under-enforced Constitutional Norms' (1978) 91 *Harvard Law Review* 1212, 1213.
99. D Levison 'Rights Essentialism and Remedial Equilibration' (1999) 99 *Columbia Law Review* 857, 861.
100. Michael Bishop surveys the Court's body of remedial orders and concludes: '[I]t seems very likely that the Court would have reached a different conclusion at the rights stage if the option of limiting retrospectivity or suspending the order had not been available'. Bishop 'Remedies' (supra) Chapter 9, 9-26 citing, amongst other cases, *Mashavha v President of the Republic of South Africa* 2005 (2) SA 476 (CC), 2004 (12) BCLR 1243 (CC) (Order of invalidity would have left government no legal authority to make social security grants); *Matatiele Municipality v President of the Republic of South Africa* 2006 (5) SA 47 (CC), 2006 (5) BCLR 622. (Order of invalidity would have invalidated election that had taken place five months earlier.)
101. M Nussbaum 'Finely Aware and Richly Responsible: Moral Attention and the Moral Task of Literature' (1985) 57 *The Journal of Philosophy* 516. Nussbaum demonstrates how justice is truly served when we work back and forth between standards and the actual contours of the relationships that demand our ethical engagement. (Standards and principles are to be preferred to rules that dictate outcomes without reflection or perception.)
102. Levison (supra) at 884.
103. P Gewirtz 'Remedies and Resistance' (1983) 92 *Yale Law Journal* 585.
104. Ibid at 678–679.
105. See R Post & R Seigal 'Roe Rage: Democratic Constitutionalism and Backlash' (2007) 42 *Harvard Civil Rights-Civil Liberties Law Review* 373.
106. As I have already noted in Chapter 3, this account of experimentalism draws upon J S. Mill's pragmatic theory of ethical empiricism. See JS Mill *On Liberty* (1851). See also J Dewey *Reconstruction in Philosophy* (1921)(On the consequences of pragmatism for politics). My account of experimentation is somewhat more diffuse. Instead of viewing experimentation as the product of individual reflection, I view it as a set of reciprocal social processes that creates the conditions for individuals, communities and the state to engage critically both the ends pursued and the means employed to pursue those ends. In *On Liberty*, Mill argued that the only way for individuals and groups within a given polity to come to know that in which the 'good life' consists, is for as many individuals and groups as is possible – given the limits of resources and the inevitable potential for conflict – to be given the space to engage in 'experiments in living'. See E Anderson 'John Stuart Mill and Experiments in Living' (1991) 101 *Ethics* 4. For Mill, the optimal condition for fostering experimentalism was through a through-going commitment to the protection of individual liberty. Mill's experimentalist model was premised on a direct, relatively unmediated vertical relationship between individual citizens and government. Given my recasting of freedom in terms of flourishing in Chapter 2, and Chapter 3's recognition of the inevitable bottlenecks in social formations that block change, we can identify three obvious shortcomings in Mill's model.

First, while cognizant of the conformist pressures that customs are capable of exerting, Mill did not fully appreciate the mutually reinforcing and restrictive roles that social norms, and legal institutions and political power play in determining individual identity. Second, Mill failed to recognize the extent to which highly conditioned individual action, constrained by inflexible social norms and rigid legal arrangements, make significant shift in value formation extremely difficult. Third, Mill overestimated the ability of individual reflection to yield optimal or novel results.

107. As I have intimated above, an adequate theory of South African constitutionalism must satisfy a number of conflicting demands. First, it cannot ignore the ineradicable textual tension between a commitment to constitutionalism and private ordering on the one hand and a commitment to social transformation through direct public action on the other. Second, such a constitutional theory cannot be committed to any specific comprehensive vision of the good. [The Constitution's vision of the good is thick enough.] Within the bounds dictated by commitments to tolerance, dignity rough equality and the rule of law, it must set out to promote a broad array of forms of human flourishing. One would think that the commitment to individual flourishing is so ingrained a feature of constitutionalism that it hardly bears mentioning. Yet many powerful traditions of humanistic thought committed to the idea of rational autonomy tend to overlook the value of human happiness. See B Fay *Critical Social Science* (1986)(Fay argues that an important drawback of many 20th century critical theories, such as that of Herbert Marcuse, is the failure to appreciate the value of happiness or to subsume happiness under the idea of autonomy.) Third, for reasons that I have already made clear, although such a constitutional theory does not provide an interpretation of rights contingent upon individual freedom, it still must provide some justification for taking rights seriously. Flourishing and experimentalism do just that. Fourth, it must present an account of how a strong system of rights can assist in social transformation and not hinder it. In Chapter 3, I noted that while John Stuart Mill's notion of 'experiments in living' unearths the potential for experimentation within private ordering, Mill himself dramatically overestimates the extent of our capacity for rational reflection on our experience and fails to appreciate fully the tenacity of social norms in resisting conscious change because of the manner in which social norms, legal rules, political power and individual identities are linked in contemporary societies. As I also noted in Chapter 3, entrenched private power creates a two-fold barrier to experimentalism. First, it aligns existing custom and practices with one's individual identity. It thereby makes critical self-reflection difficult and redefinition painful. It thwarts attempts at reflection and adjustment by increasing its costs. That is, entrenched private power forces individuals to choose *between* preserving their membership in a community by muting their demands *or* alienation if they choose to speak up. Second, it enables individuals or institutional practices supported by entrenched authority to suppress new ideas and alternative points of views on the basis of authority instead of merit. Entrenched private power creates a bottleneck and prevents individual experimentation from leading to corresponding changes in social norms. Mill's insistence on the private order as the engine for social transformation fails to account for this inevitable brake on change. One can, however, reject Mill's classically liberal politics while retaining the essential spirit of his experimentalist vision. I explore methods of breaking such bottlenecks through a doctrinal commitment to remedial equilibration. See S Woolman 'Seek Justice Elsewhere: An Egalitarian Pluralist's Reply to David Bilchitz on the Distinction between Differentiation and Domination' (2012) 28 *South African Journal of Human Rights* 243.

108. See M Dorf & C Sabel 'A Constitution of Democratic Experimentalism' (supra).

109. The Constitutional Court has warmed to the idea that an effective democracy is contingent upon the participation of an engaged and critical citizenry in the process of law-making. As Justice Sachs writes in *Doctors for Life v The Speaker of the National Assembly*: 'This constitutional matrix makes it clear that although regular elections and a multi-party system of democratic government are fundamental to our constitutional democracy, they are not exhaustive of it. Their constitutional objective is explicitly declared at a foundational level to be to ensure accountability, responsiveness and openness. The express articulation of this triad of principles would be redundant if it was simply to be subsumed into notions of electoral democracy. Clearly it is intended to add something

fundamental to such notions. It should be emphasised that respect for these three inter-related notions in no way undermines the centrality to our democratic order of universal suffrage and majority rule, both of which were achieved in this country with immense sacrifice over generations. Representative democracy undoubtedly lies at the heart of our system of government, and needs resolutely to be defended... Yet the Constitution envisages something more. True to the manner in which it itself was sired, the Constitution predicates and incorporates within its vision the existence of a permanently engaged citizenry alerted to and involved with all legislative programmes. The people have more than the right to vote in periodical elections, fundamental though that is. And more is guaranteed to them than the opportunity to object to legislation before and after it is passed, and to criticize it from the sidelines while it is being adopted. They are accorded the right on an ongoing basis and in a very direct manner, to be (and to feel themselves to be) involved in the actual processes of law-making. Elections are of necessity periodical. Accountability, responsiveness and openness, on the other hand, are by their very nature ubiquitous and timeless. They are constants of our democracy, to be ceaselessly asserted in relation to ongoing legislative and other activities of government. Thus it would be a travesty of our Constitution to treat democracy as going into a deep sleep after elections, only to be kissed back to short spells of life every five years. Although in other countries nods in the direction of participatory democracy may serve as hallmarks of good government in a political sense, in our country active and ongoing public involvement is a requirement of constitutional government in a legal sense. It is not just a matter of legislative etiquette or good governmental manners. It is one of constitutional obligation.' 2006 (6) SA 416 (CC), 2006 (12) BCLR 1399 (CC) at paras 228–232 (footnotes omitted).

110. See SH Orzack and E Sober 'Introduction' in SH Orzack and E Sober (eds) *Adaptionism and Optimality* (2001) 1, 5 (Orzack and Sober warn that even in the biological sciences, where natural selection is viewed by most practitioners as having some role in the evolution of all traits, the thesis that the evolution of individual traits inevitably tends toward optimality – that is, greater and greater adaptive fit with the environment – is articulated with caution and often viewed with scepticism.)

111. A friend in the Office of the President of South Africa, who must remain anonymous, calls this state of affairs, 'the 15% problem'. By this clever locution, he means that the 15% of the bureaucracy that does work effectively is so overwhelmed with its current responsibilities that it lacks the time and the energy to respond creatively to new problems or to implement well-conceived policies designed (by others) to address new and pressing problems.

112. W Simon 'Toyota Jurisprudence: Legal Theory and Rolling Rules Regimes' in G de Búrca & J Scott (eds) *Law and New Governance in the EU and the US* (2006) 267.

113. See S Choudhry '"He Had a Mandate": Constitutionalism in a One Party Dominant Democracy' (2009) 2 *Constitutional Court Review* 1; T Roux 'Principle and Pragmatism on the Constitutional Court of South Africa' (2009) 7 *International Journal of Constitutional Law* 106; H Klug 'Finding the Constitutional Court's Place in South Africa's Democracy: The Interaction of Principle and Institutional Pragmatism in the Court's Decision-making' (2010) 3 *Constitutional Court Review* 1.

114. For example, several provincial government departments in Gauteng lack the internal capacity to do their own commercial legal work or to represent themselves effectively within government structures. As a result, they hire private counsel, at significant expense, to represent their interests and to discharge their constitutional duties.

115. The Rastafarians, whose religious freedom to use cannabis was denied in *Prince*, represent as good an example as any of the type of out-group whose interests and rights require judicial solicitude. As Chaskalson CJ observed: '[T]he Rastafari community is not a powerful one. It is a vulnerable group.' *Prince* (supra) at para 26.

116. See S Woolman 'Is Xenophobia the Right Legal Term of Art? A Freudian and Kleinian Response to Loren Landau on Township Violence in South Africa' (2011) 22 *Stellenbosch Law Review* 285. I do not rule out the possibility of actual large-scale political rebellion in South Africa that might bring about dramatic shifts in policy. Hints of such a possibility have been part of the political landscape

since 2007. Tunisia toppled an autocratic leader because of high unemployment. Egypt has tossed out Hosni Mubarak, largely in response to broad disenchantment with state sanctioned police violence, amounting to torture, against large portions of civil society. Moamar Gaddafi, Libya' former tyrant, is still dead. Large scale demonstrations and rebellions have unsettled Jordan and led to a severe, deadly military crackdown in Syria. With the support of both Iran and Russia, the crackdown in Syria shows no sign of abating after almost two years. The Mahgreb Spring has turned from fall into winter in a number of states. Seventy per cent of Mali is now controlled by Al Queda in Islamic Maghreb. Four hundred thousand refugees have fled to the South. (More will follow as AQIM finds itself incapable of managing the distribution of basic goods such as electricity or water for more than once a week.) South Africa's revolution, were one to occur, might trace the Rwandan model of large scale unemployment, a political vacuum, dire prospects giving rise to violence amongst the most volatile segment of our society, 18–24 year old men without jobs and easily overheated. The cultural and political revolutions of the 1960s in industrialized Western states and the decolonized nations in Asia and Africa suggest how easily ideological shifts can occur – for different reasons – when the general population sees such shifts occurring elsewhere. Let's hope that this analysis does not extend to South Africa after the time of writing. However, unless the state, big business and the unions prove more responsive to the large numbers of the truly disenfranchized and dispossessed in South Africa, it's possible that we shall see similar claims that the Constitution's social contract has been breached and that rebellion is justified. See S Woolman 'My Tea Party, Your Mob, Our Social Contract: Freedom of Assembly and the Constitutional Right to Rebellion in *Garvis v SATAWU (Minister for Safety & Security, Third Party)* 2010 (6) SA 280 (WCC)' (2011) 27 *South African Journal on Human Rights* 469. One difference, as Heinz Klug has pointed out, is that South Africa remains a democracy. Unlike the states experiencing the Maghreb revolution, our fellow citizens are not primarily concerned with throwing off the strictures of authoritarian rule. We simply expected the kind of liberation long promised and the delivery of those basic goods necessary for to all South Africans to flourish. However as the Marikina Massacre reflects, the citizenry, emboldened by more and more militant miners and farm workers, may decide that the deal between ANC elites, big business and powerful unions no longer serve their interests. For more on how the deal that resulted in our constitutional democracy blocks genuine liberation for the majority of South Africans, see S Sibanda 'Not Yet Uhuru: How Constitutional Democracy has Blocked the Promise of South Africa's Liberation Movements' (PhD Thesis, in process, University of the Witwatersrand, 2012.)

117. See H Botha 'Freedom and Constraint in Constitutional Adjudication' (2004) 20 *South African Journal on Human Rights* 249.

118. See *S v Mhlungu* 1995 (3) SA 867 (CC), 1995 (7) BCLR 793 (CC) at para 129 (Constitutional interpretation takes the form of 'a principled judicial dialogue, in the first place between members of this Court, then between our Court and other courts, the legal profession, law schools, Parliament, and, indirectly, with the public at large.') See also P Hogg & A Bushell 'The Charter Dialogue between Courts and Legislatures (or Perhaps the Charter of Rights Isn't Such a Bad Thing after All)' (1997) 35 *Osgoode Hall Law Journal* 75; H Botha 'Rights, Limitations, and the (Im)possibility of Self-government' in H Botha, A Van der Walt & J Van der Walt (eds) *Rights and Democracy in a Transformative Constitution* (2003) 13, 24–25.

119. See J De Waal, I Currie & G Erasmus (eds) *The Bill of Rights Handbook* (2001) 37 quoting *S v Mhlungu* 1995 (3) SA 867 (CC), 1995 (7) BCLR 793 (CC) at para 59: 'It must be stated at the outset, however, that in practice the indirect application of the Bill of Rights must always be considered before its direct application to law or conduct. The reason for this is the principle, laid down by the Constitutional Court in an early decision, that 'where it is possible to decide a case without reaching a constitutional issue, that is the course that should be followed.' Where a legal dispute cannot be resolved without reference to the Constitution, the principle clearly prefers indirect application ... over direct application.' The logical incoherence of Currie and De Waal's position need not detain us. A full critique of that position has already been offered eslewhere. See S Woolman 'Application'

in S Woolman & M Bishop (eds) *Constitutional Law of South Africa* (2nd Edition, OS, March 2005) Chapter 31 (Appendix). In any event, it does not follow from the Court's doctrine of avoidance as articulated in *Mhlungu*. Of greater concern, however, is the lack of analytical precision and an almost casuistic approach to constitutional interpretation that flows from this doctrine. The jurisprudence of avoidance is most dangerous when it becomes, as it has, not just an approach to constitutional adjudication, but a preferred form of constructing judgments. The thinness associated with such judgments makes it more difficult to anticipate the kinds of arguments – and reasons – that would lead the Court to conclude that a right has been infringed or that the limitation of a right is (or is not) reasonable and justifiable. The absence of rules of law to which political and non-political actors must align their behaviour 'could' undermine the ability of other branches of government to comply with the Bill of Rights – and places the Court in the unnecessarily uncomfortable position of having to reject or to accept government's positions in any given case as if they were ruling ab initio. So I originally argued in 2007. See S Woolman 'The Amazing, Vanishing Bill of Rights' (2007) 124 *South African Law Journal* 762. Frank Michelman's reply led me to reconsider whether the problem was best described as a 'flight from substance' – which he denied – or 'thinness'. See F Michelman 'On the Uses of Interpretive Charity: Some Notes on Application, Equality and Objective Unconstitutionality from the 2007 Term of the Constitutional Court of South Africa' (2008) 1 *Constitutional Court Review* 165. See, then, the subsequent colloquy, S Woolman Between Charity and Clarity: Kibitzing with Frank Michelman on How to Best Read the Constitutional Court (2010) 25 *Southern Africa Public Law* 491; F Michelman 'Old Kibitzes Never Die: A Rejoinder to Stu Woolman' (2010) 25 *Southern Africa Public Law* 514. I accept Professor Michelman's claim that my original charge was too strong, based upon too limited a sample, and that my argument supported a less controversial charge of 'thinness', here and there. While a sufficiently large number of cases handed down since 2007 suggest that the first assault on the citadel possessed at least some merit, the Court has handed down too many important, thick and substantive decisions for a pure 'flight from substance' argument to stick. Professor Michelman himself seems to have recently arrived at a more cautious, but not entirely dissimilar, conclusion. His most recent argument, in short, is that South African courts, including the Constitutional Court, still remain in the thrall of common law regimes that do not take sufficient cognizance of the changes brought about to the entire legal system by the Interim Constitution and the Final Constitution. See F Michelman 'Expropriation, Eviction and the Dignity of the Common Law' (2013) 24 *Stellenbosch Law Review* – (forthcoming) (manuscript available from myself, the author and on the SSRN at http://papers.ssrn.com/sol3/papers.cfm?abstract_id=2116643). In fairness to Professor Michelman, a critical bite of difference between us remains, even as my position on the matter has shifted dramatically as a result of his sustained engagement with my texts and the case law.

120. K Roach & G Budlender 'South African Law on Mandatory Relief and Supervisory Jurisdiction' (2005) 122 *South African Law Journal* 325.
121. It might be contended that what I have written elsewhere about the need for rule-governed decisions emanating from our Constitutional Court is inconsistent with the standard-based approach articulated here. They are not inconsistent positions. Even if we accept the priority of well informed perception by persons 'upon whom nothing is lost.' – a la Nussbaum and Aristotle – both acknowledge that somewhat thickly described norms are necessary to get a constitutional, or ethical, project off the ground. See M Nussbaum 'Constitutions and Capabilities: "Perception" against Lofty Formalism' (2007) 121 *Harvard Law Review* 4.
122. I Chipkin 'Beyond the Popular Discourse: Capacity Constraints in the Public Service in South Africa' (2011) Public Affairs Research Institute, available at www.pari.org (accessed on 1 July 2011). See also I Chipkin 'The Public Sector: Is It Alive and Do We Need It?' (2011) Public Affairs Research Institute, available at www.pari.org, (podcast)(accessed on 1 October 2011).
123. See S Woolman 'On the Fragility of Associational Life: A Response to Patrick Lenta' (2009) 25 *South African Journal on Human Rights* 280.

124. See S Woolman '"I am Large": Sachs, Whitman and Democracy' (2010) 25 *Southern Africa Public Law* 57.
125. The contemporary literature on flourishing is vast. Reintroduced into the philosophical canon by the neo-Aristotelian writings of Alisdair MacIntyre, it has been readily, and, quite naturally, absorbed,into the liberal canon. See A MacIntyre *After Virtue: A Study in Moral Theory* (1984); A McIntyre *Whose Justice, Which Rationality* (1987). The philosopher most responsible for that renewed interest is Martha Nussbaum. See, e.g., M Nussbaum *Love's Knowledge* (1991); M Nussbaum *Women and Human Development: The Capabilities Approach* (2000); M Nussbaum 'The Discernment of Perception: An Aristotelian Conception of Private and Public Rationality' (1985) 1 *Proceedings of the Boston Areas Colloquium in Ancient Philosophy*' 151; M Nussbaum 'Aristotelian Social Democracy' in R Bruce Douglass (ed) *Liberalism and the Good* (1990); M Nussbaum 'The Good as Discipline, the Good as Freedom' in D Crocker and T Linden (eds) *The Ethics of Consumption: The Good Life, Justice and Global Stewardship* (1998) 320. Nussbaum's capabilities approach aims at securing the political environment necessary for flourishing. Only two points need be made here. First, Nussbaum's notion of 'flourishing' – from the Greek 'eudemonia' – can be defined as living a life worth valuing or living life in all its fullness. Indeed, '[t]he failure to flourish' she has said, 'is a kind of death.' See J Cowley 'Twelve Great Thinkers of Our Time' (2003) 132 *New Statesman* 1. However, the form that flourishing takes will vary across societies, across cultures and across individuals. What ought not to vary across societies, across cultures and across individuals is the capacity to flourish. That leads Nussbaum to assert a second axiom for her project. Her political commitment to the capabilities approach – developed with Amartya Sen – rests on the assumption that 'a human life lacking the identified capabilities would be guaranteed less than a fully human life.' B Butler 'Nussbaum's Capabilities Approach: Political Criticism and the Burden of Proof' (2001) 1(1) *International Journal of Politics and Ethics* 71. The consequences of flourishing, and capabilities theory, for South African constitutional jurisprudence are explored at greater length below in Chapter 7. Suffice it to say that Nussbaum's Decalogue of essential capabilities required for flourishing, and Sen's general theory of development, are consistent with the jurisprudence of experimental constitutionalism.
126. Aristotle *Nicomachean Ethics*, Book II, 36.
127. R Bellah *Habits of the Heart* (1985).
128. *Stanford Encyclopeadia of Philosophy* (2010)('SEP') Much of what Aristotle has to say about the world about us, and our beliefs about that world, accords with what I have already claimed, and will reassert, about truth propositions when discussing Donald Davidson's work: most of our beliefs are true, that our way of understanding the world is parasitic on 'endless true beliefs' and that error, where it occurs, is, as Davidson says: what gives truth its point. As the SEP notes: Aristotle's 'attitude towards *phainomena* does betray a preference to conserve as many appearances as is practicable in a given domain—not because the appearances are unassailably accurate, but rather because, as he supposes, appearances tend to track the truth. We are outfitted with sense organs and powers of mind so structured as to put us into contact with the world and thus to provide us with data regarding its basic constituents and divisions. While our faculties are not infallible, neither are they systematically deceptive or misdirecting. Since philosophy's aim is truth and much of what appears to us proves upon analysis to be correct, *phainomena* provide both an impetus to philosophize and a check on some of its more extravagant impulses.'
129. Aristotle *Ethics* (supra) Book 6, 150.
130. I would be misrepresenting Aristotle entirely if I did not acknowledge the teleological nature of his thought. Each thing has its purpose, its end, its perfection. Though we moderns may tend to put certain moral beliefs beyond contestation, we do not, generally, share Aristotle's teleological view of nature and of human action. However, contemporary socio-biology and neuroscience have staked a claim on the degree to which many ostensibly 'constructed' norms can be traced to the hard-wiring of our brains. This book makes such claims. In *Braintrust: What Neuroscience Tells Us About Morality* (2011), Patricia Churchland outlines a compelling hypothesis for how 'ethics or morality' is

'a four dimensional scheme for social behaviour that is shaped by interlocking brain processes': '(1) *caring* (rooted in attachment to kith and kin and care for their well-being); (2) *recognition of others' psychological states* (rooted in the benefits of predicting the behaviour of others); (3) *problem-solving in a social context* (e.g., how we should distribute scarce resources …); (4) *learning social practices* (by positive and negative reinforcement, by trial and error, by various kinds of conditioning, and by analogy.)' Ibid at 9 (emphasis added).

131. Nussbaum alludes to the following observation by Wittgenstein: 'Is there such a thing as 'expert judgment' about the genuineness of expressions of feeling? Even here, there are those whose judgment is 'better' and those whose judgment is 'worse'. Corrector prognoses will generally issue from the judgments of those with better knowledge of mankind. Can one learn this knowledge? Yes; some can. Not, however, by taking a course in it, but through experience. Can someone else be a man's teacher in this? Certainly. From time to time, he gives him the right *tip*. This is what 'learning' and 'teaching' are like here. What one learns here is not a technique; one learns correct judgments. There are also rules, but they do not form a system, and only experienced people can apply them right.' L Wittgenstein *Philosophical Investigations*, (1953) Book II, xi.

132. M Nussbaum '"Finely Aware and Richly Responsible': Literature and the Moral Imagination' *Love's Knowledge* (1990) 148, 149, 156, 157, 160, 164 citing H James *The Art of the Novel* (1907).

133. See J Rawls *A Theory of Justice* (1973). Interestingly enough, Rawls – a Kantian constructivist – traces 'reflective equilibrium' back to Aristotle, but not without making several significant adjustments inconsistent with Aristotle's, Nussbaum's and Sen's notion of perceptive equilibrium. Nussbaum identifies 3 primary qualities of Rawl's notion: 'balance, an absence of inconsistency or tension, and the dominance of intellectual judgment.' Nussbaum 'Perceptive Equilibrium' (supra) at 174. These three features alone put Rawls' outside conventional wisdom about ethics – though not perhaps beyond conventional Kantian ethical theory. He further demands that his principles be 'general in form', 'universal in application', 'public', 'impose a general ordering on conflicting claims' and 'be taken as final and conclusive.' Rawls (supra) at 47 and 135.

134. See A Sen *The Idea of Justice* (2009): 'One question that can be asked about John Rawl's formulation of justice is this: if behavioural patterns vary between different societies … how can Rawls use the same principles of justice, in what he calls the constitutional phase, to establish basic institutions in different societies? In answering this question, it must be noted that Rawls' principles for just institutions do not, in general, specify particular, physical institutions, but identify rules that should govern the choice of actual institutions. The choice of actual institutions can take as much notice as may be needed of the actual parameters of standard social behaviour. Consider, for example, Rawls' second principle of justice: 'Social and economic inequalities must satisfy two conditions: first, they are to be attached to offices and positions open to all under conditions of fair equality of opportunity; and second, they are to be to the greatest benefit for the least advantaged members of the society.' Even though the first part may suggest a straightforward demand for non-discriminatory institutions, which need not be behavioural norms, it is plausible to think that the requirement of 'fair equality of opportunity' could give a much greater role to behavioural features … in determining the appropriate choice of institutions. When we turn to the second part of this principle for institutional choice ('the Difference Principle'), we have to examine how the different potential institutional arrangements would mesh with, and interact with, behavioural norms standard in a society. Indeed, even the language of the difference principle reflects the involvement of this criterion with what would actually happen in the society … Again this gives Rawls much more room to build in sensitivity to behavioural differences.' Ibid at 77. Sen's charge is that Rawls – in pursuit of perfectly just institutions – is tone-deaf to how his rules would work themselves out in practice. This failure to take practice and perceptive equilibrium seriously may lie exactly at the root of why theorists rebel when it comes down to swallowing Rawls' two principles whole hog. They simply fail to take heterogeneous behavioural states, standards of development and variable individual capabilities seriously. Sen later rounds on Rawls as follows: 'Understanding the demands of justice is no more a soloist exercise

than any other human discipline. When we should try to assess how we should behave, and what kinds of societies should be patently unjust, we have reason to listen and pay attention to the views and suggestions of others, which might or might not lead us to revise some of our own conclusions. We also attempt ... to make others ... pay attention to our priorities ... and in this advocacy we sometimes succeed, while at other times we fail altogether. ... A theory of justice that rules out the possibility that our best efforts could still leave us locked into one mistake or other, however hidden it might be, makes a pretension that would be hard to vindicate. Indeed, it is not defeatist for an approach to allow incompleteness of judgments, and also to accept the absence of once and for all finality. It is particularly important for a theory of practical reason (phronesis) to accommodate a framework for reasoning within the body of a capacious theory – that ... is the approach to the theory of justice this work pursues.' Ibid 88 – 89. Sen gives us some very good reasons to prefer his robust, highly socially differentiated account of practical reason and of 'perceptive equilibrium' – following Aristotle and Nussbaum – to Rawls' somewhat desiccated commitment to 'perfect' principles of justice and 'reflective equilibrium'. Rawls, he contends, 'ignor[es] the discipline of answering comparative questions about justice; ... [ignores] the broader perspective of social relationships; [i]gnore the potential for adverse effects on people beyond the borders of each country from the actions and choices of this country; ... [fails] to have any systematic procedure for correcting the influence of parochial values to which any individual country may be vulnerable; ... [does not allow] that even in the original position that different persons could continue to take, even after much public discussion, some very different principles as appropriate for justice because of the plurality of their reasoned political norms and values (rather than because of their differences in vested interests.) Ibid at 90. On the fifth point, Rawls does appear somewhat at a loss as to explain how Condorcet, then Arrow, and then Sen himself could identify the fundamental problem of social choice theory – how A could defeat B; B defeat C; and C defeat A. The hyper-rationalism of Rawls does not permit – or even engage – nuanced problems of social choice. See KJ Arrow *Social Choice and Individual Values* (1951); A Sen 'The Possibility of Social Choice' (Nobel Prize Lecture)(1999) 89 *American Economic Review* 1.

135. Again, Aristotle did view the life of the mind as the highest form of human activity. It is not my intention to mischaracterize his intentions.

136. However, while Aristotle's commitment to the heterogeneity of goods might make him more palatable to moderns, he did not quite believe that virtue could be attained in a multiplicity of different ways. Ancient in outcome, if modern in method, Aristotle viewed the combination of theoretical wisdom and practical wisdom – two essential parts of a single whole – as the core drivers of virtue, excellence and flourishing. At the end of Book Six, Aristotle writes: 'Virtue or excellence is not only a characteristic which is guided by [theoretical reason], but also a characteristic of right reason; and right reason in moral matters is practical wisdom. So while, Socrates [and Plato] believed that the virtues are rational principles – [they] said that all of them are forms of knowledge – we, on the other hand, think that [virtues] are united with a rational principle. Our discussion, then, has made it clear that it is impossible to be good in the full sense of the word without practical wisdom, or to be a person of practical wisdom without moral excellence or virtue.' *Ethics* (supra) at 170 – 171.

137. M Nussbaum 'Form and Content, Philosophy and Literature' *Love's Knowledge* (supra) at 19-20.

138. Ibid at 20 – 21.

139. Michael Dorf, Charles Sabel, William Simon, Susan Sturm and Barry Friedman have been the primary exponents of this school of legal thought. Most of their primary contributions have been repeatedly cited in these pages. Others pieces that warrant notice include: M Dorf '1997 Supreme Court Term Foreword: The Limits of Socratic Deliberation' (1998) 112 *Harvard Law Review* 4 (1998); S Sturm 'Second Generation Employment Discrimination: A Structural Approach' (2001) 101 *Columbia Law Review* 452; S Sturm 'The Promise of Participation' (1993) 78 *Iowa Law Review* 981, 987-991, 1002-1010; S Sturm 'A Normative Theory of Public Law Remedies' (1991) 79 *Georgetown LJ* 1357; A Fung & EO Wright 'Deepening Democracy: Innovations in Empowered Participatory Governance' (1998) 29(1) *Science & Society* 5. I have previously employed this school's approach to

South African constitutional doctrine. See, eg, S Woolman 'Application' in S Woolman & M Bishop (eds) *Constitutional Law of South Africa* (2nd Edition, OS, March 2005) Chapter 31; S Woolman & H Botha 'Limitations' in S Woolman & M Bishop (eds) *Constitutional Law of South Africa* (2nd Edition, OS, July 2006) Chapter 34: S Woolman & B Fleisch *The Constitution in the Calssroom: Law and Education in South Africa, 1994–2008* (2009). For a leftist critique of experimental constitutionalism, see M Tushnet *After Bureaucracy: The New Constitutional Order* (2004).

140. See M Walzer *Spheres of Justice: A Defense of Pluralism and Equality* (1983). See also S Woolman 'Freedom of Association' in S Woolman & M Bishop (eds) *Constitutional Law of South Africa* (2nd Edition, OS, December 2003) Chapter 44; S Woolman 'Dignity' in S Woolman & M Bishop (eds) *Constitutional Law of South Africa* (2nd Edition, OS, February 2006) Chapter 36.

141. Experimental Constitutionalism is meant to draw our attention to the kinds of functional arrangements that are most likely to realize three basic ends of the South African state. Those ends, to the extent they are not made expressly clear above or in Chapter 7 below, are as follows. 1. If one accepts the radical givenness of the ends of individuals and groups, the South African state is under a constitutional obligation to protect those ways of being in the world that do not vitiate its concomitant core commitments to such goods as rough equality, tolerance, dignity the rule of law and democratic participation. Civil and political rights protect extant ways of being in the world. South Africa's history of radical inequality in resource allocation requires a particular form of redress. 2. The South African state is under a constitutional obligation to ensure that historically marginalized groups have access to the requisite stocks of political, economic and social capital necessary to sustain extant sources of the self. Consistent with the Final Constitution's core commitments, the South African state must ensure that its citizens are not held hostage by ways of being in the world that diminish individual flourishing. This concern turns primarily on the ability of individuals to exit repressive communities than it does on creating novel conditions for flourishing. But that does not mean that state intervention, and remedies that require support from traditional associations found to have engaged in unfair discrimination, will not have such a secondary or knock-on effect. 3. State intervention, along with remedies the ensure that private parties have some obligation to members compelled to exit, may just shake up existing social hierarchies in a manner that creates new ways of being in the world. This commitment to experimentalism and remedial equilibration is predicated upon the notion that a large number of existing ways of being in the world – extant cultural formations – will, for many individuals, fail to recognize those ends upon which the happiness of those individuals truly rests.

142. S Woolman & D Davis 'The Last Laugh: Classical Liberalism, Creole Liberalism and the Application of Fundamental Rights under the Interim and the Final Constitutions' (1996) 12 *South African Journal on Human Rights* 361, 363 ('[T]he state has an essential role to play in determining the contours of those 'private' relationships which so fundamentally shape individual identity and in making possible a variety of life choices through support for those associations and organizations which make up society writ large. Creole liberalism envisages a state which does not exhaust the possibilities of individual lives, but helps to make real those possibilities. In addition, creole liberalism requires that the state occupy a crucial, if not always central place in the debate about and construction of values at the same time as it supports a variety of different ways of being in the world.') See also A Sen *Development as Freedom* (1999) 24 (Describes these normative commitments as 'substantive freedom'.)

143. This slowly evolving enhancement and expansion of the conditions of being is fundamentally pragmatic, as opposed to deontological, in spirit. See M Dorf and C Sabel 'Democratic Constitutionalism' (supra) at 284 ('The backdrop of our design is the pragmatic account of thought and action as problem-solving in a world.') Chapter 7 shows that this shift of ideals in light of experience is rooted in the kinds of 'trial and error' mechanisms that have been revealed in recent studies of consciousness and contemporary theories about the social order (discussed in Chapters 1, 2 and 3). Moreover, ideals are not discovered through the revelation of idealized forms, but as Martha Nussbaum would have it in her Aristotelian phase, through practices in which individuals achieve virtue and come to

understand the truth, by active engagement, and not arid reflection. M Nussbaum '"Finely Aware and Richly Responsible: Moral Attention and the Moral Task of Literature' (1985) 82 *The Journal of Philosophy* 516. Amartya Sen makes this point even more powerfully in development theory. For Sen, no priority of norms pre-exist lived reality. [I share Nussbaum's skepticism about the strength of this claim. Moreover, I'm not certain Sen himself can commit himself to development without some prior ordering of norms, however limited that priority might be.] A Sen *An Idea of Justice* (2009). Justice and injustice can be measured – quantitatively – by what happens on the ground. One hundred million women (from the world's population) were missing – as Sen famously wrote in 1992 – because of some readily identifiable problems on the ground: infanticide (with respect to girls) and a general lack of access of women to adequate education, food, and healthcare. A Sen 'More Than 100 Million Women are Missing' (1990) 37 *New York Review of Books* 61; A Sen 'More Than 100 Million Women are Missing' 367 *The Lancet* 185. Such a shift away from Rawlsian (and Kantian) first principles developed behind a veil of ignorance has profound consequences for advocates, say, of the disabled, who would argue that the disabled would readily forsake many basic liberties in return for the kind of health care that would enable them to live lives worth pursuing. Another aspect of experimental constitutionalism's commitment to pragmatism is worth emphasizing here. Dorf and Sabel write: 'Pragmatism guides us in coming to grips with that which we have come to anticipate: That experience will again and again disrupt our habits and the understandings that rest upon them.' M Dorf and C Sabel 'Democratic Constitutionalism' (supra) at 285. That constant disruption, and our ability to respond to novel circumstances with novel practices, is exactly what underwrites this book's description of consciousness, the radically heterogeneous (densely populated) self, and various social and political systems as 'problem-solving' constructs (in Chapters 1, 2, 3, 4 and 5).

144. C Sabel & W Simon 'Destabilization Rights: How Public Law Litigation Succeeds' (2004) 117 *Harvard Law Review* 1015.
145. Ibid.
146. Ibid.
147. Ibid at 1023.
148. G Rosenberg *The Hollow Hope: Can Courts Bring about Social Change* (1991).
149. H Herskoff 'Positive Rights and State Constitutions: The Limits of Federal Rationality Review' (1999) 112 *Harvard Law Review* 1131, 1190 (Describing *Harper v Hunt*, No. CV-91-0117-R (Ala Cir Ct Montgomery County, Apr. 1, 1993)).
150. Ibid. See also M Rebell & R Hughes 'Schools, Communities, and the Courts: A Dialogic Approach to Education Reform' (1996) 14 *Yale Law & Policy Review* 99, 114–136.
151. I do not want to be accused of gilding the lily. As Michael Bishop notes, not all adequacy litigation has taken this sort of approach. Many state courts still address reform as a purely financial issue. These courts attempt to determine how much additional money will be required to realize 'adequate' outcomes, then order the state to make such funds available. In some instances, the court order comes down with no oversight structures in place. The result, in many instances, is that court allocated funds go to waste. Funds allocated to New York City schools as a result of adequacy litigation reflect a quintessential example of the limits of current school reform litigation. For a conservative take on the limits of the adequacy movement and court-directed spending, see E Hanushek & A Lindseth *Schoolhouses, Courthouses, and Statehouses: Solving the Funding-Achievement Puzzle in America's Public Schools* (2009). Hanushek and Lindseth contend that court rulings requiring states to increase public-school funding has done little to improve student achievement. They propose a performance-based system that directly links funding to success in raising student achievement. Not all commentators are so quick to dismiss the importance of both the financial equity and adequacy litigation. Michael Rebell defends the courts' authority and responsibility to pursue the goal of educational equity. See M Rebell *Courts and Kids: Pursuing Educational Equity through the State Courts* (2009). As Rebell notes, litigants, since 1973, have challenged the constitutionality of the education finance systems in 45 of 50 states on the grounds that they deprive many poor and minority students of adequate

access to a sound education. Those efforts cannot be blithely dismissed – even if the long term benefits to historically disadvantaged students in successful litigation has not been exactly what its advocates had envisaged. Consistent with Michael Bishop's point above, Rebell finds that the absence of court supervision ultimately led to disappointing results. Consistent with Sabel and Simon's call for 'new governance', Rebell prescribes a system in which courts collaborate with the executive and the legislature, as well as local school systems, parents and learners, in a forward and lateral looking manner designed to realize educational equity. So – despite conservative critiques – it would appear that lawyers and educators have learned valuable lessons from the previous waves of reform. Bishop notes that those courts that have successfully employed experimental remedies that set basic goals and monitored attempts to achieve them (while bringing in a variety of stakeholders to discuss different policy options) remain a minority. E-mail Correspondence with Michael Bishop (10 August 2011.)

152. For an excellent South African assessment on the relative success of, and changing strategy behind, public impact litigation, see S Wilson & J Dugard 'Constitutional Jurisprudence: The First and Second Waves' in M Langford, B Cousins, J Dugard & T Madlingozi (eds) *Symbols or Substance: The Role or Impact of Socio-Economic Rights Strategies in South Africa* (2011).
153. Sabel & Simon (supra) at 1019 and 1020.
154. L Fuller 'The Forms and Limits of Adjudication' (1978) 92 *Harvard Law Review* 358.
155. I must thank Columbia Law School Professors Jane Spinak and Philip Genty for giving me the opportunity to work as a children's advocate for two years at Morningside Heights Legal Services.
156. K Noonan, C Sabel & W Simon 'Legal Accountability in the Service-Based Welfare State: Lessons from Child Welfare Reform' (2009) 34 *Law & Social Inquiry* 523 citing J Handler *Social Citizenship and Workfare in the United States and Europe: The Paradox of Inclusion* (2004); J Handler *The Conditions of Discretion: Autonomy, Community, Bureaucracy* (1986).
157. K Noonan, C Sabel & W Simon (supra) at 524 citing ABA Center on Children and the Law *Child Welfare Consent Decrees: Analysis of Thirty-Five Court Actions from 1995 to 2005* (2005) 1.
158. K Noonan, C Sabel & W Simon (supra) at 525.
159. Ibid.
160. Ibid.
161. Ibid at 526.
162. See M Dorf & C Sabel 'Drug Treatment Courts and Emergent Experimentalist Government' (2000) 53 *Vanderbilt Law Review* 831.
163. Ibid at 832.
164. Ibid.
165. See *Prince* (supra).
166. Dorf & Simon 'Drug Treatment Courts' (supra) at 837.
167. We have our own specialized courts and fora in South Africa: the Competition Commission, the Competition Tribunal, the Commission for Conciliation, Mediation and Arbitration, the Land Claims Court, and various Labour Courts (to name but a few of the most prominent emergent experimental institutions that we possess.)
168. Ibid.
169. Dorf & Simon 'Drug Treatment Courts' (supra) at 837.

Chapter Five

Experimental Constitutionalism in South Africa: Institutions and Doctrines

I speak without exaggeration when I say that I have constructed 3,000 different 'theories' in connection with the electric light, each one of them reasonable ... Yet only in two cases did my experiments prove the truth of my theory.

Thomas Edison

[Meaningful engagement] is less costly, in both financial and emotional terms, and can only result in improved collectivism to tackle issues as a country . ... It is preferable to settle all demarcation differences through open, frank, inclusive and transparent dialogue as opposed to the courts. ... [When] all parties commit to co-operation as opposed to conflict there tends to emerge a progressive outcome that takes our country forward.

Landiwe Mahlangu

A. The South African Constitution as an Experimental Constitution

In this chapter, the rubber finally hits the road. Having defended the multi-pronged thesis that:

- (a) consciousness as experienced by radically heterogeneous selves, (b) social formations and (c) constitutional orders are best understood, and operate most effectively, when thought of in terms of trial and error and feedback mechanisms;
- the most successful of these entities are selves, associations and polities able to run as many experiments as possible, with results that both identify the best practices for realizing extant ends and work to shift the ends themselves towards ways of being in the world that we come to deem more and more optimal; and
- an experimentalist cast to theories of mind, social networks and politics are rendered more plausible when we reflect upon the fact that human beings never reach that imagined stasis of happiness, because life always works to disrupt that stasis.

We can now ask whether the institutions and doctrines identified with experimental constitutionalism are likely to improve, or at least nudge forward, the decision-making both within the halls of South African government and the broader radically heterogeneous society of which we are members.

My first response is that we are already moving in that direction.

My second response is that the very moments of crisis that cause unwarranted despondency amongst my fellow South Africans can be best addressed through the pragmatic, experimentalist tools that we already have at hand. Too much good will, too much skill exists within this land for us to squander the opportunity that we have now to re-think the ways we engage one another and the manner in which we go about solving the manifold problems that this ever-so-rich country faces.

In the chapter that follows I track quite explicitly the two dominant theses of experimental constitutionalism: (a) that virtually any constitutional democracy can accommodate a doctrine of shared constitutional interpretation; and (b) any modern democratic state – be it in the developed world or the developing world – can make use of the notion of participatory bubbles in order to resolve local problems and to share information about successful and unsuccessful attempts to work out solutions to similar problems across a nation.[1] However, shared constitutional interpretation and participatory bubbles are but two facets of experimental constitutionalism (or what some now describe as 'new governance' theory). Chapter Four identified a number of other features of experimental constitutionalism that undergird this book's analysis – reflexivity, the status of truth propositions in radically heterogeneous constitutional orders, chastened deliberation, destabilization rights, disentrenchment of private ordering through remedial equilibration, and flattened hierarchies rather than top-down systems of command and control. Where and when possible, these facets of experimental constitutionalism will inform this chapter's analysis of South Africa's own emergent experimental institutions and doctrines.

It is somewhat arbitrary to divide experimental constitutionalism up into two discrete, if dominant, components. Both notions rest on the dual assumption that multiple actors applying their minds to similar problems in different ways will elicit greater information about the kinds of rule-based legal principles and more adaptive legal standards that 'work', and that by continually attempting to test what works best, we may, ultimately, come to change our consensus about the ends that we wish our polity (and the individuals in it) to pursue or to forswear.

The justification for this bifurcation lies in the difference of emphasis and purpose of each concept.

Shared constitutional interpretation tends to emphasize both the various spheres of government and how their relationship shapes our understanding and the content of the norms generated by our basic law. Shared constitutional interpretation succeeds when as many experiments as possible are run in as many publics and subpublics as possible. The following section takes cognizance of the roles which Chapter 9 Institutions, participatory democratic fora and various organizations in civil society play in determining the shape of constitutional norms.

Participatory bubbles tend to emphasize the function of grass-roots movements, and often spatially and temporally more limited spaces of self-government. Such a description risks oversimplification. Bubbles will occur in the highest spheres of government – Parliament and the Constitutional Court. Bubbles must occur in the upper tiers of government because we want our representatives and our judges to pool information and to take cognizance of what works best when local actors fix problems that affect them directly. The substantial overlap of shared constitutional interpretation and participatory bubbles is borne out by the appearance of Chapter Nine Institutions in the discussion of both conceptual frameworks.

In the next section on shared constitutional interpretation, we will see that minor adjustments to existing doctrine create: (1) courts that employ an invigorated limitations analysis open up the manner in which facts are assesed *and* promotes a more fastidious approach to rights interpretation; (2) a deeper understanding of the principle of democracy and its relationship to rights interpretation; (3) a meaningful acceptance by the executive and the legislature of the Constitutional Court's invitation to have them assist the Court in shaping the contours of all rights; (4) an appreciation for the role Chapter 9 Institutions have to play in giving various constitutional norms greater content; (5) how socio-economic rights litigation has, perhaps by its very nature, led to the acceptance of various features of shared constitutional interpretation without any grand theorizing by the Constitutional Court as to its virtues; and, (6) the promise that provincial constitutions (might) offer with respect to fundamental rights guarantees and to political structures not afforded by the Final Constitution.

In the section on participatory bubbles, the adjustments to (existing) doctrines required by experimental constitutionalism encompass: (1) an understanding of constitutional jurisdiction that facilitates more challenges to common law doctrines that inhibit radical reformation; (2) rules of procedure that promote greater access to court for those who wish to pursue fundamental rights challenges; (3) the creative use of such remedies as structural injunctions and meaningful engagement, and a shift from rights essentialism and automatic remedialism to remedial equilibration; (4) cost orders that promote broader participation in constitutional litigation; (5) an enhanced role for public participation in legislative processes; and (6) greater roles for Chapter 9 Institutions with respect to investigation, information-sharing and norm-setting.

B. Shared Constitutional Interpretation: Design & Doctrines

1. *Limitations Analysis*

a. *Theory*

Important invitations to engage in shared constitutional interpretation can be found in the interpretation clause, the remedies clause and the limitations clause of the Bill of Rights. However, the emphasis of this work on the resolution of polycentric social conflicts justifies an initial narrowing of focus to the phrasing, structure and meaning of the limitations clause.[2]

The limitation clause directs a court to ask whether a given law of general application constitutes a reasonable or justifiable infringement of a fundamental right. As I have argued elsewhere, the clause is something more than an effort to soften the counter-majoritarian dilemma created by a justiciable Bill of Rights.[3] One the one hand, it invites the legislature or the executive to try again if previous efforts to solve a particular socio-legal problem are found to be constitutionally infirm. On the other hand, it reminds the courts that they are obliged to take the law-making efforts of the co-ordinate branches seriously and to afford them a significant degree of latitude.

The holdings in *Miranda* and *Dickerson* – and *Satchwell I and II*[4] – suggest how we are to understand the relationship between these two propositions. First, the mere re-assertion by Parliament or the Executive of the exact legal position found to be unconstitutional by the Constitutional Court warrants no judicial solicitude. Second, as in *Fourie* or *Joe Slovo II*, the law-making efforts by Parliament or the Executive to address the same issue in a different way, and in a manner not obviously (or entirely) at odds with the previous findings of the Court, warrants judicial solicitude.[5]

Perhaps the clearest articulation of a standing invitation to share power with respect to constitutional interpretation occurs in *First Certification Judgment*.[6] While the Constitutional Court states that its mandate with respect to the certification of the Final Constitution is legal and not political, the role it carves out for itself is not dissimilar from that articulated by the US Supreme Court in *Miranda*. Its job was to say, in quite general terms, what the Interim Constitution – specifically the 34 Constitutional Principles – allowed. Within those extremely generous parameters, the Constitutional Assembly was said to be free to craft any constitution it liked. To put it differently, the Constitutional Court recognized that the Constitutional Assembly could draft a well-nigh infinite number of constitutions that complied with the 34 Constitutional Principles. It was not the job of the Constitutional Court to say which of these legally compliant Final Constitutions was to be preferred.[7]

b. Practice

In a typical piece of commercial or private law litigation, a court will decide preliminary issues, interpret the facts in terms of the applicable law and render a decision. Despite the fact that the scope of judicial discretion is often extensive as to factual determinations, and only constrained by the (quite expansive) bounds of analogical reasoning, it rarely occasions major complaints. Most judicial decisions in private litigation are accepted for two reasons relevant for this argument. First, commercial actors accept the possibility of an adverse outcome. Second, courts are credited with a degree of generalized knowledge that legitimates their factual conclusions.

A similar degree of deference attaches to judicial opinions that are able to tie well-entrenched social mores to constitutional rights. Traditional constitutional law adjudication bears a sufficient resemblance to ordinary conceptions of the judicial function to escape excessive criticism.[8] But not all constitutional cases present straightforward application of principle to problem.

For example, a piece of super-ordinate legislation – The Promotion of Equality and Prevention of Unfair Discrimination Act ('PEPUDA') – is designed to give content to FC s 9 (the equality clause) in a manner that enables the state and private actors to challenge existing structures of authority, domination and tyranny within private institutions.[9] PEPUDA's Equality Courts must acknowledge the revolutionary intent of the legislation at the same time that they demonstrate their appreciation for the fact that many social practices protected by the Constitution amount to 'fair' discrimination.[10] Progressive readings of PEPUDA – and concomitant incursions into the private ordering of individual and communal relationships – will raise, quite crisply, questions about the possibility for judicially-initiated social change.[11] Cases such as *Prince* and *Jordan* pose dilemmas for traditional models of adjudication because courts comfortable with zero-sum outcomes tend to link their analysis of a complex nexus of facts and law with an often equally challenging assessment as to whether an effective remedy exists. The burden of assessing complicated fact scenarios and the judiciary's innate resistance to imposing novel solutions on the body politic has, in a range of similar cases, led the Court to accept the state's justification for the law as it currently stands.

The three-part structure of Bill of Rights analysis provides the courts with a measure of relief. By explicitly separating out the process of (a) defining the ambit of a right, (b) determining the appropriateness of any limitation, and (c) fashioning an appropriate remedy, the Bill of Rights avoids creating a binary world where the outcome of the dispute is tied entirely to rights essentialism. For example, in American constitutional law, several types of law deemed to limit the equal protection clause or the freedom of speech clause are likely to be invalidated under a strict scrutiny standard.[12] The three-part structure of South African Bill of Rights analysis, as practised, has enabled the Constitutional Court to avoid such rigid categories. While the Court has often resisted giving rights sufficiently definitive content (that would guide other actors), nothing in the text or this theory of experimental constitutionalism demands such avoidance. A relatively precise, if nuanced, approach to limitations analysis actually creates the space for a fairly fastidious treatment of rights analysis.[13]

A more emphatic embrace of an experimentalist approach would enable a South African court to use the open-ended, fact-driven framework of limitations analysis (in concert with a commitment to remedial equilibrium) to invite litigants – and other stakeholders – to participate more directly in the vetting of possible solutions to the legal problem confronting the court. Such an invitation to the parties to get their hands dirty enables the courts to overcome both their limited administrative capacity and their often enervating reliance on the good faith of the various parties. More importantly, the invitation to the parties to expand the basis of their competing claims from zero-sum outcomes to solutions in which all parties believe they may benefit enables courts to reap the problem-solving benefits inherent in well-directed collective action.

An experimentalist perspective on limitations analysis proceeds from the recognition that the determination of the reasonableness of a limitation and the identification of the best of all possible remedies are interdependent processes. This experimentalist perspective also recognizes how exceedingly difficult it is to discover the right answer – or remedy – from an outsider's perspective.[14] The notion of a single right answer in a complex context – in advance of any attempt to mediate the competing positions – is itself suspect.[15] As Susan Sturm has observed in connection with workplace discrimination, changes in legal doctrines shape people's expectations.[16] The new legal doctrine thereby reconstructs identities, beliefs and behaviour. Such an evolutionary process – a function of the law as an experimental feedback mechanism – can gradually transform the nature of the problem as originally perceived.[17]

Confronted with complexity, the task for the courts is neither to undertake Herculean quests for perfect theoretical answers nor to retreat into the political quietism of deference to administrative decisions and private ordering. An experimentalist perspective possesses two important advantages. First, by acknowledging the difficulty of finding the right answer, *ex ante*, courts with a problem-solving perspective must create mechanisms (including legal doctrines) that gather relevant information, generate proposed reforms and relay feedback quickly. Second, given the potential for the unintended consequences which flow from adaptive processes (and preferences) triggered by shifting legal principles, a problem-solving perspective implements each set of solutions tentatively and is ready to modify its solutions on the basis of new empirical evidence.[18]

Over the past several years, the Court has demonstrated a willingness to seek out critical information from organizations not initially party to the litigation. In cases such as *Juma Musjid*, the Court recognized that if didn't possess all the relevant facts, it could neither arrive at just conclusion nor fashion an adequate remedy.[19] The *Juma Musjid* Court invited the Centre for Child Law and the Socio-Economic Rights Institute as true friends of the court to provide Brandeis briefs on the actual conditions faced by learners caught up in a longstanding quarrel between a School Governing Body, a private trust that owned the land upon which the school was located and a provincial Department of Education that had failed both to adequately follow procedure and to safeguard the needs of learners.

Joe Slovo I and *Joe Slovo II* offer even further evidence of a Court willing to recognize the unintended consequences that flow from adaptive processes triggered by shifting legal principles, and to modify its solutions on the basis of new empirical evidence (as supplied by the various parties to the matter.) The flexibility and reflexivity on display in *Joe Slovo I* and *Joe Slovo II* is noteworthy. The *Joe Slovo I* Court exhibited a firm normative hand in constructing the participatory bubble that would shape subsequent (fact-driven) negotiations. It then gave its imprimatur of approval to an outcome that would enable community dwellers to secure better housing elsewhere. A *Joe Slovo II* Court was then somewhat surprised when the multiple parties to the litigation returned and stated that they wished to alter the previous order because they had discovered, through ongoing negotiations and further analysis of the lay of the land, that the original settlement would have sub-optimal outcomes for all parties concerned. With some quite understandable hesitation, the *Joe Slovo II* Court recognized that the adaptive process it had initiated had to be followed through to its logical conclusion: changing an initial settlement where that settlement failed to solve the problem that originally seized the Court. The *Joe Slovo I* and *Joe Slovo II* Courts reflect an institution that truly shares constitutional interpretation with coordinate branches of governments and its citizens.

The decade-long line of cases from *Ntuli* to *Steyn* to *Shinga* demonstrates just how flexible the Court has become and the extent to which it abides by Lord Aktin's credo: 'Finality is a good thing, but justice is better.'[20] The Constitutional Court shifts over these three cases from a semi-arid separation of powers doctrine to a more rough and tumble engagement with Parliament over the kinds of amendments to the Criminal Procedure Act that would vouchsafe a fair trial.

Early on in its existence, the Constitutional Court demonstrated a significant reluctance to alter its original orders because of the standard trope that the uncertainty which would ensue from the possibility of such variance would leave the litigants and society at large incapable of determining the appropriate course of action in the future. The question of how long a ruling would remain good law clearly vexed a court consciously developing a robust rule of law jurisprudence. In *Ntuli II*, the Court held that the principle of finality in litigation meant that an intolerable degree of uncertainty would arise if courts could be readily approached to reconsider final orders declaring provisions of statute invalid.[21] Still, the *Ntuli II* Court left open the door to the reconsideration of final orders. It wrote: 'For the purposes of this judgment [the Court is] prepared to assume that in an appropriate case an order for the suspension of the invalidity of the provisions of a statute may subsequently be varied by a Court for good cause. But if this is so, such a power, ... would be one that should be very sparingly exercised.'[22] It declined, on this basis, to grant the requested extension by Parliament to cure the infirm provisions in the Criminal Procedure Act. The Court's finding of invalidity, as promised, kicked in.[23] In declining Parliament's request for an extension beyond the 17 months already granted, the *Ntuli II* Court wrote:

> [This Court] has had to ask counsel to establish how much time will be necessary, and to make an order in the light of such information and its own evaluation of what may be necessary. In future more will be required. It is the duty of the Minister responsible for the administration of the statute who wishes to ask for an order of invalidity to be suspended, whether under the interim or the 1996 Constitution, to place sufficient information before the Court to justify the making of such an order, and to show the time that will be needed to remedy the defect in the

> legislation. This should be done with due regard to the importance of the fundamental rights enshrined in the Constitution, and to the fact that it is an obligation of the government to ensure that such rights are upheld and that the suspension of rights consequent upon the difficulties of the transition is kept to a minimum. This Court has the responsibility of ensuring that the provisions of the Constitution are upheld and enforced. It should not be assumed that it will lightly grant the suspension of an order made by it declaring a statutory provision to be invalid and of no force and effect or, if it does so, that it will allow more time than is necessary for the defect in the legislation to be cured.[24]

In *S v Steyn*, the Court demonstrates that it has drawn a number of lessons regarding institutional comity from its decisions in *Ntuli I* and *Ntuli II*.[25] Once again, the constitutionality of ss 309B and 309C of the Criminal Procedure Act, now amended by Parliament, seized the Court.

Parliament, on the *Steyn* Court's account, had failed (wilfully) to see the damage that a finding of invalidity might do the court system as a whole. In the absence of 'hard data' that ought to have been provided by Parliament with respect to the ability of the courts to handle an increasing caseload, the Court refused to grant an immediate declaration of invalidity. This time, however, it did not give Parliament a leisurely 17 months to fix the problems. The Court expressly noted the 17 month suspension granted in *Ntuli I* had proved of benefit to no one. In *Steyn*, it gave Parliament five months to get its house and the Criminal Procedure Act in order. The Court noted, again, that Parliament had failed to offer any evidence that more time was required.[26]

By the time that *Shinga v the State & Another (Society of Advocates, Pietermaritzburg Bar, as Amicus Curiae); O'Connell & Others v the State* arrived at the courthouse steps, the Constitutional Court was more than passing familiar with the various provisions of the Criminal Procedure Act at issue.[27] Over ten years, three important developments had taken place. The Court itself – through its interactions with lower courts and Parliament – had a better grip on the problems associated with appeals from Magistrates' Courts to the High Court. That familiarity enabled the Court to assess for itself which provisions were beyond redemption and which could be ameliorated without a finding of unconstitutionality. As a result, the Court could hand down judgment on the constitutionality of the provisions under scrutiny and not feel obliged to consult Parliament by deferring its order of invalidity.

2. *The Principle of Democracy and its Relationship to Rights Interpretation*

I have described in the preceding pages an approach to righs, limitations and remedies analysis that simultaneously answers deep questions about institutional comity in a constitutional democracy and adumbrates an analytical framework that responds to concerns about judicial usurpation of legislative prerogatives and the alleged inability of courts to resolve polycentric social problems. What I have not yet described is how our courts go about determining the normative content necessary for rights, limitations and remedies analysis.

The normative content for such interpretation, at least in part, turns on the phrase 'an *open* and *democratic* society based on *human dignity, equality and freedom*'. Determining the meaning of this phrase is fraught with difficulties as old as political theory itself. There are, for starters, the tensions between democracy and rights, between equality and freedom, and the deeply contested nature of each of these five terms.

For the most part, the Court has viewed the four other values (found in FC s 36 and FC s 39) largely through the lens of human dignity.[28] According to the Court, dignity provides a common measure of value which can help bridge the division between equality and freedom, between negative and positive rights, and between individual and collective forms of mutual concern and respect. However, a close examination of the Court's jurisprudence reveals that dignity does not adequately address all conflicts of right, value and interest nor does a reliance on dignity appear to do justice to those out-groups whose participation in our democratic decision-making remains marginal at best.

It is particularly surprising that the Constitutional Court has not done more to develop the meaning of 'openness' and 'democracy' – two features of our society that clearly demarcate the boundary between apartheid South Africa and post-apartheid South Africa.[29] (But that is not say that they have said nothing compelling at all.[30]) A greater elaboration of the meaning of 'an open and democratic society', and a closer connection of these values to dignity (especially dignity qua self-governance), might result in a jurisprudence more inclined to accommodate plurality and difference and therefore, the heteregenous forms of flourishing to be found in our republic. Similarly, an engagement with 'democracy' may strengthen our commitment to securing spaces in which 'counter-publics' or subpublics can challenge dominant ideas and engage in alternative discourses.[31]

In this section, I consider the possibility of a complementary understanding of the 'big five' values underlying the Bill of Rights that flows from a greater appreciation for the kind of democratic society to which the Final Constitution commits us. It is an understanding of democracy that, consistent with a commitment to shared constitutional interpretation, loosens the Gordian knot of most facile characterizations of the counter-majoritarian dilemma.

In *United Democratic Movement v President of the Republic of South Africa*, the Constitutional Court issued a challenge of sorts to the academic community: tell us what 'democracy' means, and more importantly, tell us how it ought to inform, in a principled manner, our understanding of various provisions in the text of the Final Constitution.[32] Some South African academics, and in particular, Theunis Roux, have done just that.[33] Roux pulls together the political theory out of which our particular South African conception of democracy arises, the textual provisions of the Final Constitution that shape that conception, and the extant case law of our courts to generate a 'principle of democracy'.[34] I will not rehearse all of Roux's arguments in support of that principle here. I will, however, draw down on several of his arguments, especially those that serve part (2) of his 'principle of democracy'.

The argument that lends the greatest force to a theory of shared constitutional interpretation is Roux's contention that, read together, FC ss 7(1), 36(1), and 39(1) 'structure the way in which the tension between rights and democracy is to be managed in South African constitutional law'.[35] FC ss 36(1) and 39(1) require a value-based approach to fundamental rights analysis and limitations analysis in part because they invoke the same linguistic trope – 'an open and democratic society based upon human dignity, equality and freedom'. However, Roux's connection of the oft-ignored FC s 7(1) to both fundamental rights interpretation (FC s 39) and limitations analysis (FC s 36) enables me to make four new critical points.

First, FC s 7(1) reads: 'The Bill of Rights is a cornerstone of democracy in South Africa. It enshrines the rights of all people in our country and affirms the democratic values of human dignity, equality and freedom.' Notice that democracy is treated as an independent value. Notice that the values of human dignity, equality and freedom are 'democratic' values. At a minimum, the language of FC s 7(1) should give pause to those interpreters of the basic law who privilege, reflexively, the value of human dignity. One can press this point further and argue that FC s 7(1), in fact, reverses the spin placed by the Constitutional Court on the phrase 'an open and democratic society based upon human dignity, equality and freedom'. It makes a democratic society, and not dignity, foundational.

Second, it is unnecessary to read the language of FC s 7(1) in a manner that privileges democracy over dignity. Roux rightly suggests that we should be just as wary of overly simplistic reductions (rights service democracy) as we are chary of claims that rights and democracy stand in irreconcilable tension with one another (the counter-majoritarian dilemma). I think that it is enough to suggest, as Roux does, that FC s 7(1) delinks the phrase 'an open and democratic society' from 'human dignity, equality and freedom'. That is, whereas the phrase 'open and democratic society based upon human dignity, equality and freedom' suggests a miasma of big ideas that could exhaust the entire universe of modern political theory, delinking the two phrases forces the reader of FC ss 36(1) and 39(1) to stop and to attend to the meaning, as well as the desiderata, of an 'open and democratic society'. Even if it does nothing else, by reading FC s 7(1) together with FC s 36(1), we are forced to concede that the principle of democracy is of equal weight as the value of dignity when it comes to the justification of a limitation of a fundamental right.

Third, Roux's arguments support my contention that balancing is an inapt metaphor for limitations analysis. Such metaphors block one from drawing the conclusion to which FC s 7(1) has already committed us: namely, that rights stand not in opposition to democracy, but that they are, instead, constitutive of it. Without the rights to equality, dignity, life, belief, expression, assembly, association, voting, political party membership, citizenship, access to information, access to courts, and just administrative action, we could not enjoy a meaningful democracy. These rights are themselves the preconditions for an 'open and democratic society'.[36]

Fourth, the principle of democracy gets read back into these rights. The virtues of belonging and participating – identified first and foremost with democracy – attach not just to the political realm, but to an array of associational forms – religious, traditional, linguistic, commercial, labour, intimate, cultural – that are part of, but not identical to, our political order. Although Roux might not make this fourth claim, I do. It is an appreciation for these democratic values of membership and participation that underwrites my defence of pluralism, marginal social groups and oppositional counter-publics.[37] We should value pluralism, and thus marginal social groups and oppositional counter-publics, not simply because they serve as reminders of the emancipatory potential of robust democratic discourse, but because these groups, and others like them, are where democracy takes place every day for the vast majority of us.[38]

Finally, no one can gainsay Roux's contention that 'no South African political system claiming to be democratic would be worthy of that name unless it respected the democratic values which the Bill of Rights affirms.'[39] This view firmly reinforces my own view about the relationship between courts, legislatures and citizens in a regime of shared constitutional interpretation. In such a regime, as in the political system contemplated by FC ss 7(1), 36(1) and 39(1), neither the courts nor the political branches of government have a privileged position with regard to the making and re-making of our basic law.

3. *Socio-Economic Rights*

The Final Constitution contains a sizeable portion of the world's remarkably small number of genuinely justiciable socio-economic rights. These rights run from housing to health care, from water and food to social security, from children's rights to the specific material entitlements of prisoners.[40] The content of these rights has been fleshed out by the courts in a number of important cases.[41] For my immediate purposes, we can extract the following principles from this complex body of jurisprudence:

- Socio-economic rights do not, generally speaking, embrace an entitlement to the immediate award of a remedy in the event of a breach (the rights of children and the right to a basic education are interesting anomolies);[42]
- Most socio-economic rights simply requires the state to progressively realise the access to a particular good for individual members of the polity and to do so within 'available resources';[43]
- Whether the state has discharged its duty to progressively realise a right will be evaluated by the courts in terms of the 'reasonableness' of the plan;[44]
- To be found reasonable, a comprehensive and coordinated programme to realise access to a particular socio-economic right: (1) must ensure that 'the appropriate financial and human resources are available'; (2) 'must be capable of facilitating the realisation of the right'; (3) must be reasonable 'both in their conception and their implementation'; (4) must attend to 'crises'; (5) must not exclude 'a significant segment' of the affected population; and (6) must 'respond to the urgent needs of those in desperate situations;'[45]
- The requirement to respond to persons 'in desperate situations' has given socio-economic rights (at least with respect to housing) some degree of minimum core content.[46]

One cannot find a better express example in South African jurisprudence of shared constitutional interpretation regarding the meaning of fundamental rights than our extant socio-economic rights jurisprudence. The Constitutional Court has refused, as a general matter, to identify a minimum core (content) for each socio-economic right.[47] (In this respect, our socio-economic rights jurisprudence reflects a marked departure from the jurisprudence of the UN Committee on Social, Economic and Cultural Rights.) Instead, the Court has set out, with the odd exception, general norms that govern the progressive realization of socio-economic rights and that leave the political branches ample room to experiment with policies intended to realize those rights.[48]

The invitation by the Court to the political branches to assist it in shaping the contours of socio-economic rights has been accepted by the legislature and the executive in a number of different domains. (It has been resisted in others.) Perhaps the best example of a principled dialogue between the courts and the political branches – as I will discuss at greater length in Chapter 6 below – can be found in housing policy. After the Constitutional Court handed down its decision in *Grootboom* in 2001, the government was obliged to revisit its housing policy. The first important consequence of this review – for my theoretical purposes – is that the National Department of Housing eventually generated a new policy document – *Breaking New Ground* – that quite consciously echoes the language of *Grootboom* and reorients government imperatives in light of the general norms articulated by the Court.

The relative open-endedness of many of the *Grootboom* norms ensures that the Court will likely accept good faith government efforts to execute the policies enunciated in *Breaking New Ground*. That said, the Constitutional Court will not accept policy pronouncements alone as evidence of good faith. Where, as in *Modderklip*, the state makes no meaningful effort to accommodate the housing rights, property rights and procedural rights of citizens, the Court will not only find the government conduct unconstitutional, it may take, as it did in *Modderklip*, the highly unusual step of imposing constitutional damages.[49] Shared constitutional competence has its limits. A refusal by the political branches to take seriously the Court's gloss on the Final Constitution will result in a revocation of the initial invitation.

In the second important development in housing law under s 26, the Constitutional Court has crafted a doctrine that it calls 'meaningful engagement'. The *51 Olivia Road* Court's ingenuities distinguish the matter from virtually all of its housing case predecessors.[50] Rather than impose a decision on the parties framed by *Grootboom*-based criteria, the Court ordered the residents and the city of Johannesburg to repair to the negotiating table in order to reach a settlement that would lead to a more optimal outcome for both sides. The parties did. Their settlement then became an order of the Court.

While the judgment arrived with various legal and constitutionally accepted justifications for its order, the most fascinating part of the decision – from the perspective of experimental constitutionalism – is that the Court held that, in addition to any other duties s 26(2)'s right to access to adequate housing might impose, 'a municipality that ejects people from their homes without first meaningfully engaging with them acts in a manner that is broadly at odds with the spirit and purpose of [its] constitutional obligations'.[51] What does this mean? First, it appears that the courts may not be the right branch of government to determine how some 63,000 persons – living in dangerous conditions – are to be best accommodated when a municipality determines that their current housing constitutes a threat to their lives. Second, having decided that persons who live in dangerous conditions must be removed, the Court also held that a municipality must simultaneously determine where they are to be otherwise accommodated. The right to adequate housing cannot be reconciled with a decision of the state to make people 'homeless'. Third, in deciding on how to accommodate this endangered class of persons, the city or some other sphere of government is obliged to engage the effected parties. That's 63,000 persons most immediately affected by *Occupiers of 51 Olivia Road.* As Yacoob J writes:

> Engagement has the potential to contribute towards the resolution of disputes and to increased understanding and sympathetic care if both sides are willing to participate in the process. People about to be evicted may be so vulnerable that they may not be able to understand the importance of engagement and may refuse to take part in the process. If this happens, a municipality cannot walk away without more. It must make reasonable efforts to engage and it is only if these reasonable efforts fail that a municipality may proceed without appropriate engagement. It is precisely to ensure that a city is able to engage meaningfully with poor, vulnerable or illiterate people that the engagement process should preferably be managed by careful and sensitive people on its side.[52]

No small task. The Court held, in addition, that the city had an obligation to engage meaningfully all 63 000 evictees in a systematic fashion.[53] A scheme had to be put in place to ensure that each individual or each family was heard and accommodated to the best of the state's capacity. The obligation placed upon the state did not mean that the occupants could employ obstructionist tactics to delay a move. The Court warned that '[e]ngagement is a two-way process'[54] that 'will work only if both sides act reasonably and in good faith.'[55] Consistent with the precepts of experimental constitutionalism, the *51 Olivia Road* Court places a premium on sharing (or pooling) information and on reaching accommodations that place all parties in a better position than they might find themselves if the Court were to act as the final arbiter in a zero-sum game. In sum, the enforced settlement obliged the parties to produce a range of housing alternatives for those in danger – rather than merely allowing the residents to remain endangered by living in derelict buildings or living in less than adequate shelter had they been forcibly removed to the outskirts of the city.

As doctrine, meaningful engagement has shown legs in housing, education and political participation cases. The Court used the doctrine to dispose of its next meaningful housing matter – *Residents of Joe Slovo Community, Western Cape v Thubelisha Homes & Others.*[56] Whether the doctrine of 'meaningful engagement' has sufficient content to do the experimentalist work it promises is matter taken up in greater detail, and on a case-by-by case basis, in Chapters 6 and 8. (The Court's most recent housing judgment at the time of the completion of writing (*Blue Moonlight*) suggests that the doctrine may have the kind of long-twitch muscles to allow it to go the distance.[57])

4. *Chapter 9 Institutions*

In *Grootboom*, the Constitutional Court made a modest contribution towards the design of peculiarly South African experimental institutions. It did so by charging the South African Human Rights Commission (SAHRC) with the dual responsibilities of monitoring compliance with the Court's order and of facilitating information-gathering about housing policy. (That the SAHRC failed to discharge its mandate is another (not inconsequential) matter.) Good reasons exist – as the decade after *Grootboom* suggests – for the Court to retain jurisdiction to ensure implementation of an order in such matters. At a minimum, the SAHRC would not have to waste valuable time and resources in launching a fresh application in the High Court. Moreover, if we are to take the pooling of information seriously, assistance by government agencies or independent institutions operating outside the courtroom most must have its place. Whether any given case requires a hot-line to the Court and whether an order can be appropriately monitored by the Court will turn on a mix of experience of the Court's 11 members and subsequent doctrinal developments.

There is absolutely no reason why other Chapter 9 Institutions Supporting Constitutional Democracy – the Commission on Gender Equality, the Public Protector, the Auditor-General, the Commission for the Promotion and the Protection of the Rights of Cultural, Religious and Linguistic Communities, or the Independent Electoral Commission – cannot play similar roles with regard to their areas of competence. Chapter 9 Institutions do, without prompting by the Constitutional Court, often undertake institutional roles commensurate with a commitment to experimental constitutionalism.[58] (Unfortunately, the straitened circumstances of these institutions, and the often outright hostility of the government toward their efforts, have curtailed their ability to provide the polycentric fora and feedback that might assist the state and its citizens in solving some of the many problems this 18-year-old Republic daily confronts. Should the Public Protector really find herself in a position in which she must request special protection *from the police* because a significant number of the police force's members are under investigation?)

a. Auditor-General

By virtue of its position as 'the supreme audit institution of the Republic',[59] the Auditor-General must produce financial audits and compliance audits with respect to all national and provincial departments, all municipalities, all public entities and a host of other institutions.[60] The filing of these audits with Parliament and the National Treasury is meant to ensure the proper use of public funds.[61]

These audits – some 1600 annually – provide critical information about how various arms of government are managing their budgets, enable the legislature (and the judiciary) to exercise meaningful oversight over the executive,[62] and offer the promise of a government that operates in an accountable, transparent and equitable manner.[63] As the Constitutional Court noted in *President of the Republic of South Africa v South African Rugby Football Union*, the Final Constitution is

> committed to establishing and maintaining an efficient, equitable and ethical public administration which respects fundamental rights and is accountable to the broader public. The importance of ensuring that the administration observes fundamental rights and acts both ethically and accountably should not be understated. In the past, the lives of the majority of South Africans were almost entirely governed by labyrinthine administrative regulations which, amongst other things, prohibited freedom of movement, controlled access to housing, education and jobs and which were implemented by a bureaucracy hostile to fundamental rights or accountability. The constitutional goal [of ensuring that the administration observes fundamental rights and acts both ethically and accountably] is supported by a range of provisions in the [Final] Constitution ... [including the establishment of] the Auditor-General whose responsibility it is to audit and report on the financial affairs of national and provincial State departments and administrations as well as municipalities.[64]

The Auditor-General's powers extend beyond the coercive power of shame and embrace the threat of forensic audits.[65] Its reports and its forensic audits expose malfeasance, corruption, and incompetence in the discharge of public office that enable other law enforcement agencies to launch criminal investigations.[66] Existing case law suggests that the Auditor-General may even possess standing to seek rescission of decisions or contracts that manifest fraud.[67]

As a general rule, the Auditor-General carries out audits, but does not opine on the merits of particular government programmes. However, while the Auditor-General will not 'question policy laid down by the legislative and executive authority, the arrangements for the implementation thereof, the controls applied, the cost incurred and the results achieved are all legitimate subjects for auditing.'[68] In other words, although the government's 'objectives' fall beyond the purview of the Auditor-General, the Auditor-General can interrogate the means that the government employs to realize its objectives. When it comes to the expenditure of public monies, the Auditor-General has an obligation to state whether the financial audits and the compliance audits reflect a problem with the implementation of a policy or the delivery of services.[69]

In my ideal world of shared constitutional interpretation, the Auditor-General is a gigantic feedback mechanism. It tells us what works in government and what doesn't. (When only 7 municipalities in an entire country (as of 2011) receive a clean audit, we know that something has gone terribly awry.) In addition, the Auditor-General's power to shed light on the efficacy of policy implementation plays a significant role on the future formation of policy and the discharge of constitutional duties. These Auditor-General's reports – and the problems the reports identify – have a critical role to play in the creation of a polity committed to the rule of law and for the restoration of society's faith in a government of, by and for the people.[70] The power of these reports to shame some government officials into taking appropriate action is reflected in a brace of cases that have arisen out of normal audits and forensic investigations.[71] It is also echoed in constructive responses to criticism from the Auditor-General[72] and promises to root out sources of corruption and inefficiency.[73] More worrisome, of course, has been the need for the National Government to intervene in provincial and municipal affairs when the Auditor-General has reached the conclusion that local officials cannot discharge their responsibilities.

Some might contend that the Auditor-General's ability to assess the efficacy of policies is limited to waste – and not waste that can be fixed, but waste rooted in corruption or systemic deficiencies in the state's SCM policies and its ability to manage its assets and liabilities. If, the argument continues, the Auditor General is not pooling the information uncovered into reports that can be used by the state to remedy those systemic problems, then one might be inclined to ask whether its reports are as forward and lateral looking as we might expect from an emergent experimental institution.

The critique suggests that for the information to be valuable from an experimental perspective, the Auditor-General must make it so. Why should that be? First, repeated reports of malfeasance regarding the same institutions and political structures are sent to Parliament virtually every year. Second, Parliament possesses the power to interrogate public officials, assess the value of policy initiatives and turn the spigots on or off. With respect to municipal fiscal failures at alarming rates, the Auditor-General's reports indicate which municipalities ought to be placed under provincial or national control.

Yes, it's true that a sophisticated central clearing house would be more valuable from an experimentalist perspective. But it's equally true that when such vast amounts of information enter the public domain, private actors can determine where not to invest, and the national government (and to a lesser extent provincial government) can decide which organs of state are failing and thus in greatest need of further state intervention. Finally, South African citizens can decide for themselves whether the state is genuinely committed to keeping up its end of the social contract.

The courts have reinforced this power to shame – and to reconstruct policy – by expressly recognizing that the Auditor-General is the most appropriate arbiter of disputes over the use or the misuse of public funds.[74] Moreover, in *Glenister v President of the Republic of South Africa & Others*, the Court identified the Auditor-General as one of several institutions designed to prevent rent-seeking behaviour and outright corruption from undermining both democratic rule and the obligation of the state to fulfil the promise of the Bill of Rights.[75] Whether the directly accountable branches of government – Parliament and the provincial legislatures – will heed the Auditor-General's words – or reduce it over time to the role of a mere Cassandra remains to be seen.[76] [77] However, the public response to the Auditor-General's 2009 scathing report regarding the general incompetence and the rent seeking behaviour of the police force, and the Auditor-General's conclusion that an underfunded, unskilled police force could not discharge its constitutional responsibility to protect the general population,[78] suggests that at least one of the Chapter 9 Institutions has been allowed to discharge its responsibilities.[79]

b. Public Protector[80]

Like most ombudsman around the globe, the Public Protector monitors the conduct of state officials and agencies with the aim of ensuring an effective and ethical public service.[81] The office reflects, in both conception and execution, a profound improvement upon its precursor: the Advocate-General. The Advocate-General's brief was limited to investigations into the unlawful or the improper use of public money.[82] The Public Protector's brief, as initially adumbrated in the Interim Constitution, and as now determined by the Final Constitution and the Public Protector Act ('PPA'), is to watch the watchers and to guarantee that the government discharges its responsibilities without fear, favour or prejudice.[83]

The Public Protector's role in a scheme of shared constitutional interpretation can be profitably compared with the duties discharged by the judiciary. Constitutional courts handle discrete disputes about law and conduct – even as they craft general norms designed to govern the behaviour of the state and private actors. They rely on correct procedure and solid, sometimes intricate, legal argument. Constitutional courts are not, however, designed to handle the large number of complaints that arise from simple misunderstandings or bureaucratic red-tape, nor do they lend themselves to the resolution of injustices that turn more on under-capacity than illegality.[84]

The Public Protector occupies a middle space in the politico-constitutional landscape. It assists the courts by addressing those complaints about the administration of justice that fall beyond the courts' purview. It assists the legislature by monitoring the performance of the executive and answering those complaints that elected representatives are unable to address.[85]

The Public Protector performs these functions, in theory at least, free from political pressure. It is not, however, entirely independent. For while the Public Protector enjoys priority over other institutions in the exercise of its functions,[86] it must still often act together with the courts, the executive and other Chapter 9 Institutions to fulfil its mandate.

One of the most common criticisms levelled against the Public Protector is that the institution lacks the power to make binding decisions. In point of fact, the ability of the Public Protector to investigate and to report effectively – without making binding decisions – is the real measure of its strength.[87] Stephen Owen explains this apparent paradox as follows:

> Through the application of reason, the results are infinitely more powerful than through the application of coercion. While a coercive process may cause a reluctant change in a single decision or action, by definition it creates a loser who will be unlikely to embrace the recommendations in future actions. By contrast, where change results from a reasoning process, it changes a way of thinking and the result endures to the benefit of potential complainants in the future.[88]

The publication of the Public Protector's findings can shame a body into accepting the validity of its recommendations.[89] Its reports to Parliament should enable the national legislature to exercise effectively its oversight function and shape important debates on policy and budgetary matters.[90] Whether our Public Protector has sufficient funds to maintain the high standards of investigation and reporting required in order to be the 'voice of reason' is matter assayed above. However, the Public Protector does fulfil its role in a scheme of shared constitutional interpretation by ensuring that the members of the executive 'understand' their constitutional responsibilities and that the other branches of government – the courts and the legislature – 'understand' when those norms are not being fulfilled in practice.

The current Public Protector, Thuli Madonsela, has demonstrated just how effective thorough investigations of public officials and the consequent shaming of members of cabinet can be. In March 2011, she released a damning report on irregularities related to the lease of two properties by the SAPS in Pretoria and Durban.[91] The report – *Against the Rules* – strongly suggests that the leases for the buildings were executed because of an untoward relationship between SAPS National Commissioner Bheki Cele and a private property owner. However, the Public Protector's findings of a potentially corrupt relationship are not nearly as important as her conclusions regarding the manifold constitutional breaches reflected in this 'property deal'.

With respect to the SAPS, the Public Protector identified the following constitutional and statutory improprieties:

1. 'Although the SAPS did not sign the lease agreement, its involvement in the procurement process was improper, as it proceeded beyond the demand management phase and it further failed to implement proper controls, as required by the PFMA and relevant procurement prescripts.[92]
2. 'The SAPS failed to comply with section 217 of the Constitution, the relevant provisions of the PFMA, Treasury Regulations and supply chain management rules and policies. This failure amounted to improper conduct and maladministration.'[93]
3. 'The conduct of the accounting officer of the SAPS was in breach of those duties and obligations incumbent upon him in terms of section 217 of the Constitution, section 38 of the PFMA and the relevant Treasury Regulations. These provisions require from an accounting

> officer to ensure that goods and services are procured in accordance with a system that fair, equitable, transparent, competitive and cost effective. This conduct was improper, unlawful and amounted to maladministration.'[94]

Based upon these findings, the Public Protector recommended that the National Treasury determine whether there had been any wasteful expenditure, that the Minister of Police should take action against the responsible official and that the SAPS should take steps to ensure that the same types of contraventions do not occur again.[95] One can take some solace in the fact that the Public Protector's Report ultimately resulted in the dismissal of two senior members of cabinet.

c. *Complementarity, Reflexivity and Inclusivity in Constitutional Norm Generation by Chapter 9 Institutions*

Jonathan Klaaren offers astute observations regarding the status of the SAHRC and other Chapter 9 Institution that resonate strongly with my more general theses about shared constitutional interpretation and participatory bubbles.[96] He notes that:

> [T]he six institutions listed and established in terms of FC s 181(1) are not mere creatures of statute. As creatures of the Final Constitution, the SAHRC and the other Chapter 9 Institutions enjoy a status and an authority that can potentially override unconstitutional legislative provisions.[97]

In short, Chapter 9 Institutions have the power to find legislation 'inconsistent' with the terms of the Final Constitution. (It does not follow that these institutions have the power to declare, in terms of the supremacy clause in FC s 2, law or conduct to be constitutionally infirm.[98])

Klaaren observes that since both 'the SAHRC and the Constitutional Court are designed to protect and to promote respect for human rights', a principle of complementarity governs the relationship between the Chapter 9 Institutions, the courts and other branches of government.[99] According to Karthy Govender, complementarity should be understood as follows:

> [I]nternational standards require that the [national human rights] institutions do more than simply function as a surrogate court of law. Their role is to actively protect and promote human rights and not to exist simply as an investigative mechanism which reacts to human rights violations. The institutions must work systematically and holistically towards the attainment of internationally recognized human rights.[100]

The Constitutional Court, in *New National Party*, acknowledged this role of Chapter 9 Institutions in determining the contours of South Africa's constitutional order. Then Deputy President Langa wrote, on behalf of the Court, that '[t]he Constitution places a constitutional obligation on [all] ... organs of state to assist and protect the [Independent Electoral] Commission in order to ensure its independence, impartiality, dignity and effectiveness.'[101]

FC s 181 through FC s 194 identify a fourth indispensable branch of government that has responsibility for determining the meaning of the Final Constitution. The other branches of government have an obligation not only to take heed of the activity of the Chapter 9 Institutions, but a duty to take their interpretations of the basic law seriously.[102]

5. *Provincial Constitutions*

A danger exists when one is in the thrall of a theory of any given kind. One is apt to see evidence for it everywhere.

Take provincial constitutions. The Constitution invites provinces to draft constitutions of their own.[103] While a provincial constitution may not contradict the Final Constitution, it can offer protections that the Final Constitution does not.[104] In addition, provinces may alter some of the provincial legislative and executive structures and procedures established by the Final Constitution.[105] These constitutional invitations may seem relatively trivial. But they still afford the provinces the space to experiment with fundamental rights and political institutions. Such experiments could, in theory, influence decisions taken in other provinces or by the national government.

Only two provinces have attempted to craft provincial constitutions. The Western Cape succeeded. Kwa-Zulu Natal failed.[106]

The Western Cape Constitution has made little difference. One might attribute the current Democratic Alliance's control of the province and the Cape Town metropole to subtle changes in provincial architecture. That would be something of a stretch.

As for Kwa-Zulu Natal, it failed twice in the mid to late 1990s to contrive a text that would pass constitutional muster. Slightly more recent efforts largely died out as the ANC asserted political dominance over the province, while the efforts of the IFP to use a constitutionally-mandated 'King' to block the ANC's ascension simultaneously withered.

Given the centralization of power in the NEC of the ANC, provincial constitutions must, for the time being, be viewed as failures in experimental design. Whether, at some moment in the future, when the ANC no longer controls the national government, eight of nine provinces and most of the major metropoles, provincial constitutions can fulfil their potential as experimental institutions must be viewed as an entirely speculative query. (Indeed, at the time of writing, the failure of several provinces to discharge adequately their duties has led to a different set of questions about institutional design: whether we should have nine provinces at all.)

C. Participatory Bubbles

Because my naturalized account of the self and the social takes seriously the limits on our capacity for rational reflection and collective deliberation, it is inaccurate and obscurantist to ground our politics in an alleged capacity of individuals and groups to engage in profound reflection over critical existential questions. (Again: politics as reasoned discourse remains a lovely ideal even as we recognize – doctrinally and institutionally – that it is not common practice.) My naturalized account of the self does not deny our capacity to engage in meaningful deliberation. In fact, without a commitment to unearthing 'the truth' and what we call the scientific method, neither experimentalism nor flourishing would make any sense at all.[107]

Other non-experimentalist constitutional theorists acknowledge our significant limitations with regard to rational deliberation. Bruce Ackerman has offered an understanding of error-correction and political change that is restricted to a few key constitutional moments.[108] However, rather than concentrating on earth-shaking moments of crisis, the design proposals here concentrate on narrow, subject matter specific, and often time-sensitive, institutional contexts.

The physical metaphor of bubbles is meant to convey three qualities of small-scale institutional processes. First, participatory processes become a natural part of ongoing social interactions. They originate when challenges to a given institutional authority accumulate and finally come to a boil: just as bubbles form after pressure builds up and escape to the surface of a liquid. Second, bubbles are meant to suggest limits on the scope of deliberation. Bubbles only enclose a small amount of space – both in terms of the issues debated and the number of participants. Third, bubbles are ephemeral. After satisfactory resolutions emerge from participatory processes, the raison d'etat for a particular process of engagement ceases to exist. Participants can return to their more routine lives.

But the virtue of participatory bubbles need not be so modestly cast. As we saw in our discussion of drug treatment courts and family courts in the United States, the information produced in these bubbles has the capacity both to shape the means by which we pursue particular ends and to alter the ends we pursue as we see what works best.

1. *Remedies*[109]

a. *Theory*

Conflicting interpretations of the application of constitutional principles to the practices of a given institution or person leads to litigation. Those parties challenging existing norms seek to make the institutional practices or personal conduct consonant with their preferred interpretation of a norm. One solution in such circumstances, as Owen Fiss has argued, is for the courts to initiate a process of structural reform. In these court initiated processes, 'the judge tries to give meaning to our constitutional values in the operation of those organizations.'[110] The preferred tool for such judicial intervention is, as Fiss suggests, a structural injunction. Structural injunctions permit courts to engage in a 'long, continuous relationship between the judge and the institution: it is concerned not with the enforcement of a remedy already given, but with ... shaping the remedy itself.'[111]

A number of South African scholars have argued in favour of greater use of structural injunctions.[112] They recognize that one of a structural injunction's virtues is that it does not assign the task of constitutional interpretation exclusively to the courts. Structural injunctions should, preferably, create the space for determination of the meaning of constitutional principles by members of a given political (or private) institution and the citizen-stakeholders challenging the institution's authority. Within such a bubble, all those whose interests are at stake (within reasonable limits) are offered a chance to participate in the process of norm-setting and problem-solving. Furthermore, an injunction so fashioned maximizes the legitimacy of the process by ensuring a greater degree of openness to competing points of view and placing the parties within the process on a more equal footing.

The promise of such a process is genuinely meaningful engagement. Each participant adopts a reflexive stance toward their own views and attempts 'to make the interests of others their own, [and to recognize] the circumstances in which they should give moral priority to what is good for others or for the polity as a whole.'[113] Participatory bubbles facilitate processes of institutional reform that proceed within the vocabulary and the norms of the relevant institutions and communities, instead of via imposition by judicial authority. The reflexive stance of the bubbles' participants should both foster a deeper commitment to active citizenship and enhance individual and group aptitudes for experimentation and error-correction.[114]

The foregoing discussion should make clear why participatory bubbles are important experimental feedback mechanisms. First, they enable state actors responsible for the creation of policy to benefit from insider information about the problem the parties aim to solve. Second, state actors and citizens who are not participants in a given bubble at a given moment have an opportunity to benefit – down the line – from the experimentation and experiences of their predecessors. Third, the outcomes should have an additional knock on effect. The outcomes should create incentives for political institutions to pro-actively open up their decision-making processes to affected stakeholders in advance of conflict so as to seek out non-adversarial solutions.

Of course, courts called upon to perform limitations analysis and to fashion remedies cannot avoid settling conflicts that are not readily susceptible to deliberative solutions. Here again experimental constitutionalism offers the inspired proposal of provisional adjudication. Provisional adjudication puts alternative possible remedies to the test of experience without necessarily elevating such remedies to the level of established doctrine. Provisional adjudication promises two additional benefits. It may facilitate compromise: affected parties may learn from practical experience and adjust their beliefs and conduct accordingly. It gives parties that may still feel aggrieved with a final *non-provisional* outcome the opportunity to experiment with a remedy of their own making.[115] A loss maybe just as likely to generate a creative response as a positive outcome.

b. Practice

In the beginning, the Constitutional Court's approach to structural injunctions (or similar remedies) was lukewarm at best. The Constitutional Court stated that although a structural interdict might be an appropriate and valid remedy for some constitutionally infirm law or conduct,[116] it repeatedly stressed that such an order must only be made where it is 'necessary'.[117]

Up to and through 2004, the Court remained reluctant to employ this remedy.[118] Times change. From 2005 onwards, the case law reflects a significant softening of this stance – and an acknowledgement that it might serve the ends of an experimentalist constitution.

Reluctance was never refusal. The Constitutional Court employed a fairly stringent structural interdict in *August v Electoral Commission.* After finding that both the Department of Correctional Services and the Independent Electoral Commission had failed to take the requisite steps to ensure that prisoners could exercise their constitutionally enshrined entitlement to the franchise, the *August* Court turned its attention to the appropriate remedy for this constitutional infirmity. It wrote:

> The Commission must therefore make the necessary arrangements to enable them to vote. This Court does not have the information or expertise to enable it to decide what those arrangements should be or how they should be effected. During the hearing of this matter, counsel for the Commission was invited to indicate what arrangements for registration and voting would best suit the Commission in order to assist the Court in making a precise order. The Commission did not provide the information. The determination of what arrangements should be made remains a matter pre-eminently for the Commission. It is important that there should be certainty as to what these arrangements will be. In the light of the fact that this Court is not in a position in the circumstances of the present case to give specific direction as to what is to be done, it is appropriate that the Commission be required to indicate how it will comply with the order that has been made.[119]

The Court then ordered the Commission to deliver an affidavit that stated the manner in which the Commission would comply with its edict.[120] The Constitutional Court followed *August* with a similarly strict structural interdict in matter that once again engaged the disenfranchisement of prisoners: *Minister of Home Affairs v National Institute for Crime Prevention and the Reintegration of Offenders (NICRO) & Others.*[121]

Lower courts followed suit. In *Kiliko and Others v Minister of Home Affairs and Others,* the Cape High Court heard an application by asylum seekers from the Democratic Republic of the Congo.[122] The application contended that the procedures adopted by the Western Cape refugee reception office were unlawful and unconstitutional.[123] Van Reenen J concluded that the policy of limiting the number of asylum applicants to twenty per day constituted an unjustifiable infringement of the FC s 10 and the FC s 12 rights to dignity and to freedom and security of the person. As to the remedy, Van Reenen J held that the present case was an appropriate one for the granting of a structural interdict. The interdict required the respondents to provide the Court with a report on improvements to the reception of asylum-seekers in the Western Cape. According to Van Reenen J, the purpose of the order was to 'ensure that the manner in which the respondents receive and process applications for asylum in the future does not offend against any of the State's obligations under international law, the Constitution and statutes.'[124]

In *Centre for Child Law v MEC for Education, Gauteng*, a High Court in the Transvaal Provincial Division handed down an invitation that goes significantly beyond the standard form of a structural interdict.[125] Having found that the school of industry and the MEC in question had failed to provide the most basic living conditions for its charges – and having founded that they had thus violated FC s 28, FC s 10 and FC s 12 – Judge Murphy put the school and the MEC on the strictest of terms. His order begins by requiring that the state arrange for the immediate provision of sleeping bags that would ensure sleeping temperatures of no lower than 5 degrees Celsius. The order then requires that:

> a. The MEC provide, within a month of the decision, a plan to ensure perimeter and access control to the school;
>
> b. The MEC and the school create, within a month of the decision, a quality assurance programme, in concert with relevant government bodies and non-governmental organizations, designed to ensure appropriate residential care and treatment;

c. The MEC, the school and a multi-disciplinary task team (made up of child care experts) produce, within a month of the decision, a report on their initial findings and the progress made in the intervening period;
d. The MEC and the school put in immediate place psychological and therapeutic support structures to ensure the well-being of the students;
e. The MEC would appear in court, five weeks after the judgment, to describe the aforementioned plans and how it intends to go about their implementation;
f. The applicants participate in the construction of the aforementioned plans and that they retain the ability to return to court seeking appropriate relief for any failure to carry out the court's order.

While legitimate doubts have been raised as to whether a structural interdict was the appropriate remedy in *Kiliko*, the facts of *Centre for Child Law* for – the straitened circumstances of the children in question – did not afford the High Court much latitude. However, the *Centre for Child Law* for court is also quite clear that the order handed down has at least as much to do with its great displeasure with the state. Judge Murphy writes:

> While I am minded to commend the first respondent for its concessions about the poor state of affairs, I express the concern, I am sure shared by many, about the bureaucratic prevarication intrinsic to the department's litigation strategy. Section 195(1) of the Constitution requires the public administration to respond to public needs quickly and effectively. Increasingly one is witness to public statements made by politicians and community activists about the slow pace of the delivery of social services to the vulnerable and marginalized sectors of our society. There is a growing sense arising in the general public that bureaucrats are failing us. I therefore venture the tentative suggestion that in many cases government departments defend litigation against them unnecessarily, and in doing that, use resources that might be better applied elsewhere.[126]

After detailing the parlous state of affairs at the school, and noting that the state had abdicated its responsibility to provide even marginally better care for these children than their parents currently could, Judge Murphy proceeded to announce the need for a structural interdict:

> The need for a developmental quality assurance process is patently obvious. Matters appear to have come adrift at the school. They need to be remedied immediately. The process is a useful, investigative, diagnositic and remedial tool which will identify organizational weaknesses and a way forward. Given the dilatory and lackadaisical approach taken so far, it is a good idea that this court retains a supervisory role to ensure progress. Violations of constitutional rights invite innovative remedies and the present case calls for such.[127]

The High Court's order creates the conditions for a paradigmatic participatory bubble. While the High Court finds that the general norms set out in FC s 10, FC s 12 and FC s 28 have been violated, the judge has left it up to the parties – under his supervision – to work out a plan that will leave all parties better off. Should this initial plan fail to provide the requisite levels of redress, the court retains the jurisdiction to ensure that the requirements of FC s 10, FC s 12 and FC s 28 are met. Thus, though the judgment stands as a scathing indictment of bureaucratic lassitude, it also invites the state and the school to meet their respective obligations. Moreover, by requiring the state to engage non-state actors in the construction of its plans, the court's invitation enables it to draw upon expertise it simply does not possess and allows it to avoid the articulation of principles that might look pretty on paper but wind up being rather empty in practice.

The High Court's creative response is also consistent with the idea of remedial equilibration introduced in Chapters 3 and 4. Although the *Centre for Child Law* court is not engaged in the disentrenchment of private ordering that reinforces the stratification of South African society, it does employ remedies that enable the various parties to the case to arrive at the best 'fit' between state capacity, non-state actor capacity and the needs of the effected children. The High Court eschews both rights essentialism and automatic remedialism.

In 2005, the Constitutional Court suggested that it might be inclined to use reflexive and polycentric forms of engagement to mediate constitutional conflicts and to adduce the (provisionally) true meaning of various constitutional norms. The Constitutional Court began its shift with a detailed supervisory process in *Sibiya v The Director of Public Prosecutions, Johannesburg.* In the absence of government action to revise the sentences of people still sitting on death row after the death penalty was abolished, the Court was pressed to devise an appropriate form of relief.[128] The Court required the government, and the responsible minister, to provide all pertinent information on all prisoners still on death row, to explain why their sentences had not yet been altered, and to alter the sentences post haste. As Michael Bishop notes, the Court did not justify its supervision of the process in its original judgment, but later explained that it was based on 'the delay that had occurred since [the death penalty was declared unconstitutional] coupled with the pressing need for the sentences to be replaced'.[129] The shared process of review was, quite notably, both engaged and flexible:

> The Court eventually considered five reports by the government until the process was finalized. The first report set out the number of sentences that still needed to be converted while each subsequent report indicated what steps had been taken and what still remained to be done. The entire Court considered in detail each report and identified what problems remained and ordered a further report to be made. At the completion of the process, the Court issued a judgment reflecting on the supervisory process in generally positive terms.[130]

The *Sibiya* Court draws four conclusions from its experience with supervisory orders: '(a) Successful supervision requires that detailed information be placed at the disposal of a court; (b) Supervision entails a careful analysis and evaluation of the details provided; (c) Supervision cannot succeed without the full co-operation of others in the process; (d) Courts should exercise flexibility in the supervisory process.'[131] Bishop also offers another insight into this collaborative process. He surmises that the Court was pleased that it did not have 'to substitute its own opinion for that of the government, but merely to ensure that the government completed a process to which it had already committed itself.'[132]

A myriad of subsequent cases over the past five years reflect the Constitutional Court's increased level of comfort in creating remedial structures designed to realized the best empirical and normative outcome possible. In housing cases, from *Occupiers of 51 Olivia Road* to *Joe Slovo I* and *II* to *Blue Moonlight*, the Court has demonstrated a remarkable propensity to allow the parties – including interveners and amici – to work out a veritable pareto-optimal outcome for themselves. More compelling still is the Court's willingness to allow the parties to reach settlements endorsed by the Court, and then later work out a new arrangement that better fits the needs of all concerned.

Flexible settlements are not all that's new and noteworthy. In two education cases, *Ermelo* and *Juma Musjid*, the Court has alighted upon mechanisms that ensure that what appears to work in terms of the order delivered at the end of an initial judgment continues to work over time. In *Ermelo*, the Court required both the school governing body and the provincial department of education to report back to the Court at regular intervals so it could assess the progress the parties had made in realizing learners' right to receive an adequate basic education. In *Juma Musjid*, the genius of the Court's shaping of the bubble of parties lies (a) in its willingness to treat the applicants and the respondents (learners and a private trust) as natural and juristic persons engaged in a horizontal dispute over the right to a basic education and (b) in its invitation to the Centre for Child Law and the Socio-Economic Rights Institute into a dauntingly complex polycentric matter requiring subtle non-partisan analysis. Here too, the Court requested feedback from the state and other parties regarding the manner in which learners had been accommodated.

In *Nyathi I* and *II,* the Court confronted a challenging set of cases that raised both technical financial issues regarding the payment of debts and subtle institutional politics. Instead of treating the cases in a binary fashion – outright winners and abject losers – the Court solicited participation from a broad array of parties. The Court sought out the views of the Minister of Finance and made those views a part of the Court's remedy. The *Nyathi II* Court also took on board suggestions by the applicant, the intervener and the amici about how best to ensure that state judgment debts are paid and, moreover, discharged with alacrity. Finally, the Court requested that the state report back and provide an account of all the outstanding judgment debts on its books and adumbrate a plan as to how the state would acquit itself of such arrears in the future.

2. *Rules and Procedures in Constitutional Matters*

The rules and procedures of the Constitutional Court reflect another, perhaps less obvious, set of court-created participatory bubbles. Rules and procedures regarding direct access, legal aid referrals, intervenors and amici all enhance the quality of the information available to the court and the normative legitimacy of its decisions. The greater participation and reflexivity these rules and procedures allow further enables the Court to more closely approximate an experimentalist's agenda of rolling best practices.

As Kate Hofmeyr notes, 'direct access applications are increasingly being used by parties where the relief they seek is substantially similar to the relief sought by other parties in a matter already before the Constitutional Court.'[133] The Constitutional Court is inclined to grant many of these applications where the applicants' submissions relate to substantive issues that are already before the Court and where the insights offered by the applicants may help to resolve difficult issues before the Court. The Court is especially interested in submissions that help it to fashion more appropriate remedies[134] or enable it to fill in doctrinal gaps in matters already before the Court.[135]

Legal aid referrals also possess the capacity to enhance the quality of the Court's deliberations by increasing the amount of litigation.[136] In two decisions, *De Kock v Minister of Water Affairs and Forestry* and *Mnguni v Minister of Correctional Services*, the Constitutional Court, despite refusing to grant direct access to the unrepresented applicants in both cases, directed the Registrar to bring the judgments to the attention of the Law Society of the Northern Provinces.[137] The purpose of this procedure is to ensure that unrepresented applicants have the capacity to raise 'important yet difficult issues which may well require adjudication' by the Court.[138]

Interveners represent – in terms of Constitutional Court Rule 8 – a second class of party that may enhance the Court's critical capacity.[139] In *Minister of Public Works and Others v Kyalami Ridge Environmental Association and Another (Mukhwevho Intervening)*, an application was made by an Alexandra flood victim – who was offered temporary accommodation at Leeuwkop – for leave to intervene as a party.[140] The Court noted the applicant's 'direct and substantial interest in the proceedings' – the test articulated in the case law surrounding rule 12 of the Uniform Rules of Court – and determined that it entitled him to be joined.[141] On its face, Rule 8 envisages leave being sought from the Court by a party wishing to intervene in proceedings before it. By adding the requirement that leave be sought, the Court would appear to retain the discretion to determine the right of a party to intervene. However, the Court's own doctrine of objective unconstitutionality should limit that discretion. Despite the apparent desuetude of this doctrine, the Court reaffirmed its existence in *National Director of Public Prosecutions v Mohamed NO*[142] and recommitted itself to its original articulation in *Ferreira v Levin NO Others*:

> a statute is either valid or 'of no force and effect to the extent of its inconsistency'. The subjective positions in which parties to a dispute may find themselves cannot have a bearing on the status of the provisions of a statute under attack. The Constitutional Court, or any other competent Court for that matter, ought not to restrict its enquiry to the position of one of the parties to a dispute in order to determine the validity of a law. The consequence of such a (subjective) approach would be to recognise the validity of a statute in respect of one litigant, only to deny it to another. Besides resulting in a denial of equal protection of the law, considerations of legal certainty, being a central consideration in a constitutional state, militate against the adoption of the subjective approach. [143]

The class of applicants with a direct and substantial interest in a declaration of invalidity that reaches the Constitutional Court for confirmation is potentially vast. (Indeed, the Court often speaks, quite rightly, of all South Africans as having an interest in the outcome of every constitutional matter because all constitutional matters engage the basic principles of a just and fair political order.) As I have argued elsewhere, while the specific circumstances of the original applicants – or those seeking to intervene – may shed further light on some of the implications of the impugned law or conduct, the doctrine of objective unconstitutionality, logically, makes the position of the applicants and interveners immaterial to the Court's ultimate determination.[144] While such a logical consequence of the doctrine may trouble a Court concerned with the manner in which it controls its docket, the doctrine takes seriously the demands for increased stakeholder participation required by theories of experimental constitutionalism.[145]

Amici constitute – in terms of Constitutional Court Rule 10 – a third class of party that may enhance the Court's informational resources and participatory legitimacy. While the

Constitutional Court's regularly warns amici that they incur unique responsibilities,[146] this warning is generally softened by the Court's express recognition of the invaluable role the amicus curiae play in broadening – and thereby reshaping – the Court's analysis.[147]

At the same time that we recognize the virtues of adding these additional parties, with their added expertise, we need to acknowledge the mixed results. On the one hand, the Constitutional Court loves interveners and amici and has embraced extremely broad principles of standing. On the other hand, the Court has made it not made it easier for impoverished individuals to secure direct access. The Court has not adopted the Indian Supreme Court's creative and caste-sensitive practice of accepting postcards from the impecunious as applications for a hearing on the papers or in the court. The mechanism for sorting, filtering, and litigating legal claims on behalf of those persons in our society without the means to carry a battery of attorneys and advocates all the way up to the Constitutional Court (99% of us) has become the responsibility of small coterie of legal NGOs and committed members of the bar steeped in public law advocacy. As Jackie Dugard notes, an individual without the good fortune to find such support has no chance whatsoever of having her claim heard.[148]

3. *Costs*[149]

In ordinary civil litigation, the general rule is that costs orders should indemnify a party against expenses that were incurred as a result of litigation that he should not have been required to initiate or to defend. As Michael Bishop has written: 'The rationale behind the rule in civil litigation is that, if a private person is brought to court to defend a claim with insufficient merit, it would hardly be fair to expect him to pay legal costs simply to defend an action that, objectively, ought not to have been brought in the first place.'[150]

However, the Constitutional Court has departed from the loser pays approach in a number of extremely significant ways. In many instances it does not award costs to a successful defendant. Why? Because, given the nature of constitutional litigation, the matters raised are important to the entire commonweal and not just the parties before the Court. This practice makes complete sense if the respondent is a government entity.[151] A sphere of government or an organ of state that successfully defends law or conduct alleged to be unconstitutional has not, in fact, incurred unnecessary expenses. The Court has made it clear that all parties – especially the most impecunious South Africans – ought to be able to bring challenges designed to vindicate fundamental rights.[152] As Michael Bishop observes, the rationale for this significant departure from the rule in civil litigation is two-fold.[153] First, all constitutional matters, even when initiated to serve the immediate needs of individuals, always reflect a public interest in the creation and the maintenance of a legal order that conforms to the requirements of the basic law. Second, the capacity to vindicate one's common-law rights has, unfortunately, long been dependent in commonwealth jurisdictions on one's available resources. The Constitutional Court's approach to costs mitigates the very real, and often insuperable, fiscal barriers to effective vindication of constitutional rights by and for all South Africans.

For the purposes of this chapter, the departure from the ordinary rule in civil litigation is important for two additional reasons. First, though some might think the proposition a bit tendentious, the relaxation of costs orders enhances the chances for experimental constitutionalism to gain some traction in South Africa. It enables poor applicants, (assisted by a limited number of legal NGOs and committed attorneys and advocates working pro bono), who might not otherwise get to court, to launch challenges that force the judiciary and the state to make an assessment as to whether law or policy reflects best practices and conforms to basic dictates of justice. A negative finding should force both the judiciary and the state to consider alternative means of pursuing constitutional imperatives. Second, flourishing is, in the South African legal order, inextricably bound up with the vindication of fundamental rights. Individuals and communities incapable of asserting their constitutional rights because of the costs and the risks that attach to litigation are individuals and communities far less likely to flourish. The Constitutional Court's relaxed position on cost orders with respect to successful respondents (ie, the state) and unsuccessful applicants (ie, the citizens) ensures that more of an admittedly limited class of less-well-off applicants will have their fundamental rights challenges heard.

4. *Constitutional Jurisdiction*

In a number of cases, the Constitutional Court and the Supreme Court of Appeal have deployed the doctrine of *stare decisis* in a manner that dramatically curtails the ability of High Courts to use the Bill of Rights, generally, and FC s 39(2), in particular, to develop the common law or to re-interpret legislation in ways that depart from Constitutional Court, Supreme Court Appeal, or Appellate Division precedent. In short, the Courts' doctrines make it difficult for lower courts to revisit incorrect decisions and to revise them accordingly. The existing doctrine on constitutional precedent undermines efforts to make the basic law part of a more effective rights-based feedback mechanism.

The Constitutional Court in *Walters* restricted its conclusions about *stare decisis* to precedent handed down by the Constitutional Court, the Supreme Court of Appeal and the Appellate Division in the (rather ambiguously described) 'constitutional era.'[154] The Supreme Court of Appeal in *Afrox* extended binding precedent – backwards – past the very beginning of even the most controversial understanding of the 'constitutional era'.[155] The *Afrox* Court recognized that High Courts could retain constitutional jurisdiction for any direct attack on a rule of law grounded in a pre-constitutional decision of the Appellate Division. However, where a High Court is persuaded that a pre-constitutional decision of the Appellate Division should be developed, through FC s 39(2), so that it accords with the spirit, purport and objects of the Bill of Rights (true indirect application), its hands are tied.[156] The High Court is bound to follow the pre-constitutional decisions of the Appellate Division.

As Danie Brand and I have argued elsewhere, the problems with *Walters* and *Afrox* on the issue of *stare decisis* and the constitutional jurisdiction of the High Courts are legion.[157] What is particularly troublesome for the purposes of a theory of experimental constitutionalism is that the Constitutional Court and the Supreme Court of Appeal have said that FC s 39(2) is the appropriate vehicle for development of the common law – both directly and indirectly – but that the High Courts may not disturb settled precedent through FC s 39(2).[158] This result effectively bars our trial courts from offering litigants new opportunities to explore the meaning of our basic law and the most effective ways of realizing its ends. The most obvious solution – and one consistent with the commitment to shared constitutional interpretation – is to relax the rule on precedent grounded in FC s 39(2) and permit High Courts to hear, at a minimum, direct (as opposed to indirect) constitutional challenges to precedent established under apartheid.

5. *Public Participation in Law-Making*[159]

As one might expect, and as Theunis Roux has discussed elsewhere,[160] the Final Constitution's most obvious commitment to democracy is to be found in the provisions dealing with the powers and functions of Parliament, provincial legislatures and municipal councils.[161] Of particular import for any discussion of participatory bubbles is the extent to which the Final Constitution creates space for participation by minority parties and the general public and the degree to which the need for direct participation has been recognized by the Court.

For starters, FC s 57(1)*(b)* provides that the National Assembly may 'make rules and orders concerning its business, with due regard to representative and *participatory democracy*, accountability, transparency and public involvement.'[162] In *De Lille & Another v Speaker of the National Assembly*, the Cape High Court held that the 'suspension of a Member of the Assembly from Parliament for contempt is not consistent with the requirements of representative democracy [in FC s 57(1)*(b)*, read with FC s 57(1)*(a)* and FC s 57(2)*(b)*]'.[163] The primary grounds for the High Court's conclusion was that such a sanction not only hurt the Member of Parliament in question, 'but also his or her party and those [members] of the electorate who voted for that party who are entitled to be represented in the Assembly by their proportionate number of representatives.'[164] As Roux recognizes, *De Lille*'s gloss on FC s 57(1)*(b)* 'is a classic instance of what John Hart Ely has called the 'democracy-reinforcing' function of judicial review.'[165]

FC s 57(2)*(b)* states that the National Assembly's rules and orders must allow for 'participation in the proceedings of the Assembly and its committees of minority parties represented in the Assembly, in a manner consistent with democracy'. This language is rehearsed with respect to the procedures of the National Council of Provinces, provincial legislatures, and municipal councils.[166] Two important decisions have been handed down on minority party participation in the proceedings of a municipal council and its committees (in terms of FC s 160(8).) In *Democratic Alliance v ANC & Others*, the reconstitution of three committees of the City of Cape Town was challenged under FC s 160(8).[167] The applicant, a minority political party, alleged that its representation on the City's reconstituted executive committee and two other committees was adversely disproportional to the number of seats it held in the municipal council. In oral argument, counsel for the applicant conceded that FC 160(8)*(b)* participation requirement would be satisfied by a first-past-the-post system in which the majority party took all the seats on the executive committee.[168] The decision turned on the court's interpretation of FC s 160(8)*(a)*. FC s 160(8)*(a)* provides that parties must be 'fairly represented' on committees of the Municipal Council.[169] On this issue, the Cape High Court held that FC s 160(8)*(a)* confers a right to participate in such committees, rather than a right to demand that the composition of each committee be proportional to the parties' representation in the municipal council.[170]

The Constitutional Court had an opportunity to consider FC s 160(8) in *Democratic Alliance & Another v Masondo NO & Another*.[171] In *Masondo*, the issue was whether a mayoral committee established under s 60 of the Local Government: Municipal Structures Act[172] was a committee as contemplated in FC s 160(8). Langa DCJ, writing for the majority, held that it was not. The Court found that the functions of mayoral committees under the Structures Act were 'executive' not 'deliberative',[173] and that since a mayoral committee was not elected by the municipal council, but appointed by the executive mayor, it was not a committee contemplated by FC s 160(8).[174]

The real action, however, lies not in the majority opinion but in Justice O'Regan's dissent. O'Regan J agreed that FC s 160(8)*(b)* connotes simple majority rule. However, she felt obliged to dissent because, on her reading of FC s 160(8)*(a)*, the Final Constitution requires a procedure in which the views of minority parties should at least be taken into account. In O'Regan J's view, 'the obligation of fair representation means that [majority] decisions [under FC s 160(8)*(b)*] are made only once the interests of non-majority parties have been aired.'[175] O'Regan J summarized her position as follows:

> [S]ection 160(8)*(b)* is clear that the principle of fair representation is always subject to democracy and the will of the majority. Members of the mayoral committee must therefore submit to that principle, as must all councillors. The principle established by section 160(8) is a principle which requires inclusive deliberation prior to decision-making to enrich the quality of our democracy. It does not subvert the principle of democracy itself.[176]

As Roux observes, O'Regan J's dissent echoes the theoretical literature's accepted view on the value of participation in political decision-making. While deliberation ought not to override the commitment to majority-rule – and no democratic regime 'should be beholden to the impossible ideal of decision-making by consensus' – 'deliberation and participation in decision-making are stressed for the contribution these processes can make to better informed and more legitimate decisions.'[177] Justice O'Regan's dissent emphasizes the value of participation at the same time as it recognizes that this virtue can, when a decision must be taken, become counterproductive.

Although a minority in *Masondo*, O'Regan J's view ultimately carried the day in *Matatiele II* and *Doctors for Life*.[178] *Matatiele II* and *Doctors for Life* provide a much more expansive and nuanced understanding of FC s 59(1)*(a)*, FC s 72(1) and FC s 118(1). The *Matatiele II* Court was asked whether the Twelfth Amendment to the Final Constitution was unconstitutional because it re-demarcated the boundary of the municipality of Matatiele, removed it from KwaZulu-Natal and placed it in the Eastern Cape, without sufficient public consultation.[179]

Justice Ngcobo, writing for a majority of the *Matatiele II* Court, held that a provincial legislature, whose provincial boundary is being altered, is required by the Final Constitution to approve such an alteration. Moreover, when a provincial legislature takes a decision of this nature, it clearly invokes its law-making powers. As such, the provincial legislature is required to facilitate public participation in making its decision-making process. The Court's test for sufficient facilitation is that of reasonableness: a standard not to be dismissed lightly given that the Court could have lowered the threshold to that of mere rationality.[180]

When determining whether a provincial legislature has acted reasonably, the Constitutional Court will have regard to factors such as the intensity of the impact of the legislation on the public. Ngcobo J writes:

> The more discrete and identifiable the potentially affected section of the population, and the more intense the possible effect on their interests, the more reasonable it would be to ensure that the potentially affected section of the population is given a proper opportunity to have a say.[181]

Ngcobo J found that *Matatiele II* satisfied the factual predicate required by the test: the proposed amendment would have moved an entire, identifiable community from one province to another province. Moreover, the consequences of the proposed amendment were more than symbolic. The move of the municipality from KwaZulu-Natal to the Eastern Cape would have significant effects on the provision to the constituents of Matatiele of welfare payments, health services and education. (No one would argue that KwaZulu-Natal benefits from a more professional civil service. The Eastern Cape, on the other hand, is an unmitigated disaster. Its administrative failure has led to the direct constitutionally-mandated intervention of the National Government. Population flows out of the Eastern Cape and into KwaZulu-Natal have been so significant that they may play a significant role in the 2012 ANC Presidential nomination process.) Given the test to be applied, and the salient facts, the Court concluded that KwaZulu-Natal, in not holding any public hearings or inviting any written submissions, had acted unreasonably. As a result, that part of the Twelfth Amendment that altered the boundary of KwaZulu-Natal was declared unconstitutional.

In *Doctors for Life*, the Constitutional Court was asked to address a comparable question: whether the Traditional Health Practitioners Act and the Choice on Termination of Pregnancy Amendment Act were unconstitutional because they had been passed without the requisite level of public participation. Ncgobo J, again writing for a majority of the Court, began by noting that the National Council of Provinces ('NCOP') enabled the provinces to have a say in the national law-making process. NCOP delegations are generally obliged to secure voting mandates from their respective provincial legislatures. This direct influence of the provincial legislatures on their NCOP delegations meant that both Parliament and the provincial legislatures had a constitutional obligation to facilitate public involvement. Once again, the Court in *Doctors for Life* employed a reasonableness test for determining whether citizens possessed a meaningful opportunity to be heard in the making of law.

The papers and oral argument made it abundantly clear that although the Traditional Health Practitioners Act and the Choice on Termination of Pregnancy Amendment Act had – as Bills – generated great public interest, and the NCOP had decided that public hearings would be held in the provinces, in the end, the majority of the provinces did not hold hearings. Given that the majority of provinces, and the NCOP itself, had failed to hold public hearings, and thus abdicated their respective responsibilities to provide the opportunity for the public participation contemplated by FC 72(1)(a), the *Doctors for Life* Court held that both pieces of legislation had failed the test for reasonableness and were, consequently, constitutionally infirm.

For my purposes, *Matatiele II* and *Doctors for Life* stand for the proposition that public participation is not a good because it enhances deliberation, but rather that public participation – depending upon the issued concerned – will elicit information deemed critical for decision-making in a robust constitutional democracy. Moreover, the kind of participation contemplated by the *Matatiele II* and *Doctors for Life* Courts resonates quite profoundly with previous discussions about the nature and the purpose of participatory bubbles: better data and greater legitimacy. Public participation in South Africa – after *Matatiele II* and *Doctors for Life* – is meant to address specific problems that have a direct bearing on the lives of the would-be participants. Once the contested matter has been resolved, the bubble bursts and legislators and citizens alike return to other matters that occupy them.[182]

6. *Chapter 9 Institutions*

I have discussed above the manner in which Chapter 9 Institutions share constitutional competence for interpreting the Final Constitution. However, it may well be that in a one party dominant democracy, with an extremely thin civil society, the most important role of the Chapter 9 Institutions is to create space for debate, discussion, mediation, negotiation and reconciliation between all South Africans with an interest in a pressing public issue. These organizations can, when effective, play a critical part in resolving disputes between the state and citizens as well as conflicts between private parties. The disputes are often of limited duration and easy disposition. Marginal voices are heard. Claims by discrete and largely disenfranchised minorities are treated seriously. Resolutions – even nonbinding resolutions – allow many of the participants to leave feeling at least partially vindicated.

Take the Public Protector. The Public Protector must take those steps necessary to make its ombudsman services 'accessible to all persons and communities.'[183] While meaningful access dictates that the services provided be free – which the Public Protector's services are – they must also be geographically accessible and expeditiously dispatched. The Public Protector has offices in every province and a national office in Pretoria.[184]

More importantly, although aggregate numbers of complaints and resolutions can suggest an overwhelmed and understaffed Public Protector's office, the public appears to be getting good value for money. In 2002, 10% of finalised cases found in favour of the complainant.[185] In 99% of these cases, the state rectified the wrong.[186] When a well-founded and properly registered claim is made, the Public Protector appears to be a very accessible and a highly effective alternative to the courts.[187]

The South African Humna Rights Commission ('SAHRC')[188] and the Commisssion of Gender Equality ('CGE')[189] have held regular hearings about legal and political issues of moment. Together, these institutions have created participatory bubbles in which various constituencies can engage one another in public debate regarding current crises and deeper fissures in South African society.

As Cathi Albertyn notes, the CGE's (previous) range of monitoring activities – and its invitations to a broad range of state and social actors – went beyond mere report writing and entered the realm of law and policy-making:[190]

> Although the scope of the Commission's monitoring function extends across the entire spectrum of the state and civil society, much of its work has been aimed at the state. It has been especially engaged in the development of the government's legal and policy framework. In 1998, it commissioned an audit of discriminatory legislation to identify gaps in laws. It has also made regular submissions to

> the South African Law Commission and to Parliament on laws affecting gender equality, including customary laws. More recently, it has addressed the issue of implementing law through the idea of an Annual Report Card of progress by various government departments. The Commission has evaluated the participation of women in politics, and the gender policies of political parties. It has monitored national and local elections to assess the participation of women in political parties and in voting. ... [T]he CGE's oversight responsibilities capture relationships within civil society. The CGE monitors traditional practices that are harmful to women: it has conducted research and engaged in dialogue with communities and traditional leaders on issues such as witchcraft and virginity testing. The CGE has also developed a particular focus on gender equality in the private sector. It has recently undertaken a survey of the sector and produced a report entitled 'Best Practice Guidelines for Creating a Culture of Gender Equality in the Private Sector'.

The CGE's activities enabled it to undertake a broad array of short-term and long-term problem-solving activities that require some form of polycentric decision-making. The independence of the CGE enabled it to attract participants from multiple sectors of society. Finally, the absence of the need for a final resolution of a conflict has enabled the CGE to assist the courts and the legislature in general norm-setting without being beset by the zero-sum outcomes of constitutional litigation. At the time of writing, however, the CGE's status remains unclear. Only two full-time commissioners remain. The lack of government support, and shortage of qualified personnel has left the CGE's ability to discharge it experimental constitutional mandate in doubt.

The SAHRC's range of activities is equally broad. Indeed, its subject matter competence, human rights, knows (virtually) no limits. With respect to its monitoring activities, Jonathan Klaaren writes:

> The investigations undertaken by the Commission reflect proactive enforcement of human rights. The Commission has produced, at the end of its investigations, reports on a wide range of topics: from the effect of road closures on the right to movement to the conflict between the right to equality and the freedom to associate. These investigations, and the subsequent reports, have occasionally provoked intense controversy. The Investigation of Racism in the Media led to the issuance of subpoenas by the SAHRC and equally unusual litigation-like responses from members of the media. The Commission's early reports on the lack of respect for the rights of non-nationals in post-apartheid South Africa and on the conditions of detention at an official repatriation facility, Lindela, were greeted with harsh words by government and department officials (especially the Department of Home Affairs).[191]

But report writing constitutes the least provocative and the least innovative of the SAHRC's constitutionally-mandated activities. The SAHRC's brief embraces the protection of human rights through mediation,[192] adjudication,[193] litigation,[194] and interpretation[195] and enforcement.[196] It is, moreover, empowered to undertake these activities through a 'variety of dispute resolution mechanisms'.[197] Each power and each of these dispute resolution mechanisms enables the SAHRC to tailor its responses both to problems and the affected constituencies. Given the mediating role that the SAHRC plays between state and civil society and between groups within civil society, its emphasis has been on finding solutions to problems that leave all parties better off and able to return to the rest of their lives heard, if not entirely happy.

Unfortunately, the SAHRC, like other Chapter 9 institutions, has been denuded by the government's persistent underfunding, an absence of truly qualified appointments and the resistance to policy recommendations inconsistent with the firmly entrenched interests of the ruling tripartite alliance. The government has yet to implement the 2007 Asmal Report's recommendation that Parliament radically rationalize the Chapter 9 Institutions.[198] (The report would have collapsed seven independent institutions into a single umbrella body. Better, it seems to let them slowly expire without any attempts by the state at resuscitation.) While many Chapter 9 Institutions may have as yet failed to fulfil their anticipated role in fleshing out civil society and deepening our democracy, the Public Protector and the Auditor General have – with occasional assistance from other branches of the security forces – at least been able to reveal systemic corruption and widespread bureaucratic incompetence.[199]

Endnotes

1. It is worth connecting again the parallel structures of consciousness as trial and error with the political structures of trial and error. See, eg, PA Howard 'The Neural Mechanisms of Learning from Competitors' (2010) 53 (2) *Neuroimage* 1 ('Learning from competition is not learning to act like your competitor, it is learning not to act like your competitor when they fail.') Howard may be correct with respect to competition, but in the search for the provision of common goods, most of us want to see the state and other actors identify best practices for all concerned.
2. In two stage Bill of Rights analysis, if the party challenging a law should lose at the first stage, a demonstration that a right has been abridged, then the litigation never moves on to the second stage, limitations analysis. However, the Constitutional Court prefers do the majority of its heavy lifting under the limitations clause. Limitations analysis allows the Court to arrive at a conclusion as to a law's infirmity or constitutionality based largely on the facts before it and without having to determine the actual contours of the right. For a critique of this notional approach to rights analysis, as opposed to a value-based approach to rights analysis, see S Woolman 'The Right Consistency: *Benaish v Ernst and Young* (1999) 15 *South African Journal on Human Rights* 166. The other mechanism that allows the Court to avoid determining the actual content of a right is s 39(2). See S Woolman 'The Amazing, Vanishing Bill of Rights' (2007) 125 *South African Law Journal* 762. Under s 39(2), the Court need only develop the common law or interpret a statute in light of 'the spirit, purport and objects of the Bill of Rights.'
3. On limitations analysis generally, see S Woolman & H Botha 'Limitations' in S Woolman & M Bishop (eds) *Constitutional Law of South Africa* (2nd Edition, OS, July 2006) Chapter 34.
4. In *Satchwell v President of the Republic of South Africa II*, the Constitutional Court was asked to assess the constitutionality of a statutory and regulatory framework almost identical to one that it had declared unconstitutional only a year earlier in *Satchwell v President of the Republic of South Africa I*. 2003 (4) SA 266 (CC), 2004 (1) BCLR 1 (CC)('*Satchwell II*'); 2002 (6) SA 1 (CC), 2002 (9) BCLR 986 (CC)('*Satchwell I*'). In *Satchwell I*, the Constitutional Court had declared ss 8 and 9 of the Judges' Remuneration and Conditions of Employment Act unconstitutional because they discriminated against homosexual Judges' same-sex partners. The *Satchwell I* Court ordered that the words 'or partner in a permanent same-sex life partnership in which the partners have undertaken reciprocal duties of support' be read into the provisions after the word 'spouse'. Subsequent to the judgment in *Satchwell I*, Parliament promulgated a new Act, the Judges' Remuneration and Conditions of Employment Act. This Act took no notice of the *Satchwell I* Court's order. In *Satchwell II*, the Constitutional Court refused to accord Parliament any deference, declared the new provisions discriminatory, and read into the new legislation the words 'or partner in a permanent same-sex life partnership in which the partners have undertaken reciprocal duties of support.'

5. *Minister of Home Affairs & Another v Fourie & Another (Doctors for Life International & Others, Amici Curiae); Lesbian and Gay Equality Project & Others v Minister of Home Affairs & Others* 2006 (1) SA 524 (CC), 2006 (3) BCLR 355 (CC); *Residents of Joe Slovo Community, Western Cape v Thubelisha Homes & Others* [2009] ZACC 16, 2010 (3) SA 454 (CC), 2009 (9) BCLR 847 (CC) (*'Joe Slovo I'*); *Residents of Joe Slovo Community, Western Cape v Thubelisha Homes & Others* [2011] ZACC 8 (*'Joe Slovo II'*).
6. *Ex Parte Chairperson of the Constitutional Assembly: In Re Certification of the Constitution of the Republic of South Africa, 1996* 1996 (4) SA 744 (CC), 1996 (10) BCLR 1253 (CC).
7. S Woolman 'Humility, Michelman's Method and the Constitutional Court: Rereading the *First Certification Judgment* and Reaffirming a Distinction between Law and Politics' (2013) 24 *Stellenbosch Law Review* – (forthcoming). What is true of the certification process must certainly be true of the normal process of law-making and judicial review. The role of the Constitutional Court is not to find optimal solutions but to stake out a range of constitutional solutions. One way in which the courts recognize their role and their obligation to share responsibility for constitutional interpretation is in terms of a remedy of temporary validity. While the Parliament or another branch of government goes about redrafting an infirm piece of legislation, the courts may, in the interest of good governance, suspend a declaration of invalidity. See M Bishop 'Remedies' in S Woolman & M Bishop (eds) *Constitutional Law of South Africa* (2nd Edition, OS, June 2008) Chapter 9. Matthew Chaskalson and Dennis Davis ask whether the Constitutional Court did not narrow the space for constitutional design created by the Interim Constitution's 34 principles when it rejected the first text drafted by the Constitutional Assembly. See M Chaskalson & D Davis 'Constitutionalism, the Rule of Law and the First Certification Judgment' (1997) 13 *South African Journal on Human Rights* 430. The 34 principles certainly did not demand special super-majorities for the amendment of the Bill of Rights or the removal of the Auditor-General or Public Protector. But as I argue in the article above, the Court's intervention hardly counts as political in the conventional sense. The *First Certification Judgment* Court, acting with appropriate humility, simply confined its objections to obvious gaffes and those provisions necessary if, in fact, the Final Constitution was to vouchsafe judicial review under a justiciable Bill of Rights and the basic law's express commitment to the rule of law.
8. The *Makwanyane* Court, despite the ANC's longstanding opposition to capital punishment, enjoyed no more than 30% support from the general public on this issue and others circa 1995. 1995 (3) SA 391 (CC), 1995 (6) BCLR 665 (CC), 1995 (2) SACR 1 (CC)(*'Makwanyane'*). The Court in 2012 enjoys roughly the same level of support. Despite occasional threats made by the Executive not to abide by a decision – see *Treatment Action Campaign* – and intermittent attempts to bring the judiciary within the executive's remit, the Court has maintained a significant degree of autonomy. Whether it retains such autonomy turns to a great extent on future appointments. (The most recent spate of selections bodes ill.) While that prospect may fill avid court watchers with concern, it's pretty much constitutional politics as usual. That's another point in favour of experimental constitutionalism: it does not place all of its eggs in the judicial basket. Indeed, it emphasizes the desirability of norm generation processes that take place outside the courtroom and even beyond the confines of the legislative.
9. See C Albertyn, B Goldblatt & C Roederer *Introduction to the Promotion of Equality and Prevention of Unfair Discrimination Act 4 of 2000* (2001). For a critique of the manner in which PEPUDA stacks the deck in favour of claims of discrimination, as opposed to countervailing associational concerns, see S Woolman 'Freedom of Association' in S Woolman & M Bishop (eds) *Constitutional Law of South Africa* (2nd Edition, OS, December 2003) Chapter 44.
10. See P Lenta 'Taking Diversity Seriously: Religious Association and Work-Related Discrimination' (2009) *South African Law Journal* 925; S Woolman 'On the Fragility of Associational Life: A Constitutive Liberal's Response to Patrick Lenta' (2009) 25 *South African Journal on Human Rights* 280.
11. In such circumstances, the illegitimacy of the conduct challenged is less than clear. The problem of putting private institutional norms to the PEPUDA test bears a good deal of similarity to what Professor Susan Sturm has identified as the "second-generation" problems of protecting workers' civil

rights from discrimination in the workplace in the United States. See S Sturm 'Second Generation Employment Discrimination: A Structural Approach' (2001) 101 *Columbia Law Review* 452. In the context of employment discrimination, Sturm observes that the most pressing problems have evolved from obvious, intentional discrimination of yester-years: "'first-generation' problems exemplified by 'smoking guns' such as 'the sign on the door [declaring] that 'Irish need not apply' or the rejection [of an applicant] explained by the comment that 'this is no job for a woman.'" Ibid at 459–60. Instead, individuals from historically disadvantaged groups in America and South Africa encounter discrimination that 'involve social practices and patterns of interaction among groups within the workplace that, over time, exclude non-dominant groups,' which are reinforced by 'structures of decision-making, opportunity, and power'. Ibid at 460. My account owes much to Susan Sturm's insights on the differences between traditional models of adjudication concerned with findings of liability and adjudication geared towards the creative structuring of remedies to systemic problems. See S Sturm 'The Promise of Participation' (1993) 78 *Iowa Law Review* 981, 987–991, 1002–1010. My embrace of remedial equilibrium reflects the recognition that such discrimination is difficult to attack successfully in a constitutional order committed to a significant degree of private ordering. See S Woolman 'Seek Justice Elsewhere (supra).

12. For a compelling account of the dilemmas posed by one-stage fundamental rights analysis, see L Tribe & M Dorf 'Levels of Generality in the Definition of Rights' 57 *University of Chicago Law Review* 1057 (1990).
13. See S Woolman '*Coetzee*: The Limitations of Justice Sachs' Concurrence' (1996) *South African Journal on Human Rights* 99.
14. See M Dorf '1997 Supreme Court Term Foreword: The Limits of Socratic Deliberation' (1998) 112 *Harvard Law Review* 4 (1998).
15. This recognition is one of the hallmarks of the sociological concepts of complexity and emergence. To observe that social systems are complex is not tantamount to rejecting the possibility of systematic, scientific understanding. Rather, as Lee McIntyre notes, complexity relates to our knowledge of the world at a particular level of description. It does not rebut the possibility of (social) scientific explanations at another level. See L McIntyre 'Complexity and Social Scientific Laws' (1993) 97 *Synthese* 209.
16. See Strurm 'Second Generation' (supra) at 452.
17. See Dorf 'The Domain of Reflexive Law' (supra) at 399–400 (Observes the dynamic character of social change resulting from new legal protections.) As the partial success of 'rational expectations' theory in macroeconomics demonstrates, some adaptive processes can be modelled very effectively (some of the time). See also S Sheffrin *Rational Expectations* (1996). However, there are good reasons for doubting whether models of similar precision can be designed for contexts as diverse and unpredictable as personal intimacy (*Jordan*) or religious worship (*Prince*). The experimentalist approach, however, does demand that one size of social scientific inquiry fits all.
18. See Dorf 'Legal Indeterminism and Institutional Design' (supra) at 960-970. See also J Klaaren 'A Second Look at the South African Human Rights Commission, Access to Information, and the Promotion of Socio-economic Rights' (2005) 27 *Human Rights Quarterly* 539 (Drawing on experimentalist principles in EU regulatory regimes, Klaaren suggests that the SAHRC could be responsible for gathering and disbursing information regarding the government's progress in fulfilling the promise of socio-economic rights.)
19. *Governing Body of the Juma Musjid Primary School & Others v Ahmed Asruff Essay N.O. & Others* [2011] ZACC 13, 2011 (8) BCLR 761 (CC).
20. *Ras Bahari Lal v King Emperor* (1933) 60 IA 354, 361.
21. 1997 (3) SA 772 (CC), 1997 (6) BCLR 677 (CC)('*Ntuli II*').
22. *Ntuli II* (supra) at para 30.
23. See *S v Ntuli* 1996 (1) SA 1207 (CC), 1996 (1) SACR 94 (CC), 1996 (1) BCLR 141 (CC)('*Ntuli I*') (Constitutional Court declared unconstitutional s 309(4)(a) of the Criminal Procedure Act 51 of

1977. The provision provided that a person who was serving a period of imprisonment imposed by a lower court could only prosecute any review of those proceedings if a Judge had certified that there were reasonable grounds for review.)

24. *Ntuli II* (supra) at paras 41–42.
25. *S v Steyn* 2001 (1) SA 1146 (CC), 2001 (1) SACR 25 (CC), 2001 (1) BCLR 52 (CC)('*Steyn*').
26. Ibid at para 46.
27. 2007 (4) SA 611 (CC), 2007 (2) SACR 28 (CC) 2007 (5) BCLR 474 (CC)('*Shinga*')
28. See S Woolman & H Botha 'Limitations' (supra). See also S Woolman 'The Architecture of Dignity' in D Cornell, S Woolman, M Bishop, J Brickhill & S Fuller (eds) *The Dignity Jurisprudence of the Constitutional Court of South Africa* (2012).
29. The dissenting judgment of Sachs J in *Prince* resonates with Roux's understanding of democracy, and sounds themes similar to my own thoughts about the relationship between democracy and the other values that ought to inform limitations analysis. In his dissent in *Prince*, Sachs J stressed the need in an 'open and democratic society' faced with seemingly intractable conflicts – between the state and religious communities – for a 'reasonable accommodation' of interests. This accommodation requires mutual recognition and 'a reasonable measure of give and take from all sides'. Sachs J, not surprisingly, finds that the majority's refusal to carve out an exemption for bona fide religious use of cannabis offends this very principle. The majority judgment, he writes, 'puts a thumb on the scales in favour of ease of law-enforcement, and gives insufficient weight to the impact the measure will have, not only on the fundamental rights of the appellant and his religious community, but on the basic notion of tolerance and respect for diversity that our Constitution demands for and from all in our society'. The majority's suppression of cultural and religious differences harms not only the individuals and the communities concerned, but society as a whole. He continues: '[F]aith and public interest overlap and intertwine in the need to protect tolerance as a constitutional virtue and respect for diversity and openness as a constitutional principle. Religious tolerance is accordingly not only important to those individuals who are saved from having to make excruciating choices between their beliefs and the law. It is deeply meaningful to all of us because religion and belief matter, and because living in an open society matters.' For Sachs J, freedom of belief and the freedom to express such belief are fundamental not only to the freedom and the dignity of the believers concerned, but also to the diversity and the openness that are the lifeblood of a democracy. Democracy, Sachs J seems to be saying, presupposes the capability of marginalized and vulnerable minorities to challenge the normative closure into which political communities tend to lapse. A political community can only remain free if it values plurality and difference, and allows out-groups to disturb and to challenge deeply held majoritarian beliefs and practices. For this reason, the critical challenge for our constitutional democracy consists 'not in accepting what is familiar and easily accommodated, but in giving reasonable space to what is unusual, bizarre or even threatening.' See *Prince v President of the Law Society of the Cape of Good Hope* 2001 (2) SA 388 (CC), 2001 (2) BCLR 133 (CC) at paras 146, 147, 155–156 161, 170 and 172. Sachs J's views on openness carried the day on same-sex marriage in *Fourie*. The Court remarked that '[t]he hallmark of an open and democratic society is its capacity to accommodate and manage difference of intensely-held world views and lifestyles in a reasonable and fair manner.' *Minister of Home Affairs & Another v Fourie & Another (Doctors for Life International & Others, Amici Curiae); Lesbian and Gay Equality Project & Others v Minister of Home Affairs & Others* 2006 (1) SA 524 (CC), 2006 (3) BCLR 355 (CC) at para 95. See also S Woolman '"I am Large": Sachs, Whitman and Democracy' (2010) 25 (1) *Southern African Public Law* 57.
30. See *Matatiele Municipality & Others v President of the RSA & Others* 2006 (5) SA 47 (CC), 2006 (5) BCLR 622 (CC)('*Matatiele II*').
31. The Constitutional Court has, in *Matatiele II* and *Doctors for Life*, given greater content to the principle of democracy. They have as yet not tied that understanding closely to their analysis of fundamental rights or limitations analysis. See J Brickhill & R Biabuch 'Political Rights' in S Woolman & M Bishop (eds) *Constitutional Law of South Africa* (2nd Edition, OS, March 2007) Chapter 45.

32. See *United Democratic Movement v President of the Republic of South Africa & Others (African Christian Democratic Party & Others Intervening; Institute for Democracy in South Africa & Another as Amici Curiae)* (No 2) 2003 (1) SA 495 (CC)('*UDM*').

33. See T Roux 'Democracy' in S Woolman & M Bishop (eds) *Constitutional Law of South Africa* (2nd Edition, OS, July 2006) Chapter 10.

34. This principle, in its clearest form, holds: 'Government in South Africa must be so arranged that the people, through the medium of political parties and regular elections, in which all adult citizens are entitled to participate, exert sufficient control over their elected representatives to ensure that: (a) representatives are held to account for their actions, (b) government listens and responds to the needs of the people, in appropriate cases directly, (c) collective decisions are taken by majority vote after due consideration of the views of minority parties, and (d) the reasons for all collective decisions are publicly explained. (2) The rights necessary to maintain such a form of government must be enshrined in a supreme-law Bill of Rights, enforced by an independent judiciary, whose task it shall be to ensure that, whenever the will of the majority, expressed in the form of a law of general application, runs counter to a right in the Bill of Rights, the resolution of that tension promotes the values of human dignity, equality and freedom.' See Roux 'Democracy' (supra) at § 10.5(b)(Italics removed.) The Court has begun to provide an answer of its own to the question posed in *UDM*. Within the last several years, a number of justices have articulated accounts of 'democracy' that suggest that Roux's principle was nascent, and is now ascendant, in our constitutional jurisprudence. Roux notes that in her powerful dissent in *New National Party v Government of the Republic of South Africa*, 'O'Regan J stressed the centrality of the right to vote with respect to the consolidation of South African democracy, remarking that: "The right to vote is foundational to a democratic system. Without it, there can be no democracy at all."' Roux (supra) at § 10.5(c) quoting *New National Party v Government of the Republic of South Africa* 1999 (3) SA 191 (CC), 1999 (5) BCLR 489 (CC) at para 122. O'Regan J's dissent, Roux continues, 'also supports the second element of the principle of democracy ... [I]t is integral to the Final Constitution's conception of democracy that rights be capable of trumping the will of the majority where such a result better serves "the democratic values of human dignity, equality and freedom".' Roux (supra) at § 10.5(c). Roux acknowledges that Sachs J's remarks in *Masondo* 'articulate many of the elements of the principle of democracy that [this chapter has] argued [are] immanent in the constitutional text.' Roux (supra) at § 10.5(c) citing *Democratic Alliance v Masondo* 2003 (2) SA 413 (CC), 2003 (2) BCLR 128 (CC) at paras 42–43. The Constitutional Court, in *Doctors for Life*, articulated an account of democracy that closely approximates Roux's reading of the Final Constitution. In *Doctors for Life,* Sachs J writes: 'True to the manner in which it itself was sired, the Constitution predicates and incorporates within its vision the existence of a permanently engaged citizenry alerted to and involved with all legislative programmes. The people have more than the right to vote in periodical elections, fundamental though that is. And more is guaranteed to them than the opportunity to object to legislation before and after it is passed, and to criticise it from the sidelines while it is being adopted. They are accorded the right on an ongoing basis and in a very direct manner, to be (and to feel themselves to be) involved in the actual processes of law-making. Elections are of necessity periodical. Accountability, responsiveness and openness, on the other hand, are by their very nature ubiquitous and timeless. They are constants of our democracy, to be ceaselessly asserted in relation to ongoing legislative and other activities of government. Thus it would [make] a travesty of our Constitution to treat democracy as going into a deep sleep after elections, only to be kissed back to short spells of life every five years.' *Doctors for Life* (supra) at para 231.

35. Roux (supra) at § 10.3(c).

36. *Merafong Demarcation Forum & Others v President of the Republic of South Africa & Others* [2008] ZACC 10, 2008 (5) SA 171 (CC), 2008 (10) BCLR 968 (CC). For a nuanced analysis of the case and its location in the Court's 'meaningful engagement' jurisprudence, see M Bishop 'Vampire or Prince? The Listening Constitution and *Merafong Demarcation Forum & Others v President of the Republic of South*

Africa & Others (2009) 2 *Constitutional Court Review* 313. See also G Quinot 'Snapshot or Participatory Democracy? Political Engagement as Fundamental Human Right' (2009) 25 *South African Journal on Human Rights* 392.

37. See K Thomas 'Racial Justice' in A Sarat, G Bryant & R Kagan (eds) *Looking Back at Law's Century* (2002) 78, 87. See also H Botha 'Rights, Limitations, and the (Im)possibility of Self-Government' in H Botha, A Van der Walt and J Van der Walt *Rights and Democracy in a Transformative Constitution* (2003) 13; H Botha 'Freedom and Constraint in Constitutional Adjudication' (2004) 20 *South African Journal on Human Rights* 249.

38. The Constitutional Court itself has, for the moment, come around to this very position. In *Fourie*, the Court remarked that '[t]he hallmark of an open and democratic society is its capacity to accommodate and manage difference of intensely-held world views and lifestyles in a reasonable and fair manner.' *Fourie* (supra) at para 95.

39. Roux (supra) at § 10.3(c).

40. See FC s 26, FC s 27(1) and FC s 27(3), FC s 28 and FC s 35. On the right to water, see M Langford & R Stacey 'Water' in S Woolman & M Bishop (eds) *Constitutional Law of South Africa* (2nd Edition, RS3, May 2011) Chapter 56B. On the right to housing, see K McLean 'Housing' in S Woolman & M Bishop (eds) *Constitutional Law of South Africa* (2nd Edition, OS, July 2006) Chapter 55. On the right to healthcare, see D Bilchitz 'Health' in S Woolman & M Bishop (eds) *Constitutional Law of South Africa* (2nd Edition, OS, December 2005) Chapter 56A. On the right to food, see D Brand 'Food' in S Woolman & M Bishop (eds) *Constitutional Law of South Africa* (2nd Edition, OS, March 2005) Chapter 56C. On the right to social security, see M Swart 'Social Security' in S Woolman & M Bishop (eds) *Constitutional Law of South Africa* (2nd Edition, RS4, January 2012) Chapter 56D. On children's rights, see A Friedman, A Pantazis and A Skelton 'Children's Rights' in S Woolman & M Bishop (eds) *Constitutional Law of South Africa* (2nd Edition, RS1, June 2009) Chapter 57. On prisoners' rights, see F Snyckers & J Le Roux 'Criminal Procedure: Rights of Detained, Arrested and Accused Persons' in S Woolman & M Bishop (eds) *Constitutional Law of South Africa* (2nd Edition, OS, July 2006) Chapter 51.

41. The leading Constitutional Court cases are: *Soobramoney v Minister of Health, Kwazulu-Natal* 1998 (1) SA 765 (CC)('*Soobramoney*'); *Government of the Republic of South Africa v Grootboom* ('*Grootboom*') 2001 (1) SA 46 (CC); *Minister of Health v Treatment Action Campaign* ('*TAC*') 2002 (5) SA 721 (CC); *Khosa v Minister of Social Development* 2004 (6) SA 505 (CC)('*Khosa*'). *Port Elizabeth Municipality v Various Occupiers* 2005 (1) SA 217 (CC), 2004 (12) BCLR 1268 (CC)('*Port Elizabeth Municipality*'); *Fuel Retailers Association of Southern Africa v Director-General Environmental Management, Department of Agriculture, Conservation and Environment Mpumalanga Province* [2007] ZACC 13, 2007 (10) BCLR 1059 (CC), 2007 (6) SA 4 (CC)('*Fuel Retailers*'); *Minister of Public Works & Others v Kyalami Ridge Environmental Association* [2001] ZACC 19, 2001 (3) SA 1151 (CC), 2001 (7) BCLR 652 (CC) ('*Kyalami Ridge*'); *Occupiers of 51 Olivia Road, Berea Township and 197 Main Street Johannesburg v City of Johannesburg & Others*; [2008] ZACC 1, 2008 (3) SA 208 (CC), 2008 (5) BCLR 475 (CC)('*Occupiers*'); *Residents of Joe Slovo Community, Western Cape v Thubelisha Homes & Others;* [2009] ZACC 16, 2010 (3) SA 454 (CC), 2009 (9) BCLR 847 (CC)('*Joe Slovo*'); *Abahlali Basemjondolo Movement SA & Another v Premier of the Province of Kwazulu-Natal & Others* [2009] ZACC 31, 2010 (2) BCLR 99 (CC)('*Abahlali Basemjondolo*'); *Governing Body of the Juma Musjid Primary School & Others v Ahmed Asruff Essay N.O. and Others* [2011] ZACC 13, 2011 (8) BCLR 761 (CC). For some early critiques of various parts of this ever growing body of jurisprudence, see D Bilchitz 'Giving Socio-Economic Rights Teeth: The Minimum Core and Its Importance' (2001) 119 *South African Law Journal* 484; D Bilchitz 'Towards a Reasonable Approach to the Minimum Core: Laying the Foundations for Future Socio-Economic Rights Jurisprudence' (2003) 19 *South African Journal on Human Rights* 1; (2003); T Roux 'Legitimating Transformation: Political Resource Allocation in the South African Constitutional Court' (2003) 4 *Democratization* 10 (Discusses the different standards of review adopted by the Court in socio-economic rights cases); M Pieterse 'Resuscitating Socio-Economic Rights: Constitutional

Entitlements to Health Care Services (2006) 22 *South African Journal on Human Rights* 473. See also S Liebenberg 'The Value of Human Dignity in Interpreting Socio-Economic Rights' (2005) 21 *South African Journal on Human Rights* 22; M Pieterse 'Coming to Terms with the Judicial Enforcement of Socio-Economic Rights' (2004) 20 *South African Journal on Human Rights* 383; D Moellendorf (1998) 'Reasoning About Resources: *Soobramoney* and the Future of Socio-Economic Rights Claims' (1998) 14 *South African Journal on Human Rights* 327; M Wesson '*Grootboom* and Beyond: Reassessing the Socio-Economic Rights Jurisprudence of the South African Constitutional Court' (2004) 20 *South African Journal on Human Rights* 284. For accounts that generally approve of the court's deferential approach, see C Sunstein 'Social and Economic Rights? Lessons from South Africa' (2001) 11 *Constitutional Forum* 123 (Defending the Court's administrative law model of socio-economic rights); D Davis 'Adjudicating the Socio-Economic Rights in the South African Constitution: Towards 'Deference Lite'? (2006) 22 *South African Journal on Human Rights* 301 (From a realist's perspective, defending reasonableness review by the Constitutional Court.) The burgeoning body of critical analysis is of our socio-economic rights jurisprudence is too voluminous to capture here. To those authors who have contributed to this discourse but go uncited here, you have my appreciation and my apology.

42. See *Soobramoney* (supra); *Grootboom* (supra); *TAC* (supra).

43. See *Soobramoney* (supra).

44. See *Khosa* (supra) at para 43 ('In determining reasonableness, context is all-important. There is no closed list of factors involved in the reasonableness enquiry and the relevance of various factors will be determined on a case by case basis.')

45. See *Grootboom* (supra) at paras 39–46, 52, 53, 63–69, 74, 83.

46. See *City of Johannesburg Metropolitan Municipality v Blue Moonlight Properties 39 (Pty) Ltd & Another* [2011] ZACC 33, 2012 (2) SA 104 (CC), 2012 (2) BCLR 150 (CC).

47. For the two leading monographs on the subject, see D Bilchitz *Poverty and Fundamental Rights* (2006)(Steadfastly defending minimum core arguments); S Liebenberg *Adjudicating Socio-Economic Rights under a Transformative Constitution* (2010)(Nudging the Court toward a notion of 'substantive reasonableness'.)

48. Pace Marius Pieterse, this invitation is not simply a function of the Court's gloss on FC s 26 and FC s 27. The text of both rights are crafted in a manner that gives the government ample space to decide what policies meet the constitutional desiderata of 'progressive realization'. The Court's gloss on FC s 26(2) and FC s 27(2) might be said to narrow the space within which government can determine the content of the rights to housing, health food, water and social security. See M Pieterse 'Resuscitating Socio-Economic Rights: Constitutional Entitlements to Health Care Services (2006) 22 *South African Journal on Human Rights* 473; E-Mail Correspondence with Marius Pieterse (14 March 2007). On the other hand, Kathleen Noonan, Charles Sabel and William Simon have, somewhat remarkably, identified the open-endedness of the Court's jurisprudence with the kind of politics required by experimental constitutionalism. Noonan, Sabel and Simon 'Child Welfare' (supra). This troubling proposition underscores the dangers of undertaking comparative constitutional law. Noonan, Sabel and Simon are insufficiently critical of *Grootboom* and *TAC*. Neither case leveraged forward and lateral looking change as far as one might have hoped. As we shall see in Chapter 6, however, the 'meaningful engagement' cases litigated a decade later more closely approximate their expectations.

49. In *Modderklip*, the Supreme Court of Appeal had found that the state's failure to act on the occupation of private land by an informal settlement amounted to an expropriation under FC s 25(1) read with FC s 7(2) and ordered the state to compensate Modderklip Boerdery for the violation. *Modderfontein Squatters, Greater Benoni City Council v Modderklip Boerdery (Pty) Ltd (Agri SA and Legal Resources Centre, amici curiae); President of the Republic of South Africa and Others v Modderklip Boerdery (Pty) Ltd (Agri SA and Legal Resources Centre, amici curiae)* 2004 (6) SA 40 (SCA), 2004 (8) BCLR 821 (SCA). See also *Modderklip Boerdery (Pty) Ltd v Modder East Squatters and Another* 2001 (4) SA 385 (W). The Constitutional Court declined to decide the case on the

same basis. The *Modderklip* Court relies instead, for reasons that cannot be interrogated here, on FC s 1(c) and FC s 34. No longer simply a stand-alone principle, FC s 1(c) and the rule of law doctrine, when read with the right of access to courts, FC s 34, generates the proposition that the rule of law, properly conceived, imposes an 'obligation [on] ... the state to provide the necessary mechanisms for citizens to resolve disputes that arise between them.' See, further, *Chief Lesapo v North West Agricultural Bank and Another* 2000 (1) SA 409 (CC), 1999 (12) BCLR 1420 (CC). The *Chief Lesapo* Court hints at some of the concerns raised in *Modderklip.* Mokgoro J writes that FC s 34 and the rule of law doctrine are 'foundational to the stability of an orderly society. It ensures the peaceful, regulated and institutionalised mechanisms to resolve disputes, without resorting to self-help.' Ibid at para 22. However, it is one thing to inveigh against individualized acts of self-help, and quite another to find the state culpable for the social disintegration that flows from a generalized failure of the state's legal dispute mechanisms to resolve conflict effectively. But the sting in *Modderklip* is not that FC s 34 secures for the citizenry the legal institutions required to mediate conflict. Now read in concert with FC s 1(c), FC s 34 requires more than 'the *mere* provision of the mechanisms' for dispute resolution. *President of the Republic of South Africa & Another v Modderklip Boerdery (Pty) Ltd* 2005 (5) SA 3 (CC), 2005 (8) BCLR 786 (CC)('*Modderklip*') at para 42 (emphasis added). It demands that the state take *'reasonable steps ... to ensure that large-scale disruptions in the social fabric do not occur in the wake of the execution of court orders, thus undermining the rule of law.'* Ibid (Emphasis added). If such language alone is not striking enough – the spectre of a Zimbabwe-like constitutional crisis looms large – then three subtle shifts in language are. The access to courts is no longer primarily concerned with the existence of formal legal structures. It is now concerned with 'effective remedies'. Effective remedies turn our attention to *substantive* outcomes. Substantive outcomes are to be measured by the state's compliance with rather murky notions of the 'reasonable steps' required to turn back the forces of entropy. It also seems clear that this new reasonableness test is not derived from FC s 34. It flows from FC s 1(c) and our commitment to the rule of law. As Justice Langa writes: 'The precise nature of the state's obligation in any particular case and in respect of any particular right will depend on what is reasonable, regard being had to the nature of the right or interest that is at risk as well as on the circumstances of each case.' Ibid at para 43. FC s 1(c) will tell us, in the context of various rights, what reasonable, *substantive* steps the state – and the courts – must take to maintain order. The challenges of meeting such a reasonableness requirement in similar kinds of cases are not to be underestimated. Although the Court describes these circumstances as extraordinary, they are, indeed, the circumstances in which many South Africans find themselves now. See *Modderklip* (supra) at paras 46–49 ('[C]ourt orders must be executed in a manner that prevents social upheaval. Otherwise the purpose of the rule of law would be subverted by the very execution process that ought to uphold it. ... The circumstances of this case are extraordinary in that it is not possible to rely on mechanisms normally employed to execute eviction orders. This should have been obvious to the state. It was not a case of one or two or even ten evictions where a routine eviction order would have sufficed. To execute this particular court order and evict tens of thousands of people with nowhere to go would cause unimaginable *social chaos* and *misery* and *untold disruption.* In the circumstances of this case, it would also not be consistent with the rule of law. The question that needs to be answered is whether the state was, in the circumstances, obliged to do more than it has done to satisfy the requirements of the rule of law and fulfil the [FC s] ... 34 rights of Modderklip. I find that it was unreasonable of the state to stand by and do nothing in circumstances where it was impossible for Modderklip to evict the occupiers because of the sheer magnitude of the invasion and the particular circumstances of the occupiers.') (Emphasis added.) In the space of several paragraphs, the *Modderklip* Court has moved from an apparently procedural gloss on the rule of law – consistent with the legality principle enunciated in *Fedsure* and *Pharmaceutical Manufacturers* – to something far more robust. The state – in order to comply with the dictates of the rule of law doctrine – must create and maintain courts that provide 'effective remedies'. Again, the rule of law requires not just any remedy, but an effective remedy. What is an effective remedy? An effective remedy must reflect a serious attempt to prevent 'large-scale disruptions in the social fabric' and their attendant 'chaos and misery'. Failure of the state to plan adequately for such contingencies risks censure by the courts. Moreover, such censure is no longer limited to a terse statement at the end of a judgment castigating the responsible Minister for a failure to discharge constitutional obligations. A failure to take those reasonable steps necessary to safeguard the rule of law may result in an award of *constitutional damages* against the state. In South Africa, we are concerned, not with mere violations of freedom of contract – as was the US Supreme Court in *Lochner* – but with state action or inaction that risks 'large-scale disruptions in the social fabric'. See S Woolman 'My Tea Party, Your Mob, Our Social Contract: Freedom of Assembly and the Constitutional Right to Rebellion in *Garvis v SATAWU (Minister For Safety & Security, Third Party)*' 2010 (6) SA 280 (WCC) (2011) 27 *South African Journal On Human Rights* 346. The Constitutional Court has retained, for itself, the right to intervene when it believes such disruptions pose an imminent and pronounced danger to the general welfare of the commonweal. Such a danger revealed itself quite recently in *Glenister v President of the Republic of South Africa.* [2011] ZACC 6, 2011 (3) SA 347 (CC), 2011 (7) BCLR 651 (CC). The failure to provide adequately independent security services compromises the state's ability to ensure governance under the rule of law and protection, in terms of s 7(2), of those fundamental rights necessary to secure our democracy. In one of its most dramatic statement regarding South Africa's crony capitalist order, the Court suggests that this abrogation of our social contract reflects a more general failure to protect the security, safety and pursuit of happiness of most South Africans. The Marikana massacre of some 35 striking miners by the police nearly a year later in 2012 bears out the Court's (and Public Protector's and Auditor General's) concern about an inadequately trained, poorly supervised and corrupt police force. According to some government officials, the police force lacks a functional chain of command. Officers cannot issue instructions to the rank and file and expect them to be followed. (Conversation with Steven Sachs regarding the Johannesburg Metropolitan Police Department, 1 October 2012). See also *South African Association of Personal Injury Lawyers v Heath* 2001 (1) SA 883 (CC), 2001 (1) BCLR 77 (CC) at para 4 ('Corruption and maladministration are inconsistent with the rule of law and the fundamental values of our Constitution ... If allowed to go unchecked and unpunished they will pose a serious threat to our democratic state.') What all of these cases share in common is the fear of a Hobbesian war of all against all.

50. *Occupiers of 51 Olivia Road, Berea Township and 197 Main Street Johannesburg v City of Johannesburg & others*; [2008] ZACC 1, 2008 (3) SA 208 (CC), 2008 (5) BCLR 475 (CC)('*Occupiers*').
51. Ibid at para 16.
52. Ibid at para 15.
53. Ibid at para 19.
54. Ibid at para 14.
55. Ibid at para 20.
56. [2009] ZACC 16, 2010 (3) SA 454 (CC), 2009 (9) BCLR 847 (CC)(*'Joe Slovo')*.
57. *City of Johannesburg Metropolitan Municipality v Blue Moonlight Properties 39 (Pty) Ltd & Another* [2011] ZACC 33, 2012 (2) SA 104 (CC), 2012 (2) BCLR 150 (CC).
58. Parliament's consistent under-funding of Chapter 9 Institutions and an executive policy of malign neglect make effective operation of these institutions difficult, if not impossible. See H Corder, S Jagwanth & F Soltau 'Report on Parliamentary Oversight and Accountability' Report to the Speaker of the National Assembly (1999), available at www.pmg.org.za/docs/2001/viewminute.php?id=811 (accessed 10 January 2005)('Corder Report'). Corder, Jagwanth and Soltau write that: 'In their submissions to us, many constitutional institutions have also pointed out that the present arrangement may result in a very low priority being given to constitutional institutions as government departments may be slow in recognising the interests of an institution which does not form part of the core business of the department. The very direct control by the executive of constitutional institutions can have a devastating

effect on the independence and credibility of these offices. ... In the first place, to make institutions dependent on budget allocations received through the very departments that they are required to monitor is not desirable. Secondly, these institutions must be seen by the public to be independent and free of the possibility of influence or pressure by the executive branch of the government. Approval by the executive of budgets, or other issues such as staffing, is thus inconsistent with independence, as well as the need to be perceived as independent by the public when dealing with their cases. This executive power could render impotent state institutions supporting constitutional democracy through the potential denial of both financial and human resources. Furthermore, the special constitutional features of these institutions are not recognised as executive priorities are set. 'Corder Report' (supra) at paras 7.2 and 7.2.1. The Corder Report suggests that, at a minimum, the budget of each Chapter 9 Institution be subject to a separate vote – a vote distinct from that for the budget for the department with line authority, and a vote distinct from that for the budget of other Chapter 9 Institutions. Ibid at para 7.3. To meet other constitutional imperatives, the Corder Report advocates the passage of legislation – an Accountability and Independence of Constitutional Institutions Act – and the creation of a parliamentary oversight committee – a Standing Committee on Constitutional Institutions. Ibid at paras 1.1, 7.3, 7.4, 8. Parliament has not acted on any of the Corder Report recommendations. Other Chapter 9 Institutions have noted this failure to act with dismay. See B Pityana 'South African Human Rights Commission Presentation to the Justice Portfolio Committee – Budget Review and Programmes 2001/2002' (8 June 2001), available at http://www.sahrc.gov.za (accessed on 11 January 2005). Chairperson Pityana writes: 'After five years of operations, it is very discouraging to have to report that questions about the independence of the Commission have not been resolved. ... National Treasury continues to relate to the Commission through the Justice Department. This means that we have no direct means of having queries and problems resolved. ... Since inception, the Commission has constantly raised concerns about the manner in which its budget was set. We pointed out ad nauseum that at no stage was there a proper assessment of the mandate of the Commission and the appropriate level of resources necessary to execute the mandate.' Ibid at 4-5. For more on the under-funding of Chapter 9 Institutions, generally, and the under-funding of the Commission for the Promotion and Protection of the Rights of Cultural, Religious and Linguistic Communities, in particular, see S Woolman & J Soweto-Aullo 'Commission for the Promotion and Protection of the Rights of Cultural, Religious and Linguistic Communities' in S Woolman & M Bishop (eds) *Constitutional Law of South Africa* (2nd Edition, OS, March 2005) Chapter 24F. Such under-funding is one of the rate-limiting factors with respect to experimental constitutionalism in South Africa.

59. PAA s 1 defines 'the supreme audit institution of the Republic' as 'the institution which, however designated, constituted or organized, exercises by virtue of the law of a country, the highest public auditing function of that country'. Public Audit Act 25 of 2004.

60. See FC s 188. Unlike most of the other Chapter 9 Institutions, the unique legislative environment within which the Auditor-General operates makes this institution the most likely to retain its independence and to discharge its responsibility to ensure that our government fulfils its mandate to operate in an accountable, transparent and equitable manner. Whilst the breadth of its investigatory powers may distinguish the Auditor-General from other Chapter 9 Institutions, the most unique feature of the Auditor-General is its fiscal independence. The Auditor-General's ability to generate significant revenue streams from fees charged for audit services ensures that it has the money necessary to discharge its constitutional duties. These financial resources immunize the Auditor-General from some of the budgetary pressures that have undermined the independence of other Chapter 9 Institutions. See PAA s 36; Office of the Auditor-General *Activity Report for 2003– 2004* RP 211/2004 (2005)('*Activity Report*') 11. However, the fiscal independence promised by these fees is only as good as the ability or the willingness of the audited entitees to make good. Local government has been notorious for its failure to pay its statutorily required fees. See L Loxton 'Fakie Seeks R100m from Municipalities' *Business Report* (12 March 2003).

61. See, eg, *Lebowa Mineral Trust v Lebowa Granite (Pty) Ltd* 2002 (3) SA 30 (T)(Enabling legislation for Trust requires annual audit by Auditor-General and tabling of report before the legislature); *Esack No & Another v Commission on Gender Equality* 2001 (1) SA 1299 (W), 2000 (7) BCLR 737 (W)(Commission transactions subject to audit by Auditor-General); *New National Party of South Africa v Government of the Republic of South Africa* 1999 (3) SA 191 (CC), 1999 (5) BCLR 489 (CC) at para 77 (Court notes that the Independent Electoral 'Commission's necessary expenditure is to be defrayed out of money appropriated by Parliament ... and its records are to be audited by the Auditor-General. Comprehensive reporting duties are imposed on the Commission and in particular it is required annually to submit to Parliament ... an audited statement on income and expenditure and a report in regard to its functions, activities and affairs in respect of such financial year.') See also I Rautenbach & E Malherbe *Constitutional Law* (2002) 212.
62. The lack of a meaningful distinction between legislative authority and executive authority in our parliamentary democracy places severe constraints on Parliament's oversight capacity.
63. See *Rail Commuter Action Group & Others v Transet Ltd t/a Metrorail & Others* 2005 (2) SA 359 (CC), 2005 (4) BCLR 301 (CC) at para 72 ('Accountability of those exercising public power is one of the founding values of our Constitution and its importance is repeatedly asserted in the Constitution.' The Court cites FC ss 1, 41(1) and 195(1)(f) in support of this proposition.) See also *South African Association of Personal Injury Lawyers v Heath* 2001 (1) SA 883 (CC), 2001 (1) BCLR 77 (CC) at para 4 ('Corruption and maladministration are inconsistent with the rule of law and the fundamental values of our Constitution ... If allowed to go unchecked and unpunished they will pose a serious threat to our democratic state.')
64. *President of the Republic of South Africa v South African Rugby Football Union* 2000 (1) SA 1 (CC), 1999 (10) BCLR 1059 (CC) at para 133.
65. See Office of the Auditor-General *Activity Report for 2003– 2004* RP 211/2004 (2005) 23 (*'Activity Report'*)('Forensic auditing is an independent process aimed at preventing or detecting economic crime in the public sector. The process mainly comprises an objective assessment of the measures instituted by accounting officers and other relevant role players to prevent and detect economic crime, but it can also include economic crime investigations when this is appropriate and seems necessary ... [T]he term "economic crime" is used to describe various crime categories, including fraud, forgery, theft and other contraventions of applicable statutes (e.g. corruption).')
66. The term 'corruption' here is to be broadly construed. As Sole notes, '[c]orruption may vary from the clearly illegal – such as fraud – to more subtle forms of unethical rent-seeking, patronage and abuses of power that may be just as damaging to the social fabric of a nation.' S Sole 'The State of Corruption and Accountability' in J Daniel, R Southall & J Lutchman (eds) *State of the Nation: South Africa 2004 - 2005* (2005) 86. Sole suggests the following definition – one that fits the broad brief of the Auditor-General's Office: 'Corruption is the wilful subversion (or attempted subversion) of a due decision-making process with regard to the allocation of any benefit.' Ibid at 87. See, generally, J Hyslop 'Political Corruption: Before and After Apartheid' *Conference on State and Society in South Africa* (University of the Witwatersrand 2004) 17 ('[G]overnment policy [has] encouraged rent-seeking behaviour by black entrepreneurs through the economic preferences they were given through a whole gamut of policies, especially those relating to the awarding of state contracting and corporate ownership. The tendency of such policies [is] to create a climate in which the line between legal forms of rent-seeking and outright corruption and cronyism [is] ... blurred.') Nothing much has changed in the intervening seven years. See S Woolman 'Security Services' in S Woolman & M Bishop (eds) *Constitutional Law of South Africa* (2nd Edition, RS3, May 2011) Chapter 23B (Covers the investigations of the police for this kind of malfeasance undertaken by the Public Protector, the Auditor General and the Special Investigations Units during 2009, 2010 and 2011.)
67. See *Minister of Local Government and Land Tenure & Another v Sizwe Development & Others: In re Sizwe Development v Flagstaff Municipality* 1991 (1) SA 677, 678–679 (Tk).

68. *Office of the Auditor-General Report on the Financial Statements of the Provincial Administration of the Northern Cape* (31 March 1998) 7.

69. The Auditor-General in its *Report on the Financial Statements of the Provincial Administration of the Northern Cape* found that only 1 of 17 provincial departments warranted an unqualified financial audit report – 7 were qualified and 9 had disclaimers. These findings stood as a scathing indictment of provincial administration and raise serious doubts about the capacity of current personnel asked to carry out extant policy. Ibid at 9 – 19. Provinces (and municipalities) brought under national administration have increased over the past decade, through 2011, for this very reason. Such reports remain the norm. The reasons for the qualifications ranged from 'limited or no audit performed, resulting in a disclaimer of opinion or adverse opinion; liabilities and creditors that could not be verified; loans, debtors and investments that were either misstated, or of which the recovery was doubtful; assets, including stock, stores and inventory, that could not be verified; misstatement of income; irregularities in disclosing expenditure; unacceptable financial statements for trading accounts.' Office of the Auditor-General *General Report for 1999 – 2000* RP 75/2000 (2001) 15 ('*General Report 2000*') 3, 15–21. The national departments fared even more poorly with respect to compliance audits: over 57% of national departments received qualified reports because of 'serious shortcomings in internal checking and control; non-compliance with other prescripts, including legislation and Treasury regulations; unauthorised expenditure that was incurred; insufficient control over personnel expenditure; and serious deficiencies in provisioning administration.' Ibid at 4, 22–30. The financial state of provincial government and local government is still abysmal. So few adequate controls exist at the provincial level that the Auditor-General could not issue a report on the 1999–2000 fiscal year. He was obliged to limit his assessments to completed audits from the previous financial year. Even with respect to these audits, the majority had to be qualified because internal departmental audits were largely unreliable and asset registers were either non-existent or incomplete. *General Report 2000* (supra) at 6, 36–45. See also T Keenan 'Auditor-General: Fighting Fraud with the Best of Them' *Finance Week* (12 July 2002) 16. Unfortunately, the position of municipalities has weakened even further. *Only 7 municipalities in the entire country received unqualified audits in 2011.*

70. Experts ranked the Auditor-General second, after the Special Investigating Unit, with respect to their perceived success in combating official corruption. See L Camerer *Corruption in South Africa: Results of an Expert Panel Survey Institute for Security Studies* Monograph 65 (2001) Chapter 6 ('A significant proportion (48%) of the respondents saw the office of the Auditor-General as effective in fighting corruption.')

71. See *Mthembi-Mahanyele v Mail & Guardian Ltd & Another* 2004 (6) SA 329 (SCA), 2004 (11) BCLR 1182 (SCA)(Auditor-General's report of irregularities in tender for housing contract and a call for a commission of inquiry into improper benefits bestowed upon friends of the Minister supported Court's finding that published criticism of the appellant was reasonable under the circumstance and thus not defamatory); *Young v Shaikh* 2004 (3) SA 46 (C)(Arms deal report by the Auditor-General, the Public Protector, and the Director of Public Prosecutions led to accusations, in the media, of corruption. Court finds accusations – made by the defendant – based in part on the report, but otherwise not fully corroborated, to be defamatory.) See also *Kruger v Johnnic Publishing (Pty) Ltd & Another* 2004 (4) SA 306 (T)(Findings by Auditor-General of mismanagement and irregularities at a school led to allegations of corruption that prompted an ultimately unsuccessful suit for defamation.) As this book goes to print, in 2013, President Zuma – a thus far acquitted suspect in arms deal corruption – has felt sufficient pressure from potential/impending 'new' court review of the arms deal to call for a special investigation.

72. Yearly criticism of the South African Revenue Service ('SARS') by the Auditor-General in annual reports tabled before SCOPA ultimately led SARS to overhaul its internal auditing systems and to procure the technology necessary to manage its assets. The tabling of an unqualified financial audit of SARS before SCOPA was hailed by a SARS commissioner, Pravin Gordan, as a clear indication

that SARS is a 'service organization that handles taxpayers' money efficiently.' L Loxton 'Gordhan Delighted with SARS Clean Bill of Health' *Business Report* (24 September 2004).

73. After receiving disclaimers in two consecutive years by the Auditor-General in reports to Parliament, and in the face of mounting evidence that the Unemployment Insurance Fund had failed to comply with the PFMA, the Minister of Labour committed himself to the appointment of managers who would ensure future compliance with the PFMA. See C Terrblanche 'Minister under Pressure over UIF' *The Mercury* (20 September 2004). Similarly, a forensic audit by the Auditor-General that revealed millions of rands in losses at Transnet due to an irregular scrap metal contract that had by-passed normal procurement procedures was hailed by SCOPA – which had called for the investigation – as evidence that corruption could be effectively rooted out of government. See 'Audit Finds Transnet Lost Millions through Irregular Scrap Metal Deal' *Business Report* (18 July 2003).

74. See *Ritchie & Another v Government, Northern Cape, & Others* 2004 (2) SA 584 (NC) at paras 21–23 (State's decision to fund the private defamation actions of public officials was an internal provincial government matter not susceptible of review by the courts, and that the matter fell within the domain of the Auditor-General for a determination as to whether the expenditure had been authorized.)

75. [2011] ZACC 6, 2011 (3) SA 347 (CC), 2011 (7) BCLR 651 (CC).

76. The Office of the Auditor-General has been quite critical of the government's lassitude with respect to the Office's reports of egregious, and often wilful, maladministration by national and provincial departments, municipalities and public entities: 'The extent to which audit information effectively contributes toward accountability and transparency not only depends on the quality of the information provided in the various audit reports. It is also critically dependent on the success with which such information is further processed and the response it evokes in the concluding phase of the accountability process. In this respect the role of the public accounts committee is vital. ... The Standing Committee on Public Accounts (SCOPA) is the mechanism through which the National Assembly exercises oversight over the receipt and expenditure of public money. The extent to which the committee appreciates the issues raised in the respective audit reports and pursues them through effective oversight practices will determine whether appropriate and sufficient pressure will be brought to bear on the various accountable authorities. ... The committee also did not always succeed in following up unresolved matters. Given the reconsideration of roles and processes, to a large extent brought about by the Public Finance Management Act, it may be prudent to examine the weaknesses of SCOPA's post-review processes in order to ensure that its recommendations have the desired impact on financial management in the public sector at national level. As it will be in the interests of accountability and useful for the committee and the public, and given the lack of resources of the committee, I shall in future report periodically on the status of implementation of the committee's recommendations. This is in line with international practice.' Office of the Auditor-General *General Report of the Auditor-General: Year Ended 31 March 2000* (2001) 10. Some reports in the media suggest that that SCOPA's post-review process is improving as a result of the pressure applied by the Auditor-General. See L Loxton 'Gordhan Delighted with SARS Clean Bill of Health' *Business Report* (24 September 2004)(After years of qualified reports, and criticism from SCOPA, SARS received an unqualified financial audit.) The United Nations Report on Drugs and Crime underwrites the Auditor-General's scepticism about the capacity of Parliament to rein in errant members of the executive and officials in the state apparatus. See United Nations *Drugs and Crime: Country Corruption Assessment Report on South Africa* (2003)('*UN Corruption Report*'), available at http://www.info.gov.za/reports/2003/corruption.pdf (accessed on 5 November 2005)('Members of Parliament, who are aware of corruption within the ranks, feel they are supposed to act but, all too often, when a corrupt official is exposed, party discipline is imposed.')

77. Unfortunately such hopes have been undercut by external assessments of the South African government to solve the many problems of governance that beset the country and address the ravages of apartheid that remain with us today. In 2012, Moody's downgraded South Africa to Baal, and our sovereign debt to BBB, just two grades above junk status: the first downgrade since the

inception of the democratic era. Standard and Poor's downgrad followed not long thereafter. These downgrades will make solution of the problems identified by Moody's and S & P even more difficult as South Africa will find it harder to secure the loans necessary to build infrastructure and to supply basic services. The World Bank further complicated matters when it declared the socio-economic landscape of South Africa 'unsustainable'. The World Bank Group 'South Africa: Focus on Inequality of Opportunity' (July 2012) (3) Africa Region Poverty Reduction and Economic Management 11. The truth as reflected in both the AG's reports and the World Bank's analysis, hurts. As it should.

78. See Auditor-General Report on a Performance Audit of Service Delivery at Police Stations and 10111 Call Centres at the South African Police Service 2007-2008 (March 2009)('A-G's Report') 2, available at http://www.agsa.co.za/audit-reports/SAR.aspx">http://www.agsa.co.za/audit-reports/SAR.aspx> (accessed on 10 April 2011). The Auditor-General's investigation took place during 2007 and 2008 and assessed the 'basic measures, processes or systems that should be in place at police stations and the police emergency phone line 10111'. By 'basic measure", the Auditor-General's report means sector policing, vehicle management, training, community service centres, and the provision of bullet-proof vests. The report concluded that the existing practices in all of these areas fell short of the standards required by the Constitution. The short-falls ranged from the lack of an approved policy for sector policing to inadequate training and inadequate recording of cases of domestic violence. The Auditor-General found that many of these shortfalls are a result of inadequate training, a lack of funds, or both. The Auditor-General concluded that an underfunded, unskilled police force could not discharge its constitutional responsibility to protect the general population.

79. The Marikana Massacre of 16 August 2012, and the ongoing country-wide unrest in and around mining concessions and large commercial farms can hardly come as a surprise in light of these consistent warnings from the government itself.

80. See M Bishop & S Woolman 'Public Protector' in S Woolman & M Bishop (eds) *Constitutional Law of South Africa* (2nd Edition, OS, December 2005) Chapter 24A. This section is largely drawn from, and inspired by, our mutual collaboration. New material on the Public Protector is drawn from my recent work on the security services. See S Woolman 'Security Services' in S Woolman & M Bishop (eds) *Constitutional Law of South Africa* (2nd Edition, RS3, May 2011) Chapter 23B.

81. The Public Protector was originally established in terms of the Constitution of the Republic of South Africa, Act 200 of 1993 ('Interim Constitution' or 'IC') ss 100 – 114. FC ss 182 reads: (1) The Public Protector has the power as regulated by national legislation (a) to investigate any conduct in state affairs, or in the public administration in any sphere of government, that is alleged or suspected to be improper or to result in any impropriety or prejudice; (b) to report on that conduct; and (c) to take appropriate remedial action. (2) The Public Protector has the additional powers and functions prescribed by national legislation. (3) The Public Protector may not investigate court decisions. (4) The Public Protector must be accessible to all persons and communities. (5) Any report issued by the Public Protector must be open to the public unless exceptional circumstances, to be determined in terms of national legislation, require that a report be kept confidential. See also *Ex Parte Chairperson of the Constitutional Assembly In Re: Certification of the Constitution of the Republic of South Africa, 1996* 1996 (4) SA 744 (CC), 1996 (10) BCLR 1253 (CC)('*First Certification Judgment*') at para 161 ('The Public Protector is an office modelled on the institution of the ombudsman.'). See, further, M Oosting 'The Ombudsman and His Environment: A Global View' in L Reif (ed) *The International Ombudsman Anthology* (1999)('*Reif Anthology*') 5.

82. Ombudsman Act 118 of 1979.

83. Act 23 of 1994.

84. See S Owen 'The Ombudsman: Essential Elements and Common Challenges' in *Reif Anthology* (supra) at 51, 54–55. See also M Zacks 'Administrative Fairness in the Ombudsman Process' (1967 to 18987) 7 *The Ombudsman Journal* 55, 55 ('Complainants come to Ombudsmen for help to cut through red tape and to deal expeditiously with their concerns. If they wanted technical, legal arguments and approaches, one can say with some justification that they should hire a lawyer and go to court.')

85. See Owen (supra) at 53 (Ombudsmen enable politicians to address failures in the state bureaucracy.)
86. *Special Investigating Unit v Ngcinwana & Another* 2001 (4) BCLR 411, 413B (E)(When interpreting the competence of tribunals under the Special Investigating Units and Special Tribunals Act 74 of 1996 with respect to the investigation of maladministration and corruption, the court held that '[c]onstitutional priority would thus seem to lie with the institution of the Public Protector. Any interpretation of the Act's purposes must pay heed to that reality.')
87. See Owen (supra) at 52; Oosting (supra) at 10.
88. Owen (supra) at 52.
89. See Oosting (supra) at 12 ('[T]he mobilisation of shame can constitute a powerful weapon in his arsenal.')
90. Ibid ('In this world, the sweet voice of reason – a well-formulated argument, based on meticulous research – does not always fall on attentive ears. Political support for the ombudsman is therefore essential.')
91. Public Protector *Against the Rules: Report of the Public Protector in terms of Section 182(1) of the Constitution of the Republic of South Africa, 1996 and Section 8(1) of the Public Protector Act, 1994 on an Investigation into Complaints and Allegations of Maladministration, Improper and Unlawful Conduct by the Department of Public Works and the South African Police Service relating to the Leasing of Office Accommodation in Pretoria* (2011) Report Number 33 of 2010/2011, available at http://www.info.gov.za/view/DownloadFileAction?id=142293 (accessed on 6 May 2011)('*Against the Rules*').
92. T Madonsela *Address by the Public Protector During a Media Briefing on the Release of the SAPS Lease Report* (22 February 2011) available at http://www.pprotect.org/media_gallery/2011/23022011_sp.asp (accessed on 6 May 2011).
93. Ibid.
94. Ibid.
95. Ibid.
96. J Klaaren 'South African Human Rights Commission' in S Woolman & M Bishop (eds) *Constitutional Law of South Africa* (2nd Edition, OS, December 2005) Chapter 24C. See also J Klaaren 'A Second Look at the South African Human Rights Commission, Access to Information, and the Promotion of Socio-Economic Rights' (2005) 27 *Human Rights Quarterly* 539.
97. FC s 181, read together with FC ss 193 and 194, provide the general constitutional framework for (almost) all Chapter 9 Institutions. Although these provisions do not establish ICASA, Chapter Nine does govern the Independent Authority to Regulate Broadcasting. See J White-Limpitlaw 'Independent Communications Authority of South Africa' in S Woolman & M Bishop (eds) *Constitutional Law of South Africa* (2nd Edition, OS, March 2005) Chapter 24E (Noting that the independent authority to regulate broadcasting is not listed in FC s 181(1).)
98. J Klaaren 'South African Human Rights Commission' (supra) citing C Roederer 'Founding Provisions' in S Woolman & M Bishop (eds) *Constitutional Law of South Africa* (2nd Edition, OS, December 2005) Chapter 13. See also M Pieterse 'Coming to Terms with Judicial Enforcement of Socio-Economic Rights' (2004) 20 *South African Journal on Human Rights* 383; J Klaaren 'Structures of Government and the 1996 Constitution: Putting Democracy Back into Human Rights' (1997) 13 *South African Journal on Human Rights* 3.
99. The Chapter 9 Institutions, much like the three primary branches of government, undertake investigations into matters of public interest and issue reports on their findings. The investigations undertaken by the Commission reflect proactive enforcement of human rights. See, eg, SAHRC 'Report on the Public Hearings into the Use of Boom Gates and Road Closures' available at http://www.sahrc.org.za/sahrc_cms/publish/article_132.shtml (accessed on 8 February 2006); SAHRC 'Report on the Public Hearings into Equality and Voluntary Associations' (July 2006) available at http://www.sahrc.org.za/sahrc_cms/publis. See also K Govender 'The South African Human Rights Commission' in P Andrews & S Ellmann (eds) *The Post-Apartheid Constitutions: Perspectives on South Africa's Basic Law* (2001) 571, 584–586. Perhaps the most surprising outcome of all is the

extent to which other branches of government and private parties treat these findings as binding. Of equal import is the SAHRC's capacity for adjudication and litigation. With respect to its powers of adjudication, a three member panel chaired by an SAHRC Commissioner held that the chanting of a slogan 'kill the farmer, kill the boer' did, indeed, amount to hate speech. *Freedom Front v South African Human Rights Commission* 2003 (11) BCLR 1283 (SAHRC). With respect to its powers of litigation, the SAHRC has been an amicus or party in numerous cases. See eg, *Welkom High School & Another v Head, Department of Education, Free State Province, & Another* 2011 (4) SA 531 (FB); *Director of Public Prosecutions, Transvaal v Minister of Justice and Constitutional Development & Others* 2009 (4) SA 222 (CC); *Brümmer v Minister For Social Development & Others* 2009 (6) SA 323 (CC); *Bhe & Others v Magistrate, Khayelitsha & Others; Shibi v Sithole & Others; South African Human Rights Commission & Another v President of the Republic of South Africa* 2005 (1) SA 580 (CC), 2005 (1) BCLR 1 (CC); *Bekker & Another v Jika* 2002 (4) SA 508 (E), [2002] 1 All SA 156 (E); *S v Twala (South African Human Rights Commission intervening)* 2000 (1) SA 879 (CC), 2000 (1) BCLR 106 (CC), 1999 (2) SACR 622 (CC); *National Coalition for Gay & Lesbian Equality & Another v Minister of Justice* 1998 (12) BCLR 1517 (CC), [1998] 3 ALL SA 26 (W); *Minister of Justice v Ntuli* 1997 (3) SA 772 (CC), 1997 (6) BCLR 677 (CC); *Government of the Republic of South Africa v Grootboom & Others* 2001 (1) SA 46 (CC), 2000 (11) BCLR 1169 (CC)('*Grootboom*'). The SAHRC has even acted against a vacation resort that evicted a family accompanied by two black children. See 'Settlement of the Equality Court case against the Broederstroom Holiday Resort' available at http://www.sahrc.org.za/media (accessed 3 Februrary 2006). In the magistrate's court, the SAHRC won a case on behalf of a learner who was assaulted and subject to racist remarks. See 'Landmark Victory: Edgemead Race Case' available at http://www.sahrc.org.za/media (accessed 3 February 2006).

100. Govender 'SAHRC' (supra) at 572.

101. *New National Party of South Africa v Government of the Republic of South Africa & Others* 1999 (3) SA 191 (CC), 1999 (5) BCLR 489 (CC)('*New National Party*') at para 78.

102. Of the Chapter 9 Institution's 'shared' powers of constitutional interpretation, the Constitutional Court, in *S v Jordan*, wrote: 'In determining whether the discrimination is unfair, we pay particular regard to the affidavits and argument of the Gender Commission. It is there constitutional mandate to protect, develop, promote respect for and attain gender equality. This Court is of course not bound by the Commission's views but it should acknowledge its special constitutional role and its expertise. In the circumstances, its evidence and argument that [the legal provision at issue] is unfairly discriminatory on grounds of gender reinforces our conclusion.' 2002 (6) SA 642 (CC), 2002 (11) BCLR 1117 (CC) at para 70.

103. FC s 142.

104. FC s 143.

105. Ibid.

106. For more on the actual space for innovation afforded by the Final Constitution with respect to provincial constitutions, as well as the significant constraints the Final Constitution imposes upon provincial constitutions, see S Woolman 'Provincial Constitutions' in S Woolman & M Bishop (eds) *Constitutional Law of South Africa* (2nd Edition, OS, March 2005) Chapter 21. South Africa's nine provinces have only undertaken two serious attempts to promulgate a provincial constitution. The Western Cape ultimately succeeded. *Ex Parte Speaker of the Western Cape Provincial Legislature: in Re First Certification of the Constitution of the Western Cape* , 1997 (4) SA 795 (CC), 1997 (9) BCLR 1167 (CC) at para 15 ('[C]hapter 6 provides a complete blueprint for the regulation of government within provinces which provides adequately for the establishment and functioning of provincial legislatures and executive.' The first draft failed to meet Chapter 6's standards on three separate grounds. First, the geographic multi-member constituencies endorsed by the provincial constitution could neither be squared with the closed list proportional representation system found in the Final Constitution nor saved by the legislative structure exception found within FC s 143(1)(a). Second, the WC text's insistence that the Judge President (now Chief Justice) of the High Court of the Western Cape

perform certain ceremonial functions and administer various oaths of office was inconsistent with the Final Constitution's requirement that that the President (now Chief Justice) of the Constitutional Court discharge these same duties. Third, WC text s 46(3) did not simply restate the Final Constitution's bar on paid work by MECs: it went on to grant the provincial legislature the power to promulgate legislation governing the meaning of paid work. The Constitutional Court held that ethical concerns about unpaid work by MECs did not fall within FC s 143(1)(a)'s executive structure or procedure exception. The Constitutional Court then found that FC s 136(2) proscribed paid work by MECs, that 'paid work' could only have one meaning and that any debate over the meaning of 'paid work' would have to be decided by the courts. The WC text's assertion that the province could weigh in on the meaning of 'paid work' created the possibility that each province would arrive at a different conclusion about the meaning of 'paid work'. The Constitutional Court held that because 'paid work' under the Final Constitution could have only one meaning, any potential for deviation from that univocal – but still undetermined – definition created the conditions for inconsistency.) The Western Cape cured the defects of the first draft and succeeded the second time around. *Certification of the Amended Text of the Constitution of the Western Cape 1997* 1998 (1) SA 655 (CC), 1997 (12) BCLR 1653 (CC) ('Second Certification of the Constitution of the Province of the Western Cape'). For a brief account of the drafting history of the WC text, see D Brand 'The Western Cape Provincial Constitution' (2000) 31 *Rutgers Law Journal* 961. Kwa-Zulu Natal has failed in court and in the political arena. 1996 (4) SA 1098 (CC), 1996 (11) BCLR 1419 (CC) at para 4 ('Certification of the Constitution of the Province of KwaZulu-Natal'). At the time of writing 8 of 9 provinces are currently under ANC control. A true test of provincial autonomy – and perhaps of provincial constitution-making power – will only occur when provinces possess the political independence and the political will to test the centre. Kwa-Zulu Natal took another stab at drafting a provincial constitution. Three drafts – by the ANC, the IFP and the DA – were tabled. See Draft Constitution of Kwa-Zulu Natal, 2004, Kwa-Zulu Natal Provincial Gazette No 6300, Notice A (10 November 2004). The desire to accord some form of permanent recognition for the King appeared to drive this project. Although the IFP has, historically, identified itself as the party of the Zulu people, the ANC has maintained close political ties with the reigning King. Thus both parties had a horse in this race. Nothing came of it. Interview with Professor W Freedman, University of Kwa-Zulu Natal (15 March 2005). I am indebted to Professor Freedman for his patient explanation of KZN constitutional politics.

107. See S Woolman 'Language, Power and the Margin: Eliot's Philosophy of Language, Wittgenstein on Following a Rule & Statutory Construction in *Thembekile Mankayi v Anglogold Ashanti Limited* (2012) 128 *South African Law Journal* 434.

108. See B Ackerman *We The People* (1991). However, Ackerman's subsequent work with James Fishkin, *Deliberation Day* (2005) appears to over-valorize the capacity of a limited period of discussion to meaningfully alter views. At this particular historical moment, crisis would seem to be a far more powerful engine for change than deliberation. As of 2012, the shock to the world's capitalist system post-2008 has yet to ignite substantial reform. It may have to get worse before it gets better. The Great Depression – Ackermann's second moment – seems to suggest as much. South Africa has yet to experience such a crisis – though all the conditions for one certainly exist. Violent mining sector strikes and labour unrest on farms in 2012 may work to consolidate existing, widespread discontent regarding the large scale failure to deliver basic services across the country into social movements that force a 'New Deal' between the ANC government, business, unions and the rest of the denizens of South Africa. In the short term, however, the three parties who made the deal in the 1980s that set South Africa 'free' – the ANC, big business and the unions – are likely to arrive at a new via media that enables them to continue to control the economic and political levers of power.

109. See M Bishop 'Remedies' in S Woolman & M Bishop (eds) *Constitutional Law of South Africa* (2nd Edition, OS, October 2008) Chapter 9.

110. See O Fiss 'The Supreme Court 1978 Term Foreword: Forms of Justice' 93 *Harvard Law Review* 1, 2 (1979).
111. Ibid at 28. See also C Diver 'The Judge as Political Powerbroker: Superintending Structural Change in Public Institutions' (1979) 65 *Virginia Law Review* 43, 82. For more skeptical views of court supervision, see DL Horowitz 'Decreeing Organizational Change: Judicial Supervision of Public Institutions' (1983) *Duke Law Journal* 1265. 1267; M Schlanger 'Beyond the Hero Judge: Institution Reform Litigation as Litigation' (1999) 97 *Michigan Law Review* 1994.
112. See S Budlender 'Making Socio-Economic Rights Effective: Judicial Remedies for Breaches of the State's Duty to Respect, Protect, Promote and Fulfil Socio-Economic Rights' (2002)(LLB dissertation, manuscript on file with author).
113. See J Mansbridge 'A Deliberative Theory of Interest Representation' in MP Petracca (ed) (1992) *The Politics of Interests: Interest Groups Transformed* 37, 46.
114. See A Fung and EO Wright 'Deepening Democracy: Innovations in Empowered Participatory Governance' (1998) 29(1) *Science & Society* 5, 32 (Suggests that people may become more reasonable and reflexive after 'seeing that cooperation mediated through reasonable deliberation yields benefits not accessible through adversarial methods.')
115. It is worth noting that US experimental constitutionalists are less interested in standard structural injunctions – as means of eliciting information and securing greater, reflexive, normative value – and more intent at uncovering specialist courts or reform movements that are capable of enhanced pooling of information and of more significant adaptive behaviour over time. See Chapter 4 above.
116. *August v Electoral Commission* 1999 (3) SA 1 (CC), 1999 (4) BCLR 363 (CC)('*August*').
117. The first mention of the use of structural interdicts appeared in *Pretoria City Council v Walker* 1998 (2) SA 363 (CC), 1998 (3) BCLR 257 (CC)('*Walker*') at para 96 (my emphasis))('Instead of withholding amounts lawfully owing by him to the council, [Mr Walker] could, for instance, have applied to an appropriate court for a declaration of rights or a mandamus in order to vindicate the breach of his [right to equality]. By means of such an order the council could have been compelled to take appropriate steps as soon as possible to eliminate the unfair differentiation and to report back to the court in question. *The court would then have been in a position to give such further ancillary orders or directions as might have been necessary to ensure the proper execution of its order.*')
118. Cf *Minister of Health & Others v Treatment Action Campaign & Others (No 2)* 2002 (5) SA 721 (CC) at paras 96 – 114; *Sibiya & Others v Director of Public Prosecutions, Johannesburg, & Others* 2005 (5) SA 315 (CC); 2005 (8) BCLR 812; 2006 (1) SACR 220 (CC).
119. *August* (supra) at paras 38 – 39.
120. As Steven Budlender notes, the *August* Court was motivated by the fact that 'just two months remained from the time of judgment to the time of the election, and was concerned that if there were any further dispute or uncertainty, the only way to allow prisoners to vote would be to delay the election. The court therefore very sensibly took matters into its own hands, demanding a timetable of arrangements from the Electoral Commission.' Budlender (supra) at 64.
121. 2005 (3) SA 280 (CC), 2004 (5) BCLR 445 (CC)('*NICRO*').
122. 2006 (4) SA 114 (C)('*Kiliko*').
123. Section 21 of the Refugees Act 130 of 1998 provides that an application for asylum must be made to a refugee reception officer at any refugee reception office. Five such offices exist throughout the country. The applicants contended in their own interest and in the public interest that the Western Cape refugee reception office was not providing them with a proper opportunity to apply for asylum. It permitted no more than 20 applicants to enter the office to apply for asylum on any given day. Vast numbers of asylum-seekers were effectively barred from applying for apply for asylum.
124. *Kiliko* (supra) at para 32. Van Reenen J relied heavily on the Cape High Court judgment in *Rail Commuters Action Group and Others v Transnet Ltd t/a Metrorail and Others (No 1).* But as Steven Budlender has pointed out, Van Reenen J appears to have overlooked the fact that the structural interdict granted by the Cape High Court in *Metrorail* was overturned by the Constitutional Court

in *Rail Commuters Action Group and Others v Transnet Ltd t/a Metrorail and Others.* 2005 (2) SA 359 (CC), 2005 (4) BCLR 301 (CC) at para 109. 'While any number of factors could justify the granting of a structural interdict ... and may well have justified the granting of such an order in the *Kiliko* case, it is necessary for courts to enunciate these factors when determining whether such an order is indeed 'necessary'.' Budlender (supra) at 75.

125. *Centre for Child Law & Others v MEC for Education, Gauteng, & Others* 2008 (1) SA 223 CT) ('*Centre for Child Law*').
126. *Centre for Child Law* (supra) at 3–4.
127. Ibid at 11. In a theme already engaged in Chapter 4, the under-capacity of the current public administration in South Africa practically begs for greater court intervention. The common critique that courts cannot handle polycentric social disputes does little work under conditions that one might describe as polity (as opposed to market) failure. A friend in the office of the President calls it the 15% problem. That is, since only 15% of the bureaucrats operate effectively the government finds it difficult to follow through on creative policy solutions to endemic problems.
128. 2005 (5) SA 315 (CC), 2005 (8) BCLR 812 (CC)('*Sibiya I*'). The death penalty had been abolished a decade earlier in *S v Makwanyane & Another* 1995 (3) SA 391 (CC), 1995 (6) BCLR 665 (CC).
129. *Sibiya & Others v DPP, Johannesburg High Court & Others* 2006 (2) BCLR 293 (CC)('*Sibiya III*') at para 6.
130. Bishop 'Remedies' (supra) at Chapter9, 9-185.
131. Bishop 'Remedies' (supra) at Chapter9, 9-185 citing *Sibiya II* at para 22.
132. Bishop 'Remedies' (supra) at Chapter9, 9-186.
133. K Hofmeyr 'Rules and Procedure in Constitutional Matters' in S Woolman & M Bishop (eds) *Constitutional Law of South Afriça* (2nd Edition, OS, March 2007) Chapter 5. The above discussion relies heavily upon Hofmeyr's superb analysis. For some more recent apposite cases, see *S v Marais* 2011 (1) SA 502 (CC), 2010 (12) BCLR 1223 (CC), 2010 (2) SACR 606 (CC); *Glenister v President of the Republic of South Africa & Others* [2011] ZACC 6, 2011 (3) SA 347 (CC), 2011 (7) BCLR 651 (CC); *Minister of Home Affairs & Another v Fourie & Another; Lesbian and Gay Equality Project & Others v Minister of Home Affairs & Others* 2006 (1) SA 524 (CC), 2006 (3) BCLR 355 (CC) See also *Bhe and Others v Magistrate, Khayelitsha, and Others (Commission for Gender Equality as Amicus Curiae)* 2005 (1) SA 580 (CC), 2005 (1) BCLR 1 (CC); *Shibi v Sithole and Others; South African Human Rights Commission and Another v President of The Republic of South Africa and Another* 2005 (1) SA 580 (CC); *Mkontwana v Nelson Mandela Metropolitan Municipality and Another; Bissett and Others v Buffalo City Municipality and Others; Transfer Rights Action Campaign and Others v MEC, Local Government and Housing, Gauteng, and Others (KwaZulu-Natal Law Society and Msunduzi Municipality as Amici Curiae)* 2005 (1) SA 530 (CC), 2005 (2) BCLR 150 (CC). For a more up-to-date treatment of the subject see K Hofmeyr & N Ferriera 'Rules and Procedures in Constitutional Matters' in S Woolman & M Bishop (eds) *Constitutional Law of South Africa* (2nd Edition, RS 6, Forthcoming) Chapter 5.
134. See *Bhe* (supra) at para 33.
135. See *Minister of Home Affairs & Another v Fourie & Another; Lesbian and Gay Equality Project & Others v Minister of Home Affairs & Others* 2006 (1) SA 524 (CC), 2006 (3) BCLR 355 (CC) at para 42. However, where the issues raised in the application for direct access are quite complex, the Court will tend to privilege the value of another court's views on the topic over the interests of the applicant in securing direct access. In *Mkontwana*, the Court granted the WLD applicants direct access in relation to the constitutionality of section 118(1) of the Local Government: Municipal Systems Act 32 of 2000. *Mkontwana v Nelson Mandela Metropolitan Municipality and Another; Bissett and Others v Buffalo City Municipality and Others; Transfer Rights Action Campaign and Others v MEC, Local Government and Housing, Gauteng, and Others (KwaZulu-Natal Law Society and Msunduzi Municipality as Amici Curiae)* 2005 (1) SA 530 (CC), 2005 (2) BCLR 150 (CC)('*Mkontwana*'). However, it declined to grant the applicants direct access in relation to other aspects of their challenge. Ibid at para 14.

136. In terms of Rule 4(11), the Constitutional Court's Registrar refers an unrepresented party to the nearest office or officer of the Human Rights Commission, the Legal Aid board, a law clinic or such other appropriate body or institution that may be willing and in a position to assist such party.
137. See *De Kock v Minister of Water Affairs and Forestry* 2005 (12) BCLR 1183 (CC)('*De Kock*'); *Mnguni v Minister of Correctional Services* 2005 (12) BCLR 1187 (CC)('*Mnguni*').
138. *De Kock* (supra) at para 5; *Mnguni* (supra) at para 7.
139. The 2003 Rules' inclusion of a specific provision relating to the procedure to be adopted by parties seeking leave to intervene in proceedings before the Court marks a change from the position under the 1998 Rules. Although the Court has yet to interpret Rule 8 itself, the Court's previous case law on intervention, as well as the case law surrounding Rule 12 of the Uniform Rules of Court, provide a rough and ready guide about what to expect from the Court under Rule 8. See K Hofmeyr 'Rules and Procedure in Constitutional Matters' in S Woolman & M Bishop (eds) *Constitutional Law of South Africa* (2nd Edition, OS, February 2007) Chapter 5.
140. 2001 (3) SA 1151 (CC), 2001 (7) BCLR 652) (CC)('*Kyalami Ridge*').
141. Ibid at para 30.
142. 2003 (4) SA 1 (CC), 2003 (5) BCLR 476 (CC) at para 58.
143. 1996 (1) SA 984 (CC), 1996 (4) BCLR 1 (CC) at para 26. For more on the doctrine of objective unconstitutionality, see C Loots 'Standing, Ripeness & Mootness' in S Woolman & M Bishop (eds) *Constitutional Law of South Africa* (2nd Edition, OS, March 2005) Chapter 7; S Woolman 'Application' in S Woolman & M Bishop (eds) *Constitutional Law of South Africa* (2nd Edition, OS, March 2005) Chapter 31.
144. For more on the relationship between the doctrine of objective unconstitutionality and rights interpretation, see S Woolman & H Botha 'Limitations' in S Woolman & M Bishop (eds) *Constitutional Law of South Africa* (2nd Edition, OS, July 2006) Chapter 34.
145. The Court exercises enormous amounts of discretion with respect to direct access, legal aid referrals, intervenors and amici and uses that discretion to control the kinds of cases it hears. Such discretion, readily employed, invariably undercuts its commitment to objective unconstitutionality. The absence of a written record of this exercise of discretion, as both Marius Pieterse and Michael Bishop have pointed out, makes it difficult to assess the seriousness of the Court's invitation to non-state actors to approach it for relief. The real sting in Pieterse's critique is that a Court genuinely interested in adjudicating socio-economic rights would have heard more than four cases in its first ten years (at the time of our correspondence). E-mail correspondence with Michael Bishop (5 February 2006); E-mail correspondence with Marius Pieterse (15 February 2006). The Constitutional Court, over the past six years (2006 – 2012) has indeed taken socio-economic rights matters more seriously – hearing roughly four to five cases a year.
146. In *In Re Certain Amicus Curiae Applications: Minister of Health & Others v Treatment Action Campaign & Others*, the Constitutional Court discussed the particular duty which amici owe to the Court: 'In return for the privilege of participating in the proceedings without having to qualify as a party, an amicus has a special duty to the Court. That duty is to provide cogent and helpful submissions that assist the Court. The amicus must not repeat arguments already made but must raise new contentions; and generally these new contentions must be raised on the data already before the Court.' 2002 (5) SA 713 (CC) at para 5. For more on the rules governing amici, see G Budlender 'Amicus Curiae' in S Woolman & M Bishop (eds) *Constitutional Law of South Africa* (2nd Edition, OS, July 2006).
147. See, eg, *Bannatyne v Bannatyne (Commission for Gender Equality, as Amicus Curiae)* 2003 (2) SA 363 (CC), 2003 (2) BCLR 111 (CC) at para 3; *Moise v Greater Germiston Transitional Local Council: Minister of Justice and Constitutional Development Intervening (Women's Legal Centre as Amicus Curiae)* 2001 (4) SA 491 (CC), 2001 (8) BCLR 765 (CC) at para 4; *Minister of Defence v Potsane and Another; Legal Soldier (Pty) Ltd and Others v Minister of Defence and Others* 2002 (1) SA 1 (CC), 2001 (11) BCLR 1137 (CC) at para 9.

148. J Dugard 'Court of First Instance? Towards a Pro-Poor Jurisdiction for the South African Constitutional Court' (2006) 22 *South African Journal on Human Rights* 261 (Argues that the South African Constitutional Court has not functioned as an institutional voice for the poor because its jurisdictional requirements make access difficult if not impossible for indigent plaintiffs pressing fundamental rights claims – and suggests that this difficulty could be remedied if the Court made that greater use of its power to grant direct access.)
149. For the ur-text on constitutional costs upon which my views are entirely parasitic, see M Bishop 'Costs' in S Woolman & M Bishop (2nd Edition, RS2, September 2010) Chapter 6.
150. M Bishop 'Costs' (supra) at 6-1.
151. See *Bel Porto School Governing Body and Others v Premier, Western Cape, & Another* 2002 (3) SA 265 (CC), 2002 (9) BCLR 891 (CC)('*Bel Porto School Governing Body*') at para 132. *Motsepe v Commissioner for Inland Revenue* 1997 (2) SA 898 (CC), 1997 (6) BCLR 692 (CC)('*Motsepe*') at para 30; *Ex Parte Gauteng Provincual legislature: In re Dispute concerning the constitutionality of certain provision of the Gauteng School Education Bill* 1996 (3) SA 165 (CC), 1996 (4) BCLR 537 (CC) (*'Gauteng School Education Bill'*) at para 36. See also *Pretoria City Council v Walker* 1998 (2) SA 363 (CC), 1998 (3) BCLR 257 (CC) at para 98; *Oranje Vrystaatse Vereniging vir Staatsondersteunde & Another v Premier, Province of the Free State & Other* 1998 (6) BCLR 653 (CC) at para 4. However, where the successful respondent is a private individual, the Court will often order the applicant to pay the respondent's costs. For example, in *Omar v Government, RSA & Others*, the Constitutional Court found that although the applicant's challenge to the Domestic Violence Act was 'to a considerable extent ill-conceived', no costs order should be made in favour of the governmental entities defending the Act. 2006 (2) SA 289 (CC), 2006 (2) BCLR 253 (CC)('*Omar*'). At the same time, however, the *Omar* Court ordered the applicant to pay the costs of the third respondent – the applicant's ex-wife under Islamic law who had been obliged had to acquire various protection orders against the applicant in terms of the Domestic Violence Act. *Omar* (supra) at para 64.
152. See *Motsepe* (supra) at para 30; *SACCAWU v Irvin & Johnson Ltd (Seafoods Division Fish Processing)* 2000 (3) SA 705 (CC), 2000 (8) BCLR 886 (CC)('*SACCAWU*') at para 51; *Gauteng Education Bill* (supra) at para 36.
153. M Bishop 'Costs' (supra). Unsuccessful applicants who raise important constitutional issues will generally not be mulcted in costs. However, the Constitutional Court routinely awards costs to applicants who have successfully pressed constitutional challenges. See, eg, *Jaftha v Schoeman and Others; Van Rooyen v Stoltz & Others* 2005 (2) SA 140 (CC), 2005 (1) BCLR 78 (CC) at para 66; *Bannatyne v Bannatyne & Another* 2003 (2) SA 363 (CC), 2003 (2) BCLR 111 (CC) at para 41; *Larbi-Odam v Member of the Executive Council for Education, North-West Province* 1998 (1) SA 745 (CC), 1997 (12) BCLR 1655 (CC) at para 48; *Laugh It Off Promotions CC v SAB International (Finance) BV t/a Sabmark International* 2006 (1) SA 144 (CC), 2005 (8) BCLR 743 (CC) at para 68.
154. 2002 (4) SA 613 (CC), 2002 (7) BCLR 663 (CC)('*Walters*') at para 61.
155. 2003 (6) SA 21 (SCA)('*Afrox*').
156. For more on the difference between direct application and indirect application, and why the former must, as a logical matter, precede the latter, and why as a matter of clarity with respect to Court's jurisprudence, it should be accorded priority, see S Woolman 'The Amazing, Vanishing Bill of Rights' (2007) 124 *South African Law Journal* 742; S Woolman 'Application' in S Woolman & M Bishop (eds) *Constitutional Law of South Africa* (2nd Edition, OS, March 2005) Chapter 31.
157. See S Woolman & D Brand 'Is There a Constitution in This Courtroom? Constitutional Jurisdiction after *Walters* and *Afrox*' (2003) 18 *SA Public Law* 38.
158. At least one space remains within which to contest existing precedent. The *Afrox* Court states that High Courts will be able to deviate from SCA, AD and CC precedent with respect to how they understand such open-ended notions as boni mores and public interest. *Afrox* (supra) at para 28. A second line of attack may be open to the High Courts. Where the Supreme Court of Appeal has assiduously avoided the constitutionalization of an issue of law, then the Constitutional Court's

doctrines of legality, the unity of the law, constitutional supremacy and an objective normative value system suggests that the High Courts should have an opportunity to test such a rule of law against the basic law's dictates. See *S v Boesak* 2001 (1) SA 912 (CC), 2001 (1) SACR 1 (CC), 2001 (1) BCLR 36 (CC) at para 15 ('The development of, or the failure to develop, a common-law rule by the Supreme Court of Appeal may constitute a constitutional matter. This may occur if the Supreme Court of Appeal developed, or failed to develop, the rule under circumstances inconsistent with its obligation under s 39(2) of the Constitution or with some other right or principle of the Constitution. The application of a legal rule by the Supreme Court of Appeal may constitute a constitutional matter. This may occur if the application of a rule is inconsistent with some right or principle of the Constitution.')

159. While the constitutional structures for 'public participation in the process of law-making' seem to me to belong, more properly, here under the discussion of participatory bubbles, a reasonably compelling case can be made for the proposition that public participation in the process of law-making forms a part of a regime of shared constitutional interpretation. In the discussion of *Matatiele II* and *Doctors for Life* below, I emphasize the extent to which the Court was concerned with deepening democracy and creating space for citizens to address specific problems that have a direct bearing on their lives. In participatory bubble-speak, once a specific conflict has been resolved, the bubble bursts and legislators and citizens alike return to other matters that occupy them. But, as Marius Pieterse has made clear to me, there need not be such a neat cleavage between the immediate outcomes of participatory bubbles and the long term effects of shared constitutional interpretation. Immediate outcomes of participatory bubbles can have at least two roles to play in the domain of shared constitutional interpretation. First, if our courts have created the space for meaningful participation by the citizenry in the law-making process, then citizens will have a role to play in shaping the meaning of constitutional norms through the legislative (as opposed to the judicial) process. Citizens, through the drafting of some kinds of legislation, will play a direct role in giving the basic law content. Second, even where the law fails to reflect the interventions of the citizenry, the 'burst' participatory bubble leaves behind a residue of active political engagement. The failure to influence the setting of norms (constitutional and statutory) in one set of circumstances need not, indeed cannot, prevent any future influence of civil society on norm setting. Just as neuronal networks that fail to rise to the level of consciousness may yet form a winning coalition in later cognitive battles over 'awareness', citizen networks that fail to carry one vote in Parliament or a provincial legislature may yet build upon their current strength and win a future battle in the legislature. Pieterse's point, fleshed out thus, is that the space created by participatory bubbles in legislatures holds out the promise that citizens will have an ongoing role to play in the formation of constitutional norms and that such an ongoing role has the capacity to create community based organizations that ultimately share responsibility for constitutional interpretation with various branches of government. Many people involved in the organization of social movements around litigation designed to secure basic entitlements have noted that losses tend to undermine efforts to organize the historically disadvantaged members of our society. The citizens who helped shape *Mazibuko* are a case in point. See *Mazibuko & Others v City of Johannesburg & Others* 2010 (4) SA 1 (CC), 2010 (3) BCLR 239 (CC). Many citizens described themselves as dispirited by the results. However, in a country with over 6,000 demonstrations a year, a vibrant core of social activists and doggedly committed legal NGOs, such as SERI, CALS Section 27, Equal Education, the Centre for Child Law and the LRC will likely ensure that new challenges are brought in a manner more likely to yield positive results and to ensure that the litigants understand the role of litigation as part of an overall political strategy to deliver basic services to those persons in most urgent need.

160. T Roux 'Democracy' in S Woolman & M Bishop (eds) *Constitutional Law of South Africa* (2nd Edition, OS, July 2006) Chapter 10.

161. As Sachs J remarked in *Matatiele I*, '[d]emocratically elected by the nation, Parliament is the engine-house of our democracy.' *Matatiele I* (supra) at para 109. FC s 42(3) confirms that the primary form of

democracy in South Africa is representative democracy. It reads: 'The National Assembly is elected to represent the people and to ensure government by the people under the Constitution. It does this by choosing the President, by providing a national forum for public consideration of issues, by passing legislation and by scrutinizing and overseeing executive action.' See also *King & Others v Attorneys Fidelity Fund Board of Control & Another* 2006 (1) SA 474 (SCA), 2006 (4) BCLR 442 (SCA) at para 20. The main function of the National Council of Provinces, in turn, is to represent provincial interests. FC s 42(4). Provincial legislatures and local governments fulfil similar functions. See T Madlingozi & S Woolman 'Provincial Legislative Authority' in S Woolman & M Bishop (eds) *Constitutional Law of South Africa* (2nd Edition, OS, March 2005) Chapter 19; N Steytler & J de Visser 'Local Government' in S Woolman & M Bishop (eds) *Constitutional Law of South Africa* (2nd Edition, OS, March 2007) Chapter 21.

162. Emphasis added. This formulation is reiterated, in virtually identical terms, with respect to the National Council of Provinces and the provincial legislatures in FC s 70(1)*(b)* and FC s 116(1)*(b)*. The latter provision was cited but not judicially considered in *In re: Constitutionality of the Mpumalanga Petitions Bill, 2000.* 2002 (1) SA 447 (CC), 2001 (11) BCLR 1126 (CC) at para 17. The equivalent provision in respect of municipal councils, FC s 160(6) makes no reference to democracy. FC s 160(6) was considered in *Executive Council, Western Cape v Minister of Provincial Affairs and Constitutional Development & Another; Executive Council, KwaZulu-Natal v President of the Republic of South Africa & Others.* 2000 (1) SA 661 (CC), 1999 (12) BCLR 1360 (CC) at paras 96–112.

163. 1998 (3) SA 430 (C), 1998 (7) BCLR 916 (C) at para 27.

164. Ibid.

165. Roux (supra) at § 10.3 citing JH Ely *Democracy and Distrust: A Theory of Judicial Review* (1980).

166. See FC s 70(2)*(c)*, FC s 116(2)*(b)*, FC s 160(8). See also FC s 61(3)(Providing that national legislation determining how provincial legislatures' delegates to the National Council of Provinces are to be selected must ensure minority party participation); FC s 70(2)*(b)* (Rules and orders governing participation of provinces in proceedings of National Council of Provinces must be 'consistent with democracy'.)

167. 2003 (1) BCLR 25 (C).

168. *Democratic Alliance v ANC & Others* 2003 (1) BCLR 25, 31 (C)(*'Democratic Alliance v ANC'*).

169. Ibid at 31.

170. Ibid at 37. Roux draws 'two provisional conclusions' from *Democratic Alliance v ANC:* 'First, it is clear that, where the Final Constitution refers to democracy *tout court*, rather than any particular form of democracy, there is a danger that the term 'democracy' will be understood as a reference to the majority-rule principle, rather than the deeper principle of democracy that appears to underlie the constitutional text as a whole. Secondly, the Court's reluctance to super-impose its own conception of democracy on FC s 160(8) illustrates the inherent difficulty in all cases where the principle of democracy is implicated. As the Court notes, cases of this type are by definition 'political', and therefore subject, if not to a formal political question doctrine, at least to more than the ordinary degree of deference. When this deferential approach is coupled with the contested nature of democracy itself, it may be expected that non-specific or unqualified references to democracy in the Final Constitution will rarely give rise to determinate rules, other than the requirement that the dispute should be resolved according to the wishes of the majority. On the other hand, where references to democracy *are* qualified, there may be a basis for more robust judicial intervention.' Roux (supra) at § 10.3.

171. 2003 (2) SA 413 (CC), 2003 (2) BCLR 128 (CC)(*'Masondo'*).

172. Act 117 of 1998.

173. *Masondo* (supra) at para 19.

174. Ibid at para 20.

175. Ibid at para 63.

176. Ibid at para 78.

177. Roux (supra) at § 10.3.

178. In *Matatiele I*, the Constitutional Court remarked, as obiter, that FC s 118(1)*(a)* may impose a duty on provincial legislatures, when considering a constitutional amendment under FC s 74(8), to entertain oral or written representations by the public. *Matatiele I* (supra) at para 65. Because the issue was not properly argued, the *Matatiele I* Court declined to decide it. To understand FC ss 59(1), 72(1) and 118(1), as Theunis Roux notes, one must first understand FC ss 59(2), 72(2) and 118(2). FC s 59(2) states that the National Assembly 'may not exclude the public, including the media, from a sitting of a committee unless it is reasonable and justifiable to do so in an open and democratic society'. This provision is repeated, virtually verbatim, with respect to the National Council of Provinces, in FC s 72(2), and provincial legislatures, in FC s 118(2). Roux contends that 'these provisions ... acknowledge the value not so much of public participation in legislative decision-making as access to information about the inner workings of the democratic process.' Roux (supra) at § 10.3.

179. *Matatiele Municipality & Others v President of the RSA & Others* 2006 (5) SA 47 (CC), 2006 (5) BCLR 622 (CC)('*Matatiele II*').

180. On the difference between rationality review and reasonableness review, see M Bishop 'Rationality is Dead! Long Live Rationality! Saving Rational Basis Review' in S Woolman & D Bilchitz (eds) *Is This Seat Taken? Conversations at the Bar, the Bench and the Academy about the South African Constitution* (2012) 1; A Price 'The Content and Justification of Rationality Review' in S Woolman & D Bilchitz (eds) *Is This Seat Taken? Conversations at the Bar, the Bench and the Academy about the South African Constitution* (2012) 37.

181. Ibid at para 68.

182. These two decisions shook up political practices in all 9 provincial legislatures. None of the legislatures knew how much participation was 'reasonable' for any given decision. But they do know now that they are obliged to consider public participation when reaching decisions that will have some demonstrable effect on a discrete and identifiable portion of the community. Panel Discussion on *Matatiele II* and *Doctors for Life*, South African Human Rights Commission and the South African Institute for Advanced Constitutional, Public and International Law (11 October 2006). For another decision that has extended the Court's view's on polycentricity and public participation in legislative and judicial processes, see *Merafong Demarcation Forum & Others v President of the Republic of South Africa & Others* [2008] ZACC 10, 2008 (5) SA 171 (CC), 2008 (10) BCLR 968 (CC).

183. FC s 182(4) and PPA s 6(1)(b).

184. See *2004 – 2005 Annual Report* (supra) at 128 – 129. The Public Protector has also instituted an outreach programme to improve access for people in remote areas. Ibid at 14–15.

185. *2001– 2002 Annual Report* (supra) at 16.

186. Ibid. 98% were finalised before the case closed and a further 1% after the case closed. In only one case did the state refuse to follow the recommendation: it chose to take an alternative route to address the problem.

187. The Office of the Public Protector increases access through its acceptance of complaints in numerous formats. Personal interviews ensure that persons who are illiterate or who lack sufficient education to draft a document stating the alleged wrong can lay a complaint. Complaints registered by telephone interview ensure that those persons who lack the resources (time or money) needed to travel to a Public Protector's office are still able to file a complaint. Complaints can be also be initiated by letter. See *Office of the Public Protector Public Protector: South Africa* (2003), available at http://www.publicprotector.org/brochure_faq/11_lang/english.pdf (accessed on 1 November 2005). The brochure is available in all 11 official languages. A toll free number – 0800 11 20 40 – enables members of the public to speak directly with a member of the Public Protector's office. The Public Protector's relatively high rate of success in securing adequate redress for complainants raises the question of when, and whether, the Public Protector ought to be treated as the preferred forum for ventilation of disputes between a citizen and the state. As it stands, the law provides only limited disincentives with respect to forum shopping. On the one hand, the PPA permits the Public Protector

to refuse to investigate any matter in which the complainant has not exhausted his legal remedies. PPA s 6(3)(b). On the other hand, the complainant has no obligation to approach the Public Protector for assistance prior to filing suit in a court of law. See *Ngxuza v Permanent Secretary, Department of Welfare, Eastern Cape* 2001 (2) SA 609, 625 (E), 2000 (12) BCLR 1322, 1333 (E)('[The Public Protector and the Auditor-General] are bodies constitutionally mandated to pursue matters of this kind, but where the State fails to provide them with the means to do so it seems almost bizarre to insist that the courts are precluded from coming to the assistance of the applicants.') See also *Dabalorivhuwa Patriotic Front & Another v Government, RSA & Others* [2004] JOL 12911 (T)('*Dabalorivhuwa*') at para 30.2. If anything, the current case law suggests that a complainant might be well advised to adopt a two-pronged approach to the resolution of a dispute with a public entity. See *Mothibeli v Western Vaal Metropolitan Substructure* [1999] JOL 5678 (LC) at para 18 ('While the applicant may well have been entitled to approach the Public Protector for assistance, that clearly would have been a parallel exercise to the course of legal proceedings ... In any event, he could not reasonably have understood that his referral of the dispute to the Public Protector could excuse him from pursuing the matter under the Labour Relations Act, including the filing of the necessary statement of claim in this Court.') See also *Prinsloo v Development Bank of Southern Africa Pension Fund & Another* [1999] 12 BPLR 439, 443 (PFA)(Condonation of late application denied despite earlier application to Public Protector.) *Mothibeli* makes the Public Protector a somewhat less attractive substitute for litigation. However, the Public Protector remains a free and an effective mechanism for dispute resolution. Those complainants who believe that their best chance at securing the required relief is to be found in the courts are not barred from filing in both forums simultaneously.

188. See J Klaaren 'South African Human Rights Commission' in S Woolman & M Bishop (eds) *Constitutional Law of South Africa* (2nd Edition, OS, March 2006) Chapter 24C; K Govender 'The South African Human Rights Commission' in P Andrews & S Ellmann (eds) *The Post-Apartheid Constitutions: Perspectives on South Africa's Basic Law* (2001) 571.

189. Cathi Albertyn writes: 'The CGE's most important function is to act as a watchdog for gender equality, and hence of democracy. This watchdog role extends beyond the state to the private sector and civil society. Section 11(1)(a) of the Act explicitly authorises the CGE to monitor and to evaluate the policies and practices of all organs of state, statutory bodies or functionaries, public bodies and authorities and private business, enterprises and institutions. Section 11(1)(c) requires the CGE to evaluate any Act of Parliament or aspect of the common law, with particular emphasis on systems of personal, family and customary law. In terms of s 11(1)(h), the CGE is expected to monitor compliance with relevant international instruments, especially the Convention on the Elimination of All Forms of Discrimination Against Women.' C Albertyn 'Commission for Gender Equality' in S Woolman & M Bishop (eds) *Constitutional Law of South Africa* (2nd Edition, OS, June 2004) Chapter 24D.

190. Ibid (footnotes omitted).

191. J Klaaren 'South African Human Rights Commission' (supra).

192. Human Rights Commission Act, s 8, grants the SAHRC the power to resolve by mediation, conciliation or negotiation any dispute or to rectify any act or omission in relation to a fundamental right. Section 20(5) of the Promotion of Equality and Prevention of Unfair Discrimination Act ('PEPUDA') – Act 4 of 2000 – empowers an equality court to refer disputes to an alternative forum.

193. The SAHRC has been loath to exercise its power of adjudication. But see *Freedom Front v South African Human Rights Commission* 2003 (11) BCLR 1283 (SAHRC)(Commission finds that slogan 'Kill the farmer, kill the Boer' – articulated at an ANC rally – constitutes hate speech.) Perhaps one reason for this reluctance is that its decisions are often understood not to be binding on the parties to the dispute.

194. While loath to exercise its power of adjudication, the SAHRC has initiated litigation or participated as an amicus on numerous occasions. The virtue of its appearance as an amicus – as I noted in the endnotes above – is that it gives the courts, and especially the Constitutional Court, an additional perspective on a dispute.

195. See *Jordan* (supra) at para 70 (Recognizes role of Chapter 9 Institutions in shaping the Court's understanding of the content of a constitutional norm: 'This Court is of course not bound by the Commission [of Gender Equality]'s views but it should acknowledge its special constitutional role and its expertise.')
196. The *Grootboom* Court endorsed a significant monitoring role for the SAHRC and further requested that the SAHRC adopt a supervisory role to ensure the state's compliance with the Court' order. As note, the SAHRC failed to discharge this supervisory role.
197. Klaaren (supra) at Chapter 24C.
198. Report of the Ad Hoc Committee on the Review of Chapter 9 and Associated Institutions: A Report to the National Assembly of the Parliament of South Africa (31 July 2007)('The Asmal Report'): 'The Committee finds that the multiplicity of institutions created to protect and promote the rights of specific constituencies has in practice resulted in an uneven spread of available resources and capacities, with implications for effectiveness and efficiency. This has created fragmentation, confounding the intention that these institutions should support the seamless application of the Bill of Rights. The Committee therefore recommends the establishment of an umbrella human rights body to be called the South African Commission on Human Rights and Equality, into which the National Youth Commission, the Commission for the Promotion and Protection of Cultural, Religious and Linguistic Communities (together with the Pan South African Language Board) and the Commission for Gender Equality should be incorporated together with the Human Rights Commission.' The 'fragmented' quality of that last sentence reflects the terribly underwhelming quality of the report. It leaves the reader with misapprehension that the failure of the Chapter 9 Institutions is a failure of institutional design. It most certainly is not. The failure rests entirely with a government unwilling to brook any form of contestation of its will. Parliament seems to have decided that actual amalgamation – which would have required significant changes to the Constitution – was less desirable than letting the Chapter 9 Institutions die on the vine. If the report is an insult to our intelligence, Parliament's continued inaction is slap in the face of creative institutional designers (and South Africa's citizenry) who had hoped to strengthen our democracy through the bodies that would mediate different kinds of discussions across our society and deepen our democracy and civil society in the process.
199. See S Woolman 'Security Services' in S Woolman & M Bishop (eds) *Constitutional Law of South Africa* (2nd Edition, RS3, May 2011) Chapter 24C.

Chapter Six

Experimental Constitutionalism in South Africa: The Evolution of Law and Policy in Housing & Education

Policies are stated in general terms and cannot provide for all situations. Our legacy of injustice and mistrust continuously throws up problems which need the wisdom of Solomon to settle. In this protracted transitional period, in which new policies for a democratic society are being developed and implemented, the chances are that we shall collectively make many mistakes, either in conception or execution. They must be recognised and corrected. The possibility of damage will be reduced if new policies are based on knowledge of our charter of fundamental rights and on sufficient consultation with those who are affected by them, if conflicts are negotiated, and if principled compromises are sought.

Sibusiso Bengu

A. Introduction

The previous chapter framed the possibilities of experimental constitutionalism rather broadly. It asked whether the South African Constitution can produce the institutions, and whether those institutions have already articulated the doctrines, that make experimental constitutionalism (when wedded to flourishing) a plausible approach to our basic law. The answer is that the rudiments of an experimentalist order certainly exist. However, questions remain as to whether they would qualify as emergent experimentalist institutions and experimentalist doctrines in terms of the existing body of literature on the subject. My hope is that by narrowing our focus to two important and well-ventilated areas of public law – housing and education – we shall place ourselves in a better position to understand the benefits and the limitations of experimental constitutionalism in South Africa.

B. Experimental Constitutionalism in South African Housing Law and Policy

1. *Grootboom and the Reconstruction and Development Programme*

One way to begin to interrogate the possibilities of experimental constitutionalism is to review the surrounding circumstances of, the Court's opinion in, and the political response to, *Republic of South Africa v Grootboom*. Kirsty McLean offers the following account:

> *Grootboom* began with an informal community's occupation of private land. The community named their new settlement 'New Rust' – and it was, all things being equal, an improvement upon the deplorable conditions of their previous settlement. The owner of the land, however, sought and obtained an order for the community's eviction under the Prevention of Illegal Eviction from and Unlawful Occupation of Land Act.[1] The community then sought shelter on a municipal sports field. After requesting assistance, but receiving none, from the relevant local government authorities, the community sued the local municipality in the Cape High Court for an order granting temporary shelter. In so doing, they relied on FC s 26 and FC s 28. Davis J granted an order in terms of FC s 28(1)(c), instructing the State to provide shelter for the children in the community, as well as their parents. The State appealed against this order to the Constitutional Court. After the intervention of an amicus curiae, the original claim based on FC s 26(1) and (2) was also reargued.[2] The Constitutional Court held that the rights in FC s 26 and FC s 28 did not entitle 'the respondents to claim shelter or housing immediately upon demand'.[3] At the same time, the Court emphasized that socio-economic rights are justiciable and that the right to housing is enforceable.[4] That enforcement, as a general matter, takes the form of direct regulation of State policy. Proper enforcement, according to the *Grootboom* Court, required the State to have in place a reasonable plan to realize the right to housing over time and within its budgetary constraints, including a plan to provide relief to those in desperate need. The declaratory order of the *Grootboom* Court reads as follows:
>
> (a) Section 26(2) of the Constitution requires the State to devise and implement within its available resources a comprehensive and co-ordinated programme progressively to realise the right of access to adequate housing;
>
> (b) The programme must include reasonable measures such as, but not necessarily limited to, those contemplated in the Accelerated Managed Land Settlement Programme, to provide

relief for people who have no access to land, no roof over their heads, and who are living in intolerable conditions or crisis situations.

(c) As at the date of the launch of this application, the State housing programme in the area of the Cape Metropolitan Council fell short of compliance with the requirements in para (b), in that it failed to make reasonable provision within its available resources for people in the Cape Metropolitan area with no access to land, no roof over their heads, and who were living in intolerable conditions or crisis situations.[5]

2. *An Immediate Critique of Grootboom*

On one view, *Grootboom* represents a classic instance of judicial deference in the face of extraordinarily difficult institutional reform.[6] As the Constitutional Court made clear, it could not, in good faith, have credited the government response to the housing situation as adequate under the circumstances. At the same time, the Court was concerned about its ability to intercede effectively in the legislative or administrative process for housing delivery. It therefore left the structure of the remedy almost entirely up to the government's discretion.

As Susan Sturm points out, while a court's concern regarding its institutional competence is entirely legitimate, that concern ought not dictate deference.[7] The difficulty with structural reform can be addressed through institutional mechanisms such as court-guided negotiation between stakeholders: that is, the creation of a participatory bubble. The immediate criticism of *Grootboom* is really two-fold. In addition to the government's failure to address the desperate plight of the homeless, the case raises serious questions about the accountability of those government institutions responsible for housing to those persons most in need.[8] By deferring to the government, by accepting its good faith commitment to put a plan in place, the Court sidestepped the issue of accountability.[9]

Instead of deferring entirely to the government, the Constitutional Court could have taken a more forceful stance. A judicially monitored structure that created cognizable 'destabilization rights' for the *Grootboom* community might have secured the applicants as least some of the relief that they sought. Had the Court retained jurisdiction, it could have appointed representatives for affected citizens in the *Grootboom* community and enjoined government agencies, both national and local, to engage in earnest engagement about an effective solution. Using a structural injunction to create such a participatory bubble would have had several beneficial consequences:

1. Government agencies would have had to come up with a remedy particularly tailored to the needs of the *Grootboom* community.
2. This participatory bubble could have become the model for other similarly situated groups around the country. By multiplying such bubbles, the public and the private actors charged with responsibility for housing policy would be required to take into account the saliency and the variance of the housing needs of different groups. The information gathered would allow government to allocate, more efficiently, scarce available resources and to fulfil the FC s 26 rights violated in *Grootboom*.
3. Such a polycentric process would generate experimentalist responses to the resource constraints confronted by both government agencies and those persons most in need of adequate housing. A structural injunction coupled with the replication of participatory bubbles throughout the

> country would give the Court, the government and the public the ability to share information about the kinds of strategies that work to alleviate homelessness.

The *Grootboom* Court did make a modest contribution toward developing an experimentalist model of fundamental rights adjudication. It charged the South African Human Rights Commission with the responsibility of monitoring compliance and facilitating information-gathering.[10] The SAHRC's enhanced supervisory role was designed to allow for flexibility in the implementation processes in various locales, ensure participation by stakeholders in such processes, guarantee compliance with the basic norms articulated by the *Grootboom* Court and permit constant forward and lateral looking comparison in housing policy outcomes around the country.[11] In other words, as an information-gathering and pooling body in this nation-wide experiment, the South African Human Rights Commission would report on local housing initiatives and publicize best practices.[12]

As the aforementioned benefits should make clear, the most compelling consequence of an experimentalist revision of *Grootboom* would be its systemic effect. *Grootboom* would come to represent a classic example of citizens securing government accountability through court and Chapter 9 Institution oversight. We might then have seen a *Grootboom* effect. That effect would flow from its trend-setting use of innovative injunctive relief to create participatory bubbles that facilitate wide-spread experimentation. The revised *Grootboom* effect would place other government agencies responsible for delivering basic necessities or transforming social institutions on notice. The revised *Grootboom* would tell government agencies that they are best served by finding stakeholder representatives to secure the necessary feedback on the community's needs before the government agencies design new and better forms of service delivery.[13]

But as Billy Joel wrote: 'That's just a fantasy, it's not the real thing.' An honest appraisal of *Grootboom* must acknowledge that the Court issued a detailed order setting out the facilities that ought to be provided to the *Grootboom* residents.[14] Nothing happened. The SAHRC failed to monitor adequately the Court's order. The conditions for the *Grootboom* community never improved.

3. *Breaking New Ground: The Reformation of Housing Policy in Light of Grootboom*

Despite this criticism, and the failure of many a municipality to effect co-ordinated and comprehensive programmes to address severe housing crises, *Grootboom* and its legacy have not been an unmitigated disaster. As McLean notes, '[f]rom 1 April 1994 until December 2005, the South African government subsidized the construction of 1 916 918 houses and in so doing, at an average of 4.1 people per household, provided housing to approximately 7 859 363 people in South Africa.'[15] As of the end of December 2010, the government claims to have created 2.7 million homes and given shelter to 13 million people.[16] (The annual spend on housing increased from R4.8 billion in 2005 to R10.9 billion in 2010.) Such accomplishments could only be achieved, as Kecia Rust contends, because:

> South Africa *has* tackled issues of housing finance, social housing, and consumer protection. It has institutionalised the concept of 'people's housing', made space for women in the construction

> industry, and supported the role of emerging builders. It has built a single, non-racial department of housing out of a previously fragmented and inefficient system. And, perhaps most importantly, it has entrenched the right to adequate housing in its constitution. Each of these developments is a significant achievement. Their combination, especially given South Africa's history, is unparalleled.[17]

This extremely good news must be read against the background of the lived reality of millions of South Africans who remain homeless. So, as Rust notes elsewhere, while the financial year ending in 2011 saw 121 879 subsidized units added to a housing market in which a *truly remarkable* 24% of all registered housing units have been created via subsidy, informal settlements have tripled in the last decade (to 2 628) and the backlog of housing units in 2012 stands at 2.1 million units.[18] Delivery is currently insufficient to meet demand.[19]

These reports from the NGO sector and various social movements have placed the state on notice of both (a) the crisis associated with the delivery backlog; and (b) the specific manner in which the current housing subsidy policy creates an affordability gap that effectively excludes many workers (350,000) and their families from entering the market. The Department of Human Settlement and the Office of the Presidency have responded with a 'triad of interventions' to 'address the "gap" market – the 20% too rich to afford a subsidy, but too poor to afford a house on the open market'.[20] These innovative responses to feedback from the market and potential homeowners embrace (a) a 'New Finance Linked Individual Subsidy … for households earning between R3501 and R 15 000 a month'; (b) a tax incentive for developers to promote delivery of housing units costing less than R300,000; and (c) a 'R1 Billion mortgage insurance initiative' administered by the National Housing Finance Corporation designed to enable wholesale financiers to take on greater risk with the respect to the provision of capital to non-bank housing lenders (micro-financiers) who target 'low-income earners'.[21] The state is listening to those persons who seek affordable housing (think participatory bubbles) and adroitly responding to previous mistakes by altering both means and ends (sounds very much like reflexivity).

The last several years of the post *Grootboom*-era also signal the capacity of the South African state to meet (some of) the doctrinal demands of shared constitutional interpretation. The state and the Constitutional Court appeared, for some time after *Grootboom*, to fail to engage one another in a systematic fashion about much needed reformation of housing law and policy. As matters currently stand, and as the aforementioned developments evince, a pragmatic, empirically grounded dialogue – based upon successful and unsuccessful action – has begun to take place.

Recall that the *Grootboom* Court held that to be found reasonable, a comprehensive and co-ordinated programme to realise access to housing (and the other socio-economic rights found in FC s 26 and FC s 27): (1) must ensure that 'the appropriate financial and human resources are available'; (2) 'must be capable of facilitating the realisation of the right'; (3) must be reasonable 'both in their conception and their implementation'; (4) must attend to 'crises'; (5) must not exclude 'a significant segment' of the affected population; and (6) must 'respond to the urgent needs of those in desperate situations.'[22] Evidence for the claim that the National Housing Department has responded to *Grootboom*'s call can be found in the recent promulgation of a policy document long held in abeyance, *Breaking New Ground*,[23] and an array of new amendments to the national *Housing Code*. McLean writes:

> Since 2000, and the decision in *Grootboom*, several shifts have occurred in housing policy. First, 'sustainability' has emerged as a key concept ... and within the national Department of Housing.[24] Second, as the Medium Density Housing Programme reflects, *Grootboom* has been the catalyst for two significant policy developments: the recognition that the State must cater for 'all' housing needs (which resulted in the addition of Chapter 12 of the Housing Code 'Housing Assistance in Emergency Housing Circumstances' and Chapter 13 of the Housing Code 'Upgrading of Informal Settlements'); and the State's commitment to use both market-driven and non-market-driven mechanisms to diversify housing delivery.[25]

Additional evidence for the evolution (as opposed to revolution) of housing policy in response to *Grootboom* can be found in an amendment to the Housing Code that aims to 'provide temporary assistance in the form of secure access to land and/or basic municipal engineering services and/or shelter in a wide range of emergency situations of exceptional housing need'.[26] Finally, the *Grootboom* Court's nostrum that a 'reasonable programme must clearly allocate responsibilities and tasks to the different spheres of government and ensure that the appropriate financial and human resources are available' is reflected in a more recent document entitled 'Accreditation Framework for Municipalities to Administer National Housing Programmes'. The programme is designed to enable local government to carry out their housing responsibilities by providing accreditation and long-term financial support.

4. *The Constitutional Court's Novel Commitment to Meaningful Engagement*

Does the *initial* give and take (between various branches and spheres of government) on South Africa's housing policies immediately after *Grootboom* satisfy the requirements of an experimental constitutional order? Probably not. That the government eventually responded to *Grootboom* is all to the good. However, neither the Court's first few subsequent decisions nor the government's initial policy responses can be described as a part of a robust, reflexive system designed to effect a normatively more legitimate and information rich set of rolling best practices. To make the point more poignant, Mrs Grootboom died almost a decade after the judgment without an appreciable improvement in her housing conditions.

As we have seen, however, Mrs Grootboom's fate is only part of the story.

Over the past several years, the Court, the government, the NGO housing community, impact litigators and social activists have stepped up their activities.[27] The Constitutional Court itself has grown increasingly bold, in terms of its interventions in, and construction of, the space in which housing law, policy and reality take shape. However, as the Court's first post-*Grootboom* effort in *Minister of Public Works & Others v Kyalami Ridge Association & Another* suggests, its development of doctrine was deliberately passed.[28]

The gravamen of the complaint in *Kyalami Ridge* was that the committee charged with finding appropriate space and building necessary shelter had created a transit camp on the Leeuwkop prison farm to accommodate flood-victims in Alexandra Township (in Johannesburg). The respondent, an association that represented residents in the vicinity of Leeuwkop, challenged the committee's decision. It contended that the transit camp would adversely affect property values and the long-term habitability of the surrounding environment.

In a complex matter in which the right to housing played but a supporting role, the Court held (again) that the rights of the displaced persons in need of urgent shelter and housing after the occurrence of a national disaster trumped other considerations. Ought the Court to have done more? Without displacing the more detailed commentary that appears in Chapter 8, the primary problems with the judgment – from an experimentalist perspective – are three-fold. First, the Court notes, without comment, a lack of engagement by the government with other affected actors: 'No discussions were held with residents in the vicinity of Leeuwkop.'[29] But the Court made little of this lack of meaningful engagement. Second, Chief Justice Chaskalson rather laconically remarks that

> It may have been better and more consistent with salutary principles of good government if the government had found an appropriate method to inform the neighbouring residents of its intentions before contractors went onto the site, and if it had engaged them in discussion and the planning at an early stage of the project. However, for the reasons that I have given, the absence of such consultation and engagement did not invalidate the decision.[30]

Third, the Court writes:

> When the proceedings were commenced the government contemplated that the flood victims would be accommodated on the prison farm temporarily and that they would be allocated permanent accommodation elsewhere within 6 to 12 months. Later it was said that the time would at most be 12 to 24 months. Nearly a year has passed since then. In the meantime the flood victims have been living in deplorable circumstances, and there is no word as to when permanent accommodation will become available. It is time that attention be paid to their needs.[31]

Yet the Court still does not put the government or other actors on discernable terms: via structural injunction or a substantive, automatic remedy for a rights violation. From an experimentalist perspective, *Kyalami Ridge* fails in two important respects: (a) to bring all the affected parties together in order to reach as optimal an outcome as possible; and (b) to ensure that the government respects the norms articulated by the Court so that all the affected parties – in the present and an easily imagined future – might benefit from the Court's otherwise thoughtful judgment.[32]

The result in *Port Elizabeth Municipality* suggests more of the same in s 26 matters.[33] The Port Elizabeth Municipality sought an eviction order against 68 persons living in shacks on privately owned land. The occupants agreed to move to 'suitable alternative land'. However, the space offered by the Council – in Walmer Township – provided no security of occupation and was controlled by criminal networks. The municipality contended that no other alternative existed and that making a special exception for the occupiers would be tantamount to 'queue-jumping' with respect to the municipality's comprehensive and co-ordinated housing scheme.

This background and the municipality's failure to take *any* steps – let alone all reasonable steps – to solve this polycentric problem meant that the municipality had failed to discharge its constitutional obligations. Given this abdication of responsibility, the Court held that it was neither just nor equitable for the eviction order to be granted. *Port Elizabeth Municipality* looks like a quintessentially easy case. Not so.

The Constitutional Court noted, relatively early in its judgment, that the polycentric nature of the problem – homeless persons in need of shelter, private land owners who wished to use the occupied land, municipalities charged with creating a coherent housing scheme for all its inhabitants, sheriffs charged with executing an eviction, inhabitants of other communities to which the homeless persons might be moved – posed significant challenges for the Court:[34]

> The court is thus called upon to go beyond its normal functions, and to engage in active judicial management according to equitable principles of an ongoing, stressful and law-governed social process. This has major implications for the manner in which it must deal with the issues before it, how it should approach questions of evidence, the procedures it may adopt, the way in which it exercises its powers and orders it might make.[35]

The Court first appeared as if it might rise to the challenge. It suggested that cases that affected the lives of so many parties might be best resolved through face-to-face discussions – what it describes as 'mediation'. The Court writes:

> [O]ne potentially dignified and effective mode of achieving sustainable reconciliations of the different interests involved is to encourage and require the parties to engage with each other in a pro-active and honest endeavour to find mutually acceptable solutions. Wherever possible, respectful face-to-face engagement or mediation through a third party should replace arms-length combat by intransigent opponents.[36] ... Not only can mediation reduce the expenses of litigation, it can help avoid the exacerbation of tensions that forensic combat produces. By bringing the parties together, narrowing the areas of dispute between them and facilitating mutual give-and-take, mediators can find ways round sticking-points in a manner that the adversarial judicial process might not be able to do. Money that otherwise might be spent on unpleasant and polarising litigation can better be used to facilitate an outcome that ends a stand-off, promotes respect for human dignity and underlines the fact that we all live in a shared society.[37]

Despite these largely unassailable observations, the *Port Elizabeth Municipality* Court balks when it comes down to ordering mediation and retaining jurisdiction to ensure that a just and equitable outcome occurs. *Port Elizabeth Municipality* reflects an opportunity for shared constitutional interpretation and the aggressive use of a participatory bubble gone to waste.

However, mediation as a mechanism for the resolution of polycentric conflicts in housing cases clearly remained firmly in the minds of various members of the Constitutional Court. Thanks in large part to the continued, irrepressible efforts of housing advocates at the Centre for Applied Legal Studies, and now SERI, neither the Court nor the public remained stuck in the post-*Grootboom* purgatory of a court-dictated planning requirement without court-enforced delivery mechanisms.

In *Occupiers of 51 Olivia Road, Berea Township and 197 Main Street Johannesburg v City of Johannesburg & Others*, the Court was asked to determine whether the City of Johannesburg had acted constitutionally in attempting to evict residents from derelict – and dangerous – inner-city buildings.[38] In some instances, the eviction notice came without any plan to provide comparable housing. In other cases, the eviction notice contemplated the forced removal of a building's residents to the city's outskirts.

The *Occupiers of 51 Olivia Road* Court's initiatives at the outset of the hearing distinguishes the matter from virtually all of its predecessors. Rather than impose a decision on the parties framed by *Grootboom*-based criteria, the Court ordered the residents and the city of Johannesburg to repair to the negotiating table in order to reach a settlement that would lead to a more optimal outcome for both sides. The parties did. Their settlement then became an order of the Court. The fact that Court facilitated negotiation by all the relevant stakeholders – and more informed parties – constitutes a dramatic break with its previous rubric for housing rights analysis.

The most fascinating part of the judgment – from the perspective of experimental constitutionalism – is that the *Occupiers* Court held that, in addition to any other duties s 26(2)'s right to access to adequate housing might impose, 'a municipality that ejects people from their homes without first meaningfully engaging with them acts in a manner that is broadly at odds with the spirit and purpose of [its] constitutional obligations'.[39] What does this mean? First, it appears that the courts may not be the right branch of government to determine how some 63,000 persons – living in dangerous conditions – are to be best accommodated when a municipality determines that their current housing constitutes a threat to their lives. Second, having decided that persons who live in dangerous conditions must be removed, the Court also resolved that a municipality must determine where they are to be otherwise accommodated: a right to housing cannot be reconciled with a decision of the state to make people 'homeless'. Third, in deciding on how to accommodate this endangered class of persons, the city or the state is obliged to engage the affected parties – in this case all 63,000 persons. As Yacoob J writes:

> Engagement has the potential to contribute towards the resolution of disputes and to increased understanding and sympathetic care if both sides are willing to participate in the process. People about to be evicted may be so vulnerable that they may not be able to understand the importance of engagement and may refuse to take part in the process. If this happens, a municipality cannot walk away without more. It must make reasonable efforts to engage and it is only if these reasonable efforts fail that a municipality may proceed without appropriate engagement. It is precisely to ensure that a city is able to engage meaningfully with poor, vulnerable or illiterate people that the engagement process should preferably be managed by careful and sensitive people on its side.[40]

The *Occupiers* Court held, in addition, that the city had an obligation to engage meaningfully all 63 000 evictees in a systemic fashion[41] and that '[e]ngagement is a two-way process'[42] that 'will work only if both sides act reasonably and in good faith.'[43] Thus, consistent with the precepts of experimental constitutionalism, the *Occupiers* Court places a premium on sharing (or pooling) information and on reaching accommodations that place all parties in a better position than they might find themselves if the Court were to act as the final arbiter in a zero-sum game.

The Court built upon its semi-experimentalist model for dispute resolution in *Residents of Joe Slovo Community, Western Cape v Thubelisha Homes & Others* (*'Joe Slovo I'*).[44] The *Joe Slovo I* Court addressed the constitutionality of the state's controversial N2 Gateway project. The project, as planned, would have moved the residents of existing informal settlements along the N2 highway to Delft – a community some 15 km away. The residents resisted the removal. The government sought support for the removal through an eviction order. As we shall see in Chapter 8, the *Joe Slovo I* Court split on the question as to whether the state had 'meaningfully engaged' the community regarding the removal. For our immediate purposes, the opinion that best connects shared constitutional interpretation between the courts and other branches of government in terms of (a) setting rather rarefied norms and (b) creating the participatory bubbles that enable greater participation and greater extraction of information relevant for optimal decision-making, is penned by Justice Sachs:

> This case compels us to deal in a realistic and principled way with what it means to be a South African living in a new constitutional democracy. It concerns the responsibilities of government to secure the ample benefits of citizenship promised for all by the Constitution. It expands the concept of citizenship beyond traditional notions of electoral rights and claims for diplomatic protection, to include the full substantive benefits and entitlements envisaged by the Constitution for all the people who live in the country and to whom it belongs. At the same time it focuses on the reciprocal duty of citizens to be active, participatory and responsible and to make their own individual and collective contributions towards the realisation of the benefits and entitlements they claim for themselves, not to speak of the well-being of the community as a whole. When all is said and done, and the process has run its course, the authorities and the families will still be connected in ongoing constitutional relationships. It is to everyone's advantage that they be encouraged to get beyond the present impasse and work together once more.[45]

Even after the participatory bubble of a particular conflict has burst, and the various stakeholders have returned to their regular lives, the residue of active citizenship and responsive government remains: (1) the parties have learned more about the particular problems that forced the immediate litigation and engagement; (2) the state has learned something more about the communities that they govern and the stakeholders have learned more about the political and social processes that govern their lives; and (3) politicians, bureaucrats and citizens throughout the country should take away lessons on housing and evictions that can be profitably applied to future conflicts. So, although Sachs J refers to a two-way street of engagement, the better metaphor is, perhaps, a piazza, where the public meets again and again, shares new information, and reflects upon the community's collective wisdom – as active citizens and politicians in a republic do.[46] In Chapter 8's discussion of *Joe Slovo II*, we'll see the community and the state re-entering tha piazza and moving beyond the solutions that the Court in *Joe Slovo I* had approved during the original impasse.

In *Abahlali Basemjondolo Movement SA & Another v Premier of the Province of Kwazulu-Natal & Others,*[47] Abahlali Basemjondolo – a radical shack dweller movement – challenged the KwaZulu-Natal Elimination and Prevention of Re-emergence of Slums Act ('Slums Act').[48] The Act itself seemed little more than a craven attempt to 'clean up' Durban prior to the influx of foreign visitors for the 2010 World Cup.[49] The Court's response suggests that the framework for meaningful engagement with bite has, in fact, taken hold. From the perspective of experimental constitutionalism, the most important challenge to the Slums Act flowed from the Act's willingness to allow eviction without engagement. Because the majority found that the Act could not be reasonably read to *require* engagement, it declared the Act invalid. (Only Yacoob J read the Act in a manner that would require engagement.) As Moseneke DCJ writes:

> No evictions should occur until the results of the proper engagement process are known . . . . Proper engagement would include taking into proper consideration the wishes of the people who are to be evicted; whether the areas where they live may be upgraded *in situ*; and whether there will be alternative accommodation. The engagement would also include the manner of eviction and the timeframes for the eviction.[50]

In short, engagement extracts information that might not, as yet, appear in the heads of argument. It requires all of the various stakeholders concerned – and perhaps not just the original parties, given the Court's generous approach to standing – to put all their cards on the table. Moreover, engagement should make the outcome (the settlement) less contingent on well-drafted heads, voluminous records and courtroom theatrics. What the state and other parties can do – and what the potentially homeless will and will not accept – becomes the measure of a settlement's mettle. The openness of the negotiation and the settlement process, as Yacoob J notes, makes engagement more than mere window dressing:

> If it appears as a result of the process of engagement, for example, that the property concerned can be upgraded without the eviction of the unlawful occupiers, [then] the municipality cannot institute eviction proceedings. This is because it would not be acting reasonably in the engagement process.[51]

At the very least, meaningful engagement would now have to precede any attempt to secure an eviction notice – thus, at first blush, reversing the spin of a statutory scheme designed to sweep communities away or place them out of sight and out of mind.

5. *Two Unintended Consequences of Meaningful Engagement*

Insufficient time has passed in which to assess the efficacy of the meaningful engagement requirement with respect to scripted housing law and policy. However, indications exist that the Court's insistence on forcing parties to enter into settlement agreements which are then ratified by the Court, could have a perverse effect on the quality of inner city dwellings.

An easy eviction process would create incentives for landlords to improve housing stock with a view toward increasing the rental price per unit and the overall value of the apartment complex. Tougher eviction laws combined with a requirement that alternative housing be provided in the event of a finding that an eviction ought to take place invariably means that the landlord in possession of apartment stock in need of significant repair has a diminished incentive to make living conditions habitable. The landscape the landlord now sees is one in which it is easier to simply walk away, or extract as much value as can be had from the existing tenants. At least one free-wheeling, high octane High Court judgment, *Emfuleni Local Municipality v Builders Advancement Services CC*, has confirmed these suspicions.[52]

This conclusion requires some teasing out.

Why would meaningful engagement backfire so?

The landlord must first secure an eviction notice from the city. Meaningful engagement by the municipality with tenants and the provision of alternative housing in the event of an eviction notice in the event of a finding of inhabitability means the municipality has little reason to investigate the conditions of a given building: a finding of inhabitability will have the knock on effect of costing the city more than just the cost of removing the tenants.

The municipality is now on the hook for finding reasonable alternative housing after what will often require a long and protracted negotiation with groups of tenants who actually want the housing they possess improved and not forced removal to some distant site that possesses neither access to basic services nor easy and inexpensive transportation to work or to school. The expense of the alternative accommodation and the cost of potential likelihood of litigation in the event that the apartment building's current inhabitants are dissatisfied with the city's offer of alternative housing generate an incentive to do nothing at all.

Now imagine the scene again from landlord's perspective. She is faced not only with housing stock of diminishing value, but a municipality that has little interest in initiating eviction proceedings. The landlord must press two sets of parties into proceedings that neither of them wishes to enter. In short, the landlord must be willing to bear the cost (in court) of forcing the city to act and of negotiating (with the disinterested city)(again in court) the removal of the existing tenants to some alternative, acceptable site. As Willis J writes in *Emfuleni*: 'Why buy or build housing to let to tenants, if the fundamental link between tenancy and the payment of rentals to landlords is undermined? Why invest in property if there is a serious risk that the 'investment' will be worthless?'[53]

Town planners, housing analysts and the lawyers for the inner city apartment inhabitants have all taken cognizance of and commented upon the increasing ennui of landlords and municipalities to act under such circumstances. The result – and it remains to be seen whether this initial response is the long term response – is the further deterioration of many inner city dwellings and a deepening descent into chaos for the apartment buildings' inhabitants.

Such a turn of events should come as no surprise. Exactly the same unintended consequences followed strict rent control laws in New York City. Landlords refused to attend to buildings from which they could not extract increased rent and which they found themselves unable to sell. Who, after all, wants to purchase a building with depreciating value? (Arsonists perhaps.) While landlords in middle class neighbourhoods could be pressed into making de minimus repairs, the situation in the city's poorest neighbourhoods was especially bleak. Certain Bronx neighbourhoods in the 1980s took on a Dresden-like appearance.

South African cities, their landlords and their inhabitants – working off of an even lower budget and income base – might expect an even more deleterious set of consequences. The housing stock is already uninhabitable in many instances. It only stands to get worse unless some as yet unforeseen intervention takes place.

But it's the cause of this chain of events that is of interest. As I shall contend at greater length in the case analyses found in Chapter 8, meaningful engagement without any normative framework (regarding minimum core content of the right of access to adequate housing) that forces all of the interested parties to accept that certain conditions will obtain *ex ante* for rent, for eviction notices, for the improvement of existing housing stock and the provision of alternative housing where necessary, will create significant disincentives – for the three main bodies of stakeholders – to do anything about this parlous state of affairs. The irony is that the doctrine of meaningful engagement (with respect to housing) could lead to absence of engagement. Only a state of chaos scenario – with which the Court found itself confronted in *Modderklip* – seems to have moved the Court off its acquiescent duff. But even

Modderklip did little to develop the law on adequate housing. While the Supreme Court of Appeal grasped the nettle of attempting to harmonize s 26's right to adequate housing with section 25's right to property, the Constitutional Court avoided giving content to both rights and instead grounded its decision on a s 34 right of access to court claim married to a chaos theory of the rule of law. Put somewhat differently, where the state's failure to act courts social disintegration and a descent into chaos, the Constitutional Court may find what I have previously described as a 'substantive' breach of the rule of law.[54]

But that apparent one-off scenario will become a more and more regular occurrence if the quiescence of all of the key role players in urban rental settings becomes the negative default setting. Such a turn of events cannot be what the Constitutional Court intended when it turned to 'meaningful engagement' as a solution to apparently intractable housing disputes. But as my colleague David Bilchitz would likely agree, it is a problem of the Court's own making.[55] The failure flows from a refusal to give the right of access to adequate housing the kind of normative (minimum core) content that would clearly indicate the duties and the responsibilities of all of the parties affected by such polycentric problems.[56]

The news, however, is not all bad. Quite the opposite. Where the parties subject to an order for meaningful engagement both know and trust one another, their regular engagement in meaningful engagement settlements generally results in close to optimal outcomes. Parties without the requisite trust, or, in many instances, the wherewithal to solve the polycentric problem, do not appear to succeed as often.[57]

That meaningful engagement as a form of experimental constitutionalism in a developmental state such as South Africa should be so patchy is hardly a surprise. Both the state bureaucracy and civil society remain quite thin. However, should such unevenness in outcomes continue, the Constitutional Court and lower courts may be forced to reconsider the extent to which they rely upon meaningful engagement as a bottoms up solution to South Africa's housing problems. Brian Ray has reached largely the same conclusions.[58] In comparing *51 Olivia Road* with *Mamba*,[59] he writes:

> In *Olivia Road*, the High Court's initial injunction put a stop to the City's eviction process. Additionally, while the SCA's judgment permitted the City to resume evictions, it still placed restrictions on that ability and imposed certain costs that required revising the original policy. Once the case reached the Constitutional Court, the City was already well on its way to instituting a revised policy, and the engagement order gave the residents and the groups representing them sufficient leverage to force the City to take seriously their views on the policy. *Mamba* presented precisely the opposite situation. The High Court found no basis for a challenge to the closures; there was no intermediate appellate review and the refugees asked the Constitutional Court to address a fluid situation with almost no substantive record. Under those circumstances, it was quite easy for the Gauteng government to treat engagement as nothing more than the equivalent of a formal notification requirement rather than the real consultation that the Court plainly expected. These differences highlight the political nature of engagement and its dependence on sufficient incentives for the political branches to take the process seriously. The ambiguity inherent in engagement provides ample opportunity for resistance and, without additional

political constraints, allows the government to fail to take it seriously in many situations without real political cost.[60]

In late 2011, the *Blue Moonlight* Court finally recognized the deleterious consequences of placing insufficient strictures on the parties entering meaningful engagement negotiations. The state, the property owners and the occupants not only have a procedural obligation to reach a potentially pareto-optimal solution, the municipality has substantive obligations to provide urgent shelter should the persons subject to eviction require accommodation prior to the provision of appropriate alternative lodging.[61] (Whether the rather meagre cover currently offered as 'urgent shelter' suffices for the purposes of encouraging further challenges to otherwise inadequate housing or creates another perverse *disincentive* for poor litigants who wish to press the state and other non-state actors to make good on s 26 obligations remains to be seen.)

C. Experimentalism and Flourishing in South African Education Law and Policy[62]

1. *The State's Consciously Experimentalist Approach to Education Law and Policy*

Education law and policy might initially appear to constitute a somewhat less obvious and fruitful context in which to test hypotheses regarding experimental constitutionalism. It may seem so because the Constitutional Court and lower courts have had less opportunity to engage in general norm setting and the kinds of experimentation on display in the housing cases discussed above.

But it only seems less transparent. For as various expositors on a theory of experimental constitutionalism have made clear, an experimental constitutional order need not rely solely on judicial pronouncements as to the meaning of constitutional provisions or on court monitored enforcement of judicial edicts as to what constitutional norms, in fact, require various parties to do. Experimental constitutionalism can take place effectively so long as the various stakeholders participate in running manifold experiments designed to make good on the promise of a given constitutional (or statutory) provision. Litigation is not a prerequisite for experimentation. The outcome of litigation in the highest courts can actually block more creative solutions to complex social problems. [Indeed, most experimentalists would argue that other institutions and actors, state and non-state, engaging in simultaneous forward and lateral looking trials will produce a more useful body of information about what works and what doesn't.] Rather than waves of litigation, what we have seen in education law and policy is the devolution of power from the centre to the provinces, to school governing bodies, to unions, to principals, to teachers, to parents and to learners. With that devolution has come an array of responses to the same issues: admission criteria, language policy, school governing body autonomy, access to schools, school fees and access to an adequate basic education.

So despite the relative paucity of case law, constitutional education law is not underdeveloped. The constitutional discourse is simply located elsewhere.[63] The best example of a nuanced and reflexive engagement between state and society over the meaning of education-related constitutional norms has occurred in a line of cases that have engaged linguistic and cultural autonomy in our public schools.[64] The cases reflect the kind of trial-and-error responses consistent with an experimentalist approach to statecraft.

The Department of Education's second white paper supports the proposition that the state has quite expressly adopted an experimentalist approach to education policy. Recall this a forementioned passage from Minister of Education Bengu:

> Policies are stated in general terms and cannot provide for all situations. Our legacy of injustice and mistrust continuously throws up problems which need the wisdom of Solomon to settle. In this protracted transitional period, in which new policies for a democratic society are being developed and implemented, the chances are that we shall collectively make many mistakes, either in conception or execution. They must be recognised and corrected. The possibility of damage will be reduced if new policies are based on knowledge of our charter of fundamental rights and on sufficient consultation with those who are affected by them, if conflicts are negotiated, and if principled compromises are sought.[65]

The Minister acknowledges that the Department's various imperatives pull in numerous directions and that no amount of expert analysis could anticipate the manner in which a complex set of policy initiatives would interact with a dynamic social environment. More importantly, he makes it abundantly clear that the state would revisit its experiments in education at some later date and revise them as circumstances required.

Another way to describe this experimental political space is in terms of its open texture. The education landscape circa 1994 was a function of negotiated settlements between political parties, state bureaucracies, national government, provincial government, unions, local communities, principals, teachers, parents and learners. The negotiated settlements invariably led to open spaces – such is the nature of constitution-making and law-making that are a function of compromise. Controversial questions are not fully answered by the law. They are instead left open-ended or rather abstract. Rarefied language secures agreement because all parties hope that the subsequent resolution of open-ended questions about the content of a given provision, at some later date, will incline in their favour. Within the last 17 years, plenty of open questions have been answered (sometimes repeatedly, and with different outcomes.) Experimentalists would be inclined to say that policy interventions have rolled with the times, new political exigencies, and feedback from participants in the education system about what works and what does not.

Not everyone views matters this way. The standard account begins with the widely accepted, but radically incomplete, story of how the National Party's belated attempts to decentralise control over public school education, and subsequent concerns about Afrikaner succession, resulted in the rather diffuse degree of constitutional and statutory control exercised by provincial governments, unions, principals, parents, learners and school governing bodies (SGBs).[66] To put it more pointedly, the standard account emphasises how the fragility of the ANC-led government in 1994 required it to cede authority to multiple groups in order to avoid concentrating power in a group that might contest the government's new agenda.

My preferred historical account, culled from the *travaux preparatoires* of both the Interim Constitution and the Final Constitution, as well as extant education framework legislation

(SASA), the National Education Policy Act (NEPA) and the Educators' Employment Act (EEA), suggests that appeasing the privileged or the provincial bureaucracy or the unions is but a small part of this story. SGB autonomy, for example, was driven to a very large extent by the fundamentally democratic commitments of the African National Congress ('ANC') to grassroots politics.[67] The drafting history discloses how the multiple constituencies with whom the state had to contend, and the conflicting imperatives within the state's own agenda, led to significant decentralisation of decision-making.[68] Three points need to be made about this commitment to decentralisation. First, the decentralisation of decision-making had less to do with a belief that local is always lekker and more to do with the state's need to ensure that no one interest group would be able to use the law as a means of organising in opposition to the state. Second, the decentralisation of decision-making flows from inevitable conflicts between the egalitarian, utilitarian, democratic and communitarian commitments clearly manifest in the ANC's political agenda and the two new Constitutions (as it would in any well-developed, non-reductionist social democratic political theory.) Third, and most importantly from an experimentalist perspective, the new government realised that various political and legal choices would have a number of unintended consequences. (The inevitability of unintended consequences is one reason pragmatists and experimentalists embrace the notions of reflexivity and rolling best practices.) The drafting history is replete with references to the 'provisional' nature of the structures being created by the state and the state's commitment to revisiting and to revamping those structures as it consolidated its power and shifted its policy imperatives.[69] This narrative arc correlates with the state's attempt to use the variable space of the law to experiment quite consciously with changes in education policy so that education policy might be both more effective and more closely aligned to a progressive political agenda.[70]

2. *Constitutional and Statutory Norms regarding Linguistic and Cultural Autonomy in Public Schools and Private Schools*

a. The Basic Framework

Before our velvet revolution of 1994, most political claims based on culture, language, ethnicity and religion were greeted with suspicion, and, sometimes, outright hostility.[71] From the passive resistance of Gandhi, through worker movements of the early 20th century to the Freedom Charter, the preferred language of liberation was that of universal human rights discourse.[72] The liberation movement's utilization of rights discourse reflected a considered rhetorical response to romantic assertions of white, Christian, English and Afrikaner hegemony.

The liberation movement's universalist turn provides a partial explanation for the failure of group-based claims during CODESA and the MPNF. The African National Congress rejected every attempt to entrench what it termed 'racial group rights'.[73] Political power would have to be traded for peace. That peace, and the retention of economic power by a white minority, would be vouchsafed by a firm ANC commitment to a justiciable Bill of Rights.[74] But all was not lost for advocates of community rights. The Interim Constitution's and Final Constitution's rejection of group political rights[75] was at least partially compensated by the 'notable levels of constitutional significance' to which cultural, linguistic and religious matters were elevated.[76] The Final Constitution contains six different provisions concerned with culture, eight with language and four with religion.[77] The Final Constitution, read as a liberal political document, carves out both public and private space within which cultural, linguistic and religious formations might flourish.

The public space and private space within which cultural, linguistic and religious formations might flourish is – in terms of FC s 29(2) and FC s 29(3), respectively – reflected in the constitutional recognition of single medium public schools and culturally, linguistically, and religiously-based independent schools. However, whereas public schools can, under FC s 29(2) maintain their linguistic homogeneity only when they meet strict constitutional criteria for equity, practicability and historical redress,[78] FC s 29(3) permits linguistically and culturally restrictive admissions policies at independent schools so long as these policies do not discriminate, intentionally, upon the basis of race. The Constitutional Court, in *Gauteng Education Bill*, made it quite clear that comprehensive visions of the good are more appropriately accommodated in private schools and not in our public schools.[79] As Kriegler J notes in *Gauteng School Education Bill*, IC s 32 (c), soon to be FC s 29(3), and then extant national and provincial education legislation collectively constitute

> a bulwark against the swamping of any minority's common culture, language or religion. For as long as a minority actually guards its common heritage, for so long will it be its inalienable right to establish educational institutions for the preservation of its culture, language or religion … . There are, however, two important qualifications. Firstly, … there must be no discrimination on the ground of race . … A common culture, language or religion having racism as an essential element has no constitutional claim to the establishment of separate educational institutions. The Constitution protects diversity, not racial discrimination. Secondly, … [the Constitution] … keeps the door open for those for whom the State's educational institutions are considered inadequate as far as common culture, language or religion is concerned. They are at liberty harmoniously to preserve the heritage of their fathers for their children. But there is a price, namely that such a population group will have to dig into its own pocket.[80]

Justice Kriegler offers no comment on, and certainly no support for, the contention that communities bound by common culture, language or religion have some entitlement to state support.[81] While sympathetic to the belief that communities bound by common culture, language or religion are an important source of meaning for many South Africans, Justice Kriegler makes it clear that the post-apartheid state can no longer support public institutions that privilege one way of being in the world over another. Here, as in *Fourie*, is another place where the Constitutional Court's jurisprudence is not so radically under-theorized that it leaves us with no useful guidance as to how the state ought to engage the religious, cultural and linguistic communities that co-exist within our polity and how those communities ought to engage one another. Public schools are public, not private, entities, and the state has an overriding obligation to ensure equal treatment of *all* of its citizens by *all* of its state officials (including teachers and principals.) The Final Constitution's answer to those parents who wish to school their children in the language, culture or religion of their choice is pretty straightforward: you may 'dig into your own pocket' and build the 'independent school' on your own time.[82]

b. Government Efforts to Control Private Power and to Eliminate De Facto Racially, and Exclusionary Language Policies in Public Schools

Over the last decade, the South African government has started to flex its muscle. Concerns about consolidating power through reconciliation have receded. The current ANC administration is now in a better position to consolidate its power through policy initiatives closer to its heart – say those that pursue redress – and to challenge existing patterns of privilege. The open texture of the law in this area (of admissions policies and equity requirements) anticipated such political contestation.[83]

The shift is not news. By the fin de siècle, the government quite obviously shifted from a state of anxiety about its quiescence, to apprehension about the speed of transformation. The subtle change in the government's objectives did not, so it seemed, require dramatic alterations to the law. The government sought to achieve its more egalitarian ends through the very same legal structures that it had created to promote reconciliation: new policy experiments were undertaken without a significant change in the legal equipment.[84] When there was change in the legal apparatus, that change went largely unannounced.[85]

The body of case law built up over the past 15 years evinces the government's desire to advance transformation efforts more quickly and to control the exercise of private power in public spaces. At the same time, the decisions acknowledge that certain kinds of associational interests merit continued solicitude even in the face of the state's pursuit of more egalitarian educational arrangements. The cases discussed below engage the state's and parent and learner group's attempts to experiment with public school admissions requirements facially designed to protect linguistic community rights.

Stated at a relatively high level of generality, the government has stepped into the breach created by those who assert a constitutional entitlement to single medium public schools and those who assert the constitutional right to be educated in the official language of one's choice. Not surprisingly, the state has weighed in on the side of black students who wish to receive instruction in English, but who have found themselves excluded from predominantly Afrikaans-speaking public schools. (That English has not suffered the same setbacks (as yet) can be attributed to such contingent facts as the acknowledged hegemony of English as the language of business (and thus success) and the identification of Afrikaans with the imposition of that language as a medium of instruction in the 1970s, the Soweto school uprisings of 1976, and consequent use of schools as a site of struggle against the apartheid state.)

Matukane & Others v Laerskool Potgietersrus addressed the attempt by the parent of three learners, Mr Matukane, to enroll his three children (13, 13 and 8) at the Laerskool Potgietersrus.[86] Laerskool Potgietersrus was then, and remains still, a state-aided dual-medium primary school. In the High Court, Laerskool Potgietersrus argued that it was unable to accommodate more children and that it had not rejected the children on racial grounds. At the time of the hearing, Laerskool Potgietersrus had 580 Afrikaans students and 89 English students. (The applicants were black.) The Laerskool Potgietersrus expressed concern that if it admitted these children, it would be swamped by English-speaking children who would destroy the Afrikaans ethos of the school.

Our law uniformly prohibits discrimination on grounds of race. Despite the school's assertion that the refusals were based on overcrowding, not race, the facts clearly painted a different picture. No black children had been admitted to the school. There were no black children on the waiting list. Room existed to accommodate more English-speaking children. Little danger existed of the school's Afrikaans culture and ethos being destroyed even if every black applicant were to be accepted. The ratio of Afrikaans-speaking students to English-speaking students would remain 5:1. The *Matukane* court held that it could draw no other inference as to the actual intent of the school's admissions policy other than that it had discriminated directly on the basis of race, ethnic and social origin, culture and language. The *Matukane* court was driven by the facts to conclude that the ostensible promotion of language and culture were operating as surrogates for racial discrimination and that the respondent had failed to discharge its burden of proving the fairness of its admissions policies.

Laerskool Middelburg en 'n ander v Departementshoof, Mpumalanga Departement van Onderwys, en andere extended the holding in *Matukane* from dual medium to single medium schools.[87] However, in *Laerskool Middelburg*, the High Court was clearly more troubled by the conflict between the right to a single medium school and the right to be educated in the official language of one's choice.

After chiding the state for failing to take cognizance of FC s 29's commitment to linguistic and cultural diversity, the *Laerskool Middelburg* court conceded that the right to a single medium public educational institution was subordinate to the right of every South African to a basic education and the need for linguistic and cultural communities to share education facilities with one other. The *Laerskool Middelburg* court was unwilling to allow the needs of 40 English-speaking – and largely black – learners to be prejudiced by the state's failure to play by the rules and the school's intransigence on the issue of dual-medium education.[88] So while the state's actions had, in fact, been mala fide, it was still able to secure a victory for educational equity by getting the proper parties – namely the children – before the court.

At issue in *Minister of Education, Western Cape, Another & Others v Governing Body, Mikro Primary School* was the refusal of an Afrikaans medium public school to accede to a request by the Western Cape Department of Education ('WCDoE') to change the language policy of the school so as to convert it into a parallel medium school.[89] Acting on behalf of 21 learners, the WCDoE had directed the primary school to offer instruction in their preferred medium: English. The WCDoE had interpreted the Norms and Standards issued by the National Department of Education under SASA as requiring all primary schools with 40 learners who preferred a particular language of learning to offer instruction in that language. The Supreme Court of Appeal summarily rejected both the WCDoE's reading of the Norms and Standards and the WCDoE's gloss on FC s 29(2).[90] The decision is notable in two important respects. First, it diminished the ability of the state to determine admissions policy with regard to language. Such power continued to vest in the SGB. Second, while affirming the rights of learners to instruction in a preferred language, it simultaneously confirmed that individual schools retain the privilege of offering instruction in a single medium.

Mikro brought temporary relief to the SGBs of single medium Afrikaans-speaking schools.

In *Seodin Primary School v MEC Education, Northern Cape*, the High Court held that the three SGBs of three primarily Afrikaans speaking public schools could not use language preference to exclude black, primarily English-speaking learners, from admittance.[91] Moreover, public pronouncements by the MEC for Education on the need for greater integration in the public schools system could not be interpreted as an *ultra vires* act aimed at the elimination of single medium (ie, Afrikaans) public schools. *Seodin*'s reading of the Final Constitution makes it clear that considerations of equality and transformation would, more often than not, trump considerations of associational freedom within public institutions. Put slightly differently, while the language of the Final Constitution appears to reflect a compromise between the two parties, FC s 29(2) clearly eliminates any 'right' to single medium public schools, grants the state ultimate authority over language policy and makes any demand for single medium schools subject to threshold tests for equity, practicability and historical redress.[92]

The Constitutional Court's decision in *Head of Department, Mpumalanga Department of Education & Another v Hoërskool Ermelo & Another* puts that last set of propositions beyond dispute.[93] Although *Ermelo* addresses a mixed bag of legal irregularities, opaque statutory provisions and complex constitutional issues, Deputy Chief Justice Moseneke's opinion makes transparent the Court's lack of patience with Hoërskool Ermelo's intransigence with respect to language policy and to the admission of black students who wish to be taught in English:

> The case arises in the context of continuing deep inequality in our educational system, a painful legacy of our apartheid history. The school system in Ermelo illustrates the disparities sharply. The learners-per-class ratios in Ermelo reveal startling disparities which point to a vast difference in resources and of the quality of education. … [F]ormerly black public schools have been and by and large remain scantily resourced. They were deliberately funded stingily by the apartheid government. Also, they served in the main and were supported by relatively deprived black communities. That is why perhaps the most abiding and debilitating legacy of our past is an unequal distribution of skills and competencies acquired through education … [FC s 29(2)] is made up of two distinct but mutually reinforcing parts. The first part places an obvious premium on receiving education in a public school in a language of choice [but] … is available only when it is 'reasonably practicable'.. … The second part of s 29(2) of the Constitution protects the right to be taught in the language of one's choice. It is an injunction on the State to consider all reasonable educational alternatives which are not limited to, but include, single medium institutions. In resorting to an option, such as a single or parallel or dual medium of instruction, the State must take into account what is fair, feasible and satisfies the need to remedy the results of past racially discriminatory laws and practices.[94]

Thus does the Deputy Chief Justice shut the window of autonomy granted SGB's with respect to the determination of language policy (and the discharge of any other function) ostensibly vouchsafed by the Supreme Court of Appeal in *Mikro*. While the Head of Department of the Mpumalanga Department of Education may not have followed the correct statutory procedures, and had his decision reversed accordingly, a provincial HoD clearly possesses the power to withdraw, with good reason, a function currently discharged by an SGB. In this matter, the Constitutional Court found that the necessary grounds existed for the withdrawal of the SGB's restrictive language policies. It required that both the HoD and the SGB revisit the existing language policy of the Hoërskool Ermelo in light of the needs of learners in the Ermelo circuit and then report back to the Court with regard to their findings.[95]

From an experimental constitutional perspective, it is important that we read the Final Constitution and the subsequent litigation around language policy in public schools as part of an on-going dialogue between various spheres of government and members of civil society about the meaning of FC s 29(2). After 15 years of experimentation with single medium public schools, dual medium public schools and parallel medium public schools, South African case law, education statutes and sector specific regulations support the dual proposition that (a) linguistic interests may occasionally trump equity where there is no sign of overt discrimination and (b) Afrikaans-speaking learners and their parents have *no* constitutional right to single medium public schools.

The next experiment in language in South African public schools? Multilingualism. It's already here. So read on.

2. *School Governing Bodies as a Flexible, Reflexive Form of Government*

a. *Democracy and Education and Experimentalism*

The national government, provincial government, principal, teachers, parents, learners, engagement with School Governing Bodies and the judiciary over language policy and reasonable accommodation can, as we have just seen, be viewed as an on-going experiment (trial and error) about the place of cultural autonomy, linguistic pluralism and race in our radically heterogeneous state.[96] That experiment began, as the politics of the time dictated, with fairly radical devolution of power over language policy to local communities. Over time, the state and other stakeholders identified at least two problems with such autonomy and reflexively read several limits on that autonomy back into the governing constitutional and statutory norms. A rolling basic practice analysis suggests that the state and other stakeholders *first* found racial exclusion masquerading as cultural autonomy in a sizeable number of public schools. Neither the Constitution nor SASA tolerate such behaviour. It remained for national government, provincial government, SGBs, parents and learners to work out a set of procedures (employing the extant constitutional and statutory framework) which provincial governments and public schools could follow when assessing, substantively, exactly when racial discrimination had occurred under the guise of cultural and linguistic autonomy. That first experiment turned the broad standards articulated in the Constitution and SASA into a richer set of principles regarding the relationship between recognizing our racist past and the on-going demand for cultural pluralism. I intimated above that by the time the issues in play had percolated up to the Constitutional Court, a *second* experiment had been placed, ever so gently, on the table. As we shall see in the extended discussion of *Ermelo* in Chapter 8, Deputy Chief Justice Moseneke 'ironic' [his word] aside tantalizingly suggests that the hegemony of English, at the expense of the ten other official languages, should become a space for fruitful contestation. As matters stood in 2011 in Grades 1, 2, and 3, learners were taught three subjects: language, numeracy, life skills. A second language was introduced orally in grades 2 and 3. However, in terms of the national Department of Education's new Curriculum and Assessment Policy, learners in Grades 1, 2, and 3 should receive tutelage in four subjects: numeracy, life skills and two languages.[97] The instruction in both languages embraces conversation, reading and writing skills development. The policy has sent ripples of concern throughout the public school system. How are schools meant to accommodate this new requirement? We can now ask ourselves, without a hint of irony, how much mother tongue instruction ought we to expect in our primary, secondary and tertiary levels of education? Educators and learners alike are apt to test Deputy Chief Justice Moseneke's intuitions and the government's policy. Such an experiment will yield at least three findings: (a) the type of multicultural society we wish to be, (b) whether language can be turned into a much needed instrument for mutual respect and integration and (c) what sorts of educational practices will realize an integrated sociey based on equal citizenship. It should, in addition, produce a set of best practices around how language instruction affects (the disturbingly poor) literacy and numeracy rates among South Africa learners.[98]

In this section, I will look at another experiment undertaken by national government, provincial government, parents and learners over the first 17 years of South Africa's new dispensation: the extent to which school governing bodies (SGBs) offer South African parents and learners the opportunity to participate in a particular form of self-governance. A close and careful reading of the enabling statutes governing SGBs demonstrates a clear commitment to various forms of democracy – representative, participatory, direct. More importantly for the argument propounded by this book, the broad array of participants in the SGB decision-making process is consistent with the bottom-up, reflexive, polycentric and flexible commitments that we associate with emergent, experimental institutions. The following analysis of SASA Chapter 4 supports two primary propositions: (1) SGBs operate as a flexible, polycentric tier of self-governance; (2) the state has regularly tweaked the powers of SGBs [as we saw above with respect to FC s 29(2)] in order to make them more transparent, more responsive and more accountable to the broad South African community of learners that they are meant to serve.

b. Are SGBs Flexible, Polycentric Sites of Emergent Experimental Decision-Making?

Not all educators or commentators would buy the premise that SGBs operate as a new, flexible, reflexive sphere of government. Perhaps it is safer, and more accurate, to describe them as emergent experimental institutions.

One set of commentators contends that the powers granted to school governing bodies (SGBs) in the South Africa Schools Act (SASA) obscures the real intention of the government in creating such bodies.[99] This conspiratorial reading of the law suggests that its underlying motive is to provide communities with the illusion that they have genuine control over the governance of their schools.[100] SASA, when read with constitutional rights to equality, to religion, and to freedom of expression, leaves little scope for SGB's to take decisions that reflect a comprehensive – or even partial – conception of the good held by a majority of the members of their community.[101]

Another set of commentators reply that the creation of school governing bodies in SASA and other pieces of legislation was part and parcel of a global neo-liberal agenda. In sum, the state granted certain democratic political rights to communities, parents and learners over their individual schools in return for the parents' acceptance – especially in elite public schools – of significant financial responsibility for their children's education.[102] These critics assert that the hollowing out of the state – that flowed from a neoliberal agenda (the demands of global capital for a cheaper, less tax-intensive economic environments) and golden handshakes to apartheid era bureaucrats – made cost recovery initiatives such as SGB autonomy and school fees an attractive answer to budgetary constraints and the need to attract foreign direct investment. The consequences, according to the critics, are clear. Like so much else about neo-liberal, Washington consensus policies, these cost recovery programmes, and the grant of political authority to SGBs to create and to enforce them, has only re-inscribed pre-existing patterns of social and economic inequality.[103] (The irony of the World Bank's recent description of South Africa as 'unsustainable' due to rather mundane, and seemingly intractable, features of our educational landscape, our 15% bureaucracy and our sluggish implementation of other programmes essential for the success of our developmental state should not lost upon these critics.[104] As Tony Judt, in a recent posthumously published essay, rightly opines: It's very easy to point the finger regarding anti-democratic and anti-human rights practices elsewhere. It's the obligation of intellectuals to concentrate their efforts on solutions to problems here at home.[105])

The problem with both accounts of SGB power is that they offer very selective readings of the SASA provisions and the constitutional norms that govern this emergent experimental institution. This section offers a third line of interpretation regarding SGB autonomy.[106] This reading takes seriously all of the provisions of SASA that determine the powers and the functions of SGBs. It also relies on a particularly thick conception of democracy made expressly manifest in the text of the Constitution, as well as in recent case law that more clearly delineates the political, communal, cultural and associative rights of South Africa's citizens. A careful reading of the Constitution, SASA and the case law reveals the lineaments of this emergent experimental institution.

No-one has, as yet, challenged – in toto – the constitutionality of SGBs or the enabling legislation that breathed life into them. (We have indeed seen their power curbed with respect to language policies and admissions criteria by the Constitutional Court; and incredibly powerful resistance by the Supreme Court of Appeal to the Constitutional Court's construction of SASA and the basic law.[107] After the SCA's most recent judgments in *Welkom* and *Rivonia*, many SGBs may feel emboldened to engage in unconstitutional behaviour knowing that their decisions can only be reversed if the provincial Head of Department undertakes a 'reasonable' review process and as necessary, secures a High Court finding in his or her favour.) This comparative lack of litigation, especially at the level of the Supreme Court of Appeal and the Constitutional Court, is instructive.[108]

Visible public debate and manoeuvring regularly takes place between state administrators, SGB boards and learners. The state and other stakeholders have – through the original legislation in SASA, in subsequent amendments to that legislation and in a significant number of court cases – attempted to place significant limits on what this emergent experimental institution can and cannot do. At the same time, other amendments and cases have expanded the realm of the SGB. Experiments with SGB form and function have taken place unceasingly – as SGBs and other parties confront new problems and attempt to solve old ones. Even with their uneven success, SGB's provide a vehicle for popular political participation that is quite real. That participation is made no less real by the strictures imposed upon them by our basic law and the subordinate statutory order. Despite concerns about their lack of capacity, SGBs enjoy popular acceptance and participation across race, class and language divides. SGBs are one of the few institutions that have the makings of a great, new and rather unique South African political tradition.[109]

Brahm Fleisch and I have offered elsewhere a comprehensive reading that cuts the Gordian knot that binds, perversely, those who view SGBs as little more than a thin form of compensatory legitimation for a state with little regard for communitarian concerns, and those who view SGBs as an unfortunate consequence of the need for a negotiated settlement between the apartheid state, big business, the ANC and the unions that took place in the 1980s. Some 27 discrete sections of SASA, when read together, support the contention that SGBs enjoy genuine autonomy – at the same time as they are subject to meaningful curbs on their power by other spheres of government, most notably the provincial government and the national government. This reading of SASA puts paid to the dual contentions identified above: (1) that SGBs are mere extensions of provincial departments of education or (2) that most SGBs operate like private, gilded associations.

But the point of the argument in these pages – as opposed to a book on education law – is to demonstrate the presence of *reflexivity* with respect to the norms governing SGBs and the practices engaged in by SGBs. An examination of SGBs as democratic institutions is ancillary to an understanding of the process of engagement by various stakeholders in the formation and reformation of SGBs themselves. Put slightly differently, I am less interested in the content of the legislative amendments to SASA or court judgments that have restricted the power of SGBs, than I am in showing how (through a constantly renegotiated process of legislation, regulation and other legal standards) SGBs, provincial governments and national government have effectively institutionalised shared constitutional competence over education in a variety of settings. The case law has granted SGBs broad authority to take community-based decisions on a range of school governance issues: from the hiring to the firing of teachers, to the right-sizing of school staff, to decisions about the content of their curriculum. At the same time, our jurisprudence has subjected these considerable powers to two powerful provisos: (1) no decision may block the ability of learners and parents from historically disadvantaged communities to become members of a school's community (should they meet all of the accepted statutory and regulatory criteria);[110] and (2) codes of conduct must be designed in a manner that enhances inclusion and diversity and does not unfairly limit the expressive, religious, cultural or linguistic rights of individual learners.[111] Such grants of authority and the two powerful provisos on that authority show significant evidence of the shared constitutional interpretation and participatory bubbles that are my quarry here.

i. SGBs as Emergent, Experimental Institutions

A careful examination of amendments to the legislation over the past fifteen years, as well as the case law, demonstrates that the state has, in fact, remained deeply committed to the process of representative, participatory and direct democracy in SGBs. Again: Most of the express changes in the legislation and the clarification of the legislation through case law reflect attempts to limit arbitrary use of power by SGBs, to clarify rules regarding the internal workings of SGBs and its relationships with various spheres of government, and to enhance the quality of education of as many of South Africa's learners as possible. These changes can hardly be viewed as full frontal attacks on the citadel of the SGB. (At the same time, it's important to remember that while the *Ermelo* Court has left the provincial HoD with the final say regarding a host of critical decisions that might be taken over the governance and the management of public schools, the Supreme Court of Appeal has resisted this alleged usurpation of power.)

The background against which the experiments take place is the South African Schools Act. One cannot understand the material changes made to the SGB's capacity to act as a site for experimentation without first getting a feel for the manner in which SASA creates this space. As Brahm Fleish and I have written elsewhere:

> The Preamble not only calls for the 'democratic transformation of society' but calls on 'learners, parents and educators' to take 'responsibility for the governance and funding of schools in partnership with the State'. SGBs, in sections 6, 7, and 8 are granted the power to determine the language policy of a school, to set up the conditions for religious observation and to create a binding code of conduct for learners. Section 11 sets up a representative council of learners – an entity that wields power unlike student bodies in other jurisdictions. Chapter 3, while notionally entitled Public Schools, contains provisions – from section 16 through section 32 (80 per cent of the Chapter) – devoted to the role and the responsibilities of SGBs. SASA Chapter 4 – which engages the funding of public schools – is, from start to finish, about the complex decision-making structure that exists between SGBs, school officials, learners, parents and the state. [This] delineation of SASA's provisions demonstrates that the Act welcomes public participation in school affairs in any number of different ways.[112]

a. Inclusion

Some of the most exceptional provisions of SASA, and those provisions that continue to receive considerable international attention, are the statutory provisions for learner participation in school governance.[113] Three distinct provisions underwrite this unique power of participation. In addition to articulating the legal requirement of all public schools that enrol learners in Grade 8 or higher to establish a representative council of learners (RCLs), section 11 demands that provinces develop guidelines concerning the establishment, election and function of the learner councils. SASA section 23(2)*(d)* recognises that learners in the eighth grade or higher at school are a category of persons that must be represented on the SGB. SGB section 8(1) requires that SGBs consult with learners (and other stakeholders) prior to the adoption of a school code of conduct for learners. According to Karlsson, SASA provides learners with an opportunity to 'experience democracy in student affairs, and through their representatives on the governing body, to engage in democratic structures and practices involving all relevant constituencies of the school community'.[114] Such inclusion of learners in the process of decision-making – as we saw in Dorf and Sabel's analysis of drug treatment courts and the virtues of the participation of drug users – enables SGBs to take account of the wisdom of learners without acceding to the dictates, of learners.[115]

The incorporation of learners into the governance of schools through RCLs is but one experiment in the law. SASA promotes broader, polycentric and flexible decision-making in other important respects by expanding the definition of 'parent' and ensuring that older learners, teachers, non-teaching staff and members of the community have a voice (if not voting rights).[116]

b. Decision-Making: Shared Powers of Interpretation

SASA expressly grants a wide range of specific decision-making functions and responsibilities to SGBs.[117] The SGB, in the hotly contested domain of SASA Chapter 4, takes decisions that have an enormous impact on school finance: the raising of fees, the drafting of annual budgets and the oversight of bank accounts. Many of these functions are circumscribed by national and provincial law, regulation and policy. How could it be otherwise? As matters currently stand, both national government and provincial government share legislative competence over primary schools and secondary schools. More importantly, the powers granted SGBs demonstrate the extent to which learning what works, and what doesn't, is built into this polycentric arrangement of decision-making.

c. Forms of Participation, and Forms of Participants

The primary form of democratic participation envisaged by SASA – across a range of school institutions – is conventional representative democracy. So, for example, in terms of SASA section 28, the MEC is required to issue regulations that specify how elections of members to the SGB are to be conducted. SASA section 29 then requires that the newly appointed members of the SGB elect office-bearers (e.g., the chairperson of the SGB must be a parent). SASA section 30 outlines rules related to the establishment of committees or subcommittees that could include non-elected members. (However, the chairperson of any such structure must be an elected member of the SGB.) On a slightly more mundane level, SASA specifies the composition of the governing body (section 23), the term of office of members (section 31), the status of minors on the body (section 32), and the legal standing of the body (section 15). SASA likewise articulates the procedures that need to be followed in the event that a legally constituted SGB fails to perform its function (section 25).

Learners are, as we have seen, also introduced to the practices of representative democracy through learner representative councils (section 11). When read closely, SASA provides a comprehensive set of guidelines for the exercise of representative democracy in and over public schools. But representative democracy alone would be insufficient to give full expression to a government based on the will of the people. SASA provides for two instances of direct forms of democracy. SASA section 8(a) states that the SGB must adopt a code of conduct for learners 'after consultation with learners, parents and educators of the school'. Why the requirement for a higher standard of democratic participation for the adoption of a code of conduct? If we are to follow the logic of *Matatiele II* and *Doctors for Life*, consultation, particularly with learners and parents, is likely to deepen the commitment to the democratic rules by which learners and parents are to be governed and create greater space for experimentation with critical school policies (say, the new debates over beginning genuine bilingual education at grade 1). Such direct democracy is a first step toward experimental self-governance. Direct democracy is also required for approval of a school budget and, by extension, a schedule of compulsory fees (section 38(2)). In this case, the final authority for approval lies with a simple voting majority of parents present at an annual meeting. Here again, the drafters of the legislation thought it prudent to ensure that every potential payee could give voice to her views about how money has been spent in the past and whether better pedagogy warrants changes in school expenditures. The annual meeting offers members of the school community an opportunity (a) to reflect upon their own school's performance; (b) to look laterally at the achievements of other schools and (c) to look forward and to take decisions with respect to how their own school might provide a better education for its learners.

d. Experimentation with Polycentric Participation in SGBs

In the 16 years since the adoption of SASA, Parliament has amended the legislation eight times. This section's analysis of the amendments underscores the general thesis that the state has used its power to increase access to better schools for learners from historically disadvantaged communities and to broaden participation in the governance of schools.

The 1999 Education Laws Amendment Act[118] contains two significant changes that have had a direct impact on the majority of schools. The first relates to the role of the governing body in suspension decisions. In terms of the original version of SASA s 9(1)(b), SGBs had the right, after a fair hearing, to suspend a learner from school pending the outcome of that fair expulsion hearing. In the amended legislation, SGBs can not take the decision alone – no matter how fair the process. The amendment now requires the SGB to 'consult with the [provincial] Head of Department' prior to suspending a learner awaiting an expulsion decision. The 1999 Amendment also changes the rules related to co-opted members. The 1999 Amendment adds to SASA s 23 a number of provisions that enable SGBs to continue to function when elected parents drop out of the governing body. The amendment allows the SGB to co-opt parents, temporarily, and grants these parents voting rights pending the outcome of a by-election. What is the significance of these two amendments? The first amendment, by shifting some of the SGBs authority to the provincial HoD, makes SGB decision-making more accountable. The second amendment addresses a situation in which an SGB may be rendered dysfunctional by a mid-term resignation and provides a practical solution that enables SGBs to continue to function with a parental majority. If anything, this amendment increases SGB authority and the ability of parents to exercise meaningful control over the governance of their children's school.

In 2000, s 20(1)*(k)* was amended in such a way as to give the provincial Head of Department (HoD) the right to determine what constituted reasonable and fair use of school facilities for educational programmes not actually conducted by the school.[119] The story behind this amendment is that some schools were refusing to grant provincial government the right to use parts of educational campuses to establish new schools or to provide additional classroom accommodation for nearby schools that were overcrowded. In the original formulation, schools were required to allow reasonable use under fair conditions. The question of ultimate legal authority – 'who would define what constituted reasonable use and fair conditions' – was left unspecified (until *Ermelo*?). Schools could have contested the meaning of these terms and in the process delayed the state's attempt to make use of the facilities indefinitely. The post-*Ermelo* shift in ultimate decision making power to the provincial HoD (rightly) expands the community of learners to whom any given SGB will ultimately be held accountable.

The 2001 Amendment to s 11 added the phrase: 'and such a council is the only recognised and legitimate representative body at the school'.[120] How are we to interpret the addition of this restriction? In many institutions, residual practices of the prefect system had been retained. In such cases, duly elected representative councils of learners did not receive the respect and the authority that SASA had granted them. The amendment provided a mechanism by which the state could signal to schools the importance that they attached to democratic decision-making bodies – not just for adults, but for learners as well.

The 2005 Education Laws Amendment Act contained a number of significant and far-reaching changes.[121] The most significant change was the creation of a new institution: the 'no fee' school. In the original 1996 version of SASA, all schools could charge fees and SGBs would determine the fees to be charged. As a rule of thumb, the bottom three quintiles of schools are now 'no fee schools'.' This new power to determine that a school be made a 'no fee school' came at a price. Any ministerial determination that a school could not charge school fees imposed upon the state an obligation to provide sufficient funding to such a school so as to compensate for the loss of funds associated with foregone fees. As an experiment, the state had finally come to the conclusion that fees charged by a substantial number of schools had no appreciable effect on their quality and constituted an unconstitutional barrier to access. The matter never had to be litigated.

Yet another change in legislation speaks to the experimental nature of education policy. The original formulation of SASA s 41 – which provided for the enforcement of payment of fees – has been substantially revised. The 1996 formulation simply states that the governing body may legally enforce payment of school fees. In the 2005 amendments, SASA s 41 was re-written in an attempt to clamp down on a range of abusive practices that had emerged around the enforcement of the payment of fees. For example, enforcement of payment can only take place after it has been determined that parents do not qualify for exemptions and all due process requirements have been satisfied. The new law also prohibits schools from placing an attachment on dwellings in any effort to recover unpaid school fees. While fees may still have their place, abuse of the fee system – and a concomitant denial of access to basic education – does not. Again: The matter never had to be litigated.

The pace of change to the South African Schools Act gained momentum in 2007.[122] The amendment gives the Minister the right to prescribe minimum norms and standards around a range of issues related to school infrastructure. These issues embrace class size and classroom utilisation, first and foremost. New draft norms set minimum standards for the provision of electricity, water, sanitation, libraries, labs, and sports facilities. (As matters currently stand four years later, the norms have not been promulgated and are the subject of litigation initiated by the NGO Equal Education designed to force the Minister to meet the draft those standards.) The amendment also envisages regulations regarding the provision of learning support materials of all kinds. The most significant amendment can be found in SASA s 5A(3) and (4). One would anticipate that the responsibility to meet the minimum standards would primarily fall on the provincial department. However, the amendment stresses instead that the SGB bears the responsibility of compliance with the norms and standards. The SGB must review any school policy that may have a deleterious effect on compliance with these provisions. The School Governance Foundation's interpretation suggests that: '... these norms and standards will create a basis for the state to attempt to become prescriptive concerning the number of learners in a school in relation to teacher numbers, class size and utilisation of classrooms.'[123] Given the strong emphasis on compliance by SGBs, it is difficult *not* to read this amendment against the background of battles between provincial departments and SGBs over class-size and oversubscription. As I have noted elsewhere, cases such as *Sunward Park* demonstrate that the provinces regularly struggle to deal with large learner flows around and across provinces.[124] Given the holding of the Constitutional Court in *Ermelo*, it's hard to gainsay the School Governance Foundation's interpretation. The new norms could provide provincial governments with standards against which they could measure school compliance and a legal basis to increase learner enrolment in an individual school. (One problem, and the subject of current litigation regarding the power of SGBs to control classroom numbers and enrolment, is that the provinces have not promulgated the necessary regulations.[125]) That said, Parliament has split the baby three ways: retaining for itself the power to determine adequacy standards, leaving SGBs with the power to govern themselves properly, and providing the provinces with the ultimate authority to ensure that standards are met and to solve problems that any given individual SGB might throw up with respect to access and to adequacy. (Now, for reasons that have as much to do with the economics and politics of legal NGOs, and the unqualified right to a basic education, the draft norms and standards are finally being used to leverage change through litigation around such issues as libraries, class size, teacher deployment and exclusionary practices. I am, at best, agnostic about the virtue of this new litigation frenzy.[126] As Mary Metcalfe, former Provincial MEC for Education, recently pointed out, roughly 93% of provincial education budgets are allocated to salaries. Legal NGOs seem relatively oblivious to the extent to which resource constraints, married to a widespread administrative failure of provincial governance, place discernable limits on what litigation might actually achieve.)

But before one reads these norms solely as an effort to restrict the autonomy of SGBs, one must recognise that the new norms likewise provide a relatively flexible set of standards against which the efforts and the achievements of provincial governments can be measured. The continual failure of provincial governments to respond timeously to demands for more teachers and buildings will (once the norms are promulgated) be viewed as a failure to comply with SASA's norms and standards. With the requisite legal support, parents can just as easily hold the provincial government's feet to the fire as can the state an obstreperous SGB. (However, the contestation by parents flows in both directions: many parents (through their SGBs) are attempting to hold the line against the imposition of the new norms and standards.) Sharing competence in this manner keeps the parties accountable to one another. Moreover, the publication of individual school scores ensures that information about effective teaching practices will be viewed in a rolling, lateral and forward looking fashion.

One would have to be a flak – and a very disingenuous flak at that – to conclude that 15 years' worth of amendments (and court decisions) have not altered the balance of power between the state and SGBs over the control of our classrooms. The amendments demonstrate the extent to which the state has used its power, through law-making, to challenge and to force more privileged schools to open up their gates to historically disadvantaged learners. The amendments have reinforced fee exemptions and come to grips with other exclusionary practices of a few elite public schools. The new norms enable provincial governments and parents to take firmer stands against schools that turn away learners when they are clearly undersubscribed. Once again, these restrictions on SGB power do not come at the cost of democratic processes or the creation of new stores of social capital. In fact, these amendments look remarkably like what John Hart Ely has called representative democracy reinforcing actions. When a majority fails to adequately cater for the equal participation of all community members (because the majority can always, by virtue of the franchise, effectively exclude meaningful minority participation), then it falls to the courts to ensure that the representative democratic processes work as they were intended.[127] The enforcement of fee exemptions, the power to ensure admittance to undersubscribed institutions and the move to expand the powers of RCLs all ensure greater inclusion of various members of the community in the decision-making processes that shape the school environment.

c. *Does the Evidence Support SGBs as an Emergent Experimental Institution?*

SASA, the amendments to SASA and the case law litigated under SASA (and other laws) demonstrate that SGBs have come to be accepted, over time, and through trial and error, as a legally legitimate emergent, experimental institution that enhance a bottoms-ups, reflexive (sometimes reactive), broad-based participatory form of public decision-making. SGBs clearly possess the requisite authority to take community-based decisions on a range of school governance issues: from the hiring to the firing of teachers, to the right-sizing of school staff, to decisions on language policy and curriculum offerings.[128] These immense SASA-based grants of power – as the amendments to SASA have shown – do not simply preserve the status quo. Through SASA's oft-renewed and oft-revised commitment to fee exemptions, to learner representation on SGBs and to a generally tougher legal regime that holds out the promise of new face-to-face relationships in schools, the state has charted an intelligent course between maintaining bonding networks that possess large stores of social capital and creating new social networks that deepen cross-racial, cross-creed, and cross-class collaboration. The goal: that every learner receives an education that allows her to flourish.

Some critics, however, might ask whether the reflexive activity described above counts as truly experimental. It's a legitimate question. I have pulled this punch, until now, because of an important ambiguity in theories of emergent experimental governance.

The critique elicits three primary responses. First, experimentalism does not require *formal* structures that pool information, that then reflect back to all participants best practices and suggest appropriate rolling norms. Social practices need not work in a Cartesian manner to qualify as experimental.[129] Second, the evidence regarding the manner in which school policy takes shape suggests that information about what works and what does not, in fact, occurs through consistent exchanges between national government, provincial governments, municipalities, SGBs, NGOs and a variety of other social actors. The exchanges may be imperfect and the solutions proposed limited: but to experiment is to fail more often than one succeeds. Third, the change that occurs is often driven by political concerns. In South Africa, the move from reconciliation to redress means that some policies must go. Here the critiques have some bite. And yet the distinction between policy and experiment is not always clear. Nor can it be. What is a policy but an attempt to realize some good by some means? What some experimentalists appear to want, it would seem, are pre-planned structures that arrange for different policy interventions, collect the data on those interventions and then decide which of the various interventions constitutes a best practice. However, given the commitment to reflexivity inherent in experimentalism, it's hard to know how a highly structured experimentalist regime can determine – in advance – what should count as a best practice or what should count as a new and preferred norm. The argument presumes that experimentalism requires conscious planning of all school environments and relatively conscious ex ante assessments of optimal individual and collective outcomes. As I noted in Chapter 3's discussion of Donald Campbell's views on evolutionary epistomology, no empirically-based discipline really works in that manner.

1. *The Cartesian Error as Manifest in Political and Social Experimentation*

In the first place, it's simply not true that all policies are the spawn of trial and error. Plenty of policies reflect deeply ingrained norms that lie at the very core of a community's self-understanding. Dorf and Friedman establish this very point in their discussion of *Miranda* and *Dickerson*. *Miranda* expressly invited experimentation within the rarified norms articulated by the Supreme Court. However, the *Dickerson* Court found that because (a) the community had formed legitimate expectations about their rights vis-à-vis the *Miranda* holding and (b) that co-ordinate branches of the state had failed to take up the offer to experiment for some 34 years meant that (c) the time-frame to experiment with Court's gloss on the constitutional norm had passed. The amendments to SASA that have affected the powers of SGBs, along with the holding in *Ermelo*, suggest a fluidity consistent with reflexivity and rolling basic norms.

Second, its simply not true that experimentalism must involve an expressly conscious trial and error approach in which politicians and other non-state actors create space for decentralized decision-making and feedback mechanisms that analyse the results of local actions and distil best practices that inform the next round of large-scale policymaking. This Cartesian error is exactly what this book has called into question from the outset.

Third, some readers make this Cartesian error because the experimentalist literature itself describes different kinds of forward and lateral looking reflexive feedback mechanisms. Not all experimentalist frameworks look like drug treatment courts.

However, to bring us back to the heart of this book, not all behaviour, and not even all conscious behaviour, is or ought to be structured in this manner. From the discussion of the self and consciousness, to various descriptions of social formations, to the adumbration of a number of different kinds of democratic experimental constitutional design, we see that most learning is the product of human action, *not* human design. Consciousness itself is about problem-solving: it allows for recollection of what has worked and what hasn't, and uses such recollection, and other natural and social endowments, to predict what may work effectively, or better, in the future. Recall that markets and Linux operate in a similar fashion. Experimental solutions are not worked out through armchair reflections or even dialogue: that is exactly why Dorf's pathbreaking article is called 'The Limits of Socratic Deliberation'. Moreover, not all experimental solutions begin with court-initiated litigation, or even wind up as court-sanctioned decisions: that is why Dorf and Sabel's seminal contribution is called 'A Constitution of Democratic Experimentalism'. Courtrooms have their place. But as I have suggested, they may not generate the most useful forward and lateral looking learning nor provide the greatest normative legitimacy for an outcome arrived at through extended assessment and experimentation by the parties most affected by the social problem in question. The pooling of information is essential, but it need not occur through the formal structures of a courtroom. Other institutions – as we have seen in Chapters 4 and 5 – may do just as well, if not better. South Africa and the United States are constitutional democracies. That alone skews the experimentalist pitch toward the courts. European scholars – who, for the most part, are not distracted by apex courts armed with wide-ranging powers of judicial review – have described these very same processes as 'emergent experimental governance'.

Another set of responses turns on a re-engagement with errant theories of consciousness, the desire of some critics for formal dialogical decision-making structures, and the recurring reification of Cartesian modalities of thought in the legal academy. To re-engage these well-entrenched modalities of thought, let's head back to the lab – the quintessential space for experimentation.

The 2011 Nobel Prize in physics went to three astrophysicists for their discovery of dark energy. What's truly interesting about this discovery is that the astronomers and physicists in question literally stumbled on this truly game changing finding. The three astrophysicists had – on two competing teams of astronomers – been locked in a race to discover how fast the universe was expanding by using data on a particular kind of supernova. Both teams had assumed that the data captured would indicate how fast the universe (we inhabit) was slowing down (some 13.7 billion years after the Big Bang.) The two primary theories about the expansion of the universe had held that the components of the universe, as they slowed down, would either fall back on themselves in what was described as the Big Crunch or simply continue to drift ever more slowly apart. As Dennis Overbye wrote: 'Instead, the two teams found … that the expansion of the universe was actually speeding up, a conclusion no one would have believed if not for the fact that both sets of scientists wound up with the same answer.'[130] The scientific community *did* believe the results. They did so because the findings were based on evidence, the same evidence, not mere argumentation and conjecture.

Once firmly established – after severely shaking up the overlapping communities of physicists and astronomers – other scientists were off to the races. What they found has actually told us that, as powerful as relativity theory and quantum mechanics are, they explain the behaviour of only a small amount of matter and energy in the universe. We now know that 70% of the universe is made up of dark energy and 25% is comprised of dark matter – the former speeds the universe's acceleration up, the latter slows it down. Both forces currently remain largely mysterious to us. We moved from three dimensions to four in the 20th century – and have found ourselves flummoxed by the apparent incompatibility of relativity theory (which works just fine in world of objects with substantial mass) and quantum mechanics (which works quite well at the sub-atomic level). Yet the two theories continue to do more than enough heavy lifting in everyday science and technology.

Why are we contemplating supernovas almost 13.7 billion light years away? They have shed light on the meaning and the virtues of experimentation. First, the experience of these prize-winning astrophysicists tells us that hypotheses are just that: and that unexpected meaningful data, confirmed and reconfirmed, provide new insights into our understanding of the universe. Second, and more importantly, the story above should serve as a break on the notion of 'conscious', pre-determined structures of information pooling. To be sure, the scientists in question work in communities with substantially shared visions of the universe (or what little we know of it.) However, the discovery and its consequences (to be left with just a complicated 5% solution) does not take the form of a stable, conscious, feedback mechanism that some critics have in mind. Not only were the teams in question unprepared for what they found, the discovery undermined the two basic views that astronomers and physicists had previously adopted as the best explanations for the phenomena already known to them.

These discoveries suggest that we bracket the formalism some legal theorists and even scholars familiar with experimentalism would impose. Instead, the story above should cultivate a strong degree of modesty about the power (and the limits) of legal reasoning (and how information is pooled and reflected back to the community.) Cartesian consciousness and feedback is rigid and hierarchical. Experimental consciousness is not. (And remember from Chapter 2 – what is 'conscious' is but the tip of the cognitive iceberg – other players wait in the wings for 'conscious' attention with respect to any given problem. Many of the most important neurological actors never set foot on the stage.) Dorf and Sabel understood this thesis well enough when they wrote [regarding the insights that pragmatist business management theory has to offer constitutional theory]:

> Pragmatist information pooling provides an alternative solution to the problem[s] of mass production [and] hierarchical specialization. Resources specific to one project in such a system [of hierarchical specialization] have only scrap value if put to another use, and expertise is so fragmented and specialized that the doings of one actor or group are inscrutable to others. Hence, in hierarchical firms, vertical integration, possession of residual control rights by a unitary owner, and the corresponding direction of the integrated enterprise by authority and incentives are a response to the temptations of holdups and deception. The new institutions, in contrast, so transform the conditions of cooperation that these incitements to trickery do not exist in anything like their accustomed form, and new forms of trickery can be countered by the very exchanges of information required for the exploration of ambiguity. The master resource in the new system is the ability

> to redeploy resources fluidly, as demonstrated in both the command of the novel search routines and in the capacity to reuse an increasingly high percentage of the physical equipment committed to one project in subsequent ones. The latter is accomplished, for example, by extensive use of flexible capital equipment that can be reconfigured by reprogramming the computers that guide its operation and changing one type of tool-bearing module for another. Moreover, the greater a work team's command of the search routines and problem-solving disciplines, the more accomplished the team becomes at such redeployment.[131]

Modern physics, contemporary pragmatist management theory and experimental constitutionalism demonstrate the importance of remaining extremely flexible when it comes to problem-solving. Too many legal theorists fall in love with their own brilliance. They take Dworkinian maximalism as their model, even when they profoundly disagree with his conclusions. Shouldn't that observation alone impose a certain degree of modesty about what we can legitimately claim in the domain of constitutional theory?

2. *The Desire to Experiment, the Ability to Experiment, and the Experiments Carried Out by National Government, Provincial Government and SGBs*

We can return now to Minister Bengu's statement and ask whether more than a decade of experimentation with SGB power rightly qualifies as experimentation with the decision-making structures of our public schools. A sufficient amount of change – as opposed to mere policy churn – suggests that the answer is a qualified 'yes'.

The pooling of information that has led to shifts in policy and law resides in three different locales: the SGBs, national government and provincial government. The School Governance Association pools information from its 2000 member constituency. The information, while public, is not shared with government in a fully collaborative fashion. National government has pooled information from schools throughout the country – often relying on provincial structures. This information has had a direct effect on changes in both law and policy. As for provincial governments: Left with the responsibility of managing schools, given virtually no control over their budgets (dictated as they are by the national government) and caught between powerful entities, as well as unpredictable learner demands, they have tried their best. Have education MINMECS (National Minister and Provincial Members of the Executive Council Forum) provided truly effective fora for information sharing and policy formation between the national government and provincial governments? In most instances, MINMECS do not discharge their essential function.[132] However, I have noted that the engagement between these three parties – not always friendly or truly co-operative – has led to limited litigation at the same time as constructive change has taken place. (The new drive towards litigation flows from parties – mostly legal – who wish to bend the will of all three of the dominant players toward a nascent social movement's rather vague (and often undercooked) notion of equal education. Not surprisingly the rush to usher in change – and change is certainly necessary in our ailing and often tailing public schools – does not address the most fundamental problems in our system of public education.)

The problem with the education sector MINMEC is worth teasing out for our current purposes. The MINMEC, by design, brings together the parties with shared constitutional competence for education: the national government and the provincial governments. By design, the education MINMEC should pool information from 9 very different provinces and one national government. The problem is not the experimental constitutional design contemplated by Final Constitution Schedule 4. The problem is the Big Dog that we last saw in Chapter 4. The President has no interest in actually learning about the problems in primary and secondary education in South Africa. The President (ostensibly) needs to be seen by his party and the other members of the current tripartite alliance – as well as the public – to be an engine for change. Thus, he demands that the Minister produce a document – say new 'draft' Norms and Standards about learners per classroom. These standards, once employed will ostensibly reduce the appalling illiteracy and innumeracy rates that are the hallmarks of South African school system. The Minister then produces a draft that is circulated to the provinces for their 'feedback'. The feedback from these policy interventions (well-conceived or ill-conceived) is invariably provincial education department blowback. The reason for the blowback is simple. The primary and secondary education sector, one of the three most heavily funded sectors in the national budget, spends 97% of the national outlay on labour and the maintenance of extant structures. That leaves roughly 3% for discretionary spending (read 'new initiatives'). Two immediate outcomes are possible. One. The national government can, and often does, go ahead and promulgate new regulations. Since the budget remains the same, the result of such new policies with no new funding is your standard 'unfunded mandate'. In short, the national government dictates policy initiatives but does not supply the funding necessary to make them reality. Two. The national government can make a big production of the draft – and then sit on it because it knows that the provinces oppose having to do more with less.

In the case of the new draft norms and standards, the Minister has done just that. For better or worse, however, the national government has been taken to court by Equal Education and the Legal Resources Centre (LRC) for failing to make good on the draft. The case looks like a winner from a litigator's perspective because the government has already promised to produce the new norms. Conversations with members of the LRC suggest that they have a less than optimal understanding of the actual political and financial dynamics at play, and thus, a limited appreciation for what implementation of the new standards would accomplish. However, for a lawyer a win is a win however pyrrhic. I'm not suggesting that the national government or the provinces are always in the right. Far from it. Provincial underspend has been a persistent problem. Moreover, the provinces consistently game the system when it comes to alleged markers of success such as matric results. (It's common knowledge that schools hold back students who will likely fail their final year exams.) And only recently has the public become aware that only 1 out of 3 students who bein Grade 1 graduate from high school.

So we have exchange of information and change in policy.[133] Despite the significant limitations noted above, we have it here in a form that seems far less crushingly destructive than the information pooling, feedback driven and ultimately punitive No Child Left Behind Act in the United States.

(In the year 2014, some 80% of US public schools will likely be found to fail to have adequately educated their learners.[134]) Put slightly differently, national government invariably has the power (because of our largely centralized polity) to make or to float policy. The provinces, in turn, can create quite a ruckus and can ultimately fail to make good on promises that they know cannot be kept. Or they can reach a compromise. Reformation of the schools fee regime is a good example of a halfway decent compromise.[135] National government was under substantial public pressure (from NGOs) to eliminate fees entirely. The provinces – without independent sources of raising revenue – asked how they were going to make up for the significant shortfall. (Many provincial departments of education and SGBs were on the same page on this issue.) The result, after much discussion between these three entities, was an agreement that only the poorest three quintiles of schools became fee free.

This give and take doesn't look all that bad when viewed through the prism of experimentalism. The MINMECs are fora for policy formulation – even if national government gets to be the 'big dog in the room'. The back and forth between provincial governments and SGBs looks like relatively healthy engagement – even when one brackets the line of racially motivated exclusion cases that ended in *Ermelo.* The Constitutional Court entered the fray at exactly the right juncture – where substantial SGB autonomy had run its course and racist policies suggested that provincial governments must have the final say on any given SGB policy. (Of course, provincial departments of education have repeatedly proven incapable of following the proper procedures for altering policy or taking decisions. As a result, the effect of *Ermelo* is to put the issue of SGB autonomy formally to bed, knowing full well that (the most powerful) SBGs will retain day-to-day, year-on-year operational control over most school management and policy decisions. Plus ça change.)

From my experimentalist perspective, the Constitutional Court's quiescence on issues educational has been all to the good. However, when a class of SGBs (and the Supreme Court of Appeal) proved incapable of reading FC s 29(2) properly, the Court rightly intervened on behalf of learners of colour.

From my experimentalist perspective, the host of new legal interventions is somewhat more troublesome. While a vibrant social movement around education cannot but be of great moment – for we have no future if we fail a third generation of learners – the issues chosen thus far for litigation suggest the lack of a thorough investigation of what happens inside schools themselves. Libraries for everyone would be lovely if our teachers could effectively teach our learners to read or to think critically. They certainly don't now. The reasons for this failure have become apparent to many educators and policy-makers (call it the 'Missionary Position'.[136]). The attempt to fix the limitations of our current stock of teachers has already secured meaningful monetary support (as an experiment undertaken in Gauteng.) If litigators drive the movement, as matters currently stand, then getting teachers and learners to sing from the correct hymn sheet will prove decidedly more difficult as money is shifted from one policy to another. Show me the money – and the evidence that libraries will truly change the game. The same holds for the norms and standards. Show me the money – and evidence that these new norms will truly change the game.[137]

From my experimentalist perspective, the primary virtue of this under-theorized, extremely formal approach to education litigation is that it will – like *Brown v Board of*

Education – have unintended positive consequences down the line. *Brown*'s faux sociological arguments regarding the benefits of desegregated classrooms are not its true legacy. The shift in racial relations (regarding more general social relations) unrelated to the classroom is. *Brown* ultimately delivered a two-term African-American President in Barack Obama because the US Supreme Court initiated a shift in perception that has led a sufficient large number of white Americans to view black Americans as their equals and affirmative action programmes as justifiable.[138] Missteps in litigation strategy in South Africa are acceptable so long as litigators learn from their mistakes and take cognizance of the policies that actually make a difference.

3. *The Tension between Politics and Experimentalism*

I must give the critics of my experimentalist gloss on education policy their due. Change has, to a significant degree been driven by politics – a shift from reconciliation to redress. (That the small number of schools affected by the shift to redress is not at issue here.)

For the purposes of understanding experimentalism better, and making the theory of experimental constitutionalism better, we need to understand the extent to which 'the banishment of politics' limits our understanding of experimentalism's aims. I have already suggested in this book that the social democratic (Deweyan) cast of experimental constitutionalism – or at least its primary proponents – seems to go largely unmentioned. Indeed, such silence gives Tushnet's critique of experimental constitutionalism its bite: namely, it's the best technical or instrumental approach to constitutional law in a welfare state. What's missing, again, is a clear expression of the progressive political commitments of experimental constitutionalism's primary expositors.

I fail, as before, to see why that should be so. You can nudge – as the politically progressive Sunstein would have us do. You can experiment – as the politically progressive Dorf, Freidman, Sable, Simon and Sturm would have us do. Both nudging and experimenting in law and politics must begin with at least some deeply shared normative pre-commitments. Even in his most minimalist phase, Sunstein acknowledged the need for such shared normative pre-commitments. Indeed, they are what allows either minimalism or its cousin, experimentalism, to get off the ground. (I take this same point up a third time in Chapter 7 when a substantive view of constitutional politics – flourishing – is once again ushered into the discussion.)

So politics, messy, sometimes venal, sometimes virtuous, cannot be banished. Law is meluctably though not entirely, norm driven. Yet the presence of politics is what exorcises experimentalists who want the theory limited to conscious, information pooling, feedback mechanisms, and who believe that anything but such a neutral approach fails to take the rolling, reflexive nature of experimentalism seriously. For some, describing the changes to SGB autonomy looks like nothing more than politics as usual experimentalist.

However, experimentalism makes no sense unless it rests upon a progressive core of norms. What, after all, are we trying to improve but the institutions that structure our lives? Indeed, the kinds of examples of institutions that reflect experimental constitutionalist's aspirations are dead giveaways of a progressive disposition. Drug treatment courts that have, as Dorf and

Sabel hypothesized, enabled us to revise our view of drug use as deviant and criminal and supplant it with a less judgmental view of substance abuse as an illness that requires a degree of care and understanding that proves to be both more humane and far less expensive than incarceration. Articles on child welfare and education reform reveal a similar bias toward improving the lot of the most vulnerable amongst us. All three objects of study reflect a concern with individual flourishing – the very reason experimentalism is actually so easily married with development theory and the capabilities approach.

c. *Polycentricity, Participatory Bubbles, Shared Constitutional Interpretation and the Right to a Basic Education in the Province of the Eastern Cape*

Mud huts. No ablution facilities. No electricity. No chalkboards. No seats. No desks. No books. A place one could hardly call home. And yet government officials had the temerity to call these buildings, and what happened in them, schools. The High Court in Bisho was not fooled. In *The Centre for Child Law & Others v Government of the Eastern Cape & Others*, the High Court found that the Government of the Eastern Cape Province, the OR Tambo Municipality and the Government of the Republic of South Africa had failed to deliver an adequate basic education in terms of FC s 29(1) to a large number of Eastern Cape learners.[139] The case, initiated by the Centre for Child Law and the infrastructure crisis committees of several primary schools in the Bisho district is a watershed event in South African education law and policy. A paradigmatic example of a well-designed instance of public impact litigation, the eight applicants created a record of such abject neglect that a finding of a violation of FC s 29 was ineluctable. Given this pre-ordained outcome, the culpable three tiers of government were obliged to enter into settlement talks with the applicants. From an experimentalist perspective, the settlement agreement – although not an order of the High Court – is particularly interesting because it reflects the combined wisdom of the High Court, the Centre for Child Law, the infrastructure crisis committees for seven primary schools and, of course, the government respondents.

Despite persistent averments by the Constitutional Court in a slew of socio-economic rights cases that courts in South Africa should eschew decisions that determine directly the budget of any co-ordinate branch of government, the national government was compelled to make a financial commitment of R8.2 billion from 1 April 2011 to 1 March 2014 'to replace inadequate structures, including mud structures, at schools throughout South Africa, and to provide basic services to those schools.' This amount would be delivered in three successive tranches of R700,000, R2.3 billion and R5.2 billion. R6.36 billion of this amount would flow to schools in the Eastern Cape. Of that amount, the seven applicant schools would receive amounts ranging from R10 million to R13.5 million. In addition, the national government committed itself to securing service providers within three months of the order that would ensure that the seven schools received 'water tanks, mobile classrooms, and sufficient desks and chairs for learners.' The provincial government was obliged, in the interim, to ensure that the local municipality in which the schools are located provided interim supplies of water. Unfortunately, non-compliance with any part of the order by the respondents can only immediately be brought to the attention of the High Court by the applicant's attorneys. So while the parties may approach the High Court, they may only do so through the ordinary process. The settlement agreement does, however, reflect consent by the parties to an 'expedited process' in the High Court should something go awry.

An extraordinary achievement by any measure, this settlement agreement (even without a supervisory order) sets the stage for similar forms of engagement between learners, parents, schools and all three tiers of government throughout South Africa. Should these cases continue to be brought before High Courts throughout the country, the government – at all three levels – and schools and learners will find themselves challenged to make good on these agreements. (Indeed, the national government is already in hot water for intervening in the educational affairs of the Eastern Cape, but failing to actually solve the problem of inadequate teacher post provisioning.) What we should see, in the short term and the long term, is varying degrees of success that the state, in co-operation with civil society, realizes in carrying out these orders.

This case, as well as any other, establishes the virtues of an experimentalist approach to constitutional interpretation. The High Court provided a general normative framework (as courts must do) within which the various actors had to proceed in concluding a settlement. This act of shared constitutional interpretation created the participatory bubble for negotiation. Having concluded negotiations, and having reached a settlement, the bubble has burst. However, should any of the government respondents fails to discharge its obligations in terms of the order, a new bubble may take shape. But let us assume that in this matter the bubbles entirely lose their cohesion. (This possibility cannot be assessed until April 2014.) What remains – in addition to better schools – is the enhanced legitimacy of the Constitution and the political order in the eyes of the litigants. This cardinal virtue of experimental constitutionalism – the legitimacy secured by participation – cannot be overemphasized.

This participatory bubble in the Eastern Cape foreshadows the appearance of new bubbles across the Republic. These bubbles may raise roughly identical issues. Or they may form as other parent-learner-NGO led structures identify other kinds of pressing issues best addressed by courts in terms of FC s 29(1). In each case, or any case, we shall witness a reflexive filling out of the right to a basic education, and, as a result of that reflexivity, a set of rolling best practices as determined by the parties to all such future education litigation. Here, at any rate, we can imagine participatory bubbles and shared constitutional interpretation working hand in glove to give FC s 29(1) increasingly greater, though far from inflexible, content. An experimental constitutionalist could not ask for anything more.

Endnotes

1. Act 19 of 1998.
2. *Grootboom* (supra) at paras 3–16.
3. Ibid at para 95. Analyses of the Constitutional Court's distinction between a child's unqualified guarantee to shelter under s 28 and the qualified right of access to adequate housing under s 26 were justifiably scathing. Kirsty McLean identifies three decidedly problematic contentions. First, the *travaux preparetoires* reflect an express intent that the rights of children to adequate shelter remain unqualified because children's 'vulnerability, lack of maturity and comparative innocence render them deserving of more effective protection.' *Travaux Preparatoires* Memorandum of the Panel of Constitutional Experts on 'Children' (5 February 1996). Second, the Constitutional Court conflates

shelter for children under s 28 with adequate housing for everyone under s 26. No basis for such an elision exists in the text. Shelter on the plainest of meanings is rarely confused with housing. Thirdly, the Constitutional Court's reasoning 'subsumed' the unqualified rights of children to protection from the elements under the highly qualified protections afforded adults. By making the rights to children subordinate to the rights of adults, the Constitutional Court has left us with the absurd outcome that only children without parents are entitled to immediate relief from the elements. Otherwise vulnerable minors are left to the wits of their parents or the alacrity of the state in providing sufficient shelter. K McLean *Constitutional Deference, Courts and Socio-Economic Rights in South Africa* (2009) 134-135. Davis J's analysis in the High Court suffers from none of these infirmities and is, undoubtedly, a better statement on how the relationship between s 28 and s 26 should be understood. *Grootboom v Oostenberg Municipality* 2000 (3) BCLR 277 (C). See L Stewart 'Interpreting and Limiting the Basic Socio-Economic Rights of Children in Cases where They Overlap with the Socio-Economic Rights of Others' (2008) 24 *South African Journal on Human Rights* 472. Stewart contends that one set of socio-economic rights ought not to be made subordinate to another set of socio-economic rights, nor should an unqualified socio-economic right (as in s 28) be subject to the internal limitations clause found in ss 26(2) or 27(2). Stewart argues that courts ought to employ s 36, the general limitations clause, to work out conflicts between rights and to harmonize them where possible. While Stewart's argument sounds good at a certain level of abstraction, it relies entirely on the Constitutional Court's willingness to give identifiable content to various socio-economic rights. In the absence of such content, it's hard to know exactly 'what' the Constitutional Court will be asked to compare, contrast and reconcile under s 36.

4. Ibid at para 94.
5. K McLean 'Housing' in S Woolman & M Bishop (eds) *Constitutional Law of South Africa* (2nd Edition, OS, July 2006) Chapter 55 (Provides the factual substratum for the analysis that follows.)
6. See S Sturm 'A Normative Theory of Public Law Remedies' (1991) 79 *Georgetown Law Journal* 1357, 1367–1368 (Describes the approach embraced in *Holt v Sarver* 309 F Supp 362, 383 (ED Ark 1970). In *Holt*, a finding of grave constitutional violations in an Arkansas prison system was followed by a remedial order requiring a 'prompt and reasonable start toward eliminating the conditions that have caused the court to condemn the system and to prosecute their efforts with all reasonable diligence to completion as soon as possible.')
7. Ibid at 1407–1408.
8. See Sabel & Simon (supra) at 1062-63 (Note that political blockage, i.e., the lack of accountability from the public bodies in question to certain stakeholders, is often an implicit element of the *prima facie* case for destabilization rights.)
9. Sturm (supra) at 1411 (Remedial orders must provide effective remedies 'reasonably calculated to produce compliance with the underlying substantive norm'.)
10. See *Grootboom* (supra) at para 97 ('Commission indicated during argument that the Commission had the duty and was prepared to monitor and report on the compliance by the State of its section 26 obligations. In the circumstances, the Commission will monitor and, if necessary, report in terms of these powers on the efforts made by the State to comply with its section 26 obligations in accordance with this judgment.')
11. See Sabel & Simon (supra) at 1069–1071 (The remedies, which take 'the form of a rolling-rule regime', are provisional rules that are evaluated according to their success in achieving the desired outcomes and can be supplanted with more successful rules.)
12. See Klaaren (supra) at Chapter 24C (Klaaren argues that the Human Rights Commission has the capacity to play an 'important independent role in interpreting, influencing and critiquing the state's obligations with respect to socio-economic rights.')
13. See Sabel & Simon (supra) at 1080-82 (Destabilization rights tend to spin a 'web' of social networks that extend far beyond the litigants affected by the positive outcome of the litigation.)

14. The detailed order in *Grootboom* is available at http://www.saflii.org/za/cases/ZACC/2000/14.html. The SAHRC's failure to discharge its responsibilities in terms of the order partially undercuts Professor Klaaren's hopes, and my own, with regard to how Chapter 9 Institutions can provide structures for information pooling and greater normative legitimacy for any order or settlement through continual and broad engagement with the communities most effected. Other Chapter 9 institutions have proved more robust. For example, the Public Protector, with the assistance of the Special Investigations Unit, has proved successful in identifying patterns of corruption in the security services and, in particular, the police force.
15. K McLean 'Housing' (supra) citing National Department of Housing *Ten Year Review* (2003).
16. South African Government Information *Department of Human Settlements on Housing through 2010* (2011) available at http://info.gov.za/aboutsa/housing.html (accessed on 28 August 2011).
17. K Rust 'No Shortcuts: South Africa's Progress in Implementing its Housing Policy, 1994–2002' (Unpublished paper, Institute for Housing of South Africa, 2006, on file with the author) 7.
18. K Rust and the Centre for Affordable Housing in Africa (FinMark Trust) *2012 Yearbook on Housing Finance in Africa: A Review of Some 42 of Africa's Housing Finance Markets* (2012).
19. Ibid at 125.
20. Ibid at 124.
21. Ibid at 124–125.
22. See *Grootboom* (supra) at paras 39–46, 52, 53, 63–69, 74, 83.
23. It took some time for *Breaking New Ground* to become official policy. Roughly six years. The national Department of Human Settlements notes that Cabinet approved the *Comprehensive Housing Plan for the Development of Integrated Sustainable Human Developments (Breaking New Ground)* in February 2010. (Available at www.info.gov.za, accessed 27 August 2011) Many housing analysts were unaware of the decision as of 2011.
24. See S Charlton, M Silverman & S Berrisford *Taking Stock: Review of the Department of Housing's Programme, Policies and Practice (1994–2003)*(Unpublished paper, Department of Housing, 2003)(On file with author) 31.
25. K McLean 'Housing' (supra) 55–14.
26. See National Housing Code, Part 3: National Housing Programmes: Chapter 12 Housing Assistance in Emergency Housing Situations, 12.2.1., available at http://www.housing.gov.za/Content/legislation_policies/Emergency%20%20Housing%20Policy.pdf (accessed on 25 January 2006). Many municipalities have failed to put the policy into practice. According to McLean, *City of Cape Town v Rudolph* reflects the ongoing gap between rhetoric and reality. *City of Cape Town v Rudolph & Others* 2004 (5) SA 39 (C), 2003 (11) BCLR 1236 (C), [2003] 3 All SA 517, 547 (C)(In *Rudolph I*, the primary application was for eviction under the Prevention of Illegal Eviction from and Unlawful Occupation of Land Act 19 of 1998 by the Cape Town Metropolitan Municipality. The respondents brought a counter-application for an order by the Court that the applicants were in breach of their constitutional and statutory duties.) McLean draws particular attention to the remarkable similarity between the factual circumstances in *Grootboom* and *Rudolph*: 'Both involved an attempt to evict a group of illegal occupiers from state-owned land by the Cape Town municipality. Both groups were living with 'no access to land, no roof over their heads . . . in intolerable conditions' or crisis situations. *Rudolph*, however, was decided almost three years after *Grootboom* and Selikowitz J took great care to apply the holding of the *Grootboom* Court to the facts of *Rudolph*. The *Rudolph* Court found that 'despite the clear statement by the Constitutional Court, applicant has still not implemented the AMLSP [Accelerated Managed Land Settlement Programme] or any equivalent programme' and that 'applicant has displayed and continues to display, an unacceptable disregard for the order of the Constitutional Court — and therefore the Constitution itself.' McLean (supra) at 55-22 quoting *Rudolph I* (supra) at 553, 554. Of greater import is the *Rudolph I* Court's order: 'The circumstances and, in particular, the attitude of denial expressed by applicant in failing to recognise the plight of respondents as also its failure to have heeded the order in *Grootboom* . . . makes this an appropriate

situation in which an order, which is sometimes referred to as a structural interdict, is 'necessary', 'appropriate' and 'just and equitable'.' *Rudolph I* (supra) at 553. As McLean notes, the *Rudolph I* Court was obliged to hand down such a far-reaching order -- requiring the City of Cape Town to deliver a report within four months which outlined the 'steps it has taken to comply with its constitutional and statutory obligations' – because the City had been afforded numerous opportunities to craft an appropriate response to the housing crisis and had failed to do so. McLean (supra) at 55-22 quoting *Rudolph I* (supra) at 560. The City of Cape Town barely managed to avoid being cited for contempt by making some effort to discharge their constitutional duties. *City of Cape Town v Rudolph & Others* (Unreported decision of the Cape High Court, 5 December 2005)('*Rudolph II*') 2.

27. For a superb overview of Johannesburg housing litigation from 2004 – 2008 and the limits of such litigation, see S Wilson 'Litigating Housing Rights in Johannesburg's Inner City' (2011) 27 *South African Journal on Human Rights* 127. See also B Ray 'Proceduralisation's Triumph and Engagement's Promise in Socio-Economic Rights Litigation' (2007) 27 *South African Journal on Human Rights* 107.
28. [2001] ZACC 19, 2001 (3) SA 1151 (CC), 2001 (7) BCLR 652 (CC)('*Kyalami Ridge*').
29. *Kyalami Ridge* (supra) at para 6.
30. Ibid at para 111.
31. Ibid at para 112.
32. For support for this claim, see L Feris 'Constitutional Environmental Rights: An Underutilized Resource' (2008) 24 *South African Journal on Human Rights* 29 (Finds that the content and the value of s 24 remains largely undefined and radically indeterminate.)
33. *Port Elizabeth Municipality v Various Occupiers* 2005 (1) SA 217 (CC), 2004 (12) BCLR 1268 (CC)('*Port Elizabeth Municipality*'). The usefulness of this case was brought to my attention by Professor Andre van der Walt. See A van der Walt *Constitutional Property Law* (2005).
34. L Fuller *The Morality of Law* 106 (1964).
35. *Port Elizabeth Municipality* (supra) at para 35.
36. Ibid at para 39.
37. Ibid at para 42.
38. [2008] ZACC 1, 2008 (3) SA 208 (CC), 2008 (5) BCLR 475 (CC).
39. Ibid at para 16.
40. Ibid at para 15.
41. Ibid at para 19.
42. Ibid at para 14.
43. Ibid at para 20.
44. [2009] ZACC 16, 2010 (3) SA 454 (CC), 2009 (9) BCLR 847 (CC). As always, I am indebted to Michael Bishop for his account of this case and other related matters.
45. Ibid para 408 (Sachs J, concurring).
46. Ibid para 407 (Sachs J, concurring) ('[T]hose who have been compelled by poverty and landlessness to live in shelters, should be discouraged from regarding themselves as helpless victims, lacking the possibilities of personal moral agency. ... The achievement of a just and equitable outcome required an appropriate contribution not only from the municipal authorities but from the residents themselves.')
47. [2009] ZACC 31, 2010 (2) BCLR 99 (CC).
48. Act 6 of 2007.
49. The riots in Khutsong, Merafong and Durban reflect a conscious response to the underlying repression of pain and suffering experienced by the majority of South Africans under apartheid and in the 16 intervening years of post-liberation one party dominant democratic rule. See T Madlingozi 'The Constitutional Court, Court Watchers and the Commons: A Reply to Professor Michelman on Constitutional Dialogue, 'Interpretive Charity' and the Citizenry as Sangomas' (2009) 1 *Constitutional Court Review* 63. For an additional, largely consistent explanation of this phenomena, see S Woolman

'Is Xenophobia the Correct Legal Term of Art? A Freudian and Kleinian Response to Loren Landau on Township Violence in South Africa' (2011) 22 *Stellenbosch Law Review* 185.

50. *Abahlali* (supra) at para 97.

51. Ibid at para 69.

52. 2010 (4) SA 133 (GSJ). At the same time, Willis J casts significant doubt about whether single judges sitting on the High Court can play the role of meaningful engagement facilitators envisaged by the Constitutional Court, and in these pages. With respect to that part of the opinion, the learned judge is not sufficiently precise. Many individual High Court judges, on their own, are not well placed to assess complex polycentric matters. I have suggested exactly why this contention may be so in Chapter 4 and Chapter 5.

53. Ibid at para 19.

54. See M Bishop and S Woolman 'Freedom and Security of the Person' in S Woolman & M Bishop (eds) *Constitutional Law of South Africa* (2nd Edition, OS, July 2006) Chapter 40.

55. D Bilchitz *Poverty and Fundamental Rights* (2006).

56. Of course, some more radical solutions, that depart from the standard liberal constitutional framework, are on offer. We could treat certain spaces within urban areas as commons. See E Ostrom and TK Ahn 'The Meaning of Social Capital and Its Link to Collective Action' in GT Svendsen and GLH Sendsen (eds*) The Handbook of Social Capital: The Troika of Sociology, Political Science and Economics* (2010) 17. Moreover, the notion of a commons connecting upper class Sandton and the township of Alexandria has been put on the table in the recent past.

57. The idea was mooted – and rejected. I am grateful to Michael Bishop and Jason Brickhill for extended discussions regarding this outcome.

58. Brian Ray's recent work sounds strikingly similar themes – though we have worked separately, without meaningful engagement, a continent apart. I want to thank Professor Ray for sharing his work with me as this book went to bed. See, e.g., B Ray '*Residents of Joe Slovo Community v Thubelisha Homes & Others*: The Two Faces of Engagement' (2010) 10 *Human Rights Law Review* 360; B Ray 'Policentrism, Political Mobilization, and the Promise of Socioeconomic Rights' (2009) 45 *Stanford Journal of International Law* 151.

59. See *Mamba v Minister of Social Development* 2008, Case No. 36573/08 (Northern Gauteng High Court); *Mamba v Minister of Social Development* CCT 65/08 (August 2008). *Mamba* is not your standard eviction matter. *Mamba* turned on the closure of camps for internees who had been subject to so-called xenophobic violence. For a discussion of *Mamba*, and the Constitutional Court's response, see S Woolman 'Is Xenophobia the Right Legal Term of Art? A Freudian and Kleinian Response to Loren Landau on the Violence in South African Townships' (2011) 27 *Stellenbosch Law Review* 285.

60. B Ray 'Engagement's Possibilities and Limits as a Socioeconomic Rights Remedy' (2010) 9 *Washington University Global Studies Law Review* 399, 407–408.

61. *City of Johannesburg Metropolitan Municipality v Blue Moonlight Properties 39 (Pty) Ltd & Another* [2011] ZACC 33, 2012 (2) SA 104 (CC), 2012 (2) BCLR 150 (CC). Michael Bishop and Jason Brickhill point out that the most significant part of the court's reasoning and order in relation to the eviction and provision of alternative accommodation is the principle that these two orders must be 'linked' so as to avoid the prospect of action leading to homelessness: 'The date of eviction must be linked to a date on which the City has to provide accommodation. Requiring the City to provide accommodation 14 days before the date of eviction will allow the Occupiers some time and space to be assured that the order to provide them with accommodation was complied with and to make suitable arrangements for their relocation. Although *Blue Moonlight* cannot be expected to be burdened with providing accommodation to the Occupiers indefinitely, a degree of patience should be reasonably expected of it and the City must be given a reasonable time to comply. The date should not follow too soon after the date of the judgment.' M Bishop & Jason Brickhill 'Juta Quarterly Reports: Constitutional Law 2011 (4)' (December 2011) quoting Blue Moonlight (supra) at para 100. Having reached these conclusions conjoining (1) engagement, (2) accommodation and (3) eviction, the Constitutional

Court handed down in swift succession three further judgments that put further flesh on the still largely procedural right to housing. In *Pheko,* the Constitutional Court addressed the powers of municipalities to evacuate individuals in terms of the Disaster Management Act and the extent to which both constitutional and statutory protection against eviction limited these powers. *Pheko v Ekurhuleni Metropolitan Municipality* [2011] ZACC 34, 2012 (2) SA 598 (CC), 2012 (4) BCLR 388 (CC). While the Constitutional Court held that the forcible removal of the applicants amounted to an eviction and thereby infringed the applicants' rights under s 26(3) and s 1 of the Constitution, the Court held that the evacuation of the community from an imminent sinkhole that would swallow the community was justified in terms of s 36 so long as – per *Blue Moonlight* – the municipality arranged suitable temporary accommodation between evacuation and relocation. *Skurweplaas* further extends the learning in *Blue Moonlight. Occupiers of Skurweplaas 353 JR v PPC Aggregate Quarries (Pty) Ltd* [2011] ZACC 36, , 2012 (4) BCLR 382 (CC). The Court found that since PPC Quarries had demonstrated little interest in using the land for profit in the near future and the municipality had the capacity to take reasonably quick steps to provide 'bridging' accommodation, the connection between engagement, eviction and relocation obliged the municipality to provide a clear link between the date of eviction and the date for provision of alternative accommodation. Ibid at para 13. In *Occupiers of Mooiplaats 355 JR v Golden Thread & Others,* the Court builds on its new linkage jurisprudence in two distinct ways. [2011] ZACC 35, 2012 (2) SA 337 (CC), 2012 (4) BCLR 372 (CC). First, a High Court must assess the viability and the desirability of the proposed alternative accommodation. Second, in order to undertake such an assessment, the municipality that seeks an eviction and relocation order must report back to the High Court on both issues before an order will be granted. See also *City of Tshwane Metropolitan Municipality v Mamelodi Hostel Residents Association* [2011] ZASCA 227, available at http://www.saflii.org/za/cases/ZASCA/2011/227.html.)(Supreme Court of Appeal confirmed the extant prohibition on eviction without a court order in terms of s 26(3) of the Constitution.) Of greater interest, however, with respect to issues of shared constitutional interpretation is Claassen J's approach to contempt of court in *Mthimkulu v Mahomed.* 2011 (6) SA 147 (GSJ). Claassen J writes: 'Where, however, enforcement of a court order is sought civilly without any criminal sanction, proof of contempt of court may be established on a preponderance of probability. A court may issue a declarator that a respondent is in contempt of court, established only on a balance of probabilities, together with associated civil relief such as barring a contemnor from access to civil courts until the contempt is purged. In the present case the appellants did not seek a committal, only a suspended fine.' Ibid at para 18. The High Court found that the respondents to be in contempt of court and fined them R 100,000 (suspended for 20 years, and contingent upon the state's commitment not to evict the residents during that period of time.)

62. See, generally, S Woolman and B Fleisch *The Constitution in the Classroom: Law and Education in South Africa, 1994 – 2008* (2009).

63. A notable exception occurred in the Eastern Cape in early 2011. In *The Centre for Child Law & Others v Government of the Eastern Cape & Others* (Case No 504/10, Eastern Cape High Court (Bisho))(2 February 2011). I discuss the basis for the FC 29(1) constitutional challenge and the settlement in *The Centre for Child Law & Others v Government of the Eastern Cape & Others* in the text below.

64. For a close reading of the constitutional provisions and the statutes governing equity requirements at independent schools, see S Woolman 'Defending Discrimination: On the Constitutionality of Independent Schools that Promote A Particular, If Not Comprehensive, Vision of the Good' (2007) 18 *Stellenbosch Law Review* 31 (Constitutional, legislative and regulatory framework for admissions policies at non-state-aided independent schools appears to afford learners, parents, educators and school governing bodies (SGBs) a substantial degree of autonomy.) For a close reading of the constitutional provisions and the statutes governing equity requirements at public schools, see B Fleisch and S Woolman 'On the Constitutionality of Single Medium Public Schools' (2007) 23 *South African Journal on Human Rights* 34. In *Ex Parte Gauteng Provincial Legislature: In Re Dispute Concerning the Constitutionality of Certain Provisions of the Gauteng School Education Bill of 1995*, Justice Kriegler

claimed that IC s 32 (c), FC s 29(3) and then extant national and provincial education legislation and subordinate legislation collectively constitute 'a bulwark against the swamping of any minority's common culture, language or religion ... But there is a price, namely that such a population group will have to dig into its own pocket.' *Ex Parte Gauteng Provincial Legislature: In re Dispute Concerning the Constitutionality of Certain Provisions of the Gauteng School Education Bill of 1995* 1996 (3) SA 165 (CC), 1996 (4) BCLR 537 (CC)(Kriegler J)('*Gauteng Education Bill*') at paras 39—42.

65. Department of Education draft *White Paper 2: The Organisation, Governance and Funding of Schools* (Gen 1229, 1995) 7.

66. That account, as John Pampallis writes, turns primarily on the rear-guard actions of the apartheid state to maintain white, privileged public schools. He first notes that: 'In its dying days, the apartheid government took a significant step towards decentralising the white education system. After the government's unbanning of the liberation movements in 1990, pressures began to build for the desegregation of white state schools ... In 1990, the Minister responsible for white education ... announced that white state schools would be allowed to change their status from the beginning of 1991. Three new school models were available: (1) Choosing Model A would result in the privatisation of the school; (2) A Model B school would remain a state school but could admit black students up to a maximum of 50% of its total enrolment; (3) A Model C school would receive a state subsidy but would have to raise the balance of its budget through fees and donations.' J Pampallis 'The Nature of Educational Decentralisation in South Africa' (Centre for Education Policy Development, Evaluation and Management) Decentralisation and Education Conference, Johannesburg, South Africa (11 - 14 June 2002) 3, citing Department of Education 'Education and Training in a Democratic South Africa: First Steps to Develop a New System' GN 16312 (March 1995) 8. See also S Badat 'Educational politics in the Transitional Period' in P Kallaway et al (eds) *Education after Apartheid: South African Education in Transition* (1997) 9. Pampallis continues: 'By early 1992, most of the 1 983 white state schools had chosen to retain their old status ... The following year, however, the government announced that all the formerly white schools ... would become Model C schools unless parents voted by a two-thirds majority to retain the status quo or become Model B schools, and that subsidies to all school models would be cut. As a result, ... 96% of the former white state schools became Model C schools, thus giving themselves the possibility of raising additional funds from parents to make up for the decrease in state funding . ... The parent body in each Model C school elected a governing body. Title to the fixed property and equipment of the school was given by the state to the school, to be administered by the governing body. The schools became juristic persons with the right to enter into contracts and to sue and be sued. They gained a high degree of autonomy, including the right to charge compulsory school fees and to determine their own admissions policy. The reasons for this change in the status of the white schools appear to have been twofold. First, the state was increasingly unable to provide the same level of financial support to white schools as previously. ... [T]he changing political climate ... obliged [the] government to move to greater equality in spending on black and white education. ... Second, the change to Model C was an attempt to ensure that white communities could continue to control their schools rather than allowing them to fall into the hands of a democratically-elected government, which was (rightly) seen as imminent.' Pampallis (supra) at 4 – 5. See, further, Education Affairs Act (House of Assembly) Act 70 of 1988. What was truly surprising was how few schools and parents opted for Model A. The sense of entitlement to government largesse in large sectors of the white community was so ingrained that most white parents could not foresee a future without access to state-funding. This lack of foresight explains *(a)* why advocates for historically privileged schools continue to misread FC sec 29(2) as protecting continued access to state funding for single-medium public schools and *(b)* why so few cases have turned on the protection afforded independent schools under FC sec 29(3). The need to reverse this sense of entitlement was recognised in one of the first new ANC government's white papers. See Department of Education *White Paper II: The Organisation, Governance and Funding of Schools* GN 1229 (November 1995) 6.23 ('*White Paper II*')('The provision of

state aid to a semi-privatised school system ... served to entrench existing privileges and retain the best schools, the best facilities and the most highly qualified teaching staff in the interest of those who had historically been most advantaged by the policy ... of racial preference in this country.') See also J Samuel 'The State of Education in South Africa' in B Nasson & J Samuel (eds) *Education in South Africa: From Poverty to Liberation* (1990) 17.

67. See S Woolman & B Fleisch 'Democracy, Social Capital and School Governing Bodies in South Africa' (2008) 20 *Education and the Law* 37. Extant SGB autonomy has its roots in the practices of South Africa's liberation movements. Many of the ANC government's early educational initiatives were predicated on the assumption that sustained school improvements must develop organically out of community participation and that community participation is contingent upon stronger (read autonomous) school governance structures. See Gauteng Department of Education 'Gauteng School Renovation Programme Implementation Plan' (1994)('Physical reconstruction and visible improvement in conditions at schools are tied to an incentive for strengthened school governance structures'). See also Gauteng Department of Education 'Circular No 2' (1995)('The key to successful school development lies in the capacity of communities at all levels to guide and manage their own development. ... [and] the revitalisation of participatory structure[s]'); Gauteng Department of Public Works 'Evaluation of the Gauteng Schools *Toilet Building Project*' (1997) 10–11 ('It was envisaged that community participation would prompt greater civil society participation in school governance, and stimulate emerging builders. ... It was believed that the toilet project would help to transfer power from the State to school governing bodies.') See, generally, African National Congress *The Reconstruction and Development Programme* (1994)('[T]he people affected must participate in decision-making. ... Democracy is not confined to periodic elections. It is, rather, an active process enabling everyone to contribute to reconstruction and development'); ANC National Education Co-ordinating Committee *National Education Policy Initiative* (1992)(Calls for dual structures of power: the state, on the one hand, community stakeholders on the other). It is, among other things, a testimony to the ANC's commitment to democracy that a party without a real opposition would divest itself of decision-making power based upon its belief that local schools and local communities would be best served by local political structures – in this case the SGB. However, the ANC's belief in the need of a strong central government to effect transformation may have militated against giving too much power to the community. See Y Sayed 'Discourses of the Policy of Educational Decentralisation in South Africa since 1994: An Examination of the South African Schools Act' (1999) 29 *Compare* 141, 143 (Sayed notes that community representatives – unlike parents – do not possess voting status on SGBs in terms of SASA. It seems reasonable to ask, however, why community representatives, who have no direct tie to the school, should enjoy such status.) But see R Malherbe 'Centralisation of Power in Education: Have Provinces Become National Agents?' (2006) 2 *Tydskrif vir Suid-Afrikaanse Reg* 237 (Malherbe contends that the ANC believed that 'political power should be centralised as far as possible.') Jonathan Jansen offers his own complex historical narrative to explain the constitutional choices and the educational policies that we have today. For Jansen, the trade union movement, the ANC's National Education Crisis Committee, the international aid community, the business community, the NGO sector and the National Education and Training Forum constitute the seven most important bodies with respect to educational policy development in the run-up to and aftermath of the 27 April 1994 elections. See J Jansen 'The Race for Education Policy after Apartheid' in Y Sayed & J Jansen (eds) *Implementing Educational Policies: The South African Experience* (2001) 12.

68. Sophie Oldfield describes this process of decentralisation of power in terms of a 'fragmentation' of state policy that had not, prior to 1994, been anticipated by those parties who would govern the post-apartheid state. See S Oldfield 'The South African State: A Question of Form, Function and Fragmentation' in E Motala & J Pampallis (eds) *Education and Equity: The Impact of State Policies on South African Education* (2001): 'The broader dismantling of the apartheid legacies has involved a process of rereading and rewriting the legal and social contracts that govern relationships between

state and society. However, the process of making society legible to post-apartheid imperatives of equity and then simplifying these realities into social policy to redress inequality has been fraught with difficulties. … The reconstruction of education [through state policy] lies at the heart of this transformation [of South Africa] because education marks a path for individual, community and collective development. … To give effect to these policies, Parliament has passed a host of legislative measures … to reconfigure educational structures from the level of the school, to the district, the provinces and the national state. In the process of constructing … solutions to post-apartheid transformation, the state's role in development has rotated in orientation. This rotation has altered the development process itself – so much so that the agenda of the post-apartheid state has fragmented from one of prioritising reconstruction and redistribution … to one of facilitating the delivery of social services beyond the ambit of state responsibility.' Oldfield (supra) 32–33.

69. Put somewhat differently, the fragile state that drafted the Final Constitution, SASA, NEPA and EEA could never have withheld the authority that it had granted. At best, the state could hedge its bets. Whether the issue was basic education, or school fees, or admissions policies (or even school choice), a fragile state crafted legislation and regulation that divided management, governance and policy-making responsibilities between national government, provincial government, provincial Heads of Department, teachers, principals, unions, SGBs, parents and learners without establishing clear hierarchies of authority. The result was that local and private actors in the mid-1990s were able to assert their interests through legal channels without having to worry about being rebuffed by the state. The price the state paid for such assertions of private power was small by comparison to the compensatory legitimation that it secured through *de jure* and *de facto* decentralization. H Weiler 'Comparative Perspectives on Educational Decentralization: An Exercise in Contradiction?' (1990) 12 *Education Evaluation and Policy Analysis* 433.

70. The ANC's complex political agenda mirrors, but does not always match, the egalitarian, utilitarian, democratic and communitarian commitments found within the Constitution. The ANC as a governing party in the 21st century, and no longer a liberation movement in the 20th century, must pursue: (a) an egalitarian agenda that aims to provide a substantively, equal start for all its citizens; (b) a libertarian agenda that recognises the formal freedoms enjoyed of its citizens; (c) a utilitarian agenda designed to create the greatest good for the greatest number of its denizens; and (d) a democratic and a communitarian agenda that privileges, in some important respects, the face-to-face relationships found in kin, clan and commune over the more abstract relationships that bind us, at a highly abstract level, as citizens of the Republic of South Africa.

71. A Sachs 'Opening Remarks' Konrad Adenauer Stiftung Seminar on Multiculturalism (1999) 9, available at http://www.kas.org.za/Publications/SeminarReports/Multiculturalism/SACHS1.pdf, (accessed on 1 April 2005); H Giliomee 'The Majority, Minorities and Ex-Nationalities in South Africa and the Proposed Cultural Commission' KAS Seminar on Multiculturalism (1999) 37, available at www.kas.org.za/Publications/SeminarReports/Multiculturalism/GILIOMEE (accessed on 6 January 2005).

72. Some might argue that these movements were more group oriented than this sentence admits. Gandhi's work in South Africa focused almost exclusively on rights for South Africa's Indian population and was later translated into an anti-colonialist movement when he returned to India. Worker's rights would – in the South African context – have been described as class rights for white workers. The Freedom Charter has a decidedly communitarian cast. Its language describes the land (and its fruits) as belonging to all South Africans and is decidedly focused on redistribution and reclamation. The displaced and disenfranchised South Africans were primaily people of colour.

73. See S Woolman 'Community Rights: Religion, Language and Culture' in S Woolman & M Bishop (eds) *Constitutional Law of South Africa* (2nd Edition, OS, March 2007) Chapter 58.

74. See Giliomee (supra) at 40. The ANC insisted that minority rights *qua* static, non-demographically representative levels of political representation were unacceptable. The ANC proposed a compromise between two political positions: the demand for unfettered majority rule on the one hand, and the

insistence of some whites for structural guarantees that 'majority rule will not mean domination by blacks' on the other. The Bill of Rights is, in large part, the content of that compromise.

75. See Sachs (supra) at 13 ('The instruments and the institutions of government are not based on cultural groups, cultural communities or representation in terms of membership of a particular community.')

76. See F Venter 'The Protection of Cultural, Linguistic and Religious Rights: The Framework Provided by the Constitution of the Republic of South Africa, 1996' KAS Seminar on Multiculturalism (1999) 19, available at http://www.kas.org.za/Publications/SeminarReports/Multiculturalism/VENTER.pdf, (accessed on 1 April 2005).

77. Ibid. Provisions of the Final Constitution dealing with culture, language and religion include, but are not limited to: (a) ss 9, 30, 31, 235 (culture); (b) ss 6, 29, 30, 31, 35, 235 (language); and (c) ss 9, 15, 30, 31, 224 (religion).

78. IC s 32 read quite generously. It states that 'educational institutions based on a common culture, language or religion' can be established, 'provided that there shall be no discrimination on the ground of race.' FC s 29(2) reads: 'Everyone has the right to receive education in the official language or languages of their choice in public educational institutions where that education is reasonably practicable. In order to ensure the effective access to, and implementation of, this right, the state must consider all reasonable educational alternatives, including single medium institutions, taking into account: a. equity; b. practicability; and c. the need to redress the results of past racially discriminatory laws and practices.' FC s 29 (3) reads 'Everyone has the right to establish and maintain, at their own expense, independent educational institutions that a. do not discriminate on the basis of race; b. are registered with the state; and c. maintain standards that are not inferior to standards at comparable public educational institutions.' Rassie Malherbe contends that FC s 29(2) provides a strong guarantee – a rebuttal presumption – that linguistic communities can create and maintain publicly funded single medium public schools. See R Malherbe 'The Constitutional Framework for Pursuing Equal Opportunities in Education' (2004) 22 *Perspectives in Education* 9. With the greatest respect, Malherbe misreads FC s 29(2). He collapses the distinction between the right to instruction in a mother tongue or preferred language (where practicable) with the obligation imposed upon the state to consider a range of options as to how to offer such instruction. Malherbe privileges single medium schools. FC s 29(2) does not. Ibid at 21. It only mentions them as only one in a range of alternatives that the state has an obligation to consider. Moreover, any option considered by the state for delivering mother-tongue instruction – *one* of which is single medium schooling – must satisfy the three criteria of equity, practicability and historical redress. Malherbe claims that because the Final Constitution specifically refers to 'single medium institutions' that 'whenever they [single medium institutions] are found to be the most effective way to fulfill the right to education in one's preferred language, single medium institutions should be the first option'. Ibid at 22. This analysis places the cart before the horse. Because Malherbe collapses the distinction between mother-tongue instruction and single medium schools, he fails to recognize that the right to the preferred language instruction is subject to 'practicability', and that the privilege of maintaining a single medium public school can only be retained if the school's continued existence satisfies the three-fold criteria of equity, practicality and redress. Finally, Malherbe asserts that 'right to education in one's preferred language is guaranteed unequivocally in the South African Bill of Rights.' Ibid. This statement is clearly false. As the above language of FC s 29(2) indicates, the right to receive education in the official language or languages of one's choice in 'public educational institutions' is subject to a powerful internal modifier. That dimension of the right exists only where the provision of 'that education is reasonably practicable.' See also R Malherbe 'Submission to President Nelson Mandela on behalf of a group of Afrikaans Organizations' (15 May 1996); R Malherbe 'A Fresh Start: Education Rights in South Africa' (2000) 4 *European Journal for Education Law and Policy* 49. In any event, the Constitutional Court's judgment in *Ermelo* has put paid to this line of argument.

79. See *Ex parte Gauteng Provincial Legislature: In re Dispute Concerning the Constitutionality of Certain Provisions of the Gauteng School Education Bill of 1995* 1996 (3) SA 165 (CC), 1996 (4) BCLR 537

(CC)(Justice Sachs argues that the religious, linguistic and cultural rights found in the Interim Constitution are best understood as efforts to 'concretis[e] ... a certain measure of cultural/ linguistic autonomy in the private sphere. ... Section 32(c) appears, ... to be an explicit, if limited, acknowledgement of the need in certain circumstances to allow for a departure from the general principles of [non-discrimination]... What appears to be provided for ... is not a duty on the State to support discrimination, but a right of people ... to further their own distinctive interests.')

80. Ibid at paras 39–42.

81. Others, such as Iain Benson, have argued that I Benson the Final Constitution's permission to create a Religious Charter does just that 'Religious Freedom and South Afrikca's Charter of Religion' *SAIFAC Conference on Equalityand Religious Freedom* (June 2010). (On file with another).

82. Of course, the historical and legal record regarding community rights and public schools is somewhat more complex. See S Woolman & B Fleisch 'South Africa's Unintended Experiment in School Choice: How the National Education Policy Act, the South Africa Schools Act and the Employment of Educators Act Create the Enabling Conditions for Quasi-Markets in Schools' (2006) 16 *Education and the Law* 37.

83. Cf J Beckmann 'The Emergence of Self-Managing Schools: Devolution of Authority or Disguised Centralism' (2002) 14 *Education and the Law* 153, 161.

84. A good example of this shift in goals is on display in the state's efforts to bring independent schools to heel by attempting to control the age of admittance for learners at independent schools. The state seemed to assume that it could go after independent schools in this manner without having to worry about alienating a particular constituency – a constituency that would mobilize around ascriptive identifiers such as language, religion or culture. What the state failed to take sufficiently seriously was the ability of individual parents to mobilize around the interests of their own children. In *Harris v Minister of Education*, the High Court found that the state's age restrictions on admission to Grade 1 constituted an unjustifiable impairment of Tayla Harris' right to equality. 2001 (8) BCLR 796 (T) ('*Harris HC*')(The King David Schools refused to admit Talya to Grade 1 in 2001 – even though her parents believed she was ready. The refusal to admit Talya was based upon a notice issued by the Minister of Education stating that independent schools could only admit learners to Grade 1 at the age of 7. Unwilling to take the risk that Talya might experience a developmental deficit after being held back a year, Tayla's parents decided to challenge the constitutionality of the notice so that their daughter could be admitted to Grade 1 in 2001.) The *Harris High Court* found that the state had failed to tender any adequate justification for its policy. The Minister was afforded an opportunity to rebut the presumption of unfair discrimination. First, the Minister argued that six-year old children were more likely to fail than seven-year old children and such failure rates had serious financial consequences for the state. Second, the Minister argued that the diversity of cultures and languages within South Africa produced insuperable difficulties for the creation of a school readiness test. Third, the Minister argued that sound pedagogical reasons exist for starting formal education at age 7. The *Harris High Court* rejected all three arguments tendered by the Minister because the state had failed to adduce any evidence in support of its claims. As a result, the state failed to rebut the presumption that unfair discrimination on the grounds of age had taken place. More importantly, the result thwarted state efforts, on apparently neutral grounds, to control private power as exercised through private institutions. *Harris* stands for the proposition that the associational rights of the parents who send their children to independent schools trump alleged state interests in equality where the equality interest asserted cannot be backed up by any compelling pedagogical rationales. The Constitutional Court did not confirm the ratio or the holding of the High Court, but found instead that found that the Minister lacked the requisite authority under NEPA s 3(4) to create such a rule. *Minister of Education v Harris* 2001 (4) SA 1297 (CC), 2001 (11) BCLR 1157 (CC)('*Harris CC*') at paras 11–13.

85. The biggest legal challenge to the exercise of private power in private institutions has been the promulgation of the Promotion of Equality and Prevention of Unfair Equality Act 4 of 2000.

PEPUDA constrains private power in ways the courts, and those who run public schools and non-state-aided independent schools, have yet to fully appreciate. Indeed, it seems fair to say that the government itself – in the form of national and provincial departments of education – remains largely unaware of the power this particular tool has to reshape admissions policies – along more egalitarian lines – at both public schools and non-state-aided independent schools. PEPUDA makes it clear that its provisions prevail over all other law – save where an Act expressly amends PEPUDA or the Employment Equity Act applies. However, recent Equality Court judgments have slowly drawn attention to the manner in which PEPUDA can be used to constrain private power that impairs the dignity of employees of private religious schools. See, eg, *Strydom v Nederduitse Gereformeerde Gemeente, Moreleta Park* 2009 (4) SA 510 (EqC)(The applicant was an independent contractor appointed by the church to teach music to the learners that participated in the church's arts academy. When the church discovered that Mr Strydom was gay, they dismissed him from his job. The Equality Court found that the church had unfairly discriminated against Mr Strydom on grounds of sexual orientation. It ordered the church to apologize to Mr Strydom and awarded damages for loss of earnings, the impairment of dignity, and emotional and psychological suffering.)

86. *Matukane and Others v Laerskool Potgietersrus* 1996 (3) SA 223 (T).
87. 2003 (4) SA 160 (T).
88. FC s 28(2)'s guarantee that the best interests of the child are always of paramount importance was held by the *Laerskool Middelburg* court to trump the language and cultural rights of the school's Afrikaans-speaking learners. In deciding that the 'minority' students must be accommodated, the *Laerskool Middelburg* court correctly concludes that the right to a single-medium public educational institution is clearly subordinate to the right which every South African had to education in a similar institution is to a clearly proven need to share education facilities with other cultural communities. The *Laerskool Middelburg* court seems to be on far shakier grounds when it suggests that a claim to a single-medium institution is probably best defined as a claim to emotional, cultural, religious and social-psychological security. This trivializes the desire to maintain basic, constitutive attachments. It seems clear that the desire to sustain a given culture as it stands – read contemporary Afrikaner culture – is best served by single medium institutions that reinforce implicitly and expressly the importance of sustaining the integrity of that community. As a result, the *Laerskool Middelburg* court must be wrong when it claims that the conversion of a single-medium public institution to a dual-medium school cannot *per se* diminish the force of each ethnic, cultural and linguistic communities' claim to a school organized around its language and culture. Ibid at 173. That is exactly what the conversion does. Whether such insularity is good for learners in a multicultural society is another matter. I, like Professor Jansen and others, tend to think that it leaves them ill-prepared to engage the radically heterogeneous world that they will enter upon graduation. See J Jansen *Knowledge in the Blood: Confronting Race and the Apartheid Past* (2009).
89. *Minister of Education Western Cape & Others v Governing Body, of Mikro Primary School & Another* 2006 (1) SA 1 (SCA)('*Mikro*'). See also *Governing Body, Mikro Primary School, & Another v Minister of Education, Western Cape & Others* 2005 (3) SA 504 (C), [2005] 2 All SA 37 (C), 2005 (10) BCLR 973 (C).
90. It did so on three primary grounds. First, the Supreme Court of Appeal overturned Bertelsmann J's finding in *Laerskool Middelburg* that the Norms and Standards provided a mechanism for the alteration of the language policy of a public school. At best, the Supreme Court of Appeal said, the Norms and Standards constituted a guideline for members of the department and those parties responsible for the governance of public schools. Second, the Supreme Court of Appeal held that SASA s 6(1) granted neither the national Minister of Education nor the provincial MEC or HoD the authority to determine the 'language policy of a particular school, nor does it authorize him or her to authorize any other person or body to do so'. The power to determine language policy vests solely with the SGB of a given public school and is subject only to the Final Constitution, SASA and any applicable provincial law. Third, the Supreme Court of Appeal rejected the applicant's contention that FC s 29(2) could be 'interpreted to mean that everyone had the right to receive education in the

official language of his or her choice at each and every public educational institution where this was reasonably practicable'. *Mikro* (supra) at para 30.

91. *Seodin Primary School v MEC Education, Northern Cape* 2006 (1) All SA 154 (NC).

92. Brahm Fleisch and I believe that the extant jurisprudence, post-*Ermelo*, supports the following reading of FC s 29(2): 1. FC s 29(2) grants all learners 'the right to receive education in the official language or languages of their choice in public educational institutions where that education is reasonably practicable.' First note that the right to receive education in the official language or languages of one's choice is not, as the Supreme Court of Appeal in *Mikro* noted, an unqualified right. The right is subject to a standard of reasonable practicability. How should this internal limitation of the right be read? Where sufficient numbers of learners request instruction in a preferred language – and, as we shall see below, we do possess regulations, as well as standards and norms, that make clear what those numbers are – and no *adequate alternative* school exists to provide such instruction, then a public school is under an obligation – with assistance from the state – to provide instruction in the language of choice. However, when we proceed to the second sentence in FC s 29(2), it is worth taking another look at the meaning of 'reasonably practicable'. As an evidentiary matter, the learner or the learners or the state must be able to show that instruction in the language of choice is 'reasonably practicable' at the institution where the learner or the learners has applied for admission. So, for example, a single learner who requests instruction in Sepedi in a single medium Zulu school may be hard pressed to demonstrate that it is reasonably practicable to accommodate her at a single medium Zulu school. An inability to establish reasonable practicability would be even more pronounced where the learner who preferred instruction in Sepedi had access to an adequate school that offered Sepedi instruction. Finally, a failure to demonstrate that a request for instruction is reasonably practicable ends, as the *Mikro* Court found, the FC s 29(2) inquiry. Assume, however, that the learner has shown that instruction in the language of choice is reasonably practicable at the institution where she has applied for admission. Only then do we consider the import of the second sentence of FC s 29(2). The second sentence of FC s 29(2) states that '[i]n order to ensure the effective access to, and implementation of, this right, the state must consider all reasonable educational alternatives, including single medium institutions, taking into account: a. equity; b. practicability; and c. the need to redress the results of past racially discriminatory laws and practices.' The second sentence of FC s 29(2) makes it patently clear that single medium institutions are but one way of accommodating the right of a learner to instruction in the language of choice. Moreover, the mere mention of single medium schools in no way privileges such institutions over dual medium schools, parallel medium schools, or schools that accommodate the multilingualism of the student body in some other way. All that this section of FC s 29(2) requires is that the state consider 'all reasonable educational alternatives' that would make mother tongue or preferred language instruction possible. However, even if single medium schools are found to be one of the reasonable alternatives for preferred language instruction, the single-medium school must be able to satisfy a three factor test. That is, for a single medium school to be preferred to another reasonably practicable institutional arrangement – say dual medium instruction or parallel medium instruction – it must demonstrate that it is more likely to advance or to satisfy the three listed criteria of equity, practicability and historical redress. 7. This constitutional concession to single medium schools is a very weak right indeed. It is, perhaps, best described as right to have reasons or an entitlement to justification. Such an entitlement is not without value for proponents of single medium schools. What the second sentence of FC s 29(2) ultimately requires is that the state be able to justify its preference for one form of school over another. Given the Final Constitution's recognition of single-medium schools as a legitimate means of providing preferred language education, the state will find itself under an obligation to demonstrate why another form of instruction – dual-medium, parallel-medium, special tutoring – will better serve the learners in question. Moreover, the Final Constitution's recognition of community rights, associational rights, religious rights, cultural rights and linguistic rights creates a set of background conditions against which claims for single-medium schools must be

taken seriously. For where preferred language instruction is reasonably practicable, and where single medium schools satisfy the desiderata of equity, practicability and historical redress, the state cannot simply invoke an overriding commitment to 'equality' or 'transformation' in order to dismantle single medium institutions. The Final Constitution is, ultimately, a post-apartheid constitution. Thus, at the same time as it sets its face against exclusion and discrimination, it rejects the kind of totalizing view of the state that marked and marred apartheid. Space remains – within both the private realm and the public realm – for the accommodation of multiple ways of being in the world. That public space, as we have seen, is extremely narrow for single medium public schools. However narrow it may be, it cannot be entirely wished away. The Constitutional Court, in *Ermelo*, has largely confirmed this reading. See *Head of Department, Mpumalanga Department Of Education & Another v Hoërskool Ermelo & Others* 2010 (2) SA 415 (CC), 2010 (3) BCLR 177 (CC).

93. Ibid. The High Court had heard the matter twice. *Hoërskool Ermelo & Others v Departementshoof van die Mpumalanga* [2007] ZAGPHC 4 (2 February 2007)('*Hoërskool Ermelo I*'); *Hoërskool Ermelo & Others v Departementshoof van die Mpumalanga* [2007] ZAGPHC 232 (12 October 2007)('*Hoërskool Ermelo II*'). In *Hoërskool Ermelo I*, Judge Prinsloo, of the Pretoria High Court, suspended a decision of the Mpumalanga education department to dissolve the school's governing body and to replace it with a departmentally appointed committee. The dissolution would have enabled the Mpumalanga education department to alter the school's language policy and allowed English-speaking pupils to receive instruction in English. On appeal, Transvaal Judge President Ngoepe, and Judges Seriti and Ranchod set aside the High Court ruling in *Hoërskool Ermelo I.* The *Hoërskool Ermelo II* Court found that the Afrikaans-medium public school must admit English-speaking pupils. Of particular moment for the *Hoërskool Ermelo II* Court was the under-subscription of Hoërskool Ermelo. Given that Hoërskool Ermelo was operating at only half-capacity, the Full Bench found that it was 'reasonably practicable' – as contemplated by FC s 29(2) – for the high school to accommodate the 113 Grade 8 learners. The mere fact that all the classrooms were being employed and that the existing curriculum turned on the current availability of classrooms did not constitute sufficient grounds for excluding English learners and maintaining Hoërskool Ermelo as a single medium Afrikaans-speaking public school. Equity, practicability and historical redress – the three express grounds for assessment of existing language policy in terms of FC section 29(2) – justified the transformation of Hoërskool Ermelo from a single-medium public school into a parallel medium public school. The Supreme Court of Appeal reversed the judgment of the High Court in *Hoërskool Ermelo II. Hoërskool Ermelo and Another v Head, Department of Education, Mpumalanga, and Others* 2009 (3) SA 422 (SCA). The Supreme Court of Appeal found the that HoD lacked the requisite statutory authority to alter the SGB's language policy. It did not contemplate the constitutional implications of the matter. The Constitutional Court upheld some aspects of the SCA's judgment – namely the rebuke of the HoD with regard to a brace of procedural irregularities that undermined the Department's attempt to alter Hoërskool Ermelo's language policies. At the same time, the Constitutional Court indicated that it wanted to hear – after appropriate consideration – how the HoD planned to engage the issue of a parallel instruction school or an English only instruction school in the Ermelo circuit. It also made clear that Hoërskool Ermelo must revisit its language policies in light of the Constitutional Court's clear finding that the SGB did not possess the unmitigated authority to determine the school's language policy and that it was obliged, in terms of s 29(2), to take the needs of all learners into account when it determined the language of instruction: the right to instruction in a language of choice (where reasonably practicable), fairness, feasibility and the need to remedy the results of past racially discriminatory laws and practices must play a critical role in their decision-making.

94. Ibid at paras 2, 46, 49 – 53.

95. Although *Ermelo* constitutes the first instance in which the Constitutional Court opined upon the meaning of s 29(2) of the Constitution, it is, perhaps, the Deputy Chief Justice's 'ironic' aside regarding the hegemony of colonial languages in Africa that packs the greater charge. In policy circles, a consensus may be building around the belief that the de facto default position of English

as the primary language of instruction from primary school onwards has not served South African learners well. As I note above, we may be on the verge of witnessing a new experiment: namely that educators have come to believe that multilingualism in schools is essential for the success of most South African learners (because they will only learn effectively if mother tongue instruction is offered). Although this new experiment may not save single medium Afrikaans schools, it may save Afrikaans as a living language. Multilingual schools might not necessarily have to accept English as a default language. One could easily imagine schools in which Afrikaans and Sepedi were both taught to the same, or to distinct, cohorts of learners. Indeed, single-medium Afrikaans schools may well come to see dual medium or parallel medium education as a saving grace – and get out in front of intrusive provincial Heads of Department. Such a strategic move has already occurred at the tertiary level. The University of Johannesburg (formerly Rand Afrikaans University) made a strong play for black students in 1990s – and thus the provision of tuition in English – as a strategy for growth. The University of Pretoria has embraced English as matter of survival. (Indeed far more students at the faculty of law study in English than in Afrikaans. The vast majority of these students are black.) Whether the actual needs of learners can displace the call of the marketplace will prove an interesting test for educators: a decision to pursue multilingualism would constitute South Africa's largest experiment in education.

96. When ensuring that people are not prevented from securing access to existing educational resources, FC s 29 operates much like an ordinary civil and political right. Any interference with the legitimate exercise of the right can be justified only in terms that meet the test set out in FC s 36(1). *Matukane & Others v Laerskool Potgietersrus* 1996 (2) SA 223 (T)('*Matukane*). Schools may not refuse to admit learners of a particular race, or expel learners for trivial non-compliance with dress codes. In number of cases, the exclusion flows from a school's code of conduct, which although seemingly neutral, excludes or punishes members of particular communities. In *Antonie v Governing Body, Settlers High School & Others*, a learner had been found guilty of 'serious misconduct' for attending school with dreadlocks and a cap she deemed to be essential parts of the practice of her Rastafarian faith. 2002 (4) SA 738 (C). In the High Court, Van Zyl J held that codes of conduct should not be rigidly enforced. They must instead be read in 'a spirit of mutual respect, reconciliation and tolerance. The mutual respect, in turn, must be directed at understanding and protecting, rather than rejecting and infringing, the inherent dignity, convictions and traditions of the offender.' Ibid at para 17. The student's conduct was ultimately held to fall well short of the definition of 'serious misconduct', and the High Court set aside the School Governing Body's decision. In *KwaZulu-Natal MEC for Education v Pillay*, the Constitutional Court had to decide whether a Hindu learner was entitled to wear a nose stud to school as an expression of her Tamil culture and Hindu religion. [2007] ZACC 21, 2008 (1) SA 474 (CC), 2008 (2) BCLR 99 (CC)('*Pillay*'). The school had refused to permit her to wear the stud on the grounds that the wearing of the stud did not fall within the core belief set of the religion. The Constitutional Court held that the 'norm embodied by the Code is not neutral, but enforces mainstream and historically privileged forms of adornment, such as ear studs which also involve the piercing of a body part, at the expense of minority and historically excluded forms.' Chief Justice Langa found, in addition, that voluntary religious and cultural practices were entitled to the same protection as obligatory practices. While recognizing the importance of codes of conduct and the need to ensure discipline, Chief Justice Langa concluded that a mere appeal to uniformity was insufficient grounds to refuse a learner's request for an exemption from a code. A school that wished to enforce a code of conduct under the kind of circumstances that brought Ms Pillay to court would have to show that a particular exemption was more than likely to cause a palpable disruption to school activities. Given the absence of any such evidence, the Court found that the learner ought to have been granted an exemption.

97. Department of Education *The National Curriculum and Policy Statements* (2010)(Discusses language policy at 4.6) available at www.education.gov.za and www.info.gov.za (accessed 11 September 2011).

98. See S Woolman 'The Problem of the 'Other' Language: Official Languages, Equal Citizenship and an Integrated South Africa' (Plenary Paper for Legal Resources Centre Conference on Education and Constitutional Litigation, 2012)(forthcoming *Education and the Law*). Seventy years ago, T J Haarhoff wrote: 'There is increasing ignorance of the second language; ignorance brings a feeling of inferiority, and that in turn brings aggressive assertion that it is a good thing to be unilingual and that strength lies in isolationism. Let us save our children from isolationism. The adult, with all the worries of a busy life and the handicap of an unfavourable environment, finds it difficult to acquire a new language and to break down group barriers; to a child it is "child's play". The world is moving away from the isolationist principle. ... Fullness of life, educationally or spiritually is not comparable with the barbed-wire fences of racial politics. With the sun of a new world rising over the grandeur of our limitless veld, the darkness of estranging barriers will yield; it will yield before the creative inspiration of giving ourselves to South Africa – ourselves undivided to her undivided.' T J Haarhoff 'Foreword' in EG Malherbe *The Bilingual School* (1941). The above words, written at a very different time, in a vastly different context, contain a contemporary resonance. Haarhoff and Malherbe should be read as maintaining that genuine reconciliation, dignity and equal citizenship can only be achieved in multilingual, radically heterogeneous societies when groups learn the language of the other groups with whom they share political sovereignty. That Haarhoff and Malherbe understood reconciliation, race and the 'other' solely in terms of English and Afrikaans give their words a bitterly ironic bite. As I have already noted, that bitter ironic bite has not been lost on present day commentators and the current members of the Constitutional Court, such as Deputy Chief Justice Moseneke, in *Head of Department, Mpumalanga Department of Education & Another v Hoërskool Ermelo & Another.* Haarhoff's (apt if odd) observations about race, language and understanding the 'other' retain their force with respect to the promise of national reconciliation and genuinely equal citizenship. Only the players and the petitioners have changed. Most black South Africans have done their share of heavy lifting when it comes to overcoming problems associated with race, language and understanding the 'other'. The same cannot be said for most white South Africans. We take the *Ermelo* Court's concerns seriously and refract them through current, lively and difficult debates in our public schools about how 'we', as School Governing Bodies (SGBs), provincial Heads of Department (HoDs), members of the national Department of Education, interested academics, lawyers, teachers, parents and learners should decide which two official languages should be taught at any given public school. This question is by no means a philosophical abstraction about how one should order a just and fair society. The new Curriculum and Assessment Policy Statement [CAPS] has quite consciously reinvigorated language policy deliberations and led to a growing number of disputes over the languages taught in our public schools. Curriculum and Assessment Policy Statement, Department of Basic Education, 2012. Rather than introducing the First Additional Language [FAL] at the end of the Foundation Phase, the Department of Basic Education decided to shift FAL to the first year of schooling: 'Children come to school knowing their home language. They can speak it fluently, and already know several thousand words. Learning to read and write in Grade 1 builds on this foundation of oral language. Therefore, it is easier to learn to read and write in your home language. When children start to learn an additional language in Grade 1, they need to build a strong oral foundation. They need to hear lots of simple, spoken English which they can understand from the context. Listening to the teacher read stories from large illustrated books (Big Books) is a good way of doing this as it also supports children's emergent literacy development. As children's understanding grows, they need plenty of opportunities to speak the language in simple ways. This provides the foundation for learning to read and write in Grades 2 and 3. In South Africa, many children start using their additional language, English, as the Language of Learning and Teaching (LoLT) in Grade 4. This means that they must reach a high level of competence in English by the end of Grade 3, and they need to be able to read and write well in English. For these reasons, their progress in literacy must be accelerated in Grades 2 and 3.' Ibid. To address this specific challenge of ensuring that African language speakers become sufficiently proficient in English, CAPS requires all schools identify a

First Additional Language. In most instances schools would choose English, and thus teach oral language and English reading and writing explicitly from Grade 1. The new curriculum policy explicitly allocated between two and three hours per week for the First Additional Language in Grades 1 and 2, and between three and four hours per week for the First Additional Language in Grade 3. The primary purpose of this significant portion of the school week is to develop 'listening and speaking, thinking and reasoning and language structure and use, which are integrated into all 4 languages skills (listening, speaking, reading and writing), reading and phonics, writing and handwriting.' More specifically, the CAPS Foundation Phase document specifies that Grade 1 teachers should teach listening and speaking for one and half hours a week, and half an hour on reading and phonics for the First Additional Language. By Grade 3, the policy requires one hour on listening and speaking, one hour on reading and phonics, and half hour respectively on writing and language use. Ibid. The new policy raises, at least, two new education and constitutional law questions. First, do parents have a right to choose the First Additional Language their children will learn? Second, what are the legal and constitutional strictures restrictions placed upon SGBs decisions with regard to First Additional Language policies for their schools? This decision is not merely of consequence for those elite public schools which have generally chosen English and Afrikaans as primary mediums of instruction, and a third 'African' language as something akin to an extra-curricular activity. Prior to the introduction of CAPS, most South African schools tended to teach in their home language: that is, in one or two of the nine African languages. A small percentage of disadvantaged schools shifted to English as the 'default' home language and medium of instruction. Ibid at 20. Although most quintile 1 – 3 schools introduced English towards the end of the Foundation Phase, many children in South African schools do not acquire an adequate vocabulary and the reading and the writing proficiency necessary to cope with the language demands of English medium teaching in Grade 4. Ministry of Education *Problems with English as a Medium of Instruction in Primary Schooling* (2009). Aware of this deficit, the Department of Basic Education has shifted the introduction of the first additional language to the first year of schooling. The department reasoned as follows: 'Children come to school knowing their home language. They can speak it fluently, and already know several thousand words. Learning to read and write in Grade 1 builds on this foundation of oral language. Therefore, it is easier to learn to read and write in your home language. When children start to learn an additional language in Grade 1, they need to build a strong oral foundation. They need to hear lots of simple, spoken English which they can understand from the context. Listening to the teacher read stories from large illustrated books (Big Books) is a good way of doing this as it also supports children's emergent literacy development. As children's understanding grows, they need plenty of opportunities to speak the language in simple ways. This provides the foundation for learning to read and write in Grades 2 and 3. In South Africa, many children start using their additional language, English, as the Language of Learning and Teaching (LoLT) in Grade 4. This means that they must reach a high level of competence in English by the end of Grade 3, and they need to be able to read and write well in English. For these reasons, their progress in literacy must be accelerated in Grades 2 and 3.' So far so good: it would appear at first blush an eminently reasonable manner in which to retool of the early school environment of most South African learners. To address the specific challenge of ensuring that African language speakers become sufficiently proficient in English, CAPS made a First Additional Language (FAL) mandatory at *all* public schools. In most instances, schools would choose English. They would expressly require instruction in oral language and English reading and writing from Grade 1. While an appropriate curriculum policy decision for most 1 to 3 quintile schools, it has had an unanticipated consequence for a growing number of quintile 5 English home language schools. Over the past fifteen years, privileged public schools like Parkview Junior Primary in Johannesburg and Grove Primary School in Cape Town had begun teaching two additional languages in the Foundation Phase. In Johannesburg, the two additional languages tended to be Afrikaans and isiZulu. Western Cape schools were inclined to teach Afrikaans and isiXhosa. The teaching of these additional languages was initially limited to the oral language. By Grade 3, schools introduced a limited degree of reading and writing tuition. A new irony, that Deputy Chief Justice Moseneke could have easily anticipated, arose. As a result of the new FAL requirement, a sizeable number of English home language schools (a) correctly assumed that they were obliged to make a choice and (b) opted to drop African languages and select Afrikaans as the First Additional Language. The choice of Afrikaans as the First Additional Language is, evidently, based on a range of practical considerations. First, these schools have Foundation Phase teachers that have been trained to teach Afrikaans as a second language. Any given African language is often taught by a specialist SGB paid teacher. (These staff members are often part-time employees paid by the SGB, as opposed to the state, to offer this additional tutelage.) Second, if a school adopted an African language as a FAL, the new two to three hours a week FAL requirement would have staffing consequences and increase overall school expenditures. (New teachers would be required – not simply to teach the FAL, but to teach other subject matter (math, science or geography) in the FAL African language.) As matters stood, these schools already possessed the existing resources – books and teachers – to provide instruction in Afrikaans as a second language. Few schools enjoy comparable resources for African language instruction. Most publishers have not produced systematic materials in African languages for young second language speakers. Third, many parents expressed anxiety regarding the extremely high demands that IsiZulu and other African language matriculation examinations would place on their children. Even exceptional African language students fair poorly on their exams. Afrikaans, by contrast, was widely viewed as an 'easy' language that offered the opportunity for excellent matric results. For learners in elite public schools competing for limited number of places in first rate university programmes, a mediocre FAL mark could well prejudice their chances. Given the 'locked-in' systemic advantages of English and Afrikaans, the SGBs of many top quintile schools chose Afrikaans as the FAL and dropped African language instruction. The irony of which Deputy Chief Justice spoke is no longer collateral. Diminished African language instruction, in a growing cohort of schools, is a direct function of teaching materials, qualified teachers, additional expenses and potentially difficult matric exams. These disheartening consequences raise a number of thorny legal questions. We know that s 6(1) of SASA grants an SGB the power to determine the language policy of the school subject 'to the Constitution, this Act and any applicable provincial law.' For some SGBs, this grant of power answers any questions that one might have about an FAL. But the learning of *Ermelo* suggests that the answer is not so straightforward. Although the answers to the tricky statutory and constitutional questions raised in *Ermelo* engaged SGB initiated admissions policies, the broader concerns in the matter turned on who possessed the ultimate authority to assess the 'reasonableness' of these policies. *Ermelo* found that such power vested with the provincial HoD once it had undertaken appropriate reasonable review of (a) the SGB's decision-making process and (b) the 29(2) rights of the learners in question. We will suggest that a similar, but by no means identical, set of issues are raised by FAL decisions taken by SGBs. Both the *Ermelo* Court and the state wish to ensure that the nine official African languages are treated with same degree of respect accorded English and Afrikaans in our public schools. Fair enough. It's taken long enough. For sound pedagogical reasons, they want to ensure that mother tongue instruction and dual medium tuition is offered from initial entrance into our primary schools. However, as one must be aware, the state's purse, the resources of individual schools, the availability of appropriately trained teachers and the adequacy of existing textbooks across all 11 languages place cognizable, constitutionally-recognized limits on our capacity to deliver immediately upon this promise. Thorny and difficult questions do not preclude an initial response. First, we can ask where SASA places ultimate authority for FAL decisions? Second, we can ask whether the statute, as read in light of s 29 of the Constitution, and a panoply of other rights – to citizenship, official languages, equality, dignity and community practices – does not warrant a reading of the FAL policies consistent with the need, recognized in *Ermelo,* for creating conditions in which we are truly capable of speaking to one another in languages we all eventually come to understand. Rights to equality, dignity, community rights, official languages, citizenship and a basic, adequate education, as well as a mother tongue education, all support the proposition that a truly agonistic South African democracy will never bloom until we all make an effort to understand one another as best as we possibly can. By limiting instruction to English and Afrikaans, many learners are denied access to basic capabilities and the opportunity to flourish. Second class linguistic skills invariably entrench or reinforce second class status. The state and the Constitutional Court understand that our radically, heterogeneous society will never coalesce into a single nation until we are able to speak rationally and respectfully to one another. The new policies allow us to look *inward* and protect our particular community's linguistic heritage, while demanding that we also look *outward* toward the broader South African landscape and come to appreciate that learning another language is essential if we are ever to truly understand one another and to build a 'rainbow nation' truly deserving of the appellation.

99. J Beckman 'The Emergence of Self-Managing Schools in South Africa: Devolution of Authority or Disguised Centralism?' (2002) 14(3) *Journal of Education and the Law* 1. See also J Jansen 'The Ties that Bind: Race and Restitution in Education Law and Policy in South Africa and the United States' (2006) 105 *Yearbook of the National Society for the Study of Education* 211.

100. See R Malherbe 'Centralisation of Power in Education: Have Provinces Become National Agents?' (2006) 2 *Tydskrif vir Suid-Afrikaanse Reg* 237 (Argues that ANC believed that 'political power should be centralised as far as possible'.) See also J Prinsloo 'State Interference in the Governance of Public Schools' (2006) 26 *South African Journal of Education* 355.

101. This contention is only partially true with respect to single medium public schools and entirely false with respect to independent schools. See S Woolman 'Defending Discrimination' (supra); B Fleisch & S Woolman 'Single Medium Public Schools' (supra).

102. See Y Sayed 'Democratising Education in a Decentralised system: South African Policy and Practice. (2002) 32(1) *Compare* 35–46; Y Sayed 'Discourses of the Policy of Educational Decentralisation in South Africa since 1994: An Examination of the South African Schools Act' (1999) 29(2) *Compare* 141 at 143; *Y Sayed* 'Understanding Educational Decentralisation in Post-Apartheid South Africa' (1997) 66(4) *The Journal of Negro Education* 354; Y Sayed & N Carrim 'Democracy, Participation and Equity in Educational Governance' (1997) 17(3) *South African Journal of Education* 91.

103. See F Veriava 'The Amended Legal Framework for School Fees and School Funding: A Boon or a Barrier?' (2007) 23 *South African Journal on Human Rights* 180. See also J Karlsson 'The Role of Governing Democratic Bodies in South African Schools' (2002) 38(3) *Comparative Education* 327 (Karlsson argues that while the use of democratic institutions in school governance has much to recommend it, several studies, though largely anecdotal, have suggested that these institutions have merely re-enacted traditional South African relations of race, class and gender.) Cf S Woolman & M Bishop 'Education' in Woolman and Bishop (eds) *Constitutional Law of South Africa* (2 Edition, RS4, December 2011) Chapter 57.

104. World Bank 'The Challenge of Inequality: South Africa' (supra).

105. T Judt 'On Intellectuals and Democracy' (March 22, 2012) 59 *The New York Review of Books* 7.

106. Dietlin and Enslin contend that participatory governance by SGBs block significant change in public schools, especially in those communities with limited resources, and that we would be better served by direction and intervention by our representatives at the national level of government. See V Dieltiens & P Enslin 'Democracy in Education or Education in Democracy: The Limits of Participation in South African School Governance' (2002) 28 *Journal of Education* 5. Piper responds directly to Dietlin and Enslin and suggests that they may have 'reached their conclusions too hastily' and that they have thrown out 'the participatory baby with the School Governing Body bathwater'. See L Piper 'Participatory Democracy, Education, Babies and Bathwater: A Reply to Dietlins and Enslin (2002) 28 *Journal of Education* 28.

107. See, especially, *Head, Department of Education & Another, Free State Province v Welkom High School* 2012 (6) SA S25 (CSA) [2012] ZASCA 150; Rivonia. Given the Supreme Court of Appeal's holdings in *Mikro* and *Welkom* and *Rivonia* , it's fair to expect more cases that test the boundaries of the

Constitutional Court's holding in *Ermelo*. In *Welkom*, the Supreme Court of Appeal held that a provincial HoD could not reverse, by mere departmental instruction, a decision taken by an SGB with respect to the governance of the school within the SGB's realm of statutorily granted powers (ie, 'student conduct' such as falling pregnant), even when the SGB knows that its decision effectively constitutes an unconstitutional encroachment on a learner's rights. A fair and rational review process undertaken by the provincial HoD will be deemed insufficient to overturn an SGB decision or to withdraw an SGB power or function. *Welkom* constitutes a powerful challenge to *Ermelo*'s apparent shift in the balance of power to provincial Heads of Departments of Education. Given the vast number of complaints that land on an HoD's desk regarding the behaviour of various SGBs, it is patently inconceivable that HoDs will continually retain outside counsel to litigate – in the High Court – each and every facially unconstitutional SGB action.

108. I must, however, hedge my bets at the outset of 2012. New education and law social movements led, in part, by Equal Education, the Legal Resources Centre, the Centre for Child Law and the Socio-Economic Rights Institute (to identify but a few of the NGOs litigating education cases) have brought new issues to the fore. One can fully expect both national government, provincial government and SGBs to feel increasing heat inside and outside the courtroom.

109. The tradition of local control dates back to the earliest schools on the subcontinent and has continued in various forms ever since. See EG Malherbe *Education in South Africa* (1934). See also L Tikly 'Governmentality and the Study of Education Policy in South Africa' (2003) 18 *Journal of Educational Policy* 161.

110. *Ermelo* (supra).

111. *MEC for Education, KwaZulu-Natal, and Others v Pillay* 2008 (1) SA 474 (CC), 2008 (2) BCLR 99 (CC); *Antonie v Governing Body, Settlers High School & Others*. 2002 (4) SA 738 (C).

112. Woolman & Fleisch *The Constitution in the Classroom* (supra) at 177. Other commentators demur on the meaning of the provisions and the power afforded by those provisions to SGBs under SASA: See, eg., M Smit '"Collateral Irony" and "Insular Construction" – Justifying single medium schools, Equal Access and Quality Education' (2011) 27 *South African Journal on Human Rights* 398 (With respect, the author both erroneously describes the learning of *Ermelo* and mischaracterizes the clearly articulated positions adopted by Professor Fleisch and I in various publications.) Such arguments have already been decisively engaged and rebottles by Professor Fleisch and I, and will be re-engaged again, in another place and at another time. However, it is worth noting here that Jennifer Karlsson contends that the original school governance legislation – and SASA in particular – was overly ambitious. J Karlsson 'The Role of Democratic School Governing Bodies in South African Schools' (2002) 38 (3) *Comparative Education* 327. As a result, SGB authority was largely symbolic and SGBs did not – according to Karlsson – deepen the Constitution's commitment to democracy. She reads two empirical studies as supporting two conclusions: (1) the weakness of SGB governance tends to reinforce principal and teacher authority, and (2) SGB authority – as reflected in the quality of tuck shops – tends to reproduce existing patterns of inequality. However, a substantially different picture of school governance emerges in Zolani Ngwane's study: '"Real Men Reawaken Their Fathers' Homesteads, the Educated Leave Them in Ruins": The Politics of Domestic Reproduction in Post-Apartheid Rural South Africa.' (2001) 31 *Journal of Religion in Africa* 402. Ngwane studied intergenerational conflict and social reproduction in the context of school governance in the rural Eastern Cape. Ngwane found, *pace* Karlsson, that the openness and the inclusivity of school governance turned them into sites of political opposition to the patriarchal structures of local traditional leaders. Women – who had, and continue to be, excluded from traditional centres of power – found that they could use the SGB as a vehicle for articulating grievances, making themselves heard, and changing the way things have been traditionally done. He notes: 'unpredictable as they were, these [SGB] meetings were ... important sources of legitimacy for the school and gave indispensable stamps of approval for its projects.' Ibid at 410. *Grove Primary School v Minister of Education & Others* offers another opportunity to assess complex, but competing, claims about the virtues and the vices of SGB

power. Jonathan Jansen, in a carefully reasoned and nuanced article, recognises that Grove Primary was – in 1998, in the Western Cape – part of the vanguard of the revolution in historically white, former Model C schools. J Jansen 'Grove Primary: Power, Privilege and the Law in South African Education' (1998) 23 *Journal of Education* 5. It hired black teachers and attempted to 'give effect to government priorities for transformation'. When it attempted to recruit additional black teachers, the schoool found that only two of 70 applicants met the criteria in its advertisements. It then had to head-hunt black graduates of the University of Cape Town in order to advance its transformative goals. Jansen accepts the proposition that Grove Primary's actions, in resisting the government's redeployment plan, were not motivated by racism. Jansen adamantly defends Grove on this ground. At the same time, he notes that 80 other white schools joined Grove in its contestation of the government's redeployment plan. He refuses to defend the bona fides of these other schools. For Jansen, it is clear that historically white schools wished to maintain their position of privilege and that such privilege, in South Africa, meant that schools in wealthy white communities could maintain their substantial funding and teaching advantages over schools in poor historically disadvantaged black communities. *Grove Primary*, on Jansen's reading, stands for the proposition that existing SGB powers and general funding norms invariably re-inscribe racial privilege. Jansen's reading does not go uncontested. Maree and Lowenherz, while sympathetic to many of Jansen's conclusions, express dismay with Jansen's 'unsupported claims' that Grove Primary became the object of black ridicule. H Maree and A Lowenherz 'Grove Primary: A Response to Professor Jonathan Jansen' (1998) 23 *Journal of Education* 31. They note that public support for Grove's efforts appeared evenly divided amongst black and coloured residents in the Western Cape, that black and coloured applicants for admission had increased substantially in the aftermath of the litigation and that a large number of black teachers sent their children to Grove Primary. Moreover, they argued that Jansen's tarring of Grove Primary's opposition to the VSP/Redeployment Scheme by associating it with three Wynberg schools (that had decided to spend R2 million on Astroturf fields) constituted an *ad hominem* attack that did not do justice to Jansen's otherwise balanced account. In the end, Maree, a member of Grove's SGB, and Lowenherz, the school's Principal, argue that the existing structures of school governance were, in fact, what enabled them to pursue a first class education for their learners at the same time as they pursued the government's – and the country's – transformation agenda.

113. See C Harber & B Trafford 'Democratic Management & School Effectiveness in Two Countries: A Case of Pupil Participation?' (1999) 27(1) *Educational Management, Administration and Leadership* 45.

114. See Karlsson (supra) at 329.

115. While the law opens up considerable space for participation in line with the best practices of democratic governance, the actual practices of RCLs are, at best, uneven. Nongubo has found evidence of continued autocratic tendencies among educators regarding learner involvement in school governance. See MJ Nongubo 'An Investigation into Perceptions of Learner Participation in the Governance of Secondary Schools' (Unpublished Master's thesis, Rhodes University, 2005). However, as learners became aware of the new legislation – and their increased powers – they have gradually been brought into school governance. As of 2003, their involvement tended to focus on sports policies, fundraising and discipline. See I Carr 'From Policy to Praxis: A Study of the Implementation of Representative Councils of Learners in the Western Cape, from 1997 to 2003' (Unpublished PhD dissertation, University of the Western Cape, 2005).

116. The definition of parent (SASA section 1, xiv) extends the normal definition beyond the conventional definition: a parent is a biological parent *or* legal guardian, and embraces 'the person who undertakes to fulfil the obligation referred to in (a) and (b) towards the learner's education'. In other words, an individual who may be neither a biological parent nor legal guardian, but who has taken on a major role in the education of a learner's life, may participate in school governance on an equal basis to persons that have conventional legal claims to parental status. Given long historical patterns of informal fostering, this recognition of the complexity of parenting in South Africa also represents

an important effort to extend participation in school citizenship. See F Zimmerman 'Cinderella Goes to School: The Effect of Child Fostering on School Enrolment in South Africa' (2003) 38 (3) *Journal of Human Resources* 557; K Anderson 'Relatedness and Investment in Children in South Africa' (2005) 16 (1) *Human Nature* 1; K Anderson 'Family Structure, Parent Investment, and Educational Outcomes amongst Black South Africans' (2000) *University of Michigan Population Studies Centre Research Report* 461.

117. These powers include: (1) Determine the school admissions policy (SASA s 5(5)); (2) Determine the language policy (SASA s 6(2)); (3) Issue rules regarding religious observance at school (SASA s 7); (4) Adopt a code of conduct after consultation (SASA s 8(1)); (5) Suspend learners (SASA s 9(1)); (6) Function in terms of a constitution (SASA s 18); (7) Adopt a constitution (SASA s 20(1)(b)); (8) Develop a mission Statement (SASA s 20(1)(c)); (9) Determine times of the school day (SASA s 20(1)(f)); (10) Administer and control school property (SASA s 20(1)(g)); (11) Recommend the appointment of educators (SASA s 20(1)(i)); (12) Recommend the appointment of non-educator staff (SASA s 20(1)(j)); (13) Give permission to use school facilities including the charge of a fee (SASA s 20(2)); (14) Take reasonable measures to supplement the resources of the school (SASA s 36(1)); (15) Establish a school fund (SASA s 37(1)); (16) Open and maintain a bank account (SASA s 37(3)); (17) Prepare an annual budget for parent approval (SASA s 38 (1); (18) Implement resolution parent meeting (SASA s 38(3)); (19) Enforce the payment of school fees (SASA s 41); (20) Keep financial records (SASA s 42(a)); (21) Draw up an annual financial statement (SASA s 42(b)); (22) Appoint a registered auditor (SASA s 43(1)). In addition, SGB's that have been allocated additional functions may undertake: (23) Improvement of the school's property (SASA s 21(1)(a)); (24) Determine the extra-mural curriculum (SASA s 21(1)(b)); (25) Make choices of subject options (SASA s 21(1)(b)); (26) Purchase textbooks, education materials and equipment (SASA s21(1)(c)); (27) Pay for services (SASA s 21(1)(d)).

118. Education Laws Amendment Act 48 of 1999.

119. Education Laws Amendment Act 53 of 2000.

120. Education Laws Amendment Act 57 of 2001.

121. Education Laws Amendment Act 24 of 2005.

122. Education Laws Amendment Act 31 of 2007.

123. 'Newsletter' School Governance Foundation (2007).

124. *Sunward Park High v MEC, Education, Province of Gauteng* (Case 05/2937, unreported, Witwatersrand Local Division, 6 June 2005).

125. See *The Governing Body of Rivonia Primary School & Another v Gauteng Province MEC of Education & Others* Case No: 11/08340 (Heard, October 2011). I am grateful to Michael Bishop and Jason Brickhill for their insight into this matter and to the parties for providing their heads of argument.

126. While the truly important issues in education policy tend to lie elsewhere, and a significant number of the rather new easy cases will make for meaningless 'development' of constitutional education law, some of the new actions will clarify and confirm previous Constitutional Court and High Court decisions.

127. JH Ely *Democracy and Distrust* (1985).

128. Over the first 15 years after liberation and the passage of SASA, the state regularly lost battles with SGBs in which the matter turned on identifying the party with the ultimate authority to take a decision. Whether these cases are simply evidence of a general disregard for the demands of due process by provincial officials, or whether they signify the conscious intent to challenge private power on all fronts, the cases of administrative overreach certainly suggest the willingness of the state to push up against the limits of the law in order to achieve its objectives. On hiring, see *Observatory Girls Primary School & Others v Head of Department of Education, Gauteng* 2003 (4) SA 246 (W). A contest of wills broke out between the SGB of Observatory Girls Primary School and the GDoE. The former needed an educator to teach Mathematics to Grade 5 and Grade 6 learners. The Personnel Administration Measures of the DoE required that the SGB first appoint an interview committee. The regulations then obliged the SGB to submit a list of preference to

the DoE. The SGB attempted to comply with the various regulatory and statutory requirements. Prior to forwarding the name of the candidate with the most points in the selection process to the GDoE HoD, the SGB learned that the preferred candidate lacked the requisite experience for the post and had not admitted such at her interview. Two members of the selection committee then took it upon themselves to forward the name of the candidate with the second highest point total to the GDoE HoD. The GDoE HoD received the recommendation. But he declined to reject or to confirm the SGB's new preferred candidate. The school pressed for a decision. The HoD continued to stall. This stalemate persisted for several months. The school eventually decided to institute court proceedings to force the HoD to make a decision. The HoD finally justified his refusal to act on the grounds that an applicant, who had received the third highest mark, had filed a complaint. The HoD stated that he could not make an appointment until the complaint had been resolved. The *Observatory Girls Primary* Court found that although the HoD was obliged to hear the complaint, the applicant had produced no evidence to support his claim. A thorough enquiry by the HoD would have revealed the baselessness of the charges – that the complainant had failed to make even a *prima facie* showing for a negative finding as delineated in the EEA. The heart of the matter, as the statutory language above suggests, was who, ultimately, had the authority to recommend and to ratify the appointment. Under both SASA and the Personnel Administration Measures regulations, the SGB makes the apposite recommendations. The HoD appears to retain the power to confirm or to deny. But the EEA narrows the HoD's discretion to instances in which the SGB acted *ultra vires*. The *Observatory Girls Primary* Court held that substantial compliance with procedural provisions is sufficient. The purpose of the procedures is manifestly not to provide grounds 'to stymie the process of appointing suitable candidates to teaching'. The High Court found that the HoD's intransigence did just that, and that the SGB had, in fact, followed a fair and equitable procedure. Another attempt by a Provincial Education Department to bring the personnel and the SGB of a school to heel is on display in *Schoonbee v MEC for Education, Mpumalanga*. 2002 (4) SA 877 (T). On 25 September 2001, the HoD sent a letter to the principal of the school asking him to provide reasons why he should not be suspended. (The letter was, presumably, based on the auditor-general's findings.) The principal – with the assistance of his trade union – replied that the HoD was obliged to give reasons for the suspension prior to any response by the principal. A meeting was held on 12 October 2001 between the principal, the HoD and representatives of the SGB to discuss and to resolve the matter. The SGB contended that the parties had agreed to release the principal from any obligation to respond to the HoD's letter. The HoD demurred. A flurry of further exchanges followed. The High Court held that the suspension of the senior deputy principal violated one of the most fundamental tenets of natural justice and just administrative action: the *audi alteram partem* rule. In addition to being denied the opportunity to make representations to the trier of fact and to being given no notice of the HoD's intention to suspend him, the *Schoonbee* Court found that the auditor-general's analysis provided no factual basis for a legal finding of malfeasance. The HoD's refusal to give the SGB an opportunity to address the HoD's concerns, to notify the SGB of an intention to take a decision, or to inform the SGB of the decision-making procedure or the consequences of a negative finding – the hallmarks of a fair hearing – was deemed inconsistent with the values of rationality, reasonableness, fairness and openness that underlie our Constitution and the basic tenets of administrative law. As a result, the *Schoonbee* court held that the HoD's dissolution of the SGB was invalid. Much ink has been spilled about the meaning of *Grove Primary School v Minister of Education & Others* and the power it ostensibly accords to SGBs. 1997 (4) SA 982 (C). In short, an attempt by the national government to right-size and to redeploy educators failed in the face of an SGB's refusal to allow the national government to control the process of redeployment and its willingness to use and to defend the authority vested in it by legislation – in this case, SASA and EEA. However, the state did not walk away entirely empty-handed. The court noted that while the power to recommend educators to fill posts was vested, in terms of section 4(2) of the EEA, solely in the schools and their SGBs, this power was subject to two constraints. First, the qualifications required for appointment, or promotion, as an educator were prescribed by section 4(1) of the EEA. Second, the SGB's power of appointment with regard to subsidised posts was subject to the approval of the MEC. Even here the state's victory was largely pyrrhic. The state's power was limited to formal matters – such as the nature of advertising posts. As the law stood in 1996, the Minister could not 'impose his will as regards the selection of a particular educator for appointment (or non-appointment), and thus override that of the SGB and the MEC concerned'. Given the recent outcome in *Ermelo*, it is highly unlikely that a strengthening state will sit on the fence in the face of such defeats. The Constitutional Court in *Ermelo* was quite clear that the provincial government possessed the power to withdraw an SGB function as necessary and where the HoD's decision satified criteria of reasonableness and practicability. The *Ermelo* Court's legitimate concerns regarding an HoD's procedural fairness with respect to review of an SGB's decisions did not undermine the Court's commitment to substantive fairness. One may have to revisit the above judgments in light of the *Ermelo* Court's conclusions. However, as I have already noted, the ability of the SGBs and the SGB Foundation to litigate such cases means that our Constitutional Court, after the Supreme Court of Appeal decisions in *Welkom* and *Rivonia*, will likely encounter a number of cases as they percolate upwards to test just how far SGBs can push their statutorily granted powers without fear of contradiction or usurpation by a provincial Head of Department.

129. FA Hayek 'Competition as a Discovery Procedure' *New Studies in Politics, Philosophy, Economics and the History of Ideas* (1978) 256.
130. D Overbye 'Nobel in Physics Goes to Perlmuttter, Schmidt and Riess' *The New York Times* (5 October 2011) available at www.nytimes.com/article?a=850127&f=25.
131. Dorf and Sabel 'Democratic Experimentalism' (supra) at 304.
132. S Woolman & T Roux 'Co-operative Government and Intergovernmental Relations' in S Woolman & M Bishop (eds) *Constitutional Law of South Africa* (2nd Edition, RS2, June 2010) Chapter 14.
133. Unfortunately Mary Metcalfe has noted, information often flows to the centre but not back out to the provinces or the schools. ('School Textbooks & Workbooks') Paper delivered by Mary Metcalfe, Legal Resources Centre Law and Education Conference, Webber Wentzel 14 November 2012) (On file with author.)
134. Diane Ravitch, one of the most esteemed commentators on American public schools, opines: 'Because of its utopian goals, coupled with harsh sanctions, NCLB has turned out to be the worst federal education legislation ever passed.' D Ravitch '"School Reform": A Failing Grade' (2012) 58 (14) *The New York Review of Books* 32. The harshest assessment of the Act, however, comes not, originally, from Ravitch, but from the US Department of Education Secretary Anne Duncan. Duncan writes that '*No Child Left Behind* is broken and we need to fix it now ... This law has created a thousand ways for schools to fail and very few ways to help them succeed.' 'No Child Left Behind?' *Teach Along with Me* (19 March 2010) available at http://www.teachalongwithme.blog (accessed on 10 September 2011).
135. See Woolman & Fleisch *The Constitution in the Classroom* (supra) at Chapter 7 ('Conclusion: On the Constitutionality of School Fees and the Narrative Arc of Law and Education in South Africa').
136. One problem, identified by Brahm Fleisch and others, is that teachers still work with a pedagogical system inherited from missionary schools. In short, only a few students actually learn how to read: they then function as instructors to the remainder of the class, who simply rehearse what they have heard without learning how to read from the book in front of them.
137. If I had to spend money on schools, then I would first concentrate on proper ablution facilities. As I make clear in my discussion of flourishing, development theory philosophers, political scientists and economists such as Amartya Sen regularly invoke the notion – echoing Adam Smith – that the state's first obligation to all its citizens is to give them the ability to enter the public realm without fear of embarrassment or shame.
138. One cannot comprehend the alacrity in growth and the vitriolic nature of the new powerful reactionary base of the Republican Party (the Tea Party) without looking at this phenomenon through the prism of race: namely, a black man is suddenly in the White House. For a subtle analysis of race, law and

politics in the United States, see R Kennedy *The Persistence of the Colour Line: Racial Politics and the Obama Presidency* (2011). That said, the change in demographics in the United States will, ultimately, undermine the success of the Tea Party's craven appeal to older white Americans' racist sentiments.

139. Case No 504/10, Eastern Cape High Court (Bisho)(2 February 2011).

Chapter Seven

Flourishing and Fundamental Rights under the South African Constitution

Our highest and hardest task is to make ourselves people 'upon whom nothing is lost'. ... [A] person armed only with ... general principles and rules ... would, even if she managed to apply them to the concrete case, be insufficiently equipped to act rightly ... It is not just that all by themselves they might get it all wrong; they do not suffice to make the difference between right and wrong. ... Obtuseness is a moral failing; its opposite can be cultivated. ... To respond 'at the right times, with reference to the right objects, towards the right people, with the right aim, and in the right way, is what is appropriate and best ...' [James' writings] allows us to see more deeply into the relationship between the finely tuned perceptions of particulars and a rule governed concern for general obligations; how each, taken by itself, is insufficient for moral accuracy; how the particular, if insufficient, is nonetheless prior; and how a dialogue between the two [characters], prepared by love, can find a common basis for moral judgment. ... James' talk ... of 'getting the tip' shows us what moral exchange and moral learning can be, inside a morality based upon perception. Progress comes not from the teaching of an abstract law but by leading the friend, or child, or loved one – by a word, by a story, by an image – to see some new aspect of the case at hand, to see it as this or that.

Martha Nussbaum

Divided selves are best accommodated by complex equality in domestic society and different versions of self-determination in domestic and international society. ... Even in my normal condition, I hear voices, I play parts, I identify myself in different ways – and so I must aim at a society that makes room for this divided self.

Michael Walzer

A. Flourishing Roughly Defined

1. *Experimentalism for Whom and for What?*

My original commitment to recasting the outré an unmooredmetaphysical notion of freedom in terms of the substantially more grounded concepts problem-solving, trail and error, feedback mechanisms and radically determined a heterogeneous selves of required an equally modest conception of a political – constitutional order – appropriate for South Africa. To that end, this book has thus far offered an intentionally partial theory best described as experimental constitutionalism. Even that consciously partial constitutional theory would be insufficient if it could not answer the question: experimental constitutionalism for whom and for what? The first half of the answer is relatively obvious: the individuals, groups, associations, communities and subpublics that constitute present day South Africa. This chapter responds primarily to the second half of the question: experimentalism for what? The answer, as already discussed and allooded to through out this work, is flourishing.

I return here to the notion that the individual, though fundamentally conditioned by the world, can still use the wide array of critical tools at her disposal to engage in more optimal forms of behaviour (as she understands them now, or reconceives them later). In the preceding pages, experimental constitutionalism has been shown to provide a method for *creating* institutions and doctrines that expand our ability to participate in a greater assortment of ways of being in the world. This extension of the range of ways of being in the world, the material conditions and immaterial norms that make their exercise possible and the realization of the plethora of ends toward which we direct ourselves (under the two preceding conditions) define flourishing.

Have we any reason to think that South Africa's Final Constitution is similarly committed to human flourishing? We do. The basic law expressly recognizes the right to dignity, a panoply of civil and political rights, a host of collective or community rights and a brace of socio-economic rights that serve the ends of both traditional and revolutionary forms of flourishing.

This chapter's overall goal then is to tie the constitutional text, superordinate legislation and the Constitutional Court's jurisprudence on dignity, civil rights, community rights and socio-economic rights more tightly to my account of flourishing. If this endeavor succeeds, then flourishing ought to be recognized as an implicit feature of our basic law. Flourishing does not qualify as the remaining foundation for a full blown theory of constitutionalism. Indeed, it cannot. But then again, that's not my aim. It's simply an important piece, along with experimental constitutionalism, of a larger puzzle.

To make the necessary connections between flourishing and constitutional norms requires one brief detour. In the next full section, I return briefly to the arguments, made in Chapters 1, 2, 3 and 4, that selves, as theoretical constructs, are best understood in terms of flourishing. Only then does it make sense to tie the concept of flourishing to our Constitutional Court's understanding of dignity, civil rights, community rights and socio-economic rights.

2. *Social Democracy and Experimentalism*

As I noted above in Chapter 4, one thing that I have never quite understood is the reluctance of experimental constitutionalists to marry their largely process driven theorizing to a more substantive view of justice. (Would Dorf and Friedman, for example, have been happy with a radically different outcome in *Dickerson*?) One of experimentalism's great strengths is reflexivity. That rolling norms might cause us to alter our initial normative framework has never struck me as a particularly compelling reason not to articulate a relatively clear normative baseline.

The most obvious baseline – without spelling out its details in full – would be what philosophers and political scientists tend to call social democracy. Post-war Western Europe has provided many variations on such a model of the state. It's a politics marked by extremely low Gini-coefficients, well regulated markets, flattened hierarchies between owners, managers and workers, and strong commitments to the provision of such public goods as housing, education, food, healthcare, environmental protection and participation in law-making processes.[1]

The early works in experimental constitutional theory prove even more mystifying when one realizes that the epistemology and political philosophy out of which it has arisen is expressly socially democratic. The exponents' failure to announce such a political programme is equally perplexing given that the objects of study – emergent experimental institutions – would appear to be the objects of a shared commitment to social democracy. Thus far, this book has offered a sample of institutions and processes designed to provide primary goods: we have looked at child welfare agencies, education reform, drug treatment courts, housing, and family courts. One possible answer is the wooliness of Dewey's pragmatism, or his refusal to ground it in some form of moral realism. Similarly, a contemporary pragmatic reluctance – read Rorty[2] and Fish[3] – to describe their social democratic politics as anything more than contingent may have something to do with this silence. Mark Tushnet correctly contends that a refusal to hold fast to a strong progressive line limits what one can expect from experimental constitutionalism. Experimental constitutionalism, without a stronger normative baseline, might offer no more than a tweaked version of the status quo. The end of the cold war brought about the end of a twentieth century conversation between centrally planned communism and welfare state capitalism. However, recent events suggest that a new conversation may be in the offing – one between unbridled Ayn Randian capitalism,[4] social democrats attempting to hold the line,[5] a law and order model of capitalism in the east,[6] advocates of liberation politics who rightly decry the failure of constitutional democracy to make good on its many promises,[7] crony capitalism from Italy to Japan (to South Africa), mercantilism in China, and theocracies from the Maghreb to the Middle East to Southeast Asia.[8] Experimental constitutionalists surely deserve a place at the table of political discourse. The process of experimentalism in politics invariably makes my betters in this domain of legal theory *strong democrats*. Information is pooled between multiple parties, lasting solutions arise when we acknowledge that our peers elsewhere may have alighted upon better means of realizing shared ends, hierarchies are flattened (as we saw in Simon's 'Toyota Jurisprudence') and citizens and workers have relationships that tend to be far more horizontal and equal (and thus socially democratic) than the political and economic arrangements on display in Communist China or Walmart. Its odd, as an acolyte of Michael Dorf and company, to feel a bit like the grouchy old man in Frank Capra's *It's a Wonderful Life*, who says to Jimmy Stewart's character: 'Stop talking her to death and kiss her already!'

3. *Two Modern (Covalent) Definitions of Flourishing: Development and Capabilities*

Two contemporary philosophers revived the literature on flourishing and gave birth to two new (often covalent) fields of study: Amartya Sen (development theory) and Martha Nussbaum (the capabilities approach).[9] Their extended collaboration makes development theory and the capabilities approach, when merged, the most powerful response to John Rawls' justice as fairness in the modern, western philosophical canon. (Their extended collaboration does not mean that they have ended their analysis at identical terminus points.)

Sen's classic work 'More than 100 Million Women are Missing' galvanized an entire generation of academics in philosophy, political science, cultural anthropology, sociology, economics and feminist theory by demonstrating how a socio-economic analysis of cultural and political practices in East Asia, South Asia, Sub-Saharan Africa and South America could explain why, 20 years ago, the world's human population contained 100 million fewer women than it should.[10] (Our genetic bias favors female births. Yet population studies show a proportion of 108,000 males to 100,000 females.) Infanticide, limited education, lack of access to adequate health care, less food and a host of what can be best described as entrenched patriarchal social formations have contributed, Sen shows, to significantly higher mortality rates for women. The numbers speak volumes with respect to the limited space within which women (and other vulnerable groups) have had the space to flourish.

Sen's relationship to classical schools of political philosophy is far too subtle and complicated to be explicated meaningfully here – as is his on-going pre-occupation with Rawls.[11] However, a précis of his positions may suggest why Sen, of all contemporary theorists, offers an account of dignity, equality and freedom that provides the best fit with our own Constitution's take on these 'three conjoined, reciprocal and covalent values' and my own commitment to flourishing.[12] Sen rejects Rawls' (Kantian and deontological) contention in *A Theory of Justice* that 'there are certain primary goods – civil liberties such as expression, assembly, the franchise – that cannot be compromised in any way.'[13] Sen has even less time for utilitarian frameworks that make the greatest good for the greatest number the measure of justice. In addition to offering the standard criticisms of utilitarianism – the inability to arrive at an acceptable metric for interpersonal comparisons of happiness, the general indifference to radical inequality in the distribution of happiness,[14] and their neglect of rights, freedoms and other non-utility concerns – Sen inveighs against the general inclination amongst economists to measure utility or happiness in terms of wealth (eg, GNP) and wealth in terms of income (per capita).(The world's top ten GDP/PPP countries do not map on to the OECD's quality of life list of 'happiest' countries – as measured by indices such as health, education, leisure time, basic amenities, housing, the actual exercise of civil and political rights, and life (read job) opportunities.[15]) Neither wealth nor income provides adequate information about the material well-being and the substantive opportunities available to individuals (or groups within the larger community). Both liberals and utilitarians fail to take account of how individual differences – in physical ability or disability, in environment, in social practices, in family structure – create significant asymmetries in the manner in which primary goods and incomes can be exploited.[16]

Sen asks us to take account, in any theory of distributive justice, of how the heterogeneity amongst individuals (both within societies and across societies) shapes the meaning of primary goods and incomes. For example, a primary political good like freedom of assembly will have demonstrably different meanings for a person who is ambulatory and for a person who is not ambulatory, but housebound. Similarly, the utility of an income of R200 000 will have demonstrably different value for a person who is ambulatory and for a person who requires expensive medication for a debilitating illness. At a minimum, says Sen, quoting Adam Smith, our primary concern ought to be with providing individuals with those necessities of life that will, in fact, give them '"the ability to appear in public without shame".'[17] That, in just a few well-chosen words, sounds very much like South African discourse on the right to and the value of dignity – and arguments over ablution facilities such as enclosed toilets or open pit latrines.

Sen thus shifts our focus to the actual 'freedom generated by commodities', and away from 'commodities seen on their own,' to the actual freedom generated by civil liberties, and away from formal constitutional rights viewed in the abstract.[18] Sen argues that the best measure of equality or freedom or dignity is the ability of individuals to *convert* such primary goods as *income* or *civil liberties* into the capability 'to choose a life one has reason to value' – or in simpler terms, the ability to pursue one's own ends.[19] That's how I understand flourishing. The virtue of Sen's approach is that it recognizes (a) the heterogeneity of capacity that people possess by virtue of biology, custom, or class; (b) the heterogeneity of critical functions – from nourishment to civic participation – that may be required to live a life one has reason to value; and (c) the heterogeneity of capabilities that people employ to pursue different visions of the good. Because Sen refuses to reduce human flourishing to a single basic unit, he is quite the pluralist when it comes to recognition of the kinds of goods and lives which individuals ought to be free to pursue. Because Sen recognizes that the pursuit of various ways of being in the world requires significant material means, and not just an absence of external constraints, he is committed to a rough form of egalitarianism.

As we saw in Chapter 4, Nussbaum shares Sen's disdain for reducing moral and political choices to a utilitarian algorithm or a Kantian constructivist's list of rights and obligations. Similarly, her interest lies in the ability of individuals to *convert* primary goods as such as *income* or *civil liberties* into the capability 'to choose a life one has reason to value'. Nussbaum has been less agnostic than Sen in her willingness to identify a 'core set' of primary goods that can be converted into capabilities. In *Women and Human Development*, Nussbaum offers the following Decalogue of primary goods and capabilities that must obtain in order for most individuals to flourish:

1. Life: Being able to live to the end of a human life of normal length; not dying prematurely, or before one's life is so reduced as to be not worth living;
2. Bodily Health. Being able to have good health, including reproductive health; to be adequately nourished; to have adequate shelter;
3. Bodily Integrity. Being able to move freely from place to place; having one's bodily boundaries treated as sovereign, i.e. being able to be secure against assault, including sexual assault, child

sexual abuse, and domestic violence; having opportunities for sexual satisfaction and for choice in matters of reproduction;

4. Senses, Imagination, and Thought. Being able to use the senses, to imagine, think, and reason–and to do these things in a "truly human" way, a way informed and cultivated by an adequate education, including, but by no means limited to, literacy and basic mathematical and scientific training.
5. Emotions. Being able to have attachments to things and people outside ourselves; to love those who love and care for us, to grieve in their absence.
6. Practical Reason. Being able to form a conception of the good and to engage in critical reflection about the planning of one's life: liberty of conscience.
7. Affiliation. Being able to live with and toward others, to recognize and show concern for other human beings, to engage in various forms of social interaction; to be able to imagine the situation of another and to have compassion for that situation; to have the capability for both justice and friendship; protecting this capability means protecting institutions that constitute and nourish such forms of affiliation, freedom of association, freedom of assembly and political speech.
8. Non-Discrimination. Having the social bases of self-respect and non-humiliation; being able to be treated as a dignified being whose worth is equal to that of others. This entails, at a minimum, protections against discrimination on the basis of race, sex, religion, caste, ethnicity, or national origin.
9. Play. Being able to laugh, to play, to enjoy recreational activities.
10. Control over one's Environment. Political Control: Being able to participate effectively in choices that govern one's life; having the right of political participation, protections of free speech and association. Material Control: Being able to hold property (both land and movable goods), not just formally but in terms of real opportunity; and having property rights on an equal basis with others; having the right to seek employment on an equal basis with others.[20]

Consistent with Sen's refusal to be normatively reductive, this Decalogue reflects deontological, utilitarian, communitarian and relational commitments (found throughout our own basic law). The difference between Sen and Nussbaum, for those who practice (or write about) constitutional law, is that the Decalogue provides a basis by which to assess whether or not a political community is providing an environment within which individuals can flourish. Nussbaum has recently gone so far as to assess and to critique the US Constitution, Supreme Court precedents and the current Robert's Court in terms of both the capabilities approach and this list of convertible goods.[21] Nussbaum writes that, in terms of the capabilities approach, the primary purpose of any nation's constitution should be to 'secure for all citizens the prerequisites of a life worthy of human dignity – a core of capabilities – in areas of central importance to human life.'[22] Not surprisingly, while the US Constitution and the current US Supreme Court maintain a commitment to certain entitlements consistent with the capabilities approach ('CA'), the US Constitution and the current Supreme Court come up short in a large number of striking ways:

> On the whole, [the American] constitutional tradition has done very well protecting some capabilities – namely, those enumerated in the Bill of Rights – although even here, interpretation has fluctuated between an analysis that focuses on capabilities or substantial freedoms and a more minimalist analysis. The tradition of heightened scrutiny under the Equal Protection Clause and,

> on occasion, the recognition of fundamental rights under the Due Process Clause have also led to a focus on substantive opportunities – what people are actually able to do and to be. Equal Protection Clause jurisprudence, like the modern uses of the CA in the areas of gender, race, and disability, has focused on areas affected by traditional discrimination. Our tradition, however, has been far more reluctant than many to offer constitutional protection, through judicial interpretation, to human capabilities in the areas covered by social and economic rights, although a beginning was made in the late 1960s and 1970s. ... This reluctance (which distinguishes the United States from most of the nations of Europe and the developing world) is made more complicated by disputes over institutional competence and the proper scope of judicial action. Sometimes, when courts refuse to protect a given entitlement (refusing, for example, to give education the status of a fundamental right), the reason may be that judges do not believe that the existing constitution is plausibly interpreted to protect a certain entitlement. At other times, judges may simply oppose the recognition of such a right.[23]

My purpose here is not been to identify the flaws of any given constitutional order, but to answer the question, 'Experimentalism for Whom and for What?' in the manner most congenial to both experimentalism and flourishing in South Africa. Notice one of the first things that the two constructs have in common: reflexivity. As we have seen from previous chapters, and Nussbaum's epigram at the outset, rolling best practices allow for knowledge about the most effective means to realize an end to flow back to participants for regular readjustment, for better fit. At the same time, the success (or failure) of our means may cause us to reassess the norms we pursue. Drugs users may be seen as threats to themselves, requiring rehabilitation, not incarceration. Undocumented immigrants who cause no harm may come to be viewed as valued members of the community, and not as criminals who must be repatriated to their mother countries.[24] A second commonality is a disentrenchment of private ordering where such ordering blocks individuals from securing those basic capabilities necessary for a life worth valuing. A third virtue is that both theories of the human condition are forward and lateral looking. They do not disdain the experience or the wisdom of our betters. Instead they seek out 'the progress that comes not from the teaching of an abstract law but by leading the friend, or child, or loved one – by a word, by a story, by an image – to see some new aspect of the case at hand, and thus better ways of doing things.'[25] The learning here is shot through with normativity. An experimental constitutionalist would do well to take away from development theory the realization that a commitment to a 'core of capabilities' need not undercut our ability, over time, to alter and to improve who we are – either through experiments, or through relationships with others.

B. Flourishing and Selves

Flourishing is an essential feature of this book's overall argument for four primary reasons: (1) it provides an understanding of human agency and morality that is not contingent on an outré metaphysics of free will; (2) it takes account of the heterogeneity of ways of being in the world that give life meaning; (3) it fills a gap in experimentalist thought that makes experimental constitutionalism more coherent; and (4) it provides the most compelling account of why these core basic law entitlements can best be squared with the aspirations of our own constitutional democracy.

This section rehearses Chapter 2's account of selves and Chapter 3's account of the social so that we may more readily connect those two accounts to the ultimate pay-off: a theory of the constitutional that embraces both flourishing and experimentalism. Again: Flourishing recognizes the centrality of granting individuals the capabilities 'to choose a life one has reason to value'. Various social endowments may have already made us who we are (or want to be) – a the capabilities approach should ensure that *the meaning that makes us* continues to do so. The densely populated or radically heterogeneous self may already possess the tools for critical self-engagement, for internal friction, and thus change that will better allow for our round pegs to fit into round holes. However, a commitment to the capabilities approach and development theory that undergird flourishing should create the material and immaterial conditions for sustained, constructive and progressive change (as measured by our own selves).

1. *The Situated Self*

This self is neither the rational chooser of classical economics nor the autonomous moral agent of classical liberalism or even most egalitarian forms of politics. Each self is best understood, in Dennett's terms, as a centre of narrative gravity (or in Walzer's idiom, a densely populated 'me'). Each such centre unifies a set of dispositional states (and a physical body) that draw down on the practices of the various communities – religious, cultural, linguistic, national, familial, ethnic, economic, sexual, racial, social (and so on) – into which that centre is born. As Heidegger writes:

> [That shared practices are constitutive of our being] implies that the world is already given as the common world. It is *not* the case that there are first individual subjects which are at any given time have their own world; and that the task of putting them together, by virtue of some sort of arrangement, ... one would have a common world. This is how philosophers imagine things when they ask about the constitution of the intersubjective. We say instead that the first thing that is given is the common world. ... We take pleasure and enjoy ourselves as one takes pleasure, we speak ... about something as one speaks.[26]

This view of the self (and the social) supports a number of pretty straightforward conclusions about the individual in South African constitutional politics.[27]

My account of self, consciousness and freedom, rightly understood, forces us to attend to the *arationality* of our most basic attachments and to think twice before we accord *our* arational attachments preferred status to the arational attachments of *others*.[28] As Wittgenstein writes: 'What has to be accepted, the given, is, one could say – forms of life.'[29] Moreover, these theses regarding the self and the nature of consciousness buttress my general contention that our constitutive attachments or particular ways of being in the world or forms of life possess a rebuttable presumption of legitimacy in our constitutional order. The freedom to be what we already are is often flourishing and freedom properly understood.

2. *The Experimental Self*

The recognition of the self as a function of arational, constitutive attachments does not mean that we must give each of these attachments our imprimatur of constitutional approval. As Walzer contends above, within the constraints of these social and natural endowments, we still possess the capacity to make critical assessments. Within the constraints of these social and natural endowments, we still possess the capacity to make reasoned judgments about right and wrong, good and evil.[30] Indeed, the well-nigh innumerable attachments and dispositions that make up an individual provide each of us, and our society collectively, with at least some of the critical leverage necessary for discriminating between more and less valuable forms of behaviour. Sen has put the matter thus:

> In some versions of communitarian thinking, it is presumed ... that one's identity with one's community must be the principal or dominant (perhaps even the only significant) identity a person has. This conclusion can be linked to two alternative – related but distinct – lines of reasoning. One line argues that a person does not have access to other community-independent conceptions of identity and to other ways of thinking about identity. Her social background, firmly based in 'community and culture', determines the feasible patterns of reasoning and ethics available to her. The second line of argument does not anchor the conclusion to perceptual constraints, but to the claim that ... communitarian identity will invariably be recognized to be of paramount importance.[31]

Just as I argued in Chapter One, Sen rightly rejects the acritical, homogenizing communitarian account of the self on two grounds:[32]

> First, even though certain cultural attitudes and beliefs may influence the nature of our reasoning, they cannot invariably determine it fully. There are various influences on our reasoning, and we need not lose our ability to consider other ways of reasoning just because we identify with, and have been influenced by membership in, a particular group. ... Second, the so-called cultures need not provide any uniquely defined set of attitudes or beliefs that can shape our reasoning. Indeed, many of these 'cultures' contain considerable internal variations, and different attitudes and beliefs may be entertained within the same broadly defined culture.[33]

And so, if what Sen contends holds true about the capacity of the self for critical reflection within individual cultures, then the self who lives, contemporaneously, amidst multiple communities will almost certainly possess (at least formally) somewhat greater capacity for critical reflection.

Both Sen and Nussbaum reject the acritical, homogenizing communitarian (as well as the utilitarian rational chooser) account of the self on a third, critical ground:

> If we ask what people are actually capable to do and to be, we come much closer to understanding the barriers societies have erected against full justice for women [and other marginal groups.] [We] criticize approaches that measure well-being in [solely] terms of utility [or tradition values] by pointing to the fact that women [and persons in marginal groups] frequently exhibit adaptive preferences, preferences that have adjusted to their second class status. [Utilitarian] frameworks, which ask people what they prefer and how satisfied they are, prove inadequate to confront the most pressing questions of ... justice.[34]

It is this kind of person, the second-class person in society, made up of multiple selves with their varying narratives and dispositions, who truly requires the space created by experimental constitutionalism. For just as experimental constitutionalism is predicated upon the belief that best practices are more likely to surface within institutions and through doctrines designed to promote social experimentation, so too is our experimental self grounded in a belief that an individual is more likely to alight on a preferred way of being in the world if provided the conditions – material and immaterial – under which to compare, contrast and critique different ways of being in the world.

3. *The Radically Heterogeneous Self*

The self understood as situated (or radically given) married to an experimentalist self – one that recognizes the multiple selves that make us up – leads to a self already recognized (albeit obliquely) in our constitutional jurisprudence: the radically, heterogeneous self. As Justice Albie Sachs writes in *Fourie*:

> South Africans come in all shapes and sizes. The development of an active rather than a purely formal sense of enjoying a common citizenship depends on recognising and accepting people with all their differences, as they are. The Constitution thus acknowledges the variability of human beings (genetic and socio-cultural), affirms the right to be different, and celebrates the diversity of the nation. Accordingly, what is at stake is not simply a question of removing an injustice experienced by a particular section of the community. At issue is a need to affirm the very character of our society as one based on tolerance and mutual respect. The test of tolerance is not how one finds space for people with whom, and practices with which, one feels comfortable, but how one accommodates the expression of what is discomfiting.[35]

Read correctly, Sachs J recognizes that our differences do not separate us, or merely require tolerance. They form the basis for a profound recognition that individually we are *radically heterogeneous creatures* and that absorbing that challenge leads to richer more varied lives. The radically heterogeneous self demands a commitment to pluralism and its deep and profound appreciation for difference. From this commitment to a roughly egalitarian pluralist democracy, the politics not of the majority but of the individual, we derive a commitment to democratic solidarity. How so? Once we recognise our own difference, and demand its recognition by others, we have no coherent choice but to recognise the difference of others. To put it more pointedly, once we recognise the otherness of others and demand such recognition for ourselves, we are committed to a society in which every member can comfortably live out that difference.

4. *The Egalitarian Pluralist Self*

Does democratic solidarity commit us to egalitarian pluralism or some particular political order? Since labels tend to bar understanding, I would simply say, *again*, that this account of the self, the social and the constitutional commits us to a political order in which the space we demand for ourselves is fundamentally equal to the space required by others. If such space for flourishing requires – at this particular historical moment – significant redistribution of wealth, then so be it. But the bottom line, once you embrace a Senian, Nussbaumian, Sachsian, Whitmanian, Walzerian or Deweyite commitment to democratic solidarity, is that you must be willing to afford others the material conditions in which they can recognise and express their difference. It is only through such a commitment, Sachs tells us, that we can forge a new nation.[36]

C. Flourishing, Development, Capabilities and Constitutions

My rather modest account of flourishing flows from both conservative strains and revolutionary features found in our Final Constitution and from my accounts of the situated, experimental, radically heterogeneous and egalitarian pluralist selves (found in a situated, experimental, radically heterogeneous, and socially democratic polity.) These pre-commitments further commit me to the following propositions.

The conservative strain in this account emphasizes the fact that only in light of the various practices, forms of life, or language games which social groups provide that we become anything that remotely approximates what we understand to be human. We often, incorrectly, speak of the social practices, endowments and associations that make up our lives as if we were largely free to choose them or make them up as we go along. I have suggested why such a notion of choice is not true of us as individual selves and is equally untrue of social formations. To acknowledge that there is a 'radical givenness' to our social world and that 'meaning makes us' explains why 'conditioned choice' results in little or no explanatory power being lost when we substitute flourishing for freedom. As Walzer suggests, we ought to call such decisions to reaffirm our conditioned commitments 'freedom simply, without qualification'. We may even wish to follow Walzer at least part of the way when he concludes that such 'freedom' is 'the only "freedom" that free men and women can ever have.'[37]

The revolutionary strain in this account of flourishing recognizes that the social practices from which we derive meaning in our lives also constrain our actions and often limit our ability to act in manner that we believe will enhance our own well-being and human flourishing generally. The revolutionary dimension of flourishing requires that issues of access, of coercion, of choice, of voice, of exit must be constantly negotiated in order to ensure that all members of our society have a meaningful opportunity to flourish. A reasonably equal and democratic society must mediate the radical givenness of our social life, on the one hand, and the aspirations of all of us to discriminate between those social forms of life which still fit and those which no longer reflect our (self)conception of flourishing and which continue to reinforce the social hierarchies that turn many of us into second-class citizens.

The constitutional insights to be drawn from the conservative and the revolutionary account of flourishing are much the same as those drawn from the naturalized account of the self in Chapter 2 and the naturalized account of the social in Chapter 3. Flourishing requires us to pay particular attention to the unchosen conditions of flourishing as well as the real space in which conditioned choice obtains. This understanding in no way diminishes our responsibility to engage in case-by-case analysis of rights claims made on behalf of those who inhabit such unchosen worlds. It does, however, sound a cautionary note that ought to be heeded by those who identify freedom – and not flourishing – as the ultimate trump and by those who would treat all such unchosen social associations as suspect and therefore as instruments to advance radically egalitarian (and non-pluralist) ends.

Experimental constitutionalism serves both strains of flourishing. First, all constitutional orders recognize the ineradicable 'private ordering' of social affairs. To that extent, constitutions are inherently conservative documents. (Our own Constitution conserved both the peace and the institutions that enable individuals to flourish while simultaneously realizing a democracy designed to enable all South Africans to pursue, finally, 'a life one has reason to value'.) Second, while this account begins with the premise that individual flourishing occurs primarily within the many communities into which an individual is born and within which she remains a member, experimental constitutionalism envisages a heterogeneous society made up innumerable ways of being in the world and a state that does not aim to exhaust the possibilities of individual lives. At a minimum, the experimental state enables individuals and groups to fully realize extant sources of the self. For just as experimental constitutionalism is predicated upon the belief that best practices are more likely to surface within institutions designed to promote social experimentation, so too is our experimental self grounded in a belief that an individual is more likely to alight on a preferred way of being in the world if provided the conditions under which to compare, contrast and critique different ways of being in the world. Put another way, at a minimum, an experimental constitutional state bears the dual responsibility of ruling out ways of being which threaten the core values of our polity – pluralism, dignity, rough equality, the rule of law and democratic participation – and of providing a framework within which competing notions of the good can coexist – if inevitably uncomfortably. To meet these minimal requirements, such a state must ensure that each individual denizen possesses the most basic material and immaterial entitlements and core of capabilities that would enable that person to flourish.

Does the above amount to a plausible account of flourishing under the South African Constitution? Sen's developmental politics tends to dominate my discussion of dignity, political rights, collective entitlements and socio-economic rights because his concerns about distributive justice in radically heterogeneous societies fit my own concerns. However, Nussbaum's Decalogue, and her direct application of the capabilities approach to constitutions is somewhat more congenial to rights discourse. It is impossible to read Nussbaum's Decalogue above and not see South African constitutional rights to Life; Freedom and Security of the Person; Equality; Housing; Land; Property; Freedom of Trade, Occupation and Profession; Freedom of Association; Freedom of Religion, Conscience, Thought and Belief; Freedom of Assembly; Freedom of Association; Political Rights; Freedom of Expression; and Socio-Economic Rights to Education, Health, Food, Water and Social Security. This partial list recognizes both the conservative flavor and the revolutionary character of flourishing: most of the rights above can service both conservative and revolutionary ends. This confluence of capabilities and fundamental rights sets the stage for an argument which ties flourishing ever more tightly to our South African constitutional project.

D. Flourishing and Fundamental Rights: Between Conservation and Revolution

1. *Dignity and Flourishing*

Trying to map 'dignity' on to 'flourishing' is fraught with danger. After all, 'dignity' is a constitutional grundnorm most readily associated with the deontological and reason-based ethics of Immanuel Kant. Flourishing, on the other hand, is most readily identified with Aristotle and his ethics of practical wisdom. Trying to ensure that these two views sing off the same hymn sheet courts contradiction. That need not be the case. It would be more surprising if these two schools of thought did not share common features and prescribe common outcomes. (For it to be otherwise would mean that the Western political tradition is tied to two thoroughly incompatible traditions.) Moreover, as the work of Martha Nussbaum has shown, a neo-Aristotelian philosopher can translate flourishing into the patois of rights discourse in a modern constitutional order. We should recall that Nussbaum has argued that the primary purpose of any nation's constitution should be to 'secure for all citizens the prerequisites of a life worthy of *human dignity* – a core of capabilities – in areas of central importance to human life.'[38]

If we are not fully autonomous rational choosers or fully determined arational non-choosers, then what are we? We are creatures with the capacity to flourish. And that is to say, we are creatures endowed with worlds of meaning who possess the capacity for self-actualization and self-governance within those multiple worlds of meaning.

Notice again that freedom – strong metaphysical freedom – does not feature in the aforementioned account. Flourishing is freedom shorn of the latter's unhelpful metaphysical baggage.

As fate would have it, freedom – strong metaphysical freedom – is also not what the Final Constitution requires in order for human beings to flourish. What it requires, the text of the basic law and the Constitutional Court tell us, is, first-off, a commitment to human dignity. The Court has spent the first seventeen years of operation spinning out a jurisprudence of dignity that begins with very modest premises, but ultimately bursts into a constellation of definitions and uses substantially richer and more robust.

One question, noted above, is whether dignity and flourishing can function as synonyms, or whether dignity is, in fact, a condition for flourishing. The answer must be the latter. One cannot flourish without first being accorded some minimal level of dignity. The more demanding requirements of our dignity jurisprudence – dignity *qua* self-actualization, dignity *qua* self-governance, dignity *qua* material conditions of existence – reflect three of the most important features of this account of flourishing. The Constitutional Court's commitment to these more maximal accounts of dignity leads me to conclude that a robust constitutional defence of dignity is a precondition for flourishing in an experimental constitutional state.

(a) Dignity Defined

The Constitutional Court has proffered five related, but distinct definitions of dignity.[39] These five definitions draw down on the same basic insight: that all individuals are to be recognized as and to be treated as ends-in-themselves (radically heterogeneous and determined creatures that they are.)

(i) Dignity as a Condition for Flourishing

The first two definitions of dignity are primarily negative. That is, they concern the conditions that prevent individuals from flourishing.

(aa) *Individual as an end-in-herself*[40]

In working out the meaning of dignity, the Constitutional Court consciously shadows one iteration of Kant's the categorical imperative:[41] 'Act in such a way that you always treat humanity, whether in your own person or in the person of another, never simply as a means, but always at the same time as an end.'[42] Stated in Kant's uncompromising terms, such an ethical algorithm might seem impossible to enact.[43] We all know that, even with the best of intentions, many of the myriad interactions we have with our fellow human beings will be almost entirely instrumental. We know that whether we are taking decisions for a family, a classroom of students, a neighbourhood, a town, a province or a nation, some form of a utilitarian calculus – the greatest good for the greatest number – will enter into our considerations. And we know that the relational or communitarian quality of ethics is such that we will often privilege the claims of family, kin, neighbourhood or nation over more universal deontological or utilitarian claims.

How then to understand this injunction in a way that is neither sentimental nor woolly? Consider Oscar Schachter's gloss: 'Respect for the intrinsic worth of every person should mean that individuals are not to be perceived or treated *merely* as instruments or objects of the will of others.'[44] Dignity, on this account, sets a floor below which ethical – and legal – behaviour may not fall. Although some relationships will be purely instrumental, no individual person can be treated as a mere instrument over the *entire* domain of her social interactions. This floor supports – as the *Dawood* Court suggests – the Bill of Rights' express prohibitions on slavery, servitude and forced labour.[45] This definition of dignity also bars punishments that either extinguish entirely the humanity of another – say, through the death penalty – or through the disproportionality reduction of a human being to a mere signal – a punishment that functions as a disincentive – within a large and impersonal system of social control.[46]

(bb) *Equal concern and respect*

Under South Africa's Constitution, dignity as an entitlement to equal concern and to equal respect has led to the construction of two different, though not entirely distinct, tests in terms of s 9 (the right to equality): (1) a right to equal treatment which ensures (a) that the law does not irrationally differentiate between classes of person and (b) that the law does not reflect the 'naked preferences' of government officials; and (2) a right to equal treatment that guarantees that individuals are not subject to unfair discrimination on the basis of largely ascriptive characteristics.[47] Of this demand for equal respect, Justice Ackermann writes:

> [A]t the heart of the prohibition of unfair discrimination lies the recognition that the purpose of our new constitutional and democratic order is the establishment of a society in which all human beings will be accorded equal dignity and respect regardless of their membership in particular groups. The achievement of such a society in the context of our deeply inegalitarian past will not be easy, but that that is the goal of the Constitution should not be forgotten or overlooked.[48]

(ii) Dignity as Constitutive of Flourishing

While the third and the fourth dimensions of dignity provide political conditions for flourishing, they are, in fact, constitutive of flourishing itself.

(aa) *Self-actualization*

An individual's capacity to create meaning generates an entitlement to respect for the unique set of ends that the individual pursues. In *Ferreira v Levin*, Justice Ackermann writes:

> Human dignity cannot be fully valued or respected unless individuals are able to develop their humanity, their 'humanness' to the full extent of its potential. Each human being is uniquely talented. Part of the dignity of every human being is the fact and awareness of this uniqueness. An individual's human dignity cannot be fully respected or valued unless the individual is permitted to develop his or her unique talents optimally. Human dignity has little value without freedom; for without freedom personal development and fulfilment are not possible. Without freedom, human dignity is little more than an abstraction. Freedom and dignity are inseparably linked. To deny people their freedom is to deny them their dignity.[49]

Dignity, properly understood, secures the space for self-actualisation.[50]

Dignity qua self-actualisation, consistent with my view of self and consciousness, describes only a political or an economic status, and not an outré metaphysical state.[51] Justice Ngcobo adopts this materialist and constitutive view in *Affordable Medicines*.[52] In elucidating the appropriate contours of the right to freedom of trade, occupation and profession, he writes:

> What is at stake is more than one's right to earn a living, important though that is. Freedom to choose a vocation is intrinsic to the nature of a society based on *human dignity* as contemplated by the Constitution. One's work is part of one's identity and is constitutive of one's *dignity*. Every individual has a right to take up any activity which he or she believes himself or herself prepared to undertake as a profession and to make that activity the very basis of his or her life. And there is a relationship between work and the human personality as a whole. It is a relationship that shapes and completes the individual over a lifetime of devoted activity; it is the foundation of a person's existence.[53]

(bb) *Self-governance*

Our capacity for self-governance is largely what makes democracy the only acceptable secular form of political organization in modernity. For if we are capable of shaping our own ends as individuals, equal treatment demands that we be able to shape the contours of our community as citizens. At a minimum, it means that we must be able to participate in some of the collective-decision making processes that determine the ends of our community. As Justice Sachs notes in *August v Electoral Commission:*

> The universality of the franchise is important not only for nationhood and democracy. The vote of each and every citizen is a badge of *dignity* and of personhood. Quite literally, it says that everybody counts.'[54]

Dignity qua self-governance ought to promote the Court's commitment to representation reinforcing processes – most notably where our democratic institutions cannot be profitably exploited by vulnerable minorities, historically disadvantaged individuals and other out-groups. While *Prince*, *Jordan*, *Robinson* and *De Reuck* sound cautionary notes about the extent to which the Court will extend itself on behalf of non-traditional associations, vocations or professions,[55] more recent cases such as *Fourie* and *Shilubana* suggest that the Court may be willing to walk the 'extra-mile' in order to accommodate non-traditional and even revolutionary ways of being in the world.[56]

(iii) Dignity and the Material Conditions for Flourishing

In a series of unfair discrimination and socio-economic rights cases, the Constitutional Court has made it clear that our commitment to dignity does not flow entirely from the inalienable rights of individuals. Whether it has engaged the stigma associated with HIV/AIDS, the urgent need for shelter, the entitlement of all to adequate food and water, or the desperation associated with summary evictions, the Constitutional Court has, over the past several years, repeatedly emphasized the fact that

> It is not only the *dignity* of the poor that is assailed when homeless people are driven from pillar to post in a desperate quest for a place where they and their families can rest their heads. Our society *as a whole* is demeaned when state action intensifies rather than mitigates their marginalization.[57]

Dignity is not simply a constellation of negative duties owed by the state to each human subject, or a set of positive entitlements that can be claimed by each member of the polity. Dignity is also that which binds us together as a community of equals – and it occurs only under conditions of mutual recognition. Moreover, such mutual recognition is not merely formal.[58] Justice Mokgoro, writing for the Court in *Khosa*, notes that the Final Constitution commits us to an understanding of dignity in which

> wealthier members of the community view the minimal well-being of the poor as connected with their personal well-being and the well-being of the community as a whole.[59]

The Court's account of dignity, which has, heretofore, offered various desiderata for individual moral agency, now appears to describe dignity as a collective good. How then to comprehend dignity as a collective concern? What the Court wishes us to understand is that for dignity to be meaningful in South Africa, the political community as a whole must provide that basket of goods – from the social security at issue in *Khosa* to such basic civil and political rights as expression and association – which each member of the community requires in order to exercise a fairly basic level of agency. This conception of dignity possesses striking similarities to Amartya Sen's development theory and Martha Nussbaum's capability approach.

For Sen, as for our Constitutional Court, the primary concern of the polity is not with wealth maximization. 'Wealth' as Aristotle wrote, 'is evidently not the good we are seeking; for it is merely useful and for the sake of something else.'[60] That something else, as Sen writes, is

> [t]he expansion of the 'capabilities' of persons to lead the kinds of lives they value – and have reason to value. ... Having freedom to do the things one has reason to value is (1) significant in itself for the person's overall freedom, and (2) important in fostering the person's opportunity to have valuable outcomes.[61]

However, Sen's aims are not limited to fostering the agency of the individual. Individual agents should be understood both as ends-in-themselves and as the 'basic building blocks' of [aggregate social] development. The 'greater freedom' of individuals not only 'enhances the ability of people to help themselves and ... to influence the world,' it is essential to the development of society as a whole.[62] For Sen, the link between individual capabilities and development is part of a virtuous circle. Enhancement of individual flourishing – by both political and material means – leads to greater social development, which, in turn, further enhances the possibilities for individuals to lead the kinds of lives we have reason to value.[63]

This virtuous circle would appear to be what the Constitutional Court in *Khosa* has in mind when it ties the well-being of the worst off to the well-being of the wealthy. The enhancement of individual capabilities of the poorest members of our political community enhances the development of South Africa as a whole. Or put slightly differently, the greater the agency of the least well-off members of our society, the greater the agency of all the members of our society. This gloss on *Khosa* emphasizes not the subjective sense of well-being that the well-off might experience by tying their well-being to that of the poor. Rather it emphasizes an increase in an objective measure of well-being (say, on an OECD *Better Life Index* that measures the quality of life) that flows from the enhancement of the agency of each individual member of our society.

2. *Widening Gyres of Dignity and Flourishing*

We may be able to see, now, how dignity builds upon a simple premise, the refusal to turn away from suffering, and yields, ultimately, a realm of ends. The refusal to turn away marks the very beginning of our moral awareness – the first time we come to understand that others are not mere instruments for the realization of our desires, but beings who are ends in themselves. This moral awakening leads, almost ineluctably, to two further insights: (a) that others are entitled to the same degree of concern and respect that we would demand for ourselves; and (b) that others are entitled to that equal respect and equal concern because they, like us, are possessed of faculties and talents that enable them to pursue ends which give their lives meaning.[64] The ability to give our lives meaning, and to determine the course by which we give our lives meaning, leads to the recognition that we are able to govern our selves. At a minimum, this mutual recognition of our ability to govern our selves supports the more formal political recognition that just as each one of us is capable of and entitled to govern our individual self, so too are we equally capable of legislating on behalf of the broader community of which we each are a member. This mutual recognition of one another as beings capable of ordering the ends both of our own lives and of the larger community underwrites the final insight: that we not only live in a realm of ends, but that if such a realm is to have real meaning, we must be willing to order our community in a manner that enables each individual to realize her status as an end. It is simply not enough to (a) not turn away from suffering, (b) end discrimination, and (c) grant all citizens the franchise. Once we recognize others as ends we must be committed to the provision of those material means necessary to live as ends. To refuse them such means might render meaningless the more formal guarantees found in the Final Constitution. As the Court notes in *Grootboom:*

> The Constitution will be worth infinitely less than its paper if the reasonableness of state action concerned with housing is determined without regard to the fundamental constitutional value of human dignity. Section 26, read in the context of the Bill of Rights as a whole, must mean that the respondents have a right to reasonable action by the state in all circumstances and with particular regard to human dignity. In short, I emphasise that human beings are required to be treated as human beings.[65]

The transformation of the Court's dignity jurisprudence – from an initial, basic concern with the manner in which the law denied the majority of South Africans their dignity to a more robust set of doctrines designed to foster the flourishing of each and every person – is, perhaps, nowhere more evident than in the courts' sexual orientation case law. Our courts began slowly, dispatching laws proscribing sodomy as a violation of intimate or private space.[66] The courts go on to reject laws that impair the ability of same-sex partners to live – private lives – within South Africa.[67] They then abolish laws that refuse to extend public benefits to the surviving same-sex life partner of a judicial officer.[68] Until finally, the dignity of same-sex partners is understood to be as important a public matter as it is private, and the basic law sanctions heterosexual and homosexual unions alike.[69]

It seems reasonable to ask, at this juncture, whether the Constituional Court's jurisprudence on sexual orientation reflects a genuine commitment to flourishing or the mere logical extension of Court's liberal commitment to state non-intervention (and the actual pressures of the text.) One can accept the truth of the proposition that the Constitutional Court recognizes the link between dignity and the need for individual liberty from state intervention without acceding to the proposition that dignity is *only* about the need for individual liberty from state intervention.

Amartya Sen ties his notion of 'development as freedom' to the provision of a basic basket of goods – both real and figurative – that enable human beings to develop those capabilities necessary for each individual to achieve those ends that each has reason to value.[70] Sen contends that dignity and freedom and equality, rightly understood, are meant neither to achieve definitive outcomes nor to prescribe a univocal understanding of the good. What these covalent values do require is a level of *material* support (eg, food) and *immaterial* support (eg, civil liberties) that enable individuals to pursue a meaningful and comprehensive vision of the good – as they understand it.[71] Put another way, these covalent values describe the political and material conditions for individual flourishing – as well as some of the polity's general features.[72] Martha Nussbaum is not content to let matters rest there. Her Decalogue of capabilities is meant to take the fight to constitutional lawyers. Her list, as she acknowledges, will not secure universal consent. But the use of the capabilities approach to ground constitutional theory alters the terrain of constitutional debate and forces other scholars to show how their preferred list of capabilities would lead to flourishing. By so doing, she secures a degree of acceptance for capabilities as a departure point for future arguments about the content of constitutional norms.

In the pages above, we saw that the Court has moved beyond a minimalist understanding of dignity, and a negative conception of liberty, to something richer and more substantial: flourishing. In *Grootboom*, the Constitutional Court announced: 'A society must seek to ensure that the basic necessities of life are provided to all if it is to be a society based on dignity, equality, and freedom.'[73] In *Khosa v Minister of Social Development*, the Court commits the state to the provision of actual resources, social assistance, to an identifiable class of persons – permanent residents. In so doing, the Court moves well beyond dignity as negative liberty to a vision of dignity in which 'wealthier members of the community view the minimal well-being of the poor as connected with their personal well-being and the well-being of the community as a whole.'[74]

Dignity qua collective responsibility for material agency moves us towards a Sen-like development theory and a Nussbaum-like capabilities approach. Moreover, it does so without being susceptible to the critique of dignity qua negative liberty leveled by exponents of substantive equality. Development theory and the capabilities approach each define equal treatment in terms of the provision of differently situated persons with the material and immaterial means that they, in particular, require to pursue some specific vision of the good.[75] For example, Sen argues that since pregnant women need more nutrition than men, any basic food program is obliged to recognize this difference in a basic nutritional package.[76]

Dignity qua collective responsibility modeled on a capabilities approach also appears to answer the charge that a commitment to rough equality re-inscribes the disadvantage of those who find themselves in a state of injury. A capabilities approach does not underscore the lack of freedom of our fellow citizens, nor call undue attention to their injury, so much as it demands that we recognize that all of us require a relatively unique basket of goods in order to pursue our preferred way of being in the world.

3. *Civil Rights and Flourishing*

As with dignity, political and civil rights make possible both the conservative and the revolutionary dimensions of flourishing. Take 'Freedom of Assembly'. I have argued that this modest freedom actually allows citizens a space to stand outside the Constitution, and where the Constitution qua social contract has been breached, vouchsafes the people a constitutional right to rebellion.[77] Organized labour, landless people, anti-privatisation movements, students, squatters, and advocates for every form of socio-economic good continue to use demonstrations to press their demands for delivery on the Constitution's promises (at a rate of almost 6,000 protests per year.)

The continued vitality of assembly in the still newish South Africa bespeaks its essential role in any democracy.[78] Assemblies and demonstrations, on the standard account, generate debate and thereby improve our deliberative processes. (Nor is it frankly, an accurate reflection of post-1994, post-apartheid South Africa.) That they may do. But an emphasis on the ostensibly deliberative nature of our democracy is simply not in keeping with this book's dominant mode of analysis. What assemblies and demonstrations really force us to do is attend to situations where power – inequality in power, abuse of power – has distorted our capacity to engage in meaningful discourse, and has valorised the interests (and conceptions of flourishing) of one segment of our polity over another. Arid, academic arguments often miss much of that which makes assemblies, demonstrations, pickets, processions and marches truly dynamic and powerful. That is the nature of the crowd. The crowd draws its power, as Cannetti notes, from its erasure of borders between individuals, the gravitational pull that an expanding, living, moving group has on those around it, and the incipient threat of violence that causes all around to sit up and take notice.[79] Crowd action – loud, noisy, disruptive, and sometimes dangerous – ought to be viewed, as Larry Kraemer persuasively argues, as a direct expression of popular sovereignty.[80] By creating space for crowd action, FC s 17 vouchsafes a commitment to a form of democracy in which the will of the people is not always mediated by political parties and the elites that run them. Cannetti's and Kraemer's observations, and my insistence upon a constitutionally recognized right to rebellion, suggest why, in South Africa, assemblies remain a potent tool for revolutionary flourishing.

On the flip-side stands 'Freedom of Association'. Associations serve both conservative strains of flourishing and revolutionary dimensions of flourishing. Because associations are essential for both the creation and the maintenance of identity – and the heterogeneity and arationality of choice in the domain of identity formation – we should tread very carefully when we decide which associations merit constitutional solicitude. The conservative dimension protects the existing stores of social capital in various forms of bonding networks.[81] It allows them to determine rules for entry, for membership for voice, and for exit – so that that they may (largely unencumbered) pursue the ends that give their lives meaning. The revolutionary dimension ensures that out-groups – say Rastafarians – are able to challenge (as sub-publics) the dominant mode in which members of our polity see themselves and others. These counter-republics or sub-publics contain the seeds for growth and the means for change – for individuals and society alike. The revolutionary dimension also allows, as discussed above in Chapters 3 and 4, courts that adopt a remedial equilibration approach to rights analysis to (a) find private conduct anathema to considerations of equality and dignity unconstitutional, (b) require traditional communities and conservative associations, along with the state, to provide their 'second-class' members a meaningful (read material) opportunity to exit and to create or to join other sub-publics more likely to facilitate their flourishing, (c) without necessarily dismantling these communities or associations by substantially altering their rules regarding membership, voice and exit.

'Freedom and Security of the Person' may well be described as a prerequisite for flourishing. The Constitutional Court and lower courts have certainly viewed it as such as they gone about revolutionizing two distinct bodies of law: (a) the common law of delict in the context of state liability for wrongful behaviour; and (b) the state's regulation of abortion. In both *Carmichele v Minister of Safety and Security*[82] and *K v Minister of Safety and Security*,[83] the Constitutional Court found that that the right to dignity and the right to freedom and security of the person imposed positive duties on the state to prevent violations of physical integrity, in particular rape and other forms of sexual abuse. The *Carmichele* Court writes:

> In addressing these obligations in relation to dignity and the freedom and security of the person, few things can be more important to women than freedom from the threat of sexual violence.

> ... Sexual violence and the threat of sexual violence goes to the core of women's subordination in society. It is the single greatest threat to the self-determination of South African women.[84]

What ties both *Carmichele* and *K* together, and what distinguishes them from other instances in which the state fails to discharge its responsibilities in terms of FC s 12, is the Court's concern with the dignity of women and the systemic violence to which they continue to be subject. The Court recognizes that so long as the law permits women to be treated as objects, and in particular, allows the state itself to indulge in this kind of abuse, women will never be able to flourish fully.[85]

The Final Constitution's concern for the dignity and the security of women takes a very specific form in s 12(a). FC s 12(a), unlike its predecessor in the Interim Constitution, embraces a women's right 'to make decisions concerning reproduction'.[86] Although the Constitutional Court has yet to expressly vindicate the right to an abortion, two High Courts have heard, and rebuffed, challenges to the statutory expression of this right in the Choice on Termination of Pregnancy Act.[87] In *Christian Lawyers II*, Mojapelo J held that FC s 12(2)(a) and (b) guarantees the right of every woman to determine the fate of her pregnancy.[88] Without the requisite reproductive control over their bodies – against a landscape of systemic sexual violence – one cannot discuss seriously the capacity of the majority of South African women to flourish.

Our right to privacy draws down on two notions associated with dignity: (a) the entitlement of the individual to be treated as an end-in-herself and (b) the right to pursue some semblance of self-actualization. The former dimension of the right to privacy provides a floor below which no form of flourishing is possible. The second dimension constitutes, especially in Western society, a significant feature of flourishing itself: the freedom – especially from state intervention – to be what we want to be and to do what we want to do. Didcott J, writing for a majority in *Case & Curtis*, stated that:

> What erotic material I may choose to keep within the privacy of my home, and only for my personal use there, is nobody's business but mine. It is certainly not the business of society or the state. Any ban imposed on my possession of such material for that solitary purpose invades the personal privacy which .... the ... Constitution guarantees that I shall enjoy.[89]

3. *Community Rights and Flourishing*

In the heady days following the fall of the Berlin Wall in 1989, it seemed possible that we might be able to have our cake and eat it too. Velvet revolutions in Eastern Europe and South Africa offered evidence that we were all 'social democrats' now. More amazing still, separatist claims were resolved either through partition – as occurred with the (not so) neat cleavage of Czechoslovakia into the Czech Republic and Slovakia – or through public referenda in which minority communities concluded that it would be best if they did not withdraw from the polity of which they were currently members – as occurred in French-speaking Quebec in Canada and in the white populations South Africa. The two great strains of political enlightenment thought – the individualism of Locke and the American Revolution and the romanticism of Rousseau and the French Revolution – seemed to have finally played themselves out with the end of the Cold War. We suddenly found our selves free to be 'me' and 'we': the very definition of flourishing (without the Aristotelian overlay of virtue.) That is, each individual could freely be her many selves (in an order of priority largely left to the citizen herself), maintain her affiliations with the associations that made such selves possible, and not have to worry that the state would force her to choose one of her identities over all others.

But within five years, from 1989 to 1994, the cheery, non-postmodernist, optimism with which we (global citizens) greeted placards in Prague and Pretoria bearing the words 'Freedom', 'Truth' and 'Justice' morphed into something decidedly more modest.[90] Yugoslavia disintegrated into a war of all against all. In Rwanda, Hutus only agreed to beat their machetes into ploughshares after they had already hacked almost a million Tutsis to death. Something had changed. Or more accurately, we had missed something – in this brief epoch – along the way. Today, too many nations still seemed inclined to use the machinery of the state to eliminate alternative and non-dominant ways of being in the world: read China (a militant, security state, mercantilism), the United States (captured, in party, virulent, libertarian capitalism) and Mali or Afghanistan (where al-Queda and/or the Taliban brook virtually no contest to the most violent forms of Sharia married to totalitarian rule.)

Three hundred and fifty years ago, Locke's *A Letter on Toleration* suggested that we could end civil wars and other kinds of internecine strife by denying the state the right to dictate that its citizens conform their behaviour to a comprehensive (and totalizing) vision of the good and by ensuring that the state accorded religious, cultural and linguistic groups sufficient autonomy to pursue their own preferred way of being in the world. Was he wrong? Again, what had we missed? What he missed is the difference between a politics of respect that issues from claims grounded in individual human dignity and a politics of difference that issues from claims grounded in equal group recognition. And that is exactly the difference between a politics that can accommodate both the right to be 'me' and the right to be 'we' – and one that fails to do both. It may well be that, in many societies, individual liberty, multicultural recognition and nation-building are incompatible. Indeed, for a society in transition, multicultural recognition and national identity formation appear to pull in opposite directions. For even if individual identities are formed in open dialogue, these identities are, as I have argued in this book, largely shaped and limited by a pre-determined set of scripts. Collective recognition becomes important, in large part, because the body politic has denied the members of some group the ability to form – on an individual and collective basis – a positive identity. In a perfect world, the elimination of group-based barriers to social goods would free individuals to be whatever they wanted to be.

But even in a perfect world, claims for group recognition and flourishing do not dissipate so readily. What about the demand for group recognition – for collective flourishing? In any multicultural society, two different kinds of claims for equal respect and two different senses of identity sit uncomfortably alongside one another. The first emerges from what Charles Taylor calls a politics of equal dignity.[91] This form of politics is prededicated on the idea that each individual human being is equally worthy of respect. The second issues from a politics of difference. This form of politics tends to revolve primarily around the claim that every group of people ought to have the right to maintain its own equally respected community. The important distinction between the two is as follows. The first focuses on what is the same in all of us – that we all have lives and hopes and dreams, and that we should all be granted the opportunity and the means to pursue them. The second focuses on a specific aspect of our identity, our membership in a group. According to this second demand, the body politic ought to nurture or foster that particularity. The power of this second form of liberal politics springs largely from its involuntary character – the sense that we have no capacity to choose this aspect of our identity. It chooses us.[92] One of the problems South Africa faces is that it is difficult, if not impossible, to accommodate both kinds of claim. As Taylor himself notes, while 'it makes sense to demand as a matter of right that we approach ... certain cultures with a presumption of their value ... it can't make sense to demand as a matter of right that we come up with a final concluding judgment that their value is great or equal to others.'[93]

But the demand for political recognition of distinct religious, cultural and linguistic communities often amounts to that second demand. Moreover, such recognition often reinforces a narcissism of minor difference that, in turn, provokes anxiety about the extent to which members of other groups secure access to the most important goods in a polity. Such anxiety about a just distribution of goods – and the manner in which group affiliation distorts that distribution – necessarily interferes with national identity formation. The African National Congress (ANC) has, for both historical reasons and for reasons associated with its vision of transformation, refused to lend significant support to group politics. (Whatever their failings may be in execution, Black Economic Empowerment and Broad-Based Black Economic Empowerment initiatives are clearly designed to secure redress for the large-scale disenfranchisement of the majority of South Africans under apartheid. They are largely protected by s 9(2) of the Constitution.) The Constitutional Court is also predisposed towards claims of equal respect grounded in a politics of equal dignity.[94]

Should we, like the ANC, the Constitutional Court, and Sen, be group identity sceptics? Sen contends that:

> Our shared humanity gets savagely challenged when the manifold divisions in the world are unified into one allegedly dominant system of classification – in terms of religion, or community, or culture, or nation, or civilization (treating each as uniquely powerful in the context of that particular approach to war and peace.) The uniquely partitioned world is much more divisive than the universe of plural and diverse categories that shape the world in which we live. It goes not only against the old-fashioned belief that 'we human beings are all much the same' ... but also against the less discussed but much more plausible understanding that we are diversely different. The hope of harmony in the contemporary world lies to a great extent in a clearer understanding of the pluralities of human identity, and in the appreciation that they cut across each other and work against a sharp separation along one single hardened line of impenetrable division.[95]

That much seems incontestable. Totalizing views of identity (with their ostensibly comprehensive visions of the good) have led to a hardening of boundaries between groups. The hardening of boundaries has led, in turn, to a hardening of hearts that enables many nations (and many communities or groups with claims to nationhood) to pillage, bomb and plunder with increasingly greater abandon.

The more difficult question for group identity sceptics in South Africa is how to draw down on our constitutive attachments in a manner that both protects the social capital we require to build the many institutions that make us human and simultaneously prevents specific religious, cultural, and linguistic communities from using that social capital to undermine our 'more perfect union'. Here Sen knows that he is in trouble, but can only state the problem thus:

> The sense of identity can make an important contribution to the strength and the warmth of our relations with others, such as our neighbours, or members of the same community, or fellow citizens, or followers of the same religion. Our focus on particular identities can enrich our bonds and make us do things for each other and can help us to take us beyond our self-centred lives ... [But] ... [t]he well-integrated community in which residents do absolutely wonderful things for each other with great immediacy and solidarity can be the very same community in which bricks are thrown through the windows of immigrants who move into the region from elsewhere. The adversity of exclusion can be made to go hand in hand with the gifts of inclusion.[96]

Sen's last sentence is telling – '*can* be made to go hand in hand'. Not must, not inevitably, and certainly not ought. But again, Sen's invocation of diverse difference (within individuals, as within nations) and his ringing defence of the freedom to think critically about our multiple identities does not do the hard work – the line-drawing and the rule-making – that constitutional law requires.[97] Here, at least, is one place where the Constitutional Court's jurisprudence offers us useful guidance as to how the state ought to engage the religious, cultural and linguistic communities that make up the state and how those communities ought to engage one another. In *Fourie*, the Constitutional Court found that while the state could not continue to enforce common-law rules and statutory provisions that prevented same-sex life partners from entering civilly-sanctioned marriages, the Final Constitution had nothing immediate to say about religious prohibitions on gay and lesbian marriage and could not be read to require religious officials to consecrate a marriage between members of a same-sex life partnership.[98] The *Fourie* Court writes:

> [The amici's] arguments ... underline the fact that in the open and democratic society contemplated by the Constitution ... the religious beliefs held by the great majority of South Africans must be taken seriously. For many believers, their relationship with God or creation is central to all their activities. ... It concerns their capacity to relate in an intensely meaningful fashion to their sense of themselves, their community and their universe. ... For believers, then, what is at stake is not merely a question of convenience or comfort, but an intensely held sense about what constitutes the good and proper life and their place in creation. ... Religious bodies play a large and important part in public life, through schools, hospitals and poverty relief programmes... In the open and democratic society contemplated by the Constitution there must be mutually respectful coexistence between the secular and the sacred. The function of the Court is to recognise the sphere which each inhabits, not to force the one into the sphere of the other. Provided there is no prejudice to the fundamental rights of any person or group, the law will legitimately acknowledge a diversity of strongly-held opinions on matters of great public controversy. I stress the qualification that there must be no prejudice to basic rights. Majoritarian opinion can often be harsh to minorities that exist outside the mainstream. It is precisely the function of the Constitution and the law to step in and counteract rather than reinforce unfair discrimination against a minority. The test, whether majoritarian or minoritarian positions are involved, must always be whether the measure under scrutiny promotes or retards the achievement of human dignity, equality and freedom ... . The objective of the Constitution is to allow different concepts about the nature of human existence to inhabit the same public realm, and to do so in a manner that is not mutually destructive and that

at the same time enables government to function in a way that shows equal concern and respect for all.[99]

The *Fourie* Court commits itself to five propositions that are fundamental for flourishing, generally, and for religious, cultural and linguistic community rights, in particular. First, religious, cultural and linguistic communities are a critical source of meaning for the majority of South Africans. Second, religious, cultural and linguistic communities create institutions that support the material, intellectual, ethical and spiritual well-being of many South Africans. Third, religious, cultural and linguistic associations, as part of civil society, play an essential role in mediating the relationship between the state and its citizens. Fourth, while religious, cultural and linguistic associations are entitled to articulate – and make manifest through action – their 'intensely held world views', they may not do so in a manner that unfairly discriminates against other members of South African society. Fifth, although the 'intensely held world views' and practices of various religious, cultural and linguistic associations must, by necessity, exclude other members of South African society from various kinds of membership and of participation, such exclusion may not necessarily constitute unfair discrimination.

The easy question is whether communities possess the power to exclude members who initially agree to follow the rules of the community, but then subsequently refuse to do so.[100] Of course they do.

The hard question is whether South African society as a whole would be better off if it eliminated those exclusionary practices that not only remove non-compliant individuals but prevent other individuals – who begin as outsiders – from gaining entrance into the community? The answer to this hard question turns primarily on access to those goods which individuals require in order to flourish. In 21st-century social democratic constitutional, states – such as South Africa – there are no hard and fast lines between the public sphere and the private sphere (and the various goods they provide to individuals.) The result is that the Final Constitution affords no easy answers about what remains in the private domain and thus subject to some constitutional pre-commitment to non-interference. (Even questions of sexual intimacy, as the *Jordan* Court made clear, are matters of public interest.) Instead, the Final Constitution and super-ordinate legislation such as the Promotion of Equality and Prevention of Unfair Discrimination Act are primarily concerned with questions about individual and group access to the kind of goods that enable us to lead lives worth living.

Sen, for his part, is sceptical of the value of many forms of exclusionary and discriminatory behaviour practised by some religious, cultural and linguistic communities. The virulence of these practices led Sartre to remark that the anti-Semitism of European Christianity and Nazi Germany 'makes the Jew'.[101] (By this, Sartre meant that the dominant and the discriminatory script of Christian Europe denied the Jew the most basic features of humanity: not that Sartre had much sympathy for the Jewish community.) But this critical stance toward the exclusionary practices of many communities does not commit us to the proposition that all of these exclusionary practices are constitutionally infirm. (Nor does it commit us to the proposition, relatively transparent in Sartre's tepid brief against anti-Semitism, that there is nothing of value left in Judaism once one dispenses with the discriminatory script of Christian Europe.) As I have argued at length elsewhere,[102] and as Sen recognizes,[103] no form of meaningful human association – marriages, nuclear families, extended families, friendships, burial societies, trade unions, neighbours, neighbourhood security watches, political parties, bowling clubs, political action groups, stokvels, corporations, non-governmental organizations, professional regulatory bodies, charities, guilds, churches, synagogues, mosques, temples, schools, parent-teacher committees, school governing bodies, co-op boards, landless people's movements, internet forums, foundations, trusts – is possible without some form of discrimination.[104]

The critical question – as the *Fourie* Court notes – is whether such discrimination rises to the level of an unjustifiable impairment of the dignity – and thus the impairment of the capabilities and the flourishing of some of our fellow South Africans. Again: *this question turns on access to the kinds of goods that enable us to lead lives that allow us to flourish.* It is easy to conclude that golf clubs that have been the bastion of white male Christian privilege must open their doors to persons of all colours, all sexes and all religions. But what of the large stores of social (and hard) capital that have been invested in such institutions, and what of that capital which continues to offer the possibility of significant returns to the original members (and future members)? What of stokvels that provide access to capital to members of a community – but not to outsiders? What of religious secondary schools that discriminate on the basis of an applicant's willingness to accept a prescribed religious curriculum and, at the same time, offer a better education than that generally available in our public schools? It would be foolish to dismantle such institutions solely on the grounds that either some form of exclusion takes place or that some re-inscription of privilege occurs.[105] Almost all meaningful human labour occurs within the context of self-perpetuating social networks of various kinds. We must be alive, as Nancy Rosenblum contends, to the problem of moral and cognitive 'spillover': not all associations possess the same virtues and vices, and to assume that they do leaves us open to charges of transmission belt sociology (ie, if it's bad there, it must be bad everywhere).[106] Taking a sledgehammer to social institutions that create and maintain large stores of real and figurative capital is a recipe for a very impoverished polity. The hard question thus turns on the extent to which religious, cultural and linguistic communities – or any strong bonding network – can engage in justifiable forms of discrimination in the furtherance of constitutionally legitimate ends and the extent to which the state and other social actors can make equally legitimate claims on the kinds of goods made available in these communal formations that cannot be accessed elsewhere.

This concern about inegalitarian arrangements found within various religious, cultural and linguistic communities is not limited to exclusionary practices. Quite often, or often enough, members of religious or cultural communities will complain that their own community's 'traditional practices', when married to a constitutionally-recognized claim of group autonomy, perpetuate systemic discrimination and structural disadvantage. In other words, the rules of entrance and voice and exit of a community may well preclude the flourishing of various extant members of the community – in the main, women. Take, for example, the experience of women within the federally and legally autonomous Pueblo tribe in the United States. Under Pueblo law, Pueblo women – but not Pueblo men – are expelled if they intermarry;

only women who intermarry lose residency rights (for themselves and their children), voting rights, and rights to pass their tribal membership on to their children, along with related welfare benefits that are tied to tribal membership.[107]

Julia Martinez and other women within the Santa Clara Pueblo community challenged these tribal laws as violations of both the federal equal protection clause and the Indian Civil Rights Act. The latter reads as follows: 'No Indian tribe in exercising powers of self-government shall ... deny to any person within its jurisdiction the equal protection of the laws.'[108] What is remarkable about the US Supreme Court's judgment in *Santa Clara Pueblo v Martinez* is that although the Court refused to grant tribal authorities absolute sovereignty over affairs within their jurisdiction, the *Martinez* Court was still willing to grant them sufficient autonomy to deny half of their members the equal protection of the law.[109]

The Constitutional Court has had somewhat greater success in mediating the individual flourishing and the communal flourishing at odds in a number of challenges to rules of customary law. (However, a sizeable number of South Africans differ on whether these new constitutional norms justifiably displace traditional – read African – forms of life.) In *Bhe v Magistrate, Khayelitsha & Others*, the Court found that the customary law rule of male primogeniture impaired the dignity of, and unfairly discriminated against, the deceased's two female children because the rule and the other impugned provisions prevented the children from inheriting part of the deceased's estate.[110] However, it is the manner in which the *Bhe* Court negotiates two different kinds of claims for equal respect, and two different forms of flourishing, that is most instructive for our current purposes.

The *Bhe* Court begins with the following bromide: customary law provides a comprehensive vision of the good for many South African communities that warrants some level of constitutional solicitude. However, the new-found constitutional respect for traditional practices does not immunize them from constitutional review.[111] Everyone – whether traditional leader or Constitutional Court judge – must locate any putatively valid justification of extant customary law in the provisions of the Final Constitution. Customary law has not, the *Bhe* Court then ruefully observes, evolved to meet either the changing needs of the community or the dictates of the Constitution. It fails African widows because: '(a) ... social conditions frequently do not make living with the heir a realistic or even a tolerable proposition; (b) ... the African woman does not have a right of ownership; and (c) the prerequisite of a good working relationship with the heir for the effectiveness of the widow's right to maintenance', as a general matter, no longer exists.[112] The Court takes care to note that the fault for this arrested development lies outside traditional communities. Ruptures within traditional ways of life – caused by apartheid, the hegemony of western culture, and capitalism – have prevented the law's evolution.[113] This aside sets the stage for the delivery of the *Bhe* Court's coup de grace: that 'the official rules of customary law of succession are no longer universally observed.'[114] The trend within traditional communities is toward new norms that 'sustain the surviving family unit' rather than those norms that re-inscribe male primogeniture. By showing that the spirit of succession lies in its commitment to family cohesion, that the traditional family no longer coheres as it once did, and that the 'distorted' rules of customary law are frozen in apartheid-era statute and case law that 'emphasises ... patriarchal features and minimises its communitarian ones,' the *Bhe* Court closes the gap between constitutional imperative and customary obligation.[115] Had customary law been permitted to develop in an 'active and dynamic manner,' it would have already reflected the *Bhe* Court's conclusion that 'the exclusion of women from inheritance on the grounds of gender is a clear violation of ... [FC s] 9(3).'[116] Had customary law not been allowed to ossify, traditional communities would have noted how male primogeniture entrenched 'past patterns of disadvantage among a vulnerable group' and endorsed the *Bhe* Court's re-working of customary understandings of the competence 'to own and administer property' in a manner that vindicates a woman's right to dignity under FC s 10. In this way, the *Bhe* Court is able to assert that traditional communities have conceptions of dignity worth protecting without being obliged to endorse a rule that quite clearly offends the (ostensibly Western inflected) dignity interests of many women and female children within those communities.

These inquiries into both the physical coercion and the non-physical coercion of children and adults by the practices of conservative religious and cultural communities are united by considerations of exit. The Constitutional Court has shown itself to be quite adept at distinguishing circumstances in which neither child nor adult can meaningfully vote with their feet, and thereby flourish, from those instances in which adults willingly remain members of traditional communities in which their rights and privileges may well be subordinate to the rights and the privileges of other members of the community.[117] The Court's ability to distinguish the objective conditions of second-class citizenship from the subjective decisions of equal citizens has blunted critics of religious and cultural communities who attribute 'false consciousness' to any individual or group of individuals, subject to discrimination, who remain within their community's traditional confines.[118]

Finally, I have repeatedly noted how the disentrenchment of private ordering through remedial equilibrium offers the Court a broad array of remedies when mediating discriminatory practices and relationships within a given community or association. The use of remedial equilibration recognizes that the road from the totalizing, degrading and criminal policies of the apartheid state to the social democracy or egalitarian pluralist regime anticipated by our Final Constitution is not straight. We will have unadulterated successes. We will experience shameful false starts: (a) our long-standing blindness to the ravages of HIV/AIDS,[119] (b) our propping up of a totalitarian regime across the Limpopo,[120] and (c) the creation of a crony capitalist one party dominant state apparatus too hollow to deliver adequate basic services to the majority of its denizens and so inured to the suffering of it citizens that its response to the expression of legitimate grievances is the jackboot and the bayonet.[121]

4. *Flourishing and Socio-Economic Rights*

In the Constitutional Court's preferred mode of rights discourse, rights are 'interdependent', 'overlap' and 'interpenetrate' one another. So great is the ostensible coherence of the constitution's objective, normative value order that one may be forgiven for thinking that all rights (and fundamental values) are in play in every constitutional matter.[122] For example, Sachs J writes in *Sidumo* that:

> [S]ome guidance can be sought from the manner in which this court has emphasised the intersection and interrelatedness of different protected rights in particular matters, and highlighted the influence of overarching values. Thus, when dealing with capital punishment in *Makwanyane*, the court stressed the overlap and interaction between the rights to life and dignity on the one hand, and the right not to be subjected to cruel, inhuman or degrading punishment on the other; far from being mutually exclusive, each of these protected rights was seen as reinforcing and adding substance to the others. Similarly in the sodomy case, emphasis was put on the interconnection between the rights to equality, dignity and privacy, respectively. A choice between them was not required. *Grootboom* expressly referred to the indivisibility and interrelated character of protected rights, emphasising that the determination of what was reasonable in relation to the right of access to adequate housing had to take account of the right to dignity, and the gender and racial dimensions involved. In *Khosa* the question was whether withdrawal of certain welfare entitlements for permanent residents who were not South African citizens, raised a question of equality (non-discrimination), or of the right of access to social welfare, and whether the rights of the child also featured. Mokgoro J stated: 'In this case we are concerned with these intersecting rights [socio-economic rights and the founding values of human dignity, equality and freedom] which reinforce one another at the point of intersection.'[123]

The decidedly mushy nature of such analysis blocks our understanding of the individual rights themselves. That the Court's mushiness regarding the actual content of specific provisions of a Bill of Rights – whose decidedly conflicting aims are instead magically squared by the alleged existence of some 'objective, normative value order' – is not my quarry here. I want to argue against the grain, and claim that a hierarchy of rights does indeed exist. It begins, as Nussbaum's list does with 'life' or what I would translate into South African rights discourse as 'health', 'food', 'water', 'social security', 'housing', 'education' and a clean and sustainable 'environment'. More importantly, I am going to deny the proposition articulated by a majority of members of the legal academy that the Constitutional Court's approach to socio-economic rights analysis is to a significant degree responsible for the ongoing denial of the basic goods and capabilities to a significant proportion of South Africans.

It's not that I think the Court's mode of reasoning about such matters is correct. It can often be quite thin, as we shall see in the case analysis in Chapter 8. It's simply hard to conceive of how a Court with no history of socio-economic rights analysis upon which to rely (domestic or foreign), no budget to make good a desired remedy, no independent power to enforce a judgment, and no institutional, political and social support upon which it could safely draw down could have done something utterly different than it has (without courting its own demise).[124] I have suggested above and below how the Court might have engineered more optimal outcomes – through shared constitutional interpretation and participatory bubbles – without appearing overly deferential or courting its own demise. But the owl of Minerva flies furthest at dusk, and academic cavils about the Constitutional Court's 'neo-liberal framework' seem more interested with arguing on the side of the angels then pressing down on the problems (both doctrinal and institutional) with which the Court has been confronted.[125]

This Court has, from the very beginning, shown itself to be alive to the tragedies with which it is confronted, the specific traumas experienced by the plaintiffs, the defendants and the judges themselves when the Court is asked to resolve this type of legal dispute, and the general depredations of apartheid and colonial rule. In *Soobramoney*, the Court wrote:

> We live in a society in which there are great disparities in wealth. Millions of people are living in deplorable conditions and in great poverty. There is a high level of unemployment, inadequate social security, and many do not have access to clean water or to adequate health services. These conditions already existed when the Constitution was adopted and a commitment to address them, and to transform our society into one in which there will be human dignity, freedom and equality, lies at the heart of our new constitutional order. For as long as these conditions continue to exist that aspiration will have a hollow ring.[126]

The notion that Court has, over time, become desensitized to the conditions of South Africans who continue to live in straitened circumstances is inconsistent with clear developments in our socio-economic rights jurisprudence as we saw in a string of recent meaningful engagement housing judgments (e.g., *Joe Slovo I* and *Joe Slovo II*, *Occupiers of 51 Olivia Road*) and the commitment to equal access to an adequate basic educations in our public schools (e.g., *Ermelo* and *Juma Musjid.*)

The responsibility for delivering on the promise of liberation and the delivery of basic goods lies elsewhere: with the politically accountable branches of government, with those parties who control the public fiscus, and with those members of society (natural persons and juristic persons such as our largest firms) with sufficient capital to contrive solutions to the widespread deprivations that beset *all* of us. The ongoing contempt that the coordinate branches of government and organs of state have shown for court-declared remedies in this arena suggests that it is our politics and politicians – and those individuals and juristic persons that run our largest corporations – that remain culpable (in large part) for this failure to deliver the goods. Delivery of these basic goods, as the Court itself has repeatedly recognized constitutes the minimal material conditions for flourishing.

Endnotes

1. Of course, we can now see, post-2008, exactly what happens when individual states move away their commitments to a strong social democracy. Iceland, which once possessed near end of history status, imploded immediately (in 2008) after a decade long binge of free-market fueled deregulation and a collective indebtedness 10 times the annual GNP of $13 billion. See *Inside Job* (2010). However, with its longstanding egalitarian roots, strong public sector, relative homogeneaity and small population, Iceland was able to rewrite its social contract in a manner that would reverse its current course and restore its strong social democratic moorings. More importantly for this work, we can see what happens when a formal commitment to the creation of a social democracy in South Africa (our aspirational Constitution), yields to a market-driven desire to secure foreign direct investment and a failure to put the development of its historically disadvantaged communities first. As of 2012, South Africa's social compact – a deal done by big business, the ANC and the unions in the 1980s – shows discernible signs of fragmentation. In the short term, those three actors will likely strike a 'new deal' that will temporarily shore up the status quo. However, the failure of post 1994 South Africa to live up to the promise of its social contract, as reflected in the Final Constitution, makes the short term outlook for South Africa appear 'unsustainable'. The World Bank Group '*Economic Update on South Africa: Focus on Inequality of Opportunity*' (2012)
2. R Rorty *Contingency, Irony and Solidarity* (1989).

3. S Fish *Doing What Comes Naturally: Change Rhetoric and the Practice of Theory in Literary and Legal Studies* (1989).
4. M Friedman 'The Social Responsibility of Business is to Increase its Profits' *The New York Times Magazine* (September 1970).
5. See, eg, A Sen; *The Idea of Justice* (2009); A Sen *Development as Freedom* (1999); J Cohen *Philosophy, Politics, Democracy: Selected Papers* (2009); A Gutmann & D Thompson *Why Deliberative Democracy?* (2004); A Gutmann *Identity in Democracy* (2003); M Nussbaum *Women and Human Development: The Capabilities Approach* (2001); J Habermas *Facts and Norms* (1996); J Rawls *Political Liberalism* (1993); C Larmore *Patterns of Moral Complexity* (1986); B Barber *Strong Democracy* (1984); M Walzer *Spheres of Justice* (1983). Virtually all members of the South African legal academic community engaged in writing monographs on South African constitutional law hew to a fairly strong social democratic line. See S Liebenberg *Socio-Economic Rights: Adjudication under a Transformative Constitution* (2010); K McLean *Constitutional Deference, Courts & Socio-Economic Rights in South Africa* (2009) D Bilchitz *Poverty and Fundamental Rights* (2006) AJ van der Walt *Constitutional Property Law* (2005); D Davis *Democracy and Deliberation* (2000); D Meyerson *Rights Limited* (1997). See, further, T Roux *The Politics of Pragmatism: The First 15 Years of the South African Constitutional Court* (forthcoming 2013).
6. M Mahatir & I Shintaro (eds) *The Voice of Asia: Two Leaders Discuss the Coming Century* (1995)(Mahatir, then Prime Minister of Malaysia, and Shintaro, then governor of Tokyo, argue that a special mix of culture and community, married to capitalism, offer a third way. Of course, they wrote and edited this tract before the Asian financial collapse of 1998.)
7. S Sibanda *Not Yet Uhuru: How Constitutional Democracy Has Blocked the Promise of Liberation in South Africa* (PhD, in process, University of the Witwatersrand, 2012.)
8. D Fauvre *China and Capitalism: A History of Business Enterprise in Modern China* (2006).
9. See M Nussbaum and A Sen (eds) *The Quality of Life* (1993).
10. A Sen 'More Than 100 Million Women are Missing' (1992) 37 *New York Review of Books* 61; A Sen 'More Than 100 Million Women are Missing' (1992) 367*The Lancet* 185.
11. A Sen *The Idea of Justice* (2009).
12. *S v Mamabolo* 2001 (3) SA 409 (CC), 2001 (5) BCLR 449 (CC), 2001 (1) SACR 686 (CC) at para 41.
13. Sen *Development* (supra) at 64.
14. But see P Singer 'Famine, Affluence and Morality' (1972) 1 *Philosophy and Public Affairs* 229 (1972). Singer's radical utilitarian challenge – to choose to act in a manner that would benefit others where no meaningful moral cost attaches to an agent's own life – and its rejection by most individuals intuitively inclined toward utilitarian thought – shows up a limit in one strand of utilitarian thought. Put slightly differently, when you confront most individuals with Singer's stringent test, the demands of such an account invariably cause individuals previously committed to utilitarianism to fall back on deontological or communitarian justifications that limit their obligations to persons they know or persons within their political community. As I noted above in Chapter 2 fn 159, the diverse philosophical approaches of Amartya Sen (development theory), Charles Larmore (moral philosophy) and Patricia Churchland (political philosophy) all arrive at roughly the same place: a hybrid of virtually all the major schools of modern ethical and political philosophy. See *Patterns of Moral Complexity* (1986); P Churchland *Braintrust: What Neuroscience Has to Tell Us about Morality* (2011). Each, in their own way, make the case for a non-reductive approach to deontological, utilitarian and communitarian thought. Each school of thought identifies salient features of moral and political dilemmas. We are not wired, physically or socially, in such a manner that one school of thought invariably wins out. Unsatisfying as that might seem, we are, as this book has argued all along, radically heterogeneous creatures.
15. OECD *The Better Life Index* (2011)(The top eleven Quality of Life countries are: Australia, Canada, Sweden, New Zealand, Norway, Denmark, the United States, Switzerland, Finland, Netherlands and Luxemburg. The United States, Luxemburg, Norway, Switzerland and Australia appear on both the top 11 Quality of Life list and the top 11 GDP/PPP list.)

16. Sen *Development* (supra) at 73.
17. Ibid at 73 quoting Adam Smith *The Wealth of Nations* (1776)(RH Campbell and AS Skinner (eds) 1976) 469 – 471 (By "necessities", Smith means 'not only the commodities which are indispensably necessary for the support of life, but whatever the customs of the country renders it indecent for creditable people, even the lowest order, to be without.')
18. Ibid at 74.
19. Ibid at 75.
20. M Nussbaum *Women and Human Development: The Capabilities Approach* (2000) 78 - 80; M Nussbaum, *Frontiers of Justice: Disability, Nationality, Species Membership* (2006) 76 -78. For reflections on Nussbaum's capabilities approach, see B Giovanola 'Personhood and Human Richness: Good and Well-Being in the Capability Approach and Beyond' (2005) 63 *Review of Social Economy* 1 (Offers a defence of flourishing and the Aristotelian concept of *eudaimonia*, and engages the question of whether capabilities theory offers a partial, and thus liberal, account of the good or something closer to a comprehensive Aristotelian account); A Kaufman 'Capabilities and Freedom' (2006) 14 *The Journal of Political Philosophy* 289; AM Jaggar 'Reasoning about Well-Being: Nussbaum's Methods of Justifying Capabilities (2006) 14 *The Journal of Political Philosophy* 301; K Dowling 'Can Capabilities Reconcile Freedom and Equality?' (2006) 14 *The Journal of Political Philosophy* 323.
21. M Nussbaum 'Constitutions and Capabilities: "Perception" against Lofty Formalism' (2007) 121 *Harvard Law Review* 4.
22. Ibid at 7.
23. Ibid at 57.
24. J Henry 'US Issues New Deportation Policy's First Reprieves' *The New York Times* (23 August 2011) (In a dramatic reversal, policy employs prosecutorial discretion to suspend deportation proceedings for most undocumented immigrants in United States (300,000 cases) who have committed no crime.)
25. M Nussbaum's essay '"Finely Aware and Richly Responsible": Moral Attention and the Moral Task of Literature' (1986) 82 *The Journal of Philosophy* 516, 536.
26. M Heidegger *Lectures on the History of the Concept of Time* (1924).
27. As I have already maintained, at the same time this account of the self demonstrates the extent to which associations are constitutive of the self, it dispels the notion that individuals are best understood as 'rational choosers' of the ends they seek. The self should be seen as the inheritor and the executor of a rather heterogeneous set of social practices and natural predispositions – of ways of responding to or acting in the world. Despite the dominance of the enlightenment vision of the self as a rational agent, the truth of the matter is that the majority of our responses to the world are *arational.* They are not reflective. They are not critical. They are not chosen. They just are.
28. As I noted in Chapter 3, the constitutive nature of our attachments also forces us to attend to another often overlooked feature of associations. We often speak of the associations that make up our lives as if we were largely free to choose them or make them up as we go along. I have suggested why such a notion of choice is not true of us as individual selves. It is also largely not true of associational life generally. I placed significant emphasis on Michael Walzer's contention that there is a 'radical givenness to our associational life.' M Walzer 'On Involuntary Association' in A Gutmann (ed) *Freedom of Association* (1998) 64, 67. What he meant, in short, is that most of the associations that make up our associational life are involuntary associations. The emphasis on involuntariness in associational life is meant to bracket any conception of freedom which intimates that *any* impediment to free association is a denial of that which is most fundamentally human. It is often the case that not choosing to leave an association, but to stay, is what we truly cherish as freedom. Ibid at 73.
29. L Wittgenstein *Philosophical Investigations* (1953, GEM Anscombe (ed)) Book II xi 226.
30. The emphasis in this section on the arational sources of the self invariably brackets the place of reason in ethical, political and legal thought (or most fields of human inquiry for that matter). However, bracketing reason and diminishing its efficacy to the vanishing point are two entirely different things. First, the place of instrumental reason and the ability of human beings to recognize

regularities in the world means, at the very least, that we are able to discriminate between better and worse ways of realizing our preferred ends. Second, the more de-centered the self, the more varied forms of life the individual draws upon, the more tools the individual will have when deciding upon his or her preferred vision of the good. Third, this account is not averse or opposed to the existence of some deep grammar of human reason – married to long-standing social conventions – that commits us to such varied ends as the family, the nation, a religion, a marriage and individual happiness. Some may think it convenient that such a species of naturalism results in a commitment to such imperfectly reconcilable goods as freedom, equality, dignity and democracy. However, putting aside the current dominance of social democratic thought in the academy, these values have competed with one another for primacy of place for several millennia. How one settles, in a rational manner, the differences between these values is the very meat of ethical and political thought. Fourth, though there may be plenty of instances in which the evidence for our beliefs about the world leaves room for a certain amount of theoretical indeterminacy, I take it as given that most of our beliefs about the world are true and that we, humans, share most of those beliefs. Only under such general conditions of shared understanding does it even begin to make sense to talk about disagreement. See R Rorty 'Solidarity or Objectivity' *Objectivity, Relativity & Truth: Philosophical Papers I* (1991) 21, 31. My use of the term arational may likewise strike some as deeply counterintuitive. It may seem to sweep into the ambit of the arational, various processes most people are apt to describe as falling within the domain of the rational. The point is the authorship of the processes themselves. We did not, as individuals, or as groups, consciously create most of these processes. As I argued in Chapter 3, they are not the product of any one person's capacity to reason. In this respect, they are arational. So when I say the ends we pursue 'just are' the ends we pursue, I am not denying that there might not be good reasons for our pursuit. I only deny that the ultimate source of these ends is a function of rational, freely-willed individual choice. Again: that does mean we are incapable of critique of current moral, legal and political arrangements, or the improvement of these arrangements by our own lights. See S Pinker *The Better Angels of Our Nature* (2011)(Pinker, employing findings in cognitive science and marrying them to a close reading of history, shows that we, as a species, are far less barbaric than we were several centuries ago (by an order of magnitude), and contends that our innate capacity for empathy and literacy, combined with the growth of such social institutions and artefacts such as good governance, trade and cosmopolitanism, have been the key drivers of human progress (as measured by virtually any matrix).)

31. A Sen *Identity and Violence: The Illusion of Destiny* (2006) 33.
32. See Chapter One-B, endnote 18, for extend critique of the epistomology that underlies communitarian thought.
33. Ibid at 34–35. For further argument along these same lines, see my discussion of Michael Walzer's account of the ineradicability and the virtues of the divided self in Chapter 2 and 3. See M Walzer *Thick and Thin: Moral Arguments at Home and Abroad* (2002) 85, 99–104.
34. M Nussbaum 'Capabilities as Fundamental Entitlements: Sen and Social Justice' (2003) 9 *Feminist Economics* 33.
35. *Fourie* (supra) at paras 60–61.
36. Benjamin Barber articulates a similarly strong conception of democratic politics, but, as an American, is able to locate this solidarity in over two centuries of a largely uninterrupted commitment to a democratic constitutional order (even taking into account limits placed on the franchise and the long-standing disenfranchisement of women and African-Amaericans). B Barber *Strong Democracy: Participatory Politics for a New Age* (1984). (As the Tea Party Movement suggests, I don't however believe that many older white Americans (in 2012) have yet to fully come to grips with slavery, the Civil War or the limited emancipation of African-Americans (even as Americans begin the sesquicentennial celebration of Abraham Lincoln's 'Emancipation Proclamation'.)) Barber extends the insights of pluralism into democratic theory: 'Democracy understood as self-government in a social setting is not a terminus for individually held rights and values; it is their starting place. Autonomy is not the

condition of democracy, *democracy is the condition of autonomy*. Without participating in the common life that denies them and in the decision-making that shapes their social habitat, women and men cannot become individuals. Freedom, justice, equality and autonomy are all products of common thinking and common living; democracy creates them.' Barber (supra) at xv (emphasis added). As for any difficulties that might face the framing of constitutional rights in terms of democratic solidarity, Barber responds with equal vigour: 'The rights we often affect to hurl impudently into the face of [our democratic] government are rights we enjoy only by virtue of government. The private sphere we guard so jealously from the encroachments of the public sector exists entirely by dint of law, which is the public sector's most significant creation.' Ibid. Barber turns the ostensible 'individualistic, liberal, atomistic' bases for constitutional democracy on its head. Likewise, the Constitution we praise so highly – in South Africa – exists only because virtually all South Africans (or at least their representatives) gave the Interim Constitution their imprimatur of approval. If 87% of the freely-elected Constitutional Assembly endorsed the Final Constitution then it seems fair to say, as Barber argues, that our constitutional rights flow from a democratically-determined social compact endorsed by a radically heterogeneous South African society and that they retain their force only by virtue of the democracy – and the solidarity of a citizenry – that supports them.

37. Walzer 'On Involuntary Association' (supra) at 73.
38. Nussbaum's Decalogue is both relational and hierarchal. See C Gilligan *In a Different Voice* (1982)(On the centrality of relationships in determining appropriate ethical); A Maslow 'A Theory of Human Motivation' (1943) 50 (4) *Psychological Review* 370. Nussbaum's core of capabilities, like Maslow's hierarchy of needs, looks very much like a ladder that climbs toward greater self-actualization, even as it emphasizes the importance of Gilligan-like relationships for human flourishing.
39. See S Woolman 'Dignity' in S Woolman & M Bishop (eds) *Constitutional Law of South Africa* (2nd Edition, OS, March 2006) Chapter 36.
40. Justice Ackermann, the Court's original exponent of dignity, grounds the first definition of dignity in two sources: the history of apartheid and the work of Immanuel Kant: '[I]t is permissible and indeed necessary to look at the ills of the past which [the Constitution] seeks to rectify and in this way try to establish what equality and dignity mean ... What lay at the heart of the apartheid pathology was the extensive and sustained attempt to deny to the majority of the South African population the right of self- identification and self-determination ... Who you were, where you could live, what schools and universities you could attend, what you could do and aspire to, and with whom you could form intimate personal relationship was determined for you by the state ... That state did its best to deny to blacks that which is definitional to being human, namely the ability to understand or at least define oneself through one's own powers and to act freely as a moral agent pursuant to such understanding of self-definition. Blacks were treated as means to an end and hardly ever as an end in themselves; an almost complete reversal of the Kantian imperative and concept of priceless inner worth and dignity.' Ackermann (supra) at 540. See also *Dawood & Another v Minister of Home Affairs & Others* 2000 (3) SA 936 (CC), 2000 (8) BCLR 837 (CC)('*Dawood*') at para 35 (O'Regan J writes: 'The Constitution asserts dignity to contradict our past in which human dignity for black South Africans was routinely and cruelly denied. It asserts it to inform the future, to invest in our democracy respect for the intrinsic worth of all human beings.')
41. The categorical imperative ought not to be conflated with the golden rule. Kant actually rejects the golden rule as a maxim for ethical action. See I Kant *Groundwork of the Metaphysics of Morals* (trans and ed AW Wood, 2002)('Groundwork') 46 – 47. He does so because the golden rule permits our individual inclinations to determine outcomes ('as *you* would have them do onto *you*') and does not require the attempt at moral perfection (through reason) demanded by the procedures associated with the categorical imperative. See TW Pogge 'The Categorical Imperative' in P Guyer (ed) *Critical Essays on Kant's Groundwork of the Metaphysics of Morals* (1998) 189, 191 (For Kant, 'the categorical imperative is not a version of the Golden Rule.') See also J Rawls *Lectures on the History of Moral Philosophy* (2000)('*Lectures*') 199.

42. Kant *Groundwork* (supra) at 45 – 46. See also D Meyerson *Rights Limited* (1997) 12 (Refers to this formulation of the categorical imperative as a heuristic device through which we might better understand our own basic law.) See, further, AW Wood 'Humanity as an End in Itself' in P Guyer (ed) *Critical Essays on Kant's Groundwork of the Metaphysics of Morals* (1998) 165, 170)(Defines the term 'individual as an end-in-itself' as 'an end with absolute worth or (as Kant also says) dignity, something whose value cannot be compared to, traded off against, or compensated for or replaced by any other value.')
43. Kant did not view this principle as impossible to enact. As Rawls notes, Kant found moral pietism offensive and conceived of the categorical imperative as a 'mode of reflection that could order and moderate the scrutiny of our motives in a reasonable way.' Rawls *Lectures* (supra) at 149. Perhaps the best way to characterize Kant's categorical imperative is as a reflective check – albeit a demanding one – on our moral intuitions. A contemporary example of such a reflective check – and one that continues to do a great deal of heavy lifting – is Rawls' own 'veil of ignorance'. See J Rawls *A Theory of Justice* (1972). Like the categorical imperative, the veil of ignorance serves as an intuition pump for claims about distributive justice by forcing us to forsake any knowledge of our current position in society before we begin debate on how various social goods are to be allocated. Both intuition pumps are designed to eliminate illicit information that might otherwise skew (or justify) the criteria for the distribution of various goods in favour of those who already satisfy the conditions for the distribution of those goods people tend to value most and which can be rather easily converted into other material and immaterial goods: e.g., health, wealth, intelligence, strong familial ties, influence, beauty, creativity. See, e.g., Pogge (supra) at 206 ('The categorical imperative is … a general procedure for constructing morally relevant thought experiments… [T]he categorical imperative amplifies my conscience by transforming the decision from one of marginal significance into one concerning the world at large, and also isolates my conscience by screening out personal considerations that might affect my choice of maxims but are irrelevant to my decisions about how through legislation to specify a realm of ends.') For example, when South African law students are asked whether they would be willing to step behind a veil of ignorance (I often use the lottery as an example) and trade their current elite position for one of 50 million other positions in South Africa (subject to the strictures of the veil of ignorance), they invariably drop their resistance to affirmative action or offer complaints about reverse discrimination.
44. O Schachter 'Human Dignity as a Normative Concept' (1983) 77 *American Journal of International Law* 848, 849.
45. For more on the relationship between dignity and the prohibitions of slavery, servitude and forced labour, see S Woolman 'Dignity' (supra) at § 36.4(e). See also S Woolman & M Bishop 'Slavery, Servitude and Forced Labour' in S Woolman & M Bishop (eds) *Constitutional Law of South Africa* (2nd Edition, OS, March 2005) Chapter 64.
46. For more on the relationship between dignity and sentencing, see S Woolman 'Dignity' (supra) at § 36.4(c)(iii) infra, and D Van Zyl Smit 'Sentencing and Punishment' in S Woolman & M Bishop (eds) *Constitutional Law of South Africa* (2nd Edition, OS, December 2003) Chapter 49.
47. See *President of the Republic of South Africa v Hugo* 1997 (4) SA 1 (CC), 1997 (6) BCLR 708 (CC)('*Hugo*') at para 41 ('[T]he purpose of our new constitutional and democratic order is the establishment of a society in which all human beings will be accorded *equal respect* regardless of their membership in particular groups.')
48. LWH Ackermann 'Equality under the 1996 South African Constitution' in R Wolfrem (ed) *Gleichheit und Nichtdiskriminierung im Nationalalen und Internationalen Mesenchenrechtssschutz* (2003) 547. See also *Law v Canada (Minister of Employment and Immigration)* [1999] 170 DLR 4th 1 (SCC).
49. *Ferreira v Levin* 1996 (1) SA 984 (CC), 1996 (4) BCLR 1 (CC) at para 49.
50. The majority in *Ferreira v Levin* rejected Justice Ackermann's view that IC s 11(1) and FC s 12(1) contain a robust, self-standing freedom right. Ibid at paras 170 – 185 The Constitutional Court accepted, subsequently, Justice Ackermann's thesis that dignity is meant to secure the space for

self-actualisation (autonomy). See, eg, *Hugo* (supra) at para 41 ('[D]ignity is at the heart of individual rights in a free and democratic society.') See also N Haysom 'Dignity' in H Cheadle, D Davis & N Haysom (eds) *South African Constitutional Law: The Bill of Rights* (2002) 131–132.

51. See D Cornell 'A Call for a Nuanced Constitutional Jurisprudence: Ubuntu, Dignity and Reconciliation' (2004) 19 *SA Public Law* 666, 667 ('[I]f we give Kantian dignity its broadest meaning, it is not associated with our actual freedom but with the postulation of ourselves as beings who not only can, but must, confront ... ethical decisions, and in making those decisions ... give value to our world.')

52. *Affordable Medicines Trust & Others v Minister of Health & Others* 2006 (3) SA 247 (CC), 2005 (6) BCLR 529 (CC).

53. Ibid at para 59 (citation omitted, emphasis added).

54. See *August v Electoral Commission* 1999 (3) SA 1 (CC), 1999 (4) BCLR 363 (CC) at para 17 (emphasis added).

55. *Prince v Law Society* 2002 (2) SA 794 (CC), 2002 (3) BCLR 231 (CC)('*Prince*') at para 149 ('[W] here there are [religious] practices that might fall within a general legal prohibition, but that do not involve any violation of the Bill of Rights, the Constitution obliges the State to walk the extra mile' and to find adequate means – perhaps a carefully constructed exemption – of accommodating the practice at issue); *S v Jordan & Others (Sex Workers Education and Advocacy Task Force & Others as Amici Curiae)* 2002 (6) SA 642 (CC), 2002 (11) BCLR 1117 (CC)('*Jordan*'); *De Reuck v Director of Public Prosecutions, Witwatersrand Local Division* 2004 (1) SA 406 (CC), 2003 (12) BCLR 1333 (CC) ('*De Reuck*'); *Volks v Robinson* 2005 (5) BCLR 466 (CC)('*Volks*'). Cf *Minister of Home Affairs & Another v Fourie & Another; Lesbian and Gay Equality Project & Others v Minister of Home Affairs & Others* 2006 (1) SA 524 (CC), 2006 (3) BCLR 355 (CC)('*Fourie*').

56. See *Fourie* (supra) at paras 60 – 61 (Sachs J)('Equality ... does not presuppose ... suppression of difference ... Equality ... does not imply ... homogenisation of behaviour .... [T]here are a number of constitutional provisions that underline the constitutional value of acknowledging diversity and pluralism in our society, and give a particular texture to the broadly phrased right to freedom of association contained in section 18. Taken together, they affirm the right of people to self-expression without being forced to subordinate themselves to the cultural and religious norms of others, and highlight the importance of individuals and communities being able to enjoy what has been called the 'right to be different'. In each case, space has been found for members of communities to depart from a majoritarian norm.')

57. *Port Elizabeth Municipality v Various Occupiers* 2005 (1) SA 217 (CC), 2004 (12) BCLR 1268 (CC) at para 18 (emphasis added).

58. Concrete, mutual recognition of the other as essential for the recognition of one's own self lies at the core of African philosophical thought and the concept of uBuntu. See D Cornell 'Is There a Difference that Makes a Difference between uBuntu and Dignity? (2010) 25 *SA Public Law* 382; Y Mokgoro and S Woolman 'Where Dignity Ends and Ubuntu Starts: An Amplification of, and a Tension in, Drucilla Cornell's Thoughts' (2010) 25 *SA Public Law* 400; T Metz 'African Ethics' *International Encyclopaedia of Ethics* (2010); T Metz 'African Moral Theory and Public Governance: Nepotism, Preferential Hiring and Other Partiality' in J Murove (ed) *African Ethics: An Anthology for Comparative and Applied Ethics* (2009) 335.

59. *Khosa* (supra) at para 74. The Court's language echoes Rawls' description of a Kantian 'realm of ends' in which 'everyone recognizes everyone else as not only honouring their obligation of justice and duties of virtue, but also, as it were, legislating law for their moral commonwealth. For all know of themselves and of the rest that they are reasonable and rational, and that this fact is mutually recognized.' Rawls *Lectures* (supra) at 209. See also S Doctor 'Dignity, Criminal Law and the Bill of Rights' (2004) 121 *South African Law Journal* 265, 315 ('Dignity has a communitarian aspect: by requiring respect for others' claims to dignity, vindication of the human dignity of all is better assured, and a community of mutual co-operation and solidarity is fostered.')

60. See Aristotle *Nichomachean Ethics* (trans D Ross 1980) Bk I, § 5, 7.
61. A Sen *Development as Freedom* (1999) 18.
62. Ibid.
63. For a more detailed discussion of the relationship between our dignity jurisprudence and Sen's views on capabilities and development, see Woolman 'Dignity' (supra) at § 36.5(a)(ii).
64. See Laurie WH Ackermann 'The Significance of Human Dignity for Constitutional Jurisprudence' (Lecture, Stellenbosch Law Faculty, 15 August 2005)(Manuscript on file with author) § 4 quoting T Dürig 'Der Grundrechtssatz von der Menschenwürde' (1956) 81 *Archiv für öffentliches Recht* 117, 125 ('All humans are human by virtue of their intellectual capacity ("kraft seine Geistes") which serves to separate them from the impersonality of nature and enables them to exercise their own judgment, to have self-awareness, to exercise self-determination and to shape themselves and nature.' (Ackermann's translation).)
65. *Government of the Republic of South Africa & Others v Grootboom & Others* 2001 (1) SA 46 (CC), 2000 (11) BCLR 1169 (CC)('*Grootboom*') at para 83 (Emphasis added).
66. *National Coalition for Gay and Lesbian Equality v Minister of Justice* 1999 (1) SA 6 (CC), 1998 (12) BCLR 1517 (CC).
67. *National Coalition for Gay and Lesbian Equality v Minister of Home Affairs* 2000 (2) SA 1 (CC), 2000 (1) BCLR 39 (CC)('*NCGLE II*'); *Satchwell v President of the Republic of South Africa* 2002 (6) SA 1 (CC), 2002 (9) BCLR 986 (CC)('*Satchwell I*'); *Satchwell v President of the Republic of South Africa* 2003 (4) SA 266 (CC), 2004 (1) BCLR 1 (CC)('*Satchwell II*')
68. *Satchwell v President of the Republic of South Africa* 2002 (6) SA 1 (CC), 2002 (9) BCLR 986 (CC) ('*Satchwell I*'); *Satchwell v President of the Republic of South Africa* 2003 (4) SA 266 (CC), 2004 (1) BCLR 1 (CC)('*Satchwell II*')
69. See *Minister of Home Affairs & Another v Fourie & Another; Lesbian and Gay Equality Project & Others v Minister of Home Affairs & Others* 2006 (1) SA 524 (CC), 2006 (3) BCLR 355 (CC).
70. See A Sen *Development as Freedom* (1999); A Sen *Inequality Re-examined* (1992); A Sen *The Idea of Justice* (2010).
71. Sen *Development* (supra) at 75.
72. One of the defining features of the South African state – as would be the case in any liberal constitutional state – is that the very conditions for individual flourishing – self-governance and self-actualization – are also two of the goods which individuals generally seek.
73. K van Marle 'No Last Word: Reflections on the Imaginary Domain, Dignity and Intrinsic Worth' (2002) 13 *Stellenbosch Law Review* 299, 306.
74. *Khosa* (supra) at para 74.
75. See D Cornell *Defending Ideals: War, Democracy, and Political Struggles* (2004).
76. See Sen *Development* (supra) at 189 – 203.
77. Six thousand demonstrations take place annually. That one thousand demonstrations are denied permission to proceed – for few, if any good reasons – is a matter I take up elsewhere. See S Woolman 'My Tea Party, Your Mob, Our Social Contract: Freedom of Assembly and the Constitutional Right to Rebellion in *Garvis v SATAWU (Minister for Safety & Security, Third Party)* 2010 (6) SA 280 (WCC)' (2011) 27 *South African Journal on Human Rights* 346.
78. See *S v Mamabolo (E TV and others Intervening)* 2001 (3) SA 409 (CC), 2001 (1) SACR 686 (CC), 2001 (5) BCLR 449 (CC) at para 50 ('That freedom to speak one's mind is now an inherent quality of the type of society contemplated by the Constitution as a whole and is specifically promoted by the freedoms of conscience, expression, assembly, association and political participation protected by ss 15 - 19 of the Bill of Rights.' (Emphasis added).) See also *South African National Defence Union v Minister of Defence* 1999 (4) SA 469 (CC), 1999 (6) BCLR 615 (CC) at para 8 ('[F]reedom of expression [FC s 16]... freedom of religion, belief and opinion [FC s 15], the right to dignity [FC s 10], as well as the right to freedom of association [FC s 18], the right to vote and to stand for public office [FC s 19] and the right to assembly [FC 17] ... taken together protect the right of individuals not only

individually to form and express opinions, of whatever nature, but to establish associations and groups of like-minded people to foster and propagate such opinions.')

79. E Cannetti *Crowds and Power* (1962) 22: '[E]ruption ... the sudden transition from a closed into an open crowd ... is a frequent occurrence. ... A crowd quite often seems to overflow from some well-guarded space into the squares and streets of a town where it can move about freely, exposed to everything and attracting everyone. But more important than this external event is the corresponding inner movement: the dissatisfaction with the limitation of the number of participants, the sudden will to attract, the passionate determination to reach all men.' See also *In Re Munhumeso and Others* 1995 (1) SA 551, 557 (ZS), 1995 (2) BCLR 130 (ZS), 1994 (1) ZLR 49 (SC)(Court dryly observes that: 'A procession, which is but an assembly in motion, is by its very nature a highly effective means of communication, and one not provided by other media. It stimulates public attention and discussion of the opinion expressed. The public is brought into direct contact with those expressing the opinion.')

80. See L Kraemer *The People Themselves: Popular Constitutionalism and Judicial Review* (2005). This book presses a thesis of shared constitutional interpretation – a collective effort that embraces non-political actors. Kraemer's view is that such ecstatic expressions of the will of the people transform constitutional interpretation into an enterprise shared with the people themselves.

81. See S Woolman 'Freedom of Association' in S Woolman & M Bishop (eds) *Constitutional Law of South Africa* (2nd Edition, OS, December 2003) Chapter 44. For other views on entrance, voice and exit, see A Hirschman *Exit, Voice and Loyalty* (1970); E Brody 'Entrance, Voice and Exit: The Constitutional Bounds of Freedom of Association' (2002) 35 *University of California Davis Law Review* 821.

82. 2001 (4) SA 938 (CC), 2001 (10) BCLR 995 (CC)('*Carmichele*').

83. 2005 (6) SA 419 (CC), 2005 (9) BCLR 835 (CC)('*K*').

84. *Carmichele* (supra) at para 62.

85. See S Woolman 'Security Services' in S Woolman & M Bishop (eds) *Constitutional Law of South Africa* (2nd Edition, RS3, May 2011) Chapter 23B.

86. FC s 12(2): 'Everyone has the right to bodily and psychological integrity which includes the right-(a) to make decisions concerning reproduction.' For more on the relationship between FC s 12, FC s 10 and abortion, see M O'Sullivan 'Reproductive Rights' in S Woolman & M Bishop (eds) *Constitutional Law of South Africa* (2nd Edition, OS, March 2005) Chapter 37.

87. Act 92 of 1996.

88. *Christian Lawyers Association v Minister of Health & Others* (Reproductive Health Alliance as Amicus Curiae) 2005 (1) SA 509, 526 (T), 2004 (10) BCLR 1086, 1103 (T)('*Christian Lawyers II*'); *Christian Lawyers Association & Others v Minister of Health & Others* 1998 (4) SA 1113 (T), 1998 (11) BCLR 1434 (T)('*Christian Lawyers Association I*').

89. *Case v Minister of Safety and Security; Curtis v Minister of Safety and Security* 1996 (3) SA 617 (CC), 1996 (5) BCLR 609 (CC) at para 91 (Privacy protects 'the inner sanctum of a person' that lies within 'the truly personal realm.') For the leading statement on privacy, see *Bernstein & Others v Bester NO & Others* 1996 (2) SA 751, (CC), 1996 (4) BCLR 449 (CC) at paras 67, 73, 79 (Ackermann J quotes, with approval, the Council of Europe's gloss on the right to privacy: '[The right to privacy] consists essentially in the right to live one's own life with a minimum of interference. It concerns private, family and home life, physical and moral integrity, honour and reputation, avoidance of being placed in a false light, non-revelation of irrelevant and embarrassing facts, unauthorised publication of private photographs, protection from disclosure of information, given or received by the individual confidentially.') See also *Investigating Directorate: Serious Economic Offences v Hyundai Motor Distributors (Pty) Ltd: In re Hyundai Motor Distributors (Pty) Ltd v Smit* NO 2001 (1) SA 545 (CC), 2000 (10) BCLR 1079 (CC) at para 18 (Right to privacy protects intimate space because such a space is a prerequisite for human dignity, and thus flourishing.)

90. For more on the non-relativist, shared (if necessarily narrow), understanding of such basic political terms as freedom, justice and truth in substantially different contexts, see M Walzer *Thick and Thin:*

Moral Argument at Home and Abroad (2002). Walzer claims that we (global citizens) share a minimalist account of justice with those persons marching and revolting in Prague and Pretoria. And what is that? Walzer writes: 'What they meant by ... justice ... was simple enough: an end to arbitrary arrests, equal and impartial law enforcement; the abolition of the privileges and prerogatives of the party elite and common, garden variety justice.' Ibid at 2.

91. See C Taylor 'The Politics of Recognition' in A Gutmann (ed) *Multiculturalism and the Politics of Recognition* (1996) 1
92. See M Walzer 'On Involuntary Association' in A Gutmann (ed) *Freedom of Association* (1998) 64, 67.
93. Taylor 'The Politics of Recognition' (supra) at 16.
94. See *National Coalition for Gay and Lesbian Equality v Minister of Justice* 1999 (1) SA 6 (CC), 1998 (12) BCLR 1517 (CC) at paras 28–30 ('[I]t is clear that the constitutional protection of dignity requires us to acknowledge the value and the worth of all individuals as members of society.') See also *President of the Republic of South Africa v Hugo* 1997 (4) SA 1 (CC), 1997 (6) BCLR 708 (CC) at para 41 ('[E]quality means nothing if it does not represent a commitment to each person's equal worth as a human being, regardless of their differences.')
95. A Sen *Identity and Violence: The Illusion of Destiny* (2006) xiv.
96. Ibid at 2-3.
97. For a substantially more optimistic view about our capacity to recognize diverse difference, and our ability to sustain political institutions, in heterogeneous societies, through rational discourse, see KA Appiah *Cosmopolitanism: Ethics in a World of Strangers* (2006) 113, 144 ('We do not need, have never needed, settled community, a homogenous system of values. The odds are that, culturally speaking, you already live a cosmopolitan life, enriched by literature, art, and film that comes from many places, and that contains influences from many more. And the marks of cosmopolitanism in [my] Asante village soccer, Muhammed Ali, hip-hop entered [our] lives, as they entered yours, not as work, but as pleasure. ... One distinctly cosmopolitan commitment is to pluralism. Cosmopolitans [therefore] think that there are many values worth living by and that you cannot live by all of them. So we hope and expect that different people and different societies will embody different values. But they have to be values worth living by.')
98. *Minister of Home Affairs v Fourie (Doctors For Life International & Others, Amici Curiae); Lesbian & Gay Equality Project & Others v Minister of Home Affairs* 2006 (1) SA 524 (CC), 2006 (3) BCLR 355 (CC) ('Fourie') at paras 90–98. See also *Fourie v Minister of Home Affairs* 2005 (3) SA 429 (SCA), 2005 (3) BCLR 241 (SCA) at paras 36–37 (No religious denomination would be compelled to marry gay or lesbian couples.)
99. *Fourie* (supra) at paras 90-98.
100. S Scheffler *Equality and Tradition: Questions of Value in a Moral and Political Theory* (2010); S Scheffler *Boundaries and Allegiences: Problems of Justice and Responsibility in Liberal Thought* (2001); N Rosenblum *Membership and Morals: The Personal Uses of Pluralism in America* (1998).
101. See JP Sartre *Portrait of the Anti-Semite* (trans E de Mauny 1968) 57 ('The Jew is a man whom other men look upon as a Jew; ... it is the anti-Semite who makes the Jew.')
102. S Woolman 'Freedom of Association' in S Woolman & M Bishop (eds) *Constitutional Law of South Africa* (2nd Edition, OS, December 2003) Chapter 44; S Woolman 'Dignity' in S Woolman & M Bishop (eds) *Constitutional Law of South Africa* (2nd Edition, OS, December 2005) Chapter 36. For more on how to resolve the tension between associational and egalitarian imperatives, see also P Lenta 'Religious Liberty and Cultural Accommodation' (2005) 122 *South African Law Journal* 352 P Lenta 'Taking Diversity Seriously: Religious Associations and Work-Related Discrimination' (2009) 125 (4) *South African Law Journal* 828; S Woolman 'On the Fragility of Associational Life: A Constitutive Liberal's Response to Patrick Lenta' (2009) 25 *South African Journal on Human Rights* 280; See also S Woolman 'Seek Justice Elsewhere: An Egalitarian Pluralist's Reply to David Bilchitz on the Distinction between Differentiation and Domination' (2012) 28 *South African Journal*

on Human Rights 273; D Bilchitz 'Why Courts Should Not Sanction unfair Discrimination in the Private Sphere: A Reply (2012) 28 *South African Journal on Human rights* 296.

103. Sen (supra) at 151 ('[S]ometimes a classification that is hard to justify may nevertheless be made important by social arrangements. That is what competitive examinations do (the 300th candidate is still something, the 301st is nothing). In other words, the social world constitutes differences by the mere fact of designating them.')

104. Why defend the parochial, the partial, the provincial? Why defend any community that excludes others by virtue of genealogy, rules, beliefs, traditions or practices? Edmund Burke wrote: '[T]o love the little platoon we belong to is the first principle, (the germ as it were) of public affections. It is the first link in the series by which we proceed towards love of country and to mankind.' E Burke *Reflections on the Revolution in France* (JCD Clark (ed), 2001) 202. Burke thereby connects the parochial with the universal. K Anthony Appiah comes at the problem from a slightly different direction. K Anthony Appiah defends cosmopolitanism – what he calls universality plus difference – on the grounds that cosmopolitanism is committed to (a) pluralism, the notion that there are different values worth living by and (b) fallibilism, the notion that our knowledge and our values are imperfect, provisional, subject to revision in the face of new evidence. Appiah (supra) at 144. So, for Appiah, religious, cultural and linguistic communities retain their value when they provide us with values worth living by, (as they almost all do to some extent), and when the members of those communities do not insist that there is one right way for human beings to live and do not then insist on imposing that one right way on others so as to truly set them free. Ibid. The members of religious, cultural and linguistic communities must commit themselves as citizens of a republic, or citizens of the world, to some significant degree of value or ethical laissez-faire.

105. See S Dersso 'The Need for Constitutional Accommodation of Ethno-Cultural Diversity in the Post-Colonial State' (2008) 24 *South African Journal on Human Rights* 565. Dersso argues that the large number of failed states in post-colonial Africa can be traced, in part, to the failure to provide institutional arrangements that can accommodate group-based diversity. South Africa's constitutional order and its commitment to various associational and community rights (and, therefore, the private ordering of substantial amounts of South African social space), Dersso contends, is one of the primary reasons for South Africa's ongoing success as a constitutional democracy.

106. Rosenblum *Membership and Morals* (supra) at 48–49.

107. A Gutmann *Identity in Democracy* (2003) 45.

108. *Martinez v Santa Clara Pueblo* 540 F2d 1039, 1042 (10th Cir 1976).

109. US 49 (1978). But see *Santa Clara Pueblo v Martinez* 436 US 49, 83 (1978)(Justice White, in dissent, writes: 'The extension of constitutional rights to citizens is intended to intrude upon the authority of government.')

110. *Bhe v Magistrate, Khayelitsha & Others* 2005 (1) SA 580 (CC), 2005 (1) BCLR 1 (CC)('*Bhe*').

111. See *Bhe* (supra) at paras 42–46 ('[T]he question in this case is not whether a rule or provision of customary law offers similar remedies to the Intestate Succession Act. The issue is whether such rules or provisions are consistent with the Constitution.') See also *Alexkor Ltd & Another v The Richtersveld Community & Others* 2004 (5) SA 460 (CC), 2003 (12) BCLR 1301 (CC)('*Richtersveld*') at para 51 ('While in the past indigenous law was seen through the common law lens, it must now be seen as an integral part of our law. Like all law it depends for its ultimate force and validity on the Constitution. Its validity must now be determined by reference not to common-law, but to the Constitution'); *Mabuza v Mbatha* 2003 (4) SA 218 (C), 2003 (7) BCLR 743 (C)('*Mabuza*') at para 32 ('It bears repeating … that the constitutional validity of … principles of customary law depend on their consistency with the Constitution and the Bill of Rights.')

112. See South African Law Reform Commission *The Harmonisation of the Common Law and the Indigenous Law: Succession in Customary* Law Issue Paper 12, Project 90 (April 1998) 6-9. See also TW Bennett *Human Rights and African Customary Law under the South African Constitution* (1997) 126–127.

113. See, eg, *Richtersveld Community & Others v Alexkor Ltd & Another* 2003 (6) SA 104 (SCA), 2003 (6) BCLR 583 (SCA) at paras 85–105.
114. *Bhe* (supra) at para 84.
115. Ibid at para 89.
116. Ibid at para 83.
117. *Shilubana & Others v Nwamitwa* 2009 (2) SA 66 (CC), 2008 (9) BCLR 914 (CC)(Valoyi traditional authorities may develop customary law in accordance with norms and values of the Constitution so that tenable women may become Hosi – community leaders. Such development outstrips the need for 'legal certainty' about succession.)
118. However, many South Africans believe the Constitutional Court to be out of step with the traditional mores of many communities. Thus no matter how objectionable lobolo might appear to me – or Nussbaum or Sen (as a chattel transaction) – many South African men and women identify lobolo with (a) a tightening of communal bonds, and (b) a recognition of the dignity of the woman for whom the lobolo is offered. They view lobolo as designed to preserve the cohesion and stability of the extended family unit and, ultimately, the entire community.
119. E Cameron *Witness to Aids* (2005).
120. On the relationship between South Africa and Zimbabwe over the last 15 years, see S Chan *Southern Africa: Old Treacheries and New Deceits* (2011).
121. This book went to print hot on the heels of the massacre at Marikana. But the inability of our (corrupt and bankrupt) security services to achieve its most basic function – the freedom and security of all South Africans – that made Marikana possible hardly counts as news. S Woolman 'Security Services' in S Woolman & M Bishop (eds) *Constitutional Law of South Africa* (2nd Edition, RS3, May 2011) Chapter 23. The murders at Marakana were not only foreseeable, but inevitable. See S Woolman 'Is Xenophobia the Right Legal Term of Art? A Freudian and Kleinian Response to Loren Landau on the Violence in South African Townships (2011) 11(2) *Stellenbosch Law Review* 285; S Woolman 'My Tea Party, Your Mob, Our Social Contract: Freedom of Assembly & the Constitutional Right to Rebellion in *Garvis & Others v Satawu (Minister for Safety and Security, Third Party)*' (2011) 27 *South African Journal on Human Rights* 346. Perhaps, no better example of just how blinkered the South African political and business establishment has been with respect to the breakdown of South Africa's social contract exists than Chief Justice Mogoeng Mogoeng's closing remarks to COSATU and SATAWU's counsel, Advocate Wim Trengove, at the end of oral argument in *SATAWU & COSATU v Garvis & Others* [2012] ZACC 13: 'If the organizers cannot ensure that no damage to person or to property will occur during a demonstrations, then perhaps the demonstrators should stay at home.' (Notes taken by author during Constitutional Court oral argument in *Garvis*.)
122. For a critique of the notion of 'an objective, normative value order', see S Woolman 'Application' in S Woolman & M Bishop (eds) *Constitutional Law of South Africa* (2nd Edition, OS, June 2005) Chapter 31.
123. *Sidumo & Another v Rustenburg Platinum Mines Ltd & Others* 2008 (2) SA 24 (CC), 2007 (12) BCLR 1097 (CC).
124. See T Roux 'Principle and Pragmatism on the Constitutional Court of South Africa' (2009) 7 *International Journal of Constitutional Law* 106. In addition, the absence of the identification of a minimum core often makes it hard (for all stakeholders) to make sense of what individual rights are actually designed to do. In *Blue Moonlight*, the Constitutional Court has begun to flesh out a minimum core. [2012] ZACC 33, 2012 (2) SA 104 (CC), 2012 (2) BCLR 150 (CC). *Blue Moonlight*, and three other recent housing judgments, are discussed at some length in Chapter 6.
125. In his blog, *Constitutionally Speaking*, my friend and colleague Pierre De Vos charges that the *Mazibuko* Court was somehow beholden to a 'neo-liberal framework'. It's a hefty charge, and Professor De Vos offers no basis for this ad hominem attack on O'Regan J or the rest of the Court.
126. *Soobramoney v Minsiter of Health, KwaZulu Natal* 1998 (1) SA 765 (CC), 1997 (12) BCLR 1696 (CC) ('*Soobramoney*') at para 8.

Chapter 8

Tweaking Doctrine: Constitutional Court Cases Revisited and Revised

Do not judge me by my successes, judge me by how many times I fell down and got back up again.

Nelson Mandela

A foolish consistency is the hobgoblin of little minds, adored by little statesmen and philosophers and divines.

Ralph Waldo Emerson

TWEAKING DOCTRINE: CONSTITUTIONAL COURT CASES REVISITED AND REVISED

At the outset of this work, I claimed that the Constitutional Court's initial emphasis on freedom-talk, rather than flourishing, and on the deference reflected in an often arid separation of powers doctrine, rather than a more fluid inter-institutional and inter-personal theory of experimental constitutionalism, has had several untoward consequences for our constitutional jurisprudence. In this section, I revisit and recast twenty important and representative Constitutional Court judgments in terms of the modest theory developed thus far: experimentalism married to flourishing. Some critiques take their aim at rights analysis, others toward remedies. Some re-appraisals take stock of a tendency toward an overweening effort toward institutional comity, while some accounts chide the Court for a failure to envisage ways in which co-operation between the branches and the pooling of information of potential stakeholders might advance the interests of all of our polity's denizens.

Over the course of this survey, readers will see a gratifying pattern emerge. They will appreciate a trend in more recent judgments toward an experimentalist approach: from pre-trial orders for meaningful engagement, to expanded grounds for standing, to rights analysis that invites comment from all interested stakeholders, to remedies that grant suspended orders while parties (including the legislature and the executive) work out the appropriate contours of a legislative 'fix' that falsl within the broadly framed constitutional norms articulated by the Court, to structural injunctions that ensure that an ongoing conversation between the Court and interested stakeholders effectively rights the wrong identified by the Court in a manner that allows the parties to work out solutions over time by seeing what works and what doesn't. Indeed, these cases reflect a mature Court possessed of an increasingly bold vision that takes seriously the possibility of a greater collective imagination that exists beyond the chambers of 11 women and men. We can glimpse a Court that wants to 'learn aggressively' – as my friend Frank Michelman might put it – from the parties before the Court and from individuals, associations and institutions not initially party to a given matter.[1]

Two riders attach to the organization of the case studies that follow.

It would be convenient if the development of the Constitutional Court's jurisprudence (along the lines this book has espoused) occurred in perfect chronological fashion. It hasn't. It would be the rare court at the apex of a legal system that moved in logical lock-step with its own or some academic's deeply theoretical musings. So while the case studies begin at a time when hints of experimentalism and flourishing might have been difficult to discern, they do track the evolution of the Court's jurisprudence in a manner that is quasi-linear and subject matter driven. It makes greater sense to group later cases together in terms of subject matter – say, customary law or education – than strict adherence to the date the judgment was handed down. By grouping the later case studies thematically, one actually gains a greater appreciation for the subtle shifts that have occurred over time.

It would serve the ends of writerliness if the following cases struck you as entirely fresh and simply served as additional proof of the most contentious arguments proffered in the preceding chapters. However, many, though not all, of this score of cases will have been discussed and analysed over the past 400 pages. Some cases rehearsed here performed very different ends in earlier passages. Some aided my initial explication of experimental constitutionalism and flourishing, and simply receive more expansive treatment now: often in an attempt to show how both experimental constitutionalism and flourishing work in tandem. In either case, some repetition is inevitable. Skip, rather than march, where necessary. It's your book after all.

A. The Tenets of a Theory of Experimentalism and Flourishing Rehearsed

Before we begin this exercise in reconstruction, it is worth recalling the content of the flourishing and experimentalist criteria by which the cases will be reassessed.

1. *Flourishing*

The conservative strain in my account emphasizes the manner in which various social practices and natural dispositional states determine that which makes us human. Our recognition that there is a radical givenness to our ways of being in the world both and that 'meaning makes us' explains why the metaphysical commitment to conditioned choice results in little or no explanatory power being lost when we substitute the notion of flourishing for the outré metaphysics of freedom.[2]

The revolutionary strain in my account of flourishing recognizes that these same social practices and forms of life from which we derive the better part of meaning in our lives may, unnecessarily, limit our ability to act in a manner that we believe will enhance our own well-being. The revolutionary dimension of flourishing requires that issues of access, of coercion, of choice, of voice, of exit must be constantly negotiated – by the state and other actors – in order to ensure that all members of our society have a meaningful opportunity to flourish. A meaningful opportunity to flourish will, in turn, require the provision of those basic goods (material and immaterial) that individuals must possess in order to pursue lives worth valuing.[3]

This revolutionary understanding in no way diminishes our responsibility to engage in case-by-case analysis of rights claims made on behalf of those who prefer to inhabit unchosen worlds that we view as anathema to our own conception of the right and the good. Flourishing *persse* and the underlying nostrum that 'meaning makes us' should sound a cautionary note that ought to be heeded by those who identify freedom as the ultimate trump, as well as by those who reify equality and tend to treat all unchosen social institutions as suspect and in need of reformation along sweeping and radically egalitarian lines.[4]

Experimental constitutionalism serves both strains of flourishing. First, all constitutional orders recognize an ineradicable private ordering of social affairs. To that extent, constitutions are inherently conservative documents. Second, while this account begins with the premise that individual flourishing occurs primarily within the many communities into which an individual is born and within which she remains a member, experimental constitutionalism envisages a heterogeneous society made up of radically heterogeneous selves[5] and a state that does not aim to determine or to exhaust the possibilities of individual lives.[6] At a minimum, the experimental state enables individuals and groups to fully realize extant sources of the self. At the same time, experimental constitutionalism is predicated upon the belief that best practices are more likely to surface within institutions designed to promote social experimentation, and that, as a result of such experimentation, individuals are more likely to alight on a preferred way of being in the world if provided with roughly equal and mutually respectful conditions – political, social and economic – under which to compare, contrast and critique different ways of being in the world.[7]

Recall that a broad array of principles undergirds experimental constitutionalism. First, the judiciary, as well as the legislature and the executive, can act as an agent of social change, even as it moves from top-down command and control models to flattened hierarchies that invite broad participation and rolling best practices that are both forward and lateral looking.[8] Second, difficult cases, especially those cases that turn on limitations analysis of prima facie abridgements of constitutional rights, become somewhat easier to resolve when courts move away from traditional models of adjudication and adopt such experimentalist, problem-solving modalities as meaningful engagement orders, structural injunctions and remedial equilibration.[9] Third, for experimental constitutionalism to succeed, courts and other fora – including non-political institutions – must facilitate the sometimes rough and tumble debates between stakeholders are often essential for information-gathering, information-pooling, information-sharing, collective action and collective norm-setting.[10] Fourth, these processes, forward and lateral looking, are reflexive and committed to rolling best norms. It's not that a baseline or core for constitutional rights does not exist – flourishing helps us to establish such first principles – but that constant reassessment of the means by which we pursue our ends often has the consequence of changing both our means and our ends. Moreover, courts and non-traditional problem solving fora can – when they balance the playing field – destabilize existing social hierarchies and produce new 'experiments in living' that may enhance individual and group flourishing.[11]

Experimental constitutionalism can also be explained in terms of two overlapping emergent modes of governmental design: (i) shared constitutional interpretation; and (ii) participatory bubbles. Shared constitutional interpretation (a) supplants the 'arid' notion of judicial supremacy with respect to constitutional interpretation,[12] and grants all branches of government a relatively equal stake in giving our basic law content; (b) contemplates courts that consciously limit the reach of their holdings regarding the meaning of a given provision and, as already suggested, invite co-ordinate branches, other organs of state and other social actors, to come up with their own alternative gloss on the text;[13] (c) views these invitations as mechanisms to flatten political hierarchies, to increase the opportunities to see how different doctrines operate in different spaces, and to make revision of constitutional doctrines possible in light of new experience and novel demands; (d) ratchets down the conflict between co-ordinate branches and levels of government[14] and frees the court of the burden of having to provide a theory of everything; (e) assumes the different means employed by different actors may shed new light on – or change our understanding of – the very constitutional norms we seek to promote.[15]

The notion of participatory bubbles directs our attention to experimentation in smaller units: at the level of the individual or the local community.[16] As I have already noted, my naturalized account of the self and the social takes seriously the limits on our capacity for rational reflection and collective deliberation. But my naturalized account of the self never denies our capacity to engage in meaningful and careful rationation.[17] However, rather than limiting our collective conversations to a few earth-shaking moments of universal participation[18] – think of the Multi-Party Negotiating Forum of 1993, the elections of 27 April 1994 or the Constitutional Assembly circa 1996 – small-scale bubbles of limited participation can regularly experiment with and challenge the conventional understanding of individual constitutional norms and their application to subject matter specific, and often time-sensitive, institutional contexts.[19]

The physical metaphor of bubbles is meant to convey four (or more) qualities of small-scale experimental institutional processes. First, processes of brass-knuckled engagement between parties with different interests are a natural part of on-going social interactions. They originate when challenges to a given authority accumulate and finally come to a boil: just as bubbles form after pressure builds up and escape to the surface of a liquid. Second, bubbles are meant to suggest limits on the scope of engagement. Bubbles enclose a small number of contested issues. Third, bubbles are (often, but not always) ephemeral. After satisfactory resolutions emerge from multi-party participatory processes, the raison d'etre for such process generally ceases to exist. Yet courts and other oversight fora may wish to retain jurisdiction until we can be assured that a novel practice has succeeded. Fourth, a court creating a bubble must be willing to articulate norms or frameworks – as departure points – that enable less powerful stakeholders to have a meaningful role to play in the polycentric decision-making process initiated by the court.[20] The promise of such a process is *successful action*. Each participant adopts a reflexive stance toward their own views and attempts 'to make the interests of others their own, [and to recognize] the circumstances in which they should give moral priority to what is good for others or for the polity as a whole.'[21] Thus, participatory bubbles facilitate processes of institutional reform that proceed within the vocabulary and inside the norms of the relevant institutions and contested communities, instead of via top-down imposition by a judicial authority. The reflexive stance should both foster a deeper commitment to public political participation and enhance individual and group aptitudes for experimentation and error-correction.

Put another way, participatory bubbles are important experimental feedback mechanisms.[22] First, they enable state actors (and other private actors) responsible for the creation of policy to benefit from insider information about the problem the parties aim to solve. Second, state actors and citizens who are not participants in a given bubble at a given moment have an opportunity to benefit – down the line – from the forward and lateral looking experimentation of their predecessors. Third, both the process and the outcome of bubble-making should have a knock on effect. It should create incentives for political institutions to pro-actively open up their decision-making processes to affected stakeholders in advance of conflict so as to seek out non-adversarial solutions.

In addition, courts called upon to perform limitations analysis and to fashion remedies cannot avoid adjudicating conflicts that are not readily susceptible to straightforward doctrinally essentialist solutions.[23] Here again experimental constitutionalism offers two additional constructs: (a) provisional adjudication and (b) remedial equilibration. Provisional adjudication promises two primary benefits. Provisional adjudication puts alternative possible remedies to the test of experience without necessarily elevating such remedies to the level of established doctrine. It gives parties that may have been aggrieved with a final non-provisional outcome the opportunity to experiment with a remedy of their own making. Remedial equilibration may facilitate compromise. By enabling individuals to exit communities that treat them as second class members, without dismantling entire communities in the process, remedial equilibration should enable affected parties, learn from practical experience and adjust their beliefs and conduct accordingly as they maintain existing subpublics or create new subpublics.

B. Experimentalism and Flourishing Applied

1. *Prince v President, Cape Law Society and Others*[24]

There is, perhaps, no better example of the limits of the Constitutional Court's basic approach to rights analysis than its judgment in *Prince*.[25] A narrowly divided Court found itself doctrinally incapable of extending the protections of religious freedom to the kind of vulnerable minority most in need of judicial solicitude.[26] How might the judgment have differed if the Court had followed the outlines of the slightly altered jurisprudence described in these pages?

The most significant outcome-determinative difference would have been to supplant 'freedom-talk' with 'flourishing'. The *Prince* Court ought to have been disposed towards viewing the actions of the members of the Rastafarian community in terms of social endowments that largely determine the meaning of individual lives – and not through the lens of rational, autonomous moral agents that freely-will their ends (or rather, the ends of a hide-bound majority.) Had it been so inclined, the Court might have taken more time to explore legal structures that would take the Rastafarian way of being in the world seriously.[27]

A shared constitutional interpretation approach to limitation's analysis might have also altered the outcome. The *Prince* Court did ask for the government's assistance in making a difficult instance of limitations analysis easier. The Court asked the government to furnish facts regarding (1) practical difficulties with granting an exemption for the sacramental use of cannabis and (2) the differential impact on law enforcement posed by a religious ritual exemption as compared with medical and scientific exemptions. But the information provided, to the extent it was provided, did little to shape the Court's approach to its limitations analysis. The majority of the Court accepted the state's contention that a feasible exemption could not be crafted.

But what if the Court had adopted an experimentalist approach toward limitations analysis – linked to a remedial equilibration doctrine that proceeds from the recognition that the determination of the reasonableness of a limitation and the identification of the best of all possible remedies are interdependent processes. Remedial equilibration might have led the Court to recognize how difficult it is to discover the 'right' answer – or remedy – from an outsider's perspective: a difficulty with respect to which the Court was already partially aware. Had they acted on this awareness, instead of simply relying on the good faith of the government, it could have used a number of mechanisms to mediate the competing positions.

The experimentalist approach to limitations and remedies analysis – with its explicit commitment to eliciting better information from all the relevant parties – might have led the

Court to issue a structural injunction or one of the creative panoply of partial and temporally limited remedies it now employs. A structural injunction or an order for meaningful engagement that brought law enforcement officials and Rastafarian leaders together might have (a) elicited the relevant information for more precise limitations analysis and (b) generated proposals for remedies that might diminish – to the vanishing point – the constitutional conflict.[28] At a minimum, the participatory bubble created by the order might have led the Rastafarian stakeholders and the state to find a short-term answer to the problem of the ritual use of cannabis. The Court would *not* then have been in the uncomfortable position of imposing its will by fiat through rights essentialism and automatic remedialism. Moreover, retention of jurisdiction through a structural injunction (or what would become hard-nosed orders for 'meaningful engagement') would have allowed the *Prince* Court to track any unintended consequences that might flow from adaptive processes triggered by shifting legal principles and would have allowed it to modify the remedy – say, through some form of exemption for the use of cannabis – on the basis of new empirical evidence.[29] The disentrenching powers of such a remedy might have also led, over time, to a general social acceptance of Rasterfarianism as just one of many of South Africa's religious orders. (Here again it's worth recalling how drug treatment courts have led to a more and more widely shared view (in the United States) of drug use as a form of treatable addiction, rather than a *criminal* offense that warrants sustained incarceration that provides little hope of rehabilitation. Don't believe me? Two US states have, by recent referendum, in 2012, decriminalized marijuana use.)

As the last several paragraphs suggest, a doctrine of shared constitutional interpretation ought not be limited to colloquies between the legislature and the courts. Shared constitutional interpretation – especially in a constitutional order that places constitutional duties on both private actors and public actors – would require both law enforcement officials and citizen-stakeholders to offer their respective gloss on constitutional norms. Such shared competence enables parties at the coal-face to assist the Court in developing constitutional norms and to facilitate experiments in the application of such norms to novel sets of circumstances.[30]

The recast-experimentalist *Prince* judgment suggests how the original *Prince* Court, with the assistance of others, could have gone Justice Sachs' 'extra mile' in order to safeguard the constitutive attachments of a vulnerable minority. It also shows how experimental constitutionalism steers a path between a conservative constitutional politics committed to extant understandings of individual and group flourishing and a revolutionary politics committed to error-correction and the increased acceptance of out-groups through novel institutional arrangements.

2. *S v Jordan*[31]

Jordan warrants recasting for two distinct reasons.

(a) Flourishing, not Freedom

As I have already discussed at length in Chapters 1, 2 and 7, the *Jordan* Court rejected equality, dignity, privacy and freedom of profession challenges to those sections of the Sexual Offences Act that criminalise prostitution.[32] The majority reasoned as follows:

> If the public sees the recipient of reward as being 'more to blame' than the 'client', and a conviction carries a greater stigma on the 'prostitute' for that reason, that is a social attitude and not the result

> of the law. The stigma that attaches to prostitutes attaches to them, not by virtue of their gender, but by virtue of the conduct they engage in. That stigma attaches to female and male prostitutes alike. I am not persuaded by the argument that gender discrimination exists simply because there are more female prostitutes than male prostitutes, just as I would not be persuaded if the same argument were to be advanced by males accused of certain crimes, the great majority of which are committed by men.[33]

The majority's commitment to a very strong form of metaphysical autonomy – a form of autonomy that makes all individuals morally and legally culpable for actions that issue ineluctably from their circumstances – fails dramatically many sex workers. (It seems particularly inapt for the many sex workers who ply this trade only because they are victims of sexual trafficking.[34]) The majority approaches the circumstances of such prostitutes – to use classic metaphysical parlance – as if they 'could have done otherwise'. That is the kind of 'freedom talk' that does no meaningful work.

The *Jordan* majority and minority's approach may hold for some sex workers who are attracted to this profession. But such circumstances are rare. First, as I have argued above, the attribution of culpability to those who act under circumstances of severe economic duress is suspect. Prostitution generally involves the sale of sexual services by women (controlled and exploited by syndicates). This exploitation of women, of people who have little chance, and virtually no choice, in life's wheel of fortune, to pursue lives worth valuing, seems to do the argument from autonomy little favour. It may be true that a free market might make decriminalized prostitution more appealing than starvation. But that argument hardly seems to work to the Court's advantage.[35] Second, the *Jordan* majority and minority's approach cannot be applied, without real violence being done to the word 'voluntary', to the large cohort of prostitutes who are the victims of sexual slavery.

The *Jordan* Court has left us with the impression that this most vulnerable and marginalised class of individuals is not especially deserving of our solicitude and that they have, somehow, brought this fate upon themselves. This errant belief constitutes a cultural – and not just a legal – practice that makes the manumission of sexual slaves – and other prostitutes who work under some form of duress – that much more difficult.

A later judgment hints at a way out of the kind of autonomy trap on display in *Jordan*. In *Khosa v Minister of Social Development; Mahlaule v Minister of Social Development*, the Constitutional Court found unconstitutional, as a violation of both FC s 9 and FC s 27 (1), the exclusion of permanent residents from the class of persons entitled to a variety of social security grants: old age, disability, veterans, child-support and foster care. Mokgoro J writes:

> The exclusion of permanent residents in need of social-security programmes forces them into relationships of dependency upon families, friends and the community in which they live, none of whom may have agreed to sponsor the immigration of such persons to South Africa ... Apart from the undue burden that this places on those who take on this responsibility, it is likely to have a serious impact on the dignity of the permanent residents concerned who are cast in the role of supplicants.[36]

Mokgoro J could well have added that permanent residents are, as supplicants, not merely dependent on family members, but quite literally at their mercy.[37] Many prostitutes would consider themselves fortunate to be supplicants. They are not just excluded from the protection of the law. Many sex workers do not speak the language, do not know the lay of the land, do not have the resources to engage corrupt immigration officials or to escape criminal syndicates. Many are enslaved by their own families.

The point is not that sex workers are excluded from some particular benefit to which another class of persons is entitled. *Khosa* stands for the broader proposition that FC s 7(2) places the state under an obligation to protect and to fulfil the rights of all persons in South Africa.[38] As the *Khosa* Court rightly recognises, legal regimes that offer incentives to become members of the political community but that punish inhabitants who cannot act on such incentives – by withholding benefits or through incarceration – are perverse. These disincentives deny the affected person exactly that which the state is obliged to provide. *Khosa* indicates that where meaningful opportunities for flourishing are curtailed, the state bears part of the burden for bringing the material conditions for flourishing into being.[39]

(b) Experimentation, not Deference

Could we also use structural injunctions, meaningful engagement or remedial equilibration, and any consequent participatory bubble, to recast the outcome in *Jordan*? Perhaps. Law enforcement officials and streetwalkers might yet be able to reach some consensus on the kind of framework necessary for the de-criminalization of prostitution. [They already 'work' together.] If concerns about coercion, disease transmission and trafficking lie at the heart of criminalization of the sex trade, then one can easily imagine setting up structures that would permit the state or entrusted non-state actors (NGOs) to supervise the industry. The affected parties might agree that a requirement that commercial sex take place at brothels in a set area of a city would enable the state and entrusted non-state actors (NGOs) to conduct regular inspections. Such regulation of the profession would enable the responsible authorities to track the health, age and (relative) autonomy of many sex workers.

Another benefit of experimentalism is that by recasting the law in a manner that allows for limited state sanction and greater state control of commercial sex workers is that the general population may, over time, come to view prostitution itself as less morally repugnant. That may seem like a stretch in as conservative and religious society as South Africa. But previously well-embedded practices, say speeding, or a refusal to wear condoms, do change as laws, policies and enforcement mechanisms surrounding traffic safety and HIV/AIDs alter the social landscape.[40]

The *Jordan* Court could have moved beyond deference – with its rather unfortunate consequences for the Court's dignity jurisprudence – to norm setting that recognized the intrinsic worth of prostitutes as human beings. That does not, of course, mean that the Court would be obliged to craft a remedy other than it did. It only means that a participatory bubble might have offered the Court a broader array of institutional arrangements with which to work.

3. *Government of the Republic of South Africa v Grootboom & Others*[41]

I have, in Chapter 6, already suggested how *Grootboom* has led to a minor revolution in South African housing law and policy. I will rehearse that discussion here only to demonstrate in a rather step-by-step fashion how the analytical tools provided by experimental constitutionalism can be used to re-think similar sorts of socio-economic rights cases.[42]

(a) *Structural Injunctions and Participatory Bubbles*

The *Grootboom* Court could have issued a structural injunction (or mediation) that required representatives for affected citizens in the Cape Flats and parties responsible for housing in national, provincial and local government to engage in talks aimed at an effective solution. Using a structural injunction to create such a participatory bubble would have had several beneficial consequences. First, government agencies would have had to come up with a remedy particularly tailored to the needs of the *Grootboom* community. Second, this participatory bubble could become the model for other similarly situated groups around the country. Third, such a polycentric process of political participation would generate other experimentalist responses to the resource constraints confronted by both government agencies and those persons and communities in need of adequate housing. A structural injunction, coupled with the replication of participatory bubbles throughout the country, would give the courts, the government and the public the ability to share information about the kinds of strategies that work to alleviate homelessness.[43] [As I noted above in Chapter 5 and 6, the Court did order – in a separate judgment – the South African Human Rights Commission to monitor the implementation of its holdings in *Grootboom*. One can only speculate as to whether that monitoring injunction would have been more effective had it been made part of the original judgment. That the SAHRC failed to discharge its obligations might well have been a function of the Constitutional Court's inability to foresee the consequences of not using the structural injunction to bring *all* parties together from the outset.]

That such an approach is possible is reflected in the subsequent Cape High Court cases of *Rudolph I* and *Rudolph II*.[44] The High Court in *Rudolph I* and *Rudolph II* noted the lack of responsiveness on the part of government. The High Court's structural injunction forced the state to come up with a housing plan that – if implemented – would meet its constitutional obligations. It is rather more heartening to see my writing (very) slowly being overtaken by time. The approach advocated above has, to some degree, now been adopted a decade later by the Court itself. As we shall see below, the Court's novel notion of 'meaningful engagement' creates the conditions for the kinds of creative solutions that can only be achieved within an experimentalist framework.

(b) *Experimentalism, Systemic Feedback Effects and Transformation*

Perhaps the most compelling consequence of an experimentalist revision of *Grootboom* would be its replication. *Grootboom* would come to represent a classic example of citizens emboldened with a set of 'destabilization rights' that would secure greater accountability from government and other social actors. We would see a *Grootboom* effect. That effect would flow from its trend-setting use of innovative injunctive relief to create participatory bubbles that facilitate widespread experimentation. The *Grootboom* effect would place other government agencies responsible for delivering basic necessities or transforming social institutions on notice that they are best served by finding stakeholder representatives who can provide the necessary feedback on new and better forms of service delivery. The decisions of the High Court in *Rudolph I* and *Rudolph II* suggest that putting such feedback loops in place is both possible and desirable.

(c) Shared Constitutional Interpretation

The *Grootboom* Court's approach to socio-economic rights suggests a deep-seated fear of ordering relief that would require sustained judicial oversight of a complex remedial apparatus that would appear to displace the policy-making prerogatives of the political branches of government. By retaining jurisdiction through a structural injunction, but allowing responsible government officials and citizen stakeholders the opportunity to craft an appropriate remedy, the Court would obviate the need to allocate scarce administrative resources to remedial management or to wade into complex terrain through which it feels ill-equipped to move. (Such a flexible response is a paradigmatic example of the experimentalist commitment to remedial equilibration adumbrated in Chapter 4.)

As we shall see in some of the most recent cases, the Court can go about setting out general norms to guide various government actors and non-governmental stakeholders. It can invite, a la the *Miranda* Court, other government actors to provide effective means of realizing the right in question. General norm-setting (even the minimalist minimum core now taking shape within the parameters of s 26)[45] married to such an open-ended invitation services experimental constitutionalism by creating a body of doctrine and experience that is flexible enough to address new challenges.[46] The flexibility of shared constitutional competence frees the Court from its ever-present anxiety that it will say too much and thus bind its hands in the future. Likewise, it frees the Court from the doctrinal dead-end of one-case-at-a-time land, where the future is always now and no guiding principles can ever be affirmed. As I noted above in Chapter 6, the National Department of Housing's new policy document, *Breaking New Ground*, various amendments to the *Housing Code*, and even more supple recent developments in the delivery of housing units suggest that the Court's general norm setting has had the intended effect of motivating those parties with greater expertise to generate social, economic, political and legal responses consistent with newly articulated constitutional norms.[47]

However, as the judgments in both *Modderklip* and in *Rudolph I* and *Rudolph II* suggest, the state may not always respond with alacrity to the Court's invitation to create new policy.[48] (It may well often be that a government department (with 15% capacity) lacks the requisite capacity to implement a meaningful response.[49]) If the state fails to respond to the Court's invitation, then de facto constitutional damages – as in *Modderklip* – or threats of citation for contempt – as in *Rudolph* – become necessary and appropriate judicial responses.

4. *Minister of Health & Others v Treatment Actions Campaigne & Others (No 2)*[50]

Treatment Action Campaign is often considered both a significant victory for advocates of a more robust approach to socio-economic rights and an easy case for those commentators who view the Court as rather reluctant to put the government on specific terms in the event of an adverse ruling.[51] After just over a decade, *Treatment Action Campaign* warrants a re-appraisal.[52]

From the perspective of flourishing, *Treatment Action Campaign* promised an easy solution to the problem of intra-partum transmission of HIV. Moreover, the Court's order held that the government must 'make provision if necessary for counsellors based at public hospitals and clinics other than the research and training sites to be trained for the counselling necessary for the use of nevirapine to reduce the risk of mother-to-child transmission of HIV [and] take reasonable measures to extend the testing and counselling facilities at hospitals and clinics throughout the public health sector to facilitate and expedite the use of nevirapine for the purpose of reducing the risk of mother-to-child transmission of HIV.'[53] Implementation of these portions of the Court's order would have gone some distance towards solving the problem of sero-conversion that takes places if HIV-positive mothers breastfeed their children after birth. From the perspective of experimental constitutionalism, the order looked tough enough to guarantee the desired result – provision of Nevirapine to HIV-positive pregnant women in order to prevent intra-partum transmission of HIV from mother to child (MTCT) – while flexible enough to allow government to shift its policies should a more efficacious, safer and cheaper solution to the problem of MTCT be found.[54]

a. *Failure to Flourish*

There can be little doubt that the Constitutional Court believed that its order requiring Nevirapine to be provided at all public hospitals would be carried out and that a clear consequence of its order bei would be a significant diminution in MTCT and a concomitant decrease in infant mortality. The statistics tell another story. [55]

Five years after the *TAC* judgment, roughly 94,900 HIV-infected children were born each year. That number reflects an overall 40% increase. Moreover, only 13,134 of these 94,900 children received any antiretroviral treatment (ART).[56] In sum, over the first five year post-*TAC* period, 400,000 children who urgently required access to ARVs did not receive them. The majority of these children did not reach the age of two.[57] Yet, as the *TAC* Court was aware at the time of its judgment, and as the World Health Organization continues to emphasize:

> Paediatric HIV is almost entirely preventable. It has been virtually eliminated in high-income countries.[58]

One doesn't require a particularly sophisticated account of flourishing or capabilities to conclude that the South African government under former President Mbeki failed to take the Constitutional Court's order seriously.[59] Many of the HIV/AIDs policies of the Mbeki Presidency were patently retrogressive – a clear violation of s 27 of the Constitution and South Africa's international law obligations.[60] While the HIV/AIDs policy regime under President Zuma reflects a palpable improvement, retrogressive measures remain in place.[61]

b. *Not Tough Enough*

Part of the responsibility for this failure surely lies with the Court itself.[62] After surveying the foreign literature on structural interdicts, the Court concluded that no good jurisprudential reason existed for making them a routine remedy.[63] The Court held that it could employ a structural interdict that forced the government to alter its policies as the exigencies of the moment so dictated:

> A factor that needs to be kept in mind is that policy is and should be flexible. It may be changed at any time and the executive is always free to change policies where it considers it appropriate to do so. The only constraint is that policies must be consistent with the Constitution and the law. Court orders concerning policy choices made by the executive should therefore not be formulated in ways that preclude the executive from making such legitimate choices.[64]

However, despite incontrovertible evidence that the government's reasons for refusing to supply Nevirapine were internally incoherent and factually incorrect, the Court decided that the government deserved the benefit of the doubt.[65] Had it retained the jurisdiction that normally attaches to a structural injunction, it might have found itself in a position to address what appears to be a persistent pattern of malign neglect around MTCT of HIV/AIDS. As Courtenay Sprague, Vivian Black and I have argued elsewhere:

> .... [I]n something of a break with ... current academic commentary – which only presses the point that the government should not be held to the rather amorphous dictates of the 'reasonableness' standard – we believe that the institutionalised use of poorly remunerated, marginalised 'lay counsellors' to discharge the responsibilities of healthcare professionals (doctors and nurses who had previously undertaken counselling and testing) constitutes a *'retrogressive measure'*. In short, despite the government's commitment to an expanded, more efficacious rollout, it is currently delivering less health care – not more – and less adequate health care – not better – to this particular cohort of patients with HIV. Such retrogressive measures violate international covenants to which South Africa is bound. At the same time, these measures would also seem to offend the Court's own understanding of the delivery of this constitutionally-mandated public good to pregnant women with HIV and their infants.[66]

5. *Port Elizabeth Municipality v Various Occupiers*[67]

The Port Elizabeth Municipality sought an eviction order against 68 persons living in shacks on privately owned land. The occupants agreed to move to 'suitable alternative land'. However, the space offered by the Council, in Walmer Township, provided no security of occupation and was controlled by criminal networks. The municipality contended that no other alternative existed and that making a special exception for the occupiers would be tantamount to queue-jumping with respect to the municipality's comprehensive and co-ordinated housing scheme.

After having won in the High Court and lost in the Supreme Court of Appeal, the municipality sought a ruling from the Constitutional Court that would confirm that it was not constitutionally obliged to find alternative accommodation or land when seeking an order evicting unlawful occupiers. The Court denied the appeal. It held that although a municipality was not generally under an obligation to provide alternative accommodation or land, the municipality's failure to take any steps – let alone all reasonable steps – to solve this social problem meant that the municipality had failed to discharge its constitutional obligations. Given this abdication of responsibility, the Court held that it was neither just nor equitable for the eviction order to be granted.

The Constitutional Court noted, relatively early in its judgment, that the polycentric nature of the problem – homeless persons in need of shelter, private land owners who wished to use the occupied land, municipalities charged with creating a coherent housing scheme for all its inhabitants, sheriffs charged with executing an eviction, inhabitants of other communities to which the homeless persons might be moved – posed significant challenges:[68]

> The court is thus called upon to go beyond its normal functions, and to engage in active judicial management according to equitable principles of an ongoing, stressful and law-governed social process. This has major implications for the manner in which it must deal with the issues before it, how it should approach questions of evidence, the procedures it may adopt, the way in which it exercises its powers and orders it might make.[69]

The Court first appeared as if it might rise to the challenge. It noted that cases that affected the lives of so many parties might be best resolved through face-to-face meetings. It introduces the term: 'mediation'. On the virtues of such participatory bubbles, the Court writes:

> In seeking to resolve the above contradictions, the procedural and substantive aspects of justice and equity cannot always be separated. The managerial role of the courts may need to find expression in innovative ways. Thus one potentially dignified and effective mode of achieving sustainable reconciliations of the different interests involved is to encourage and require the parties to engage with each other in a pro-active and honest endeavour to find mutually acceptable solutions. Wherever possible, respectful face-to-face engagement or mediation through a third party should replace arms-length combat by intransigent opponents.[70]

The *Port Elizabeth Municipality* Court elucidates two further benefits of participatory bubbles: the internalization of constitutional norms by the participants in the negotiations; and the ability of such bubbles to make up for the information deficits that top-down statecraft or adversarial legal proceedings tend to generate:

> Not only can mediation reduce the expenses of litigation, it can help avoid the exacerbation of tensions that forensic combat produces. By bringing the parties together, narrowing the areas of dispute between them and facilitating mutual give-and-take, mediators can find ways round sticking-points in a manner that the adversarial judicial process might not be able to do. Money that otherwise might be spent on unpleasant and polarising litigation can better be used to facilitate an outcome that ends a stand-off, promotes respect for human dignity and underlines the fact that we all live in a shared society.[71]

Despite these largely unassailable observations, the *Port Elizabeth Municipality* Court balks when it comes down to ordering mediation and retaining jurisdiction to ensure that a just and equitable outcome occurs. Its reasons for not putting mediation and a structural injunction in place range from the intransigence of the parties, the small likelihood of success given the failure to reach any agreement earlier in the process, the failure of lower courts to employ this dispute resolution mechanism and the idiosyncratic nature of the community effected. With respect, these justifications for refusing to issue a structural injunction are extremely good reasons for doing so.[72] A structural injunction that sets out the general norms that will shape the outcome of the dispute, but leaves the parties to discover the best possible remedy, is exactly the kind of remedy that might overcome existing intransigence, idiosyncrasies of circumstance and previous failures to generate an outcome that both sides might prefer (to the zero-sum outcome of a court order.) As it turns out, the parties are left pretty much where they started: the Municipality has 'illegal' occupants that it cannot move, as yet, and the occupiers remain, for the moment, on private land to which they can stake no meaningful claim. Despite its high minded rhetoric about novel judicial interventions, the *Port Elizabeth Municipality* Court looks, ultimately, to be more concerned with saving its political capital than with creating the conditions that might present a lasting solution to a particularly pressing social problem.[73]

One can speculate, in a meaningful way, as to the basis for the strong rhetoric, and the absence of action: disagreement within the Court. Whereas some may have pressed for mediation, others resisted. On a Court institutionally and politically committed to unanimity, the result is hardly surprising. Ultimately, as we shall see, the pragmatism of unanimity yields to the pragmatism of meaningful engagement.

6. *The Minister of Public Works & Others v Kyalami Ridge Association & Another*[74]

In 1999, unseasonable rains caused floods across South Africa. These floods, in a country rife with informal housing, resulted in widespread homelessness. To address this national calamity, the national government established a committee to address the urgent need for shelter. It committed R557 million to the provision of temporary and permanent housing.

The gravamen of the complaint in *Kyalami Ridge* was that the committee charged with finding appropriate space and building necessary shelter had created a transit camp on the Leeuwkop prison farm to accommodate flood-victims in Alexandra Township (in Johannesburg). The respondent, an association that represented residents in the vicinity of Leeuwkop, challenged the committee's decision. It contended that the transit camp would adversely affect property values and the long-term habitability of the surrounding environment.

The High Court and then the Supreme Court of Appeal accepted the association's contention that the committee's actions were indeed invalid. Not only was the decision taken absent authorizing legislation, but it was found to have infringed statutory and constitutional rights regarding land and the preservation of the environment. Moreover, given the polycentric nature of the decision, the High Court and the SCA accepted the association's claim that that they should have at least been consulted.

The Constitutional Court, in a detailed and nuanced response, reversed the SCA and High Court's decisions and upheld the government's appeal. Sadly, the Court's decision comes up short in ways we have seen occur in two of the cases surveyed thus far – *Grootboom* and *PE Municipality*.

After holding, not uncontroversially, that the government has the same rights as other land owners,[75] the Constitutional Court traversed the applicable township ordinances, development statutes, environmental legislation and apposite rights in the Constitution – the right to housing, s 26, and the right to a safe and healthy environment, s 24. In the end, the Court held that the rights of the displaced persons in need of urgent shelter and housing after the occurrence of a national disaster trumped other considerations. The decision had to be taken quickly – and the Government did so within its available resources and after appropriate consideration. But ought the Court to have done more?

As Basson and Van der Linde have observed:

> Some commentators have argued that *Kyalami Ridge* would have been an ideal opportunity for the Court to discuss the principle of sustainable development and to tackle an alleged conflict between economic development and environmental protection.[76] Although the Court could have considered sustainable development, this argument does not properly appreciate the scope and application of sustainable development. The case only raised competing commitments to adequate housing and environmental protection: economic development did not feature.[77]

Is the last statement entirely true? Surely the homeowners association was far more concerned with the economic value and the capacity for economic development of the land of its members than it was with the environmentally detrimental effects of the effluents emitted by the transit camp.

a. The Failure to Create a Participatory Bubble

The real problem with the judgment – from an experimentalist perspective – is two-fold.

First, the Court notes, without comment, a lack of engagement with other affected actors: 'No discussions were, however, held with residents in the vicinity of Leeuwkop.'[78] Residents learned of the government's decision at a press conference:

> Mr Paul Mashatile, the Gauteng MEC for Housing … stress[ed] that a transit camp was being established, and that the persons to be accommodated there would move to permanent housing when that became available, and that the transit camp would then be dismantled.[79]

After finding that the failure to engage or to consult with the residents of *Kyalami Ridge* violated neither statute nor the constitutional norm of legality, then Chief Justice Chaskalson shrugged his shoulders and remarked:

> It may have been better and more consistent with salutary principles of good government if the government had found an appropriate method to inform the neighbouring residents of its intentions before contractors went onto the site, and if it had engaged them in discussion and the planning at an early stage of the project. However, for the reasons that I have given, the absence of such consultation and engagement did not invalidate the decision.[80]

C'est dommage.[81]

b. The Consequences of a Failure to Create a Participatory Bubble[82]

An equally important failure – perhaps one of greater import – seems to have been the inability or the lack of interest on the part of the state to honour its commitment to wind up the transit camp as soon as possible and provide adequate permanent housing to its occupants. The *Kyalami Ridge* Court writes, as it delivers its remedy:

> This has been a most unfortunate case. When the proceedings were commenced the government contemplated that the flood victims would be accommodated on the prison farm temporarily and that they would be allocated permanent accommodation elsewhere within 6 to 12 months. Later it

> was said that the time would at most be 12 to 24 months. Nearly a year has passed since then. In the meantime the flood victims have been living in deplorable circumstances, and there is no word as to when permanent accommodation will become available. It is time that attention be paid to their needs.[83]

But the Court's concerns do not lie with the homeless alone. They acknowledge the interests – statutory and constitutional – that rest with the members of the association that brought the matter to Court:

> In responding to the application for leave to appeal, the Kyalami residents said that if there is no other place in the vicinity of Alexandra Township for the flood victims to be given temporary accommodation, they would be willing to consent to this being done on the prison site if they are consulted and if their concerns relating to access to the site from the main road and the sewerage system to be installed are addressed. They also seek greater certainty as to when and where the permanent housing will be provided for the victims.[84]

The government promises that such housing will be provided. It fails, as the *Kyalami Ridge* Court notes, to say how and when that will happen, and whether such development will accord with the statutory and constitutional analysis laid out in the Court's judgment:

> The constitutional rights of the flood victims and the corresponding obligations on the government are clearly relevant to any consent that may be required for the development to take place. The government must, however, discharge its constitutional obligations lawfully. If the law requires it to secure such consent it must seek and obtain it, or pass legislation that either exempts it from the provisions of such legislation, or enables it to override its provisions in cases of emergency. It cannot, however, on the basis of its rights as owner of the land and a constitutional obligation to provide access to housing, claim the power to develop its land contrary to legislation that is binding on it. Whether there are such constraints is a matter which is left open in this judgment and on which I express no opinion. The order to be made cannot anticipate this issue.[85]

But why not? The Court has acknowledged the amount of time that has passed. The government's silence is deafening. As many a South African knows, Ms Grootboom died, almost a decade after the judgment (in her favour?), without ever receiving the kind of shelter to which she had thought she was constitutionally entitled. Such regular failures to carry out in full the judgments of the courts in these cases casts something of a pall over the positive outcomes bestowed upon the homeless, and the long forgotten promises made to other members of the community – such as the Kyalami residents – that their concerns will be taken into account.

In sum: from an experimentalist perspective, *Kyalami Ridge* disappoints in two important respects. It fails: (a) to bring all the affected parties together in order to reach as optimal an outcome within the law as possible; and (b) to ensure that the government respects the norms articulated by the Court so that all the affected parties – in the present and an easily imagined future – might benefit from the Court's otherwise thoughtful judgment.[86]

7. *Fuel Retailers Association of Southern Africa v Director-General Environmental Management, Department of Agriculture, Conservation and Environment Mpumalanga Province*[87]

This decision provides something of a corrective to its predecessor – *Kyalami Ridge*. As we saw in *Kyalami Ridge*, the Court deferred to government officials, left, right and centre, when it came to virtually any determination the government had made regarding urgency, temporariness of shelter, the building of permanent structures, consultation, the control of effluents and the willingness of affected members of the two communities in question to work together in order to better solve the problems with which they were both confronted. While it can be fairly said that the *Kyalami Ridge* Court took the plight of the flooding victims seriously, the same cannot be said of the bona fides of the association contesting the government's immediate response or the government officials charged with implementing a plan: a plan that at the time of writing of the Constitutional Court's judgment was already substantially delayed.

a. A Few Participatory Bubbles

Fuel Retailers offers us an opportunity to re-think *Kyalami Ridge* in three respects.[88] First, the Court does not defer to the local government's analysis of the need for a new petrol station either in terms of environmental impact or in terms of socio-economic development (shared constitutional interpretation). Second, the Court effectively recalls the parties to the table (albeit through heads of argument and oral argument) to determine whether the prior decision complied with extant environmental law and the imperative of economic development (participatory bubbles). Third, the Court is clearly engaged by the need to vouchsafe a clean environment in order to secure greater long-term economic benefits (flourishing). In short, the Court takes its responsibilities as a shared interpreter of the basic law and statutes seriously and is willing to recall the parties affected in order to arrive at a more optimal outcome for all concerned.

b. Shared Constitutional Interpretation

No other right creates more internal tension than s 24.[89] The tripartite alliance of environmental protection, economic development and local community participation is fragile indeed. While the three domains may occasionally overlap, they are just as likely to come into conflict. The Court appreciates that decision-makers confronted with development applications have no easy task, and yet in order to do justice to all concerned, they must attempt to assess the competing virtues of a plan all the same. As Justice Ncgobo writes:

> Unsustainable developments are in themselves detrimental to the environment. … It is … not enough to focus on the needs of the developer while the needs of the society are neglected. One of the purposes of the public participation provision of NEMA is to afford people the opportunity to express their views on the desirability of a [development] that will impact on socio-economic conditions affecting [a local population] . … [S]ocio-economic development must be justifiable in the light of the need to protect the environment. The Constitution and environmental legislation introduce a new criterion for considering future developments. Pure economic factors are no longer

> decisive. The need for development must now be determined by its impact on the environment, sustainable development and social and economic interests. The duty of the environmental authorities is to integrate these factors into decision-making and make decisions that are informed by these considerations. This process requires a decision-maker to consider the impact of the proposed development on the environment and socio-economic conditions. … [Similarly, the developer must] identify and predict the actual or potential impact on socio-economic conditions and consider ways of minimizing negative impact while maximizing benefit.[90]

These words bring us back to one of the primary goals of constitutional (and democratic) experimentalism: rolling norms based upon empirical findings. The kind of analysis required of decision-makers faced with s 24 decisions should, over time, build up a base of knowledge that enables all parties to make more informed evaluations of specific cases and allow courts to better determine how environmental concerns, economic development and community empowerment relate to one another as interlocking principles. The more s 24 cases heard, the better idea we shall have of what s 24 means.[91]

8. *Occupiers of 51 Olivia Road, Berea Township and 197 Main Street Johannesburg v City of Johannesburg & Others*[92]

Thus far, we have re-analyzed cases in terms of shared constitutional interpretation, participatory bubbles, rolling norms and flourishing. At the time that I began writing in 2004, such imaginative reconstructions of the cases were all the Court's decisions afforded us. However, over the last couple of years the Court itself has moved from a model of standard binary conflict to – depending on the case with which it is confronted – a model of judicial review better suited to polycentric conflicts and rolling constitutional norms. (In other cases, as I have noted elsewhere,[93] it has moved away from norm setting, multiple-stakeholder engagement and rolling yet still coherent precedents – leaving the legal community and the community at large in the most uncomfortable position of having to imagine the state of the law and what the future will bring. In short, it has, in more cases than it should, left us without the guidance required by a constitutional order committed to the rule of law.)

While some degree of multi-stakeholder participation appears in such housing cases as *Kyalami*,[94] *Grootboom*[95] and *Port Elizabeth Occupiers*,[96] the Court was, by and large, content to accept the facts placed before it. Whether the new polycentric approach actually fits this book's theories about shared constitutional interpretation, participatory bubbles, flattened hierarchies, reflexivity, remedial equilibration and rolling norms model will be interrogated later. Suffice it to say that a Court with a largely new bench has begun to experiment with a new manner of adjudicating cases.[97]

In *Occupiers of 51 Olivia Road, Berea Township and 197 Main Street Johannesburg v City of Johannesburg & Others*, the Court was asked to determine whether the City of Johannesburg had acted constitutionally in attempting to evict residents from derelict – and dangerous – inner-city buildings.[98] In some instances, the eviction notice came without any plan to provide comparable housing. In other cases, the eviction notice contemplated the ejection of a building's residents and their *forced removal* to the city's outskirts.

a. A Participatory Bubble: The Dawn of 'Meaningful Engagement'

The *Occupiers of 51 Olivia Road* Court's ingenuity at the outset of the hearing distinguishes itself from its many predecessors. Rather than impose a decision on the parties framed by *Grootboom*-based criteria, the Court ordered the residents and the City of Johannesburg to repair to the negotiating table in order to reach a settlement that would lead to a more optimal outcome for both sides. The parties did. Their settlement then became an order of the Court.

While the judgment arrived with generally well-established justifications for its order, the most fascinating part of the judgment – from the perspective of experimental constitutionalism – is that the Court held that, in addition to any other duties s 26(2)'s right to access to adequate housing might impose, 'a municipality that ejects people from their homes without first meaningfully engaging with them acts in a manner that is broadly at odds with the spirit and purpose of [its] constitutional obligations'.[99] What does this mean? First, it appears that the courts may not be the right branch of government to determine how some 63,000 persons – living in dangerous conditions – are to be best accommodated when a municipality determines that their current housing constitutes a threat to their lives. Second, having decided that persons who live in dangerous conditions must be removed, the Court also resolved that a municipality must determine where they are to be otherwise accommodated. A right to housing cannot be reconciled with a decision of the state to make people 'homeless'. Third, in deciding on how to accommodate this endangered class of persons, the city or the stare is obliged to engage all of the affected parties – in this case 63,000 persons. As Yacoob J writes:

> Engagement has the potential to contribute towards the resolution of disputes and to increased understanding and sympathetic care if both sides are willing to participate in the process. People about to be evicted may be so vulnerable that they may not be able to understand the importance of engagement and may refuse to take part in the process. If this happens, a municipality cannot walk away without more. It must make reasonable efforts to engage and it is only if these reasonable efforts fail that a municipality may proceed without appropriate engagement. It is precisely to ensure that a city is able to engage meaningfully with poor, vulnerable or illiterate people that the engagement process should preferably be managed by careful and sensitive people on its side.[100]

No small task. The Court held, in addition, that the city had an obligation to engage meaningfully all 63 000 evictees in a systemic fashion.[101] In short, a scheme had to be put in place to ensure that each individual or each family was heard and accommodated to the best of the state's capacity. Of course, the obligation placed upon the state did not mean that the occupants could employ obstructionist tactics to delay a move. The Court noted that '[e]ngagement is a two-way process'[102] that 'will work only if both sides act reasonably and in good faith.'[103]

Consistent with the precepts of experimental constitutionalism, the *51 Olivia Road* Court places a premium on pooling information and on reaching accommodations that place all parties in a better position than they might find themselves if the Court were to act as the final arbiter in a zero-sum game. The court-enforced settlement obliged the parties to produce a range of alternatives for housing those in danger, rather than merely allowing the residents to remain endangered by living in derelict buildings or living in less than adequate shelter had they been forcibly removed to the outskirts of the city.

b. An Absence of Norms?

Although *51 Olivia Road* looks attractive from the perspective of polycentric problem-solving, a significant question looms over the judgment. What will the ratification of the judgment mean for future housing judgments or any judgments in which the Court calls for meaningful engagement (prior to preceding with any hearing should the engagement fail)?

One answer is that the ratification of a settlement lets the Court off the hook for the development of even the most basic norms when eviction orders are accessed against the backdrop of the right to access to adequate housing. After all, if the Court accepts the settlement, then it is not bound to develop the law. It need not force the hand of any given party to the litigation. The result – from one point of view – is that future litigants in similar cases will not know how to go about structuring their arguments regarding evictions. Neither side will know the contours of their obligations prior to entering into negotiations.

A second answer might reflect the legal realist view of adjudication that animates both experimental constitutionalism and South African socio-economic rights jurisprudence.[104] One will come to know what is expected of the state, an occupant, another land-holder or other interested parties as more and more cases come before the Court for review and for settlement. We will learn, one, two, or three cases at a time, exactly what the Court requires from the state in terms of meaningful engagement and the satisfaction of other *Grootboom*-based criteria.

A third answer exists. Victories in housing cases in South Africa have been notoriously difficult to enforce. Court findings of a breach of FC s 26 have not necessarily resulted in changes on the ground. Why? Two reasons. First, as a rule, violations of s 26 only require the state to conceive of a programme likely to realize the right to housing in the short-term, mid-term and long-term. Second, by refusing to retain jurisdiction of most housing cases, the courts have relied on the good faith of the government to discharge its constitutional obligations. Too often, the government has failed to do so. The use of settlements, and court enforced 'meaningful engagement' to reach them, may offer the best opportunity for the dispossessed or the homeless to wring immediate benefits from s 26.

Meaningful engagement in the case at hand dramatically turned matters around. Upon further inspection, all the parties agreed that the dangerous buildings could be upgraded – to the requisite standards – and that the residents could stave off eviction. What would have likely been a loss-loss for all parties (in cost and result), turned into a win-win when the parties were forced to reapply their minds to the various problems of collective action with which they had been confronted.[105]

9. Abahlali Basemjondolo Movement SA & Another v Premier of the Province of Kwazulu-Natal & Others[106]

In *Abahlali Basemjondolo Movement SA & Another v Premier of the Province of Kwazulu-Natal & Others,* Abahlali BaseMjondolo, a radical shack dweller movement, challenged the KwaZulu-Natal Elimination and Prevention of Re-emergence of Slums Act ('Slums Act').[107] The Act itself seemed little more than a craven attempt to 'clean up' Durban prior to the influx of foreign visitors for the 2010 World Cup.[108]

From the perspective of experimental constitutionalism, the most important challenge to the Slums Act flowed from the Act's willingness to allow eviction without engagement. The entire bench found that the Act, to pass constitutional muster, had to be read so that engagement is required. Moseneke DCJ wrote:

> No evictions should occur until the results of the proper engagement process are known .... Proper engagement would include taking into proper consideration the wishes of the people who are to be evicted; whether the areas where they live may be upgraded *in situ*; and whether there will be alternative accommodation. The engagement would also include the manner of eviction and the timeframes for the eviction.[109]

Engagement extracts information that might not, as yet, appear in the heads of argument. It requires the various stakeholders concerned – and perhaps not just the original parties, given the Court's generous approach to standing – to put all their cards on the table. Engagement should make the outcome (the settlement) less contingent on well-drafted heads, voluminous records and courtroom theatrics. What the state and other parties can do – and what the potentially homeless will and will not accept – becomes the measure of a settlement's mettle. The openness of the negotiation and settlement process – as Yacoob J notes – makes engagement more than mere window dressing:

> If it appears as a result of the process of engagement, for example, that the property concerned can be upgraded without the eviction of the unlawful occupiers, the municipality cannot institute eviction proceedings. This is because it would not be acting reasonably in the engagement process.[110]

The requirement of engagement might explain the difference between the majority and the minority opinion on the validity of s 16 of the Act. Section 16 gave the Member of the Executive Council of the Province power to determine the period within which an owner or person in charge of land or a building that is occupied by unlawful occupiers must institute proceedings to evict the occupiers under the PIE Act; where the owner or person in charge failed to comply, the municipality was obliged to institute proceedings to evict the occupiers.

The majority may have ultimately arrived at the conclusion that s 16 of the Act violated s 26 of the Constitution because it so loaded any conversation between the disputants in favour of the state or person responsible for the land by: (a) enabling an owner of a building or land to institute eviction proceedings against unlawful occupiers even in circumstances where the requirements of the PIE Act, which protects unlawful occupiers against arbitrary evictions, are not met by the land owner; and (b) making residents of informal settlements, who are invariably unlawful occupiers, more vulnerable to evictions should an MEC decide to issue a notice under section 16. Given a legal backdrop against which eviction notices can be secured with little difficulty, the state or other land owner has little reason to reach a somewhat more amicable solution with illegal occupiers. The ease of issuance of such orders constituted a blunt cudgel that might cause even the most radical social movement to search for (alternative) cover. By eliminating the possibility of easily obtained arbitrary eviction notices or the promulgation of potentially arbitrary and irrational notices by an MEC, the majority put illegal occupiers – the inevitable, unenviable inhabitants of South African slums – on a slightly more even footing with the state or another landowner. At the very least, meaningful engagement would now have to precede any attempt to secure an eviction notice – thus reversing the spin of a statutory scheme designed to sweep communities away or place them out of sight and out of mind.

10. Merafong Demarcation Forum & Others v President of the Republic of South Africa & Others[111]

(a) Participatory Bubbles and Popular Sovereignty

In August of 2005, the Municipal Demarcation Board took an ostensibly straightforward decision to consolidate the town of Merafong and to place it entirely within the North West Province. Its various parts had previously cut across the borders of the provinces of Gauteng and North West. A single cross-border municipality served by two provincial governments had created administrative confusion, led to the unnecessary replication of responsibilities and, not surprisingly, resulted in the failure to deliver the most basic of basic services.

The citizens of Merafong, however, were less than an impressed with this rationalization of resources and made their displeasure known through on-going protests in the streets. The gravamen of their complaint: Provincial services in Gauteng were deemed far superior to those services found in North West. The citizens of Merafong had little interest in moving in with the poorer provincial cousin.

The government could not ignore this clear expression of popular sovereignty and responded accordingly. It moved Merafong back into Gauteng. For a day. It then moved Merafong back into North West.

Merafong exploded. People burned tyres in the streets. The police responded with measured forced. The violence resulted in a meeting with the Minister for Provincial and Local Government and a promise of more face to face discussion.

Meaningful engagement could not prevent political chaos. Bills in both Houses of Parliament had been prepared with the cross border move in mind. At the same time, the Gauteng Provincial Legislature's (GPL) Local Government Portfolio Committee and the North West legislature held a joint session at which the majority of constituents present elected to remain in Gauteng. In an about face, Gauteng charged its NCOP select committee with an obligation that would allow it to approve the 12th Amendment Bill subject to the requirement that Merafong remain in Gauteng.

Unfortunately, the GPL then received poor legal advice. The GPL was informed that it could neither amend nor propose amendments to a bill in the National Council of Provinces. So rather than query this initial counsel, the GPL reversed course and recommended a final mandate that would support the entire bill. The NCOP passed the 12th Amendment Bill and Merafong was placed on the schedule for a cross-border move to North West on 1 March 2006.

Not surprisingly, the people of Merafong refused to accept the outcome. The streets were, once again, set alight. The insurrection continued up to and through the local elections. On

1 March 2006, a mere 232 members of 29 540 Merafong's citizenry cast their votes. The resistance to reincorporation continued throughout 2006 and 2007.

At the same, the Merafong Democratic Forum initiated litigation. This round of MDF-inspired litigation failed to postpone the 2006 elections. However, following the Constitutional Court's decision in *Matatiele* – in which the Court had found that a provincial legislature had failed to create the proper space for public consultation – the MDF approached the Court for a different form of relief.[112] As Michael Bishop writes:

> The main issue ... was whether the GPL had fulfilled their duty under s 118(1)(a) of the Constitution to 'facilitate public involvement in the legislative and other processes of the legislature and its committees'. The Court recognized in *Doctors for Life v Speaker of the National Assembly & Others* that s 118(1)(a) imposed a justiciable obligation on provincial legislatures and that 'legislative processes' encompassed determining mandates for votes in the NCOP. If the duty was not fulfilled, then the legislation would be invalid. *Matatiele Municipality & Others v President of the Republic of South Africa & Others* confirmed that this obligation applied not only to ordinary legislation, but also to constitutional amendments. But what is the nature of the obligation imposed on the legislature? Restating s 118(1)(a) in new language, the *Doctors for Life* Court tells us it 'means taking steps to ensure that the public participate in the legislative process. The legislature must, however, have 'considerable discretion to determine how best to fulfil their duty'. Nonetheless, the Court would review the specific measures taken to enhance involvement for individual pieces of legislation. The standard that government must meet in fulfilling both parts of the duty is reasonableness.[113] Expanding on this theme [of reasonableness], Justice Ngcobo writes: 'Whether a legislature has acted reasonably in discharging its duty to facilitate public involvement will depend on a number of factors. The nature and importance of the legislation and the intensity of its impact on the public are especially relevant. Reasonableness also requires that appropriate account be paid to practicalities such as time and expense, which relate to the efficiency of the law-making process. Yet the saving of money and time in itself does not justify inadequate opportunities for public involvement. In addition, in evaluating the reasonableness of Parliament's conduct, this Court will have regard to what Parliament itself considered to be appropriate public involvement in the light of the legislation's content, importance and urgency.'[114]

Ngcobo J held that 'the duty to facilitate public involvement will often require Parliament and the provincial legislatures to provide citizens with a meaningful opportunity to be heard in the making of the laws that will govern them. Our Constitution demands no less.'[115] Whatever their shortcomings, the GPL, the NCOP and other government entities – including the courts – had allowed the citizens of Merafong just that: a meaningful opportunity to be heard and to have their interests taken into account. That the citizens of *Merafong* had neither persuaded the state nor the Court to alter the decision to move *Merafong* back into Gauteng does not count against the open-ended, experimentalist cast of the case. Virtually every form of democratic engagement – participatory, direct and representative – had played some role in the ultimate outcome. Experimentalism means that all the right questions are asked and answered, and that future litigants and stakeholders will have an opportunity to learn from the case decided. To that end, the citizens of Merafong, the MDF and the Constitutional Court all played their roles in advancing our understanding of the Constitution and in contributing to appreciation of how such volatile public conflicts ought to be handled in the future.

(b) When Bubbles Run Up Against the Limits of Shared Constitutional Interpretation

Until now, I have spoken as if participatory bubbles and shared constitutional interpretation were two sides – or perhaps the bottom and the top – of experimental constitutionalism. It is, perhaps, important to distinguish between the two once again: (1) shared constitutional interpretation relies upon conflicting constructions that an array of governmental and non-governmental actors place upon a given constitutional norm and the results that such conflicting constructions generate; (2) participatory bubbles depend upon the creation of space in which a variety of stakeholders in a given constitutional or legal dispute are able to bring as much information to the table as possible so that either the stakeholders themselves or the court or forum obliged to render a judgment can reach the most informed decision possible. Shared constitutional interpretation engages the basic law's norms at a relatively high level of abstraction and allows contested readings of the law's meaning to play themselves out over time. Participatory bubbles are, in effect, the experiments themselves. They provide the kind of feedback that enables courts and the other co-ordinate branches to pool information on the kinds of policy strategies and legal regimes that work best over a broad range of individual cases.

The notion, then, of a participatory bubble is to give various stakeholders a say in the outcome of a dispute. Participatory bubbles do not supplant the established roles of the courts, the legislatures or the executives; nor do they displace representative democracy and participatory democracy with popular sovereignty. Whatever mistakes might have been made in *Merafong* – and there were quite a few – the case should not be viewed as one in which the Court turned a deaf ear to the petitioners.

At the end of this drama, the *Merafong* Court decided not to give disappointed parties license to extend the debate over the proper location of Merafong. The people and the government had had their say, and their day, in court. Why then is *Merafong* different – in terms of a structural interdict or continued court oversight – than previous cases?

The Court was largely unmoved (even if incorrectly so) by the substantive arguments made by the citizens of Merafong. In some sense, nothing remained to be done. From the first word of the potential move, through the rioting in the streets, to the less fraught contentions made in court, the parties had been heard and various solutions to the problem tabled. *Merafong* was not a case which required greater ventilation.

Not all commentators agree. For Michael Bishop, the system was rigged in a manner that gave Merafong's denizens a mere semblance of voice, but no meaningful participation in the outcome. Neither the GPL's misreading of its legislative obligations, nor the Constitutional Court's endorsement of that reading, truly allowed Merafong's citizens the opportunity to alter the course of the decision-making process. Bishop's contention undercuts the notion that *Merafong* can readily be read as part of the Court's evolution toward greater stakeholder participation.

11. Bhe v Magistrate, Khayelitsha[116]

In *Bhe v Magistrate, Khayelitsha & Others*, the Constitutional Court found that the customary law rule of male primogeniture – and several statutory provisions that reinforced the rule –

unfairly discriminated against the deceased's wife and her two female children because the rule and the other impugned provisions prevented the children from inheriting the deceased's estate. On an initial reading, the *Bhe* Court's strategy for reconciling this rule of customary law with the dictates of s 9 (equality) and s 10 (dignity) of the Bill of Rights struck me as masterful, and the decision a model for finessing the radical disjunction between the ideals of a Western-style constitutional democracy and the traditions and the lived experience of many South Africans.

(a) *Whose Norms, Whose Flourishing?*

The *Bhe* Court begins with the following bromide. While customary law provides a comprehensive vision of the good for many South African communities, the new-found constitutional respect for traditional practices does not immunize them from constitutional review.[117] The Court locates any ongoing justification of customary law in the provisions of the Final Constitution. The *Bhe* Court then goes on to characterize the customary law of succession in terms that validate its spirit without necessitating that the Court be beholden to its letter. The customary law of succession is, according to the Court, a set of rules

> designed to preserve the cohesion and stability of the extended family unit and ultimately the entire community . ... The heir did not merely succeed to the assets of the deceased; succession was not primarily concerned with the distribution of the estate of the deceased, but with the preservation and perpetuation of the family unit. Property was collectively owned and the family head, who was the nominal owner of the property, administered it for the benefit of the family unit as a whole. The heir stepped into the shoes of the family head and acquired all the rights and became subject to all the obligations of the family head. He inherited the property of the deceased only in the sense that he assumed control and administration of the property subject to his rights and obligations as head of the family unit. The rules of the customary law of succession were consequently mainly concerned with succession to the position and status of the deceased family head rather than the distribution of his personal assets.[118]

By recasting the justification for customary rules of succession in terms of family and community stability, rather than patriarchy and property, the Court softens its critique of this traditional way of life. It then notes that the conditions of family and community which gave rise to the challenged rules no longer obtain. The *Bhe* Court writes:

> Modern urban communities and families are structured and organised differently and no longer purely along traditional lines. The customary law rules of succession ... determine succession to the deceased's estate without the accompanying social implications which they traditionally had. Nuclear families have largely replaced traditional extended families. The heir does not necessarily live together with the whole extended family which would include the spouse of the deceased as well as other dependants and descendants. He often simply acquires the estate without assuming, or even being in a position to assume, any of the deceased's responsibilities. In the changed circumstances, therefore, the succession of the heir to the assets of the deceased does not necessarily correspond in practice with an enforceable responsibility to provide support and maintenance to the family and dependants of the deceased.[119]

Customary law has not, the *Bhe* Court ruefully observes, evolved to meet the changing needs of the community. It fails African widows because '(a) ... social conditions frequently do not make living with the heir a realistic or even a tolerable proposition'; (b) '... the African woman does not have a right of ownership'; and (c) 'the prerequisite of a good working relationship with the heir for the effectiveness of the widow's right to maintenance', as a general matter, no longer exists.[120] Again the Court takes care to note that the fault for this arrested development lies outside traditional communities. Ruptures within traditional ways of life – caused by apartheid, the hegemony of Western culture and capitalism – had, according to the Court, prevented the law's evolution.[121] This aside actually sets the stage for delivery of the *Bhe* Court's coup de grace: that 'the official rules of customary law of succession are no longer universally observed'.[122] The trend within traditional communities is toward new norms that 'sustain the surviving family unit' without re-inscribing male primogeniture.

By having shown that the spirit of succession lies in its commitment to family cohesion, that the traditional family no longer coheres as it once did, and that the 'distorted' rules of customary law, as frozen in time by apartheid-era statute and case law, that 'emphasise ... patriarchal features and minimise ... communitarian ones,' the *Bhe* Court closes the gap between constitutional imperative and customary obligation.[123] Had customary law been permitted to develop in an 'active and dynamic manner', it would have already reflected the *Bhe* Court's conclusion that 'the exclusion of women from inheritance on the grounds of gender is a clear violation of ... [FC s] 9(3).'[124] Had customary law not been fossilised, traditional communities would have noted how male primogeniture entrenched 'past patterns of disadvantage among a vulnerable group' and endorsed the *Bhe* Court's re-working of customary understandings of the competence 'to own and administer property' in a manner that vindicates a woman's right to dignity under [FC] s 10.[125]

The decision in *Bhe* makes manifest the related virtues of reliance on objective characterizations of the subordinate position of women in traditional communities and avoidance of thorny issues of false consciousness. As I have written elsewhere:

> It seems trite, but still worth noting, that when faced with physical coercion, the rights of women to freedom and security of the person, to freedom from servitude, to equality and to dignity all trump any and all benefits that might accrue from sustaining traditional ways of life that re-inscribe such abuse. Female genital mutilation and forced labour are obvious candidates for the trash-heap of history. But polygamy and lobola? It is easy – and in most cases quite right – to identify such practices with the continued subordination of women. ... The more difficult question is whether such practices can be reconfigured so as to sustain legitimately both intimate familial associations and cultural practices. ... With adults, one difficulty is the paternalistic presumption that government can substitute its judgment of what is best for that of its citizenry. Inquiries into non-physical coercion of children and adults are united by considerations of exit. One must take great care, however, when we interfere in associational life that we are not too quick to allow attributions of false consciousness to masquerade as concerns about the inability of children or adults to vote with their feet.[126]

Caution with respect to such attribution does not mean abdication. Where reliable qualitative studies and statistical analyses can show that lobolo-like exchange correlate closely with lower levels of education, higher incidents of domestic violence, lower wages, higher rates of morbidity and lower levels of life expectancy for women, then caution ought to be overcome.[127] That, at least, was my initial response to *Bhe*. And from the Sen-like development perspective adopted in this work, I'm not entirely convinced that my immediate response was wrong. However, other voices in our constitutional democracy demand to heard.

(b) Rolling Norms or Riding Roughshod Over Tradition?

It did not take long for me to find out that my Manhattanite, Northern Suburb, 'White-tendency, little thingy' weltanschaunng (as so aptly described by Julius Malema) was dramatically out of step with the beliefs and the lived experiences of many South Africans. In this case, my teachers were my students at the University of Pretoria and the University of the Witwatersrand and my colleagues at the South African Institute for Advanced Constitutional, Public, Human Rights and International Law.

I should not have been surprised. I had, after all, been forewarned by Justice Ngcobo's weighty caesura in *Bhe*. It was, however, the vehemence of the response to these decisions, and most especially the reaction of female students who might have been thought opposed to the stipulation of lobolo or other biases in customary law that caught me short. Justice Ngcobo's dissent best captures the disjunction between the sentiments of many South Africans still tied to traditional moorings and the western-trained academics such as myself. Justice Ngcobo writes:

> Ours is not the only country that has a pluralist legal system in the sense of common, statutory and indigenous law. Other African countries that face the same problem have opted not for replacing indigenous law with common law or statutory laws. Instead, they have accepted that indigenous law is part of their laws and have sought to regulate the circumstances where it is applicable. In my view this approach reflects recognition of the constitutional right of those communities that live by and are governed by indigenous law. It is a recognition of our diversity, which is an important feature of our constitutional democracy. The importance of diversity in our country was emphasised by this Court in *Christian Education South Africa v Minister of Education*, where the Court said: '[t]here are a number of other provisions designed to protect the rights of members of communities. They underline the constitutional value of acknowledging diversity and pluralism in our society and give a particular texture to the broadly phrased right to freedom of association contained in s 18. Taken together, they affirm the right of people to be who they are without being forced to subordinate themselves to the cultural and religious norms of others, and highlight the importance of individuals and communities being able to enjoy what has been called the 'right to be different'. In each case, space has been found for members of communities to depart from a general norm. These provisions collectively and separately acknowledge the rich tapestry constituted by civil society, indicating in particular that language, culture and religion constitute a strong weave in the overall pattern. It seems to me therefore that the answer lies somewhere other than in the application of the Intestate Succession Act only. It lies in flexibility and willingness to examine the applicability of indigenous law in the concrete setting of social conditions presented by each particular case. It lies in accommodating different systems of law in order to ensure that the most vulnerable are treated fairly. The choice of law mechanism must be informed by the need to: (a) respect the right of communities to observe cultures and customs which they hold dear; (b) preserve indigenous law subject to the Constitution; and (c) protect vulnerable members of the family.[128]

One need not agree with Ngcobo J's inclination to allow customary law to develop unfettered in our 'newish' constitutional democracy to recognize the coherent line that he adopts on associational and community rights in a radically heterogeneous society and that he speaks for any number of different communities – traditional, religious, linguistic and cultural – in contemporary South Africa. If we are to take flourishing seriously as a foundation for South Africa's basic law, then Ncgobo J's arguments cannot be ignored. Indeed, eighteen years into our constitutional democracy, the clarion call of tradition is making itself heard and the practices behind the protests are making their presence felt.

(c) How Experimental Constitutionalism Addresses Conflicts between Conservative Flourishing and Revolutionary Flourishing

How, if at all, can Ngcobo J's conservative breed and Langa's revolutionary strain of flourishing – as manifest in the Constitution and our nascent jurisprudence – be squared with one another? As we saw in Chapter 7, we will struggle to reconcile them at the purely conceptual level of constitutional case law. More likely than not, the resolution of these conflicting strains of flourishing will be worked out through the actual lived experience of individuals and communities shaped by both well-entrenched tradition and the pressures of modernity.

Still, something remains to be said of our empirical inquiries into both the physical coercion and the non-physical coercion of children and adults by the practices of traditional, religious and cultural communities that are united by considerations of exit. On my initial reading of Langa DCJ's judgment in *Bhe*, the Constitutional Court proved itself quite adept at distinguishing circumstances in which neither child nor adult can meaningfully vote with their feet, from those instances in which adults willingly remain members of traditional communities in which their rights and privileges may well be subordinate to the rights and the privileges of other members of the community. The Court appeared able to distinguish the objective conditions of second-class citizenship from the attribution of false consciousness to any individual or group of individuals who remain within their community's traditional confines. The Court might have been aided by placing an experimentalist twist on how we can accommodate the close bonds Justice Ngcobo rightly associates with traditional communities, while, at the same time, ensuring that individuals and groups within the community possess an opportunity to form revised or alternative associations. My preferred mode of analysis suggests the following five-fold conclusion:

(1) Obvious abuses of the 'dignity' of any South African cannot be tolerated. Dignity – not equality – is the primary 'groundnorm' of South African constitutional law.

(2) However, where, as in *Bhe*, different communities may have different responses to rules of male primogeniture or lobolo or ritual circumcision, and where *clear* empirical life outcomes can be established, the Constitutional Court must set clear norms about what will and will not be tolerated.

(3) The Court – and other political institutions, from Parliament through the CGE, SAHRC and CRLC to CONTRALESA – can also help to establish the contours for meaningful engagement between members of the same traditional community can take place and allow for some settlement that might enable individuals heretofore treated as second class citizens of the sub-public to remain members of the community. Or, the 'meaningful engagement' might

enable different constituencies within the same traditional community to conceive of a manner in which the various parties can dissolve the links between them with a minimum of animus.

(4) The dissolution of a traditional community is no easy matter. The social capital built up by a community might be its most important asset. Moreover, communities with large stores of social capital are apt to possess similarly large stores of real capital. Courts or other mediating institutions may be required to determine how an appropriate divorce – and a concomitant dissolution of assets – occurs.

(5) The analysis of cases in the Constitutional Court, as well as our Equality Courts, suggest how remedial equilibration allows for (1) public sanction of retrogressive practices out of step with generally accepted norms of dignity and equal treatment, (2) remedies that enable second-class members of such communities to exit such communities as necessary and with adequate support to join and to create new sub-publics, and (3) recognition that as outré as the mores of some communities may be, they still supply the meaning that makes so many South African lives worth pursuing (even if others would rather not have them pursued.) Change, as I discuss in the Preface, and Chapters 1, 2, 3, is an ineradicable part of the human condition. Unfortunately, progress – even for hard-nosed realists like myself – never takes a linear path. We must do, as my father sagely said, the very best that we can with the resources and the capacity for creative solutions available to us. To expect more, of ourselves and others, is hubris.

12. *Minister of Home Affairs & Another v Fourie & Another*[129]

(a) *Finessing Flourishing*

Fourie engaged the question of whether same-sex couples were constitutionally entitled to enjoy the same status, entitlements and responsibilities as marriage law accords to heterosexual couples. The *Fourie* Court found that granting such status to same-sex couples would in no way attenuate the capacity of heterosexual couples to marry in the form they wished and according to the tenets of their religion. The Court then concluded that the common law and section 30(1) of the Marriage Act were inconsistent with [FC] s 9(1) and [FC] s 9(3) and [FC] s 10 to the extent that they made no provision for same-sex couples to enjoy the status, entitlements and responsibilities that they accord to heterosexual couples.

Of immediate moment is the remedy crafted by a majority of the Court. It has been summarized by the *Fourie* Court as follows:

- The common law definition of marriage is declared to be inconsistent with the Constitution and invalid to the extent that it does not permit same-sex couples to enjoy the status and the benefits coupled with the responsibilities it accords to heterosexual couples.
- The omission from section 30(1) of the Marriage Act 25 of 1961 after the words "or husband" of the words "or spouse" is declared to be inconsistent with the Constitution, and the Marriage Act is declared to be invalid to the extent of this inconsistency.
- These declarations of invalidity are suspended for 12 months from the date of this judgment to allow Parliament to correct the defects.

- Should Parliament not correct the defects within this period, Section 30(1) of the Marriage Act 25 of 1961 will forthwith be read as including the words "or spouse" after the words "or husband" as they appear in the marriage formula.[130]

From the perspective of the doctrine of shared constitutional interpretation, it might be argued that the Court's refusal to follow the simple proposal found in the papers of the Equality Project – or in Justice O'Regan's partial dissent – to 'read in' the words 'or spouse' after the words 'or husband' in the Marriage Act was correct.[131] Parliament, if one takes the Court's majority seriously, was invited to craft a remedy of its own device that will ensure that legal unions of same-sex life partners are accorded the same respect by the state as opposite-sex life partners.[132] Even if one agrees with Justice O'Regan – as I do – that no such invitation was warranted (given the precedents set by the Court on the rights of same sex couples) – the broader, normative 'Coverian' legitimacy afforded by Parliament's Civil Unions Act may have been worth the cost imposed by suspending the order of invalidity for a year while constitutionally compliant legislation was passed.[133] In short, the Republic of South Africa, and its citizens, were confronted with, and had to come to terms with, the revolutionary understanding of flourishing that informs the *Fourie* Court's judgment(s).[134]

(b) Negotiating between Conservative Flourishing and Revolutionary Flourishing[135]

Parliament appears to have had little interest in passing the Civil Union Act. It waited almost a full year (the period allotted by the Court) to come to terms with *Fourie*'s dictates. Parliament's resistance – a relatively clear function of its members' reluctance to recognize gay marriage as a constitutional entitlement – raises again the question of how the conservative breed and revolutionary strain of flourishing manifest in our Constitution can be squared with one another.

The *Fourie* Court captures much of what is at stake in all matters associational, and conservative and revolutionary forms of flourishing, when it writes:

> A democratic, universalistic, caring and aspirationally egalitarian society embraces everyone and accepts people for who they are. At the very least, it affirms that difference should not be the basis for exclusion, marginalisation and stigma. At best, it celebrates the vitality that difference brings to any society. ... The acknowledgment and acceptance of difference is particularly important in our country where for centuries group membership based on supposed biological characteristics such as skin colour has been the express basis of advantage and disadvantage. South Africans come in all shapes and sizes. The development of an active rather than a purely formal sense of enjoying a common citizenship depends on recognising and accepting people with all their differences, as they are. The Constitution thus acknowledges the variability of human beings (genetic and socio-cultural), affirms the right to be different, and celebrates the diversity of the nation. Accordingly, what is at stake is not simply a question of removing an injustice experienced by a particular section of the community. At issue is a need to affirm the very character of our society as one based on tolerance and mutual respect. The test of tolerance is not how one finds space for people with whom, and practices with which, one feels comfortable, but how one accommodates the expression of what is discomfiting. As was said by this Court in *Christian Education*, there are a number of constitutional provisions that underline the constitutional value of acknowledging diversity and pluralism in our society [ss 10, 15, s 16, 29, 30 and 31], and give a particular texture to the broadly

phrased right to freedom of association contained in s 18. Taken together, they affirm the right of people to self-expression without being forced to subordinate themselves to the cultural and religious norms of others, and highlight the importance of individuals and communities being able to enjoy what has been called the 'right to be different'. ... The strength of the nation envisaged by the Constitution comes from its capacity to embrace all its members with dignity and respect.[136]

This portion of the holding signals a significant victory for communities – traditional, cultural, linguistic, and religious – whose mores might not be on all fours with many of the other rights and values articulated in the Final Constitution.

However, as I have just noted in Chapter 7, the Constitutional Court's jurisprudence answers hard questions about the extent to which group identity in our many sub-publics should be tolerated and offers us useful guidance as to how the state ought to engage the religious, cultural and linguistic communities that make up the state and how those communities ought to engage one another. The *Fourie* Court writes:

[The amici's] arguments raise important issues concerning the relationship foreshadowed by the Constitution between the sacred and the secular. They underline the fact that in the open and democratic society contemplated by the Constitution, although the rights of non-believers and minority faiths must be fully respected, the religious beliefs held by the great majority of South Africans must be taken seriously. ... For many believers, their relationship[s] with God or [other transcendental entities] is central to all their activities. It concerns their capacity to relate in an intensely meaningful fashion to their sense of themselves, their community and their universe. ... [The associations they form] play a large and important part in public life, through schools, hospitals and poverty relief programmes. ... The test, whether majoritarian or minoritarian positions are involved, must always be whether the measure under scrutiny promotes or retards the achievement of human dignity, equality and freedom. The hallmark of an open and democratic society is its capacity to accommodate and manage difference of intensely-held world views and lifestyles in a reasonable and fair manner. The objective of the Constitution is to allow different concepts about the nature of human existence to inhabit the same public realm, and to do so in a manner that is not mutually destructive and that at the same time enables government to function in a way that shows equal concern and respect for all.[137]

As noted in Chapter 7, the *Fourie* Court commits itself to five propositions that are fundamental for our understanding of flourishing: (1) traditional, religious, cultural and linguistic communities are a critical source of meaning for the majority of South Africans; (2) traditional, religious, cultural and linguistic communities create institutions that support the material, intellectual, ethical and spiritual well-being of many South Africans; (3) religious, cultural and linguistic associations, as part of civil society, play an essential role in mediating the relationship between the state and its citizens; (4) traditional, religious, cultural and linguistic associations are entitled to articulate – and make manifest through action – their 'intensely held world views', they may not do so in a manner that unfairly discriminates against other members of South African society; (5) since the 'intensely held world views' and practices of various traditional religious, cultural and linguistic associations invariably excludes other members of South African society from some forms of membership and diminishes the nature of their participation when they are granted membership, such exclusion necessarily constitutes a *prima facie* case of unfair discrimination.

Can the *prima facie* burden of unfair discrimination be overcome? Should it? If we accept the *Fourie* Court's fifth proposition – which goes to the heart of the matter in conflicts between egalitarian concerns and associational rights – then South Africans, as members of a socially democratic constitutional state, are obliged to ask a number of other questions about the effects of exclusionary practices.

The easy question is whether communities possess the power to exclude members who initially agree to follow the rules of the community, but then subsequently refuse to do so. Of course they do.

The hard question contains multiple parts. Would South African society as a whole be better off if it eliminated those exclusionary practices that not only remove non-compliant individuals but prevent other individuals – who begin as outsiders – from gaining entrance into the community? What remedies do we have at the ready, if we are to take the hard question seriously?

The first part of the answer to the hard question turns primarily on access to those goods which individuals require in order to flourish. In 21st-century social democratic states – such as South Africa – there are no hard and fast lines between the public sphere and the private sphere (and the various goods they provide to individuals.) The result is that the Final Constitution affords no easy answers about what remains in the private domain and thus subject to some constitutional pre-commitment to non-interference. Instead, the Final Constitution – and super-ordinate legislation such as the Promotion of Equality and Prevention of Unfair Discrimination Act – is or should be primarily concerned with questions about individual and group access to the kind of goods that enable us to lead lives worth valuing, as we each come to understand them.

It is easy to conclude that clubs, associated and communities that have been the bastion of white male Christian privilege must open their doors to persons of all colours, all sexes and all religions. But what of the large stores of social capital that have been invested in such institutions, and what of that capital which continues to offer the possibility of significant returns to the original members (and future members)? Almost all meaningful actions occurs within the context of such self-perpetuating social networks of various kinds. As I have already contended, the wholesale trashing institutions that create and maintain large stores of real and figurative capital is a recipe for a very impoverished polity.

The answer to the first part of the hard question thus turns on features of both traditional subpublics and the broader Republic grounded in our basic law. We must interrogate the extent to which the practices of religious, cultural and linguistic communities are justifiable forms of discrimination in the furtherance of constitutionally legitimate ends, and, with somewhat greater discernment, assess the extent to which the state and other social actors can make equally legitimate claims on the kinds of goods available in these communal formations that cannot be accessed elsewhere.

The answer to the second part of the hard question arises when, as I argue elsewhere,[138] the state and other social actors cannot secure access to or make legitimate claims upon the kinds of goods made available in these communal formations. At this juncture, a court may, as has been noted above, have to rely upon forms of remedial equilibration in order to square both conservative strains and revolutionary forms of flourishing. In short, the subpublic engaged in the discriminatory behaviour and a Republic that sets its face squarely against such discrimination may be obliged to ensure ease of exit and the real and figurative capital necessary to ensure that otherwise second class citizens possess the material conditions and the immaterial goods necessary to 'seek justice elsewhere'.

13. Shilubana v Nwamitwa[139]

(a) The Facts, Findings and Holdings in Shilubana

In 1968 Ms Shilubana's father, Hosi Fofoza Nwamitwa, died without a male heir. Customary law at the time did not permit a woman to become Hosi. As a result, Ms Shilubana did not succeed him. Instead, Hosi Fofoza's brother, Richard Nwamitwa, succeeded him. However, some thirty years and a peaceful constitutional revolution later, the traditional authorities of the Valoyi community passed resolutions in 1996 and 1997 that held that Ms Shilubana would succeed Hosi Richard. Her succession was subsequently approved by the provincial government. Hosi Richard died in 2001. Not everyone was pleased to see Ms Shilubana's ascension to Hosi. Sidwell Nwamitwa, Richard's son, sought an interdict to prevent Ms Shilubana's installation. He claimed that he, as Hosi Richard's eldest son, was entitled to succeed his father. Both the Pretoria High Court and the Supreme Court of Appeal ruled in favour of Mr Nwamitwa.

The Constitutional Court reversed the rulings of both the Pretoria High Court and the Supreme Court of Appeal. The Court held that the High Court and the Supreme Court of Appeal had failed to acknowledge, appropriately, the power of and the manner in which traditional authorities could interpret and alter customary law. The Court placed particular emphasis on s 211(2) of the Constitution's injunction that all courts and state institutions must respect the right of traditional communities to develop their own law. Courts must come to understand the present practice (as well as the past practice) of traditional communities and ratify those developments that remain consistent with constitutional dictates. The *Shilubana* Court articulated the following multi-part test for constitutionally-influenced development of traditional norms and practice:

i. 'Where there is a dispute over the legal position under customary law, a court must consider both the traditions and the present practice of the community.'
ii. 'If development happens within the community, then the court must strive to recognise and [to] give effect to that development, to the extent consistent with adequately upholding the protection of rights.'
iii. 'The imperative of section 39(2) must be acted on when necessary, [but] deference should be paid to the development by a customary community of its own laws and customs where … possible.'
iv. 'Customary law must be permitted to develop, and the enquiry must be rooted in the contemporary practice of the community in question. Section 211(2) of the Constitution requires this. The legal status of customary law norms cannot depend simply on their having been consistently applied in the past, because that is a test which any new development must necessarily fail. Development implies some departure from past practice. A rule that requires absolute consistency with past practice before a court will recognise the existence of

> a customary norm would therefore prevent the recognition of new developments as customary law. [C]ourts applying laws which communities themselves no longer follow ... would stifle the recognition of the new rules adopted by the communities in response to the changing face of South African society. This result would be contrary to the Constitution and cannot be accepted.'[140]

The *Shilubana* Court, in applying this test to the instant matter, found that while the succession to the leadership of the Valoyi had operated in the past according to the principle of male primogeniture, the traditional authorities retained the authority to develop customary law. After promulgation of the Interim Constitution and the Final Constitution, the Valoyi authorities altered the traditional law in a manner consistent with the constitutional right to equality. The value of recognising the development by a traditional community of its own law in accordance with the Constitution was not outweighed by the need for legal certainty or the protection of communal rights. The Court found that the immediate change in Valoyi customary law did not create legal uncertainty. As a result, Mr Nwamitwa did not have a vested right to be Hosi. The Court concluded that the traditional authorities had the authority to develop their customary law under the Constitution, to ensure Ms Shilubana's ascension to Hosi and to conclude that Mr Nwamitwa did not have a right to be declared Hosi.

(b) A Nuanced Response to Flourishing when the Analysis is Driven by an Experimentalist Approach

Yes, *Shilubana* concerns a gender-inflected leadership succession battle in a traditional community. But the one thing that jumps out for experimental constitutionalist are the number and variety of applicants and amici, in addition to the respondent (who is not without support amongst the amici): (1) Tinyiko Lwandhlamuni Philla Nwamitwa Shilubana, First Applicant; Walter Mbizana Mbhalati, Second Applicant; District Control Officer, Third Applicant; The Premier: Limpopo Province Fourth Applicant; MEC for Local Government and Housing, Limpopo Fifth Applicant; House for Traditional Leaders, Sixth Applicant; Christina Somisa Nwamitwa, Seventh Applicant; Mathews T N Nwamitwa, Eighth Applicant; Ben Shipalana Ninth Applicant; Ernest Risaba, Tenth Applicant; Stone Ngobeni, Eleventh Applicant; Sidwell Nwamitwa, Respondent; Commission for Gender Equality, First Amicus Curiae; National Movement of Rural Women, Second Amicus Curiae; The Congress of Traditional Leaders of South Africa Third Amicus Curiae. No one can claim that the *Shilubana* Court lacked the benefit of hearing from numerous participants, with varying perspectives, and relatively unique access to information relevant to any final decision taken.

The second revelation is the bottom up quality of the Court's analysis. Having established the parameters for constitutional analysis – the right to equality, the right to dignity, the right to language and culture, the right to community practice of religion, culture and language, the power of traditional authorities to develop customary law and the manner in which customary law engages constitutional law – the Court spends the better part of its time tracing the factual and historical narrative behind Ms Shilubana's rise to Hosi of the Valoyi community. The Court does not deny that the Constitution remains the supreme law and the law by which all other law is measured.[141] However, in reaching its decision in *Shilubana*, the Court allows for various voices beyond its chambers to shape the constitutional norms at play.

The third pleasant surprise is that the Court's use of experimentalist tools enables it to chart successfully a path from conservative understandings to revolutionary conceptions of traditional law that stay true to the original moorings of customary norms and practices. I have no doubt that some readers of *Shilubana* will find its conclusion repugnant to their conception of African customary law. Could it be otherwise when so many voices are heard and when the conception of ascension to Hosi remains contested territory? Yet I have little doubt that in the context of constitutional adjudication, the *Shilubana* Court's method of analysis is largely beyond reproach. It takes the commitment to (traditional and revolutionary forms of) flourishing and experimentalist modes of investigation seriously.

(c) On Rolling Constitutional Norms: Mind the Gap between the Doctrine Rehearsed and the Doctrine Applied

Shilubana looks, on first blush, to be a textbook example of an experimentalist's approach to the determination of constitutional norms that cabin customary law. It does not take a top down approach – say, employing s 9(4) equality analysis to assess the validity of Valoyi practices past and present. In addition to its direct invitation to CONTRALESA and the National House of Traditional Leaders to participate in the proceedings, the Constitutional Court also allowed the Commission of Gender Equality and the National Rural Women's Movement to join the matter. It's difficult to imagine the Court engaging any more stakeholders as it strived to determine the contours of the Valoyi's living law. This exercise enables the *Shilubana* Court to arrive – without saying as much – at a truism about monarchy and passage of the throne: the Valoyi are no different than any other tribe, say the English, when it comes down to the passage of the crown from one generation to another. Just as the British crown was bathed in blood and subject to regular contestation, the Valoyi royal tradition, while less gruesome in many respects, has been equally hotly contested. Finally, the careful parsing of the Valoyi tradition allows the *Shilubana* Court to arrive at a conclusion that permits what I have called revolutionary flourishing.

The question that hangs over the final judgment is what work it will do for future courts and communities confronted with comparable conflicts over ascension to the leadership of a traditional community. The Court, rightfully so, looks to steer a careful path between the Scylla of tradition and the Charybdis of revolution. It acknowledges that customary norms develop over time and that they cannot be locked into past practice – especially under a Constitution that requires courts to consider present 'lived' practice when determining what the apposite rule is and what the outcome ought to be. Beyond that, the Court says little more. Such silence about what women in traditional, cultural and religious communities can expect from political authorities naturally lead commentators such as Cathi Albertyn to inveigh against 'the stubborn persistence of patriarchy' in traditional, cultural and religious communities.[142] And well she should: at the same time as she remembers that she is but one voice in a radically heterogeneous, quite conservative, hotly contested social order. South Africa is a densely populated, radically heterogeneous 'we'.

14. *Nyathi v Member of the Executive Council for the Department of Health Gauteng ('Nyathi I')*[143] *and*

15. *Minister for Justice and Constitutional Development v Nyathi ('Nyathi II')*[144]

(a) *Modelling Participatory Democracy and Institutional Comity in the Face of Contempt*

In *Nyathi I*, Mr Nyathi, the applicant, sought confirmation of a declaration that section 3 of the State Liability Act was inconsistent with the Constitution. The impugned portion of section 3 barred the execution, the attachment or any similar process against a state defendant or respondent or against any property of the state for the satisfaction of judgment debts. Mr Nyathi had, by the State's own admission, been treated negligently at Pretoria Academic Hospital. Mr Nyathi sued the MEC for Health, Gauteng for an amount of R1 496 000 and asked for an interim payment of R 317 700 to cover his medical and legal expenses pending the determination of the quantum of the state's liability. The Pretoria High Court approved this interim payment. Gauteng's MEC for Health failed to comply with the High Court's interim order. Mr Nyathi asked the High Court to declare section 3 of the State Liability Act unconstitutional and to force the MEC to execute the interim order. The High Court held that the Act's blanket ban on execution and attachment unjustifiably limited the right to equality and the right to access to courts and unjustifiably impaired ss 165(5) and 195(1)(f) of the Constitution. After finding section 3 of the State Liability Act unconstitutional, the High Court sought confirmation of the order in the Constitutional Court. The Constitutional Court, subsequent to an urgent hearing, ordered the Gauteng MEC for Health make good the applicant's request for interim costs and to demonstrate that it had discharged this debt. After a full hearing, the Court held that s 3 of the Act violated the right to equal protection of the law (in terms of s 9(1)), the right to dignity, right of access to courts, and the constitutional principles of judicial authority the accountability of the administrative arms of the state to the greater South African public. However, in confirming (and extending) the declaration of constitutional invalidity, the *Nyathi I* Court suspended the order for 12 months. It gave Parliament 12 months to promulgate legislation that would create an effective means of enforcement of money judgments against the state. The *Nyathi I* Court censured the state severely for its abject failure to discharge over 200 outstanding judgment debts. The *Nyathi I* Court then placed the state on strict terms (a) to provide it with details of all outstanding judgment debts and (b) to submit a plan to discharge all outstanding debts with alacrity.[145]

(b) *Shared Constitutional Interpretation and a Participatory Bubble*

The Executive undertook its responsibilities with some zeal, if not zest. Several reports from the Director-General and other parties, at the insistence of the Court, ensured that all outstanding debts were paid and that the state had a plan in place to avoid any future dereliction of duty.

The *Nyathi I* Court had, according to some commentators, placed upon Parliament an obligation to pass new legislation. But that reading misconstrues the actual content of the *Nyathi I* Court's judgment. Consistent with *Nyathi I*, the state could have adopted the position that it did not need new legislation, but preferred instead to adopt the proposition that state property could be as easily attached as private property with respect to the discharge of outstanding debts. Parliament chose not to adopt that route.

Instead, the Minister for Justice and Constitutional Development approached the *Nyathi II* Court with a request for an extension of the suspended order of invalidity handed down in *Nyathi I*. After noting the irony of being asked by the state for an extension for the promulgation of legislation designed to curb the failure of the state to respond with the appropriate degree of institutional comity, let alone alacrity, to court orders, the *Nyathi II* Court granted the request. It gave Parliament two more years to enact effective legislation. In the interim, it put in place a set of procedures that would enable judgment creditors to attach moveable state property owned by the responsible state party 'for the purposes of a sale in execution to satisfy the judgment debt'.[146] The Court also made it clear that it had tired both of waiting for Parliament in the instant matter and of the implicit contempt that various state institutions had generally demonstrated for court orders (including orders of the Constitutional Court itself.) The *Nyathi II* Court did not respond with a diktat. It invited the original parties, the intervenor and the amici – Mr Nyathi, the Minister for Justice and Constitutional Development, the Law Society of South Africa, the Legal Resources Centre, Freedom under Law, the Aids Law Project – as well as the Minister of Finance to provide more effective alternatives than the Court's preferred interim solution. The Court – unless it received more useful procedures – would craft an order that created a tailored attachment and execution procedure against state assets similar to that it had already articulated.

The Minister for Finance suggested that judgment creditors could approach the national treasury or the provincial treasury for the satisfaction of their judgment debts if the relevant state department failed to discharge its judgment debts. The Minister for Finance then recommended that that any amount paid by the treasury in question be set off against the budget allocation of the debtor department for the current or future financial year. Despite eliciting the ire of the amici and the intervening party – who accused various state parties of having violated repeatedly the rule of law in this case and others – the Court received useful advice from all concerned. The Court cobbled together a viable order from the best of the suggestions on offer from the Minister for Finance, Mr Nyathi, the amici and the intervening party.[147] From the perspective of shared constitutional interpretation, it is also worth noting that the new State Liability Act closely tracks the remedy the Court adopted in *Nyathi II*.

(c) On Shared Constitutional Interpretation and Participatory Bubbles: Mind the Gap between the Doctrine Rehearsed and the Doctrine Applied

Again, the Court's solicitation of participation from a broad array of parties looks like a paradigmatic example of shared constitutional interpretation. The Court, on its own steam, sought out the views of the Minister of Finance and made those views a part of the Court's remedy. The *Nyathi II* Court also took on board suggestions by the applicant, the intervenor and the amici about how best to ensure that state judgment debts are paid and, moreover, discharged with alacrity. In addition, the Court requested that the state provide an account of all the outstanding judgment debts on its books and a plan as to how the state would acquit itself of such future arrears.

Could one ask for more? One could look back at the degree of contempt shown for court orders in a broad array of housing cases and easily arrive at the conclusion that that we are likely to see continuing contempt by various state parties in this arena. Recent reports by the Auditor-General give us little reason to expect otherwise. Moreover, the failure of Parliament to address the Court's concerns in *Nyathi I* places a question mark over the state's commitment to following the weakest branch's instructions.[148]

That said, it would seem churlish to fail to acknowledge the steps the Court has taken to devise optimal solutions to the persistent disdain displayed by the co-ordinate branches for its edicts. As Michael Bishop has shown in his incisive discussion of meaningful engagement, the Court has maintained on-going supervision in recent housing cases in large part because multiple stakeholder arrangements could overcome information deficits and secure greater normative legitimacy. Political doctrine cases are an altogether different matter and turn more appropriately on a clear conception of the form of democracy the Constitution requires. While Bishop may disagree with the substantive outcome in such politically charged matters as *Merafong*, supervisory orders are an inappropriate mechanism for their resolution. As Theunis Roux has made clear, some cases offer the Court the opportunity to establish clear and compulsory principles, while other cases suggest caution, and a case-by-case accretion of binding precedent. Such acknowledgement of the Court's ability to establish general norms at the same time as it takes account of changing circumstances seems very much of a piece – and at peace – with the theory of experimental constitutionalism adumbrated in these pages.

16. *Residents of Joe Slovo Community, Western Cape v Thubelisha Homes & Others ('Joe Slovo I')*[149]

17. *Residents of Joe Slovo Community, Western Cape v Thubelisha Homes & Others ('Joe Slovo II')*[150]

Another one or two housing cases have enabled the Court to further refine the requirements of meaningful engagement and, in so doing, to inch ever closer to what a truly experimentalist court might be expected to do. In *Residents of Joe Slovo Community, Western Cape v Thubelisha Homes & Others* (*'Joe Slovo I'*), the Court addressed the constitutionality of the state's controversial N2 Gateway project. The project, as planned, would have moved approximately 20 000 residents in existing informal settlements along the N2 highway to Delft – a community some 15 km away. The residents resisted the removal. The government sought support for the removal through an eviction order.

The Western Cape High Court granted the eviction. Hlophe J held that the government agencies seeking the eviction had complied with the requirements of the Prevention of Illegal Eviction from and Unlawful Occupation of Land Act 19 of 1998 ('PIE').[151] The High Court action succeeded, in large part, because the government claimed that the eviction's primary purpose was to enable the government to upgrade and redevelop the settlement (a) for the current occupants and (b) in terms of the government's housing policy. The residents appealed directly to the Constitutional Court.

In many respects, the *Joe Slovo I* Court's various members allowed the facts to speak eloquently for themselves. The Court found that many of the residents of the Joe Slovo settlement had lived there for as long as 15 years, that the City of Cape Town had never previously tried to remove them or intimated that they might be removed, and that the City had, in terms of its constitutional and legislative obligations, provided substantial on-going permanent services (streets, electricity, and basic municipal services.) The City's own actions reflected its recognition of the settlement's relative permanence and the obligation to treat its denizens in a humane manner until more adequate housing (and services) could be provided.[152]

While the *Joe Slovo I* Court – in a five opinion judgment – reversed the High Court's ruling, its members split on the question as to whether the state had 'meaningfully engaged' the community regarding the removal. The different takes on this new requirement are reflected in the opinions of Ngcobo J, O'Regan J and Sachs J. According to Ngcobo J:

> The requirement of engagement flows from the need to treat residents with respect and care for their dignity. ... It enables the government to understand the needs and concerns of individual households so that, where possible, it can take steps to meet their concerns. ... . The goal of meaningful engagement is to find a mutually acceptable solution to the difficult issues confronting the government and the residents in the quest to provide adequate housing. This can only be achieved if all sides approach the process in good faith and with a willingness to listen and, where possible, to accommodate one another. ... Ultimately, the decision lies with the government. The decision must, however, be informed by the concerns raised by the residents during the process of engagement.[153]

In sum, while the ultimate decision may lie with the government, and be upheld if reasonable, a court undertaking reasonableness analysis must assess whether the process of engagement treated potential evictees with dignity and whether the government made sincere efforts to meet the concerns of the persons to be removed. By tying the process of engagement to the value of dignity, Ngcobo J places a weighty thumb – the Court's dignity jurisprudence – on the scale in favour of the persons opposing eviction.

Justice O'Regan's approach to meaningful engagement is somewhat more formal or process-driven, and may appear to leave applicants with little more than the right to be heard:

> Th[e] purpose [of engagement] is to give affected parties an opportunity to be heard on a decision before it is finally made. Fair process improves the quality of decisions and establishes their legitimacy. However, it should not result in unnecessary and prolix requirements that may strangle government action.[154]

In fairness to Justice O'Regan, by requiring a hearing, or multiple hearings, the Court creates a richer administrative record that forces the state to take cognizance of the needs of the potentially dispossessed and gives the Court a fuller record against which to assess the reasonableness of the government's plans for post-eviction housing.

However, the opinion that best connects (a) shared constitutional interpretation between the courts and other branches of government in terms of setting norms and (b) the participatory bubbles that enable enhanced participation and greater extraction of information relevant for optimal decision-making is penned by Justice Sachs:

> This case compels us to deal in a realistic and principled way with what it means to be a South African living in a new constitutional democracy. It concerns the responsibilities of government to secure the ample benefits of citizenship promised for all by the Constitution. It expands the concept of citizenship beyond traditional notions of electoral rights and claims for diplomatic protection, to include the full substantive benefits and entitlements envisaged by the Constitution for all the people who live in the country and to whom it belongs. At the same time it focuses on the reciprocal duty of citizens to be active, participatory and responsible and to make their own individual and collective contributions towards the realisation of the benefits and entitlements they claim for themselves, not to speak of the well-being of the community as a whole. When all is said and done, and the process has run its course, the authorities and the families will still be connected in on-going constitutional relationships. It is to everyone's advantage that they be encouraged to get beyond the present impasse and work together once more.[155]

Sachs J captures, better than virtually anyone, anywhere else in the Court's entire oeuvre, the on-going reciprocal relationship between citizens and a truly robust democratic state. Sachs J emphasizes how, after the participatory bubble of a particular conflict has burst, and the various stakeholders have returned to their regular lives, the residue of active citizenship and responsive government remains. First, the parties have not only learned more about the particular problems that forced the immediate litigation and engagement. The state has learned something more about the communities that they govern. The stakeholders have learned more about the political and social processes that govern their lives. Second, in keeping with the commitment to experimentalism, governments and citizens throughout the country should take away lessons on housing and evictions that can be profitably applied to future conflicts. So, although Sachs J refers to a two-way street of engagement, the better metaphor, as I noted in Chapter 6, is a piazza. In the piazza, members of the public, governed alike, meet again and again, shares new information and reflects upon the community's collective wisdom – as active citizens and politicians in a republic do.[156]

Despite their difference in views, notice how – in their order – the various members of the *Joe Slovo* Court push the opposing parties into the piazza. Although the Court granted the eviction, it did so subject to a range of conditions that required continued interaction between the residents and the government. The Court framed the conditions for meaningful engagement over relocation between the parties as follows:

- ascertainment of the names, details and relevant personal circumstances of those who are to be affected by each relocation;
- the exact time, manner and conditions under which the relocation of each affected household will be conducted;
- the precise temporary residential accommodation units to be allocated to those persons to be relocated;
- the need for transport to be provided to those to be relocated;
- the need for transport of the possessions of those to be relocated;

- the provision of transport facilities to the affected residents from the temporary residential accommodation units to amenities, including schools, health facilities and places of work;
- the prospect in due course of the allocation of permanent housing to those relocated to temporary residential accommodation units, including information regarding their current position on the housing waiting list, and the provision of assistance to those relocated with the completion of application forms for housing subsidies; and
- a report back to Court on the implementation of the order and on the allocation of permanent housing opportunities to those persons affected by this order by 1 December 2009.[157]

As Michael Bishop and Jason Brickhill note, while the meaningful engagement component of the order appears

> procedural in nature, the Court's order as to engagement has a clearly substantive aim: to minimise the prospect of homelessness or other hardship for the individuals being evicted, relocated and, eventually, permanently housed by building in safeguards to ensure that individuals do not fall through programmatic cracks. The order develops the importance already assigned to engagement as an element of the s 26 right to housing.[158]

The eviction order is made contingent upon two conditions: (a) meaningful engagement with respect to the relocation; (2) court-determined standards for any temporary accommodation prior to permanent re-settlement. A failure to meet either condition would result in a withdrawal of the order of eviction. Appropriate pressure is placed upon the state to create a scheme – a la *51 Olivia Road* – to accommodate individuals and families. The individuals and families concerned have a reciprocal obligation to participate in the structures designed to address the problem with which they are confronted. The order then compels the parties to agree to a timetable and any outstanding issues that might block the settlement. Although an eviction order dangles over the heads of the applicants, no removal could take place until 'alternative' accommodation that met the 'specific requirements' of the Court's order had been arranged. The respondents were, in addition, required to go over the details of the relocation and to provide assistance with any move. But the move was not necessarily a foregone conclusion for the Joe Slovo residents. The respondents were further 'directed to allocate 70% of the "Breaking New Ground" houses to be built at the site of Joe Slovo to the current and former residents of Joe Slovo who apply for and qualify for this housing.'[159] Thus the *Joe Slovo I* Court ensured that a significant cohort of the current residents would benefit from the planned permanent housing to be built on the site. To ensure that meaningful engagement resulted in meaningful action, the Court retained supervision over the order and required the parties to report back to the Court within a year regarding progress made and compliance with the Court's dictates. In short, any order of eviction (a) had to guarantee appropriate provision for the safe, dignified and humane relocation of the settlement's residents and (b) had to promise that the settlement's residents must be allocated a significant proportion of the new houses to be built on the site of the current Joe Slovo settlement and (c) that the preceding two processes had to occur in terms of meaningful engagement between the occupants of the settlement and the government agencies responsible for adequate housing and municipal services.[160]

The process of meaningful engagement did not result in a meaningful agreement between all the parties concerned. After one deadline passed, another was requested. During these discussions, the MEC for Housing suggested that the relocation order might be prohibitively expensive and that an upgrade to the existing settlement would make eviction unnecessary. For the next half year, negotiations between the parties turned on the possibility of an in situ upgrade. Indeed, a joint steering committee was created to work out the technical features of the government's proposal. The eviction order originally sought by the government and granted by the Court apparently no longer lay on the table.

In *Joe Slovo II,* the Court requested that both the residents and the MEC lodge affidavits that stated that the eviction order was no longer necessary. So they did. The *Joe Slovo II* Court noted that it possessed the power to vary orders as necessary, and where justice and equity so required. But it added the following qualifier:

> There may be some force in the argument that there is no reason in logic or policy why an order that is made because it is just and equitable to make it should not be susceptible to rescission when justice and equity require that course. Indeed, it seems illogical for this Court to have the power to vary an order issued on the basis that it was just and equitable when changing circumstances require, but not to have the power to discharge an order when the dictates of justice and equity require. Common sense tells us, and we must emphasise, that there is a fundamental difference between the variation of an order and its rescission. That difference requires that orders of this Court ought not to be discharged lightly. In our view, something more than a change in circumstances pointing to a different justice and equity conclusion is required.[161]

The order in *Joe Slovo II* reads:

> (a) There have been no adequate steps by the government to carry out the supervised eviction order made by this Court. The order has for all intents and purposes been left in abeyance.
> (b) There is no intention to proceed with the supervised eviction order as granted.
> (c) The order cannot be executed absent agreement between the parties or a complex amendment to the order.
> (d) The order relates to thousands of people.
> (e) The circumstances that motivated this Court to grant the supervised eviction order have ceased to exist.
> (f) There is no reason why the threat of eviction, in all the circumstances, should continue to disturb the applicants.[162]

Joe Slovo I and II demonstrate, collectively, virtually all the virtues of experimental constitutionalism and the potential power of court-supervised polyarchy.

a. Shared Constitutional Interpretation

In the true spirit of shared interpretation, the Constitutional Court first handed down a detailed order that created a framework within which the parties could meaningfully engage the constitutional and statutory rights in play as well as reach a concrete outcome with which all the parties would be satisfied. Surprisingly, the grant of power to the denizens of the settlement and the MEC to work out an accord resulted in an outcome that the *Joe Slovo I* Court did not anticipate – a rejection of the framework. In keeping with dictates of an experimentalist regime, the Court noted that while a discharge of an order is not a matter to be taken lightly, should the parties to a matter arrive at a conclusion that serves the ends of justice better, then the Court should rescind its original order. Rather than forcing the parties to accept a solution – and a reading of the Act and the Constitution – that the other spheres of government and the citizenry affected deemed suboptimal, the Court acknowledged that the parties might, ultimately, have a better, birds-eye view of what worked best.

One must take note of the disaggregation between interpretation and remedy. Nothing in *Joe Slovo II* suggests that the Constitutional Court had reconsidered its reading of PIE or s 26 of the Constitution. What became clear, after a year, was that Court's anticipated remedy – forced engagement on the condition of humane relocation – had led the parties to reconsider their original positions. Given the flexible nature of meaningful engagement, however, it is reasonable to conclude that the Court, other spheres of government and similarly situated communities will, in the future, come to consider their constitutional and statutory positions *differently* in light of the *different* outcomes in *Joe Slovo I* and in *Joe Slovo II*.

b. Participatory Bubbles

Joe Slovo I and in *Joe Slovo II* possesses all the hallmarks of a functional participatory bubble. First, they may not (necessarily) be limited to the initial parties to the litigation. Other interested stakeholders – amici et al – may participate. The aim, again, is two-fold: greater elicitation of information; greater normative legitimacy of any decision ultimately taken. Second, the other feature of these participatory bubbles is that they may not remain within the domain of the courts. The parties to *Joe Slovo I* and in *Joe Slovo II* ultimately arrived at a mutually beneficial agreement provoked, but not determined, by the Court. Third, participatory bubbles lose their cohesion – and the pressure to produce better than zero-sum outcomes – if courts fail to articulate the norms within which a preferred solution is meant to occur and refuse to maintain some degree of oversight over the deliberative process. In *Joe Slovo I* and in *Joe Slovo II*, the parties could only reach an agreement because (a) the Court placed them under fairly strict, procedural cum substantive requirements and (b) the Court required and responded to regular reports from the parties after the initial order was put in place. Ultimately, the Court's decision to discharge its order is consistent with a legal system that is both forward and lateral looking – and not focused on placing parties back in their original position:[163]

c. Chastened Deliberation and Destablization Rights

The destabilization rights in *Joe Slovo I* and in *Joe Slovo II* were shaped by the Court's initial order. While the order was only partially implemented – in terms of the report process – the rest of the order placed the state and the inhabitants of the settlement on relatively equal footing. The requirement of engagement (with conditions attached) forced the state back to the table. Moreover, the Court's order possessed sufficient substance that only fairly generous terms for relocation would satisfy the terms for eviction. The Court's order shook up the status quo.

It seems clear – from the history of both *Joe Slovo I* and in *Joe Slovo II* – that deliberation did not drive the resolution. Action did. Were deliberation the primary driver, one would have expected pre-litigation engagement to provide an optimal response. Instead, the power of government to secure an eviction order in the High Court was countered by the Constitutional Court's substantive meaningful engagement requirements. The two remedies, in tandem, eviction on the one hand, appropriate alternative accommodation on the other, forced the two parties to knock heads and come up with a solution in which both came out better off. Less an ideal speech situation than a squeeze play.

d. Reflexivity and Flattened Hierarchies

Both *Joe Slovo I* and in *Slovo II* began as rather top-down command and control operations. In the first instance, the state sought evictions in order to realize its vision of an optimal housing scheme. The courts followed suit: either through the grant of an eviction order, or a fairly rigid set of procedures for meaningful engagement. Once the eviction orders were tied to strict terms of meaningful engagement and humane alternative accommodation, the hierarchy of state and citizenry was partially flattened if not entirely levelled.

Reflexivity appears a number of related forms. For example, although the state secured an unencumbered eviction order in the High Court, the *Joe Slovo I* Court, the settlement dwellers and the amici forced the state to reconsider its original position. The Court, fascinatingly enough, was then pressed by the state and the settlement dwellers to reconsider its own original position in *Joe Slovo I*. In *Joe Slovo II,* the Court found itself in a rather unprecedentted self of circumstances: having handed down a fairly restrictive meaningful engagement order (designed to push the parties to a particular outcome), only to have to discharge the order when the parties arrived at a more optimal solution. Parties in future eviction and houses cases have much to learn from the forward and lateral looking manner in which *Joe Slovo II* was resolved.

e. A Court that Aggressively Learns

At the time of writing, the Constitutional Court continues to experiment with shared constitutional interpretation and the use of participatory bubbles with respect to its housing jurisprudence. The Constitutional Court has extended its housing jurisprudence beyond meaningful engagement to 'linkage'. Linkage recognizes, on the basis of past learning, that (1) meaningful engagement, (2) alternative accommodation and (3) eviction, cannot be treated as discrete pieces of South Africa's housing puzzle. No eviction order can be granted without a municipality (and/or a private land owner) first ensuring that *proper* alternative accommodation has been arranged prior to the eviction and, as necessary, before the relocation accommodation has been put in place.[164].

18. *Head of Department, Mpumalanga Department of Education & Another v Hoërskool Ermelo & Another*[165]

Hoërskool Ermelo seems me to be one of the perfect places with which to begin to wind up this analysis of recent case lae through the prism of constitutional theory founded upon experimentalism and flourishing. *Ermelo*, for that purpose, serves as the terminus point for a decentralized 15 year national experiment conducted by numerous stakeholders (the national government, the provincial governments, school governing bodies, principals, parents and learners) with respect to the question of whether South Africa and the Constitution are committed to single medium schools that rebuff learners on the ostensible basis of cultural and linguistic autonomy. As we have seen in Chapter 6, the answer is 'No!' At the same time, the Constitutional Court and the national government, with its first additional language policies, have initiated related if belated enquiring into the potential virtues of multilingualism as the basis for a society of truly equally citizens. With respect to individual flourishing, this new experimental hypothesizes that most learners are best served by not 'reading the market' and opting for English tuition alone. Instead, the new hypothesis could suggests that our learners will likely flourish in an educational environment that provides access both to mother tongue instruction and what many parents believe to be the language of life-time opportunity.

(a) Procedural Issues and Substantive Issues

As discussed at length in Chapter 6, *Hoërskool Ermelo* raised two discrete sets of issues. Did the Head of Department (HoD) of the Mpumalanga Department of Education follow the correct procedures in addressing the language policy and the admissions criteria adopted by the School Governing Body of Hoërskool Ermelo? The Constitutional Court found – as is often the case in education cases – that the correct procedure had not been followed. Did the HoD possess the power, under s 22(1) of the South African Schools Act, to withdraw a function of the SGB if he had good reason to believe that such powers were not reasonably exercised? Yes. It did not follow, however, that the withdrawal of an SGB could occure in the absence of due process. As a consequence, the HoD's decision to alter the language policy of Hoërskool Ermelo – while substantively sound – was reversed because of procedural irregularities. The *Hoërskool Ermelo* Court did, however, invite the HoD to report back to the Court on the language needs of learners in the Ermelo school district before the 2010 school year. The invitation – found in the Court's remedy – indicated the Court's interest in ensuring that all learners received instruction in their language of choice where it was both reasonably practical to do so and other critical desiderata of fairness and historical redress had been met. The Hoërskool Ermelo SGB was likewise invited to offer new proposals on its language policy in light of the Court's finding that the current policy of the undersubscribed single medium school was manifestly unconstitutional. It is to the meaning of this second finding that I now turn.

(b) Flourishing and Shared Constitutional Interpretation

As previously noted in Chapter 6, the most litigated line of education cases (thus far) has turned on the ability of single medium schools to rebuff students on 'cultural' and 'linguistic' grounds. In virtually every case, black learners had requested admission to single medium Afrikaans speaking public schools and asked that they receive instruction in English. In virtually every case, the refusal of admission on 'cultural' and 'linguistic' grounds looked to be a place holder for exclusion on 'racial' grounds.

After a decade of experimentation with single medium public schools and parallel or dual medium public schools, South African case law, education statutes, sector specific regulations and education department directives support the following three-fold proposition: (1) the Constitution clearly bars the refusal of admission on the basis of race; (2) linguistic and associational interests may occasionally trump equity concerns where there is no sign of overt discrimination and where learners who wish to receive instruction in another language, say English, Zulu or Sepedi, have meaningful access to (say, Sepedi-speaking, Zulu-speaking or English-speaking) schools that provide a roughly equal and generally adequate education as compared to the schools (say, Afrikaans-instruction only) from which the students have been turned away; and (3) learners have *no* constitutional right to single medium public schools under s 29(2) of the Constitution.

The Constitutional Court's decision in *Hoërskool Ermelo* put that three-fold proposition beyond dispute.[166] Deputy Chief Justice Moseneke's opinion makes transparent the Court's lack of patience with the school's intransigence with respect to language policy – and its refusal of admission of black students who wish to be taught in English:

> The case arises in the context of continuing deep inequality in our educational system, a painful legacy of our apartheid history. The school system in Ermelo illustrates the disparities sharply. The learners-per-class ratios in Ermelo reveal startling disparities which point to a vast difference in resources and of the quality of education. ... And therefore, an unequal access to education entrenches historical inequity since it perpetuates socio-economic disadvantage. ... [W]hite public schools were hugely better resourced than black schools. They were lavishly treated by the apartheid government. ... On the other hand, formerly black public schools have been, and by and largely remain, scantily resourced. ... That is why perhaps the most abiding and debilitating legacy of our past is an unequal distribution of skills and competencies acquired through education. ... Of course, vital parts of the 'patrimony of the whole' are indigenous languages which, but for the provisions of s 6 of the Constitution, languished in obscurity and underdevelopment with the result that, at high-school level, none of these languages have acquired their legitimate roles as effective media of instruction and vehicles for expressing cultural identity. ... And that perhaps is the collateral irony of this case. Learners whose mother tongue is not English, but rather one of our indigenous languages, together with their parents, have made a choice to be taught in a language other than their mother tongue. This occurs even though it is now well settled that, especially in the early years of formal teaching, mother-tongue instruction is the foremost and the most effective medium of imparting education. ... *However, I need say no more about this irony because the matter does not arise for adjudication.* For purposes of this case, the crucial provision is s 29(2) of the Constitution. ... The provision is made up of two distinct but mutually reinforcing parts. The first part places an obvious premium on receiving education in a public school in a language of choice. That right, however, is

> internally modified because the choice is available only when it is 'reasonably practicable'. When it is reasonably practicable to receive tuition in a language of one's choice will depend on all the relevant circumstances of each particular case. These would include the availability of and accessibility to public schools, their enrolment levels, the medium of instruction of the school that its governing body has adopted, the language choices that learners and their parents make, and the curriculum options offered. In short, the reasonableness standard built into s 29(2)(a) imposes a context-sensitive understanding of each claim for education in a language of choice. ... The second part of s 29(2) of the Constitution protects the right to be taught in the language of one's choice. It is an injunction on the State to consider all reasonable educational alternatives which are not limited to, but include, single-medium institutions. In resorting to an option, such as a single or parallel or dual medium of instruction, the State must take into account what is fair, feasible and satisfies the need to remedy the results of past racially discriminatory laws and practices.[167]

However, as noted in Chapter 6, the Deputy Chief Justice does not pin the possibility of learner flourishing solely upon their ability to secure instruction in English. In a remarkable aside, the Deputy Chief Justice questions whether the majority of South African learners are well-served by choosing English as their primary language of instruction. He contends that they would be better served by pursuing dual medium instruction that embraces their African mother tongue.

Again: this 'collateral irony', as the Deputy Chief Justice puts it, is not meant to be ironic at all. The Deputy Chief Justice recognizes the possibility of a second lost generation of learners – not through the imposition of a language of instruction, but through an understandable misapprehension amongst many parents regarding the language instruction that will serve their children best. In reading 'the market', a significant percentage parents of learners have concluded that the flourishing of their child hinges on a mastery of English from the very entry of learners into school. The Deputy Chief Justice calls that reading into question. As I previously noted, in policy circles a consensus is building around the conclusion that the de facto default position of English as the primary language of instruction from primary school onwards has not served South African learners well. But the Deputy Chief Justice's remark appeals to the two different conceptions of flourishing identified earlier – the traditional and the revolutionary. The Deputy Chief Justice is clearly concerned that the majority of young South Africans are, because of new form of hegemony (cultural, as opposed to political), losing touch with who they are and the communities from which they (can) draw meaning. He is also rightly alarmed by illiteracy and innumeracy rates that place South Africa 45th out of 45 developing countries and where only 1 out of 3 learners who begin garde one actually graduate from grade 12 with a high school degree.[168]

The causes of such woeful results cannot be traced to a single source. The Deputy Chief Justice is quite aware that students and teachers alike are ill-served by a system that makes the already arduous task of teaching and learning that much more difficult. No revolutionary form of flourishing – where new vistas open up to learners once they have mastered a complex array of symbolic tools – can occur under conditions where the language used to convey these tools remain largely impenetrable.

A third, largely unstated ground for Moseneke DCJ's remarks exist. He takes subtle aim at first language English speakers. Just as Jonathan Jansen has criticized first language Afrikaans-speaking communities for reinforcing their isolation and leaving their children ill-equipped to live a multi-lingual society,[169] so too must the Deputy Chief Justice be read as calling the lassitude and commitment of white English speakers into question. Some 70 years ago, T J Haarhoff, wrote:

> There is increasing ignorance of the second language; ignorance brings a feeling of inferiority, and that in turn brings aggressive assertion that it is a good thing to be unilingual and that strength lies in isolationism. Let us save our children from isolationism. The adult, with all the worries of a busy life and the handicap of an unfavourable environment, finds it difficult to acquire a new language and to break down group barriers; to a child it is "child's play". The world is moving away from the isolationist principle. … Fullness of life, educationally or spiritually is not comparable with the barbed-wire fences of racial politics. With the sun of a new world rising over the grandeur of our limitless veld, the darkness of estranging barriers will yield; it will yield before the creative inspiration of giving ourselves to South Africa – ourselves undivided to her undivided.[170]

The above words, written at a very different time, in vastly different context, contain a contemporary resonance. Haarhoff and Malherbe can be read as maintaining that genuine reconciliation, dignity and equal citizenship can only be achieved in multilingual, heterogeneous societies when groups learn the language of the other groups with whom they share political sovereignty. (That Haarhoff and Malherbe understood reconciliation, race and the 'other' solely in terms of English-Afrikaans give their words a bitterly ironic bite.)

Seventy years later, the idea that understanding the 'other' through language retains its force with respect to the as yet unfolfilled promise of national reconciliation and genuinely equal citizenship. Only the players and the petitioners have changed. Most black South Africans have done their share of heavy lifting when it comes to overcoming problems associated with race, language and understanding the 'other'. The same cannot be said for most white South Africans.

However, now that black South Africans control the political levers of power, and possess significantly increased economic and social clout, this barrier to mutual understanding and equal concern and respect is under challenge. Over the past several years, the state and the Constitutional Court have turned their attention to public school language policy. Although their respective legal and policy aims differ somewhat in scope and target, their underlying motivations remain much the same.

Both the Court and the government wish to ensure that the 9 official African languages are treated with same degree of respect accorded English and Afrikaans in our public schools. Fair enough. It's taken long enough.

For sound pedagogical reasons, they want to ensure that mother tongue instruction and dual medium tuitionis offered from initial entry into our primary schools. At the same time, all parties are aware that the state's purse, the availability of appropriately trained teachers and the adequacy of existing textbooks across all 11 languages currently place cognizable and constitutionally-recognized limits on our capacity to deliver immediately upon this promise.

Despite how *Ermelo* and the 2012 First Additional Language Policy Statement may read, both the State and our highest court clearly want School Governing Bodies to take responsibility for the determination and the execution of language policy. Most SGBs have.

The bottom line is that if all citizens are to enjoy the full benefits afforded us by our Constitution, then we need to secure an education that provides for that possibility. By limiting instruction to English and Afrikaans, many learners are denied these entitlements. Second class linguistic skills invariably re-entrench second class status.

The state and the Constitutional Court understand that our radically, heterogeneous society will never coalesce into a single nation until we are able to speak rationally and respectfully to one another. The new policies allow us to look *inward* and protect our particular community's linguistic heritage, while demanding that we also look *outward* toward the broader South African landscape and come to appreciate that learning another language is essential if we are ever to truly understand one another and build a 'rainbow nation' truly deserving of the appellation.

Thus, as I noted earlier, as one experiment in education seems to have reached its denouement (the end of the autonomy of single medium public schools), the Court proposes a new experiment: multilingualism as a mechanism for both the transmission of knowledge to learners and the connection of learners to the communities from whence they come and to communities with whom they must inevitably engage. Moreover, *Ermelo* offers the possibility of flourishing in both its conservative strain and its revolutionary form.

19. *Governing Body of the Juma Musjid Primary School & Others v Ahmed Asruff Essay N.O. and Others*[171]

Ermelo might have been a great place to end our analysis of the case law had *Juma Musjid Primary School* not come along. *Juma Musjid Primary School* tests – and expands – our notions of flourishing, shared constitutional interpretation and participatory bubbles in ways no other Constitutional Court judgment has to date.

The constitutional matter arose out of a dispute between the Juma Musjid Trust (Trust), the owner of the private property, the Member of the Executive Council for Education for KwaZulu-Natal (MEC), the School Governing Body (SGB) for Juma Musjid Primary School and the learners and parents at the school. The trust, a private entity, had for some time leased the land to the government. The government had, in turn, used the property for maintaining a primary school.[172] The dispute arose when the Trust and the MEC of Education for KwaZulu-Natal could not conclude an agreement under the South African Schools Act regarding continued tenancy by the province and the school. The Trust then secured an eviction order in the High Court. The Supreme Court of Appeal upheld the order.

Unlike the courts below, the Constitutional Court was not so ready to allow private interests to trump public interests. In addition, the polycentric nature of the conflict – trust, school, SGB, teachers, parents and learners – made any possibility of a simple binary resolution impossible. So, instead of hearing the merits of the matter immediately, and because the new school year was relatively close at hand (April 2010), the Court issued a provisional order that directed the MEC to engage meaningfully with the Trustees and the SGB in an effort to resolve the dispute and permit the continued operation of the school.[173] More importantly for my analysis, the Court framed the discussions to be had by all the concerned parties within the following normative rubric:

- The Trustees had a negative obligation in terms of s 8 of the Constitution – (direct horizontal application) – and a constitutional duty in terms of s 29(1) of the Constitution not to infringe the right of the learners to access to a basic education.
- Given that obligation, the Trustees had acted reasonably in approaching the High Court for an eviction order – however its reasonable behaviour did not constitute sufficient reason for the High Court to grant the eviction order; the High Court had failed to consider properly the best interests of the learners and their right to a basic education.
- The MEC had a primarily positive obligation to provide access to schools with respect to the learners' right to a basic education, and had thus far failed to discharge that duty.
- If meaningful engagement between the parties – subject to this framework – failed, the MEC was obliged to take steps to secure alternative placements for the learners. In addition, the MEC was required to file a report setting out, among other things, the steps that she had taken to ensure the learners' right to a basic education had been secured.

The Constitutional Court then asked the parties to reach a resolution in light of the above gloss placed upon the constitutional and common law rights and obligations of the parties. The parties could not meet the Court's desiderata. As of 25 November 2010, the parties, having failed to reach an accommodation, reported back to the Court as to the steps that had been taken to discharge their various obligations. The Court first noted that the closure of the school had become inevitable. However, it then observed that the MEC's report was insufficient to the assigned task of ensuring adequate placement for the learners in 2011. It requested a second report. Upon receipt of the second report, the Court reached the following conclusions: (1) the learners' rights under FC s 29(1) had, finally, been satisfied, given that alternative arrangements for the placement of the children for the 2011 school-year had been made; (2) given the alternative accommodation, the Court then granted the eviction order requested by the Trust and ordered the eviction to take place at the end of the school year - 11 December 2010; and (3) with the institutional comity that shared constitutional interpretation requires firmly in mind, the Court expressed its displeasure with MEC's conduct in the matter and ordered the MEC to pay the (substantial) costs of the litigation in the High Court, Supreme Court of Appeal and the Constitutional Court.[174]

(a) Flourishing

The Court made the connection between education and flourishing, and the material means required for flourishing, in the following manner:

> The significance of education, in particular basic education for individual and societal development in our democratic dispensation in the light of the legacy of apartheid, cannot be overlooked. The inadequacy of schooling facilities, particularly for many blacks was entrenched by the formal institution of apartheid, after 1948, when segregation even in education and schools in South Africa was codified. Today, the lasting effects of the educational segregation of apartheid are discernible in the systemic problems of inadequate facilities and the discrepancy in the level of basic education for the majority of learners. … [B]asic education is an important socio-economic right directed, among other things, at promoting and developing a child's personality, talents and mental and physical

> abilities to his or her fullest potential. Basic education also provides a foundation for a child's lifetime learning and work opportunities. To this end, access to school – an important component of the right to a basic education guaranteed to everyone by section 29(1)(a) of the Constitution – is a necessary condition for the achievement of this right.[175]

However, it's fair to say that one of the most compelling features of the judgment is the Court's recognition that a variety of public and private actors have obligations – positive and negative – regarding the basic education of learners at primary and secondary public schools (through to the age of 15). Of course, the Court's path-breaking finding is that the a private party – the Trust – had a clear obligation in terms of s 29(1) not to impair the access of learners to public schools. As a result, the eviction order granted by the High Court and upheld by the Supreme Court of Appeal had to be supplanted with an order that first ensured that learners at the school had continued access to the school until alternative arrangements for their education could be put in place. But other parties, with different interests, also had their feet held to the fire. No party more so than the MEC. Her department had not only ignored a request by the Trust to transform the public school back into an independent Islamic school, but had repeatedly failed to pay its bills for use of the land and acted in bad faith in negotiations over an increased tariff that would allow the public school to continue operating in its current form – an Islamic-inflected public primary school. What of the SGB? Surely the role of community-managed school boards is to ensure that nine years of legal wrangling do not place the education of learners (usually their children) in jeopardy. Ultimately, belatedly, and under pressure from the Constitutional Court, the responsible parties were obliged to give students adequate time to finish the school year (the Trust) and to organize alternative schooling for 2011 (the MEC). The big takeaway is that we all – to some degree – have negative obligations and positive obligations to ensure that all learners have access to one of the primary material goods or capabilities that makes a life worth valuing possible – a basic education.

(b) Shared Constitutional Interpretation and Participatory Bubbles

This case offers one of the best possible examples of how shared constitutional interpretation and participatory bubbles are meant to function – even when the parties to the polycentric process refuse to play nicely with one another. The Court created a framework, grounded in various constitutional norms (FC ss 8, 28, and 29), that allowed the various parties to creatively resolve the problem before them: ensuring continued access to a basic education. It did not prescribe the outcome. Given the circumstances, the school could have remained as it was (with proper payment to the Trust), become an independent school (as the Trust had previously requested) or wrapped up its affairs and found appropriate new placement for its learners (as turned out to be the case).

From the perspective of shared constitutional interpretation, all the parties, from the highest court in the land, to a provincial DoE, to an SGB, to a private trust, to individual learners, to the two amici (the Centre for Child Law and the Socio-Economic Rights Institute) had a voice in determining the best possible outcome under the circumstances. When the parties failed to move with alacrity, the Court pushed harder and ultimately secured a desirable outcome.

While this participatory bubble may have burst, the lessons to be learned are forward and lateral looking. So long as various parties remain within the existing flexible framework, new options may present themselves. Aside from the Court's guarantee to learners, *Juma Musjid* does not prescribe how access to basic education under such complex circumstances is to be secured. What we do see is the *Juma Musjid* Court inviting all interested parties to come up with novel solutions (remember *Miranda*), while using its muscle to ensure that a baseline or core of the right (to basic education) is protected (again: remember *Miranda*).

20. *Khumalo v Holomisa*[176]

As compared with *Ermelo*, *Juma Musjid* or *Joe Slovo I* and *Joe Slovo II*, *Khumalo v Holomisa* might appear to be an odd place to end our assessment of the fruitfulness of experimentalism and flourishing. It most assuredly is not.

(a) *Facts and the Holding of Khumalo v Holomisa*

Bantu Holomisa, the leader of the United Democratic Movement, sued the *Sunday World* over an article that alleged that Mr Holomisa was involved with a gang of bank robbers and was therefore under police investigation. In the High Court, the *Sunday World* averred, by way of exception, that because the contents of the article 'were matters in the public interest' and that the respondent had failed 'to allege in his particulars of claim that the article was false', Mr Holomisa had failed to satisfy the requirements for a cause of action in defamation. The High Court dismissed the applicant's exception.[177] The High Court did so on the grounds that it was bound by the Supreme Court of Appeal's decision in *National Media Ltd v Bogoshi*.[178]

Given that there could be no appeal to the Supreme Court of Appeal in terms of a dismissal of an exception, the applicants had no choice but to seek leave to appeal to the Constitutional Court. To succeed, the applicants had to show that the common-law rules of defamation as they stood post-*Bogoshi* violated the Final Constitution. The applicants relied primarily on FC s 16. In the alternative, the applicants sought relief in terms of FC s 39(2). Either way, asserted the applicants, the role of the mass media in an open and democratic society vindicated their position that the current law of defamation had to be altered. The Constitutional Court rejected the applicant's claims. While noting the value of a robust exchange of ideas in any democracy, the Court found that the Final Constitution's commitment to human dignity – and thus to self-worth and reputation – was of greater import under the circumstances. The *Khumalo* Court held that the defence of reasonableness developed in *Bogoshi*, rather than a requirement that the plaintiffs prove an allegedly defamatory statement false, better struck the desired balance between these competing interests.

Changes in the law of defamation hold limited interest for an exercise designed to tease out the benefits of experimentalism and flourishing for our jurisprudence. It is the *Khumalo* Court's break with a traditional mode of Bill of Rights adjudication – the state action doctrine – that warrants our attention. By exploding the cramped binary opposition of state and subject found in most constitutional democracies, the *Khumalo* Court's reassessment of the vexed question of whether the common law of defamation was subject to the direct application of the substantive provisions of the Bill of Rights held out the promise that all citizen-subjects are responsible for the material enhancement of all other citizen-subjects and that holding private parties accountable for violations of constitutional rights would, in many cases, require a host of state and non-state actors to apply their minds in creative and instructive ways to polycentric social problems.

Recall, however, that the *Khumalo* Court had not only to break with constitutional traditions in Canada, Germany and the United States, but with its own initial pronouncement on the subject in *Du Plessis v De Klerk*. Justice Kentridge, writing for a majority of the Court in *Du Plessis*, had rejected direct horizontal applications of the substantive provisions of the Bill of Rights because the 'judiciary' was neither mentioned nor ostensibly bound by the Bill of Rights in terms of the Interim Constitution s 7(1) and that the binding of 'all law' in IC s 7(2) ostensibly referred solely to actions of the 'legislative and executive'. Together IC s 7(1) and IC s 7(2) were read to exclude emanations of law from the judiciary (in particular, rules of common law) and disputes between private persons (since no 'state actor' was allegedly present) from the direct application of the substantive provisions of the Bill of Rights. (Let's forget the sturm und drang surrounding the merits of the majority's many arguments in favour of a traditional, vertical reading of the reach of a bill of rights. In short, the traditional position maintains constitutions ostensibly concern themselves with power relations between the state and its citizens.[179] That claim is patently false.)

So: *Du Plessis* effectively foreclosed debate on the direct application of the substantive provisions of the Interim Constitution's Bill of Rights to rules of common law governing private disputes. The drafters of the Final Constitution, in the interim, had reconsidered the Interim Constitution's provisional language on application.

In *Khumalo*, the Constitutional Court accepted the Final Constitution's invitation to broaden its conception of the law and the relationships to which the substantive provisions of the Bill of Rights apply directly. The application provisions of the Bill of Rights now read as follows:

> 8 (1) The Bill of Rights applies to all law, and binds the legislature, the executive, the judiciary and all organs of state.
>
> 8 (2) A provision of the Bill of Rights binds a natural or a juristic person if, and to the extent that, it is applicable, taking into account the nature of the right and the nature of any duty imposed by the right.
>
> 8 (3) When applying a provision of the Bill of Rights to a natural or juristic person in terms of subsection (2), a court
>
> *(a)* in order to give effect to a right in the Bill, must apply, or if necessary develop, the common law to the extent that legislation does not give effect to that right; and
>
> *(b)* may develop rules of the common law to limit the right, provided that the limitation is in accordance with section 36(1).

Unlike the Interim Constitution, the Final Constitution's Bill of Rights points unequivocally toward a much broader conception of direct application: FC s 8(1) states that the Bill applies to 'all law' and binds 'the judiciary'; FC s 8(2) states that the provisions of the Bill will bind natural and juristic persons where appropriate.

The *Khumalo* Court read these provisions in a rather idiosyncratic manner. The *Khumalo* Court held that, contrary to the applicants' contention, and the plain meaning of the text, FC s 8(1) did not subject the law that governed disputes between private parties to the direct application of the substantive provisions of the Bill of Rights. It held *instead* that FC s 8(2) determined the conditions under which direct application of the substantive provisions of the Bill of Rights to disputes between private parties would occur. Under FC s 8(2), the substantive provisions of the Bill of Rights apply directly to disputes between private parties where a specific provision is interpreted by a court to bind the private party or non state actor against whom the right is asserted. In the instant case, the *Khumalo* Court found that FC s 16 bound the private party relying upon the existing common law rules of defamation. The signal difference between *Du Plessis* and *Khumalo* is that the *Khumalo* Court reads FC s 8(2) to mean that some of the specific provisions of the Bill of Rights will apply directly to some disputes between private parties some of the time.[180] The *Khumalo* Court quite consciously crosses over the public-private divide. The text of the Final Constitution left it little choice. Let's forget the *sturm und drang* surrounding the merits of the Court's textually-mandated reversal of course.[181] Post-*Khumalo*, the South African Constitution must be understood to recognize that the basic law concerns itself with more than traditional public power relations between the state and its citizens, and directly engages more complex issues regarding the exercise of private power or quite often polycentric 'private-private-public' disputes between citizens, juristic persons, other denizens of South Africa, and the state.

(b) Slip Sliding Away?

For almost seven years, the Constitutional Court neither confirmed *Khumalo* nor employed s 8(2). Where had the commitment to horizontal application gone? As it turns outs, the Court simply preferred to conduct its analysis under the interpretation provision of the Bill of Rights, s 39 Section 39 (2) reads as follows: 'When interpreting any legislation and when developing the common law and customary law, every court, tribunal or forum must promote the spirit, purport and objects of the Bill of Rights.' About the reach of s 39(2), the Constitutional Court, in *Carmichele*, wrote as follows:

> It needs to be stressed that the obligation of Courts to develop the common law in the context of the s 39(2) objectives, is not purely discretional. On the contrary, it is implicit in s 39(2) read with s 173 that where the common law as it stands is deficient in promoting the s 39(2) objectives, the Courts are under a general obligation to develop it appropriately. We say a 'general obligation' because we do not mean to suggest that a court must, in each and every case where the common law is involved, embark on an independent exercise as to whether the common law is in need of development and, if so, how it is to be developed under s 39(2).[182]

As to what the FC s 39(2) inquiry requires of any tribunal, the *Carmichele* Court wrote:

> [T]here are two stages to the inquiry a court is obliged to undertake ... The first stage is to consider whether the existing common law, having regard to the s 39(2) objectives, requires development in accordance with these objectives. This inquiry requires a reconsideration of the common law in the light of s 39(2). If this inquiry leads to a positive answer, the second stage concerns itself with how such development is to take place in order to meet the s 39(2) objectives.[183]

Note the word 'objectives' – a term somewhat discussed, derisively, in Chapter 1. The amorphous nature of these 'objectives' has led, on more than one occasion to thinly reasoned judgments. Moreover this preferred approach can, on occasion, fail to take constitutional rights – as opposed to common law rights – as seriously as they should.[184] The *Thebus* Court's gloss on FC s 39(2) obligation 'to develop the common law in the context of the s 39(2) objectives' is even more perplexing. It turned out to be the thin edge of the wedge. Justice Moseneke, for the *Thebus* Court, writes:

> It seems to me that the need to develop the common law under s 39(2) could arise in at least two instances. The first would be when a rule of the common law is inconsistent with a constitutional provision. Repugnancy of this kind would compel an adaptation of the common law to resolve the inconsistency. The second possibility arises even when a rule of the common law is not inconsistent with a specific constitutional provision but may fall short of its spirit, purport and objects. Then, the common law must be adapted so that it grows in harmony with the 'objective normative value system' found in the Constitution.[185]

Fulfilling FC s 39(2) objectives is not about direct challenges to laws that conflict with specific provisions of the Bill of Rights. That is why we have the various provisions of FC s 8. This gloss of the *Thebus* Court on FC s 39(2) offends the 'no surplusage' canon of constitutional interpretation (as articulated by O'Regan J) by making parts (if not the entirety) of FC s 8 redundant. The approach of the *Thebus* Court does not merely suffer from a lack of analytic precision. The over-determination of the textual bases for changing the common law contradicts the Constitutional Court's own distinctions between (1) direct application and indirect application and (2) those remedies that flow from findings of constitutional invalidity and those remedies that flow from a re-formulation or a re-interpretation of the law in light of the spirit, purport and objects of the Bill of Rights. If the Constitutional Court's judgments in *National Coalition for Gay and Lesbian Equality v Minister of Justice*[186] or *Khumalo* tell us anything, it is that FC ss 8(1) and s 8(2) engage rules of common law directly, and that remedies for any violation of a specific provision take place in terms of FC ss 172*(a)* and 172*(b)* or 8(3). The Constitutional Court in *Amod* addressed directly the distinction between changes to the common law via FC ss 8(2) and (3) and changes to the common law via FC s 39(2). The *Amod* Court writes:

> Section 8(2) makes the Bill of Rights [directly] binding on natural and juristic persons ... Section 8(3) requires Courts in giving effect to s 8(2) to 'apply, or if necessary develop, the common law to the extent that legislation does not give effect to that right ...' The development of a coherent system of law may call for the development of the common law under ... s 39(2) of the 1996 Constitution to be done in a manner consistent with the way in which the law will be developed under s 8(2) and (3) of the 1996 Constitution ... When a constitutional matter is one which turns on the direct application of the Constitution ... considerations of costs and time may make it desirable that the appeal be brought directly to this Court. But when the constitutional matter involves the development of the common law, the position is different. The Supreme Court of Appeal has jurisdiction to develop the common law in all matters including constitutional matters. Because of the breadth of its jurisdiction and its expertise in the common law, its views as to whether the common law should or should not be developed in a 'constitutional matter' are of particular importance.[187]

The *Amod* Court recognizes that the unitary system of law contemplated by the Final Constitution 'may' require both the development of the law as a result of s 39(2)'s indirect application of the Bill of Rights as well as the development of the law that flows from the direct application of the Bill of Rights. It is difficult to make any sense of this observation unless FC s 8 analysis and FC s 39(2) analysis are different in kind.[188]

Extra-curial remarks made by Deputy Chief Justice Moseneke in 2009 reflected the by-then obvious proposition that s 39(2) constituted the preferred mechanism for engagement to disputes between parties governed the common law – irrespective of whether a specific substantive provision of the Bill of Rights could be directly applied. What he wrote in support of this proposition was truly disconcerting:

> In *Khumalo v Holomisa,* which was decided under the new Constitution, the Court refused the invitation to overrule *Du Plessis v De Klerk.* It nonetheless decided that the right to freedom of expression is of direct horizontal application, even when the invasion of the right could have been occasioned by a person other than the state or one of its organs.[189]

The Final Constitution expanded expressly the direct application, in terms of FC s 8, of the substantive provisions of the Bill of Rights to cover disputes between private parties governed by common law. A unanimous Constitutional Court in *Khumalo*, on law and facts identical in all meaningful ways to the law and facts at issue in *Du Plessis,* held, unequivocally, that s 8 of the Final Constitution does what s 7 of the Interim Constitution did not. In terms of s 8(2) and 8(3), rules of common law governing disputes between private parties are subject to the direct application of the specific substantive provisions of the Bill of Rights (where appropriate).

Several questions arise. Obvious answers follow.

(1) Can the silence of the Court about the status of *Du Plessis* be read to mean that the central holding of *Khumalo* did not overturn the central holding of *Du Plessis? No.*

(2) Can *Du Plessis* still be good law when the constitutional provisions upon which it was grounded no longer exist, and have been completely supplanted by new provisions in the altered? *No.*

(3) Does not FC s 8(2) expressly reject the claim in *Du Plessis* that the Bill of Rights does not apply directly to disputes between private parties governed by common law? *Yes.*

(4) Didn't a unanimous Constitutional Court in *Khumalo* expressly recognise that the substantive provisions of the Bill of Rights of the Final Constitution applies to private disputes, where appropriate, through ss 8(2) and 8(3)? *Yes.*

(5) Is it still correct, as a matter of law, to say that *Du Plessis* was *not* overturned by *Khumalo* read with the text of the Final Constitution? *No.*

(6) Should we be satisfied with the Deputy Chief Justice's contention that the Constitutional Court's approach circa 2009/2010 to the development of the common law remains the same as it did under the Interim Constitution? *No.*

The Deputy Chief Justice's remarks are that much more disconcorting given that the Technical Committee charged with drafting the Bill of Rights of the Final Constitution expressly intended for ss 8(1) and 8(2) to capture all matters involving direct application of a substantive provision of the Bill of Rights (including, specifically, the direct application of substantive provisions to disputes between private parties governed by the common law). Section 39 was intended to be exactly what it says it is – a guide to interpretation of all law in light of the spirit, purport and objects of the Bill of Rights.[190]

(c) Back in Black: The Promise of 8(2) for Flourishing and Experimentalism

As it turns out, *Du Plessis vs De Klerk* is dead: as official doctrine anyway.[191] In *Governing Body of the Juma Musjid Primary School & Others v Ahmed Asruff Essay N.O. & Others,* the Constitutional Court, confirmed the holding in *Khumalo*, and held that one private party in a dispute with another private party governed by common law – a trust seeking to evict learners from a public school so that it might use the property more profitably – was subject to the formal terms of the Bill of Rights through s 8(2) – and could not deny learners access to a basic education in terms of s 29(1)(the righ to a basic education) and s 28 (Children's Rights) of the Bill of Rights. While the judgment expressly confirms the holding in *Khumalo v Holomisa*, it takes care to limit the duty of the private trust: while it may not negatively impair the learner's right to a basic education, it is under no apparent positive duty to provide the means for that education.[192] The positive obligation is borne by the state.

Juma Musjid holds out two distinct promises. First, by refusing to grant the trust an eviction order that negatively impaired a learner's right to a basic education at a public school, the Court holds private parties materially responsible for the material conditions necessary for natural persons to flourish. The Court writes: 'basic education is ... directed, among other things, at promoting and developing a child's personality, talents and mental and physical abilities to his or her fullest potential.'[193] Second, by expanding the range of a right's obligations to embrace private parties who might negatively interfere with the exercise of right, at the same time as it holds the state accountable for the discharge of a positive obligation, the Court in *Juma Musjid* forced the various parties – the Trust, the MEC, the SGB and the parents – to engage one another in a manner that ensured that they would arrive at solution in which virtually all the parties' rights were honoured and their duties discharged. The Trust – by honouring the s 29(1) rights of learners – ultimately secured its s 25 rights to property. The MEC – by finding new schools for its learners – discharged its statutory and constitutional obligations to its learners. The learners – by holding both the Trust, the MEC and the SGB accountable – were able to maintain their right of access to a basic education during 2010 and ensure that appropriate schools were found for them in 2011. The Court's use of s 8(2) allowed it to craft a meaningful engagement order that compelled the parties to come up with an optimal resolution to a conflict that had dated back almost a decade. The experimentalist cast of the Court's handling of the matter enabled the parties to arrive at optimal means to ensure that rights were protected at the same time as the resolution had the reflexive effect of telling other schools, MECs, SGBs and private property owners what they might legitimately expect the content of ss 25, 28, and 29 to take in future matters. So while some jurists and commentators might be inclined to view operational sections such as these as s 8 or s 39 as no more than guidelines as to how a court should think about rights and the development of the basic law, the *Juma Musjid* demonstrated that horizontal application has teeth and can be used to promote the development and capabilities of rights bearers at the same time as it compels various parties confronted with a seemingly intractable problem to come up with a creative solution.

Endnotes

1 See F Michelman 'On the Uses of Interpretive Charity: Some Notes on Application, Avoidance, Equality and Objective Unconstitutionality from the 2007 Term of the Constitutional Court of South Africa' (2008) 1 *Constitutional Court Review* 1, 3 ('The aim is to learn. It is aggressively to learn what there is to be learnt from puzzles … interlocutors pose to us, by assuming there is method in their madness and doing our best to ferret that out, using everything else we know or can guess (in part from their likeness and kinship to us) about where they are coming from.')

2 See M Heidegger *Being and Time* (1927)(On 'throwness', 'facticity' and 'ways of being'); L Wittgenstein *Philosophical Investigations* (1953)(On 'forms of life').

3 See A Sen *Development as Freedom* (1999); A Sen *The Idea of Justice* (2009)(In both works, Sens argues – pace Rawls – that we have no reason to assume that a lexical ordering or a priority of goods, norms or principles will apply across all individuals, publics, societies or states.) See also C Taylor 'The Diversity of Goods' in C Taylor *Philosophical Papers II: Philosophy and the Human Sciences* (1985).

4 See M Walzer *Spheres of Justice: A Defence of Pluralism and Equality* (1983).

5 See S Woolman 'I am Large': Sachs, Whitman & Democracy' (2010) 25 *Southern African Public Law* 58 (On the relationship between radically heterogeneous selves and democratic solidarity.)

6 See S Woolman & D Davis 'The Last Laugh: Classical Liberalism, Creole Liberalism and the Application of Fundamental Rights under the Interim and the Final Constitutions' (1996) 12 *South African Journal on Human Rights* 361 (Contends that the Final Constitution tolerates reasonably significant differences in conceptions of the good (within the broad but substaintive parameters of 'the good' reflected in the basic law) and commits the state to providing the material means for making these competing visions possible.)

7 See JS Mill *On Liberty* (1863)(Experiments in living enable individuals to discovery lives that provide for a better fit – in large part by seeing the results of 'experiments in living' undertaken by others.)

8 For moral, political and legal arguments that question the virtue of constitutional orders committed to justiciable, court-enforced bills of rights, see T Pogge *World Poverty and Human Rights* (2nd Edition, 2008); J Waldron *The Dignity of Legislation* (1999); J Waldron *Law and Disagreement* (1999); J Waldron 'The Core of the Case against Judicial Review' (2006) 115 *Yale Law Journal* 1346; M Tushnet *The New Constitutional Order* (2003); B Flanagan 'Judicial Rights Talk: Defects in the Liberal Challenge to Constitutional Review' (2006) 22 *South African Journal of Human Rights* 173. But see M Dorf 'Review of Mark Tushnet's *The New Constitutional Order*' (2004) 71 *University of Chicago Law Review* 1245.

9 See S Woolman and H Botha 'Limitations' in S Woolman & M Bishop (eds) *Constitutional Law of South Africa* (2nd Edition, OS, July 2006) Chapter 34 (Limitations analysis gives the Court an opportunity to place its gloss on a constitutional right or norm while simultaneously inviting a co-ordinate branch of government to provide an alternative reading of the right.) .

10 See C Sunstein *Infotopia* (2007)(On the biases present in deliberation that inevitable limit what we can expect of deliberative democracy.)

11 See R Thaler and C Sunstein *Nudge: Improving Decisions about Health, Wealth and Happiness* (2008) (Argue that social policy experiments can elicit information that will allow decision-makers to create policies or structures that will 'nudge' individuals and groups into making better decisions); R Post & R Seigel 'Roe Rage: Democratic Constitutionalism and Backlash' (2007) 42 *Harvard Civil Rights-Civil Liberties Law Review* 373 (Contend that rights conflicts have the capacity to animate an otherwise passive citizenry, and in so doing promote more informed engagement regarding important issues.) Perhaps Post and Seigal are on to something. However, as Tony Judt notes, most contemporary western democracies witness plunging appearances at the polls over time. 'On Intellectuals and Democracy' (2012) 58 *The New York Review of Books* 7. Recent findings report that those persons inclined to discuss matters are *less* likely to be politically active. The former tend toward tolerance – and need not win. More intolerant citizens see the battle in terms of high stakes, and can be moved to vote in higher percentages by campaigns that employ demagogy and rely on lies both big and small.

12 K McLean *Constitutional Deference: Courts and Socio-Economic Rights in South Africa* (2009).

13 Of course, as I have pointed out repeatedly – in this text and elsewhere – in many areas of law and social life, we do not want the state or other actors to experiment. Flourishing, and freedom, as Walzer notes above, often means embracing fully who we already are. Moreover, in that truly constitutional orders with a justiciable Bill of rights, commitment to private ordering allows other publics, and the individuals within them, the ability to carry on living as they wish. Experimentalism is consistent with this commitment to flourishing and largely concerns itself with solving problems within the broader framework of the basic law, subordinate bodies of law and legal disputes. Of course, matters will invariably arise in which the commitment to experimentalism and flourishing knock heads – but only to the extent that some social actors will prefer to maintain the status quo and others will attempt to use the basic law to leverage change. Experimentalism seeks to ratchet down those conflicts by allowing the parties ultimately affected to work out solutions for themselves. *Joe Slovo I and II*, and *Shilubana*, as discussed below, offer opportunities to understand our evolving constitutional discourse in terms of both the overcoming of informational deficits in polycentric disputes and the normative legitimacy that resolution of those disputes secure.

14 See *Ex parte Chairperson of the Constitutional Assembly: in re Certification of the Constitution of the Republic of South Africa, 1996* 1996 (4) SA 744 (CC).

15 See M Dorf 'The Domain of Reflexive Law' (2003) 103 *Columbia Law Review* 384; M Dorf & B Friedman 'Shared Constitutional Interpretation' (2000) *Supreme Court Review* 61; M Dorf '1997 Supreme Court Term Foreword: The Limits of Socratic Deliberation' (1998) 112 *Harvard Law Review* 4.

16 See M Dorf and C Sabel 'A Constitution of Democratic Experimentalism' (1998) 98 *Columbia Law Review* 267.

17 See D Dennett *Freedom Evolves* (2004).

18 See B Ackermann *We the People* (1991).

19 See H Klug *Constituting Democracy: Law, Globalism and South Africa's Political Reconstruction* (2000).

20 J Dugard 'Court of First Instance? Towards a Pro-Poor Jurisdiction for the South African Constitutional Court' (2006) 22 *South African Journal on Human Rights* 261 (Argues that the South African Constitutional Court has not functioned as an institutional voice for the poor because its jurisdictional requirements make access difficult if not impossible for indigent plaintiffs pressing fundamental rights claims – and suggests that this difficulty could be remedied if the Court made that greater use of its power to grant direct access.)

21 R Cover 'The Supreme Court, 1982 Term: Foreword: Nomos and Narrative' (1983) 97 Harvard Law Review 4.

22 See, eg, R Thaler & S Sunstein *Nudge* (supra).

23 See S Woolman and H Botha 'Limitations' (supra) (Limitations analysis by the Court offers but one answer for hard constitutional questions and leaves the door open to alternative justifications for alternative normative assessments arrived at by co-ordinate branches of government). See also M Bishop 'Remedies' in S Woolman & M Bishop (eds) *Constitutional Law of South Africa* (2nd Edition, OS, July 2008) Chapter 9.

24 *Prince v President, Cape Law Society and Others* 2002 (2) SA 794 (CC), 2001 (2) BCLR 133 (CC).

25 One might argue that *Pillay* reflects a shift that takes difference more seriously. *MEC for Education: KwaZulu-Natal & Others v Pillay* 2007 ZACC 21, 2008 (1) SA 474 (CC), 2008 (2) BCLR 99 (CC)

26 See the discussion of the facts and the law at issue in *Prince* above in Chapter 1.

27 S Dersso 'The Need for Constitutional Accommodation of Ethno-Cultural Diversity in the Post-colonial African State (2008) 24 *South African Journal on Human Rights* 565 (Addresses post-colonial nation-building and constitutional discourse in Africa and draws on South African institutions and practices in sketching out an alternative constitutional framework that facilitates the accommodation of the interests and identity of members of various groups in the process of national integration.)

28 See C Mbazira 'From Ambivalence to Certainty: Norms and Principles for the Structural Interdict in Socio-economic Rights Litigation in South Africa' (2008) 24 *South African Journal on Human Rights* 1 (Offers justifications for the use of interdicts because they can elicit information from experts, interested parties not before the court, reports on progress from government officials and further constructive engagement between the parties.)

29 As the Court itself has come to appreciate, the interaction between rights interpretation, limitations analysis and remedies ought to be principled, but fluid. For example, the *Prince* Court could/should have found the state's limitation unjustifiable for principled reasons, but then employed a structural interdict or an order for meaningful engagement that enabled the parties to arrive at a workable solution. Once the Court approaches matters thus, it frees itself of the dual burden of an arid, deferential separation of powers doctrine or grand theorizing about the meaning and the ambit of a given constitutional norm – say, freedom of religion. A more imaginative experimentalist take on remedies possesses the added benefit of extracting information from all interested stakeholders that might just place the Court's ultimate decision on firmer footing.

30 See C Sabel & W Simon 'Destabilization Rights: How Public Law Litigation Succeeds' (2004) 117 *Harvard Law Review* 1015. See also M Dorf 'Legal Indeterminism and Institutional Design' (2004) 78 *New York University Law Review* 875.

31 *S v Jordan (Sex Workers Education and Advocacy Task Force and others as Amici Curiae)* 2002 (6) SA 642 (CC), 2002 (11) BCLR 1117 (CC).

32 See s 20(1)(aA) of the Sexual Offences Act 23 of 1957.

33 *Jordan* (supra) at para 16 – 17.

34 See S Woolman & M Bishop 'State as Pimp: Sexual Slavery in South Africa' (2006) 23 *Development Southern Africa* 385; S Woolman & M Bishop 'Slavery, Servitude & Forced Labour' in S Woolman & M Bishop (eds) *Constitutional Law of South Africa* (2nd Edition, OS, December 2006) Chapter 64.

35 This critique of *Jordan* cannot be read as an implicit denial of women's agency. While we must recognise that material and legal conditions exist that impair the ability of women to shape their preferred way of being in the world, and that such obstacles to agency ought to be removed, we should be leery of the argument that to live life within the transgressive frame of a brothel makes a woman's life undignified or demonstrates a lack of agency. See Woolman 'Dignity' (supra) at § 36.5.

36 *Khosa* (supra) at para 76. See also S Woolman 'The Widening Gyre of Dignity' in S Woolman & M Bishop (eds) *Constitutional Conversations* (2008) 149.

37 See M Swart 'Social Security' in S Woolman & M Bishop (eds) *Constitutional Law of South Africa* (2nd Edition, OS, July 2006) Chapter 54D; C Albertyn and B Goldblatt 'Equality' in S Woolman & M Bishop (eds) *Constitutional Law of South Africa* (2nd Edition, OS, July 2007) Chapter 35.

38 For more on the state's obligations under s 7(2), see *Glenister v President of the Republic of South Africa & Others* 2011 (3) SA 347 (CC); *Democratic Alliance v President of the Republic of South Africa & Others* 2012 (1) SA 417 (SCA).

39 To the extent that the *Jordan* Court does operate with an appreciation for flourishing, it distinguishes invidiously between the ways of being in the world of sex workers and the ways of being in the world of other human beings who have ostensibly non-commercial sex. The manifold motivations for sex – and the bewilderingly complex forms of exchange that underlie so much of it – make the Court's distinctions between protected forms of intercourse and unprotected forms of intercourse unpersuasive. See S Woolman 'Freedom of Association' in S Woolman & M Bishop (eds) *Constitutional Law of South Africa* (2nd Edition, OS, December 2003) Chapter 44. See also N Fritz 'Crossing *Jordan*: Constitutional Space for (Un)Civil Sex?' (2004) 20 *SAJHR* 230; V Barolsky.

40 See M Dorf and C Sabel Drug 'Drug Treatment Courts and Emergent Experimental Government' (1999) 53 *Vanderbilt Law Review* 831, 832 ('Variations in nomenclature and precise details of their operations aside, treatment courts ... share the same basic pattern. ... In the treatment court, the plaintiff pleads guilty or otherwise accepts responsibility for a charged offense and accepts placement in a court mandated program of drug treatment ... The judge and court personnel closely monitor

the defendant's performance in the program and the program's capacity to serve the mandated client. If progress in the treatment regime is unsatisfactory, courts offering various programs may require the offender to choose another, more intensive one. Upon successful completion of the treatment program the conviction is typically expunged. The drug court, however, will cease directing defendants to programs that show signs of incompetence and increase referrals to others that show greater promise. ... In changing our conception of addiction and how treatment can respond to it, drug courts will likely reshape the background ideas that crucially influence what we regard as criminal behaviour and how we respond to it.')

41 2001 (1) SA 46 (CC), 2000 (11) BCLR 1169 (CC)('*Grootboom*').

42 See K Mclean 'Housing' in S Woolman & M Bishop (eds) *Constitutional Law of South Africa* (2nd Edition, OS, July 2006) Chapter 55.

43 See C Mbazira *Litigating Socio-Economic Rights in South Africa: A Choice between Corrective and Distributive Justice* (2009).

44 For more on *Rudolph I* and *Rudolph II*, see *City of Cape Town v Rudolph & Others* 2004 (5) SA 39 (C), 2003 (11) BCLR 1236 (C), [2003] 3 All SA 517, 547 (C)('*Rudolph I*'); *City of Cape Town v Rudolph & Others* (Unreported decision of the Cape High Court, 5 December 2005)('*Rudolph II*').

45 See *City of Johannesburg Metropolitan Municipality v Blue Moonlight Properties 39 (Pty) Ltd & Another* [2011] ZACC 33, 2012 (2) SA 104 (CC), 2012 (2) BCLR 150 (CC)(On adequate shelter, a minimal minimum core and other recent housing cases, see Chapter 6).

46 See M Dorf & B Friedman 'Shared Constitutional Interpretation' (2000) *Supreme Court Review* 61 citing *US v Dickerson* 530 US 428 (2000) citing *Miranda v Arizona* 384 US 436 (1966)(The *Miranda* Court's gloss on the 4th Amendment came with a clear invitation to the Federal Government and the states to revisit how law enforcement agencies conducted searches in a constitutionally permissible manner.)

47 National Department of Housing *Breaking New Ground* (2011)(Department revisits its policies to deliver adequate housing in light of the criticism of the *Grootboom* Court and the evidence that the initial conception of Reconstruction and Development Programme housing had failed to take into account a variety of related needs of new home-owners – to be near places of employment, decent schools, hospitals and environments with access to adequate water, food and electricity.)

48 See *President of the Republic of South Africa & Another v Modderklip Boerdery (Pty) Ltd (Agri SA & Others, Amici Curiae)* 2005 (5) SA 3 (CC).

49 See JD Mujuzi 'Don't Send Them to Prison Because They Can't Rehabilitate Them! The South African Judiciary Doubts the Executive's Ability to Rehabilitate Offenders: A Note on *S v Shilubane* 2008 (1) SACR 295 (T) (2008)' 24 *South African Journal on Human Rights* 330. The national government's decision in 2011 to intervene with respect to the political and administrative functions of the province of Limpopo suggests that the Constitutional Court and any other court must be sensitive to the actual capacity of a municipality or a province to respond meaningfully to an order of engagement or a structural injunction. The repeated failures of the Eastern Cape with respect to the payment of social security grants has been met with calumny and contempt by the High Court and the Supreme Court of Appeal. See M Swart 'Social Security' in S Woolman & M Bishop (eds) *Constitutional Law of South Africa* (2nd Edition, OS, March 2011) Chapter 54C. Failed provinces, or ineffective Chapter Nine Institutions, hold out little promise of making good on a bona fide commitment to experimental governance. They fail both as a participant in an extended problem-solving exercise and as a comparator for other state and social actors looking laterally for guidance as to 'best practices' in the discharge of constitutional and statutory obligations.

50 *Minister of Health & Others v Treatment Action Campaign & Others (No 2)* 2002 (5) SA 721 (CC)('*TAC*')

51 See S Liebenberg *Socio-Economic Rights Adjudication under a Transformative Constitution* (2010). See also B Ray 'The Interpretation of Socio-Economic Rights' in S Woolman & M Bishop (eds) *Constitutional Law of South Africa* (2nd Edition, RS7, forthcoming, July 2013) Chapter 33.

52 But see *Biowatch Trust v Registrar Genetic Resources and Others* [2009] ZACC 14, 2009 (6) SA 232 (CC), 2009 (10) BCLR 1014 (CC)(Court adopts a new approach to costs in constitutional litigation aimed at facilitating, rather than chilling, litigation of this nature.) For an extended analysis of the new *Biowatch* model, see M Bishop 'Costs' in S Woolman & M Bishop (eds) *Constitutional Law of South Africa* (2nd Edition, RS2, 2010) Chapter 9. See also T Humby 'The *Biowatch* Case: Major Advance in South African Law of Costs and Access to Environmental Justice: Trustees for the Time Being, *Biowatch Trust v Registrar, Genetic Resources and Others* (2010) 22 *Journal of Environmental Law* 125.

53 *TAC* (supra) at para 135.

54 See C Sprague and S Woolman 'Moral Luck: Exploiting South Africa's Policy Environment to Produce A Sustainable National Antiretroviral Treatment Programme' (2006) 22 *South African Journal on Human Rights* 337 (State's best hope for discharging the duties imposed by the Constitution is a systematic, structural intervention: the implementation of a socio-industrial policy that leverages existing industrial capacity and voluntary licenses in a manner that generates price reductions and offers an uninterrupted sustainable local supply.)

55 See S Woolman, C Sprague and V Black 'Why State Policies that Undermine HIV Lay Counsellors Constitute Retrogressive Measures that Violate the Right of Access to Health Care for Pregnant Women And Infants' (2009) 25 *South African Journal on Human Rights* 102. As Courtenay Sprague notes elsewhere: 'Although ARV medicines became freely available through the public health system in April 2004, pregnant women and children for whom treatment is indicated face significant barriers to accessing antiretroviral medicines (ARVs).' C Sprague 'Cui Bono: Barriers to Access for HIV-Infected Women and Children' (PhD, 2009, manuscript on file with author.) As of 2005, only 10% of infected children and 14.6% of pregnant women had access to life-saving Anti-retroviral Treatment. See WHO *Summary Country Profile for HIV/AIDS Treatment Scale-Up* (June 2005), available at http://www.who.int/3by5/countryprofiles/en. Sprague argues that 'the most visible manifestation of this complex problem is the high mortality rates exhibited in children under age five in South Africa' and that 'these death rates are preventable'. Sprague (supra) at 6 citing World Health Organization *The World Health Report 2006* (Estimates from 2004 data); World Health Organization *National Guide to Monitoring and Evaluating Programmes for the Prevention of HIV in Infants and Young Children* (2006); World Health Organization *Antiretroviral Therapy of HIV Infection in Infants and Children in Resource-Limited Settings: Towards Universal Access: Recommendations for a Public Health Approach.* World Health Organization *Antiretroviral Drugs for Treating Pregnant Women and Preventing HIV* (2006); World Health Organization *Infection in Infants in Resource-Limited Settings Towards Universal Access: Recommendations for a Public Health Approach* (2006); Médecins sans Frontières *New MSF Data Shows Treatment of Children Works in Resource PoorSettings but Scale Up is Hampered by Ill-Adapted Tools and Exorbitant Costs* (August 2006), available at http://www.msf.org.

56 According to Courtenay Sprague, these numbers must be used, and viewed, with caution. Email correspondence with Courtenay Sprague (27 February 2008). For the source of these numbers, see F Hassan et al 'AIDS Law Project Monitoring Unit, Joint Civil Society Monitoring Forum' (September 2006), available at http://www.alp.org.za/modules.php?op=modload&name=News&file=article&sid=318.

57 UNICEF South Africa *Impact on Children: Paediatric Testing and Treatment* (2006), available at http://www.unicef.org/southafrica; G Gray Global AIDS: HIV Prevention and Care in Children, Treatment Access and Challenges Among Children in Resource-Limited Settings. *Management of Pediatric HIV Infection, and Prevention of Mother-to-Child HIV Transmission* (2006) available at http://www.medscape.com/viewarticle/544610.

58 World Health Organization *Infection in Infants in Resource-Limited Settings Towards Universal Access: Recommendations for a Public Health Approach* (2006); UNICEF *The State of the World's Children: 2002* (2002).

59 Even if I don't offer a particularly full account of flourishing or capabilities, it seems clear that if health is impaired, then 'most other human capabilities will remain out of reach.' Sprague (supra) at 6. Ruger, who argues that the state's obligation to improve health 'rests on the ethical principle of human flourishing – or human capability', contends that: 'Policies that deny antiretroviral drugs to patients with HIV/AIDS, as happens in sub-Saharan Africa and other parts of the world, are morally troubling not only because they constitute subminimal healthcare, reduce individuals' opportunity for employment and require cosmopolitan duty ... The moral concern is the reduced capability for physical and mental functioning or even for being alive. Deprivations in the capability to function rob individuals of the freedom to be what they want to be.' JP Ruger 'Ethics and Governance of Global Health Inequalities' (2006) 60 *Journal of Epidemiological and Community Health* 998, 999.

60 S Woolman, C Sprague & V Black 'Why the State's Treatment of HIV/AIDS Lay Counsellors for ART and PMTCT Programmes Constitutes Retrogressive Measures that Violate the Right to Adequate Healthcare' (2009) 24 *South African Journal on Human Rights* 102.

61 S Woolman & C Sprague 'Mixed Messages and Retrogressive Measures: Policies on Breast Feeding and Formula Use Lead to Higher Prevalence of *Mother-to-Child HIV Transmission*' (2013, Draft on file with authors.)

62 See D Bilchitz *Poverty and Fundamental Rights* (2006); D Bilchitz 'Towards a Reasonable Approach to the Minimum Core: Laying the Foundations for Future Socio-Economic Rights Jurisprudence' (2003) 19 *South African Journal on Human Rights* 1; D Bilchitz (2001) 'Giving Socio-Economic Rights Teeth: The Minimum Core and Its Importance' 119 *South Africa Law Journal* 484; D Bilchitz 'Health' in S Woolman & M Bishop (eds) *Constitutional Law of South Africa* (2nd Edition, OS, December 2005) Chapter 54A; M Pieterse 'Resuscitating Socio-Economic Rights: Constitutional Entitlements to Health Care Services' (2006) *South African Journal on Human Rights* 473.

63 See *TAC* (supra) at paras 112 – 113 ('What this brief survey makes clear is that in none of the jurisdictions surveyed is there any suggestion that the granting of injunctive relief breaches the separation of powers. The various courts adopt different attitudes to when such remedies should be granted, but all accept that within the separation of powers they have the power to make use of such remedies particularly when the state's obligations are not performed diligently and without delay. South African courts have a wide range of powers at their disposal to ensure that the Constitution is upheld. These include mandatory and structural interdicts. How they should exercise those powers depends on the circumstances of each particular case. Here due regard must be paid to the roles of the legislature and the executive in a democracy. What must be made clear, however, is that when it is appropriate to do so, courts may and if need be must use their wide powers to make orders that affect policy as well as legislation.')

64 Ibid at para 114.

65 C Mbazira 'From Ambivalance to Certainty: Norms and Principles for the Use of Structural Interdicts in Socio-Economic Right' (2008) 24 *South African Journal on Human Rights* 1. Mbazira bashes the Constitutional Court for its general abstention from using structural interdicts to ensure that broad policy based remedies are carried out. He notes, in addition, that structural interdicts possess the virtues of increased stakeholder participation and flexibility with respect to both the means and the ends reflected in the Court's initial judgment. Neither administrative burdens nor the argument that the Constitutional Court is ill-equipped to be a consistent 'trier of fact' (as circumstances change) seem particularly compelling.

66 S Woolman C Sprague & V Black 'Why State Policies that Undermine HIV Lay Counsellors Constitute Retrogressive Measures that Violate the Right of Access to Health Care for Pregnant Women And Infants' (2009) 25 (supra). See also S Woolman, C Sprague & V Black 'Some are More Equal than Others: The Constitutional Justification and Ethical Arguments Granting Enhanced Antiretroviral Therapy to Selected Priority Groups' (2011) *Journal of South African Law* 496.

67 *Port Elizabeth Municipality v Various Occupiers* 2005 (1) SA 217 (CC), 2004 (12) BCLR 1268 (CC)('*Port Elizabeth Municipality*'). The usefulness of this case was brought to my attention by Professor Andre van der Walt. See A van der Walt *Constitutional Property Law* (2005).

68 L Fuller *The Morality of Law* 106 (rev ed 1964).

69 *Port Elizabeth Municipality* (supra) at para 35.

70 Ibid at para 39.

71 Ibid at para 42.

72 M Bishop 'Remedies' in S Woolman & M Bishop (eds) *Constitutional Law of South Africa* (2nd Edition, OS, 2010) Chapter 9.

73 See T Roux 'Tactical Adjudication' *Kwa-Zulu Natal School of Law Conference on Democracy and Judicial Review* (Draft copy, 9 February 2007)(Manuscript on file with author).

74 [2001] ZACC 19, 2001 (3) SA 1151 (CC), 2001 (7) BCLR 652 (CC)('*Kyalami Ridge*').

75 Does the Government have the same rights and responsibilities as other land owners – especially private owners? Or does the Government hold and dispose of all state land for the benefit of all members of the polity? One would have thought that the latter proposition was true (regardless of the outcome in this matter.)

76 See L Ferris & D Tladi 'Environmental Rights' in D Brand & C Heyns (eds) *Socio-Economic Rights in South Africa* (2004).

77 E Basson & M Van Der Linde 'Environment' in S Woolman & M Bishop (eds) *Constitutional Law of South Africa* (2nd Edition, RS2, 2010) Chapter 50.

78 *Kyalami Ridge* (supra) at para 6.

79 Ibid.

80 Ibid at para 111.

81 S Woolman 'The Amazing, Vanishing Bill of Rights' (2007) 124 *South African Law Journal* 762 (Lack of explanatory reach of the Court's decisions undermines the value of Court's precedents, prevents state and non-state actors from orienting future actions in light of a discernable rule of law and thus undermines the rule of law itself.) But F Michelman 'On the Uses of Interpretative Charity' (supra) note 1. Arguments from urgency do no work here. Even if an initial decision had to be taken, nothing prevented the Court from retaining jurisdiction and setting up engagement processes that might have arrived at more optimal solution down the line. Indeed, *Joe Slovo I* and *Joe Slovo II* indicate just how flexible the Court's remedial powers are.

82 Loretta Feris would seem to agree with my general assessment of the Court's hollowing out of specific provisions, at least in so far as that thesis speaks to FC s 24. L Feris 'Constitutional Environmental Rights: An Underutilised Resource' (2008) 24 *South African Journal on Human Rights* 29.

83 *Kyalami Ridge* (supra) at para 112.

84 Ibid at 113.

85 Ibid at 115.

86 As I have already noted in Chapter 6 and the outset of this chapter, one can read the housing cases from *Grootboom*, *Modderklip*, *PE* and *Kyalami*, through to *51 Olivia Road* and *Abahlali* and *Blue Moonlight* – as an ongoing experiment conducted by the Court as to how to build a jurisprudence of general principles from first principles (an exercise more Cartesian and foundationalist than some may allow): from legality, to the rule of law, to rationality review, to reasonableness, to meaningful engagement (with teeth). While academics including myself have been quick to chastise the Chaskalson Court's minimalist approach, perhaps a more charitable reading would have them establish basic, relatively uncontroversial principles first – can anyone take issue with a commitment to the rule of law – and thereby allow more subtle developments of doctrine over time. Here then, the basic tenets of the constitutional theory expounded here, experimental governance as generally read, and Sunsteinian minimalism could as previously and properly understood, be said to dovetail to a significant degree.

87 [2007] ZACC 13, 2007 (10) BCLR 1059 (CC), 2007 (6) SA 4 (CC).

88 The facts and the law as issue in *Fuel Retailers* are described by Chief Justice Ngcobo as follows: 'This application for leave to appeal against the decision of the Supreme Court of Appeal concerns the nature and scope of the obligations of environmental authorities when they make decisions that may have a substantial detrimental impact on the environment. In particular, it concerns the interaction between social and economic development and the protection of the environment. It arises out of a decision by the Department of Agriculture, Conservation and Environment, Mpumalanga province (the Department), the third respondent, to grant the Inama Family Trust (the Trust) authority in terms of section 22(1) of the Environment Conservation Act, 1989 (ECA) to construct a filling station on a property in White River, Mpumalanga (the property). Section 22(1) of ECA forbids any person from undertaking an activity that has been identified in terms of section 21(1) as one that may have a substantial detrimental impact on the environment without written authorisation by the competent authority. It was not disputed that the MEC Agriculture, Conservation and Environment, Mpumalanga, (the MEC) the second respondent, is the competent authority designated by the Minister. Before authorisation can be granted, a report concerning the impact of the proposed development on the environment must be furnished. The relevant authority has a discretion to grant or refuse such authorisation. In granting it, the relevant authority may impose such conditions as may be necessary to ensure the protection of the environment. ... The Fuel Retailers Association of Southern Africa (incorporated in terms of section 21 of the Companies Act), the applicant, challenged the decision to grant authorisation in the Pretoria High Court on various grounds. However, the only ground that concerns us in this application is that the environmental authorities in Mpumalanga had not considered the socio-economic impact of constructing the proposed filling station, a matter which they were obliged to consider. In resisting the application on this ground the Department contended that need and desirability were considered by the local authority when it decided the rezoning application of the property for the purposes of constructing the proposed filling station. Therefore it did not have to reassess these considerations.' Ibid at paras 1–5

89 On the ability, or lack thereof, of the Court to harmonize the three elements of the triple bottom line or sustainable development as mandated by s 24, see L Feris 'Sustainable Development in Practice: *Fuel Retailers Association of Southern Africa v Director-General Environmental Management, Department of Agriculture, Conservation and Environment, Mpumalanga Province*' (2008) 1 *Constitutional Court Review* 235; D Tladi '*Fuel Retailers*, Sustainable Development & Integration: A Response to Feris' (2008) 1 *Constitutional Court Review* 255.

90 *Fuel Retailers* (supra) at paras 44–45, 58–59, 61, 72, 74, 76 and 79–80. In *BP Southern Africa (Pty) Limited v MEC for Agriculture, Conservation, Environment & Land Affairs*, Judge Claassen had held that the constitutional right to an environment is on par with the rights to freedom of trade, occupation, profession and property. 2004 (5) SA 124, 143 (W)('*BP Southern Africa*'). As such, when a court engages – often contemporaneously – rights to property, land and freedom of trade and environmental rights, the court must enter into a normative and often empirical assessment of how the rights can best be harmonized. If the rights cannot be harmonized, then the court must offer a compelling account of why one right must be given precedence over any other right given the facts in play. Such an ineradicable tension between s 24 and other rights is inevitable. Judge Claassen writes: 'By elevating the environment to a fundamental justiciable human right, South Africa has irreversibly embarked on a road, which will lead to the goal of attaining a protected environment by an integrated approach, which takes into consideration *inter alia* socio-economic concerns and principles.' Ibid at 144.

91 I don't want to gild the lily. As I have noted elsewhere, while some informal pooling and distribution of information in s 24 cases will occur, in the absence of a proper system for collating all the information and deducing best practices based on the results, and then distributing that information to decision-makers, the system may not be as efficient as possible in terms of learning from past experience. The Minister of Water Affairs and Forestry, in collaboration with NGOs, is probably

best placed to provide the kind of watering hole that parties interested in s 24(b)(iii) best practices require.

92 [2008] ZACC 1, 2008 (3) SA 208 (CC), 2008 (5) BCLR 475 (CC).

93 See S Woolman 'Application' in S Woolman & M Bishop (eds) *Constitutional Law of South Africa* (2nd Edition, OS, 2005) Chapter 31; S Woolman 'The Amazing, Vanishing Bill of Rights' (2007) 124 *South African Law Journal* 762; F Michelman 'On the Uses of Interpretive Charity' (2009) 1 *Constitutional Court Review* 1; S Woolman 'Between Charity and Clarity: Kibitzing with Frank Michelman on How Best to Read the Constitutional Court' in S Woolman & D Bilchitz (eds) *Is This Seat Taken? Conversations at the Bar, the Bench and the Academy about the South African Constitution* (2012) 391; F Michelman 'Old Kibitzes Never Die: A Rejoinder to Stu Woolman' in S Woolman & D Bilchitz (eds) *Is This Seat Taken? Conversations at the Bar, the Bench and the Academy about the South African Constitution* (2012) 417 ; F Michelman 'Eviction, Expropriation and the Dignity of the Common Law' (2013) 24 *Stellenbosh Law Review* – (forthcoming). Professor Michelman's most recently articulated concerns stem from our courts' conservative enthrallment with the existing state of the common law and the manner in which enthrallment retards the development of that law in a manner consistent with the revolutionary spirit of most of the substantive provisions of the Bill of Rights.

94 *Minister of Public Works & Others v Kyalami Ridge Environmental Association and Others (Mukhwevho Intervening)* 2001 (3) SA 1151 (CC), 2001 (7) BCLR 652 (CC) at para 111.

95 *Government of the Republic of South Africa & Others v Grootboom & Others* 2001 (1) SA 46 (CC), 2000 (11) BCLR 1169 (CC) at para 87.

96 *Port Elizabeth Municipality v Various Occupiers* 2005 (1) SA 217 (CC), 2004 (12) BCLR 1268 (CC) at para 39.

97 It must be noted that this novel approach to adjudication started to take shape in the last years of the *Langa* Court and thus came about after reassessments of doctrine by several justices appointed to the original 11 member bench of the Constitutional Court in 1995.

98 [2008] ZACC 1, 2008 (3) SA 208 (CC), 2008 (5) BCLR 475 (CC).

99 Ibid at para 16.

100 Ibid at para 15.

101 Ibid at para 19.

102 Ibid at para 14.

103 Ibid at para 20.

104 See D Davis 'Adjudicating the Socio-Economic Rights in the South African Constitution: Towards 'Deference Lite?' (2006) 22 *South African Journal on Human Rights* 301.

105 Of course, from the perspective of *Blue Moonlight* and recent 2011/2012 Constitutional Court cases discussed in Chapter 6, the jurisprudence looks to be ever more experimentalist when: (a) the Court establishes some minimum core content, say adequate temporary housing, that frame the engagement; and (b) that meaningful engagement can work effectively when occupiers receive decent representation. (The work of the Socio-Economic Rights Institute, the Centre for Applied Legal Studies and the Legal Resources Centre has been noteworthy in this regard.) In addition, and as I have noted in Chapter 6 and in this chapter, polycentric problem solving in this arena also requires the creation of positive relationships between counsel, municipalities, other organs of state, different spheres of government and private property owners. For a pre-*Blue Moonlight* discussion, see L Chenwi 'A New Approach to Remedies in Socio-Economic Rights Adjudication: *Occupiers of 51 Olivia Road and Others v City of Johannesburg and Others*' (2009) 2 *Constitutional Court Review* 371.

106 [2009] ZACC 31, 2010 (2) BCLR 99 (CC).

107 Act 6 of 2007.

108 The riots in Khutsong, Merafong and Durban reflect a conscious response to the underlying repression of pain and suffering experienced by the majority of South Africans under apartheid and in the 15 intervening years of post-liberation one party dominant democratic rule. See T Madlingozi 'The Constitutional Court, Court Watchers and the Commons: A Reply to Professor Michelman on

Constitutional Dialogue, 'Interpretive Charity' and the Citizenry As *Sangomas*' (2009) 1 *Constitutional Court Review* 63, 68–71 citing, amongst others, D McKinley 'Democracy and Social Movements in SA' (2004) 28 *Labour Bulletin* 39, 40. Madlingozi writes: 'On 20 August 2007, the Court was hearing *Merafong Demarcation Forum v President of the Republic of South Africa*. After a long period of struggle in which they had employed both institutional and extra-institutional mechanisms of democracy, the people of Khutsong decided to take their case to the Constitutional Court. Why? 'The government does not want to listen.' On that day more than a 1 000 protesters gathered outside the court room *toyi toying* and singing liberation songs. During the course of the day, things turned nasty when protesters started burning tyres, brandishing dangerous weapons and allegedly pelting the police with stones. For me, this episode vividly demonstrates the fragile state of South Africa's constitutional culture. ... Khutsong – during this period of struggle – is both a reminder of the fragility of South Africa's new political order and an indictment of its ability to respond effectively to those persons and communities in the greatest need. As one of the leaders of the Khutsong anti-demarcation movement wrote: "The struggle of the people of Greater Merafong is not just about forceful incorporation into North West, but about fighting for truth from government, people's rights and democracy." Khutsong is not a singular, if continuous, event in a long but peaceful transition from a fascist apartheid state to a democratic constitutional order. Every week some poor community engages in illegal and often violent actions to back up demands for a more responsive government. ... The time bomb ticking away inside our polity is the disillusionment of the overwhelming majority of South Africans with the politics and the policies of our post-apartheid democracy.' Madlingozi (supra) at {Find Cite} On the corrosive effects of extended one party dominant democratic rule, see S Choudhry "He Had a Mandate": The South African Constitutional Court and the African National Congress in a Dominant Party Democracy' (2009) 2 *Constitutional Court Review* 1.

109 *Abahlali* (supra) at para 97.

110 Ibid at para 69.

111 [2008] ZACC 10, 2008 (5) SA 171 (CC), 2008 (10) BCLR 968 (CC).

112 For further discussion of this case upon which my own views are partially parasitic, see M Bishop 'Vampire or Prince? The Listening Constitution and *Merafong Demarcation Forum & Others v President of the Republic of South Africa & Others* (2009) 2 *Constitutional Court Review* 313.

113 Bishop 'Vampire or Prince?' (supra) at 327. See also G Quinot 'Snapshot or Participatory Democracy? Political Engagement as Fundamental Human Right' (2009) 25 *South African Journal of Human Rights* 392.

114 *Doctors for Life* (supra) at para 128 (as cited in M Bishop 'Vampire or Prince? (supra) at 327 – 328.)

115 Ibid.

116 2005 (1) SA 580 (CC), 2005 (1) BCLR 1 (CC).

117 Ibid at para 42 ('At the level of constitutional validity, the question in this case is not whether a rule or provision of customary law offers similar remedies to the Intestate Succession Act. The issue is whether such rules or provisions are consistent with the Constitution. This status of customary law has been acknowledged and endorsed by this Court.') See also *Alexkor Ltd & Another v the Richtersveld Community & Others* 2004 (5) SA 460 (CC), 2003 (12) BCLR 1301 (CC) *('Richtersveld')* at para 51 ('While in the past indigenous law was seen through the common law lens, it must now be seen as an integral part of our law. Like all law it depends for its ultimate force and validity on the Constitution. Its validity must now be determined by reference not to common-law, but to the Constitution'); *Pharmaceutical Manufacturers Association of SA & Another: In re Ex Parte President of the Republic of South Africa & Others* 2000 (2) SA 674 (CC); 2000 (3) BCLR 241 (CC) at para 44; *Mabuza v Mbatha* 2003 (4) SA 218 (C), 2003 (7) BCLR 743 (C) at para 32 ('[These rules] provide a setting which contributes to the unity of family structures and the fostering of co-operation, a sense of responsibility in and of belonging to its members, as well as the nurturing of healthy communitarian traditions such as ubuntu. These valuable aspects of customary law more than justify its protection by the Constitution. It bears repeating, however, that as with all law, the constitutional validity of

rules and principles of customary law depend on their consistency with the Constitution and the Bill of Rights.')

118 *Bhe* (supra) at para 75.

119 Ibid at para 80.

120 See South African Law Reform Commission *The Harmonisation of the Common Law and the Indigenous Law: Succession in Customary Law* Issue Paper 12, Project 90 (April 1998) 6-9. See also TW Bennett *Human Rights and African Customary Law under the South African Constitution* (1997) 126–127. See, further, TW Bennett & C Murray 'Traditional Leaders' in S Woolman & M Bishop (eds) *Constitutional Law of South Africa* (2nd Edition, OS, December 2005) Chapter 28.

121 See, eg, *Richtersveld Community and Others v Alexkor Ltd & Another* 2003 (6) SA 104 (SCA) at paras 85–105.

122 B*he* (supra) at para 84.

123 *Bhe* (supra) at para 89.

124 Ibid at para 83.

125 Ibid at para 86. Judge Hlophe employs a similar disabling strategy in *Mabuza v Mbatha. Mabuza v Mbatha* 2003 (4) SA 218 (C), 2003 (7) BCLR 743 (C). He recognizes the supremacy of the Final Constitution at the same time as he asserts the protean features of customary law that enable it to conform, as necessary, to the dictates of the Bill of Rights. His nuanced assessment of the role of ukumekeza reconfigures siSwati marriage conventions in a manner that (a) refuses to allow ukumekeza to be used by the groom's family as a means of control over the bride and (b) consciously places the husband and wife on an equal footing with respect to subsequent determinations of whether a valid marriage under siSwati customary law has taken place. Constitutional challenges to lobola should be able to exploit the schema developed in *Bhe* and *Mabuza*. Those familiar with and committed to customary law acknowledge that: (a) the conditions under which lobola served to unite families and create security for women and their children no longer obtain; (b) cash lobolo transactions, which result in the purchase of such transient goods as home furnishings, can hardly be said to benefit the clan or the community; and (c) the present practice of lobola serves the pecuniary interests of a few men. By showing that the spirit of lobola lies in its commitment to family cohesion and that the 'distorted' rules of customary marriage emphasise male domination at the expense of communitarian concerns, a party challenging the centrality of lobola in customary marriages can close the gap between constitutional imperative and customary obligation. Following *Bhe,* a court can feel confident that in so far as lobolo remains an obstacle either to an exchange of vows or to the disengagement from a failed relationship, the practice constitutes a violation of a woman's rights to equality and dignity. More importantly for our immediate purposes, *Bhe* supports the proposition that neither the living customary law nor the Final Constitution can be squared with an institution that ultimately reduces to the purchase of a women's reproductive capacity or to compensation for the loss of female labour in the father's household. Following *Mabuza*, a court can ameliorate the burden of lobola by making its legal status as a marker of marriage contingent upon evidence of genuine mutual consent. The requirement of genuine mutual consent introduced by *Mabuza* means that lobolo can be waived as a condition for recognition of marriage. The *Mabuza* court makes clear that traditional institutions such as lobola can only survive as legally binding rites of marriage when shorn of all those asymmetries that reduce women to chattel. Even the South African Law Reform Commission recognizes the possibility that 'payment or non-payment of bridewealth' can be removed as a matter of legal consequence when assessing the validity of marriage, the spouses' marital obligations or the custodial rights to children. The Law Reform Commission observes that in customary law, payment of bridewealth is often deferred and the status of a marriage is seldom placed in doubt through failure to pay timeously. SALC Report on Customary Marriage I (supra) at para 4.3.1. It further observes after promulgation of the General Law Fourth Amendment Act, husbands lost the traditional marital power they exercised over their wives. Act 132 of 1993, s 29. The facts and the holding of *Republic v Kadhi, Kisumu Ex Parte Nasreen* provide a useful departure

point for analysis of religious rites of marriage. [1973] EALR 153 (High Court of Kenya). The High Court of Kenya was asked to enforce a Kadhi order that held that Islamic law required the return of a wife to her husband. The High Court rejected the request on the grounds that the 'Kadhi order would ... subject the [wife] to the effective dominion of the plaintiff to an extent constituting "servitude" ... and in a manner inconsistent with the intendment of s 73(1) of the [Kenyan] Constitution.' Ibid at 161. While South African courts must treat non-Christian religious rites with a relatively high degree of solicitude, a South African court would, we think, be obliged to reach an identical conclusion under the Final Constitution. Compare *Amod v Multilateral Motor Vehicle Accidents Fund (Commission for Gender Equality Intervening)* 1999 (4) SA 1319 (SCA) and *Ryland v Erdos* 1997 (2) SA 690 (C), 1997 (1) BCLR 77 (C)(Holding that Muslim religious rites of marriage are not presumptively contra bonos mores) with *Ismail v Ismail* 1983 (1) SA 1006 (A)(Holding that Muslim religious rites of marriage are contra bonos mores). The Final Constitution reflects the Lockean discomfort with using the profane power of the state to alter what others believe to be the contours of sacred space by subjecting its protection of customary law to FC s 31(2)'s proviso that a rule of customary law inconsistent with a provision of the Bill of Rights is prima facie unconstitutional, but not forcing a rule of religious community practice protected by FC s 15 and FC s 31 to operate under any such disability. See also *Taylor v Kurtstag No & Others* 2005 (2) SA 362 (W) [2004] 4 All SA 317 (W)(Court upheld the right of the Beth Din to issue a Cherem – an excommunication edict – against a member of the Jewish community who had violated the terms of the Beth Din's child maintenance order, but refused to enforce the maintenance order itself.)

126 S Woolman 'Freedom of Association' in S Woolman & M Bishop (eds) *Constitutional Law of South Africa* (2nd Edition, OS, December 2003) Chapter 44, §§ 44.3(c)(ii) and 44.2(d). See, especially, S Woolman 'Seek Justice Elsewhere: An Egalitarian Pluralist's Reply to David Bilchitz on the Distinction between Differentiation and Domination' (2012) 28 *South African Journal on Human Rights* 273; and S Woolman 'On the Fragility of Associational Life: A Constitutive Liberal's Response to Patrick Lenta' (2009) 25 *South African Journal on Human Rights* 280. See also P Lenta 'Taking Diversity Seriously: Religious Associations and Work-Related Discrimination' (2009) 125 (4) *South African Law Journal* 828; P Lenta 'Cultural and Religious Accommodation to School Uniform Regulations' (2008) 1 *Constitutional Court Review* 259; P Lenta 'Religious Liberty and Cultural Accommodation' (2005) 122 *South African Law Journal* 352. See, further, G Pienaar 'The Effect of Equality and Human Dignity on the Right to Religious Freedom' (2003) 66 *THRHR* 579 D Bilchitz *South African Journal on Human Rights.*

127 See S Woolman and M Bishop 'Down on the Farm and Barefoot in the Kitchen: Farm Labour and Domestic Labour as Forms of Servitude' (2007) 24 *Development Southern Africa* 595; S Woolman and M Bishop 'Slavery, Servitude and Forced Labour' in S Woolman & M Bishop (eds) Constitutional Law of South Africa (2nd Edition, OS, December 2005) Chapter 64.

128 *Bhe* (supra) at para 235 – 238.

129 *Minister of Home Affairs & Another v Fourie & Another; Lesbian and Gay Equality Project & Others v Minister of Home Affairs & Others* 2006 (1) SA 524 (CC), 2006 (3) BCLR 355 (CC)('*Fourie*'). See also *Fourie v Minister of Home Affairs* 2005 (3) SA 429 (SCA), 2005 (3) BCLR 241 (SCA) at paras 36–37 (No religious denomination would be compelled to marry gay or lesbian couples.)

130 For the actual order of the Court, see *Fourie* (supra) at para 162. The order, as it appears in the text above, was crafted by the Court for public consumption in its media summary. The entire media summary is available at http://www.constitutionalcourt.org.za/fourie/summary.

131 My use of the word 'correct' must come with a rider. The legitimacy that the Court provides for same sex marriages comes with a cost that my colleagues in the South African legal academy have been quick to identify. They have, to a man and a woman, roundly criticized the Constitutional Court for effectively ratifying (and reinforcing) traditional, conservative views of same-sex relationships and family structures by kicking responsibility for rectifying wrongs back to Parliament. See P de Vos 'The Inevitability of Same-Sex Marriage in South Africa's Post-Apartheid State' (2007) *South African Journal on Human Rights* 432. Pierre de Vos notes that the victory was not inevitable, but largely a function of the inclusion of 'sexual orientation' in the constitutional text and the careful

public impact litigation strategy of the National Coalition for Gay and Lesbian Equality. However, the victory did little to displace the ongoing systemic discrimination that homosexuals and lesbians face in South African society writ large. The decision holds out symbolic hope for broad-based social reform. I agree with Professor De Vos' analysis, but can only point to the 'long time coming' view of how legal decisions realize social change. Fifty-four years passed between *Brown v Board of Education* and the election of Barack Hussein Obama for two consecutive terms as President of the United States. No one would claim that race relations in the United States are suddenly relationships between equals. (The Tea Party Movement's recent success suggests the opposite is true amongst a statistically significant portion of the population. At the same time, the symbolic 9-0 vote of the US Supreme Court in *Brown* set off a process of social change that has been slow, but dramatic. Just not dramatic enough. As to the success of the NCGLE strategy culminating in *Fourie*, Justice Edwin Cameron, Advocate Gilbert Marcus and Judge Fayeeza Kathree all confirmed the decision taken in the mid-90s to proceed carefully, and to build on expected success in easy cases, before bringing a challenge to various common law rules and statutory provisions that barred gay and lesbian marriages. See 'Notes on Public Impact Litigation: Sexual Orientation and Children's Rights' (Seminar on South African Institute for Advanced Constitutional, Public, Human Rights and International Law, April 2010, On file with author.) See also D Bilchitz and M Judge 'For Whom Does the Bell Toll? The Challenges and Possibilities of the Civil Union Act for Family Law' (2007) 23 *South African Journal on Human Rights* 466 (Act does little to disentrench existing norms around the meaning of 'family' – though the law possesses the power, if properly constructed, to disentrech existing heterosexual, and anti-homosexual, biases.) See, further, AJ Barnard 'Totalitarianism, Same-Sex Marriage and Democratic Politics in Post-Apartheid South Africa' (2007) 23 *South African Journal on Human Rights* [Find Cite] (Views *Fourie* as only a partial success, given Parliament's repeated attempts to evade the dramatic democratic moment reflected in the judgment); R Robson 'Sexual Democracy' (2007) 23 *South African Journal on Human Rights* 409 (Ties reconceptualization of sexuality to the possibility for more profound forms of democratization in South Africa.)

132 Justice O'Regan, in a partial dissent, found that the Court's clear commitment to ensuring that same-sex couples and opposite-sex couples receive the same treatment by the State required the Court to 'read in words to section 30 of the Act that would ... permit gays and lesbians to be married by civil marriage officers' and to develop the common law to realize the same ends. *Fourie* (supra) at paras 169 – 170. Unfortunately, the Civil Union Act passed by Parliament retains a commitment to 'separate but equal' treatment of same-sex life partners that the Court held, quite clearly, to be manifestly inconsistent with FC s 9 and FC s 10. (While same sex partners may now have the same duties and responsibilities as opposite sex couples that enter civil unions, the status of the new institution – civil union – does not seem on par with that of marriage.) Parliament does not appear to have taken the Court's invitation to revisit the marriage laws in light of the demands of the basic law as seriously as the court might have liked.

133 See T Roux 'Principle and Pragmatism on the Constitutional Court of South Africa' (2009) 7 *International Journal of Constitutional Law* 106.

134 See B Goldblatt 'Different Routes to Relationship Recognition Reform: A Comparative Discussion of South Africa and Australia' Law and Society Association Australia and New Zealand (LSAANZ) *W(h)ither Human Rights Conference* (December 2008)(Manuscript on file with author).

135 See S Woolman and M Bishop 'Community Rights: Language, Culture and Religion' in S Woolman & M Bishop (eds) *Constitutional Law of South Africa* (2nd Edition, OS, March 2007) Chapter 58.

136 *Fourie* (supra) at para 61 citing *Christian Education South Africa v Minister of Education* 2000 (4) SA 757 (CC), 2000 (10) BCLR 1051 (CC) at para 24 and *S v Lawrence; S v Negal; S v Solberg* 1997 (4) SA 1176 (CC) (1997 (10) BCLR 1348) at paras 146 – 147.

137 *Fourie* (supra) at paras 90–98.

138 S Woolman 'Seek Justice Elsewhere' (supra).

139 2008 (9) BCLR 914 (CC); 2009 (2) SA 66 (CC).

140 *Shilubana* (supra) at paras 54 and 55.

141 See *Pharmaceutical Manufacturers Association of South Africa and Another: In re Ex Parte President of the Republic of South Africa and Others* [2000] ZACC 1; 2000 (2) SA 674 (CC); 2000 (3) BCLR 241; *Fedsure Life Assurance Ltd and Others v Greater Johannesburg Transitional Metropolitan Council and Others* [1998] ZACC 17; 1999 (1) SA 374 (CC); 1998 (12) BCLR 1458. See, further, F Michelman 'The Rule of Law, Legality and Constitutional Supremacy' in S Woolman & M Bishop (eds) *Constitutional Law of South Africa* (2nd Edition, OS, December 2005) Chapter 11; D Dyzenhaus 'The Past and Future of the Rule of Law in South Africa' (2007) 124 *South African Law Journal* 734.

142 For a critical take on *Shilubana*, see C Albertyn 'The Stubborn Persistence of Patriarchy? Gender Equality and Cultural Diversity in South Africa' (2009) 2 *Constitutional Court Review* 163. See also C Rautenbach, W du Plessis & G Pienaar 'Is Primogeniture Extinct like the Dodo, or is there any Prspect of it Rising from the Ashes? Comments on the Evolution of Customary Law' (2006) 22 *South African Journal on Human Rights* 99; C Rautenbach 'Therapeutic Jurisprudence in the Customary Courts of South Africa (Traditional Authority Courts as Therapeutic Agents)' (2005) 21 *South African Journal on Human Rights* 323. If Traditional Authority Courts were intended to soften the transition to and conflict with the institutions of a Western-style constitutional democracy, then we have good reason to doubt whether they have played such a role. Resistance to the Court's engagement with traditional norms seems to have increased over the intervening years. Whether a Constitutional Court currently led by Chief Justice Ngcobo will soften the conflict between traditional norms and constitutional norms – as suggested by CJ Ngcobo's earlier writings as a member of the Court – remains to be seen.

143 [2008] ZACC 8, 2008 (5) SA 94 (CC), 2008 (9) BCLR 865 (CC)('*Nyathi I*').

144 [2009] ZACC 29, 2010 (4) BCLR 293 (CC), 2010 (4) SA 567 (CC)('*Nyathi II*').

145 The minority in *Nyathi I* took issue with the need to put the state on such stringent terms. Nkabinde J noted that: 'The problem of non-compliance with court orders has frequently confronted our courts in recent times and various solutions have been devised to ensure the satisfaction of judgment debts. In some cases, courts have opted for contempt proceedings to enforce money judgments against the state.' The Justice cited *Mjeni v Minister of Health and Welfare, Eastern Cape* 2000 (4) SA 446 (TkH); *East London Transitional Council v MEC for Health, Eastern Cape and Others* 2001 (3) SA 1133 (Ck); [2000] 4 All SA 443 (Ck); *Federation of Governing Bodies of South Africa (Gauteng) v MEC Education, Gauteng* 2002 (1) SA 660 (T) at 678G-679H; *Lombard v Minister van Verdediging* 2002 (3) SA 242 (T) In other cases, structural interdicts have been granted. The Justice cited *Magidimisi and Others v The Premier, Eastern Cape and Others* Case No. 2180/04, 25 April 2006. The solutions in those cases appear to have been effective in satisfying the judgment debts in question. *Nyathi I* (supra) at para 95. The Justice then rehearsed Nugent JA's words on behalf of a unanimous Supreme Court of Appeal in *MEC, Department of Welfare, Eastern Cape v Kate* 2006 (4) SA 478 (SCA); [2006] 2 All SA 455 (SCA): 'It goes without saying that a public functionary who fails to fulfil an obligation that is imposed upon him or her by law is open to proceedings for a *mandamus* compelling him or her to do so. That remedy lies against the functionary upon whom the statute imposes the obligation, and not against the provincial government. If *Jayiya* has been construed as meaning that the remedy lies against the political head of the government department, as suggested by the Court below, then that construction is clearly not correct. The remarks that were made in *Jayiya* related to claims that lie against the State, for which the political head of the relevant department may, for convenience, be cited nominally in terms of s 2 of the State Liability Act 20 of 1957, though it is well established that the government might be cited instead. Moreover, there ought to be no doubt that a public official who is ordered by a court to do or to refrain from doing a particular act, and fails to do so, is liable to be committed for contempt, in accordance with ordinary principles, and there is nothing in *Jayiya* that suggests the contrary. '*Kate* (supra) at para 30. Justice Nkabinde further noted that, according to Nugent J's dictum': … a judgment creditor is free to seek a *mandamus* against the public official who fails to comply with a court order. What the judgment creditor is precluded from doing is

seeking committal of the state official concerned for failure to satisfy a judgment debt without first obtaining a *mandamus* because, in the view of the Supreme Court of Appeal, that would constitute the creation of a crime that does not exist under the common law. It must be stressed however that the remarks by the Supreme Court of Appeal must not be construed as meaning that a *mandamus* cannot be sought against political heads of state departments. The remarks were made in the context of the case before that Court. It follows that the remedy of *mandamus* is available against, any public official who is obliged to do something by a statute but fails to act promptly or diligently.' *Nyathi I* (supra) at para 95.

146 *Nyathi II* (supra) at para 57.

147 Ibid.

148 This concern is hardly new. See M Swart 'Left Out in the Cold? Crafting Constitutional Remedies for the Poorest of the Poor' (2005) 21 *South African Journal on Human Rights* 163. Swart contends that the Constitutional Court ought to be more 'adventurous' in dealing with government departments and officials who fail to execute court orders. She too cites *Kate* as an example of an appropriate remedy. How adventurous courts can be without guns, butter or budgets is a question well worth considering.

149 [2009] ZACC 16, 2010 (3) SA 454 (CC), 2009 (9) BCLR 847 (CC). As always, I am indebted to Michael Bishop and his account of this case and other related matters.

150 [2011] ZACC 8, 2011 (7) BCLR 723 (CC)(*'Joe Slovo II'*).

151 *Thubelisha Homes v Various Occupants* 2008 JDR 0257 (C).

152 *Joe Slovo I* (supra) at paras 155–156, 180, 280 and 358.

153 Ibid at paras 238 and 244 (Ngcobo J, concurring).

154 Ibid at para 296 (O'Regan J, concurring).

155 Ibid at para 408 (Sachs J, concurring).

156 Ibid at para 407 (Sachs J, concurring) ('[T]hose who have been compelled by poverty and landlessness to live in shelters, should be discouraged from regarding themselves as helpless victims, lacking the possibilities of personal moral agency. … The achievement of a just and equitable outcome required an appropriate contribution not only from the municipal authorities but from the residents themselves.')

157 *Joe Slovo I* Order at para 11 as described by M Bishop & J Brickhill 'Constitutional Law' 2009 (2) *Juta Quarterly Report*.

158 M Bishop & J Brickhill 'Constitutional Law' 2009 (2) *Juta Quarterly Report*.

159 *Joe Slovo I* Order (supra) at para 11.

160 Ibid at paragraphs 114, 175, 260–261, 313, 326 and 409.

161 *Joe Slovo II* (supra) at para 24.

162 Ibid at para 37.

163 The notion that meaningful engagement might do some work in the formation of participatory bubbles is given credence by those opinions on the *Joe Slovo* bench that require the court-imposed engagement to be meaningful: failure to meet this requirement could result in a finding that the state had acted unreasonably in terms of FC s 26. (A failure on the part of a member of the community to make appropriate use of engagement structures might support a finding that she is owed no remedy that might better suit her needs.) However, the connection between meaningful engagement and participatory bubbles only makes sense on the thicker account of engagement offered by Justice Sachs. The thicker or the more demanding the engagement required, the more likely it is to generate the kind of information necessary to resolve a dispute more optimally a dispute. No party has an interest in sitting on information in such negotiations, only to have its silence ratified by a Court finding – against the party – that the engagement was meaningful and the settlement reasonable in terms of s 26. The notion of 'engagement as bubbles' is given greater purchase when it comes to a court order – signed by the entire bench – that (even while upholding the eviction) mandates on-going, court-supervised discussions between the residents and the state in order to realize a mutually

acceptable, if not pareto optimal, solution. The on-going supervision and reports back to the Court is – as we saw in US drug treatment courts – one of the hallmarks of emergent experimentalism in American constitutional law. By retaining jurisdiction and supervision, a court can ensure that both parties operate with the rules of the game – reasonableness under s 26 – without imposing an outcome in a situation where the 'facts' on the ground are likely to determine whether one would find the state's behaviour reasonable or unreasonable.

164 See, eg, *City of Johannesburg Metropolitan Municipality v Blue Moonlight Properties 39 (Pty) Ltd & Another* [2011] ZACC 33, 2012 (2) SA 104 (CC); *Occupiers of Skurweplaas 353 JR v PPC Aggregate Quarries (Pty) Ltd* [2011] ZACC 36, *Occupiers of Mooiplaats 355 JR v Golden Thread & Others,* [2011] ZACC 35, 2012 (2) SA 337 (CC), 2012 (4) BCLR 372 (CC)('*Ermelo*').

165 2010 (2) SA 415 (CC), 2010 (3) BCLR 177 (CC).

166 The High Court had heard the matter twice. *Hoërskool Ermelo & Others v Departementshoof van die Mpumalanga* [2007] ZAGPHC 4 (2 February 2007)(*'Hoërskool Ermelo I'*); *Hoërskool Ermelo & Others v Departementshoof van die Mpumalanga* [2007] ZAGPHC 232 (12 October 2007)(*'Hoërskool Ermelo II'*). In *Hoërskool Ermelo I*, Judge Prinsloo, of the Pretoria High Court, suspended a decision of the Mpumalanga education department to dissolve the school's governing body and to replace it with a departmentally appointed committee. The dissolution would have enabled the Mpumalanga education department to alter the school's language policy and allowed English-speaking pupils to receive instruction in English. On appeal, Transvaal Judge President Ngoepe, and Judges Seriti and Ranchod set aside the High Court ruling in *Hoërskool Ermelo I.* The *Hoërskool Ermelo II* court found that the Afrikaans-medium public school must admit English-speaking pupils. Of particular moment for the *Hoërskool Ermelo II* Court was the under-subscription of Hoërskool Ermelo. Given that Hoërskool Ermelo was operating at only half-capacity, the Full Bench found that it was 'reasonably practicable' – as contemplated by FC s 29(2) – for the high school to accommodate the 113 Grade 8 learners. The mere fact that all the classrooms were being employed and that the existing curriculum turned on the current availability of classrooms did not constitute sufficient grounds for excluding English learners and maintaining Hoërskool Ermelo as a single-medium Afrikaans-speaking public school. Equity, practicability and historical redress – the three express grounds for assessment of existing language policy in terms of FC s 29(2) – justified the transformation of Hoërskool Ermelo from a single-medium public school into a parallel-medium public school. The Supreme Court of Appeal reversed the judgment of the High Court in *Hoërskool Ermelo II. Hoërskool Ermelo & Another v Head, Department of Education, Mpumalanga, & Others* 2009 (3) SA 422 (SCA) ('*Ermelo III*'). The Supreme Court of Appeal found the that HOD lacked the requisite statutory authority to alter the SGB's language policy. It did not contemplate the constitutional implications of the matter. The Constitutional Court upheld some aspects of the SCA's judgment – namely the rebuke of the HoD with regard to a brace of procedural irregularities that undermined the Department's attempt to alter Hoërskool Ermelo's language policies. At the same time, the Constitutional Court indicated that it wanted to hear – after appropriate consideration – how the HOD planned to engage the issue of a parallel instruction school or an English only instruction school in the Ermelo circuit. It also made clear that Hoërskool Ermelo must revisit its language policies in light of the Constitutional Court's clear finding that the SGB did not possess the unmitigated authority to determine the school's language policy and that it was obliged, in terms of FC s 29(2), to take the needs of all learners into account when it determined the language of instruction: the right to instruction in a language of choice (where reasonably practicable), fairness, feasibility and the need to remedy the results of past racially discriminatory laws and practices must play a critical role in their decision-making.

167 *Ermelo* CC (supra) at paras 2, 46, 49 – 53.

168 B Fleisch *Primary Education in Crisis* (2010).

169 J Jansen *We Need to Talk* (2011).

170 TJ Haarhoff 'Foreword' in EG Malherbe *The Bilingual School* (1941).

171 [2011] ZACC 13, 2011 (8) BCLR 761 (CC). But see *United Apostolic Faith Church v Boksburg Christian Academy* 2011 (6) SA 156 (GSJ) at para 16 ('Even if it were accepted that ownership of the property remained vested in the English church or the governing body thereof, a person in bona fide possession of immovable property acquired a right in rem which gave rise to the right to apply for an eviction order. The church was clearly the bona fide possessor of the property and, as such, entitled to apply for the ejectment of others occupying it.' The difference is that the learners here were deemed to lack a constitutional trump, in terms of FC s 29(1) vis-à-vis the property rights of the church.)

172 *Juma Musjid* (supra) at para 11 ('The school was officially established in 1957 as a government-aided school, and a Madressa, an Islamic school established to offer education with a distinctive religious character, for children in Grades 1 to 9. During 1997, the Trust permitted the Department to enlist the school as a public school with an Islamic religious ethos on its property in terms of section 14(1) of the [South African Schools] Act.)

173 The provisional order read: 'Having heard argument on behalf of the applicants, respondents and amici curiae, and having considered the application for leave to appeal, the Court is satisfied that— (a) The Trustees (first to ninth respondents) have a constitutional duty to respect the learners' right to a basic education in terms of section 29(1) of the Constitution; (b) Having regard to all the circumstances of the case, including this obligation, the Trustees acted reasonably in seeking an order for eviction; and (c) In considering the Trustees' application and in granting the order of eviction, the High Court did not properly consider the best interests of the learners under section 28(2) and their right to a basic education under section 29(1) of the Constitution. .... In view of the urgency of the matter, the following provisional order is made, for which reasons will in due course be furnished: (a) The Tenth Respondent, Member of the Executive Council for Education for the Province of KwaZulu-Natal (MEC), is ordered to engage meaningfully with the first to ninth respondents (Trustees) and the first applicant (School Governing Body) in an effort to resolve the questions arising from the dispute before the Court, and the options available for its resolution, including— (i) whether it is possible for the MEC to conclude an agreement in terms of section 14 of the South African Schools Act 84 of 1996 with the Trustees for the continued operation of the school; and, if not, (ii) what steps the MEC has taken to secure alternative placements for the learners enrolled at the school in accordance with the learners' right to a basic education. (b) The MEC is required to file a written report with this Court by no later than Friday 8 October 2010 setting out— (i) the efforts undertaken in terms of paragraph (a) of this order; (ii) the conclusions to which the MEC has come; and (iii) the reasons for those conclusions. (c) In the light of the MEC's report, the Trustees are granted leave to apply directly to this Court before Friday 29 October 2010, on the papers as suitably supplemented, and on notice to the other parties, for an order that will be just and equitable, including an order for eviction.' *Juma Musjid* (supra) at para 3, fn 5.

174 The province had – in 1997 – denied the desire of the Trust to establish an independent Islamic school on the property. In addition, it had continually failed to make payments to the Trust for the use of the property from 2004 onwards – despite repeated undertakings to do so.

175 Ibid at paras 42 and 43. The Court also quoted, with approval, General Comment 13 of the UN Committee on Economic, Social and Cultural Rights, on the meaning of the right to in terms of the ICESCR: 'Education is both a human right in itself and an indispensable means of realizing other human rights. As an empowerment right, education is the primary vehicle by which economically and socially marginalized adults and children can lift themselves out of poverty and obtain the means to participate fully in their communities. Education has a vital role in empowering women, safeguarding children from exploitation and hazardous labour and sexual exploitation, promoting human rights and democracy, protecting the environment, and controlling population growth. Increasingly, education is recognised as one of the best financial investments States can make. But the importance of education is not just practical: a well-educated, enlightened and active mind, able to wander freely and widely, is one of the joys and rewards of human existence.' ICESCR Committee

General Comment 13 (21st Session, 1999) "The Right to Education (art 13)" UN Doc E/C.12/1999/10 at para 1 cited at *Juma Musjid* (supra) at para 41.

176 *Khumalo v Holomisa* 2002 (5) SA 401 (CC), 2002 (8) BCLR 771 (CC)('*Khumalo*').

177 *Holomisa v Khumalo* 2002 (3) SA 38 (T).

178 1998 (4) SA 1196 (SCA), 1999 (1) BCLR 1 (SCA)('*Bogoshi*').

179 Elsewhere I have offered several demurrals to the *Du Plessis* doctrine. S Woolman 'Application' in S Woolman & M Bishop (eds) *Constitutional Law of South Africa* (2nd Edition, OS, March 2005) Chapter 31. As three dissenting justices in *Du Plessis* note, the text did not settle the debate. But it did lead the *Du Plessis* Court to the jurisprudentially untenable conclusion that while rules of common law that govern disputes between private parties are not subject to direct application of the substantive provisions of the Bill of Rights, (because constitutions traditionally do not apply to relations between private parties), rules in statutes or regulations that govern disputes between private parties are subject to direct application of the substantive provisions of the Bill of Rights. So the 'fact' that a legal dispute is between private parties would appear to be a necessary *but not a sufficient* condition for the *Du Plessis* Court's conclusion. Indeed, it is hard to know whether it should be called a 'condition' at all. As to whether the law governing a dispute between private parties was subject to direct application under the Interim Constitution was entirely and fortuitously contingent upon the form the law took. Embedded in the *Du Plessis* Court's differential treatment of these two bodies of law is the premise that the common law – unlike legislation – protects a private ordering of social life that is neutral between the interests of various social actors. That premise is not only false. It runs directly against the commitment to flourishing (and the social democratic jurisprudence of experimentalism) articulated in these pages. Put slightly differently, abstention from constitutional review of common-law rules functions as a defence of deeply entrenched and radically inegalitarian distributions of wealth and power in South Africa by immunizing from review those rules of property, contract and delict that sustain those inegalitarian distributions. The differential treatment of the two bodies of law also rests on a traditional distinction between the public realm and the private realm. At a minimum, this distinction fails to recognize the extent to which the state structures all legal relationships. With the ineluctable erosion of the public-private divide, one of the last justifications for treating common law and legislation differently disintegrates as well. What we are left with is a doctrine that traditionally produces an incoherent body of decisions and that cannot explain why courts, perfectly capable of vindicating autonomy interests when asked to review statutory provisions governing private relationships for consistency with the Bill of Rights, prefer not to subject common-law rules governing private relationships to the same form of scrutiny.

180 The black letter law on application in terms of *Khumalo* takes the following form. FC s 8(1) stands for the following two propositions: (a) All law governing disputes between the state and a natural or juristic person is subject to the direct application of the Bill of Rights; (b) All state conduct that gives rise to a dispute between the state and a natural or juristic person is subject to the direct application of the Bill of Rights. FC s 8(2) stands for the following proposition: Disputes between natural and/or juristic persons *may* be subject to the direct application of the Bill of Rights if the specific right asserted is deemed to apply. FC s 8(3) stands for the following proposition: Where direct application of the right asserted occurs in terms of FC s 8(2), and the court further finds a non-justifiable abridgment of that right, then the court must develop the law in a manner that gives adequate effect to the right infringed. For reasons the judgment does not adequately explain, the *Khumalo* Court chose to ignore FC s 8(1)'s injunction that the Bill of Rights applies to 'all law' and binds 'the judiciary'. One might have thought that such an explanation was warranted, given that it was precisely the absence of these phrases – 'all law' and binds 'the judiciary' – in a comparable section of the Interim Constitution that led the *Du Plessis* Court to reach the conclusion that the Interim Constitution's Bill of Rights did not apply directly to disputes between private parties governed by the common law. The *Khumalo* Court claims instead that had it given FC s 8(1) a gloss that ensured that the substantive provisions of the Bill of Rights applied to all law-governed disputes

between private parties – regardless of the provenance of the law – it would have rendered FC s 8(3) meaningless. That particular assertion is unfounded – and contradicted by the Court's own s 8(3) jurisprudence. See Woolman 'Application' (supra). My preferred reading on application takes the following form. FC s 8(1) covers 'all law' – regardless of provenance, form, and or the parties before the court. FC s 8(1) also covers all government conduct – by all branches of government and all organs of state – whether that conduct takes the form of law or reflects some other manifestation or exercise of state power. In sum, FC s 8(1) should be understood to stand for the following proposition: *All* rules of law and every exercise of state power are subject to the direct application of the Bill of Rights. FC s 8(2) covers dispute-generating conduct between private actors not 'adequately' governed by an express rule of law. There are two basic ways to read 'not governed adequately by an express rule of law.' First, it could contemplate the possibility of a dispute over an aspect of social life that is not currently governed by any rule of law at all. Such instances will be rare. Indeed, there is good reason to believe that such instances do not exist at all. The second and better reading views non-rule governed conduct in a much narrower sense. In many instances, a body of extant rules – or even background norms – may be said to govern a particular set of private relationships. FC s 8(2) calls our attention to the fact that these rules of law may not give adequate effect to the specific substantive provisions of the Bill of Rights and may require the courts to develop a new rule of law that does give adequate effect to a particular provision in the Bill of Rights in so far as a dispute between private persons requires it to do so. In sum, FC s 8(2) should be understood to stand for the following proposition: While, on the Hohfeldian view, a body of extant rules – or background norms – will always govern a social relationship, those same rules will not always give adequate effect to a provision in the Bill of Rights. FC s 8(2) calls attention to the potential gap between extant rules of law and the prescriptive content of the Bill of Rights, and, where necessary, requires the courts to bridge that gap by bringing the law into line with the demands of the particular constitutional right or rights deemed to apply. If we decide that the right invoked engages the conduct in question and that the right has been unjustifiably infringed, then we move on to FC s 8(3). FC ss 8(3)*(a)* and *(b)* enjoin the court to develop new rules of law and remedies designed to give effect to the right infringed. Thus, where FC s 8(2) acknowledges gaps in existing legal doctrine, FC s 8(3) aims to fill those gaps. In sum, FC s 8(3) should be understood to stand for the following proposition: If the court finds that the right relied upon warrants direct application to the conduct that has given rise to the dispute, and further finds a non-justifiable abridgment of the right, then FC ss 8(3)*(a)* and *(b)* guide the court's development of the law in a manner that gives adequate effect to the right infringed. It may be, however, that the prescriptive content of the substantive provisions of the Bill of Rights does not engage the rule of law or conduct at issue. Two things can happen. A court can decide that the Bill of Rights has nothing at all to say about the dispute in question. A court can decide that although no specific provision of the Bill of Rights is offended by the law or the conduct in question, the Bill of Rights warrants the development of the law in a manner that coheres with the general spirit, purport and objects of Chapter 2. In sum, FC s 39(2) should be understood to stand for the following: Where no specific right can be relied upon by a party challenging a given rule of law or the extant construction of a rule of law, the courts are obliged to interpret legislation or to develop the law in light of the general objects of the Bill of Rights. See Woolman 'Application' (supra).

181 In *Du Plessis*, the traditional view of constitutional review was used to *suppress* direct application of the Bill of Rights with respect to disputes between private parties governed by the common law. In *Khumalo*, the traditional view of constitutional review is used to *defer* – and potentially suppress – direct application of the Bill of Rights with respect to disputes between private parties. Here's the rub. Direct application is deferred – and by that I simply mean turned into a question of interpretation – with respect to *all* disputes between private parties. It matters not whether the law governing disputes between private parties is grounded in statute, subordinate legislation, regulation, common law or customary law. Put slightly differently, whereas the Interim Constitution's Bill of Rights was understood to apply directly, and unequivocally, to legislation that governed private disputes, the

Final Constitution's Bill of Rights (ostensibly) does not. Technically, less law is subject to the direct unqualified application of the Bill of Rights under the *Khumalo* Court's reading of the Final Constitution than it was under the *Du Plessis* Court's reading of the Interim Constitution. (The Court has not followed the logic of its own judgment. It would be surprising indeed if a statute governing private disputes were not held subject to the direct application of the Bill of Rights.) Doctrinal tension generates a second objection. The Constitutional Court has constructed a powerful set of doctrines in which (1) every exercise of state power is subject to constitutional review and (2) every law is subject to the objective theory of unconstitutionality. See *Ingledew v Financial Services Board: In re Financial Services Board v Van der Merwe & Another* 2003 (4) SA 584 (CC), 2003 (8) BCLR 825 (CC) at para 20 ('This court has adopted the doctrine of objective constitutional invalidity.') Much is rightly made of the Constitutional Court's bold assertion in *Fedsure*, *Pharmaceutical Manufacturers* and their progeny that all law derives its force from the basic law – the Final Constitution – and that all law, and all conduct sourced in the law, must as a logical matter be consistent with the basic law. *Fedsure Life Assurance Ltd v Greater Johannesburg Transitional Metropolitan Council* 1999 (1) SA 374 (CC), 1998 (12) BCLR 1458 (CC); *Pharmaceutical Manufacturers Association of SA: In Re Ex Parte President of The Republic of South Africa* 2000 (2) SA 674 (CC), 2000 (3) BCLR 241 (CC). In its most general form, the doctrine of objective unconstitutionality holds that the validity or the invalidity of any given law is in no way contingent upon the parties to the case. If a provision of legislation would be deemed to be unconstitutional when invoked by an individual in a dispute between the State and an individual, then it must likewise be unconstitutional when invoked by an individual in a dispute between that individual and another individual. However, the Court's differentiation between FC s 8(1) disputes that are invariably subject to the direct application of the Bill of Rights and FC s 8(2) disputes that are not invariably subject to the direct application of the Bill of Rights is logically incompatible with the doctrine of objective unconstitutionality. The *Khumalo* application doctrine relies upon the ability to distinguish constitutional cases – and thus the constitutionality of laws – upon the basis of the parties before the court. The doctrine of objective unconstitutionality denies the ability to distinguish constitutional cases – and thus the constitutionality of laws – upon the basis of the parties before the court. This contradiction is a direct consequence of the *Khumalo* Court's refusal to give the term 'all law' in FC s 8(1) it's most obvious construction and the Court's ostensible preference for making FC s 8(2) the engine that drives the analysis of all disputes between private parties. Not even the good faith reconstruction of *Khumalo* can meet this second objection. The third objection flows from the *Khumalo* Court's refusal to say anything about FC s 8(1)'s binding of the judiciary. Perhaps the most damning consequence of this structured silence is that it offends a canon of constitutional interpretation relied upon by Justice O'Regan in *Khumalo* itself: 'We cannot adopt an interpretation which would render a provision of the Constitution to be without any apparent purpose.' *Khumalo* (supra) at para 32. Not only does Justice O'Regan refuse to give the phrase 'any apparent purpose', we cannot, even on the good faith reconstruction, give it any apparent purpose. The good faith reconstruction gains its traction through a distinction between a constitutional norm's range of application and that same norm's prescriptive content. That creates the interpretational space to argue that while FC s 8(1) speaks to each specific constitutional norm's range of application – and does not distinguish one genus of law from another – FC s 8(2) speaks to the prescriptive content of each specific constitutional norm and directs us to consider whether that prescriptive content ought to be understood to govern the private conduct of the private parties that constitutes the gravamen of the complaint. This good faith reconstruction does no work with respect to the phrase 'binds the judiciary' because the distinction between 'range' and 'prescriptive content' engages the relationship between constitutional norms and ordinary law. It does not speak to the provenance of a given law. The reason it cannot be recast in a manner that speaks to the differing concerns of FC s 8(1) and FC s 8(2) is that FC s 8(2) does not concern itself with our different law-making institutions – legislative, executive or judicial. What is left? A weak reading in which the judiciary is bound – not in terms of the 'law' it makes – but purely in terms of its 'conduct' (or 'non-law-making conduct'). It seems to me to defy both logic and common sense to argue that when FC s 8(1) binds the legislature and the judiciary, it means to bind the actions of legislators or judges solely in their personal capacity. When we bind the legislature, we must bind both the law it makes and the non-law-making actions it takes. The text offers no reason to treat the judiciary any differently. While we do want state actors – legislators and judges alike – to care about the manner in which they comport themselves, we care primarily about the law they make. But that is not what *Khumalo* says, nor can it be reconstructed in such a manner as to say so. The final objection to *Khumalo*'s construction of FC s 8 turns on the style of the argument. In short, before Justice O'Regan decides whether to engage the applicant's exception to the action in defamation in terms of freedom of expression, she has already concluded: *(a)* that the law of defamation is in pretty good shape post-*Bogoshi*; *(b)* that freedom of expression is important but not central to an open and democratic society; and *(c)* that dignity – especially as viewed through the lens of reputation – is of paramount concern. Only after having reached these conclusions does Justice O'Regan decide that this matter warrants direct application of freedom of expression to the common law of defamation in a dispute between private parties. The judgment looks, in manner of delivery, much like the kind of judgment in which, under FC s 39(2), the common law is developed via indirect application of the Bill of Rights. The style of the judgment suggests that the *Khumalo* Court considers it relatively unimportant to engage this dispute as if, in fact, direct application takes place. Or more accurately, by packaging *Khumalo* as if it were simply a common law judgment, the *Khumalo* Court intimates that the difference between direct application and indirect application of the Bill of Rights is minimal, if not entirely absent. It is this style or mode of reasoning that blocks the kind of experimentalism and flourishing jurisprudence that a bold horizontal application doctrine would invite. I might be inclined to accept this elision of the analytical processes required by FC s 8 and FC s 39(2) were it not for the fact that the Supreme Court of Appeal and the Constitutional Court have handed down judgments regarding constitutional jurisdiction, *stare decisis* and indirect application under FC s 39(2) that manifest a clear desire not to disturb settled bodies of common law precedent and that cannot help but immunize a substantial body of apartheid-era decisions from reconsideration by lower courts. This claim requires some amplification. Leaving aside the problem of surplusage raised by our courts' occasional interchangeable use of FC s 8 and FC s 39(2), the Supreme Court of Appeal in *Afrox*, extending the reasoning of the Constitutional Court in *Walters*, has held that there is at least one critical difference between direct application under FC s 8 and indirect application under FC s 39(2). *Afrox Healthcare Bpk v Strydom* 2002 (6) SA 21 (SCA)('*Afrox*'); *Ex parte Minister of Safety and Security & Others: In re S v Walters & Another* 2002 (4) SA 613 (CC), 2002 (2) SACR 105 (CC), 2002 (7) BCLR 663 (CC)('*Walters*'). A High Court may revisit pre-constitutional Appellate Division precedent only where a party has a colourable claim grounded in the direct application of a substantive provision of the Bill of Rights. High Courts may not alter existing common law precedent (whether pre-constitutional or post-constitutional) through indirect application of FC s 39(2). (The rest of our appellate courts' novel doctrine of constitutional *stare decisis* further constrains the High Courts' constitutional jurisdiction.) What happens when our appellate courts' marry this restrictive doctrine of *stare decisis* to an incrementalist gloss on indirect application in terms of FC s 39(2)? It spawns an application doctrine that effectively disables the High Court from undertaking meaningful constitutional review of existing common law precedent (as well as all other constructions of law) and thereby protects 'traditional' conceptions of law and existing legal hierarchies. This observation about the manner in which our existing array of application doctrines – as well as related doctrines of *stare decisis* and constitutional jurisdiction – conspire to blunt the experimental and flourishing potential of the basic law is one of the strongest rejoinders to those jurists and commentators who have suggested that whether one relies upon FC s 8 (1) or FC s 8 (2), or FC s 39(2), the song remains the same: namely, how should the law governing a dispute be developed, re-formulated or re-interpreted? For the most compelling argument that I have, above and elsewhere, elevated form over function (offered by the same person who assisted me in making my argument as persuasive as it could possibly be), see F Michelman 'On the Uses of Interpretive Charity' (supra). For some evidence that Professor Michelman has come to the conclusion that the South African courts' predilection for common law review undermines the progressive political purpose of the Bill of Right's substantive provisions, see F Michelman 'Eviction Expropriation and the Dignity of the Common Law' (2013) 24 *Stellenbosch Law Review* – (fortchcoming).

182 *Carmichele v Minister of Safety and Security* 2001 (4) SA 938 (CC), 2001 (10) BCLR 995 (CC) ('*Carmichele*').

183 Ibid at para 40.

184 See D Davis & K Klare 'Transformative Constitutionalism, the Common Law and Customary Law' (2010) 26 *South African Journal on Human Rights* 403.

185 *Thebus* (supra) at para 28.

186 1999 (1) SA 6 (CC), 1998 (12) BCLR 1517 (CC) at paras 90 and 96.

187 *Amod v Multilateral Motor Vehicle Accidents Fund* 1998 (4) SA 753 (CC), 1998 (10) BCLR 1207 (CC) at paras 31–33. See also *De Freitas & Another v Society of Advocates of Natal (Natal Law Society Intervening)* 1998 (11) BCLR 1345 (CC) at paras 20–21.

188 FC s 39(2), although not engaged expressly in *Khumalo*, now stands, under a secondary body of black letter law, for the following two propositions: (a) Where an asserted right is, under FC s 8(2), deemed not to apply directly to a dispute between private parties, the court may still develop the common law or interpret the provision of legislation in light of the more general objects of the Bill of Rights; (b) Even where a right is asserted directly, the court may still speak as if a finding of inconsistency or invalidity requires that a new rule of common law be developed in terms of FC s 39(2). See *Minister of Home Affairs v National Institute for Crime Prevention* 2005 (3) SA 280 (CC), 2004 (5) BCLR 445 (CC)(On the difference between how constitutional norms operate as values and how they operate as rules.) Professor Frank Michelman and I have been round and round about whether much turns on this conceptual confusion. I have, in large part, deferred to Professor Michelman's super-pragmatic account of s 39(2) jurisprudence – that sense can be made of it, and that it does not reflect a wholesale flight from substantive engagement with the specific provisions of the Bill of Rights. At the same time, I maintain, and believe the decisions and the weight of academic authority show, that the Court's preference for s 39(2) 'objectives' analysis, over actual rights analysis, has allowed for a creeping thinness in the Court's jurisprudence. See Woolman 'Application' (2005)(supra); Woolman 'The Amazing, Vanishing Bill of Rights' (2007) (supra); Michelman 'On the Uses of Interpretive Charity' (2008)(supra); Woolman 'Between Charity and Clarity' (2010)(supra); Michelman 'Old Kibitzes Never Die' (2010)(supra).

189 D Moseneke 'Transformative Constitutionalism: Its Implications for the Law of Contract' (2009) *Stellenbosch Law Review* 1, 8.

190 See M Tushnet 'The Issue of State Action/Horizontal Effect on Comparative Constitutional Law' (2003) 1 *Journal of International Constitutional Law* 79. Tushnet thought, a decade ago, that two factors – with respect to South Africa – might influence the extent to which a given set of application provisions will be more or less likely to result in the constitutional transformation of existing bodies of private law: (1) a specialized Constitutional Court that lacks powers of general jurisdiction has a limited capacity to change non-constitutional bodies of law and concomitantly less control over courts of general jurisdiction; and (2) a commitment to strong social democracy – through either socio-economic rights or state policy or both – diminishes the impact of public-private distinctions in constitutional law because the ends of social transformation are likely to be secured through either socio-economic rights or government programmes. Tushnet was correct about proposition one, but, given the weakness of remedial government programmes and the Court's socio-economic rights jurisprudence, incorrect about proposition two. See also S Ellmann 'A Constitutional Confluence: American State Action Law and the Application of Socio-Economic Rights Guarantees to Private Actors' in P Andrews & S Ellmann (eds) *The Post-Apartheid Constitutions: Perspectives on South Africa's Basic Law* (2001) 444 (Argues that a broad understanding of FC s 8(1)'s application of the Bill to

organs of state, FC s 8(2)'s invitation to apply the Bill of Rights to private disputes, and the presence of socio-economic rights should narrow the gap between constitutional and non-constitutional bodies of law.)

191 See C Sprigman & M Osborne '*Du Plessis* is not Dead: South Africa's 1996 Constitution and The Application of the Bill of Rights to Private Disputes' (1999) 15 *South African Journal of Human Rights* 25 (Authors looked relatively prescient for some time, and, until *Juma Musjid*, the Court's continued reliance on FC s 39(2) provided empirical support for their claims.)

192 *Juma Musjid* (supra) at paras 57 – 59 ('It is clear that there is no primary positive obligation on the Trust to provide basic education to the learners. That primary positive obligation rests on the MEC. There was also no obligation on the Trust to make its property available to the MEC for use as a public school. A private landowner may do so, however, in accordance with section 14(1) of the Act which provides that a public school may be provided on private property only in terms of an agreement between the MEC and the owner of the property. This Court, in *Ex Parte Chairperson of the Constitutional Assembly: In re Certification of the Constitution of the Republic of South Africa*, made it clear that socio-economic rights (like the right to a basic education) may be negatively protected from improper invasion. [1996] ZACC 26, 1996 (10) BCLR 1253 (CC), 1996 (4) SA 744 (CC) at para 78. Breach of this obligation occurs directly when there is a failure to respect the right, or indirectly, when there is a failure to prevent the direct infringement of the right by another or a failure to respect the existing protection of the right by taking measures that diminish that protection. It needs to be stressed however that the purpose of section 8(2) of the Constitution is not to obstruct private autonomy or to impose on a private party the duties of the state in protecting the Bill of Rights. It is rather to require private parties not to interfere with or diminish the enjoyment of a right. Its application also depends on the "intensity of the constitutional right in question, coupled with the potential invasion of that right which could be occasioned by persons other than the State or organs of State". The Trust permitted the Department to enlist the school as a public school on its property with a distinctive religious character in accordance with sections 56 and 57 of the Act. It also performed the public function of managing, conducting and transacting all affairs of the Madressas in the most advantageous manner, including the payment of the costs of various items which the SGB and the Department ought to have provided. By making contributions towards expenses associated with the running of a public school, the Trust acted consistently with its duties: to erect, maintain, control and manage the school in terms of the Deed of Trust. Notably, counsel for the Trustees conceded during oral argument that the Trust had a duty not to impair the learners' right to a basic education. This concession was properly made.') On the obligation of private persons (natural and juristic) not to engage in actions that would negatively impair another person's ability to exercise their socio-economic rights, the *Juma Musjid* Court cited, amongst other cases, *Jaftha v Schoeman & Others, Van Rooyen v Stoltz and Others* [2004] ZACC 25, 2005 (1) BCLR 78 (CC), 2005 (2) SA 140 (CC) at paras 33-34; *Rail Commuters Action Group and Others v Transnet Ltd t/a Metrorail & Others* [2004] ZACC 20, 2005 (4) BCLR 301 (CC), 2005 (2) SA 359 (CC) at paras 68-71; *Minister of Health & Others v Treatment Action Campaign & Others (1)* [2002] ZACC 15, 2002 (10) BCLR 1033 (CC), 2002 (5) SA 721 (CC) at para 46; *Government of the Republic of South Africa & Others v Grootboom & Others* [2000] ZACC 19, 2000 (11) BCLR 1169 (CC), 2001 (1) SA 46 (CC) at para 34.

193 *Juma Musjid* (supra) at para 43.

Chapter 9

Coda
The Book as a Framing Device & the Crooked Timber of Democracy

If they don't believe me now, will they ever believe me?

Morrissey

I am constantly preparing for the last judgment, for the highest court from which nothing can be hidden, which will appreciate everything that should be appreciated, and which will of course notice anything that is not in its place. . . . But why does this final evaluation matter so much to me? After all, at that point, I shouldn't care. But I do care, because I am convinced that my existence – like everything else that has happened – had ruffled the surface of Being, and that after my little ripple, however marginal, insignificant and ephemeral it may be, Being is, and always will be different than it was before.

Vaclav Havel

We take care of our own. Wherever this flag is flown. We take care of our own.

Bruce Springsteen

If you look at the history of nations that maximized the virtues that we associate with democracy, you notice that what came first was constitutionality, rule of law, and the separation of powers. Democracy almost always came last. If by democracy we mean the right of all adults to take part in the choice of government that's going to rule over them, that came very late—in my lifetime in some countries that we now think of as great democracies, like Switzerland, and certainly in my father's lifetime for other European countries like France. So we should not tell ourselves that democracy is the starting point. ... Democracy bears the same relationship to a well-ordered liberal society as an excessively free market does to a successful, well-regulated capitalism. Mass democracy in an age of mass media means that on the one hand, you can reveal very quickly that Bush stole the 2000 election, but on the other hand, much of the population doesn't care. ... So we pay a price for the massification of our liberalism, and we should understand that. That's not an argument for going back to restricted suffrage. ... But it is an argument for understanding that democracy is not the *only* solution to the problem of unfree societies. ... Democracy has been the best short-term defense against undemocratic alternatives, but it is not a defense against its own genetic shortcomings. The Greeks knew that democracy is *not* likely to fall to the charms of totalitarianism, authoritarianism, or oligarchy; it's much more likely to fall to a corrupted version of itself. Democracies corrode quite fast; they corrode linguistically, or rhetorically, if you like—that's the Orwellian point about language. They corrode because most people don't care very much about them. Notice that the European Union, whose first parliamentary elections were held in 1979 and had an average turnout of over 62%, is now [in 2012] looking to a turnout of less than 30%, even though the European Parliament matters more now and has more power. The difficulty of sustaining voluntary interest in the business of choosing the people who will rule over you is well attested. And the reason why we need intellectuals ... is to fill the space that grows between the two parts of democracy: the governed and the governors.

Tony Judt

Generalissimo Francisco Franco is *still* dead.

Chevy Chase

We have always understood that when times change, so must we; that fidelity to our founding principles requires new responses to new challenges, that preserving our individual freedoms requires collective action. Being true to our founding documents does not require us to agree on every contour of life. It does not mean that we all define liberty in the same way or follow the same precise path to happiness. Progress does not compel us to settle centuries' long debates about the role of government for all time, but it does require us to act in our time. For now decisions are upon us and we cannot afford delay. We cannot mistake absolutism for principle, or substitute spectacle for politics, or treat name calling as reasoned debate. We must act, knowing that today's victories will be only partial, and that it will be up to those who stand here four years and forty years and 400 hundred years hence to advance the timeless spirit [of dignity, equality and freedom] conferred upon us in a spare hall in Philadelphia.

Barack Obama

Overcoming poverty is not a task of charity; it is an act of justice. Like slavery and apartheid, poverty is not natural. It is man-made and can be overcome by the actions of human beings.

Nelson Mandela

(a) The Book as a Framing Device

I don't expect the majority of readers to believe me now. However, good reasons exist to believe that many of empirical claims propounded herein about the self will become accepted facts about our brains and bodies as neuroscientists and philosophers effectively challenge the erroneous folk psychology that underpins current conceptions of regarding free will and consciousness. The same holds true for empirically-based social thought. Both social capital theory and choice architecture are no more than twenty years old and ten years old respectively: advances in both disciplines will increase our appreciation of the manner in which our (diverse, heterogeneous) communities operate and how we can nudge them in a direction best for all of their respective inhabitants. Whether democratic experimental constitutionalism (predicated on shared interpretation, participatory bubbles, reflexivity, rolling norms, remedial equlibration and polyarchy, while wedded to a politics of flourishing) will overtake – or even challenge – dominant forms of constitutional theory and practice is far from evident. As it stands now, most countries are neither genuinely democratic nor committed to constitutionalism. Within the clutch of constitutional democracies that function as such, a theory grounded in experimentalism and flourishing has a vast number of competitors that it will find difficult to displace.

Here's the real clue for unlocking the meaning and the purpose of this work: *The book is an extended framing device.*

Though long on length, the scale upon which this book operates is quite modest. It means to engage primarily my fellow South Africans for whom such ideas matter. The ultimate purpose of this book *qua* framing device has been to challenge some basic assumptions about the self, the social and the political in the service of a non-dominant (but perhaps helpful) argument as to how we should work with the South African Constitution. Yes, it's a bit of cheat. Just as the trolley car cases are constructed to drive one's moral intuitions in a particular direction (or to unearth disconcerting presuppositions), this book pushes its readers to reconsider previously held positions on a range of constitutional doctrines and the design of political institutions intended to make good on the promises of our basic law. Whether you believe me now or not, if you have drawn back the cover back, *kept your head down and followed through*, then this experiment has been a success.

(b) The Crooked Timber of Democracy

The path to democracy is never straight. As Tony Judt notes above, the kind of egalitarian pluralist democracy so often held out in South Africa as an oh-so proximate ideal is quite often the very last staging post, much as the final emotion to meekly crawl out of Pandora's box is hope. But hope, as both Nelson Mandela and Baracck Obama observe, is no substitute for action. While the success of any course of action may seem partial at the time, and thus a source of frustration, history again cautions us against all or nothing wagers. Who better than Mandela and to Obama, riding their respective waves from Robben Island and Rosa Parks to Soweto and Selma, to remind us how long, centuries long, it has taken various polities to design and redesign their institutions so that each and every denizen might rise in value from nothing to 3/5ths to 1 to first among equals.

Judt's, Mandela's, Havel's and Obama's words serve a five-fold purpose for this work.

First. Readers should pause before they consider this work out of step or out of time with contemporary South African politics. It most certainly is not. As the drafters of our constitution and our Constitutional Court sagely recognized, constitutionality, the rule of law, and the separation of powers come first. We have, somewhat successfully, arrived at this first staging post.

Second. To the extent that some ideal perfect democracy – in which we are all constantly engaged in debates in our piazzas and public squares on issues of great moment – holds philosophers and theorists of various stripes in its thrall, we should again take heed of the lessons of history. People, being people, have other, more pressing matters (by their lights) going on in their lives. While advancing an egalitarian pluralist agenda, this book takes cognizance of the limited energy any given citizen placing politics at the core of her day-to-day life: children must be fed and sent to school, dignified work ought to occupy our hands, engagement with others, in the various associations and communities into which we are born and give our lives meaning, fill our hearts and minds. Just getting through such a day is often the most meaningful measure of success. That's why 'participatory bubbles', with their emphasis on engagement between multiple parties with respect to a rather narrow political issue over a short duration of time matters play such a central role in this work. We attempt to solve the 'problem' – as set by a Mandela or an Obama, or any of their surrogates -- as best we can – and then get on with life.

Third. We ought to bracket the inclination toward Springsteen's bitterly ironic pessimism: that our common South African flag masks a common tendency in South African politics for kin and clan to take care only of their own. Eighteen years after liberation, the majority of South Africans feel a grave sense of disappointment that we still have such a long road to travel before reaching our second staging post: the provision of those basic entitlements that will enable all South Africans to appear in public without shame. Neither cock-eyed optimism nor abject pessimism (flip-sides of the same coin) constitutes an appropriate response. An optimist will usually have her head in the sand and her arse in the air. A pessimist will throw up her hands and feel naught but despair. Ironically, both seem stuck in what Klein might call a paranoid-schizoid position: fear, anger, ennui and paralysis dominate the landscape. Havel, just like my father, had it right: to understand that as a result of your 'little ripple' - treating others as subjects of equal worth - 'however marginal, insignificant and ephemeral it may be, "Being" is, and always will be different than it was before.'

Fourth. If this book has a single unifying theme, then it is that life is series of constant disruptions. The measure (or mettle) of a person, a society or a democratic state is how creatively she, he, them or it responds to the problems with which she, he, them or it are confronted: what we both need and want is a resourceful and imaginative realism. Here, an example from recent South African history casts the proper light on the problems that currently beset us. In April 1993, Chris Hani was assassinated. This tragedy could have been easily exploited by demagogues out to destabilize the country to such a degree that civil war became the inevitable outcome (as it did in Yugoslavia and Rwanda.) Nelson Mandela, and the liberation movement he led, chose a different path. In public pronouncements immediately following

Chris Hani's murder, Mandela leveraged the calamity to secure a commitment to an election on 27 April 1994 and the drafting of an Interim Constitution that would bind South Africa until an elected, representative Constitutional Assembly could devise a new scheme of norms, principles, standards, doctrines and institutions. This book does not place its faith in another messianic 'Mandela Moment'. Rather it recognizes that when we accord fellow members of our society the dignity, equal respect, tolerance, trust, care, loyalty and other material and immaterial goods that we demand for ourselves, then we also possess the resources, hard as it might be to summon them up, to solve the problems with which we are all daily confronted.

Fifth. However imperfect our current union may be, however ill-equipped our current party dominant democracy might be to deliver *fully* upon the aspirations of our basic law, we ought to view the Cassandra-like predictions of political scientists and comparative constitutional law scholars with a healthy dose of scepticism. That's not to say that my peers and betters who engage in comparative constitutionalism are wrong. Their bracing assessments of how recently created constitutional courts have failed to operate as hedges against democratic authoritarianism are often spot on the mark. The problem is the framing of the picture, of zooming in too tight. These scholars inevitably concentrate on too limited a period of time in assessing the merits of newly minted constitutional democracies and the demerits of what we, in the West tradition, have long acknowledged as 'the weakest branch': a constitutional court without the arms to execute its orders or the bread and butter for those who require such sustenance in order to pursue lives worthy valuing. Chevy Chase's laugh line in 1975 – 'Generalissimo Francisco Franco is *still* dead' – should give critics pause. If Spain's modern democracy, roughly 40 years old, and teetering on the brink of financial collapse brought on by the government's irresponsible spending and blinkered (de)regulation of the economy, is not viewed through the same prism as the South African state, then we might want to ask 'why?' It would seem, as Chevy Chase often pronounced for the next two years, that 'Generalissimo Francisco Franco is fighting to remain dead.' Even academics can find themselves trapped in a seemingly endless news-cycle of dread and woe.

Sixth. I am a South African, American-born. This double-consciousness regularly reminds me that our limitations have more to do with a lack of imagination and a failure to recognize that the partial contributions we each make, in good faith, every day, still count as progress. The problems that we confront, as Mandela reminds us, are solvable. If apartheid can be overcome, than so can an education system that graduates but a third of its entrants, or a bureaucracy so riven by politics that no line of authority exists (save in name only), and so undisciplined that women fear the very police charged with their protection. The solutions at which we arrive for such problems may not, as Obama declares, make our imperfect union perfect. But the novel experiments that show us the way to regular, successful action, in some, but not all, domains of human affairs, are certainly to be preferred to just kicking the can down the road. Finally, we are nowhere in the vicinity of 'the end of history', here, in South Africa, or there, in the United States. This book then is a blueprint for polities at various staging posts – be they a score, or two hundred years more, in age. It's a Judtian-inflected work 'that fills in the space that grows between the two parts of democracy: the governed and the governors' and *suggests how we move from one staging post to another* – by revealing a little bit more about (a) radically heterogeneous determined selves still capable of change and flourishing; (b) socially constructed creatures adept at breaking traditional bottlenecks, and who figure out, experimentally and collectively, how to continue to fit square pegs into square holes, whilst they carve out radically new holes for radically new pegs; and (c) citizens, politicians and jurists committed both to the provision of those predicate conditions necessary for all to appear in public without shame and to the meaningful engagement with one another required to solve the most immediate problems on our horizon.

Modest, creative folk – Judt, Mandela, Havel and Obama – much like my ancestors in Tiahuanaco. They have neither ignored the problems confronting them in the hopes that they would go away, nor have they blithely assumed that some outside beneficent force would save them at the 11th hour. All endorse a modest form of collective self-reliance: the experimental method. Moreover, neither Judt, nor Mandela, nor Havel, nor Obama reject the various bodies of knowledge that had been bestowed upon them, nor did they disavow the obvious benefits of the social capital that grounded their society and allowed (some of) them to work together towards solving collective concerns. They also recognize that only a decidedly significant degree of common beliefs and common property – a 'commons' – will allow all to flourish. This two-fold recognition regarding the benefits of and the conditions for experimentalism and flourishing lies at the heart of their thinking. It is also the two-fold recognition that lies at the heart of this work on South African constitutionalism. I could not ask for better company, or stronger endorsements.

Bibliography:
Books, Articles, Chapters, Reports & Tables of Cases, Covenants & Legislation

... Years later I
Encounter them on the road –
Words dry and riderless,
The indefatigable hoof-taps.
Sylvia Plath

BOOKS

Ackerman B (1991) *We The People: Foundations* Cambridge: Belknap Press/Harvard University Press

Adair R (2002) *The Physics of Baseball* (3rd Edition) New York: Harper Collins

Albertyn C, Goldblatt B & Roederer C (2001) *Introduction to the Promotion of Equality and Prevention of Unfair Discrimination Act 4 of 2000* Johannesburg: Wits University Press

Alexander J (2006) *The Civil Sphere* Oxford: Oxford University Press

American Heritage Dictionary (2010). Boston: Houghton Mifflin

Andrews P & Ellmann S (eds) (2001) *The Post-Apartheid Constitutions: Perspectives on South Africa's Basic Law* Johannesburg: Witwatersrand University Press

Appiah K A (2006) *Cosmopolitanism: Ethics in a World of Strangers* New York: Norton

Appiah K A (2008) *Experiments in Ethics* Cambridge: Harvard University Press

Arendt H (1961) *The Human Condition* Chicago: University of Chicago Press

Arrow KJ (1951) *Social Choice and Individual Values* New Haven: Yale University Press

Ayala FJ & Dobzhansky T (eds) (1974) *Studies in the Philosophy of Biology* London: Macmillan

Baars BJ (1988) *A Cognitive Theory of Consciousness* New York: Cambridge University Press

Baars BJ (1997) *In the Theatre of Consciousness: The Workspace of the Mind* New York: Oxford University Press

Baars BJ, Banks W & Newman JB (edo) (2003) *Essential Sources in the Scientific Study of Consciousness* Cambridge: MIT Press

Baier A (1991) *A Progress of Sentiments: Reflections on Hume's Treatise* Boston: Harvard University Press
Baker GP & Hacker PMS (1984) *Scepticism, Rules & Language* New York: Blackwell
Barber B *Strong Democracy* (1984) Berkeley: University of California Press
Barolsky V et al *Understanding the Dimensions of Human Trafficking in Southern Africa* (2010) Pretoria: National Prosecuting Authority and Human Sciences Research Council
Bellah R *Habits of the Heart* (1985) Berkeley: University of California Press
Benhabib S (1992) *Situating the Self* New York: Routledge
Bennett M, Dennett D, Hacker P, Searle J (2007) *Neuroscience & Philosophy: Brain, Mind, Language* New York: Columbia University Press
Bennett TW (1997) *Human Rights and African Customary Law under the South African Constitution* Cape Town: Juta Law
Bilchitz D (2006) *Poverty and Fundamental Rights* Oxford: Oxford University Press
Blackburn S (2008) *How to Read Hume* (2008) London: Granta
Blackmore C & Greenfield S (eds) (1987) *Mindwaves* Oxford: Blackwell
Blackmore S (2004) *Consciousness* New York: Oxford University Press
Bock GR and Marsh J (eds) (1993) *Experimental and Theoretical Studies of Consciousness* New York: Wiley
Botha H, Van der Walt A & Van der Walt J (eds) (2003) *Rights and Democracy in a Transformative Constitution* Stellenbosch: SUN Press
Burke E (2001) *Reflections on the Revolution in France* (JCD Clark (ed)) Stanford: Stanford University Press
Busaki G (eds) (1994) *Temporal Coding in the Brain* New York: Springer-Verlag
Calvin WH (1996) *How Brains Think: Evolving Intelligence, Then and Now* New York: Basic Books
Campbell D & Russo J (1999) *Social Experimentation* Thousand Oaks, California: Sage Publications
Cannetti E (1962) *Crowds and Power* New York: Viking Press
Chalmers D (1996) *The Conscious Mind* New York: Oxford University Press
Chalmers D (2010) *The Character of Consciousness* Oxford: Oxford University Press
Cheadle H, Davis D & Haysom N (eds) (2002) *South African Constitutional Law: The Bill of Rights* Durban: Butterworths
Christensen SM & Turner DR (eds) (1993) *Folk Psychology and the Philosophy of Mind* Hillsdale, N.J: L. Erlbaum
Churchland P (2011) *Braintrust: What Neuroscience Tells Us about Morality* Princeton: Princeton University Press
Claxton G (1994) *Noises from the Darkroom* London: Acquarian
Cohen J *Philosophy, Politics, Democracy: Selected Papers* (2009) Cambridge: Harvard University Press
Cohen J (1986) *Rules of the Game* Boston: South End Press
Cohen J, Fung A and Elgar E (eds) (1996) *Constitutionalism, Democracy, and State Power: Promise and Performance* Brookfield: E Elgar

Cohen J & Rogers J (1995) *Associations and Democracy* New York: Verso
Connolly WE (1988) *Political Theory and Modernity* New York: B. Blackwell
Cornell D (2000) *Just Cause: Freedom, Identity and Rights* Lanham, MD: Rowman & Littlefield Publishers
Cornell D (2004) *Defending Ideals: War, Democracy, and Political Struggle* New York: Routledge
Cornell D, Woolman S, Bishop M Brickhill J (eds) (2010) *The Dignity Jurisprudence of the Constitutional Court of South Africa* New York: Fordham University Press
Crick F (1994) *The Astonishing Hypothesis* New York: Maxwell Macmillan International
Crocker D & Linden T (eds) (1998) *The Ethics of Consumption: The Good Life, Justice and Global Stewardship* Lanham, MD: Rowman & Littlefield
Currie I & De Waal J (2005) *The Bill of Rights Handbook* Cape Town: Juta
Cziko G (1995) *Without Miracles: Universal Selection Theory and the Second Darwinian Revolution* Cambridge: MIT Press
Dahl RA (1989) *Democracy and Its Critics* New Haven: Yale University Press
Damasio A (2010) *Self Comes to Mind: Constructing the Conscious Brain* New York: Pantheon Press
Damasio A (1999) *The Feeling of What Happens: Body, Emotion and the Making of Consciousness* New York: Harcourt Brace
Damasio A (1994) *Descartes' Error: Emotion, Reason and the Human Brain* New York: Putnam
Davidson D (1984) *Inquiries into Truth and Interpretation* New York: Oxford University Press
Davis D (1999) *Democracy and Deliberation* Cape Town: Juta Law
Dawkins R (1976) *The Selfish Gene* New York: Oxford University Press
Dawkins R (1982) *The Extended Phenotype* San Francisco: Freeman
De Búrca G & Scott J (eds) (2006) *Law and New Governance in the EU and the US* Oxford: Hart
De Toqueville A *Democracy in America* (1835). Cambridge: Sever and Francis
De Waal J, Currie I & Erasmus G (2001) *The Bill of Rights Handbook* Cape Town: Juta
Dehaene S & Naccache L (2001) *The Cognitive Neuroscience of Consciousness* Cambridge: MIT Press
Dennett D (1991) *Consciousness Explained* Boston: Little, Brown and Co
Dennett D (1978) *Brainstorms* Montgomery, Vt: Bradford Books
Dennett D (1984) *Elbow Room: The Varieties of Freedom Worth Wanting* New York: Oxford University Press
Dennett D (2003) *Freedom Evolves* New York: Viking
Dennett D (1986) *Elbow Room: The Varieties of Free Will Worth Wanting* Boston, MA: Harvard University Press
Dennett D (1996) *Kinds of Minds* New York, NY: Basic Books
Dennett D (2003) *Freedom Evolves* New York: Viking
Dennett D (2005) *Sweet Dreams: Philosophical Obstacles to a Science of Consciousness* Cambridge: MIT Press
Descartes R (1641) *Meditations on First Philosophy* Paris: J Vietch
Dewey J (1916) *Democracy and Education* Radford, Virginia: Wilder
Dewey J (1920) *Reconstruction in Philosophy* Boston: Beacon Hill Press

Dinnerstein D (1976) *The Mermaid and the Minotaur* New York: Harper and Row
Douglass RB (ed) (1990) *Liberalism and the Good* New York: Routledge
Eccles JC (1965) *The Brain and the Unity of Conscious Experience* Cambridge: Cambridge University Press
Eccles JC (1994) *How the Self Controls Its Brain* New York: Springer-Verlag
Edelman GM & Tononi G (2000) *A Universe of Consciousness* New York: Basic Books
Edwards M (2004) *Civil Society* Cambridge: Polity Press
Elster J (1992) *Ulysses and the Sirens* Cambridge: Cambridge University Press
Elton M (2003) *Daniel Dennett: Reconciling Science and Our Self-Conception* Cambridge, U.K.: Polity Press
Eysenck HJ (1995) *Genius: The Natural History of Creativity* New York: Cambridge University Press
Fauvre D (2006) *China and Capitalism: A History of Business Enterprise in Modern China* Hong Kong: Hong Kong University Press
Fay B (1987) *Critical Social Science* Ithaca: Cornell University Press
Fay B (1996) *Contemporary Philosophy of Social Science* Cambridge: Blackwell
Feyerabend P (1975) *Against Method* Atlantic Highlands, NJ: Humanities Press
Feyerabend P (1987) *A Farewell to Reason* London: Verso
Fish S (1989) *Doing What Comes Naturally: Change Rhetoric and the Practice of Theory in Literary and Legal Studies* Durham: Duke University Press
Fish S (1999) *The Trouble with Principle* Boston: Harvard University Press
Fischer JM & Ravizza M (eds)(1992) *Ethics: Problems and Principles* Fort Worth: Harcourt, Brace Jovanovich
Fleisch B (2002) *Managing Educational Change: The State and School Reform* Johannesburg: Heinemann
Fleisch B (2008) *Primary Education in Crisis* Johannesburg: Wits University Press
Fletcher G (1993) *Loyalty* New York: Oxford University Press
Fuller L (1964) *The Morality of Law* 106 (rev ed) New Haven: Yale University Press
Gadamer HG (1961, 2nd edition 1989) *Truth & Method* New York: Continuum International Publishing Group
Galston W (1992) *Liberal Pluralism: The Implications of Value Pluralism for Political Theory and Practice* Cambridge: Cambridge University Press
Gazzaniga MS (1992) *Nature's Mind* New York: Basic Books
Gilligan C (1982) *In a Different Voice: Psychological Theory and Women's Development* Cambridge: Harvard University Press
Gittler R and Vidal A (1998) *Community Organizing: Building Social Capital as a Development Strategy* London: Sage
Gray J (1995) *Enlightenment's Wake: Politics and Culture at the Close of the Modern Age* New York: Routledge
Greenfield S (2000) *Brain Story* New York: Dorling Kindersley
Gutmann A (2003) *Identity in Democracy* Princeton: Princeton University Press

Gutmann A & Thompson D (2004) *Why Deliberative Democracy?* Princeton: Princeton University Press

Gutmann A (ed) (1998) *Freedom of Association* Princeton: Princeton University Press

A Gutmann (ed) (XXXX) *Multiculturalism and the Politics of Recognition* (1996) Princeton: Princeton University Press

Guyer P (ed) (1998) *Critical Essays on Kant's Groundwork of the Metaphysics of Morals* Lanham, MD: Rowman & Littlefield

International Encyclopaedia of Ethics (2010) New York: Wiley

Habermas J (1996) *Between Facts and Norms: Contributions to a Discourse Theory of Law and Democracy* (trans W Rehg) Cambridge: MIT Press

Hardin G (1977) *The Limits of Altruism: An Ecologist's View of Survival* Bloomington: Indiana University Press

Hauser M (2000) *Wild Minds: What Animals Really Think* New York: Henry Holt

Hayek FA (1952) *Counter-Revolution in Science* Glencoe, III: Free Press

Hayek FA (1952) *The Sensory Order* Chicago: University of Chicago Press

Hayek FA (1967) *Studies in Philosophy, Politics and Economics* Chicago: University of Chicago Press

Hayek FA (1973) *Law Legislation & Liberty (Volume 1): Rules and Order* Chicago: University of Chicago Press

Hayek FA (1979) *Law Legislation & Liberty (Volume 3): The Political Order of a Free People* Chicago: University of Chicago Press

Heidegger M (1923) *Lectures on the History of the Concept of Time* Bloomington: Indiana University Press

Heidegger M (1927) *Being and Time* New York: Harper Perenial Modern Thought

Halpern D (2005) *Social Capital* Cambridge, UK: Polity

Hamann R, Woolman S & Sprague C (eds) (2008) *The Business of Sustainable Development in Africa: Human Rights, Partnerships and Alternative Business Models* New York: United Nations University Press

Handler J (2004) *Social Citizenship and Workfare in the United States and Europe: The Paradox of Inclusion* Cambridge, UK: Cambridge University Press

Handler J (1986) *The Conditions of Discretion: Autonomy, Community, Bureaucracy* New York: Russell Sage Foundation

Hanushek E & Lindseth A (2009) *Schoolhouses, Courthouses, and Statehouses: Solving the Funding-Achievement Puzzle in America's Public Schools* Princeton: Princeton University Press

Hardin G (1977) *The Limits of Altruism: An Ecologist's View of Survival* Bloomington: Indiana University Press

Heyes C & Hull D (eds) (2001) *Selection Theory and Social Construction* Albany: State University of New York Press

Hayek FA (1952) *Counter-Revolution in Science* New York: Free Press

Hayek FA (1973) *Law Legislation & Liberty (Volume 1): Rules and Order* Chicago: University of Chicago Press

Hayek FA (1979) *Law Legislation & Liberty (Volume 3): The Political Order of a Free People* Chicago: University of Chicago Press

Hayek FA (1952) *The Sensory Order* London: Routledge and Kegan Paul

Heidegger M (1927) *Being and Time* Oxford: Blackwell

Heidegger M (1923) *Lectures on the History of the Concept of Time* Indianapolis: Indiana University Press

Hirschman A (1970) *Exit, Voice and Loyalty* Cambridge: Harvard University Press

Hobson JA & Brazier MAB (eds) (1980) *The Reticular Formation Revisted* New York: Raven Press

Hofstadter DR & Dennett D (eds) (1985) *The Mind's I: Fantasies and Reflections on Self and Soul* New York: Basic Books

Hull DL (2001) *Science and Selection: Essays on Biological Evolution and the Philosophy of Science* New York: Cambridge University Press

Hume D (1739) *A Treatise of Human Nature* Oxford: Oxford University Press

Hume D (1748) A*n Enquiry Concerning Human Understanding* Oxford: Oxford University Press

Hume D (1777) *An Enquiry Concerning the Principles of Morals* La Salle: Open Court Press

Hutchinson A & Green L (eds) (1994) *Law and the Community: The End of Individualism?* Toronto: Carswell

James H (1907) *The Art of the Novel* New York: Scribner

James W (1890) *The Principles of Psychology: Volume I* New York: H. Holt & Company

James W (1907) *Pragmatism* Indianapolis: Hackett

James W (2011) *The Heart of William James* (R Richardson (ed)) Cambridge: Harvard University Press

Jansen J (2009) *Knowledge in the Blood: Confronting Race and the Apartheid Past* Stanford, CA: Stanford University Press

Kant I (1754) *Investigation of the Question as to Whether the Rotation of the Earth on its Axis Has Undergone Any Modification* Cambridge: Cambridge University Press

Kant I (1754) *Question as to Whether the Earth is Growing Old from the Angle of Physics* Chicago: Open Court

Kant I (1755) *A Brief Outline of Some Meditations on Fire* Cambridge: Cambridge University Press

Kant I (1755) *Universal Natural History and Theory of the Heavens* Cambridge: Cambridge University Press

Kant I (1756) *Consideration of Recently Perceived Earthquakes* Cambridge: Cambridge University Press

Kant I (1764) *Enquiry into Diseases of the Head* Cambridge: Cambridge University Press

Kant I (1785) *Concerning the Volcanoes on the Moon* Cambridge: Cambridge University Press

Kant I (1785) *Definition of the Concept of a Human Race* Cambridge: Cambridge University Press

Kant I (1785) *Groundwork of the Metaphysics of Morals* (trans and ed AW Wood) New Haven: Yale University Press

Kant I (1790) *Critique of Judgment* (trans JC Meredith) Oxford: The Clarendon Press

Kant I (1798) *Anthropology from the Pragmatic Viewpoint* Cambridge: Cambridge University Press

Kennedy R (2011) *The Persistence of the Colour Line: Racial Politics and the Obama Presidency* New York: Pantheon

Klein M (1986) *Love, Guilt and Reparation and Other Works 1921–1945* New York: Free Press

Klein M (1986) *Selected Work* Mitchell J (ed) New York: Hogarth

Klug H (2000) *Constituting Democracy: Law, Globalism and South Africa's Political Reconstruction* Cambridge: Cambridge University Press

Knobe J and Nichols S (eds) (2008) *Experimental Philosophy* Oxford: Oxford University Press

Koch C (2004) *The Quest for Consciousness: A Neurobiological Approach* Denver, Colo: Roberts and Co

Kommers D (1997) *The Constitutional Jurisprudence of the Federal Republic of Germany* Durham, N.C: Duke University Press

Kraemer L (2005) *The People Themselves: Popular Constitutionalism and Judicial Review* New York: Oxford University Press

Kuhn (1970) *The Structure of Scientific Revolutions* Chicago: University of Chicago Press

Lakoff G & Johnson M (1980) *Metaphors We Live By* Chicago: University of Chicago Press

Larmore C (1987) *Patterns of Moral Complexity* New York: Cambridge University Press

Liebenberg S (2010) *Adjudicating Socio-Economic Rights under a Transformative Constitution* Cape Town: Juta

Libet B (2004) *Mind Time: The Temporal Factor in Consciousness* Cambridge: Harvard University Press

Lin N (2001) *Social Capital: A Theory of Social Structure and Action* New York: Cambridge University Press

Locke J (1690) *An Essay Concerning Human Understanding* London: Thomas Bassett

Locke J (1689) *A Letter Concerning Toleration* New York: Routledge

MacIntyre A (1984) *After Virtue: A Study in Moral Theory* Notre Dame, Indiana: University of Notre Dame Press

McIntyre A (1987) *Whose Justice, Which Rationality?* Notre Dame, Indiana: University of Notre Dame Press

Mahatir M & Shintaro I (eds)(1995) *The Voice of Asia: Two Leaders Discuss the Coming Century* Tokyo: Kodansha International

Malherbe EG (1934) *Education in South Africa* Pretoria: The New Education Fellowship

Malherbe EG (1941) *The Bilingual School* Pretoria: The New Education Fellowship

Martin LH, Gutman H & Hutton PH (1988) *Technologies of the Self: A Seminar With Michel Foucault* Amherst: University of Massachusetts Press

Mates B (1981) *Skeptical Essays* Chicago: University of Chicago Press

McGinn C (2011) *The Meaning of Disgust* New York: Oxford University Press

McGinn C (1999) *The Mysterious Flame: Conscious Minds in a Material World* New York: Basic Books

McClelland JL & Rummelhart DE (eds) (1986) *Parallel Distributing Processing* Cambridge: MIT Press

McKenna T, Davis J & Zornetzer ZF (eds) (1992) *Single Neuron Computation* Boston: Academic Press
McLean K (2009) *Constitutional Deference, Courts & Socio-Economic Rights in South Africa* Pretoria: Pretoria University Law Press
Mead G (1934) *Mind, Self, and Society: From the Standpoint of a Social Behavioralist* Chicago: University of Chicago Press
Meredith F (2005) *Experiencing the Post-metaphysical Self: Between Hermeneutics and Deconstruction* New York: Palgrave Macmillan
Metzinger T (2003) *Being No-One: The Self Model Theory of Subjectivity* Cambridge: MIT Press
Metzinger T (ed) (2000) *Neural Correlates of Consciousness* Cambridge: MIT Press
Meyerson D (1997) *Rights Limited* Cape Town: Juta Law
Michelman, FI (1999) *Brennan and Democracy* Princeton: Princeton University Press
Mill JS (1863) *On Liberty* Boston: Ticknor and Fields
Moore GE (1903) *Principia Ethica* Cambridge: Cambridge University Press
Mouffe C (1996) *Deconstruction and Pragmatism* New York: Routledge
Nagel T *Moral Luck* (1979) New York: Cambridge University Press
Nietzsche F (1887) *On the Genealogy of Morals* (trans D Smith) Oxford: Oxford University Press
Nordhaus W (2003) *Warming the World: Economic Models of Global Warming* Cambridge: MIT Press
Nordhaus W (1994) *Managing the Global Commons: The Economic Models of Climate Change* Cambridge, MA: MIT Press
Nussbaum M (2011) *Creating Capabilities: The Human Development Approach* Cambridge, Mass: Belknap Press of Harvard University Press
Nussbaum, M (2006) *Frontiers of Justice: Disability, Nationality, Species Membership* Cambridge, Mass: Belknap Press of Harvard University Press
Nussbaum M (2001) *Upheavals of Thought: The Intelligence of Emotions* Cambridge: Cambridge University Press
Nussbaum M (2000) *Women and Human Development: The Capabilities Approach* New York: Cambridge University Press
Nussbaum M (1990) *Love's Knowledge* New York: Oxford University Press
Nussbaum M and Sen A (eds) (1993) *The Quality of Life* New York: Oxford University Press
OECD (2011) *The Better Life Index* Paris: OECD
Orzack SH & Sober E (eds) (2001) *Adaptionism and Optimality* New York: Cambridge University Press
Overman ES (ed) (1988) *Methodology and Epistemology for Social Science: Selected Papers* Chicago: University of Chicago Press
Parfit D (1984) *Reasons and Persons* Oxford: Clarendon Press
Peirce C (1978) *How To Make Our Ideas Clear* Indianapolis: Indiana University Press
Pitkin HF (1972) *Wittgenstein and Justice* Berkeley: University of California Press
Plato (2007) *The Republic* London: Penguin
Plous S (ed) (2003) *Understanding Prejudice and Discrimination* Boston: McGraw-Hill
Pogge T (2008) *World Poverty and Human Rights* (2nd Ed) Cambridge: Polity.

Popper K and Eccles JC (1977) *The Self and Its Brain* New York: Springer International

Posner R (2008) *How Judges Think* Cambridge: Harvard University Press

Prior A (1949) *Logic and the Basis of Ethics* Oxford: Clarendon Press

Putnam R (1993) *Making Democracy Work: Civic Traditions in Modern Italy* (1993). Princeton: Princeton University Press

Putnam R (2002) *Democracy in Flux: The Evolution of Social Capital in Contemporary Society* New York: Oxford University Press

Putnam R (2000) *Bowling Alone: The Collapse and Revival of American Community* New York: Simon & Schuster

Quine WVO (1960) *Word and Object* Cambridge: MIT Press

Ramachandram VS (2010) *The Tell-Tale Brain: A Neuroscientist's Quest for What Makes Us Human*

Rawls J (1971) *A Theory of Justice* Cambridge: Belknap Press of Harvard University Press

Rawls J (1993) *Political Liberalism* New York: Columbia University Press

Rawls J (2000) *Lectures on the History of Moral Philosophy* Cambridge: Harvard University Press

Rawls J (2007) *Lectures on the History of Political Philosophy* Cambridge: Harvard University Press

Rebell M (2009) *Courts and Kids: Pursuing Educational Equity through the State Courts* Chicago: University of Chicago Press

Rehg W (2000) *Insight & Solidarity: The Discourse Ethics of Jurgen Habermas* Berkeley: University of California Press

Rehg W (2009) *The Cogent Science in Context* Cambridge: MIT Press

Report of the Senate Select Committee on Intelligence on Weapons of Mass Destruction in Iraq (2004) Washington, DC: United States Congress Senate Select Committee on Intelligence

Rorty R (1982) *Consequences of Pragmatism* Minneapolis: University of Minnesota Press

Rorty R (1989) *Contingency, Irony and Solidarity* New York: Cambridge University Press

Rorty R (1979) *Philosophy and the Mirror of Nature* Princeton: Princeton University Press

Rorty R (1991) *Objectivity, Relativism & Truth: Philosophical Papers I* New York: Cambridge University Press

Rorty R (1991) *Essays on Heidegger & Others: Philosophical Papers II* New York: Cambridge University Press

Rosenberg G (1991) *The Hollow Hope: Can Courts Bring about Social Change?* Chicago: University of Chicago Press

Rosenblum N (1998) *Membership and Morals: The Personal Uses of Pluralism in America* Princeton: Princeton University Press

Royal and Ancient Golf Association (2010) *Rules of Golf* St Andrews: The R&A Association

Roux T *The Politics of Pragmatism: The First 15 Years of the South African Constitutional Court* (2013) Cambridge: Cambrisge Univerty Press

Rudomin P (edP) (1993) *Neuroscience: From Neural Networks to Artificial Intelligence* New York: Springer-Verlag

Ryle G (1949) *The Concept of Mind* New York: Hutchinson's University Library

Sachs O (1985) *The Man Who Mistook His Wife for His Hat* South Yarmouth: J. Curley

Sandel M (1982) *Liberalism and the Limits of Justice* New York: Cambridge University Press
Sandel M (2010) *Justice: What's the Right Thing to Do?* Harvard University Press
Sartre JP (1968) *Portrait of the Anti-Semite* (trans E de Mauny) London: Secker & Warburg
Scheffler S (2001) *Boundaries and Allegiances: Problems of Justice and Responsibility in Liberal Thought* New York: Oxford University Press
Scheffler S (2010) *Equality and Tradition: Questions of Value in a Moral and Political Theory* New York: Oxford University Press
Schlipp PA (ed) (1974) *The Philosophy of Karl Popper* La Salle, Illinois: Open Court
Searle J (2010) *Making the Social World: The Structure of Human Civilization* New York: Oxford University Press
Searle J (1984) *Minds, Brains and Science* Cambridge: Harvard University Press
Searle J (ed) (1997) *The Mystery of Consciousness* New York: New York Review of Books
Sen A (1985) *Commodities and Capabilities* New York: Oxford University Press
Sen A (1992) *Inequality Re-examined* Cambridge, Mass: Harvard University Press Nussbaum M and Sen A (eds) (1993) *The Quality of Life* New York: Oxford University Press
Sen A (1999) *Development as Freedom* New York: Oxford University Press
Sen A (2006) *Identity and Violence: The Illusion of Destiny* New York: WW Norton & Co
Sen A (2010) *The Idea of Justice.* London: Penguin
Sinnot-Armstrong Walter (ed) (2008) *Moral Psychology (Vol 2), The Cognition Science of Morality: Intuition and Diversity* Cambridge: MIT Press
Sinnot-Armstrong Walter (ed) (2008) *Moral Psychology (Vol 3), The Neuroscience of Morality: Emotion, Brain Disorders and Development* Cambridge: MIT Press
Smith A (1759) *A Theory of Moral Sentiments* Indiana: Liberty Classics
Smith A (1776) *The Wealth of Nations* (RH Campbell and AS Skinner (eds)) New York: Oxford University Press
Sommers C (2000) *The War against Boys: How Misguided Feminism is Harming Our Young Men* New York: Simon & Schuster
Spinoza B (2000) *Ethics* Oxford: Oxford University Press
Stanford Encyclopeadia of Philosophy (2010) Stanford: Stanford University Press
Strozier RM (2002) *Foucault, Subjectivity, and Identity: Historical Constructions of Subject and Self* Detroit: Wayne State University Press
Sunstein C (2010) *On Rumours: How Falsehoods Spread, Why We Believe Them, What Can Be Done* New York: Penguin Books
Sunstein C and Thaler R (2008) *Nudges: Improving Decisions about Health, Wealth & Happiness* Cambridge: Harvard University Press
Sunstein C (2007) *Infotopia* Cambridge: Harvard University Press
Sunstein C, D Schkade, L Ellman and A Sawicki (2006) *Are Judges Political?* Washington, D.C.; Brookings Institute Press
Sunstein C (1999) *One Case at a Time* Cambridge: Harvard University Press
Suskind R (2006) *The One Percent Doctrine: Deep Inside America's Pursuit of Its Enemies since 9/11* New York: Simon & Schuster

Svendsen GT and Swendsen GLH (2010) *Handbook of Social Capital: The Troika of Sociology, Political Science and Economics* Chelthanham: Edward Edgar

Tancredi L *Hard-Wired Behaviour: What Neuroscience Reveals about Morality* (2005) New York: Cambridge University Press

Taylor C (1985) *Philosophical Papers I: Human Agency and Language* New York: Cambridge University Press

Taylor C (1985) *Philosophical Papers II: Philosophy and the Human Sciences* New York: Cambridge University Press

Taylor C (1991) *The Ethics of Authenticity* Cambridge: Harvard University Press

Taylor JG (ed) (1993) *Mathematical Approaches to Neural Networks* New York: North-Holland

Taylor R (1966) *Action and Purpose* Englewood Cliffs: Prentice-Hall

Tulving E & Craik FIM (eds) (2000) *The Oxford Handbook of Memory* New York: Oxford University Press

Tancredi L (2005) *Hardwired Behaviour: What Neuroscience Reveals about Morality* New York: Cambridge University Press

Tribe L (1985) *Constitutional Choices* Cambridge: Harvard University Press

Unger RM (1987) *False Necessities: Anti-Necessitarian Social Theory in the Service of Radical Democracy* New York: Cambridge University Press

Unger RM (1987) *Plasticity into Power: Comparative Historical Studies on the Institutional Conditions of Economic and Military Societies* New York: Cambridge University Press

Unger RM (1987) *Politics: A Work in Constructive Social Theory* New York: Cambridge University Press

Unger RM (1987) *Social Theory: Its Situation and Its Task* New York: Cambridge University Press

UNICEF *The State of the World's Children: 2002* (2002) Paris: UNICEF

Van der Walt AJ (2005) *Constitutional Property Law* Cape Town: Juta Law

Van Der Walt J (2006) *Law and Sacrifice* Johannesburg: Wits University Press

Van Iwagen P (1983) *An Essay on Free Will* New York: Oxford University Press

Waldron J (1999) *The Dignity of Legislation* New York: Cambridge University Press

Waldron J (1999) *Law and Disagreement* New York: Oxford University Press

Watson G (ed) (2003) *Free Will* New York: Oxford University Press

Wegner D (2002) *The Illusion of Conscious Will* Cambridge: MIT Press

Weiskrantz L (1997) *Consciousness Lost & Found: A Neuropsychological Exploration* New York: Oxford University Press

Werth B (1995) *The Billion Dollar Molecule: One Company's Quest for the Perfect Drug* New York: Simon & Schuster

Williams B (1985) *Ethics and the Limits of Philosophy* Cambridge: Harvard University Press

Wittgenstein L (1953) *Philosophical Investigations* (GEM Anscombe, trans. 3rd Ed) New York: Prentice Hall

Wittgenstein L (1921) *Tractatus Logico-Philosophicus* New York: McGraw-Hill

Wolfrem R (ed) (2003) *Gleichheit und Nichtdiskriminierung im Nationalalen und Internationalen Mesenchenrechtssschutz* New York: Springer

Wolin S (1960) *Politics and Vision: Continuity and Innovation in Western Political Thought* Boston: Little, Brown

Woolman S & Fleisch B (2009) *The Constitution in the Classroom: Law and Education in South Africa, 1994 – 2008* Pretoria: Pretoria University Law Press

Woolman S & Bishop M (eds)(2003 – 2012) *Constitutional Law of South Africa, 2nd Edition* Cape Town: Juta

Woolman S & Bilchitz D (eds)(2012) *Is This Seat Taken? Conversations at the Bar, the Bench and the Academy about the South AfricanConstitution* Pretoria: Pretoria University Law Press

Woolman S & Bishop M (eds)(2008) *Constitutional Convesations,* Pretoris: Pretoria University Press

United Nations Inter-agency Commission (1990) *World Declaration On Education for All and a Framework for Action to Meet Basic Learning Needs* New York: United Nations University Press

World Health Organization (2006) *Antiretroviral Drugs for Treating Pregnant Women and Preventing HIV* Geneva: WHO

World Health Organization (2006) *Antiretroviral Therapy of HIV Infection in Infants and Children in Resource-Limited Settings: Towards Universal Access: Recommendations for a Public Health Approach.* Geneva: WHO

World Health Organization (2006) *Infection in Infants in Resource-Limited Settings Towards Universal Access: Recommendations for a Public Health Approach* Geneva: WHO

World Health Organization (2006) *National Guide to Monitoring and Evaluating Programmes for the Prevention of HIV in Infants and Young Children* Geneva: WHO

World Health Organization (2006) *The World Health Report* Geneva: WHO

Wringham R & Peterson D (1996) *Demonic Males: Apes and the Origins of Human Violence* Boston: Houghton Mifflin

Young IM (1990) *Justice and the Politics of Difference* Princeton: Princeton University Press

Young IM (1991) *Throwing Like a Girl and Other Essays* Bloomington: Indiana University Press

ARTICLES

Adelstein R 'Institutional Function and Evolution in the Criminal Process' (1981) 76 *Northwestern University Law Review* 1

Albertyn C 'The Stubborn Persistence of Patriarchy? Gender Equality and Cultural Diversity in South Africa' (2009) 2 *Constitutional Court Review* 165

Anderson E 'John Stuart Mill and Experiments in Living' (1991) 101 *Ethics* 4

Anderson K 'Family Structure, Parent Investment, and Educational Outcomes amongst Black South Africans' *University of Michigan Population Studies Centre Research Report* (2000) 461

Anderson K 'Relatedness and Investment in Children in South Africa' (2005) 16 *Human Nature* 1

Armstrong F 'The CIA and WMDs: The Damning Evidence' (2010) 57 (13) *The New York Review of Books* 53

'Audit Finds Transnet Lost Millions through Irregular Scrap Metal Deal' *Business Report* (18 July 2003)

Baars BJ 'In the Theatre of Consciousness: Global Workspace Theory, A Rigorous Scientific Theory of Consciousness' (1997) 4(4) *Journal of Consciousness Studies* 292

Baars BJ 'There are No Known Differences in Fundamental Brain Mechanisms of Sensory Consciousness Between Humans and Other Animals' (2001) 10 *Animal Welfare* 31

Barnard AJ 'Totalitarianism, Same-Sex Marriage and Democratic Politics in Post-Apartheid South Africa' (2007) 23 *South African Journal on Human Rights* 500

Beckmann J 'The Emergence of Self-Managing Schools: Devolution of Authority or Disguised Centralism' (2002) 14 *Education and the Law* 153

Belluck P 'In Study, Fatherhood Leads to Drop in Testosterone' *The New York Times* (12 September 2011)

Berger L, Ruiter D, Churchland S, Schmid G, Carlson K, Dirks P & Kibii J 'Australopithecus Sediba: A New Species of Homo-Like Australopith from South Africa' (2010) 328 *Science* 195

Bhana D 'The Law of Contract and the Constitution: *Napier v Barkhuizen*' (2007) 124 *South African Journal on Human Rights* 269

Bilchitz D 'Giving Socio-Economic Rights Teeth: The Minimum Core and Its Importance' (2001) 119 *South African Law Journal* 484

Bilchitz D 'Towards a Reasonable Approach to the Minimum Core: Laying the Foundations for Future Socio-Economic Rights Jurisprudence' (2003) 19 *South African Journal on Human Rights* 219 1

Bilchitz D and Judge M 'For Whom Does the Bell Toll? The Challenges and Possibilities of the Civil Union Act for Family Law' (2007) 23 *South African Journal on Human Rights* 219

Bilchitz D 'Is the Constitutional Court Wasting Away the Rights of the Poor?' (2010) 127 *South African Law Journal* 591

Bilchitz D and Tuovinen J 'Theory, Practice and the Legal Enterprise: A Reply to Stu Woolman' (2010) 25 *Southern African Public Law* 544

Bilchitz D 'Should Religious Associations Be Allowed to Discriminate?' (2011) 27 *South African Journal on Human Rights* 219

Bilchitz D 'Why Courts Should Not Sanction Unfair Discrimination in the Private Sphere' (2012) 28 *South African Journal on Human Rights* 296

Bilgrami A 'Notes toward a Definition' (2006) 135 (4) *Daedulus: Journal of the American Academy of Arts & Sciences* 5

Bishop M 'Vampire or Prince? The Listening Constitution and *Merafong Demarcation Forum & Others v President of the Republic of South Africa & Others* (2009) 2 *Constitutional Court Review* 313

Bishop M and J Brickhill 'Constitutional Law' 2009 (2) *Juta Quarterly Report*

Biskowski LJ 'Reason in Politics: Arendt and Gadamer on the Role of the *Eide*' (1998) 31 *Polity* 1

Biswas-Diener R, E Diener & Taya M 'The Psychology of Subjective Well-Being' (2004) 133 *Daedelus* 18

Bond P 'Rejoinder: Collaborations, Co-optation & Contestation in Praxis-based Knowledge Production' (2008) 35 *Review of African Political Economy* 271

Botha H 'Freedom and Constraint in Constitutional Adjudication' (2004) 20 *South African Journal on Human Rights* 249

Brody E 'Entrance, Voice and Exit: The Constitutional Bounds of Freedom of Association' (2002) 35 *University of California Davis Law Review* 821.

Brand D 'The Western Cape Provincial Constitution' (2000) 31 *Rutgers Law Journal* 961.

Brassey M 'Back Off, but Back Up: Administrative Law Rightly Yields to Labour Law (2009) 2 *Constitutional Court Review* 209

Brickhill J 'Precedent and the Constitutional Court' (2010) 3 *Constitutional Court Review* 79

Burham T, Chapman J, Gray P, McIntyre M, Lipson S & Ellison E 'Men in Committed, Romantic Relationships have Lower Testosterone' (2003) 44 *Hormones and Behaviour* 119.

Butler B 'Nussbaum's Capabilities Approach: Political Criticism and the Burden of Proof' (2001) 1 *International Journal of Politics and Ethics* 71

Calvin WH 'The Brain as Darwin Machine' (1987) 330 *Nature* 33

Campbell D 'Blind Variation and Selection Retention in Creative Thought as in Other Knowledge Processes' (1960) 67 *Psychological Review* 380

Carey B 'Psychoanalytic Therapy Wins Backing' *The New York Times* (30 September 2008).

Carr I 'From Policy to Praxis: A Study of the Implementation of Representative Councils of Learners in the Western Cape, from 1997 to 2003' (Unpublished PhD dissertation, University of the Western Cape, 2005)

Chalmers D 'Facing Up to the Problem of Consciousness' (1995) 3(1) *Journal of Consciousness Studies* 200

Chalmers D 'First-Person Methods in the Science of Consciousness' (1999) *Consciousness Bulletin*, available at http://www.u.arizona.edu/chalmers/papers/firstperson.html

Charlton S, Silverman M & Berrisford S *Taking Stock: Review of the Department of Housing's Programme, Policies and Practice (1994–2003)*(Unpublished paper, Department of Housing, 2003)(On file with author)

Chaskalson M and Davis D 'Constitutionalism, the Rule of Law and the First Certification Judgment' (1997) 13 *South African Journal on Human Rights* 430

Chayes A 'The Role of the Judge in Public Law Litigation' (1976) 89 *Harvard Law Review* 1281

Chenwi L 'A New Approach to Remedies in Socio-Economic Rights Adjudication: *51 Olivia Road v City of Johannesburg*' (2009) 2 *Constitutional Court Review* 371

Cherniak C 'Rationality and the Structure of Human Memory' (1983) 57 *Synthese* 163

Chipkin I & B Ngqulunga 'Friends and Family: Social Cohesion in South Africa' (2007) 34(1) *Journal of Southern African Studies* 310

Choudhry S '"He Had a Mandate": Constitutionalism in a One Party Dominant Democracy' (2009) 2 *Constitutional Court Review* 1

Clarke R 'Toward a Credible Agent-Causal Account of Free Will' (1993) 27 *Nous* 191

Clough M 'Reflections on Civil Society' (1999) 268 *The Nation* 18

Cohen J 'Review of Michael Walzer's *Spheres of Justice: A Defense of Pluralism and Equality* (1986) 82 *The Journal of Philosophy* 457

Cornell D 'A Call for a Nuanced Constitutional Jurisprudence: Ubuntu, Dignity and Reconciliation' (2004) 19 *SA Public Law* 666

Cornell D 'Is there a Difference that makes a Difference between uBuntu and Dignity? (2010) 25 *SA Public Law* 382

Cornell D 'The Significance of the Living Customary Law for an Understanding of Law: Does Custom Allow for a Woman to be Hosi' (2009) 2 *Constitutional Court Review* 395

Cover R '1982 Term Foreword: Nomos and Narrative' 97 *Harvard Law Review* 4

Cover R 'Violence and the Word' (1986) 95 *Yale Law Journal* 1601

Cowan S 'Can Dignity Guide Our Equality Jurisprudence?' (2001) 17 *South African Journal on Human Rights* 34

Cowley J 'Twelve Great Thinkers of Our Time' (2003) 132 *New Statesman* 1

Crick F and Koch C 'A Framework for Consciousness' (2003) 6 *Nature Neuroscience* 119

Crick F and Koch C 'Consciousness and Neuroscience' (1998) 8 *Cerebral Cortex* 97

Crick F and Koch C 'Why Neuroscience May Be Able to Explain Consciousness' (1995) 273 *Scientific American* 84

Currie I 'Judicious Avoidance' (1999) 15 *South African Journal on Human Rights* 138

Damasio A 'Time-Locked Multi-Regional Retro-activation: A Systems Proposal for the Neural Substrates of Recall and Recognition' (1989) 33 *Cognition* 25

Damasio A, Everitt B and Bishop D 'The Somatic Marker Hypothesis of the Brain and the Possible Functions of the Prefrontal Cortex' (1996) 351 *Philosophical Transactions of the Royal Society of London – Series B, Biological Sciences* 1413

Dandalides G 'The Patentability of Isolated DNA Sequences' (2011) 14 *Tulane Journal of Technology and Intellectual Property* 283

Davidson D 'On the Very Idea of a Conceptual Scheme' (1974) 47 *Proceedings and Addresses of the American Philosophical Association* 1

Davis D 'Equality: The Majesty of Legoland Jurisprudence' (1999) 116 *South African Law Journal* 398

Davis D 'Adjudicating the Socio-Economic Rights in the South African Constitution: Towards 'Deference Lite'?' (2006) 22 *South African Journal on Human Rights* 301

Davis D 'Private Law after 1994: Progressive Development or Schizoid Confusion?' (2008) 24 *South African Journal on Human Rights* 318

Davis D & Klarke K 'Transformative Constitutionalism, the Common Law and Customary Law' (2010) 26 *South African Journal on Human Rights* 403

De Búrca G and Scott J 'Introduction to Narrowing the Gap? Law and New Approaches to Governance in the European Union 13 *Columbia Journal of European Law* 513, 514 (2007)

De Dreu C 'The Neuropeptide Oxytocin Regulates Parochial Altruism in Intergroup Conflict among Humans' (2010) 328 *Science* 1408

Dehaene M & Changeux JP 'A Hierarchical Neuronal Network for Planned Behaviour' (1997) 94 *Proceedings of the National Academy of Sciences USA* 13293

Dehaene M, Kerzberg M & Changeux JP 'A Neuronal Model of a Global Workspace in Effortful Cognitive Tasks' (1998) 95 *Proceedings of the National Academy of Sciences USA* 14529

Deschenes M, Madariage-Domich A & Steriade M 'Dendrodendritic Synapses in the Cat Reticularis Thalami Nucleus: A Structural Basis for Thalmic Spindle Synchronization' (1985) 334 *Brain Research* 165

Dersso S 'The Need for Constitutional Accommodation of Ethno-Cultural Diversity in the Post-Colonial State' (2008) 24 *South African Journal on Human Rights* 565.

De Vos P 'The Inevitability of Same-Sex Marriage in South Africa's Post-Apartheid State' (2007) *South African Journal on Human Rights* 432

Dieltiens V & P Enslin 'Democracy in Education or Education in Democracy: The Limits of Participation in South African School Governance' (2002) 28 *Journal of Education* 5

Diver C 'The Judge as Political Powerbroker: Superintending Structural Change in Public Institutions' (1979) 65 *Virginia Law Review* 43

Doctor S 'Dignity, Criminal Law and the Bill of Rights' (2004) 121 *South African Law Journal* 265

Dorf M '1997 Supreme Court Term Foreword: The Limits of Socratic Deliberation' (1998) 112 *Harvard Law Review* 4

Dorf M & Friedman B 'Shared Constitutional Interpretation' (2000) *Supreme Court Review* 61

Dorf M 'Legal Indeterminism and Institutional Design' (2004) 78 *New York University Law Review* 875

Dorf M 'Review of Mark Tushnet's *After Bureaucracy: The New Constitutional Order*' (2004) 71 *University of Chicago Law Review* 1245

Dorf M & Sabel C 'A Constitution of Democratic Experimentalism' (1998) 98 *Columbia Law Review* 267

Dorf M & Friedman B 'Shared Constitutional Interpretation' (2000) 2000 *Supreme Court Review* 61

Dorf M & C Sabel 'Drug Treatment Courts and Emergent Experimentalist Government' (2000) 53 *Vanderbilt Law Review* 831

Dowling K 'Can Capabilities Reconcile Freedom and Equality?' (2006) 14 *The Journal of Political Philosophy* 323

Dugard J 'Courts and the Poor in South Africa: A Critique of Systemic Judicial Failures to Advance Transformative Justice' (2009) 25 *South African Journal on Human Rights* 214

Dugard J 'Court of First Instance? Towards a Pro-Poor Jurisdiction for the South African Constitutional Court' (2006) 22 *South African Journal on Human Rights* 261

Dürig T 'Der Grundrechtssatz von der Menschenwürde' (1956) 81 *Archiv für öffentliches Recht* 117

Dyzenhaus D 'The Past and Future of the Rule of Law in South Africa' (2007) 124 *South African Law Journal* 734

English R 'Ubuntu: The Quest for an Indigenous Jurisprudence' (1996) 12 *South African Journal on Human Rights* 641

Eysenck HJ 'Creativity and Personality: Suggestions for a Theory' (1993) 4 *Psychological Inquiry* 147

Fagan A 'The Confusions of K' (2009) 126 *South African Law Journal* 154

Feiberg T 'Our Brains, Our Selves' (2006) 135 (4) *Daedulus: Journal of the American Academy of Arts & Sciences* 72

Feris L 'Constitutional Environmental Rights: An Underutilized Resource' (2008) 24 *South African Journal on Human Rights* 29

Feris L 'Sustainable Development in Practice: *Fuel Retailers Association of Southern Africa v Director-General Environmental Management, Department of Agriculture, Conservation and Environment, Mpumalanga Province*' (2009) 1 *Constitutional Court Review* 235

Fiss O 'The Supreme Court 1978 Term Foreword: Forms of Justice' (1979) 93 *Harvard Law Review* 1

Flanagan B 'Judicial Rights Talk: Defects in the Liberal Challenge to Constitutional Review' (2006) 22 *South African Journal of Human Rights* 173

Fleisch B 'Social Scientists as Policy Makers: EG Mahlerbe and the National Bureau for Social and Educational Research, 1929 -1943' (1995) 21 *Journal of Southern African Studies* 349

Fleisch B & S Woolman 'On the Constitutionality of Single Medium Public Schools' (2007) 23 *South African Journal on Human Rights* 34

Fleisch B & Woolman S 'South Africa's Education Legislation, Quasi-Markets and School Choice' (2006) 24 (2) *Perspectives in Education* 1

Frankfurt H 'Alternative Possibilities and Moral Responsibility' (1969) 66 *Journal of Philosophy* 829

Frederick W 'The Growing Concern over Business Responsibility' (1960) 2 *California Management Review* 54

Friedman M 'The Social Responsibility of Business is to Increase its Profits' *The New York Times Magazine* (September 1970)

Fritz N 'Crossing Jordan: Constitutional Space for (Un)Civil Sex?' (2004) 20 *South African Journal on Human Rights* 230.

Fuller L 'The Forms and Limits of Adjudication' (1978) 92 *Harvard Law Review* 358

Fung A & Wright EO 'Deepening Democracy: Innovations in Empowered Participatory Governance' (1998) 29 (1) *Science & Society* 5

Gettler L, T McDade, A Feranil & C Kuzawa 'Longitudinal Evidence that Fatherhood Decreases Testosterone in Human Males' (2011) 108 *Proceeding of the National Academy of Sciences* 1

Gewirtz P 'Remedies and Resistance' (1983) 92 *Yale Law Journal* 585

Giovanola B 'Personhood and Human Richness: Good and Well-Being in the Capability Approach and Beyond' (2005) 63 *Review of Social Economy* 1

Galasso A & M Schankerman 'Patent Thickets, Courts and the Market for Innovation' (2008) 41 *Rand Journal of Economics* 472

Goldblatt B 'Different Routes to Relationship Recognition Reform: A Comparative Discussion of South Africa and Australia' Law and Society Association Australia and New Zealand (LSAANZ) *W(h)ither Human Rights Conference* (December 2008)(Manuscript on file with author)

Goldman-Radic PS 'Topography of Cognition: Parallel Distributed Networks in Primate Association Cortex' (1988) 11 *Annual Review of Neuroscience* 137

Gray G 'Global AIDS: HIV Prevention and Care in Children, Treatment Access and Challenges Among Children in Resource-Limited Settings' *Management of Pediatric HIV Infection, and Prevention of Mother-to-Child HIV Transmission* (2006), available at http://www.medscape.com/viewarticle/544610

Green J, Nystrom L, Engell A, Darley J and Cohen J 'The Neural Basis for Cognitive Conflict and Control in Moral Judgment' (2004) 44 *Neuron* 389

Green J, Sommerville R, Nystrom L, Darley J & Cohen J 'An MRI Investigation of Emotional Engagement in Moral Judgment' (2001) 293 *Science* 2105

Green JR and S Scotchmer 'On the Division of Profit in Sequential Innovation' (1995) 26 (1) *Rand Journal of Economics* 20

Grindley PC and DJ Teece 'Managing Intellectual Capital: Licensing and Cross-Licensing in Semiconductors and Electronics' (1997) 39 *California Management Review* 8

Harber C and B Trafford 'Democratic Management & School Effectiveness in Two Countries: A Case of Pupil Participation?' (1999) 27 *Educational Management, Administration and Leadership* 45

Hastings I Dynamic Innovative Inefficiency in Pharmaceutical Patent Settlements, 13 *North Carolina Journal of Law & Technology* 31 (2011)

Hayek FA 'The Use of Knowledge in Society' (1945) 35 (4) *American Economic Review* 519

Hayek FA 'The Results of Human Action, but not of Human Design' *Studies in Philosophy, Politics and Economics* (1967) 96, 97

Heise M 'State Constitutions, School Finance Litigation and the "Third Wave": From Equity to Adequacy' (1995) 68 *Temple Law Review* 1151

Heller M & Eisenberg R 'Can Patents Deter Innovation? The Anticommons in Biomedical Research' (1998) 280 *Science* 5364

Henry J 'US Issues New Deportation Policy's First Reprieves' *The New York Times* (23 August 2011)

Hershkoff H 'Positive Rights and State Constitutions: The Limits of Federal Rationality Review' (1999) 112 *Harvard Law Review* 1131

Hiochberg L, Serruya M, Friehs G, Mukland J, Saleh M, Caplan A, Branner A, Chen D, Penn R & Donoghue JP 'Neuronal Ensemble Control of Prosthetic Devices by a Human with Tetraplegia' (2006) 442 *Nature* 164

Hoexter C 'Clearing the Intersection? Administrative Law and Labour Law in the Constitutional Court (2008) 1 *Constitutional Court Review* 209

Hogg P and Bushell A 'The Charter Dialogue between Courts and Legislatures (or Perhaps the Charter of Rights Isn't Such a Bad Thing after All)' (1997) 35 *Osgoode Hall Law Journal* 75

Horowitz DL 'Decreeing Organizational Change: Judicial Supervision of Public Institutions' (1983) *Duke Law Journal* 1265

Howard PA 'The Neural Mechanisms of Learning from Competitors' (2010) 53 (2) *Neuroimage* 1

Humby T 'The *Biowatch* Case: Major Advance in South African Law of Costs and Access to Environmental Justice: Trustees for the Time Being, *Biowatch Trust v Registrar, Genetic Resources and Others* (2010) 22 *Journal of Environmental Law* 125

Jackson K 'A Colony with a Conscience' *The New York Times* (27 December 2007)

Jaggar AM 'Reasoning about Well-Being: Nussbaum's Methods of Justifying Capabilities (2006) 14 *The Journal of Political Philosophy* 301

Jansen J 'Grove Primary: Power, Privilege and the Law in South African Education' (1998) 23 *Journal of Education* 5

Jansen J 'The Ties that Bind: Race and Restitution in Education Law and Policy in South Africa and the United States' (2006) 105 *Yearbook of the National Society for the Study of Education* 211

Kapindu R 'The Desperate Left in Desperation: A Court in Retreat – *Nokotyana v Ekurhuleni Metropolitan Municipality* Revisited' (2010) 3 *Constitutional Court Review* 201

Karlsson J 'The Role of Governing Democratic Bodies in South African Schools' (2002) 38(3) *Comparative Education* 327

Kaufman A 'Capabilities and Freedom' (2006) 14 *The Journal of Political Philosophy* 289

Keenan T 'Auditor-General: Fighting Fraud with the Best of Them' *Finance Week* (12 July 2002) 16

Kim KM 'DT Campbell's Social Epistemology of Science: Vicarious Selection, Epistemological Fallabilism, and Sociology of Scientific Validity' (1997) 3 *Evolution and Cognition* 75

Klaaren J 'A Remedial Interpretation of the *Treatment Action Campaign* Decision' (2003) 19 *South African Journal of Human Rights* 539

Klaaren J 'A Second Look at the South African Human Rights Commission, Access to Information, and the Promotion of Socio-Economic Rights' (2005) 27 *Human Rights Quarterly* 539

Klaaren J 'Structures of Government and the 1996 Constitution: Putting Democracy Back into Human Rights' (1997) 13 *South African Journal on Human Rights* 3

Klare K 'Legal Subsidiarity and Constitutional Rights: A Reply to AJ Van Der Walt' (2008) 1 *Constitutional Court Review* 129

Klug H 'Finding the Constitutional Court's Place in South Africa's Democracy: The Interaction of Principle and Institutional Pragmatism in the Court's Decision-making' (2010) 3 *Constitutional Court Review* 1

Nichols S & Knobe J 'Moral Responsibility and Determinism: The Cognitive Science of Folk Psychology' *Nous* 1.

Koch C A "Complex" Theory of Consciousness *Scientific American* (18 August 2009)

Koch C and Laurent G 'Complexity and the Nervous System' (1999) 284 *Science* 96

Koch C and Tootell RB 'Stimulating Brain, But No Mind' (1996) 383 *Nature* 301

Kozin A 'Bernstein on the Mystery Behind the Music' *The New York Times* (February 15, 2011)

Kroeze IG 'Doing Things with Values (Part 2): The Case of Ubuntu' (2002) 13 *Stellenbosch Law Review* 252

Lenta P 'Judicial Constraint and Overreach' (2004) 20 *South African Journal on Human Rights* 544

Lenta P 'Religious Liberty and Cultural Accommodation' (2005) 122 *South African Law Journal* 352

Lenta P Taking Diversity Seriously: Religious Associations and Work-Related Discrimination' (2009) 125 *South African Law Journal* 828

Libet B 'The Experimental Evidence for Subjective Referral of Evidence Backward in Time: Reply to PS Churchland' (1981) 48 *Philosophy of Science* 182

Libet B 'Time of Conscious Intention to Act in Relation to the Onset of Other Cerebral Activities (Readiness Potential): The Unconscious Initiation of a Freely Voluntary Act' (1983) 106 *Brain* 623

Libet B 'Unconscious Cerebral Initiative and the Role of Conscious Will in Voluntary Action' (1985) 8 *Behavioural and Brain Sciences* 529

Libet B et al 'Time of Conscious Intention to Act in Relation to the Onset of Other Cerebral Activities (Readiness Potential): The Unconscious Initiation of a Freely Voluntary Act' (1983) 106 *Brain* 623

Liebenberg S 'The Value of Human Dignity in Interpreting Socio-Economic Rights' (2005) 21 *South African Journal on Human Rights* 22

Leichsenring F & S Rabung 'Effectiveness of Long-term Psychodynamic Psychotherapy ('LTPP'): A Meta-Analysis' (2008) 300 (13) *Journal of the American Medical Association* 1551

Leichsenring F & S Rabung 'Analyzing Effectiveness of Long-Term Psychodynamic Psychotherapy: A Reply' (2009) 301 (9) *Journal of the American Medical Association* 932

Levison D 'Rights Essentialism and Remedial Equilibration' (1999) 99 *Columbia Law Review* 857

Llinas RR and Pare D 'Of Dreaming and Wakefulness (1991) 44 (3) *Neuroscience* 521

Loxton L 'Fakie Seeks R100m from Municipalities' *Business Report* (12 March 2003)

Loxton L 'Gordhan Delighted with SARS Clean Bill of Health' *Business Report* (24 September 2004)

Madlingozi T 'The Constitutional Court, Court Watchers and the Commons: A Reply to Professor Michelman on Constitutional Dialogue, 'Interpretive Charity' and the Citizenry as Sangomas' (2009) 1 *Constitutional Court Review* 63

Makker A 'The Nanotechnology Thicket and the Path to Commercialization' (2011) 84 *Southern California Law Review* 1163

Malherbe R 'Centralisation of Power in Education: Have Provinces Become National Agents?' (2006) 2 *Tydskrif vir Suid-Afrikaanse Reg* 237

Malherbe R 'Constitutional Framework for Pursuing Equal Opportunities in Education' (2004) 22(3) *Perspectives in Education* 9

Malherbe R 'Fresh Start: Education Rights in South Africa' (2000) 4 *European Journal for Education Law and Policy* 49

Mansbridge J 'A Deliberative Theory of Interest Representation' in MP Petracca (ed) (1992) *The Politics of Interests: Interest Groups Transformed* 37

Maree H & Lowenherz 'Grove Primary: A Response to Professor Jonathan Jansen' (1998) 23 *Journal of Education* 31

Maslow A 'A Theory of Human Motivation' (1943) 50 (4) *Psychological Review* 370

Mazur A and Michalek J 'Marriage, Divorce and Male Testosterone' (1998) 77 *Social Forces* 315

Maurer SM 'Inside the Anticommons: Academic Scientists' Struggle to Build a Commercially Self-Supporting Human Mutations Database, 1999-2001' (2006) 35 (6) *Research Policy* 839

Mbazira C 'Appropriate, Just and Equitable Relief in Socio-Economic Rights Litigation: The Tension between Corrective and Distributive Forms of Justice' (2007) 125 *South African Law Journal* 71

Mbazira C 'From Ambivalance to Certainty: Norms and Principles for the Use of Structural Interdicts in Socio-Economic Rights Cases' (2008) 24 *South African Journal on Human Rights* 1

McCabe ME & Kile LJ 'Recent Developments in Patent Law and Their Impact on the Pharmaceutical and Biotechnology Industries' (2011) 19 *University of Baltimore Intellectual Property Law Journal* 75

McCauley RN 'Folk Psychology is Here to Stay' (1985) 94 *The Philosophical Review* 197

McGinn C 'The Tell-Tale Brain: An Exchange with VS Ramachandram' (2011) 58 (11) *New York Review of Books* 68

McGinn C 'VS Ramachandram's *The Tell-Tale Brain*' (2011) 58 (5) *New York Review of Books* 8

McIntosh AR, MN Rajah & NJ Lobaugh 'Interactions of the Prefrontal Cortex in Relation to Awareness in Sensory Learning' (1999) 284 *Science* 1531

McKinley D 'Democracy and Social Movements in SA' (2004) 28 *Labour Bulletin* 39, 40

Merges RP and Nelson RR 'On the Complex Economics of Patent Scope' (1990) 90 *Columbia Law Review* 839

McIntyre L 'Complexity and Social Scientific Laws' (1993) 97 *Synthese* 209

Michelman F 'Expropriation, Eviction and the Gravity of the Common Law' (Constitution Hill, 21 July 2012) and (2013) 25 (2) *Stellenbosch Law Review* – (forthcoming)

Michelman F 'Old Kibitzes Never Die: A Rejoinder to Stu Woolman' (2010) 25 *Southern African Public Law* 515

Michelman F 'On the Uses of Interpretive Charity: Some Notes on Application, Equality and Objective Unconstitutionality from the 2007 Term of the Constitutional Court of South Africa' (2008) 1 *Constitutional Court Review* 165

Michelman F 'Law's Republic' (1988) 97 *Yale Law Journal* 1438

Mirowski P 'A Visible Hand in the Marketplace of Ideas: Precision-Measurement as Arbitrage' (1994) 7 *Science in Context* 563

Miyawaki Y, Uchida H, Sato O, Morito Y, Tanabe H, Sadato N & Kamitani Y 'Decoding the Mind's Eye – Visual Image Reconstruction from Human Brain Activity using a Combination of Multiscale Image Decoders' (2008) 60 *Neuron* 915

Moellendorf D (1998) 'Reasoning About Resources: *Soobramoney* and the Future of Socio-Economic Rights Claims' (1998) 14 *South African Journal on Human Rights* 327

Mokgoro Y 'Ubuntu and the Law in South Africa' (1998) 4 *Buffalo Human Rights Law Review* 15

Mokgoro Y and Woolman S 'Where Dignity Ends and Ubuntu Starts: An Amplification of, and a Tension in, Drucilla Cornell's Thoughts' (2010) 25 *Southern African Public Law* 400

Moseneke D 'Transformative Constitutionalism: Its Implications for the Law of Contract' (2009) *Stellenbosch Law Review* 1

Mujuzi JD 'Don't Send Them to Prison Because They Can't Rehabilitate Them! The South African Judiciary Doubts the Executive's Ability to Rehabilitate Offenders: A Note on *S v Shilubane* 2008 (1) SACR 295 (T)' (2008) 24 *South African Journal on Human Rights* 330

Muller M, Marlowe F, Bugumba R and Ellison P 'Testosterone and Parental Care in East African Foragers and Pastoralists' (2009) 276 *Proceedings of the Royal Academy: Biological Sciences* 347

Musaliam S, Corniel B, Gregor B, Shermberger H and R Anderson R 'Cognitive Control Signals for Neural Prosthetics' (2004) 305 *Science* 258

Nagel T 'What Is It Like to be a Bat?' *Mortal Questions* (1979) 165

Neely RB 'The Hearsay Speech Understanding System: An Example of the Recognition Process' (1973) *Proceedings of the International Conference on Artificial Intelligence* 185

Nelson RR 'The Market Economy and the Scientific Commons' (2004) 33 (3) *Research Policy* 455

Newman JB 'Reticular-Thalamic Activation of the Cortex Generates Conscious Contents' (1995) 18 (4) *Behavioral and Brain Sciences* 691

Newman JB, Baars BJ and Cho SB 'A Neural Global Workspace Model for Conscious Attention' (1997) 10 *Neural Networks* 1195

Ngwane Z '"Real Men Reawaken Their Fathers' Homesteads, The Educated Leave Them in Ruins": The Politics of Domestic Reproduction in Post-Apartheid Rural South Africa' (2001) 31 *Journal of Religion in Africa* 402

Nichols S and Knobe J 'Moral Responsibility and Determinism: The Cognitive Science of Folk Psychology' (2007) 41 *Nous* 663

Noel MD & Schankerman M 'Strategic Patenting and Software Innovation' CEPR Discussion Paper 5701 (2006)

Nongubo MJ 'An Investigation into Perceptions of Learner Participation in the Governance of Secondary Schools' (Unpublished Master's thesis, Rhodes University, 2005)

Noonan K, Sabel C and Simon W 'Legal Accountability in the Service-Based Welfare State: Lessons from Child Welfare Reform' (2009) 34 *Law & Social Inquiry* 523

Nussbaum M 'Capabalities Approach: Sen and Social Justice' (2010) 9 *Feminist Economics* 33

Nussbaum M 'Constitutions and Capabilities: Perception against Lofty Formalism' (2007) 121 *Harvard Law Review* 4

Nussbaum M 'Discernment of Perception: An Aristotelian Conception of Private and Public Rationality' (1985) 1 *Proceedings of the Boston Areas Colloquium in Ancient Philosophy*' 151

Nussbaum M '"Finely Aware and Richly Responsible": The Moral Task of Literature' (1985) 82 *The Journal of Philosophy* 10

Overbye D 'Nobel in Physics Goes to Perlmuttter, Schmidt and Riess' *The New York Times* (5 October 2011)

Parker-Hope T 'Rick Perry's Brain Freeze' *The New York Times* (10 November 2011)

Palmer S (1999) 'Colour, Consciousness, and the Isomorphism Constraint' (1999) 22 *Behavioral and Brain Sciences* 923

Parvisi J & Damasio A 'Consciousness and the Brain Stem' (2001) 79 *Cognition* 135

Paslick M '"Exclusive" No Longer Means Exclusive in the Context of Patent Licenses' (2011) 19 *University of Baltimore Intellectual Property Law Journal* 167

Penfold G & Milo D'Media Freedom and the Law of Privacy: *NM v Smith (Freedom of Expression Institute as Amicus Curiae)* 2007 5 SA 250 (CC)' (2008) 1 *Constitutional Court Review* 311

Pienaar G 'The Effect of Equality and Human Dignity on the Right to Religious Freedom' (2003) 66 *THRHR* 579

Pieterse M 'Coming to Terms with Judicial Enforcement of Socio-Economic Rights' (2004) 20 *South African Journal on Human Rights* 383

Pieterse M 'Finding the Applicant? Individual Claimants and Group-Based Disadvantage' (2008) 24 *South African Journal on Human Rights* 39

Pieterse M 'Indirect Horizontal Application of the Right to Have Access to Health Care Services' (2007) 23 *South African Journal on Human Rights* 157

Pieterse M 'Resuscitating Socio-Economic Rights: Constitutional Entitlements to Health Care Services (2006) 22 *South African Journal on Human Rights* 473

Piper L 'Participatory Democracy, Education, Babies and Bathwater: A Reply to Dietlins and Enslin (2002) 28 *Journal of Education* 28

Poppel E, Held R & Frost D 'Residual Visual Function after Brain Wounds Involving the Central Visual Pathways in Man' (1973) 243 *Nature* 295

Post R & Siegal R 'Popular Constitutionalism, Departmentalism and Judicial Supremacy' (2004) 92 *California Law Review* 1027

Post R and Siegal R 'Roe Rage: Democratic Constitutionalism and Backlash' (2007) 42 *Harvard Civil Rights-Civil Liberties Law Review* 373

Prinsloo S 'State Interference in the Governance of Public Schools' (2006) 26 *South African Journal of Education* 355

Putnam R 'Tuning In, Tuning Out: The Strange Disappearance of Social Capital in America' (1995) 28 *Political Science and Politics* 1

Quinot G 'Snapshot or Participatory Democracy? Political Engagement as Fundamental Human Right' (2009) 25 *South African Journal on Human Rights* 392

Rae-Dupree J 'Can You Become a Creature of New Habits?' *The New York Times* (4 May 2008)

Rautenbach C 'Therapeutic Jurisprudence in the Customary Courts of South Africa (Traditional Authority Courts as Therapeutic Agents)' (2005) 21 *South African Journal on Human Rights* 323

Rautenbach C, Du Plessis W and Pienaar G 'Is Primogeniture Extinct like the Dodo, or Is there Any Prospect of it Rising from the Ashes? Comments on the Evolution of Customary Law' (2006) 22 *South African Journal on Human Rights* 99

Ravitch D '"School Reform": A Failing Grade' 58 (14) *The New York Review of Books* 32. 'No Child Left Behind?' *Teach Along with Me* (19 March 2010) available at http://www.teachalongwithme.blog

Rawling A 'The AIDS Virus Dispute: Awarding Priority for the Discovery of the Human Immunodeficiency Virus' (1994) 19 *Science, Technology & Human Values* 342

Rawls J 'The Domain of the Political and Overlapping Consensus' (1989) 64 *New York University Law Review* 23

Ray B 'Engagement's Possibilities and Limits as a Socioeconomic Rights Remedy' (2010) 9 *Washington University Global Studies Law Review* 399

Ray B 'Policentrism, Political Mobilization, and the Promise of Socioeconomic Rights' (2009) 45 *Stanford Journal of International Law* 151

Ray B 'Proceduralisation's Triumph and Engagement's Promise in Socio-Economic Rights Litigation' (2007) 27 *South African Journal on Human Rights* 107

Ray B '*Residents of Joe Slovo Community v Thubelisha Homes & Others*: The Two Faces of Engagement' (2010) 10 *Human Rights Law Review* 360

Rebell M and Hughes R 'Schools, Communities, and the Courts: A Dialogic Approach to Education Reform' (1996) 14 *Yale Law & Policy Review* 99

Reiss D and Marino L 'Self-Recognition in the Bottlenose-Dolphin: A Case of Cognitive Convergence' (2001) 98 (10) *Proceedings of the National Academy of Sciences* 5937

Renault B, Signoret JL, Debouille B, Breton F & Bolgert F ' Brain Potentials Reveal Covert Facial Recognition in Prosopagnosia' (1989) 27 *Neuropsychologia* 905

Roach K and Budlender G 'Mandatory Relief and Supervisory Jurisdiction: When Is It Appropriate, Just and Equitable?' (2005) 122 *South African Law Journal* 325

Robson R 'Sexual Democracy' (2007) 23 *South African Journal on Human Rights* 409

Rodriguez E, George N, Lachaux JP, Martinerie J, Renault B and Varela FJ 'Perception's Shadow: Long-Distance Synchronization of Human Brain Activity' (1999) 397 *Nature* 430

Roithmayr D 'Lessons from *Mazibuko*: Persistent Inequality and the Commons' (2010) 3 *Constitutional Court Review* 347

Rosenblueth A, Wiener N and Bigelow J 'Behavior, Purpose and Teleology' (1943) 10 *Philosophy of Science* 18

Roux T 'Principle and Pragmatism on the Constitutional Court of South Africa' (2009) 7 *International Journal of Constitutional Law* 106

Roux T 'Legitimating Transformation: Political Resource Allocation in the South African Constitutional Court' (2003) 4 *Democratization* 10

Roux T 'Pro-Poor Court, Anti-Poor Outcomes: Explaining the Performance of the South African Land Claims Court (2004) 20 *South African Journal on Human Rights* 511

Rovane C 'Why Do Individuals Matter?' (2006) 135 (4) *Daedulus: Journal of the American Academy of Arts & Sciences* 49

Ruger JP 'Ethics and Governance of Global Health Inequalities' (2006) 60 *Journal of Epidemiological and Community Health* 998

Sabel C and Simon W 'Destabilization Rights: How Public Law Litigation Succeeds' (2004) 117 *Harvard Law Review* 1015

Sabel C and Zeitlin J 'Learning from Difference: The New Architecture of Experimentalist Governance in the EU' 14 *European Law Journal* 271(2008)

Sager L 'Fair Measure: The Legal Status of Under-enforced Constitutional Norms' (1978) 91 *Harvard Law Review* 1212

Sayed Y 'Democratising Education in a Decentralised System: South African Policy and Practice' (2002) 32(1) *Compare* 35

Sayed Y 'Discourses of the Policy of Educational Decentralisation in South Africa since 1994: An Examination of the South African Schools Act' (1999) 29 *Compare* 141

Sayed Y 'Understanding Educational Decentralisation in post-apartheid South Africa' (1997) 66(4) *The Journal of Negro Education* 354

Sayed Y & Carrim N 'Democracy, Participation and Equity in Educational Governance' (1997) 17(3) *South African Journal of Education* 91

Schachter O 'Human Dignity as a Normative Concept' (1983) 77 *American Journal of International Law* 848

Schedler J 'The Efficacy of Psychodynamic Psychotherapy' (2010) 65 *American Psychologist* 98

Schlanger M 'Beyond the Hero Judge: Institution Reform Litigation as Litigation' (1999) 97 *Michigan Law Review* 1994

Scott J & Sturm S 'Courts as Catalysts: Re-Thinking the Judicial Role in New Governance' (2007) 13 *Columbia Journal of European Law* 565

Searle J 'Reply to Barclay Martin on Antonio Damasio's *Self Comes to Mind*' (2011) 58 (14) *New York Review of Books* 101

Segal E 'The Court: A Conversation with Judge Richard Posner' (2011) 58 (14) *The New York Review of Books* 47

Segal R 'Dead or Alive: Originalism as Popular Constitutionalism in *Heller*' (2008) 122 *Harvard Law Review* 191

Segal R 'Heller and Originalism's Dead Hand – in Theory and Practice' (2009) 56 *University of Southern California Law Review* 1399

Seligman M 'Can Happiness be Taught? (2004) 133 *Daedelus* 87

Sen A 'More Than 100 Million Women Are Missing' 20 December 1990 *The New York Review of Books*

Sen A 'The Possibility of Social Choice' (Nobel Prize Lecture)(1999) 89 *American Economic Review* 1

Sen A 'The Profit Motive' (1983) 147 *Lloyds Bank Review* 1

Shinji N, Vu A, Naseralis T, Yu B & Gallant J'Reconstructing Visual Experiences from Brain Activity Evoked by Natural Movies' (2011) 10 *Current Biology* 1016

Silberman S 'Don't Even Think About Lying: How Brain Scans are Re-Inventing the Science of Lie Detection' (2006) 14 (1) *Wired* 1

Singer P 'Famine, Affluence and Morality' (1972) 1 *Philosophy and Public Affairs* 229

Singer W and Gray C 'Visual Feature Integration and Temporal Correlation Hypothesis' (1995) 18 *Annual Review of Neuroscience* 555

Smart JCC 'Free Will, Praise and Blame' (1961) 70 *Mind* 291

Smiley M 'Pragmatic Inquiry and Democratic Politics' (1999) 43 *American Journal of Political Science* 639

Sokolove M 'For Derek Jeter, on His 37th Birthday' *The New York Times* (23 June 2011)

Soros G 'My Philanthropy' *The New York Review of Books* (23 June 2011) 4

Sperry RW 'Hemisphere Deconnection and Unity in Conscious Awareness' (1968) 23 *American Psychologist* 723
Sprague C and Woolman S 'Moral Luck: Exploiting South Africa's Policy Environment to Produce a Sustainable National Antiretroviral Treatment Programme' (2006) 22 *South African Journal on Human Rights* 337
Sprigman C and Osborne M '*Du Plessis* is not Dead: South Africa's 1996 Constitution and The Application of the Bill of Rights to Private Disputes' (1999) 15 *South African Journal of Human Rights* 25
Strawson G 'The Self' (1997) 4 *Journal of Consciousness Studies* 405
Stewart L 'Interpreting and Limiting the Basic Socio-Economic Rights of Children in Cases Where They Overlap with the Socio-Economic Rights of Others' (2008) 24 *South African Journal of Human Rights* 472
Struber I 'Framing Pragmatic Aspirations' (2003) 35 *Polity* 491.
Sturm S 'A Normative Theory of Public Law Remedies' (1996) 79 *Georgetown Law Journal* 1357
Sturm S 'Second Generation Employment Discrimination: A Structural Approach' (2001) 101 *Columbia Law Review* 452
Sturm S 'The Promise of Participation' (1993) 78 *Iowa Law Review* 981
Sunstein C 'Incompletely Theorized Agreements in Constitutional Law' *John M Olin Law & Economics Working Paper* no 322 (January 2007)
Sunstein C 'Leaving Things Undecided' (1996) 110 *Harvard Law Review* 4
Sunstein C 'Lochner's Legacy' (1987) 87 *Columbia Law Review* 873
Sunstein C 'Social and Economic Rights? Lessons from South Africa' (2001) 11 *Constitutional Forum* 123
Sunstein C, Schkade D, & Ellman L 'Ideological Voting on the Federal Courts of Appeals: A Preliminary Investigation' (2004) 90 *University of Virginia Law Review* 304.
Swart M 'Left Out in the Cold? Crafting Constitutional Remedies for the Poorest of the Poor' (2005) 21 *South African Journal of Human Rights* 163
Szyszczak E 'Experimental Governance: The Open Method of Coordination' (2006) 12 *European Law Journal* 486
Tallon-Baudry C and Betrand O 'Oscillatory Gamma Activity in Humans and Its Role in Object Representation' (1999) 3 *Trends in Cognitive Science* 151
Terrblanche C 'Minister under Pressure over UIF' *The Mercury* (20 September 2004)
Thombs BD, Bassel M & Jewett LR 'Analyzing Effectiveness of Long-Term Psychodynamic Psychotherapy' (2009) 301 *Journal of the American Medical Association* 930
Tikly L 'Governmentality and the Study of Education Policy in South Africa' (2003) 18 *Journal of Educational Policy* 161
Tladi D '*Fuel Retailers*, Sustainable Development & Integration: A Response to Feris' (2009) 1 *Constitutional Court Review* 255
Tononi G & Edelman GM 'Consciousness and Complexity' (1998) 282 *Science* 1846
Tribe L & Dorf M 'Levels of Generality in the Definition of Rights' (1990) 57 *University of Chicago Law Review* 1057

Tulving E 'Memory and Consciousness' (1985) 26 *Canadian Psychology* 1

Turing A 'Computing Machinery and Intelligence' (1950) 59 *Mind* 433

Tushnet M 'The Issue of State Action/Horizontal Effect on Comparative Constitutional Law' (2003) 1 *Journal of International Constitutional Law* 79

Ullmann-Margalit E 'Invisible-Hand Explanations' (1978) 39 *Synthese* 263

Van Der Walt A 'Normative Pluralism and Anarchy: Reflections on the 2007 Term' (2008) 1 *Constitutional Court Review* 77

Van Marle K 'Law's Time, Particularity and Slowness' (2003) 19 *South African Journal on Human Rights* 239

Van Marle K 'No Last Word: Reflections on the Imaginary Domain, Dignity and Intrinsic Worth' (2002) 13 *Stellenbosch Law Review* 299

Veriava F 'The Amended Legal Framework for School Fees and School Funding: A Boon or A Barrier?' (2007) 23 *South African Journal on Human Rights* 180

Waldron J 'The Core of the Case Against Judicial Review' (2006) 115 *Yale Law Journal* 1346

Wegner D & Wheatley T 'Apparent Mental Causation: Sources of the Experience of Will' (1999) 54 *American Psychologist* 480

Weiler H 'Comparative Perspectives on Educational Decentralization: An Exercise in Contradiction?' (1990) 12 *Education Evaluation and Policy Analysis* 433

Wermiel S 'Law and Human Dignity: The Judicial Soul of Justice Brennan' (1998) 7 *William and Mary Bill of Rights Law Journal* 223

Wesson M 'Grootboom and Beyond: Reassessing the Socio-Economic Rights Jurisprudence of the South African Constitutional Court' (2004) 20 *South African Journal on Human Rights* 284

Whalen PJ, Rauch SL, Etcoff NL, McInerney SC, Lee MB & Jenike MA 'Masked Presentations of Emotional Facial Expressions Modulate Amygdala Activity Without Explicit Knowledge' (1998) 18 *Journal of Neuroscience* 411

Wilkinson M 'Three Conceptions of Law: Towards a Jurisprudence of Democratic Experimentalism' (2010) *University Of Wisconsin Law Review* 673

Williamson OE 'The Economics of Organization: The Transaction Cost Approach' (1981) 87(3) *American Journal of Sociology* 548

Wilson S 'Breaking the Tie: Evictions from Private Land, Homeslessness and a New Normality' (2009) 126 *South African Law Journal* 270

Wilson S 'Litigating Housing Rights in Johannesburg's Inner City' (2011) 27 *South African Journal on Human Rights* 127

Woolman S 'Humility, Michelman's Method and the Constitutional Court: Rereading the *First Certification Judgment* and Reaffirming a Distinction between Law and Politics' (2013) 25 *Stellenbosch Law Review* – (forthcoming)

Woolman S, Fishman E & Fischer M 'Evidence of a Patent Thickets in Complex Biopharmaceutical Technologies' (2013) 53 *IDEA: The International Journal of Intellectual Property Law* 1

Woolman S 'Language, Power and the Margin: Eliot's Philosophy of Language, Wittgenstein on Following a Rule, and Statutory Construction in *Thembekile Mankayi v Anglogold Ashanti Limited*' (2012) 128 *South African Law Journal* 434

Woolman S '"Seek Justice Elsewhere": An Egalitarian Pluralist's Reply to David Bilchitz on the Distinction between Differentiation and Domination' (2012) 28 *South African Journal on Human Rights* 271

Woolman S and Zeffertt D 'Judging Jews: Court Interrogation of Rule-Making and Decision-Taking by Jewish Ecclesiastical Bodies' (2012) 28 *South African Journal on Human Rights* 196

Woolman S 'My Tea Party, Your Mob, Our Social Contract: Freedom of Assembly and the Constitutional Right to Rebellion in *Garvis v SATAWU (Minister for Safety & Security, Third Party)* 2010 (6) SA 280 (WCC)' (2011) 27 *South African Journal on Human Rights* 450

Woolman S, Sprague C & Black V 'Some are More Equal than Others: The Constitutional Justification and Ethical Arguments Granting Enhanced Antiretroviral Therapy to Selected Priority Groups' (2011) 3 *Journal of South African Law* 496

Woolman S & Sprague C VidaGás: Delivering Better Health in Mozambique with Liquid Petroleum Gas' (2011) 5 *Journal of Enterprising Communities* 41

Woolman S 'Is Xenophobia the Right Legal Term of Art? A Freudian and Kleinian Response to Loren Landau on Township Violence in South Africa' (2011) 22 *Stellenbosch Law Review* 285

Woolman S '"I am Large": Sachs, Whitman and Democracy' (2010) 1 *Southern African Public Law* 57

Woolman S 'On the Common Saying "What's True in Golf is True in Law": The Relationship between Theory and Practice across Forms of Life' (2010) 25 *Southern African Public Law* 520

Woolman S 'Between Charity and Clarity: Kibbitzing woth Frank Michelmann on How Best to Read the Constitutional Court' (2010) *South African Public Law* 491

Woolman S 'On the Fragility of Associational Life: A Constitutive Liberal's Response to Patrick Lenta' (2009) 25 *South African Journal on Human Rights* 280

Woolman, S, Sprague C & V Black "Why the State's Treatment of HIV/AIDS Lay Counselors for ART & PMTCT Programmes Constitutes Retrogressive Measures that Violate the Right to Access to Adequate Health Care Services for Pregnant Women & Infants with HIV/AIDS' (2009) 25 *South African Journal on Human Rights* 102

Woolman S 'Category Mistakes and the Waiver of Constitutional Rights: A Response to Deeksha Bhana on *Barkhuizen*' (2008) 125 *South African Law Journal* 10

Woolman S and Fleisch B 'Democracy, Social Capital and School Governing Bodies in South Africa' (2008) 20 *Education and the Law* 47

Woolman S 'Amazing, Vanishing Bill of Rights' (2007) 124 *South African Law Journal* 762

Woolman S & Bishop M 'Down on the Farm and Barefoot in the Kitchen: Farm Labour and Domestic Labour as Forms of Servitude' (2007) 24 *Development Southern Africa* 595

Woolman S 'Defending Discrimination: On the Constitutionality of Independent Schools that Promote a Particular, If Not Comprehensive, Vision of the Good' (2007) 18 *Stellenbosch Law Review* 31

Woolman S & Fleisch B 'On the Constitutionality of Single Medium Public Schools' (2007) 23 *South African Journal on Human Rights* 34

Woolman S & Sprague C 'Moral Luck: Exploiting South Africa's Policy Environment to Produce a Sustaintable National Antiretroviral Treatment Programme' (2006) 22 *South African Journal on Human Rights* 357

Woolman S & Fleisch B 'South Africa's Unintended Experiment in School Choice: How the National Education Policy Act, the South Africa Schools Act and the Employment of Educators Act Create the Enabling Conditions for Quasi-Markets in Schools' (2006) 16 *Education and the Law* 37.

Woolman S & Bishop M 'State as Pimp: Sexual Slavery in South Africa' (2006) 23 *Development Southern Africa* 385

Woolman S 'Metaphors and Mirages: Some Marginalia on Choudhry's "The *Lochner* Era and Comparative Constitutionalism"' (2005) *Southern Africa Public Law* 28

Woolman S & Fleisch B 'On the Constitutionality of School Fees: A Reply to Roithmayr' (2004) 22 (1) *Perspectives in Education* 111

Woolman S & Brand D 'Is There a Constitution in This Classroom? Constitutional Jurisdiction after *Walters* and *Afrox*' (2003) 18 *Southern African Public Law* 38

Woolman S 'The Right Consistency: *Benaish v Ernst and Young* (1999) 15 *South African Journal on Human Rights* 166

Woolman S 'A Question of Spatial and of Temporal Location: *Zantzi v Council of State, Ciskei*' (1996) *South African Journal on Human Rights* 151

Woolman S '*Coetzee*: The Limitations of Justice Sachs' Concurrence' (1996) *South African Journal on Human Rights* 99

Woolman S & Davis D 'The Last Laugh: Classical Liberalism, Creole Liberalism and the Application of Fundamental Rights under the Interim and the Final Constitutions' (1996) 12 *South African Journal on Human Rights* 361

Zacks M 'Administrative Fairness in the Ombudsman Process' (1967 to 1987) 7 *The Ombudsman Journal* 55

Zimmerman Z 'Cinderella Goes to School: The Effect of Child Fostering on School Enrolment in South Africa' (2003) 38(3) *Journal of Human Resources* 557

CHAPTERS

Ackermann LWH 'Equality under the 1996 South African Constitution' in R Wolfrem (ed) *Gleichheit und Nichtdiskriminierung im Nationalalen und Internationalen Mesenchenrechtssschutz* (2003) New York: Springer

Albertyn C 'Commission for Gender Equality' in S Woolman & M Bishop (eds) *Constitutional Law of South Africa* 2nd Edition (2003) Chapter 24D, Cape Town: Juta Law

Albertyn C and Goldblatt B 'Equality' in S Woolman & M Bishop (eds) *Constitutional Law of South Africa* 2nd Edition (2007) Chapter 35, Cape Town: Juta Law

Baars BJ 'How Does a Serial, Integrated and Very Limited Stream of Consciousness Emerge from a Nervous System that is Mostly Unconscious, Distributed, Parallel and of Enormous Capacity' in GR Bock and J Marsh (eds) *Experimental and Theoretical Studies of Consciousness* (1993) New York: Wiley

Baddeley AD 'Short-term and Working Memory' in E Tulving and FIM Craik (eds) *The Oxford Handbook of Memory* (2000) New York: Oxford University Press

Baier A 'Trust and Antitrust' in *Moral Prejudices* (1995) Cambridge: Harvard University Press

Badat S 'Educational politics in the Transitional Period' in P Kallaway et al (eds) *Education after Apartheid: South African Education in Transition* (1997) Chapter 9, Cape Town: University of Cape Town Press

Basson E & Van Der Linde M 'Environment' in S Woolman & M Bishop (eds) *Constitutional Law of South Africa* (2nd Edition, RS2, 2010) Chapter 50, Cape Town: Juta Law

Bennett TW & Murray C 'Traditional Leaders' in S Woolman & M Bishop (eds) *Constitutional Law of South Africa* (2nd Edition, OS, December 2005) Chapter 28, Cape Town: Juta Law

Bilchitz D 'Health' in S Woolman & M Bishop (eds) *Constitutional Law of South Africa* 2nd Edition (2005) Chapter 56A, Cape Town: Juta Law

Bishop M 'Costs' in Woolman S & Bishop M (eds) *Constitutional Law of South Africa* (2nd Edition, OS, October 2010) Chapter 6, Cape Town: Juta Law

Bishop M 'Remedies' in Woolman S & Bishop M (eds) *Constitutional Law of South Africa* 2nd Edition (2008) Chapter 9, Cape Town: Juta Law

Bishop M, Raboshakga N & Budlender S 'National Legislative Authority' in S Woolman & M Bishop (eds) *Constitutional Law of South Africa* 2nd (2004, Revised 2011) Chapter 17, Cape Town: Juta Law

Bishop M (2011) 'Rationality is Dead! Long Live Rationality! Saving Rational Basis Review' in Woolman S & Bilchitz D (eds) *Is This Seat Taken? Conversations at the Bar, the Bench & the Academy* (2010) National Executive Authoroty Pretoria: Pretoria University Law Press.

Bishop M & Woolman S 'Freedom and Security of the Person' in S Woolman & M Bishop (eds) *Constitutional Law of South Africa* (2nd Edition, OS, July 2006) Chapter 40, Cape Town: Juta Law

Bishop M & Woolman S 'Public Protector' in S Woolman & M Bishop (eds) *Constitutional Law of South Africa* (2nd Edition, OS, December 2005) Chapter 24A, Cape Town: Juta Law

Botha H 'Rights, Limitations, and the Impossibility of Self-government' in H Botha, A Van der Walt & J Van der Walt (eds) *Rights and Democracy in a Transformative Constitution* (2003) Stellenbosch: SUN Press

Bourdieu P 'Forms of Capital' in JC Richards (ed) *Handbook of Theory and Research for the Sociology of Education* (1986), New York: Greenwood

Brand D 'Food' in S Woolman & M Bishop (eds) *Constitutional Law of South Africa* 2nd Edition (2005) Chapter 56C, Cape Town: Juta Law

Brickhill J & Biabuch R 'Political Rights' in S Woolman & M Bishop (eds) *Constitutional Law of South Africa* (2nd Edition, OS, March 2007) Chapter 45, Cape Town: Juta Law

Budlender G 'Amicus Curiae' in S Woolman & M Bishop (eds) *Constitutional Law of South Africa* 2nd (2006) Chapter 8, Cape Town: Juta Law

Budlender S (2002) *Making Socio-Economic Rights Effective: Judicial Remedies for Breaches of the State's Duty to Respect, Protect, Promote and Fulfil Socio-Economic Rights* (LLB dissertation, manuscript on file with author)

Campbell D 'Downward Causation in Hierarchically Organized Biological Systems' in FJ Ayala & T Dobzhansky (eds) *Studies in the Philosophy of Biology* (1974) London: Macmillan

Campbell D 'Evolutionary Epistemology' in PA Schlipp (ed) *The Philosophy of Karl Popper* (1974) La Salle: Open Court

Campbell D 'The Experimenting Society' in ES Overman (ed) *Methodology and Epistemology for Social Science: Selected Papers* (1988) Chicago: University of Chicago Press

Charlton S, Silverman M & Berrisford S (2003) *Taking Stock: Review of the Department of Housing's Programme, Policies and Practice (1994–2003)*, (Unpublished paper, Department of Housing, on file with the author)

Chipkin I 'Social Cohesion as a Factor in Development' in K Gupta, G Svendsen & P Maiti (eds) *Social Capital, Volume II* (2008) Chapter 8.

Chisholm R 'Human Freedom and the Self' in G Watson (ed) *Free Will* (2003) Oxford: Oxford University Press

Churchland P 'Eliminative Materialism and Propositional Attitudes' in SM Christensen & DR Turner (eds) *Folk Psychology and the Philosophy of Mind* (1993) Hillsdale: L. Erlbaum

Claxton G 'The Light's On, But There's Nobody Home: The Psychology of No-Self' in G Claxton (ed) *Beyond Therapy: The Influence of Eastern Religions on Psychological Theory and Practice* (1986) London: Wisdom Publications

Cohen J & CF Sabel 'Sovereignty and Solidarity: EU and US' in J Zeitlin & DM Trubek (eds) *Governing Work and Welfare in A New Economy: European and American Experiments* (2003) New York: Oxford University Press

Crick F 'Forward' in Koch C *The Quest for Consciousness: A Neurobiological Approach* (2004) Denver, Colo: Roberts and Co

Cziko G 'Universal Selection Theory and the Complementarity of Different Types of Blind Variation and Selective Retention' in C Heyes and D Hull (eds) *Selection Theory and Social Construction* (2001) Albany: State University of New York Press

Davidson D (1984) 'Thought and Talk' in *Inquiries into Truth and Interpretation* New York: Oxford University Press

Davidson D (1984) 'On the Very Idea of a Conceptual Scheme' *Inquiries into Truth and Interpretation* New York: Oxford University Press

Davidson D (1984) 'Introduction' *Inquiries into Truth and Interpretation* New York: Oxford University Press

Dehaene S & Naccache L 'Towards a Cognitive Neuroscience of Consciousness: Basic Evidence and a Workspace Framework' in S Dehaene (ed) *Cognitive Neuroscience of Consciousness* (2001) Cambridge: MIT Press

Descartes R *The Passions of the Souls* (1649) in *Selected Writings* (trans. J Cottingham, R Stoothoff and D Murdoch, 1988) New York: Cambridge University Press

Driver J and Vuilleumer P 'Perceptual Awareness and Its Loss in Unilateral Neglect and Extinction' in S Dehaene and L Naccache (eds) *The Cognitive Neuroscience of Consciousness* (2001) Cambridge: MIT Press

Du Plessis L 'Interpretation' in S Woolman & M Bishop (eds) *Constitutional Law of South Africa* (2nd Edition, OS, December 2008) Chapter 32, Cape Town: Juta Law

Dürig T 'Der Grundrechtssatz von der Menschenwürde' (1956) 81 *Archiv für öffentliches Recht* 117, 125

Durfee EH 'Cooperative Distributed Problem Solving between (and within) Intelligent Agents' in P Rudomin et al (eds) *Neuroscience: From Neural Networks to Artificial Intelligence* (1993) New York: Springer-Verlag

Dworkin R 'Pragmatism, Right Answers and True Banality' in M Brint and W Weaver (eds) *Pragmatism in Law and Society* (1991) Boulder: Westview Press

Ellmann S 'A Constitutional Confluence: American State Action Law and the Application of Socio-Economic Rights Guarantees to Private Actors' in P Andrews & S Ellmann (eds) *The Post-Apartheid Constitutions: Perspectives on South Africa's Basic Law* (2001) Columbus: Ohio University Press

Ferris L & Tladi D 'Environmental Rights' in D Brand & C Heyns (eds) *Socio-Economic Rights in South Africa* (2004). Pretoria: Pretoria University Law Press

Feyerabend P 'Materialism and the Mind-Body Problem' in SM Christensen & DR Turner (eds) *Folk Psychology and the Philosophy of Mind* (1993) Hillsdale: L. Erlbaum

Fish S 'The Jurisprudence of Richard Posner, Richard Rorty and Ronald Dworkin' in *There's No Such Thing as Free Speech, And It's a Good Thing Too!* (1994) New York: Oxford University Press

Fleisch B (2002) 'State Formation and the Origins of Bantu Education' in P Kallaway (ed) *The History of Education under Apartheid* Johannesburg: Pearson South Africa

Friedman A, Pantazis A & Skelton A 'Children's Rights' in S Woolman & M Bishop (eds) *Constitutional Law of South Africa* 2nd Edition (2004) Chapter 57, Cape Town: Juta Law

Friedman A 'Costs' in S Woolman & M Bishop 2nd Edition (2007) Chapter 6B, Cape Town: Juta Law

Fegbeutel JP (1990) *An Ombudsman for South Africa* (Unpublished LLD thesis, University of South Africa, on file with author).

Folkwes J 'Founding Provisions' in Woolman S & Bishop M (eds) *Constitutional Law of South Africa* 2nd Edition (2013) Chapter 13, Cape Town: Juta Law

Gigerenzer G 'Moral Intuition = Fast and Frugal Heuristics' in W Sinnott-Armstrong (ed) *Moral Psychology, Volume II-The Cognitive Science of Morality: Intuition and Diversity* (2008) Boston: MIT Press

Govender K 'The South African Human Rights Commission' in P Andrews & S Ellmann (eds) *The Post-Apartheid Constitutions: Perspectives on South Africa's Basic Law* (2001) Johannesburg: Witwatersrand University Press

Graeff P 'Social Capital: The Dark Side' in GT Svendsen and GLH Svendsen (eds) *Handbook of Social Capital: The Troika of Sociology, Political Science and Economics* (2009) Cheltenham: Edward Elgar

Greene J 'The Secret Joke of Kant's Soul' in W Sinnot-Armstrong (ed.) *Moral Psychology, Volume 3: The Neuroscience of Morality: Emotion, Brain Disorders and Disorder* (2008) Boston: MIT Press

Hayek FA 'Competition as a Discovery Procedure' in *New Studies in Philosophy, Politics and Economics* (1978) London: Routledge

Hayek FA 'The Legal and Political Philosophy of David Hume' in FA Hayek *Studies in Philosophy, Politics and Economics* (1967) Chicago: University of Chicago Press

Hayek FA 'The Results of Human Action, But Not of Human Design' in FA Hayek *Studies in Philosophy, Politics and Economics* (1967) Chicago: University of Chicago Press

Haysom N 'Dignity' in H Cheadle, D Davis & N Haysom (eds) *South African Constitutional Law: The Bill of Rights* (2002) Durban: Butterworths

Hofmeyr K 'Rules and Procedure in Constitutional Matters' in S Woolman & M Bishop (eds) *Constitutional Law of South Africa* 2nd Edition (2007) Chapter 5, Cape Town: Juta Law

Holmes OW (1920) 'The Path of the Law' in *Collected Papers* Clark: The Lawbook Exchange Limited 173

James W 'Does Consciousness Exist' in *Essays in Radical Empiricism* (1912) New York: Cosimo Inc.

Jansen J 'The Race for Education Policy after Apartheid' in Y Sayed & J Jansen (eds) *Implementing Educational Policies: The South African Experience* (2001) Lansdowne: UCT Press

Kant I 'On the Common Saying: While It is True in Theory, It is Not Necessarily True in Practice' in A Wood (ed) *Basic Short Writings of Immanuel Kant* New York: Random House

Kim KM 'Nested Hierarchies of Vicarious Selectors' in C Heyes and D Hull (eds) *Selection Theory and Social Construction* (2001) Albany: State University of New York Press

Klaaren J 'South African Human Rights Commission' in S Woolman & M Bishop (eds) *Constitutional Law of South Africa* 2nd Edition (2005) Chapter 24C, Cape Town: Juta Law

Knobe J and S Nichols 'An Experimental Philosophy Manifesto' in J Knobe and S Nichols (eds) *Experimental Philosophy* (2008) Oxford: Oxford University Press

Koch C and Poggio T 'Multiplying with Synapses and Neurons' in T McKenna, J Davis and SF Zornetzer (eds) *Single Neuron Computation* (1992) Boston: Academic Press

Lanford M and Stacey R 'Water' in S Woolman & M Bishop (eds) *Constitutional Law of South Africa* 2nd Edition (2011) Chapter 56B, Cape Town: Juta Law

Liebenberg S 'The Interpretation of Socio-Economic Rights' in S Woolman & M Bishop (eds) *Constitutional Law of South Africa* 2nd Edition (2003) Chapter 33, Cape Town: Juta Law

Llinas RR, Ribary U, Joliot M and Wang XJ 'Content and Context in Temporal Thalmocortical Binding' in G Busaki et al (eds) *Temporal Coding in the Brain* (1994) New York: Springer-Verlag

Loots C 'Standing, Ripeness & Mootness' in S Woolman & M Bishop (eds) *Constitutional Law of South Africa* 2nd (2005) Chapter 7, Cape Town: Juta Law

McCarthy J 'Pandemonium: A Paradigm for Learning' in *Symposium on the Mechanization of Thought Processes* (1959) London: HMSO

MacKay D 'Divided Brains – Divided Minds?' in C Blackmore and S Greenfield (eds) *Mindwaves* (1987) Oxford: Blackwell

Madlingozi T & Woolman S 'Provincial Legislative Authority' in S Woolman & M Bishop (eds) *Constitutional Law of South Africa* 2nd Edition (2005) Chapter 19, Cape Town: Juta Law

Mansbridge J 'A Deliberative Theory of Interest Representation' in MP Petracca (ed) (1992) *The Politics of Interests: Interest Groups Transformed* Boulder: Westview Press

McClelland JL 'The Programmable Blackboard of Reading' in JL McClelland and DE Rummelhart (eds) *Parallel Distributing Processing* (1986) Cambridge: MIT Press

McLean K 'Housing' in S Woolman & M Bishop (eds) *Constitutional Law of South Africa* 2nd Edition (2006) Chapter 55, Cape Town: Juta Law

Metz T 'African Moral Theory and Public Governance: Nepotism, Preferential Hiring and Other Partiality' in J Murove (ed) *African Ethics: An Anthology for Comparative and Applied Ethics* (2009) Pietermaritzburg: University of Kwa-Zulu Natal Press

Michelman F 'The Rule of Law, Legality and the Supremacy of the Constitution' in S Woolman & M Bishop (eds) *Constitutional Law of South Africa, 2nd Edition* (2006) Chapter 11, Cape Town: Juta Law

Michelman F 'Old Kibitzes Never Die: A Rejoinder to Stu Woolman' in S Woolman & D Bilchitz (eds) *Is This Seat Taken? Conversations at the Bar, the Bench & the Academy* (2012) Pretoria: Pretoria University Law Press

Nagel T 'What Is It Like to be a Bat?' (1979) *Mortal Questions* Cambridge: Cambridge University Press

Nedelsky J 'Reconceiving Autonomy: Sources, Thoughts and Possibilities' in A Hutchinson & L Green (eds) *Law and the Community: The End of Individualism?* (1989) Toronto: Carswell

Newman JB, BJ Baars and SB Cho 'A Neural Global Workspace Model for Conscious Attention' as reprinted in BJ Baars, W Banks and JB Newman *Essential Sources in the Scientific Study of Consciousness* (2003) Cambridge: MIT Press

Nussbaum M 'Aristotelian Social Democracy' in R Bruce Douglass (ed) *Liberalism and the Good* (1990) New York: Routledge

Nussbaum M 'The Good as Discipline, the Good as Freedom' in D Crocker and T Linden (eds) *The Ethics of Consumption: The Good Life, Justice and Global Stewardship* (1998) Lanham: Rowman & Littlefield

Oakeshott M (1961) 'Political Education' *Inaugural Lecture at the London School of Economics*

Oldfield S 'The South African State: A Question of Form, Function and Fragmentation' in E Motala & J Pampallis (eds) *Education and Equity: The Impact of State Policies on South African Education* (2001) Cape Town: Heinemann

Oosting M 'The Ombudsman and His Environment: A Global View' in L Reif (ed) *The International Ombudsman Anthology* (1999) Boston: Kluwer Law International

Orzack SH and Sober E 'Introduction' in SH Orzack and E Sober (eds) *Adaptionism and Optimality* (2001) New York: Cambridge University Press

Ostrom E & Ahn TK 'The Meaning of Social Capital and Its Link to Collective Action' in GT Svendsen and GLH Svendsen (eds) *The Handbook of Social Capital The Troika of Sociology, Political Science and Economics* (2010) Cheltenham: Edward Elgar

Ostrovick J (2004) 'The Timing Experiments of Libet and Walters' (Unpublished, manuscript on file with author)

O'Sullivan M 'Reproductive Rights' in S Woolman & M Bishop (eds) *Constitutional Law of South Africa* (2nd Edition, OS, March 2005) Chapter 37, Cape Town: Juta Law

Owen S 'The Ombudsman: Essential Elements and Common Challenges' L Reif (ed) *The International Ombudsman Anthology* (1999) Boston: Kluwer Law International

Palmer S 'Consciousness and Isomorphism: Can the Colour Spectrum Really be Inverted?' in B Baars, W Banks & J Newman (eds) Essential S*ources in the Scientific Study of Consciousness* (2003) 185 Boston: MIT Press

Parfit D 'Divided Minds and the Nature of Persons' in C Blackmore and S Greenfield (eds) *Mindwaves* (1987) Oxford: Blackwell

Pieterse M 'Traditional African Jurisprudence' in C Roederer & D Moellendorf (eds) *Jurisprudence* (2004) Cape Town: Juta Law

Plotkin H 'Social Constructions and Evolution' in C Heyes and D Hull (eds) *Selection Theory and Social Construction* (2001) Albany, NY: State University of New York Press

Pogge TW 'The Categorical Imperative' in P Guyer (ed) *Critical Essays on Kant's Groundwork of the Metaphysics of Morals* (1998) Lanham: Rowman & Littlefield

Price A 'The Content and Justification of Rationality Review' in S Woolman & D Bilchitz (eds) *Is This Seat Taken? Conversations at the Bar, the Bench & the Academy* (2010) Pretoria: Pretoria University Law Press

Ray B 'The Interpretation of Socio-Economic Rights' in S Woolman & M Bishop (eds) *Constitutional Law of South Africa* 2nd Edition (2013) Chapter 33, Cape Town: Juta Law

Roederer C 'Founding Provisions' in S Woolman & M Bishop (eds) *Constitutional Law of South Africa* 2nd Edition (2005) Chapter 13, Cape Town: Juta Law

Rorty R 'Heidegger, Contingency and Pragmatism' in *Essays on Heidegger & Others: Philosophical Papers 2* (1991) Cambridge: Cambridge University Press

Rorty R 'Pragmatism without Method' in *Objectivity, Relativism and Truth: Philosophical Papers 1* (1991) New York: Cambridge University Press

Rorty R 'Solidarity or Objectivity' in R Rorty *Objectivity, Relativism & Truth: Philosophical Papers I* (1991) New York: Cambridge University Press

Rorty R 'Unger, Castoriadis and a National Future' in R Rorty *Essays on Heidegger & Others: Philosophical Papers I* (1991) New York: Cambridge University Press

Roux T 'Democracy' in S Woolman & M Bishop (eds) *Constitutional Law of South Africa* 2nd Edition (2006) Chapter 10, Cape Town: Juta Law

Sabel C & W Simon 'Epilogue: Accountability without Sovereignty' in G de Búrca & J Scott (eds) *Law and New Governance in the EU and the US* (2006) Oxford: Hart

Schiebel AB 'Anatomical and Physiological Substrates of Arousal: A View from the Bridge' in JA Hobson and MAB Brazier (eds) *The Reticular Formation Revisited* (1980) New York: Raven Press

Searle J 'Putting Consciousness Back in the Brain' in M Bennett, D Dennett, P Hacker and J Searle (eds) *Neuroscience and Philosophy: Brain, Mind & Language* (2003) New York: Columbia Univerisity Press

Shapiro C 2001 'Navigating the Patent Thicket: Cross Licenses, Patent Pools, and Standard-Setting' in A Jaffe et al (eds) *Innovation Policy & the Economy (Vol I)* Boston: MIT Press

Simon W 'Toyota Jurisprudence: Legal Theory and Rolling Rules Regimes' in G de Búrca & J Scott (eds) *Law and New Governance in the EU and the US* (2006) Oxford: Hart Publishers

Snyckers F & Le Roux J 'Criminal Procedure: Rights of Detained, Arrested and Accused Persons' in S Woolman & M Bishop (eds) *Constitutional Law of South Africa* 2nd Edition (2006) Chapter 51, Cape Town: Juta

Sole S 'The State of Corruption and Accountability' in J Daniel, R Southall & J Lutchman (eds) *State of the Nation: South Africa 2004-2005* (2005) Pretoria: Human Sciences Research Council

Steytler N & de Visser J 'Local Government' in S Woolman & M Bishop (eds) *Constitutional Law of South Africa* (2nd Edition, OS, March 2007) Chapter 21, Cape Town: Juta

Swart M 'Social Security' in S Woolman & M Bishop (eds) *Constitutional Law of South Africa* 2nd Edition (2012) Chapter 56D, Cape Town: Juta

Taylor C 'Agency and the Self' in C Taylor *Philosophical Papers I: Human Agency and Language* (1985) New York: Cambridge University Press

Taylor C 'Atomism' in C Taylor *Philosophical Papers II: Philosophy and the Human Sciences* (1985) New York: Cambridge University Press

Taylor C 'The Diversity of Goods' in C Taylor *Philosophical Papers II: Philosophy and the Human Sciences* (1985) New York: Cambridge University Press

Taylor C 'The Politics of Recognition' in A Gutmann (ed) *Multiculturalism and the Politics of Recognition* (1996) Princeton: Princeton University Press

Taylor C 'What's Wrong with Negative Liberty' in C Taylor *Philosophy and the Human Sciences: Philosophical Papers* 2 (1985) New York: Cambridge University Press

Taylor JG and Alavi FN 'Mathematical Analysis of a Competitive Network for Attention' in JG Taylor (ed) *Mathematical Approaches to Neural Networks* (1993) New York: North-Holland

Thomas K 'Racial Justice' in A Sarat, G Bryant & R Kagan (eds) *Looking Back at Law's Century* (2002) Ithaca: Cornell University Press

Van Iwagen P 'An Argument for Incompatabilism' in P Van Iwagen *An Essay on Free Will* (1983) New York: Oxford University Press

Van Zyl Smit D 'Sentencing and Punishment' in S Woolman & M Bishop (eds) *Constitutional Law of South Africa* 2nd Edition (2003) Chapter 49, Cape Town: Juta Law

Walters WG *Presentation to the Osler Society* (1963) as reported in D Dennett *Consciousness Explained* (1991) Harmansworth: Penguin

Walzer M 'On Involuntary Association' in A Gutmann (ed) *Freedom of Association* (1998) Princeton: Princeton University Press

White J 'Independent Communications Authority of South Africa' in S Woolman & M Bishop (eds) *Constitutional Law of South Africa* 2nd Edition (2005) Chapter 24E, Cape Town: Juta Law

White-Limpitlaw J 'Independent Communications Authority of South Africa' in S Woolman & M Bishop (eds) *Constitutional Law of South Africa* (2nd Edition, OS, March 2005) Chapter 24E Cape Town: Juta

Williams B 'The Idea of Equality' in P Laslett & WG Runciman (eds) *Philosophy, Politics and Society* (1962) Oxford: Blackwell

Wilson S and Dugard J 'Constitutional Jurisprudence: The First and Second Waves' in Malcolm Langford, Ben Cousins, Jackie Dugard and Tshepo Madlingozi (eds) *Symbols and Substance: The Role and Impact of Socio-Economic Rights Strategies in South Africa* Cambridge: Cambridge University Press

Wood AW 'Humanity as an End in Itself' in P Guyer (ed) *Critical Essays on Kant's Groundwork of the Metaphysics of Morals* (1998) Lanham: Rowman & Littlefield

Woolman S 'Application' in S Woolman & M Bishop (eds) *Constitutional Law of South Africa* 2nd Edition (2005) Chapter 31, Cape Town: Juta Law

Woolman S 'Community Rights: Religion, Language and Culture' in S Woolman, T Roux, J Klaaren, A Stein, M Chaskalson & M Bishop (eds) *Constitutional Law of South Africa* 2nd Edition (2007) Chapter 58, Cape Town: Juta Law

Woolman S 'Dignity' in S Woolman & M Bishop (eds) *Constitutional Law of South Africa* 2nd Edition (2005) Chapter 36, Cape Town: Juta Law

Woolman S 'Freedom of Association' in S Woolman & M Bishop (eds) *Constitutional Law of South Africa* 2nd Edition (2003) Chapter 43, Cape Town: Juta Law

Woolman S 'Freedom of Assembly' in S Woolman & M Bishop (eds) *Constitutional Law of South Africa* 2nd Edition (2005) Chapter 44, Cape Town: Juta Law

Woolman S 'Provincial Constitutions' in S Woolman & M Bishop (eds) *Constitutional Law of South Africa* 2nd Edition (2007) Chapter 21, Cape Town: Juta Law

Woolman S 'Security Services' in S Woolman & M Bishop (eds) *Constitutional Law of South Africa* 2nd Edition (RS3, May 2011) Chapter 23B, Cape Town: Juta Law

Woolman S 'On the Common Saying "What's True in Golf is True in Law": The Relationship between Theory and Practice across Forms of Life' in S Woolman & D Bilchitz (eds) *Is This Seat Taken? Conversations at the Bar, the Bench and the Academy about the South African Constitution* (2012) Pretoria: Pretoria University Law Press

Woolman S 'Between Charity and Clarity: Kibitizing with Frank Michelman about How to Best Read the Constitutional Court' in S Woolman & D Bilchitz (eds) *Is This Seat Taken?*

Conversations at the Bar, the Bench and the Academy about the South African Constitution (2012) Pretoria: Pretoria University Law Press

Woolman S 'The Architecture of Dignity' in D Cornell, S Woolman, M Bishop, J Brickhill & S Fuller (eds) *The Dignity Jurisprudence of the Constitutional Court of South Africa* (2012) New York: Fordham University Press

Woolman S & Bishop M 'Education' in S Woolman and M Bishop (eds) *Constitutional Law of South Africa* 2nd Edition (2007) Chapter 57, Cape Town: Juta Law

Woolman S & MBishop M 'Slavery, Servitude and Forced Labour' in S Woolman & M Bishop (eds) *Constitutional Law of South Africa* 2nd Edition (2005) Chapter 64. Cape Town: Juta Law

Woolman S & Botha H 'Limitations' in S Woolman & M Bishop (eds) *Constitutional Law of South Africa* 2nd Edition (2006) Chapter 34, Cape Town: Juta Law

Woolman S & Roux T 'Co-operative Government & Intergovernmental Relations' in Woolman S & Bishop M (eds) *Constitutional Law of South Africa* 2nd Edition (2009) Chapter 14, Cape Town: Juta Law

Woolman S, Roux T and Bishop M 'A Baedeker to Constitutional Law of South Africa' in Woolman S & Bishop S (eds) *Constitutional Law of South Africa* 2nd Edition (2008) Chapter 1, Cape Town: Juta Law

Woolman S & Swanepoel J 'Constitutional History' in S Woolman & M Bishop (eds) *Constitutional Law of South Africa* 2nd Edition (2008) Chapter 2, Cape Town: Juta Law

Woolman S & Soweto-Aullo J 'Commission for the Promotion and Protection of the Rights of Cultural, Religious and Linguistic Communities' in S Woolman & M Bishop (eds) *Constitutional Law of South Africa* 2nd Edition (2005) Chapter 24F, Cape Town: Juta Law

Woolman S & Shutte Y 'Auditor-General' in S Woolman & M Bishop (eds) *Constitutional Law of South Africa* 2nd Edition (2005) Chapter 24E, Cape Town: Juta Law

Young IM 'The Ideal of Community and the Politics of Difference' in IM Young *Throwing Like a Girl and Other Essays* (1991) Bloomington: Indiana University Press

INTERNET SOURCES, GOVERNMENT REPORTS, ACADEMIC PAPERS, NEWSPAPER ARTICLES & GOVERNMENT

Ackermann LWA 'The Significance of Human Dignity for Constitutional Jurisprudence' (Lecture, Stellenbosch Law Faculty, 15 August 2005)(Manuscript on file with author)

Adams S 'Scorpions Probe Medical Aid Fraud' *The Mercury* (5 October 2004)

African National Congress *The Reconstruction and Development Programme* (1994)

African National Congress, National Education Co-ordinating Committee *National Education Policy Initiative* (1992)

Camerer L *Corruption in South Africa: Results of an Expert Panel Survey Institute for Security Studies* Monograph 65 (2001)

Centre for Applied Legal Studies (1998) *Audit of Legislation that Discriminates on the Basis of Sex/Gender*

Commission on Gender Equality (1999) 'Gender and the Private Sector'

Commission on Gender Equality (1999) 'Redefining Politics–Women and Democracy in South Africa'

Commission on Gender Equality (1999) 'Report on the 1999 General Elections: A Gender Perspective'

Commission on Gender Equality (2000) *Annual Report 2000*

Commission on Gender Equality (2001) *Annual Report 2000/2001*

Chipkin I 'Beyond the Popular Discourse: Capacity Constraints in the Public Service in South Africa' (2011) Public Affairs Research Institute, available at www.pari.org

Chipkin I 'The Public Sector: Is It Alive and Do We Need It?' (2011) Public Affairs Research Institute, available at www.pari.org, (podcast).

Chipkin I 'Social Cohesion as a Factor in Development' Symposium for Office of the President (11-12 June 2007)

Corder H, Jagwanth S & Soltau F *Report on Parliamentary Oversight and Accountability' Report to the Speaker of the National Assembly (1999)*, available at <www.pmg.org.za/docs/2001/viewminute.php?id=811> (accessed 10 January 2005)

Department of Education General Notice 1229 'White Paper 2: The Organization, Governance and Funding of Schools' (1995)

Department of Education 'Education and Training in a Democratic South Africa: First Steps to Develop a New System' GN 16312 (March 1995)

Department of Education *The National Curriculum and Policy Statements* (2010)

Department of Human Settlements: *Comprehensive Housing Plan for the Development of Integrated Sustainable Human Developments (Breaking New Ground)* (2010),

Equal Education *We Can't Afford Not To: Costing the Provision of Functional Libraries in South African Public Schools* (2011)

Freeman RE, Velamuri, SR & Moriarty B 'Company Stakeholder Responsibility: A New Approach to CSR' *Bridge Paper: Business Roundtable Institute for Corporate Ethics* (2006), available at http://www.corporate-ethics.org/pdf/csr.pdf.

Friedman M 'The Social Responsibility of Business is to Increase its Profits' *The New York Times Magazine* (September 1970)

Gauteng Department of Education 'Circular No 2' (1995)

Gauteng Department of Education 'Gauteng School Renovation Programme Implementation Plan' (1994)

Gauteng Department of Public Works 'Evaluation of the Gauteng Schools Toilet Building Project' (1997)

General Electric *Annual Report* (2009) available at http://www.ge.com/ar2009/

General Electric *Ecomagination Report* (2010) available at http://ge.ecomagination.com

General Electric 'GE Announces Largest Single Electric Vehicle Commitment, Commits to Convert Half of Global Fleet by 2015' (New York Stock Exchange, Press Release, November 11, 2010)

Giliomee H 'The Majority, Minorities and Ex-Nationalities in South Africa and the Proposed Cultural Commission' KAS Seminar on Multiculturalism (1999) 37, available at <www.kas.org.za/Publications/SeminarReports/Multiculturalism/GILIOMEE>

Gray G 'Global AIDS: HIV Prevention and Care in Children, Treatment Access and Challenges Among Children in Resource-Limited Settings' *Management of Pediatric HIV Infection, and Prevention of Mother-to-Child HIV Transmission* (2006) available at <http://www.medscape.com/viewarticle/544610>

Hassan F AIDS Law Project Monitoring Unit, Joint Civil Society Monitoring Forum (September 2006), at http://www.alp.org.za/modules.php?op=modload&name=News&file=article&sid=318

Hyslop J 'Political Corruption: Before and After Apartheid' *Conference on State and Society in South Africa* (University of the Witwatersrand 2004) 17

ICESCR Committee General Comment 13 (21st Session, 1999) 'The Right to Education (art 13)' UN Doc E/C.12/1999/10

Madonsela T *Address by the Public Protector, Adv Thuli Madonsela, During a Media Briefing on the Release of the SAPS Lease Report* (22 February 2011) available at http://www.pprotect.org/media_gallery/2011/23022011_sp.asp (accessed on 6 May 2011).

Médecins sans Frontières New MSF Data Shows Treatment of Children Works in Resource PoorSettings but Scale Up is Hampered by Ill-Adapted Tools and Exorbitant Costs (August 2006), available at <http://www.msf.org> (accessed on 10 December 2006)

Media summary of *Minister of Home Affairs v Fourie (Doctors for Life International and others, amici curiae); Lesbian and Gay equality project and others v Minister of Home Affairs* available at http://www.constitutionalcourt.org.za/fourie/summary

Montgomery J 'Here Comes Conscious Capitalism: Part IV' (August 13, 2010), available at http://www.pehub.com/76857/here-comes-conscious-capitalism

National Housing Code, Part 3: National Housing Programmes: Chapter 12 Housing Assistance in Emergency Housing Situations, 12.2.1., available at <http://www.housing.gov.za/Content/legislation_policies/Emergency%20%20Housing%20Policy.pdf> (accessed on 25 January 2006)

Naravan D 'Bonds and Bridges: Social Capital and Poverty' Poverty Group, World Bank (July 1999).

National Department of Housing (2004) *Breaking New Ground*

National Department of Housing (2003) *Ten Year Review*

National Health Council's Committee on Health, Environmental and Other External Costs and Benefits of Energy Production and Consumption, *Hidden Costs of Energy: Unpriced Consequences of Energy Production and Use* (2011).

National Housing Code, Part 3: National Housing Programmes: Chapter 12 Housing Assistance in Emergency Housing Situations, 12.2.1., available at http://www.housing.gov.za/Content/legislation_policies/Emergency%20%20Housing%20Policy.pdf (accessed on 25 January 2006)

Office of the Auditor-General *Activity Report for 2003– 2004* RP 211/2004 (2005) 23

Office of the Auditor General *'Against the Rules' Report of the Public Protector in terms of Section 182(1) of the Constitution of the Republic of South Africa, 1996 and Section 8(1) of the Public Protector Act, 1994 on an Investigation into Complaints and Allegations of Maladministration, Improper and Unlawful Conduct by the Department of Public Works and the South African Police*

Service relating to the Leasing of Office Accommodation Pretoria Report No. 33 of 2010/11 (22 February 2011)

Office of the Auditor-General *General Report for 1999 – 2000* RP 75/2000 (2001) 15

Office of the Auditor-General (2001) *General Report of the Auditor-General: Year Ended 31 March 2000*

Office of the Auditor-General (2003) *General Report on Local Government*

Office of the Auditor-General *Report on a Performance Audit of Service Delivery at Police Stations and 10111 Call Centres at the South African Police Service 2007-2008* (March 2009)('A-G's Report') 2, available at http://www.agsa.co.za/audit-reports/SAR.aspx

Office of the Auditor-General *Report on the Financial Statements of the Provincial Administration of the Northern Cape* (31 March 1998) 7.

Office of the Public Protector *Public Protector: South Africa* (2003), available at http://www.publicprotector.org/brochure_faq/11_lang/english.pdF

Office of the Public Protector' *'Against the Law'* Media Release, available at www.pprotect.org.za/media_gallery/2011/2302211

Public Protector *Against the Rules: Report of the Public Protector in terms of Section 182(1) of the Constitution of the Republic of South Africa, 1996 and Section 8(1) of the Public Protector Act, 1994 on an Investigation into Complaints and Allegations of Maladministration, Improper and Unlawful Conduct by the Department of Public Works and the South African Police Service relating to the Leasing of Office Accommodation in Pretoria* (2011) Report Number 33 of 2010/2011, available at http://www.info.gov.za/view/DownloadFileAction?id=142293

Ostrovick J (2004) *The Timing Experiments of Libet and Walters* (Unpublished manuscript on file with author).

Pampallis J *'The Nature of Educational Decentralisation in South Africa'* (Centre for Education Policy Development, Evaluation and Management) Decentralisation and Education Conference, Johannesburg, South Africa (11-14 June 2002) 3

Pityana NB *South African Human Rights Commission Presentation to the Justice Portfolio Committee – Budget Review and Programmes 2001/2002* (8 June 2001), available at www.sahrc.gov.za

Roux T 'Tactical Adjudication' *Kwa-Zulu Natal School of Law Conference on Democracy and Judicial Review* (Draft copy, 9 February 2007, on file with author.)

Rust K and the Centre for Affordable Housing in Africa (FinMark Trust) *2012 Year book on Housing Finance in Africa: A Review of same 42 of Africa's Housing Finance Markets* (2012)

Rust K (2003) *No Shortcuts: South Africa's Progress in Implementing its Housing Policy, 1994 – 2002* (Institute for Housing of South Africa, Manuscript on file with author)

Sachs A 'Democracy, Dignity and Deliberation', paper delivered at the *Conference on the Dignity Jurisprudence of Laurie Ackermann* (University of Cape Town, 27 July 2007)(Notes of conference on file with author.)

Sachs A Opening Remarks' *Konrad Adenauer Stiftung Seminar on Multiculturalism* (1999) available at http://www.kas.org.za/Publications/SeminarReports/Multiculturalism/SACHS1.pdf

South African Government Information *Department of Human Settlements on Housing through 2010* (2011) available at http://info.gov.za/aboutsa/housing.html (accessed on 28 August 2011).

SAHRC *'Landmark Victory: Edgemead Race Case'* available at http://www.sahrc.org.za/media (accessed 3 February 2006).
SAHRC *'Report on Equality and Voluntary Associations'* available at www.sahrc.org.za
SAHRC *'Report on the Public Hearings into Equality and Voluntary Associations'* (July 2006) available at http://www.sahrc.org.za/sahrc_cms/publis
SAHRC *'Report on the Public Hearings into the Use of Boom Gates and Road Closures'* available at http://www.sahrc.org.za/sahrc_cms/publish/article_132.shtml
SAHRC *'Settlement of the Equality Court Case against the Broederstroom Holiday Resort'* available at http://www.sahrc.org.za/sahrc_cms/publish/ article_132.shtml
Sibanda S *How Constitutional Democracy Has Blocked the Promise of Liberation Movements in South Africa* (PhD, in process, University of the Witwatersrand, 2011.)
Silberman S *Don't Even Think About Lying: How Brain Scans are Re-inventing the Science of Lie Detection* (2006) 14 (01) *Wired* 1, available at www.wired.com/wired/archive/14.01/lying.html
South African Law Reform Commission *The Harmonisation of the Common Law and the Indigenous Law: Succession in Customary* Law Issue Paper 12, Project 90 (April 1998)
Sprague C *'Cui Bono: Barriers to Access for HIV-Infected Women and Children'* (PhD, 2009, manuscript on file with author or available at Wits Business School)
The Sustainable Scale Project *Understanding Human Happiness and Well-Being* (2003), available at www.sustainable.scale.org./attractive solutions
Transparency International *Country Enforcement of the OECD Anti-Bribery Convention, Progress Report for 2012* (2012) available at http://www.transparency.org/
UNICEF South Africa *Impact on Children: Paediatric Testing and Treatment* (2006), available at http://www.unicef.org/southafrica
UNICEF (2002) *The State of the World's Children: 2002*
United Nations *Drugs and Crime: Country Corruption Assessment Report on South Africa* (2003) available at http://www.info.gov.za/reports/2003/corruption.pdf
Venter F 'The Protection of Cultural, Linguistic and Religious Rights: The Framework Provided by the Constitution of the Republic of South Africa, 1996' *KAS Seminar on Multiculturalism* (1999) available at http://www.kas.org.za/Publications/SeminarReports/Multiculturalism/VENTER.pdf
WHO Summary Country Profile for HIV/AIDS Treatment Scale-Up (June 2005), available at http://www.who.int/3by5/countryprofiles/en
World Health Organization *Antiretroviral Therapy of HIV Infection in Infants and Children in Resource-Limited Settings: Towards Universal Access: Recommendations for a Public Health Approach*
World Health Organization *Antiretroviral Drugs for Treating Pregnant Women and Preventing HIV* (2006)
World Health Organization *National Guide to Monitoring and Evaluating Programmes for the Prevention of HIV in Infants and Young Children* (2006)
World Health Organization *Infection in Infants in Resource-Limited Settings Towards Universal Access: Recommendations for a Public Health Approach* (2006)

WHO *Summary Country Profile for HIV/AIDS Treatment Scale-Up* (June 2005), available at http://www.who.int/3by5/countryprofiles/en.) at 6 citing

The Work of Donald Campbell, at http:en.m.wikipedia.org/wiki/Donald_T._Campbell#cite_ref-1

The World Bank *Economic Update on South Africa: Focus on Inequality of Opportunity* (2012) 3 *Africa Region – Poverty Reduction & Economic Management* viii: 'The State of Human Opportunity in South Africa

World Bank *Poverty and Social Capital* (1999), available at www.worldbank.org/poverty/capital.

World Health Organization (2006) *Infection in Infants in Resource-Limited Settings Towards Universal Access: Recommendations for a Public Health Approach*

World Health Organization (2006) *Antiretroviral Drugs for Treating Pregnant Women and Preventing HIV*

World Health Organization (2006) *Antiretroviral Therapy of HIV Infection in Infants and Children in Resource-Limited Settings: Towards Universal Access: Recommendations for a Public Health Approach*

World Health Organization (2006) *Infection in Infants in Resource-Limited Settings Towards Universal Access: Recommendations for a Public Health Approach*

World Health Organization (2006) *National Guide to Monitoring and Evaluating Programmes for the Prevention of HIV in Infants and Young Children*

World Health Organization (2006) *The World Health Report 2006*

CONSTITUTIONS AND COVENANTS – INTERNATIONAL

Constitution of the Republic of South Africa Act 200 of 1993 (Interim Constitution or IC)

Constitution of the Republic of South Africa, 1996 (Final Constitution or FC)German Basic Law art 1.1

International Covenant on Civil and Political Rights

International Covenant on Economic, Social and Cultural Rights

LEGISLATION, REGULATIONS & POLICY DOCUMENTS – NATIONAL

Choice on Termination of Pregnancy Act 92 of 1996

Civil Union Act 17 of 2006

Department of Education *White Paper on Education and Training* GN 196 (March 1995)

Department of Education *White Paper II: The Organisation, Governance and Funding of Schools* GN 130, *GG* 16987 (February 1996)

Department of Housing *Comprehensive Housing Plan for the Development of Integrated Sustainable Human Developments (Breaking New Ground)* (2010)

Department of Housing *Ten Year Review* (2003)

Department of Human Settlements *Housing through 2010* (2011)

Domestic Violence Act 116 of 1998

Education Labour Relations Act 146 of 1993 sec 6(1); sec 12(6)

Education Laws Amendment Act 100 of 1997

Education Laws Amendment Act 48 of 1999

Education Laws Amendment Act 53 of 2000
Education Laws Amendment Act 57 of 2001
Education Laws Amendment Act 50 of 2002
Education Laws Amendment Act 1 of 2004
Education Laws Amendment Act 24 of 2005
Education Laws Amendment Act 31 of 2007 sec 6A; sec 16A
Education Laws Amendment Bill B23-2005
Educators' Employment Act 1994 (Proc 138 of 1994) ('EEA') sec 1; sec 4(1); sec 4(2); sec 4(4)
Employment Equity Act 55 of 1998
Employment of Educators Act 76 of 1998 sec 4; sec 6(3)
Employment Equity Act 55 of 1998
Fourth General Law Amendment Act 132 of 1993
Gauteng Department of Education Personnel Administration Measures GN R222 *PG* 19767 (18 February 1999)
Gauteng Department of Education Regulations passed under the Gauteng School Education Act, sec 11(1)
Gauteng School Education Bill 1995
Gauteng Education Policy Act 12 of 1998 ('GEPA') Regulations on admission of learners to public schools GN 4138, *PG* 129 (13 July 2001) 3(1); 4(a)(i)
Gauteng Local Government Ordinance 17 of 1939
Gauteng School Education Act 6 of 1995 ('GSEA') Chap 3 sec 11; Chap 8 sec 68
Human Rights Commission Act 54 of 1994
Judges' Remuneration and Conditions of Employment Act 88 of 1989
Judges Remuneration Act 47 of 2001
Labour Relations Act 55 of 1995
Local Government: Municipal Structures Act 117 of 1998
Local Government: Municipal Systems Act 32 of 2000
National Education Policy Act 27 of 1996 ('NEPA') sec 3(4) Regulations on admission policy for ordinary public schools 6-10, 33, 34 sec 1; sec 5; sec 5(1); sec 6; sec 13; sec 14; sec 14(3); Schedule sec 2
Ombudsman Act 118 of 1979
Prevention of Illegal Eviction from and Unlawful Occupation of Land Act 19 of 1998
Promotion of Access to Information Act 2 of 2000
Promotion of Equality and Prevention of Unfair Discrimination Act 4 of 2000
Public Audit Act 25 of 2004
Public Finance Management Act 1 of 1999
Public Protector Amendment Act 113 of 1998
Public Protector Amendment Act 22 of 2003
Public Protector Act 23 of 1994
Public Service Laws Amendment Act 47 of 1997
Refugees Act 130 of 1998
Sexual Offences Act 23 of 1957

SALC Report on Customary Marriage I

South African Law Reform Commission *The Harmonisation of the Common Law and the Indigenous Law: Succession in Customary Law* Issue Paper 12, Project 90 (April 1998)

South African Schools Act 84 of 1996 ('SASA') Preamble; Chap 2; Chap 3; Chap 4; sec 1; sec 2(1); sec 3(1); sec 4; sec 5; sec 5(1); sec 5(2); sec 5(3); sec 5(4); sec 5(5); sec 5A; sec 5A(1); sec 5A(1); sec 5A(3); sec 5A(4); sec 6; sec 6(1); sec 6(2); sec 7; sec 8; sec 8(1); sec 9(1); sec 11; sec 12(1); sec 15; sec 16-32; sec 20(1); sec 20(2); sec 21(1); sec 23; sec 23(2); sec 25; sec 28; sec 29; sec 30; sec 31; sec 32; sec 34-41; sec 36; sec 36(1); sec 37(1); sec 37(3); sec 38(1); sec 38(2); sec 38(3); sec 39; sec 39(4); sec 41; sec 42(b); sec 43(1); sec 46(3); sec 61; National norms and standards for school funding GN 2362, *GG* 19347 (October 1998) Amended national norms and standards for school funding GN 869, *GG* 29179 (31 August 2006): Amended national norms and standards for school funding: correction GN 1282, *GG* 29473 (15 December 2006); Norms and standards regarding language policy published in terms of section; 6(1) of the South African Schools Act, 1996, GN 383 Vol 17997 (9 May 1997) Norms and standards regarding language policy published in terms of section 6(1) of the South African Schools Act, 1996

TABLE OF CASES

Dabalorivhuwa Patriotic Front & Another v Government, RSA & Others 2004 JOL 12911 (T). .
Daniels v Campbell NO 2004 (5) SA 331 (CC), 2004 (7) BCLR 735 (CC). . . . .
Dawood & Another v Minister of Home Affairs & Others 2000 (3) SA 936 (CC), 2000 (8) BCLR 837 (CC). . . . .
De Freitas & Another v Society of Advocates of Natal (Natal Law Society Intervening) 1998 (11) BCLR 1345 (CC) . . . .
De Kock v Minister of Water Affairs and Forestry 2005 (12) BCLR 1183 (CC) . . . .
De Lille & Another v Speaker of the National Assembly 1998 (3) SA 430 (C), 1998 (7) BCLR 916 (C) . . . .
De Reuck v Director of Public Prosecutions, Witwatersrand Local Division 2004 (1) SA 406 (CC), 2003 (12) BCLR 1333 (CC). . . . .
Democratic Alliance & Another v Masondo NO & Another. 2003 (2) SA 413 (CC), 2003 (2) BCLR 128 (CC) . . . .
Democratic Alliance v ANC & Others 2003 (1) BCLR 25 (C) . . . .
Doctors for Life International v Speaker of the National Assembly 2006 (6) SA 416 (CC), 2006 (12) BCLR 1399 (CC) . . . .
Du Plessis v De Klerk 1996 (3) SA 850 (CC), 1996 (5) BCLR 658 (CC) . . . .
East London Transitional Council v MEC for Health, Eastern Cape and Others 2001 (3) SA 1133 (Ck); [2000] 4 All SA 443 (Ck). . . . .
Edgewood Independent School District v Kirby SW 2d 391 (Tex 1991) . . . .
Edwards v Aguillard 482 US 578, 107 SCt 2573 (1987). . . . .
EN & Others v Government of RSA & Others 2007 (1) BCLR 84 (D). . . . .
Epperson v Arkansas 397 US 97 (1968). . . . .
Esack No & Another v Commission on Gender Equality 2001 (1) SA 1299 (W), 2000 (7) BCLR 737 (W). . . . .
Ex Parte Chairperson of the Constitutional Assembly: In Re Certification of the Constitution of the Republic of South Africa, 1996 1996 (4) SA 744 (CC), 1996 (10) BCLR 1243 (CC). . . . . . .
Ex Parte Minister of Safety and Security & Others: In re S v Walters & Another 2002 (4) SA 613 (CC) 2002 (7) BCLR 633 (CC) . . . .
Ex Parte Gauteng Provincial Legislature: In Re Dispute Concerning the Constitutionality of Certain Provisions of the Gauteng School Education Bill of 1995, 1995 1996 (3) SA 165 (CC), 1996 (4) BCLR 537 (CC) . . . .
Executive Council, Western Cape v Minister of Provincial Affairs and Constitutional Development & Another; Executive Council, KwaZulu-Natal v President of the Republic of South Africa & Others 2000 (1) SA 661 (CC), 1999 (12) BCLR 1360 (CC) . . . .
Federation of Governing Bodies of South Africa (Gauteng) v MEC Education, Gauteng 2002 (1) SA 660 (T) . . . .
Fedsure Life Assurance Ltd & Others v Greater Johannesburg Transitional Metropolitan Council and Others [1998] ZACC 17, 1999 (1) SA 374, 1998 (12) BCLR 1458. . . . .
Ferreira v Levin NO & Others 1996 (1) SA 984 (CC), 1996 (4) BCLR 1 (CC) . . . .
First Certification of the Constitution of the Province of the Western Cape (1997) (4) SA 795 (CC), 1997 (9) BCLR 1167. . . . .

In Re: The Gauteng School Education Bill 1996 (3) SA 165 (CC), 1996 (4) BCLR 537 (CC). . . .

In Re Munhumeso and Others 1995 (1) SA 551 (ZS), 1995 (2) BCLR 130 (ZS), 1994 (1) ZLR 49 (SC) . . . .

Investigating Directorate: Serious Economic Offences v Hyundai Motor Distributors (Pty) Ltd: In re Hyundai Motor Distributors (Pty) Ltd v Smit NO 2001 (1) SA 545 (CC), 2000 (10) BCLR 1079 (CC). . . . .

Islamic Unity Convention v Independent Broadcasting Authority 2002 (4) SA 294 (CC), 2002 5 BCLR 433 (CC) . . . .

Ismail v Ismail 1983 (1) SA 1006 (A). . . . .

Jaftha v Schoeman and Others; Van Rooyen v Stoltz and Others 2005 (2) SA 140 (CC), 2005 (1) BCLR 78 (CC) . . . .

Khosa & Others v Minister of Social Development & Others; Mahlaule & Others v Minister of Social Development & Others 2004 (6) SA 505 (CC), 2004 (6) BCLR 569 (CC) . . . .

Khumalo v Holomisa 2002 (5) SA 401 (CC), 2002 (8) BCLR 771 (CC) . . . .

King & Others v Attorneys Fidelity Fund Board of Control & Another 2006 (1) SA 474 (SCA), 2006 (4) BCLR 442 (SCA) . . . .

KwaZulu-Natal MEC for Education & Others v Pillay [2007] ZACC 21 (CC), 2008 (1) SA 474 (CC). . . . .

Kiliko and Others v Minister of Home Affairs and Others 2006 (4) SA 114 (C). . . . .

Kimberley Girls' High School and Another v Head, Department of Education, Northern Cape Province & Others 2005 (5) SA 251(NCD) . . . .

King & Others v Attorneys Fidelity Fund Board of Control & Another 2006 (1) SA 474 (SCA), 2006 (4) BCLR 442 (SCA) . . . .

Kruger v Johnnic Publishing (Pty) Ltd & Another 2004 (4) SA 306 (T) . . . .

Laerskool Middelburg en 'n ander v Departementshoof, Mpumalanga Departement van Onderwys, en andere 2003 (4) SA 160 (T) . . . .

Larbi-Odam v Member of the Executive Council for Education, North-West Province 1998 (1) SA 745 (CC), 1997 (12) BCLR 1655 (CC) . . . .

Laugh It Off Promotions CC v SAB International (Finance) BV t/a Sabmark International 2006 (1) SA 144 (CC), 2005 (8) BCLR 743 (CC). . . . .

Law v Canada (Minister of Employment and Immigration) [1999] 170 DLR 4th 1 (SCC). . . . . .

Lebowa Mineral Trust v Lebowa Granite (Pty) Ltd 2002 (3) SA 30 (T) . . . .

Lesbian and Gay Equality Project & Others v Minister of Home Affairs & Others 2006 (1) SA 524 (CC), 2006 (3) BCLR 355 (CC) . . . .

Lombard v Minister van Verdediging 2002 (3) SA 242 (T) . . . .

Lufuno Mphaphuli & Associates (Pty) Ltd v Andrews & Another 2009 (4) SA 529 (CC). . . . . . .

M v The State [2007] ZACC 18 (CC), 2008 (3) SA 232 (CC) . . . .

Mabuza v Mbatha 2003 (4) SA 218 (C), 2003 (7) BCLR 743 (C) . . . .

Magidimisi and Others v The Premier, Eastern Cape and Others Case No. 2180/04, 25 April 2006 . . . .

Makhanya v University of Zululand 2010 (1) SA 62 (SCA). . . . .

Mkontwana v Nelson Mandela Metropolitan Municipality and Another; Mitchells Plain Town Centre Merchants Association v Mcleod 1996 (4) SA 159 (A) . . . .
Mnguni v Minister of Correctional Services 2005 (12) BCLR 1187 (CC) . . . .
Modderfontein Squatters, Greater Benoni City Council v Modderklip Boerdery (Pty) Ltd (Agri SA and Legal Resources Centre, Amici Curiae) 2004 (6) SA 40 (SCA). . . . .
Modderklip Boerdery (Pty) Ltd v Modder East Squatters & Another 2001 (4) SA 385 (W) . . . . .
Moise v Greater Germiston Transitional Local Council: Minister of Justice and Constitutional Development Intervening (Women's Legal Centre as Amicus Curiae) 2001 (4) SA 491 (CC), 2001 (8) BCLR 765 (CC). . . . .
Moseneke & Others v Master of the High Court 2001 2 SA 18 (CC), 2001 3 BCLR 103 (CC). . .
Mothibeli v Western Vaal Metropolitan Substructure 1999 JOL 5678 (LC). . . . .
Motsepe v Commissioner for Inland Revenue 1997 (2) SA 898 (CC), 1997 (6) BCLR 692 (CC) . .
Mthembi-Mahanyele v Mail & Guardian Ltd & Another 2004 (6) SA 329 (SCA), 2004 (11) BCLR 1182 (SCA) . . . .
Mthimkulu v Mahomed 2011 (6) SA 147 (GSJ), 2011 BCLR (GSJ). . . . .
Murray v SA Tattersall's Subscription Rooms 1910 TH 35 . . . .
National Coalition for Gay & Lesbian Equality & Another v Minister of Justice 1998 (12) BCLR 1517 (CC), [1998] 3 ALL SA 26 (W). . . . .
National Coalition for Gay & Lesbian Equality & Another v Minister of Justice 1999 (1) SA 6 (CC), 1998 (12) BCLR 1517 (CC). . . . .
National Coalition for Gay & Lesbian Equality & Another v Minister of Home Affairs 2000 (2) SA 1 (CC), 2000 (1) BCLR 39 (CC). . . . .
National Director of Public Prosecutions v Mohamed NO 2003 (4) SA 1 (CC), 2003 (5) BCLR 476 (CC). . . . .
Nederduitse Gereformeerde Kerk in Afrika (OVS) v Verenigende Gereformeerde Kerk in Suider-Afrika 1999 (3) SA 156 (SCA). . . . .
New National Party of South Africa v Government of the Republic of South Africa 1999 (3) SA 191 (CC), 1999 (5) BCLR 489 (CC) . . . .
National Institute for Crime Prevention and the Reintegration of Offenders (NICRO) 2005 (3) SA 280 (CC), 2004 (5) BCLR 445 (CC) . . . .
Ngxuza v Permanent Secretary, Department of Welfare, Eastern Cape 2001 (2) SA 609 (E), 2000 (12) BCLR 1322 (E) . . . .
Nokotyana v Ekurhuleni Metropolitan Municipality [2009] ZACC 33, 2010 (4) BCLR 312 (CC). . . . .
Nyathi v Member of the Executive Council for the Department of Health Gauteng and Another [2008] ZACC 8; 2008 (5) SA 94 (CC), 2008 (9) BCLR 865 (CC) . . . .
Observatory Girls Primary School & Others v Head of Department ofEducation, Gauteng 2003 (4) SA 246 (W) . . . .
Occupiers of 51 Olivia Road, Berea Township, & 197 Main Street, Johannesburg v City of Johannesburg & Others [2008] ZACC 1, 2008 3 SA 208 (CC), 2008 5 BCLR 475 (CC). . .
Occupiers of Skurweplaas 353 JR v PPC Aggregate Quarries (Pty) Ltd [2011] ZACC 36, 2012 (4) SA (CC), 2012 BCLR 382 (CC). . . . .

S v Baloyi 2000 2 SA 425 (CC), 2000 1 BCLR 86 (CC) . . . .

S v Boesak 2001 (1) SA 912 (CC), 2001 (1) SACR 1 (CC), 2001 (1) BCLR 36 (CC) . . . .

S v Dube 2000 (2) SA 583 (N) . . . .

S v Jordan & Others (Sex Workers Education and Advocacy Task Force & Others as Amici Curiae) 2002 (6) SA 642 (CC), 2002 (11) BCLR 1117 (CC). . . . .

S v Makwanyane 1995 (3) SA 391 (CC), 1995 (6) BCLR 665 (CC), 1995 (2) SACR 1 (CC). . .

S v Mamabolo (E TV & Others, Intervening) 2001 (3) SA 409 (CC), 2001 (1) SACR 686 (CC), 2001 (5) BCLR 449 (CC) . . . .

S v Marais 2011 (1) SA 502 (CC), 2010 (12) BCLR 1223 (CC) . . . .

S v Mhlungu 1995 (3) SA 867 (CC), 1995 (7) BCLR 793 (CC) . . . .

S v Ntuli 1996 (1) SA 1207 (CC), 1996 (1) SACR 94 (CC), 1996 (1) BCLR 141 (CC) . . . . . .

S v Ntuli 1997 (3) SA 772 (CC), 1997 (6) BCLR 677 (CC) . . . .

S v Steyn 2001 (1) SA 1146 (CC), 2001 (1) SACR 25 (CC), 2001 (1) BCLR 52 (CC). . . . .

S v Twala (South African Human Rights Commission intervening) 2000 (1) SA 879 (CC), 2000 (1) BCLR 106 (CC), 1999 (2) SACR 622 (CC) . . . .

SACCAWU v Irvin & Johnson Ltd (Seafoods Division Fish Processing) 2000 (3) SA 705 (CC), 2000 (8) BCLR 886 (CC) . . . .

San Antonio Independent School District v Rodriguez (1973) 411 US 1, 93 SCt 1278 . . . .

Sanderson v Attorney-General, Eastern Cape 1998 (2) SA 38 (CC), 1998 (1) SACR. . . . . 227 (CC), 1997 (12) BCLR 1675 (CC). . . . .

Santa Clara Pueblo v Martinez 436 US 49 (1978) . . . .

Satchwell v President of the Republic of South Africa 2002 (6) SA 1 (CC), 2002 (9) BCLR 986 (CC). . . . .

Satchwell v President of the Republic of South Africa 2003 (4) SA 266 (CC), 2004 (1) BCLR 1. .

Schoonbee v MEC for Education, Mpumalanga 2002 (4) SA 877 (T). . . . .

Seodin Primary School v MEC Education, Northern Cape 2006 (1) All SA 154 (NC), 2006 (4) BCLR 542 (NC). . . . .

Shibi v Sithole & Others; South African Human Rights Commission & Another v President of the Republic of South Africa & Another 2005 (1) SA 580 (CC), 2005 (1) BCLR 1 (CC) . . . .

Shilubana v Nwamitwa 2009 (2) SA 66 (CC), 2008 (9) BCLR 914 (CC) . . . .

Shinga v the State & Another (Society of Advocates, Pitermaritzburg Bar, as Amicus Curiae 2007 (4) SA 611 (CC), 2007 (2) SACR 28 (CC) 2007 (5) BCLR 474 (CC). . . . .

Sibiya & Others v Director of Public Prosecutions, Johannesburg & Others 2003 (5) SA 518 (C) . . .

Sibiya & Others v Director of Public Prosecutions, Johannesburg & Others 2005 (5) SA 315 (CC), 2005 (8) BCLR 812 (CC) . . . .

Sibiya & Others v Director of Public Prosecutions, Johannesburg & Others [2006] ZACC 22, 2006 (2) BCLR 293 (CC). . . . .

Sidumo & Another v Rustenburg Platinum Mines Ltd & Others 2008 (2) SA 24 (CC), 2007 (12) BCLR 1097(CC). . . . .

South African Association of Personal Injury Lawyers v Heath 2001 (1) SA 883 (CC), 2001 (1) BCLR 77 (CC) . . . .